Cisco Router Firewall Security

Richard A. Deal

D1328133

Cisco Press

800 East 96th Street
Indianapolis, Indiana 46240 USA

Cisco Router Firewall Security

Richard A. Deal

Copyright© 2005 Cisco Systems, Inc.

Published by:
Cisco Press
800 East 96th Street
Indianapolis, IN 46240 USA

Printed in the United States of America 1 2 3 4 5 6 7 8 9 0

First Printing August 2004

Library of Congress Cataloging-in-Publication Number: 2003111982

ISBN: 1-58705-175-3

Warning and Disclaimer

This book is designed to provide information about using Cisco routers as perimeter firewall solutions. Every effort has been made to make this book as complete and as accurate as possible, but no warranty or fitness is implied.

The information is provided on an "as is" basis. The authors, Cisco Press, and Cisco Systems, Inc., shall have neither liability nor responsibility to any person or entity with respect to any loss or damages arising from the information contained in this book or from the use of the discs or programs that may accompany it.

The opinions expressed in this book belong to the author and are not necessarily those of Cisco Systems, Inc.

Trademark Acknowledgments

All terms mentioned in this book that are known to be trademarks or service marks have been appropriately capitalized. Cisco Press or Cisco Systems, Inc., cannot attest to the accuracy of this information. Use of a term in this book should not be regarded as affecting the validity of any trademark or service mark.

Corporate and Government Sales

Cisco Press offers excellent discounts on this book when ordered in quantity for bulk purchases or special sales.

For more information, please contact: **U.S. Corporate and Government Sales**   1-800-382-3419, corpsales@pearsontechgroup.com.

For sales outside the U.S. please contact: **International Sales**   international@pearsoned.com

Feedback Information

At Cisco Press, our goal is to create in-depth technical books of the highest quality and value. Each book is crafted with care and precision, undergoing rigorous development that involves the unique expertise of members from the professional technical community.

Readers' feedback is a natural continuation of this process. If you have any comments regarding how we could improve the quality of this book or otherwise alter it to better suit your needs, you can contact us through e-mail at feedback@ciscopress.com. Please be sure to include the book title and ISBN in your message.

We greatly appreciate your assistance.

Publisher	John Wait
Editor-in-Chief	John Kane
Executive Editor	Brett Bartow
Cisco Representative	Anthony Wolfenden
Cisco Press Program Manager	Nannette M. Noble
Acquisitions Editor	Michelle Grandin
Production Manager	Patrick Kanouse
Development Editor	Andrew Cupp
Project Editor	Marc Fowler
Copy Editor	Krista Hansing
Technical Editors	Scott Clayton, Stephen Marcinek, Umar Shafiq
Team Coordinator	Tammi Barnett
Book and Cover Designer	Louisa Adair
Composition	Interactive Composition Corporation
Indexer	Tim Wright

CISCO SYSTEMS

Corporate Headquarters
Cisco Systems, Inc.
170 West Tasman Drive
San Jose, CA 95134-1706
USA
www.cisco.com
Tel: 408 526-4000
800 553-NETS (6387)
Fax: 408 526-4100

European Headquarters
Cisco Systems International BV
Haarlerbergpark
Haarlerbergweg 13-19
1101 CH Amsterdam
The Netherlands
www-europe.cisco.com
Tel: 31 0 20 357 1000
Fax: 31 0 20 357 1100

Americas Headquarters
Cisco Systems, Inc.
170 West Tasman Drive
San Jose, CA 95134-1706
USA
www.cisco.com
Tel: 408 526-7660
Fax: 408 527-0883

Asia Pacific Headquarters
Cisco Systems, Inc.
Capital Tower
168 Robinson Road
#22-01 to #29-01
Singapore 068912
www.cisco.com
Tel: +65 6317 7777
Fax: +65 6317 7799

Cisco Systems has more than 200 offices in the following countries and regions. Addresses, phone numbers, and fax numbers are listed on the
Cisco.com Web site at www.cisco.com/go/offices.

Argentina • Australia • Austria • Belgium • Brazil • Bulgaria • Canada • Chile • China PRC • Colombia • Costa Rica • Croatia • Czech Republic
Denmark • Dubai, UAE • Finland • France • Germany • Greece • Hong Kong SAR • Hungary • India • Indonesia • Ireland • Israel • Italy
Japan • Korea • Luxembourg • Malaysia • Mexico • The Netherlands • New Zealand • Norway • Peru • Philippines • Poland • Portugal
Puerto Rico • Romania • Russia • Saudi Arabia • Scotland • Singapore • Slovakia • Slovenia • South Africa • Spain • Sweden
Switzerland • Taiwan • Thailand • Turkey • Ukraine • United Kingdom • United States • Venezuela • Vietnam • Zimbabwe

About the Author

Richard A. Deal, CCSP, CCNP, and CCNA, attended Grove City College, where he majored in mathematics, computers, and English, and graduated with a bachelor of science degree. For the past seven years, Richard has operated his own company, which provides consulting and technical training. Richard has 17 years of experience in the computing and networking industry, including networking, training, systems administration, and programming.

Besides teaching various Cisco certification courses, Richard has published many books, the most recent of which is CCNP BCMSN Exam Cram 2 (642-811) by Que Publishing. Richard actively is writing Cisco certification self-preparation tests for Boson, including one for the SECURE exam (SECURE #3). Boson Software, Inc., is a software and training company specializing in test preparation and hands-on skills acquisition product development. Boson has been a profitable software company focused on adult learning and network utilities since 1998. Their mission is to provide high-quality practice tests and study supplements in a cost-effective manner. Boson was among the first software vendors to support Cisco certifications and is now an authorized Cisco Learning Partner and Premier Reseller. Other Boson study aids are available at http://www.boson.com.

Richard currently lives with his wife, Natalie, and their new daughter, Emily, in Oviedo, Florida, just outside of Orlando.

About the Technical Editors

Scott Clayton, CCIE No. 10064, is a systems engineer specializing in security and VPN designs. He currently works supporting several Fortune 100 companies, as well as local and state government customers. Before holding this position, Scott worked in the Cisco TAC supporting customers on a wide range of security, VPN, and content service products and technologies. Scott was among the first group of people to take and pass the Security CCIE exam in October 2002. Scott holds a bachelor of science degree from the College of William and Mary in Williamsburg, Virginia.

Stephen Marcinek, CCIE No. 7225, is a technical trainer for Boson Training. He develops the course content and delivers numerous classes in Cisco networking and security, from introductory to CCIE level. Steve also consults for numerous large organizations. He holds a bachelor of arts degree from Rutgers University and is a member of American Mensa.

Umar Shafiq, CCIE No. 7119, has worked as a customer support engineer at Cisco Systems since 1998. His team handles highly technical troubleshooting of multiprotocol networks, network security, and VPNs for all of Cisco's installed bases worldwide. He received his bachelor of science degree in electronics engineering at the University of Engineering and Technology in Lahore, Pakistan, and he received his masters in business administration at California State University. He resides in Fremont, California.

Dedications

This book is dedicated to Natalie and Emily. Thank you for bringing so much joy to my life.

Acknowledgments

I'd like to give special recognition to Michelle Grandin for providing the opportunity to write this and future books with Cisco Press, as well as the team from Cisco Press for making the writing of this book a very smooth process.

Special thanks goes out to the technical editors of this book: Umar Shafiq, Scott Clayton, and especially Steve Marcinek. I have personally known Steve for quite some time and can always count on him as a co-worker and friend.

A big "thank you" goes out to the production team for this book. Marc Fowler and Krista Hansing have been incredibly professional and a pleasure to work with. And a really special thanks to Drew! I couldn't have asked for a finer team.

Last and most important, this book would not have been possible without the support of my wife, Natalie. A book of this size is very time consuming, especially when you have to balance a book, a job, and, most important, a family. My wife provided endless encouragement to keep me writing when I was pressed to meet deadlines for the book.

Best wishes to all! And cheers!

Contents at a Glance

Introduction   xxxii

Part I   **Security Overview and Firewalls   3**
Chapter 1   Security Threats   5
Chapter 2   Introduction to Firewalls   41

Part II   **Managing Access to Routers   109**
Chapter 3   Accessing a Router   111
Chapter 4   Disabling Unnecessary Services   161
Chapter 5   Authentication, Authorization, and Accounting   201

Part III   **Nonstateful Filtering Technologies   235**
Chapter 6   Access List Introduction   237
Chapter 7   Basic Access Lists   259

Part IV   **Stateful and Advanced Filtering Technologies   349**
Chapter 8   Reflexive Access Lists   351
Chapter 9   Context-Based Access Control   381
Chapter 10 Filtering Web and Application Traffic   425

Part V   **Address Translation and Firewalls   471**
Chapter 11 Address Translation   473
Chapter 12 Address Translation Issues   509

Part VI   **Managing Access Through Routers   549**
Chapter 13 Lock-and-Key Access Lists   551
Chapter 14 Authentication Proxy   567
Chapter 15 Routing Protocol Protection   597

Part VII   **Detecting and Preventing Attacks   633**
Chapter 16 Intrusion-Detection System   635

Chapter 17 DoS Protection 661

Chapter 18 Logging Events 705

Part VIII **Virtual Private Networks 745**

Chapter 19 IPSec Site-to-Site Connections 747

Chapter 20 IPSec Remote-Access Connections 785

Part IX **Case Study 807**

Chapter 21 Case Study 809

Index 845

Table of Contents

Introduction   xxxii

Part I   Security Overview and Firewalls   3

Chapter 1   Security Threats   5

Planning for Security   6
   Diverse Platforms   6
   Security Goals   7

Causes of Security Problems   8
   Policy Definitions   9
      Policies: Business and Security   9
      People   10
      Enforcement   10
      Change Management   11
      Disaster Recovery   11
   Computer Technologies   13
      Network Protocol Weaknesses   13
      Operating System Weaknesses   14
      Network Equipment Weaknesses   15
   Equipment Configurations   15

Types of Security Threats   16
   External and Internal Threats   16
   Unstructured and Structured Threats   17

Categories of Threats   18
   Reconnaissance Attacks   19
      Scanning Attacks   19
      Eavesdropping Attacks   20
   Access Attacks   22
      Unauthorized Access Attack   23
      Data-Manipulation Attack   24
      Session Attacks   25
      Virus, Trojan Horse, and Worm Attacks   29
   Denial of Service Attacks   31
      Types of DoS Attacks   31
      DoS Attack-Prevention Methods   33

Security Solutions   34
   Designing a Security Solution   34

The Cisco Security Wheel   35
   Secure Your Network   36
   Monitor Your Security   36
   Test Your Security   37
   Improve Your Security   37
Security Checklist   37
Additional Information   38

Summary   38

Chapter 2   Introduction to Firewalls   41

Firewall Overview   41
   Definition of a Firewall   42
   Firewall Protection   43

Controlling Traffic and the OSI Reference Model   45
   OSI Reference Model Overview   45
   Firewalls and the OSI Reference Model   46

Firewall Categories   47
   Packet-Filtering Firewalls   47
      Filtering Actions   48
      Filtering Information   49
      Advantages of Packet-Filtering Firewalls   51
      Limitations of Packet-Filtering Firewalls   52
      Uses for Packet-Filtering Firewalls   53
   Stateful Firewalls   53
      Problems with Packet-Filtering Firewalls   54
      State Table   59
      Advantages of Stateful Firewalls   61
      Limitations of Stateful Firewalls   61
      Uses for Stateful Firewalls   64
   Application Gateway Firewalls   64
      Authentication Process   65
      Authentication Methods   66
      Application Gateway Firewall Types   67
      Cut-Through Proxy Firewalls   69
      Advantages of Application Gateway Firewalls   70
      Limitations of Application Gateway Firewalls   70
      Other Types of Application Proxy Devices   71
      Uses for Application Gateway Firewalls   72
   Address-Translation Firewalls   72
      Filtering Process   72
      Advantages of Address-Translation Firewalls   75
      Limitations of Address-Translation Firewalls   75
      Uses for Address-Translation Firewalls   76

Host-Based Firewalls   76
    Advantages of Host-Based Firewalls   77
    Limitations of Host-Based Firewalls   78
    Uses for Host-Based Firewalls   79
Hybrid Firewalls   79
Firewalls and Other Services   80

Firewall Design   81
Design Guidelines   81
    Developing a Security Policy   81
    Designing Simple Solutions   82
    Using Devices Correctly   82
    Creating a Layered Defense   83
    Dealing with Internal Threats   84
DMZ   85
    DMZ Rules and Traffic Flow   85
    DMZ Types   87
Components   91
    Perimeter Router Component   91
    Firewall Component   92
    VPN Component   92
    IDS Component   92
Component Placement   94
    Simple Firewall System Design   95
    Enhanced Firewall System Design   96
    Design Considerations   98
Firewall Implementation   99
    Security Device Manager   99
    Implementing Firewall Features   101
Firewall Administration and Management   101

Cisco IOS Security   102
Cisco IOS Uses   102
Cisco IOS Security Features   103
Cisco IOS Devices and Their Uses   105
When to Use a Cisco IOS Firewall   105

Summary   107

Part II   Managing Access to Routers   109

Chapter 3   Accessing a Router   111

Types of Authentication   111
    No Password Authentication   112
    Static Password Authentication   112
    Aging Password Authentication   113

One-Time Password Authentication   114
Token Card Services   115

Methods of User EXEC Access   117
Local Access: Console and Auxiliary   118
Login Authentication Methods   119
Login Connection Timeouts   120
Remote Access   121
VTY (Telnet)   121
Secure Shell   123
Web Browser   127
HTTP with SSL   130
SNMP   139

Privileged EXEC Access   146
Passwords   146
Privilege Levels   146
Restricting Levels   146
Password Levels   149
Local Authentication Database   150

Other Access Items   152
Encrypting Passwords   152
Banners   153
Banner Guidelines   153
Banner Configuration   154

Example Configuration   156

Summary   159

Chapter 4   Disabling Unnecessary Services   161

Disabling Global Services   161
Cisco Discovery Protocol   162
TCP and UDP Small Servers   163
Finger   164
IdentD   165
IP Source Routing   166
FTP and TFTP   167
HTTP   167
SNMP   168
Name Resolution   169
BootP   170
DHCP   171
PAD   172
Configuration Autoloading   172

Disabling Interface Services   173
    CDP on Insecure Interfaces   173
    Proxy ARP   174
    Directed Broadcasts   176
    ICMP Messages   177
        ICMP Unreachables   177
        ICMP Redirects   178
        ICMP Mask Replies   180
    Maintenance Operation Protocol   181
    VTYs   181
    Unused Interfaces   182

Manual Configuration Example of Disabling Services on a Perimeter Router   183

AutoSecure   184
    Securing Planes   185
        The Management Plane   185
        The Forwarding Plane   186
    AutoSecure Configuration   187
        Starting up AutoSecure   187
        Going Through a Sample Script   188
        Verifying AutoSecure's Configuration   198
        Using Additional Commands   198

Summary   199

Chapter 5   Authentication, Authorization, and Accounting   201

AAA Overview   201
    AAA Functions   202
    Enabling AAA   202
    Security Protocols   203
        TACACS+   203
        RADIUS   205
        Server Groupings   208
        Troubleshooting TACACS+ and RADIUS   209
        Server Protocol Example Configuration   211
        Comparison of TACACS+ and RADIUS   212

Authentication   213
    Methods of Authentication   213
    Authentication Configuration   216
        User EXEC Authentication   216
        Privileged EXEC Authentication   217
        Username and Password Prompts   218
        Login Banners   218
        Login Attempts   219

Authentication Troubleshooting   219
Authentication Example   220

Authorization   221
Methods of Authorization   222
Authorization Configuration   222
Executing Commands   223
Executing Configuration Commands   224
Authorization Troubleshooting   224
Authorization Example   225

Accounting   226
Methods of Accounting   226
Accounting Configuration   227
Enabling Accounting   227
Suppressing Null Username Records   229
Enabling Broadcast Accounting   229
Accounting Troubleshooting   230
Accounting Example   230

Secure Copy   231
Preparation for SCP   231
SCP Configuration   232
SCP Troubleshooting   232
SCP Example   232

Summary   233

Part III   Nonstateful Filtering Technologies   235

Chapter 6   Access List Introduction   237

Access List Overview   237
ACLs and Filtering   238
Simple ACL Example   238
Types of ACLs   239
Processing ACLs   241
Conditions   241
Matches on Conditions   241
ACL Flowchart   242
Statement Order in ACLs   243
ACL Rules and Restrictions   246
Placement of ACLs   247

Basic ACL Configuration   249
Creating ACLs   250
Activating ACLs   251
Editing ACLs   252

Wildcard Masks   254
Converting a Subnet Mask to a Wildcard Mask   254
Wildcard Mask Mistakes   256

Summary   257

Chapter 7   Basic Access Lists   259

Types of ACLs   259
Standard ACLs   260
Numbered Standard ACLs   261
Named Standard ACLs   262
Standard ACL Examples   263
Extended ACLs   264
Numbered Extended ACLs   264
Named Extended ACLs   273
Extended ACL Examples   273
ACL Verification   278
Fragments and Extended ACLs   280
Fragmentation Process   280
Fragmentation and Filtering Issues   281
Filtering Fragments   282
Fragment Filtering Example   283
Timed ACLs   285
Creating Time Ranges   285
Activating Time Ranges   287
Using Distributed Timed ACLs   287
Example of Timed ACL   288

Additional ACL Features   289
ACL Remarks   290
Logging Updates   291
IP Accounting and ACLs   292
Configuration of Accounting   292
Restriction of Accounting Information   293
Turbo ACLs   295
Sequenced ACLs   296
ACLs and Sequencing   297
Resequencing ACLs   298
Deleting an Entry in a Sequenced ACL   299
Inserting an Entry in a Sequenced ACL   299

Protection Against Attacks   301
Bogon Blocking and Spoofing   301
Ingress Filtering   302
Egress Filtering   305

DoS and Distributed DoS Attacks   307
    TCP SYN Floods   307
    Smurf and Fraggle Attacks   308
Simple Reconnaissance Attacks   314
    Ingress Filtering of ICMP Traffic   314
    Egress Filtering of ICMP Traffic   315
    Traceroute   316
Distributed DoS Attacks   317
    DDoS Components   317
    DDoS Process   317
    The Five Main DDoS Attacks   319
Trojan Horses   325
    Trojan Horse ACLs   325
    Other Prevention Methods   327
Worms   327
    Solutions to Worm Problems   328
    SQL Slammer Worm   328
    Deloder Worm   330
    The Microsoft RPC Service and Worms   330

Blocking Unnecessary Services   332
    An Uphill Battle   332
    Instant-Messenger Products   333
        AOL Instant Messenger   333
        ICQ   334
        Microsoft MSN Messenger   335
        Yahoo! Messenger   336
        Apple iChat   338
    File Sharing: Peer-to-Peer Products   338
        Prevention and Detection   339
        Napster   340
        Kazaa and Morpheus   341
        Gnutella   343
        IMesh   343
        WinMX   344
        AudioGalaxy   345
        eDonkey2000   346

Summary   347

Part IV   Stateful and Advanced Filtering Technologies   349

Chapter 8   Reflexive Access Lists   351

Overview of Reflexive ACLs   351
    Extended Versus Reflexive ACLs   352
        How Extended ACLs Handle Returning ICMP Traffic   352

How Extended ACLs Handle Returning UDP Traffic   353
How Extended ACLs Handle Returning TCP Traffic   354
How RACLs Handle Returning Traffic   355
Reflexive ACLs in Action   357
Steps in Processing Traffic   357
Traffic Leaving the Network   358
Building the RACL   358
Traffic Returning to the Network   359
Removing RACL Entries   360
Limitations of Reflexive ACLs   361
Stateful Issues   362
Application Issues   362

Configuring Reflexive ACLs   365
Interface Selection   365
Two-Interface Example   365
Three-Interface Example   366
Configuration Commands   368
Building the RACL   368
Referencing the RACL   371
ACL Activation   372
Optional Commands   373
RACL Verification   373

Reflexive ACL Examples   374
Simple RACL Example   374
Two-Interface RACL Example   375
Three-Interface RACL Example   375

Summary   379

Chapter 9   Context-Based Access Control   381

Cisco IOS Firewall Features   381

CBAC Functions   382
Filtering Traffic   382
Inspecting Traffic   383
Detecting Intrusions   383
Generating Alerts and Audits   383

Operation of CBAC   383
Basic Operation   384
CBAC Enhancements over RACLs   385
TCP Traffic   385
UDP Traffic   386
ICMP Traffic   386
Extra Connections   387

Embedded Addressing Information   387
Application Inspection   389
DoS Detection and Prevention   389

Supported Protocols for CBAC   390
RTSP Applications   390
H.323 Applications   392
Skinny Support   393
SIP Support   394

CBAC Performance   395
Throughput Improvement Feature   396
Connections Per Second Improvement Feature   396
CPU Utilization Improvement Feature   397

CBAC Limitations   397

CBAC Configuration   398
Step 1: Interface Selection   399
Step 2: ACL Configuration   399
Step 3: Global Timeouts   400
Step 4: Port Application Mapping   401
PAM Table   402
PAM Configuration   403
PAM Verification   404
PAM Examples   404
Step 5: Inspection Rules   405
Inspection Rule Components   405
Generic TCP and UDP Inspection   406
ICMP Inspection   407
HTTP Inspection   407
RPC Inspection   408
SMTP Inspection   408
Fragment Inspection   409
Skinny Inspection   409
Step 6: Inspection Activation   410
Step 7: Troubleshooting CBAC   410
show commands   411
debug commands   413
Alerts and Audits   414
CBAC Removal   415

CBAC Examples   415
Simple Example   415
Two-Interface CBAC Example   417
Three-Interface CBAC Example   418

Summary   423

Chapter 10   Filtering Web and Application Traffic   425

Java Applets   425
  Java Inspection   425
  Java Blocking 426
  Java Blocking Example   426

URL Filtering   428
  Operation of URL Filtering   429
  Advantages and Limitations of URL Filtering   430
    Advantages of URL Filtering   430
    Restrictions of URL Filtering   431
  URL Filtering Implementation   432
    Content Server Location   432
    URL Filtering Setup   433
  URL Filtering Verification   439
    show Commands   440
    debug Commands   442
  URL Filtering Example   442

Network-Based Application Recognition   444
  Components of QoS   444
  NBAR and Classification   445
    Classification Process   445
    NBAR and Traffic Filtering   447
    Supported Protocols and Applications   447
  NBAR Restrictions and Limitations   451
  Basic NBAR Configuration   451
    Step 1: Enable CEF   452
    Step 2: Specify Nonstandard Ports   452
    Step 3: Classify Traffic   454
    Step 4: Download PDLMs   457
    Step 5: Define a Traffic Policy   458
    Step 6: Activate the Traffic Policy   459
    Step 7: Filter Marked Traffic   459
  NBAR Verification   460
    Class Maps   460
    Policy Maps   460
    Traffic Flow and NBAR   462
  NBAR Examples   463
    NBAR and Code Red   463
    NBAR and Nimda   466
    NBAR and P2P Programs   467

Summary   469

Part V   Address Translation and Firewalls   471

Chapter 11   Address Translation   473

Address Translation Overview   473
  Private Addresses   473
  Address Translation   474
    Advantages of Address Translation   475
    Disadvantages of Address Translation   475

How Address Translation Works   476
  Terms Used in Address Translation   476
  Performing Address Translation   477
    Network Address Translation   477
    Overlapping Addresses   479
    Address Overloading   480
    Traffic Distribution and Load Balancing   482
  Limitations of Address Translation   483

Address Translation Configuration   484
  Configuration of NAT   484
    Static NAT   485
    Dynamic NAT   487
  Configuration of PAT   489
  Configuration of Port Address Redirection   491
  Dealing with Overlapping Addresses   493
    Static Translation   494
    Dynamic Translation   496
  Configuration of Traffic Distribution   497
  Configuration of Translation Limits   499
    Setting Connection Limits   500
    Setting Timeout Limits   500
  Verifying and Troubleshooting Address Translation   501
    show Commands   501
    clear Commands   503
    debug ip nat Command   504

NAT and CBAC Example   505

Summary   507

Chapter 12   Address Translation Issues   509

Embedded Addressing Information   509
  Problem with Embedding Addressing Information   510
  Supported Protocols and Applications   511
  Nonstandard Port Numbers   512
    IP NAT Service Configuration   513
    IP NAT Service Example   513

Controlling Address Translation   514
    Using ACLs   514
    Using Route Maps: Dynamic Translations   515
        Problems with ACLs and Address Translation   516
        Route Map Configuration   517
    Using Route Maps: Static Translations   520

Address Translation and Redundancy   521
    Static NAT Redundancy with HSRP   522
        HSRP Redundancy Process   522
        HSRP Redundancy Configuration   524
        HSRP Redundancy Example   525
    Stateful Address Translation Failover   526
        Stateful Failover Features and Restrictions   526
        SNAT with HSRP   527
        SNAT Without HSRP   531
        SNAT Verification   534

Traffic Distribution with Server Load Balancing   535
    SLB Process   536
        Load-Balancing Algorithms   538
    SLB Advantages and Limitations   540
    SLB Configuration   540
        Required SLB Commands   541
        Optional SLB Commands   542
    SLB Verification   544
    SLB Example   545

Summary   546

Part VI   Managing Access Through Routers   549

Chapter 13   Lock-and-Key Access Lists   551

Lock-and-Key Overview   551
    Lock-and-Key and Normal ACLs   551
    When to Use Lock-and-Key   552
    Lock-and-Key Benefits   552
    Lock-and-Key Process   553

Lock-and-Key Configuration   554
    Configuration Steps   555
        Step 1: Create Your Extended ACL   555
        Step 2: Define Your Authentication Method   558
        Step 3: Enable Lock-and-Key Authentication   559
    Allowing Remote Administration Access   560
        Telnet Solution   560

SSH Solution   561
Local Database Solution   562
Verification and Troubleshooting   562

Lock-and-Key Example   563

Summary   565

Chapter 14   Authentication Proxy   567

Introduction to AP   567
AP Features   568
AP Process   569
AP Process Example   570
AP Authentication and JavaScript   572
AP Usage   573
When to Use AP   573
Where to Use AP   573
Limitations of AP   574

AP Configuration   575
Configuring AAA on Your Router   576
Configuring AAA on Your Server   576
AP Service   577
User Authorization Profiles   578
Preparing for HTTP or HTTPS   579
HTTP Configuration Tasks   579
Configuration Tasks for HTTPS   579
Configuring AP Policies   580
AP Policy Definitions   580
AP Policy Activation   581
Tuning AP   582
Protecting Against Access Attacks   583

Verifying and Troubleshooting AP   584
show Commands   584
clear Commands   586
debug Commands   587

AP Examples   587
Simple AP Example   587
Complex AP Example: CBAC and NAT   590

Summary   595

Chapter 15   Routing Protocol Protection   597

Static and Black Hole Routing   597
Static Routes   597

Null Routes   598
Policy-Based Routing   601

Interior Gateway Protocol Security   604
Authentication   604
Supported Routing Protocols   605
Authentication Process   605
RIPv2   606
EIGRP   608
OSPF   608
IS-IS   609
Group 1 Steps: Authentication Keys   610
Group 2 Steps: IS-IS Authentication   610
Group 3 Steps: Using Authentication   610
IS-IS Authentication Example   611
Other Tools   612
Passive Interfaces   612
ACL Filters   613
HSRP   614

BGP Security   617
Authentication   617
Route Flap Dampening   618
BGP Routing Example   620

Reverse-Path Forwarding (Unicast Traffic)   625
RPF Process   625
ACL Enhancements   626
Statistics   627
RPF Usage   627
RPF Limitations   628
RPF Configuration   629
RPF Verification   630
Unicast RPF Example   631

Summary   631

Part VII   Detecting and Preventing Attacks   633

Chapter 16   Intrusion-Detection System   635

IDS Introduction   635
IDS Implementations   635
Profiles   636
Signatures   636
Complications with IDS Systems   637

IDS Solutions   637
    Network-Based Solutions   638
    Host-Based Solutions   639
    Host-Based Versus Network-Based   640
IDS Concerns   640
    Installed Components   640
    Detecting Intrusions   641
    Responding to Intrusions   641

IDS Signatures   642
    Signature Implementations   642
    Signature Structures   642
    Basic Classification   643
    Cisco Signature Categories   643

Cisco Router IDS Solution   644
    Signature Support   644
    Router IDS Process   651
    Memory and Performance Issues   652

IDS Configuration   652
    Step 1: Initialization Configuration   652
    Step 2: Logging and PostOffice Configuration   653
    Step 3: Audit Rule Configuration and Activation   654
        Global Policies   655
        Specific Policies   655
        Signature Policies   655
        Protection Policies   656
        Policy Activation   656
    IDS Verification   657

IDS Example   658

Summary   659

Chapter 17   DoS Protection   661

Detecting DoS Attacks   661
    Common Attacks   661
    Symptoms of Attacks   662
    Examining CPU Utilization to Detect DoS Attacks   663
    Using ACLs to Detect DoS Attacks   665
        ACL Counters   665
        Specific ACL Entries   666
        ACL Logging   668
        Smurf Example   668

Damage Limitations   670
Finding the Attacker   670
Using NetFlow to Detect DoS Attacks   672
NetFlow Overview   672
NetFlow Configuration   673
Examining and Clearing NetFlow Statistics   673
NetFlow and DoS Attacks   675

CEF Switching   678

TCP Intercept   679
TCP SYN Flood Attacks   679
TCP Intercept Modes   679
Intercept Mode   680
Watch Mode   681
TCP Intercept Configuration and Verification   681
Enabling TCP Intercept   681
Defining the Mode   682
Changing the Timers   682
Changing the Thresholds   683
Changing the Drop Method   684
Verifying Your Configuration   684
TCP Intercept Example   686

CBAC and DoS Attacks   687
Timeouts and Thresholds   687
Setting Connection Timeouts   688
Setting Connection Thresholds   688
CBAC DoS Prevention Verification   690
CBAC Example Configuration   690

Rate Limiting   692
ICMP Rate Limiting   692
Using Other Solutions   692
Using the ICMP Rate-Limiting Feature   693
CAR   694
CAR Configuration   694
Verifying CAR   696
Rate Limiting for ICMP and Smurf Attacks   697
Rate Limiting for TCP SYN and Other TCP Floods   698
How to Choose a Rate Limit   698
Rate Limiting for W32.Blaster Worm   699
NBAR   700
Smurf Example   700
W32.Blaster Worm Example   702

Summary   703

Chapter 18   Logging Events   705

Basic Logging   705
  Log Message Format   706
  Basic Logging Configuration   706
    Enabling Logging   706
    Configuring Synchronous Logging   706
  Logging Destinations   708
    Severity Levels   708
    Line Logging   709
    Internal Buffer Logging   710
    Syslog Server Logging   710
    SNMP Logging   713
  Other Logging Commands   713
    Date and Time Stamps   714
    Sequence Numbers   714
    Rate Limits   715
  Logging Verification   716
    show logging Command   716
    show logging history Command   717
  Logging and Error Counts   718

Time and Date and the Cisco IOS   718
  Router Time Sources   719
    Hardware Clock   719
    Software Clock   719
  Manual Time and Date Configuration   720
    Time Zone   720
    Daylight Saving Time   720
    Software Clock Settings   721
    Hardware Clock Settings   722
  Network Time Protocol Overview   722
    Time Distribution   722
    Simple Network Time Protocol   723
  Router Client Configuration for NTP   723
    Poll-Based Configuration   724
    Broadcast-Based Configuration   725
    SNTP Configuration   725
  Router Server Configuration for NTP   725
    Distributing Timing Information   726
    Configuring an External Clock   726
    Setting Up the NTP Server   727
  NTP Security   727
    Access Groups   728
    Authentication   728

Other NTP Commands   729
NTP Verification   730
NTP Commands   730
SNTP Command   731
NTP Configuration Example   731

Embedded Syslog Manager   732
ESM Overview   733
ESM Filter Modules   733
Input Process   734
Filtering Process   736
Example Filter Modules   737
Introduction to ESM Setup and Configuration   738
Specifying Filter Modules   739
Using Filter Modules   739
Verifying Your ESM Configuration   740

Additional Logging Information   740
What to Look For   741
Additional Tools   741
Rotating Syslog Log Files   741
Examining Log File Contents   742

Summary   743

Part VIII   Virtual Private Networks   745

Chapter 19   IPSec Site-to-Site Connections   747

IPSec Preparation   747
Basic Tasks   747
External ACL   749

IKE Phase 1: Management Connection   750
Enabling ISAKMP/IKE   750
Defining IKE Phase 1 Policies   751
Policy Commands   751
Policy Verification   753

IKE Phase 1 Peer Authentication   753
Identity Type   754
Authentication with Preshared Keys   754
Authentication with RSA Encrypted Nonces   755
RSA Manual Key Generation   755
Peer Key Configuration   756
Authentication with Certificates   757
Certificates and CAs   757

Simple Certificate Enrollment Protocol   758
Certificate Revocation List   759
Certificate Enrollment and Configuration Process   759
Removing Your Router's Certificate   765
Removing Your Router's RSA Keys   765

IKE Phase 2: Data Connection   766
Step 1: Building a Crypto ACL   766
Step 2: Creating a Transform Set   767
Transform Set Protection Parameters   767
Transform Set Connection Modes   768
Transform Set Verification   769
Step 3: Creating a Crypto Map   770
Crypto Map Rules   770
Crypto Map Types   771
Static Crypto Map Entries   771
Entry Commands   772
Step 4: Activating a Crypto Map   773
Step 5: Verifying a Crypto Map Configuration   774

IPSec Connection Troubleshooting   775
Examining SAs   775
Using debug Commands   778
Clearing Connections   780

L2L Example   780

Summary   783

Chapter 20   IPSec Remote-Access Connections   785

Remote Access Overview   785
EasyVPN Introduction   786
EasyVPN IPSec Support   787
EasyVPN Features   787

IPSec Remote-Access Connection Process   789
Step 1: The EVC Initiates an IPSec Connection   789
Step 2: The EVC Sends the IKE Phase 1 Policies   790
Step 3: The EVS Accepts an IKE Phase 1 Policy   790
Step 4: The EVS Authenticates the User   790
Step 5: The EVS Performs IKE Mode Config   791
Step 6: The EVS Handles Routing with RRI   791
Step 7: The IPSec Devices Build the Data Connections   793

IPSec Remote-Access EVS Setup   793
Configuration Process   793
Task 1: Authentication Policies   793

Task 2: Group Policies   794

Task 3: IKE Phase 1 Policies   797

Task 4: Dynamic Crypto Maps   798

Overview of Dynamic Crypto Maps   798

Creating a Dynamic Crypto Map   799

Using a Dynamic Crypto Map   800

Verifying a Dynamic Crypto Map   800

Task 5: Static Crypto Map   801

Task 6: Remote-Access Verification   802

IPSec Remote Access Example   802

Summary   805

Part IX   Case Study   807

Chapter 21   Case Study   809

Company Profile   809

Corporate Office   809

Perimeter Router   809

Internal Router   811

Branch Office   812

Remote-Access Users   812

Proposal   812

Case Study Configuration   813

Basic Configuration   813

Unnecessary Services and SSH   815

AAA   817

Access Control Lists   820

CBAC and Web Filtering   825

Address Translation   827

Routing   830

Intrusion-Detection System   832

Connection Attacks and CBAC   832

Rate Limiting   833

NTP and Syslog   835

Site-to-Site VPN   836

Remote-Access VPNs   839

Summary   842

Index   845

Icons Used in This Book

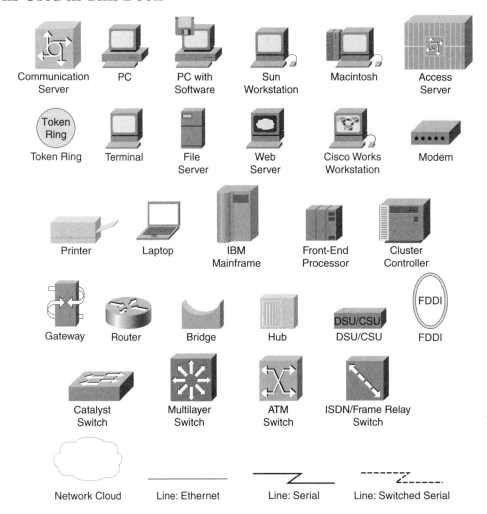

Command Syntax Conventions

The conventions used to present command syntax in this book are the same conventions used in the Cisco IOS Command Reference. The Command Reference describes these conventions as follows:

- **Boldface** indicates commands and keywords that are entered literally as shown. In actual configuration examples and output (not general command syntax), boldface indicates commands that are input manually by the user (such as a **show** command).

- *Italics* indicate arguments for which you supply actual values.

- Vertical bars (|) separate alternative, mutually exclusive elements.

- Square brackets [ ] indicate optional elements.

- Braces { } indicate a required choice.

- Braces within brackets [{ }] indicate a required choice within an optional element.

Introduction

Cisco has been an important part of the networking industry for many years and will continue to become more important. The first router product that I worked on, back in 1993, was a Cisco AGS+. I have seen many flavors of the Cisco IOS Software, including the introduction of most of the security features you see today in the Cisco IOS Software operating system. Over the past several years, I have seen security becoming a key component in network design. And with more companies using the Internet as a business tool today, security is more important than ever.

Goals and Methods

Three years ago, I realized that there were many certification books to help people pass Cisco security certification exams; however, I found no books of any substance that brought Cisco security features together to be applied in a real-life situation. I continually monitor various Cisco newsgroups and constantly see questions related to how to implement various Cisco security features. This was the foundation of my first security book, *Cisco PIX Firewalls*.

The purpose of this book, *Cisco Router Firewall Security*, is to show you how to implement a perimeter firewall solution using Cisco routers. To that end, this book focuses on important features of the Cisco IOS Software, and how to use them to secure your perimeter router and provide a secure solution for traffic entering and leaving the perimeter of your network. Of course, many of the topics I discuss in this book can be applied to any Cisco router in your network; however, because most mid- to large-size networks have a Cisco router on their perimeter, I focus this text on perimeter security problems and how to use a Cisco router to deal with these problems. This is not a certification book, but a "how to" book. I've included the following methods to help you with the "how to" process:

- Providing explanations and information to fill in your knowledge gaps
- Explaining advantages and disadvantages of the various Cisco IOS Software security features, to help you understand when they should be used
- Using small examples from my personal consulting experience to illustrate the issues related to security
- Supplying many examples, including a detailed case study at the end of the book, to show you how Cisco's security features should be implemented

Who Should Read This Book?

This book is intended to provide the necessary framework for using a Cisco router as a perimeter firewall solution. With this goal in mind, this is a "how-to" book. Although other objectives can be achieved from using this book, such as preparing for Cisco's CCSP SECUR exam, this book is written with one main goal in mind: to secure your perimeter network using Cisco routers.

This book assumes that you have a basic understanding of Cisco routers and the Cisco IOS Software operating system and command-line interface (CLI). I assume that you have an intermediate to advanced level of knowledge of Cisco routers and, minimally, that you have Cisco's CCNA certification to understand and make best use of the material in this book.

Because this book focuses on using Cisco IOS Software features to enhance the security of your perimeter routers, it will be very useful for any network administrator or engineer who currently must provide security for the perimeter of a network, as well as anyone who needs to enhance the security of other routers in a network.

How This Book Is Organized

Although this book can be read cover to cover, it is designed to allow you to move easily among chapters and sections of chapters to cover just the material that you are interested in. However, each part and each chapter in each part builds upon the others. There are nine parts to this book. Each part deals with an important component of perimeter router security, and each chapter covers Cisco IOS Software features that you can use to implement your perimeter router security. The following topics are covered in the chapters of this book:

- **Part I, "Security Overview and Firewalls"**
  - **Chapter 1, "Security Threats"**—This chapter contains a brief overview of the kinds of threats that you'll face in securing your network, as well as some generic solutions that you can use to deal with these threats. The chapter begins with a discussion of the causes of security problems. It also categorizes security threats and lists some common and not so common security threats you'll face: how they're implemented and a quick overview of how you can deal with them. This chapter lays the groundwork for the rest of the book, which focuses on firewall technologies to protect the perimeter of your network.
  - **Chapter 2, "Introduction to Firewalls"**—This chapter contains an introduction to firewall technologies and the different types of firewall implementations. It includes a brief overview of the OSI Reference Model and uses this model to explain how different types of firewall technologies provide different levels of protection. This chapter also has an introduction to firewall design, including the components typically used to provide a firewall solution. Finally, it introduces the technologies that are discussed in this book.

- **Part II, "Managing Access to Routers"**
  - **Chapter 3, "Accessing a Router"**—This chapter is the first in the book that deals with Cisco IOS Software features and their implementation. Chapters 3, 4, and 5 discuss how to use Cisco IOS Software features to protect access to the router itself. This chapter focuses on securing basic access to your perimeter router. It discusses the different access methods to a router and the solutions you can use to secure these types of access; it also offers warnings about using certain kinds of access methods. In addition, it discusses how to set up different levels of EXEC access on your perimeter router and how to assign accounts to the different levels of access.
  - **Chapter 4, "Disabling Unnecessary Services"**—This chapter covers how to disable global services, how to disable interface services, and how to use the AutoSecure feature. AutoSecure is a new Cisco IOS Software feature, similar to the System Configuration Dialog script, and is used to automate the basic securing of your router.

— **Chapter 5, "Authentication, Authorization, and Accounting"**—This chapter discusses the use of AAA to secure your perimeter router. AAA has many features, but this chapter focuses only on those to secure your perimeter router, including the use of local and remote AAA.

- **Part III, "Nonstateful Filtering Technologies"**

  — **Chapter 6, "Access List Introduction"**—This chapter contains an introduction to access control lists (ACLs). If you already have your CCNA, you should be familiar with this material.

  — **Chapter 7, "Basic Access Lists"**—This chapter includes coverage of the following types of basic ACLs: numbered, named, standard, extended, and timed. It also discusses some new ACL features, such as sequenced ACLs (with the capability to delete any ACL entry or insert a new ACL entry anywhere into an existing list), ACL remarks, logging of ACL information, and turbo ACLs (compiling ACLs to improve router processing efficiency). The last part of the chapter focuses on using ACLs to block various types of security threats and attacks, such as spoofing, DoS, Trojan horses, and worm attacks, as well as unnecessary or nuisance services, such as Peer-to-Peer (P2P) file-sharing and instant messenger (IM) programs.

- **Part IV, "Stateful and Advanced Filtering Technologies"**

  — **Chapter 8, "Reflexive Access Lists"**—This chapter discusses the use of reflexive ACLs (RACLs). RACLs are a precursor to Cisco's CBAC technology, and this is a semistateful firewall feature. This chapter discusses the advantages and disadvantages of using RACLs for perimeter routers in implementing a stateful firewall function. The end of the chapter has an example of using RACLs with a two- and three-interface perimeter router.

  — **Chapter 9, "Context-Based Access Control"**—This chapter covers Cisco's recommended stateful firewall feature: CBAC. Because this is the first chapter that introduces a feature from the Cisco IOS Software Firewall feature set, it includes a brief overview of these features. Following this, the chapter discusses the advantages and limitations of CBAC and then its implementation. Some of CBAC's components, such as DoS protection, are left for later chapters. The end of the chapter has a few examples, including a complex three-interface router example.

  — **Chapter 10, "Filtering Web and Application Traffic"**—This chapter covers the filtering of application layer traffic, including web traffic. The first part of the chapter deals with web traffic filtering, including the filtering of Java applets and URLs embedded in HTTP requests. The second half of the chapter introduces Network-Based Application Recognition (NBAR). NBAR normally is used to implement QoS functions on a router; however, it also can be used to implement bandwidth *and* security policies. Other places in this book also discuss the use of NBAR, which is a very useful and flexible Cisco IOS Software feature.

- **Part V, "Address Translation and Firewalls"**
  - **Chapter 11, "Address Translation"**—This chapter covers address translation on routers. It begins with an overview of what address translation is and the various types of translation and their limitations. The last half of the chapter discusses the implementation of these types of address translation.
  - **Chapter 12, "Address Translation Issues"**—This chapter focuses on some key issues with address translation and solutions for dealing with these issues. It first discusses issues with embedded addresses and how the Cisco IOS Software can deal with these when performing address translation. Then it covers how you can incorporate redundancy in your network when you use address translation, specifically for the address-translation device. In addition, it discusses various methods of load balancing, such as HSRP and server load balancing (SLB).

- **Part VI, "Managing Access Through Routers"**
  - **Chapter 13, "Lock-and-Key Access Lists"**—This chapter covers the use of lock-and-key ACLs to authenticate users connections before you grant them access through your perimeter router. This was Cisco's first developed solution for this problem and originally was meant for dialup access; however, it also can be used to authenticate users passing traffic through a perimeter router.
  - **Chapter 14, "Authentication Proxy"**—This chapter covers the use of another Cisco IOS Software Firewall feature set: Authentication Proxy (AP). AP is Cisco's recommended feature for authenticating users before allowing them to pass traffic through a router. This chapter covers the many advantages that AP has over lock-and-key, as well as its implementation.
  - **Chapter 15, "Routing Protocol Protection"**—This chapter discusses the protection of the routing process on your router, which, in turn, controls the router's traffic flow. This chapter focuses on authentication for routing protocols, as well as how to protect your router from routing and spoofing attacks. These concepts include black hole routing, interior gateway protocol (IGP) security, BGP security, and reverse-path forwarding (RPF).

- **Part VII, "Detecting and Preventing Attacks"**
  - **Chapter 16, "Intrusion-Detection System"**—Another component of the Cisco IOS Software Firewall feature set is detecting attacks with a rudimentary IDS component. This chapter contains an introduction to IDS, including signatures, and then follows with the configuration of IDS on a perimeter router.
  - **Chapter 17, "DoS Protection"**—This chapter contains solutions to protect a router and network from DoS attacks. The first part of the chapter discusses how to detect DoS attacks; the last half discusses tools that you can use for protection, including TCP Intercept, CBAC, and rate limiting.

- **Chapter 18, "Logging Events"**—This chapter discusses how to set up logging on your perimeter router. It covers basic logging, as well as logging to an external server using syslog. It also covers the use of time stamps with logging records and your options of defining time on your router, including manually doing so and using the Network Time Protocol (NTP). The Embedded Syslog Manager (ESM) discusses how you can customize the Cisco IOS Software syslog functions, including e-mail alerts. The last part of the chapter briefly discusses the kinds of things that you should look for in your log files for attacks against your router and network.

- **Part VIII, "Virtual Private Networks"**
  - **Chapter 19, "IPSec Site-to-Site Connections"**—This chapter discusses the use of a perimeter router to terminate a site-to-site IPSec connection. The chapter begins by discussing preparation needs and then continues to discuss the configuration of the management connection in IKE Phase 1, including device authentication options. The second half of the chapter covers the setup of the data connections in IKE Phase 2, including troubleshooting of your IPSec connections.

  - **Chapter 20, "IPSec Remote-Access Connections"**—This chapter discusses the use of a perimeter router to terminate IPSec remote-access connections. The chapter begins with an overview of remote access, including how remote-access connections are established. The rest of the chapter discusses the use of the Easy VPN feature to establish remote-access connections.

- **Part IX, "Case Study"**
  - **Chapter 21, "Case Study"**—This last chapter contains a case study and implements many of the features discussed throughout this book. It presents solutions to as well as explanations of a company's problems for protecting its perimeter network.

Additional Information

Many of the features discussed in this book are supported only on various router models or Cisco IOS Software versions. To learn whether a Cisco IOS Software feature is supported on a specific router platform or Cisco IOS Software version, use the Cisco Feature Navigator at http://www.cisco.com/go/fn. You need a CCO account to use this feature.

For a list of product security advisories and notices for Cisco products and Cisco IOS Software releases, visit http://www.cisco.com/warp/public/707/advisory.html.

TIP   I highly recommand that you *carefully* view this list before loading a specific Cisco IOS Software version on your perimeter router.

If your router or network has been attacked, you can find a list of law-enforcement contacts at http://www.cisco.com/warp/public/707/LE-contacts.html.

For a list of additional security tools that you can use to detect weaknesses in your network, as well as secure your network, you can visit the following websites:

- http://www.packetstormsecurity.nl
- http://www.insecure.org/nmap
- http://www.laurentconstantin.com/en/lcrzoex
- http://www.hping.org

Security Overview and Firewalls

Chapter 1   Security Threats

Chapter 2   Introduction to Firewalls

Security Threats

With the increase of hacking attacks, worms, viruses, and other networking threats, security is a major problem in today's networks. 10 to 15 years ago, security was a simple problem requiring simple solutions; in those days, the Internet was small and had only a small number of universities and government agencies connected to it. Aging passwords were used to protect accounts, and simple packet-filtering firewalls were used to restrict traffic flows. However, today is a different world from more than a decade ago. With the explosion of the Internet, the proliferation of software applications, and the ingenuity of hackers, security has become a complex problem that requires a well-thought-out security solution to deal with it. The security solution must be capable of dealing with the security threats that your network will face, but it also must allow your company to reach its business goals and must be flexible enough to adapt to network topology and technology changes.

This chapter contains a brief overview of the kinds of threats that you will face in securing your network, as well as some generic solutions that you can use to deal with these threats. Understanding these topics will greatly help you choose and implement the correct Cisco security feature on your router. The main purpose of this book is to explain how to use a Cisco perimeter router as a complete firewall solution or as a component of a firewall solution. The end of the chapter explains the Cisco Security Model, which is used to implement security solutions.

TIP   Most hackers are intimate with UNIX operating systems; thus, most hacking, as well as security tools, is done in UNIX. Many tools are available for Windows platforms, but most of these are expensive commercial products. Therefore, if you are interested in becoming a security specialist, I highly recommend that you become familiar with the UNIX operating system, network administration with UNIX, and how to use many of the different security tools in a UNIX environment. At a minimum, most security job positions require this level of expertise. One of my favorite UNIX system administration books is *Unix Systems Administration Handbook* (3rd Edition), by Evi Nemeth, Garth Snyder, Scott Seebass, and Trent T. Hein (Prentice Hall PTR, August 2000). I used the first edition of this book to help me with my UNIX skills more than a decade ago; it is simple to read and easy to understand.

Planning for Security

Probably the most difficult task when dealing with security is the planning stage, in which you need to develop a solution to meet your company's business and security needs. When examining your network and identifying critical and insecure areas and components, you need to approach a security plan from various perspectives:

- Business goals and user needs
- People and politics
- Technical issues

First, you have to remember that your company has business goals outlined in a business plan. These are used as a roadmap to increase your company's success. A good security solution should help, not hinder, a company in reaching its business goals. The company's users have needs that are related to the company's business plan. Whereas the business plan is a general guideline, users have specific needs to reach the company's business goals.

You must deal with all kinds of users from different departments and divisions when determining what assets and resources your company is using to reach its business goals. This means that you need to be intimate with the corporate organization ladder and have political savvy when dealing with various users and departments, as well as their diverse needs.

When you understand what resources either are being used by or are required by users to reach the company's business goals, you need to determine what kind of security solution should be implemented that will protect your company yet allow it to achieve its goals. A solution that is completely secure yet prevents a company from reaching its goals is counterproductive and useless.

Diverse Platforms

Probably one of the most difficult things you face when designing a security solution is trying to find a one-size-fits-all solution—in other words, trying to find all your security products from one vendor with a management system that easily enables you to implement your security polices across all your security products.

For example, your security solution must encompass many types of hardware devices and software applications. Here is a small list of some of the types of devices that your security solution might have to deal with:

- PCs and laptops running Windows 95, 98, Me, 2000, XP, and 2003, as well as UNIX desktops and Macintoshes
- Servers running NT, 2000, 2003, NetWare, Linux, Solaris, HP-UX, and other operating systems

- Mainframes running Multiple Virtual Storage (MVS) and Virtual Machine (VM)
- Routers from Cisco, Juniper, Nortel, Lucent, and others
- Switches from Cisco, Foundry, Extreme, and others

This list is not all encompassing, by any means: Many more types of hardware devices, as well as dozens, if not hundreds, of software applications, play a role in your network.

NOTE   In many situations, you might have to buy security products from different vendors to implement a security solution that will meet your company's policies and goals. In this situation, take care when determining a management solution that will be used to maintain your security implementation. I have found that the more products that you have from different vendors, especially as related to security, the more difficult it becomes to manage the solution.

Security Goals

A security solution can become complex quickly, especially in large enterprise networks. To help simplify the process, a good security solution should meet these goals:

- A single cohesive security policy should be created, based on your company's business plan and goals.
- Security policies should dictate the choice of security solutions and products, not vice versa.
- Security management should be centralized under a single umbrella.

First, you should create a single, cohesive, company-wide security policy. This policy should be based on your company's business plans and goals. It should be flexible enough to allow your company to meets its business objectives, while still protecting your company's assets at a cost-effective price.

Second, the security products that you purchase should complement your security plan. You should never try to force a particular product into a role that it was not meant to be used in. Instead, develop a security solution with general components, and then find specific products that will meet the design guidelines for the included components.

Third, ongoing management and support of your products is critical, especially as they relate to detecting and dealing with security threats in a real-time manner. Some companies like to purchase all of their security products from one vendor, which makes management integration of the products easier: It is easier to deploy, manage, and support platforms from a single vendor than from multiple vendors. Of course, this approach might not be an option, based on the kinds and types of products that you need for your security solution.

If you need to purchase equipment and software from different vendors to develop a cohesive security solution, remember that you must manage these products after you implement them. Therefore, you should choose a security-management software product(s) that will ease the management and monitoring of your security devices. Choosing the right management solution will allow you to scale your security solution to a large size. It is also important to point out that even if you buy all of your security products from one vendor, that vendor might not have a single security-management platform to manage your security.

TIP   When developing a security solution, keep in mind that there is a total dollar cost for implementing any type of security measure, which includes equipment purchases, installation, training, management, and ongoing support. You need to carefully weigh the costs of a particular security measure with its benefits to determine whether the cost of the security measure outweighs the cost of the asset(s) being protected. There is no such thing as a completely secure network. Therefore, you need to examine your company's business plan, the needs of your users, and your critical resources to find a solution that adequately will protect these items.

Causes of Security Problems

Literally thousands of elements can pose security threats to your company's network, as well as to your company itself:

- Outside people and hackers
- The people who work for your company
- The applications that your users use to perform their business tasks
- The operating systems that run on your users' desktops and your servers, as well as the equipment employed
- The network infrastructure used to move data across your network, including devices such as routers, switches, hubs, firewalls, gateways, and other devices

In a large network, these elements might include thousands of devices and hundreds of applications. When tackling security, at first a large number like this sounds daunting, if not impossible to tackle. However, if you use a divide-and-conquer approach, you can break up your network into areas and components, making the development of a solution easier.

To help simplify the security process, security problems are divided into three general categories:

- **Weaknesses in policy definitions**—These weaknesses include both business and security policy weaknesses. A simple example of this type of weakness is not having a written security policy. If you do not have a policy, how can you enforce it?

- **Weaknesses in computer technologies**—These weaknesses include security weaknesses in protocols, such as TCP/IP and IPX, as well as operating systems, such as UNIX, Novell NetWare, and Windows. An example of a computer technology weakness is the BackOrifice attack, which allows a hacker to remotely control a Windows-based system.

- **Weaknesses in equipment configurations**—These weaknesses include the setup, configuration, and management of your networking devices. An example of equipment configuration weakness is not assigning a password to a Windows 2000 server's Administrator account or to a Cisco router's console port.

The following sections cover these three weaknesses in more depth.

Policy Definitions

The first weakness relates to definitions of business and security policies. Many times I have walked into small and some medium-size companies to face this problem: lack of a written security policy or business policy, or, in the worst case, both. For a company to develop and meet business goals, it needs a well-written business plan that includes the company's goals *and* policies. Likewise, to implement and maintain a good security solution that will help a company meet the objectives outlined in its business plan, you need to develop a well-written security policy. The security policy should be based on the company's business plan. This ensures that the security plan follows the restrictions placed on how the company performs its day-to-day business, and that the security plan allows the company to meet its business objectives.

Policies: Business and Security

At a minimum, a well-written security policy should address the following questions:

- What should be protected?
- How you will protect it?
- How much protection should be used?

Even though these three questions are simple, in enterprise networks, the "what" and "it" mentioned can refer to 10,000 PCs, 400 servers, 2 minicomputers, 5 UNIX database servers, remote and Internet access, and many other items. However, as you are answering each of these three questions for important hardware and software components in your network, you should refer back to your company's business policies and plans, to ensure that your proposed security solution will not hinder your company in meeting its business objectives.

As an example, a corporation might have 30 remote offices that connect to a corporate office. This corporation sells widgets as its primary business. The remote offices contain sales staff who access the corporate office's database software to place orders and check the status of orders for their local customers. If you implemented a security solution that would protect the corporation's database contents, you would need to ensure that the remote offices could access this information (in a secure manner). If you could not meet this business goal, your security solution actually would create a hindrance to the company's business plan.

NOTE   I cannot begin to stress how important a security policy is. However, it is beyond the scope of this book to discuss all the components that are involved, as well as how to put one together. However, here is an excellent starting place that you can visit to learn more about security policies and see some sample policies: http://infosyssec.master.com/texis/master /search/+/Top/Computers/Security/Policy/.

People

One of the most difficult issues to face with the development of a cohesive security policy is people and their politics. This is especially true in large companies in which each division or department has its own agenda: Each has certain goals and has tunnel vision concerning what is and what is not important for the company as a whole. As long as each department meets its goals, it is happy. You will have to deal with many people who have different ideas about what is and is not important in the network.

Each of these people is different—and, be forewarned, you cannot treat them the same. It would be convenient if each was a computer running Windows 2000 Professional; each would react in an expected manner based on the questions that you ask. However, this is not a world filled with computers; it's a world filled with people. You must consider this when you are interacting with them to learn about their issues and problems so that you can develop a cohesive security policy that meets not only their needs, but also the needs of the company as a whole.

Enforcement

Another weakness in policy definition is exposed when you have created all of these business and security policies but do not enforce them or follow through with them. In other words, having a security policy and then not implementing it completely (or at all), or not enforcing it, will not help you with your security problems; it actually creates security problems for you.

Here is a simpler example of policy enforcement. You might have written guidelines for choosing passwords for accounts in your security policy. To test your system, you might use a password-cracking program against your users' accounts to make sure that they do not use their names, addresses, or other easy-to-guess passwords. If you are able to break a password, you might talk to the user, explain the guidelines in the security policy, and have that user change the password to something less easy to guess.

Being Sued

I once dealt with a company that had both business and security policies in place; however, they were not very consistent in the enforcement of their policies. If you have policies, you need to enforce them equally. This company had a written policy that prohibited the downloading of visually offensive material, but they did not enforce it equally among their employees. In most instances, an employee got a verbal warning. However, in one instance, a person was fired instead of getting a verbal warning. This was actually not the real reason for firing the individual, but the company was not happy with this person's performance and needed an excuse for firing him. The fired employee sued the company for discrimination—he was not treated in the same manner as the other employees who broke the same rule— and won a lot of money in the suit. This is an extreme example of inconsistent policy enforcement (or a lack of one), but it is better to be prepared. I have found that when you actually enforce polices and follow through with the specified consequences, your company's employees quickly find out that they are being paid to do a job and to follow the rules, even though they might not like the policies.

Change Management

A lack of a change-management policy also will cause security problems in your network. A change-management policy typically is used to ensure that when changes are made in your network, such as upgrading a file server or changing an access control list on a router (used for filtering traffic), you do not inadvertently affect services for employees or resources, or create a security problem.

Therefore, before any change is made to the network, you should document it and take it before a committee that usually comprises network administrators and employees from various departments. This committee can discuss the proposed change and determine its impact on the network. Based on this information, the committee might modify the change request or might specify that the change occur at 2:00 A.M., to minimize its impact.

Having a change-management system in place enables other people to examine the proposed changes for problems, especially those related to security, and to catch them before they become a problem. Too often I have seen situations in which people haphazardly change the configurations on their networking equipment, typically without documenting those changes. It becomes almost impossible in this type of environment to determine what security holes these unapproved changes have created.

Disaster Recovery

When you think of a disaster-recovery plan, thoughts of natural disasters such as tornados, floods, hurricanes, and fires come to mind first. A disaster-recovery plan is used to implement a backup solution when the absolute worst case occurs.

Disaster-recovery plans also should apply to security threats and attacks. For example, your company might be selling products through its e-commerce servers. Perhaps this is your company's only line of revenue. What would happen if a hacker flooded your network with garbage traffic, possibly affecting the service that you are providing and maybe even crashing some or all of your web servers? What ramifications would occur if your e-commerce servers are hacked and it takes two or three days to bring them back online? Is your company prepared to deal with this? Do you have a plan of action that details what steps to take to deal with the problem?

A good disaster-recovery plan, in this instance, would have a redundant system in place at a different location that could be switched to easily in less than an hour, if not minutes. By placing the resources in a separate building, you are protecting yourself against natural disasters. Also, a good disaster-recovery plan lists, in detail, steps that should be taken to simplify the problem of cutting over to the new system. This reduces the likelihood of errors occurring during the cutover.

TIP	Before you actually cut over to your backup system, if your primary system was hacked, make sure that you know how it was hacked, and implement protection measures on the backup system before bringing it online. Otherwise, the hacking attack will be repeated and you will have run out of backup options.

The Headless Chicken Syndrome

Too often I run into what I call the *headless chicken syndrome*, which causes people to act rashly without consulting a prepared plan of action. For example, I was performing consulting work for a company to completely redesign its network. We were taking inventory of their equipment and looking at the topology of their current network. One afternoon, we were in their data center tracing cables to see what was and was not attached to their backbone, when one of the administrators came in with a very worried expression on his face. Apparently, some external hacker was flooding a part of the network with ICMP packets, and it was affecting this company's remote sites that were trying to access the data center over the Internet through a VPN. The administrator's first action, without thinking, was to disconnect the cable from the router that was connected to the service provider, thinking that this would reduce congestion on the network. Unfortunately, in this process, the remote sites completely lost access to the corporate site, and the administrator damaged the serial cable when pulling it out (the company did not have another serial cable as a spare part). As you can see from this example, the administrator actually made things a lot worse than the problems that the hacker had caused. This whole problem occurred because the company had no documented plan of action for what to do in this kind of event.

Computer Technologies

The second security weakness relates to computer technologies. Weaknesses in computer technologies deal with the protocols and software that use these protocols. Computer technology weaknesses are divided into three general categories:

- Network protocols
- Operating systems
- Network equipment

The following sections discuss the weaknesses that these three categories face.

Network Protocol Weaknesses

Networking protocol weaknesses deal with the weaknesses in the networking protocols and applications that use these protocols. The most popular and most implemented networking protocol is TCP/IP. TCP/IP is actually a suite of protocols, including IP, TCP, UDP, ICMP, OSPF, IGRP, EIGRP, ARP, RARP, and others.

Some of these protocols have weaknesses that hackers exploit. A good example is TCP, which uses a three-way handshake process to set up a connection before transmitting data. During the three-way handshake, three exchanges occur between the source and destination, as shown in the top part of Figure 1-1. With TCP, the source sends a segment with the SYN flag set, indicating that it wants to establish a connection. The destination responds with a segment in which the SYN and ACK flags are set in the segment header, indicating that the connection can proceed. The source then acknowledges receipt of the destination's segment by sending the ACK flag in a segment to the destination. When this process is complete, the source can begin transmitting data.

One weakness in TCP is that the destination expects the source to send a final ACK back to the destination, completing the setup of the connection. Hackers can exploit this weakness by flooding a service with TCP SYNs, without following through and completing the setup of these connections, as shown in bottom part of Figure 1-1. These connections sometimes are referred to as *embryonic*, or half-open, connections. The hacker's goal is to tie up finite resources on the target server and thus disrupt valid connection attempts. For example, some lower-end Windows machines can handle only 128 half-open connections before they run out of resources, which then makes new connection attempts fail.

Many TCP/IP applications also have weaknesses. Probably the four most common ones that hackers like to attack are HTTP, SMTP, SNMP, and finger. On many occasions, hackers have used exploits to gain unauthorized access to a server or to crash it by focusing on TCP/IP application attacks.

Figure 1-1 *TCP's Three-Way Handshake*

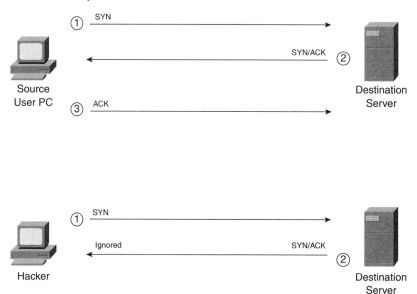

Operating System Weaknesses

For users and servers to support applications, their respective devices run an operating system to control hardware functions. Each operating system that you have deployed is guaranteed to have one or more security holes in it. This is especially true of operating systems that are used widely because hackers have a tendency to target these in their attacks. A hacker's thought process is that if he can find a security hole in an operating system such as Windows XP, he has just opened up hacking possibilities to tens of thousands of PCs. On the other hand, if a hacker spent time trying to find security weaknesses in DOS, he would be very hard pressed to find PCs connected to the Internet that still use this operating system.

When I refer to operating system weaknesses, I am talking specifically about operating systems that run on a server, PC, or laptop. These are some of the most popular operating systems that hackers focus on:

- Microsoft Windows 95, 98, NT, Me, 2000, XP, and 2003
- The many flavors of UNIX, including Linux
- Novell NetWare

One of the most targeted platforms is UNIX because the source code for many UNIX flavors, such as Linux and FreeBSD, is free. This makes it easier for a hacker to find security weaknesses and holes because the hacker can scrutinize the source code for possible problems. Because of Microsoft's popularity as a desktop solution, hackers also focus on Microsoft's many different operating systems. As an example, I use Microsoft Windows 2000 Professional for my personal and business use. On a semiweekly basis, I download security patches for this operating system, which gives you an idea of how busy hackers are in finding exploits of security holes in Windows.

Network Equipment Weaknesses

Network equipment weaknesses refer to security vulnerabilities in equipment such as routers, switches, firewalls, and others that also run an operating system. Typically, you are dealing with the security mechanisms that are built into this equipment, such as how passwords are implemented, how authentication is performed, and what security features they support and have been implemented. However, sometimes, based on a protocol, or an application that uses a protocol such as finger or SNMP, you must scrutinize your networking equipment, look at the default configurations, and make adjustments to provide for tighter security.

TIP   When security weaknesses are discovered in a protocol, an operating system, or a particular piece of networking equipment, the person who discovered the weakness should notify the Computer Emergency Response Team (CERT). CERT then verifies the vulnerability, notifies the vendor about the problem, and publishes the problem to make sure that everyone is aware of the security weakness so that they can obtain the appropriate patch from the vendor. You can view a list of the past and current security problems at http://www.cert.org. Other popular sites include http://www.infosyssec.com/ and http://www.securityfocus.com/.

Equipment Configurations

The third security weakness relates to equipment configuration problems. Weaknesses in equipment configurations are some of the hardest security problems to deal with because these weaknesses are a result of human error in the configuration or a misunderstanding about how the equipment should be configured. When I talk about networking equipment, I am talking about pretty much everything that you connect to your network, from a PC or file server to a router, switch, firewall, or other product.

You should be most concerned about controlling access to your network equipment. All user accounts should have secured passwords. This means that, for some equipment that uses default accounts, you either should change these passwords or should deactivate the accounts. You also should be concerned about the passwords that are assigned to these accounts:

- Do they have easily guessed passwords?
- How often are passwords changed?
- Do passwords travel across the network in clear text?

If you are concerned about authentication and authorization—what users access and what they are doing on a piece of network equipment—you might want to centralize authentication and authorization into a central security server. Chapter 5, "Authentication, Authorization, and Accounting," discusses how this is done on Cisco IOS routers.

One of the most difficult tasks that you will face with an Internet connection and the configuration of network equipment is exposing the applications and services running on them to the entire world. Many of these applications, such as WWW and SMTP, are known to be sure targets of hackers because of hackers' past successes in exploiting these common applications. Another example of applications that can give a hacker a way into your network is Java and ActiveX scripts that typically are embedded within web pages. One of your users might download and inadvertently run one of these scripts, giving a hacker access to your network.

To reduce the threats to your network, disable any unnecessary services on all of your networking devices. For instance, if you have a DNS server, you should disable FTP, SMTP, and other services. Likewise, on a web server, you should disable SMTP, FTP, and other services. If you have a Cisco router, you should disable all unnecessary services, such as finger and chargen. Many of these tasks are tedious work, especially if you have 300 routers and 300 servers running in your network. The work that you put into securing these services will make it that much harder for a hacker to gain a foothold into your network, however. Disabling services on a Cisco IOS router is discussed in Chapter 4, "Disabling Unnecessary Services."

CAUTION   You should run only the applications that are absolutely necessary on a device. All unnecessary applications and services should be disabled, to minimize your threat exposure.

Types of Security Threats

Now that you have a basic understanding of the kinds of weaknesses that you have to deal with in a security solution, this section turns to some of the many security threats that your network faces. As I mentioned earlier, your network might face thousands of threats daily. The Computer Security Institute (CSI) conducted a study on network security threats and security breaches and discovered that, out of all of the companies polled, 70 percent have had some type of security breach. These security threats can be categorized as external versus internal, and unstructured versus structured.

External and Internal Threats

Security threats can come from two locations:

- External users
- Internal users

An external security threat occurs when someone outside your network creates a security threat to your network. If you are using an intrusion-detection system (IDS), which detects attacks as they occur, you probably will be mildly shocked at the number of probes and attacks that occur against your network daily.

An internal security threat occurs when someone from inside your network creates a security threat to your network. Interestingly, the CSI study has found that, of the 70 percent of the companies that had security breaches, 60 percent of these breaches come from internal sources. Some of these security breaches were malicious in intent; others were accidental. Therefore, you should not just be concerned about protecting the perimeter of your network, you should also aim to protect every key resource and service. This topic is discussed in more depth in Chapter 2, "Introduction to Firewalls."

CAUTION   Most security threats are internal. Therefore, when you design a security solution, you must address this issue by using internal measures to protect important resources.

Unstructured and Structured Threats

General methods of security threats fall under two categories:

* Unstructured threats
* Structured threats

An unstructured security threat is one created by an inexperienced person who is trying to gain access to your network—a wannabe hacker. A good security solution easily should thwart this kind of attack. Many tools available to anyone on the Internet can be used to discover weaknesses in a company's network. These include port-scanning tools, address-sweeping tools, and many others. Most of these kinds of probes are done more out of curiosity than with a malicious intent in mind. This is especially true of internal users who are interested in what kinds of devices exist in their own network.

A structured security threat, on the other hand, is implemented by a technically skilled person who is trying to gain access to your network. This hacker creates or uses some very sophisticated tools to break into your network or to disrupt the services running in your network. A good example of a structured attack is a distributed ICMP flood. A person with very little hacking skill probably would send a flood of pings from the same source machine, making it fairly easy to track down the culprit. A sophisticated hacker, on the other hand, will try to hide the source of the ICMP packets by changing the source address inside the packets (called spoofing), as well as executing the attack from several different sources. Tracking down the culprit of this kind of attack takes a lot of work and patience.

Figure 1-2 shows a simple example of a sophisticated spoofing attack. In this example, the hacker changes the source address in ICMP packets to those of Server C, which is the device that the hacker is attacking. He sends these packets to both Server A and Server B.

These servers respond to the ICMP messages to the destination listed as the source in the packets, Server C. In this example, with the hacker flooding packets to both Server A and Server B, which, in turn, hit Server C twice as hard, it becomes more difficult, from Server C's perspective, to figure out who the real culprit of the attack is: the hacker.

Figure 1-2 *Sophisticated Spoofing Attack*

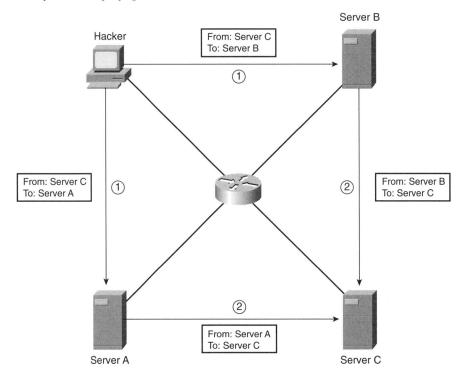

NOTE Even though you might be able to determine both the source (external versus internal) and the type of attack (structured versus unstructured), you should take each event seriously.

Categories of Threats

Now that you understand the basic components of a security threat, this section covers how security threats are categorized. When talking about a specific type of a security threat, it typically is categorized by using one of the following terms:

- Reconnaissance attacks
- Access attacks
- Denial of service (DoS) attacks

The following sections cover these three categories more thoroughly, including some specific attacks that fall under these categories and solutions that can be used to deal with these threats.

Reconnaissance Attacks

In a reconnaissance attack, a hacker tries to gain information about your network, including its topology, the devices that reside inside it, the software running on them, and the configuration that has been applied to these devices. The hacker then uses this information to execute further attacks, such as DoS or access attacks. Reconnaissance attacks come in different types, including the following:

- Scanning
- Eavesdropping

The following sections cover the basics of these types of reconnaissance attacks.

Scanning Attacks

The most common type of reconnaissance attack is a scanning attack. A *network scanning* attack occurs when a hacker probes the machines in your network. He might do this by sending an ICMP ping to every IP address in your network, or he might use a network ping, in which he pings the IP address of the directed broadcast of every network. As an example, if you have a network of 200.200.200.0/24, the hacker would ping 200.200.200.255. There are other ways to scan networking devices, but these two methods are the most popular.

Of course, a network scan tells the hacker only that there are machines in your network with a configured IP address; it does not tell what services are running on these machines. To find out what services are running on a machine, a hacker uses a port-scanning utility. A *port-scanning* utility probes the port numbers of a machine to detect whether a service is running. Using this approach, a hacker can determine whether the machine is running SMTP, Telnet, FTP, WWW, or other services. The hacker then can use this to plan further attacks against your device.

TIP   Many scanning tools are available—freeware, shareware, and commercial. One of my favorites, GFI's LANguard Network Security Scanner, is a feature-rich network-scanner tool. It comes with a 30-day trial, after which certain features are disabled unless you purchase the full version. It can be downloaded from http://www.gfi.com/. I use this tool a lot when examining networks to see what services are running, which is helpful in determining whether devices are exposed. I also use a product called Nessus, available at http://www.nessus.org/, and Cisco Scanner (formerly known as NetSonar), available at http://www.cisco.com/univercd/cc/td/doc/pcat/nssq.htm.

The most common method of stopping networking and port-scanning attacks is to use filtering devices. This can be something as simple as using Cisco routers with access control lists or a sophisticated firewall. These concepts are discussed in much more depth in Chapter 2.

Of course, you always should play it safe and disable all services that are not necessary on all of your resources. For instance, if you have a web server, you should disable services such as Telnet, SMTP, finger, and FTP on it. You want to make it as hard as possible for any hacker to get even the smallest of footholds in your network. Performing these tasks on a Cisco router is discussed in Chapter 4.

Eavesdropping Attacks

Another form of reconnaissance attack is eavesdropping. *Eavesdropping* is the process of examining packets as they are in transit between a source and destination device. A hacker typically uses a protocol-analyzer tool to perform eavesdropping. Figure 1-3 shows how eavesdropping works. In step 1 of this example, the hacker is examining traffic between the user and the server. The hacker notices that the user is establishing a Telnet connection and authenticates with a username and password. Because Telnet passes this information in clear text, the hacker now knows how to log into the Telnet server, spoofing the identity of the user. In step 2, the hacker uses this information to log into the Telnet server.

Figure 1-3 *Eavesdropping Attack*

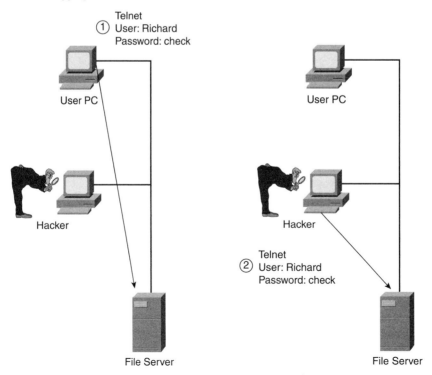

The protocol analyzer used for eavesdropping, sometimes referred to as a *packet sniffer*, might be a sophisticated hardware-based protocol analyzer, such as the Network Associates Sniffer products, or it might be a software-based application running on a PC (Network Associates also sells a software-based Sniffer version). For software applications, the hacker needs a promiscuous network interface card (NIC); this is a NIC that processes all frames, not just frames with a destination MAC address that matches the one on the NIC. Many commercial, shareware, and freeware protocol-analyzer products are available.

To execute this attack, the hacker typically must be connected physically to the network somewhere between the source and the destination, and must see the actual packets. Another approach that a hacker more typically uses is to compromise a PC in the network and download a packet-sniffing program to it. When eavesdropping, the hacker looks for account names and passwords, such as these:

- Microsoft Windows login
- Novell Netware login
- Telnet login
- FTP login
- HTTP login

Hackers also use eavesdropping to examine other information, perhaps database or financial transactions.

To prevent eavesdropping, your best solution is to use some form of encryption on your packets. VPNs, which are discussed in Part VIII, "Virtual Private Networks," allow you to use Data Encryption Standard (DES), 3DES, and AES encryption algorithms to protect your data. For terminal access, you should use a Secure Shell (SSH) program, which is an encrypted form of Telnet. For web access, you should use HTTP with Secure Socket Layer (HTTPS), which uses Secure Socket Layer (SSL) encryption.

You always should encrypt the following types of information:

- Passwords (and sometimes usernames)
- Personal information, such as telephone numbers, medical information, driver's license numbers, and social security numbers
- Credit card information
- Financial transactions
- Company trade secrets and sensitive information

Two basic methods of implementing encryption exist:

- **Link encryption**—The entire frame (Ethernet, token ring, Frame Relay, HDLC, and so on) is encrypted. This method of encryption can be used only on point-to-point connections in which both sides are configured for encryption.

- **Packet encryption**—Only the packet contents, such as the TCP or UDP segments in an IP packet (the payload), are encrypted; the addressing information (IP addresses in the IP header) is not. This method of encryption is used on connections that traverse multiple hops, such as internal networks, public networks, and the Internet.

NOTE   Because encryption is very process intensive, it typically is used for external connections; in other words, it typically is not used inside your network. For internal security, you might want to include in your security policy a statement that prohibits eavesdropping, with severe penalties applied. However, for sensitive information, encryption should be used to protect it. Obviously, certain network administrators should be allowed to perform eavesdropping in certain situations, such as troubleshooting connectivity issues. Any other type of eavesdropping by anybody else (other employees), however, should not be tolerated and should be dealt with immediately.

Another solution is to employ a switched infrastructure, giving every device its own switch port connection. Using this design, even if a hacker has compromised one of the PCs in your network and loads a packet-sniffing tool onto the PC, the hacker will be able to see only traffic directed at the compromised PC or multicast or broadcast traffic. However, one concern to consider is the security of the switches themselves. If the hacker can compromise both a PC and the switch connected to the PC, the hacker can set up port mirroring, to have the switch mirror traffic from other ports to the port of the compromised PC. Cisco calls this mirroring process SPAN, short for switched port analyzer.

Access Attacks

Another common type of attack is an access attack. In an access attack, a hacker attempts to gain unauthorized or illegal access to your network and its resources, particularly resources such as file, e-mail, and web servers. He typically does this by trying to access password files, using password-cracking programs, or examining traffic on your network for packets that contain clear-text passwords (eavesdropping attack). Other types of attacks include exploiting weaknesses in operating systems and applications, such as buffer overflows, that can allow a hacker access without first authenticating.

After a hacker has broken into one of your networking devices, he usually tries to raise his privilege level to the highest possible degree and then uses this account to break into other networking devices. He also might modify files on your resources or, in the worst possible scenario, erase everything on the disk drive and laugh as he tells his story to his friends. The following sections cover the basics of these types of access attacks.

Unauthorized Access Attack

In the most basic form of an access attack, a hacker tries to gain illegal access to equipment in your network. This is called an *unauthorized access* attack. To accomplish this kind of attack, a hacker can use many tools, including the following:

- Guessing passwords for well-known accounts, such as root and Administrator
- Using a protocol analyzer and executing an eavesdropping attack to examine clear-text passwords in packets
- Accessing a password file and using a password-cracking program on it
- Using social engineering

The last item, social engineering, is probably the hacker's easiest method of gaining unauthorized access to resources in your network. With social engineering, a hacker calls various users in your network, pretending to be a network administrator. The hacker tells the user about some fictional network security problem and, using guile and ingenuity, gathers information from the user that the hacker then can use to access resources on your network. This can go the other way, too; the hacker can pretend to be a user and can call a network administrator, acting as if he has forgotten his password.

The solution that you implement to restrict unauthorized access attacks depends on the method the hacker is using to gain unauthorized access. For instance, if the hacker is trying to gain illegal access to your network through your network's remote access (dialup) server, you probably would want to implement the following solutions:

- Use the Challenge Handshake Authentication Protocol (CHAP) with PPP (Point-to-Point Protocol), where the password is not sent across the wire, is tied to a specific user, and is verified by a security server
- Use double authentication. Cisco IOS routers have two features: Lock-and-key access control lists (ACLs) and authentication proxy. Lock-and-key works hand-in-hand with PPP's CHAP. The user is authenticated first through CHAP and then through lock-and-key. However, lock-and-key also works over nondialup links. Lock-and-key is discussed in Chapter 13, "Lock-and-Key Access Lists." Authentication proxy (AP) is the preferred method of authenticating users and is discussed in Chapter 14, "Authentication Proxy." It also has the capability to authenticate users before allowing them access to network resources. As you will see in Chapter 14, Cisco recommends using AP over lock-and-key because it is more flexible, supporting Telnet, FTP, HTTP, and HTTPS for authentication.

For application security, if your applications support additional security mechanisms, you definitely should implement them. For some applications, you might consider replacing them. For instance, the standard Telnet application uses clear-text passwords when performing authentication. You might want to consider replacing your standard Telnet application with a secure one that encrypts the password before sending it across the network, such as SSH. You also should disable all unnecessary services and consider using a host-based firewall. Host-based firewalls are discussed in more depth in Chapter 2.

Centralizing Authentication Functions

I once worked with a client that had to manage more than 1000 Cisco routers. This client was using the standard user EXEC and privileged EXEC passwords on these devices for authentication. When the company hired contractors, it hired them only to perform monitoring functions on the network: They never performed configuration tasks. This was because every week a new contractor was hired and an old contractor's time was up, and the old contractor moved on to the next job. The networking department did not want to have to change all of the privileged EXEC passwords on the routers every time a contractor left the company. Therefore, the solution was simple: Give only permanent employees the privileged EXEC password for the routers.

One of the biggest problems that you will face is the management of your security solution. A much better and more manageable solution than the one discussed in the previous sidebar is to use a centralized security server; Cisco has one called Cisco Secure ACS. You configure all of your user accounts and security policies on this server, and you have your routers and other networking devices use this security server to perform authentication functions. By centralizing the authentication process, you have more control over who is accessing your devices and what they are doing on them, making it easier to determine whether unauthorized access attacks are occurring. Centralizing authentication functions is discussed in Chapter 5.

One often-neglected prevention method, but one that is easy to implement, is user training. By training users not to write their passwords on their desk, to use passwords that do not have common words and that have a mixture of letters and numbers, and to be careful about what they say to people over the telephone or in person, you make your security job easier.

Data-Manipulation Attack

Data manipulation is simply the process of a hacker changing information. These changes could be something as simple as modifying file contents on a file server or something as sophisticated as changing packet contents as they are in transit from a source to a destination machine.

A common attack that hackers employ is to break into your web server and change the content (web pages). This form of attack is called *graffiti*. This type of attack has happened to many organizations, typically government resources; a hacker breaks into a web server and replaces the web content with pornography or "interesting" political content. To execute this kind of attack, a hacker typically first performs a reconnaissance attack, such as eavesdropping, to discover user accounts and passwords, and then executes an unauthorized access attack. A more ingenious hacker might use Java or ActiveX scripts either to learn information about a client's device or to break into it. Likewise, a hacker might try to take advantage of known vulnerabilities in a web server application or operating system.

The best method of preventing data-manipulation attacks is to implement a centralized and robust authentication and authorization system, such as Cisco Secure ACS, which is discussed briefly in the previous section. With this solution, you can restrict what users can access, restrict what they can do on the service that they access, and record the event for security purposes.

For file servers, tools are available to take a snapshot of your files, and the snapshot then is stored in a secured location. You periodically should compare the critical files on your server to the snapshot that you took previously. If there is a difference between the two, you might be a victim of a data-manipulation attack. One of the most common security tools that performs this function is Tripwire, which can be accessed from http://www.tripwire.com/.

To prevent Java and ActiveX attacks on your users, and possibly your web servers, you should use a filtering solution that can filter Java and ActiveX scripts that are embedded in HTML pages. Many solutions are available, including the use of Cisco IOS routers and the PIX firewall. If you are concerned about the actual content that users access or what Internet sites that they can view, you might want to put in place a web filtering solution, such as WebSense or N2H2. Many sites have inappropriate material for business purposes, as well as hacking and cracking tools. Cisco IOS routers and the PIX firewall can work hand in hand with WebSense and N2H2. Both of these products enable you to enter policy information about what URLs a user can or cannot access. When the Cisco IOS router or PIX sees a web access request from a user, it first verifies it with the policy server before permitting it. Filtering of Java and ActiveX scripts, as well as URL filtering, is discussed in Chapter 10, "Filtering Web and Application Traffic."

To prevent a hacker from using known vulnerabilities to access your system, you should make sure that your applications and operating systems have the latest security patches applied. Microsoft Windows products simplify this process with the Windows Update tool, which automates the process.

Session Attacks

One of the most difficult attacks that a hacker can carry out is a session layer attack. In a session attack, a hacker attacks a session layer connection, hoping either to use this information to mount another attack, or, through subterfuge, to take over the session in which he pretends to be either the source or the destination device. Four general categories of session attacks exist:

- Masquerading
- Session replay
- Session hijacking
- Repudiation

The following sections cover these session attacks in more depth.

Masquerading Attack

Masquerading is an attack method that a hacker uses to hide his identity. He pretends to be a different machine by changing his source address in his IP packets. An example of this attack is discussed earlier in the chapter in the "Unstructured and Structured Threats" section and in Figure 1-2.

In TCP/IP, this form of an attack is called *IP spoofing*. To carry out an IP spoofing attack, a hacker typically uses a software program that changes the source address of packets (and even the TCP sequence numbers for TCP segments). Many programs are available on the Internet to perform this process, including Hping (http://www.hping.org/) and Nemesis (http://www.packetfactory.net/Projects/nemesis/), as well as others. In some instances, the hacker can do this at the operating system level in certain versions of Linux.

A hacker typically implements a reconnaissance attack that involves the use of a port scanner to discover open ports, and possibly even an eavesdropping attack, using a protocol analyzer, to see the actual traffic flow, including usernames and passwords. Sophisticated hackers use a source IP address that resides inside your network to execute a masquerading attack. They combine this with a routing attack so that the packets sent to a destination are returned not to the source inside your network, but to the hacker himself. This requires excellent technology skills on the hacker's part.

NOTE Most DoS attacks use IP spoofing, which makes tracking down the hacker difficult. I discuss this issue in more depth in Chapter 17, "DoS Protection."

Session-Replay Attacks

When a hacker executes a session-replay attack, he captures (actually, eavesdrops on) packets from a real session data transfer between two devices with a protocol analyzer. Then he uses this information to execute an attack on the source device, the destination, or both, at a later time. Sometimes a hacker downloads Java or ActiveX scripts to clients that capture web transactions—possibly even online order information such as credit card numbers—and then uses this for his own purposes. Another favorite method of hackers is to use cookies to masquerade as a site, and then to get the client device to believe that the hacker's computer is the real web destination.

Session-Hijacking Attacks

In a session-hijacking attack, a hacker attempts to take over an existing session between two computers. As an example, the hacker might cut the source device out of the picture and pretend to be the source, tricking the destination device into believing that the destination still is communicating with the original source. A sophisticated hacker even might be able to insert himself into the middle of the session, pretending to be the source to the real destination, and pretending to be the destination to the real source device.

A session-hijacking attack typically involves a handful of other attacks, such as masquerading, eavesdropping, and data manipulation. You might think that executing this type of attack would be very complicated; however, some protocols, such as TCP, are fairly predictable, especially in their use of sequence numbers for TCP segments. With a good hacking software program, a skilled hacker can insert himself into the middle of an existing connection. The top part of Figure 1-4 shows what a session looks like from the perspective of the source and destination that have been hijacked. The bottom of Figure 1-4 shows the actual data path of a hijacked session.

Figure 1-4   *Session-Hijacking Attack*

One of the easiest attacks that hackers like to employ involves masquerading and session hijacking. Almost all TCP/IP services use the Domain Name System (DNS) to resolve names to IP addresses. A skilled hacker can intercept DNS replies from servers and replace the IP addresses for the requested names with addresses of machines that the hacker controls, thus providing an easy method for ongoing session attacks.

Repudiation Attacks

Repudiation is a process in which you cannot prove that a transaction took place between two entities. The goal of the hacker is to perform repudiation when executing session layer attacks. Nonrepudiation, on the other hand, is having absolute proof of the identities of the parties in a transaction that has taken place. As an example, certain types of transactions need a nonrepudiation process. For instance, signing electronic documents, transferring money electronically, and buying a product online with your credit card all must have a nonrepudiation process, or else they cannot be legally binding.

Hackers typically use a repudiation attack when users are accessing web information. Hackers like to use Java or ActiveX scripts, port-scanning utilities, masquerading, and eavesdropping to carry out their repudiation attack. Perhaps one of the simplest forms of repudiation attacks is to use public e-mail systems such as hotmail.com, yahoo.com, and others to generate garbage mail and execute a DoS attack against a company's e-mail server. Getting a free e-mail account from these systems is usually a simple process, with little identity proof required. This makes it easy for a hacker to get an e-mail account and hide his activities behind a cloud of anonymity.

Two common issues with e-mail are spamming and e-mail bombs. Spamming is the process by which you receive unsolicited e-mail. This is perhaps one of the biggest complaints of anyone who has an Internet e-mail account; I am constantly getting spam e-mails. Another security problem is an e-mail bomb, an e-mail that contains code that is executed either automatically upon receipt or when a user clicks something, like a hyperlink or an attachment. The most common form of an e-mail bomb is a virus or worm. My Internet provider constantly scans for these types of e-mails, as does the antivirus software that I run on my PC.

Preventing Session Attacks

You can use many solutions to prevent session layer attacks against your user and service connections:

- Using VPNs
- Using SSL for web browser connections
- Authenticating with digital signatures
- Filtering Java and ActiveX scripts
- Blocking e-mail from public e-mail sites

Probably the most important is using a Virtual Private Network (VPN) to encrypt information going across the connection. With a VPN, a hacker cannot see the actual data that is being transferred between the source and destination devices. Part VIII covers an overview of VPNs using IPSec and discusses how to configure IPSec connections on a Cisco IOS router. Secure Sockets Layer (SSL) provides security in web transactions. The main difference between IPSec and SSL is that IPSec can protect any type of IP traffic, whereas SSL can protect only web application traffic.

Another popular method used for providing identity verification is to use digital signatures. A digital signature is similar to a written signature, a person's thumbprint, a retinal scan of a person's eye, or a DNA profile of a person. In other words, it is used to uniquely identify the user. In the online world, a special third-party device called a *Certificate Authority* (CA) is used to handle the repository of identities. A CA performs a similar function to what a notary does in real life: It handles and validates identities of individuals. For instance, if you wanted to set up a connection to a remote site, but you wanted some kind of proof of the remote site's identity, your networking device could get the digital signature of the remote site from the CA and then request the remote site's own digital signature. Your networking device then would compare the two signatures. If they matched, you would know that you were dealing with the correct device; if they did not match, you would know that a session attack is occurring.

Another tool that you should consider using is a router or firewall that can filter Java and ActiveX scripts from untrusted sites. By filtering these scripts and applets, you are reducing the likelihood of a hacker performing a session layer attack. To make your life easier, your networking devices always should have logging enabled, and they should transfer this logging information to a central repository where you can keep an audit trail of important connections and transaction.

CAUTION Be very careful if you decide to filter Java and ActiveX. Many, if not most, web sites take advantage of this technology to provide enhanced web features. Therefore, I recommend filtering these scripts only from networks in which known security threats exist.

To prevent spamming and e-mail bombs, as well as to reduce the likelihood of a hacker using a public e-mail site to execute a repudiation attack, you should block all e-mail access from public e-mail sites. This might mean that some legitimate people might not be able to send you e-mail any longer, but, on the other hand, you are greatly reducing the likelihood of exposure to reconnaissance, DoS, and repudiation attacks against your e-mail system. Many commercial products on the market help deal with spamming. The next section discusses some other solutions to e-mail bombs.

TIP I use a program called MailWasher that scans my e-mail before downloading it. It is excellent for detecting spam messages and bouncing these back to the sender. Information about this excellent freeware product can be found at http://www.mailwasher.net/. However, this tool is for end-user use only; you also should have a good server tool to detect and remove SPAM.

Virus, Trojan Horse, and Worm Attacks

Viruses, worms, and Trojan horses are probably the most well-known attacks on computer systems because these are the most publicized, as well as the most likely to affect the general user public. Many different views actually exist regarding the definition of these three types of attacks. Generally, a virus is a program or a piece of code that is loaded onto and run on your computer without your knowledge. Many viruses also replicate themselves to spread their damage. Unlike bugs, viruses are manmade. A worm is a program that replicates itself over a network with some malicious intent in mind, such as crashing a system or using up all the resources on the system. Many people view viruses and worms as the same type of attack. A Trojan horse is a program loaded onto your computer that acts as a benign application, waiting for the user to activate it through normal computer and application activity. Unlike viruses and worms, Trojan horses do not replicate themselves. Sometimes Trojan horses pretend to be your antivirus software or replace it, hoping to add instead of remove viruses from your system.

These kinds of attacks might be something as simple as an e-mail attachment that you click or something as sophisticated as a software program that is executed because of a security problem with your e-mail program.

Typically, most of these attacks are exploited through the e-mail system, although there are other methods, such as executing an infected program. When executed as a reconnaissance attack, these attacks can send your e-mail's address book or your password file back to the hacker. When executed as a DoS attack, these attacks can affect the CPU cycles, memory, disk space, or bandwidth of a networking device, such as a PC.

You can employ three different methods in combating these kinds of attacks:

- User training
- Antivirus software
- Application-verification software

One of the best defenses is to train your user population. For instance, you should warn your users never to open e-mails or attachments from individuals whom they do not know. Any suspicious e-mail should be reported immediately to a network administrator.

Of course, one of the most popular methods of dealing with these kinds of attacks is to deploy antivirus software. Many packages are available on the market, with the most popular being antivirus software packages from Network Associates and Norton (I use Norton on my PC). When deploying these in an enterprise network, you need to make absolutely sure that all of your desktops and servers have the most recent data files that contain the list of known viruses. You definitely will want to explore some type of automation process, in which a client's software is updated periodically (all commercial antivirus packages that I have dealt with support automatic updates of virus information on clients and servers).

Another typical solution for file servers is to use application verification software. This type of software takes a snapshot of existing files and keeps it in a secure place (usually on a separate, secure device). You typically include files such as executables, batch scripts, and configuration files in this snapshot. You then run a periodic analysis with the application-verification software, comparing the current files on the server with the secured ones. If there is a difference, the application alerts you to this. A difference might indicate that an access attack has taken place, possibly with a worm or Trojan horse attack, and that one of your files has been replaced with a hacker's file.

NOTE   To see an encyclopedia of viruses, worms, and Trojan horses, visit Symantec's site at http://securityresponse.symantec.com/avcenter/vinfodb.html.

Denial of Service Attacks

Besides reconnaissance attacks, the second most common form of security threat and attack is the DoS attack. With a DoS attack, a hacker attempts to deny legitimate traffic and user access to a particular resource, or, at the very least, reduce the quality of service for a resource. Many kinds of DoS attacks exist; the simplest to implement is a flood attack, in which the hacker overwhelms a device or network with a flood of ICMP packets. The next two sections cover some common DoS attacks, as well as methods used to prevent these kinds of attacks.

Types of DoS Attacks

Hackers can use many types of DoS attacks against your network. Some of these affect the performance of a particular service running on a server, and some drastically can affect the performance of all the machines on a particular network segment. Because there are literally hundreds of DoS attacks, the following list is limited to some of the most common ones:

- An *application attack* is simply an attack against an application running on a server. Hackers typically attack such popular applications as Microsoft's IIS web server, web browsers such as Microsoft Internet Explorer and Netscape Navigator, and e-mail applications such as Sendmail and Microsoft Exchange and Outlook because of their widespread use. Hackers try various methods, such as buffer overruns and e-mail bombs, to disable a system or to send information back to the hacker to be used for other types of attacks.

- An *e-mail bomb* is a form of an attack that a hacker uses to tie up e-mail resources on your system or possibly even compromise the security of your e-mail server. An unsophisticated hacker typically sends large messages to your e-mail server, hoping to fill up the disk space and crash it. A sophisticated hacker, on the other hand, includes Trojan horses, viruses, or worms that either are embedded in the e-mail or are included as an attachment. If a user activates these, they can cause damage to your system or open a security hole that will allow a hacker into the networking device.

- *CPU hogging* is a type of attack that affects the CPU cycles of a service. This is a general category of a DoS attack in which more specific attacks, such as packet fragmentation or chargen, are used.

- *Chargen* is a character generator that produces serialized character output. Typically, chargen uses UDP, but it can be implemented with TCP. Chargen runs on port 19 and usually is enabled on most operating systems. Hackers sometimes send garbage data to this port, hoping that your resource will process this information and thus take away CPU cycles from other legitimate processes on the resource.

- A *packet fragmentation and reassembly attack* is an ingenious attack in which a hacker sends hundreds of fragments to a destination service, hoping that the destination device will perceive these as valid connections and thus waste both buffer space and CPU cycles to process them. A good hacker makes this flood of fragments appear as a set of legitimate connections, which can cause a buffer overrun on the destination and possibly crash the machine. Even if the machine does not crash, the hacker is tying up buffer space, which prevents legitimate traffic from being processed.

- *Land.c* is a program that sends TCP segments to a destination where both the source address and destination are the same in the packet. Upon receiving the packet, the destination tries to forward the packet to itself. To make it even more confusing for the destination device, the packet might contain the same port number for both the source and the destination. In some instances, this can cause the device to try repeatedly to establish connections to itself, tying up resources.

- Hackers sometimes use Java or ActiveX scripts to create malicious applets. When downloaded to user's desktop, these applets sometimes can damage the user's file system or send information back to the hacker that he then can use to attempt further attacks.

- A *ping of death* attack is one of my favorite attacks because of its simplistic beauty. A hacker sends a single ICMP message with an offset field indicating that the data is larger than 65,535 bytes. On some systems, this crashes the device. When this bug was discovered, for a period of two or three days, many companies were disconnecting their connection to the Internet to prevent hackers and curious people from bringing down their resources.

- One of the most difficult attacks to implement is an attack on your router's routing protocols, called a *rerouting attack*. In this type of attack, a hacker tries to feed your routers with either bad routing information that will cause your packets to be routed to a dead end, or misinformation that will cause your packets to be routed back to the hacker so that he can perform eavesdropping and use this information to execute another attack. Typically, a hacker uses a protocol analyzer and special software to implement this type of attack.

- *TCP SYN flood attacks* occur when a hacker floods a particular service with TCP SYN segments without any intent of completing the connection. With this kind of attack, the hacker basically is tying up the connection resources on a particular server.

- *Smurf attacks* occur when a hacker sends ICMP traffic to a destination (a directed broadcast address) but replaces its own source IP address in the packet header with the IP address of the device that it wants to attack. When the ICMP traffic reaches the destination network, the devices respond to the spoofed source address, which is the device that the hacker wants to flood.

- *WinNuke* is a program that was developed to take advantage of a bug in certain versions of Microsoft operating systems, including 95, 98, Me, XP, NT, and 2000. The hacker sends out-of-band information to port 139, hoping to bring down the server.

An enhanced form of DoS attacks are Distributed DoS (DDoS) attacks. With a DDoS attack, a hacker subverts or controls multiple sources and uses these sources to attack one or more destinations. Tracing the culprit in these kinds of attacks can be difficult, especially if the hacker is using many different ISPs as the source of the attack. For more information on common DDoS attacks and tools, visit Dave Dittrich's site at http://staff.washington.edu/dittrich/misc/ddos/.

DoS Attack-Prevention Methods

Just as hackers use many DoS attacks to hamper your network's performance, you can use many solutions to prevent or at least hinder a hacker's DoS attack. The following are common solutions used to detect and prevent DoS attacks:

- Performing packet filtering
- Using an intrusion-detection system (IDS)
- Using routing protocols with authentication
- Running detailed audits and logs

The first solution that you should implement is filtering. You can use something as simple as ACLs on a Cisco router, or you can use a firewall system such as the PIX or the Cisco IOS Firewall feature set available on Cisco routers. The Cisco IOS Firewall feature set supports a feature called Context-based Access Control (CBAC), which implements a firewall system on a router. To protect yourself from malicious applets, you should use a firewall system, such as the Cisco IOS router or PIX, to filter Java and ActiveX scripts and applets. CBAC is discussed in Chapter 9, "Context-Based Access Control."

You also should consider using an IDS. An IDS solution examines traffic and, based on its contents, classifies the traffic as either an attack or not an attack. One large advantage of using an IDS is that these can detect reconnaissance attacks and probes, alerting you to the fact that possible hacking problems are looming. More sophisticated IDS solutions even can interact with your network equipment, such as routers and firewalls, and automatically configure them to filter the offending traffic when it is detected. Cisco has a range of IDS solutions, which enable you to implement a feature called IP blocking or shunning. With IP blocking, when a Cisco IDS detects an attack, it can log into a Cisco PIX or router and add a temporary filtering rule to block the attack. IDS and IP blocking are discussed in Chapter 16, "Intrusion-Detection System."

To prevent routing attacks, you can use a routing protocol that has built-in authentication, such as RIPv2, EIGRP, OSPF, IS-IS, or BGP. These use the MD5 hashing algorithm, which creates a unique digital signature that is added to all routing information. The MD5 hashing algorithm, which also is used by PPP's CHAP and by IPSec's AH and ESP, is discussed in Chapter 19, "IPSec Site-to-Site Connections." You also might want to configure filters to allow routing update traffic from only certain routing sources; however, if the hacker is smart about this process, he typically changes the source address to match an address that is specified in your allowed list. If your router is located at the perimeter of your network, you might want to consider using static routes instead of using a dynamic routing protocol. Routing protocol protection is discussed in Chapter 15, "Routing Protocol Protection."

At the very least, your networking equipment should keep extensive audits and logs to keep track of security issues. You should peruse these periodically, looking for DoS attacks. Or, if you are smart, you will use a system that parses the logs and does all of this work for you. Logging is discussed in Chapter 18, "Logging Events."

NOTE   For more information on DoS attacks, visit http://www.infosyssec.com/infosyssec/secdos1.htm.

Security Solutions

It is beyond the scope of this book to cover every type of security solution that is available on the market. This section covers some basic solutions that you should be aware of, as well as a security checklist to help strengthen your company's network security. The rest of this book focuses on the Cisco IOS routers for firewalls in implementing security in your network.

Designing a Security Solution

As you have seen throughout this chapter, a hacker can cause damage to your network in many ways (and this chapter barely skims the surface on the different kinds of attacks that your network will face). Therefore, you need to design a solid security solution to deal with these threats. This solution also should be easy to maintain and should be flexible enough to handle changes in your network. Here is a simple checklist that should describe your security solution:

- **It should be easy to use and implement**—It also should be easy to monitor and maintain. If a security solution is complex, with a lot of configuration tasks to perform and management systems to monitor, you might be making your security worse. Misconfigurations easily can create security holes, and if you have too many management platforms to monitor, the administrators might miss key events or might become lax in their monitoring duties.

- **It should enable your company to develop and deploy new applications in your network**—In other words, you should not have to change your security system completely to accommodate new applications. Remember that your security solution should meet the outline created in your security policy, and your security policy should allow your company to meet the goals that were developed in its business plan.

- **It should enable your company to use the Internet in a secure manner**—The company should feel secure that its key resources are protected and that the Internet can be used to further the company's business goals.

NOTE   Chapter 2 goes into more depth on developing a security solution, particularly the roles that firewalls play in protecting your network and different design philosophies in the use of firewalls.

The Cisco Security Wheel

As you quickly will learn, network security is not a one-time implementation. You do not implement your security solution and walk away from it. Instead, network security is a continuous process that is built around your company's security policy. Cisco developed a concept called the *security wheel* that outlines a four-step process that is repeated continuously. Here are the four steps in the security wheel, shown in Figure 1-5:

1 Secure your network.

2 Monitor your network's security.

3 Test your network's security.

4 Improve your network's security, based on your monitoring and testing results in Steps 2 and 3.

Figure 1-5   *Cisco Security Wheel*

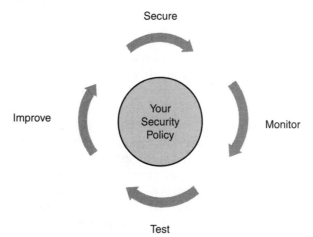

The next four sections cover these four steps in more depth.

Secure Your Network

In the first step, you should do what is necessary to secure your network. This includes many of the prevention methods that I mentioned in this chapter, but it also includes physical security (locking up key components and removing the likelihood that users or strangers physically can get their hands on key resources in your network). Some of the solutions that you might consider implementing are authenticating through the use of one-time passwords, smart cards, and authentication servers; using firewalls to filter traffic; using VPNs to encrypt your traffic; and keeping up-to-date on security holes in your equipment and ensuring that they have the latest security patches applied. Chapter 2 goes into the design philosophy in a lot more depth.

Monitor Your Security

When you have put your security solution in place, your next step is to monitor your network to ensure that no security breaches take place. One very common tool that many companies use is an IDS. These devices enable you to monitor traffic and look for attacks, alerting you through a management station, e-mail, or a pager for a quick response. A security solution is no good if you do not monitor it.

Importance of Monitoring

As an example of the importance of monitoring, I was hired by a company to redesign its network, and one of the components of the design included the existing Internet connection. In the current network, the company had contracted with its ISP to handle all of the security functions. This basically consisted of a firewall sitting at the ISP's site that was responsible for basic filtering functions. Even though the company was trying to save money by taking this approach, I strongly warned of the kinds of problems this could create. About a month later, I was fooling around on the Internet back at my office when, out of curiosity, I tried to access a UNIX server sitting at this company's site. I was somewhat surprised when I got a Telnet prompt. I then proceeded to check what other resources were available to me. I was able to access every single resource in the company's network, including the IBM mainframe.

What made this situation worse is that this was a medical facility containing information about people and patients. I immediately notified the data center administrator, and he was absolutely furious with the ISP. Apparently, the ISP had made some changes in the network topology and moved the firewall, never testing whether the move impacted the security of the companies that it was supposed to protect. The CIO of this company learned a very valuable lesson that day: When it comes to security, do not trust other people to do it for you. Fortunately, no hackers noticed this major breach in security, and no harm came of it. As you can see, vigilance in your monitoring duties is extremely important.

Test Your Security

As the previous sidebar example points out, it is also important to follow the third step: Test your security periodically. The company in my example should have been at least attempting certain kinds of tests on the ISP's security periodically, not just to verify that its assets are protected, but also to ensure that the money that it is paying the ISP is being well spent. These tests should include reconnaissance attacks (network scanning and port probing), as well as checks on the security logs of networking devices.

Improve Your Security

The last step is to examine the results of your monitoring and testing events, and use this information either to make changes to your security system or to improve upon your security system. Likewise, you should use this information to make adjustments to your security policy.

After you have completed these four steps, your job is not over yet. Instead, you should go back to Step 1 and start over. You will repeat this process continually, adjusting your security policy and security solution to meet all existing and newly developing security threats.

Security Checklist

Internet Security Systems (ISS) has developed a similar concept to the Cisco security wheel. I have summarized it in the following security checklist:

- ☐ Create a well-defined security policy that is complementary to your company's business objectives.

- ☐ Create an easy-to-read security handbook that will be distributed to all of your employees, to help educate and train them in your company's security policies and procedures.

- ☐ Adequately protect your mission-critical resources and services.

- ☐ Develop a security plan of action that lays out what actions and responses your company will take if a security breach or problem occurs.

- ☐ Develop a disaster-recovery plan that deals with the worst-case situations for security breaches, such as if a hacker reformats the hard drives on all of your web servers, or if an arsonist torches your company's headquarters.

- ☐ Purchase damage insurance for the software and hardware that you own, in case an individual intentionally physically damages your company's computer and networking assets. You might even want to include insurance for lost data and downtime requirements to restore your system to its previous state.

☐ Train your networking employees so that they can implement and monitor your proposed security solution.

☐ Use an IDS to detect security attacks.

☐ Use a firewall system to filter *all* unnecessary traffic as it comes into your network.

☐ Use a VPN solution to protect data between sites and devices in a remote access network.

☐ Implement a corporate-wide antivirus solution that incorporates your PCs, laptops, and file servers.

☐ Disable all unnecessary services on your devices.

This is not meant to be a comprehensive checklist, but it contains some of the basic things that you should be doing and implementing in your network. More information about ISS and their products can be found at http://www.internetsecuritysystems.com/.

Additional Information

If you are a novice to security, you will soon find that you have a lot to learn about security, threats, and solutions. To help you with this process, I have included some links to additional information that you will find useful:

- For an overview of security, visit http://www.cisco.com/univercd/cc/td/doc/cisintwk/ ito_doc/security.htm.

- For information about CERT and published security threats, visit http://www.cert.org.

- For information concerning the security life cycle and checklist, visit this ISS document at http://documents.iss.net/whitepapers/securityCycle.pdf.

- For an overview of Cisco security products, visit either of these two URLs:

  — http://www.cisco.com/univercd/cc/td/doc/product/vpn/ciscosec/index.htm

  — http://www.cisco.com/en/US/netsol/index.html

- For an overview of Cisco security features, visit http://www.cisco.com/univercd/cc/ td/doc/product/iaabu/newsecf/index.htm.

- Other important security sites that I commonly use include these:

  — http://www.infosyssec.com/

  — http://www.securityfocus.com/

Summary

This chapter discussed some of the basics of security. Planning for security can be a complex process, but having a security policy simplifies it. A security policy is one of the most important tools that you will use to design and implement a security solution.

Causes of security problems include weaknesses in policy definitions, computer technologies, and equipment configurations. Security threats can come from internal as well as external sources and are either structured or unstructured. Most security threats originate inside your network.

Security threats are categorized as a reconnaissance, DoS, or access attack. In a reconnaissance attack, the hacker it trying to learn information about your network, including its weaknesses. The hacker then uses this information to implement a DoS or access attack.

Cisco has developed a four-step security wheel to help deal with the implementation and maintenance of a security solution. Security is a never-ending process, so you will be repeating the four steps quite often.

Next up is Chapter 2, which discusses what a firewall is, the types of firewalls, and how to design networks with firewalls.

## CHAPTER 2

Introduction to Firewalls

One of the main purposes of this book is to discuss how to secure your Cisco IOS router—more specifically, how to use your Cisco IOS router to protect your network from threats. Basically, this entails using your router as a firewall solution. As you will see in this chapter and throughout the rest of the book, the Cisco IOS supports many technologies and features that will enable you to do this.

Before I start discussing the many security features that Cisco routers support, as well as when and how to deploy them, it is important to give you a basic understanding of firewall technologies—what they are and how they can be used to protect your network. That will make it easier to determine how you will use your router to protect your network infrastructure.

The beginning of this chapter covers what a firewall is and what its purpose is. As you will see, there are many definitions and many types of firewalls; this makes it difficult to put an exact definition on them or to place them into a specific category. One of the first things I do is discuss what a firewall is and how it operates. I also discuss some general design guidelines on using firewall products to protect your network infrastructure.

These subjects are discussed in this chapter:

- Firewall overview
- Traffic control and the OSI reference model
- Firewall categories
- Firewall design
- Cisco IOS security

Firewall Overview

Firewall technologies have undergone substantial changes since their entry into the marketplace in the early 1990s. These first firewalls were simple packet-filtering devices. Since those days, firewalls have become much more sophisticated in their filtering features, adding such capabilities as stateful filtering, Virtual Private Networks (VPNs), intrusion-detection systems (IDS), multicast routing, connection authentication, Dynamic Host Configuration Protocol (DHCP) services, and many others. One of the driving forces of these enhancements, besides vendor competition, was the explosion of Internet usage in the mid- to late 1990s. This huge growth brought many beneficial services to individuals and companies, but it also brought its own set of problems, including hacking, break-ins, and other types of undesirable actions. Given these problems and the need to protect a company's assets, firewalls have become a common technology for not only enterprise companies, but also small businesses and personal computers that have Internet access.

As you will see in this chapter, many components make up a firewall solution; naturally, a firewall, or filtering device, is an important part of that solution. Normally, firewalls are seen as your first layer of defense when protecting company or personal assets. However, a complete firewall solution involves many components that are used to protect not only the perimeter of your network, but also your internal network infrastructure.

Definition of a Firewall

People use many descriptions when defining a firewall. Its first use had to do not with network security, but with controlling actual fires. A firewall is a method of constructing walls so that when a real fire breaks out, it can be contained easily within one part of a building instead of spreading to other parts.

Of course, when we talk about network security, the term *firewall* means something different, but the original essence is carried over: It is used to protect your network from malicious people and to stop their illicit actions at defined boundary points.

Basically, a firewall is a device or systems that control the flow of traffic between different areas of your network. Notice something important about this definition: The definition can include one or more devices. In simple, small network designs, such as a small office/home office (SOHO) environment, this typically is done with one device. For example, I use a wireless Linksys router at home to protect my home network. In an enterprise network, the firewall system includes many components, such as perimeter firewalls, stateful firewalls, VPNs, IDS solutions, and others.

Many people assume that firewalls are used to protect assets from external threats, such as those from the Internet, where the protocol used is TCP/IP. However, most malicious network threats and attacks occur, interestingly enough, within the interior of your network; in many instances, they come from a company's own employees. Many studies have found that between 60 and 70 percent of network attacks are internal, not external. On top of this, you might have more than one protocol running on your internal network, such as TCP/IP, IPX, AppleTalk, SNA, NetBIOS, and others. A comprehensive firewall solution must be capable of dealing not only with both internal and external threats, but also with multiple protocols.

Firewall Protection

Firewall systems can perform many functions and offer many solutions. However, one of its primary purposes is to control access to resources. You can use many methods to perform this task.

For instance, you could physically secure all of your servers and PCs by making sure that they all have the most up-to-date patches, have unnecessary services disabled, use a robust form of authentication and authorization for accessing and using resources, and have security software installed on them, as shown in Figure 2-1. In this example, firewall software is installed on each PC and file server, and is configured to allow only certain types of traffic to enter or leave the machine. This works well in a small office with only a handful of devices that need to be secured. In this example, the devices might need only file and print sharing, as well as Internet access, so setting up this security policy on each device is straightforward.

Figure 2-1   *Securing All Network Devices*

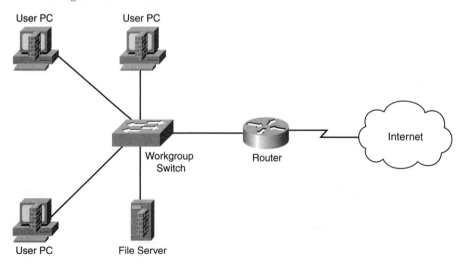

In a network with tens of thousands of devices, this becomes problematic: It would be very difficult to manage all of these devices to ensure that they were secured properly. Besides offering file and print sharing services, you might want to implement different levels of Internet access for different groups of users, you might need to protect certain internal resources based on a user's group membership, and you might allow only certain types of Internet traffic into your network.

A more scalable approach would be to centralize your security solution, as shown in Figure 2-2. I used the same example in Figure 2-1, but instead of using a firewall solution on each internal device, I placed it on the perimeter router. In this example, because the firewall solution is implemented in one device, it becomes much easier to manage security policies and their implementation. With a single device, it becomes easier to restrict traffic entering and leaving the network: You set up the policies only once instead of on all the internal devices. This also reduces the total cost of the solution.

Figure 2-2   *Securing All Network Devices*

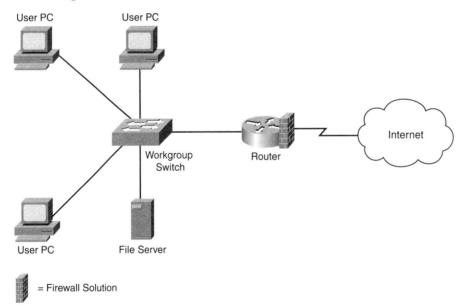

This is not to say that you must use just one of these two solutions. However, it does begin to make you think about design issues as well as the types of access that you need to address. You must balance security, functionality, and cost in your design. For example, you still need to be concerned about internal threats to internal resources, so some of your critical internal resources might implement a firewall solution. I discuss design issues in much more depth in the "Component Placement" section.

Controlling Traffic and the OSI Reference Model

Before I can begin discussing the various firewall categories and their functions, I need to cover some basics of firewall operations: how firewalls deal with traffic. A good place to start is to review the Open System Interconnection (OSI) reference model, developed by the International Organization for Standardization (ISO). The ISO is a standards body that defines standards for interoperability, including networking standards. Using the OSI reference model will help you understand how firewalls process traffic. Many different categories of firewall solutions exist; each functions differently. This is particularly true of firewalls that filter traffic.

OSI Reference Model Overview

The ISO developed the OSI reference model to describe how devices communicate with each other. This model was developed to help instruct people on the communication process, simplify troubleshooting tasks, break related components into a modular structure, and ease development and implementation tasks for vendors.

The OSI reference model breaks up the communication process into seven layers, shown in Figure 2-3. It defines the general process that takes place when a user sitting at a keyboard types in information, and how it is transported across the network and processed at a destination device.

Figure 2-3   *OSI Reference Model*

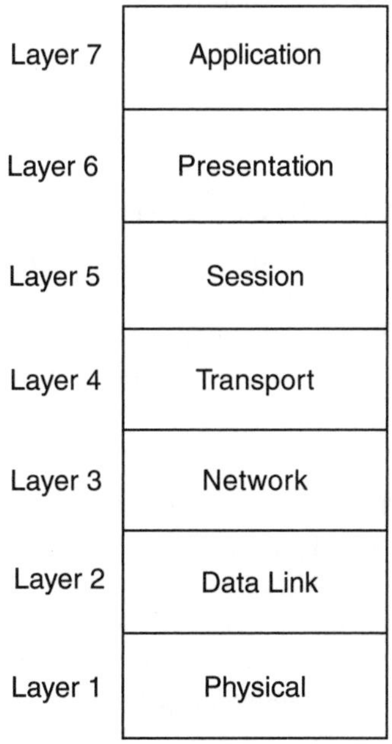

Layer 7	Application
Layer 6	Presentation
Layer 5	Session
Layer 4	Transport
Layer 3	Network
Layer 2	Data Link
Layer 1	Physical

Table 2-1 shows the seven layers and their descriptions. When talking about protocols and the OSI reference model, not all protocols used today have seven layers. The OSI reference model is just that: a model used generically to describe interactions between layers. For example, in TCP/IP, the application, presentation, and session layer functions are grouped into one generic layer, called the *application* layer. The transport, network, data link, and physical layers are used to handle the mechanics of the transmission of data between devices.

Table 2-1 *OSI Reference Model Description*

Layer	Name	Description
7	Application	Handles the command-line or graphical user interface (CLI or GUI) that an individual uses to interact with the device
6	Presentation	Identifies how data types, such as text, pictures, sound, and movies, are presented on an individual's monitor
5	Session	Sets up, monitors, and tears down network connections between devices
4	Transport	Provides a reliable or unreliable delivery mechanism for connections, as well as optional flow control
3	Network	Defines a logical topology for the network through the use of logical addressing schemes, such as IP and IPX
2	Data link	Defines how devices on a specific media type, such as Ethernet, communicate with each other, and hardware addresses, such as MAC addresses
1	Physical	Defines the physical characteristics and properties used to transmit data across a physical medium, such as copper, fiber, or air

Firewalls and the OSI Reference Model

As shown in Figure 2-4, a firewall system can operate at five of the seven layers of the OSI reference model. However, most firewall systems operate at only four layers: the data link, network, transport, and, possibly, application layers. Based on the simplicity or complexity of a firewall product or solution, the number of layers covered varies. For example, a standard IP access control list (ACL) on a Cisco router functions at OSI Layer 3, and an extended IP ACL functions at Layers 3 and 4.

The more layers that a firewall product or solution can cover, the more thorough and effective it can be in restricting access to and from devices. For example, a firewall that operates at only Layers 3 or 4 can filter only on IP protocol information, IP addresses, and TCP or UDP port numbers; it cannot filter on application information such as user authentication or commands that a user enters. Therefore, the more layers a firewall can process information from, the more granular it can be in its filtering process.

Figure 2-4   *Firewalls and the OSI Reference Model*

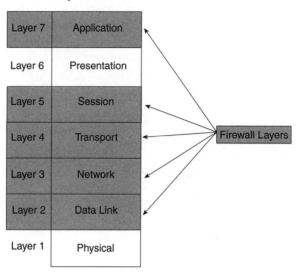

Firewall Categories

A firewall system can be composed of many different devices and components. One of those components is the filtering of traffic, which is what most people commonly call a firewall. Filtering firewalls come in many different flavors, including the following:

- Packet-filtering firewalls
- Stateful firewalls
- Application gateway firewalls
- Address-translation firewalls
- Host-based (server and personal) firewalls
- Hybrid firewalls

The following sections cover these different firewall categories, explaining how they function and describing the advantages and disadvantages each of them have.

Packet-Filtering Firewalls

The simplest form of a firewall is a packet-filtering firewall. A packet-filtering firewall is typically a router that has the capability to filter on some of the contents of packets. The information that the packet-filtering firewall can examine includes Layer 3 and sometimes Layer 4 information, as shown in Figure 2-5. For example, Cisco routers with standard ACLs can filter information at Layer 3, and Cisco routers with extended ACLs can filter information at both Layers 3 and 4.

Figure 2-5 *Packet Filtering Firewalls and the OSI Reference Model*

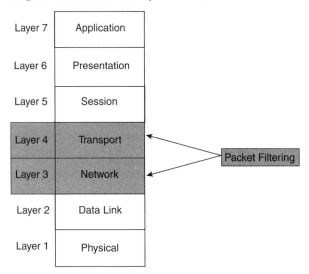

My First Firewall

The very first firewall product that I worked with, back in late 1993, was called the TIS Firewall Toolkit. From my recollection, it was the first commercial firewall product available. At that time, TIS was developing a UNIX-based version of the product, and the beta versions were available for free download to encourage use of the product and to help find and remove any bugs. This firewall could perform only simple packet filtering. It is a freely available source product, although TIS holds the rights to sell it as a commercial product.

Because TCP/IP is the de facto standard of communications protocols in today's networks, most packet-filtering firewalls support at least this protocol. However, packet-filtering firewalls can support other protocols as well, including IPX, AppleTalk, DECnet, and Layer 2 MAC address and bridging information. Cisco routers with standard and extended ACLs support many protocols, including the ones mentioned.

Filtering Actions

When implementing packet filtering, packet-filtering rules are defined on the firewall. These rules are used to match on packet contents to determine which traffic is allowed and which is denied. When denying traffic, two actions can be taken: notify the sender of traffic that its data was dropped or discard the data without any notification. This can be important when implementing a firewall solution. With the first option, the user knows that traffic was filtered by a firewall. If this is an internal user trying to access an internal resource, the user can call the administrator and discuss the problem. The administrator then can change the filtering rules to allow the user access if the user has the appropriate privileges. If the packet-filtering firewall did not send back a message, the user would have no idea why the connection could not be set up and would have to spend more time troubleshooting the problem.

On the other hand, if a hacker on the Internet is trying to access internal resources in your network, and the hacker gets back a message that the information is being filtered, this gives the hacker information about your network that might tell him how you are protecting it. In this situation, you might want to have your packet-filtering firewall silently drop the filtered traffic. As an example, you might have an internal web server running on port 80 of a device. You have a filtering rule that blocks port 80 traffic for most outside users except for your remote office locations. When a hacker tries to reach port 80 while doing a port scan, if your packet-filtering firewall sends back a message that port 80 is being filtered, the hacker now knows that you are using a filtering device to protect internal resources, and he will spend more time investigating the reaction to different kinds of packets that he tries to slip through the firewall.

Filtering Information

A packet-filtering firewall can filter on the following types of information:

- Source and destination Layer 3 address
- Layer 3 protocol information
- Layer 4 protocol information
- Interface of sent or received traffic

For example, a Cisco router can be used to filter on specific ICMP messages (Layer 3), or source and destination IP addresses (Layer 3) and TCP port numbers (Layer 4). Table 2-2 displays some of the things that a TCP/IP packet-filtering firewall can filter on.

Table 2-2   *TCP/IP Packet Filtering Information*

Layer	Filtered Information
3	IP addresses
3	TCP/IP protocols, such as IP, ICMP, OSPF, TCP, UDP, and others
3	IP precedence (type of service [ToS]) information
4	TCP and UDP port numbers
4	TCP control flags, such as SYN, ACK, FIN, PSH, RST, and others

As you can see, you can use a lot of information when making filtering decisions on your packet-filtering firewall. For example, examine the filtering table that the packet-filtering firewall (a router, in this example) is using in Figure 2-6. Table 2-3 shows the router's packet-filtering rules. Assume that these rules are activated on the WAN interface connected to the Internet as traffic comes *into* the interface.

Figure 2-6   *Packet-Filtering Firewall Example*

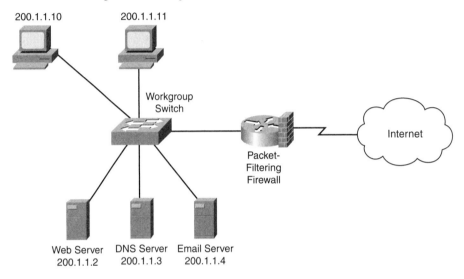

Table 2-3   *Packet-Filtering Table*

Rule	Source Address	Destination Address	IP Protocol	IP Protocol Information	Action
1	Any	200.1.1.2	TCP	Port 80	Allow
2	Any	200.1.1.3	UDP	Port 53	Allow
3	Any	200.1.1.4	TCP	Port 25	Allow
4	Any	Any other address	Any	Any	Drop

In this example, rule 1 states that if traffic from any device on the Internet is sent to TCP port 80 of 200.1.1.2, the packet-filtering firewall should allow it. Likewise, if any traffic is sent to UDP port 53 of 200.1.1.3 or TCP port 25 of 200.1.1.4, the traffic should be allowed. Any other type of traffic should be dropped.

It is important to point out that if you omit rule 4, you might have issues with a packet-filtering firewall. A packet-filtering firewall will make one of two assumptions:

- If there is no match in the rule set, allow the traffic.
- If there is no match in the rule set, drop the traffic.

For example, assume that you have a packet-filtering firewall that used the first process. In this example, if you omitted rule 4 in Table 2-3, if there were no matches in rules 1 through 3, all other traffic would be permitted.

If your packet-filtering firewall uses the second process, if you omitted rule 4 in Table 2-3, any traffic that did not match the first three rules would be dropped (Cisco uses this process with its ACLs).

CAUTION   Understanding the rule sets that your packet-filtering firewall uses, as well as understanding how the rules are processed, is extremely important. You need to be very careful when creating or changing your rules: An inadvertent configuration mistake can create a huge security hole in your packet-filtering firewall.

Another important item to point out is how packet filters are activated on the firewall. Typically, they are activated on an interface, with a direction specified for traffic flow. For example, a packet-filtering firewall might enable you to filter traffic as it comes into an interface, leaves an interface, or both. If it enables you to filter in both directions, this gives you more flexibility in creating your rule sets: You can restrict traffic coming into your network as well as user traffic trying to leave it. Typically, inbound rules for external users filter on both Layers 3 and 4 information. When setting up policies about Internet access, in many situations, a simple Layer 3 packet filter can be used to restrict which of your internal users have the right to access the Internet. Of course, you always can apply Layer 4 filtering to your users' traffic, to be more granular about what sites and applications they are allowed to access.

Advantages of Packet-Filtering Firewalls

Packet-filtering firewalls have two main advantages:

- They can process packets at very fast speeds.
- They easily can match on most fields in Layer 3 packets and Layer 4 segment headers, providing a lot of flexibility in implementing security policies.

Because packet-filtering firewalls examine only Layer 3 and/or Layer 4 information, many routing products support this type of filtering; this includes Cisco routers with the use of standard and extended ACLs. Depending on the router model that you purchase, you can scale your filtering to very high speeds.

Because routers are typically at the perimeter of your network, providing WAN and MAN access, you can use packet filtering to provide an additional layer of security. These routers commonly are called *perimeter* or *boundary* routers, and they were shown previously in Figure 2-6. Even with simple Layers 3 and 4 filtering, packet-filtering firewalls can provide protection against many types of attacks, including certain types of denial-of-service (DoS) attacks, and can filter out unnecessary, unwanted, and undesirable traffic. This allows an internal firewall to deal with other types of threats and attacks that the packet-filtering firewall cannot detect or deal with.

Limitations of Packet-Filtering Firewalls

Despite their advantages, packet-filtering firewalls have these disadvantages:

- They can be complex to configure.
- They cannot prevent application-layer attacks.
- They are susceptible to certain types of TCP/IP protocol attacks.
- They do not support user authentication of connections.
- They have limited logging capabilities.

As mentioned earlier, one of the disadvantages of packet-filtering firewalls involves the creation and maintenance of their rule sets. For TCP/IP, you must be familiar with the operation of various TCP/IP protocols and the fields in their headers, including IP, TCP, UDP, and ICMP, to name a few. Without this knowledge, you inadvertently could block traffic that you are supposed to allow, or allow traffic that you are supposed to block. In either situation, if you are not careful with your configuration, you could be creating a lot of problems for yourself. Plus, any changes that you do make must be tested thoroughly to ensure proper configuration.

Packet-filtering firewalls cannot prevent all types of attacks. For example, you might be allowing traffic to port 80 to a specific web server in your network. By doing this, the packet-filtering firewall is examining the destination address in the Layer 3 packet and the destination port number in the segment. If there is a match, the packet-filtering firewall allows the traffic. One problem with this approach is that the packet-filtering firewall does not examine the actual contents of the HTTP connection. One of the most popular methods of hacking a network is to take advantage of vulnerabilities found in web servers. A packet-filtering firewall cannot detect these attacks because they occur over TCP connections that have been permitted.

Also, packet-filtering firewalls cannot detect and prevent certain kinds of TCP/IP protocol attacks, such as TCP SYN floods and IP spoofing. If a packet-filtering firewall allows traffic to an internal web server, it does not care what kind of traffic it is. A hacker can take advantage of this and flood the web server with TCP SYNs to port 80, pretending to want resources on the server, but tying up resources on it instead. As another example, a packet-filtering firewall cannot detect all kinds of IP spoofing attacks. If you allow traffic from an external network, such as 201.1.1.0/24, your packet-filtering firewall can only examine the source IP address in the packets; it cannot determine whether this is the real source (or destination) of the packet. A hacker can take advantage of this to implement a DoS attack against your internal network by flooding it with allowed traffic from an allowed source.

These two problems, IP spoofing and DoS attacks, typically can be dealt with by causing an individual first to authenticate traffic before allowing it through the firewall. Unfortunately, a packet-filtering firewall examines only Layers 3 and 4 information. Performing authentication requires a firewall that processes authentication information, which is a Layer 7 (application layer) process.

Finally, packet-filtering firewalls typically support logging functions. However, their logging functions are limited to just Layers 3 and 4 information. If someone was executing a specific type of web server attack on port 80 and you were denying port 80 traffic, your packet-filtering firewall could log the deny action, but, unfortunately, the firewall wouldn't log the application-layer data encapsulated in the HTTP transport segment. Therefore, you, as an administrator, would know that someone was attempting to access port 80 on your server, but you would not know what that person was trying to do.

Uses for Packet-Filtering Firewalls

Because of these limitations, packet-filtering firewalls typically are used in the following areas:

- As a first line of defense (perimeter router)
- When security policies can be implemented completely in a packet filter and authentication is not an issue
- In SOHO networks that require minimal security and are concerned about cost

Many companies use packet-filtering firewalls as a first line of defense, with some other type of fully functioning firewall behind it providing additional security. An example of this is a Cisco PIX.

Likewise, packet-filtering firewalls can be used for internal access control between different subnets and departments where authentication is not necessary. In this example, you are concerned about controlling access to specific internal resources from your users; you are not as concerned about sophisticated hacking attacks from your users.

Many SOHO networks employ packet-filtering firewalls because of their simplicity and cost when compared to other types of firewalls. SOHOs are interested in basic security at a reasonable cost. You must realize, of course, that packet-filtering firewalls do not provide complete protection for the SOHO, but they do provide at least a minimal level of protection to keep out many types of network threats and attacks.

Stateful Firewalls

Unlike packet-filtering firewalls, stateful firewalls keep track of the state of a connection: whether the connection is in an initiation, data transfer, or termination state. This is useful when you want to deny the initiation of connections from external devices, but allow your users to establish connections to these devices and permit the responses to come back through the stateful firewall.

Many security people disagree on what layer of the OSI reference model stateful firewalls function at: Layers 3 and 4 (transport), or Layers 3, 4, and 5 (session). From a transport layer perspective, the stateful firewall examines information in the headers of Layer 3 packets and Layer 4 segments. For example, it looks at the TCP header for SYN, RST, ACK, FIN, and other control codes to determine the *state* of the connection.

However, because the session layer establishes and tears down the connection—the transport layer handles the actual mechanics of the connection—some say that stateful firewalls operate at Layer 5, as shown in Figure 2-7. In either case, remember that stateful firewalls know about a connection and its state.

Figure 2-7   *Stateful Firewalls and the OSI Reference Model*

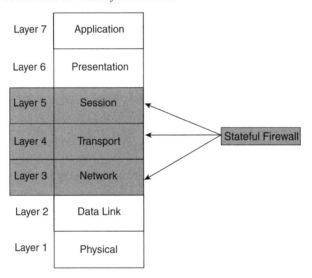

Problems with Packet-Filtering Firewalls

This section and the next one examine one of the issues that packet-filtering firewalls have with traffic and how stateful firewalls can deal with it.

Refer to Figure 2-8 for the example. In the figure, the packet-filtering firewall has a rule placed on its inbound interface from the Internet stating that any external traffic sent to 200.1.1.10 (a user's PC) is denied. As shown in Figure 2-8, when 170.1.1.1 tries to access 200.1.1.10, the packet-filtering firewall drops the traffic, as it is supposed to do.

Figure 2-8   *Packet-Filtering Firewall Example—Initiating Connections*

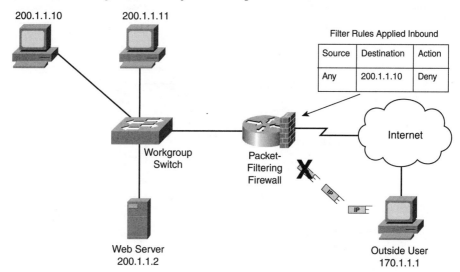

However, what happens if someone inside the network, such as 200.1.1.10, tries to access this external device (170.1.1.1)? Assume that this is an HTTP request to 170.1.1.1, which has a web server running on it. HTTP uses TCP, and TCP goes through a three-way handshake to establish a connection before data is transferred: SYN, SYN/ACK, and ACK. Initially, 200.1.1.10 sends a SYN to establish a connection. With TCP (and UDP), a source port number is chosen that is greater than 1,023, which represents this specific connection. The destination is port 80, telling 170.1.1.1 that this is an HTTP request for web services.

As the packet-filtering firewall receives the traffic on its internal interface, it checks to see if the traffic for 200.1.1.10 is allowed to leave the network. In this case, no filtering rules prevent this, so traffic for 200.1.1.10 traffic is sent to the 170.1.1.1.

170.1.1.1 now responds back to the TCP SYN message of 200.1.1.10 with a SYN/ACK (the second step in the three-way handshake), as shown in Figure 2-9. However, when the packet-filtering firewall examines the packet, it determines that because the destination is 200.1.1.10, the packet should be dropped, according to its packet-filtering rules. Therefore, the connection cannot be set up to the external web server, denying the internal user's web access.

Figure 2-9   *Packet-Filtering Firewall Example—Handling Responses*

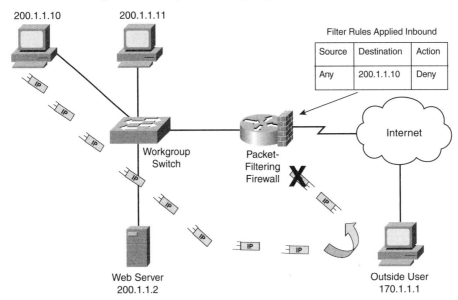

Opening Ports

You can solve this problem with packet-filtering firewalls in two ways:

- Open destination ports greater than 1023 as traffic comes back to the source
- Examine the TCP control bits to determine whether this is returning traffic

Take a look at the first solution. In this situation, the source originally opened a source port greater than 1023, such as 10,000, and used a destination port of 80 for HTTP. Therefore, to allow the traffic to return from 170.1.1.1, the packet-filtering firewall needs a rule that will allow port 10,000. Of course, the problem with this is that the source can use *any* source port number greater than 1023: Whichever one is free and is chosen by the operating system is the one assigned. Therefore, you would have to allow all ports greater than 1023 to allow the returning traffic to 200.1.1.10, as shown in Figure 2-10.

CAUTION   Opening ports greater than 1023 is not a recommended practice to allow returning traffic from an originating connection: You are creating a huge security hole in your firewall that will open your internal devices to all kinds of attacks.

Figure 2-10 *Packet-Filtering Firewall Example—Opening Ports*

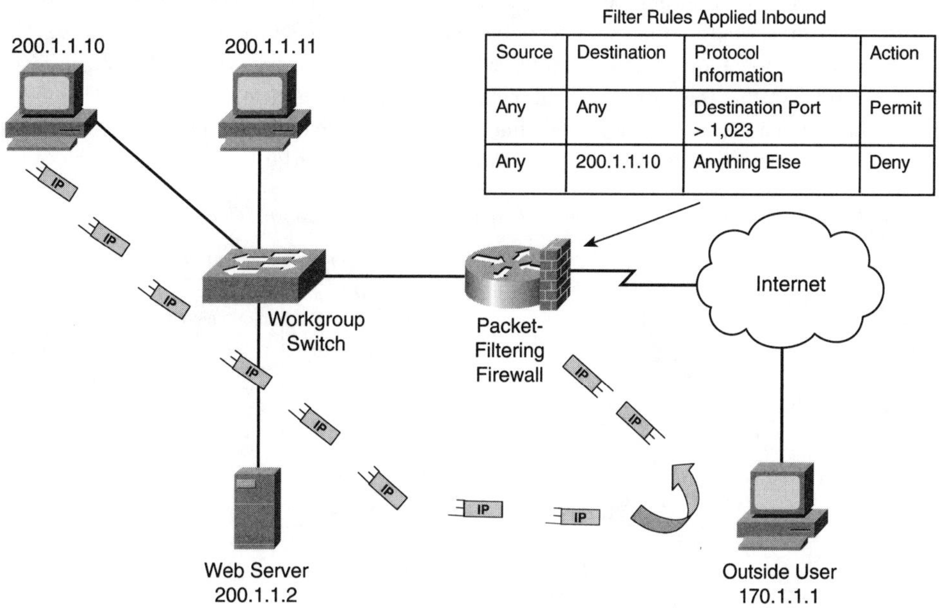

Filter Rules Applied Inbound

Source	Destination	Protocol Information	Action
Any	Any	Destination Port > 1,023	Permit
Any	200.1.1.10	Anything Else	Deny

Examining TCP Control Bits

The second approach is to examine transport layer information about the connection to determine whether it is part of an existing connection and, if so, allow the returning traffic back to 200.1.1.1. With TCP, this can be done by examining the control flags in the TCP segment header. These are shown in Table 2-4 and are defined in RFC 793. Note that multiple codes, commonly called *flags*, can be sent in the same segment header, such as SYN and ACK (SYN/ACK), or FIN and ACK (FIN/ACK).

Table 2-4 *TCP Control Information*

TCP Message	Explanation
ACK	Acknowledges receipt of data
FIN	Terminates a connection
PSH	Acts as the push function
RST	Resets the connection
SYN	Initiates a connection and synchronizes sequence numbers
URG	Points to urgent data in the segment payload

In this situation, the packet-filtering firewall examines not only the source and destination addresses and port numbers, but, for TCP connections, it also examines the code bits to determine whether this is traffic being initiated from a device or traffic being sent in response to a request. For example, when the internal user (200.1.1.10) sends a TCP SYN, you know that the 170.1.1.1 will respond with a SYN and ACK in the TCP segment header. Therefore, if you know what kind of response control flags TCP uses, you could configure your packet-filtering firewall to allow this traffic, as shown in Figure 2-11.

Figure 2-11 *Packet-Filtering Firewall Example—Examining Transport Control Codes*

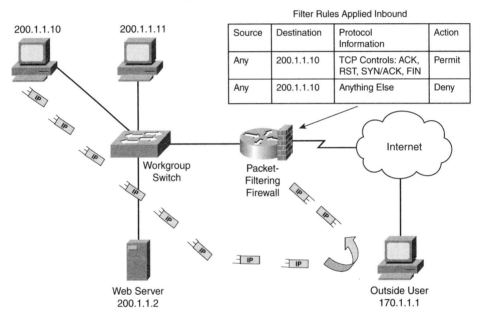

Two problems exist with examining control codes at the transport layer:

- Not all transport layer protocols support control codes.
- Control codes can be manipulated manually to allow a hacker to slip packets through a packet-filtering firewall.

One of the biggest problems of having the packet-filtering firewall examine the control codes is that, in the TCP/IP protocol suite, TCP has control codes, but UDP doesn't. Therefore, for a UDP connection, you do not know whether this is the beginning, middle, or end of a connection unless you examine the data encapsulated in the UDP segment.

The other problem is that, even for transport-layer protocols that support control codes, such as TCP, these control codes can be manipulated manually. For example, the packet-filtering router in Figure 2-11 allows traffic to 200.1.1.10 if certain control codes, such as SYN and ACK, are set in the TCP header. The assumption here—and it is a big assumption—is that the data is a response to information that 200.1.1.10 requested from an external device, such as 170.1.1.10. However, the packet-filtering firewall cannot distinguish between a valid response and a fake response. With a fake response, a hacker generates TCP segments with certain code flags set, trying to gain access through your firewall. A packet-filtering firewall, cannot distinguish between the two types of traffic.

CAUTION   The **established** Cisco parameter for TCP extended ACLs examines the code flags and allows returning traffic into the network. However, a hacker can manipulate this returning traffic, opening you to reconnaissance, DoS, and other types of attacks.

State Table

Unlike packet-filtering firewalls, stateful firewalls use a mechanism to keep track of the state of a connection. See Figure 2-12 and Figure 2-13 for an illustration of this. Figure 2-12 uses the same network discussed in the last section with a packet-filtering firewall. In this example, the packet-filtering firewall has been replaced by a stateful firewall, but the filtering rule is unchanged: Any traffic sent to 200.1.1.10 is dropped.

Figure 2-12 *Stateful Firewall Filtering Example—Part 1*

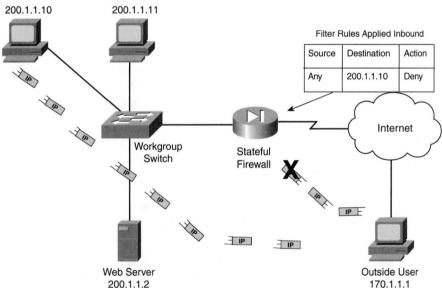

Assume that 170.1.1.1 sends traffic to 200.1.1.10. As shown in Figure 2-12, this traffic is dropped. Now assume that 200.1.1.10 opens a web connection to 170.1.1.1, as shown in the bottom part of Figure 2-12. When 200.1.1.10 does this, it uses a TCP segment with a source port of 10,000 and a destination port of 80. It uses a SYN flag in the control field.

Figure 2-13 *Stateful Firewall Filtering Example—Part 2*

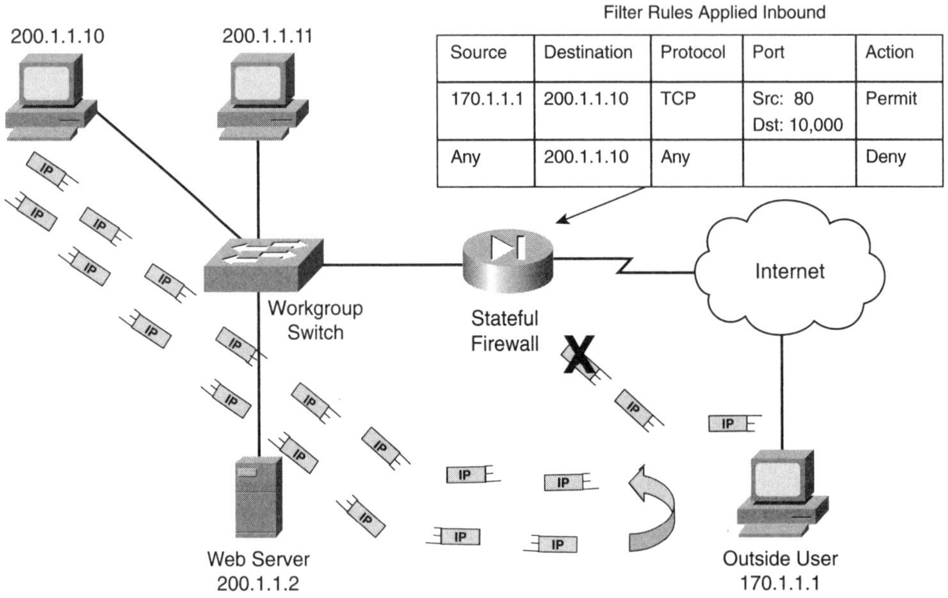

Filter Rules Applied Inbound

Source	Destination	Protocol	Port	Action
170.1.1.1	200.1.1.10	TCP	Src: 80 Dst: 10,000	Permit
Any	200.1.1.10	Any		Deny

200.1.1.10   200.1.1.11

Workgroup Switch

Stateful Firewall

Internet

Web Server 200.1.1.2

Outside User 170.1.1.1

When the stateful firewall receives this traffic, it first checks to see whether the 200.1.1.10 connection is allowed out. In this case, no filtering rules prevent this. Unlike a packet-filtering firewall, which just forwards the packet to 170.1.1.1, a stateful firewall adds a filtering rule to its configuration. This information either is added to the top of the existing filtering rule set or is placed into a *state* table. This table is used to keep track of the state of connections. The former process is shown in Figure 2-13.

After 170.1.1.1 receives the connection request, it responds to 200.1.1.1 with a SYN/ACK. When this segment reaches the stateful firewall, the firewall looks in its state table first (if the second method discussed previously is used) to see if the connection exists. Then it processes the filtering rules on the interface. In this example, only one table was used, but the connection entry was placed at the top. Because the connection information was added when 200.1.1.1 initiated the connection, the stateful firewall knows that the response from 170.1.1.1 (TCP port 80) to 200.1.1.1 (TCP port 10,000) is part of an existing connection and, therefore, that should allow the traffic, as shown in Figure 2-13.

One advantage of the stateful process is that when the connection terminates, the source or destination device tears down the connection and the stateful firewall notices this by examining the TCP header control flags and dynamically removes the connection from the state table (or filtering rules table).

Therefore, when comparing packet-filtering firewalls and stateful firewalls, stateful firewalls are more intelligent because they understand the state of a connection: initiating a connection, transferring data, or terminating a connection. Basically, a stateful firewall contains a superset of packet-filtering functions.

Advantages of Stateful Firewalls

As you learned in the previous explanation, stateful firewalls have advantages over packet-filtering firewalls:

- Stateful firewalls are aware of the state of a connection.

- Stateful firewalls do not have to open up a large range of ports to allow communication.

- Stateful firewalls prevent more kinds of DoS attacks than packet-filtering firewalls and have more robust logging.

First, stateful firewalls are aware of a connection's state: Stateful firewalls typically build a state table and use this table to allow only returning traffic from connections currently listed in the state table. After a connection is removed from the state table, no traffic from the external device of this connection is permitted. Therefore, these types of connections are more difficult to spoof. For instance, with HTTP, connections are very short lived, so if a hacker noticed the connection being torn down and tried to sneak in some data by spoofing the TCP port numbers and IP addresses, the data would be stopped because the connection entry already would have been removed.

However, if this was a Telnet connection, which might last many minutes or hours, the hacker could attempt to spoof the connection. To do this, the hacker would not only have to spoof the port numbers in the transport layer segment, but he also would have to spoof the IP addressing information, which is a difficult process if the hacker wants this information returned to his desktop. Even so, when the real source or destination terminated the connection, the stateful firewall would remove the entry.

Second, stateful firewalls do not require you to open a large range of port numbers to allow returning traffic back into your network: The state table is used to determine whether this is returning traffic; otherwise, the filtering table is used to filter the traffic.

Third, by using a state table, the stateful firewall can prevent more kinds of DoS attacks than a packet-filtering firewall. Plus, the stateful firewall can log more information than a packet-filtering firewall, such as when a connection was set up, how long it was up, and when it was torn down.

Limitations of Stateful Firewalls

You would think that with these advantages, stateful firewalls are a great tool, and they are. But stateful firewalls have these limitations:

- They can be complex to configure.

- They cannot prevent application-layer attacks.

- They do not support user authentication of connections.

- Not all protocols contain state information.

- Some applications open multiple connections, some of which use dynamic port numbers for the additional connections.
- Additional overhead is involved in maintaining a state table.

The first three items I already discussed in the section on packet-filtering firewalls. As with packet-filtering firewalls, most of the filtering is done by specifying rule sets with Layers 3 and 4 information, which can be complex. Plus, because stateful firewalls really only process Layers 3, 4, and 5 (depending on whom you speak with) information, they can't detect application-layer attacks or perform any type of user authentication to allow the setup of a connection.

Stateful Firewall Problem: Nonstateful Protocols

In addition to these problems, stateful firewalls have issues with nonstateful protocols. Protocols that go through a defined process to establish, maintain, and tear down a connection are called stateful; mechanics are defined as to how these processes occur. TCP is an example of a stateful protocol.

However, not all protocols are stateful: UDP and ICMP are not. For example, UDP has no defined process for how to set up, maintain, and tear down a connection; this is defined on an application-by-application basis. A simple example is a DNS resolution: A source generates a DNS request to resolve a name, and a DNS server responds with a reply with the IP address for the name. In this example, keeping track of the state of the connection is simple: The stateful firewall looks for a DNS request, adds an entry to the state table to allow the reply, and then removes the entry when the DNS server sends the reply.

Not all UDP applications are this simple, however. In most of these applications, many packets are sent between the source and destination, typically at a constant rate. Most stateful firewall solutions treat UDP traffic as stateful by assigning an idle timer to these connections in the state table. As an example, a stateful firewall might use an idle timer of 30 seconds; if after 30 seconds no UDP traffic is seen for a UDP entry in the state table, the stateful firewall removes it. The main problem with this approach is that if a hacker sends spoofed packets into your network, this would keep the entry in the table indefinitely. Of course, a hacker must be quick about this because most UDP connections are temporary.

Like UDP, ICMP also presents problems. A simple example is a ping test. Depending on the ping program, it might generate 1, 3, 5, or even 10 echo test requests. Given this discrepancy, how should a stateful firewall handle this nonstateful protocol? As with UDP, one solution is to use an idle timer, but this entry in the state table can be spoofed. As with UDP, ICMP connections are very brief, so spoofing this connection is unlikely. Another solution would be to put a separate entry in the state table for each echo request. The problem with this is that if you are doing a congestion test by generating thousands of echo requests, your stateful firewall can become overburdened by trying to manage all of these short, temporary connections.

Stateful Firewall Problem: Multiple Application Connections

Another problem that stateful firewalls have involves dealing with applications that open additional connections to transmit information. These can include FTP, multimedia, NetBIOS, and many others. FTP is used as an example here. FTP supports two different modes:

- Standard (or active)
- Passive

Both modes set up two TCP connections. An example of these connections is shown in Figure 2-14. With passive-mode FTP, as long as the user is inside the network establishing connections going out, you have no problems: Both outbound connections are placed in the state table, and the returning traffic for these automatically is allowed. However, if the client device is outside the stateful firewall, you would need a specific filtering rule to allow the port 21 connection (called the control channel) and a very expansive filtering rule to allow the second connection (the data channel).

NOTE   Packet-filtering firewalls have the same problem with external users and passive FTP.

Figure 2-14 *FTP Connections*

Standard FTP

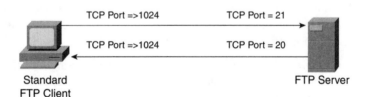

Passive FTP

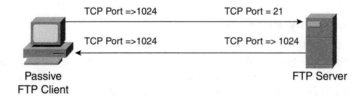

With standard FTP, if the client is inside the network and the server is outside, both stateful and packet-filtering firewalls would have problems dealing with the data connection that the FTP server was establishing to the client: You would have to open a whole range of ports to allow this second connection.

Stateful Firewall Problem: Size of State Table

When it comes to the state table, it is a double-edged sword for stateful firewalls. Yes, it does provide a lot of advantages. But in large networks, the stateful firewall might be busy building and maintaining the state table, putting an extra burden on its processing capacity. The more connections your stateful firewall must monitor, the more horsepower your stateful firewall needs to maintain the table, thus increasing its cost. Unlike stateful firewalls, packet-filtering firewalls typically have small filtering tables, which has much less impact on its processing than a stateful firewall has with its state table.

Uses for Stateful Firewalls

Because of its increased intelligence over packet-filtering firewalls, stateful firewalls typically are used in the following areas:

- As a primary means of defense
- As an intelligent first line of defense (perimeter router with stateful capabilities)
- Where more stringent controls over security than packet filtering are needed, without adding too much cost

In most situations, a stateful firewall is used as a primary means of defense by filtering unwanted, unnecessary, or undesirable traffic. Its main advantage over packet-filtering firewalls is that it opens dynamic, temporary holes in the filter rule set to allow returning traffic from connections that originated inside your network.

In some situations, certain routing products support a stateful function and can be used as either a primary line of defense or, more typically, as an additional security boost on your perimeter router. In a design with two firewalls—main and perimeter—a router typically is not used as the main stateful firewall because of performance issues; instead, a dedicated firewall appliance is used as the main firewall device.

Also, stateful firewalls provide more control over packet-filtering firewalls, typically at not too much additional cost. If you are more concerned about security, you might consider purchasing a stateful firewall or upgrading a router that supports stateful features to take advantage of more intelligent packet filtering.

Application Gateway Firewalls

Application gateway firewalls (AGFs), commonly called *proxy firewalls*, filter information at Layers 3, 4, 5, and 7 of the OSI reference model, as shown in Figure 2-15. Because AGFs process information at the application layer, most of the firewall control and filtering is done in software, which provides much more control over traffic than packet-filtering or stateful firewalls.

Sometimes AGFs support only a limited number of applications, or even just one application. Some of the more common applications that an AGF might support include e-mail, web services, DNS, Telnet, FTP, Usenet news, LDAP, and finger.

Figure 2-15 *Application Gateway Firewalls and the OSI Reference Model*

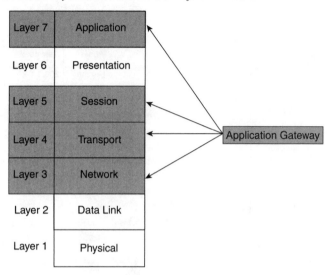

TIP   When choosing an AGF, one of the issues to evaluate is the applications supported and the applications needed to send through it.

Authentication Process

One of the features of AGFs is that they typically allow you to authenticate connection requests before allowing the traffic to an internal or external resource. This enables you to authenticate the user requesting the connection instead of the device. This is one disadvantage that packet-filtering and stateful firewalls have: They examine only Layers 3 and 4 information and, thus, can authenticate only the Layer 3 address of a device.

Figure 2-16 shows a simple example of an AGF using an authentication process. In this example, the user first must authenticate to the AGF. This can be done by having the user open a special connection—perhaps a web browser connection to the AGF, or the AGF can intercept the user's initial connection request and send the user a request for authentication information, like a web browser pop-up window. The AGF or an authentication server then authenticates the user's identity. The authentication process occurs in software at the application layer. In Figure 2-16, the authentication database is on the AGF and uses a username and password. In this database, the AGF allows Richard to access web server A upon successful authentication, but it will not allow Richard to access web server B. As you can see from this example, when Richard authenticates, he can access web server A; however, he cannot access any other resource. In Figure 2-16, when Richard tries to send information to web server B, the AGF drops that information.

Figure 2-16 *AGF Authentication Process*

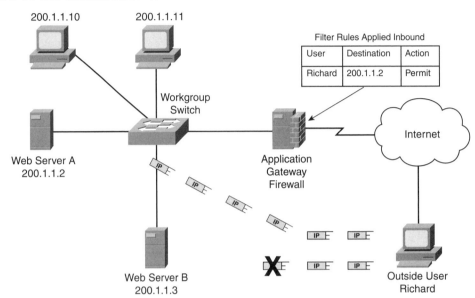

User	Destination	Action
Richard	200.1.1.2	Permit

NOTE   To make the authentication and connection process more efficient, many AGFs authenticate a user once and then use authorization information stored in the authentication database to determine what resources a person can access. The authorization then is used to limit the additional resources that the user is allowed to access, if any, instead of requiring the user to authenticate for each resource that he wants to access. Also note that the AGF can be used to authenticate both inbound and outbound connections.

Authentication Methods

An AGF can use many methods to authenticate a connection request, including username and passwords, token card information, Layer 3 source addresses, and biometric information. Typically, Layer 3 source addresses are not used for authentication, unless they are combined with one of the other methods. Authentication information can be stored locally or on a security server or directory service. An example of a security server is Cisco Secure ACS. Examples of directory services include Novell NDS, Microsoft Active Directory, and LDAP.

CAUTION   You should not rely on the use of just Layer 3 source addresses to perform authentication because Layer 3 addresses are susceptible to masquerading and spoofing attacks.

If you are using a username and password for authentication, the AGF prompts for the username and password. Then it does a lookup for the username and compares the password to what the person typed. If both are the same, the user is validated. One problem with this authentication method is that if the username and password are sent across the connection in clear text, this information is susceptible to eavesdropping; a hacker then can use this information to execute a masquerading attack. Therefore, this information should be encrypted. Typically, this is done through the Secure Socket Layer (SSL) protocol within a web browser connection. This means that the person must open an HTTP SSL (HTTPS) connection to the AGF to perform the authentication. Another method is to have the person use an encrypted Telnet application, such as Secure Shell (SSH). In either method, though, the person first must access the AGF directly to perform the authentication.

Biometric information is more secure than a username and password because usernames and passwords are guessed more easily. With biometrics, some unique physical characteristic of a person, such as a fingerprint or retinal scan, is examined. However, when sending this information to the AGF, it, like usernames and passwords, is susceptible to eavesdropping. Therefore, a secure connection should be used to transmit this authentication information.

Of all of the authentication methods, token cards are the most secure. Token cards create a one-time password, a password that can be used only once. After the password has been used, it is no longer valid. The advantage of token cards is that they are not susceptible to eavesdropping: If the hacker eavesdrops and sees the token card information, it is of no use to him because it will have expired by the time the hacker tries to use it. The downside of token cards is that they can be expensive to deploy on a large scale and are more difficult to troubleshoot and set up.

Application Gateway Firewall Types

AGFs fall under two categories: connection gateway firewalls (CGFs) and cut-through proxy (CTP) firewalls. The next two sections compare the two different types.

Connection Gateway Firewalls

CGFs offer more protection than CTP firewalls. Figure 2-17 shows the process that a person goes through when setting up a connection through a CGF. In Step 1, Richard attempts to set up a connection to the internal web server (200.1.1.2). The CGF intercepts the connection and authenticates it, if this has been configured. After authentication, the CGF opens a separate connection to the internal web server (Step 2). At this point, any web traffic sent by Richard to 200.1.1.2 first is processed by the CGF and then is redirected to the internal web server, as shown in Step 3. Any other traffic from Richard is dropped unless it has been authorized by the first authentication request or unless the CGF asks for authentication for any additional connections. If Richard does not authenticate successfully, the CGF terminates the connection.

Figure 2-17 *Connection Gateway Firewall Process*

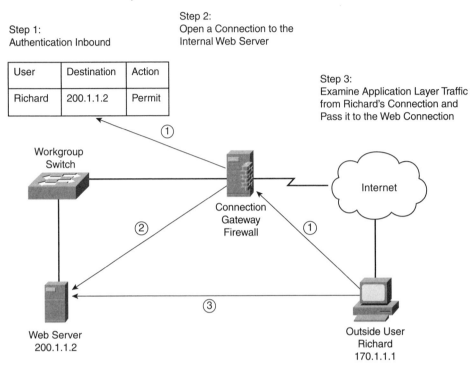

NOTE   Many CGFs (and CTPs) enable you to configure multiple authorization rules for a single user. Therefore, when the user successfully authenticates, all the authorization rules are put into effect without requiring the user to authenticate for each connection request.

One nice feature of a CGF is that it can examine all data that Richard sends to the web server, even specific URL requests. This allows the CGF to examine what pages Richard tries to access and whether Richard is trying to sneak malformed URLs or data that might try to crash the server or open the server because of a security weakness. Basically, any character that Richard types in for the connection is visible to the CGF. This type of examination is not possible by a packet-filtering or stateful firewall because these devices operate, for the most part, at Layers 3 and 4.

With a CGF, you can be creative in your filtering. For example, you can restrict what Java applets or ActiveX scripts a user has access to. With a Telnet connection, you can monitor and restrict what commands a person can execute on a networking device, such as a Cisco router. With an FTP server, you can restrict what directories a person can see and what files he can download. As you can see, you can create some very powerful filtering rules to secure your network with a CGF.

Cut-Through Proxy Firewalls

One of the main problems of a CGF is that, for the applications that it supports, all traffic is processed at the application layer; this is very process-intensive. In some cases, you might be interested only in performing authentication of a connection at the application layer; after that, you are not really interested in monitoring the activities on the connection—you want just the authentication features. Of course, you could perform this function with a CGF; however, a CGF always processes information at Layer 7, which can introduce a noticeable delay in individuals' connections, especially on an CGF that handles thousands of connections.

Cut-through proxy (CTP) firewalls are a modified version of CGF that deals with this inefficiency. Figure 2-18 shows a simple example of the process that a CTP uses to allow connections into a network. In this example, Richard tries to access the internal web server (200.1.1.2). The CTP intercepts the connection request and authenticates Richard, shown in Step 1. After authentication, this connection and any other authorized connections are added to the filtering rules table, shown in Step 2. From here, any traffic from Richard to the web server is handled by the filtering rules at Layers 3 and 4.

Figure 2-18 *Cut-Through Proxy Firewall Process*

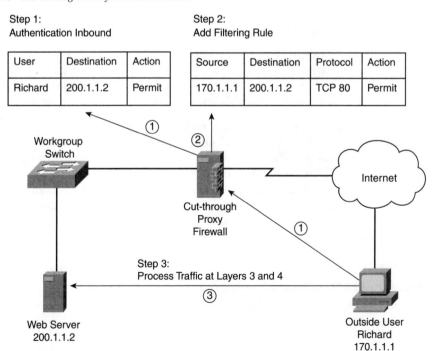

As you can see from this example, the authentication process is handled at Layer 7; after being authenticated, however, all traffic is processed at Layers 3 and 4. Therefore, the advantage that CTP has over CGF is a huge boost in throughput. However, because CTP does not examine application-layer data, it cannot detect application-layer attacks.

Typically, the CTP supports Telnet, HTTP, and HTTPS for handling the initial authentication. This is done by having the individual set up an authentication to the CTP itself. Optionally, some CTPs can intercept certain connections and respond with authentication prompts. After authentication, the CTP allows the connection initiation request to the internal resource.

Advantages of Application Gateway Firewalls

AGFs have many advantages over packet-filtering and stateful firewalls, including the following:

- They authenticate individuals, not devices.
- Hackers have a harder time with spoofing and implementing DoS attacks.
- They can monitor and filter application data.
- They can provide detailed logging.

One of the advantages of an AGF (CGF and CTP) is that it enables you to authenticate the individual who is trying to access internal resources. This enables you to prevent most spoofing attacks. Plus, DoS attacks are limited to the AGF itself: The AGF can detect these, reducing the burden on your internal resources.

With a CGF, you can monitor all data on a connection, which enables you to detect application attacks such as malformed URLs, buffer overflow attempts, unauthorized access, and more. You even can control what commands or functions an individual is allowed to perform based on the authentication and authorization information.

Finally, with an AGF, you can generate very detailed logs. With a CTP, you can log only the authentication process and any filtering done at Layers 3 and 4; with a CGF, you can monitor the actual data that the individual is sending across a connection. This can be extremely useful if a hacker finds a new type of attack: You can monitor what he does and how he does it so that you can address the problem. Besides using logging for security purposes, you can use it for management purposes by keeping track of who is accessing what resources, how much bandwidth is used, and how often the resources are accessed.

Limitations of Application Gateway Firewalls

Even with their advantages, AGFs have the following limitations:

- They process packets in software.

- They support a small number of applications.
- They sometimes require special client software.

The main limitation of AGFs is that they are very process intensive. They require a lot of CPU cycles and memory to process every packet that they see, which sometimes creates throughput problems. Plus, the detailed logging can create disk space problems. To address these issues, you can use one of these two solutions:

- Use a CTP
- Have the AGF monitor only key applications

For the first solution, using a CTP enables you to do authentication and authorization only; you cannot monitor data on the connection. With the second solution, you limit the AGF to processing only certain application types, such as e-mail, Telnet, FTP, or web services—and then, perhaps, processing just connections to specific internal resources. The problem with this approach is that you are not monitoring all applications and connections, creating a security weakness.

AGFs also typically do not support all applications. They generally are limited to one or a handful of connection types, such as those listed at the beginning of this section. Therefore, you cannot monitor data on all connections.

Finally, AGFs sometimes require you to install vendor-specific software on the client, which is used to handle the authentication process and any possible connection redirection. This can create scalability and management issues if you need to support thousands of clients.

Other Types of Application Proxy Devices

Other types of application gateway devices exist besides AGFs. AGFs are used mainly for security purposes; however, other application gateways (commonly called *proxies*) can be used to help with throughput issues.

For example, a common type of proxy is an HTTP proxy. With an HTTP proxy, an individual configures the web browser to point to the proxy. Whenever the individual requests a web page, the request goes to the proxy first. The proxy examines its local cache to see if the information was retrieved previously. If it is in the cache, the proxy responds with the information; otherwise, the proxy generates a request to pull the information from the real web server, caches that information, and forwards it to the client. This is similar to a CGF, but without the security functions.

Sometimes these proxies are used to help reduce logging functions on the AGF itself. The AGF monitors connections and creates logging records for security events, but the application proxy handles the detailed logging of all connection data. Likewise, application proxies are useful for tracking your internal users' Internet and remote resource access. This is important if you have acceptable use and abuse policies and need to monitor resource requests so that you can enforce these policies.

Uses for Application Gateway Firewalls

Because of its increased intelligence over packet-filtering and stateful firewalls, AGFs typically are used in the following areas:

- A CGF commonly is used as a primary filtering function.
- A CTP commonly is used as a perimeter defense.
- An application proxy is used to reduce the logging overhead on the CGF, as well as to monitor and log other types of traffic.

In many situations, a CGF is used as a primary filtering defense. In this situation, a perimeter router might or might not be used as a first line of defense; however, the CGF functions as the main line of defense and protection. The CGF performs authentication, but this can be offloaded to a CTP perimeter device. The CGF also performs application filtering and monitoring, and is used to prevent many types of application layer attacks.

A CTP commonly is used as a perimeter defense tool. It performs initial authentication but processes filtering at Layers 3 and 4, thereby reducing its load and allowing a smaller-end device to handle perimeter connectivity.

If too much traffic needs to be monitored or logged, an application proxy is used to offload these functions from the CGF. This allows the CGF to handle important security screening tasks, but it still enables you to keep a detailed record of all connections.

Address-Translation Firewalls

Address translation was developed to address two issues with IP addressing:

- It expands the number of IP addresses at your disposal.
- It hides network addressing designs.

The main reason that address translation (RFC 1631) and private addresses (RFC 1918) were developed was to deal with the concern of the shortage of addresses that was seen on the horizon in the mid- to late 1990s. I thoroughly discuss this topic in Chapter 11, "Address Translation," and Chapter 12, "Address Translation Issues."

Basically, address translation translates the source/destination address(es) and/or port numbers in an IP packet or TCP/UDP segment header. Because of this, address-translation firewalls (ATF) function at Layers 3 and 4 of the OSI reference model, as shown in Figure 2-19.

This section focuses on the second reason: hiding network addressing designs.

Filtering Process

Most people assume that address translation is used to translate private to public addresses or vice versa, so you might be wondering how you can use address translation as a security function. Examine Figure 2-20, which illustrates the usefulness of address translation in protecting your network. In this example, two web servers have private addresses assigned to their NICs, 192.168.11.2 and 192.168.12.2. Because private IP addresses are nonroutable in public networks, a public address must be associated with these two devices, and a DNS server needs to send the public address in response to DNS queries for the addresses of these devices.

Figure 2-19 *Address-Translation Firewalls and the OSI Reference Model*

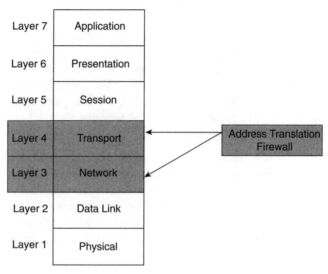

Figure 2-20 *Address-Translation Firewall Example*

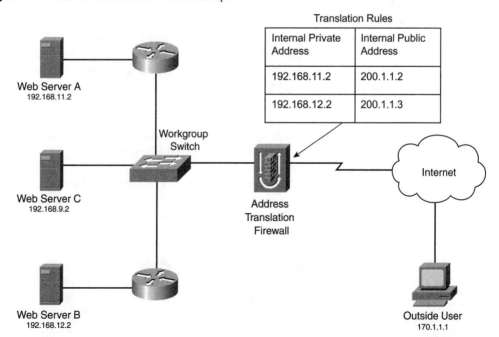

The ATF defines the translation rules. Traffic heading to 200.1.1.2 is translated to 192.168.11.2, and traffic to 200.1.1.3 is translated to 192.168.12.2, and vice versa. This process serves two functions. First, an outside person cannot decipher anything about the IP address structure of your network: That person knows only that 200.1.1.2 and 200.1.1.3 are reachable addresses and appear to be on the same segment. The outside person does not know that these web servers are on two different physical segments behind two different routers.

Second, traffic sent to any other device in your network cannot be reached it unless it first is translated; remember that your internal devices are using private addresses. If an outside person sends traffic to an address of 192.168.x.x, his ISP (or some other ISP) will drop it. If the outside person sends traffic with a public address in it, only the public addresses listed in your translation table will allow the translation to take place so that the data can reach the internal resource. For example, there is no way that 170.1.1.1 can reach web server C because there is no translation in the ATF.

Address translation also can be used to restrict traffic leaving your network. Again, refer to Figure 2-20. In this example, if web server A sends data to 170.1.1.1, when the packets are received by the ATF, the firewall looks at its table and sees that this should be translated to 200.1.1.2 and forwarded to the Internet. However, there is a problem if web server C tries to send data to 170.1.1.1. When the ATF sees these packets from web server C, it looks in its translation table and does not find a match. At this point, the ATF can take one of two actions:

- Drop the packets
- Forward the packets

If the ATF takes the first approach, you definitely have restricted Internet access for devices that are not listed in the translation table. If the address-translation firewall forwards the packets but does not perform any address translation, the same result occur, but when these packets are received by your ISP. In this instance, because they are private addresses, your ISP should drop them.

CAUTION   I am assuming that you are using private addresses inside your network. Address translation can translate private addresses to public addresses (and vice versa), private addresses to private addresses, and public addresses to public addresses. If you are using public addresses on inside devices and you do not have translation rules on your ATF for these devices, you need to ensure that your ATF drops all packets without configured rules (assuming that you want to implement a drop policy when no match occurs).

Given these two scenarios—traffic heading into your network or leaving your network—the ATF serves as an access-control point. As a control point, the ATF controls which traffic enters or leaves by the nature of its function: translating addresses. Therefore, because traffic must go through this device to enter or leave your network, it becomes easier to centralize your security policies as well as to implement them.

NOTE   These two examples used simple network address translation: translating one IP address to another. However, this can be expanded easily to include TCP or UDP ports in the translation process, allowing you to restrict translations for specific applications.

Advantages of Address-Translation Firewalls

ATFs provide these advantages:

- They hide your network-addressing design.
- They control traffic entering and leaving your network.
- They allow for the use of private addressing.

As already mentioned, ATFs hide your IP addressing design. Plus, you easily can control traffic as it enters and leaves your network if your internal devices are using private addresses: Your address translation firewall serves as a choke-point. Only through the configuration of address-translation rules can traffic enter or leave the network. Plus, with the capability to use private addresses, you have millions of IP addresses at your disposal: 1 Class A, 16 Class B, and 256 Class C network numbers.

Limitations of Address-Translation Firewalls

Just like any firewall solution, address translation firewalls have limitations, including the following:

- Delay is introduced because of packet manipulations.
- Some applications do not work with address translation.
- Tracing and troubleshooting become more difficult.

Because address translation must change the IP address(es) in the IP header, the header checksum must be recomputed; plus, if port address translation is performed on TCP or UDP segment headers, the checksums in these headers also must be recomputed. This process of changing packet and segment contents, as well as recomputing checksums, is very process intensive and adds delay to your data stream. In addition, the more connections that you have defined in your address table, the longer it takes to find a match and the more processing it takes to maintain the table.

The second issue with address translation is that not all protocols function correctly or at all when address translation is performed on the packet and segment contents. Some applications embed addressing information in the data payload of TCP and UDP segment payloads, which typically is not translated by an ATF. This can create reachability issues. Multimedia and NetBIOS applications are notorious for embedding addressing information in data payloads. This topic is covered in more depth in Chapter 12.

The third issue with address translation is a double-edged sword. Yes, by hiding your addressing scheme, you are making your network more secure. On the other hand, hackers can use this to their advantage by hiding their source addressing information. Therefore, when you are being attacked by a hacker, it becomes much more difficult for you to track down the actual culprit. Plus, troubleshooting is not an easy process when dealing with address translation because you must know both the IP address assigned to a device on its NIC and its translated address when trying to find the source and destination of a connection.

Uses for Address-Translation Firewalls

ATFs are somewhat different when compared to other types of firewalls, such as application gateways, stateful firewalls, and packet-filtering firewalls. These latter firewalls filter traffic based on filtering rules that you define, which can be very specific. ATFs are more general in their filtering process because they can filter only on address (and sometimes port) information. Therefore, ATFs typically are used in the following situations:

- When you have a private IP addressing scheme in your internal network
- When you need to easily separate two or more networks

If you are using private IP addresses, you need to use some type of address-translation device to allow traffic into and out of your network. An ATF provides extra security when performing this process.

An ATF also can separate two or more networks and control traffic between these through the use of address translation easily. Again, this typically is done when address translation is required. For example, one of the networks might be using private addresses, or the two networks might be using an overlapping address space.

Host-Based Firewalls

A host-based firewall is basically firewall software running on a PC or file server. When running on a personal PC, this commonly is called a *personal* firewall. This typically is used to enhance your security solution or to provide additional protection to your desktop. You can use literally dozens of free, shareware, and premium software-based firewall products to protect Microsoft Windows, Apple Macintosh, and the many flavors of UNIX that you might have running as your operating system.

Host-based firewalls usually do not have the same capabilities of the other firewall categories that I already discussed. They are typically a simplified packet-filtering firewall that filter on the IP protocol, such as TCP or UDP, source and destination IP addresses, and protocol information such as TCP or UDP port numbers. Host-based firewalls were built to provide a low-cost alternative to other firewall categories yet still provide a decent level of protection: They typically have fewer filtering and logging capabilities.

Figure 2-21 shows two examples of using host-based firewalls. On the left, the file server has firewall software loaded on it, providing an additional layer of protection along with the packet-filtering router/firewall. At the bottom right is a user who is connected directly to the Internet and who has a host-based firewall installed on his desktop.

Figure 2-21 *Host-Based Firewall Example*

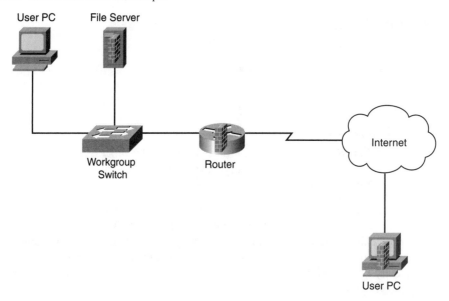

Advantages of Host-Based Firewalls

Host-based firewalls have the following advantages:

- They can be used to enhance your security.
- Some can provide host-based authentication.
- Their cost is typically less than $100—and sometimes they even are free.

Typically, host-based firewalls are used to enhance the security of a device and typically are used as just one component in a firewall system. Other firewall solutions also are used, but the host-based software provides an additional layer of protection for critical resources. You never should assume that by having a main firewall between your internal devices and the network that you are now completely safe. Remember that 60 to 70 percent of attacks come from within your network. Therefore, for select resources, installing this software on critical resources provides a higher level of security.

With some host-based firewall products, user authentication is built in, allowing authentication of users before they can access resources. One advantage that this provides is that if you don't have an AGF, you can still perform user authentication at the host level.

In small networks, such as SOHO environments, purchasing one of the other firewalls from the categories that I mentioned might be cost-prohibitive. Many SOHO packet-filtering and stateful firewalls exist in the $150 to $500 range, but for a small company just beginning, it is cheaper to load a freeware host-based firewall. This is typically true for the home user who needs to protect his PC from only the casual Internet hacker.

Limitations of Host-Based Firewalls

Host-based firewalls have the following limitations:

- They are software-based firewalls.
- They are simplified packet filters.
- They have weak logging capabilities.
- They are difficult to manage on a large scale.

The first limitation of a host-based firewall is that it adds processing overhead to your PC or server: It requires more memory and CPU cycles to process traffic, and it requires a larger disk drive to log information.

For the most part, host-based firewalls are generic packet-filtering firewalls. They typically filter on IP addresses, TCP and UDP port numbers, and ICMP messages. Because they are meant for the casual user, care must be taken in their configuration, or you might create more security problems than you solve. In addition, the information that they log is typically generic in nature and will not help a lot when trying to determine whether an application layer attack is occurring or has occurred.

One of the main limitations of host-based firewalls is that they run on top of a commercial operating system, such as Windows 2000, 2003, or XP; Linux; or some other common operating system. Each of these operating systems has had security issues in the past, and you can bet that all will have security issues in the future. Therefore, these systems are more vulnerable to attack than firewall appliances. Firewall appliances, such as the PIX, typically use a proprietary operating system, which makes them more difficult to attack. Plus, these appliances were built to do one thing: implement access control, which typically is done by application-specific integrated circuits (ASICs) instead of processors. This allows firewall appliances to handle a high number of connections compared to host-based firewalls, which use a generic processor. Given this advantage of firewall appliances, as well as their low cost (between $100 and $500), many people opt to use a firewall appliance instead of host-based software. For example, I used a PIX 501 for my home network until I went wireless and installed a Linksys 54G wireless firewall appliance.

Host-based firewalls are also difficult to administer on a large scale. If you want to protect 50 web servers, all with the same security policies, ensuring that each server has the same firewall software configuration and patches becomes a difficult management process. Imagine trying to manage 50 firewalls—a simple rule change would have to be replicated 50 times. In this situation, it would be easier to use a central solution that handles firewall functions for all your servers. Plus, the more individual devices you need to secure, the more expensive a host-based system becomes, making a central solution more attractive.

Another concern is ensuring that all host-based firewalls have the appropriate rules defined on them. You might have two or three different rule sets for your various servers, and two or three more rule sets for your users. Managing the rule sets—adding, changing, and deleting rules—would be a difficult process.

NOTE   Because of management issues, you need to carefully examine the management capabilities of any host-based firewall solution that you might be considering, especially when it comes to being able to manage a wide range of rule sets across different types of hosts.

Uses for Host-Based Firewalls

Host-based firewalls offer a decent level of protection at a low cost. Because of their limitations, they typically are used in the following situations:

- With home users or telecommuters with Internet access
- In small SOHO environments
- To add an extra level protection to critical resources, such as e-mail and database servers

Hybrid Firewalls

Because of the many advances in technology, the widespread use of the Internet, and the explosion of e-commerce and e-business, the need for security has increased greatly. Therefore, classifying a firewall product is a difficult, if not impossible, process. To provide robust security features to compete against other vendors, many of the firewall categories that I discussed previously are incorporated into a single product that sometimes is referred to as a *hybrid* firewall. An example of this is the Cisco PIX firewall. It supports a stateful firewall, a cut-through proxy, a minimal form of a connection gateway firewall, and address translation, as well as many other features.

Cisco IOS Routers

When I started working with Cisco routers in 1993, access control lists had just been introduced to the Cisco IOS. This allowed the Cisco IOS to perform very basic packet filtering. From there, Cisco continually has added features to the Cisco IOS. Currently, the Cisco IOS supports many of the same security features that the Cisco PIX firewalls support, including stateful filtering, cut-through proxy (called authentication proxy), address translation, and many other features.

Actually, in today's market place, it is almost impossible to find a firewall that neatly fits into one of the categories I previously discussed. To improve their security and market appeal, today's firewall products contain many innovative features and functions.

TIP   When evaluating a firewall solution, you should closely examine the additional features and functions of the firewall, as well as its primary function. For example, if you are interested in wire-speed stateful filtering, you would consider a Cisco PIX over a Cisco router with the Cisco IOS firewall feature set. However, when examining hardware-based firewalls such as the PIX and other vendors, scrutinize their additional features and functions to see how they best fit into your security design.

Firewalls and Other Services

Just because a firewall is branded "firewall" doesn't mean that it *only* performs firewall functions. Many vendors' products include a host of other features that ease administration of your network and secure it better:

- Dynamic Host Configuration Protocol (DHCP) server and client functions
- Virtual Private Networks (VPNs)
- Intrusion detection
- Fully functioning unicast and multicast routing protocols
- Enhanced content filtering

Most firewalls support Dynamic Host Configuration Protocol functions. For SOHO environments, this is very important. A firewall might need to support a DHCP server to assign addressing information dynamically to clients. Likewise, the firewall might be connected directly to the ISP, and the ISP might use DHCP or Point-to-Point Protocol over Ethernet (PPPoE) to assign addressing information dynamically to the firewall.

Also, it is becoming more popular to use the Internet to connect various remote sites and users. The problem of using the Internet is that all information is susceptible to eavesdropping. Many firewalls support VPN functions that enable you to encrypt traffic between devices or networks. Cisco IOS-based VPNs are discussed in Part VIII, "Virtual Private Networks."

Some firewalls support intrusion-detection capabilities, which allow them to detect certain kinds of attacks. In most cases, the intrusion-detection system (IDS) included is a simplified implementation. This feature typically enables you to detect common networking attacks, such as popular DoS attacks, and is more suitable for SOHO environments or as an added measure of security in enterprise networks. To detect hundreds of network threats and attacks, a real IDS solution, such as Cisco's 4200 series sensors or IDS modules (IDSMs) for the Catalyst 6500 switches, should be used.

Many firewalls now can filter on some content, typically web-based. For example, some firewalls can filter Java and ActiveX scripts, which can contain dangerous code; some firewalls even can filter URL information. Chapter 10, "Filtering Web and Application Traffic," discusses how the Cisco IOS can filter web content.

As you can see, firewalls have come a long way and will face many new challenges in the future to adapt to new technologies and to deal with new security threats.

Firewall Design

As mentioned at the beginning of the chapter, a firewall is a device or devices that control traffic between different areas of your network. In a more robust design you typically see two or three firewall devices, as well as many other security components to protect company resources. In a firewall design, I refer to the security solution as a *firewall system*, indicating that many devices are being used to protect your resources.

As you will see in this section, you should follow some practical guidelines when developing a firewall system. These can include packet and application firewalls, application gateway and ATFs, host-based firewalls, and, more than likely, hybrid firewalls, as well as many other security devices, such as VPN concentrators, IDS devices, authentication security servers, and many other components.

After briefly covering the components in a security solution, I discuss some various designs that commonly are used to protect resources. Then I discuss their advantages and disadvantages and cover management issues.

Design Guidelines

You should follow five basic guidelines when designing a firewall system:

- Develop a security policy.
- Create a simple design solution.
- Use devices as they were intended.
- Implement a layered defense to provide extra protection.
- Consider solutions to internal threats that should be included in your design.

The following subsections cover these five key design points.

Developing a Security Policy

One of the first things you do when designing a firewall system is to create a security policy. The policy should define acceptable and unacceptable behavior, should state restrictions to resources, and should adhere to the company's business plan and policies. Without a security policy, it is practically impossible to develop a security solution that will meet your company's needs.

The key to a good design is basing it on a security policy. Basically, a policy defines who is allowed to access resources, what they are allowed to do with resources, how resources should be protected (in general terms), and what actions are taken when a security issue occurs. Without a security policy, it is impossible to design a firewall system that will protect your assets. In other words, if you don't have a security policy, what should you protect? How much should you protect resources? Who is allowed to access resources? If your policy does not define these items, it is hard to design and implement a solution based on hunches. Actually, without a security policy, the firewall system that you put in place might be creating a security risk: It might not be providing adequate protection to your company's resources.

Designing a security policy is beyond the scope of this book. However, it minimally should address the following items:

- The resources that require access from internal and external users
- The vulnerabilities associated with these resources
- The methods and solutions that can be used to protect these resources
- A cost-benefit analysis that compares the different methods and solutions

Designing Simple Solutions

A firewall system design should be kept simple and should follow your security policy. The simpler the design is, the easier it will be to implement it, maintain it, test and troubleshoot it, and adapt it to new changes. Many people like to call this the *KISS* principle: Keep it simple, stupid. The last kind of problem you want to deal with is a design or configuration error that leaves your network open to all different kinds of attacks.

CAUTION   Complex solutions are prone to design and configuration errors, and are difficult to test and troubleshoot. The simpler you can make the design, the easier it will be to manage it.

Using Devices Correctly

Network devices have functional purposes; they were built with a specific purpose in mind. For example, a Layer 2 switch is used to break up a collision or bandwidth domain, and it also uses VLANs to break up broadcast domains: It is typically *not* a good device to use to filter traffic because the filtering is done by creating filtering rules based on MAC addresses. The problem with this approach is that MAC addresses tend to change quite a bit: NICs fail, PCs and servers are upgraded, devices are moved to different locations in the network, and so on. Filtering is done best when logical addressing is deployed.

Using the wrong product to solve a security problem can open you to all kinds of security threats. For example, assume that you want to use an IDS to detect different kinds of network threats. You notice that your Cisco router has the capability in the Cisco IOS Firewall feature set, and you decide to enable it, feeling secure that your Cisco router will generate an alarm when an attack occurs. If you had taken time to read the security material related to Cisco routers, you would have realized that Cisco routers can detect only a few dozen different kinds of networking attacks (typically, the most common ones). Therefore, for all the other hundreds of kinds of attacks, your Cisco router will not be capable of detecting them, leaving you exposed. In this example, a better solution would have been to purchase an IDS solution that can detect hundreds of different kinds of attacks.

Using Old Junk to Solve New Problems

As a consultant, I repeatedly hear from customers that they want an inexpensive (that is, "cheap") solution that reuses a lot of the networking gear that they already have in their current design. Unfortunately, with a network that has equipment that is more than 5 years old, this presents a problem because that technology is outdated and probably useless.

When designing a network, especially as it relates to security, you first must come up with a simplified design that describes the basic components that are required. Then you must determine which actual products you will use for these components, based on the features and functions you need. Never try to approach this backward by trying to fit a product to your design: You create problems by doing this instead of solving them. Also remember that there is no such thing as a networking product that will do everything: Do not force yourself to cut corners by trying to make one device do everything.

Creating a Layered Defense

A security design typically uses a layered defense approach. In other words, you usually do not want one layer of defense to protect network. If this one layer is compromised, your entire network will be exposed.

The French and a One-Layer Defense

The French learned the one-layer defense limitation the hard way during World War II with the Maginot line, a physical barrier between Germany and France. The Maginot line extended only the distance of the border between France and Germany. The Germans were smart: They went north and west and came down through the Netherlands, bypassing this fortification and allowing them to easily conquer France.

Instead, you should use a multilayer defense in your firewall system design. With multiple layers, if one layer is compromised, you still have other layers behind it protecting you.

One of the examples that I like to use to describe a firewall system is the fortification systems that kings used to protected their castles in medieval times. Figure 2-22 shows an example of this. In this figure, the first line of defense is the moat surrounding the castle. For the second line of defense, spearmen are behind the moat, preventing anyone from trying to swim across it. Behind the spearmen is the third line of defense: the castle wall, which can be as little as 3 meters high but typically was much higher than this. On the wall are swordsmen, providing the fourth layer of defense. Inside the castle wall are the castle grounds and the castle itself. The castle is built with very high stone walls and turrets, providing the fifth layer of defense. And in the windows of the wall and on top of the turrets are the archers, providing the last layer of defense. As you can see from this system, an attacker must go through many layers of defense to capture or kill the king.

Figure 2-22 *A Medieval Firewall System*

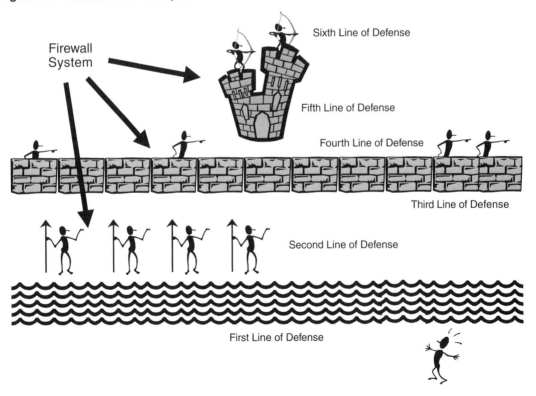

Dealing with Internal Threats

Too often, security personnel are concerned about protecting a company's resources and assets from outside threats. Remember that it is much easier to attack your assets from within; plus, most threats and attacks (60 to 70 percent) are internal attacks. Therefore, a good firewall system not only protects you from external threats, but also allows you to minimize internal threats.

DMZ

Most firewall systems use a demilitarized zone (DMZ) to protect resources and assets. A DMZ is a segment or segments that have a higher security level than that of external segments, but a lower security level than that of internal segments. DMZs are used to grant external users access to public and e-commerce resources such as web, DNS, and e-mail servers without exposing your internal network. A firewall is used to provide the security-level segmentation among the external, DMZ, and internal resources. Basically, the DMZ acts as a buffer between different areas in a network.

DMZ Rules and Traffic Flow

To help enforce security more easily, each area in the firewall system is assigned a security level. This could be something as simple as low, medium, and high, or something more sophisticated, such as a number between 1 and 100, where 1 is the lowest security level and 100 is the highest. Typically, traffic from a more secure (higher) layer is permitted to a lower layer, but not vice versa.

For traffic to go from a lower layer to a higher layer, it must be permitted explicitly: In other words, you must set up a filtering rule that allows this traffic to go from a lower level to a higher level. If two areas have the same security level, such as medium, the traffic between the two areas is either permitted or denied, based on the process that the product uses.

CAUTION   When allowing traffic to go from a lower security level to a higher one, you should be very specific about what traffic is allowed. For example, if you want Internet users to access a web server, specify both the destination IP address of the web server, such as 200.1.1.2, the protocol (TCP), and the destination port number (80), in the filtering rule. By being very specific, you are opening a hole in the firewall system for only traffic that is necessary; all other traffic (including other types of traffic to the web server) is blocked by the configuration of your security levels.

It is important to point out that these rules sometimes are built into the firewall or must be configured manually on the firewall. In either situation, this gives you a lot of flexibility in assigning a level of threat to particular areas in your network and configuring your firewall system appropriately.

NOTE   The Cisco PIX firewall uses a numbering scheme approach to security levels, providing a very flexible system for separating areas by their level of threat. Higher-number areas freely can send traffic to lower-number areas, but not vice versa, and areas with the same level cannot send traffic to each other. On Cisco IOS routers, you must configure filtering rules manually to define levels of security.

The network shown in Figure 2-23 illustrates how security levels work.

Figure 2-23   *Security Level Example*

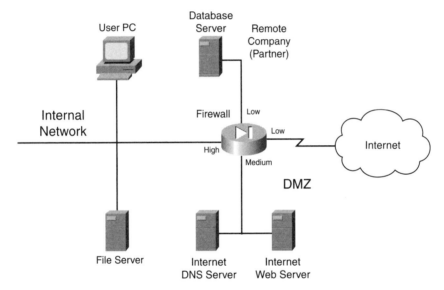

In this example, a firewall is used to separate different areas of a network. The firewall has the following four interfaces:

- A connection to the Internet, assigned a low security level
- A connection to the DMZ, where public servers are located, assigned a medium security level
- A connection to a remote company that is working on a project for them, assigned a low security level
- A connection to the internal network, assigned a high security level

This company has assigned the following rules:

- High- to low-level access: permit
- Low- to high-level access: deny
- Same-level access: deny

Given these rules, the following traffic is allowed automatically to travel through the firewall:

- Internal devices to the DMZ, the remote company, and the Internet
- DMZ devices to the remote company and the Internet

Any other type of traffic flow is restricted. One advantage of this design is that, because the remote company and the Internet are assigned the same level, traffic from the Internet cannot reach the remote company (which provides protection), and the remote company cannot use your Internet access for free (which saves you money).

Another advantage of security levels is that they create a layered approach to security. For example, for either hackers on the Internet or the remote company to access internal resources in Figure 2-23, they probably first must hack into your DMZ and then use this as a stepping stone to hack into your internal network. Using this layered approach, you make the hacker's job much more difficult and your network much more secure.

DMZ Types

DMZs come in many types of designs. You can have a single DMZ, multiple DMZs, DMZs that separate the public network from your internal network, and DMZs that separate traffic between internal networks. The following sections show some of these implementations.

Single DMZ

Single DMZs come in two types:

- Single segment
- Service-leg segment

Figure 2-24 shows an example of a single DMZ with a single segment. In this example, there are two firewalls: a perimeter firewall and a main firewall, with the DMZ segment between the two. One disadvantage of this design is that two firewalls are needed: one to protect the DMZ from the Internet and one to protect the internal network from the DMZ and the Internet.

Figure 2-24 *Single DMZ with a Single Segment*

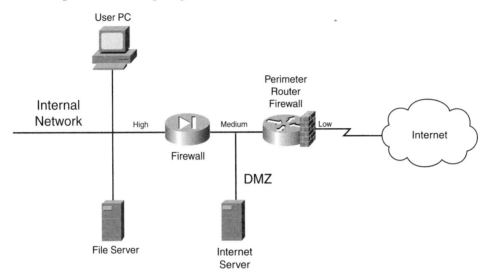

Most firewall designs use a service-leg DMZ, which is shown in Figure 2-25. In this example, a router is used to connect to the Internet. The design in Figure 2-25 has two advantages over the single-segment DMZ shown in Figure 2-24:

- The firewall sometimes can be connected directly to the Internet, removing the extra cost of the perimeter router.
- All security-level polices can be defined on one device (in a single-segment DMZ, you must define your policies on two devices).

Figure 2-25 *Single DMZ with a Service-Leg Segment*

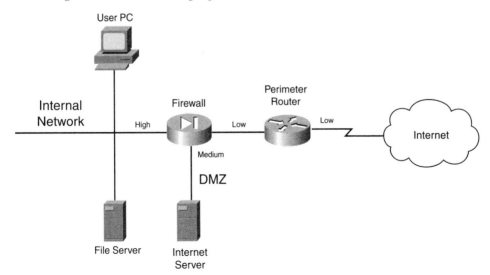

The main problem with this approach, however, is that, because a single firewall is handling all security policies, a successful DoS attack can degrade the firewall's performance. In the best case, only your throughput is affected; in the worst case, the firewall might crash. With a single-segment DMZ, because the policies are spread between the two firewalls, there is less likelihood of an overload occurring. This is especially true for traffic between the DMZ and the internal network. If a hacker is attacking a web server on the DMZ, the perimeter firewall takes the brunt of this attack, which allows the internal firewall to handle DMZ/internal traffic without affect.

Multiple DMZs

A firewall system can be used to separate multiple areas of your network, including multiple DMZs. Figure 2-26 shows an example of a network with multiple DMZs. In this example, a firewall is used to break up a network into four areas: the internal network, a DMZ for Company A's server, a DMZ for Company B's server, and the Internet. In this example, the internal network is assigned a high security level, both company servers are assigned a medium security level, and the Internet is assigned a low security level. Assume that high-to-low access is allowed by default but that same-to-same is denied. In this example, the internal network can access any resource, and each company server can access the Internet, but not the other company's server. You would need to set up security rules to allow Internet access into the two servers on the medium-security segments, as well as communication between the two servers, if this is desired.

Figure 2-26 *Multiple DMZ Example*

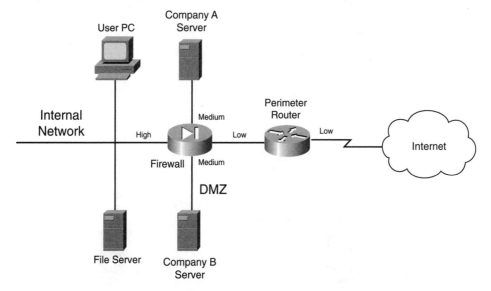

Actually, this type of design is very common in ISPs. Most ISPs offer web-hosting services and use this type of design to separate each company's server(s) from the others.

Internal DMZ

Another type of DMZ is an internal one. An internal DMZ enables you to provide separation between different parts of your internal network. Most people assume that a DMZ is used to separate your internal services from those that you offer to the public, such as a web or e-commerce server; however, they can be used effectively to protect resources in one part of your company from another.

Figure 2-27 illustrates the usefulness of an internal DMZ. In this example, a firewall is used to separate the internal network (in the right of the figure) from the engineering and accounting users. In this example, both engineering and accounting are assigned a medium level of security. Assume that same security level to the same security level is denied by default; in other words, if two interfaces have the same security level, they cannot, by default, communicate with each other. With this configuration, accounting and engineering are allowed to send traffic to the internal network but not themselves. Internal users cannot access either of these two groups because the internal users are on a lower security level interface. To allow these last types of access, you would need to configure security rules on your firewall to allow same-to-same or low-to-medium levels of access.

Figure 2-27 *Internal DMZ Example*

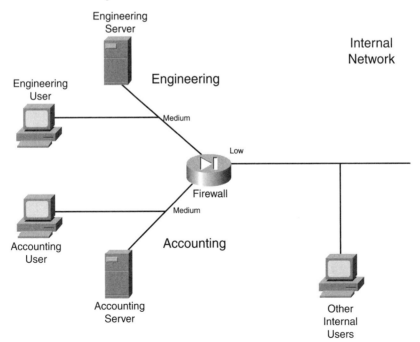

As you can see in this example, you easily can protect important resources in your network from other internal users. Internal DMZs enable you to accomplish the following:

- Control traffic between areas
- Localize security problems

I already have discussed the first bulleted point. For the second, imagine that a hacker somehow could compromise your perimeter defenses and access an internal resource such as a file server. By using an internal DMZ, you still are protecting important resources. In Figure 2-27, the accounting and engineering resources are protected from the hacker if an internal resource connected to the lower-level internal interface was compromised.

Components

Now that you have a basic understanding of firewall system design practices, this section takes a closer look at the components that make up a firewall system. A good firewall system typically contains the following components:

- Perimeter router
- Firewall
- VPN
- IDS

It is important to point out here that I used the word *component*, not *device*, to describe what is included in a firewall system. This is because many devices can support multiple components. For example, a Cisco IOS router can act as a perimeter router or a main firewall, can terminate VPN connections, and can perform IDS—all in one chassis. Remember my caution, though, if you are using a single layer for defense: Using multiple layers provides for a better design and protection. The following sections cover the different components used in a firewall system.

Perimeter Router Component

The main purpose of the perimeter router is to provide a connection to a public network, such as the Internet, or a different company. It is used to convert data-link layer media types from a LAN to either a WAN or MAN medium.

The functions of the perimeter router can include the following:

- Routing through static routes or a dynamic routing protocol
- Filtering through either packet filtering or stateful filtering
- Terminating VPN connections
- Providing address translation

TIP | Remember that the main function of the perimeter router is to access a different network: It is your first, but not your last, line of defense. Therefore, you do not want to overload it with a bunch of security functions that another component in the firewall system can handle better.

Firewall Component

The main purpose of the firewall component is to separate your network into different security levels and control traffic between these levels. Typically, you find a firewall component near the perimeter of the network, protecting you from external threats as well as providing controlled access to a public DMZ segment. However, you also might find firewall components inside your internal network, separating critical resources so that they are better protected.

The functions of the firewall can include the following:

- Stateful filtering
- User authentication of connection with CTPs
- Connection filtering with CGFs
- Address translation

VPN Component

The main purpose of the VPN component is to provide a protected connection between two devices, two networks, or a device and a network. This protection can include encryption, authentication, and packet-integrity checking, preventing eavesdrop attacks from prying eyes. VPNs are a cost-effective, remote-access solution because they enable you to use a public network, in a secure manner, to connect two private networks. This is cheaper than purchasing private WAN links to provide connectivity.

The functions of the VPN component can include the following:

- Protecting (encrypting) traffic between LAN sites and remote access users
- Assigning addressing information to remote access clients
- Using simple packet filters to restrict traffic flow

VPNs are covered in more depth in Part VIII.

IDS Component

The main purpose of the IDS component is to detect, and possibly prevent, reconnaissance, DoS, and unauthorized access attacks. To understand the different kinds of network attacks that your company is facing, you need an intimate understanding of the different kinds of traffic flowing through your network, as well as the intentions of this traffic.

Most traffic entering or traversing your network has a valid purpose: to access web pages with HTTP, resolve names to addresses with DNS, send e-mail with SMTP, and so on. However, a small percentage of traffic has malicious intentions. In these cases, a hacker might be executing a reconnaissance attack to determine what kinds of resources are available in your network, and then might execute a DoS attack to affect their level of service or carry out an unauthorized attack to open a back door into your network. An IDS solution should be capable of detecting these kinds of threats.

IDS Overlooked

IDS components often are overlooked or are seen as unnecessary in a security solution if your network has a firewall component. I once performed work for a company that took this position on IDS solutions, and it was shaken when I set up a test IDS system that detected more than 1000 network threats directed against the network system over a single day. You will not know what kinds of attacks your network is facing unless you monitor it. Plus, new types of attacks are appearing at a steady rate. A good IDS solution can help detect and prevent attacks.

IDS components fall under one of three categories:

- Anomaly-based
- Signature-based
- Hybrid-based

Anomaly-based solutions capture traffic over a period of time and use this as a reference for what is valid. These systems then compare new traffic to what is considered to be "normal" and look for anomalies. One disadvantage of anomaly-based solutions is that they tend to generate a lot of false positives (they trigger alarms that are not really attacks). This is because traffic patterns change; if you do not stay up-to-date on a database of normal traffic flows, false positives are bound to happen.

Signature-based solutions compare traffic to signatures to look for attacks. A signature is a static definition of things to examine in packet or packets; these can include header information as well as data. Signature-based solutions have a lot less false positive alarms. However, their main disadvantage is that they cannot detect new kinds of attacks unless you keep your signature database updated. This is where an anomaly-based solution shines: It can detect new kinds of attacks without a software upgrade.

In many of today's IDS solutions, a hybrid approach is used, with both signatures and anomaly detection used in tandem to provide the best possible intrusion detection.

IDS solutions come in two flavors:

- Network-based IDS
- Host-based IDS

A network-based IDS solution is a protocol analyzer on steroids: It plugs into your network at key points and monitors traffic. Network-based systems can be used to detect attacks against many different devices. A good network-based IDS solution should have the capability, when an attack is detected, to access (log into) your firewall component and configure a temporary filter to block the malicious traffic. This is an excellent tool for shutting down the hacker's access even into public areas of your network.

A host-based IDS solution is IDS software running on a host, such as a PC or file server, that detects attacks only against that host. This can provide an additional measure of protection for critical servers that are not necessarily protected by a firewall or IDS component. One downside of host-based solutions is that they require extra processing power to examine packet information sent to the host.

CAUTION IDS solutions are still in their infancy and should not be relied upon solely for security. For many IDS systems, a very wily hacker can slip by attacks without raising an alarm. Remember that a good firewall system has multiple components to it.

Your IDS component should play a key role in your firewall system. The functions of the IDS component can include these:

- Monitoring traffic for statistical purposes
- Examining traffic for network threats
- Reporting network threats and possibly taking action to prevent the threats

IDS is discussed in more depth in Chapter 16, "Intrusion-Detection System."

TIP IDS systems can generate a lot of logging information. You should review and analyze this carefully daily. By doing this, you will gain an excellent understanding of the traffic patterns in your network, as well as what hackers are currently up to.

Component Placement

Now that you understand some of the components used in a firewall system, this section talks about where these components are placed in a network design. As you will see, you can design a network in many different ways, each with advantages and disadvantages.

NOTE   It is important to point out that there is no one correct way to design a secure network. Each network is unique, and its unique characteristics must be taken into account when designing a solution. However, the examples shown here are a good starting point for creating the appropriate design for your network.

Simple Firewall System Design

To help understand where components are placed in a firewall system, I use two examples. The first example, shown in Figure 2-28, is the simpler of the two designs.

Figure 2-28 *Simple Firewall System Design*

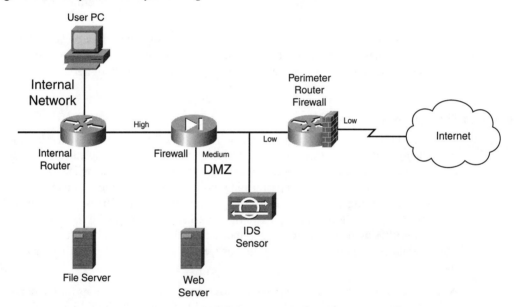

In this example, a perimeter router with basic packet filtering screens traffic as it enters the network. A standalone IDS device is used to detect attacks that the perimeter packet-filtering firewall did not filter.

The traffic then is processed by a stateful firewall. The stateful firewall has set up three security levels: low for the Internet side, medium for the DMZ, and high for the internal network. A security rule was added on the stateful firewall to allow traffic from the Internet to only the web server. All other traffic from a lower security level to a higher one is prohibited; however, higher-to-lower movement is permitted, allowing the web server administrator located on the internal network to log into the DMZ web server to update web pages.

An internal router in this design provides routing to internal segments. If you need to set up security levels and restrict access to areas of this network, you can use basic packet-filtering services on the router.

One of the advantages of this design is its simplicity: It has a minimum of three layers of defense: the packet-filtering firewall at the perimeter, the IDS, and the stateful firewall. Optionally, you can turn the internal router into a packet-filtering firewall.

This design has some disadvantages, however:

- Any attacks directed at the perimeter router/firewall are not seen by the IDS, which might be useful in determining who is trying to hack into the router and how they are trying to do it.

- No IDS exists on the inside the network, so you cannot easily determine whether internal attacks are occurring.

- The internal router might provide only simple packet filtering, which makes it difficult to implement security levels for internal users. However, this can be remedied by using a different type of firewall, such as a stateful firewall or an AGF.

Enhanced Firewall System Design

The second firewall system design is shown in Figure 2-29. As you can see, it has more components and rectifies some of the security deficiencies in the simple firewall system design. I examine the perimeter router component first. As in the last example, the perimeter router/packet-filtering firewall is performing basic filtering of traffic as it comes into the Internet. Nothing is different in this example except for what the bottom-right IDS device is doing: monitoring both the external Internet segment and the segment between the packet-filtering perimeter router and the stateful firewall. This allows the IDS to see what attacks are directed at the router, as well as what attacks are getting through the router.

Next is the VPN concentrator. It is used to provide encrypted connections for the remote office connection (from the remote office firewall to the concentrator), as well as to terminate remote-access user connections from telecommuters and SOHO users. Notice that an IDS sensor behind the VPN concentrator is examining the unencrypted traffic. This is placed here just in case one of the remote access users or the remote office becomes compromised: The IDS can view the unencrypted traffic to detect network threats, which the IDS device connected between the perimeter router and the Internet firewall cannot because the traffic is encrypted at this point.

In addition, when the unencrypted traffic is sent to the Internet firewall from the external users, it is assigned a medium level of security, which means that it can be routed back to the Internet without any filtering and to the DMZ (assuming that same-to-same level of access is allowed). To access an internal resource, the internal firewall needs a security rule configured.

Figure 2-29 *Enhanced Firewall System Design*

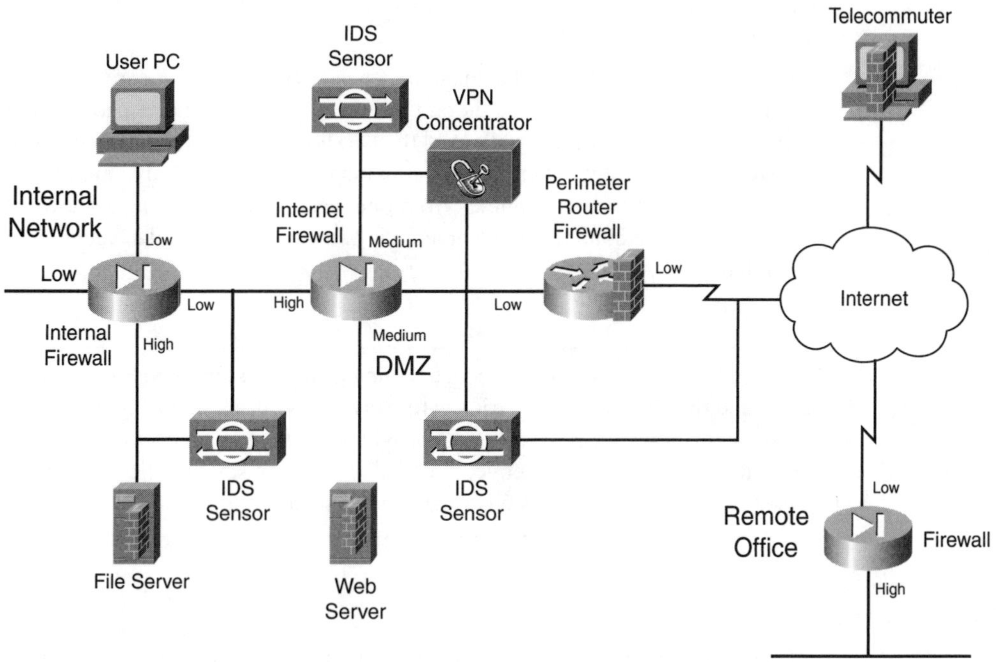

The Internet firewall provides a second layer of filtering after it passes the perimeter router/ firewall. It handles traffic from the VPN concentrator, the Internet, and the DMZ. Notice that the server in the DMZ has a host-based firewall installed, adding protection to it.

The bottom-left IDS is monitoring the Internet Firewall-to-Internal Firewall segment as well as the internal high-security segment, detecting attacks that get through the respective firewalls. Plus, the host-based firewall software is installed on the internal file server.

Inside the network, an internal stateful firewall is used to provide security levels. In this example, the file-server connection has a high security level, and all of the other connections are set to low. This means that rules must be configured on the internal firewall to allow any type of traffic to reach the internal file server.

In all, this is a good security design. It uses IDS components at key places to monitor critical traffic, and it has a layered defense approach, with a packet-filtering firewall and two stateful firewalls. Plus, host-based firewall software is used on critical servers. A VPN also is used to protect traffic across the Internet.

This design also has some disadvantages, however:

- It costs a lot more than the simple design.

- The IDS systems are monitoring a lot of traffic and are generating a lot of logging information. If someone does not take the time to examine the IDS logs carefully, attacks could slip through the cracks.

- Much more configuration and management need to be done, to ensure that the correct security policies are implemented on the firewalls: the perimeter packet-filtering firewall, the two stateful firewalls, and the two host-based software firewalls. In this scenario, you definitely want to look at management software that enables you to define all your security policies from one desktop, and then have these polices converted into the configuration commands and downloaded and executed on your firewall devices.

TIP   As I learned a long time ago, there is no such thing as network nirvana. Every solution has advantages and disadvantages. The trick is to weigh these when factoring which solution meets your security policy requirements, provides the best cohesive yet manageable solution, and is the most cost-effective. Notice that I did not say that the solution has to be the most secure—only that it needs to meet your security policies.

Design Considerations

Here are some important points to remember when placing components in a firewall system:

- Use a packet-filtering firewall for the boundary router, to provide an extra level of protection. If you are really concerned about security, use a stateful firewall for this component.

- All servers that have publicly available resources should be placed in a DMZ. Servers that handle critical processes or financial transactions should have host-based firewall software installed on them. In addition, all unnecessary services on these servers should be disabled.

- For DMZ servers with sensitive information, consider using a multiple DMZ design. This is especially true if you have a web server and a database server that it interfaces with. Put the web server on a lower security level than the database server.

- If external users or remote sites that traverse a public network want to access internal resources, require a VPN. This ensures that any sensitive data is protected.

- VPN connections, as well as remote-access connections through private networks, should be terminated on their own DMZ on the Internet firewall. An IDS system should be used to examine this traffic after it is decrypted. This also allows the traffic to go right back out to the Internet, but because it is going through the firewall, you have more control over what is allowed.

- For critical internal resources, use an IDS component to monitor key segments to detect network threats. You can add extra security by segmenting your internal network into different security levels. This can compartmentalize your network and restrict access from the general population of users to areas that they have no business being in, such as accounting and R&D.

- For e-mail, you should have a public e-mail server in the DMZ that accepts all incoming and outgoing mail services. I highly recommend that you have antivirus, spam, and host-based firewall software running on this server. I also recommend that you use a limited form of a CGF that can examine mail content and make filtering decisions on it, to catch networking threats that the antivirus software cannot deal with. After e-mail is processed, it then can be forwarded to an internal server. I also recommend that all outgoing e-mail be forwarded through the DMZ e-mail server and have the same processes performed on it (remember that someone on the inside might try to use your e-mail server for malicious purposes).

I could list probably a dozen or so more items, but these are the more important ones. As you can see from this list, you have your work cut out for you.

Firewall Implementation

Now that you have chosen your components for your firewall system, you need to set them up and configure your security policies on them. Typically, you use either a command-line interface (CLI) or a graphical user interface (GUI) to perform the configuration. Cisco products support both methods, but this book focuses on the CLI, which is the most common method used by Cisco administrators.

TIP   I have found that, at least with Cisco products, the Cisco development team for routers always implements features using the CLI first and then adds this function to GUI-based products, such as Security Device Manager (SDM) and CiscoWorks VMS. Therefore, I highly recommend that you become very comfortable with the Cisco CLI if you plan to keep your Cisco IOS routers up-to-date with the latest security technology.

Security Device Manager

Cisco has introduced a new web device manager called Security Device Manager (SDM) that provides an alternative to CLI configuration of a Cisco router. SDM is a web software component loaded into flash of a supported Cisco router that enables you to use a web browser to configure the router. Not all routers support SDM, but most routers that Cisco currently sells today do, including the 831, 836, 837, 1701, 1710, 1711, 1712, 1721, 1751, 1760, 2610XM, 2611XM, 2620XM, 2650XM, 2651XM, 2691, 3620, 3640, 3661, 3662,

3725, 3745, 7204VXR, 7206VXR, and 7301. You also need Cisco IOS 12.2(11)T6 or later on your router. If you buy one of the previously mentioned routers today, SDM automatically ships with it; however, you easily can download SDM from the Cisco web site and install it in flash on a supported router platform.

Figure 2-30 shows the main screen of SDM. With SDM, Cisco provides wizardlike functionality when configuring many Cisco IOS features, including LAN, WAN, firewall, and VPN features. The use of SDM is beyond the scope of this book; however, if you are comfortable using the CLI of a router, you will find that using SDM makes configuring a Cisco router, including its security features, a very simple process. More information about SDM can be found at http://www.cisco.com/en/US/products/sw/secursw/ps5318/index.html.

Figure 2-30 *SDM's Main Window*

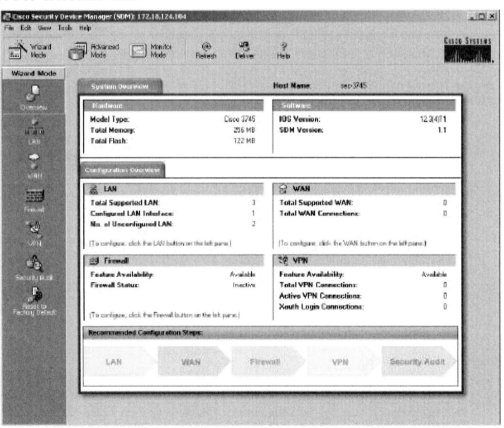

TIP	If you are not familiar with the CLI of Cisco routers, SDM is the right management tool for you. Using a GUI interface, SDM turns your input into actual router CLI commands. After you perform and apply a configuration in SDM on your router, you can use the CLI to view the actual commands that SDM implemented. This provides a training tool to help you become more familiar with the CLI.

Implementing Firewall Features

One of the first things you need to do is secure your firewall(s) itself. In other words, if a hacker breaks into your firewall, your network is wide open to a multitude of attacks. Therefore, you should be very careful about how it is administered, what services it is running, and how an administrator can access and manage it. Part II, "Managing Access to Routers," covers this information.

Most firewall devices use rule sets to set up security rules and access controls. As you will see with Cisco routers in Part III, "Nonstateful Filtering Technologies," and Part IV, "Stateful and Advanced Filtering Technologies," most of the security rules and access controls are defined by using access control lists (ACLs). As you will see, you can use many methods in the Cisco IOS to create your rule sets. These rule sets should be defined as specifically as possible: If you are permitting traffic between two machines, be specific about the type of traffic, such as TCP on port 80, or UDP on port 69. Basically, the rule-set premise should be to permit certain things and drop everything else.

Other features also should be implemented on your firewalls, if necessary: address translation (Part V, "Address Translation and Firewalls"), access authentication to your network (Part VI, "Managing Access Through Routers"), IDS (Part VII, "Detecting and Preventing Attacks"), VPNs (Part VIII, "Virtual Private Networks"), and other necessary features and services.

Firewall Administration and Management

After you have completed your firewall system implementation, you need to administer and manage it on an ongoing basis. One of the weakest links in your security setup is the people maintaining it: People are prone to making errors. Therefore, your security solution should be simple enough for your administrators to make changes to it and to troubleshoot it, yet still meet the objectives outlined in your company's security policy.

Even in this situation, configuration errors will be made in your firewall system. Therefore, before any changes are made to the firewall system, it is important that you back them up before the changes are made. After changes are made, it is of the utmost importance that you always test changes in your firewall system.

You should use two basic methods when testing the configuration. First, you should print the configuration and compare its rule set to your security policy, to double-check that the configuration it is using follows the security policy. Second, use software tools to test the change. In this situation, you, the administrator, are pretending to be the hacker. Many tools available to you enable you to perform all kinds of tricks, such as IP spoofing, DoS attacks, and others. Some of these I cover in this book as I show you how to use your Cisco IOS router to protect yourself from them. Many vendors also sell software packages geared toward security policy testing. The tools I use are either freeware or shareware.

CAUTION   Any major changes to a firewall system first should be done in a lab environment and should be tested before being configured on your production firewall system. Failure to do this can create serious security problems for your network if you make configuration mistakes.

Cisco IOS Security

The one product that has put Cisco on the face of the networking map is Cisco IOS software, which runs on a variety of platforms from routers and switches, as well as other devices. Cisco continually is enhancing the Cisco IOS to include new features and tools that enable you to deal with the networking problems you face every day.

When it comes to security, the Cisco IOS is packed with all kinds of security features that you can take advantage of in securing your network. Some security tools are part of the normal Cisco IOS packaging. Other tools require the purchase of the Cisco IOS Firewall feature set, which includes enhanced firewall tools to implement access control more securely. The following two sections discuss some of the security features you will find in the Cisco IOS software and compare two Cisco firewall products: the Cisco IOS router and the PIX.

Cisco IOS Uses

As I mentioned in the introduction to this section, the Cisco IOS is packed with many different kinds of security tools and features that enable you to implement a secure firewall system. Combined with the Cisco IOS Firewall feature set, you can set up your Cisco IOS router as a well-defended perimeter firewall or a scalable Internet firewall, providing a robust firewall solution. Here is just a small list of roles that your Cisco IOS router can play in a firewall system:

- A perimeter firewall
- An Internet firewall
- An internal firewall
- A VPN concentrator
- An IDS

Cisco IOS Security Features

The Cisco IOS Firewall feature set enhances the security of the normal Cisco IOS, adding much greater depth and flexibility to a security solution. Some of these features include address translation, authentication, encryption, stateful filtering, failover, URL content filtering, and many others. Here are some of the key benefits that the Cisco IOS Firewall software provides:

- **Flexibility**—As I already mentioned, the Cisco IOS firewall router can play many roles: VPN, filtering firewall, IDS, and others. This enables you to choose the features that you need to customize your security solution.

- **Scalability**—The Cisco IOS Firewall software is available on a wide range of router platforms and interface selection, enabling you to choose the appropriate product for your security solution.

- **Easier provisioning and investment protection**—The Cisco IOS Firewall software uses the same Cisco IOS interface that you are familiar with, reducing the learning curve in enabling Cisco IOS Firewall security features. This reduces your cost and also protects your investment by enabling you to upgrade a router product without having to completely redo the new router's configuration.

- **VPN support**—The Cisco IOS Firewall works with VPNs to enable you to use inexpensive public networks to provide secure connectivity between remote offices and users.

These are some of the many features you will find in the Cisco IOS, including the Cisco IOS Firewall feature set:

- **Address translation**—Supports many flavors of address translation, including NAT, PAT, and load distribution. With address translation, you have stricter control over traffic that enters and leaves your network, and you can keep your IP addressing design from prying external eyes.

- **Audit trail**—Supports detailed audit trails. With the Cisco IOS, you can record detailed information about transactions and denied connections, including the source and destination IP addresses and ports, and the number of bytes transmitted for the connection. This can be done on a per-application, per-feature basis.

- **Authentication proxy**—Supports per-user authentication and authorization for LAN and dialup connections. This enables you to authenticate users before they can access your resources, and then authorize which resources they can access. This can be done through Telnet, HTTP, or HTTPS. Authorization is implemented by downloading per-user access-control information.

- **Basic filtering technologies**—Supports basic Cisco IOS filtering technologies. Basic IOS filtering features, such as standard, extended, timed, lock-and-key, and reflexive ACLs, are available to you without having to purchase the Cisco IOS Firewall feature set.

- **DoS**—Supports DoS detection and prevention through features such as TCP Intercept and Context-Based Access Control (CBAC), enabling you to take actions such as logging, resetting connections, or even dropping connections.

- **Dynamic port mapping**—Supports mapping of ports to different numbers. Many applications run on ports that are different than the standard ones. For example, some web servers use ports 8080 and 8090. Dynamic port mapping allows the Cisco IOS to treat these ports as a port 80 connection and to perform special types of inspection on these connections.

- **Intrusion detection**—Supports real-time monitoring and detection of more than 100 different kinds of network threats and attacks. The Cisco IOS IDS can be used to supplement your IDS solution, as well as to provide a basic level of protection for SOHO environments.

- **Java applet filtering**—Supports filtering of Java applets. The Cisco IOS can filter Java applets that are embedded in HTTP connections, enabling you to prevent malicious applets from wreaking havoc on your users' desktops.

- **Real-time alerts**—Supports logging of real-time alerts to external devices, such as a syslog server or management platform. Real-time alerts enable you to rank security issues so that you can deal with them in an appropriate order, dealing with high-risk security issues first.

- **Router authentication**—Supports authentication of routing updates, preventing spoofing and routing attacks. With this feature, you can be assured that your routing information is protected from internal and external attacks.

- **Stateful firewall filtering**—Supports stateful filtering of traffic with CBAC, a component of the Cisco IOS Firewall feature set. CBAC implements the stateful firewall filtering feature in the Cisco IOS and can be used as a main firewall component in your network. Currently, stateful filtering is supported for TCP, UDP, and ICMP protocols.

- **URL filtering**—Supports URL filtering. With the help of an external WebSense or N2H2 web content filtering server, the Cisco IOS can filter URL content. These two servers contain your URL content-filtering policies, and the Cisco IOS acts as the filtering agent, using the policies on the servers to implement its filtering.

- **Voice connections**—Supports H.323v2, Skinny, and SIP voice connections. Certain applications, such as multimedia and voice, create problems with traditional firewalls. The Cisco IOS Firewall feature set supports a limited form of protocol fixup, which allows it to deal with dynamic connection and addressing allocations for H.323 and SIP.

This is just a small list of the security features that the Cisco IOS and Cisco IOS Firewall feature set support. Later chapters focus on all of these features, plus many more.

Cisco IOS Devices and Their Uses

One of the things you need to decide is which router platform or platforms you will use to implement your firewall system. With the Cisco IOS Firewall feature set, you have a wide range of choices of hardware platforms available for SOHO, branch office, extranet connections, and corporate office settings. Table 2-5 summarizes the Cisco recommendations for routers you should use for these environments.

Table 2-5   *Router Recommendations*

Routers	Recommendations
800, UBR 900, 1700	SOHO environments
2600, 3600, 3700	Branch offices and extranets
7100, 7200, 7400, 7500, Catalyst 6500 switches with the MSFC2	VPN and WAN aggregation points, as well as environments that need high-bandwidth throughput

NOTE   Table 2-5 contains basic recommendations. Note that every network and every situation is different. You need to carefully evaluate the needs of your network when choosing a Cisco product.

When to Use a Cisco IOS Firewall

The Cisco IOS Firewall typically is best suited when you need to integrate multiprotocol routing with security policies, providing secure firewall functions. However, there are many choices of firewall products, and many administrators and engineers have asked me which product they should choose. Answering this question is difficult:

- You must understand your company's issues and security policy.
- You must understand what products were meant to do.

I cannot help you that much with the first issue, but I can help you with the second issue, especially as it relates to choosing between a Cisco PIX or Cisco IOS firewall solution.

The PIX and the Cisco IOS router support many common security features and tools; however, I focus on just the differences so that you can develop a better understanding of what the two products cannot do or are not good at doing. Table 2-6 shows a list of these items.

Table 2-6 *Cisco IOS Firewall and PIX comparison*

Process or Feature	PIX	Cisco IOS Firewall
Operating system	Has a dedicated operating system, which minimizes security risks.	Handles many processes, providing flexibility in implementing a multitude of features.
Scalability	Offers a wide variety of platforms and speed performance of more than 1 Gbps.	Offers a wide variety of platforms and interfaces—LAN, WAN, and MAN.
Authentication	Supports cut-through proxy with HTTP, HTTPS, FTP, and Telnet.	Supports authentication proxy with only Telnet, HTTP, and HTTPS.
Training and maintenance	Uses the FOS operating system, which is similar to but not the same as the Cisco IOS.	Runs the same Cisco IOS, requiring no additional training on its configuration.
One-box solution	Acts as a dedicated firewall appliance and is one of the best security products on the market, but requires other network devices for other services.	Provides a one-box solution, enabling you to use all of its services in a single chassis.
QoS	Does not have a rate-limiting function. It can limit only the number of connections.	Supports very sophisticated QoS features, enabling to limit the rate and level of service of a connection.
Application inspection	With the Protocol Fixup feature, can perform generic inspection of certain applications for a limited number of attacks.	Supports a form of protocol fixup similar to the PIX. However, the Cisco IOS also supports NBAR, which allows for a much better solution when dealing with filtering application content.

Typically, the PIX is used as a dedicated firewall appliance for wire-speed filtering of traffic and secure VPN connections. The Cisco IOS typically is used to enhance a router's security while it performs other services, such as QoS or multiprotocol routing. The Cisco IOS Firewall feature set typically is used to increase the protection of a perimeter router. However, I have seen PIXs used as both Internet and perimeter firewalls, and I also have seen Cisco IOS routers used for both solutions. Every network and every solution is different.

Summary

This chapter showed you the basics of firewalls and firewall systems. You were introduced to the various types of firewalls and their functions, and you learned how to design a good firewall system. The remainder of this book focuses on how to secure your Cisco IOS router and use it as a component in a firewall system. This can be something as simple as setting it up as a packet-filtering firewall, to something as complex as using stateful firewall features to implement security levels, authenticating user connections, inspecting traffic for network threats, authenticating user connections, and making use of many other features.

Next up is Part II, which shows you how to protect the router itself by securing access to it and disabling all unnecessary services.

## PART II

Managing Access to Routers

Chapter 3   Accessing a Router

Chapter 4   Disabling Unnecessary Services

Chapter 5   Authentication, Authorization, and Accounting

Accessing a Router

This chapter focuses on the various methods by which you can access your Cisco router and how to provide a secure method of access without using an external security server. External security servers and authentication are discussed in Chapter 5, "Authentication, Authorization, and Accounting." Remember that this book focuses on using a Cisco router as a firewall solution, so many of the ideas presented here have disadvantages in providing secure access to your router (and some I would never recommend). However, I discuss many of the options available to you so that you can understand their disadvantages and advantages, and choose the correct solution for your particular situation.

Because many people use a Cisco router as a perimeter firewall, that router serves as a first line of defense. Therefore, restricting access to it is very important. If a hacker gains access to your perimeter router, it eases his job of gaining access to resources behind it. As you will see in this chapter, you can secure access to your router in many ways: Some of them I recommend, and some of them I would never use.

Types of Authentication

When attempting to gain management access to a Cisco router, this can be done in a variety of ways, including the following:

- Console port
- Auxiliary port
- Telnet
- Hypertext Transfer Protocol (HTTP) and HTTP with Secure Socket Layer (HTTPS)
- Secure Shell (SSH)
- Simple Network Management Protocol (SNMP)

Each of these methods presents a certain level of security risk. However, you can secure each method by using password authentication. You can authenticate access in many ways, including the following:

- No passwords
- Static passwords

- Aging passwords
- One-time passwords (OTP)
- Token card services

Each of these authentication methods has advantages and disadvantages. The following sections cover these methods in more detail.

No Password Authentication

The worst type of authentication method is to not configure passwords on your device, whether on a Cisco router or even your PC. If some networking devices do not have passwords, they prevent remote access to the device. This is true of Cisco routers with Telnet. If a virtual type terminal (VTY) line and a privileged EXEC password have not been configured on a Cisco router, you cannot Telnet to it.

CAUTION   Note that it is possible to allow VTY access to a router without a line password by using the **no login** command. Never do this on a Cisco router because anyone then can remotely Telnet to your router without authenticating.

However, I would never leave this to chance. Always configure some method of authentication for every type of access in the device—or, if possible, disable methods of access that are not used. Some type of authentication method is better than nothing.

Static Password Authentication

The most common method of authentication is to use static passwords, with or without user accounts. This is probably one of the most popular methods of securing Cisco routers. However, static passwords have the following problems:

- If the account password becomes compromised, the device is compromised. You can fix this by changing the password, but you might not detect this for a period of time, if at all.

- How static passwords are chosen can create security risks. Using names, birthdays, and common words is popular among users. A good password should have a mixture of letters, numbers, and special characters.

- The most secure form of a static password is a random string of characters, but this presents another security issue: Users write down these passwords because they are hard to remember, and they tape them to the border of their monitors, available for everyone to see.

- Some methods of access require multiple people to perform the same tasks using the same account, such as root in UNIX or Administrator in Microsoft Windows. When the administrators use the same account, it becomes more difficult to manage: More people have access to the password, making the account less secure. It becomes a management headache to manage password changes because multiple people must be notified.

- Static passwords are susceptible to eavesdropping attacks if the password information is not encrypted (such as with Telnet connections).

- These passwords are susceptible to password-cracking programs if a hacker can gain access to your password file.

Typically, static passwords are used in small environments in which access attacks are not that much of a concern; however, they are, by no means, a secure method of authentication.

TIP   I highly recommend that you not use accounts that are required on a system, such as root in UNIX or Administrator in Windows, for management purposes. Instead, create a separate management account for each administrator, and let each user assign a password to the account that falls under the guidelines defined in your security policy concerning passwords. Then disable the default management account by assigning a random string of letters, numbers, and special characters. Lock up this password in case you ever need access to these accounts in emergency situations. Plus, you always should monitor attempted access to these disabled accounts: This indicates that a probable access attack is occurring.

Aging Password Authentication

To help overcome the issues that static passwords have, some administrators use aging passwords. With aging passwords, the password is valid for a predefined period of time. When the time period expires, the password is no longer valid. Typically, a password history file is used to ensure that when a user is forced to change his password, it isn't changed to a password that the user previously used for the account.

Most administrators think that by using aging passwords, they have removed all the disadvantages of static password configurations. In reality, aging passwords are not that much more secure than static passwords. About the only advantage that aging passwords have over static passwords is that if an account was compromised and the user of the account was forced to change the passwords, the hacker then is locked out of the account.

NOTE   Most hackers are aware of this process and install keystroke-capturing programs that you install in the login script that is executed when the user logs in. In this situation, if the user is forced to change the password, the capturing script sees this information and sends it to the hacker.

Given the ingenuity of the hacker to use keystroke-capturing programs, aging password authentication does not have any real advantage over static passwords. Note that Cisco routers support static passwords, but they do not support aging passwords.

CAUTION   My main concern with static and aging password authentication is that they are susceptible to eavesdropping attacks for many types of remote-access connections, such as Telnet, FTP, HTTP, RCP, RSH, and others. Therefore, if you are using static or aging passwords, I highly recommend that you use some method that encrypts the authentication information between the user and the resource, to prevent eavesdropping attacks. Some remote-access tools that you can use include SSH, HTTPS, and Secure Copy (SCP).

Also be careful about backing up resources across the network, especially because their password files will be susceptible to eavesdropping. Chapter 5 discusses how you can centralize authentication functions and keep user and password information on a security server that you can back up locally. Chapter 5 also discusses how to securely back up a router's configuration file, to prevent eavesdropping attacks.

One-Time Password Authentication

One-time passwords (OTPs) were developed specifically to deal with the limitations and security issues of static and aging passwords. Unlike static and aging passwords, OTPs can be used only once: After a password is used, it no longer is valid.

A password-generator program is used to generate a list of passwords, with the S/Key algorithm, which uses an MD5 hash function, generating the list. This process typically is accomplished through a password calculator program in which the user enters a secret key or phrase into the program. The program then generates a file containing a list of valid OTPs. The passwords can be used for authentication purposes for resources that use the S/Key algorithm. When a password is used, it becomes invalid.

OTP authentication has a few advantages over static and aging passwords:

- The applications that users employ do not have to be changed, easing the implementation of OTP.

- These passwords are typically secure from password-cracking programs because of the nature in creating these random passwords. However, if the hacker can guess the secret key that was used to generate the list of passwords, there is a chance that he can determine the OTPs that were generated.

- OTP defeats eavesdropping attacks. Even if a hacker sees the password, it is too late to use it because the user is authenticated and the password becomes invalid.

- If a hacker is lucky enough to guess a randomly generated OTP, he is granted access to the account one time; subsequent access requires the hacker to get lucky again guessing a randomly generated OTP.

OTPs have one main disadvantage: They generate a file with the random OTPs. Because the file might contain 10, 20, or even 100 passwords, the user has a tendency to print this file and keep it on or in his desk. The user then uses this printout to log in to a device, choosing one of the passwords in the list and crossing it off after it is used. Anyone who has access to the user's desk can compromise his account.

In addition, if this file is printed to a network printer, it can be compromised through eavesdropping. Note that Cisco routers do not support OTP innately.

NOTE   The main weakness of OTPs is that they are susceptible to eavesdropping. When the hacker knows the passwords stored in the file, he easily can gain unauthorized access to this user's account; from here, the hacker can install keystroke-capturing and backdoor programs to overcome the OTP authentication method for authorizing access to the user's device or resource.

Token Card Services

Of all of the methods discussed so far, the most secure authentication method is to use token cards and token card services. When using a token card solution, a user uses a special hardware device called a token card. This card is about as small as a credit card or PCMCIA card, but it has integrated circuits and typically an LED display. This card is synchronized with a token card server by the time of day.

One of two methods is used to handle authentication with token card services:

- Time-based authentication
- Challenge-based authentication

With the first method, the user enters a password or PIN into the token card, which then is used on a one-way hash function along with the time of day. Note that the time of day is not an exact time, but it is based on a time period. Therefore, the card and the token card server must have a time defined on them that is not very different. This information, along with the account name, is sent to the service that the user is trying to log in to, as shown in Step 1 of Figure 3-1. In Step 2, the service forwards this information to a token card server. The token card server then looks up the user's account name in a local database, along with the user's password or PIN; it runs it through the same one-way hash function that the token card used, along with the time of day. The token card server authenticates the request and passes back the result, shown in Step 3. In Step 4, the service passes back the authentication success or failure to the user.

Figure 3-1 *Token Card Authentication Process*

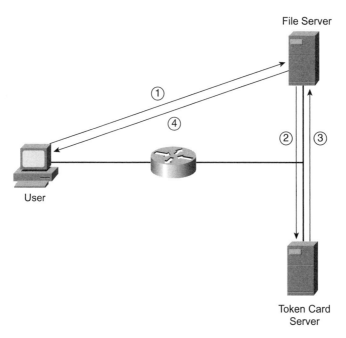

With the second method of handling authentication with token card services, instead of using the time of day, the token card solution uses a challenge, which is synchronized between the card and the token card authentication server. The challenge used with this kind of token card solution is similar to the challenge that PPP's CHAP uses. Otherwise, the authentication process is the same as that shown in Figure 3-1 with the time of day token card solutions.

The main advantage of this solution over the OTP process described in the last section is that a token card solution does not generate a file of valid random passwords: A password is generated each time that the user needs to authenticate.

However, token card solutions have their own set of problems:

- Cost
- Additional software
- Synchronization between the token card and token card server

Probably the main disadvantage of token card servers is their cost: You need a token card for each server (they run about $50 to $75), and you need a server with token card software running on it to handle authentication requests. For many companies, this can be cost prohibitive.

Second, to use a token card solution, your resources must support integration of token card software. This is not always possible, based on your service or resource. For example, a Cisco IOS router does not support authentication directly to a token card server. Instead, it requires a central authentication server, such as Cisco Secure ACS, which handles the interoperability with the token card server (again, this increases your implementation cost). In some instances, some devices, services, or resources do not support token card integration.

The Cisco Secure ACS authentication server supports integration with the following token card solutions:

- ActivCard Token Server 3.1
- CRYPTOCard CRYPTOAdmin 5.16
- PassGo (formerly AXENT) Defender version 5.16
- RSA ACE/Server version 5.0 and ACE/Client version 1.1.2 for Windows 2000
- Secure Computing PremierAccess Server version 3.1
- Vasco Vacman Server version 6.0.2

The third problem with token card solutions deals with the synchronization between the token card and the token card server. It is important to point out that because the random OTP that is generated by the token card uses the time of day or a challenge, the card and the token card server must be synchronized; otherwise, authentication will fail. This can present a manageability issue for aging cards because the battery process used on the cards might cause a synchronization problem. Troubleshooting this kind of problem is not easy. Plus, when the token card generates the random password, it is typically good for only a short period of time, such as 1 minute. Therefore, the user immediately must type in the OTP to authenticate or will have to re-enter his password or PIN on the token card to generate a new password. This can create a lot of headaches for your users, especially slow typists.

Token card servers typically are used in environments that need to use random passwords to prevent eavesdropping attacks in secure environments. In these situations, companies are very concerned about access attacks, and the additional cost of a token card solution is negligible compared with the repercussions of a hacker gaining unauthorized access to a critical resource. Also, if you need to access services and resources remotely across a public network on which passwords are susceptible to eavesdropping, a token card solution provides a secure authentication solution.

Methods of User EXEC Access

Now that you have a basic understanding of password authentication methods, this section discusses how you can secure your Cisco IOS router. This chapter focuses only on local solutions available on the router. Chapter 5 discusses how to centralize this using a security server, such as the Cisco Secure ACS security server product.

Two levels of access to a Cisco router exist:

- **User EXEC**—Used for basic troubleshooting processes
- **Privileged EXEC**—Used for detailed troubleshooting and configuration

Both of these methods support authentication. Within user EXEC access, however, the Cisco IOS differentiates between local and remote access. Local access is done through the console or auxiliary port, where you use the Cisco IOS command-line interface (CLI) to interact with the Cisco IOS and the device. Remote access can be performed in a multitude of ways. This section covers how to secure user EXEC access. Privileged EXEC access is covered in the section "Privileged EXEC Access," later in this chapter.

Cisco IOS Configuration Tips

Before I discuss any other commands, I would like to share a few side tips about router configurations. First, to prevent logging messages from showing up in your lines and disrupting your typing flow, use the **logging synchronous** line-configuration command; this is placed under your console, auxiliary, and VTY lines. This command causes the Cisco IOS to redisplay the information that you typed in after any Cisco IOS output is displayed on the terminal, such as debug output and system event messages, perhaps for when an interface goes up or down.

Second, use the **no ip domain-lookup** command to prevent the router from resolving names (including bad or invalid commands) to IP addresses. I am not the greatest typist in the world, so it's annoying to have to break out of an inadvertent Telnet attempt by the Cisco IOS when you type in a nonexistent command.

Third, as of Cisco IOS 12.2(8)T, you can execute EXEC commands from configuration mode. From configuration mode, use the **do** command followed by the EXEC command that you want to execute, like this: **do show running-config**. Many people have hoped for this capability for a long time, and Cisco finally has delivered.

Local Access: Console and Auxiliary

To assign a static password to the console line, use the following configuration:

```
Router(config)# line console 0
Router(config-line)# password password
```

The password that you enter in the **password** command is a clear-text password. When you examine the output from the **show running-config** command, you will see the actual password in the configuration:

```
line con 0
 password cisco
 logging synchronous
```

Obviously, this is a problem if someone is looking over your shoulder or if you back up your configuration to a TFTP server with the **copy running-config tftp** command. Two solutions discussed later remedy this problem: encrypting the clear-text password, and using a secure form of copying your configuration to an external server without having to use TFTP, which lacks any authentication and encryption method.

NOTE   Most passwords that you configure on your router can be from 1 to 25 characters, and the first character cannot be a number. You can have leading spaces before the password, but they are ignored. However, any trailing spaces after the password become a part of the password. You can include a ? in a password by first using the Ctrl-V sequence and then typing in the ?, like this: **alpha**Ctrl-V**?987**. This creates a password of **alpha?987**.

CAUTION   Remember that the **password** *Line Configuration* mode command does not encrypt passwords by default; it stores them in clear text. I highly recommend that you not use the **password** command as your authentication method because all administrators who access the line must use the same password. This makes accountability difficult. Typically, this is used as a last resort. I recommend either a local user and password database, discussed in the "Local Authentication Database" section later in this chapter, or a security server, discussed in Chapter 5.

If your router has an auxiliary line, you can assign it a password with basically the same configuration:

```
Router(config)# line aux 0
Router(config-line)# password password
```

Typically, this line is used for remote dial-in access for emergency situations. If you are using this line for dialup, you must implement security for dialup on your router, which is beyond the scope of this book. I recommend that you run PPP on your auxiliary port in this case, using CHAP for authentication and caller ID to restrict unauthorized access.

Password Usage

I have been teaching Cisco-related courses, including official Cisco classes, for more than 7 years. In almost all courses, I see Cisco using the passwords of cisco, san-fran or sanfran, and san-jose or sanjose as examples to secure user and privileged EXEC levels of access. You would think that something as obvious as these passwords never would be used in a production environment, but many times I have seen these used as passwords to secure company routers. Basically, the newbie Cisco IOS administrator looked at the examples in Cisco's course material and copied them verbatim. Guess what passwords a hacker first will try when gaining access to your router?

Login Authentication Methods

One main difference between the console line for user EXEC access and the auxiliary and VTY (discussed in the next section) lines is that a password on the console line is optional, whereas it is required on auxiliary and VTY lines. You must enable authentication on these two latter types of lines to allow access. If you do not, the Cisco IOS displays an error message and closes the connection:

```
Password required, but none set
[Connection to 192.168.1.254 closed by foreign host]
```

To allow access through the auxiliary or VTY lines, use one of the following two configurations:

```
Router(config)# line aux 0
Router(config-line)# [no] login [local]
```

or:

```
Router(config)# line vty 0 4
Router(config-line)# [no] login [local]
```

The **login** command, by itself, specifies the use of authentication. By default, it checks for a password configured with the **password** line-configuration command. If this does not exist, the user is not allowed access. To disable authentication checking, use the **no login** command. Note that this never is recommended for any type of connection, whether local or remote access.

NOTE   Even if the Cisco IOS does not check a password for user EXEC access, a password still must be configured for privileged EXEC access for remote-access connections. Otherwise, the user is not allowed access to user and privileged EXEC mode. This process is not true concerning the console line.

Optionally, you can override the use of the password configured on the line and use other methods, such as a local username and password database, by specifying **login local** (discussed later in this chapter in the "Local Authentication Database" section), or use external authentication using a security server (discussed in Chapter 5). Remember my earlier caution: Use either of these two methods (preferably the latter one, which is preferred for securing line access).

TIP   Always put some method of authentication on all your lines, even ones that you are not using, such as the auxiliary line. This ensures that later someone does not set up a new line connection inadvertently and forget to secure it.

Login Connection Timeouts

By default, console, auxiliary, and Telnet (VTY) sessions time out after 10 minutes of idling. You can override this with the **exec-timeout** command, shown here:

```
Router(config)# line type #
Router(config-line)# exec-timeout minutes seconds
```

You must specify the minutes and seconds for the timeout. Optionally, you can specify 0 and 0 for the minutes and seconds, specifying an infinite timeout. I never recommend this for a production router, but only for lab situations, such as practicing for the CCIE Router and Switch or Security lab exam.

This simple example sets the timeout to 5 minutes for Telnet sessions:

```
Router(config)# line vty 0 4
Router(config-line)# exec-timeout 5 0
```

To view your timeouts, use the **show line** command. Based on my previous configuration, Example 3-1 shows the partial output of this command.

Example 3-1 *Example Line Configuration*

```
Router# show line vty 0
   Tty Typ     Tx/Rx    A Modem  Roty AccO AccI   Uses   Noise  Overruns   Int
    6 VTY         -      -    -     -    -    -      2      0      0/0       -

Line 6, Location: "", Type: ""
Length: 24 lines, Width: 80 columns
Baud rate (TX/RX) is 9600/9600
Status: Ready, No Exit Banner
Capabilities: none
Modem state: Ready
Special Chars: Escape  Hold  Stop  Start  Disconnect  Activation
               ^^x     none   -     -       none
Timeouts:      Idle EXEC      Idle Session    Modem Answer  Session   Dispatch
               00:05:00         never                         none    not set
                              Idle Session Disconnect Warning
                                never
                              Login-sequence User Response
                                00:00:30
                              Autoselect Initial Wait
                                not set
←output omitted→
```

In Example 3-1, you can see that the idle timeout, below the Idle EXEC column, was set to 5 minutes. This is a common setting for Telnet sessions.

Remote Access

Compared to local access, in which you can access user EXEC mode only through the console or auxiliary line, you can access your router remotely in quite a few ways. These methods include Telnet, RSH, SSH, HTTP and HTTPS, and SNMP. The following sections cover the configurations and issues with these approaches.

VTY (Telnet)

Cisco uses VTY lines to handle incoming and outgoing Telnet connections. VTYs are basically logical lines: The Cisco IOS treats them as a physical line from a configuration and operation perspective, but they are not something that you physically can touch with your hands.

You already know how to set up basic authentication on a VTY. Here is a simple example:

```
Router(config)# line vty 0 4
Router(config-line)# password cisco
Router(config-line)# login
```

This sets up basic Telnet access to your router.

CAUTION   Now that you know how to set this up on your router, I recommend that you never use it. Why? Because Telnet sends user information across the network in clear text. Remember that if you are using this router as part of a firewall system, you want to keep it as secure as possible. You could get around the Telnet password issue by using token cards and a token card server, but all other information that you type in the Telnet router session is sent in clear text. I recommend that you use either SSH, discussed in the "Secure Shell" section later in this chapter, or a VPN, discussed in Part VIII, "Virtual Private Networks," when gaining user and privileged EXEC CLI access to your router.

Given this previous caution, however, you want to configure one thing on your VTYs, whether the access method is Telnet, SSH, or a VPN. Way back in Cisco IOS 10.0, Cisco built in the capability to filter sessions that use the VTY lines. This is accomplished by creating a standard access control list (ACL), which specifies which source address or addresses are allowed access; then the standard ACL is applied to the VTY lines. Chapter 7, "Basic Access Lists," discusses the details of standard ACLs. Figure 3-2 shows a simple example illustrating the usefulness of this feature. Here, a router is being used as a perimeter firewall. In this network, only two administrators should be allowed remote SSH access to the router. This is accomplished by setting up a standard ACL and applying it to the VTYs, as shown in Example 3-2.

Figure 3-2   *Restricting VTY Access*

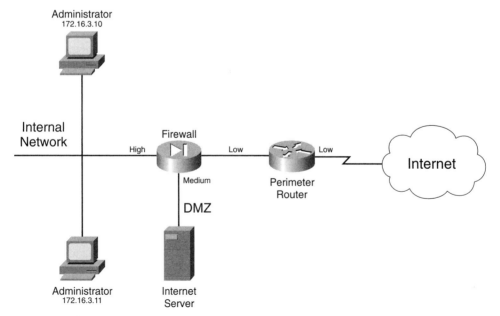

In this example, applying the standard ACL requires the use of the **access-class** command. This command requires that you specify the number of the standard ACL (1) and the direction of restriction (**in** or **out**). Using the **in** parameter restricts inbound VTY sessions;

out restricts outbound VTY sessions. When using the **out** parameter, the addresses listed in the standard ACL are viewed as destination, not source, addresses. One note on Cisco ACLs applies: If you do not explicitly permit traffic in an ACL, it is implicitly denied.

Example 3-2 *Restricting VTY Access*

```
Router(config)# access-list 1 permit 172.16.3.10
Router(config)# access-list 1 permit 172.16.3.11
Router(config)# line vty 0 4
Router(config-line)# transport input ssh
Router(config-line)# transport output ssh
Router(config-line)# access-class 1 in
```

The syntax of the **access-class** command is as follows:

```
Router(config)# line vty beginning_# ending_#
Router(config-line)# access-class standard_ACL_# in | out
```

It is important to point out that you should apply the **access-class** command to all VTYs. For a router that has five VTYs, the beginning and ending numbers are 0 and 4. If you are not sure how many VTYs you have, use the **show running-config** or **show lines** commands.

NOTE   Remember that the **access-class** command applies to VTY sessions. Telnet is not the only type of connection that uses a VTY: So does SSH. This Cisco IOS feature helps you limit which devices can establish a VTY connection, reducing the likelihood of an access attack.

The main problem of the Cisco IOS VTYs is that they allow many different types of remote access, such as Telnet, rlogin, SSH, and others. The **transport input ssh** command limits access to the VTYs to SSH access only, whereas the **transport output ssh** command restricts remote access to other devices to SSH. The syntax of the **transport** command is as follows:

```
Router(config)# line vty beginning_# ending_#
Router(config-line)# transport {input | output} {all | none |
   pad | rlogin | ssh | telnet | udptm}
```

If you want to use only SSH for remote access, use the **transport** commands displayed in Example 3-2.

Secure Shell

In the old days of UNIX when no real need existed for a secure environment, many administrators used the **rexec** and **rsh** tools to execute commands on remote systems without having to log into them. However, in today's world, these tools offer no real security: They send information across the network in clear text, which is easy to eavesdrop on, and their authentication is based on the user's source IP address, which is easy to spoof. Two versions of SSH are available: version 1 and version 2. In most Cisco IOS versions, Cisco supports an enhanced version of version 1, called 1.5; however, starting in Cisco IOS 12.3T and later versions of 12.1E, Cisco also supports SSHv2.

Two components are required for SSH to function:

- Server
- Client

The SSH server provides a secure connection, which is encrypted, to the Cisco IOS CLI. This connection is similar to an encrypted Telnet connection. The SSH client runs the SSH protocol to connect to an SSH server, and it must support the Data Encryption Standard (DES) or 3DES as well as password authentication. DES and 3DES are discussed in more depth in Chapter 19, "IPSec Site-to-Site Connections." Authentication is performed in a normal fashion: Users can be authenticated using local mechanisms or by using an external security server. Cisco routers support both server and client connections. However, SSH on Cisco IOS routers has the following restrictions:

- You cannot use RSA authentication (discussed in Chapter 19).
- You must use a Cisco IOS image that supports DES or 3DES.

TIP   Many SSH commercial client packages are available on the market. One of my favorites is Teraterm, with the TTSSH extension. Actually, Teraterm is my preferred terminal software (it's free) for console and Telnet connections as well. To download Teraterm and the TTSSH extension, visit http://www.zip.com.au/~roca/ttssh.html. I have experienced some problems with Teraterm's SSH client with certain versions of the Cisco IOS. If you experience these problems, try PenguiNet SSH, a fully functional shareware client that I have had great success with. It is free to try and less than $30 to buy. You can download it from www.siliconcircus.com.

SSH Server Configuration

Before setting up SSH, you must install a Cisco IOS image that supports DES or 3DES (this requires the image to support IPSec). For both router client and server functions to work, you need at least Cisco IOS 12.1(3)T.

When you have installed the appropriate Cisco IOS software, you can begin your Cisco IOS configuration. You should perform these six steps:

Step 1   Assign a name to the router (required).

```
Router(config)# hostname router_name
```

Step 2   Assign a domain name to the router (required).

```
Router(config)# ip domain-name DNS_domain_name
```

Step 3   Generate your encryption keys (required).

```
Router(config)# crypto key generate rsa
```

You must assign a router and domain name before executing this command; otherwise, you will get an error message. Cisco recommends that you use a key size of at least 1024 bits. When you execute this command, it does not appear in the running or saved configuration. Also, if you need to generate a new key pair, first use the **crypto key zeroize rsa** command.

Step 4   Set up your VTY access for SSH (optional, but recommended):

```
Router(config)# username name secret password
Router(config)# line vty 0 4
Router(config-line)# transport input ssh
Router(config-line)# transport input ssh
Router(config-line) login local
```

For SSH access, you must use a username and password by setting up either a local authentication database (discussed later in the "Local Authentication Database" section) or an authentication server (see Chapter 5). The **username** and **login local** commands set up local authentication. This is true of most SSH clients that I have dealt with.

Step 5   Tune the SSH server (optional).

```
Router(config)# ip ssh {[timeout seconds] | [authentication-retries
    integer]}
```

Optionally, you can specify a timeout, in seconds, for initiating an SSH connection. If the connection cannot be established in this time period, the connection fails. You also can limit the number of authentication retries for a connection upon an invalid authentication attempt (the default is 3). Other parameters exist for this command, but these are the two most common ones. If you cannot execute this command, it is because you have not generated your encryption keys with the **crypto key generate rsa** command. After the user has authenticated and established an SSH connection to the router, the Cisco IOS uses the VTY idle timeout (**exec-timeout** command) to monitor the session.

Step 6   Verify SSH server operation (optional).

```
Router# show ssh
Router# show ip ssh
```

TIP   I highly recommend that you use the VTY **access-class** line configuration command to restrict SSH access to your router. Note that after you set up SSH, devices still can Telnet to the router, even with the configuration of the **access-class** command. Therefore, use the **transport** command to limit remote access to SSH. You also can create an ACL to filter unwanted remote-access traffic to the router. This is discussed in Chapter 7.

Also, SSH client connections connect to TCP port 22 on an SSH server, so you need to allow this port through your filter, if one exists.

SSH Server Example

To help illustrate how to set up an SSH server on a Cisco IOS router, this example uses the perimeter router shown previously in Figure 3-2. Example 3-3 shows the configuration.

Example 3-3 *SSH Server Configuration Example*

```
Router(config)# hostname bullmastiff
bullmastiff(config)# ip domain-name quizware.com
bullmastiff(config)# crypto key generate rsa
The name for the keys will be: bullmastiff.quizware.com
Choose the size of the key modulus in the range of 360 to 2048 for your
  General Purpose Keys. Choosing a key modulus greater than 512 may take
  a few minutes.
How many bits in the modulus [512]: 1024
% Generating 1024 bit RSA keys ...[OK]
00:02:25: %SSH-5-ENABLED: SSH 1.5 has been enabled
bullmastiff(config)# username richard secret bigXdogYlover
bullmastiff(config)# username natalie secret BIGxDOGyLOVER
bullmastiff(config)# access-list 1 permit 172.16.3.10
bullmastiff(config)# access-list 1 permit 172.16.3.11
bullmastiff(config)# line vty 0 4
bullmastiff(config-line)# login local
bullmastiff(config-line)# access-class 1 in
bullmastiff(config-line)# transport input ssh
bullmastiff(config-line)# transport output ssh
bullmastiff(config-line)# end
```

After the RSA encryption keys were generated, notice that the Cisco IOS displayed a message that SSH 1.5 has been enabled: The SSH server function is operating. Also, I used a standard ACL and the **access-class** statement to limit the devices that can access the router's VTYs.

To verify that the SSH server is operating, as well as to verify its configuration, use the **show ip ssh** command, as shown in Example 3-4.

Example 3-4 *Verifying Your SSH Configuration*

```
bullmastiff# show ip ssh
SSH Enabled - version 1.5
Authentication timeout: 120 secs; Authentication retries: 3
```

To see the SSH client connections, use the **show ssh** command, as shown in Example 3-5.

Example 3-5 *Viewing Your SSH Client Connections*

```
bullmastiff# show ssh
Connection     Version Encryption    State              Username
    0            1.5     3DES         Session started    richard
```

In this example, you can see that someone logged into the richard account and that 3DES is being used for encryption.

SSH Client Connections

Besides functioning as a server, the Cisco IOS supports an SSH client. However, this option is available only after you have set the Cisco IOS as an SSH server (performed Steps 1 through 3 from the previous section). When you have completed these steps, you can initiate SSH client connections from your router. This is accomplished using the following EXEC command:

```
Router# ssh [-l username] [-c {des | 3des}] [-o numberofpasswdprompts #]
   [-p port_#] {IP_Address | hostname} [command]
```

The **ssh** command has many parameters. When accessing a remote resource, you might be required to give a username for authentication; this is true if you used a local authentication database or an external security server. Use the **–l** option to specify the username. You also can specify the encryption algorithm to use with the **–c** option. To change the number of password prompts, use the **–o numberofpasswordprompts** option. SSH uses port 22 by default, but you can change it with the **–p** option. The one required parameter is the address or name of the destination SSH server. Following this are optional commands that you might want to have executed (this feature is not supported if you are logging into a Cisco IOS router).

Example 3-6 shows a sample of testing the connection by establishing an SSH client connection from a router to itself, using the code configuration shown in Example 3-6.

Example 3-6 *SSH Client Connection Example*

```
bullmastiff# ssh -l richard 192.168.1.254
Password: cisco
bullmastiff>
```

CAUTION   Many versions of the Cisco IOS, up through 12.2, are vulnerable to a specific kind of SSH DoS attack in which a hacker can affect greatly the performance of a Cisco IOS device. A complete description of this attack is available at http://www.cisco.com/warp /public/707/SSH-multiple-pub.html. For software updates to limit the effect of this kind of attack, visit http://www.cisco.com/warp/public/707/SSH-scanning.shtml#Software.

Also, SSH 1.5 is less secure than SSH 2.0. Information about security issues with SSH v1 (and Cisco 1.5) can be seen at http://lwn.net/2001/0322/a/ssh-analysis.php3. Because of some of the security issues that have cropped up lately with SSH, I recommend that this be used only for internal connections if you are using an older version of the Cisco IOS. The best approach is to upgrade your Cisco IOS to a version that supports SSH 2.0. For connections across a public network, I recommend using a remote-access VPN connection, discussed in Part VIII.

Web Browser

Cisco supports the use of a web browser to access and manage a Cisco router. This is a nice feature for administrators who find the Cisco IOS CLI intimidating. This section discusses how to set up your router as an HTTP server and details some issues with using HTTP.

NOTE   Even though the GUI interface of a web browser presents a user-friendly front end to the router's Cisco IOS, you cannot perform all configuration and management options from a web browser. Therefore, in many cases, you still need to access the Cisco IOS CLI to perform configuration and management tasks.

By default, the HTTP server function on the router is disabled. To configure HTTP access, use the following steps:

Step 1   Enable the HTTP server (required).

```
Router(config)# ip http server
```

The **ip http server** command enables the HTTP server function on the router. This is the only required command to enable the server function; however, you will want to implement the security features in Steps 2 and 3. If you are using HTTPS (discussed in the next section), you should disable the standard HTTP server with **no ip http server**.

Step 2   Define an authentication method (highly recommended).

```
Router(config)# ip http authentication {aaa | enable | local}
```

Most people use three basic methods to perform authentication with HTTP. The **aaa** parameter specifies that AAA should be used (AAA is discussed in Chapter 5). The **enable** parameter specifies that the privileged EXEC password is used to authenticate HTTP access (this is discussed in the later section "Privileged EXEC Access"). The **local** parameter specifies that the local authentication database of usernames and passwords should be used for authentication (this is discussed in the later section "Local Authentication Database"). Note that the user needs level 15 access, which is privileged EXEC level. Of the three methods, I don't recommend the privileged EXEC password, and recommend either the local username database or an AAA server.

Step 3   Restrict access through HTTP (highly recommended).

```
Router(config)# ip http access-class standard_ACL_#
```

This command enables you to restrict, based on the source IP address of the client, which devices are allowed HTTP or HTTPS access to the router. The function of this command is the same as that described previously with VTY restrictions and the **access-class** command. With the **ip http access-class** command, you need to specify a standard ACL number or name that contains a list of permitted source addresses.

Step 4   Change the HTTP port number (optional).

```
Router(config)# ip http port port_#
```

By default, the Cisco IOS uses port 80 for HTTP connections; however, you can change this port to a different number with the **ip http port** command. By changing the port number to a nonstandard one, you make it more difficult for a hacker to determine that you are running a web server on the router. Most inept hackers never would figure out that you changed the HTTP port number; however, a smart hacker would scan all TCP ports to determine this, so changing the port number provides only a limited form of protection.

Step 5   Change the location of HTML files (optional).

```
Router(config)# ip http path URL_location
```

Typically, you will not use this command: It sets the base HTTP location path for HTML files on the router. By default, these files are located in Flash, but you can move them to a different location, such as a PCMCIA card, if you do not have enough space in Flash for your Cisco IOS. Here is a simple example of doing this: **ip http path slot0:**.

Step 6   Restrict the number of HTTP connections (recommended).

```
Router(config)# ip http max-connections #_of_connections
```

This command enables you to limit the maximum number of HTTP management connections to the HTTP server on the router. The default value is 5.

Step 7   Change the idle timeout for HTTP connections (optional).

```
Router(config)# ip http timeout policy idle seconds life seconds
    requests number
```

This command enables you to define how long an HTTP server connection to the router should remain open. The **idle** parameter specifies the maximum allowed idle time for an HTTP connection before it is torn down. The default is 180 seconds. The **life** parameter specifies the maximum amount of time that the connection is allowed to be established (busy or idle) before it is torn down. The default is 180 seconds, but this can be increased up to 86,400 (24 hours). The **requests** parameter restricts the maximum number of persistent requests (for the same information) before the connection is closed. This defaults to 1. Note that if the router's HTTP server is busy, it can terminate HTTP client connections to free up resources.

When you have the HTTP server set up, from a web browser, access your router by using the following URL in the address bar:

```
http://router's_IP_address
```

Now that you have a basic understanding of the setup of an HTTP server on a Cisco IOS router, take a look at a simple example, using the network shown previously in Figure 3-2.

In this example, only the two administrator devices should be allowed HTTP access to the router. Example 3-7 shows the basic configuration to accomplish this.

Example 3-7 *HTTP Server Configuration*

```
Router(config)# access-list 1 permit 172.16.3.10
Router(config)# access-list 1 permit 172.16.3.11
Router(config)# username richard privilege 15 secret bigXdogYlover
Router(config)# username natalie privilege 15 secret BIGxDOGyLOVER
Router(config)# ip http server
Router(config)# ip http authentication local
Router(config)# ip http access-class 1
```

In this example, only two devices are allowed HTTP access to the router: 172.16.3.10 and 172.16.3.11. Both administrators have accounts set up, and the router uses the local authentication database (**username** commands) to perform the authentication. One interesting thing to point out about the **username** commands is the **privilege 15** reference. Remember that you need privileged EXEC access for HTTP server connections to the router. This command is discussed in much more depth in the later section "Local Authentication Database."

Use the **show ip http client all** command to list all client connections on your router. Use the **show ip http server all** command to list all HTTP server functions on your router, including past client connections.

CAUTION   Some security issues arise when using HTTP access to manage your router. First, any usernames and passwords are sent across the wire in clear text, along with any operations or commands executed. This presents a serious problem if a hacker is implementing an eavesdropping attack. You could get around the HTTP password issue by using token cards and a token card server, but all other information that you enter in the HTTP router session is sent in clear text. Therefore, never use HTTP across a public network to manage your router. On internal networks, make sure that you use authentication and filtering to restrict HTTP access to the router itself.

Second, because of many of the issues with HTTP itself, as well as the first item, I recommend that if you want to use a web browser for management purposes, either use HTTPS (discussed in the next section) or protect the HTTP connection with a VPN (discussed in Part VIII).

HTTP with SSL

Because HTTP is susceptible to eavesdropping attacks, it is not a recommended tool for remote access management. Instead of using HTTP, you can use HTTPS, which is HTTP with Secure Socket Layer (SSL) support. Cisco supports SSL 3.0 for its router HTTP server functions. This feature is new in Cisco IOS 12.2(15)T, and it requires a Cisco IOS image that supports SSL.

RSA authentication is used to validate the identity of devices and uses certificates. The Cisco IOS image needs SSL support to sign these certificates digitally. Certificates are used for authentication purposes and, to my knowledge, never have been spoofed.

As you recall from the last section, you can use the **ip http access-class** command to restrict access to an HTTP server. However, the main limitation of this command is that because filtering is done on Layer 3 IP addresses, an ingenious hacker could spoof these and bypass the filter. Certificates are discussed in more depth in Part VIII.

HTTPS Components

Three main components play a role in an HTTPS connection:

- Server and client devices
- Cipher suites
- Certificate authority (commonly called a trustpoint)

With server and clients, HTTPS ensures that before any data is sent across the wire, it is protected through encryption and packet signing (commonly called packet authentication or integrity). This prevents all eavesdropping and session-hijacking attacks.

A cipher suite defines how the connection should be protected. Cisco commonly calls this a transform set. Minimally, an encryption algorithm is used to protect the confidentiality of the information being transmitted. Supported encryption algorithms include DES, RC4, and 3DES on Cisco routers. Each packet sent is signed digitally using a hashing function. The digital signature is used by the remote end of the connection to determine whether the encrypted packet contents were tampered with. Cisco supports MD5 and SHA to protect the integrity of packets and detect packet tampering.

A certificate authority (CA) is used to issue and manage certificates. CAs provide a trusted third-party solution to prevent repudiation attacks and to identify the parties in the transaction. HTTPS uses certificates and a CA to perform these functions. Cisco routers support two options in this regard: They can use an external CA to authenticate certificates, or they can function as the CA themselves (only for HTTPS connections, though). The first method is preferred because it is more secure. However, for small networks, setting up and maintaining a CA can be expensive and burdensome; therefore, using a router as the CA for HTTPS connections is a cost-effective solution.

TIP   If you are concerned about the amount of administration but still want to use a CA for an additional level of protection, you can purchase CA services from companies such as Verisign (see http://www.verisign.com).

Note that the details of protected connections are covered in more depth in Part VIII, which includes encryption algorithms, hash functions, and certificate authorities.

HTTPS Operation

HTTPS is based on a client/server model. When clients establish an HTTPS connection to a server, such as a Cisco router, they use TCP on port 443. To establish the connection, the client uses the following syntax in a web browser's URL address bar:

```
https://IP_address_of_server
```

When the connection is established, the server (router) sends its own certificate to the client. The server has two keys that are used by this certificate: public and private. The public key encrypts data, and only the private key decrypts it (this process is discussed in more depth in Chapter 19). The private key is kept local on the router, and no one sees it. The public key is included on the certificate. Upon receipt of the certificate, the client generates an encryption key. It uses the server's public key to encrypt it and sends this key to the server. Only the server's private key can decode this encryption. At this point, only the client and the server know about the key that the client generated: This is the key used to encrypt data between the client and the server.

NOTE   HTTP with SSL uses TCP port 443. If you are filtering traffic as it comes into your router, you need to allow this port connection.

HTTPS Configuration: No CA

As I mentioned in the section on HTTPS components, you can implement an HTTPS server function on your router in two ways: Have the router itself generate its own certificate information (less secure), or have the router use a CA and obtain a certificate from it (much more secure). This section covers how you configure the first method: The router generates its own certificate.

The configuration is straightforward and uses some of the commands discussed previously in the "Web Browser" section. Here are the steps:

Step 1   Disable the HTTP server (highly recommended).

```
Router(config)# no ip http server
```

You do not want your router accepting both HTTP and HTTPS connections; therefore, disable the HTTP function on the router.

Step 2   Assign a host name and a domain name.

```
Router(config)# hostname router_name
Router(config)# ip domain-name domain_name
```

To generate certificate information, your router needs a host name and a domain name.

Step 3   Enable the HTTPS server.

```
Router(config)# ip http server-secure
```

The **ip http server-secure** command enables HTTP with SSL 3.0.

Here are some optional items that I highly recommend you use:

- Set up user authentication with the **ip http authentication** command. For **local** authentication, create a list of usernames and passwords with the **username** command, specifying privileged EXEC access with the **privilege 15** parameter.

- Restrict HTTPS access to the router with the **ip http access-class** command, listing only the allowed IP addresses of administrator devices.

The following items enable you to tune your HTTPS server. The **ip http secure-port** command specifies which port clients will use for HTTPS:

```
Router(config)# ip http secure-port port_#
```

By default, the port number is 443.

You also can change which cipher suite(s) the router will use to protect the connection:

```
Router(config)# ip http secure-ciphersuite {[3des-ede-cbc-sha] [rc4-128-md5]
  [rc4-128-sha] [des-cbc-sha]}
```

It is recommended that you allow the client and server to negotiate which suite to use for protection. However, if you are paranoid about protection, you can specify only the most secure suite (**3des-ede-cbc-sha**) to secure your HTTPS connection.

Now take a look at a simple configuration example to illustrate how to set up HTTPS on your router without a CA, using Figure 3-2 for the network. Example 3-8 shows the configuration.

Example 3-8 *HTTPS Server Configuration with an Internal CA Function*

```
Router(config)# hostname Bullmastiff
Bullmastiff(config)# ip domain-name quizware.com
Bullmastiff(config)# access-list 1 permit 172.16.3.10
Bullmastiff(config)# access-list 1 permit 172.16.3.11
Bullmastiff(config)# username richard privilege 15 secret bigXdogYlover
Bullmastiff(config)# username natalie privilege 15 secret BIGxDOGyLOVER
Bullmastiff(config)# no ip http server
Bullmastiff(config)# ip http secure-server
Bullmastiff(config)# ip http authentication local
Bullmastiff(config)# ip http access-class 1
```

When you are finished, access the router through a web browser using HTTPS. When you do this for the first time, the router automatically generates keying information for its certificate. Here is an example of the Cisco IOS message from the CLI:

```
00:49:41: %CRYPTO-6-AUTOGEN: Generated new 768 bit key pair
00:49:45: %CRYPTO-6-AUTOGEN: Generated new 768 bit key pair
00:49:46: %SSH-5-ENABLED: SSH 1.5 has been enabled
```

Notice that because RSA keys were generated, SSH can be used. If you want a more secure connection, use the **crypto key generate rsa** command and specify a longer number of bits than 768, such as 1024.

Also, your web browser client is presented with a pop-up window about the router's certificate. You must click the Yes button to accept the certificate.

You can see the web server's status with the **show ip http server all** command, discussed in the "Web Browser" section. You can limit the output to just HTTPS information with the command displayed in Example 3-9, taken from the previous configuration.

Example 3-9   *Examining the Status of the Router's HTTPS Server*

```
Bullmastiff# show ip http server secure status
HTTP secure server status: Enabled
HTTP secure server port: 443
HTTP secure server ciphersuite: 3des-ede-cbc-sha des-cbc-sha rc4-128-md5
  rc4-128-sha
HTTP secure server client authentication: Disabled
HTTP secure server trustpoint:
```

In this example, you can see that HTTPS is enabled, and you can see the cipher suite that it is using to protect the web browser connections.

HTTPS Configuration: CA

The configuration of HTTPS using a CA server is much more complicated than what was done in the previous section. The configuration is broken into two parts: setting up access to the CA to obtain your certificate, and setting up the HTTPS server function.

The first thing that you need to do is to set up your connection to the CA server and obtain a certificate. Follow these steps to accomplish this:

Step 1   Set the correct time and date on your router (recommended).

```
Router(config)# clock timezone name offset
Router(config)# exit
Router# clock set hh:mm:ss day month year
```

The **clock timezone** command specifies the time zone that your router is in. The *name* specifies the name of the time zone, such as EDT for Eastern Daylight Saving Time. The *offset* specifies the number of hours, plus or minus, from UTC time—for EDT, it would be –5. The privileged EXEC **clock set** command sets the time—the day of the month is a number from 1 to 31; the month is a name, such as June; and the year is a four-digit year, such as 2003. I discuss the use of the Network Time Protocol, which I recommend over the **clock set** command, in Chapter 18, "Logging Events." Other clocking configurations are discussed here as well.

Step 2   Assign a host name and a domain name (required).

```
Router(config)# hostname router_name
Router(config)# ip domain-name domain_name
```

To generate certificate information, your router needs a host name and a domain name.

Step 3   Generate your RSA keys (optional).

```
Router(config)# crypto key generate rsa
```

This command generates your RSA keys for your router's certificate. This is optional because the router does this when acquiring a certificate; using this command simply enables you to control how long the keys are.

Step 4 If you are not using DNS resolution, define a static DNS resolution entry for the CA server (recommended).

```
Router(config)# ip host CA_server's_name CA_server's_IP_address
```

Your router needs to know how to reach the CA to obtain and authenticate certificate information. This can be done through DNS or a static host entry with the **ip host** command. Remember that DNS is susceptible to DNS spoofing, so I recommend using static DNS resolution with the **ip host** command.

Step 5 Set up access to the CA server (required).

```
Router(config)# crypto ca trustpoint CA_server's_name
Router(config-trustpoint)# enrollment url URL_location
Router(config-trustpoint)# primary
Router(config-trustpoint)# enrollment http-proxy
   HTTP_server's_name port_#
```

The **crypto ca trustpoint** command defines the name of the CA (what you defined in the **ip host** command) and takes you into a subconfiguration mode for further configuration. Before 12.2.8(T), you used the **crypto ca identity** command instead of the **crypto ca trustpoint** command—both do the same thing. The **enrollment url** command specifies the URL to use to access the certificate information on the CA. For example, Microsoft's CA product for Windows Server 2000 uses http://*CA_server's_name* /certsrv/mscep/mscep.dll. You need to contact the administrator of the CA to determine what URL to use. If you are specifying more than one CA server, use the **primary** command to specify which one has precedence. If you are using a proxy server to access the CA, the **enrollment http-proxy** command specifies the name or IP address of the proxy server, along with the port number. Note that the only two required commands are the first two in the previous code listing: **crypto ca trustpoint** and **enrollment url**.

Step 6 Obtain the CA's personal certificate (required).

```
Router(config)# crypto ca authenticate CA_server's_name
```

This command obtains the CA's certificate from the CA. When your router receives the certificate, it asks you whether you want to accept the certificate. Before accepting it, call the CA administrator to verify the fingerprint message that was sent to the router. If a man-in-the-middle attack occurred, validating the fingerprint can determine this.

Step 7 Obtain the router's personal certificate (required).

```
Router(config)# crypto ca enroll CA_server's_name
```

After obtaining the CA's certificate, use the **crypto ca enroll** command to have the CA generate a certificate for the router itself. You are prompted for a few pieces of information. First, you must enter a challenge password; this is used if you ever need to revoke your certificate on the CA because the CA administrator will ask for it. Next, you are prompted for what information you want to include in the certificate, such as the router's serial number and its IP addresses. After answering these questions, you are asked to obtain a certificate from the CA. The Cisco IOS displays a message with the appropriate success status. When obtaining a certificate, a delay (in seconds, minutes, or hours, depending upon how the CA is configured to respond) might occur before the router obtains its certificate.

Upon completion, save your configuration: This saves your certificate information as well as your commands. Part VIII discusses certificates and their setup in much more depth.

Now that you have configured access to the CA, you need to prepare your router as an HTTPS server. This is similar to what I described in the previous section. Here are the steps to follow:

Step 1 Disable the HTTP server (highly recommended).

```
Router(config)# no ip http server
```

You want to ensure that only the HTTPS server function is operating on your router.

Step 2 Enable the HTTPS server (required).

```
Router(config)# ip http secure-server
```

Step 3 Specify the HTTPS port and cipher suite to use (optional). This is accomplished with the **ip http secure-port** and **ip http secure-ciphersuite** commands, which were discussed in the last section.

Step 4 Configure verification of client's certificate (highly recommended).

```
Router(config)# ip http secure-client-auth
```

This command has the server request the client's certificate and validate the client's identity. Use this option only if you know that your PCs have SSL certificates installed; otherwise, the router will prevent HTTPS access. I highly recommend this option because it adds more security to the connection, verifying both endpoints of the connection: client and server.

Step 5 Specify the CA server to use for HTTPS (required).

```
Router(config)# ip http secure-trustpoint CA_server's_name
```

This command specifies who the CA server is. Enter the same name that you used with the **crypto ca trustpoint** command.

Step 6   Authenticate and restrict access to the HTTP server (highly recommended). Use the **ip http authentication** and **ip http access-class** commands to accomplish these tasks. These commands were discussed earlier in the "Web Browser" section.

Step 7   Configure other optional HTTP server commands, such as **ip http path**, **ip http max-connections**, and **ip http timeout-policy**. These commands were discussed earlier in the "Web Browser" section.

When you are finished, open a web browser connection to your router, using this syntax in the web browser's URL address bar:

```
https://Router's_IP_address
```

You must accept the router's certificate by clicking the Yes button in the certificate pop-up window.

Use the **show ip http server secure status** and **show ip http server all** commands to see your server's configuration and existing connections to it. For detailed troubleshooting of SSL connections, use the **debug ip http ssl error** command.

To illustrate how to set up HTTPS on a router so that it uses a CA for authentication, take a look at an example, using the same network shown in Figure 3-2. Example 3-10 shows the configuration.

Example 3-10 *Configuring HTTPS Authentication Using a CA*

```
Router(config)# clock timezone edt -5
Router(config)# exit
Router# clock set 16:15:00 16 sept 2003
Router# configure terminal
Router(config)# hostname bullmastiff
bullmastiff(config)# ip domain-name quizware.com
bullmastiff(config)# ip host I7500 172.16.4.253
bullmastiff(config)# crypto key generate rsa
The name for the keys will be: bullmastiff.quizware.com
Choose the size of the key modulus in the range of 360 to 2048 for your
  General Purpose Keys. Choosing a key modulus greater than 512 may take
  a few minutes.
How many bits in the modulus [512]: 1024
% Generating 1024 bit RSA keys ...[OK]
Sep 16 21:19:28.219: %SSH-5-ENABLED: SSH 1.5 has been enabled
bullmastiff(config)# crypto ca trustpoint I7500
bullmastiff(ca-trustpoint)# enrollment url
  http://I7500/certsrv/mscep/mscep.dll
bullmastiff(ca-trustpoint)# exit
bullmastiff(config)# crypto ca authenticate I7500
Certificate has the following attributes:
Fingerprint: A6A5BFDD DCA6123F 30C04693 654C1024
% Do you accept this certificate? [yes/no]: yes
Trustpoint CA certificate accepted.
Fingerprint:  00BE96B7 5F4F08C2 C9281FA4 ABD2E422
Sep 16 21:42:40.859: %CRYPTO-6-CERTRET: Certificate received from Certificate
  Authority
```

continues

Example 3-10 *Configuring HTTPS Authentication Using a CA (Continued)*

```
Bullmastiff(config)# crypto ca enroll I7500
% Start certificate enrollment ..
% Create a challenge password. You will need to verbally provide this
    password to the CA Administrator in order to revoke your certificate.
    For security reasons your password will not be saved in the configuration.
    Please make a note of it.
Password: MyI7500Cert6
Re-enter password: MyI7500Cert6
% The fully-qualified domain name in the certificate will be:
  bullmastiff.quizware.com
% The subject in the certificate will be: bullmastiff.quizware.com
% Include the router serial number in the subject name? [yes/no]: no
% Include an IP address in the subject name? [no]: no
Request certificate from CA? [yes/no]: yes
% Certificate request sent to Certificate Authority
% The certificate request fingerprint will be displayed.
% The 'show crypto ca certificate' command will also show the fingerprint.
Fingerprint:  00BE96B7 5F4F08C2 C9281FA4 ABD2E422
Sep 16 21:42:40.859: %CRYPTO-6-CERTRET: Certificate received from Certificate
  Authority
bullmastiff(config)# no ip http server
bullmastiff(config)# ip http secure-server
bullmastiff(config)# ip http secure-trustpoint I7500
bullmastiff(config)# username richard privilege 15 secret cisco
bullmastiff(config)# ip http authentication local
bullmastiff(config)# access-list 1 permit 172.16.3.10
bullmastiff(config)# access-list 1 permit 172.16.3.11
bullmastiff(config)# ip http access-class 1
```

As you can see from this configuration, it is much more involved than the configuration that did not use a CA. The first part shows the setting of the date and time on the router with the **clock timezone** and **clock set** commands. Next, the router's name and domain name are configured with the **hostname** and **ip domain-name** commands. The RSA keys then are generated. This is optional, but it adds another layer of security because you can specify a longer key length (in this example, I used 1024 bits).

After generating the keys, the configuration of the CA begins. Because this router is not using DNS, I statically resolved the CA server's name (I7500) to an IP address (172.16.4.253). Next, I defined I7500 as the CA with the **crypto ca trustpoint** command. This takes you into a subconfiguration mode where you need to specify only the URL location to access the CA server. In this instance, I'm using Microsoft's CA product, which is on a Windows 2003 server. After defining the CA, I can obtain the CA's own certificate with the **crypto ca authenticate** command. Remember to verify the fingerprint of the CA's certificate with the CA's administrator, to make sure that a man-in-the-middle attack (in which a hacker's computer pretends to be the CA) did not occur.

After verification, I obtained the router's personal certificate with the **crypto ca enroll** command. Notice that I am asking for the challenge password as well as the information that I want to include in the router's certificate. After answering these questions, the router asks me one more question: whether I am ready to acquire the router's certificate from the

CA. After I answer Yes, it might take a few seconds, to dozens of minutes to obtain the certificate from the CA server; this depends upon how the CA server is configured to respond to certificate requests. When the router has its own certificate, this completes the configuration process for the CA.

Now you're ready to proceed with the configuration of the HTTPS server on your router. First, you need to disable the HTTP (nonprotected) server with the **no ip http server** command and enable the HTTPS server with the **ip http secure-server** command. Following this, you must tell the router which CA server it should use for authentication with the **ip http secure-trustpoint** command.

The last part of the configuration is not necessary, but I highly recommend it: The **ip http authentication** sets up local authentication with the use of the **username** commands. The **username** command is discussed later in the "Local Authentication Database" section. You also can use an external authentication server, which is discussed in Chapter 5. I restricted HTTP access to the server by using the **ip http access-class** command as well.

Now you can test your configuration by opening a web browser window and entering the following in the URL:

```
https://Router's_IP_address
```

Click Yes to accept the router's certificate. Then the router prompts you for your username and password. Remember that the **username** commands must specify a privilege level of 15 to allow configuration access to the router.

As you can see from this example, setting up secure HTTPS with a CA server for authentication is not a trivial matter. A lot of planning and configuration must be done on your part to get this up and running on your router.

NOTE   For small networks, I recommend using the configuration from the last section (without an external CA). However, in large enterprise networks with a CA server already in use, I highly recommend using certificates with HTTPS because this practically removes any likelihood that a masquerading attack will occur.

Given this information, my preferred method of secure access to a router is through the console port or a VPN. Even with encrypted HTTPS, there have been exploits against HTTP servers, especially DoS attacks, that drastically have affected their performance. But if you really like using a web browser for configuration and management functions, make sure that you use either HTTPS or HTTP through a VPN connection.

SNMP

SNMP is an application that allows for communication of system events and information between devices. It is used for monitoring as well as management of devices. In SNMP, there is a manager (a workstation that gathers SNMP information), agents (devices such as routers that supply SNMP information to a manager), and MIBs (which define what information is available and in what format on an agent).

With SNMP, the agent can send unsolicited notifications, referred to as traps or informs, to the manager for when specific events occur. For example, a Cisco router can send a trap when an interface goes up or down, or when the router is rebooted. Traps are connectionless; informs are connection oriented. With traps, there is no acknowledgment that the trap on the management station has been received; with an inform, the management station replies with an acknowledgment that the agent has received the inform. The other method by which information can be shared is the manager accessing the agent and pulling data directly from the agent's MIB(s).

NOTE	SNMP typically uses UDP 161. However, SNMP notifications are sent using UDP 162. Therefore, if you need to forward SNMP information through a filtering device, you must allow these protocols through your filter.

SNMP Versions

Three different versions of SNMP exist: v1, v2, and v3. The Cisco IOS supports all three, depending on the Cisco IOS version and platform. v1 is the least secure, and v3 is the most secure. Table 3-1 compares the three different versions of SNMP.

Table 3-1 *SNMP Version Comparison*

Version	Authentication	Encryption
v1	Community string	No
v2	Community string	No
v3	Username or MD5/SHA hash functions	Yes: 56-bit DES

SNMP v1 and v2 use community strings to perform authentication: This is a simple mechanism similar to password checking. With Cisco routers, you can use ACLs to control SNMP access, similar to what you saw earlier in this chapter with VTY and HTTP/HTTPS access. Security-wise, there is no difference between these protocols. The main difference is how error conditions are handled: SNMP v2 has more intelligence in this regard.

SNMP v3 was developed because of the security limitations that SNMP v1 and v2 had. It is based on a security model that allows for authentication using both users and groups, and it can encrypt the packet contents. SNMP v3 is defined in RFC 2570 and provides three basic security functions:

- **Authentication**—Verifying that the SNMP message was received from a valid source, preventing masquerading attacks
- **Integrity**—Verifying that the SNMP message was not altered between two devices, preventing session-hijacking attacks
- **Confidentiality**—Encrypting the contents of SNMP packets, preventing eavesdropping attacks

NOTE The purpose of the next two sections is not to show you how to set up a full-blown SNMP configuration on your router. Instead, the configuration focuses only on the commands to provide the most secure form of SNMP access.

SNMP v1 and v2 Configuration

With any of the versions of SNMP, the first **snmp-server** command that you execute enables the agent on your router. Setting up and securing access for SNMP v1 and v2 is simple. Two basic commands are used for setting up SNMP v1 and v2 access on a Cisco router: **snmp-server community** and **snmp-server host**.

This is the syntax of the **snmp-server community** command:

```
Router(config)# snmp-server community string [view view-name]
  [ro | rw] [number]
```

The **snmp-server** command is a generic command. First, notice that you do not specify the version of SNMP: You can specify only the string (password), the view that is allowed by devices that know the password, the type of access (**ro** is read-only and **rw** is read-write), and a standard ACL number, restricting which devices can access the router through SNMP. If you omit the read-only or read-write parameter, the SNMP string defaults to read-only.

To have a router generate traps or informs, you can use the following two commands:

```
Router(config)# snmp-server enable traps [notification_type]
Router(config)# snmp-server enable informs
```

With the **snmp-server enable traps** command, you can limit the traps that the router generates by listing them; omitting any traps enables all of them. No option exists to enable or disable specific informs. The main problem with these two commands is that you cannot restrict on a device-by-device basis what traps or informs are directed to specific SNMP management stations.

Because of the limitations of the **snmp-server community** and **snmp-server enable** commands, the **snmp-server host** command is preferred over the **snmp-server community** command. Here is the syntax of this command:

```
Router(config)# snmp-server host SNMP_manager_IP_address
  [traps | informs][version {1 | 2c} ] community_string [udp-port port_number]
  [notification_type]
```

If you do not configure at least one **snmp-server host** command, the router cannot send SNMP notifications to a management station. With this command, you specify the IP address of the management station as well as its own personal community string. You also can specify whether notifications are sent as traps or informs. Note that v1 does not support informs.

Following this comes the SNMP version; omitting it causes the version to default to SNMP v1. You optionally can specify a different port number to use for notifications; the default is UDP 162. Finally, you can limit the types of notifications sent to the SNMP management station; omitting this causes all notifications to be sent.

TIP   Of all of the IP protocols that exist, SNMP is one of the favorites of hackers because a hacker can learn a lot of information about your network and devices if he can compromise SNMP. With SNMP v1 and v2, this easily is accomplished by using an eavesdropping attack. Therefore, I highly recommend that if you are absolutely set on using SNMP v1 or v2 on your perimeter router firewall, you should filter all unnecessary SNMP traffic and change the UDP port number, to attempt to hide the fact that the router has SNMP enabled on it. I also highly recommend that you protect the SNMP traffic by sending it through an encrypted VPN connection from the management station to the router, and vice versa.

CAUTION   If you have not configured the **snmp-server community** command before configuring **snmp-server host** commands, the router automatically adds an **snmp-server community** command with a community string from the **snmp-server host** command. This happens automatically in Cisco IOS versions 12.0(3) and later.

Take a look at an example of securing SNMP v1, using the network shown in Figure 3-3. In this example, the router needs to provide SNMPv1 access, but for only management, not configuration, purposes. Example 3-11 shows the basic configuration.

Figure 3-3   *Restricting SNMP Access*

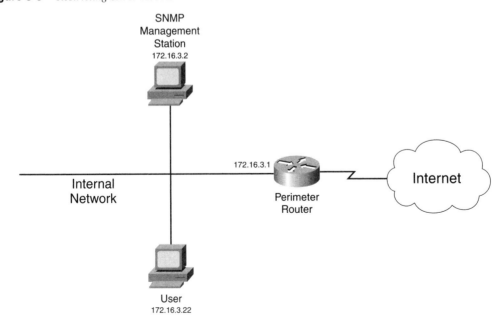

Example 3-11 *Simple SNMP Configuration Example*

```
Router(config)# access-list 1 permit 172.16.3.2
Router(config)# access-list 1 deny any log
Router(config)# snmp-server community keep935out ro 1
```

In this example, only the management station (172.16.3.2) is allowed SNMP read-only access; the ACL denies all others. One interesting thing to note about the **deny** statement in the ACL is that all unauthorized access is logged, internally as well as to a configured syslog server. If there is a deny on an SNMP packet trying to access the router, you will see the following Cisco IOS message:

```
%SEC-6-IPACCESSLOGS: list 1 denied 172.16.3.22 3 packet
```

In this example, three SNMP packets were denied from 172.16.3.22.

Configuring standard ACLs is discussed in Chapter 7, and configuring logging is discussed in Chapter 18.

If you want to allow your router to generate SNMP traps and informs, but you don't want a management station polling or directly accessing your router, use the configuration in Example 3-12, based on Figure 3-3.

Example 3-12 *Enabling SNMP Traps and Informs Only*

```
Router(config)# snmp-server community traps3997only ro 1
Router(config)# snmp-server host 172.16.3.2 traps3997only
Router(config)# access-list 1 deny any
```

In this example, the router can send SNMP traps to 172.16.3.2, but 172.16.3.2 cannot poll or access the router through SNMP. This is accomplished with the ACL associated with the **snmp-server community** command that denies all source addresses.

CAUTION   SNMP v1 and v2 are insecure protocols. Hackers love to use SNMP to learn all kinds of information about your network and its devices. I recommend never using them, especially on a router that is acting as a firewall. If you need to use these versions internally, follow these recommendations. First, don't use easy-to-guess community strings, such as public and private. Instead, make them a random string of numbers and letters. Second, use ACLs to restrict access through SNMP to the router. Third, use a VPN to protect the SNMP traffic between your agents and management devices, or use SNMP v3. Also make sure that you filter out any and all SNMP traffic from external networks; you don't want your router responding to external queries.

SNMP v3 Configuration

The configuration of SNMP v3 is different from that of v1 and v2. You use three commands to secure SNMP v3 access:

- **snmp-server group**

- **snmp-server user**

- **snmp-server host**

The combination of these three commands enables you to secure SNMP access to your router.

The **snmp-server group** command maps SNMP users to SNMP views. A view enables you to restrict the MIB or MIBs that the group is allowed to access. Here is the syntax of this command:

```
Router(config)# snmp-server group groupname v3 {auth | noauth | priv}
   [read readview] [write writeview] [notify notifyview ] [access standard_ACL_#]
```

First, you must specify the name of the group, which is configured on your management station or stations. This command actually supports all three versions of SNMP, but for the purpose of this section, I am using v3. With v3, you have three types of protection:

- **noauth**—Does not authenticate or encrypt the packet. This is the weakest form of security for SNMPv3.

- **auth**—Authenticates the packet but does not encrypt it.

- **priv**—Authenticates the packet and encrypts the packet contents. This is the strongest form of security for SNMPv3.

I highly recommend that you use the **priv** method of securing SNMP v3 traffic because the contents are not readable as they are traveling across the network.

Following the security information, you can specify the views (read, write, and notify) that you previously created, restricting the group to only certain MIB structures. Typically, you do not specify notify views in this command, but with the **snmp-server host** or **snmp-server user** commands, since the use of the **snmp-server group** command restricts notifications (notify views) for all users of the group. Finally, you can use a standard ACL to restrict which SNMP management devices can access the router.

To add a user to a group, use the **snmp-server user** command:

```
Router(config)# snmp-server user username groupname [remote IP_address]
   [udp-port port_#] v3 [encrypted] [auth {md5 | sha} password [priv des56 password]
   [access standard_ACL_#]
```

The *username* parameter specifies the username on the management station that will access the router and the group name associated with the group that the user belongs to (**snmp-server group** command). Following this is the IP address of the management station. If you omit this, the address in the **snmp-server host** command is used. You can change the port number for notifications, but it defaults to UDP 162. For the most secure access, you specify SNMP v3.

You have different options for securing the connection. The **encrypted** option specifies that any passwords are protected; that is, you cannot see the passwords in clear text when you execute the **show running-config** command. The **auth** parameter specifies that authentication should be used to verify the remote side's identity by performing packet-integrity checking. You need to specify the hashing function to use—MD5 or SHA—and the key to use for the hashing function. This key cannot exceed 64 characters. The **priv des56** parameter specifies that encryption should be performed using DES with 56-bit keys. Following this is the key value for the encryption algorithm, which cannot exceed 64 characters. For both passwords, Cisco recommends that they be at least eight characters long. The last part of the command enables you to specify a standard ACL to limit access to the router.

To specify the destination of SNMP traps, use the **snmp-server host** command:

```
Router(config)# snmp-server host IP_address [traps | informs]
   version 3 [{auth | noauth | priv} community_string [udp-port port_#]
   [notification_type]
```

This is the same command discussed with SNMP v1 and v2, but with some additions. In this example, the version is SNMP v3. The main difference is the security options: The **noauth** option specifies no security, the **auth** option specifies packet integrity checking only, and the **priv** option specifies both integrity checking and encryption for the SNMP connection.

Example 3-13 shows an insecure SNMPv3 configuration, using the network shown in Figure 3-3.

Example 3-13 *Insecure SNMP v3 Configuration Example*

```
Router(config)# snmp-server group group1 v3 noauth
Router(config)# snmp-server user user1 group1 remote 172.16.3.2 v3
Router(config)# snmp-server host 172.16.3.2 traps version 3 noauth user1
```

In this example, the management station is 172.16.3.2, and no SNMP v3 authentication is performed for user1 in group1.

Example 3-14 shows a more secure configuration.

Example 3-14 *Secure SNMPv3 Configuration Example*

```
Router(config)# snmp-server group group1 v3 priv
Router(config)# snmp-server user user1 group1 remote 172.16.3.2 v3
                          encrypt auth md5 secretpass1
                          priv des56 secretpass2
Router(config)# snmp-server host 172.16.3.2 traps version 3 priv user1
```

In this example, packet-integrity authentication is enabled, as is DES encryption. The two passwords are encrypted (using the **encrypt** parameter).

CAUTION   My personal preference is to not use any type of SNMP on a perimeter firewall router. This limits your management functions on it, but it provides for a more secure solution. In the worst case, I use a VPN to encrypt data between the management station and the router. I have found that SNMP v3 is not simple to set up and maintain across multiple platforms; I have found VPNs easier, but your mileage may vary.

Use the **no snmp-server** command to disable all SNMP functions on your router.

Privileged EXEC Access

Up to this point in the chapter, I have focused on user EXEC levels of access and remote access. The remainder of this chapter focuses on privileged EXEC access and how to secure it using static passwords, user accounts, and modification of privilege levels.

The second level of EXEC access on a router is privileged EXEC. By default, this level of access gives you complete access to all of the router's functions, including configuration, troubleshooting, and management.

Passwords

You can use two commands to statically assign passwords to privileged EXEC mode:

```
Router(config)# enable password password
Router(config)# enable secret password
```

The **enable password** command does not encrypt the password, whereas the **enable secret** command does. This affects what you can see when executing a command such as **show running-config**. The **enable secret** command uses the MD5 hashing function to encrypt the password, which is a very secure method of protection.

Privilege Levels

Cisco has 16 different levels of access to the Cisco IOS: 0 through 15. By default, only two of these are used: 1 is for user EXEC access, and 15 is for privileged EXEC access. One problem with this approach is that if you want to give an administrator access to privileged EXEC mode to use **debug** commands for troubleshooting problems, you also give him configuration rights, by default. Unfortunately, with this two-level hierarchy, if a user has access to the privileged EXEC password, he has full access to the router.

One nice feature of the Cisco IOS, however, is that you can change the access level assigned to commands from both user and privileged EXEC modes. In the example of an administrator needing only access to user EXEC and debug functions, you could assign a privilege level of 7 to **debug** commands and then set up either a privileged EXEC password or an account for your administrator that is assigned a level of 7. Therefore, when the administrator logs into the router with his account or password, he can execute commands only at level 7 or lower—in this case, **debug** commands and all user EXEC commands.

The next section covers assigning privilege levels to commands. The following two sections cover how to set up authentication for these levels of access.

Restricting Levels

To assign privilege levels to commands, the **privilege** command is used. Here is its general syntax:

```
Router(config)# privilege mode [all] {level level | reset} command_string
```

The *mode* parameter specifies the mode from which the command is executed. Table 3-2 lists some of the more important modes that you can specify. New in Cisco IOS 12.0(22)S and 12.2(13)T, you can specify the **all** keyword. This keyword functions as a wildcard and includes all commands and parameters beginning with those described by the *command_string* parameter at the end of the command. Before this feature, you had to list each command separately, which could be a time-consuming process (especially for **show** and **debug** commands).

Table 3-2   *Privilege Modes*

Command	Description
configure	Global configuration mode
controller	Controller subconfiguration mode
crypto-map	Crypto map subconfiguration mode, used for VPN configurations
crypto-transform	Crypto map transform set subconfiguration mode, used for VPN configurations
exec	EXEC mode
interface	Interface subconfiguration mode
interface-dlci	Frame Relay Interface DLCI subconfiguration mode
ipenacl	IP named extended ACL subconfiguration mode
ipsnacl	IP named standard ACL subconfiguration mode
line	Line subconfiguration mode
map-class	Map class subconfiguration mode
map-list	Map list subconfiguration mode
preauth	AAA preauthorization definitions
route-map	Router map subconfiguration mode
router	Router subconfiguration mode
sg-radius	RADIUS server group
sg-tacacs+	TACACS+ server group
subscriber-policy	Subscriber policy subconfiguration mode
tcl	TCL subconfiguration mode
template	Template subconfiguration mode
translation-rule	Translation rule subconfiguration mode
vpdn-group	VPDN remote access subconfiguration mode

The **level** keyword specifies the level of access that you assign to the command(s). This can be from 0 to 15, where 1 is user EXEC and 15 is privileged EXEC, by default. Instead of specifying the **level** keyword, you can use **reset**; this keyword resets the privilege level of the command(s) to the default privilege level and removes the **privilege** command from the router's configuration. Prefacing the **privilege** command with the **no** parameter resets the privilege level of the command(s) but does not remove it from the router's configuration.

NOTE   Five commands are actually at level 0 instead of 1 or 15: **disable**, **enable**, **exit**, **help**, and **logout**.

In the last part of the command you enter your command or partial command. When entering a partial command, make sure that you use the **all** keyword to match on all commands that begin with this string.

CAUTION   Whenever you set the privilege level for a command that has multiple words, such as **show ip access-list**, all commands beginning with the first parameter also have their privilege level changed. This makes sense because, for this example, to execute the **show ip access-list** command, you first must be able to execute **show ip**; likewise, to execute **show ip**, you must be able to execute **show**. For example, if I set the level to 7 for **show ip access-list**, all **show** and **show ip** commands also would have their levels set to 7.

Therefore, the privilege-level restriction is what it describes: It typically can restrict a specific command (unless that command has no parameters), but it typically is used to restrict a group of commands, or all commands, for a specific method of access, such as EXEC or configuration mode.

Using the **privilege** command can be tricky, so take a look at a simple example to illustrate its usage. In this example, you want an administrator to be able to execute **show** and **debug** commands, and disable and enable an interface, but only these privileged EXEC commands. Example 3-15 shows the configuration to accomplish this.

Example 3-15 *Command Restriction Example*

```
Router(config)# privilege exec level 7 show
Router(config)# privilege exec level 7 debug
Router(config)# privilege exec level 7 configure
Router(config)# privilege configure level 7 interface
Router(config)# privilege interface level 7 shutdown
```

The first two commands are straightforward. To execute any **show** or **debug** command from EXEC mode, you must be at least logged into the router at level 7 or higher.

CAUTION   In Example 3-15, all **show** commands are assigned to privileged EXEC level 7. This means that if a user has access only to user EXEC mode, he will not be able to execute any **show** commands.

Restricting the administrator to only enabling and disabling interfaces is more difficult. To do this, the user must execute the [**no**] **shutdown** command within an interface from configuration mode. First, the administrator must be able to access configuration mode; this is the EXEC level 7 access for the **configure** command (third line). Next, the user needs access to interfaces on the router from configuration mode (fourth line). Finally, the user is restricted to just the **shutdown** command within the interfaces (last line).

TIP   As you can see from the previous example, setting up restrictions is not necessarily an easy process. Therefore, I highly recommend that you not configure these on a production router without first doing them on a test router, to make sure that you are not creating any inadvertent security problems. Plus, you definitely do not want to lock yourself out of the router because of a misconfiguration. To recover from this problem, you would have to perform the password-recovery procedure, and this requires a reboot of the router.

NOTE   The configuration discussed here has the router itself performing command authorization. One problem with this approach is scalability: If you have 100 routers on which you need to implement and maintain command execution restrictions, you have your work cut out for you. Chapter 5 discusses how to centralize AAA functions, such as command authorization, on an AAA security server such as Cisco Secure ACS.

Password Levels

Now that you have set up your privilege levels for access restrictions, you need to set up your authentication so that administrators can access these privilege levels. This can be done with one of two methods: privileged EXEC passwords assigned to a specific level or a local authentication database. This section covers the former, and the next section covers the latter.

Of the two authentication methods for privilege levels, using the **enable** command is the easiest to implement. Use the following command to associate a privileged EXEC password with a specific level:

```
Router(config)# enable secret level level_# password
```

All you need to do is specify the level number for access and then specify the password.

NOTE   You also can use the **enable password** command to do this. However, in Cisco IOS 12.3, when this command is executed, the router displays a warning message:

```
% Converting to a secret.  Please use "enable secret" in the future.
```

The Cisco IOS then converts the **enable password** command to the **enable secret** command. This makes sense because the **enable secret** command uses an MD5 hash function to encrypt the password, which is very secure.

Also, using the **enable password** command stores the password on the router in clear text, which is susceptible to eavesdropping attacks. Therefore, do not use the **enable password** command; instead, use **enable secret**.

After you have set up your passwords, to test them, log out of the router and then log back in. From user EXEC mode, use this command:

```
Router> enable level_#
```

When you specify the level number with the **enable** command, the router uses the appropriate password configured with the **enable secret level** command. If you omit the level number, the Cisco IOS assumes level 15 access.

To view your privilege level after you have authenticated, use the **show privilege** command:

```
Router# show privilege
Current privilege level is 7
```

To exit to a specific level, use this command:

```
Router# disable level_#
```

Given the previous privilege command configuration, to set up level 7 authentication, use the following command:

```
Router(config)# enable secret level 7 hidden88secret
```

To test this access, use the process in Example 3-16 when logging in.

Example 3-16 *Logging into a Specific Privileged EXEC Level*

```
Router> enable 7
Password: hidden88secret
Router# show privilege
Current privilege level is 7
Router#
```

Local Authentication Database

The main problem of using the **enable secret** command to assign passwords to levels is that if multiple administrators need access to the same level, they all must use the same password, which is a security risk. A better approach is to create a local authentication database in which each user is assigned a different account name and password. Therefore, if an administrator leaves the company, you do not have to notify all the other administrators of the password change to the access level. Instead, you would just delete the old administrator's account.

TIP   The local authentication database is used best when you need to maintain only a small number of Cisco IOS routers. If you have dozens or hundreds of routers, it is not practical to replicate account changes on each router. Instead, you will want to use AAA and an external security server to centralize your authentication and authorization functions, as discussed in Chapter 5.

To create a local authentication database, the **username** command is used:

```
Router(config)# username user's_name [privilege #]
   {secret | password} password
```

The account name must be unique. If you omit the privilege level, it defaults to 1. Two options exist for specifying how the router treats the password. The **secret** parameter encrypts the password using MD5 (the same as the **enable secret** command). This option was introduced in Cisco IOS 12.0(18)S and was integrated fully into the Cisco IOS in versions 12.1(8a)E and 12.2(8)T. The **password** parameter does not encrypt the password.

Here is a simple example of creating a user with level 7 access that is encrypted with MD5:

```
Router(config)# username richard privilege 7 secret keepOUT
```

After you have built your authentication database, use the **login local** command on your lines, forcing them to use the local authentication database instead of the **password** command on the line. Example 3-17 shows a sample of setting up your lines to use the local authentication database.

Example 3-17 *Setting up Your Lines to Use the Local Authentication Database*

```
Router(config)# line con 0
Router(config-line)# login local
Router(config-line)# exit
Router(config)# line aux 0
Router(config-line)# login local
Router(config-line)# exit
Router(config)# line vty 0 4
Router(config-line)# login local
```

Based on the privilege level, the user immediately is placed in that level upon successfully logging in. You then can use the **show privilege** command to verify the privilege level.

After you have set up the connection, log into the router using the account name. Check the privilege level with the **show privilege** level command, and then test the commands allowed by this account to ensure that you have set up your **privilege** commands correctly.

CAUTION	If you configure the **login local** command on your lines and do not have any accounts defined with the **username** command, you have just locked yourself out of the router. I recommend setting up the **login local** command on the VTYs first; then test this and apply the command to the console line to prevent inadvertent lockouts.

Other Access Items

I want to discuss two other items concerning setting up basic authentication to various types of access to your router. The first item deals with unencrypted passwords, and the second deals with login banners. The following two sections cover this information.

Encrypting Passwords

Certain password commands, such as the **password** line subconfiguration mode command and the **username password** and **enable password** commands, do not encrypt their passwords. Unfortunately, this means that every time you view your configuration with the **show running-config** command or back up your configuration to a TFTP server, these clear-text passwords are susceptible to eavesdropping attacks. You can use a few solutions to limit your exposure to eavesdropping attacks for your passwords:

- Use commands that encrypt the passwords, such as **username secret** and **enable secret**.

- When backing up your configuration to a remote server, use a VPN that performs encryption, or, instead of using TFTP, use SCP (secure copy). VPNs are discussed in Part VIII, and SCP is discussed in Chapter 5.

- Encrypt the unencrypted passwords with the **service password-encryption** command.

This section focuses on the last point. The **service password-encryption** command is used to encrypt clear-text passwords in your configuration:

```
Router(config)# service password-encryption
```

Passwords are encrypted whenever you execute this command and any time after this when you enter a password in your router's configuration. This applies to all clear-text passwords, including authentication key passwords, line passwords, privileged EXEC passwords, and routing protocol passwords. However, the encryption process used for the encryption is very weak and can be reversed.

CAUTION	The main purpose of the **service password-encryption** command is to provide some level of protection from eavesdroppers. However, it should be pointed out that passwords encrypted with this command can be decrypted with the correct tool. At one time, you could download freely this tool if you had CCO access.

As an example, you can go to the website http://www.oldach.net/ciscocrack.shtml and enter the full **username password** or **enable password** command, and the website will decrypt the password for you. Here's an example of information that I entered and the output that it produced:

```
The line
          username richard privilege 7 password 7 0822455D0A16
decodes to
          username richard privilege 7 password cisco
```

That's pretty cool, yet scary. If you use the **secret** parameter, which uses MD5 to encrypt the password, this nifty utility cannot decode the password. The one limitation of this link is that it decrypts passwords only from the **username password** command. Boson software has a similar utility that you can download and freely use on your desktop. It can be found at http://www.boson.com/promo/utilities/getpass/getpass_ utility.htm. This utility decrypts any password that was encrypted with the **service password-encryption** command. Actually, I have never heard of anyone breaking an MD5-protected password, so I highly recommend that you use commands that use MD5 for password protection.

Banners

Even though this is a minor thing, you always should put a login banner on your router that is displayed before the username/password prompt. This might not seem like an important measure to take when securing your router; however, if you ever need to take someone to court over damages caused by hacking into your router, you will need proof that access to the router is limited to only authorized personnel.

Banner Guidelines

At a minimum, a good banner should contain the following:

- What company or person owns the router
- Who is authorized to use the router
- A statement that unauthorized use is illegal and in violation of state and federal laws
- A statement that users' activities will be monitored while on the system
- A statement that actions will be prosecuted to the fullest extent of the law

From a legal standpoint, your banner should address two major issues:

- Display a message that would prove that a hacker's actions were intentional, so that the hacker can't argue that his actions were inadvertent or accidental. By going past the banner to log in, the hacker should be forewarned.

- Display a message regarding the law and repercussions for breaking the law. This tells any hacker that he cannot plead ignorance of the law if he breaks into your router.

Your warnings should be spelled out but general in nature as to what type of crime a hacker is committing by gaining unauthorized access, and that federal or state law-enforcement agencies will be used to prosecute the offense. What you don't want to include in your banner are words such as *welcome*, *greeting*, and other types of friendly salutations. You want to make it distinctly clear to whom the router belongs, who is allowed to use it, and the repercussions of unauthorized access.

Here is a standard banner that I commonly see on U.S. government devices:

```
THIS UNITED STATES GOVERNMENT COMPUTING SYSTEM IS FOR AUTHORIZED
OFFICIAL USE ONLY. Unauthorized use or use for other than official
U.S. Government business is a violation of Federal Law (18 USC).

Individuals using this computing system are subject to having all
of their activities on this system monitored and recorded without
further notice. Auditing of users may include keystroke monitoring.

Any individual who uses this system expressly consents to such
monitoring and is advised that information about their use of the
system may be provided to Federal law enforcement or other authorities
if evidence of criminal or other unauthorized activity is found.
```

Of course, you should change this to fit your own company's policies.

CAUTION   Each government institution has its own laws regarding illegal access and destruction. Therefore, you first should consult your legal department about your created banner so that you have a better chance of winning in court if you must prosecute someone.

Banner Configuration

You can up a login banner on a Cisco router in a few ways:

- **banner motd** creates a message of the day (MOTD) banner. This banner is displayed to all connected terminal users before they are prompted for the username/password information.

- **banner login** creates a login banner. This banner is displayed after the MOTD banner but before the user is prompted for the username/password information. This sometimes is used to list contact information.

- **banner exec** creates an EXEC banner. This banner is displayed before an EXEC process is started. This is typically after the user has authenticated but before the CLI prompt is presented to the user. This sometimes is used to display scheduled events, such as system downtime or maintenance.

- **banner incoming** creates an incoming banner. This is used in reverse Telnet connections. This typically displays instructions on the use of reverse Telnet, such as how to suspend a session.

- **banner slip-ppp** creates a banner for incoming SLIP and PPP dialup connections.

Of the banners listed, at a minimum, you should configure the **banner motd** command. Your main concern here is to ensure that no matter what method someone uses to gain access to your router—local through the console or auxiliary lines, or remote through VTY—a banner is always displayed.

CAUTION   I know of no way of making a banner appear on an HTTP login connection through a web browser to a Cisco IOS router. Therefore, you need to take very careful measures to prevent this kind of unauthorized access to your router.

The general syntax of the banner command is as follows:

```
Router(config)# banner banner_type stop_character message stop_character
```

The banner type can be **motd**, **login**, **exec**, **incoming**, or **slip-ppp**. Following this is the stop, or delimiting, character. This indicates that when you are typing in your message and this character appears, the Cisco IOS will terminate the banner. Next you type in your banner message. Note that the stop character, not the <ENTER> key, indicates the end of the banner; therefore, banners can span multiple lines. After you type in your stop character and then type in any other character, the Cisco IOS exits the banner creation.

Within the banner message, you can insert banner tokens. A banner token is basically a variable the Cisco IOS fills in with the appropriate information. Table 3-3 lists some of the banner tokens that you can insert into all but the **incoming** banner messages.

Table 3-3   *Privilege Modes*

Banner Token	Description
$(hostname)	The name of the router configured with the **hostname** command
$(domain)	The domain name configured on the router with the **ip domain-name** command
$(line)	The VTY or TTY line number that the user is using to access the router

To illustrate the use of a login banner, Example 3-18 shows how to create a simple MOTD banner using the canned government banner shown in the previous section.

Example 3-18 *Creating a Login Banner*

```
Router(config)# banner motd $
THIS UNITED STATES GOVERNMENT COMPUTING SYSTEM IS FOR AUTHORIZED
OFFICIAL USE ONLY. Unauthorized use or use for other than official
U.S. Government business is a violation of Federal Law (18 USC).

Individuals using this computing system are subject to having all
of their activities on this system monitored and recorded without
further notice. Auditing of users may include keystroke monitoring.

Any individual who uses this system expressly consents to such
monitoring and is advised that information about their use of the
system may be provided to Federal law enforcement or other authorities
if evidence of criminal or other unauthorized activity is found.
$
Router(config)#
```

In this example, the stop character is the dollar sign ($). To test the banner, log out and back into your router.

CAUTION   In Cisco IOS 12.2 and earlier, there is an operational problem with Cisco routers: If a user attempts to log in and gives an invalid username, the router responds with a "% Login invalid" message instead of prompting the user for a password again. The problem with this message is that it tells the hacker that the account name that the hacker tried to use does not exist on the router. If the hacker does not get this message, he knows that he has found a valid account name. This greatly aids a hacker in gaining unauthorized access to your router. If you are concerned, upgrade to Cisco IOS 12.3.

Example Configuration

Now that you understand some of the basics of authentication and access, take a look at an example that uses some of the ideas discussed in this chapter. This example uses the network shown in Figure 3-4 to illustrate the configuration of the router called Skunk. In this example, there are two administrative machines: 192.168.3.10 and 192.168.3.11. Example 3-19 displays the configuration.

The two **username** commands at the beginning of the configuration use MD5 encryption to protect the passwords for the admin1 and techie1 accounts. Admin1 is given level 15 access, and techie1 is given only level 7 access. Notice that the **privilege** commands below this allow techie1 to execute **show** and **debug** commands and the **shutdown** command on an **interface**.

Figure 3-4   *Basic Configuration Example*

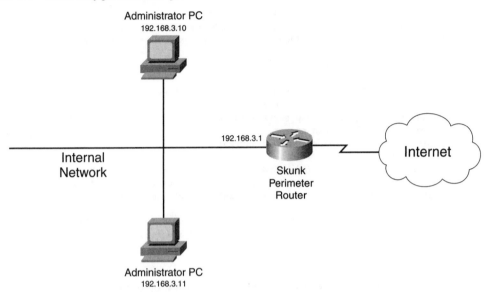

Example 3-19 *Implementing Many Concepts Covered in This Chapter*

```
Router(config)# username admin1 privilege 15 secret geekyadmin
Router(config)# username techie1 privilege 7 secret
  underpaidoverworked
Router(config)# privilege exec level 7 show
Router(config)# privilege exec level 7 debug
Router(config)# privilege exec level 7 configure
Router(config)# privilege configure level 7 interface
Router(config)# privilege interface level 7 shutdown
Router(config)# line console 0
Router(config-line)# login local
Router(config-line)# exit
Router(config)# line aux 0
Router(config-line)# login local
Router(config-line)# exec-timeout 5 0
Router(config-line)# exit
Router(config)# access-list 1 permit 192.168.3.10
Router(config)# access-list 1 permit 192.168.3.11
Router(config)# line vty 0 4
Router(config-line)# access-class 1 in
Router(config-line)# login local
Router(config-line)# transport input ssh
Router(config-line)# transport output ssh
Router(config-line)# exec-timeout 5 0
Router(config-line)# exit
Router(config)# hostname Skunk
Skunk(config)# ip domain-name quizware.com
Skunk(config)# crypto key generate rsa
```

continues

Example 3-19 *Implementing Many Concepts Covered in This Chapter (Continued)*

```
The name for the keys will be: Skunk.quizware.com
Choose the size of the key modulus in the range of 360 to 2048 for your
  General Purpose Keys. Choosing a key modulus greater than 512 may take
  a few minutes.
How many bits in the modulus [512]: 1024
% Generating 1024 bit RSA keys ...[OK]
00:02:25: %SSH-5-ENABLED: SSH 1.5 has been enabled
Skunk(config)# no ip http server
Skunk(config)# no ip http server-secure
Skunk(config)# no snmp-server
Skunk(config)# service password-encryption
Skunk(config)# banner motd $
THIS, THE DEAL GROUP, INC., COMPUTING SYSTEM IS FOR AUTHORIZED
OFFICIAL USE ONLY. Unauthorized use or use for other than official
THE DEAL GROUP, INC. business is a violation of State and Federal LAW

Individuals using this computing system are subject to having all
of their activities on this system monitored and recorded without
further notice. Auditing of users may include keystroke monitoring.

Any individual who uses this system expressly consents to such
monitoring and is advised that information about their use of the
system may be provided to State and Federal law enforcement or
other authorities if evidence of criminal or other unauthorized
activity is found.
$
Skunk(config)# do copy running-config startup-config
```

Below the last **privilege** command, I have set up authentication for the console, auxiliary, and VTY lines to use the local authentication database (**login local**). For both the auxiliary and VTY lines, I have limited their idle timeout to 5 minutes; for the VTY lines, I have restricted Telnet (and SSH) access to only the two administrative PCs. I also have restricted VTY access to SSH with the **transport** line commands.

Below this begins the configuration to allow SSH access, which gives the two administrators encrypted access to the Skunk router. Notice that you first must assign the router a name (**hostname**) and a domain name (**ip domain-name**). Next, you must generate your encryption keys with the **crypto key generate rsa** command. Even though ACLs are discussed later in the book, make sure that you set up an ACL that allows SSH (TCP 22) but denies Telnet (TCP 23) to the router.

Below the SSH configuration, I have disabled specific services: HTTP, HTTPS, and SNMP. Even though all the passwords I have used (**username secret**) are encrypted by MD5, I am providing an additional layer of protection by using the **service password-encryption** command for any other later passwords that I enter that are not encrypted. Finally, I set up a login banner using the **banner motd** command and saved the configuration.

As you can see, this example is simple and straightforward. However, as you will see throughout the rest of this book, you need to configure many more things on your router, especially a perimeter router, to make it more secure.

Summary

This chapter showed you a lot of basic tasks that you will perform to secure access to your router, including local (console and auxiliary) and remote (Telnet, SSH, web browser, and SNMP) access. Some of these access methods are more secure than others; carefully evaluate which method you want to use, and secure it appropriately. As an added measure of security, you can assign command levels and create accounts that correspond to those levels, restricting what an administrator can do on your router.

Next up is Chapter 4, "Disabling Unnecessary Services," which shows you how disable applications and protocols that typically are not necessary on a firewall-hardened router, including those that present security risks.

## CHAPTER 4

Disabling Unnecessary Services

This chapter discusses some of the different kinds of services that your router might or might not be running by default, what type of security impact they have, and how to disable them. Many of the services that I discuss here have security issues, each with its own level of risk. A hacker can use these services to his advantage by gathering information about your router, executing a denial of service (DoS) attack, or attempting to gain unauthorized access. Therefore, you need to disable all of the services on your perimeter router (or any router, for that matter) that you are not using or that are unnecessary.

I have divided chapter into three sections:

- How to disable global services
- How to disable interface services
- How to use the AutoSecure feature

The first two sections discuss how to disable services manually; the new AutoSecure security feature does this process for you dynamically.

Disabling Global Services

Depending on the Cisco IOS version that you are running, many services are enabled by default on your router. Some of these present security issues. This section covers the global services that might or might not be running on your router, and how to disable them.

TIP   I highly recommend that you manually or dynamically (with AutoSecure) disable all services that you are not using. I make this recommendation because Cisco has the habit of sometimes enabling or disabling a service automatically in a specific software release. Therefore, I take the more cautious approach and assume that the services are enabled. Plus, you never know what might happen when you upgrade your Cisco IOS. A previous service that was disabled by default might be enabled (by default) in the new release. By disabling these services manually or with AutoSecure, you are protecting yourself from this kind of issue. Never make any assumptions about what is or is not running on your router; always assume the worst-case scenario and disable all services that you are not using.

Cisco Discovery Protocol

The Cisco Discovery Protocol (CDP) is a Cisco-proprietary protocol used to share basic device information with another directly connected Cisco device. The media types supported include ATM, Ethernet, FDDI, frame relay, HDLC, PPP, and token ring. CDP messages are generated as multicasts and include the following information about your Cisco IOS device:

- The name of your Cisco IOS device (configured with the **hostname** command)
- The hardware platform of the Cisco IOS device, such as a 2600 series router or a 2950 switch
- The Cisco IOS software version running on your Cisco IOS device
- The hardware capabilities of your Cisco IOS device, such as routing, switching, or bridging
- The Layer 3 address of the device
- The interface from which the CDP multicast was sent

Example 4-1 shows some of the information that you can see from a neighboring device.

Example 4-1 *CDP Neighbor Example*

```
RouterB# show cdp neighbor detail
-------------------------
Device ID: RouterA
Entry address(es):
  IP address: 192.168.1.250
Platform: cisco 4500,  Capabilities: Router
Interface: Ethernet0/0,  Port ID (outgoing port): Ethernet0/1
Holdtime : 127 sec

Version :
Cisco Internetwork Operating System Software
IOS (tm) 4500 Software (C4500-J-M), Version 11.3.10,
    MAINTENANCE INTERIM SOFTWARE
Copyright (c) 1986-1997 by cisco Systems, Inc.
Compiled Mon 07-Apr-97 19:51 by dschwart
<--output omitted-->
```

As you can see in Example 4-1, the neighboring router, RouterA, has an IP address of 192.168.1.250, is a 4500, was advertising information from Ethernet0/1, and is running Cisco IOS 11.3.10. Normally, CDP is used to test data link layer (Layer 2) connections. If you are receiving CDP information from a neighboring Cisco device, you can be assured that at least Layer 2 is functioning correctly. If you are having Layer 3 connectivity problems, you can see your neighbor's IP address without having to log into the neighbor.

However, a hacker can use CDP information during a reconnaissance attack. The likelihood of this is small because the hacker must be in the same broadcast domain to view the CDP multicast frame. Therefore, I highly recommend that you disable CDP completely on your perimeter router, or at least on the interfaces that connect to public networks, such as your ISP or other sites that you connect to that are not part of your company's security umbrella.

I discuss how to disable CDP globally in this section, and I cover how to disable it on your interfaces later in the chapter. To globally disable CDP, use the configuration in Example 4-2.

Example 4-2   *Globally Disabling CDP*

```
Router# show cdp
Global CDP information:
        Sending CDP packets every 60 seconds
        Sending a holdtime value of 180 seconds
        Sending CDPv2 advertisements is  enabled
Router# configure terminal
Router(config)# no cdp run
Router(config)# exit
Router# show cdp
% CDP is not enabled
Router#
```

As you can see from this example, after you have disabled CDP with the **no cdp run** command, you will want to verify that it has been disabled with the **show cdp** command.

TCP and UDP Small Servers

TCP and UDP small servers are services running on ports 19 and lower on a device. All of the services are outdated: They were used a decade ago in UNIX environments to provide basic information such as the date and time (daytime, port 13), to test connectivity (echo, port 7), and to generate a stream of characters (chargen, port 19). Hackers sometimes can use these services to their advantage. For instance, if you have chargen (TCP or UDP 19) enabled on your device, a hacker could send a flood of traffic to this port, creating a DoS attack such as Fraggle. Basically, with chargen enabled, your device would process all this traffic, taking away CPU cycles from other processes, and then just discard the information.

Example 4-3 shows a connection being opened to a router with chargen enabled.

Example 4-3   *Connecting to the Chargen Port*

```
Router# telnet 192.168.1.254 chargen
Trying 192.168.1.254, 19 ... Open
 !"#$%&'()*+,-./0123456789:;<=>?@ABCDEFGHIJKLMNOPQRSTUVWXYZ[\]^_`abcdefg
 !"#$%&'()*+,-./0123456789:;<=>?@ABCDEFGHIJKLMNOPQRSTUVWXYZ[\]^_`abcdefgh
 "#$%&'()*+,-./0123456789:;<=>?@ABCDEFGHIJKLMNOPQRSTUVWXYZ[\]^_`abcdefghi
 #$%&'()*+,-./0123456789:;<=>?@ABCDEFGHIJKLMNOPQRSTUVWXYZ[\]^_`abcdefghij
 <--output omitted-->
```

As you can see from Example 4-3, a string of characters is repeated continuously. Example 4-4 shows a sample of connecting to the time port.

Example 4-4   *Connecting to the Time Port*

```
Router# telnet 192.168.1.254 daytime
Trying 192.168.1.254, 13 ... Open
Wednesday, September 17, 2003 02:01:09-UTC
[Connection to 192.168.1.254 closed by foreign host]
Router#
```

To disable these services on your router, use the configuration in Example 4-5.

Example 4-5   *Disabling Small Services*

```
Router(config)# no service tcp-small-servers
Router(config)# no service udp-small-servers
Router(config)# exit
Router# telnet 192.168.1.254 daytime
Trying 192.168.1.254, 13 ...
% Connection refused by remote host
Router#
```

After you have disabled the services, make sure that you test your configuration as shown earlier.

NOTE   In most current versions of the Cisco IOS, TCP and UDP small servers are disabled. However, do not trust the Cisco IOS default behavior; hard-code these commands to ensure that they are disabled.

Finger

Finger is an old UNIX program to determine who is logged into a host. This was used many years ago to determine, without logging into a device, who was logged in. This was useful if you were at a remote site and wanted to see if someone was at his desk before you made a long-distance phone call (I used finger quite often for this purpose).

In today's world, finger is basically a dead application because many other resources, including e-mail and instant-messenger products, can perform this function. Therefore, I recommend disabling this service to limit your exposure: You do not want hackers to know who, if anyone, is logged into your router or gain any valid user IDs for the system.

Example 4-6 shows a simple configuration of verifying that finger is enabled and how to disable it.

Example 4-6 *Determining Whether Finger Is Enabled*

```
Router# telnet 192.168.1.254 finger
Trying 192.168.1.254, 79 ... Open
    Line       User      Host(s)              Idle       Location
    0 con 0              192.168.1.254        00:00:00
*   6 vty 0              idle                 00:00:00 192.168.1.254

   Interface    User                 Mode      Idle      Peer Address
[Connection to 192.168.1.254 closed by foreign host]
Router# configure terminal
Router(config)# no ip finger
Router(config)# no service finger
Router(config)# exit
Router#
Router# telnet 192.168.1.254 finger
Trying 192.168.1.254, 79 ...
% Connection refused by remote host
Router#
```

When executing a finger against a router, the router responds with the output from the **show users** command. To prevent responses, use the **no ip finger** command; this disables the finger server. On older Cisco IOS versions, the **no service finger** command was used. In newer versions of the Cisco IOS, both commands work.

NOTE   In most current versions of the Cisco IOS, finger is disabled. However, do not trust the Cisco IOS default behavior; hard-code these commands to ensure that finger is disabled.

IdentD

IdentD (the identification daemon) allows remote devices to query a TCP port for identification purposes. IdentD is defined in RFC 1413 and is an insecure protocol. Its purpose is to help identify a device that a remote device wants to connect to. It is a very simple protocol: A device sends a request to the Ident port (TCP 113), and the destination responds with its identification, such as a host or device name. Some applications, such as SMTP and FTP (at least some of them), use this to help provide some method of authentication.

Unfortunately, IdentD does not provide any real authentication function, and it is useful to a hacker since you can learn information from it. Plus, a hacker easily can spoof this, allowing him to send a bogus reply, for instance, when an e-mail server asks for the identity of the hacker's device using IdentD. Because of these issues with IdentD, you should disable it on a Cisco router. There is no real reason for the router to be establishing a connection to a remote device that is using IdentD as an additional method of authentication verification; likewise, there is no reason for someone else trying to access the router's IdentD process. To disable it, use the following command:

```
Router(config)# no ip identd
```

You can test it by Telnetting to port 113. In newer Cisco IOS versions, IdentD is disabled by default.

IP Source Routing

Sometimes when you are experiencing routing problems, you can take advantage of the IP source routing feature to help troubleshoot the problem. With IP source routing, you can place the actual route that a packet should take in the IP header. Routers then use this information to route the packet to the destination.

Unfortunately, a hacker can use this to his advantage. Figure 4-1 shows an illustration of a hacker using ingenuity to get into your network. In this example, when all devices on the Internet want to get into your network, they send traffic to you through your ISP. You have used a router/firewall to secure your Internet access. However, in this example, you do business with another company, and you want to have a private WAN connection between your two networks. In this example, your router for the private WAN connection is not protected as well as your other router connected to the Internet; you made the colossal mistake of assuming that your partner company was doing a good job in security. The hacker takes advantage of this by using IP source routing to have the Internet and Company A's routers route his traffic through the less protected path, bypassing your main firewall.

Figure 4-1   *Source Routing Example*

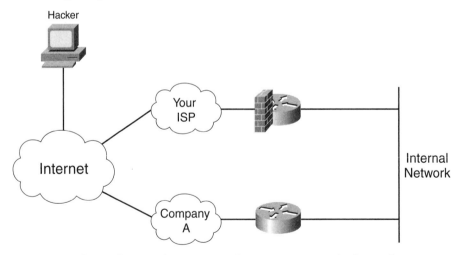

As you can see from this example, source routing can create security issues for your network and, therefore, should be disabled on *all* your routers, including your perimeter router. To disable it, use the following command:

```
Router(config)# no ip source-route
```

TIP	You can test this by using the Cisco IOS extended **ping** command and placing source routing information in your ICMP messages. With this command, choose the extended commands option; then choose either strict or loose and enter your source routing information. Strict source routing has the intermediate routers use the exact path specified in the ICMP payload; loose source routing specifies recommended paths for intermediate routers, if these paths are available. Hackers commonly use strict source routing to use alternative, less secure paths into your network. Loose source routing can be used to learn about alternative paths and the layout of your network. To see the actual path that an ICMP packet took to the destination, use the *record* option (this is useful in troubleshooting).

FTP and TFTP

Your router can function as both an FTP server and a TFTP server. Many administrators use this function to allow a quick copy of a Cisco IOS image from one router to another. I highly recommend that you not use this feature because both FTP and TFTP are insecure protocols. With TFTP, there is no security; with FTP, there is only authentication through a username and password, which is susceptible to eavesdropping attacks. The only way to enable a TFTP server on a router is to specify which file in Flash you want external devices to access. Therefore, this service is disabled unless you explicitly configure it: Do not do so.

By default, the FTP server is disabled on Cisco routers. However, I still recommend executing the following command on your router, to be safe:

```
Router(config)# no ftp-server enable
```

Test this by using an FTP client from your PC, and try to establish a connection to your router. Using Microsoft's standard FTP client, I get the following message after configuring the previous command:

```
C:\> ftp 192.168.1.254
> ftp: connect: Connection refused
```

If you get any other type of message, you have not disabled FTP on your router successfully.

TIP	If you need to copy files to and from your router, I recommend that you use Secure Copy (SCP) instead. This is discussed in Chapter 5, "Authentication, Authorization, and Accounting."

HTTP

Chapter 3, "Accessing a Router," discussed how to secure HTTP connections to your router. However, I also cautioned against this because of the many things hackers have found that allow them to use web browser–based attacks to gain unauthorized access. You could use HTTP with secure socket layer (HTTPS), which provides better security, but your router still is functioning as a web server, which presents inherent security risks. Remember that managing your router through a web browser requires the user to enter a level-15 password.

The easiest way to test this is to use a web browser and try to access your router. From a router prompt, you also can test it by using the two commands in Example 4-7.

Example 4-7 *Accessing a Router's Web Server Through the Telnet Application*

```
Router# telnet 192.168.1.254 80
Trying 192.168.1.254, 80 ... Open
Router# telnet 192.168.1.254 443
Trying 192.168.1.254, 80 ... Open
```

If you see the word "open" in either connection attempt, the HTTP and/or HTTPS service is running on your router. To disable both of these services, as well as verify that they have been disabled, perform the steps in Example 4-8.

Example 4-8 *Disabling a Router's Web Server Process*

```
Router(config)# no ip http server
Router(config)# no ip http secure-server
Router(config)# end
Router# telnet 192.168.1.254 80
Trying 192.168.1.254, 80 ...
% Connection refused by remote host
Router# telnet 192.168.1.254 443
Trying 192.168.1.254, 443 ...
% Connection refused by remote host
```

Instead of using HTTP to manage your router remotely, use the following, in order of preference: VPN, SSH, or HTTPS.

SNMP

As I mentioned in the previous chapter, SNMP can be used to monitor and administer your Cisco devices remotely. However, SNMP has many security problems, especially in SNMP v1 and v2. To completely disable SNMP on your router, do the following three things:

* Remove the default community strings from your router's configuration.
* Disable SNMP traps and the system shutdown feature.
* Disable the SNMP service.

To see whether any SNMP commands are configured on your router, execute the command in Example 4-9.

Example 4-9 *Checking Whether SNMP Commands Exist on Your Router*

```
Router# show running-config | include snmp
Building configuration...
snmp-server community public RO
snmp-server community private RW
Router#
```

For Cisco IOS 12.0 and earlier, the **include** parameter will not work, so you must view the configuration and carefully look for **snmp-server** commands. Example 4-10 shows the configuration that you should use to disable SNMP completely.

Example 4-10 *Disabling SNMP on Your Router*

```
Router(config)# no snmp-server community public RO
Router(config)# no snmp-server community private RW
Router(config)#
Router(config)# no snmp-server enable traps
Router(config)# no snmp-server system-shutdown
Router(config)# no snmp-server trap-auth
Router(config)#
Router(config)# no snmp-server
```

The first two commands remove the read-only and read-write community strings. Note that the names of the community strings might be different in your configuration. The next three commands disable SNMP traps, system shutdowns, and authentication traps through SNMP. The last command disables the SNMP service on the router. After you have disabled SNMP, use the **show snmp** command to verify your configuration, as displayed in Example 4-11.

Example 4-11 *Verifying that SNMP Is Disabled*

```
Router# show snmp
%SNMP agent not enabled
Router#
```

In this example, SNMP has been disabled successfully.

Name Resolution

Everyone with an Internet connection uses the Domain Name System (DNS) to resolve fully qualified domain names (FQDN) to IP addresses. This is especially important for Internet-based applications. Cisco routers also support name resolution with DNS, as well as static, or manual, resolution.

If you router is using DNS to resolve names, you will see something similar to Example 4-12 in your configuration.

Example 4-12 *Using DNS to Resolve Names*

```
Router(config)# hostname santa
santa(config)# ip domain-name claus.gov
santa(config)# ip name-server 200.1.1.1 202.1.1.1
santa(config)# ip domain-lookup
```

As you can see in this example, the router has a name of santa and a domain name of claus.gov. Two name servers are defined, and DNS is enabled (**ip domain-lookup**). You can use the **show hosts** command to view your resolved names.

Because DNS has no security mechanisms built into it, it is susceptible to session-hijacking attacks, in which a hacker sends a fake reply before the destination DNS server can respond. If your router gets two responses back, it typically ignores the second one. Therefore, if the hacker's fake response is received first, your hacker is now one step further in implementing his attack. If you are concerned about this, either make sure that the router has a secure path to the DNS server or do not use DNS; instead, use manual resolution. With manual resolution, you disable DNS and then statically define any common host names that you use on your router with the **ip host** command. To prevent the router from generating DNS queries either to specifically configured DNS servers (**ip name-server**) or as a local broadcast (when DNS servers were not configured), use the configuration in Example 4-13.

Example 4-13 *Disabling DNS on Your Router*

```
Router# telnet www.quizware.com 80
Translating "www.cisco.com"...domain server (255.255.255.255)
Translating "www.cisco.com"...domain server (255.255.255.255)
Translating "www.cisco.com"...domain server (255.255.255.255)
% Unknown command or computer name, or unable to find computer address
Router# configure terminal
Router(config)# no ip domain-lookup
Router(config)# end
Router# telnet www.cisco.com 80
Translating "www.cisco.com"
% Unknown command or computer name, or unable to find computer address
Router#
```

In Example 4-13, DNS resolution was enabled, but no DNS servers were configured. Therefore, the router used local broadcasts to resolve the name to an address. After DNS resolution was disabled with the **no ip domain-lookup** command, the router immediately responded with the "% Unknown command" message, indicating that no resolution was available.

NOTE   Some router configurations, such as SSH and VPN, require the router to have a host and a domain name; however, the router does not require these for DNS resolution to function correctly.

BootP

BootP is an old protocol that was used to assign addressing information to a diskless workstation and, in many cases, load the operating system on the device. In the 1980s and even the early 1990s, the use of diskless workstations was popular because of cost. Most workstations were UNIX based and cost prohibitive, and the same was true of PCs. To overcome the cost burden, many companies deployed diskless workstations. The term *diskless workstation* describes what it is—a device without a hard drive, but with all of the other components, such as a monitor, CPU, RAM, a NIC, and so on.

The diskless workstation used the BootP protocol to dynamically acquire an IP address, and, in some instances, its operating system. This is sent as a local broadcast to UDP port 67 (the same as DHCP). To accomplish this, a BootP server had to be configured to assign the IP addressing information as well as any requested files. After the diskless workstation booted up, it accessed a workstation or server to run applications. An X-terminal is an example of a diskless workstation.

Cisco routers can function as BootP servers, offering files in Flash memory to requesting devices. BootP should be disabled on your router for these three reasons:

- No one really uses it anymore.
- No authentication mechanism is built into it. Anyone can request things from the router, and the router will reply with whatever is configured on it.
- It is susceptible to DoS attacks by a hacker.

To disable BootP, use the following configuration:

```
Router(config)# no ip bootp server
```

DHCP

The Dynamic Host Configuration Protocol (DHCP) commonly is used in networks today. It allows a device to acquire all of its IP addressing information from a server, including its IP address, subnet mask, domain name, DNS server addresses, WINS server addresses, TFTP server addresses, and other information. Cisco routers can function as both DHCP clients and DHCP servers.

CAUTION   When using a Cisco router as a perimeter router, the only time you should set it up as a DHCP client is if you are connecting it to an ISP through a DSL or cable modem and your ISP is using DHCP to assign you addressing information. Otherwise, you never should set up your router as a DHCP client; a hacker easily can masquerade as a DHCP server and send your router false information. This can lead to DoS and routing attacks.

Likewise, the only time your router should function as a DHCP server is when you use your router in a SOHO environment, where it is basically the only device in the small network that can assign addresses to PCs. If you do this, make sure that you filter port UDP port 67 on your router's external interface; this blocks both DHCP and BootP requests from external people.

In many Cisco IOS versions, the DHCP server is enabled by default. If you do not use this on the router, disable it with the following configuration:

```
Router(config)# no service dhcp
```

This prevents the router from acting as a DHCP server or relay agent.

PAD

A packet assembler/disassembler (PAD) is used in X.25 networks to provide reliable connections between remote sites. In today's networks, X.25 has lost a lot of market presence to other protocols, such as frame relay, ATM, ISDN, and even Ethernet in providers' WAN and MAN networks.

However, PAD does serve a useful function to a hacker. Assuming that the hacker can gain control of a directly connected device to the router, and if the router is running the PAD service, it will accept PAD connections from anyone. This give the hacker a foothold into your router, where he can use other attacks to gain EXEC access. To disable this service, use the following command:

```
Router(config)# no service pad
```

Configuration Autoloading

When Cisco routers boot up, they go through various stages of testing, finding the Cisco IOS, and finding a configuration file before you are presented with a CLI prompt. When the router is booting up, it typically goes through five steps:

1 The router loads and executes POST, found in ROM, and tests the hardware components of the router, such as its memory and interfaces.

2 The router loads and executes the bootstrap program.

3 The bootstrap program finds and loads a Cisco IOS image. These images can come from Flash, a TFTP server, or ROM.

4 When the Cisco IOS is loaded, it finds and executes a configuration file: The configuration file is stored in NVRAM, but if this is empty, the System Configuration dialog box is started, or the router can use TFTP to acquire a configuration file.

5 The user finally is presented with the CLI EXEC prompt.

When finding a Cisco IOS image, assuming that there are no **boot system** commands in NVRAM, the router looks for the first valid Cisco IOS image in Flash. If there are no Cisco IOS images in Flash, the router performs a TFTP boot, or network boot; it sends out a local broadcast asking for an operating system file from a TFTP server. If this fails, the router loads the Cisco IOS image in ROM (some routers do not support this third option).

Booting a Cisco IOS image from a TFTP server is not a recommended solution for many reasons, including these:

- For larger images, it is a very slow process to load the image.

- You have no control over which interfaces the router sends the broadcast out; it does it to all active interfaces.

- A hacker can take advantage of this process and send his own Cisco IOS image, one with security weaknesses, to the router—or, he can send an invalid image, preventing the router from booting.

Because TFTP is used for this process, there is no security to protect the load process. Therefore, you should not allow your router to use this function. To prevent this, use the following configuration:

```
Router(config)# no boot network
```

After the Cisco IOS image has loaded, the router goes out and finds a configuration file. If there is no configuration file in NVRAM, the router can use the System Configuration dialog box to create one, or use the network configuration option: using TFTP broadcasts to find one. As with finding a Cisco IOS image with a TFTP server, this has security risks:

- If your configuration file comes from a TFTP server, it is sent across the network in clear text.

- A hacker could act as a TFTP server and send his own configuration file to your router, giving him open access to your network.

Therefore, you should disable this feature by using the following command:

```
Router(config)# no service config
```

Disabling Interface Services

Now that you have disabled all global services that are insecure or that are not necessary, you are ready to proceed to disabling unnecessary or undesirable services on your router's interfaces. This section covers the basics about disabling insecure services on your router's interfaces.

CAUTION   Subinterfaces, loopback interfaces, and null interfaces are considered physical interfaces on the router, so a lot of the things I discuss here also should be done on these interfaces. It is better to be safe than really sorry.

CDP on Insecure Interfaces

As I mentioned at the beginning of this chapter, CDP typically is used as a troubleshooting tool. However, a hacker can use this information in a reconnaissance attack to learn more information about your router. Therefore, if you do not globally disable CDP, you at least should disable CDP on insecure interfaces. Insecure interfaces are basically any interface that is not connected to your internal network:

- An insecure interface is connected to a public network, such as the Internet

- It is connected to a different private network (some other company).

- It is connected to a private WAN to a remote office.

To disable CDP on an interface, use the following configuration:

```
Router(config)# interface type [slot_#/]port_#
Router(config-if)# no cdp enable
```

After you have disabled CDP on your router's interface(s), you can verify it by using the
show cdp interface command. You should not see the disabled interfaces in the output of
this command.

Proxy ARP

IP devices use the Address Resolution Protocol (ARP) to resolve Layer 3 addresses to
Layer 2 (MAC) addresses. This allows devices to communicate with each other at Layer 2,
like Ethernet. Typically, ARP is used to help devices communicate with each other on the
same segment, subnet, or broadcast domain (virtual LAN, or VLAN).

Cisco routers can function as a proxy, giving a requesting device a MAC address of the
router. This typically happens when the device is confused about the destination. The
device thinks that the destination is on the same segment, but, in reality, the device is in a
different subnet. Figure 4-2 illustrates how proxy ARP works, as defined in RFC 1027.

Figure 4-2   *Proxy ARP Example*

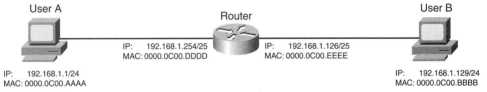

In this example, the network administrator is breaking up a Class C segment (192.168.1.0/24)
into two physically separate segments: 192.168.1.0/25 and 192.168.1.128/25. You will
notice that the router has been configured correctly for both of these subnets. However, you
now have an addressing issue for User A and User B. Both of these devices assume that they
are on the same physical segment because of their subnet mask: /24. As an example, if User A
wants to get to 192.168.1.129, it assumes that this address is on the same segment and
performs an ARP for 192.168.1.129. Obviously, the destination is not on the same segment,
so User B cannot respond with a reply. Two solutions exist for this problem:

- Readdress the clients with the correct addressing information (good solution).

- Have the router use proxy ARP (not a very good solution).

Of course, readdressing the network might not be a simple task, so the administrator in this
example decided to have the router use proxy ARP. With proxy ARP, the router responds on
behalf of User B; however, instead of sending User B's MAC address to User A, it sends its
own address: 0000.0C00.DDDD. User A then encapsulates its IP packet with a source of
192.168.1.1 and a destination of 192.168.1.129 in a frame with a destination MAC address
of the router. When the router receives the frame, it processes it because it matches its NIC's
MAC address; then it examines its routing table and routes the packet correctly. Basically,
proxy ARP is a poor man's version of routing: It allows devices to talk to each other across
subnet boundaries.

Given the example in Figure 4-2, however, there are problems with using proxy ARP.
Assume that you have gone through and readdressed the network correctly, as shown

in Figure 4-3. The administrator has set up filtering to allow traffic between the two 192.168.1.0/24 subnets, but to deny other types of traffic. An ingenious hacker has found out that the interface on the router that he is connected to supports proxy ARP. The hacker wants to execute a DoS attack against User B. The hacker takes advantage of proxy ARP by configuring an address from 192.168.1.0/25 (192.168.1.77) and pings User B. With proxy ARP enabled, the router responds with its own MAC address. The hacker then executes his DoS attack by flooding User B. The router's filtering rules allow this traffic and forward it to User B. Assuming that these were ICMP messages, User B attempts to respond by sending them to 192.168.1.77. The router receives the responses, looks at its routing table, and determines that the packets need to go to the segment where User A is. The router does one of two things at this point: either sends the responses back to the hacker (not likely because the routing information points to a different interface), or uses ARP to get the MAC address of 192.168.1.77 on User A's segment, does not get a response, and responds to each ICMP message to User B with a host unreachable message.

Figure 4-3   *Proxy ARP Hacking Example*

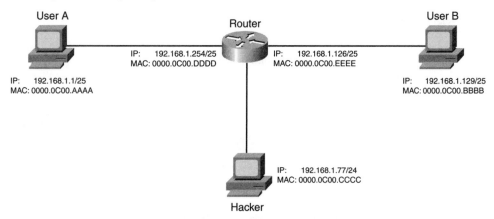

By default, Cisco routers perform proxy ARP on all their interfaces with IP addresses configured on them. I can understand why Cisco initially did this 10 years ago in the infancy of networking with TCP/IP, but this makes no sense today. Therefore, I highly recommend that you disable proxy ARP on your router's interfaces. Use the following command to do this:

```
Router(config)# interface type [slot_#/]port_#
Router(config-if)# no ip proxy-arp
```

NOTE   There is one instance where you do not want to disable proxy ARP: when your router is terminating IPSec remote access VPN connections. In this instance, the router will have to respond to a local ARP from a local device when the local device wants to access the remote access client across the VPN connection. In this instance, leave proxy ARP enabled on the router's internal interface(s).

Remember to repeat the **no ip proxy-arp** command on each interface. To verify your configuration, use the **show ip interface** command. In Example 4-14, proxy ARP has been disabled on the router's fastethernet0 interface.

Example 4-14 *Verifying That Proxy ARP Is Disabled*

```
Router# show ip interface
FastEthernet0 is up, line protocol is up
  Internet address is 192.168.1.254/24
  Broadcast address is 255.255.255.255
  Address determined by non-volatile memory
  MTU is 1500 bytes
  Helper address is not set
  Directed broadcast forwarding is disabled
  Outgoing access list is not set
  Inbound  access list is not set
  Proxy ARP is disabled
<--output omitted-->
```

Directed Broadcasts

A directed broadcast is a broadcast specific to a network. Each network or subnet has three types of addresses: a network number, host addresses, and a broadcast address, called a directed broadcast. Unlike local broadcasts, directed broadcasts are routable. Some old DoS attacks used this by flooding a specific network or subnet with directed broadcasts, typically in a spoofing attack in which the hacker replaced his own IP address with one of the devices in the subnet in the source address field of the packet header. The Smurf attack does this through the use of ICMP packets.

No application really uses the directed broadcast function, so it is highly recommended that you prevent the router from forwarding directed broadcasts by configuring the following on its interfaces:

```
Router(config)# interface type [slot_#/]port_#
Router(config-if)# no ip directed-broadcast
```

Remember to repeat the **no ip directed-broadcast** command on each interface. To verify your configuration, use the **show ip interface** command. In Example 4-15, directed broadcasts have been disabled on the router's fastethernet0 interface.

Example 4-15 *Verifying that Forwarding of Directed Broadcasts Is Disabled*

```
Router# show ip interface
FastEthernet0 is up, line protocol is up
  Internet address is 192.168.1.254/24
  Broadcast address is 255.255.255.255
  Address determined by non-volatile memory
  MTU is 1500 bytes
  Helper address is not set
  Directed broadcast forwarding is disabled
<--output omitted-->
```

ICMP Messages

A hacker can use three types of ICMP messages to create either a DoS attack or a reconnaissance attack:

- ICMP unreachables
- ICMP redirects
- ICMP mask replies

The following three sections discuss how these ICMP messages are used, how a hacker can exploit them, and how you can disable them on your routers' interfaces.

ICMP Unreachables

By default, if a Cisco router receives a nonbroadcast packet to itself with an unknown protocol, or if the router receives a packet that the router cannot forward to its destination because the host or network is not reachable, the router automatically generates an ICMP unreachable message. A hacker can use this information in two ways:

- This information tells the hacker what is not reachable in the network.
- The hacker can use a DoS attack to cause the router to respond to the ICMP unreachable messages. An intelligent hacker changes the source address in the packet to a destination that it wants to attack. This is a form of the Smurf attack.

To prevent the router from responding with ICMP unreachable messages, use this configuration on each of your router's interfaces:

```
Router(config)# interface type [slot_#/]port_#
Router(config-if)# no ip unreachable
```

Remember to repeat the **no ip unreachable** command on each interface. To verify your configuration, use the **show ip interface** command. In Example 4-16, ICMP unreachables have been disabled on the router's fastethernet0 interface.

Example 4-16 *Verifying that ICMP Unreachables Is Disabled*

```
Router# show ip interface fastethernet0
FastEthernet0 is up, line protocol is up
  Internet address is 192.168.1.254/24
  Broadcast address is 255.255.255.255
  Address determined by non-volatile memory
  MTU is 1500 bytes
  Helper address is not set
  Directed broadcast forwarding is disabled
  Outgoing access list is not set
  Inbound  access list is not set
  Proxy ARP is enabled
  Local Proxy ARP is disabled
  Security level is default
  Split horizon is enabled
```

continues

Example 4-16 *Verifying that ICMP Unreachables Is Disabled (Continued)*

```
    ICMP redirects are never sent
    ICMP unreachables are never sent
    ICMP mask replies are never sent
<--output omitted-->
```

ICMP Redirects

ICMP redirects are used to help devices intelligently find a destination. The example shown in Figure 4-4 illustrates how ICMP redirects work. In this example, User A is using Router A as a default gateway. All of User A's traffic leaving the subnet is forwarded to Router A. User A then sends some traffic to User B. When Router A receives the traffic, it realizes that Router B, on the same segment, actually has a better path. Router A thus sends an ICMP redirect message to User A, basically telling User A that Router B should be used for this particular destination. Basically, Router A is sharing routing information with User A. User A then uses Router B to reach User B.

Figure 4-4 *ICMP Redirect Hacking Example*

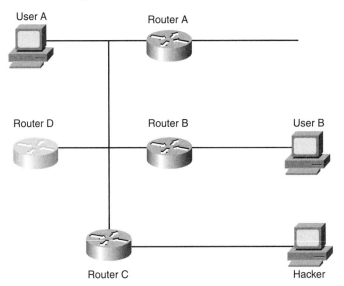

However, hackers can take advantage of this process by corrupting a device's routing table, creating a DoS attack. For example, assume that the hacker in Figure 4-4 sends ICMP redirect messages to User A concerning User B's network. In the hacker's packet, the hacker gives an imaginary router address—say, Router D—to User A. When User A tries to send traffic to User B, it forwards its traffic to Router D, the imaginary router, thus preventing the traffic from reaching User B. A more intelligent hacker would have User A forward traffic to Router C, where the hacker is connected. Of course, for Router C to forward that traffic to the hacker's PC, the hacker first would have to corrupt Router C's routing table in a routing attack.

Headaches with ICMP Redirects

About 7 years ago, I was working with a customer that was the victim of an ICMP redirect hacking attack. It actually took me a handful of days to figure out what the problem was. A few of the file servers were being sent redirect messages that pointed to invalid next-hop addresses. It was weird because sometimes things worked, and sometimes they did not. This is because of how ICMP redirects were incorporated into the file servers: Every 30 minutes, the file servers verified the reachability of the routers that they knew about. So when the attack took place, the file servers lost connectivity to certain locations; then, 30 minutes later, everything worked. The attacker repeated this process every so often, but not often enough for me to catch the problem right away. It took long hours of looking at packets with a protocol analyzer to pinpoint the culprit.

Cisco routers can prevent the router from generating ICMP redirect messages. To prevent the router from generating ICMP redirect messages, use this configuration on each of your router's interfaces:

```
Router(config)# interface type [slot_#/]port_#
Router(config-if)# no ip redirect
```

Remember to repeat the **no ip redirect** command on each interface. To verify your configuration, use the **show ip interface** command. In Example 4-17, ICMP redirects have been disabled on the router's fastethernet0 interface.

Example 4-17 *Verifying that ICMP Redirects Are Disabled*

```
Router# show ip interface
FastEthernet0 is up, line protocol is up
  Internet address is 192.168.1.254/24
  Broadcast address is 255.255.255.255
  Address determined by non-volatile memory
  MTU is 1500 bytes
  Helper address is not set
  Directed broadcast forwarding is disabled
  Outgoing access list is not set
  Inbound  access list is not set
  Proxy ARP is enabled
  Local Proxy ARP is disabled
  Security level is default
  Split horizon is enabled
  ICMP redirects are never sent
  ICMP unreachables are never sent
  ICMP mask replies are never sent
<--output omitted-->
```

ICMP Mask Replies

ICMP supports a mask request message that allows devices on a segment to learn about what the subnet mask is for the segment if this has not been configured on them. Any device, including a router, can generate an ICMP mask reply message. Hackers can use this for two purposes:

- First, it tells the hacker what the range of addresses are on the subnet.

- Second, it tells the hacker the directed broadcast for the subnet, which allows the hacker to use a DoS directed broadcast attack using a modified form of Smurf.

In some cases, the hacker can learn the identity of the device, such as what operating system it is running, with ICMP mask reply messages. For example, Sun systems respond to a mask reply that is fragmented across two ICMP packets. If a hacker gets a reply to this request, he has just found a Sun device and can start using his Sun hacking tools to exploit holes in the SunOS/Solaris operating system of this device.

ICMP mask requests and replies were meant for a local segment and should not be forwarded to other segments. Firewalls should filter them, and routers should ignore these requests; in today's world, every device on the segment either is hard-coded with a subnet mask or learns it through DHCP. To prevent the router from sending ICMP mask reply messages, use this configuration on each of your router's interfaces:

```
Router(config)# interface type [slot_#/]port_#
Router(config-if)# no ip mask-reply
```

Remember to repeat the **no ip mask-reply** command on each interface. To verify your configuration, use the **show ip interface** command. In Example 4-18, ICMP mask replies have been disabled on the router's fastethernet0 interface.

Example 4-18 *Verifying that ICMP Mask Reply Messages Are Disabled*

```
Router# show ip interface
FastEthernet0 is up, line protocol is up
  Internet address is 192.168.1.254/24
  Broadcast address is 255.255.255.255
  Address determined by non-volatile memory
  MTU is 1500 bytes
  Helper address is not set
  Directed broadcast forwarding is disabled
  Outgoing access list is not set
  Inbound  access list is not set
  Proxy ARP is enabled
  Local Proxy ARP is disabled
  Security level is default
  Split horizon is enabled
  ICMP redirects are never sent
  ICMP unreachables are never sent
  ICMP mask replies are never sent
<--output omitted-->
```

Maintenance Operation Protocol

The Maintenance Operation Protocol (MOP), popular in older Digital Equipment Corporation (DEC) equipment, is used for maintenance services such as these:

- Uploading or downloading of system software
- Remote testing
- Problem troubleshooting

Cisco routers can use this to load a Cisco IOS image from a MOP server, assuming that MOP is enabled. This process is a carryover from more than a decade ago, but many routers still have MOP enabled, by default, on their interfaces. To prevent a DoS MOP attack from occurring, disable MOP on your interfaces:

```
Router(config)# interface type [slot_#/]port_#
Router(config-if)# no mop enable
```

Remember to repeat the **no mop enable** command on each interface.

VTYs

Even though VTYs are not interfaces, this is an appropriate place to discuss them. By default, VTYs allow all types of remote access, such as Telnet, SSH, and others. For your VTYs, you will want to restrict access to your VTYs to only Telnet (not recommended) and SSH (recommended). To restrict the router's VTYs to only Telnet access, use this configuration:

```
Router(config)# line vty 0 4
Router(config-line)# transport input telnet
Router(config-line)# transport output telnet
```

To restrict the router's VTYs to only SSH access (I recommend this approach over the previous one), use this configuration:

```
Router(config)# line vty 0 4
Router(config-line)# transport input ssh
Router(config-line)# transport output ssh
```

The **transport** command restricts VTY access into and out of the router. By specifying one particular access method, such as SSH, you are preventing anyone else from using another method. Therefore, if you want to let remote administrators use only SSH (but not Telnet), use the previous configuration. Use the **show line vty** command to verify your configuration, as shown in Example 4-19.

Example 4-19 *Verifying the Configuration of the Router's VTYs*

```
Bullmastiff# show line vty 0
  Tty Typ     Tx/Rx    A Modem  Roty AccO AccI   Uses   Noise  Overruns   Int
    6 VTY               -    -     -    -    -      2      0      0/0       -

Line 6, Location: "", Type: ""
```

continues

Example 4-19 *Verifying the Configuration of the Router's VTYs (Continued)*

```
Length: 24 lines, Width: 80 columns
Baud rate (TX/RX) is 9600/9600

<--output omitted-->

DNS resolution in show commands is enabled
Full user help is disabled
Allowed input transports are ssh.
Allowed output transports are ssh.
Preferred transport is telnet.
No output characters are padded
No special data dispatching characters
Bullmastiff#
Bullmastiff# telnet 192.168.1.254
Trying 192.168.1.254 ...
% Connection refused by remote host
Bullmastiff# ssh -l richard 192.168.1.254
Password: cisco
Bullmastiff#
```

Notice in Example 4-19 that only SSH connections are allowed. I then tested this by trying to Telnet to the router itself, which was refused. I then used SSH to access the router and was successful.

You will want to put one more security measure in place, to ensure that a DoS attack against your VTYs does not tie them up and prevent remote access by a valid administrator. The following two commands help somewhat with this process:

```
Router(config)# service tcp-keepalives-in
Router(config)# service tcp-keepalives-out
```

With these two commands, the router monitors network TCP connections to and from the router by generating keepalives for connections such as Telnet and SSH. The advantage that these commands provide is that if a Telnet connection is abnormally aborted, for instance, the keepalive function detects this and removes the bad connection, allowing other devices to use the VTY line. This feature is disabled by default, and I recommend that you enable it.

Unused Interfaces

As a last precaution, disabling unused interfaces creates a more secure environment than when leaving them up and opening them to hacking attempts. You should use the **shutdown** command on all interfaces that you are not currently using, like this:

```
Router(config)# interface type [slot_#/]port_#
Router(config-if)# shutdown
```

Remember to repeat the **shutdown** command on each interface that you are not using. To verify your configuration, use the **show ip interface brief** command. In Example 4-20, ethernet0 has been disabled manually.

Example 4-20 *Verifying that Unused Interfaces Are Disabled*

```
Router# show ip interface brief
Interface        IP-Address      OK? Method Status                 Protocol
Ethernet0        unassigned      YES NVRAM  administratively down down
FastEthernet0    192.168.1.254   YES NVRAM  up                     up
```

Manual Configuration Example of Disabling Services on a Perimeter Router

To reinforce all the services that you manually should disable on your perimeter router, take a look at an example. In this example, assume that the router has only two interfaces: Ethernet0 and Ethernet1. Example 4-21 shows the router's configuration to manually disable insecure and unnecessary services.

Example 4-21 *How to Disable Insecure and Unnecessary Services*

```
Router(config)# no cdp run
Router(config)# no service tcp-small-servers
Router(config)# no service udp-small-servers
Router(config)# no ip finger
Router(config)# no ip identd
Router(config)# no service finger
Router(config)# no ip source-route
Router(config)# no ftp-server enable
Router(config)# no ip http server
Router(config)# no ip http secure-server
Router(config)# no snmp-server community public RO
Router(config)# no snmp-server community private RW
Router(config)# no snmp-server enable traps
Router(config)# no snmp-server system-shutdown
Router(config)# no snmp-server trap-auth
Router(config)# no snmp-server
Router(config)# no ip domain-lookup
Router(config)# no ip bootp server
Router(config)# no service dhcp
Router(config)# no service pad
Router(config)# no boot network
Router(config)# no service config
Router(config)# interface ethernet 0
Router(config-if)# no ip proxy-arp
Router(config-if)# no ip directed-broadcast
Router(config-if)# no ip unreachable
Router(config-if)# no ip redirect
Router(config-if)# no ip mask-reply
Router(config-if)# exit
Router(config)# interface ethernet 1
Router(config-if)# no ip proxy-arp
```

continues

Example 4-21 *How to Disable Insecure and Unnecessary Services (Continued)*

```
Router(config-if)# no ip directed-broadcast
Router(config-if)# no ip unreachable
Router(config-if)# no ip redirect
Router(config-if)# no ip mask-reply
Router(config-if)# exit
Router(config)# service tcp-keepalives-in
Router(config)# service tcp-keepalives-out
Router(config)# username admin1 privilege 15 secret geekboy
Router(config)# hostname Bullmastiff
Bullmastiff(config)# ip domain-name quizware.com
Bullmastiff(config)# crypto key generate rsa
Bullmastiff(config)# line vty 0 4
Bullmastiff(config-line)# login local
Bullmastiff(config-line)# transport input ssh
Bullmastiff(config-line)# transport output ssh
```

Notice that the bottom part of this configuration restricts access to and from the router through SSH.

AutoSecure

AutoSecure is a new security feature in Cisco IOS 12.2(18)S and 12.3(1). Up to this point in the chapter, you have had to manually disable services to protect your router. This is okay if you understand the Cisco IOS configuration process and are familiar with all the things that you must disable and why you should disable them.

However, for a novice administrator, this becomes a difficult task. AutoSecure removes the complexity by using a simple script that asks basic questions about the use of the router, and then creates a configuration file that will be used to secure the router. This is very similar to the use of the System Configuration dialog script that some administrators use to put a basic configuration on their router. The difference between this and AutoSecure is that AutoSecure focuses only on security-related services.

The AutoSecure feature provides the following security functions:

- It disables all IP services that can be exploited by an attack.
- It enables IP services that can help you prevent attacks.
- It configures minimum password-length restrictions, preventing passwords such as cisco and admin from being configured.
- It generates syslog messages when the maximum number of unsuccessful authentication attempts has been exceeded.

On the surface, the use of AutoSecure sounds simple, but you need to understand how AutoSecure works, as well as its restrictions, before you use it.

Securing Planes

AutoSecure's security focuses on two basic areas: management and forwarding. The next two sections cover these areas.

The Management Plane

AutoSecure can secure the management plane of your router by disabling global and interface services. Basically, everything I have discussed until this point of the chapter is included in the AutoSecure management plane, including securing access to the router and logging functions. Here is a list of the global services AutoSecure disables:

- BootP
- CDP
- Finger
- HTTP server
- IdentD protocol
- NTP (Network Time Protocol)
- PAD
- Source routing
- TCP small servers
- UDP small servers

NTP is the only service I have not discussed in this chapter. I discuss NTP in more depth in Chapter 18, "Logging Events."

Here is a list of the interface services that AutoSecure disables:

- Directed broadcasts
- ICMP mask replies
- ICMP redirects
- ICMP unreachables
- MOP
- Proxy ARP

Note that if you need any of these services, like HTTP, you need to re-enable them manually after running AutoSecure.

Besides disabling the previous services, AutoSecure can enable certain services to increase your security, including the following:

- The **service password-encryption** command is executed, encrypting unencrypted passwords. This command is covered in Chapter 3.

- The **service tcp-keepalives-in** and **service tcp-keepalives-out** commands are executed to remove abnormally terminated TCP connections.

- Secure Copy (SCP) is set up in tandem with SSH to provide secure access to and from the router.

- For all lines, the **login** and **password** commands are configured.

- For VTY connections, only Telnet and SSH are allowed through the **transport input** and **transport output** commands.

- If AAA is not set up, AutoSecure can create a local authentication database with usernames and passwords, to give you more control over router access.

- A login text banner is created, if one does not already exist.

- SNMP is disabled (if not needed), and community strings that are configured with either public or private are removed.

- Logging on the console port and the internal buffer is enabled, sequence numbers and time stamps are added to all logging and debug messages, and trap logging levels are set to debug (logging is discussed in Chapter 18).

From this long list of services that are disabled and enabled, you can see that AutoSecure performs a lot of tasks for you from a simple menu-driven script.

The Forwarding Plane

AutoSecure also can secure the forwarding plane of your Cisco router. This is a marketing term used to describe how AutoSecure will configure security features that affect traffic flowing through your router. Here are some of the things that AutoSecure configures for the forwarding plane:

- For routers that support Context-based Access Control (CBAC), AutoSecure enables this stateful firewall feature on your external interface. CBAC is discussed in Chapter 9, "Context-Based Access Control."

- AutoSecure implements antispoofing by blocking reserved addresses defined by the IANA. This is done by creating an extended access list. These reserved addresses can be examined at http://www.iana.org/assignments/ipv4-address-space. Note that these addresses are subject to change, so you should compare AutoSecure's list of ACL statements with those in the previous URL. Extended ACLs are discussed in Chapter 7, "Basic Access Lists."

- Private IP address spaces defined in RFC 1918 from external sources are blocked.

- CEF is enabled on CEF-supported routers, which helps the router perform better when DoS attacks such as TCP SYN flood attacks are occurring.

- Unicast Reverse Path Forwarding is implemented to help prevent packet spoofing. This feature is covered in Chapter 15, "Routing Protocol Protection."

- TCP Intercept is configured, if available, to reduce the impact of DoS attacks on your internal resources. TCP Intercept is covered in Chapter 17, "DoS Protection."

For those features that need to be implemented on your perimeter router's public interface, such as CBAC and extended ACLs, AutoSecure prompts you for the necessary configuration information.

CAUTION   AutoSecure does not guarantee that it completely secures your router. It is actually a good tool to use when you originally are setting up your router to put a base security configuration on it. However, you will want to implement the many other features in this book to completely secure your router and the traffic behind your router, especially if your router is functioning as a perimeter router or firewall solution.

AutoSecure Configuration

Now that you have a basic understanding of what AutoSecure can do for you, let us discuss how you use this script and how to verify its security configuration. You probably will perform three basic tasks:

- Execute the AutoSecure script.
- Verify the script's secured configuration.
- Use optional commands to increase your security solution.

CAUTION   Before you begin the AutoSecure script to automatically secure your router, make sure that you back up its current configuration to an SCP server. When the script completes, your old configuration is gone. I discuss the use of SCP in Chapter 5.

Starting up AutoSecure

AutoSecure is meant to be run on a router with a base, or initial configuration. If you have a router that already has a configuration on it, with many security features enabled, some features of AutoSecure might not be enabled because of configuration conflictions or restrictions. Therefore, follow these steps to ensure the proper operation of AutoSecure:

Step 1   Either put a very basic configuration on your router or use the System Configuration dialog with the **setup** privileged EXEC command.

Step 2   Use AutoSecure.

Step 3   Complete the configuration of your router, including the implementation of other security features.

To start up AutoSecure, you use the privileged EXEC **auto secure** command, shown here:

```
Router(config)# auto secure [management | forwarding] [no-interact]
```

These are the options that you can enter:

- **No options**—AutoSecure secures both the management and forwarding planes, prompting you for the necessary information.

- **management**—AutoSecure performs security configurations for only the management plane, prompting you for the necessary information.

- **forwarding**—AutoSecure performs security configurations for only the forwarding plane, prompting you for the necessary information.

For all three of these configuration options, if you include the **no-interact** parameter, the router uses all the defaults for parameters and does not prompt you for any information.

NOTE   The AutoSecure script functions basically the same as the System Configuration dialog box. As you are going through the script, the script prompts you for specific information. Information in brackets ([]) is default values and is accepted when you press the Enter key on an empty line. There is no method of returning to a question if you answer it incorrectly; in this case, abort the script with Ctrl-c.

Going Through a Sample Script

To help you understand how to interact with the AutoSecure script, this section goes through an example. This example uses a 1720 router with an internal FastEthernet0 interface and an external Ethernet0 interface. The 1720 has the Cisco IOS Firewall feature set installed. Example 4-22 shows the script configuring both the management and forwarding planes. An explanation of the most important lines follows.

Example 4-22 *How to Use AutoSecure*

```
Router# auto secure
                --- AutoSecure Configuration ---

*** AutoSecure configuration enhances the security of
the router but it will not make the router absolutely secure
from all security attacks ***

All the configuration done as part of AutoSecure will be
shown here. For more details of why and how this configuration
is useful, and any possible side effects, please refer to Cisco
documentation of AutoSecure.
At any prompt you may enter '?' for help.
Use ctrl-c to abort this session at any prompt.
```

Example 4-22 *How to Use AutoSecure (Continued)*

```
If this device is being managed by a network management station,
AutoSecure configuration may block network management traffic.
Continue with AutoSecure? [no]: yes                                    (1)

Gathering information about the router for AutoSecure

Is this router connected to internet? [no]: yes                       (2)
Interface      IP-Address    OK? Method Status                 Protocol
Ethernet0      unassigned    YES NVRAM  administratively down down
FastEthernet0 192.168.1.254 YES NVRAM  up                      up
Enter the interface name that is facing internet: Ethernet0

Securing Management plane services..                                  (3)

Disabling service finger
Disabling service pad
Disabling udp & tcp small servers
Enabling service password encryption
Enabling service tcp-keepalives-in
Enabling service tcp-keepalives-out
Disabling the cdp protocol

Disabling the bootp server
Disabling the http server
Disabling the finger service
Disabling source routing
Disabling gratuitous arp

Here is a sample Security Banner to be shown
at every access to device. Modify it to suit your
enterprise requirements.

Authorized Access only
  This system is the property of So-&-So-Enterprise.
  UNAUTHORIZED ACCESS TO THIS DEVICE IS PROHIBITED.
  You must have explicit permission to access this
  device. All activities performed on this device
  are logged and violations of this policy result
  in disciplinary action.

Enter the security banner {Put the banner between                     (4)
k and k, where k is any character}:
+
This system is the property of the Deal Group, Inc.
Unauthorized access to this device is prohibited.
You must have explicit permission to access this
device. All activities performed on this device are
logged and violations of this policy result in
disciplinary, civil, and criminal action.
+
Enable secret is either not configured or                            (5)
 is same as enable password
```

continues

Example 4-22 *How to Use AutoSecure (Continued)*

```
Enter the new enable secret: ciscocisco
Enable password is not configured or its length
is less than minimum no. of characters configured
Enter the new enable password: sanfransanfran

Configuration of local user database                          (6)
Enter the username: richard
Enter the password: EmilyAlina
Configuring aaa local authentication
Configuring console, Aux and vty lines for
local authentication, exec-timeout, transport

Configure SSH server? [yes]: yes                              (7)
Enter the hostname: Bullmastiff
Enter the domain-name: quizware.com

Configuring interface specific AutoSecure services           (8)
Disabling the following ip services on all interfaces:

 no ip redirects
 no ip proxy-arp
 no ip unreachables
 no ip directed-broadcast
 no ip mask-reply

Securing Forwarding plane services..                         (9)

Enabling CEF (it might have more memory requirements on some
     low-end platforms)
Configuring the named acls for Ingress filtering

autosec_iana_reserved_block: This block may subject to       (10)
change by iana and for updated list visit
www.iana.org/assignments/ipv4-address-space.
1/8, 2/8, 5/8, 7/8, 23/8, 27/8, 31/8, 36/8, 37/8, 39/8,
41/8, 42/8, 49/8, 50/8, 58/8, 59/8, 60/8, 70/8, 71/8,
72/8, 73/8, 74/8, 75/8, 76/8, 77/8, 78/8, 79/8, 83/8,
84/8, 85/8, 86/8, 87/8, 88/8, 89/8, 90/8, 91/8, 92/8, 93/8,
94/8, 95/8, 96/8, 97/8, 98/8, 99/8, 100/8, 101/8, 102/8,
103/8, 104/8, 105/8, 106/8, 107/8, 108/8, 109/8, 110/8,
111/8, 112/8, 113/8, 114/8, 115/8, 116/8, 117/8, 118/8,
119/8, 120/8, 121/8, 122/8, 123/8, 124/8, 125/8, 126/8,
197/8, 201/8
autosec_private_block:                                        (11)
10/8, 172.16/12, 192.168/16
autosec_complete_block: This is union of above two and       (12)
the addresses of source multicast, class E addresses
and addresses that are prohibited for use as source.
source multicast (224/4), class E(240/4), 0/8, 169.254/16,
192.0.2/24, 127/8.
```

Example 4-22 *How to Use AutoSecure (Continued)*

```
Configuring Ingress filtering replaces the existing
acl on external interfaces, if any, with ingress
filtering acl.

Configure Ingress filtering on edge interfaces? [yes]: yes          (13)

[1] Apply autosec_iana_reserved_block acl on all edge interfaces
[2] Apply autosec_private_block acl on all edge interfaces
[3] Apply autosec_complete_bogon acl on all edge interfaces
Enter your selection [3]: 3                                         (14)
Enabling unicast rpf on all interfaces connected to internet
Configure CBAC Firewall feature? [yes/no]: yes                     (15)

This is the configuration generated:                               (16)
no service finger
no service pad
no service udp-small-servers
no service tcp-small-servers
service password-encryption
service tcp-keepalives-in
service tcp-keepalives-out
no cdp run
no ip bootp server
no ip http server
no ip finger
no ip source-route
no ip gratuitous-arps
banner +
This system is the property of the Deal Group, Inc.
Unauthorized access to this device is prohibited.
You must have explicit permission to access this
device. All activities performed on this device are
logged and violations of this policy result in
disciplinary, civil, and criminal action.
+
security passwords min-length 6
security authentication failure rate 10 log
enable secret 5 $1$1q95$10TM0DLUhsUo.C37dF2WZ/
enable password 7 021505550D140E2F5F4F071F17161C
username richard password 7 03175A050C0032495D08170F18010E
aaa new-model
aaa authentication login local_auth local
line console 0
 login authentication local_auth
 exec-timeout 5 0
 transport output telnet
line aux 0
 login authentication local_auth
 exec-timeout 10 0
 transport output telnet
line vty 0 4
 login authentication local_auth
 transport input telnet
```

continues

Example 4-22 *How to Use AutoSecure (Continued)*

```
hostname Bullmastiff
ip domain-name quizware.com
crypto key generate rsa general-keys modulus 1024
ip ssh time-out 60
ip ssh authentication-retries 2
line vty 0 4
transport input ssh telnet
service timestamps debug datetime localtime show-timezone msec
service timestamps log datetime localtime show-timezone msec
logging facility local2
logging trap debugging
service sequence-numbers
logging console critical
logging buffered
int Ethernet0
 no ip redirects
 no ip proxy-arp
 no ip unreachables
 no ip directed-broadcast
 no ip mask-reply
int FastEthernet0
 no ip redirects
 no ip proxy-arp
 no ip unreachables
 no ip directed-broadcast
 no ip mask-reply
ip cef
ip access-list extended autosec_iana_reserved_block
 deny ip 1.0.0.0 0.255.255.255 any
 deny ip 2.0.0.0 0.255.255.255 any
 deny ip 5.0.0.0 0.255.255.255 any
 deny ip 7.0.0.0 0.255.255.255 any
 deny ip 23.0.0.0 0.255.255.255 any
 deny ip 27.0.0.0 0.255.255.255 any
 deny ip 31.0.0.0 0.255.255.255 any
 deny ip 36.0.0.0 0.255.255.255 any
 deny ip 37.0.0.0 0.255.255.255 any
 deny ip 39.0.0.0 0.255.255.255 any
 deny ip 41.0.0.0 0.255.255.255 any
 deny ip 42.0.0.0 0.255.255.255 any
 deny ip 49.0.0.0 0.255.255.255 any
 deny ip 50.0.0.0 0.255.255.255 any
 deny ip 58.0.0.0 0.255.255.255 any
 deny ip 59.0.0.0 0.255.255.255 any
 deny ip 60.0.0.0 0.255.255.255 any
 deny ip 70.0.0.0 0.255.255.255 any
 deny ip 71.0.0.0 0.255.255.255 any
 deny ip 72.0.0.0 0.255.255.255 any
 deny ip 73.0.0.0 0.255.255.255 any
 deny ip 74.0.0.0 0.255.255.255 any
 deny ip 75.0.0.0 0.255.255.255 any
```

Example 4-22 *How to Use AutoSecure (Continued)*

```
deny ip 76.0.0.0 0.255.255.255 any
deny ip 77.0.0.0 0.255.255.255 any
deny ip 78.0.0.0 0.255.255.255 any
deny ip 79.0.0.0 0.255.255.255 any
deny ip 83.0.0.0 0.255.255.255 any
deny ip 84.0.0.0 0.255.255.255 any
deny ip 85.0.0.0 0.255.255.255 any
deny ip 86.0.0.0 0.255.255.255 any
deny ip 87.0.0.0 0.255.255.255 any
deny ip 88.0.0.0 0.255.255.255 any
deny ip 89.0.0.0 0.255.255.255 any
deny ip 90.0.0.0 0.255.255.255 any
deny ip 91.0.0.0 0.255.255.255 any
deny ip 92.0.0.0 0.255.255.255 any
deny ip 93.0.0.0 0.255.255.255 any
deny ip 94.0.0.0 0.255.255.255 any
deny ip 95.0.0.0 0.255.255.255 any
deny ip 96.0.0.0 0.255.255.255 any
deny ip 97.0.0.0 0.255.255.255 any
deny ip 98.0.0.0 0.255.255.255 any
deny ip 99.0.0.0 0.255.255.255 any
deny ip 100.0.0.0 0.255.255.255 any
deny ip 101.0.0.0 0.255.255.255 any
deny ip 102.0.0.0 0.255.255.255 any
deny ip 103.0.0.0 0.255.255.255 any
deny ip 104.0.0.0 0.255.255.255 any
deny ip 105.0.0.0 0.255.255.255 any
deny ip 106.0.0.0 0.255.255.255 any
deny ip 107.0.0.0 0.255.255.255 any
deny ip 108.0.0.0 0.255.255.255 any
deny ip 109.0.0.0 0.255.255.255 any
deny ip 110.0.0.0 0.255.255.255 any
deny ip 111.0.0.0 0.255.255.255 any
deny ip 112.0.0.0 0.255.255.255 any
deny ip 113.0.0.0 0.255.255.255 any
deny ip 114.0.0.0 0.255.255.255 any
deny ip 115.0.0.0 0.255.255.255 any
deny ip 116.0.0.0 0.255.255.255 any
deny ip 117.0.0.0 0.255.255.255 any
deny ip 118.0.0.0 0.255.255.255 any
deny ip 119.0.0.0 0.255.255.255 any
deny ip 120.0.0.0 0.255.255.255 any
deny ip 121.0.0.0 0.255.255.255 any
deny ip 122.0.0.0 0.255.255.255 any
deny ip 123.0.0.0 0.255.255.255 any
deny ip 124.0.0.0 0.255.255.255 any
deny ip 125.0.0.0 0.255.255.255 any
deny ip 126.0.0.0 0.255.255.255 any
deny ip 197.0.0.0 0.255.255.255 any
deny ip 201.0.0.0 0.255.255.255 any
permit ip any any
```

continues

Example 4-22 *How to Use AutoSecure (Continued)*

```
remark This acl might not be up to date. Visit
    www.iana.org/assignments/ipv4-address-space
    for update list
exit
ip access-list extended autosec_private_block
 deny ip 10.0.0.0 0.255.255.255 any
 deny ip 172.16.0.0 0.15.255.255 any
 deny ip 192.168.0.0 0.0.255.255 any
 permit ip any any
exit
ip access-list extended autosec_complete_bogon
 deny ip 1.0.0.0 0.255.255.255 any
 deny ip 2.0.0.0 0.255.255.255 any
 deny ip 5.0.0.0 0.255.255.255 any
 deny ip 7.0.0.0 0.255.255.255 any
 deny ip 23.0.0.0 0.255.255.255 any
 deny ip 27.0.0.0 0.255.255.255 any
 deny ip 31.0.0.0 0.255.255.255 any
 deny ip 36.0.0.0 0.255.255.255 any
 deny ip 37.0.0.0 0.255.255.255 any
 deny ip 39.0.0.0 0.255.255.255 any
 deny ip 41.0.0.0 0.255.255.255 any
 deny ip 42.0.0.0 0.255.255.255 any
 deny ip 49.0.0.0 0.255.255.255 any
 deny ip 50.0.0.0 0.255.255.255 any
 deny ip 58.0.0.0 0.255.255.255 any
 deny ip 59.0.0.0 0.255.255.255 any
 deny ip 60.0.0.0 0.255.255.255 any
 deny ip 70.0.0.0 0.255.255.255 any
 deny ip 71.0.0.0 0.255.255.255 any
 deny ip 72.0.0.0 0.255.255.255 any
 deny ip 73.0.0.0 0.255.255.255 any
 deny ip 74.0.0.0 0.255.255.255 any
 deny ip 75.0.0.0 0.255.255.255 any
 deny ip 76.0.0.0 0.255.255.255 any
 deny ip 77.0.0.0 0.255.255.255 any
 deny ip 78.0.0.0 0.255.255.255 any
 deny ip 79.0.0.0 0.255.255.255 any
 deny ip 83.0.0.0 0.255.255.255 any
 deny ip 84.0.0.0 0.255.255.255 any
 deny ip 85.0.0.0 0.255.255.255 any
 deny ip 86.0.0.0 0.255.255.255 any
 deny ip 87.0.0.0 0.255.255.255 any
 deny ip 88.0.0.0 0.255.255.255 any
 deny ip 89.0.0.0 0.255.255.255 any
 deny ip 90.0.0.0 0.255.255.255 any
 deny ip 91.0.0.0 0.255.255.255 any
 deny ip 92.0.0.0 0.255.255.255 any
 deny ip 93.0.0.0 0.255.255.255 any
 deny ip 94.0.0.0 0.255.255.255 any
 deny ip 95.0.0.0 0.255.255.255 any
 deny ip 96.0.0.0 0.255.255.255 any
```

Example 4-22 *How to Use AutoSecure (Continued)*

```
deny ip 97.0.0.0 0.255.255.255 any
deny ip 98.0.0.0 0.255.255.255 any
deny ip 99.0.0.0 0.255.255.255 any
deny ip 100.0.0.0 0.255.255.255 any
deny ip 101.0.0.0 0.255.255.255 any
deny ip 102.0.0.0 0.255.255.255 any
deny ip 103.0.0.0 0.255.255.255 any
deny ip 104.0.0.0 0.255.255.255 any
deny ip 105.0.0.0 0.255.255.255 any
deny ip 106.0.0.0 0.255.255.255 any
deny ip 107.0.0.0 0.255.255.255 any
deny ip 108.0.0.0 0.255.255.255 any
deny ip 109.0.0.0 0.255.255.255 any
deny ip 110.0.0.0 0.255.255.255 any
deny ip 111.0.0.0 0.255.255.255 any
deny ip 112.0.0.0 0.255.255.255 any
deny ip 113.0.0.0 0.255.255.255 any
deny ip 114.0.0.0 0.255.255.255 any
deny ip 115.0.0.0 0.255.255.255 any
deny ip 116.0.0.0 0.255.255.255 any
deny ip 117.0.0.0 0.255.255.255 any
deny ip 118.0.0.0 0.255.255.255 any
deny ip 119.0.0.0 0.255.255.255 any
deny ip 120.0.0.0 0.255.255.255 any
deny ip 121.0.0.0 0.255.255.255 any
deny ip 122.0.0.0 0.255.255.255 any
deny ip 123.0.0.0 0.255.255.255 any
deny ip 124.0.0.0 0.255.255.255 any
deny ip 125.0.0.0 0.255.255.255 any
deny ip 126.0.0.0 0.255.255.255 any
deny ip 197.0.0.0 0.255.255.255 any
deny ip 201.0.0.0 0.255.255.255 any

deny ip 10.0.0.0 0.255.255.255 any
deny ip 172.16.0.0 0.15.255.255 any
deny ip 192.168.0.0 0.0.255.255 any

deny ip 224.0.0.0 15.255.255.255 any
deny ip 240.0.0.0 15.255.255.255 any
deny ip 0.0.0.0 0.255.255.255 any
deny ip 169.254.0.0 0.0.255.255 any
deny ip 192.0.2.0 0.0.0.255 any
deny ip 127.0.0.0 0.255.255.255 any
permit ip any any
remark This acl might not be up to date.
    Visit www.iana.org/assignments/ipv4-address-space
    for update list
exit
interface Ethernet0
 ip access-group autosec_complete_bogon in
exit
```

continues

Example 4-22 *How to Use AutoSecure (Continued)*

```
ip access-list extended 100
 permit udp any any eq bootpc
interface Ethernet0
 ip verify unicast source reachable-via rx 100
 exit
ip inspect audit-trail
ip inspect dns-timeout 7
ip inspect tcp idle-time 14400
ip inspect udp idle-time 1800
ip inspect name autosec_inspect cuseeme timeout 3600
ip inspect name autosec_inspect ftp timeout 3600
ip inspect name autosec_inspect http timeout 3600
ip inspect name autosec_inspect rcmd timeout 3600
ip inspect name autosec_inspect realaudio timeout 3600
ip inspect name autosec_inspect smtp timeout 3600
ip inspect name autosec_inspect tftp timeout 30
ip inspect name autosec_inspect udp timeout 15
ip inspect name autosec_inspect tcp timeout 3600
ip access-list extended autosec_firewall_acl
 permit udp any any eq bootpc
 deny ip any any
interface Ethernet0
 ip inspect autosec_inspect out
!
end

Apply this configuration to running-config? [yes]: yes        (17)
Applying the config generated to running-config
The name for the keys will be: Bullmastiff.quizware.com
% The key modulus size is 1024 bits
% Generating 1024 bit RSA keys ...[OK]
Bullmastiff#
```

The following list explains the output from the script in Example 4-22. The numbers on the right side of Example 4-22 correspond to the numbers in the following list:

1 At the beginning of the script, you are given the instructions and then asked to continue; the default is **no**.

2 If the router is connected to the Internet, answer the question **yes**; you then are shown a list of interfaces and are asked which interface is connected to the Internet. In this example, I entered **Ethernet0**. If this is an internal router, just answer **no** to the question.

3 After answering the public interface question, the AutoSecure script displays which global management services it is disabling.

4 A sample login banner is displayed, and you are given the opportunity to configure your own. This is similar to using the **banner motd** command, in which you need a

beginning and ending delimiter character. In this example, I used **+** as the delimiting character.

5   You must enter an encrypted privileged EXEC password (**enable secret**) if one is not configured or if it matches the clear-text privileged EXEC password (**enable password**). You also must enter a clear-text privileged EXEC password.

6   Next, you are asked to configure one entry in your router's local authentication database, which is used for both console and remote access. In this example, I created an account called richard.

7   If you want to use SSH, answer **yes** to this question. If you answer **yes**, you must enter a hostname and a domain name so that the Cisco IOS can generate an RSA for the SSH encryption keys.

8   Now that the global management services are completed, you are taken into the interface-specific management services. Here you can see which services automatically are disabled. You do not have to answer any questions here.

9   When the router completes the management services, it moves on to the forwarding services. If the router supports CEF, this is enabled.

10 The first filter set up is to block source addresses defined by the IANA. Note that the addresses that the Cisco IOS uses in AutoSecure might not be the most current; therefore, you periodically should check with IANA's web site to verify the Cisco IOS configuration.

11 The second filter includes private IP source addresses defined in RFC 1918.

12 The third filter combines the first two filters and adds source multicast addresses, Class E addresses, and 169.254.0.0/24, 0.0.0.0/8, 192.0.2.0/24, and 127.0.0.0/8.

13 Next, you are asked if you want to use one of the three filters in steps 10, 11, or 12 to be applied inbound on the Internet (public) interface.

14 If you answer **yes** to step 13, you are asked which filter you want to apply to the interface. If the interface is not connected directly to the Internet and you are using public addresses, choose 1. However, you will want to go back into the configuration later and add the addresses from Step 12. If you are connected to the Internet, choose option 3.

15 After unicast reverse path forwarding is enabled, you are asked if you want to configure CBAC on your router. This happens only if you have installed the Cisco IOS Firewall feature set on your router. This sets up a stateful firewall for allowing returning traffic for outbound connections.

16 You now have answered all of the questions for the AutoSecure configuration process. The script displays the actual Cisco IOS commands that it will execute. Examine these closely to make sure that this is the configuration that you want.

17   In the last step you are asked if you want to implement this configuration. Answer **yes** to do so. When you answer **yes**, if you chose to enable SSH, the Cisco IOS generates RSA encryption keys.

This completes the AutoSecure configuration script. As you can see, this is a lot easier than manually configuring all of these commands individually.

NOTE   I have not discussed many features here that AutoSecure configures for you, including CBAC, CEF, ACLs, and others. These are covered in later chapters in much more depth.

Verifying AutoSecure's Configuration

When you have implemented AutoSecure, you can view the commands that AutoSecure generated with the following command:

```
Router# show auto secure config
```

This is the same display shown in Step 16 of the previous demonstration. Note that to execute the **show auto secure config** command, you must be in privileged EXEC mode.

Using Additional Commands

Two additional commands are a part of AutoSecure:

```
Router(config)# security passwords min-length length
Router(config)# security authentication failure rate #_of_failures log
```

The **security passwords min-length** command specifies the minimum length that passwords must be; this allows you to ensure that passwords are not short, making them more secure and preventing common passwords such as *cisco* and *admin*. The default is a minimum length of six characters. If you do not configure a password of the minimum required length, you will see a message like the one in Example 4-23.

Example 4-23 *AutoSecure Can Force Passwords to Be a Minimum Length*

```
Bullmastiff(config)# username natalie secret cisco
% Password too short - must be at least 6 characters.
      Password configuration failed
```

The **security authentication failure rate** command specifies the maximum number of failed authentication attempts before the router stops any subsequent authentication requests; the router pauses for 15 seconds and then processes new authentication requests. The default threshold for this command is 10 attempts. This is a very useful command in preventing brute force password-guessing attacks.

Summary

This chapter showed you how to disable both global and interface services that can cause security problems for your network, including reconnaissance, DoS, and access attacks. The first part of the chapter discussed how to do this manually; the second part discussed how to do this dynamically with the AutoSecure configuration script. AutoSecure disables insecure services and also secures traffic as it passes through your router. It does this by enabling services such as CBAC, extended ACLs, CEF, and others.

Next up is Chapter 5, which shows you how to centralize your AAA functions on your router by using an external security server.

Authentication, Authorization, and Accounting

Chapter 3, "Accessing a Router," discussed some basic methods of securing access to your router, including using the **username** command to assign accounts to multiple administrators accessing your router. However, the authentication methods discussed in Chapter 3 do not scale well. If you have 100 routers, you probably do not want the hassle of maintaining all of these accounts on each of these routers.

Authentication, authorization, and accounting (AAA) enables you to centralize this process. Many companies centralize AAA functions by purchasing a security server that contains all of the security polices that define the list of users and what they are allowed to do. When authenticating or authorizing requests, routers forward these requests to the AAA server, which validates the requests. The AAA server then responds with its action, and the router either permits or denies the access or action.

This chapter focuses on using AAA to secure access to your router. It discusses how to use an AAA server to authenticate administrators when they access a router, authorize the commands they can execute, and keep an accounting record of their actions. The last part of this chapter discusses secure copy (SCP), which provides an encrypted and secure method of transferring files to and from a router (versus using TFTP, discussed in Chapter 3, which provides no security). SCP relies on AAA to assist in providing a secure connection.

NOTE Many components actually make up AAA (enough to fill a book by itself). However, this chapter focuses only on the AAA components necessary to authenticate users accessing a router, restrict their actions on a router, and log information related to these processes.

AAA Overview

AAA provides a cohesive framework to control who can access a router, what services they can use on a router, and what they can do on a router. The following sections cover the functions of AAA, as well as how to enable it.

AAA Functions

AAA has three main components:

- Authentication
- Authorization
- Accounting

The authentication component of AAA is responsible for providing a method to identify (authenticate) users. This can include login access, as well as other types of access, such as PPP network access. With AAA authentication, you define one or more authentication methods that the router should use when authenticating a user. For example, you could specify two authentication methods: use an external security server, and, if this is not available, use the local **username** database on the router. As you will see later in the chapter, you can use many methods to perform authentication on your router.

When authentication for a user successfully has completed, AAA's authorization is used to restrict what actions a user can perform or what services a user can access. For example, you might want a network administrator to have privileged EXEC access, but want him to use only the **debug** command. With AAA authorization, you can enforce this restriction.

AAA's accounting component is responsible for keeping a record of events of authentication and authorization actions. This can be as simple as keeping track of who logs into a router and any status changes on the router (such as an interface going down or the router being reloaded), or something as complex as keeping track of each command that a user executes on a router. The accounting of AAA keeps a log of these events. One restriction of the accounting component is that it requires an external AAA security server to store the actual accounting records.

NOTE   AAA is the recommended Cisco solution for implementing access control. Note that other solutions exist, such as those that I discussed in Chapter 3, but AAA is the preferred one.

Enabling AAA

You need to configure many things to implement AAA. This book focuses on only the router configuration (configuring an AAA security server is beyond the scope of this book). To configure AAA, you need to perform the following steps:

Step 1   Enable AAA.

Step 2   Configure the parameters for an external AAA server, if used.

Step 3   Define the method or methods you will use to perform authentication.

Step 4   Optionally, configure authorization to restrict what the user can do on the router.

Step 5   Optionally, configure accounting to keep track of what and when events
occur on the router.

By default, AAA is disabled on your Cisco router. To enable it, use the following command:

```
Router(config)# aaa new-model
```

As you can see, enabling AAA is a very simple process; however, this is only the first step
in configuring AAA on your router.

Security Protocols

If you want to centralize your AAA implementation, you use one or more AAA security
servers. Many products are available on the market, including the Cisco Secure Access
Control Server (ACS). Centralizing AAA provides these benefits:

- Scalability
- Redundancy through multiple AAA servers
- Flexibility

If you decide to use an AAA server to centralize your AAA security policies, you need to
use a security protocol between your router and the AAA server. This protocol is used
to exchange AAA messages. In most situations, three security protocols are used:

- Terminal Access Controller Access Control System Plus (TACACS+)
- Remote Authentication Dial-In User Service (RADIUS)
- Kerberos

Of these three, TACACS+ and RADIUS are the more common. The following sections
discuss and compare TACACS+ and RADIUS; Kerberos is not discussed in this book.

Scalability Example

I once dealt with a client that had 1,300 routers in its network. When I walked through
the company's door, authentication/authorization was not centralized; it was localized on
each router. The problem with this situation was that the company hired many contractors,
who came and went on a weekly basis. Because authentication was localized, contractors were
given only the user EXEC password, greatly limiting their usefulness as systems administrators
and putting a very large workload on the full-time employees. We designed a centralized
solution using Cisco's Cisco Secure ACS security server product.

TACACS+

TACACS+ is a third-generation security protocol, with roots in XTACACS and, before
that, TACACS. TACACS+ is a Cisco-proprietary protocol that facilities the use of AAA.
Basically, it defines how a router and an external AAA server communicate. TACACS+

supports all three components of AAA. It enables you to modularize the AAA components for security purposes: One or more AAA servers can be used to handle these components. For example, you could have one AAA server handle authentication and another handle authorization for a router using TACACS+.

TACACS+ provides an additional layer of security by authenticating access to the security server, as well as encrypting messages between the router and the server, protecting your AAA transactions from prying eyes.

To use TACACS+, you need a router that supports it (Cisco IOS 10.3 and later) and an AAA server with the TACACS+ daemon software. Even though TACACS+ is Cisco proprietary, Cisco has pushed its acceptance in the network marketplace by placing it in an RFC draft state with IETF. This allows other vendors to implement TACACS+ in their AAA security server solution. Cisco provides two commercial products that support TACACS+ (Cisco Secure ACS for Windows and UNIX), as well as a freeware version of TACACS+ that runs on Linux.

NOTE   Note that Cisco Secure ACS for UNIX is scheduled to be end-of-life shortly and no longer will be available. If you want to deploy Cisco Secure ACS, I recommend that you purchase the Windows version.

If you will be using TACACS+ on your router, you need to perform the following AAA tasks:

Step 1   Enable AAA with the **aaa new-model** command (required).

Step 2   Specify the location and authentication/encryption key of the TACACS+ server or servers with the **tacacs-server host** and **tacacs-server key** commands, respectively (required).

Step 3   For authentication, specify the use of the external security server using TACACS+ with the **aaa authentication** command (required).

Step 4   For authorization, specify the use of the external security server using TACACS+ with the **aaa authorization** command (optional).

Step 5   For accounting, specify the use of the external security server using TACACS+ with the **aaa accounting** command (optional).

When you have enabled AAA with the **aaa new-model** command, you are ready to set up TACACS+ so that you can communicate, through TACACS+, with your external security server. You can use two commands to set up this communication link:

```
Router(config)# tacacs-server host IP_address [single-connection]
  [port port_#] [timeout seconds] [key encryption_key]
Router(config)# tacacs-server key encryption_key
```

Of these two commands, only the first is required. The **tacacs-server host** command specifies the location of the server. You can specify either an IP address or a host name (that DNS resolves to an IP address or statically resolves with the router's **ip host** commands) for the location of the server. The **single-connection** parameter causes the router to set up a dedicated TCP connection that TACACS+ will use between the router and AAA server. This option should be used to limit the number of TCP connections that the router opens to the AAA server. As long as traffic is being passed between the router and the AAA server, the single connection remains up; however, it is brought down when the connection is idle and must be re-established when new traffic needs to be sent. Note that this option does not provide any real performance advantage, but it slightly decreases the amount of time that it takes to handle multiple successive AAA requests to the server.

The default port number that an AAA server uses for TACACS+ is TCP 49. If you change this on the security server, you also need to reflect that change with the **port** parameter. Optionally, you can change the timeout for the TACACS+ server communication with the **timeout** parameter. If this value is reached and you have other TACACS+ servers configured, your router will try using one of the other servers.

TIP   If you specify more than one AAA server for redundancy, the first server configured is used, by default. If this fails, the second server that was configured is used, and so on. Therefore, the order in which you enter the **tacacs-server host** commands is important.

Also, if you have an inbound ACL restricting traffic on the interface on which the TACACS+ server is located, you need to permit TCP port 49 in the ACL.

If you have more than one TACACS+ server and each server uses a different encryption key, you need to use the **tacacs-server host** command, along with the encryption key in the **key** parameter. However, if all your TACACS+ servers use the same encryption key, you can omit this from all your **tacacs-server host** commands and specify it once with the **tacacs-server key** command. If you have both specified, the key configured in the **tacacs-server host** command takes precedence for the specified host over the key configured in the **tacacs-server key** command.

NOTE   The encryption key that you specify on the router must match the one found on the AAA server; otherwise, the two devices will not be capable of decrypting each other's messages.

RADIUS

Like TACACS+, RADIUS is a security protocol used to communicate AAA information between a device and an external AAA security server. Many AAA products support RADIUS: Unlike TACACS+, RADIUS is an open standard, defined primarily in

RFCs 2865–2869. The Cisco IOS supports RADIUS as of Cisco IOS 11.1, and Cisco continually enhances the Cisco IOS to add additional RADIUS features and functions.

Unlike TACACS+, RADIUS uses UDP to share information between a device and the security server in a client/server manner. One downside of using UDP is that it requires extra steps to ensure that information that was sent was received by the destination. Cisco networking devices function as a client component, whereas a security server, such as Cisco Secure ACS, functions as a server component. The client is responsible for passing all authentication information to the RADIUS server, and the RADIUS server is responsible for authenticating the user and returning all necessary information to the originating device. RADIUS uses a shared key to protect password information sent between two devices. Basically, the shared key is used to encrypt and decrypt the passwords (such as a user's password for his account); password information never is sent across the network in clear text. This is different from TACACS+, which encrypts the entire AAA message, including the password information.

RADIUS typically is used in the following situations:

- You have networking devices from multiple vendors and need a single security protocol to communicate with them.

- You need to implement resource accounting, such as keeping track of how long a user was logged in to a networking device or dialed up to the network.

- Some smart card authentication systems support only RADIUS.

- You want to use preauthentication before allowing a user initial access to a device (I discuss this process in Chapter 14, "Authentication Proxy").

RADIUS has its limitations, such as the use of UDP, the encryption of only password information, and additional limitations:

- It does not support AppleTalk's Remote Access Protocol (ARAP), the NetBIOS Frame Control Protocol (NBFCP), NetWare's Asynchronous Services Interface (NASI), and X.25 PAD connections (these are all dialup services).

- RADIUS sometimes cannot be modularized. In other words, your networking device sometimes must use RADIUS for all AAA functions, not just some specific ones.

- It supports only one-way authentication: It does not support two-way authentication, as with PPP's CHAP authentication between two Cisco routers.

- Unlike TACACS+, RADIUS combines authentication/authorization functions into "authentication," giving you less flexibility in modularizing your AAA processes.

The steps involved in setting up and using TACACS+ are basically the same as those configured to use RADIUS. The main difference is the specification of RADIUS communication instead of TACACS+ when communicating to an AAA security server. Here are the basic commands for specifying your AAA servers using RADIUS:

```
Router(config)# radius-server host IP_address
  [auth-port port_#] [acct-port port_#] [timeout seconds] [retransmit retries]
  [key key_value] [alias {hostname | IP_address}]
```

```
Router(config)# radius-server timeout seconds
Router(config)# radius-server retransmit retries
Router(config)# radius-server key key_value
```

As you can see from these commands, the configuration is not that much more complex than when setting up TACACS+. The **radius-server host** command specifies the location to the AAA server running RADIUS, including access parameters. You can specify either the IP address of the AAA server or its host name. The **auth-port** parameter specifies the UDP port that the server is using to listen for RADIUS authentication messages. This defaults to UDP 1645. RADIUS accounting messages use UDP 1646, but you can change this with the optional **acct-port** parameter.

TIP	Note that you can have more than two RADIUS services running on the same device. If this is the case, at least one of the services must be using different port numbers for authentication and authorization. This sometimes is done for redundancy or separation of AAA policies on the AAA server.
	Also, if you have an inbound ACL restricting traffic on the interface where the RADIUS+ server is located, you need to permit UDP ports 1645 (authentication and authorization) and 1646 (accounting) in the ACL.

NOTE	In RFC 2026, RADIUS also uses UDP ports 1812 and 1813. Therefore, most newer RADIUS server implementations (and some client ones) listen on four UDP ports: 1645, 1646, 1812, and 1813. You need to be aware of this on intermediate routers that have ACL filters, as well as perimeter routers that have internal inbound filters. Be sure to allow the appropriate ports so that RADIUS traffic can travel between the clients and servers.

The default timeout for a RADIUS server connection is 5 seconds; this can be overridden with the **timeout** parameter (a specific AAA server) or globally with the **radius-server timeout** command. Typically, this does not need to be changed unless the traffic between the router and the AAA server must travel many hops and has packet manipulations performed on it, such as encryption or address translation.

By default, the router tries to contact the AAA server using RADIUS three times before giving up and trying another method. This can be changed with the **retransmit** parameter for a specific AAA server or globally with the **radius-server retransmit** command.

As with TACACS+, you can specify the encryption key (for passwords only) either globally or per server. If you are specifying the key globally, use the **radius-server key** command. To override the global setting for a specific server, use the optional **key** parameter in the **radius-server host** command.

You also can specify an alias or aliases for a RADIUS server—other names or IP addresses configured on it by using the **alias** parameter.

NOTE   You actually can use many more commands to set up RADIUS. Some of these are used when connecting to a server running a proprietary implementation of RADIUS; most are used for dialup functions. Because this book covers only basic AAA functions, such as login access control and command restriction, I do not go into the details of these additional commands.

Server Groupings

One of the limitations of using the previously mentioned TACACS+ and RADIUS commands is that the first server that you enter becomes the primary, and the rest are backups. In some situations, you want to divide your AAA servers into groups, with one group handling authentication and authorization functions, and another handling accounting. This can be accomplished through one of two methods:

- Set up your primary AAA server to redirect AAA requests to the appropriate AAA server.
- On your router, use server groupings to direct AAA messages to the correct group of servers.

This section focuses on the latter method.

Basically, a server grouping is a list of the AAA servers' host names or IP addresses. You need to configure two things for grouping servers together:

- Your **tacacs-server host** and **radius-server host** commands
- Your server-grouping commands

To create a grouping of servers (after configuring your **tacacs-server host** and **radius-server host** commands), use the following configuration syntax:

```
Router(config)# aaa group server radius | tacacs+ group_name
Router(config-sg)# server IP_address | hostname
  [auth-port port_#] [acct-port port_#]
```

The **aaa group server** command specifies the group of servers. Note that you cannot mix the security protocols within a group: The group contains either TACACS+ or RADIUS servers. Each server grouping must be assigned a unique name, which then is referenced in your AAA authentication, authorization, and accounting configuration. Executing the **aaa group server** command takes you into a subconfiguration mode, in which you use the **server** command to list the servers in the group. For your RADIUS configuration, if one AAA server is running multiple instances of RADIUS, with different port numbers, you need to differentiate the services by specifying the **auth-port** and **acct-port** parameters with the appropriate port numbers.

Troubleshooting TACACS+ and RADIUS

You can use a handful of commands to troubleshoot TACACS+ and RADIUS AAA problems. The following two subsections cover these commands.

Troubleshooting TACACS+

When troubleshooting TACACS+ connectivity problems, you use three commands:

- **show tacacs**
- **debug tacacs**
- **debug tacacs events**

The **show tacacs** command displays a summary status of the connections that it has to configured TACACS+ servers, as shown in Example 5-1.

Example 5-1 *Using the **show tacacs** Command*

```
Router# show tacacs
Tacacs+ Server          : 10.0.0.10/49
            Socket opens:       3
           Socket closes:       3
           Socket aborts:       0
           Socket errors:       0
         Socket Timeouts:       0
  Failed Connect Attempts:      0
       Total Packets Sent:     42
       Total Packets Recv:     41
        Expected Replies:       0
  No current connection
```

For more detailed troubleshooting, use the **debug tacacs** and **debug tacacs events** commands. The **debug tacacs** command displays information related to TACACS+ operations. The main difference between this command and the **debug tacacs events** command is that the latter displays more detailed information, including information about the TACACS+ processes running on the router.

CAUTION   The **debug tacacs events** command is very CPU intensive. Take care to use it when the CPU utilization is low and during times of inactivity.

Example 5-2 demonstrates the **debug tacacs** command.

Example 5-2 *Using the **debug tacacs** Command*

```
Router# debug tacacs
15:32:22: TAC+: Opening TCP/IP connection to 10.0.0.10 using       (1)
          source 10.0.0.1
15:32:22: TAC+: Sending TCP/IP packet number 417383154-1 to        (2)
          10.0.0.10 (AUTHEN/START)
```

continues

Example 5-2   *Using the* **debug tacacs** *Command (Continued)*

```
15:32:22: TAC+: Receiving TCP/IP packet number 417383154-2
          from 10.0.0.10
15:32:22: TAC+ (417383154): received authen response          (3)
          status = GETUSER
15:32:24: TAC+: send AUTHEN/CONT packet
15:32:24: TAC+: Sending TCP/IP packet number 417383154-3
          to 10.0.0.10 (AUTHEN/CONT)
15:32:24: TAC+: Receiving TCP/IP packet number 417383154-4
          from 10.0.0.10
15:32:24: TAC+ (417383154): received authen response          (4)
          status = GETPASS
15:32:25: TAC+: send AUTHEN/CONT packet
15:32:25: TAC+: Sending TCP/IP packet number 417383154-5
          to 10.0.0.10 (AUTHEN/CONT)
15:32:25: TAC+: Receiving TCP/IP packet number 417383154-6
          from 10.0.0.10
15:32:25: TAC+ (417383154): received authen response          (5)
          status = FAIL
15:32:27: TAC+: Closing TCP/IP connection to 10.0.0.10        (6)
```

Here is an explanation of the output in Example 5-2. The numbers on the right side of Example 5-2 correspond to the numbers in the following list:

1   In this statement, the router opens a TACACS+ connection to the AAA server.

2   In the next two statements, the router sends and receives an authentication START message, telling the AAA server that more authentication information will be sent.

3   The AAA server responds and requests a username, which the router sends to the AAA server.

4   Next, the AAA server requests the user's password, which the router sends to the AAA server.

5   In this instance, the user entered the wrong username/password combination, so the AAA server responds with a FAIL message.

6   Notice here that the router closes the TACACS+ connection, indicating that no more information needs to be transmitted.

Troubleshooting RADIUS

You can use two commands to troubleshoot RADIUS problems: **show radius statistics** and **debug radius**. The first command displays basic statistics about the packets sent and received for accounting and authentication, as displayed in Example 5-3.

Example 5-3 *Using the* **show radius statistics** *Command*

```
Router# show radius statistics
                                Auth.      Acct.      Both
       Maximum inQ length:       NA         NA         1
     Maximum waitQ length:       NA         NA         1
     Maximum doneQ length:       NA         NA         1
      Total responses seen:       5          0         5
     Packets with responses:      5          0         5
  Packets without responses:      0          0         0
 Average response delay(ms):    1880         0        1880
 Maximum response delay(ms):    6540         0        6540
   Number of Radius timeouts:     0          0         0
        Duplicate ID detects:     0          0         0
```

You can see that there are three columns of statistics. Remember that RADIUS combines authentication and authorization functions. In this example, you can see the total number of responses, as well as round-trip delays and timeouts.

For more detailed troubleshooting, use the **debug radius** [**brief**] command. The **brief** parameter creates similar output as the **debug tacacs** command; omitting this parameter creates output similar to that of the **debug tacacs events** command.

Server Protocol Example Configuration

Now you will take a look at how to set up the security protocols for AAA. In the example network in Figure 5-1, the TACACS+ servers handle authentication and authorization functions, and the RADIUS servers handle all accounting functions.

Figure 5-1 *AAA Server Configuration Example*

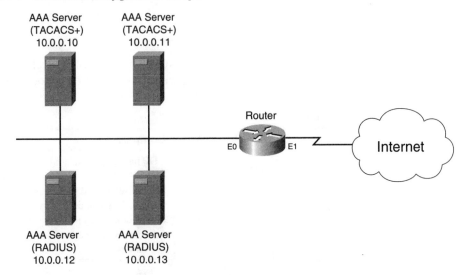

This example focuses only on enabling AAA, defining the AAA servers and setting up the server groupings. The later sections "Authentication," "Authorization," and "Accounting" discuss how to associate the server groups with the different AAA processes.

Example 5-4 shows the configuration for Figure 5-1.

Example 5-4 *Setting up AAA Security Server Connectivity*

```
Router(config)# aaa new-model
Router(config)# tacacs-server host 10.0.0.10 single-connection
  key secret10
Router(config)# tacacs-server host 10.0.0.11 single-connection
  key secret11
Router(config)# radius-server host 10.0.0.12 key secret12
Router(config)# radius-server host 10.0.0.13 key secret13
Router(config)# aaa group server tacacs aaatacgroup
Router(config-sg)# server 10.0.0.10
Router(config-sg)# server 10.0.0.11
Router(config-sg)# exit
Router(config)# aaa group server radius aaaradgroup
Router(config-sg)# server 10.0.0.12
Router(config-sg)# server 10.0.0.13
```

In this example, the **aaa new-model** command, listed first, enables AAA. The **tacacs-server host** and **radius-server host** commands specify the AAA server's location and the encryption key used for communications. With the TACACS+ server configuration, the single TCP connection option is enabled. At the bottom of the configuration, two server groupings are created. In the TACACS+ server group aaatacgroup, 10.0.0.10 is the primary server and 10.0.0.11 is the backup. In the RADIUS server group aaaradgroup, 10.0.0.12 is the primary server and 10.0.0.13 is the backup. As you can see from this example, enabling AAA and setting up your security server connections are straightforward processes.

Comparison of TACACS+ and RADIUS

Now that you have a basic understanding of TACACS+ and RADIUS, as well as their configuration, take a closer look at them by comparing the two security protocols shown in Table 5-1.

Table 5-1 *TACACS+ Versus RADIUS*

Item	TACACS+	RADIUS	Comparison
Connection	TCP	UDP	UDP has less overhead; however, with TCP, TACACS+ more quickly can detect a failed server and switch over to a backup. TCP can do this by having the router look for an RST (closed connection) message or by using TCP keepalives.

Table 5-1   *TACACS+ Versus RADIUS (Continued)*

Item	TACACS+	RADIUS	Comparison
Encryption	Payload	Passwords	TACACS+ is more secure because it encrypts the entire payload, which includes all user and AAA message information; RADIUS encrypts only passwords, so everything else, including usernames and other account information, is sent in clear text.
Authentication and authorization	Separate	Combined	RADIUS combines authentication and authorization functions, which means that you must use the same server or group for these functions. TACACS+ separates them, giving you more control over the server that handles these functions.
WAN protocols	PPP, ARAP, NetBIOS, NASI, and X.25 PAD	PPP and SLIP	TACACS+ is better suited for remote-access situations that involve multiple dialup protocols, whereas RADIUS supports only PPP and SLIP.
Router command authorization	Yes	No	TACACS+ enables you to control what commands an authenticated user can execute on a router; RADIUS does not.
Accounting	Basic	Advanced	The one big advantage that RADIUS has over TACACS+ is its robust accounting, which is why many ISPs use it to monitor PPP connections.

Authentication

This section covers the setup of authentication using one of the supported methods. A router can authenticate two basic modes of access:

- Character mode
- Packet mode

With character mode access, a user gains EXEC access to the router. This can be accomplished using one of the four lines on the router: console, auxiliary, TTY, or VTY. In packet-mode access, the user establishes a data-link layer connection by using a remote-access protocol, such as PPP, SLIP, ARAP, NASI, NetBIOS, or X.25 PAD. Because this book focuses on using a router as a firewall solution, not as a remote-access solution, this section focuses only on securing character-mode access.

Methods of Authentication

One of the first things you need to determine is how you will authenticate the different types of character-mode access. This is accomplished by using a method list, which is a sequential list of one or more authentication methods. An authentication method defines how the character mode access will be authenticated. The router processes the entries in the list in the order that you enter them. When the router successfully can use a method in the list, the other remaining methods are ignored.

For example, assume that you define two methods in your list in the following order:

1 TACACS+ server group aaatacgroup

2 Local authentication database built with **username** commands

With this list, the router first attempts to use the AAA servers in the TACACS+ aaatacgroup group. If the router cannot contact any of these servers, it then uses the **username** commands configured locally. If no **username** commands exist on the router, the authentication fails. As you can see from this example, you can specify multiple types of authentication in your method list, providing redundancy.

With method lists, the router attempts to use the first entry in the list. If this is not successful, it proceeds to the second entry. It is important to point out here that "unsuccessful" is not a failed authentication. In other words, if you configured AAA servers for authentication, but the servers were not reachable (do not respond back), this is unsuccessful. However, if your router can contact the servers and send the authentication information, but the AAA server denies the authentication access request, this is considered a successful authentication request (even though the user is denied access). Likewise, if you include in your method list that the router should use a local means of verifying authentication, but these commands (such as **username** commands, or the **enable secret** or line **password** commands) do not exist on the router, then when the router tries to use these methods, it considers them unsuccessful and proceeds to the next method in the list.

NOTE   As with ACLs, if the router attempts to use all of the methods in the list but is unsuccessful, the router automatically denies the authentication request.

Now take a look at Figure 5-2, another example that clarifies the use of method lists.

In this example, 10.1.1.1 is trying to gain EXEC access to the router. Here is the method list defined to perform authentication for EXEC access:

1 TACACS+ server group tacgroup.

2 Local authentication database built with the **username richard secret quizware** command.

In the first method, there are two AAA servers in the TACACS+ group tacgroup: 10.0.0.10 and 10.0.0.11. The second method defines one local **username** command for an account called richard.

When 10.1.1.1 tries to gain EXEC access, based on the methods configured on the router, the Cisco IOS first tries to contact AAA server 1 (10.0.0.10) to perform authentication. If this server is reachable, neither the other AAA server, nor the other method in this list, is used. Instead, 10.1.1.1 must put in a correct username/password combination that is found on the AAA server. If the user does not, the user fails authentication and is denied access to the router.

Figure 5-2   *Authentication Method List Example*

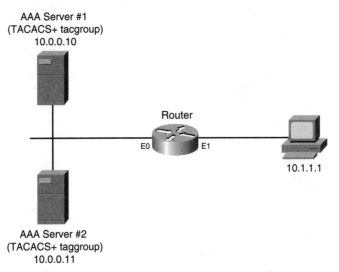

AAA Server #1
(TACACS+ tacgroup)
10.0.0.10

Router

E0   E1

10.1.1.1

AAA Server #2
(TACACS+ taggroup)
10.0.0.11

Assume that AAA server 1 has failed, though. In this situation, when 10.1.1.1 tries to access EXEC mode on the router, the Cisco IOS still uses the tacgroup method first. It attempts to contact the first AAA server; because this server is not reachable, it then attempts to contact the second server. If the second server is also not reachable, only then is the second method in the list used. In this example, because one **username** command is defined, the 10.1.1.1 user must put in this correct username/password combination to gain access to the router's EXEC mode. If I had forgotten to configure any **username** commands, and the Cisco IOS was attempting to use the second method, the Cisco IOS would realize that because no **username** commands were configured, it should go to the third method in the list. Because there is no third method defined in this example, the user automatically is denied access.

NOTE   Basically three types of statuses are shown in the previous example:

- **Success**—The method was available, and the user was authenticated.

- **Fail**—The method was available, but the user was not able to authenticate.

- **Error**—One of two things occurred:

    — The first AAA server in the group of the specified method was not reachable, so the next server in the group was used.

    — The method specified either does not exist, or, with an AAA server group, all of the servers are not reachable.

Authentication Configuration

Now that you have a basic understanding of method lists, take a look at the command used to configure AAA authentication: **aaa authentication**. The following sections expand on the use of this command.

User EXEC Authentication

Two types of authentication are discussed in this chapter for AAA: gaining access to a user and privileged EXEC shell, commonly referred to as *login authentication* and *enable authentication*, respectively. This section and the next section cover these two types of authentication.

To secure user EXEC shell access, you need to use at least the first two commands listed:

```
Router(config)# aaa new-model
Router(config)# aaa authentication login {default | list_name}
  method1 [method2...]
Router(config)# line [aux | console | tty | vty] start_line_# [end_line_#]
Router(config-line)# login authentication {default | list_name}
Router(config-line)# timeout login response seconds
```

As you already know, the **aaa new-model** command enables AAA. You must execute this command before you can configure any other AAA commands on the router. The **aaa authentication login** command is used to secure EXEC access to the router.

Following the **login** parameter is the name of the authentication reference. The Cisco IOS uses this parameter so that the appropriate **aaa authentication login** command is used for the type of access that a person is using to gain access to a line (an EXEC shell). The **default** parameter specifies that this default authentication method command should be used if a line does not specify which **aaa authentication login** command to use. You can create specific authentication methods by entering **aaa authentication login**, followed by a unique name to the authentication method, as in *telnet-access*. You then go into the appropriate line or lines, as shown in the bottom two commands in the previous syntax. Next, you specify the list name AAA authentication method that should be used with the **login authentication** command, followed by the list name found in the **aaa authentication login** command, as in *telnet-access*. Note that, on all lines, the default list is **default**, so the Cisco IOS uses the **aaa authentication login default** command's method list to verify authentication.

The last, and most important, part of the **aaa authentication login** command is the list of methods. Remember from the previous section that the method list defines how authentication should be done. You can list up to four methods. A list of valid methods is found in Table 5-2. These methods are processed in the order that you specify. Remember that if a method produces an error result, the next method in the list is used.

Table 5-2 *AAA Authentication Methods for User EXEC Access*

Method Keyword	Description
enable	The password in the **enable secret** or **enable password** commands is used to perform the authentication.
line	The line **password** command, on the line that the user is trying to access, is used to perform authentication.
local	The **username** commands are used to perform authentication.
local-case	The **username** commands are used to perform authentication. However, the username that the user enters is treated as case sensitive.
none	No authentication is performed.
group radius	All configured RADIUS servers can be used to perform authentication.
group tacacs+	All configured TACACS+ servers can be used to perform authentication.
group *group_name*	Only servers in the specified **aaa group server** command are used to perform authentication.

CAUTION   I highly recommend that you not use the **none** method for authentication, even if you list multiple methods and this is the last one, creating a back door into the router. Always perform some type of authentication, even if it is something as simple as using the enable or line passwords. Some hackers try to exploit a DoS attack against the router and AAA servers if you are using AAA servers as a method, hoping that your second method defined on the router is **none**. This would allow the hacker to sneak into your router by preventing the router and AAA servers from communicating with each other.

The **timeout** line command specifies the number of seconds that the Cisco IOS waits for login information before timing out the authentication. The default is 30 seconds, but this can range from 1 to 300 seconds.

Privileged EXEC Authentication

To secure privilege EXEC access, you need to use the following command:

```
Router(config)# aaa authentication enable default
    method1 [method2...]
```

Unlike the **aaa authentication login** command, the **aaa authentication enable** command does not allow you to specify authentication lists—you can use only the keyword **default**. This makes sense because there is only one way to access privileged EXEC mode: Execute the **enable** command from user EXEC mode. With user EXEC mode access, a user can gain access in many ways, such as with the console, auxiliary, VTY, and TTY lines. With the **aaa authentication login** command, you can set up different authentication methods for these. However, this is not necessary for privileged EXEC access because there is only one way to access it.

You can list four AAA methods in your method list for securing privileged EXEC access. These are the same ones shown previously in Table 5-2; however, the **local** and **local-case** methods are not supported with privileged EXEC authentication.

Username and Password Prompts

By default, when the Cisco IOS prompts you for a username or password when you log in, you see the following prompts:

```
Username:
Password:
```

You can override these default prompts with the following two commands:

```
Router(config)# aaa authentication username-prompt prompt_string
Router(config)# aaa authentication password-prompt prompt_string
```

The **aaa authentication username-prompt** command overrides the username prompt and enables you to specify your own prompt for the username. The **aaa authentication password-prompt** command enables you to change the password prompt presented to the user. Remember to add the : to the end of the prompt; it is not included automatically.

TIP   Sometimes I set the username prompt to Password: and leave the password prompt as the same thing. At first, this looks confusing because, even though the first prompt states "password," it actually wants the username. I do this to confuse hackers and users trying to gain unauthorized access. Just tell authorized users that no matter what they see in the prompts, they need to enter the username for the first prompt and the password for the second prompt.

NOTE   TACACS+ and RADIUS servers have the capability to override the username and password prompts. If you have configured the **aaa authentication username-prompt** and **password-prompt** commands, and have also configured these prompts on your AAA servers, the Cisco IOS uses the prompts from the AAA servers.

Login Banners

If you have enabled AAA, you can override the router's default login banner with the following command:

```
Router(config)# aaa authentication banner stop_character
  message stop_character
```

This command works the same as the **banner** command discussed in Chapter 3. The actual message can be up to 2996 characters in length. When you enter the **aaa authentication banner** command, the router displays this banner instead of the banner created with the **banner** command.

Optionally, you can display a message whenever a user enters an invalid username/ password combination by configuring the following command:

```
Router(config)# aaa authentication fail-message stop_character
   message stop_character
```

With this command, whenever the user enters an invalid username/password combination, the Cisco IOS displays the configured message. The actual message can be up to 2996 characters in length.

Login Attempts

By default, the Cisco IOS prompts you for username/password information up to three times so that you can enter the correct information. After three times, the Cisco IOS disconnects you and forces you to attempt to log in again. With AAA, you can change the number of login attempts before the router disconnects you with the following command (this is new in Cisco IOS 12.2T):

```
Router(config)# aaa authentication attempts login #_of_attempts
```

The number of login attempts can range from 1 to 25.

TIP   For a perimeter router, I recommend that you set this value to 1. This makes it more cumbersome for someone to execute an access attack against it, especially a brute-force password attack.

Authentication Troubleshooting

You use one basic command for troubleshooting AAA authentication problems: **debug aaa authentication**. Example 5-5 shows output from the **debug aaa authentication** command.

Example 5-5   *Using the* **debug aaa authentication** *Command*

```
Router# debug aaa authentication
13:21:20: AAA/AUTHEN: create_user user='' ruser='' port='tty6'      (1)
          rem_addr='10.0.0.32' authen_type=1 service=1 priv=1
13:21:20: AAA/AUTHEN/START (0): port='tty6' list=''                 (2)
          action=LOGIN service=LOGIN
13:21:20: AAA/AUTHEN/START (0): using "default" list                (3)
13:21:20: AAA/AUTHEN/START (70215483): Method=TACACS+
13:21:20: TAC+ (70215483): received authen response
          status = GETUSER
13:21:20: AAA/AUTHEN (70215483): status = GETUSER
```

continues

Example 5-5 *Using the* **debug aaa authentication** *Command (Continued)*

```
13:21:23: AAA/AUTHEN/CONT (70215483): continue_login
13:21:23: AAA/AUTHEN (70215483): status = GETUSER
13:21:23: AAA/AUTHEN (70215483): Method=TACACS+
13:21:23: TAC+: send AUTHEN/CONT packet
13:21:23: TAC+ (70215483): received authen response
          status = GETPASS
13:21:23: AAA/AUTHEN (70215483): status = GETPASS
13:21:27: AAA/AUTHEN/CONT (70215483): continue_login
13:21:27: AAA/AUTHEN (70215483): status = GETPASS
13:21:27: AAA/AUTHEN (70215483): Method=TACACS+
13:21:27: TAC+: send AUTHEN/CONT packet
13:21:27: TAC+ (70215483): received authen response
          status = PASS
13:21:27: AAA/AUTHEN (70215483): status = PASS            (4)
```

The following is an explanation of Example 5-5. The numbers on the right side of Example 5-5 correspond to the numbers in the following list:

1 A remote user from 10.0.0.32 attempts to log in to the router.

2 The router checks to see if login authentication services are enabled; they are.

3 The router sees that the default list method is used, and the corresponding method is TACACS+ (the line below this).

4 After authentication takes place, the TACACS+ server responds with a successful authentication message (status = PASS).

Authentication Example

Now that you have a basic understanding of how to configure authentication for AAA, take a look at an authentication example in Example 5-6.

Example 5-6 *AAA Authentication Example*

```
Router(config)# aaa new-model                             (1)
Router(config)# tacacs-server host 10.0.0.10 single-connection  (2)
  key secret10
Router(config)# tacacs-server host 10.0.0.11 single-connection
  key secret11
Router(config)# aaa group server tacacs aaatacgroup        (3)
Router(config-sg)# server 10.0.0.10
Router(config-sg)# server 10.0.0.11
Router(config)# aaa authentication login console           (4)
  group aaatacgroup local
Router(config)# username admin1 secret cisco1
Router(config)# username admin2 secret cisco2
Router(config)# aaa authentication login default           (5)
  group aaatacgroup
Router(config)# aaa authentication enable default          (6)
  group aaatacgroup enable
Router(config)# enable secret OutKeep
```

Example 5-6 *AAA Authentication Example (Continued)*

```
Router(config)# aaa authentication username-prompt "Password: "    (7)
Router(config)# aaa authentication password-prompt "Password: "
Router(config)# aaa authentication attempts login 1                (8)
Router(config)# line console 0
Router(config-line)# login authentication console                  (9)
```

The following is an explanation of Example 5-6. The numbers on the right side of Example 5-6 correspond to the numbers in the following list:

1 This command enables AAA.

2 These two commands specify the two TACACS+ servers used for authentication.

3 These three commands are not really necessary in this example, but I like to set up groupings for future use.

4 This command sets up a user EXEC authentication method called console, and it has two methods in its method list: Use the TACACS+ servers in the aaatacgroup (**group aaatacgroup**) and **username** commands (**local**). This statement is referenced in number 9, which authenticates console access. Note that I used the word *console* as a descriptive term; you can use anything that you want to describe this authentication method.

5 This command is the default authentication method for user EXEC access. It specifies that only the TACACS+ servers are used for authentication. If these servers are not available, the user is not allowed access to the router. This command can be used to authenticate VTY access because there is no reference to the type of authentication list that should be used on the VTY lines.

6 This command authenticates access to privileged EXEC mode. It has two methods for authentication: the TACACS+ server grouping and the **enable** command, listed below this statement.

7 These two statements are used to confuse or trick people performing access attacks: It changes the username prompt to match that of the password prompt.

8 This command restricts the number of access attempts to one for a session. If the user cannot successfully authenticate on the first try, the session is terminated, and the user must re-establish the session to try again.

9 This command references the **aaa authentication login console** command, which specifies how authentication should be done on the console line.

Authorization

Authorization occurs after authentication takes place. After a user successfully has authenticated, you can restrict what services and commands the user has access to. This section discusses how authorization works and how to configure it.

NOTE   Note that authorization is optional. You need to configure authorization only if you want to have more control over what people do on your router after they have authenticated.

Methods of Authorization

As with authentication, AAA's authorization can be used to restrict access to certain things. With authentication, I focus only on two: user and privileged EXEC access. Authorization is used to determine what resources the user has access to on the router. With AAA's authorization, the Cisco IOS can be used to restrict the following services:

- **Authentication proxy**—Authentication proxy is used to open temporary holes in your router/firewall after a user successfully has authenticated. How much access the user is given is defined on the security server. This process is discussed in Chapter 14.

- **Commands**—You can restrict what commands a user can execute on the router. The "Authorization Configuration" section of this chapter focuses on this concept.

- **EXEC**—You can restrict EXEC access to the router. At first, this sounds confusing, but this method is used in dialup situations in which the user was authenticated through PPP's PAP or CHAP. You can use the EXEC method to restrict the user's access to an EXEC prompt.

- **Network**—After a user has authenticated and gained EXEC access to the router, he can establish PPP or SLIP connections on dialup links, if these exist on the router. With authorization, you can restrict the use of these network connections. Because this primarily occurs on a dialup server, and we are using a router as a perimeter router/firewall, I do not cover the configuration of this method.

- **Reverse Telnet**—After authentication, you can restrict a user from performing reverse Telnets. These are typically done on routers set up as terminal servers, with the router emulating console connections to various devices. Again, because this is not typically done on a perimeter router/firewall, I do not cover the configuration of this method.

For a specific authorization command, you can list up to four methods in your method list that define how authorization should occur. For example, your first method could be to use a RADIUS server, and the second method could be to use the local username database. As with authentication, many authorization methods are available to you, as discussed next in the configuration section.

Authorization Configuration

To set up authorization, you first need to perform the following steps:

Step 1   Enable AAA with the **aaa new-model** command.

Step 2 If you are using an AAA security server, set up its connection with the **tacacs-server** and **radius-server** commands.

Step 3 Configure your authentication methods with the **aaa authentication** command(s).

When you have completed these three steps, you are ready to set up AAA authorization.

NOTE Actually, before you set up command authorization, you need to set up your commands and their restrictions. I briefly discussed this in Chapter 3 for using the **privilege** command. However, in most instances, you will be doing this on your AAA server. The configuration of command authorization on an AAA server is beyond the scope of this book.

Executing Commands

If you are concerned about what commands are executed on your perimeter router/firewall, you can use AAA authorization to restrict what commands the user can execute. To set up command authorization, use the following configuration syntax:

```
Router(config)# aaa authorization commands level_#
   {default | list_name} [method1 [method2...]]
Router(config)# line [aux | console | tty | vty] start_line_# [end_line_#]
Router(config-line)# authorization commands level_#
   {default | list_name}
```

With the **aaa authorization** command, you can choose from many authorization methods. However, this chapter focuses on only one: commands that you can execute (**commands**). With the **commands** parameter, you must specify which command level (0–15) you want to set up authorization for. Following this, you specify what scope the authorization command has. With command authorization, you specify **default** or an authorization list name. A list name typically is given if you are setting up other types of authorization, such as a default one, and one for users accessing a specific line on the router. Following the **default** parameter is the list of authorization methods (how authorization should be performed). Table 5-3 lists the authorization parameters for your method list.

Table 5-3 *AAA Authorization Methods*

Method Keyword	Description
local	The **username** commands are used to perform authorization.
none	No authorization is performed. This parameter is typically not used.
group radius	All configured RADIUS servers can be used to perform authorization.
group tacacs+	All configured TACACS+ servers can be used to perform authorization.
group *group_name*	Only servers in the specified **aaa group server** command are used to perform authorization.

If you want to control on a per-line basis what does or does not get authorized, you can use the **authorization** command in line subconfiguration mode. For example, you might want to enforce authorization on commands for all remote users (VTY lines), but disable this function for an administrator accessing the router through the console port.

Executing Configuration Commands

When using the **aaa authorization commands** command, AAA is used to check whether a user can execute any command on a router in user and privileged EXEC mode, as well as configuration mode. This might cause problems in some cases, especially with global configuration mode, in which the same command appears at both global configuration mode and privileged EXEC mode. You can disable authorization for all configuration mode commands with the following command:

```
Router(config)# no aaa authorization config-commands
```

Authorization Troubleshooting

You use one basic command for troubleshooting AAA authorization problems: **debug aaa authorization**. Example 5-7 displays a sample of this command.

Example 5-7   *Using the* **debug aaa authorization** *Command*

```
Router# debug aaa authorization
2:23:21: AAA/AUTHOR (0): user='admin1'                          (1)
2:23:21: AAA/AUTHOR (0): send AV service=shell                  (2)
2:23:21: AAA/AUTHOR (0): send AV cmd*                           (3)
2:23:21: AAA/AUTHOR (342885561): Method=TACACS+                 (4)
2:23:21: AAA/AUTHOR/TAC+ (342885561): user=admin1              (5)
2:23:21: AAA/AUTHOR/TAC+ (342885561): send AV service=shell
2:23:21: AAA/AUTHOR/TAC+ (342885561): send AV cmd*
2:23:21: AAA/AUTHOR (342885561): Post authorization status = FAIL (6)
```

The following is an explanation of Example 5-7. The numbers on the right side of Example 5-7 correspond to the numbers in the following list:

1 The user, admin1, is attempting to do something that requires authorization.

2 In this example, the user is attempting to gain an EXEC shell.

3 The *cmd* parameter specifies a command that the user is trying to execute. If it lists *, this refers to plain EXEC access.

4 The method used to authorize this access is TACACS+.

5 The router sends the necessary information through TACACS+ to the security server.

6 The security server verifies the authorization, determines that the user is not authorized to perform this function, and sends back a FAIL message.

Authorization Example

Now take a look at an example that uses authorization. I build upon Example 5-6 in the "Authentication Example" section. Here, I just list the authorization commands. In this example, I want to set up authorization for all privileged EXEC and configuration mode commands. Example 5-8 shows the configuration.

Example 5-8 *Adding Authorization to the Example AAA Configuration*

```
Router(config)# aaa authorization commands 15 default
  group aaatacgroup
Router(config)# aaa authorization commands 15 conauthor
  group aaatacgroup none
Router(config)# line console 0
Router(config-line)# authorization commands 15 conauthor
```

In this example, the first **aaa authorization** command defines a default method of authorization for all privileged EXEC and configuration mode commands; the AAA server group called aaatacgroup performs the authorization. If all the servers in the group are not reachable, the administrator's command on the router is denied. To allow an administrator to execute commands in an emergency situation, the second **aaa authorization** command specifies that the aaatacgroup server group should be used if the servers are reachable; if they are not reachable, no authorization is to be performed. This second command is assigned an authorization name of conauthor. Notice that there is a restriction with this command: It is activated only on the console interface. Therefore, if the AAA servers are not reachable, you still can manage the perimeter router through its console port.

CAUTION   When using authorization to determine whether a user can or cannot execute commands, you should be aware of this issue: Before the user is allowed to execute a command with AAA authorization and an external security server, the Cisco IOS sends the authorization request to the security server, the security server validates the authorization request, and the security server sends back a response. As an administrator trying to execute a command while this is going on, you will notice a slight delay during this process for each command that you execute.

Also, you will want to make sure that, in a worst-case situation, you can execute any command from the console port. Therefore, if you are using an external AAA server for authorization, make sure that you have a second method, such as **local**, listed (and possibly a third, **none**). If you are using **none** as a method and want extra protection, you might want to enable accounting to keep track of the commands that your administrators execute on your perimeter router.

TIP   In the previous example, I recommend configuring first the console authorization and then the default method, to prevent lockouts.

Accounting

After you have configured authentication or authorization, you are ready to configure accounting. AAA accounting is used to keep track of AAA transactions and events that occur on your router, such as when a user logs in or out of the router, or what commands the user has executed. This can be used as an audit trail to enhance your security as a change-management system (keeping track of the changes that people are making on your router).

NOTE   Note that accounting is optional. You need to configure accounting only if you want to keep a log file of AAA transactions and events on your router.

Methods of Accounting

As with authentication and authorization, you need to specify two things when setting up AAA accounting: what you want to capture accounting information on and the method lists that define where to send it.

Here is a list of the types of things that you can create accounting records for:

- **Commands**—This accounting method provides information about what commands a user executed, including user and privileged EXEC and configuration mode commands.

- **Connection**—This accounting method provides information about connections made from the router, such as an administrator Telnetting from the router to another device. Connections include Telnet, LAT, TN32760, PAD, and rlogin. Accounting information captured includes the user's username, the date and time that each command was executed, and the command executed.

- **EXEC**—This accounting method provides information about EXEC sessions started on the router. This information includes the user's name, the date with start and stop times, and the IP address of the user's device.

- **Network**—This accounting method provides information about dialup connections, such as PPP and SLIP (this is not covered in this book). The information captured includes the number of packets and bytes for the network connection.

- **Resource**—This accounting method is used for dialup connections and displays resource information about the phone calls (this is not covered in this book).

- **System**—This accounting method provides information about system-level events, such as an interface going up or down, the router being reloaded, or accounting being enabled or disabled.

NOTE   Cisco's implementation of RADIUS does not support command accounting; you must use TACACS+ for this function.

The previous list displays the kind of information that you can capture for accounting. What the router does with this information is defined by your method lists. With accounting, there are only two method lists:

- RADIUS
- TACACS+

Unfortunately, this means that you cannot log accounting information locally on the router or to a syslog server. Instead, the Cisco IOS uses an AAA security server to log the accounting information.

Accounting Configuration

Now take a look at setting up AAA accounting on your router. As mentioned in the last section, accounting requires the use of an external security server using either the TACACS+ or RADIUS communications security protocols. Therefore, you need to do the following things first:

Step 1   Enable AAA with the **aaa new-model** command.

Step 2   Set up your security server connection with the **tacacs-server** and **radius-server** commands.

Step 3   Set up authentication with the **aaa authentication** command.

Step 4   Set up authorization with the **aaa authorization** command (optional).

Enabling Accounting

After you have done these things, you are ready to set up accounting. Here is the command syntax to configure accounting:

```
Router(config)# aaa accounting {system | network | exec |
  connection | commands level_#} {default | list_name}
  {start-stop | stop-only | none} [method1 [method2...]]
Router(config)# line [aux | console | tty | vty] line_# [ending_line_#]
Router(config-line)# accounting {arap | commands level_# |
  connection | exec} {default | list_name}
Router(config)# interface type [slot_#/]port_#
Router(config-if)# ppp accounting {default | list_name}
```

Enabling accounting requires the use of the **aaa accounting** command. Table 5-4 lists the six services that you can enable accounting for.

Table 5-4   *AAA Accounting Services*

Service Keyword	Description
system	Enables accounting to capture system-level events, such as an interface status changing or the router reloading (only the **default** method list is supported for this service)
network	Enables accounting for all network services, such as SLIP, PPP, NCP, and ARAP
exec	Enables accounting for EXEC sessions, listing what users logged in and when they logged into and out of the router
connection	Enables accounting for outbound connections from the router, such as Telnet and TN3270
commands *level_#*	Enables accounting for commands, listing the commands (and their privilege levels) that were executed by a user
resource	Enables accounting for dialup connections, listing resource information for them

Following the service is the keyword **default** or the name of the method list. With the exception of **system**, all accounting services can be enabled or disabled on a line or interface basis. With these accounting services, you can specify a unique name for the method list and associate it with the appropriate line or interface, thereby restricting the accounting information that you gather. For example, you could enable the **commands** service for VTY connections, but not for other types of access.

After you have entered the **default** parameter or method list, you need to define how accounting records should be created. You can use these keywords:

- **start-stop**—Create an accounting record at the beginning and end of the event. For example, with an outbound Telnet, the Cisco IOS would create a starting accounting record when the user establishes a Telnet connection, and then an ending accounting record when the user terminates the connection.

- **stop-only**—Create an accounting record only at the end of the user process. For example, for an outbound Telnet connection, an accounting record is created only when the user terminates the Telnet connection.

- **none**—Disables accounting for the specified accounting service.

- **wait-start**—As with start-stop, an accounting record is generated at the beginning and end of the service; however, the service is not started until the router successfully can log the beginning accounting record with the AAA server. This is useful if you want extra protection and require a log of actions before the action takes place.

NOTE   Note that the **wait-start** parameter was removed in Cisco IOS 12.1 and later, and no longer is supported.

As mentioned in the last section, only two listed methods are supported for accounting: RADIUS and TACACS+. You can use these keywords for these methods:

- **group radius**
- **group tacacs+**
- **group** *AAA_server_group_name*

These previously were discussed in the "Authentication" and "Authorization" sections.

Using a named method list, you can associate that list with either a line or an interface. On a line, use the **accounting** command, specifying the service that you want to create accounting information for, as well as the name of the accounting service. If you do not use this command, the **default** method list is used. On interfaces, only network PPP connection information can be gathered.

Suppressing Null Username Records

In some situations, accounting generates accounting records when no username is involved—a null username. For example, you might have configured AAA for login authentication (**aaa authentication login**) and specified two methods in your list: a TACACS+ AAA server and none. In this situation, the TACACS+ server is used to perform authentication; if it is not available, authentication is not performed. Assume that you have another AAA server running RADIUS that handles all accounting functions. When a user attempts to authenticate and the TACACS+ server is not available, the user is allowed access to the router (this probably was restricted to only the console port) because of the **none** method. In this situation, the user accessing the router did not have to supply a username for this method because no authentication is required (**none** method). However, accounting still generates an accounting record, using a null username. If you desire, you can suppress these accounting records with the following command:

```
Router(config)# aaa accounting suppress null-username
```

Enabling Broadcast Accounting

One of the initial limitations of AAA accounting is that all records were sent to the primary AAA server. If you wanted multiple AAA servers to receive the accounting information, the router would send the information to the primary AAA server, and the primary server would forward it to other AAA servers. As of 12.1(1)T, the Cisco IOS simultaneously can forward accounting information to up to four AAA servers. Imagine an AAA accounting server that must handle accounting information for 2000 or 3000 routers. Using the old method would place a heavy burden on the AAA server. The new broadcast solution is especially useful because it reduces the burden on the primary accounting server and places it on the routers sending accounting information.

Enabling the broadcast function is simple. First, create a list of AAA servers of the same type. Optionally, you can put them into an AAA server group, but this is not necessary. When configuring your **aaa accounting** commands, insert the **broadcast** parameter before your list of methods, like this:

```
Router(config)# aaa accounting {system|network|exec|
   connection|commands level_#} {default|list_name}
   {start-stop|stop-only|(none} broadcast [method1 [method2...]]
```

Accounting Troubleshooting

You use two basic commands for troubleshooting AAA accounting problems: **show accounting** and **debug aaa accounting**. Note that, depending on the Cisco IOS version, you have to use either the **show accounting** command or its replacement, the **show aaa user all** command.

The **show accounting** command lists a summarized view of each accounting record in the router's buffer, as well as a summarization of the types of accounting records. For more detailed troubleshooting of accounting, use the **debug aaa accounting** command, as displayed in Example 5-9.

Example 5-9 *Using the* **debug aaa accounting** *Command*

```
Router# debug aaa accounting
Sep 17 14:48:33.011: AAA/ACCT/EXEC(00000005): Pick
        method list 'default'
Sep 17 14:48:33.011: AAA/ACCT/SETMLIST(00000005): Handle 0,
        mlist 81CA79CC, Name default
Sep 17 14:48:33.011: Getting session id for EXEC(00000005)
        : db=82099258
Sep 17 14:48:33.011: AAA/ACCT/EXEC(00000005): add, count 2
Sep 17 14:48:33.011: AAA/ACCT/EVENT/(00000005): EXEC UP
```

In this example, the default method was used, as shown in the second line of output ('default'). In the middle and bottom of the display, you can see that a user successfully gained access to the router's EXEC shell.

Accounting Example

Now that you understand how to use basic AAA accounting commands, take a look at a simple configuration. This builds upon Example 5-6 and Example 5-8 used in the "Authentication Example" and "Authorization Example" sections. Example 5-10 shows a sample configuration for accounting.

Example 5-10 *Adding Accounting to the AAA Example Configuration*

```
Router(config)# aaa accounting commands 15 default
  stop-only group aaatacgroup broadcast
Router(config)# aaa accounting system default
  stop-only group aaatacgroup broadcast
Router(config)# aaa accounting connection default
  stop-only group aaatacgroup broadcast
Router(config)# aaa accounting exec default
  stop-only group aaatacgroup broadcast
```

In this example, aaatacgroup, which contains two TACACS+ servers, is handling the accounting functions. Notice that I used the **broadcast** parameter, ensuring that the AAA accounting information is sent from the router directly to both servers. In this configuration, accounting records are created when a user executes privilege level 15 commands, a system event occurs, a user tries to connect to a remote device, or a user tries to gain access to an EXEC shell.

Secure Copy

As mentioned in Chapter 3, if you need to move configuration files between a router and a host, it is preferable that they are encrypted. One solution mentioned in Chapter 3 was secure copy (SCP). SCP relies on SSH. Therefore, before you can set up and use SCP, you must configure SSH. SCP is also relatively new to the Cisco IOS; you need Cisco IOS 12.2(2)T to use it.

It seems that SCP is out of place in this chapter and really should be covered in Chapter 3. However, SCP requires the configuration of AAA to use it, so I have decided to cover it here instead of Chapter 3.

Preparation for SCP

The configuration of SSH was discussed in Chapter 3. You need to configure at least three things:

- A hostname: **hostname**.

- A domain name: **ip domain-name**.

- RSA encryption keys: **crypto key generate rsa**. (Your router must have the crypto-enabled feature set of the Cisco IOS to execute this command.)

SCP also requires the use of AAA authorization. Therefore, you need to use some of the commands discussed in this chapter to implement SCP.

NOTE   Note that not all routers support SCP. Here is a list of currently supported routers: 1700, 2600, 3600, 7200, 7500, and 12000 series models.

SCP Configuration

After you have set up SSH, you need to configure AAA for SCP:

Step 1 Enable AAA: **aaa new-model**.

Step 2 Specify security servers, if used: **tacacs-server** and **radius-server**.

Step 3 Specify local accounts, if used: **username**.

Step 4 Configure login authentication: **aaa authentication login**.

Step 5 Configure authorization for EXEC access: **aaa authorization exec**.

The last step is to set up the router as an SCP server:

```
Router(config)# ip scp server enable
```

SCP Troubleshooting

After you have set up SCP, you can test it by copying files to and from the router. From the router, use the following syntax:

```
Router# copy source_file scp://user_name@IP_address_of_server/
Address or name of remote host [x.x.x.x]?
Destination username [username]?
Destination filename [file_name]
Writing file_name
Password:
Router#
```

As you can see, you need to use the **scp** keyword in the destination filename.

If you are having problems, use the following **debug** commands:

- **debug ip ssh**
- **debug ip ssh client**
- **debug ip scp**

Example 5-11 shows an example of the **debug ip scp** command and a successful copy.

Example 5-11 *Troubleshooting SCP Connections*

```
Router# debug ip scp
2d01h:SCP:[22 -> 10.0.0.100:1019] send <OK>
2d01h:SCP:[22 <- 10.0.0.100:1019] recv C0648 21 router.cfg
2d01h:SCP:[22 -> 10.0.0.100:1019] send <OK>
2d01h:SCP:[22 <- 10.0.0.100:1019] recv 21 bytes
2d01h:SCP:[22 <- 10.0.0.100:1019] recv <OK>
2d01h:SCP:[22 -> 10.0.0.100:1019] send <OK>
2d01h:SCP:[22 <- 10.0.0.100:1019] recv <EOF>
```

SCP Example

Example 5-12 shows a simple example of setting up SCP to use local authentication.

Example 5-12 *Setting up SCP*

```
Router(config)# hostname bullmastiff
bullmastiff(config)# ip domain-name quizware.com
bullmastiff(config)# crypto key generate rsa
The name for the keys will be: bullmastiff.quizware.com
Choose the size of the key modulus in the range of 360 to 2048 for your
  General Purpose Keys. Choosing a key modulus greater than 512 may take
  a few minutes.
How many bits in the modulus [512]: 2048
% Generating 1024 bit RSA keys ...[OK]
00:02:25: %SSH-5-ENABLED: SSH 1.5 has been enabled
bullmastiff(config)# access-list 1 permit 10.0.0.50
bullmastiff(config)# line vty 0 4
bullmastiff(config-line)# login local
bullmastiff(config-line)# transport input ssh
bullmastiff(config-line)# transport output ssh
bullmastiff(config-line)# access-class 1 in
bullmastiff(config-line)# end
bullmastiff(config)# aaa new-model
bullmastiff(config)# aaa authentication login default local
bullmastiff(config)# aaa authorization exec default local
bullmastiff(config)# username admin1 privilege 15 secret cisco
bullmastiff(config)# ip scp server enable
```

In this example, the first part sets up SSH and restricts Telnet/SSH access to only one device: 10.0.0.50. Following this is the AAA configuration to allow SCP operations. In this example, local authentication/authorization is used, and one account has been created on the router: admin1.

Summary

This chapter showed you the basics of AAA. AAA enables you to authenticate users, authorize what services they can access, and account for what happened. AAA must be enabled with the **aaa new-model** command. Cisco supports external security servers for AAA; you can use RADIUS, TACACS+, and even Kerberos to provide for a secure connection and communications between your router and the security server. When you need to manage a large number of routers, using AAA with a security server is the most scalable solution.

Next up is Part III, "Nonstateful Filtering Technologies," which shows you how to protect the router using standard and extended access control lists (ACLs).

Nonstateful Filtering Technologies

Chapter 6   Access List Introduction

Chapter 7   Basic Access Lists

Access List Introduction

Cisco access control lists (ACLs), pronounced *ackuls*, are one of the most powerful features of the Cisco IOS. This chapter is an introduction to ACLs. It covers basic guidelines when dealing with ACLs, including tips, recommendations, considerations, and cautions.

This chapter is divided into three basic sections:

- Access list overview
- Basic ACL configuration
- Wildcard masks

Each section contains many examples to illustrate the use of ACLs and their components.

This chapter covers only the basic configuration of ACLs; subsequent chapters in this book cover the operation and configuration of the different types of ACLs that the Cisco IOS supports, as well as the use of ACLs to secure a perimeter router.

Access List Overview

ACLs are a multipurpose configuration tool on your router. Typically, ACLs are seen as a filtering tool, filtering traffic as it comes into or leaves your router. This enables you to implement detailed security policies. ACLs are known mostly for their security features, but ACLs support all of the following types of actions:

- Filtering traffic entering an interface
- Filtering traffic exiting an interface
- Controlling access to the router's VTY lines (this is discussed briefly in Chapter 3, "Accessing a Router")
- Controlling what routing updates a router advertises to or receives from neighboring routers
- Triggering dial-on-demand routing (DDR) phone calls with analog or ISDN
- Classifying traffic for dealing with congestion, such as congestion avoidance, congestion management, and queuing functions
- Restricting the output from **debug** commands based on addressing or protocol information

As you can see from this list, ACLs can perform many different types of functions. This book, however, focuses on how you can use ACLs as a security filtering solution. As you will see later in this chapter and throughout the book, Cisco supports many different kinds of ACLs with different kinds of capabilities. Your task is to choose the best ACL solution, based on your policies, to implement a filtering solution.

ACLs and Filtering

ACLs are a grouping of commands that enable you to control traffic as it comes into or exits an interface. When ACLs are filtering traffic, they commonly are also referred to as *filters*. Decisions that you can apply to traffic include permitting or dropping traffic based on conditions (rules) that you define on your router. Conditions can look for matches on the contents of a packet, including the following:

- Source or destination address
- Layer 2 protocol information, such as the type Ethernet frame
- Layer 3 protocols, such as IP, IPX, and AppleTalk
- Layer 3 protocol information, such as IP, ICMP, OSPF, TCP, UDP, and others within the TCP/IP protocol suite
- Layer 4 protocol information, such as TCP and UDP port numbers

Typically, ACLs filter Layers 3 and 4 information, but as you can see from the previous list, you also can use them to filter Layer 2 information. When I discuss reflexive ACLs in Chapter 8, "Reflexive Access Lists," and Context-based Access Control (CBAC) in Chapter 9, "Context-Based Access Control," you will see that ACLs can also keep track of Layer 5 information, or session information, and higher.

NOTE   Cisco supports ACLs for many different protocols, including bridging, TCP/IP, DECnet, IPX, Vines, and XNS. This book, however, focuses only on TCP/IP–based ACLs.

ACLs can provide a base level of security for traffic flowing through your network. It is important to point out that, by default, your router does *not* filter any traffic; you must configure and apply ACLs for your router to filter traffic as it flows through the router. ACLs commonly are used to prevent different devices from accessing a specific service, a specific device, or a part of a network.

Simple ACL Example

The network in Figure 6-1 serves as an example to show the usefulness of filtering with ACLs. In this example, there are two routers: an internal router and a perimeter/firewall router.

Figure 6-1   *Filtering Example*

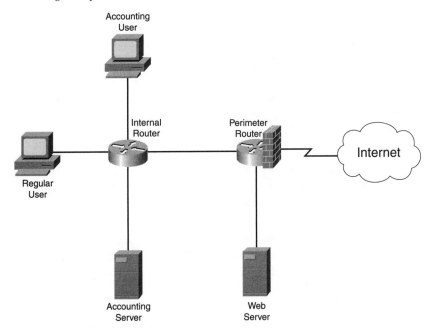

The perimeter/firewall router is using these policies:

- For traffic originating from the Internet, only traffic destined for the web server (its IP address and TCP port 80) is allowed. All other Internet traffic coming into this router is dropped.

- For internal traffic being forwarded to the Internet, only the returning traffic is allowed. (This can be accomplished with stateful firewall filtering, which is discussed in Chapter 2, "Introduction to Firewalls"; Chapter 8, "Reflexive Access Lists"; and Chapter 9, "Context-Based Access Control.")

The internal router is using these filtering policies:

- Only traffic from the accounting users is allowed to reach the accounting server.

- All other traffic between other segments is allowed.

With the filtering policies defined for the two routers in Figure 6-1, ACLs are used to implement and enforce them.

Types of ACLs

ACLs can be used in any situation to control traffic between devices, services, networks, or a combination of these. As shown in Figure 6-1, you can use ACLs to implement a firewall solution on a router, or you can use them to restrict internal usage of resources, such as an accounting server. Actually, it is very common to see a perimeter router with ACLs on it restricting the type of traffic allowed into the network. In Figure 6-1, the perimeter router is allowing only web traffic destined for the internal web server, as well as any returning traffic that internal users initiated.

You can use many types of ACLs to implement filtering solutions. Each is meant to accomplish a specific function, and each has its own advantages and disadvantages. Some types of ACLs are meant for firewall solutions; others are not. The following types of IP ACLs are discussed in this book:

- **Standard IP ACLs**—This type of ACL can filter only Layer 3 information. These ACLs are used to filter packets based on the source address in the packet header. Chapter 7, "Basic Access Lists," covers standard IP ACLs. Standard ACLs commonly are used to restrict VTY access to a Cisco router.

- **Extended IP ACLs**—This type of ACL can filter Layers 3 and 4 information. These ACLs are used to filter packets based on the source and destination IP address, the IP protocol (such as ICMP, IP, OSPF, TCP, UDP, and others), and protocol information (such as ICMP message types or TCP or UDP port numbers). Chapter 7 covers extended IP ACLs. Extended ACLs commonly are used to filter traffic, especially traffic as it enters your network.

- **Turbo ACLs**—This is an ACL feature that enables you to compile standard and extended ACLs, making them more efficient for the router to process and resulting in quicker lookup times. Chapter 7, "Basic Access Lists," covers turbo ACLs.

- **Timed IP ACLs**—This is an extended IP ACL that can filter on Layers 3 and 4 information. Unlike normal extended IP ACLs, timed ACLs can be activated based on the time of day, day of the week, or day of the month. They can be set up to filter on a recurring time period or just a single time period. Chapter 7 covers timed IP ACLs.

- **Reflexive IP ACLs**—This type of ACL can filter on Layers 3, 4, and 5 information. Some people think that reflexive ACLs implement a stateful firewall function; they do not, as you will see in Chapter 8, "Reflexive Access Lists," but they come very close. I like to refer to them as the "poor-man's firewall."

- **Context-based Access Control (CBAC) ACLs**—This type of ACL can filter on Layer 3 through Layer 7 information. This is Cisco's stateful firewall function in its Cisco IOS. Chapter 9, "Context-Based Access Control," covers CBAC ACLs.

- **Lock-and-key ACLs**—This type of ACL filters on Layer 3 and sometimes Layer 4 information. These ACLs implement double-authentication, in which, when connecting through PPP, the user authenticates first through PAP or CHAP and then at the application layer before the router allows the connection. Chapter 13, "Lock-and-Key Access Lists," covers lock-and-key ACLs. As you will see there, lock-and-key ACLs can be used to restrict any type of access to your network.

CAUTION	Each type of ACL has advantages and disadvantages. It is important that you choose the right type of ACL when dealing with security issues. It is not uncommon to see a router use different types of ACLs to implement security policies. It is important to point out that ACLs perform filtering, for the most part, at Layers 3, 4, and sometimes 5: They cannot prevent all kinds of attacks, such as application layer ones. ACLs are also susceptible to spoofing attacks. Therefore, you should combine ACLs with other Cisco IOS security features to provide for the best protection of your network from security threats.

Processing ACLs

ACL statements have two components: a condition and an action. A condition is used to match on packet contents. When a match is found for a condition, an action is taken: permit or deny the packet. Even though this sounds simple, ACLs are one of the most complex features of the Cisco IOS: Take care when you configure and activate them. A misconfigured ACL can inadvertently block traffic or open a huge security hole. The following sections cover the ACL process in more depth.

Conditions

A condition is basically a set of rules that define what to look for in a packet's contents to determine whether the packet matches. A condition can be something as simple as looking for a match on the source address in the packet, or something as complicated as looking for a match in a source address, destination address, protocol type, and protocol information.

Only one condition can be listed in each ACL statement; however, you can group ACL statements to form a single list or policy. The statements are grouped by a common number or name.

NOTE	Each protocol has its own set of conditions that you can use to match on packet contents. No real limitation exists for the number of statements that you can put in your ACL, except for the amount of RAM and NVRAM. However, the longer the ACL is, the more complicated it becomes to manage the statements in the list.

Matches on Conditions

The Cisco IOS can take two basic actions when a condition in an ACL statement matches the contents in a compared packet:

- Permit
- Deny

When there is a match in an ACL statement, no further statements are processed.

Also, there is an invisible statement at the end of every ACL, called the *implicit deny* statement. The purpose of this statement is to drop packets; if a packet was compared to every statement in the list and a match was not found, the packet is dropped. Therefore, it is only common sense to have at least one permit action in your ACL. If you have only deny actions, the Cisco IOS either will match on one of these statements and drop the packet, or it will use the implicit deny statement to drop the packet.

ACL Flowchart

To help understand how the Cisco IOS processes an ACL, examine the flowcharts shown in Figures 6-2 and 6-3. Figure 6-2 shows an example in which an ACL is applied inbound on an interface. In this example, when a packet is received on an interface, the Cisco IOS first determines whether an ACL is applied on the interface. If it is not, the Cisco IOS normally routes the packet. If it is, the Cisco IOS processes the ACL. It starts with the first statement and compares the packet contents with the condition. If there is no match, the Cisco IOS goes to the next statement in the list. If there is a match, it executes the action: permit or deny. If the Cisco IOS goes through the entire ACL and does not find a match, it drops the packet.

Figure 6-2   *Inbound ACL Flowchart*

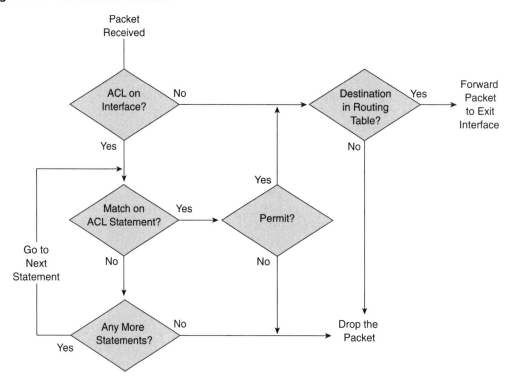

Figure 6-3   *Outbound ACL Flowchart*

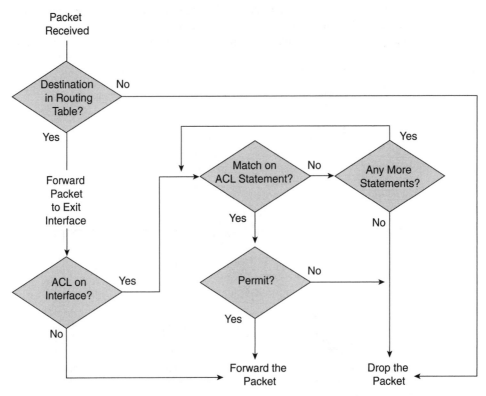

With an outbound ACL, the process is similar, as shown in Figure 6-3. When the Cisco IOS receives a packet, it first routes the packet to the outbound interface. The Cisco IOS then checks to see whether there is an outbound ACL on the interface. If not, the Cisco IOS queues up the packet to be sent out the interface. Otherwise, the packet is processed by comparing it to the ACL entries, as described previously.

Statement Order in ACLs

The order in which ACL statements are placed is very important. By default, when you add an ACL statement to the list, it is added at the bottom, or end, of the list. Until Cisco IOS 12.2(14)S and 12.3(2)T, you could not easily insert an ACL statement into the middle of an existing ACL grouping, nor could you delete a specific ACL statement (with the exception of named ACLs).

The order of the statements is important because the Cisco IOS processes the list from the top down. Starting with the first ACL statement, the Cisco IOS compares the packet contents with the condition. If there is no match, the router proceeds to the next statement, and so on and so forth. If the Cisco IOS does not find a match on any statements, the Cisco IOS drops the packet (implicit deny).

Look at a simple example in which statement ordering can create problems. In the example network shown in Figure 6-4, a router is separating two segments: One segment has users, and one segment has file servers. The goal in filtering traffic is to allow all users to reach the web server, but to allow only the Accounting user to the accounting server.

Figure 6-4 *Simple ACL Ordering Problems*

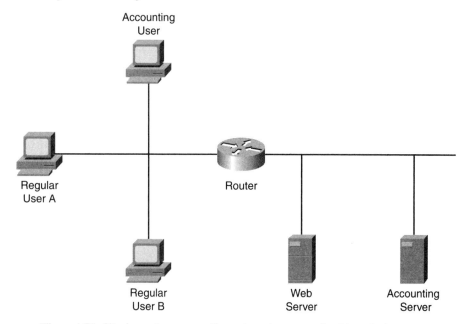

These ACL filtering rules are configured on the router (in this order):

1 Allow all users to access the server segment.

2 Deny regular User A from accessing the accounting server.

3 Deny regular User B from accessing the accounting server.

Given the order of these rules, there is a problem. Because the statements are processed from the top down, when regular User A tries to access the accounting server, he is permitted based on a match of the first statement. In this example, everyone can access all servers on the server segment. Instead, the ACL should read as follows:

1 Deny regular User A from accessing the accounting server.

2 Deny regular User B from accessing the accounting server.

3 Allow all users to access the server segment.

In this example, the regular users are denied access to the accounting server but still are allowed access to other servers on the segment.

Now look at a more complicated filtering problem by examining the network shown in Figure 6-5. The administrator must configure these policies, in no important order:

- Allow all access to the web server.
- Restrict access to the development server.
- Restrict access to the accounting server.
- Restrict access to the database server.

Figure 6-5   *Complex ACL Ordering Problems*

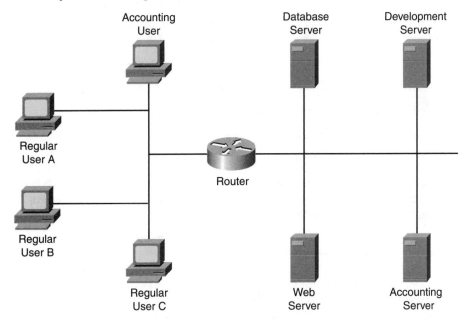

In this example, the administrator configured the following ACL rules in the specified order:

1 Allow regular Users A, B, and C access to the server segment.

2 Allow only regular Users A and B access to the development server.

3 Allow only the Accounting User access to the accounting server.

4 Only regular Users A, B, and C should access the database server.

5 Allow the Accounting user access to the web server.

In this example, there is a configuration problem. For example, based on the previous rules and processing of the ACL from the top down, regular Users A, B, and C can access any resource because the first statement allows them to do so. Now switch the first two statements and see the results of this action:

1. Allow only regular Users A and B access to the development server.

2. Allow regular Users A, B, and C access to the server segment.

3. Allow only the Accounting user access to the accounting segment.

4. Only regular Users A, B, and C should access the database server.

5. Allow the Accounting User access to the web server.

This example fixes some of the access problems, but regular Users A, B, and C can still access the accounting server. Here is how the ACL should be structured and ordered:

1. Allow the Accounting User access to the accounting server.

2. Allow regular Users A and B access to the development server.

3. Allow regular Users A, B, and C access to the database server.

4. Allow all users access to the web servers.

5. Deny all other types of access (the implicit deny).

As you can see in this example, the structure and ordering of the statements become more complicated because many policy variables come into play. The previous example is not the only way to accomplish the ordering of the list, but it does satisfy the requirements.

TIP   When you set up your filtering rules, you list them from most restrictive to least restrictive. Plus, if you want to allow everyone access to most services but deny just a few specific ones, you set up an ACL that, at the beginning, denies the specific connections and then permits everything else. This type of ACL is common within a company's network. If you want to permit only a few things and deny everything else, you specify your permit statements at the beginning and let the implicit deny drop everything else. This kind of ACL is common when providing a firewall function between two networks.

ACL Rules and Restrictions

Given the complexity that ACLs can create when implementing your security policies, you should be aware of these general rules, guidelines, and restrictions when creating your grouping of ACL statements:

- ACL statements are grouped by either a name or a number.

- Each ACL statement can have only one set of conditions and one action (permit or deny). If you need multiple conditions or multiple actions, you must create multiple ACL statements.

- If a match is not found in the condition of a statement, the next ACL statement in the list is processed.

- When a match is found on a statement in an ACL group, no further statements are processed.

- If all the statements in the list are processed and no match is found, the invisible implicit deny statement denies the packet.

- Given the implicit deny at the end of the grouping of ACL statements, you should have at least one permit action; otherwise, all packets will be denied.

- When filtering, if the Cisco IOS drops a packet, it generates an ICMP administratively prohibited message.

- Order of statements is important. The most restrictive statements should be at the top of the list, and the least restrictive should be at the bottom.

- An empty ACL grouping permits all packets. An empty ACL grouping is an ACL that has been activated on a router but that does not contain any statements. For the implicit deny statement to take effect, there must be at least one permit or deny statement in the ACL.

- You are allowed to apply one ACL per interface, per protocol, per direction. For example, you cannot have two IP ACLs applied inbound on an interface, but you can have an IP ACL applied inbound and outbound, or an IP and IPX ACL applied inbound.

- Inbound ACLs are processed before a packet is routed to another interface (see Figure 6-2).

- Outbound ACLs are processed after a packet is routed to the interface but before the packet exits the interface (see Figure 6-3).

- When an ACL is applied to an interface, which affects traffic flowing through the interface, the ACL does not filter traffic that the router itself generates. For example, if an outbound ACL is on a interface that blocks ICMP traffic, it will not filter pings that the router generates.

From this list, you can see that the processing of ACLs, as well as the configuration and management of them, is not a simple process. Care must be taken in the setup, implementation, maintenance, and troubleshooting of them. Therefore, you must be familiar with the previous bullets if you want to implement your security policies with the fewest problems and headaches.

Placement of ACLs

One of the questions that students commonly ask in my classes is where to configure ACLs—on what router or routers and on which interface or interfaces? The classic answer to this question is that it depends on your specific situation. However, two guidelines can help you with your decision:

- ACLs that filter only on the source address in a packet should be placed as close to the destination (that you are filtering) as possible.

- ACLs that filter on both the source and destination address in a packet, as well as other things, should be placed as close to the source as possible.

To demonstrate where ACLs should be placed, consider the network shown in Figure 6-6.

Figure 6-6   *Placement of ACLs*

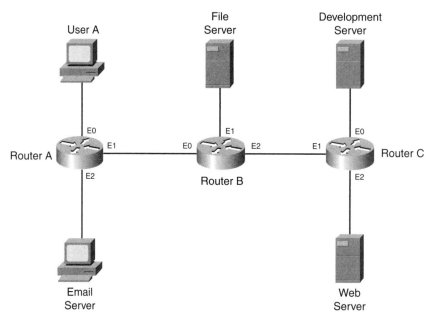

In the first situation, assume that the network administrator is using ACLs that filter only on the *source* addresses in packets. In this example, User A is allowed to access all resources except the development server. Here is the ACL rule for User A:

1 Deny User A access to the development server.

2 Allow User A access to all other servers.

3 Allow all other users access to all other servers.

The question is, on which router should the ACL be placed, and on which interface? Given the two placement rules just mentioned, the ACL should be placed as close to the destination as possible: on Router C's E0 interface in the outbound direction.

Now look at some other options with this example. If you placed it on Router A's E0 interface in the inbound direction, this definitely would stop the user from accessing the development server. However, because this ACL looks at the source address when matching the condition (it does not look at the destination), this filter would also prevent this user from accessing any other resource. If you put this ACL on Router C's E1 interface in the inbound direction, the user would be able to access the e-mail and file servers (as desired), but that user would be prevented from accessing the needed resources on the web server.

However, ACLs that filter only on source addresses in packets have two limitations:

- Even with the ACL applied outbound on E0 on Router C, any traffic from User A would be prohibited from accessing anything on this segment, including the development server.

- Traffic must go all the way to the destination. It is dropped just before reaching the destination. This is inefficient use of bandwidth.

In the second example, the network administrator is using ACLs that can filter on both source and destination addresses in packets. In this example, User A is allowed to access all resources except the development server. The question is, on which router should the ACL be placed, and on which interface? The answer is as close to the *source* as possible: Router A's E0 interface in the inbound direction. This solution solves the previous two problems. With this type of ACL, you can be specific about what resources are being accessed. In this example, you easily can set up this filtering policy to deny User A from accessing the development server and to grant access to all other services throughout the network.

NOTE   Given the advantages of ACLs that can filter only on source addresses and ACLs that can filter on both, you might wonder why you even would use the former. Before the innovations of things such as Cisco Express Forwarding (CEF) and other types of high-speed switching, simple ACLs that filtered only on source addresses had a much smaller impact on the router's CPU processing than other types of ACLs. Therefore, the preferred method was to use these types of ACLs, called standard ACLs, instead of ACLs that could filter on both the source and destination addresses, called extended ACLs. Today this is not a limitation with the type of caching that CEF supports (ACL information). Standard ACLs typically are used with VTY and HTTP restrictions to the router itself, as discussed in Chapter 3, and extended ACLs typically are used to filter traffic flowing through the router.

Basic ACL Configuration

Configuration of ACLs is a two-step process:

Step 1   Create your ACL rules.

Step 2   Activate your ACL rules.

The following sections cover the configuration of ACL rules and their activation. This is an overview process concerning ACLs. Configuring specific types of ACLs, such as extended, reflexive, CBAC, and others, is covered in later chapters.

Creating ACLs

For each protocol that you want to filter, such as IP and IPX, you need to create a separate ACL. Each ACL is basically a grouping of statements that define your filtering rules, where either a number or name is used to group the statements. When using numbers, you cannot just choose any random number to assign to the grouping of your ACL statements. Instead, Cisco has reserved ranges of numbers for different protocols. Table 6-1 lists the numbers that you can use for the various protocols that support ACLs.

Table 6-1 *ACL Numbering*

Protocol	ACL Numbers
Standard IP	1–99, 1300–1999
Extended IP	100–199, 2000–2699
Ethernet type code	200–299
Transparent bridging protocol type	200–299
Source route bridging protocol type	200–299
Ethernet MAC addresses	700–799
Transparent bridging vendor code	700–799
Source route bridging vendor code	700–799
Extended transparent bridging	1100–1199
DECnet	300–399
Standard XNS	400–499
Extended XNS	500–599
AppleTalk	600–699
Standard IPX	800–899
Extended IPX	900–999
IPX SAPs	1000–1099
Standard vines	1–99
Extended vines	100–199
Simple vines	200–299

The numbers (or names) listed in Table 6-1 are used to group multiple ACL statements in the same group. This enables you to create detailed filtering rules to enforce your security policies.

Generically, the following is the command to create a grouping of ACL statements that use numbers to differentiate between different groups:

```
Router(config)# access-list ACL_# permit|deny conditions
```

As you can see from this syntax, the number appears first, followed by the action and, finally, the conditions. Each type of ACL has its own set of valid conditions. These are covered in subsequent chapters on traffic filtering.

Here are some helpful tips when building your ACLs:

- Before creating your ACLs, make sure that you have a picture of the topology of your network in front of you, along with a list of your security policies that you will be enforcing.
- Put your list of security policies in order from most to least restrictive. Then use this list to build your ACL commands.
- With ACL statements that have the same level of restriction, put the statement(s) that are used more often before the ones used less often. This ensures that commonly matched statements are processed first, reducing the burden on your router.
- ACLs support remarks. This enables you to put a brief description before or after any command in your ACL grouping. Use this feature to make your ACL more readable and easier to reference.
- Always create your ACL and then apply it to an interface. By default, empty ACLs permit all traffic. Plus, if you have Telnetted into a router and pasted in an ACL from a text editor, your Telnet connection could break if the empty ACL already was activated on the interface you were using for the Telnet connection.

ACLs and Remarks

One of the neat and handy features of ACLs is the capability to insert a description before or after an ACL statement in a grouping. This can be useful if you are looking at an ACL later trying to figure out why certain commands are listed in that order.

As an example, one of my clients had a very extensive ACL with more than 500 lines. Administrators were modifying the ACL weekly to fit changing conditions in their network. Because many people were modifying the ACL, an administrator coming in after the fact did not know what was changed, why it was changed, and when it was changed. In one situation, an administrator added an entry in the ACL over the course of the holiday to allow users to access specific internal resources so that they could work at home while enjoying time with their families. This would allow them to complete a critical project on time. Unfortunately, another administrator noticed this apparent hole in the ACL configuration and removed it. Of course, this caused problems for users over the holiday break because they could not access their resources from home. It took more than 3 days to track down this problem and fix it.

Activating ACLs

The statements in the ACL grouping will have no impact on the router until you activate them. When you are filtering traffic traveling through the router, you do this by activating the ACL on an interface with the following command:

```
Router(config)# interface type [slot_#/]port_#
Router(config-if)# protocol_name access-group ACL_#_or_name in|out
```

For example, if you wanted to activate an IP ACL on your interface, you would use the keyword **ip** for the *protocol_name*. Following this, you must specify either the name or number of the ACL that you are activating. Finally, you must specify the direction that the Cisco IOS will use when filtering traffic. If you specify **in**, the Cisco IOS uses the ACL to filter traffic as packets come into the interface (see Figure 6-2 for the processing of inbound ACLs); if you specify **out**, the Cisco IOS uses the ACL to filter traffic before it leaves the interface (see Figure 6-3 for the processing of outbound ACLs).

Editing ACLs

You can use two methods to edit groupings of ACL statements:

- Use a text editor for Cisco IOS versions earlier than 12.2(14)S and 12.3(2)T.
- Add, modify, and delete specific ACL entries in Cisco IOS versions 12.2(14)S and 12.3(2)T.

Before Cisco IOS 12.2(14)S and 12.3(2)T, editing ACLs was not a simple process. You could not delete a specific entry (unless the ACL was named), you could not insert an ACL into a specific place in the list (entries always were added to the bottom of the list), and you could not modify an existing entry in the list. Instead, you had to follow these steps to edit your ACL:

Step 1 Either copy the active configuration to a TFTP server (**copy running-config tftp** or **scp**—the latter is more secure) and use a text editor, such as Notepad, Wordpad, or any common editor, to extract the ACL statements; or execute the **show running-config** command, select the ACL statements, and paste them into a text editor.

Step 2 From the text editor, make your ACL changes.

Step 3 Select and copy your changes in your text editor, log back into the router, and access Configuration mode (**configure terminal**).

Step 4 Go into the interface or interfaces where the ACL was applied, and remove its application (**no ip access-group**).

Step 5 Delete the access list (**no access-list**); otherwise, if you pasted in the updated ACL configuration, you would be adding your text editor ACL to the end of the existing ACL on the router. Remember that order is important.

Step 6 Paste your ACL into the router (or use the **copy tftp running-config** or **scp** commands to pull in your ACL from your TFTP server).

Step 7 Reactivate the ACL on your router's interface or interfaces (**ip access-group**).

Step 8 Test your ACL configuration.

CAUTION   One problem with the previous approach is that you briefly face a security issue: Between the time that you deactivate the old ACL and reactivate the new ACL, all traffic is allowed through the interface. If this is a concern, when fixing your ACL, give it a different name or number than the one currently being used on the router. Then you can paste your new ACL on the router, remove the old ACL on the interface, and activate the new ACL on the interface. This leaves the interface open for only a second or two between the deactivation and activation of the two ACLs.

Starting with Cisco IOS versions 12.2(14)S and 12.3(2)T, you no longer have to perform these steps when modifying ACLs. Cisco has listened to its customer base and implemented an ACL feature that enables you to modify a specific statement in an ACL, delete one, or insert one at any point in the list. (Since Cisco introduced ACLs in the early 1990s, I have been complaining to any Cisco employee who would listen to me about this annoying approach to editing existing ACLs.) With the new ACL-editing feature, if you need to make only a minor change, such as modify an incorrect line, you can do this with a single command instead of the first seven steps listed earlier. This feature, called sequenced ACLs, is discussed in Chapter 7.

CAUTION   With either method, you need to take care that you do not accidentally lock yourself out of the router when you are configuring the router through Telnet. If you Telnet into the router, delete the ACL, and paste it back in, you inadvertently could lock yourself out. For example, assume that you have an ACL in which the first statement is to permit web traffic for certain users. You have fixed this ACL and deleted the old ACL on the router. You currently are Telnetted into the router through Ethernet0, where this ACL is applied inbound. If you do not remove this empty ACL before pasting in your fixed ACL, you will lock yourself out.

When you paste in the ACL, the router processes each statement in the ACL. As soon as one valid statement is pasted into the router's configuration, the Cisco IOS immediately uses the implicit deny (the ACL is no longer empty and already has been activated on the interface). If your Telnet connection is not permitted with the first statement, you have just locked yourself out of the router through Telnet. This is a very common occurrence, and I sometimes repeat this mistake. Therefore, closely examine your ACL before pasting it in, deactivate the ACL on the interface, paste in your ACL (or make your change with sequenced ACLs), and then reactivate the ACL.

Of course, if this is a perimeter router, you should not be using the public interface when Telnetting in the router, so you should not have to remove its application. However, when you delete and paste in the ACL, the applied empty ACL briefly permits all traffic. Therefore, if you are really paranoid, disable the public interface before making any ACL changes. An absolute must is to test your changes to ensure that your ACL configuration meets your security policies.

Wildcard Masks

One of the most difficult components to grasp with ACLs is the wildcard mask. *Wildcard masks* are used to match on a range of IP addresses in a condition. For example, imagine that you want to allow a device to access any address in 192.168.1.0/24. One approach is to have 254 permit statements for these addresses: 192.168.1.1 through 192.168.1.254. This takes a lot of time to configure and places an extra burden on the router to process all of these statements. Instead, the Cisco IOS uses a feature called wildcard masks. Wildcard masks enable you to match on a range of addresses in a single condition, such as 192.168.1.0/24. A wildcard mask can match on all 256 of these addresses.

The greatest confusion involving wildcard masks concerns how they are configured to match on a range of addresses. Like IP addresses and subnet masks, wildcard masks are 32 bits in length. When comparing a wildcard mask to a subnet mask, however, the bit values used in both (0 and 1) mean different things. Table 6-2 compares the bit values in subnet and wildcard masks and tells what they represent.

Table 6-2   *Wildcard and Subnet Mask Values*

Mask	Binary 1	Binary 0
Subnet mask	A bit in the corresponding address is a network component.	A bit in the corresponding address is a host component.
Wildcard mask	A bit in the corresponding condition address is ignored.	A bit in the corresponding condition address must match.

NOTE   With standard IP ACLs, the wildcard mask is optional. If you omit it, the wildcard mask defaults to 0.0.0.0. With extended IP ACLs, the wildcard mask is required for both the source and destination addresses.

Converting a Subnet Mask to a Wildcard Mask

Probably the best way to look at a wildcard mask is to compare it to an inverted subnet mask. For example, say that you want to match on network 192.168.1.0/24. This network is a subnet mask of 255.255.255.0. To invert this mask, flip all the 1 bits to 0s and all the 0 bits to 1s. This results in twenty-four 0 bits and eight 1 bits, or 0.0.0.255. Therefore, to match on all addresses in network 192.168.1.0/24, you would use a wildcard mask of 0.0.0.255.

TIP   I have developed a quick trick to perform the conversion process from subnet mask to wildcard mask. First, write down the subnet mask in dotted decimal. Subtract each octet from 255, resulting in the corresponding wildcard mask value for that octet.

Take a look at some examples of performing the conversion. In the first example, I want to figure out the wildcard mask that will match on any packet. In IP, the default network (any address) is 0.0.0.0/0, resulting in a subnet mask of 0.0.0.0. When performing the conversion, the resulting wildcard mask for all address is 255.255.255.255 (subtract each subnet mask octet from 255). To match on any address, you would use an IP address of 0.0.0.0 and a wildcard mask of 255.255.255.255. Like a subnet mask, the context of the wildcard mask is based on the address associated with the mask.

TIP	When configuring an ACL condition and specifying a source address and a wildcard mask that will match on any address, you can either use 0.0.0.0 255.255.255.255 or the keyword **any**. Both mean the same thing.

In this example, I want to match on one specific address, 192.168.1.1. In subnetting, to represent a single address, you use a /32 (255.255.255.255) mask. To convert this to a wildcard mask, subtract each subnet mask octet from 255. This results in a wildcard mask of 0.0.0.0. Therefore, to match on this specific address, you would use 192.168.1.1 0.0.0.0 in your condition.

TIP	When configuring an ACL condition and specifying a source address and a wildcard mask that will match on a specific address, such as 192.168.1.1, you can use either 192.168.1.1 0.0.0.0 or the keyword **host** followed by the host address (**host 192.168.1.1**). Both mean the same thing.

In this third example, I want to create a wildcard mask that will match this range of address: 192.168.1.16/28 (255.255.255.240). To convert this to a wildcard mask, subtract each subnet mask octet from 255, resulting in a wildcard mask of 0.0.0.15. Therefore, to match on 192.168.1.16/28 addresses, you would use the following in your condition: 192.168.1.16 0.0.0.15. As you can see, using this simple trick makes converting subnet masks to wildcard masks an easy process.

NOTE	Unlike subnet masks, wildcard masks support discontiguous 1s and 0s, which enables you to match on a range of values with a specific octet, such as any packet that has a number of 0 to 7 in the third octet.

In this last illustration, I use an example that you might see on a CCIE Routing and Switching or Security written or lab exams. In this example, you are given the following network: 172.16.0.0/16. In this network, you want to match on the first address in each subnet, where the subnet mask is /24. You do not care about the subnet number; you care only about the first address in every subnet, such as 172.16.0.1, 172.16.1.1, 172.16.2.1, and so on. Given these requirements, what kind of address and wildcard mask would you use for your condition? Given the requirements, the address must begin with 172.16. Therefore, the first two octets in the wildcard mask are 0.0. You do not care about the subnet number in the third octet, so the wildcard mask is 255 here. But you do care about the last octet. You want to match on the first address (.1), resulting in a 0 in the fourth octet of the wildcard mask. Therefore, the resulting address and wildcard mask in the condition would be 172.16.0.1 0.0.255.0.

One interesting point to make about this partial condition is that 172.16.0.1 0.0.255.0 and 172.16.1.1 0.0.255.0 mean the same thing. Remember that the wildcard mask specifies that you do not care what is in the third octet; anything matches in this octet. Therefore, it does not matter what number you put here in the address part of the condition. This can be useful if you use the same address in a subnet for a particular type of device, such as a router, and want to match on these addresses. Of course, the example I gave here was simple; CCIEs would be expected to configure something much harder than this.

NOTE   One item to point out is that the Cisco IOS converts any value in an address to 0 if the corresponding wildcard mask value in the octet is 255. For example, if you specified 172.16.1.1 0.0.255.0, the Cisco IOS would change this to 172.16.0.1 0.0.255.0. Note that when the Cisco IOS performs matching, it ignores all values in the third octet. Cisco uses this process to remove any ambiguity about command configuration.

Wildcard Mask Mistakes

Because of the complexities of wildcard masks, many people make mistakes when configuring the wildcard mask for the address or range of addresses that they want to match on. Here are some common mistakes:

- 192.168.1.0 255.255.255.0 matches on any packet with any values in the first three octets and a 0 in the last octet. Remember that the mask that you put in is a wildcard mask, not a subnet mask!

- 192.168.1.1 255.255.255.255 matches on any address. The wildcard mask says to match on all addresses and ignores what you put in for the IP address (192.168.1.1).

- 192.168.1.0 0.0.0.0 matches on any packet that has an address of 192.168.1.0, which is a network number. Actually, if you see an address like this in a packet, it is a spoofing attack. Probably what the administrator meant to use as a wildcard mask was 0.0.0.255, which is any address in the 192.168.1.0/24 network.

Summary

This chapter showed you the basics of ACLs. Cisco uses ACLs to implement or enhance many features, including filtering of traffic, restricting access to the router, triggering DDR phone calls, classifying traffic for quality of service (QoS), and many others. ACLs can be difficult to configure and maintain. Therefore, understanding how the Cisco IOS processes ACLs is important when implementing your filters (based on your security policies). Cisco supports many different ACLs for various protocols; however, this book focuses only on the IP variety of ACLs, such as standard, extended, reflexive, lock-and-key, CBAC, and turbo ACLs.

One of the most common things misconfigured in ACLs is the wildcard mask. Wildcard masks are used to match on a range of addresses in an ACL condition. Understanding the use of wildcard masks is paramount in ensuring that you are not opening yourself to security threats.

Next up is Chapter 7, which shows you how to use standard, extended, named, timed, and turbo ACLs.

## CHAPTER 7

Basic Access Lists

Chapter 6, "Access List Introduction," introduced you to the concept of access control lists (ACLs) and their uses. An ACL most commonly is used for traffic filtering. This chapter focuses on different types of ACLs that you can use for this purpose: standard, extended, named, and timed. I also discuss some additional features of ACLs, such as ACL remarks, compiling ACLs, and sequenced ACLs.

The second half of this chapter covers some of the common types of attacks that you will face and how to use an ACL to filter this offensive traffic. I even discuss how to block some common Internet applications, such as Instant Messenger and file-sharing programs (Kazaa and the sort), to keep your users in line with work-related instead of fun-related or illegal tasks.

Types of ACLs

Since 1993, most administrators have used two basic ACLs: standard and extended ACLs. Standard IP ACLs can filter on only the source IP address in an IP packet header, whereas an extended IP ACL can filter on the following:

- Source IP address
- Destination IP address
- TCP/IP protocol, such as IP (all TCP/IP protocols), ICMP, OSPF, TCP, UDP, and others
- TCP/IP protocol information, such as TCP and UDP port numbers, TCP code flags, and ICMP messages

Given the differences between these two types of ACLs, standard ACLs typically are used for the following configuration tasks on a router:

- Restricting access to a router through the VTY lines (Telnet and SSH)
- Restricting access to a router through HTTP or HTTPS
- Filtering routing updates

Extended ACLs, on the other hand, commonly are used to filter traffic between interfaces on the router, mainly because of their flexibility in matching on many different fields at Layers 2, 3, and 4.

As you recall from Chapter 2, "Introduction to Firewalls," packet-filtering firewalls can filter traffic at Layers 3 and 4. The Cisco standard and extended ACLs fall under this category. In Chapter 2, I pointed out some of the limitations of packet-filtering firewalls, including these:

- They can be complex to configure.
- They cannot prevent application layer attacks.
- They are susceptible to certain types TCP/IP protocol attacks, such as spoofing.
- They do not support user authentication of connections.
- They have limited logging capabilities: They do not log actual packet contents that can be useful in determining what someone was attempting to do.

Standard and extended ACLs have the following advantages:

- They can process packets at very fast speeds.
- They easily can match on most fields in Layer 3 packets and Layer 4 segments, providing a lot of flexibility in implementing security policies.

NOTE   It is important to understand the use and limitations of standard and extended ACLs: They cannot prevent all kinds of attacks, but they are good at filtering out a lot of the garbage and then letting another component in your firewall system deal with application layer attacks. You will see some of these limitations in this chapter when I discuss how you can attempt to limit traffic such as that from Instant Messenger or from file-sharing programs, such as Kazaa, with the use of ACLs.

In this part of the chapter, I discuss how to use the Cisco IOS to configure standard and extended ACLs. Later in the chapter, I discuss how you can use ACLs, especially extended ACLs, to protect your network.

Standard ACLs

Originally, there was a large performance difference between standard and extended ACLs. Standard ACL information was capable of being cached in the various high-speed caches that the router supported, such as fast switching, autonomous switching, silicon switching, optimum switching, and others. Extended ACLs could be only process-switched, drastically affecting the performance of the router. Therefore, when possible, administrators attempted to use standard ACLs over extended ones, to provide the best possible performance.

Today, however, this is typically not true. With Cisco Express Forwarding (CEF), routers can cache ACL information and process traffic in hardware. However, this requires a router that supports CEF, which many routers do. Therefore, a standard ACL typically is used to restrict traffic to or from the router itself, such as through its VTY lines or routing update contents.

Numbered Standard ACLs

You can group standard ACL statements in two ways: by number or by name. This section covers how to create standard numbered ACLs; the "Named Standard ACLs" section discusses how to create named ACLs. To create a numbered standard ACL, use the following command:

```
Router(config)# access-list ACL_# {permit | deny}
   source_IP_address [wildcard_mask] [log]
```

With this command, you must specify the ACL's number, which can range from 1 to 99 or 1300 to 1999. This number is used to group statements in the same list. By default, when you enter an ACL command for the specified list, it is added at the bottom of the list. Chapter 6 discussed how to edit ACLs. In the later section "Sequenced ACLs," I discuss how you can insert, delete, or modify entries in a specific ACL grouping.

Following the ACL number is the action to take if there is a match on the condition. You can specify only two actions: **permit** or **deny**. Following the action is the condition. With standard ACLs, you can specify only a source address and wildcard mask. The wildcard mask is optional.

TIP   If you omit the wildcard mask in a standard ACL, it defaults to 0.0.0.0—a specific match. If you want to match on all addresses, replace the source address and mask with the keyword **any**.

At the end of the ACL, you optionally can configure the **log** parameter. If you configure this parameter and the Cisco IOS compares a packet and finds a match to the statement, the router logs it to any enabled logging facility, such as the console, the router's internal buffer, or a syslog server.

CAUTION   You cannot delete a specific entry in a numbered ACL unless it is sequenced first, as discussed in the later section "Sequenced ACLs." If you try to delete a specific entry by preceding the command with the **no** parameter, you actually will delete the entire ACL grouping. This applies to all numbered ACLs, both standard and extended.

After you have built your ACL, activate it on your router; until you do this, the ACL will do nothing. You can activate a traffic-filtering standard ACL on your router in two basic ways. If you want to filter traffic as it comes into or leaves an interface, use the following configuration:

```
Router(config)# interface type [slot_#/]port_#
Router(config-if)# ip access-group ACL_#_or_ACL_name {in | out}
```

With the **ip access-group** command, you need to specify the name or number of the ACL and the direction in which the router will filter information:

- **in**—As traffic enters the interface of the router from the network segment
- **out**—As traffic leaves the interface to the network segment

If you want to restrict Telnet or SSH connections to the router, activate the ACL with the following configuration:

```
Router(config)# line type line_#
Router(config-if)# access-class ACL_#_or_ACL_name {in | out}
```

Use the **access-class** command to activate an ACL on a line. This command was discussed in Chapter 3, "Accessing a Router."

Named Standard ACLs

Named ACLs were introduced in Cisco IOS 11.2. Their main advantages over numbered ACLs were these:

- They allowed an administrator to give a descriptive name to the ACL.

- They allowed an administrator to create more than 99 standard or 100 extended ACLs. This was the original limitation put on the number of ACLs that you could create.

- They allowed you to delete a specific entry in an ACL.

Today you can use other methods to do these three things besides using a named ACL. For example, you can give a description to an ACL with a remark, as discussed later in the "ACL Remarks" section. Today's standard IP ACLs also support numbers from 1 to 99 and 1300 to 1999, allowing for almost 700 ACL groupings. Therefore, named ACLs do not have any real advantage (or disadvantage) over numbered ACLs. Named ACLs still have two main advantages: They support a descriptive name, and, with the introduction of sequenced ACLS, discussed later in the "Sequenced ACLs" section, you can insert and delete specific ACL entries.

NOTE   In most situations, determining whether you want to use named or numbered ACLs is personal preference. In some instances, however, you might have to use one over another, based on any ACL extensions that you might want to add. For example, reflexive ACLs, discussed in Chapter 8, "Reflexive Access Lists," require the use of named extended ACLs. Other than implementing specific features, there is no real difference between the two types. I grew up on numbered ACLs, so I use them in most instances.

To create a named standard IP ACL, use the following configuration:

```
Router(config)# ip access-list standard name_of_ACL
Router(config-std-nacl)# deny {source [src_wildcard] | any} [log]
Router(config-std-nacl)# permit {source [src_wildcard] | any} [log]
Router(config-std-nacl)# exit
```

The first thing that you must do is specify the type of named ACL (**standard**) and the name of the ACL in the **ip access-list** command. The name actually can be a number, such as 50, but a name is more descriptive.

Executing this command takes you into a subconfiguration mode. Here you enter your **permit** and **deny** commands, which have the same basic syntax as those in the numbered standard IP **access-list** commands. Note that you can delete a specific entry in a named ACL by going into ACL subconfiguration mode and prefacing the command with the **no** parameter.

When you are done entering your ACL statements, activate the ACL on an interface with the **ip access-group** command, specifying the name of the ACL. This was discussed in the last section, "Numbered Standard ACLs." If you want to filter traffic destined to the VTYs of your router, you cannot use the **ip access-group** command to activate the ACL on the VTYs. Instead, you need to use the **access-class** command, discussed in Chapter 3.

Standard ACL Examples

Now that you have a basic understanding of the syntax of commands to create standard IP ACLs, you can take a look at a couple of examples to illustrate how they are configured. In the first example, I show you how to restrict VTY access on your router using, as an example, the network shown in Figure 7-1. In this example, only the two administrator PCs should be allowed access. Example 7-1 shows the configuration.

Figure 7-1 *Restricting VTY Access*

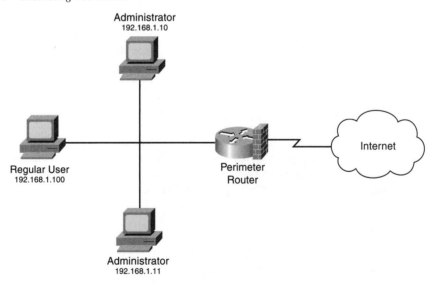

Example 7-1 *Restricting VTY Access with a Standard Numbered ACL*

```
Router(config)# access-list 1 permit 192.168.1.10
Router(config)# access-list 1 permit 192.168.1.11
Router(config)# line vty 0 4
Router(config-line)# access-class 1 in
```

In this example, notice that I omitted the wildcard mask. Whenever you omit the wildcard mask for a standard IP ACL, as I mentioned in Chapter 6, it defaults to 0.0.0.0—an exact match.

Example 7-2 shows the same configuration for Figure 7-1, except that it uses a named ACL.

Example 7-2 *Restricting VTY Access with a Standard Named ACL*

```
Router(config)# ip access-list standard restrict_VTY
Router(config-std-nacl)# permit 192.168.1.10
Router(config-std-nacl)# permit 192.168.1.11
Router(config-std-nacl)# exit
Router(config)# line vty 0 4
Router(config-line)# access-class restrict_VTY in
```

Either of the two configuration methods—numbered or named ACLs—will work.

Extended ACLs

Extended IP ACLS are much more flexible than standard ACLs because their conditions can match on many more criteria in a packet or segment header. I have divided this section into two subsections: numbered and named extended IP ACLs. Within the numbered section, I discuss some common types of extended IP ACLs, such as TCP, UDP, and fragmented packets.

Numbered Extended ACLs

Numbered extended IP ACLs were introduced in Cisco IOS 10.0. Here is the basic syntax of creating a numbered extended ACL statement:

```
Router(config)# access-list ACL_# {deny | permit} protocol_name_or_#
   source_IP_address source_wildcard_mask destination_IP_address
   destination_wildcard [protocol_options] [precedence precedence] [dscp value]
   [tos tos] [log | log-input] [fragments] [established]
```

To build an extended IP ACL statement, use the **access-list** command. The first parameter that you need to specify is the ACL number, which groups the ACL statements. IP extended ACLs can have numbers from 100 to 199 and 2000 to 2699. Following this is the name or number of the TCP/IP protocol. Here is a list of protocol names supported by the Cisco IOS:

- **ahp**—Authentication Header Protocol
- **eigrp**—The Cisco EIGRP routing protocol
- **esp**—Encapsulation Security Payload
- **gre**—Cisco GRE tunneling
- **icmp**—Internet Control Message Protocol
- **igmp**—Internet Gateway Message Protocol
- **ip**—Any Internet Protocol
- **ipinip**—IP in IP tunneling
- **nos**—KA9Q NOS–compatible IP over IP tunneling

- **ospf**—OSPF routing protocol
- **pcp**—Payload Compression Protocol
- **pim**—Protocol Independent Multicast
- **tcp**—Transmission Control Protocol
- **udp**—User Datagram Protocol

If the name of the protocol that you want to filter is not listed, you can enter the number; protocol numbers range from 0 to 255.

TIP   To match on any IP protocol, use the **ip** protocol keyword.

Following the protocol name or number is the source and destination addressing information. Unlike standard IP ACLs, with extended IP ACLs, you must specify both the source and destination addresses, as well as their corresponding wildcard masks.

TIP   In an extended IP ACL, if the wildcard mask for an address is 0.0.0.0 (exact match), the router converts it to this syntax: **host** *IP_address*. Either syntax is valid; just remember that the router performs this conversion automatically.

The rest of the information is optional. For a specific protocol, such as TCP, UDP, ICMP, and others, protocol options can be supplied to refine the condition further, assuming that the protocol supports options. I discuss these options for TCP, UDP, and ICMP in the following subsections.

The **precedence** parameter (optional) enables you to filter on a specific precedence level, ranging from 0 to 7. This field in the IP packet header typically is used to classify traffic for Quality of Service (QoS) and queuing purposes. Here is a list of names that you can use for the level instead of specifying a number:

- **critical** (0)
- **flash** (1)
- **flash-override** (2)
- **immediate** (3)
- **internet** (4)
- **network** (5)
- **priority** (6)
- **routine** (7)

The **dscp** parameter (optional) enables you to filter on the Differentiated Services Code Points (DSCPs) value in an IP packet header. DSCP is used to implement QoS by prioritizing traffic. You can specify either a value from 0 to 63 or the DSCP code name.

The **tos** parameter (optional) enables you to filter on the Type of Service field in the IP packet header. This IP option sometimes is used to implement QoS. This can be a number from 1 to 15 or the name of the service:

- **max-reliability**
- **max-throughput**
- **min-delay**
- **min-monetary-cost**
- **normal**

The optional **log** parameter causes the Cisco IOS to log a match on the condition to whatever logging facility has been enabled (console, internal buffer, and/or syslog server). The information logged includes the following:

- The action: permit or deny
- The protocol, such as TCP, UDP, or ICMP
- The source and destination addresses
- For TCP and UDP, the source and destination port numbers
- For ICMP, the message types

Log messages are generated on the first packet match and then on 5-minute intervals after that on packet matches. This is to ensure that a Denial of Service (DoS) attack does not overrun the router's logging function. You can change the update interval with the **ip access-list log-update** command, as covered later in the "Logging Updates" section.

CAUTION   Enabling the **log** (or **log-input**) parameter on a router disables CEF switching, seriously impacting the performance of your router. When logging is enabled, packets are either process- or fast-switched. Therefore, use this only if you are under a network attack and are trying to determine the culprit. In this instance, enable logging for the period for which you need to gather the appropriate information, and then disable logging.

The optional **log-input** command includes the input interface of the received packet and the Layer 2 source address in the packet, such as an Ethernet MAC address, a frame relay DLCI number, or a ATM VC number.

I discuss the optional **established** keyword in the "TCP" subsection, and I discuss the optional **fragments** parameter in the "Fragments and Extended ACLs" subsection.

When you are done entering your ACL statements, activate the ACL on an interface with the **ip access-group** command, specifying the name of the ACL. This was discussed in the "Numbered Standard ACLs" section.

TCP

You can filter TCP traffic with the following ACL statement:

```
Router(config)# access-list ACL_# {deny | permit} tcp
   source_IP_address source_wildcard_mask [operator src_port_name_or_number]
   destination_IP_address destination_wildcard [operator dest_port_name_or_number]
   [log | log-input] [precedence precedence] [dscp value] [tos tos] [fragments]
   [established] [ack] [fin] [psh] [rst] [syn] [urg]
```

For filtering TCP traffic, use the **tcp** keyword for the protocol parameter. This is followed by the source and destination addresses and wildcard masks. Optionally, you can match on source or destination port numbers. To match on a port number for an address, you must specify an operator and then a port name or number. Here is a list of operators that you can specify:

- **eq**—Must match exactly this port name or number
- **lt**—Must be lower than this port name or number
- **gt**—Must be greater than this port name or number
- **neq**—Must not be equal to this port name or number
- **range**—Must be within the specified inclusive range, where the beginning and ending port name or numbers are separated by a space, like this: 22 23.

If you specify an operator, you must follow it with a TCP port name or number. Table 7-1 lists the TCP port names supported on the router. If you do not find the name of the TCP port in Table 7-1 that you need to filter, specify the number instead. Numbers range from 0 to 65,535, where 0 represents all TCP ports.

Table 7-1   *TCP Port Names*

Name	Port Number	Description
bgp	179	Border Gateway Protocol
chargen	19	Character generator
cmd	514	Remote commands (rcmd)
daytime	13	Daytime
discard	9	Discard
domain	53	Domain Name System zone transfers
echo	7	Echo
exec	512	Remote commands/shell (rsh)

continues

Table 7-1   *TCP Port Names (Continued)*

Name	Port Number	Description
finger	79	Finger
ftp	21	File Transfer Protocol control channel
ftp-data	20	FTP data channel
gopher	70	Gopher
hostname	101	NIC host name server
ident	113	Ident protocol
irc	194	Internet Relay Chat
klogin	543	Kerberos login
kshell	544	Kerberos shell
login	513	Remote login (rlogin)
lpd	515	Remote printing
nntp	119	Network News Transport Protocol
pim-auto-rp	496	PIM Auto Rendezvous Point
pop2	109	Post Office Protocol v2
pop3	110	Post Office Protocol v3
smtp	25	Simple Mail Transport Protocol
sunrpc	111	Sun remote-procedure call
syslog	514	Logging to a syslog server
tacacs	49	TAC access control system server connection
talk	517	Talk
telnet	23	Telnet
time	37	Time
uucp	540	UNIX-to-UNIX copy program
whois	43	Nickname
www	80	World Wide Web (HTTP)
	0 to 65,535	Valid port numbers

One additional parameter that can be used with TCP connections is the **established** keyword. Basically, this allows return replies from established connections. This means that if you have an inbound ACL on your perimeter router, protecting you from the Internet, TCP traffic that your users send out will be allowed back in. The **established** keyword looks to see if the ACK, FIN, PSH, RST, SYN, or URG set TCP control flags are set. If they are, the TCP traffic is allowed in; if not, the Cisco IOS assumes that this is a new connection and does not match on this statement.

CAUTION	Many administrators think that using the **established** keyword implements a stateful firewall on a router. This cannot be further from the truth. All the **established** parameter does is allow any TCP segments with the appropriate control flag or flags set: If they are set, the action is executed (permit or deny). The parameter does not look to see if this is returning traffic from a connection that was initiated from inside your network. Remember that standard and extended ACLS are plain packet filters and do not maintain state information. Therefore, if you use the **established** keyword to allow returning traffic into your network, you are opening a large hole in your perimeter router. Hackers can take advantage of this hole by using a packet generator/scanner to sneak TCP packets into your network by hiding them as returning traffic. Hackers accomplish this by using packet-generator tools and setting the appropriate bit or bits in the TCP control field. Some packet-generator products that I use include hping, nmap, nemesis, and lcrzoex, but there are dozens out there. Some are available for Windows platforms, but most were developed for UNIX-based platforms. I highly recommend that you download and try out these tools; especially to test the packet filters that you configure on your router.

Where the **established** keyword looks for a specific control flag or flags in the TCP segment header, you can be more specific and filter on just a single control flag, including **ack**, **fin**, **psh**, **rst**, **syn**, and **urg**. The rest of the parameters for TCP ACL statements were discussed at the beginning of this section.

UDP

You can filter UDP traffic with the following ACL statement:

```
Router(config)# access-list ACL_# {deny | permit} udp
    source_IP_address source_wildcard_mask [operator src_port_name_or_number]
    destination_IP_address destination_wildcard [operator dest_port_name_or_number]
    [log | log-input] [precedence precedence] [dscp value] [tos tos] [fragments]
```

For filtering UDP traffic, use the **udp** keyword for the protocol parameter. This is followed by the source and destination addresses and wildcard masks. Optionally, you can match on source or destination port numbers. To match on a port number for an address, you must specify an operator and then a port name or number. The operators are the same as those used by TCP, discussed in the previous section.

If you specify an operator, you must follow it with a UDP port name or number. Table 7-2 lists the UDP port names supported on the router. If you do not find the name of the

UDP port in Table 7-2 that you need to filter, specify the number instead. Numbers range from 0 to 65,535, where 0 represents all UDP ports.

Table 7-2   *UDP Port Names*

Name	Port Number	Description
biff	512	Biff mail notification and comsat
bootpc	68	BootP client
bootps	67	BootP server
discard	9	Discard
dnsix	195	DNSIX security protocol auditing
domain	53	DNS queries and replies
echo	7	Echo
isakmp	500	Internet Security Association and Key Management Protocol
mobile-ip	434	Mobile IP registration
nameserver	42	IEN116 name service, which is now obsolete
netbios-dgm	138	NetBIOS datagram service
netbios-nm	137	NetBIOS name service
netbios-ss	139	NetBIOS session service
non500-isakmp	4500	ISAKMP on nonstandard port
ntp	123	Network Time Protocol
pim-auto-rp	496	PIM Auto Rendezvous Point
rip	520	Routing Information Protocol
snmp	161	Simple Network Management Protocol
snmptrap	162	SNMP traps
sunrpc	111	Sun remote-procedure calls
syslog	514	Remote logging of messages
tacacs	49	TAC Access Control System
talk	517	Talk
tftp	69	Trivial File Transfer Protocol
time	37	Time
who	513	Remote who service (rwho)
xdmcp	177	X Display Manager Control Protocol
	0 to 65,535	Valid port numbers

The one main difference between UDP and TCP is that UDP is connectionless. Thus, the **established** keyword and the TCP code flag parameters are not valid when configuring a UDP ACL statement.

ICMP

You can filter ICMP traffic with the following ACL statement:

```
Router(config)# access-list ACL_# {deny | permit} icmp
    source_IP_address source_wildcard_mask
    destination_IP_address destination_wildcard [ICMP_message_type_or_#]
    [log | log-input] [precedence precedence] [dscp value] [tos tos] [fragments]
```

For filtering ICMP traffic, use the **icmp** keyword for the protocol parameter. This is followed by the source and destination addresses and wildcard masks. Optionally, you can match on ICMP message types. Unlike TCP and UDP, there is no operator to specify a match; instead, you just configure the specific ICMP message type. If you omit the message type, it defaults to matching on any ICMP message type. To specify a message type, configure either the name of the message or its number. Table 7-3 lists the ICMP message type names supported on the router. If you do not find the name of the ICMP message type in Table 7-3 that you need to filter, specify the number instead. Numbers range from 0 to 255, where 0 represents all ICMP messages.

Table 7-3 *ICMP Messages*

Name	Description
administratively-prohibited	Administratively prohibited (packet was filtered)
alternate-address	Alternate IP address
conversion-error	Packet-conversion error
dod-host-prohibited	Host prohibited in Department of Defense network
dod-net-prohibited	Network prohibited in Department of Defense network
echo	Echo request (ping)
echo-reply	Echo reply
general-parameter-problem	Message parameter problem
host-isolated	Host isolated
host-precedence-unreachable precedence_value	Host unreachable for the given precedence value
host-redirect	Host redirect message
host-tos-redirect	Host redirect for ToS
host-tos-unreachable	Host unreachable for a given ToS
host-unknown	Host unknown
host-unreachable	Host unreachable

continues

Table 7-3   *ICMP Messages (Continued)*

Name	Description
information-reply	Reply to information
information-request	Request for information
mask-reply	Subnet mask reply message
mask-request	Subnet mask request message
mobile-redirect	Mobile host redirect message
net-redirect	Network redirect message
net-tos-redirect	Network redirect for ToS
net-tos-unreachable	Network unreachable for ToS
net-unreachable	Network unreachable
network-unknown	Network unknown
no-room-for-option	ICMP parameter required, but no space in the packet header
option-missing	ICMP parameter required, but not present in the packet header
packet-too-big	Fragmentation needed on the packet, and the DF bit is set
parameter-problem	All parameter problems for ICMP
port-unreachable	Port not available
precedence-unreachable	Precedence cutoff
protocol-unreachable	Protocol not running on the destination
reassembly-timeout	Reassembly timeout
redirect	All ICMP redirect messages
router-advertisement	Router-discovery advertisements (IRDP)
router-solicitation	Router-discovery solicitations (IRDP)
source-quench	Source quenches to throttle throughput
source-route-failed	Source routing failed
time-exceeded	All ICMP time exceeded messages
time-range	Specification of a time range
timestamp-reply	ICMP time-stamp reply messages
timestamp-request	ICMP time-stamp request messages
traceroute	Traceroute messages
ttl-exceeded	TTL in the IP packet header exceeded
unreachable	All ICMP unreachable messages
0 to 255	ICMP message type number

Named Extended ACLs

Besides using numbers to reference extended ACLs, you can use names. Named extended ACLs were introduced in Cisco IOS 11.2. Here is the general syntax of a named extended ACL:

```
Router(config)# ip access-list extended ACL_name
Router(config-ext-nacl)# {deny | permit} protocol_name_or_#
   source_IP_address source_wildcard_mask
   destination_IP_address destination_wildcard [protocol_options]
   [precedence precedence] [dscp value] [tos tos]
   [log | log-input] [fragments] [established]
```

To create a named extended ACL, use the **ip access-list extended** command, followed by the name of the ACL. When you execute this command, you are taken into a subconfiguration mode where you enter your **permit** or **deny** statements. At this point, the syntax is the same as a numbered ACL, with the same options being supported.

Remember that you can delete a specific entry in a named ACL by going into ACL subconfiguration mode and prefacing the command with the **no** parameter.

Extended ACL Examples

To help you understand the configuration of ACLs, take a look at a couple of examples. The first example uses a router with two interfaces; the second uses a router with three interfaces.

Two-Interface Router Example

The first example uses a network with a simple setup, as shown in Figure 7-2. In this example, the router has two interfaces: ethernet0 is the internal interface, and ethernet1 is the external interface.

Figure 7-2   *Simple Extended ACL Example*

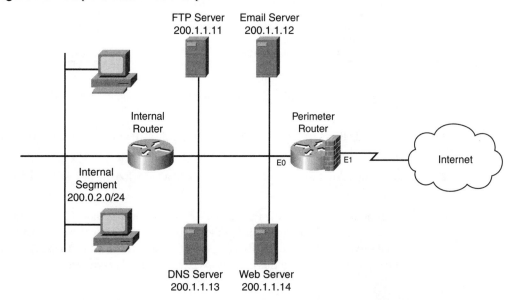

In Figure 7-2, the security policies are as follows:

- Allow web traffic to the internal web server
- Allow DNS queries to the internal DNS server
- Allow e-mail to be sent from Internet users to the internal e-mail server
- Allow FTP control connection from the Internet to the internal FTP server, as well as the data connection in an active, or standard, FTP connection
- Allow the internal users to access external DNS servers and web servers only
- Deny all other types of traffic

Example 7-3 shows the ACL configuration to accomplish these policies.

Example 7-3 *Using an Extended ACL to Implement a Two-Interface Router Solution*

```
Router(config)# access-list 100 permit tcp any              (1)
  host 200.1.1.14 eq 80
Router(config)# access-list 100 permit udp any              (2)
  host 200.1.1.13 eq 53
Router(config)# access-list 100 permit tcp any              (3)
  host 200.1.1.12 eq 25
Router(config)# access-list 100 permit tcp any eq 25
  host 200.1.1.12 established
Router(config)# access-list 100 permit tcp any              (4)
  host 200.1.1.11 eq 21
Router(config)# access-list 100 permit tcp any              (5)
  host 200.1.1.11 eq 20
Router(config)# access-list 100 permit tcp any eq 80        (6)
  200.1.2.0 0.0.0.255 established
Router(config)# access-list 100 permit udp any eq 53        (7)
  200.1.2.0 0.0.0.255
Router(config)# access-list 100 deny ip any any             (8)
Router(config)# interface ethernet1
Router(config-if)# ip access-group 100 in                   (9)
```

Take a look at this access list with reference to the numbering on the right side of Example 7-3:

1 This command allows traffic from anywhere to reach TCP port 80 of the web server (200.1.1.14).

2 This command allows traffic from anywhere to do a DNS lookup to UDP port 53 on 200.1.1.13.

3 The first command allows traffic from anywhere to send an e-mail to TCP port 25 on 200.1.1.12; the second command allows the internal e-mail server to send e-mail to external servers and get replies. Reading this statement is confusing to many users. Remember that the source, in this case, is an external e-mail server, and because

the internal server initiated the connection to port 25 on the Internet e-mail server, the source port will be 25 when the Internet server responds.

4 This command allows traffic from anywhere to set up a control connection to TCP port 21 on the FTP server.

5 This command allows the Internet user to use the FTP data port, TCP 20 (set up from the server to the Internet user), if the traffic is destined to 200.1.1.11. One problem with this ACL is that, normally, the control connection is set up first from the client to the server, and then the server sets up the data connection to the client; however, this ACL allows data connections without a corresponding control connection, which represents a security risk. This can be overcome by using a stateful firewall, such as CBAC, instead of a standard packet filter.

6 Notice in this command that the source port is TCP 80. This command allows the returning traffic from external web servers to the internal users. I also added the **established** command to provide an extra level of protection.

7 This command allows any DNS queries sent to external servers to return to the internal users. The source port is UDP 53, which is traffic coming from (the source) external DNS servers.

8 The **deny any any** command is not necessary, but I always put it in to remind me of the implicit deny at the end of the list. Plus, you can see the hit count when you display the ACL with the **show [ip] access-list** command.

9 The **ip access-group** command activates the ACL inbound on the external interface—the interface connected to the Internet.

In this example, for internal users sending traffic and allowing the replies back in, a stateful firewall, such as the use of CBAC in the Cisco IOS, would be a much better solution than the one given here (Steps 5, 6, and 7). I discuss CBAC in Chapter 9, "Context-Based Access Control."

NOTE   You can configure polices using an extended ACL in one of two ways. One approach is to use two ACLs on the external interface, with one applied inbound and the other applied outbound. You also could use two ACLs on the internal interface, with one applied inbound and the other applied outbound. I typically like to put as much as possible into a single ACL because it makes troubleshooting easier.

Three-Interface Router Example

The second example uses the network shown in Figure 7-3. Notice that this example is more complicated than that shown in Figure 7-2. In this example, the router has three interfaces: internal (ethernet0), external (ethernet1), and dmz (ethernet2).

Figure 7-3 *Complex Extended ACL Example*

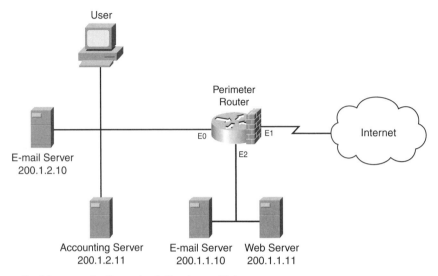

In this example, I use the following policies:

- Users from the Internet can access web pages in the DMZ web server.

- Users from the Internet can send e-mail to the SMTP server in the DMZ.

- The DMZ SMTP server can forward mail to the internal server, but no other traffic can originate from this segment to the internal network.

- Internal users should be able to perform DNS queries.

- Internal users should be able to access both servers in the DMZ.

- Internal users should be able to access all TCP services in the Internet.

Example 7-4 shows the ACL configuration to accomplish these policies.

Example 7-4 *Using an Extended ACL to Implement a Three-Interface Router Solution*

```
Router(config)# access-list 100 deny ip any                    (1)
  200.1.2.10 0.0.0.1
Router(config)# access-list 100 permit tcp any                 (2)
  host 200.1.1.11 eq 80
Router(config)# access-list 100 permit tcp any                 (3)
  host 200.1.1.10 eq 25
Router(config)# access-list 100 permit tcp any eq 25           (4)
  host 200.1.1.10 any established
Router(config)# access-list 100 permit tcp any                 (5)
  200.1.2.0 0.0.0.255 established
Router(config)# access-list 100 permit udp any eq 53           (6)
  200.1.2.0 0.0.0.255
Router(config)# access-list 100 deny ip any any                (7)
Router(config)# interface ethernet 1
Router(config-if)# ip access-group 100 in                      (8)
Router(config-if)# exit
```

Example 7-4 *Using an Extended ACL to Implement a Three-Interface Router Solution (Continued)*

```
Router(config)# access-list 101 deny ip any              (9)
  host 200.1.2.11
Router(config)# access-list 101 permit tcp any           (10)
  200.1.2.0 0.0.0.255 established
Router(config)# access-list 101 permit udp any eq 53     (11)
  200.1.2.0 0.0.0.255
Router(config)# access-list 101 permit tcp host 200.1.1.10   (12)
  host 200.1.2.10 eq 25
Router(config)# access-list 101 permit tcp host 200.1.1.10 eq 25 (13)
  host 200.1.2.10 established
Router(config)# access-list 101 deny ip any any          (14)
Router(config)# interface ethernet 0
Router(config-if)# ip access-group 101 out               (15)
Router(config-if)# exit
```

In Example 7-4, I have created two ACLs. ACL 100 is used to filter traffic to the internal network, and ACL 101 is used to filter traffic from the Internet and the DMZ to the internal segment. Compared to Example 7-3, Example 7-4 is more difficult to implement; as in Example 7-3, there is more than one solution to implement your security policies. I have broken down the policies into steps, with reference to the numbering on the right side of Example 7-4:

1 All Internet traffic is denied from reaching the internal Accounting server and the e-mail server. This is necessary because of Step 5, which allows all TCP returning traffic to the internal network. This step prevents any traffic to the Accounting and e-mail server, including returning TCP traffic and DNS replies (Step 6).

2 This step allows Internet users to request web pages from the DMZ web server.

3 This step allows external users and servers to send e-mail traffic to the DMZ web server.

4 This step allows the DMZ e-mail server to get replies to e-mail that it has sent to external e-mail servers, as long as the correct TCP flag or flags are set (**established** keyword).

5 This statement allows any returning TCP traffic to be forwarded to the inside users who requested it (except the Accounting and internal e-mail server, which was filtered in Step 1).

6 This statement allows DNS replies to be forwarded to internal users who sent DNS queries (except the internal accounting and e-mail server, which was filtered in Step 1).

7 This statement drops all remaining traffic (not necessary because the implicit deny is enforced).

8 ACL 100 is applied inbound on the interface facing the Internet.

9 ACL 101 is used to filter traffic from the DMZ and Internet to the internal segment. This statement prevents any traffic from being sent to the Accounting server.

10 This statement allows the replies of TCP connections that internal users requested to be forwarded back to them from the Internet (except the Accounting server, which was filtered in Step 9). Even though this was done in Step 1 in ACL 100, this step is necessary to prevent DMZ traffic from accessing the Accounting server.

11 This statement allows DNS replies to be forwarded to the internal users (except the Accounting server—see Step 9).

12 This statement allows the DMZ e-mail server to forward e-mail to the internal e-mail server.

13 This statement allows the internal server to forward e-mail to the DMZ server and to allow the responses back.

14 This drops all remaining traffic (not necessary because the implicit deny is enforced).

15 This activates ACL 101 as traffic comes from either the Internet or the DMZ interfaces and exits ethernet0, the internal interface.

The biggest problem in this example and the previous one is trying to implement a secure "stateful" function using packet filters. In a large network, this is either impractical or impossible. For instance, this example allows only returning TCP traffic; UDP traffic presents a problem. However, the assumption in this example is that internal users basically are using HTTP (TCP) and DNS (UDP), which are allowed.

TIP When you need to allow returning traffic into your network, using the **established** keyword, opening a specific source port, or opening a range of ports, makes you vulnerable to spoofing and DoS attacks. Therefore, I highly recommend that you use a stateful firewall function. As you will see in Chapters 8 and 9, with the Cisco IOS, you can use these two features to implement stateful features to allow returning traffic and still use extended ACLs to filter traffic originating from devices.

Therefore, use the previous examples as just that: examples in packet-filtering practice. Do not use this solution to allow returning traffic.

ACL Verification

When you have completed the configuration (**access-list** or **ip access-list standard | extended**) and activation of your ACLs (**ip access-group**), you are ready to verify your router's configuration and operation. Use the following command to list your ACLs and the statements that they contain:

```
Router> show [protocol_name] access-list [ACL_#_or_name]
```

If you enter only **show access-list**, all ACLs from all protocols are displayed, as in Example 7-5.

Example 7-5   *Using the* **show access-list** *Command*

```
Router# show access-list
Extended IP access list 109
  permit tcp 172.16.0.0 0.0.255.255 any established (189 matches)
  permit udp host 172.16.1.39 any eq domain (32 matches)
  permit icmp host 199.199.199.1 any (98 matches)
  deny ip any any (1237 matches)
IPX sap access list 1000
 deny FFFFFFFF 7
 permit FFFFFFFF 0
```

In this example, there is an extended numbered IP ACL and an IPX SAP filter (1000). If you want to view only ACLs from a specific protocol, specify the protocol, like this: **show ip access-list**. You even can be more restrictive by adding the name or number of the ACL.

I want to point out two important items in Example 7-5. First, notice that at the end of each ACL statement is a list of the number of matches that the Cisco IOS found when comparing packets to the ACL. This gives you information that your ACL has been activated on your interface and is filtering traffic. Second, notice that I manually configured the **deny ip any any** statement at the end of the list. I configured this statement so that I could see how many packets the Cisco IOS was dropping.

TIP   Any matches on the implicit deny statement are not logged and are not recorded as a match, by default. If you want to record matches, manually configure a deny all statement at the end of the ACL. I typically use this and keep a record of the number of matches on statements daily. If I see something radically different from the average, I typically inspect it to see if there is a security issue related to the anomaly.

If you want to log dropped packets, add the **log** keyword to your manually configured **deny** statement. Remember my caution, though, about using the logging feature and the impact that it has on the router's switching capabilities. Do this only to troubleshoot problems or to examine a security incident more closely.

To reset the counters that you see in the **show access-list** command, use the **clear access-list counters** command:

```
Router# clear access-list counters [ACL_#_or_name]
```

If you do not specify a specific ACL name or number, all counters for all ACLs are cleared.

If you want to see if an IP ACL is applied to an interface, use the **show ip interfaces** command:

```
Router> show ip interface [interface_name_and_#]
```

You can restrict the output of this command by specifying a particular interface. Example 7-6 shows sample output of this command.

Example 7-6 *Using the* **show ip interface** *Command*

```
Router# show ip interface fastethernet0
FastEthernet0 is up, line protocol is up
  Internet address is 192.168.1.254/24
  Broadcast address is 255.255.255.255
  Address determined by non-volatile memory
  MTU is 1500 bytes
  Helper address is not set
  Directed broadcast forwarding is disabled
  Outgoing access list is not set
  Inbound  access list is 100
<--output omitted-->
```

As you can see in this example, an extended ACL has been applied inbound on the interface fastethernet0.

Fragments and Extended ACLs

Fragments are used when the data cannot fit into the configured payload size. Typically this occurs when packets cross over between media types that use different maximum MTUs, such as token ring to Ethernet. A large packet is broken into two or more smaller packets to meet the maximum configured MTU size. There is no real restriction on how many times fragmentation can occur because it is performed on a hop-by-hop basis. The main problem with fragmentation is that it is process intensive: An intermediate device must break up the original packet into fragments, and then the destination must reassemble them.

Fragmentation Process

As an example, assume that you create a TCP segment that is 1600-bytes long and has been forwarded to a next-hop address in an IP packet. The next-hop device does not support this MTU size on the next hop, so it fragments the original packet into two or more fragments. The first, or initial, fragment is the first part of the original segment. However, the subsequent (noninitial) fragments look different.

NOTE   The first fragment has a fragment-offset value of 0. Subsequent, or noninitial, fragments have a fragment offset that is greater than 0.

In this example, the first fragment contains the TCP header and part of the data. However, the second and subsequent fragments carry only the remainder of the TCP data. This presents a problem because, when the destination receives the fragments, it knows that the first one is for a specific TCP port number, but it does not know about the port number in the remaining fragments. Plus, if the fragments are received out of order, the destination has an issue with the reassembly process.

To overcome these problems, the IP headers in all these fragments are marked as fragments. The identification field in the IP header is assigned a unique identifier for the fragments of the original packet, which helps the destination determine what protocol and port this should be forwarded to. The flags field is used to mark the fragment as either the beginning or middle part of the fragment, or the last fragment in a packet. The fragment offset field is used to mark where in the reassembly process the fragment fits into the total (completed) packet.

Fragmentation and Filtering Issues

The process that fragmentation uses can pose problems with how packet-filtering devices process packets. In this example, assume that the data being fragmented is a TCP port 80 (web) connection. The first fragment lists the IP protocol (TCP) and contains the TCP header, with port 80 as the destination. The second fragment lists the IP protocol (TCP) but does not list the port number. The TCP header was in the first fragment, and the remaining TCP data is in the second fragment. With the second fragment, a packet-filtering router or firewall knows that this is a TCP fragment, but it does not know what the port number is. How should the packet-filtering firewall treat these fragments?

With a stateful firewall, this would be easier because if a stateful firewall was set up to do so, it could keep track of the identification field and allow subsequent fragments into its interface based on the receipt of the TCP 80 fragment first. However, there is no guarantee that the first fragment will be received first. In this instance, what would happen if the second fragment arrived before the first? The stateful firewall would lack information about the connection. It could buffer fragments of a packet to determine whether they were all part of the same connection, but this requires extra resources on the firewall.

The most common solution is to allow the fragments into the network. The assumption made here is that these fragments must be part of a valid connection. Unfortunately, hackers can take advantage of this assumption and create a DoS attack by flooding your network with fragments. If your packet-filtering firewall assumes that fragments are part of a valid connection, basically any fragment, whether it is or is not a true fragment, is allowed. This can be a dangerous assumption. With a brute-force approach, a hacker just floods garbage fragments into your network that cannot be reassembled. A more intelligent hacker uses fragments that are reassembled into a valid packet, which requires more resources to process.

You can use three solutions to deal with fragmentation with your Cisco IOS:

- Use packet filters.
- Use CBAC (discussed in Chapter 9, "Context-Based Access Control").
- Use IDS shunning (discussed in Chapter 16, "Intrusion-Detection System").

All three of these solutions have advantages and disadvantages. In the following section, I discuss how you can use extended ACLs to filter packet fragments.

NOTE   RFC 1858 discusses security issues related to fragments.

Filtering Fragments

You can filter fragments for packets by using the **fragments** keyword in your extended ACL statement. Fragment filtering requires Cisco IOS versions 12.0(11) or 12.1(2) or later.

This keyword works with both numbered and named extended ACLs. Here is the syntax for a numbered ACL:

```
Router(config)# access-list ACL_# {deny | permit} IP_protocol
  source_IP_address source_wildcard_mask
  destination_IP_address destination_wildcard [log | log-input]
  [precedence precedence] [dscp value] [tos tos] fragments
```

When filtering fragments, noninitial fragments that match Layer 3 information in your ACL have the appropriate action taken against them: **permit** or **deny**. No Layer 4 information can be filtered, with the exception of the IP protocol, when filtering fragments in an ACL statement.

NOTE   By using the **fragments** keyword, only noninitial fragments are filtered: The first fragment of a packet, or packets that are not fragmented, will not match this condition. Also, with TCP and UDP, you cannot include Layer 4 information, such as port numbers, when using the **fragments** keyword. As you recall from the "Fragmentation and Filtering Issues" section, this information is not noted in noninitial fragments of a packet. Basically, only Layer 3 header information can be used in a condition. As an example, you can use the **fragments** keyword with ICMP and ICMP message types because ICMP is a Layer 3 protocol.

In this example, all IP fragments are dropped:

```
Router(config)# access-list 100 deny ip any any fragments
Router(config)# ! <rest of ACL statements in ACL 100>
```

When setting up a grouping of ACL statements, you should deny fragments at the top or toward the top of you list, and put your specific **permit** statements below them. This is especially true of internal firewalls, where you are denying specific types of access but permitting all other types.

TIP   You want to make sure that a **permit** statement in an ACL does not inadvertently permit fragments. Therefore, the fragment ACL statements are placed at the top of the list.

In this example, only TCP, UDP, and ICMP fragments are dropped:

```
Router(config)# access-list 100 deny tcp any any fragments
Router(config)# access-list 100 deny udp any any fragments
Router(config)# access-list 100 deny icmp any any fragments
Router(config)# ! <rest of ACL statements in ACL 100>
```

In this example, only TCP, UDP, and ICMP fragments are dropped, allowing other types of fragments into the router. Note that this is less secure than the first example. Even though TCP, UDP, and ICMP are the most common protocols that hackers use for DoS fragment attacks, other protocols, such as IGMP, have been exploited in the past.

When setting up ACL filters, if you do not specify that fragments should be filtered, certain rules apply to whether the fragments are permitted or denied. First, if you have an ACL statement with only Layer 3 information in it, such as the source and destination addresses and the IP protocol type (IP, TCP, ICMP, UDP, and so on), both nonfragmented, initial fragments and noninitial fragments can match against the configured condition.

If you have an ACL statement with both Layers 3 and 4 information, such as TCP or UDP port numbers, a different process is used:

- If the packet is a nonfragmented packet or an initial fragment from a packet and the condition matches, the action (**permit** or **deny**) is applied.

- If the packet is a noninitial fragment from a packet and the condition matches and the action is **permit**, the fragment is permitted. However, if the condition matches and the action is **deny**, the next ACL statement in the list is processed.

CAUTION   As you can see from this last point, the **deny** keyword in an ACL statement does not drop fragments; it drops only nonfragmented packets and the initial fragment in a packet. This is important to remember because the default action of ACLs is to allow fragments. Therefore, if you want to deny traffic from a specify device, you need two **deny** statements: one to deny nonfragmented packets and the initial packet in a fragment (not using the **fragments** keyword), and one to deny the noninitial fragments (using the **fragments** keyword). This is definitely true if you are using Cisco IOS versions earlier than 12.0(11) or 12.1(2).

Newer versions of the Cisco IOS, however, have fixed this security hole and allow the implicit deny statement to drop noninitial fragments that do not match any of the statements in the ACL grouping. In either case, I recommend following the more secure path and always specify whether fragments are permitted or denied.

Fragment Filtering Example

Take a look at a couple of examples that filter traffic to see how fragments are affected. These use the network shown in Figure 7-4.

Figure 7-4 *FTP and Fragments Example*

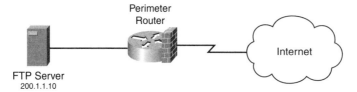

In Example 7-7, you want to allow Internet users to access an internal FTP server, so you configure the following ACL:

Example 7-7 *Configuring a Simple ACL to Allow FTP Traffic*

```
Router(config)# access-list 100 permit tcp any host 200.1.1.10 eq 21
Router(config)# access-list 100 deny ip any any
```

As you recall, FTP uses two connections: 21 for control information and 20 for data. In an active FTP session, the server opens the port 20 connection. To allow the client to send traffic across the opened port 20 connection, I assume that the router is performing as a stateful firewall. If the router were not, you would need the commands in Example 7-8 before the **deny** statement in Example 7-7.

Example 7-8 *Allowing the FTP Data Connection for Example 7-7*

```
Router(config)# access-list 100 permit tcp any host 200.1.1.10 eq 20 established
Router(config)# access-list 100 permit tcp any host 200.1.1.10 eq 21
Router(config)# access-list 100 deny ip any any
```

Remember that the use of the **established** keyword does not implement a stateful firewall function.

In either of these two configurations, if the router was running earlier versions than Cisco IOS 12.0(11) or 12.1(2), fragments would be allowed, by default. This could be a big security risk, so I have modified the ACL as displayed in Example 7-9.

Example 7-9 *Adding Fragment Filtering to Example 7-8*

```
Router(config)# access-list 100 deny ip any any fragments
Router(config)# access-list 100 permit tcp any host 200.1.1.10 eq 20 established
Router(config)# access-list 100 permit tcp any host 200.1.1.10 eq 21
Router(config)# access-list 100 deny ip any any
```

In this example, you have prevented fragments from reaching any internal device (no matter what Cisco IOS version your router is running). However, you just received an e-mail from an Internet user stating that he cannot access your FTP server. After investigating the problem, you discover that it is a fragmentation issue: He is sending IP packets that are composed of fragments. To solve this problem, you probably would allow fragments to the FTP server, as displayed in Example 7-10.

Example 7-10 *Allowing Fragments to the FTP Server from Example 7-9*

```
Router(config)# access-list 100 permit tcp any host 200.1.1.10 fragments
Router(config)# access-list 100 deny ip any any fragments
Router(config)# access-list 100 permit tcp any host 200.1.1.10 eq 20 established
Router(config)# access-list 100 permit tcp any host 200.1.1.10 eq 21
Router(config)# access-list 100 deny ip any any
```

The first statement in Example 7-10 allows any TCP fragments to be forwarded to your FTP server, but it is denying all other types of fragments. Also, by allowing TCP fragments to your FTP server, you are opening it to TCP fragmentation DoS flood attacks.

CAUTION   In most networks today, fragmentation is uncommon except for IPSec connections. Therefore, if you are not using IPSec, you typically can filter fragments without any side effects. If you are filtering fragments and certain connections are failing, it might be because of fragmentation and your filtering rules. In this situation, you might have to open your filter to allow fragments. In this case, make sure that you use an IDS solution that can detect fragmentation attacks and dynamically can log into your router and configure a filtering rule to prevent the flood of fragments. Cisco calls this process shunning, and it is discussed in Chapter 16.

Timed ACLs

Timed ACLs were introduced in Cisco IOS 12.0(1)T. Timed ACLs enable you to restrict traffic based on the time of day, the day of the week, or the day of the month. Sometimes you want to open a hole in your router's filter to allow a specific type of traffic, but you do not want to leave the hole open indefinitely. For example, you might not want your users accessing the Internet during business hours, but you might let them do so during lunch or before or after hours. Timed ACLs enable you to enforce this kind of policy.

Timed ACLs are actually an extension of numbered and named extended ACLs, and work with IP and IPX. You create your entries that are timed based and use the **time-range** parameter to specify the time period or periods that the ACL statement is valid. The time periods can be recurring, such as every day between 12 and 1 P.M., or absolute, occurring only once. Besides being an extension of extended ACLs, they can be used with reflexive ACLs and CBAC stateful filtering. They also can be used with VPNs to restrict access during certain time periods or to implement different QoS policies based on the time of day.

Creating Time Ranges

To create a time range, use the following commands:

```
Router(config)# time-range time_range_name
Router(config-time)# absolute [start_time start_date]
  [end_time end_date]
Router(config-time)# periodic day_of_the_week hh:mm  to
  [day_of_the_week] hh:mm
```

When creating a time range with the **time-range** command, you must give the time range a unique name. The name must begin with a letter and cannot contain a space. You will use this name later to associate a specific ACL statement with this range. Executing the **time-range** command takes you into a subconfiguration mode where you can specify two types of ranges: one time only (**absolute**) and recurring (**periodic**).

absolute Command

The **absolute** command specifies a single time period for which the time range is valid; the ACL statement(s) referencing this time range is not used after this period. With the **absolute** command, you can specify a beginning time period, an ending time period, or both. The time is specified in 24-hour time, like this: *hh:mm*, where the hours range from 0 to 24 and the minutes are 0 to 59. For example, 3 P.M. would be represented as 15:00. The date is specified in this format: *day month year*. The day is specified as a number from 1 to 31; the month is the name of the month, such as May; and the year is a four-digit value, such as 2003. Here is an example date: 19 November 2004. The earliest date that you can reference is 00:00 1 January 1993, and the latest date that you can reference is 23:59 31 December 2035. If you omit the starting time, it defaults to the current time on the router. If you omit the ending time, it defaults to 23:59 31 December 2035. One restriction with the **absolute** command is that you can have only one of these commands in a single **time-range** configuration.

periodic Command

The **periodic** command specifies a recurring time period for which the time range is valid. Unlike **absolute** commands, you can have multiple **periodic** commands in the same time range. With this command, you must specify a beginning and ending time; however, the ending time can be on a different day. The first parameter that you specify is the day of the week beginning time, which is one of the following values:

- **monday**
- **tuesday**
- **wednesday**
- **thursday**
- **friday**
- **saturday**
- **sunday**
- **daily** (every day)
- **weekdays** (Monday through Friday)
- **weekend** (Saturday and Sunday)

After the day of the week is the beginning time, specified as *hh:mm*. This is followed by the **to** parameter and the ending time. If you omit the day of week parameter, it defaults to the day of week that you configured for the beginning time. Following this is the ending time, specified as *hh:mm*.

Activating Time Ranges

After you have created your time range or ranges, you are ready to activate them. This is done by adding the **time-range** parameter to the ACL statement. This is supported in both named and numbered extended ACLs. Here is the configuration for a numbered ACL:

```
Router(config)# access-list ACL_# {deny | permit} protocol_name_or_#
  source_IP_address source_wildcard_mask
  destination_IP_address destination_wildcard
  [protocol_options][precedence precedence] [dscp value] [tos tos] [log | log-input]
  [fragments] [established] [time-range name_of_time_range]
```

As you can see from this command, you need to add the time range only to the ACL statement. When you do this, the ACL statement is processed only by the Cisco IOS when the router's time falls within the period specified by the **periodic** or **absolute** commands defined in the **time-range** configuration.

Using Distributed Timed ACLs

Distributed timed ACLs were introduced in Cisco IOS 12.2(2)T and are an extension to timed ACLs. One restriction with timed ACLs, however, is that they were not supported on the VIP line cards of the 7500 series of routers. If you configured a time-based ACL on one of these line cards, the Cisco IOS treated it as a normal ACL statement. In addition, if an interface was configured with a time-based ACL, packets were not distributed switched through the line card; they had to be forwarded to the Route Processor (RP) card to be processed. In other words, timed ACLs basically were broken for the 7500 series routers.

Distributed timed ACLs fix these two problems. A distributed timed ACL activated on a 7500's interface is distributed through the line card, but the software clock between the RP and the line card must be synchronized. This process is performed through the exchange of interprocess communications (IPC) messages between the two cards. Whenever you add, delete, or modify a time range for an ACL that is associated with an interface, the RP sends an IPC message to the line card.

TIP   To ensure that your router has a reliable clock source, I recommend that you use the Network Time Protocol (NTP). I discuss this protocol in Chapter 18, "Logging Events."

The configuration of distributed timed ACLS is done the same way with normal timed ACLs by using the **time-range** and the **absolute** and **periodic** commands. After you build your time range, reference it in your extended ACL with the **time-range** parameter.

After you have configured your timed ACLs on your 7500 router (with VIP line cards), you can verify that the timed ACLs are functioning properly with these commands:

- **show time-range ipc**—Use this command to verify that the clocks are synchronized between the VIP line cards and the RP. It displays statistics about the communication process.

- **clear time-range ipc**—Use this command to clear the time-range IPC statistics and counters and reset them to 0.

- **debug time-range ipc**—Use this command to display the messages shared between the RP and VIP cards.

Example of Timed ACL

To help illustrate how timed ACLs are used, take a look at an example, using the network shown in Figure 7-5. In this example, e-mail and DNS query traffic should be allowed from the Internet to the two respective DMZ servers, and vice versa. However, no other traffic should be allowed. Even users are not allowed to directly access the Internet during business hours, but management has just passed a policy that allows users to access the Internet during lunch and after hours until 7 P.M., when the office closes.

Figure 7-5 *Timed ACL Example*

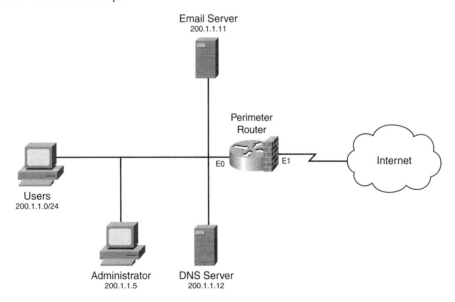

Example 7-11 displays the configuration to accomplish this.

Example 7-11 *Using Timed ACLs to Implement Filtering Policies*

```
Router(config)# time-range employee-time
Router(config-time)# periodic weekdays 12:00 to 13:00
Router(config-time)# periodic weekdays 17:00 to 19:00
Router(config-time)# exit
Router(config)# access-list 100 permit tcp any host 200.1.1.11 eq 25
Router(config)# access-list 100 permit tcp any eq 25 host 200.1.1.11 established
Router(config)# access-list 100 permit udp any host 200.1.1.12 eq 53
Router(config)# access-list 100 permit udp any eq 53 host 200.1.1.12
Router(config)# access-list 100 permit tcp any 200.1.1.0 0.0.0.255 established
   time-range employee-time
Router(config)# access-list 100 deny ip any any
Router(config)# interface ethernet 1
Router(config-if)# ip access-group 100 in
Router(config-if)# exit
Router(config)# access-list 101 permit tcp host 200.1.1.11 eq 25 any
Router(config)# access-list 101 permit tcp host 200.1.1.11 any eq 25
Router(config)# access-list 101 permit udp host 200.1.1.12 eq 53 any
Router(config)# access-list 101 permit udp host 200.1.1.12 any eq 53
Router(config)# access-list 101 permit tcp 200.1.1.0 0.0.0.255 any
   time-range employee-time
Router(config)# access-list 100 deny ip any any
Router(config)# interface ethernet 1
Router(config-if)# ip access-group 101 out
```

In this example, only e-mail and DNS traffic is allowed in and out at any time. However, employees are allowed TCP access to the Internet during lunch time and after work hours (**periodic** commands). Again, setting up this configuration is difficult because extended ACLs are packet filters and do not support stateful firewall functions. The first timed ACL entry (ACL 100) allows returning TCP traffic to employees' PCs. The second timed ACL entry (ACL 101) allows the employees to access the Internet. Two ACLs are required, based on the requirements: 100 prevents traffic from entering this company's network, and 101 prevents traffic from leaving the network.

Additional ACL Features

This section rounds out the introduction to ACLs and their configuration. This section covers five enhanced ACL features: remarks, throttling of logging updates, IP accounting, turbo ACLs, and sequenced ACLs. ACL remarks enable you to insert descriptions into your ACL statement grouping. Throttling logging information from ACL matches (with the **log** parameter) enables you to restrict the number of messages that the Cisco IOS generates on matches, reducing an overload on the router. IP accounting enables you to identify traffic that matches a **deny** statement in an ACL, providing more information about the dropped packet. Turbo ACLs allow the Cisco IOS to compile ACLs, making them more efficient and faster to process. Sequenced ACLs enable you to insert or delete a specific ACL entry in your statement grouping without having to delete the entire ACL and rebuild it. The following sections cover these enhanced features.

ACL Remarks

As of Cisco IOS 12.0(2)T, you can include remarks in your ACL statements. Before this, most administrators created a text configuration file with their ACLs, using comments to accomplish the same thing, as displayed in Example 7-12.

Example 7-12 *Using Comments in Your Configuration*

```
! This ACL is used to restrict access to the router:
access-list 1 permit 192.168.1.10
access-list 1 permit 192.168.1.11
! Activating it on the VTYs
line vty 0 4
  access-class 1 in
```

The problem with this approach is that when this was loaded into the Cisco IOS, the Cisco IOS ignored the comments. Therefore, you always had to look back to your text file to determine what an ACL was for or what a particular statement was intended to do.

Remarks are supported with both numbered and named ACLs. Here is the syntax for entering a remark in either one:

```
Router(config)# access-list ACL_# remark remark
```

or:

```
Router(config)# ip access-list {standard|extended} ACL_name
Router(config-{std|ext}-nacl)# remark remark
```

The remark that you enter can be up to 100 characters in length. If you enter a remark that is longer than 100 characters, any extra characters automatically are truncated. When you enter a remark, it is inserted after the last ACL command that you entered. However, using sequenced ACLs, you can insert a remark or multiple remarks anywhere in your ACL statement grouping. Example 7-13 shows a simple example of an ACL that is used to restrict VTY access to a router.

Example 7-13 *Using the* **remark** *Command in an ACL*

```
Router(config)# access-list 1 remark This ACL restricts administrator
Router(config)# access-list 1 remark -----access to the router for
Router(config)# access-list 1 remark -----VTY access
Router(config)# access-list 1 remark -----
Router(config)# access-list 1 remark -----Allow Richard access
Router(config)# access-list 1 permit 192.168.1.10
Router(config)# access-list 1 remark -----Allow Natalie access
Router(config)# access-list 1 permit 192.168.1.11
```

As you can see from this example, it is much easier to understand what the ACL is used for and what each statement is doing.

Using ACL Remarks

One of the topics covered during a Cisco router course that I recently taught was how to use and configure ACLs. As you have seen so far in this chapter, configuring ACLs is not an easy process: You must be very familiar with TCP/IP and its various protocols and packet contents. A student in the class asked me to review one of the ACLs being used to restrict traffic from the Internet. The student then proceeded to pull out an eight-page ACL—with no comments.

First, an ACL this long is very difficult to troubleshoot. As you recall from the last chapter, a successful ACL design is kept simple. Second, it is difficult to determine what certain statements were used for (if they even had a use). Managing this ACL was nearly impossible.

To help this student, we discussed what the network was trying to accomplish from a policy perspective and then drew up a new ACL configuration. In this ACL configuration we put in remarks, to help the student remember the discussions we had and what specific statements or grouping of statements were used for. After the class, the student sent me an e-mail saying that the best part of the class was learning all the idiosyncrasies of ACLs and their configurations and enhancements.

Logging Updates

As I mentioned earlier with standard and extended ACLs, you can add the optional **log** parameter to a specific ACL statement(s), causing the Cisco IOS to generate a log message when a packet matches the condition in the statement. This is a very useful feature when you are trying to determine what kinds of traffic you are dropping (specifically, to see what hackers and curious individuals are attempting to send into your network).

I mentioned that logging affects the performance of your router: It no longer can use high-speed switching methods such as CEF. Another issue with the default logging function is that the Cisco IOS displays a message on the first matching packet, but it displays another message on a subsequent match only after a 5-minute interval has expired. The problem with this is that if someone is probing or attacking a particular device or part of your network, you probably will see only a small number of log messages.

As of 12.0(2)T, you can change the logging threshold. To change the threshold of logging, use the following command:

```
Router(config)# ip access-list log-update threshold #_of_matches
```

This command defines a threshold for how often a log message is generated. When you specify the value for the number of matches, the Cisco IOS generates a log message after each number of matches. For example, if you set the number of matches to 5, the Cisco IOS generates a log message on the first match, then a message after five subsequent matches, then another message after another five subsequent matches, and so on. This enables you to control how much logging your router generates.

One caveat with the configuration of this command is that, even if you configure a threshold, the Cisco IOS clears its cache of counts after a 5-minute period. As an example, assume that you set a threshold of five packets. Someone sends a packet that matches on a condition with logging enabled, so, because this is the first match, the Cisco IOS generates a message. This person sends two more packets, totaling three. Because the threshold of five has not been reached no additional messages are generated. At this point, the 5-minute period expires and the Cisco IOS clears its matching count cache, setting all counts to 0 for the ACL. The person then sends his fourth packet. From the Cisco IOS perspective, this is counted as the first packet, and it causes a logging message to be generated.

CAUTION   If you are under an attack, you might want to set up this threshold to gather more logging information about what is occurring. Be careful, though, of setting the logging update threshold to a very small value, such as 1. Doing this causes your Cisco IOS to generate a lot more log messages. With a massive DoS attack by a hacker, this easily could flood your router and bring it to its knees, if not crash it. Cisco recommends not setting this to 1.

IP Accounting and ACLs

The IP accounting feature has been around since Cisco IOS 10.0. Actually, IP accounting initially was intended to gather traffic statistics for accounting purposes. However, an option was added to it to log statistics for access violations. This feature enables you to get more information about traffic that matches a **deny** statement in an ACL (available in Cisco IOS 10.3).

Configuration of Accounting

To enable accounting for logging violations, configure the following:

```
Router(config)# interface type [slot_#/]port_#
Router(config-if)# ip accounting access-violations
```

When you enable IP accounting for access violations, the Cisco IOS keeps track of the source and destination address that matched the **deny** statement, as well as the number of packets and bytes and the ACL number or name that was matched. To view your access-violation accounting information, use the **show ip accounting access-violations** command.

NOTE   One restriction with IP accounting is that it can gather accounting information for only transit information—traffic that is not destined to the router itself or traffic that the router itself generates.

IP accounting also works with process, fast, and CEF switching, but it disables autonomous and SSE switching.

Example 7-14 shows a sample of a router filtering ICMP traffic, with accounting enabled, as well as its verification.

Example 7-14 *Using IP Accounting to Log ACL Matches*

```
Router(config)# access-list 100 deny icmp any any
Router(config)# access-list 100 permit ip any any
Router(config)# interface fastethernet0
Router(config-if)# ip address 192.168.1.254 255.255.255.0
Router(config-if)# ip access-group 100 in
Router(config-if)# ip accounting access-violations
Router(config-if)# end
Router# show ip accounting access-violations
   Source            Destination         Packets      Bytes   ACL
   192.168.1.100     192.168.2.253             4        240   100

Accounting data age is 9
Router#
```

In this example, all ICMP traffic is filtered, but everything else is permitted. Notice that IP accounting is enabled on the fastethernet0 interface. In the output of the **show ip accounting access-violations** command, 192.168.1.100 tried pinging a remote destination (192.168.2.253), which was filtered by the router's ACL, and its accounting information was recorded: Four packets, totaling 240 bytes, were dropped by ACL 100.

Restriction of Accounting Information

Remember that any packet that matches a **deny** statement (or the implicit deny) generates or updates an accounting record when access violations are enabled. Because IP accounting can generate a large amount of information, you will want to restrict it to a reasonable amount that the router can handle. You can use three commands to restrict the amount of accounting information:

- **ip accounting-list**—Filters accounting information based on the addresses listed
- **ip accounting-threshold**—Defines the maximum number of accounting records that the router will create
- **ip accounting-transits**—Limits the number of transit records that the router stores

Filtering Accounting Information

To limit accounting information to just specific hosts, use the **ip accounting-list** command:

```
Router(config)# ip accounting-list IP_address wildcard_mask
```

With this command, enter an IP address or network number, and qualify it with a wildcard mask (this is the same wildcard mask used with standard and extended ACL statements). You must configure both of these parameters. You also can specify more than one record to capture traffic from a multitude of sources or destinations.

TIP

Restricting accounting data is useful if you know that an attack is occurring to or from a specific device. Normally, you might not know what device is creating the attack, but you easily can find out which internal device (or network or subnet) is bearing the brunt of the attack. Knowing this information, you can restrict accounting information with your device's IP address or your internal network number. By using this command, you can focus your accounting information on just the matches on **deny** statements for specific devices.

Defining Thresholds

By default, the Cisco IOS stores up to 512 entries in its internal accounting database. An entry is basically a source-destination address pairing. With 512 entries, this takes up 12,928 bytes of memory. This number of address pairings is actually not very much, so you can increase this using this command:

```
Router(config)# ip accounting-threshold threshold_value
```

The threshold value is the maximum number of entries that you want the Cisco IOS to store in the accounting database. It can range from 0 to 4,294,967,295!

CAUTION

Be careful not to set the accounting threshold value to too large of a size. Setting this value too high can cause a router to consume all its free memory, creating buffer overflow problems and possible crashes.

Limiting Number of Transit Records

Besides limiting the number of accounting records or the devices for which accounting records are created and maintained, you can limit the number of transit records that the Cisco IOS maintains.

One problem of using the **ip accounting-list** command is that only devices included in the list have accounting information maintained for them. In certain instances you still want accounting information displayed for other devices, but you want to control the amount of additional accounting records that this creates in memory.

The **ip accounting-transits** command accomplishes this task:

```
Router(config)# ip accounting-transits #_of_records
```

With this command, the default number of transit records kept defaults to 0. Therefore, accounting information is generated only when a device listed in the **ip accounting-list** command matches a **deny** statement. As an example, you might want to keep accounting records for certain devices, but allow up to 100 other devices to generate records. To accomplish this, use this configuration:

```
Router(config)# ip accounting-transits 100
```

In this example, up to 100 additional address-pairs are kept in the accounting database besides the ones specified in the **ip accounting-list** command(s).

NOTE   Other commands for IP accounting have nothing to do with security. This section focuses only on the ones that can be used to help with security auditing and logging.

Turbo ACLs

Normally, ACLs are searched sequentially, from the first to the last entry, when trying to find a match on a condition. However, very long ACLs can slow down the search process to find a match on a condition. In addition, depending on the packet contents, one packet might match on one of the first statements in an ACL, while another might match on one of last statements in an ACL, producing a variable delay in latency that then affects delay-sensitive traffic.

Cisco developed turbo ACLs to speed up the processing of ACLs and to produce a more defined latency period during ACL processing. This feature is available only on the 7100, 7200, 7500, and 12,000 Gigabit Switch routers. Turbo ACLs are basically ACLs that are compiled into a lookup table that still maintains first-match requirements (remember, order of statements is important). The Cisco IOS uses packet headers to match against these table entries in a small number of lookups, which is independent of the number of ACLs in the original list.

Turbo ACLs provide these two advantages:

- The time to find a match is fixed, so latency is smaller and consistent. This is important with very large ACLs and mixed types of data traffic.
- For ACLs that have three or more entries, turbo ACLs reduce the CPU processing cycles required to find a match. Actually, the CPU load to find any match is fixed, no matter how many ACL statements are in the ACL list. Therefore, the larger the list is, the better the performance gain is.

Turbo ACLS have limitations, of course. For example, you cannot use timed entries or reflexive entries in ACLs (discussed in Chapter 8). In addition, when you compile an ACL, you need an additional 2 to 4 MB of memory to hold the compiled contents. The **show access-list compiled** command displays the memory overhead used by the compiled ACL(s).

Turbo ACLs were introduced in Cisco IOS 12.0(6)S and on the 7200 in 12.1(1)E. They have been integrated into 12.1(5)T. By default, turbo ACLS are disabled on a router that supports them. To compile your ACLs on a supported router, use this command:

```
Router(config)# access-list compiled
```

This command has no parameters; in other words, you cannot choose which ACLs are compiled and which ones are not. Instead, if an ACL can be compiled, the Cisco IOS compiles it automatically. When compiling, the Cisco IOS scans the ACL and then compiles the ACL, if the Cisco IOS can. For large and complex ACLs, it might take a few seconds (or minutes) for the compilation to complete. After an ACL is compiled, any changes that you make to the ACL automatically trigger a recompilation of the ACL. While an ACL is being compiled or recompiled, the Cisco IOS uses the uncompiled ACL to filter traffic.

After you have enabled a turbo ACL on your router, you can use the **show access-list compiled** command to verify its successful configuration and operation, as displayed in Example 7-15.

Example 7-15 *Using the* **show access-lists compiled** *Command*

```
Router# show access-lists compiled
Compiled ACL statistics:
4 ACLs loaded, 4 compiled tables
  ACL        State   Tables Entries Config Fragment Redundant Memory
1          Operational   1     2      1       0         0      1Kb
100        Operational   1     15     9       7         1      1Kb
101        Operational   1     13     6       6         0      1Kb
102        Operational   1     2      1       0         0      1Kb
First level lookup tables:
Block   Use               Rows    Columns Memory used
  0     TOS/Protocol       6/16    12/16      66048
  1     IP Source (MS)    10/16    12/16      66048
  2     IP Source (LS)    27/32    12/16     132096
  3     IP Dest (MS)       3/16    12/16      66048
  4     IP Dest (LS)       9/16    12/16      66048
  5     TCP/UDP Src Port   1/16    12/16      66048
  6     TCP/UDP Dest Port  3/16    12/16      66048
  7     TCP Flags/Fragment 3/16    12/16      66048
Router#
```

An ACL can be placed in five states:

- **Operational**—The ACL has been compiled successfully.

- **Deleted**—The ACL is empty (no entries).

- **Unsuitable**—The ACL cannot be compiled because it contains time-range, reflexive, or dynamic entries.

- **Building**—The ACL is currently being compiled, which might take a few seconds to complete.

- **Out of memory**—The router does not have enough memory to compile the ACL.

Sequenced ACLs

For years, customers have been complaining about how difficult it is to maintain ACLs: adding, modifying, or deleting statements in an ACL. I detailed how this was done using a text editor, in Chapter 6. I have been using this process for more than a decade now, and I always have found it to be a tedious, error-prone process.

Hallelujah! Cisco has implemented a feature that enables you to delete specific entries in an ACL, as well as insert entries anywhere you want within an ACL. Cisco calls this feature sequenced ACLs. This makes your ACL-editing process much simpler. Actually, sequenced

ACLs are not a new ACL type: They use normal standard or extended named ACLs (numbered ACLs are not supported). This feature was introduced in Cisco IOS 12.2(14)S and has been integrated into 12.2(15)T and 12.3(2)T.

NOTE	Sequenced ACLs work only with named standard or extended ACLs. However, you can create a named ACL and give it a number as its name, such as **ip access-list extended 100**. This is common with old-school administrators who have been dealing with ACLs for years. Likewise, you can take a normal numbered ACL and treat it like a named ACL, using the **ip access-list {standard	extended}** command, where you reference the number in the name field.

ACLs and Sequencing

With sequenced ACLs, each ACL entry is associated with a sequence number. Sequence numbers then can be used to insert an ACL into the middle of an existing list or to delete an existing statement in the list. And if you do not like the sequence numbers that the Cisco IOS assigns to the list, you can resequence them with your own numbering scheme. This ensures that you always can insert ACL statements into a list.

Working with sequenced ACLs is a simple process. However, you need to be aware of some things when adding or deleting entries in a sequenced ACL. First, all ACL statements have sequence numbers—even if you did not assign them any. If you upgrade your Cisco IOS to one that supports sequenced ACLs, the Cisco IOS automatically assigns a sequence number to each statement. The first statement in the list is assigned a sequence number of 10, and every subsequent statement's sequence number is 10 more than the previous one. For example, if you had three statements in your ACL, the default sequence numbers would be 10, 20, and 30. Of course, you do not have to use the standard sequencing that Cisco assigns to ACLs. For route-processor cards and line cards, any sequencing or resequencing that you do automatically is synchronized by the route processor card to all the line cards.

You can create your own sequencing process. For example, you can have ACL sequence numbers incrementing by 100 instead of 10. However, the maximum sequence number that can be assigned is 2,147,483,647. If you exceed this number, you will see the following error message:

```
Exceeded maximum sequence number.
```

If you enter an ACL statement without specifying a sequence number, the router uses the default increment of 10 when adding the statement to the end of the list. This applies to a new ACL grouping as well. If you enter an ACL command that already is in the list but that has a different sequence number, the router ignores your input. If you enter a new ACL statement, where it is a unique command in the list, but you have specified a sequence number that is already in use, you will see the following error message:

```
Duplicate sequence number.
```

In this case, the Cisco IOS aborts your command, and you need to assign a different sequence number to your statement.

NOTE	Any sequence numbers that are applied to an ACL are not saved to NVRAM. Each time that the router boots up, the Cisco IOS applies the default sequencing scheme, assigning a sequence number of 10 for the first statement and incrementing sequence numbers by 10 for subsequent statements. Cisco did this to ensure backward compatibility for older Cisco IOS versions that do not support sequence numbers. Therefore, if you resequence your list to multiples of 100, this is not saved when you execute the **copy running-config startup-config** command.

Resequencing ACLs

Remember that you do not have to sequence a named ACL first; the Cisco IOS does this automatically by starting at 10 and incrementing each statement's sequence number by 10 for following statements. Optionally, you can implement your own sequencing method using the following command:

```
Router(config)# ip access-list resequence ACL_name
  starting_seq_# increment
```

As an example, if you want to resequence the ACL named 100, you would follow these steps. First, display the current ACL with the **show access-list** command, as shown in Example 7-16 (this is the same ACL that I used previously for the network in Figure 7-2).

Example 7-16 *Displaying the Sequence Numbers for ACLs*

```
Router# show access-list 100
Extended IP access list 100
  10 permit tcp any host 200.1.1.14 eq www
  20 permit udp any host 200.1.1.13 eq domain
  30 permit tcp any host 200.1.1.12 eq smtp
  40 permit tcp any eq smtp host 200.1.1.12 established
  50 permit tcp any host 200.1.1.11 eq ftp
  60 permit tcp any host 200.1.1.11 eq ftp-data
  70 permit tcp any eq www 200.1.2.0 0.0.0.255 established
  80 permit udp any eq domain 200.1.2.0 0.0.0.255
  90 deny ip any any
```

Notice that the ACL statements use the default sequencing. In this example, I am going to change the sequence numbers to start at 1 and increment by 1. Here is the command to change the sequencing:

```
Router(config)# ip access-list resequence 100 1 1
```

To verify the configuration, redisplay the ACL as displayed in Example 7-17.

Example 7-17 *Viewing Updated ACL Sequence Numbers*

```
Router# show ip access-list 100
Extended IP access list 100
  1 permit tcp any host 200.1.1.14 eq www
  2 permit udp any host 200.1.1.13 eq domain
  3 permit tcp any host 200.1.1.12 eq smtp
```

Example 7-17 *Viewing Updated ACL Sequence Numbers (Continued)*

```
4 permit tcp any eq smtp host 200.1.1.12 established
5 permit tcp any host 200.1.1.11 eq ftp
6 permit tcp any host 200.1.1.11 eq ftp-data
7 permit tcp any eq www 200.1.2.0 0.0.0.255 established
8 permit udp any eq domain 200.1.2.0 0.0.0.255
9 deny ip any any
```

Notice that the sequence numbers have changed. At any given time, you can resequence the numbers in your ACL.

Deleting an Entry in a Sequenced ACL

Deleting a sequenced ACL entry is just as simple as resequencing it. If you want to delete a specific entry in the ACL, first display the entries with the **show access-list** command and note the sequence number to the left of the statement that you want to delete. Next, enter the subconfiguration mode for the named ACL, and then delete the command by prefacing the sequence number of the statement with the **no** parameter. Here is a simple breakdown:

```
Router# show access-list
  <--output omitted-->
Router# configure terminal
Router(config)# ip access-list {standard|extended} ACL_name
Router(config-{std|ext}-nacl)# no sequence_#
```

As you can see from this example, deleting an entry is straightforward. To illustrate this, in Example 7-18, I delete entry number 9 from the resequencing Example 7-17.

Example 7-18 *Deleting a Specific Sequenced ACL Entry*

```
Router(config)# ip access-list extended 100
Router(config-ext-nacl)# no 9
Router(config-ext-nacl)# end
Router# show access-list 100
Extended IP access list 100
    1 permit tcp any host 200.1.1.14 eq www
    2 permit udp any host 200.1.1.13 eq domain
    3 permit tcp any host 200.1.1.12 eq smtp
    4 permit tcp any eq smtp host 200.1.1.12 established
    5 permit tcp any host 200.1.1.11 eq ftp
    6 permit tcp any host 200.1.1.11 eq ftp-data
    7 permit tcp any eq www 200.1.2.0 0.0.0.255 established
    8 permit udp any eq domain 200.1.2.0 0.0.0.255
```

As you can see in this example, deleting entry 9 was as simple as entering **no 9**.

Inserting an Entry in a Sequenced ACL

Inserting an entry in a sequenced ACL is also very simple. If you want to insert an entry in the ACL, first display the entries with the **show access-list** command and note the two sequence numbers of the statements where you want to insert your new ACL statement.

Choose a number between these two sequence numbers; if there is no room, resequence the ACL. Next, enter the subconfiguration mode for the named ACL and then enter your sequence number for the new ACL, the action (**permit** or **deny**), and the condition. Basically, this is exactly the same as adding a normal named ACL statement, with the exception of putting the sequence number at the beginning of the line. Here is a simple breakdown:

```
Router# show access-list
<--output omitted-->
Router# configure terminal
Router(config)# ip access-list {standard|extended} ACL_name
Router(config-{std|ext}-nacl)# sequence_# {permit | deny} condition
```

As you can see from this example, inserting an entry is straightforward. To illustrate this, in Example 7-19 I add back entry number 9 from the deletion example in Example 7-18, using a sequence number of 50 for this entry.

Example 7-19 *Previewing an ACL Before Inserting an ACL Statement*

```
Router# show access-list 100
Extended IP access list 100
    1 permit tcp any host 200.1.1.14 eq www
    2 permit udp any host 200.1.1.13 eq domain
    3 permit tcp any host 200.1.1.12 eq smtp
    4 permit tcp any eq smtp host 200.1.1.12 established
    5 permit tcp any host 200.1.1.11 eq ftp
    6 permit tcp any host 200.1.1.11 eq ftp-data
    7 permit tcp any eq www 200.1.2.0 0.0.0.255 established
    8 permit udp any eq domain 200.1.2.0 0.0.0.255
```

As you can see from this ACL, sequence number 50 does not exist, so in Example 7-20, I add the statement that I previously deleted back into the ACL.

Example 7-20 *Inserting an ACL Statement*

```
Router(config)# ip access-list extended 100
Router(config-ext-nacl)# 50 deny ip any any
```

As you can see, I added my new statement with a sequence number of 50. Next, I view my ACL configuration to verify the statement's placement within the ACL, as displayed in Example 7-21.

Example 7-21 *Verifying the Statement's Placement Within the ACL*

```
Router# show access-list 100
Extended IP access list 100
    1 permit tcp any host 200.1.1.14 eq www
    2 permit udp any host 200.1.1.13 eq domain
    3 permit tcp any host 200.1.1.12 eq smtp
    4 permit tcp any eq smtp host 200.1.1.12 established
    5 permit tcp any host 200.1.1.11 eq ftp
    6 permit tcp any host 200.1.1.11 eq ftp-data
    7 permit tcp any eq www 200.1.2.0 0.0.0.255 established
    8 permit udp any eq domain 200.1.2.0 0.0.0.255
    50 deny ip any any
```

In this example, my new statement is placed in the correct location.

From these last two sections, you can see that editing an ACL is a breeze when using sequence numbers. It takes the wonderful pain out of editing ACLs and reduces the number of stories that I can tell my students about stupid editing mistakes I have made using the old method.

Protection Against Attacks

Now that you have a basic understanding of ACL configuration and their additional features, the rest of this chapter focuses on some important filtering rules that you should implement on your router. In this section, I assume that your router is acting either as a perimeter router or as the main perimeter firewall.

Bogon Blocking and Spoofing

A *bogon* is a network or route prefix that should not appear in an Internet routing table. Many types of bogon addresses exist, including the following:

- Addresses that should be used only internally, such as RFC 1918 addresses.
- Loopback addresses (127.0.0.0/8).
- Reserved IANA addresses.
- Multicast addresses (224.0.0.0/4).
- Research addresses (240.0.0.0/4).
- DHCP local address (169.254.0.0/16). This is what your PC uses if it cannot find a DHCP server from which to acquire its addressing information.
- Documentation/test network (192.0.2.0/24).

TIP   This list of bullets is not all-inclusive. IANA is responsible for address assignments and has a list of all addresses that are currently in use; those that are not in use should be blocked. To see the current list of IANA addresses, visit http://www.iana.org/assignments/ipv4-address-space. One problem with this list is that it lists all addresses and, if they are used, who they are assigned to. I typically use the bogon list at the website http://www.cymru.com/Documents/bogon-list.html. This site keeps the list up-to-date and includes only bogon addresses.

You will want to check this list periodically; some addresses that were assigned to an ISP sometimes are taken back (and placed on the bogon list), and some addresses sometimes are assigned (and should be removed from the bogon list).

As a good example of a bogon, imagine that someone from the Internet is trying to forward traffic to you with an RFC 1918 source address or an address that currently is unassigned by the IANA. These commonly are used in distributed DoS (DDoS) attacks.

You can block these addresses in four common ways:

- ACL filtering
- BGP prefix filtering (discussed in Chapter 15, "Routing Protocol Protection")
- Black hole routing (discussed in Chapter 15)
- Route policy filtering with route maps (discussed in Chapter 15)

This section focuses on using ACLs and filtering bogon addresses.

The first question that you might ask is, what kind of advantage does bogon filtering provide? Rob Thomas of Team Cymru, who has done frequent work with bogons and network attacks, has found that 66 percent of DDoS attacks use bogons. Of this 66 percent, more than half of these attacks use source addresses from a Class D or E address space. Therefore, blocking these addresses will stop more than 60 percent of DDoS attacks right at your front door—your perimeter router. If you want to read more about Rob's study, "60 Days of Basic Naughtiness," visit http://www.cymru.com/Presentations/60Days.ppt.

Essentially, bogon filtering typically is used to prevent spoofing attacks. As you recall from Chapter 1, "Security Threats," in a spoofing attack, the hacker tries to hide his source IP address. Bogon filtering filters out the addresses that are basically bogus addresses or impossible addresses. RFC 2267 discusses filtering of spoofed addresses.

Ingress Filtering

As you recall from Chapter 4, "Disabling Unnecessary Services," the Cisco IOS AutoSecure feature automatically creates a bogon filter and applies it to your perimeter or firewall router's interface connected to the public network. Consider the network shown previously in Figure 7-5 as an example. Example 7-22 shows an example of an ingress ACL filtering traffic as it comes from the Internet and into your network.

Example 7-22 *Using an Ingress ACL to Filter Bogons*

```
Router(config)# ip access-list extended ingress-filter
Router(config-ext-nacl)# remark Unassigned IANA addresses
Router(config-ext-nacl)# deny ip 1.0.0.0 0.255.255.255 any
Router(config-ext-nacl)# deny ip 2.0.0.0 0.255.255.255 any
Router(config-ext-nacl)# deny ip 5.0.0.0 0.255.255.255 any
Router(config-ext-nacl)# deny ip 7.0.0.0 0.255.255.255 any
Router(config-ext-nacl)# deny ip 23.0.0.0 0.255.255.255 any
Router(config-ext-nacl)# deny ip 27.0.0.0 0.255.255.255 any
Router(config-ext-nacl)# deny ip 31.0.0.0 0.255.255.255 any
Router(config-ext-nacl)# deny ip 36.0.0.0 0.255.255.255 any
Router(config-ext-nacl)# deny ip 37.0.0.0 0.255.255.255 any
Router(config-ext-nacl)# deny ip 39.0.0.0 0.255.255.255 any
```

Example 7-22 *Using an Ingress ACL to Filter Bogons (Continued)*

```
Router(config-ext-nacl)# deny ip 41.0.0.0 0.255.255.255 any
Router(config-ext-nacl)# deny ip 42.0.0.0 0.255.255.255 any
Router(config-ext-nacl)# deny ip 49.0.0.0 0.255.255.255 any
Router(config-ext-nacl)# deny ip 50.0.0.0 0.255.255.255 any
Router(config-ext-nacl)# deny ip 58.0.0.0 0.255.255.255 any
Router(config-ext-nacl)# deny ip 59.0.0.0 0.255.255.255 any
Router(config-ext-nacl)# deny ip 60.0.0.0 0.255.255.255 any
Router(config-ext-nacl)# deny ip 70.0.0.0 0.255.255.255 any
Router(config-ext-nacl)# deny ip 71.0.0.0 0.255.255.255 any
Router(config-ext-nacl)# deny ip 72.0.0.0 0.255.255.255 any
Router(config-ext-nacl)# deny ip 73.0.0.0 0.255.255.255 any
Router(config-ext-nacl)# deny ip 74.0.0.0 0.255.255.255 any
Router(config-ext-nacl)# deny ip 75.0.0.0 0.255.255.255 any
Router(config-ext-nacl)# deny ip 76.0.0.0 0.255.255.255 any
Router(config-ext-nacl)# deny ip 77.0.0.0 0.255.255.255 any
Router(config-ext-nacl)# deny ip 78.0.0.0 0.255.255.255 any
Router(config-ext-nacl)# deny ip 79.0.0.0 0.255.255.255 any
Router(config-ext-nacl)# deny ip 83.0.0.0 0.255.255.255 any
Router(config-ext-nacl)# deny ip 84.0.0.0 0.255.255.255 any
Router(config-ext-nacl)# deny ip 85.0.0.0 0.255.255.255 any
Router(config-ext-nacl)# deny ip 86.0.0.0 0.255.255.255 any
Router(config-ext-nacl)# deny ip 87.0.0.0 0.255.255.255 any
Router(config-ext-nacl)# deny ip 88.0.0.0 0.255.255.255 any
Router(config-ext-nacl)# deny ip 89.0.0.0 0.255.255.255 any
Router(config-ext-nacl)# deny ip 90.0.0.0 0.255.255.255 any
Router(config-ext-nacl)# deny ip 91.0.0.0 0.255.255.255 any
Router(config-ext-nacl)# deny ip 92.0.0.0 0.255.255.255 any
Router(config-ext-nacl)# deny ip 93.0.0.0 0.255.255.255 any
Router(config-ext-nacl)# deny ip 94.0.0.0 0.255.255.255 any
Router(config-ext-nacl)# deny ip 95.0.0.0 0.255.255.255 any
Router(config-ext-nacl)# deny ip 96.0.0.0 0.255.255.255 any
Router(config-ext-nacl)# deny ip 97.0.0.0 0.255.255.255 any
Router(config-ext-nacl)# deny ip 98.0.0.0 0.255.255.255 any
Router(config-ext-nacl)# deny ip 99.0.0.0 0.255.255.255 any
Router(config-ext-nacl)# deny ip 100.0.0.0 0.255.255.255 any
Router(config-ext-nacl)# deny ip 101.0.0.0 0.255.255.255 any
Router(config-ext-nacl)# deny ip 102.0.0.0 0.255.255.255 any
Router(config-ext-nacl)# deny ip 103.0.0.0 0.255.255.255 any
Router(config-ext-nacl)# deny ip 104.0.0.0 0.255.255.255 any
Router(config-ext-nacl)# deny ip 105.0.0.0 0.255.255.255 any
Router(config-ext-nacl)# deny ip 106.0.0.0 0.255.255.255 any
Router(config-ext-nacl)# deny ip 107.0.0.0 0.255.255.255 any
Router(config-ext-nacl)# deny ip 108.0.0.0 0.255.255.255 any
Router(config-ext-nacl)# deny ip 109.0.0.0 0.255.255.255 any
Router(config-ext-nacl)# deny ip 110.0.0.0 0.255.255.255 any
Router(config-ext-nacl)# deny ip 111.0.0.0 0.255.255.255 any
Router(config-ext-nacl)# deny ip 112.0.0.0 0.255.255.255 any
Router(config-ext-nacl)# deny ip 113.0.0.0 0.255.255.255 any
Router(config-ext-nacl)# deny ip 114.0.0.0 0.255.255.255 any
Router(config-ext-nacl)# deny ip 115.0.0.0 0.255.255.255 any
Router(config-ext-nacl)# deny ip 116.0.0.0 0.255.255.255 any
```

continues

Example 7-22 *Using an Ingress ACL to Filter Bogons (Continued)*

```
Router(config-ext-nacl)# deny ip 117.0.0.0 0.255.255.255 any
Router(config-ext-nacl)# deny ip 118.0.0.0 0.255.255.255 any
Router(config-ext-nacl)# deny ip 119.0.0.0 0.255.255.255 any
Router(config-ext-nacl)# deny ip 120.0.0.0 0.255.255.255 any
Router(config-ext-nacl)# deny ip 121.0.0.0 0.255.255.255 any
Router(config-ext-nacl)# deny ip 122.0.0.0 0.255.255.255 any
Router(config-ext-nacl)# deny ip 123.0.0.0 0.255.255.255 any
Router(config-ext-nacl)# deny ip 124.0.0.0 0.255.255.255 any
Router(config-ext-nacl)# deny ip 125.0.0.0 0.255.255.255 any
Router(config-ext-nacl)# deny ip 126.0.0.0 0.255.255.255 any
Router(config-ext-nacl)# deny ip 197.0.0.0 0.255.255.255 any
Router(config-ext-nacl)# deny ip 201.0.0.0 0.255.255.255 any
Router(config-ext-nacl)# remark RFC 1918 private addresses
Router(config-ext-nacl)# deny ip 10.0.0.0 0.255.255.255 any
Router(config-ext-nacl)# deny ip 172.16.0.0 0.15.255.255 any
Router(config-ext-nacl)# deny ip 192.168.0.0 0.0.255.255 any
Router(config-ext-nacl)# remark Other bogons
Router(config-ext-nacl)# deny ip 224.0.0.0 15.255.255.255 any
Router(config-ext-nacl)# deny ip 240.0.0.0 15.255.255.255 any
Router(config-ext-nacl)# deny ip 0.0.0.0 0.255.255.255 any
Router(config-ext-nacl)# deny ip 169.254.0.0 0.0.255.255 any
Router(config-ext-nacl)# deny ip 192.0.2.0 0.0.0.255 any
Router(config-ext-nacl)# deny ip 127.0.0.0 0.255.255.255 any
Router(config-ext-nacl)# remark Internal networks
Router(config-ext-nacl)# deny ip 200.1.1.0 0.0.0.255 any
Router(config-ext-nacl)# remark Allow Internet to specific services
Router(config-ext-nacl)# remark permit <what you need to permit>
Router(config-ext-nacl)# deny ip any any
Router(config-ext-nacl)# exit
Router(config)# interface ethernet1
Router(config-if)# ip access-group ingress-filter in
```

The first part of the ACL blocks the IANA unassigned addresses. The second part blocks the RFC 1918 private addresses. The third part blocks other bogon addresses, such as multicast, research, network 0, DHCP local addresses, and loopback addresses. The fourth part blocks internal network addresses. This commonly is forgotten. Make sure that you prevent source addresses coming into your network that have the same addresses that you are using. This is an obvious DDoS attack. In the example in Figure 7-2, no one from the Internet should be using a source address of 200.1.1.0/24 because this is what IANA or the ISP assigned you.

One specialized form of DoS attack is called Land.c, or Land, for short. In this attack, the hacker sends traffic to a destination with a source address that matches that of the destination. When the destination receives the packet, it tries to respond to itself. In one variant of this attack, the hacker uses the same port number for the source and destination ports. For example, if a hacker was executing a Land.c attack against the e-mail server in Figure 7-2, the hacker would use a source and destination address of 200.1.1.11, and a source and destination port number of 25. In most cases, this would only eat up extra CPU cycles on the e-mail server. However, with certain TCP/IP protocol stacks, this might cause the machine to crash, especially under a heavy load. This bug was discovered a long time ago, and most operating systems that were affected have been patched. If you prevent traffic coming into your network that has a source address that you are using, you have prevented Land attacks (as I did at the bottom of the ingress ACL filter under the "Internal networks" remark).

NOTE	One question that I commonly am asked is "Why use **deny** statements to block this when the implicit deny will do this anyway?" Well, in some cases, your implicit deny will block this traffic. However, if you omit the **deny** statements that I listed in the code example, you basically are permitting anyone to send traffic to your permitted internal services with any kind of source address. Typically, these **permit** statements use the keyword **any** for the source address. Therefore, you want to put these bogon **deny** statements at the beginning, to prevent bogon DoS attacks against your internal resources.

Egress Filtering

The previous example shows you how to block bogus traffic coming into your network. However, as you recall from Chapter 1, most security threats (more than 60 percent), originate from inside your network. Therefore, you need to take precautions about restricting traffic leaving your network as well. In this case, you are concerned about two things: what address is in the source field and what address is in the destination field.

To restrict traffic leaving your network, you could use a filter similar to the one I created for ingress filtering on your Cisco IOS perimeter router/firewall in Example 7-22. However, it would be much simpler to create an ACL that specifies exactly what source addresses are allowed out and lets the implicit deny drop everything else. For example, if you allow all your internal traffic out, use a code example as shown in Example 7-23.

Example 7-23 *Using an Egress ACL to Allow Only Valid Addresses to Exit*

```
Router(config)# ip access-list extended egress-filter
Router(config-ext-nacl)# permit ip 200.1.1.0 0.0.0.255 any
Router(config-ext-nacl)# deny ip any any
Router(config-ext-nacl)# exit
Router(config)# interface ethernet1
Router(config-if)# ip access-group egress-filter out
```

Notice that this is applied on the external (public) interface in the outbound direction (see Figure 7-2).

CAUTION	You also can apply this egress filter on ethernet0 in the inbound direction. However, if your devices are using private addresses and your router is performing NAT on them, you have to allow these private addresses into the router. This is prone to error because some addresses you translate and some you do not. My personal preference is to filter the traffic as it leaves the interface. If you are using address translation, make sure that the address you specify is the public address in your extended ACL (assuming that the ACL is on the public interface applied outbound).

One problem arises with the previous egress filter. If a hacker can compromise one of your internal devices and gain unauthorized access to it, he might implement a DoS attack from it, attempting to send traffic to bogon network numbers. Some of this you already are preventing because internal routers will not forward certain kinds of traffic, such as multicasts, unless you have configured a multicast routing protocol. However, many network administrators set up a default route to route traffic to destinations that routers do not have in their routing tables. You definitely do not want a default route routing traffic to unassigned addresses. Therefore, you either can filter this in the egress filter, denying the bogon destination addresses and placing these statements before your permit statement, or you can use a static route for these bogon networks and point it to a null interface, commonly called black hole routing (I discuss this latter option in Chapter 15).

Internal Spoofing Attack

I once dealt with a company that forgot to filter destination bogon addresses from internal machines. A hacker was able to compromise one of these devices and began flooding traffic to 169.254.0.0/16, a bogon network. The routers routed this to the default gateway (perimeter) router and then out to the ISP. Besides saturating the Internet link, the company got a nasty call from the ISP asking why it was bombarding the ISP access router with bogon traffic. It took a couple of hours to figure out which internal machine was compromised and to boot out the hacker. In the mean time, the company immediately fixed its egress ACL to block this kind of traffic. One difficulty that it had in tracking the hacked device was that the hacker was using both source and destination address spoofing, continually changing his source IP address to a range of valid IP addressed used in the network. From an analytical view, that was pretty cool to see in action, but it was a real pain in tracking down the culprit device.

Example 7-24 shows a sample ACL to prevent traffic from being sent to bogon addresses for your egress filter, as well as to prevent spoofing attacks with bogon addresses as the source IP address in the packet header.

Example 7-24 *Using an Egress Filter to Block Bogons*

```
Router(config)# ip access-list extended egress-filter
Router(config-ext-nacl)# remark Unassigned IANA addresses
Router(config-ext-nacl)# deny ip any 1.0.0.0 0.255.255.255
Router(config-ext-nacl)# deny ip any 2.0.0.0 0.255.255.255
Router(config-ext-nacl)# deny ip any 5.0.0.0 0.255.255.255
Router(config-ext-nacl)# deny ip any 7.0.0.0 0.255.255.255
Router(config-ext-nacl)# deny ip any 23.0.0.0 0.255.255.255
Router(config-ext-nacl)# deny ip any 27.0.0.0 0.255.255.255
<--output omitted-->
Router(config-ext-nacl)# remark RFC 1918 private addresses
Router(config-ext-nacl)# deny ip any 10.0.0.0 0.255.255.255
Router(config-ext-nacl)# deny ip any 172.16.0.0 0.15.255.255
Router(config-ext-nacl)# deny ip any 192.168.0.0 0.0.255.255
```

Example 7-24 *Using an Egress Filter to Block Bogons (Continued)*

```
Router(config-ext-nacl)# remark other bogons
Router(config-ext-nacl)# deny ip any 224.0.0.0 15.255.255.255
Router(config-ext-nacl)# deny ip any 240.0.0.0 15.255.255.255
Router(config-ext-nacl)# deny ip any 0.0.0.0 0.255.255.255
Router(config-ext-nacl)# deny ip any 169.254.0.0 0.0.255.255
Router(config-ext-nacl)# deny ip any 192.0.2.0 0.0.0.255
Router(config-ext-nacl)# remark block bogons as source addresses
Router(config-ext-nacl)# deny ip 1.0.0.0 0.255.255.255 any
Router(config-ext-nacl)# deny ip 2.0.0.0 0.255.255.255 any
Router(config-ext-nacl)# deny ip 5.0.0.0 0.255.255.255 any
Router(config-ext-nacl)# deny ip 7.0.0.0 0.255.255.255 any
Router(config-ext-nacl)# deny ip 23.0.0.0 0.255.255.255 any
Router(config-ext-nacl)# deny ip 27.0.0.0 0.255.255.255 any
<--output omitted-->
Router(config-ext-nacl)# remark Internal networks--allow out
Router(config-ext-nacl)# permit ip 200.1.1.0 0.0.0.255 any
Router(config-ext-nacl)# deny ip any any
Router(config-ext-nacl)# exit
Router(config)# interface ethernet1
Router(config-if)# ip access-group egress-filter out
```

As you can see from the ingress and egress filters, there are a lot of ACL statements. However, these statements prevent only certain kinds of DDoS attacks. You still have a lot of ACL statements to add to prevent other types of attacks, so do not relax yet. Note that in Example 7-24, I have cut out some of the ACL commands for bogon filtering (<--output omitted-->) for brevity sake.

NOTE   Cisco IOS routers also support another solution to deal with certain kinds of address spoofing: IP unicast reverse-path forwarding verification. This provides a more efficient process in filtering spoofed packets, but it also has disadvantages. I discuss this feature in Chapter 15.

DoS and Distributed DoS Attacks

As discussed in Chapter 1, denial-of-service (DoS) attacks attempt to limit the operation of a device, possibly even causing it to crash. DoS attacks come in many flavors and can use different protocols, such as ICMP, TCP, and UDP. This section discusses some of the most common types of DoS attacks and what you can do with ACLs to prevent or, at a minimum, limit your exposure.

TCP SYN Floods

As I briefly discussed in Chapter 1, TCP SYN flood attacks are a type of DoS attack that attempts to overwhelm a resource with TCP connection requests. In this instance, the hacker typically uses either real or spoofed source IP addresses. In this kind of attack, the hacker floods a device with TCP SYN segments, with no intention of completing the connection.

I already discussed how you can prevent spoofing with ACLs. If the hacker is using a real IP address, the hacker's software basically ignores the SYN/ACK message that the service responds with. This section discusses why you cannot use an ACL to limit your exposure to a TCP SYN flood attack.

Unfortunately, an ACL solution is not fancy and does not provide much protection. Consider the network previously shown in Figure 7-5 for this example, which illustrates the limitations that ACLs have with TCP SYN flood attacks. Example 7-25 shows a snippet of code dealing with the TCP SYN flood issue.

Example 7-25 *Attempting to Use ACLs to Deal with TCP SYN Floods*

```
Router(config)# ip access-list extended tcp-syn-flood
Router(config-ext-nacl)# permit tcp any 200.1.1.0 0.0.0.255 established
Router(config-ext-nacl)# permit tcp any host 200.1.1.11 eq 25
<--output omitted-->
Router(config-ext-nacl)# deny ip any any
Router(config-ext-nacl)# exit
Router(config)# interface ethernet1
Router(config-if)# ip access-group tcp-syn-flood in
```

In this example, the configuration focuses on only the TCP SYN flood problem. Obviously, many other statements are needed in this ACL. The first **permit** command basically allows returning traffic from internal TCP connection requests to outside resources. Remember my warning about using the **established** parameter: It does not implement a stateful firewall function, so a hacker can take advantage of this and use a different type of TCP flood attack by setting the appropriate control flags in the TCP segment header, such as ACK. This provides only limited protection to network 200.1.1.0/24. However, the second statement poses more problems. Because you want to allow Internet users access to specific resources, such as an e-mail server, you must let TCP SYNs into your network.

CAUTION   Unfortunately, there is no way that an extended ACL can prevent a TCP SYN flood attack to the e-mail server in this example. However, you can use other Cisco IOS features, such as TCP Intercept and CBAC inspection, which both are covered in Chapter 17, "DoS Protection."

Smurf and Fraggle Attacks

Smurf is a DoS attack that uses ICMP echos. The name Smurf is used because this was what the original hacker application was called. A hacker using Smurf uses two things that can create a massive DoS attack against your resources.

Smurf in Action

First, the hacker puts a directed broadcast into the destination field of the IP packet header. Directed broadcasts, unlike local broadcasts, are routable. Depending on the user's device, a directed broadcast can be either the first or the last address in a network or subnet. Typically, it is the last address. For example, with network 192.168.1.0/24, the directed broadcast address could be 192.168.1.0 or 192.168.1.255. Second, instead of using his own address as the source address of the packet, the hacker replaces it with the address of the device that he wants to attack. If the destination network or networks do not filter the directed broadcast, all the destinations on the segment of the directed broadcast respond with an echo reply to the source address in the packet (the victim).

Figure 7-6 illustrates the process of a Smurf attack. In this example, the hacker wants to attack the internal server (200.1.2.1). The attacker then finds a network that allows directed broadcasts into the network. This could be the same network (not likely) or another network connected to the Internet (most likely). The hacker then sends an ICMP echo with a destination-directed broadcast to the segment that will initiate the attack and puts a source address in the packet header of the actual victim (200.1.2.1). When the destinations on 200.1.1.0/24 receive the echo-directed broadcast, each device responds to the source address with an echo reply. These devices commonly are called *reflectors* because they are being used to reflect the attack to the actual victim. In this example, only three user devices— 200.1.1.1, 200.1.1.2, and 200.1.1.3—send an echo reply to 200.1.2.1.

Figure 7-6   *Smurf Attack*

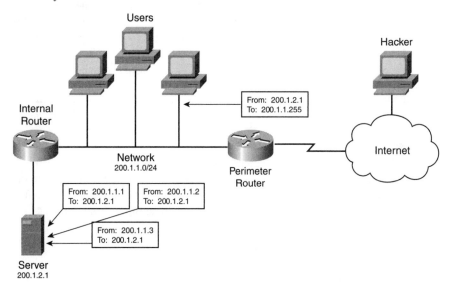

In the example in Figure 7-6, sending one echo and generating three echo replies is negligible—I would not even bat an eye about this attack. However, the hacker is not going to send one echo. Assume that, in this example, the hacker had a fractional T1 connection to the Internet, perhaps 512 kbps. He uses up all of his bandwidth sending directed broadcast ICMP echos to network 200.1.1.0/24. When these devices receive these, they respond by each generating 512 kbps of echo replies to the victim, resulting in 1.5 Mbps of echo replies flooding the internal server. The devices that respond to the echo requests commonly are called *amplifiers* because they generate x amount of more traffic than originally was sent to them, where x is the based on the number of devices in the network or subnet of the directed broadcast address. In this example, the server obviously is affected by this attack, but if it has a Fast Ethernet connection and a fast processor, the attack does not affect it that much.

However, most hackers typically use directed broadcast addresses from multiple networks. Consider a different example to illustrate how overpowering a Smurf attack can be. In this example, the hacker is using 512 kbps of bandwidth. Assume that the hacker has found three networks on the Internet that allow amplifiers (responses to directed broadcasts). Each of these network segments has 100 hosts. The hacker splits up his echo requests by sending an equal portion (about 170 kbps) to each of these amplified segments. Each host on these segments (300 in total) responds to the victim. The victim, unfortunately, is clobbered with 300 sets of echo replies at 170 kbps each, resulting in more than 51 Mbps of echo replies to the server. The server definitely will feel this. As you can see in this example, through amplification, a hacker easily can flood a network.

NOTE   Interestingly enough, Internet Relay Chat (IRC) servers are the devices most often hit with these kinds of attacks. This is probably because the hacker was banned from the server for inappropriate language or actions. Hackers like to hang out on these servers, and the hacker responds with this simple yet efficient attack. Note that in this attack there are two victims: the amplifiers and the victim, who takes the biggest brunt of the assault.

Attack Prevention

Fraggle is very similar to Smurf, but it uses UDP echos instead of ICMP echos—basically, someone recoded Smurf to work with UDP. Given the huge impact that both of these two programs have, you might be wondering what you can do to prevent these kinds of massive attacks. You can do five basic things to limit the affect of this kind of attack:

- Shut down networks with amplifiers.
- Disable directed broadcast addresses.
- Perform ingress and egress filtering of directed broadcast addresses.
- Perform rate limiting through CAR. This does not prevent the attack, but it does limit the amount of bandwidth that the ICMP and UDP echos (or replies) can use. CAR is discussed further in Chapter 17.
- Use IP unicast reverse-path forwarding verification to prevent IP spoofing. This feature is covered in Chapter 15.

RFC 2267 discusses these solutions in a general sense. The best solution to this problem is to have all networks connected to the Internet block directed broadcast traffic. You would think that everyone already is doing this, but you would be making a bad assumption. To see a list of networks that are known amplifiers, visit http://www.netscan.org. You will find that more than 8600 networks (at the time of this writing) support amplification. As you can see, until every ISP and network administrator takes this problem seriously, these kinds of amplification attacks will not disappear.

Second, you want to make sure that your network is not one of the networks that support amplification; you do not want hackers to use your network to instigate a Smurf or Fraggle attack. To prevent amplification, you can do few things. For Fraggle, disable TCP and UDP small servers on all the routers in your network. I discussed how to do this in Chapter 4. For Smurf, you can do one of two things (preferably both). I discuss these in the next two sections.

TIP	You can test whether you are an amplifier by going to http://www.powertech.no/smurf, which scans your network for amplification.

Disable Directed Broadcasts   First, on *all* your routers, disable directed broadcast processing. This is done by going into each router and, on each interface, disabling directed broadcasts with the **no ip directed-broadcast** command. If you miss a router or an interface on a router, directed broadcasts typically will be forwarded by other routers. For example, assume that you have a network, 192.168.1.0/24, that is subnetted into four networks: 192.168.1.0/26, 192.168.1.64/26, 192.168.1.128/26, and 192.168.1.192/26. All routers connected to these subnets understand what addresses are host addresses and what are broadcast addresses; however, you might have other routers in your network that are connected not to these subnets, but to others, such as 192.168.2.0/24, 192.168.3.0/24, and so on. These routers do not understand the subnetting of the 192.168.1.0/24 network unless you use a routing protocol that supports VLSM and is not performing summarization. Therefore, if you miss even one router's interface in your network with the **no ip directed-broadcast** command, you might accidentally make yourself an amplifier.

As of Cisco IOS 12.0, this is the default configuration on a Cisco router's interface: Directed broadcasts are disabled. I know of only one situation in which using the directed broadcast option is valid: In a network where Samba (an SMB server for UNIX) or NT is used, some stations use a directed broadcast to find resources on remote segments. Disabling directed broadcasts breaks connectivity. The fix for this is to implement WINS instead of using directed broadcasts.

Filter Directed Broadcasts   The second filtering solution that you want to implement is ingress and egress filtering. Sometimes you can get away with a simple filter such as the one in Example 7-26.

Example 7-26 *Using an ACL to Block Smurf and Fraggle*

```
Router(config)# ip access-list extended smurf-fraggle
Router(config-ext-nacl)# deny icmp any any echo
Router(config-ext-nacl)# deny icmp any any echo-reply
Router(config-ext-nacl)# deny udp any any eq echo
Router(config-ext-nacl)# deny udp eq echo any
Router(config-ext-nacl)# remark --> add your other ACL statements
   here as necessary
Router(config-ext-nacl)# deny ip any any
Router(config-ext-nacl)# exit
Router(config)# interface ethernet1
Router(config-if)# ip access-group smurf-fraggle in
Router(config-if)# ip access-group smurf-fraggle out
```

In this example, the first two **deny** statements drop all ICMP echos and echo requests. The second two **deny** statements drop all UDP echo requests. The problem with the first two **deny** statements is that this means you cannot get back any echo replies for testing. Therefore, you might want to tweak this configuration by allowing echo replies only to certain internal management devices.

The second solution is to use an extended ACL to filter all directed broadcast addresses. This can be a cumbersome task, especially if you have many subnets in your network. Using Figure 7-5 as an example, this is easy: Just block 200.1.1.0 and 200.1.1.255. Example 7-27 shows how to block these directed broadcast addresses.

Example 7-27 *Using an ACL to Block Directed Broadcast Addresses*

```
Router(config)# ip access-list extended no-broadcasts-in
Router(config-ext-nacl)# remark This command prevents spoofing
Router(config-ext-nacl)# deny ip 200.1.1.0 0.0.0.255 any
Router(config-ext-nacl)# remark These two commands block directed
   broadcast addresses
Router(config-ext-nacl)# deny ip any host 200.1.1.0
Router(config-ext-nacl)# deny ip any host 200.1.1.255
Router(config-ext-nacl)# remark --> add your other ACL statements
   here as necessary
Router(config-ext-nacl)# deny ip any any
Router(config-ext-nacl)# exit
Router(config)# ip access-list extended no-broadcasts-out
Router(config-ext-nacl)# deny ip any host 200.1.1.0
Router(config-ext-nacl)# deny ip any host 200.1.1.255
Router(config-ext-nacl)# deny ip host 200.1.1.0 any
Router(config-ext-nacl)# deny iphost 200.1.1.255 any
Router(config-ext-nacl)# remark --> add your other ACL statements
   here as necessary
Router(config-ext-nacl)# deny ip any any
Router(config-ext-nacl)# exit
Router(config)# interface ethernet1
Router(config-if)# ip access-group no-broadcasts-in in
Router(config-if)# ip access-group no-broadcasts-out out
```

In this example, I am filtering directed broadcasts in both directions on the public interface of the router in Figure 7-5. The first statement in the first ACL prevents spoofing of internal addresses by an Internet hacker. The second and third statements drop any traffic destined to the two internal broadcast addresses. In the second ACL, there are two sets of commands. The first two prevent your devices from sending directed broadcasts to the Internet—basically, from becoming the victim (reflector) of an amplification attack. The second two statements prevent your devices from generating packets with source-directed broadcast addresses, just in case the hacker is inside your network and wants to trick someone on the outside into sending stuff back into your network. As you can see, in a simple one-segment network, you have to set up a few filtering rules. In a large network, however, you might have a few hundred networks or subnets, which equates to twice as many filtering statements.

TIP

Even though each **deny** statement is not necessary (in other words, you probably could accomplish the same thing without all of these statements in your ACL), I typically place these commands in the ACL so that, when using the **show access-lists** command, I can see the number of matches. If they are incrementing rapidly, I know that I am the amplifier or victim of a Smurf (or Fraggle) attack. I discuss this further in the next subsection.

Are You Being Attacked?   To determine whether you are under attack, use the **show access-lists** command, which shows you the number of matches on a statement. If you see one of these **deny** statements incrementing extremely fast, you are under attack. If you see the ICMP echos incrementing, someone is trying to use you as an amplifier. If you see the ICMP echo replies incrementing, you are the intended victim. By adding the **log-input** parameter to the **deny** ACL statement(s) from the last section, you can see from which interface the packets are coming from. Here is an example of this output using the network shown in Figure 7-2:

```
%SEC-6-IPACCESSLOGDP: list smurf-fraggle denied icmp
     200.1.1.1 (Ethernet0) -> 199.1.1.1 (0/0), 1 packet
%SEC-6-IPACCESSLOGDP: list smurf-fraggle denied icmp
     200.1.1.2 (Ethernet0) -> 199.1.1.1 (0/0), 1 packet
%SEC-6-IPACCESSLOGDP: list smurf-fraggle denied icmp
     200.1.1.3 (Ethernet0) -> 199.1.1.1 (0/0), 1 packet
```

In this example, you can see that network 200.1.1.0/24 (off Ethernet0) is acting as the amplifier and is sending echo replies to the victim (199.1.1.1). In this case, the administrator now knows that he is the amplifier and can set up the necessary measures to prevent this in the future. However, if someone else was the amplifier, you could use the whois database to find the names of the administrators of the amplifiers, contact them, and hope that they will help you by fixing their security hole. It is important to remember that the amplifiers are typically ignorant victims—they do not realize that they are amplifiers causing mayhem with other people's networks. Therefore, you should be as courteous as possible.

TIP	When under attack, you first need to determine whether you are the amplifier. If you are the amplifier, contact your ISP and try to determine where the packets are coming from. In some rare instances, you might be able to track the attack back to a specific ISP, which, in turn, might be able to find the attacker; this is a really slim chance, but you might as well try. Next, find out what internal network is amplifying and prevent this with the methods I already have discussed.
	If you are the victim, implement CAR to reduce the amount of amplified traffic. Contact your ISP and have it do the same thing. You can use the whois database registry to determine who the amplifiers are (based on the source IP address in the echo replies). This database officially is called the *Internet Routing Registry (IRR)*. In the Europe, visit http://www.ripe.net /whois. In Asia-Pacific, visit http://www.apnic.net/. In the United States and the rest of the world, visit http://www.arin.net/whois. These databases list contact information of companies and ISPs that are assigned IP addresses. Contact the administrators of the source addresses in the attack and notify them that they are amplifiers. Have your ISP do the same thing. Sometimes pressure from multiple sources works better when dealing with the amplifier.

NOTE	One question that I commonly am asked is whether you can track down the hacker who instigated the Smurf or Fraggle attack. Unfortunately, in most cases, you will not be able to do this. To ultimately solve this problem, ISPs and the networks that connect to those ISPs need to perform filtering to prevent IP spoofing. When everyone performs this, almost all IP spoofing tasks will be a historical footnote in the history books.

Simple Reconnaissance Attacks

Many network threats begin with a reconnaissance attack. In a reconnaissance attack, the hacker tries to illicit information about your network, including what IP addresses are in use. Two very basic tools that are useful in this situation are ping and traceroute. Ping, which uses ICMP messages, is useful in testing connectivity, but it also can help a hacker learn what devices are reachable (and hackable) in your network. Therefore, you should limit what types of ICMP messages are allowed in and out of your network.

Ingress Filtering of ICMP Traffic

This next example uses the network in Figure 7-5 to illustrate how to restrict ICMP traffic from entering your network. For ingress filtering, you should at least configure Example 7-28 in your ingress filter.

Example 7-28 *Restricting ICMP Traffic with an Ingress Filter*

```
Router(config)# ip access-list extended ICMP-in
Router(config-ext-nacl)# remark <permit or deny other traffic>
Router(config-ext-nacl)# remark <put these statements here>
Router(config-ext-nacl)# deny icmp any any echo
Router(config-ext-nacl)# deny icmp any any redirect
Router(config-ext-nacl)# deny icmp any any mask-request
Router(config-ext-nacl)# permit icmp any host 200.1.1.5 echo-reply
Router(config-ext-nacl)# deny icmp any any echo-reply
Router(config-ext-nacl)# permit icmp any 200.1.1.0 0.0.0.255
Router(config-ext-nacl)# remark <permit or deny other traffic>
Router(config-ext-nacl)# remark <put these statements here>
Router(config-ext-nacl)# exit
Router(config)# interface ethernet1
Router(config-if)# ip access-group ICMP-in in
```

In this example, the first ACL statement blocks ICMP echos, which is also useful in preventing DoS attacks such as Smurf. The second ACL statement blocks ICMP redirects. As you recall from Chapter 4, this also can be done with the **no ip redirects** command. One issue with this command is that it needs to be configured on all interfaces of all routers on which redirect attacks are possible. Some hackers use redirect messages to corrupt routing information. The third **deny** statement prevents subnet mask requests. Hackers can use this message to learn what subnets you have, including the directed broadcasts of these addresses. When this is known, the hacker can implement a DoS Smurf or Fraggle attack.

The first **permit** statement in this ACL allows echo reply messages to be sent only to the administrator's PC—this is necessary so that the administrator can test connectivity to devices on the Internet, but no one else can (the deny statement after the **permit**). By doing this, you are dropping traffic from amplifiers in a Smurf attack. Following this, the second **permit** statement allows remaining ICMP traffic into the internal network. In this example, all other ICMP messages can be sent to the any of the devices in 200.1.1.10/24. You can be more restrictive than this, but certain message types, such as a parameter problem, a packet that is too big, and others, are needed to ensure that traffic can be sent between certain devices.

Egress Filtering of ICMP Traffic

Besides filtering traffic in the ingress direction, you want to restrict egress ICMP traffic, especially to prevent someone inside your network from executing an attack against an outside destination. You should permit certain ICMP message types so that connections can be established between certain devices. Again, this example uses Figure 7-5 to illustrate the configuration of an egress filter, which is displayed in Example 7-29.

Example 7-29 *Restricting ICMP Traffic with an Egress Filter*

```
Router(config)# ip access-list extended ICMP-out
Router(config-ext-nacl)# remark <permit or deny other traffic>
Router(config-ext-nacl)# remark <put these statements here>
Router(config-ext-nacl)# permit icmp host 200.1.1.5 any echo
Router(config-ext-nacl)# permit icmp 200.1.1.0 0.0.0.255 any parameter-problem
Router(config-ext-nacl)# permit icmp 200.1.1.0 0.0.0.255 any packet-too-big
Router(config-ext-nacl)# permit icmp 200.1.1.0 0.0.0.255 any source-quench
Router(config-ext-nacl)# deny icmp any any
Router(config-ext-nacl)# remark <permit or deny other traffic>
Router(config-ext-nacl)# remark <put these statements here>
Router(config-ext-nacl)# exit
Router(config)# interface ethernet1
Router(config-if)# ip access-group ICMP-out out
```

In this example, the first **permit** statement allows the management station (200.1.1.5) to send echo messages, through ping, to test connectivity to devices on the Internet. The second **permit** statement allows internal devices to send problems with packet headers to devices on the Internet sending traffic inbound. The **packet-too-big** parameter in the **permit** statement allows MTU discovery along the path between the source and destination, and the source quench statement allows devices to adapt to congestion. All other ICMP messages are dropped.

Traceroute

Traceroute traces the path of routers along the way to the destination. It is very useful in troubleshooting routing problems. However, hackers can use this to find what routers exist in your network. To prevent traceroute into your network, you need to block UDP ports 33,400 through 34,400, as in Example 7-30.

Example 7-30 *Filtering Traceroute Traffic*

```
Router(config)# ip access-list extended traceroute
Router(config-ext-nacl)# remark <permit or deny other traffic>
Router(config-ext-nacl)# remark <put these statements here>
Router(config-ext-nacl)# deny udp any any range 33400 34400
Router(config-ext-nacl)# remark <permit or deny other traffic>
Router(config-ext-nacl)# remark <put these statements here>
Router(config-ext-nacl)# exit
Router(config)# interface ethernet1
Router(config-if)# ip access-group traceroute in
```

Because you cannot be sure what specific port traceroute uses, you must filter the range of ports, as shown in the previous **deny** statement.

If you are concerned about internal devices performing traceroute, you can use the same **deny** command listed previously in an egress filter; however, you need to allow the external replies to the traceroute queries. This can pose a problem because the source port used is a random one. Unfortunately, when using normal extended ACLs, you must open a large range of UDP ports to allow the returning traffic back into your network in your ingress filter. Therefore, if you want to deny external users from performing traceroute but want to allow a few internal users, I recommend a stateful firewall solution, such as reflexive ACLs (see Chapter 8) or CBAC (see Chapter 9).

Distributed DoS Attacks

In a distributed DoS attack, multiple sources are flooding traffic, whether it be ICMP, TCP control flag segments (such as SYN), or UDP floods. This can be something as simple as a hacker sending multiple streams of directed broadcasts to different subnets and having those subnets respond with echo replies to the victim. However, many DDoS attacks are much more sophisticated than the simple Smurf or Fraggle attacks.

NOTE   This section covers only the most common types of DDoS attacks. For more information about DDoS attacks, visit the Packet Storm website: http://packetstormsecurity.nl/distributed/. The site has a comprehensive list of DDoS attacks, as well as the tools that hackers user to execute these attacks.

DDoS Components

Most DDoS attacks contain three components:

- Client
- Handler
- Agent

The client is the hacker who is orchestrating the attack. A sophisticated hacker might have a partner or two who join in the process. The client controls one or more handlers. A handler is a compromised device that the hacker has gained unauthorized access to and has installed a special program on. This program allows the client to control this machine remotely. The client then downloads hacking programs to the handler to use in other attacks. Handlers control agents, which also are compromised devices with special programs installed. Handlers pass down hacking software to the agents that will be used in a DDoS attack. Basically, the hacker on the client sends messages to the handler, which then tells the agents (the troops) what and how to attack the victim.

DDoS Process

Figure 7-7 illustrates the components and how they work together. In this example, the hacker has compromised three devices and is using them as handlers. He communicates to them through a special control program and has downloaded the Smurf, Fraggle, TCP SYN flood, and unauthorized access programs to each. The hacker also has compromised many agents and has set up a control relationship between certain handlers and agents. For example, in Figure 7-7, Handler A controls Agent A1 and Agent A2. The hacker has decided to gain control of a victim and convert it to an agent. In this example, it is a web server. The hacker wants to hide this unauthorized access attack, so he sets up a DDoS attack that hopefully will hide his unauthorized attempts. He sends instructions to his handlers to execute the attack. Handler A is responsible for telling his agents to implement a Fraggle attack against the server, Handler B is responsible for telling his clients to implement a Smurf attack against the server, and Handler C is responsible for implementing a TCP SYN flood and an unauthorized attack through its controlled agents. The hacker is hoping that, through this massive flood of ICMP echo replies (Smurf), UDP echo replies (Fraggle), and the TCP SYN flood, the administrators of the web server (and its network) will be so overwhelmed dealing with this attack, especially with all of the security alarms going off, that the hacker quickly can execute an unauthorized access attack and gain access to the server unnoticed.

Figure 7-7 *Common DDoS Attack*

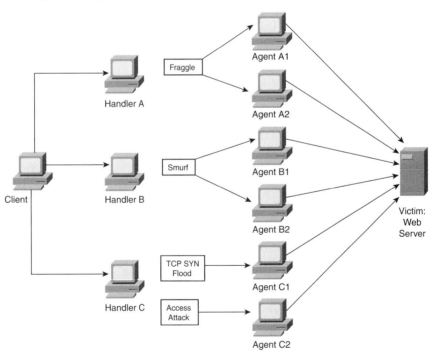

In reality, a hacker probably will use a feint attack, in which he centers his flood attack on one part of the network and tries to slip by to gain unauthorized access to other devices in the network. By gaining access to other devices, the hacker converts them to handlers and agents, expanding his DDoS army. If a hacker has compromised many hosts, it becomes very difficult to track down who actually is executing the attack, especially if the hacker can find networks that support amplification.

DDoS Experience

My first experience with a DDoS attack happened when I was performing consulting work for a company in the late 1990s. When it happened, it caught everyone off guard. No one, including myself, had ever seen anything like this. All of us thought that it was a coincidence that two Smurf attacks were happening simultaneously. But when this went from two to three and eventually up to eight networks (amplifiers) in the Smurf attack, we knew that something unusual was occurring. After examining the information on the CERT website, we realized that, besides distracting us with this huge flood of traffic, a hacker (or hackers) was trying to compromise some of our systems to join the DDoS army. This was one of my best learning experiences, especially seeing how the hacker was attempting to exploit security holes in certain systems that we were maintaining, how he was setting them up as handlers and agents, and how the handlers and agents communicated with each other. Besides being a hair-raising and hair-pulling experience, it was cool to see how well the hacker planned and executed his actions.

The Five Main DDoS Attacks

Hackers use five main DDoS programs to implement their attacks:

- Tribe Flood Network (TFN)
- Tribe Flood Network 2K (TFN2K)
- Trinoo
- Stacheldraht
- Trinity

When the hacker starts, he attempts to find devices that he can convert into handlers and agents. To do this, he scans hundreds, if not thousands, of devices, looking for specific security flaws that will allow him to gain unauthorized access. Typically, he is looking for SUN UNIX or Linux devices. When he finds devices with the security flaw, his specialized scanning software automatically executes a script that gains unauthorized access to the system and downloads the handler and agent programs, as well as any attack programs that he deems necessary. When he finds a susceptible device, breaking in and compromising the device takes less than a handful of seconds. The compromised host then does the same thing that the hacker was doing: It begins to scan and look for hosts that it can compromise. This process is repeated in the same way. As you can see from this process, in a short time, the hacker can build an army of devices. I have heard of stories of a hacker adding more than 2200 machines to his DDoS army in less than an hour, which is amazing (but not funny if you are the victim).

TFN

Two varieties of TFN exist: TFN and TFN2K. TFN is a DDoS program that was developed by a German hacker in mid-1999. When it spreads, the clients are capable of launching all types of DoS attacks, including ICMP, UDP floods, TCP SYN floods, and Smurf attacks.

After TFN is installed, the hacker can use a variety of connection methods to control the clients, including Telnet. Communication between the compromised devices is done with ICMP echo messages, in which specific header fields and the data payload contain the "instructions" for what is to be done or pass basic status information. Encryption is optional for hiding the contents, but if it is used, it is very weak.

Because ICMP echo reply messages are the heart of the TFN communication system, detecting this attack is difficult. The best way to block TFN is to restrict the flow of ICMP echo reply packets. Again, this example uses the network in Figure 7-5. Example 7-31 shows a basic ACL configuration to block this traffic.

Example 7-31 *Blocking TFN with ACLs*

```
Router(config)# ip access-list extended TFN-in
Router(config-ext-nacl)# remark <permit or deny other traffic>
Router(config-ext-nacl)# remark <put these statements here>
Router(config-ext-nacl)# permit icmp any host 200.1.1.5 echo-reply
Router(config-ext-nacl)# deny icmp any any echo-reply
Router(config-ext-nacl)# remark <permit or deny other traffic>
Router(config-ext-nacl)# remark <put these statements here>
Router(config-ext-nacl)# exit
Router(config)# ip access-list extended TFN-out
Router(config-ext-nacl)# remark <permit or deny other traffic>
Router(config-ext-nacl)# remark <put these statements here>
Router(config-ext-nacl)# deny icmp any any echo-reply
Router(config-ext-nacl)# remark <permit or deny other traffic>
Router(config-ext-nacl)# remark <put these statements here>
Router(config-ext-nacl)# exit
Router(config)# interface ethernet1
Router(config-if)# ip access-group TFN-out out
Router(config-if)# ip access-group TFN-in in
```

For the most part, this was covered in the "Ingress Filtering of ICMP Traffic" and "Egress Filtering of ICMP Traffic" sections. In Example 7-31, inbound TFN echo-reply packets are being filtered, with the exception of the management station. This allows the management station to test connectivity to the Internet. However, it also enables the management station, if infected with TFN, to allow its embedded ICMP echo reply messages to pass through the filter.

TIP   If you see the number of matches against the **permit** echo-reply statements constantly increasing, this could indicate that your management station(s) has become a client TFN device. For more information about TFN, visit http://staff.washington.edu/dittrich/misc/tfn.analysis.

TFN2K

TFN2K is an extension of TFN. Unlike TFN, TFN2K uses UDP, ICMP, and TCP packets to communicate; with TCP and UDP, the port numbers are random. To make it less detectable, two or three of these IP protocols can be used. In addition, TFN2K uses much stronger encryption to protect its messages and data on the agent. Because it uses TCP, UDP, and ICMP packets, which can be randomized, and also encrypts the messages, it is impossible to filter this traffic with a normal packet-filtering firewall, such as the Cisco IOS extended ACLs. TFN2K also has been known to use decoy packets to hide its infiltration or to point the finger to other devices.

TIP	All hope is not lost, though, in detecting and preventing TFN2K. Through an oversight of the developer, TFN2K leaves a detectible fingerprint in each packet: The hacker uses a predictable method of padding the packet payload, producing a sequence of trailing 0s followed by at least one A (and, in most cases, multiple As). A good IDS solution should be capable of picking up this fingerprint and raising an alarm. I briefly discuss some other methods that you can use to limit your exposure to TFN2K in the "Other Prevention Methods" section later. For more information about TFN2K, visit http://packetstormsecurity.nl/distributed/TFN2k_Analysis.htm.

Trinoo

Trinoo was discovered in August 1999. A hacker used more than 100 compromised systems to implement a DDoS attack from 227 amplifiers, bringing down a critical server at the University of Washington for 2 days. Speculation also has arisen that Trinoo was used to bring down Yahoo! and other major Internet sites with a flood of UDP packets. To install the client, the hacker used a buffer overrun exploit to gain unauthorized access to the agents. At one point, more than thousands of agents were suspected of being compromised. After compromising the system, the hacker installs a daemon by which he can control it remotely through a master program. The hacker then logs into the device(s) with the master program (typically through Telnet) to send his instructions to his troop of agents. His instructions are typically simple: He specifies the destination of the attack and for how long the attack takes place.

Detecting a trinoo infiltration can be very difficult. The original trinoo server (master) listened on UDP 27,655. However, modifications have been made to the port number, and known instances have included TCP and UDP ports of 1524, 27,665, 27,444, and 31,335. The hacker commonly uses ports 1524 and 27,655 to access the master. The master commonly uses port 27,444 to communicate with the clients, and the clients use 31,335 to communicate with the master. Example 7-32 shows how to filter this traffic with an ACL.

Example 7-32 *Using an ACL to Filter Trinoo*

```
Router(config)# ip access-list extended trinoo
Router(config-ext-nacl)# remark <permit or deny other traffic>
Router(config-ext-nacl)# remark <put these statements here>
Router(config-ext-nacl)# deny tcp any any eq 1524
Router(config-ext-nacl)# deny tcp eq 1524 any any
Router(config-ext-nacl)# deny udp eq 1524 any any
Router(config-ext-nacl)# deny tcp any any eq 27665
```

continues

Example 7-32 *Using an ACL to Filter Trinoo (Continued)*

```
Router(config-ext-nacl)# deny tcp any eq 27665 any
Router(config-ext-nacl)# deny udp any any eq 27444
Router(config-ext-nacl)# deny udp any eq 27444 any
Router(config-ext-nacl)# deny udp any any eq 31335
Router(config-ext-nacl)# deny udp any eq 31335 any
Router(config-ext-nacl)# remark <permit or deny other traffic>
Router(config-ext-nacl)# remark <put these statements here>
Router(config-ext-nacl)# exit
Router(config)# interface ethernet1
Router(config-if)# ip access-group trinoo out
Router(config-if)# ip access-group trinoo in
```

First, notice that I am using the same ACL statements to filter both inbound and outbound traffic. This is to block trinoo communication into the network and to prevent any affected clients from sending traffic out of the network. If you are seeing matches on these ACL statements, you might have clients or a master installed in your network.

NOTE   Because the hacker easily can change the port numbers, a good IDS solution is needed to detect and prevent this kind of attack. The previous ACL works to prevent beginner hackers from exploiting weaknesses in your network. For more information about trinoo, visit http://staff.washington.edu/dittrich/misc/trinoo.analysis.

Stacheldraht

Stacheldraht, which is German for "barbed wire," is based on the source code of TFN but combines it with features from trinoo to make it more robust. For example, it adds strong encryption to protect messages among the hacker, the handlers, and the agents, which makes it very hard to determine what actually is happening, if anything, among two or more Stacheldraht devices. Stacheldraht also supports automatic updates of the daemon programs, allowing the hacker to modify the code that it uses, to make it less susceptible to detection. Each master can control up to 1000 agents installed on unsuspecting, innocent devices. A hacker's attack begins with a massive intrusion phase, in which many computers are attacked and the hacker gains unauthorized access. The agent program daemon is installed and waits for a command to implement a DDoS attack against a victim.

The hacker originally used TCP ports 16,660 and 65,000 to communicate with the master and used echo replies to communicate between the masters and agents. You can attempt to filter this traffic by using the ACL in Example 7-33 (this uses the network in Figure 7-5).

Example 7-33 *Using an ACL to Block Stacheldraht*

```
Router(config)# ip access-list extended barb-wire-in
Router(config-ext-nacl)# remark <permit or deny other traffic>
Router(config-ext-nacl)# remark <put these statements here>
Router(config-ext-nacl)# permit icmp any host 200.1.1.5 echo-reply
Router(config-ext-nacl)# deny icmp any any echo-reply
Router(config-ext-nacl)# deny tcp any any eq 16660
Router(config-ext-nacl)# deny tcp any eq 16660 any
Router(config-ext-nacl)# deny tcp any any eq 65000
Router(config-ext-nacl)# deny tcp any eq 65000 any
Router(config-ext-nacl)# remark <permit or deny other traffic>
Router(config-ext-nacl)# remark <put these statements here>
Router(config-ext-nacl)# exit
Router(config)# ip access-list extended barb-wire-out
Router(config-ext-nacl)# remark <permit or deny other traffic>
Router(config-ext-nacl)# remark <put these statements here>
Router(config-ext-nacl)# deny icmp any any echo-reply
Router(config-ext-nacl)# deny tcp any any eq 16660
Router(config-ext-nacl)# deny tcp any eq 16660 any
Router(config-ext-nacl)# deny tcp any any eq 65000
Router(config-ext-nacl)# deny tcp any eq 65000 any
Router(config-ext-nacl)# remark <permit or deny other traffic>
Router(config-ext-nacl)# remark <put these statements here>
Router(config-ext-nacl)# exit
Router(config)# interface ethernet1
Router(config-if)# ip access-group barb-wire-out out
Router(config-if)# ip access-group barb-wire-in in
```

In this example, I have included the TFN code to filter the echo replies, and I have highlighted the ACL statements to filter stacheldraht control connections.

NOTE   Note that the port numbers in Example 7-33 can be different for a stacheldraht attack. A smart hacker will change these. Therefore, you typically need an IDS solution to detect and prevent this kind of infiltration from occurring.

Because stacheldraht uses ICMP echo replies for some of its communication and also encrypts the TCP connection used for management, it is very difficult to detect.

TIP   Probably the easiest way to detect stacheldraht without having an IDS solution is to use a packet-crafting tool that enables you to create an ICMP echo reply packet with an ID field of 668. If you see an echo reply with an ID value of 669 and a string of sicken\n in the data field, you know you are infected. Another method is, again, to use a packet-crafting tool to send an ICMP echo reply packet with a source address of 3.3.3.3, an ID value of 666, and skillz in the data field. If your packet-sniffing tools see an ICMP echo reply with an ID value of 1000 and spoofworks in the data field, you have been infected. For more information on stacheldraht, visit http://staff.washington.edu/dittrich/misc/stacheldraht.analysis.

Trinity

Trinity is one of the newest DDoS attacks discovered. Unlike the other attacks that I have discussed so far, Trinity is much more ingenious in its command-sharing method between the master and the agents. First, the hacker gains unauthorized access to a UNIX system and installs the program /usr/lib/idle.so. When activated, this program connects to an IRC server on port 6667. The client then sets its IRC nickname to the first three letters of victim's name, followed by three random letters. For example, if the victim's name was www.quizware.com, the nickname would be something such as quiabc. After setting its nickname, the client joins channel #b3ebl3br0x, using a special key. Then the client patiently waits for instructions.

By using an IRC server, the hacker hopes to hide all his control actions. The hacker accesses the appropriate IRC server and channel, and then tells the client what actions to perform. Basically, the hacker hopes that no one in the victim's network is monitoring IRC connections and that the hacker can bypass normal filtering done to prevent other types of DDoS attacks. In addition, the hacker hopes that on a very busy IRC network, all of these IRC commands are lost in the messages and traffic. From the IRC server, the hacker easily can issue commands to begin a DDoS attack. The more agents that have been compromised, the more that are listening on the IRC channel and the larger the army the hacker controls when beginning his attack.

To prevent trinity communications, you need to block a few things. First, IRC has no business application, is very insecure and vulnerable, and wastes bandwidth and employees' time; therefore, you should block this application (the last part of this chapter discusses blocking other types of programs like this, including Instant Messenger [IM] programs). IRC servers either use TCP or UDP and run on ports 6665 through 6669. Second, trinity installs a back-door root shell on the infected machine. This shell listens on TCP port 33,270 and possibly 39,168 (rumored, but not proven). Therefore, you should block all three sets of these connections. Example 7-34 shows a sample configuration, using the network shown in Figure 7-5.

Example 7-34 *Blocking Trinoo Traffic*

```
Router(config)# ip access-list extended trinoo-in
Router(config-ext-nacl)# remark <permit or deny other traffic>
Router(config-ext-nacl)# remark <put these statements here>
Router(config-ext-nacl)# deny tcp any any range 6665 6669
Router(config-ext-nacl)# deny tcp any range 6665 6669 any
Router(config-ext-nacl)# deny tcp any any eq 33270
Router(config-ext-nacl)# deny tcp any eq 33270 any
Router(config-ext-nacl)# deny tcp any any eq 39168
Router(config-ext-nacl)# deny tcp any eq 39168 any
Router(config-ext-nacl)# remark <permit or deny other traffic>
Router(config-ext-nacl)# remark <put these statements here>
Router(config-ext-nacl)# exit
Router(config)# interface ethernet1
Router(config-if)# ip access-group trinoo out
Router(config-if)# ip access-group trinoo in
```

In this example, the first two **deny** statements prevent any traffic to or from IRC servers. The next four **deny** statements prevent any communication that trinity might be using for the back-door program installed on the agent.

NOTE   It is important to point out that there are variations of trinity floating around on the Internet—all of them use IRC servers. You can prevent communication between agents and the hacker by blocking all IRC traffic. For more information about trinity, visit http://xforce.iss.net/xforce/alerts/id/advise59.

Trojan Horses

Trojan horses are programs that are executed either accidentally or inadvertently. In some cases, a user must run the program to install the Trojan. In other cases, through a security bug in the operating system, the hacker has the operating system itself install and run the Trojan. After installing and running a Trojan horse, the hacker is given partial or complete control over the system. For example, Back Orifice exploits Windows machines and gives a hacker complete control of the device, even allowing such functions as sniffing for packets or capturing keystrokes.

Literally hundreds of different types of Trojan horses exist. You can use ACLs to detect Trojan horses, but with the hundreds of entries you would have to put in your ACL, I typically leave it up to an IDS solution to perform this detection: IDS solutions are much better suited to examining the complete packet contents than is an extended ACL with its capability to examine Layers 3 and 4 information. However, if you cannot afford an IDS solution, Cisco's extended ACLs are the next best thing.

TIP   I am just as concerned about detecting Trojan horses as they come into my network as I am about detecting the ones that already exist in my network. A good detection solution examines both inbound and internal traffic.

Trojan Horse ACLs

I typically configure **deny** entries for only the most common Trojan horse attacks. Example 7-35 shows an example of an ACL configuration that blocks common Trojan horse attacks.

Example 7-35 *Using ACLs to Block Trojan Horses*

```
Router(config)# ip access-list extended trojan
Router(config-ext-nacl)# remark <permit or deny other traffic>
Router(config-ext-nacl)# remark <put these statements here>
Router(config-ext-nacl)#
Router(config-ext-nacl)# remark Block Netbus and its varieties
Router(config-ext-nacl)# deny tcp any any 6000
Router(config-ext-nacl)# deny tcp any any range 12345 123456
Router(config-ext-nacl)# deny tcp any any 20034
Router(config-ext-nacl)# remark SubSeven and its varieties
Router(config-ext-nacl)# deny tcp any any eq 1080
```

continues

Example 7-35 *Using ACLs to Block Trojan Horses (Continued)*

```
Router(config-ext-nacl)# deny tcp any any eq 1243
Router(config-ext-nacl)# deny tcp any any eq 1369
Router(config-ext-nacl)# deny tcp any any eq 1999
Router(config-ext-nacl)# deny tcp any any eq 2222
Router(config-ext-nacl)# deny tcp any any range 2772 2774
Router(config-ext-nacl)# deny tcp any any eq 5873
Router(config-ext-nacl)# deny tcp any any eq 6667
Router(config-ext-nacl)# deny tcp any any range 6711 6713
Router(config-ext-nacl)# deny tcp any any eq 6669
Router(config-ext-nacl)# deny tcp any any eq 6676
Router(config-ext-nacl)# deny tcp any any eq 7000
Router(config-ext-nacl)# deny tcp any any eq 7215
Router(config-ext-nacl)# deny tcp any any eq 16959
Router(config-ext-nacl)# deny tcp any any eq 27573
Router(config-ext-nacl)# deny tcp any any eq 54283
Router(config-ext-nacl)# remark Back Orifice
Router(config-ext-nacl)# deny udp any any eq 31337
Router(config-ext-nacl)# deny tcp any any range 31337 31338
Router(config-ext-nacl)# remark Back Orifice 2K
Router(config-ext-nacl)# deny tcp any any eq 8787
Router(config-ext-nacl)# deny tcp any any range 54320 54321
Router(config-ext-nacl)# remark Hack-a-Tack
Router(config-ext-nacl)# deny tcp any any eq 28431
Router(config-ext-nacl)# deny tcp any any range 31785 31792
Router(config-ext-nacl)# deny udp any any range 31785 31792
Router(config-ext-nacl)# remark <permit or deny other traffic>
Router(config-ext-nacl)# remark <put these statements here>
Router(config-ext-nacl)# exit
Router(config)# interface ethernet1
Router(config-if)# ip access-group trojan in
```

For a complete list of known ports that Trojan horses listen on, visit http://www.neohapsis.com/neolabs/neo-ports/neo-ports.html or http://www.simovits.com/nyheter9902.html.

TIP   By blocking these port numbers, you actually might be preventing valid traffic. If this is a concern, change all the **deny** parameters to **permit**. This at least allows you to keep track of the matches and helps you determine whether a Trojan horse is installed in your network.

NOTE   If you think that you have machines infected with Trojan horses, plenty of tools are available on the Internet to detect and remove them. I commonly use the Packet Storm website: http://packetstormsecurity.nl.

One of the best solutions when dealing with Trojan horses is a good antivirus software package. This software should be capable of detecting Trojan horses that are downloaded through popular methods, such as e-mail and HTTP.

Other Prevention Methods

To wrap up this section, you can do other things to protect yourself from DoS and Trojan horse attacks. Two key things that you want to implement are an IDS solution and antispoofing. IDS is covered in Chapter 16. An IDS solution is much better at detecting attacks than a Cisco IOS-based router with ACLs (I discuss the IDS capabilities and limitations of the Cisco IOS in Chapter 16).

Antispoofing was covered previously in the "Bogon Blocking and Spoofing" section of this chapter. This blocks invalid addresses that hackers like to use in DoS and DDoS attacks. Another antispoofing tool that you can use is IP verify unicast reverse path, which verifies the validity of the source address location. I discuss this feature in Chapter 15.

You can use other features, too, such as NBAR (a more sophisticated form of packet matching than ACLs) and CAR (which limits the rate of data streams). These features are discussed in Chapter 17.

One additional item that you will want to keep a close eye on is the use of the **rcp** command. This originally was developed for UNIX to allow files to be copied between systems. With an .rhosts file, if your system name (or address) is listed on the remote device, you could execute the **rcp** command without authenticating, which is a huge security risk. Many DoS and other hacking tools use the **rcp** command (remote copy) to download information to a victim's (agent's) computer. Therefore, you should monitor its use. With an ACL, this can be done as displayed in Example 7-36.

Example 7-36 *Using ACLs to Block RCP Connections*

```
Router(config)# ip access-list extended rcp
Router(config-ext-nacl)# remark <permit or deny other traffic>
Router(config-ext-nacl)# remark <put these statements here>
Router(config-ext-nacl)# deny tcp any any eq 514
Router(config-ext-nacl)# remark <permit or deny other traffic>
Router(config-ext-nacl)# remark <put these statements here>
Router(config-ext-nacl)# exit
Router(config)# interface ethernet1
Router(config-if)# ip access-group rcp in
Router(config-if)# ip access-group rcp out
```

Worms

A worm, in a general form, is a special type of replicating virus. Worms infect a machine and then attempt to self-replicate themselves by infecting other machines. Hackers use worms to take advantage of a security hole that they find in an application or operating system. The most common avenue of work access is through buffer overflow attacks: A hacker discovers a buffer overflow condition in an application or operating system, writes code to gain unauthorized access through the bug, and then has that code install itself and start looking for other devices that have the same bug. The most common applications that worms hit are e-mail (especially Sendmail, Exchange, and Outlook because these are the most popular), web servers (such as Apache and Microsoft IIS), and RPCs (remote-procedure calls).

Solutions to Worm Problems

When worms attack, they typically use the same port number that the application uses, so it is impossible to detect this kind of an attack with an extended ACL. For applications that you cannot filter with an extended ACL, you have other solutions:

- **ACLs**—Unfortunately, ACLs can examine only Layers 3 and 4 information. Worms typically are implemented at the application layer (Layer 7) and require a security component that can analyze this.

- **Security patches**—Because worms take advantage of poor or sloppy programming, the best solution to deal with worms is to patch the application software when the vendor has made a patch available. This slowly kills off the worm as more systems are patched.

- **Application gateways**—These solutions are beneficial for proxy services and can detect viruses and worms in certain kinds of connections. However, they add a heavy utilization load because the gateway must examine every packet for the inspected applications.

- **Antivirus software**—This solution is helpful when downloading information through e-mail or HTTP because many antivirus packages can scan this information inline. However, this requires up-to-date antivirus software on all devices.

- **IDS**—Unlike antivirus software, an IDS solution can scan network traffic, similar to a packet sniffer. This provides broader coverage because it can run on a standalone box. In addition, many IDS implementations can take a proactive approach and direct filtering devices, such as a router, to drop the malicious traffic.

- **NBAR**—NBAR is a Cisco IOS solution that can look for matches in packet contents, including the payload. This is great because it allows the router to perform IDS-type functions. However it can place a very heavy burden on the utilization of the router. I discuss how to use NBAR in Chapter 10, "Filtering Web and Application Traffic," and Chapter 16.

- **Sink-hole routing**—You can use sink-hole routing if NBAR and IDS are not available. For example, the SQL Slammer worm attempts to exploit unallocated addresses. By setting up null routes and logging this information, you can get a quick list of infected hosts. I discuss this solution in Chapter 15.

SQL Slammer Worm

The SQL Slammer worm made its introduction on January 24, 2003. Within a very short period, it infected more than 35,000 devices (some estimates place this at more than 300,000 devices), creating a very effective DoS attack on many different companies' networks.

The worm itself does not contain malicious code, but it uses a buffer overflow condition in Microsoft SQL server software (the SQL Server Resolution Service on UDP port 1434) to gain unauthorized access to the server. After gaining access, the worm installs itself and attempts to infect other hosts. One problem with the worm is that it does not check to see if it already has infected a host. Therefore, the worm easily can overwhelm a server by infecting it hundreds of times.

To make this matter worse, the worm attempts to scan all kinds of network numbers, including unallocated ones, and routers respond with a large number of ICMP unreachable messages for all these scans. From these two occurrences, many networks had brief outages while trying to deal with the amount of traffic that the worm created, as well as the load that it was placing on devices that were affected with multiple instances of the worm.

This worm affected Internet connectivity worldwide. Basically, the SQL Slammer worm doubled every 8.5 seconds, which was 100 times faster than the worse worm to that date (Code Red). At the peak of its mayhem, the worm was scanning more than 55 million hosts every second. During this period, about 20 percent of packets were dropped Internet-wide because of congestion, South Korea lost most of its Internet service, airlines using SQL Server had their airline ticketing systems crash, and many network administrators were running around trying to put out the packet storms that the worm was leaving in its wake. A more detailed discussion of the worm can be found at http://www.eeye.com/html/ Research/Flash/AL20030125.html.

Normally, users outside the network do not use the ports that Microsoft SQL server uses (TCP 1433 and UDP 1434). Therefore, you should filter these ports in the ingress direction on your perimeter firewall. However, after the worm has gained access to your network, you will have a big problem cleaning it out. Unfortunately, trying to filter these ports internally creates connectivity issues because many mission-critical applications use SQL Server (for internal usage). As an example of this, certain IP phone installations use SQL Server; blocking these ports internally would shut down the IP phone system. Most administrators tried to contain the problem by filtering the SQL Server traffic entering and leaving the network. This can be done with a simple ACL, as shown in Example 7-37.

Example 7-37 *Using ACLs to Filter SQL Server Connections*

```
Router(config)# ip access-list extended slammer
Router(config-ext-nacl)# remark <permit or deny other traffic>
Router(config-ext-nacl)# remark <put these statements here>
Router(config-ext-nacl)#
Router(config-ext-nacl)# remark Stop the Slammer!
Router(config-ext-nacl)# deny udp any any eq 1434
Router(config-ext-nacl)# deny tcp any any eq 1433
Router(config-ext-nacl)# remark <permit or deny other traffic>
Router(config-ext-nacl)# remark <put these statements here>
Router(config-ext-nacl)# exit
Router(config)# interface ethernet1
Router(config-if)# ip access-group slammer in
Router(config-if)# ip access-group slammer out
```

TIP   If your router supports NetFlow switching and this is enabled, you can use this **show** command to see if your network is infected: **show ip cache flow | include 059A**. If you see results, you are infected. At least you will know which systems are affected and can take the appropriate action to wipe out the worm on them.

Deloder Worm

The Deloder worm tries to take advantage of weak passwords configured on systems to gain unauthorized access. It uses a Remote Process Launch (RPL) application, psexec.exe, commonly used by Microsoft network administrators, to perform remote management. This process logs into port 445 (Microsoft SMB) and gives system access to file shares on a server. The worm scans this port on all systems and uses a brute-force method of password cracking, using hundreds of passwords in its own password file. After it accesses a system, it installs a back-door Trojan and an RPL application. It then attempts to copy and execute itself on other systems through its brute-force attack. It can replicate itself only from Windows NT, 2000, and XP systems, but it can install itself on 9*x* and Me systems as well.

Because you should not be allowing access to or from a public network to port 445, you should be filtering it, as shown in Example 7-38.

Example 7-38 *Filtering SMB Connections*

```
Router(config)# ip access-list extended deloder
Router(config-ext-nacl)# remark <permit or deny other traffic>
Router(config-ext-nacl)# remark <put these statements here>
Router(config-ext-nacl)#
Router(config-ext-nacl)# remark Stop Deloder!
Router(config-ext-nacl)# deny tcp any any eq 445
Router(config-ext-nacl)# remark <permit or deny other traffic>
Router(config-ext-nacl)# remark <put these statements here>
Router(config-ext-nacl)# exit
Router(config)# interface ethernet1
Router(config-if)# ip access-group deloder in
Router(config-if)# ip access-group deloder out
```

Increases on matches of the previous **deny** statement in the output of the **show access-lists** command typically indicate that a worm attack is occurring (probably Deloder, but other worms have been known to access this port also).

The Microsoft RPC Service and Worms

Many hackers have found flaws in Microsoft remote-procedure call (RPC) code and have exploited them with worm attacks. RPCs are used to share messages between remote machines, providing application functions. With the Microsoft implementation, a stack-based buffer overflow problem occurred in the Distributed Component Object Module (DCOM), allowing unauthorized access. DCOM uses ports 135, 139, and 445.

The W32/Blaster variety of worms took advantage of this hole to spread itself. Unfortunately, you cannot disable DCOM on a Windows server because it is a critical component of the Windows kernel. Applications can use DCOM to implement intercommunications. As an example of this, some Microsoft-based applications use HTTP. With the W32/Blaster worm, the hacker found out that sending a malformed RPC message to the DCOM-based application created a buffer overrun and caused the application to execute code that the hacker sent it. This allowed the hacker to run code as an administrator on the server.

The W32.Welchia worm is a derivative of the W32/Blaster worm. As with Blaster, the Welchia worm exploited weaknesses in DCOM RPC-based applications, specifically targeting Windows XP, 2000, and NT devices. Basically, the Welchia worm infiltrates the device and attempts to download the DCOM RPC patch from the Microsoft website to patch the software, to stamp out the Blaster worm. This sounds fine, but it then actively seeks out other machines to install itself on and repeat the process. Unfortunately, there is no reign mechanism to keep it in check. As with Blaster, it just spreads itself unchecked. One side effect that it creates is to flood a network with pings, attempting to find other devices that it can access and eradicate Blaster.

Other worms, including Nachi, also have exploited weaknesses in the Microsoft RPC DCOM-based implementation. The best solution for preventing these types of worms from entering your network is to filter the ports that they access. This can be done with the ACL displayed in Example 7-39, which uses Figure 7-5 as the example network.

Example 7-39 *Blocking DCOM Connections*

```
Router(config)# ip access-list extended ms-rpc
Router(config-ext-nacl)# remark <permit or deny other traffic>
Router(config-ext-nacl)# remark <put these statements here>
Router(config-ext-nacl)#
Router(config-ext-nacl)# remark block Microsoft's insecure protocols
Router(config-ext-nacl)# deny tcp any any eq 135
Router(config-ext-nacl)# deny udp any any eq 135
Router(config-ext-nacl)# deny udp any any range 137 139
Router(config-ext-nacl)# deny tcp any any eq 139
Router(config-ext-nacl)# deny tcp any any eq 445
Router(config-ext-nacl)# deny tcp any any eq 593
Router(config-ext-nacl)# remark block remote access via W32.blaster
Router(config-ext-nacl)# deny tcp any any eq 4444
Router(config-ext-nacl)# remark <permit or deny other traffic>
Router(config-ext-nacl)# remark <put these statements here>
Router(config-ext-nacl)# exit
Router(config)# interface ethernet1
Router(config-if)# ip access-group ms-rpc in
Router(config-if)# ip access-group ms-rpc out
```

Fast increases on matches of the previous **deny** statements in the output of the **show access-lists** command typically indicate that a worm attack is occurring.

NOTE   Because these varieties of worms use ICMP to find other destinations to infect, if you have disabled ICMP unreachables on all of your routers' interfaces with the **no ip unreachables** command, this can create an explosion of pings to nonexistent devices. By enabling IP unreachables, you are cutting down on the number of worm pings you will see, but you also are exposing yourself by letting internal malicious people understand the topology of your network (what addresses are and are not in use).

The best solution is disable ICMP unreachables but to put a rate limit on how many packets the router will respond to when under a heavy ICMP load. I discuss this solution in Chapter 17.

Blocking Unnecessary Services

I constantly am asked by network administrators how to block two of the most commonly used applications:

- Instant-messaging (IM) applications, such as AOL IM, ICQ, MSN Messenger, and others.

- File-sharing applications, such as Kazaa, Napster, and eDonkey.

This section focuses on filtering these two services.

Bandwidth Pigs

I was consulting with a client not too long ago that was having bandwidth problems on its T3. The company could not understand why, at times, its Internet connection was sluggish. After we put a protocol analyzer on the wire, we were shocked to find out that an average of 50 percent of the traffic was related to IM and file-sharing applications. Employees enjoyed using IM to keep in touch with their friends and family; however, some of these included audio and video functions that used up a lot of bandwidth. In addition, many employees were using file-sharing programs such as Kazaa, sharing large files such as music CDs, which is illegal. It took a while to prevent this by enforcing new policies and penalties, as well as using filtering solutions.

An Uphill Battle

Before I say anything about IM or file sharing, I want to make it absolutely clear that filtering these applications is not a simple process. Many of these applications are located on many different servers on which a different IP address is returned when a DNS query is performed. Discovering these IP addresses is not easy, and the sponsor of the IM or file-sharing application tends to change these quite often. Second, if you miss an IP address, there is a chance that the client software still can connect. You can attempt to filter port numbers, but many of these applications use a range of port numbers. In addition, if a client cannot connect to any of them, sometimes they use a common port number, such as 80 (HTTP).

Therefore, even though I show you how to use ACLs to filter this traffic, it will not be an easy task. You also will have to update your ACLs constantly to reflect changes by the IM and file-sharing sponsors. Here are the things I recommend doing to prevent these programs from running rampant over your network:

- Develop a policy prohibiting their use.
- Use ACLs to detect and filter them.
- Set up DNS to black-hole these applications.
- Use NBAR to filter them (I discuss using NBAR to filter unwanted traffic in Chapters 10 and 17).
- Use an IDS to detect their usage.

The first thing you should do to prevent this traffic is to define a policy that prohibits it, outlining punishments. This kind of software easily can eat up a lot of the bandwidth of your Internet connection, preventing valid applications from functioning correctly.

The second thing you will want to do is filter this traffic. There are two approaches to this. The less preferred method is to use a packet filter to filter the traffic. As I mentioned at the beginning of this section, this might be very difficult, if not impossible. I use this solution if my second solution is not possible. At least with ACLs, if you are blocking the first method of access that the IM or file sharing product is using, at least it will register a match on the ACL statement. This tells you that someone in your network is trying to use these banned products.

TIP	My preferred method of filtering these programs is to use DNS to spoof the responses. If your clients are using your DNS server to resolve the names, configure your DNS server to not forward the resolution request to the Internet to be resolved, but instead resolve it yourself. In this situation, return the address of 127.0.0.1 to the user's request. This prevents all of these applications. Of course, you must know the DNS names that the clients are trying to resolve. For each name, create a zone and assign the name to the zone, associating one A record with an IP address of 127.0.0.1. For some applications that have hundreds of servers, this might be a difficult task.

Instant-Messenger Products

IM products are an enhanced version of IRC. They allow the real-time exchange of messages, information, audio, video, and other information. They are actually pretty cool, but they are bandwidth pigs. Unchecked, they can create congestion problems in your network. My personal view of these products is that if you want to use them, use them at home. Your company is not paying employees to chat all day long with their friends at other locations through the IM, nor is it paying them to download live feeds of music, stock feeds, and sports updates. Even though these seem like innocent fun, they can create serious bandwidth problems if their use goes unchecked.

AOL Instant Messenger

The first new-generation IM program was AOL Instant Messenger (AIM). If you will be using DNS filtering, redirect the following name to 127.0.0.1: login.oscar.aol.com.

For an ACL filter, configure the outbound filter in Example 7-40.

Example 7-40 *Filtering AIM Connections*

```
Router(config)# ip access-list extended aol-messenger
Router(config-ext-nacl)# remark <permit or deny other traffic>
Router(config-ext-nacl)# remark <put these statements here>
Router(config-ext-nacl)# deny udp any any eq 5190
```

continues

Example 7-40 *Filtering AIM Connections (Continued)*

```
Router(config-ext-nacl)# deny tcp any any eq 5190
Router(config-ext-nacl)# deny tcp any any eq 4443
Router(config-ext-nacl)# deny ip any host 64.12.161.153
Router(config-ext-nacl)# deny ip any host 64.12.161.185
Router(config-ext-nacl)# deny ip any host 64.12.200.89
Router(config-ext-nacl)# deny ip any host 205.188.153.249
Router(config-ext-nacl)# deny ip any host 205.188.179.233
Router(config-ext-nacl)# remark <permit or deny other traffic>
Router(config-ext-nacl)# remark <put these statements here>
Router(config-ext-nacl)# exit
Router(config)# interface ethernet1
Router(config-if)# ip access-group aol-messenger out
```

Notice that I am filtering only outbound traffic in this example. This is because you want to prevent your users from accessing the IM servers at the vendor's location.

TIP   I prefer to create **deny** statements for the filtering even if the implicit deny will drop these packets: At least I will be seeing matches on these records if someone is breaking the company policy. If this occurs, I can enable logging on the ACL statement to get the source IP address of the user and remind that person of the security policy regarding network usage.

CAUTION   All the IP addresses that I mention for filtering IM applications are subject to change by the vendor at any point in time. Therefore, make sure that you periodically use a program such as aDig to look up the IP address of the vendor's name server, and then do another lookup for the name, such as login.oscar.aol.com, to get all of the IP addresses that you should be filtering. To download aDig, visit http://www.nscan.org/index.cgi?index=dns.

ICQ

ICQ previously was be owned by Mirabilis, but it was bought out by AOL. Most ICQ clients connect to login.oscar.aol.com, which is AIM's login. Therefore, the filter that I specified in the last section should catch most of your ICQ rule-breakers. However, for the other ICQ users, you need a different configuration. If you are using DNS filtering, set up login.icq.com and http.proxy.icq.com to resolve to 127.0.0.1.

For an ACL filter, configure the outbound filter in Example 7-41.

Example 7-41 *Filtering ICQ Connections*

```
Router(config)# ip access-list extended ICQ
Router(config-ext-nacl)# remark <permit or deny other traffic>
Router(config-ext-nacl)# remark <put these statements here>
Router(config-ext-nacl)# deny udp any any eq 5190
Router(config-ext-nacl)# deny tcp any any eq 5190
```

Example 7-41 *Filtering ICQ Connections (Continued)*

```
Router(config-ext-nacl)# deny tcp any any eq 4001
Router(config-ext-nacl)# deny udp any any range 4000 4001
Router(config-ext-nacl)# deny tcp any any eq 3474
Router(config-ext-nacl)# deny tcp any any eq 7320
Router(config-ext-nacl)# deny ip any host 64.12.161.153
Router(config-ext-nacl)# deny ip any host 64.12.161.185
Router(config-ext-nacl)# deny ip any host 64.12.200.89
Router(config-ext-nacl)# deny ip any host 64.12.163.130
Router(config-ext-nacl)# deny ip any host 64.12.163.132
Router(config-ext-nacl)# deny ip any host 64.12.163.134
Router(config-ext-nacl)# deny ip any host 64.12.163.136
Router(config-ext-nacl)# deny ip any host 64.12.162.57
Router(config-ext-nacl)# deny ip any host 205.188.153.249
Router(config-ext-nacl)# deny ip any host 205.188.179.233
Router(config-ext-nacl)# deny ip any host 205.188.213.228
Router(config-ext-nacl)# remark <permit or deny other traffic>
Router(config-ext-nacl)# remark <put these statements here>
Router(config-ext-nacl)# exit
Router(config)# interface ethernet1
Router(config-if)# ip access-group ICQ out
```

In this filter, you might want to try filtering 64.12.162.0/24 and 64.12.163.0/24, and see what happens. I have seen these addresses change now and then, so denying all of these addresses might fix the problem. Just be careful that you do not block a valid address, such as a DNS, e-mail, or web server, with the filter.

Microsoft MSN Messenger

Microsoft introduced an IM product late in the game. Just recently, Microsoft stated that it is discontinuing its MSN Messenger product outside the United States because of liability and legal reasons: It has been having problems with people breaking the law, such as sharing child pornography, and had issues with validating the identity of their users committing these crimes. Basically, you must have, at a minimum, only a Hotmail e-mail account to use MSN Messenger. To use DNS to black-hole access to MSN Messenger, set up DNS A records to redirect traffic for messenger.hotmail.com and gateway.messenger.hotmail.com to 127.0.0.1.

For an ACL filter, configure the outbound filter in Example 7-42.

Example 7-42 *Filtering MSN Connections*

```
Router(config)# ip access-list extended MSN-messenger
Router(config-ext-nacl)# remark <permit or deny other traffic>
Router(config-ext-nacl)# remark <put these statements here>
Router(config-ext-nacl)# deny tcp any any eq 1503
Router(config-ext-nacl)# deny tcp any any eq 1863
Router(config-ext-nacl)# deny tcp any any eq 6891
Router(config-ext-nacl)# deny udp any any eq 1863
```

continues

Example 7-42 *Filtering MSN Connections (Continued)*

```
Router(config-ext-nacl)# deny udp any any range 13324 13325
Router(config-ext-nacl)# deny tcp any any eq 569
Router(config-ext-nacl)# deny udp any any eq 569
Router(config-ext-nacl)# deny ip any 64.4.13.0 0.0.0.255
Router(config-ext-nacl)# deny ip any host 207.46.104.20
Router(config-ext-nacl)# deny ip any 207.46.96.0 0.0.0.255
Router(config-ext-nacl)# remark <permit or deny other traffic>
Router(config-ext-nacl)# remark <put these statements here>
Router(config-ext-nacl)# exit
Router(config)# interface ethernet1
Router(config-if)# ip access-group MSN-messenger out
```

In the shaded line in this example, you need to filter addresses from only 170 to 190; however, in this example, I filtered the entire subnet.

Yahoo! Messenger

Yahoo! Messenger is not as popular as the other products that I have discussed so far. However, out of all of the IM products, it is the most difficult to block. I have seen it run on all kinds of ports, including 80 (HTTP) and even 23 (Telnet). Your best approach is to black-hole DNS queries. Here is a list of names that you should redirect to 127.0.0.1:

- cs.yahoo.com
- scs.msg.yahoo.com
- scsa.msg.yahoo.com
- scsb.msg.yahoo.com
- scsc.msg.yahoo.com
- scs-fooa.yahoo.com
- msg.edit.yahoo.com
- messenger.yahoo.com
- msg.yahoo.com
- http.msg.yahoo.com
- http.pager.yahoo.com
- msg1.edit.vip.sc5.yahoo.com
- webcam.yahoo.com
- wc1.vip.sc5.yahoo.com
- filetransfer.msg.yahoo.com
- filetrans1.msg.vip.sc5.yahoo.com
- vc1.vc.scd.yahoo.com
- vc2.vc.scd.yahoo.com

- vc3.vc.scd.yahoo.com
- vc4.vc.scd.yahoo.com
- vc5.vc.scd.yahoo.com
- vc6.vc.scd.yahoo.com
- vc7.vc.scd.yahoo.com
- vc8.vc.scd.yahoo.com
- vc9.vc.scd.yahoo.com
- vc10.vc.scd.yahoo.com
- vc11.vc.scd.yahoo.com
- vc12.vc.scd.yahoo.com
- vc13.vc.scd.yahoo.com
- vc1.vip.scd.yahoo.com

As you can see from this list, your DNS work is cut out for you.

For an ACL filter, configure the outbound filter in Example 7-43.

Example 7-43 *Filtering Yahoo! Messenger Connections*

```
Router(config)# ip access-list extended Yahoo
Router(config-ext-nacl)# remark <permit or deny other traffic>
Router(config-ext-nacl)# remark <put these statements here>
Router(config-ext-nacl)# deny tcp any any eq 5050
Router(config-ext-nacl)# deny udp any any range 5100 5101
Router(config-ext-nacl)# deny tcp any any range 5100 5101
Router(config-ext-nacl)# deny udp any any range 5050
Router(config-ext-nacl)# deny udp any any range 5000 5010
Router(config-ext-nacl)# deny tcp any any range 5000 5010
Router(config-ext-nacl)# deny tcp any any range 8000 8001
Router(config-ext-nacl)# deny udp any any range 8000 8001
Router(config-ext-nacl)# deny ip any host 64.58.76.37
Router(config-ext-nacl)# deny ip any 66.163.169.0 0.0.0.255
Router(config-ext-nacl)# deny ip any 66.163.172.0 0.0.0.255
Router(config-ext-nacl)# deny ip any 66.163.174.0 0.0.0.255
Router(config-ext-nacl)# deny ip any 66.218.70.0 0.0.0.255
Router(config-ext-nacl)# deny ip any 216.109.116.176 0.0.0.1
Router(config-ext-nacl)# deny ip any host 216.136.128.128
Router(config-ext-nacl)# deny ip any 216.136.172.0 0.0.0.255
Router(config-ext-nacl)# deny ip any 216.136.173.0 0.0.0.255
Router(config-ext-nacl)# deny ip any 216.136.175.0 0.0.0.255
Router(config-ext-nacl)# deny ip any host 216.136.225.238
Router(config-ext-nacl)# deny ip any host 216.136.232.153
Router(config-ext-nacl)# remark <permit or deny other traffic>
Router(config-ext-nacl)# remark <put these statements here>
Router(config-ext-nacl)# exit
Router(config)# interface ethernet1
Router(config-if)# ip access-group Yahoo out
```

For the 66.163.169.0/24 subnet, I know that 143, 148, 149, 150, 212, and 213 are used, but I filtered the entire subnet. For the 66.163.172.0/24 subnet, I know that 51, 80 to 83, 93, 94, 99, and 100 are being used. For the 66.163.174.0/24 subnet, I know that 46 to 49, 77 to 82, 111 to 115, and 117 to 126 are being used. For the 66.218.70.0/24 subnet, I know that 32 to 46 are being used. For the 216.109.116.0 network, only 176 and 177 are used. For the 216.136.172.0 network, I know that 222, 223, 225, and 226 are being used. For the 216.136.173.0 network, 16, 141, 142, and 183 to 186 are being used. For the 216.136.175.0 network, 143 to 145 are being used.

As you can see from the ACL in Example 7-43, filtering Yahoo! Messenger is not simple. Actually, I would like to talk to the designers of this network design—it is a mess.

Apple iChat

With the introduction of the Apple Mac OS X Rendezvous, the Apple iChat program is becoming more popular. It has built-in text chat, audio, video, and file-sharing capabilities. Filtering this is much easier than filtering the others that I have discussed. Example 7-44 shows the ACL to filter this traffic.

Example 7-44 *Filtering iChat Connections*

```
Router(config)# ip access-list extended iChat
Router(config-ext-nacl)# remark <permit or deny other traffic>
Router(config-ext-nacl)# remark <put these statements here>
Router(config-ext-nacl)# deny tcp any any eq 5298
Router(config-ext-nacl)# deny udp any any eq 5298
Router(config-ext-nacl)# deny udp any any eq 5353
Router(config-ext-nacl)# deny udp any any eq 5060
Router(config-ext-nacl)# deny udp any any range 16384 16403
Router(config-ext-nacl)# remark <permit or deny other traffic>
Router(config-ext-nacl)# remark <put these statements here>
Router(config-ext-nacl)# exit
Router(config)# interface ethernet1
Router(config-if)# ip access-group iChat out
```

File Sharing: Peer-to-Peer Products

File-sharing programs, commonly called peer-to-peer (P2P) programs, allow people to share files easily: They are the next generation of FTP. Many of these services are legitimate, allowing users to share resources that provide benefits. However, many of these services allow users to trade illegal items, such as copyrighted books and music, certain kinds of pornography, software and games, and many other items. However, some users still want to install and use these programs on their desktops.

It is bad enough that a user wants to set up a client and download large files, eating up your bandwidth. It is much worse when someone gets set up as a server and lets hundreds of people download content to and from the desktop. In university environments, P2P programs have created a huge bandwidth problem. Normally, universities are fairly open in the use of the Internet, but many of them are creating and enforcing policies to reduce the congestion that these programs have on their network. Some even have developed ingenious solutions to dynamically bar users from network access if they break university policies regarding the use of these programs. In a university environment, it is not unusual to see 50 to 60 percent of Internet traffic related to P2P file sharing; I can understand why universities are taking a hard stance on the use of P2P programs.

Prevention and Detection

Many of the files shared are very large in P2P environments, so many companies have policies prohibiting users from using P2P programs. You can use four basic solutions to help prevent the use of P2P programs in your network:

- Create policies prohibiting the use of P2P programs.
- Use an IDS solution to detect P2P programs.
- Use a content-filtering solution to catch P2P programs that use port 80 (they try to hide their downloads in a web connection). I discuss content filtering in Chapter 10.
- Use ACLs to filter P2P traffic.

To do this correctly, you first need to ensure that your company implements a policy to ban the use of P2P programs: Your company's policy should have an acceptable use clause, in which P2P programs do not fall under this clause. Of the last three bullets, you typically use a combination of two or three of these to detect and prevent the use of P2P programs.

One main issue of P2P programs is that they are very dynamic in accessing P2P servers and downloading content, so detecting and preventing them is difficult (sort of like the filtering example to prevent Yahoo! Messenger). My main concern when dealing with P2P programs is not to prevent them completely; this is probably impossible. My main goal is to detect their usage and confront the person or people using them, and to enforce the penalties, if necessary, in the company's policies. Therefore, the ACLs that I am using detect and prevent most P2P program usage. You definitely will want to keep track of ACL matches on these statements to catch rule-breakers in your company.

CAUTION   Some P2P applications use ports 80 and 23 (Telnet) to run the server software. Therefore, in many instances, it might be impossible to stop the traffic. However, in most instances, the client software typically uses the well-known port number when connecting to the server. If this access is denied, these programs typically try other configured ports (such as 80 or 23, if the client software supports these). If you see a lot of **deny** statement matches on P2P ACL statements and a big increase of traffic on other port numbers, one or more people in your network are using P2P programs.

Also, some people use proxy programs, such as SOCKS, to connect to an external server, assuming that the server permits proxy connections for various applications, such as P2P. Unless you use an IDS solution, catching this kind of behavior is very difficult.

Napster

The most well known of the P2P programs is Napster. It gained its fame when the music industry sued because its customer base was illegally sharing music content without users paying for it. Because of the lawsuit, Napster closed it doors and then reopened as a pay site. Therefore, you do not need to be as concerned with this P2P program, compared to others I talk about in subsequent sections.

To block Napster traffic, you need to filter certain ports and IP addresses. Example 7-45 displays an example of a filter to prevent Napster traffic.

Example 7-45 *Filtering Napster Connections*

```
Router(config)# ip access-list extended napster-in
Router(config-ext-nacl)# remark <permit or deny other traffic>
Router(config-ext-nacl)# remark <put these statements here>
Router(config-ext-nacl)# deny tcp any any eq 6699
Router(config-ext-nacl)# deny tcp any any eq 6257
Router(config-ext-nacl)# deny udp any any eq 6699
Router(config-ext-nacl)# deny udp any any eq 6257
Router(config-ext-nacl)# deny tcp any any range 8875 8890
Router(config-ext-nacl)# deny tcp any any eq 1911
Router(config-ext-nacl)# deny tcp any any eq 2222
Router(config-ext-nacl)# deny tcp any any eq 3456
Router(config-ext-nacl)# deny tcp any any eq 4444
Router(config-ext-nacl)# deny tcp any any eq 5555
Router(config-ext-nacl)# deny tcp any any eq 56789
Router(config-ext-nacl)# deny tcp any any eq 6666
Router(config-ext-nacl)# deny tcp any any eq 7777
Router(config-ext-nacl)# deny tcp any any eq 9999
Router(config-ext-nacl)# deny tcp any any eq 35000
Router(config-ext-nacl)# deny tcp any any eq 44444
Router(config-ext-nacl)# deny tcp any any eq 56789
Router(config-ext-nacl)# remark <permit or deny other traffic>
Router(config-ext-nacl)# remark <put these statements here>
Router(config-ext-nacl)# exit
Router(config)# ip access-list extended napster-out
Router(config-ext-nacl)# remark <permit or deny other traffic>
Router(config-ext-nacl)# remark <put these statements here>
Router(config-ext-nacl)# deny tcp any any eq 6699
Router(config-ext-nacl)# deny tcp any any eq 6257
Router(config-ext-nacl)# deny udp any any eq 6699
Router(config-ext-nacl)# deny udp any any eq 6257
Router(config-ext-nacl)# deny tcp any any range 8875 8890
Router(config-ext-nacl)# deny tcp any any eq 1911
Router(config-ext-nacl)# deny tcp any any eq 2222
Router(config-ext-nacl)# deny tcp any any eq 3456
Router(config-ext-nacl)# deny tcp any any eq 4444
Router(config-ext-nacl)# deny tcp any any eq 5555
Router(config-ext-nacl)# deny tcp any any eq 56789
Router(config-ext-nacl)# deny tcp any any eq 6666
Router(config-ext-nacl)# deny tcp any any eq 7777
Router(config-ext-nacl)# deny tcp any any eq 9999
Router(config-ext-nacl)# deny tcp any any eq 35000
```

Example 7-45 *Filtering Napster Connections (Continued)*

```
Router(config-ext-nacl)# deny tcp any any eq 44444
Router(config-ext-nacl)# deny tcp any any eq 56789
Router(config-ext-nacl)# deny ip any 208.184.216.222 0.0.0.1
Router(config-ext-nacl)# deny ip any host 208.178.163.61
Router(config-ext-nacl)# deny ip any 208.178.175.128 0.0.0.7
Router(config-ext-nacl)# deny ip any 208.184.216.192 0.0.0.31
Router(config-ext-nacl)# deny ip any 208.49.239.240 0.0.0.15
Router(config-ext-nacl)# deny ip any 64.124.41.0 0.0.0.255
Router(config-ext-nacl)# remark <permit or deny other traffic>
Router(config-ext-nacl)# remark <put these statements here>
Router(config-ext-nacl)# exit
Router(config)# interface ethernet1
Router(config-if)# ip access-group napster-in in
Router(config-if)# ip access-group napster-out out
```

Notice that in this example I have two ACLs. The first one is used to filter Napster traffic coming into the network, just in case a user has set himself up as a server. The second one is used to filter the Napster client from connecting to a server. I put in the known IP addresses of Napster servers in this list, but it is subject to change at any given time.

TIP   The most important thing to include in these filters is the port numbers that I have listed. Because your first concern is detecting the Napster use, you might want to exclude the Napster servers that I have listed. The filter will keep track of the number of matches if you have users attempting to use Napster.

The ACL in Example 7-45 filters "official" Napster traffic. However, additional rogue napster servers are known to exist on the Internet. Users can download a product called Napigator that will allow them to access either set of servers. The up-to-date list of these servers is kept at http://www.napigator.com/serverlist. The last time I checked, more than 100 Napigator servers were listed. The main problem with this list is that many of the addresses I checked did not have the Napster software installed on them; furthermore, this list changes on a weekly basis. With the ACL I configured, I have included the port numbers that these servers use; you should not have to worry about filtering these addresses unless you find a specific Napster problem in your network that is related to one of these servers.

Kazaa and Morpheus

Kazaa and Morpheus are second-generation Napster applications. As with Napster, they allow the use of P2P to share files between people. Because of the legal issues Napster faced, Kazaa has become one of the most popular file-sharing programs on the Internet. Blocking these P2P applications is actually more difficult than blocking Napster. For example, when a Kazaa client accesses a Morpheus server, it first tries TCP 1214 (sometimes UDP). If this is blocked, it tries ports from 1000 to 4000. If these are blocked, it tries port 80. Therefore, because you will want your users to access port 80, it seems that blocking this P2P traffic is impossible. However, your main goal here is to detect that your users are using this application. When you know that one of your users is trying use the Kazaa, you can take the appropriate action detailed in your company's policies. Example 7-46 shows how set up an ACL to filter Kazaa traffic.

Example 7-46 *Filtering Kazaa Connections*

```
Router(config)# ip access-list extended kazaa-in
Router(config-ext-nacl)# remark <permit or deny other traffic>
Router(config-ext-nacl)# remark <put these statements here>
Router(config-ext-nacl)# deny tcp any any eq 1214
Router(config-ext-nacl)# deny udp any any eq 1214
Router(config-ext-nacl)# remark <permit or deny other traffic>
Router(config-ext-nacl)# remark <put these statements here>
Router(config-ext-nacl)# exit
Router(config)# ip access-list extended kazaa-out
Router(config-ext-nacl)# remark <permit or deny other traffic>
Router(config-ext-nacl)# remark <put these statements here>
Router(config-ext-nacl)# deny tcp any any eq 1214
Router(config-ext-nacl)# deny udp any any eq 1214
Router(config-ext-nacl)# deny ip any 213.248.112.0 0.0.0.255
Router(config-ext-nacl)# deny ip any host 24.73.55.18
Router(config-ext-nacl)# deny ip any host 24.103.112.18
Router(config-ext-nacl)# deny ip any host 65.92.89.216
Router(config-ext-nacl)# deny ip any host 68.5.8.4
Router(config-ext-nacl)# deny ip any host 68.65.238.48
Router(config-ext-nacl)# deny ip any host 68.67.210.20
Router(config-ext-nacl)# deny ip any host 68.81.141.205
Router(config-ext-nacl)# deny ip any host 68.97.116.232
Router(config-ext-nacl)# deny ip any host 68.98.62.2
Router(config-ext-nacl)# deny ip any host 68.102.79.211
Router(config-ext-nacl)# deny ip any host 205.150.0.55
Router(config-ext-nacl)# deny ip any host 205.180.85.40
Router(config-ext-nacl)# deny ip any host 205.206.22.50
Router(config-ext-nacl)# deny ip any host 206.29.192.80
Router(config-ext-nacl)# deny ip any host 206.142.53.17
Router(config-ext-nacl)# deny ip any host 206.142.53.19
Router(config-ext-nacl)# deny ip any host 206.142.53.21
Router(config-ext-nacl)# deny ip any host 208.185.90.205
Router(config-ext-nacl)# deny ip any host 209.225.0.6
Router(config-ext-nacl)# deny ip any host 213.248.112.35
Router(config-ext-nacl)# remark <permit or deny other traffic>
Router(config-ext-nacl)# remark <put these statements here>
Router(config-ext-nacl)# exit
Router(config)# interface ethernet1
Router(config-if)# ip access-group kazaa-in in
Router(config-if)# ip access-group kazaa-out out
```

Notice that in Example 7-46, I have two ACLs. The first one is used to filter Kazaa traffic coming into the network, just in case a user has set himself up as a server. The second one is used to filter the Kazaa client from connecting to a Morpheus server. I put in the known

IP addresses of Morpheus servers in this list, but it is subject to change at any given time. The most important thing to include in these filters is the port numbers that I have listed. Because your first concern is detecting Kazaa usage, you might want to exclude the Morpheus servers that I have listed. The filter will keep track of the number of matches if you have users attempting to use Kazaa/Morpheus.

Gnutella

Gnutella is another P2P file-sharing application. Many client programs are based on the Gnutella technology, including Bearshare, LimeWare, Gnucleus, ToadNode, and others. As with Kazaa, Gnutella can use many different port numbers to make its connection, making it difficult to filter. Even if you filter its main port, TCP 6346, it can use other ports, such as 80 and 21 (FTP). Again, the main concern is detecting this traffic. Example 7-47 shows an ACL configuration that greatly restricts these kinds of connections.

Example 7-47 *Filtering Gnutella Connections*

```
Router(config)# ip access-list extended gnutella
Router(config-ext-nacl)# remark <permit or deny other traffic>
Router(config-ext-nacl)# remark <put these statements here>
Router(config-ext-nacl)# deny tcp any any eq 6346
Router(config-ext-nacl)# deny tcp any any range 6345-6349
Router(config-ext-nacl)# deny udp any any range 6345-6349
Router(config-ext-nacl)# remark <permit or deny other traffic>
Router(config-ext-nacl)# remark <put these statements here>
Router(config-ext-nacl)# exit
Router(config)# interface ethernet1
Router(config-if)# ip access-group gnutella in
Router(config-if)# ip access-group gnutella out
```

Most Gnutella clients connect through TCP 6346; however, some have been know to use either TCP or UDP and port numbers from 6345 to 6349. Therefore, I have included statements for these. Even though the first **deny** statement is not necessary, I typically put it in so that I can see the number of matches on people who use the more popular Gnutella programs versus the less popular ones. If I see an increase in the less popular ones, I begin investigating further to see if the ACL that I have created is catching this traffic, especially if it is a new program.

IMesh

Like the other programs discussed so far, IMesh is a P2P program. Unlike the others, it has a neat user feature: When a user selects a file to download, the IMesh server searches the list of available sources and tells the client the source that has the fastest download access at that time. In addition, if the download is interrupted, the user can resume the download process for the same file from a different server. This is great if you have only modem access and you get disconnected constantly.

IMesh is difficult to filter, especially because it can try many ports when attempting to connect. IMesh licensed the P2P technology from Kazaa, making the ACL filter similar, as displayed in Example 7-48.

Example 7-48 *Filtering IMesh Connections*

```
Router(config)# ip access-list extended IMesh-in
Router(config-ext-nacl)# remark <permit or deny other traffic>
Router(config-ext-nacl)# remark <put these statements here>
Router(config-ext-nacl)# deny tcp any any eq 1214
Router(config-ext-nacl)# deny udp any any eq 1214
Router(config-ext-nacl)# deny icmp 216.35.208.0 0.0.0.255 any
Router(config-ext-nacl)# remark <permit or deny other traffic>
Router(config-ext-nacl)# remark <put these statements here>
Router(config-ext-nacl)# exit
Router(config)# ip access-list extended IMesh-out
Router(config-ext-nacl)# remark <permit or deny other traffic>
Router(config-ext-nacl)# remark <put these statements here>
Router(config-ext-nacl)# deny tcp any any eq 1214
Router(config-ext-nacl)# deny udp any any eq 1214
Router(config-ext-nacl)# deny icmp any 216.35.208.0 0.0.0.255
Router(config-ext-nacl)# deny ip any 216.35.208.0 0.0.0.255
Router(config-ext-nacl)# remark <permit or deny other traffic>
Router(config-ext-nacl)# remark <put these statements here>
Router(config-ext-nacl)# exit
Router(config)# interface ethernet1
Router(config-if)# ip access-group IMesh-in in
Router(config-if)# ip access-group IMesh-out out
```

The first ACL drops inbound traffic to an internal IMesh server if a rogue one has been set up. All IMesh servers that I know of are located in 216.35.208.0/24. Notice that the only **deny** statement in the inbound ACL drops any ICMP traffic from these servers. One interesting tidbit about IMesh is that the servers periodically send ICMP messages to see if the clients are connected. By putting this **deny** statement here, you are capturing matches while a client is connected (you might want to log this information). The outbound ACL drops traffic sent to the IMesh servers. I also put in a filter, just in case the client initiates the ping process (I have never seen this personally, but it might happen, based on the experience of other network administrators). Note that IMesh is smart and allows clients to connect on different ports if 1214 is filtered.

WinMX

WinMX is another Napster-type clone. However, it has included some additional functionality, similar to that of Gnutella. Filtering it also is difficult, but the ACL in Example 7-49 should prevent most, if not all, downloads through WinMX clients.

Example 7-49 *Filtering WinMX Connections*

```
Router(config)# ip access-list extended winmx-in
Router(config-ext-nacl)# remark <permit or deny other traffic>
Router(config-ext-nacl)# remark <put these statements here>
Router(config-ext-nacl)# deny tcp any any eq 6699
Router(config-ext-nacl)# deny tcp any any eq 6257
Router(config-ext-nacl)# deny udp any any eq 6699
Router(config-ext-nacl)# deny udp any any eq 6257
Router(config-ext-nacl)# deny ip 64.49.201.0 0.0.0.255 any
```

Example 7-49 *Filtering WinMX Connections (Continued)*

```
Router(config-ext-nacl)# deny ip 209.61.186.0 0.0.0.255 any
Router(config-ext-nacl)# remark <permit or deny other traffic>
Router(config-ext-nacl)# remark <put these statements here>
Router(config-ext-nacl)# exit
Router(config)# ip access-list extended winmx-out
Router(config-ext-nacl)# remark <permit or deny other traffic>
Router(config-ext-nacl)# remark <put these statements here>
Router(config-ext-nacl)# deny tcp any any eq 6699
Router(config-ext-nacl)# deny tcp any any eq 6257
Router(config-ext-nacl)# deny udp any any eq 6699
Router(config-ext-nacl)# deny udp any any eq 6257
Router(config-ext-nacl)# deny ip any 64.49.201.0 0.0.0.255
Router(config-ext-nacl)# deny ip any 209.61.186.0 0.0.0.255
Router(config-ext-nacl)# remark <permit or deny other traffic>
Router(config-ext-nacl)# remark <put these statements here>
Router(config-ext-nacl)# exit
Router(config)# interface ethernet1
Router(config-if)# ip access-group winmx-in in
Router(config-if)# ip access-group winmx-out out
```

Notice that in this example, I am blocking the two common ports that Napster uses because WinMX uses them also. However, this is no guarantee that WinMX connections will fail. Typically, the client uses other ports to connect. I also have included in my two ACLs the networks where the WinMX servers are located, hopefully shutting the door on any WinMX file sharing.

AudioGalaxy

AudioGalaxy is used to share audio files, such as music. When the client attempts to make a connection, it typically searches for higher ports (41,000 through 42,000) on the AudioGalaxy server. Filtering these ports can be an issue, especially because these might be valid source ports from Internet users accessing your internal resources. Therefore, you might not want to filter these ports, but minimally put a **permit** statement in your ACL to keep track on the number of hits on the statement. On top of this issue, AudioGalaxy uses FTP to transfer the files. If you have an internal FTP server or you want your internal users to access external FTP servers, you cannot block FTP access. Therefore, the best solution to prevent this problem is to filter traffic to and from the AudioGalaxy network, as displayed in Example 7-50.

Example 7-50 *Filtering AudioGalaxy Connections*

```
Router(config)# ip access-list extended audiogalaxy-in
Router(config-ext-nacl)# remark <permit or deny other traffic>
Router(config-ext-nacl)# remark <put these statements here>
Router(config-ext-nacl)# deny ip 64.245.58.0 0.0.1.255 any
Router(config-ext-nacl)# remark <permit or deny other traffic>
Router(config-ext-nacl)# remark <put these statements here>
Router(config-ext-nacl)# exit
Router(config)# ip access-list extended audiogalaxy-out
Router(config-ext-nacl)# remark <permit or deny other traffic>
```

continues

Example 7-50 *Filtering AudioGalaxy Connections (Continued)*

```
Router(config-ext-nacl)# remark <put these statements here>
Router(config-ext-nacl)# deny ip any 64.245.58.0 0.0.1.255
Router(config-ext-nacl)# remark <permit or deny other traffic>
Router(config-ext-nacl)# remark <put these statements here>
Router(config-ext-nacl)# exit
Router(config)# interface ethernet1
Router(config-if)# ip access-group audiogalaxy-in in
Router(config-if)# ip access-group audiogalaxy-out out
```

Notice that I did not block the port ranges from 41,000 to 42,000; I have done this in the past but have experienced problems with Internet users accessing internal resources with source port numbers in this range, thereby denying them service. Therefore, I filter only on the network where AudioGalaxy operates. Notice the 0.0.1.255 wildcard mask that I used: This is correct. I actually am matching on 64.245.58.0 and 64.245.59.0.

eDonkey2000

Unlike the other P2P programs that I have discussed so far, eDonkey2000 is a noncommercial package used by people who want to set up their own P2P service or network. It is not a simple matter to filter traffic going to a specific destination, especially because you do not know what the destinations are. To see a list of active eDonkey2000 sites, visit http://ocbmaurice.dyndns.org/pl/slist.pl.

eDonkey2000 uses three types of connections:

- TCP 4661 is used by the client to connect to the server. (I also have seen 4242 and 4243.)
- TCP 4662 is used by the client to connect to other clients.
- UDP 4665 is used by the client to send messages to servers that the client currently is not connected to.

The ACL in Example 7-51 prevents client eDonkey2000 traffic from leaving and entering your network.

Example 7-51 *Filtering eDonkey2000 Connections*

```
Router(config)# ip access-list extended edonkey
Router(config-ext-nacl)# remark <permit or deny other traffic>
Router(config-ext-nacl)# remark <put these statements here>
Router(config-ext-nacl)# deny tcp any any range 4661 4662
Router(config-ext-nacl)# deny tcp any any range 4242 4243
Router(config-ext-nacl)# deny udp any any eq 4665
Router(config-ext-nacl)# remark <permit or deny other traffic>
Router(config-ext-nacl)# remark <put these statements here>
Router(config-ext-nacl)# exit
Router(config)# interface ethernet1
Router(config-if)# ip access-group edonkey in
Router(config-if)# ip access-group edonkey out
```

TIP   If you really are concerned about P2P software, there are much better detection systems out there than using ACLs on a router. Many of these systems are sort of a hybrid IDS, enabling you to track P2P usage, the amount of bandwidth used, how much connect time is involved, what files are being downloaded, and so on. If want a detailed record of these kinds of transactions, I recommend buying one of these products. The solutions that I discussed in this section are a quick-and-dirty fix: They identify users who are using these programs, which enables you to deal with the problem directly with these people. I have never worked with any of these products personally, but a few of my customers have used them with success: AssetMetrix (http://www.assetmetrix.com/solutions/p2p/) and Packeteer (http://www.packeteer.com/).

Summary

This chapter showed you how to configure standard and extended ACLs on your router. As I have shown you throughout the chapter, ACLs, especially extended ACLs, are a very powerful tool in filtering undesirable traffic and detecting attacks. Remember, through, that extended ACLs have limitations: They cannot filter all kinds of traffic (such as P2P or IM connections, in some instances), nor are they a good solution for stateful filtering. However, you always can combine standard and extended ACLs with other solutions that I discuss in this book to create a robust, flexible, and secure firewall system.

Next up is Part IV, "Stateful and Advanced Filtering Technologies," which shows you how to protect the router itself by using stateful filtering features such as reflexive ACLs and CBAC ACLs. This next part also teaches you how to filter web traffic.

TIP   One last tip for this chapter: I typically use specific **deny** statements in an ACL even though the implicit deny would drop this traffic anyway. I do this so that I can see the number of matches on ACL statements with the **show access-lists** command. This gives me a quick view of whether certain kinds of attacks are occurring without having to create logging information, which can be a burden to the router. By comparing day-to-day numbers, I should have a good idea of what level of matches is considered normal. If I see a huge difference in matches from one day to the next, something is probably not right. If I think that I am under a specific kind of attack, or if an internal user has found a hole in my perimeter/firewall router to get around IM and P2P filtering, I add the **log** or **log-input** parameters to the ACL statement where I am getting a lot of matches. This gives me some more information about the type of attack or access.

Of course, having a good IDS system is a must in detecting and preventing attacks, but using the method I just described, you can create a "poor man's IDS" with ACLs.

Stateful and Advanced Filtering Technologies

Chapter 8   Reflexive Access Lists

Chapter 9   Context-Based Access Control

Chapter 10   Filtering Web and Application Traffic

Reflexive Access Lists

Reflexive ACLs (RACLs) first were introduced in Cisco IOS 11.3. Unlike standard IP ACLs that can filter on Layer 3 information, and extended IP ACLs that can filter on Layers 3 and 4 information, RACLs can filter on Layers 3, 4, and 5 (session layer). This chapter focuses on using RACLs to implement a stateful firewall function on your router. As you will see, RACLs have many advantages, as well as limitations. Typically, RACLs are used when you do not have access to Context-based Access Control (CBAC), which provides a better stateful firewall function and has many more enhanced features than RACLs. CBAC is discussed in Chapter 9, "Context-Based Access Control."

Overview of Reflexive ACLs

As discussed in Chapter 7, "Basic Access Lists," you can use standard and, especially, extended ACLs to provide excellent packet-filtering capabilities, protecting you from all different kinds of attacks. Every perimeter router that I have configured or seen takes advantage of extended ACLs in filtering traffic. However, as I also pointed out in Chapter 7, these ACLs have certain limitations. The biggest limitation is that they are good for filtering unidirectional but not bidirectional, connections. As you recall, standard and extended ACLs do not keep track of the state of a connection; therefore, if someone inside sends traffic to the Internet, it is very hard to safely allow the returning traffic back into your network without opening a large hole on your perimeter router. In other words, a standard or extended ACL has static entries that always filter on the information that you have configured—with no exceptions.

RACLs were developed to deal with this issue. RACLs enable you to filter on session layer information. With this type of filtering, the Cisco IOS keeps track of the connections leaving your network and allows the returning traffic of these connections back in. By default, RACLs deny traffic that originates outside of your network and attempts to connect to internal resources. RACLs basically create temporary entries in your inbound filter whenever an internal device opens a session to the outside world. This temporary entry allows the returning traffic for this session back through the perimeter firewall router.

For example, assume that an internal user generates a Telnet connection to a remote device on the Internet, and this traffic passes through your perimeter router with RACLs configured on it. The Cisco IOS would permit the outgoing connection and add a temporary, dynamic entry to allow the returning Telnet traffic back to the internal user. However, the RACLs would not allow Internet users to Telnet to the internal user's device unless you explicitly allowed this connection with an extended ACL entry.

Extended Versus Reflexive ACLs

To help you understand the advantages that RACLs provide over extended ACLs, this section compares the two different types of ACLs. As you recall from Chapter 7, extended IP ACLs can filter only on Layers 3 and 4 information, such as the IP protocol (IP, ICMP, TCP, UDP, and so on), source and destination IP addresses, IP protocol information (ICMP message types, TCP and UDP port numbers, TCP control flags, and so on), and other information related to the Layers 3 and 4 header fields.

How Extended ACLs Handle Returning ICMP Traffic

This section looks how you can deal with returning traffic for sessions from internal users when using extended IP ACLs. Refer to Figure 8-1 as an illustration of how ICMP traffic can be handled. In this example, the internal user pings an external server (200.1.1.1) using ICMP echo messages. Assume that this traffic is allowed out by the perimeter router. After the pings have been sent out of the network, and assuming that 200.1.1.1 replies to the echo requests, the echo replies make it back to the filtering router. To allow the ICMP replies back into the network, you would have to configure something like Example 8-1.

Figure 8-1   *ICMP Traffic and Extended ACLs*

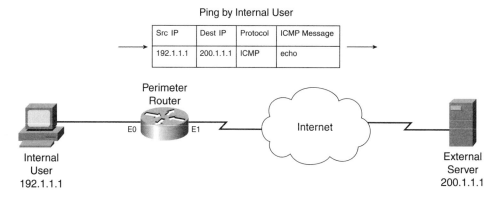

Example 8-1   *Sample Extended ACL with ICMP*

```
Router(config)# ip access-list extended perimeter-filter
Router(config-ext-nacl)# permit icmp any host 192.1.1.1 echo-reply
Router(config-ext-nacl)# deny ip any any
Router(config-ext-nacl)# exit
Router(config)# interface ethernet1
Router(config-if)# ip access-group perimeter-filter in
```

This example allows ICMP echo replies back to 192.1.1.1. A few problems arise with this solution, though:

- Because you do not know who 192.1.1.1 is pinging, you must allow all echo replies to return to this device (other devices besides 200.1.1.1).

- This filter statement is always active, so a hacker could implement a denial of service (DoS) spoofing attack against 192.1.1.1.

- This filter works only with one device: 192.1.1.1. If you want other internal devices to ping outside devices, you also must include them in the extended ACL.

As you can see from this example, using an extended IP ACL does not provide a very good solution. Probably the main problem of these three is the DoS attack that you open yourself to. If a hacker knows that ICMP echo replies are allowed to 192.1.1.1, he easily could orchestrate a Smurf attack through reflectors and overload your internal user's PC. The Smurf attack is discussed in Chapter 7.

How Extended ACLs Handle Returning UDP Traffic

Now that you know the issues that extended ACLs have when dealing with ICMP and stateful processes, you can see how an extended ACL handles UDP connections. Consider the network shown in Figure 8-2 as an illustration of how to allow returning UDP traffic into this network. In this example, a user (192.1.1.1) performs a DNS query to an external DNS server (200.2.2.2).

Figure 8-2   *UDP Traffic and Extended ACLs*

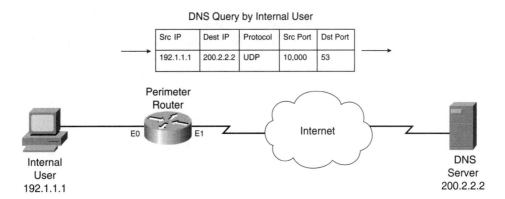

In this example, an internal user performs a DNS query and expects a response back from 200.2.2.2. Because DNS queries use UDP, the user's PC chooses a source port number greater than 1023 and a destination port number of 53. In the example, the random port number chosen was 10,000. To allow this traffic back into the network, you would have to configure the ACL as shown in Example 8-2.

Example 8-2 *Sample Extended ACL with UDP DNS Connections*

```
Router(config)# ip access-list extended perimeter-filter
Router(config-ext-nacl)# permit udp any eq 53 host 192.1.1.1 gt 1023
Router(config-ext-nacl)# deny ip any any
Router(config-ext-nacl)# exit
Router(config)# interface ethernet1
Router(config-if)# ip access-group perimeter-filter in
```

Here are some of the issues with the ACL configuration in Example 8-2:

- You probably do not know which DNS server or servers the internal user is using, so you must allow all DNS server replies back into your network.

- All port numbers greater than 1023 must be allowed because this is what the source device randomly chooses.

In this example, you have opened an even bigger hole in your firewall by allowing all UDP ports greater than 1023 to 192.1.1.1. Another problem with this ACL is that it solves (and not very well, at that) only DNS replies to 192.1.1.1. What about DNS replies (and other types of UDP traffic) to other internal devices? As you can see from this example, you would have to open ports greater than 1023 to all internal devices for the specific UDP applications that they will be accessing externally. Again, a hacker can take advantage of this with a tool such as Fraggle, creating a DoS attack (Fraggle was discussed in Chapter 7). Even if you lock down the source IP addresses that are allowed this access, a hacker easily can get around this with address spoofing.

How Extended ACLs Handle Returning TCP Traffic

When using an extended ACL to permit returning TCP traffic, you have more control on what returning traffic actually is allowed with the **established** keyword. As you recall from Chapter 7, the **established** keyword checks whether the ACK, FIN, PSH, RST, SYN, or URG TCP control flags are set. This typically indicates the return of traffic from an established session. Look at Figure 8-3 to see how returning TCP traffic is treated with an extended ACL.

Figure 8-3 *TCP Traffic and Extended ACLs*

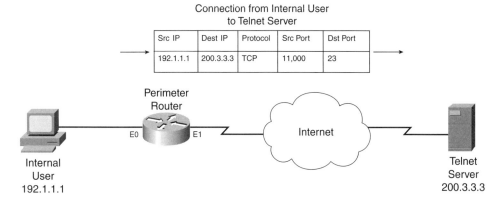

Connection from Internal User
to Telnet Server

Src IP	Dest IP	Protocol	Src Port	Dst Port
192.1.1.1	200.3.3.3	TCP	11,000	23

Perimeter
Router

E0   E1

Internet

Internal
User
192.1.1.1

Telnet
Server
200.3.3.3

In this example, I have configured the commands in Example 8-3 on the perimeter router.

Example 8-3 *Sample Extended ACL Allowing TCP Connections*

```
Router(config)# ip access-list extended perimeter-filter
Router(config-ext-nacl)# permit tcp any host 192.1.1.1 established
Router(config-ext-nacl)# deny ip any any
Router(config-ext-nacl)# exit
Router(config)# interface ethernet1
Router(config-if)# ip access-group perimeter-filter in
```

In this example, when the user establishes a Telnet connection to 200.3.3.3 and goes through the three-way handshake, the SYN/ACK from 200.3.3.3 is allowed back through the router because of the **established** ACL statement. Likewise, any traffic sent from 200.3.3.3 in response to the Telnet connection, such as sending or acknowledging the receipt of data, is also allowed through. Even the messages for the teardown of the TCP connection are allowed through.

However, even though this is more restrictive than the filters I previously showed you with ICMP and UDP in the last two sections, the **established** keyword does not look at session information for connections. In other words, it does not look to see if this traffic is part of an existing connection that originated from inside the network. Instead, any TCP segment that has the right TCP control flag or flags set is allowed through to 192.1.1.1. Again, a hacker can take advantage of this with a modified form of the TCP SYN flood attack. In this instance, the hacker might flood 192.1.1.1 with SYN/ACK messages, which the packet-filtering firewall would allow through.

How RACLs Handle Returning Traffic

As you saw in the previous three sections, you can use methods with extended IP ACLs to restrict traffic as it returns to your network. However, the solutions described in these sections open big security holes in your perimeter router firewall. Therefore, network administrators typically do not use extended IP ACLs to handle returning traffic (responses to requests that originated inside a network).

Cisco addressed this issue with the development of the RACL feature. Unlike extended IP ACLs, RACLs are aware of state information concerning a connection—at least, to a certain degree. In other words, a reflexive ACL can detect when a user initiates a connection to the outside world and can allow only returning traffic for that user's connection. Unlike extended IP ACLs that can do this somewhat for TCP connections (with the **established** parameter), RACLs can do this with all IP protocols. Basically, RACLs are a stripped-down version of Cisco's CBAC stateful firewall feature, which is part of the Cisco IOS Firewall feature set (discussed in Chapter 9).

RACLs perform a function similar to that of a true stateful firewall, like CBAC: Only when a session is initiated on the inside of your network is returning traffic allowed back in. RACLs accomplish this feat by using temporary ACL statements that are inserted into your extended ACL filter, which is applied on your router's external interface. When the session ends or the temporary entry times out, it is removed from the external interface's ACL configuration. This reduces your exposure to DoS attacks by a hacker. As you will see in the later section "Limitations of Reflexive ACLs," RACLs do have limitations; however, they at least provide a solution that is much better than one that uses only extended ACLs.

Now take a look at a basic example of how RACLs works. Figure 8-4 illustrates how the perimeter router treats a Telnet connection.

Figure 8-4   *Telnet Connection and RACLs*

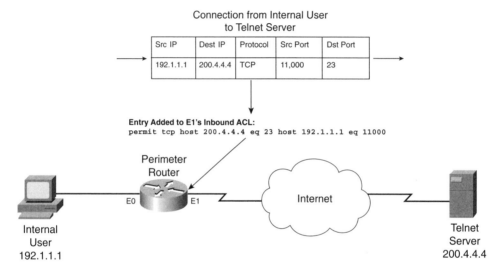

In this example, assume that RACLs already have been configured for the router and that the default behavior of the router is to drop any traffic that originates outside the router and that is trying to access internal resources. As you can see from Figure 8-4, the internal user (192.1.1.1) establishes an outbound Telnet connection to 200.4.4.4. When the router receives the packet, the Cisco IOS checks to see if a RACL has been configured, to determine whether returning traffic for this user's connection should be allowed. If this is true, the Cisco IOS creates a temporary ACL entry on the inbound external interface (E1). This ACL entry allows only Telnet traffic from the server to the client (and only returning traffic, at that). When the user terminates this connection, or if it exceeds the idle timeout for the connection, the Cisco IOS removes the temporary RACL entry from the extended IP ACL. As you can see from this example, the temporary entry allows returning traffic for a specific period of time, which limits your exposure to DoS attacks.

As you saw in the previous three sections, extended IP ACLs have problems with allowing the return of replies. With TCP, you at least can have the Cisco IOS examine the TCP control flags, such as SYN, ACK, and others, to determine whether the traffic is part of an existing connection. However, extended ACLs do not have this option for ICMP or UDP traffic (or for other types of IP traffic, for that matter). Unlike TCP, these protocols do not indicate the state of the connection, so it is difficult, if not impossible, to determine whether the connection has just started, is in the middle of transmitting data, or is ending. Plus, even with the **established** keyword in a TCP extended ACL statement, the Cisco IOS does not look at whether this traffic is part of a connection that was initiated from inside your network; it looks at just whether fields in the segment header are marked appropriately.

Reflexive ACLs, however, do look at the source (origin) of the traffic. Only when a valid source originates traffic is a temporary ACL entry created, allowing the returning traffic only for this connection. In other words, the Cisco IOS looks at who establishes a session and uses this information to allow returning traffic for that specific connection. This gives you much tighter control over the type of traffic allowed back into your network, presenting a much smaller window in your filter that a hacker can take advantage of. Plus, RACLs actually build on the ACL technology of the Cisco IOS. In other words, they are an extension of extended ACLs: You can mix and match the two features to provide a more secure perimeter defense. By combining these two filtering features, you are much less susceptible to network attacks such as IP spoofing, DoS, and access attacks.

Reflexive ACLs in Action

As you saw in the previous section, RACLs create temporary holes in your router's inbound ACL to allow returning traffic back into your network. This section discusses how RACLs perform in more detail.

Steps in Processing Traffic

RACLs require the use of two ACLs to function correctly. The first ACL is used to capture session information for outbound traffic. This information is placed in a special RACL and inserted into the inbound ACL you have applied to your router's external interface. Figure 8-5 illustrates the use of the different ACLs.

Figure 8-5   *ACLs and RACLs*

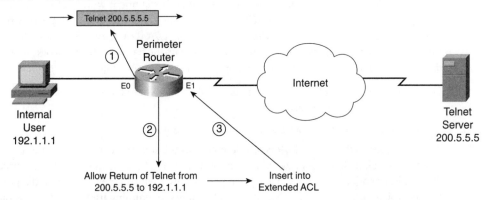

The steps for RACL processing in Figure 8-5 are as follows:

1 The internal ACL examines traffic for outbound sessions. This is a named extended ACL.

2 A statement is added to the temporary named RACL (separate access list).

3 The RACL is inserted into a third named ACL applied inbound on the router's external interface.

In this example, three ACLs are used.

When the session has been completed or timed out, the session entry in the RACL automatically is removed by the Cisco IOS.

Traffic Leaving the Network

You can break this down further. As traffic leaves your network, you have a named extended ACL that examines this traffic. This ACL can be applied inbound on an internal interface or outbound on the external interface. The latter method is more common because you need to apply it on only one interface. If you used the former method, you might have to create more than one ACL and apply them inbound on your internal interfaces.

In this "internal" ACL, you place statements that examine traffic for new sessions (with the **reflect** parameter). With these statements, you can control which connections you will build RACL entries for, where these entries will allow returning traffic back into your network. If you do not configure these statements, returning traffic is dropped, by default. This gives you much greater control over which internal users you want to access the external network and what type of connections they should be permitted. For example, you could set up your ACL statements to examine only HTTP connections, thus allowing only temporary RACL entries to be created for HTTP traffic.

Building the RACL

As traffic is leaving the network, if it matches a **permit** statement with a **reflect** parameter, a temporary entry is added to the RACL specified in the statement. For each **permit/reflect** statement you have, your router builds a separate RACL. A RACL entry is an inverted entry. Remember that these entries need to allow returning traffic back into the network; therefore, the source and destination information is flipped in the RACL statement.

For example, if a user (192.1.1.1) Telnets to 200.5.5.5, where the source port number is 11000, this RACL entry is created:

```
permit host 200.5.5.5 eq 23 host 192.1.1.1 eq 11000
```

As you can see in this example, this RACL entry has the source and destination information reversed, which includes both the address information and, because this is a TCP connection, the port information. Also note that any temporary RACL entries created contain the **permit** action, which makes sense because you want to allow the returning traffic for this session.

These are some of the characteristics of RACL entries:

- The action is always **permit**.
- The protocol of the packet, such as TCP, UDP, and ICMP, is placed in the RACL entry.
- The source and destination IP addresses are reversed in the RACL entry, to allow the return of this traffic.
- For TCP and UDP, the source and destination port numbers are switched, to allow the traffic to return from the destination device.
- For other protocols, such as ICMP and IGMP, the Cisco IOS can specify other protocol criteria, such as message types for ICMP.

Traffic Returning to the Network

To use RACLs to filter returning traffic, you must build an extended named ACL that filters traffic coming from the external network. This ACL is applied inbound on your external interface and commonly is called an external ACL.

In the external ACL, you put a placeholder (or reference) where your RACL or RACLs should be processed. Basically, you are nesting your RACL within an ACL. Whatever statement or statements exist in the RACL or RACLs logically are inserted into the specified place of your external ACL. When the Cisco IOS processes the external ACL and finds a RACL reference, it processes the statements in the RACL until it finds a match. If no match is found in the RACL, the Cisco IOS returns to the next external ACL statement after the RACL reference and continues to look for a match.

NOTE   It is important to point out that a RACL is slightly different than an ACL. With a RACL, there is no implicit deny statement at the end of the list. This is because RACL statements are inserted into the external ACL, which might have other statements below these inserted statements.

The insertion of your RACL references is done with the **evaluate** statement. Placement of these statements is important. For example, you might have the configuration in Example 8-4 for an external ACL.

Example 8-4   *Example Extended ACL and RACL Placement*

```
Router(config)# ip access-list extended inbound
Router(config-ext-nacl)# permit tcp any host 192.1.1.10 eq www
Router(config-ext-nacl)# deny ip any any
Router(config-ext-nacl)# exit
Router(config)# interface ethernet1
Router(config-if)# ip access-group inbound in
```

In Example 8-4, only web traffic is allowed to the internal web server (192.1.1.10); all other traffic is dropped.

To allow returning traffic into your network for sessions listed in your temporary RACLs, you need to put a placeholder in your external inbound ACL that specifies the use of the RACL statements. The location of the reference/placeholder is important.

Assume that you have a RACL with the following temporary statements:

```
permit host 200.5.5.5 eq 23 host 192.1.1.2 eq 10000
permit host 200.5.5.5 eq 23 host 192.1.1.1 eq 11000
```

In this example, two internal devices (192.1.1.2 and 192.1.1.1) have Telnetted to 200.5.5.5. If you put the RACL reference at the bottom of the external ACL, you actually would prevent the returning of their traffic because the **deny ip any any** statement would be processed first and would drop the returning traffic. Your RACL entries never would be processed because the packet would match this **deny** statement. In the previous example, you would need to put your RACL reference before any **deny** statement that might block it (this is accomplished with the **evaluate** statement). Example 8-5 shows a simple example for the code in Example 8-4.

Example 8-5 *Example Showing RACL Placement*

```
Router(config)# ip access-list extended inbound
Router(config-ext-nacl)# remark -> insert RACL reference or references here
Router(config-ext-nacl)# permit tcp any host 192.1.1.10 eq www
Router(config-ext-nacl)# deny ip any any
Router(config-ext-nacl)# exit
Router(config)# interface ethernet1
Router(config-if)# ip access-group inbound in
```

In this example, the RACL reference (indicated by a **remark** comment line and shaded) is placed at the beginning of the external ACL, guaranteeing that returning traffic will be allowed back through the router. This is a common placement for RACL references.

CAUTION Take care that your security policies still are being enforced by the placement of your RACL references and ACL statements.

Removing RACL Entries

Entries in a RACL are temporary. They are removed from the RACL under two conditions:

- The session terminates.
- The entry in the RACL times out (is idle for a period of time).

When a session terminates, the Cisco IOS removes the temporary entry from the RACL. However, only TCP uses a well-defined mechanism by which the Cisco IOS can detect the end of a session. UDP, ICMP, and other protocols do not have this mechanism (they are connectionless). With TCP, the Cisco IOS looks for two FIN messages, and the temporary RACL entry is removed after 5 seconds. The 5-second waiting period is used to ensure that the TCP session is allowed enough time to close gracefully. If the Cisco IOS sees an RST message instead, this indicates an abrupt session closure, causing the Cisco IOS to immediately remove the session entry from the RACL.

Otherwise, for all other conditions for TCP and all other protocols, such as UDP and ICMP, the Cisco IOS monitors each session to see if the session is idle for a period of time. If the session is idle longer than the configured timeout value, the Cisco IOS automatically removes the session entry from the RACL.

CAUTION The idle timer for all sessions defaults to 300 seconds (5 minutes). I highly recommend that you change the default for connectionless sessions, such as UDP and ICMP. In other words, you do not want a user's DNS query or a ping to stay in the RACL for 5 minutes when the session typically is done in less than 5 or 10 seconds. For these protocols, I highly recommend that you tune it to an appropriate value, such as 30 or 60 seconds. By leaving it at 5 minutes, you are putting these devices at a much higher level of exposure to DoS and other types of attacks.

NOTE As you can see from how the Cisco IOS processes RACLs, RACLs do not provide a stateful firewall solution; they provide something close to it, as I alluded to in the introduction and at the beginning of this chapter. CBAC, covered in Chapter 9, provides a more stateful solution than RACLs. However, if you do not want to or cannot afford to purchase the Cisco IOS Firewall feature set, which includes CBAC, RACLs are your next-best solution.

Limitations of Reflexive ACLs

RACLs have two main limitations:

- RACLs do not provide a complete stateful solution (the ending of a session for protocols such as UDP and ICMP is approximated by an idle timer).
- Not all applications work with RACLs.

TIP RACLs were developed for smaller environments (a few dozen users) in which the Cisco IOS Firewall feature set's cost (which includes CBAC) is deemed too much or is not necessary. However, RACLs are memory and process intensive. If you suspect that you are having performance problems, use the **show processes memory** and **show processes cpu** commands, and look for the RACL entry to see if this is your problem. (You can add the **history** parameter to the **show processes cpu** command, which displays a chart of the CPU processes, making it easier to spot CPU utilization problems.) However, if you have a large environment, steer away from RACLs and use CBAC, which is much more memory efficient.

Stateful Issues

You already know one of the limitations of RACLs: They are stateful only for TCP. With other TCP/IP protocols, RACLs use timeouts to remove idle sessions. Even with TCP traffic, there is a minor issue with returning traffic. For example, as you recall from Chapter 7, the extended ACL **established** keyword allows only TCP segments with certain control flags set, such as the ACK flag. The assumption here is that certain control flags indicate the return of traffic into the network. However, it does not restrict a RACL entry that the Cisco IOS creates for TCP sessions. This is a minor issue and probably will not cause a problem.

Even though this is a very minor issue, it does open you up to possible problems. For example, imagine that an internal host somehow was compromised. Your perimeter routers are using RACLs to prevent incoming traffic. A hacker knows about the use of RACLs and wants to gain access to the device he has hacked into, probably through a virus or worm spread through an e-mail attachment. To get around the RACLs, the hacker has the internal machine periodically open a TCP connection to his own PC. The hacker's software then disconnects the session but does not go through the hand-shake process of tearing down the connection. The hacker's software then starts up a Telnet process on the port just closed. In this situation, the RACL entry is still there until it times out. The hacker can take advantage of this by setting up a Telnet connection with the three-way TCP handshake to the internal device on the previously used port. From the Cisco IOS perspective, it looks like this is a continuation of the previous TCP connection; in reality, it is a new TCP connection, but with the same source and destination addresses and port numbers. The problem with the RACL implementation is that, for TCP, it does not examine the inbound TCP control flags to determine the direction of the flow of traffic.

This same issue can be applied to the other protocols. As long as the hacker can compromise an internal device, have that internal device initiate an outbound connection, and prematurely terminate the connection, the hacker can use the temporary RACL entry to gain access to the internal device. Therefore, even by using RACLs, you are exposing yourself, even in a limited way, to specific kinds of attacks.

Application Issues

The second problem with RACLs is that they do not work with all session layer applications. Examples of some of these applications include FTP and multimedia, such as RTSP, H.323, VoIP, and many others. With these applications more than one connection is involved in sharing information between the devices. Typically, the first connection is a control connection, and the second and subsequent connections are data, error, and synchronization connections. How these extra connections are set up is random: Sometimes the client sets them up, and other times the server sets them up. In some instances, the ports that the connections use are standardized; sometimes they fall within a range, and sometimes they are completely random.

Standard FTP Example

Unfortunately, RACLs have problems with these types of additional connections. This section looks at how FTP uses connections to illustrate this problem. Figure 8-6 displays the two types of modes that FTP supports: standard (active) and passive. With a standard connection, the FTP client chooses a random TCP port number greater than 1023 for the source and connects to port 21 on the server. This is called the control connection, and FTP commands are passed across this connection. As soon as the user wants to get data from the server or load data to the server, the client tells the server of the data exchange, as well as the port number to use to connect to on the client (higher than 1023). The server opens the data connection by connecting back to the client's specified data port from its local data port (the source port is 20).

Figure 8-6   *FTP Connections*

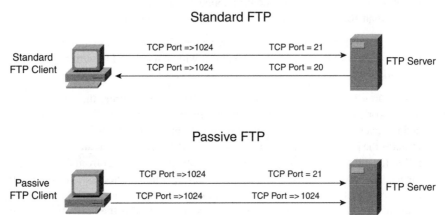

Next you will look at how this affects a router with RACLs, from two perspectives with standard FTP: with the client inside the network and the server outside, and then vice versa.

Client on the Inside   The first standard FTP example assumes that the FTP client is inside the network and that the server is outside. In this example, RACLs have been configured and the external extended ACL denies all inbound traffic by default. When the client initiates the port 21 connection to the server, a RACL entry is created to allow the returning traffic from the server for this connection. However, as soon as the client retrieves data from the server, and the server tries to open a connection back to the client, it fails. Unfortunately, the RACL entry and the extended external ACL do not allow this second connection. You could get around this problem by allowing any TCP source port 20 connection going to a destination port greater than 1023 into your network with an extended ACL entry, but this presents a security risk.

Client on the Outside   The second standard FTP example assumes that the FTP client is outside the network and that the server is inside. In this example, RACLs have been configured and the external extended ACL denies all inbound traffic, by default, with the exception of the external users trying to access the internal FTP server (TCP port 21). When the client initiates the port 21 connection to the server, the extended ACL permits the connection. When the client tries to upload or download data, the server sets up a connection back to the client; the Cisco IOS adds the RACL entry for this second connection (allowing the client to send traffic to the server on this connection). In this example, the client has no problems with bidirectionally communicating with the FTP server on a standard connection.

Passive FTP Example

With a passive connection, the FTP client chooses a random TCP port number greater than 1023 for the source port and connects to port 21 on the server. This is called the control connection, and commands are passed across this connection. As soon as the user wants to get data from the server or load data to the server, the client opens a new connection to the server from an unused random port greater than 1023. The server tells the client what destination port number to use (across the control connection), which is typically a random port number greater than 1023 that is not being used currently on the server.

Now you will look at how this affects a router with RACLs. I examine this from two perspectives with passive FTP, just as I did with standard FTP: with the client inside the network and the server outside, and then vice versa.

Client on the Inside   The first passive FTP example assumes that the FTP client is inside the network and that the server is outside. In this example, RACLs have been configured and the external extended ACL denies all inbound traffic, by default. When the client initiates the port 21 connection to the server, a RACL entry is created to allow the returning traffic from the server. When the client attempts to retrieve data from the server, the client opens up a second connection to the FTP server, which is successful (unlike with standard FTP). With passive FTP, the client initiates the second connection. When the Cisco IOS sees that the internal client is initiating a session, it adds the session information as a temporary ACL entry in the RACL, allowing the returning traffic from the server back into the network. In this example, there is no issue with passive FTP and RACLs.

Client on the Outside   The second passive FTP example assumes that the FTP client is outside the network and that the server is inside. In this example, RACLs have been configured and the external extended ACL denies all inbound traffic, by default, with the exception of the external users trying to access the internal FTP server (TCP port 21). When the client initiates the port 21 connection to the server, the extended ACL permits the connection. Then when the client tries to upload or download data, the client tries to establish the data connection to the server on the prenegotiated port numbers greater than 1023. Unfortunately, because RACLs build temporary entries for outbound traffic, and this is inbound traffic, the connection is not allowed.

NOTE   To get around the FTP access problem, you must use passive FTP for outbound client connections and standard FTP for inbound client connections. This creates a lot of confusion for users, so other solutions are preferred over using RACLs in this situation; these include the Cisco CBAC and the Cisco PIX firewall with the protocol-fixup feature.

Configuring Reflexive ACLs

Now that you have a better understanding of reflexive ACLs, their operation, and their limitations, this section discusses how to configure them on your Cisco IOS router. Configuring your router to use RACLs involves three steps:

Step 1 Create an internal named ACL that looks for new outbound sessions and creates your temporary RACLs.

Step 2 Create an external named ACL that uses the RACLs to examine returning traffic to your network.

Step 3 Activate the named ACLs on the appropriate interface or interfaces.

You must do three main things for your router to use RACLs. Some optional items, such as changing the idle timeout for sessions, also can be configured. The remainder of this section focuses on the configuration of RACLs on your router.

NOTE   It is important to point out that all ACLs used in this process are *named extended* ACLs—numbered ACLs and standard ACLs are not supported. Also, only TCP/IP supports reflexive ACLs; other protocols, such as IPX, do not support this feature.

Interface Selection

Typically, the configuration of RACLs is done on the perimeter router or firewall as traffic is entering and leaving your network. This can be a connection to the Internet or another network, such as a different company (extranet). One of the first things you need to decide is on what interface or interfaces you will be configuring your ACLs for RACLs. Take a look at two examples of where you can put your ACLs on your router's interface(s).

Two-Interface Example

Figure 8-7 illustrates how to use RACLs in a router that has two interfaces. Remember that you must set up two ACLs: one that builds RACLs as traffic leaves the network, and one that uses the RACLs to allow returning traffic into the network. When examining traffic as it leaves the network, you can apply the internal ACL in one of two ways:

- Inbound on the internal interface (E0 in)
- Outbound on the external interface (E1 out)

For the external ACL, because you typically configure RACLs on a perimeter router/firewall, you will be applying it inbound on the external interface (E1 in).

Figure 8-7 *Two-Interface RACL Example*

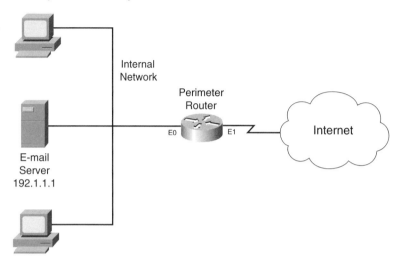

In this example, the network has two policies: allow Internet traffic to the internal e-mail server, and allow users access to the Internet. To accomplish this, you need an ACL configuration like the following:

- Internal ACL (apply outbound on E1 or inbound on E0): Examine outbound traffic and build the RACL for new sessions.

- External ACL (apply inbound on E1):
  - Reference the RACL to allow returning traffic.
  - Allow Internet traffic to the e-mail server.
  - Deny all other traffic.

TIP The most common way to set up RACLs on a two-interface router is to apply the internal ACL on the router's external interface in the outbound direction (E1 out), and to apply the external ACL on the external interface in the inbound direction (E1 in).

Three-Interface Example

Figure 8-8 illustrates how to use RACLs in a router that has three interfaces. This configuration is more difficult because of the policy rules defined by this company:

- The Internet should be capable of accessing the DMZ e-mail server.

- The Internet should be capable of accessing the DMZ DNS server.

- The Internet should be capable of accessing the DMZ web server.

- The Internet should not be capable of accessing the internal network.
- The internal e-mail server should be capable of accessing only the DMZ e-mail server, nothing else.
- The DMZ e-mail server should be capable of accessing the internal e-mail server to forward mail.
- Internal users should be able to access the Internet and receive replies.
- Internal users should not be able to access the DMZ e-mail server or any external e-mail servers.

Figure 8-8   *Three-Interface RACL Example*

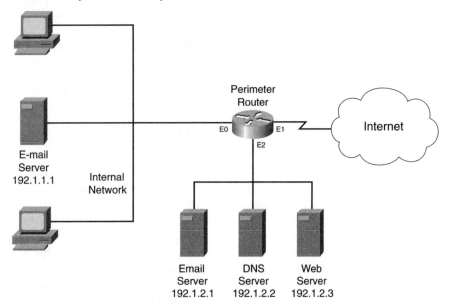

To accomplish these policies, you need three ACLs:

- Internal ACL (apply inbound on E0):
  - Allow the internal e-mail server to access the DMZ e-mail server.
  - Deny internal users access to the DMZ e-mail server and other e-mail servers.
  - Deny the internal e-mail server from accessing anything else.
  - Examine outbound traffic and build the RACL for new sessions to the DMZ.
  - Examine outbound traffic and build the RACL for new sessions to the Internet.
  - Allow internal users to access all other services (DMZ and Internet).

- DMZ ACL (apply outbound on E0)—this restricts traffic from the DMZ to the internal network:
    - Reference the internal-to-DMZ RACL to allow internal users to get their replies from the DMZ.
    - Reference the internal-to-external RACL to allow internal users to get their replies from Internet resources.
    - Allow the DMZ e-mail server to send e-mail to the internal server.
- External ACL (apply inbound on E1):
    - Reference the internal-to-external RACL to allow internal users to get their replies from the Internet.
    - Allow Internet users access to the DMZ e-mail server.
    - Allow Internet users access to the DMZ DNS server for DNS queries.
    - Allow Internet users access to the DNS web server.

As you can see from this list of policies, the setup of RACLs and ACLs is more difficult. One item that I want to point out is that I used two RACLs in this example:

- One for traffic from the internal segment to the Internet
- One for traffic from the internal segment to the DMZ segment

You actually could get away with using one RACL and reference the same RACL on interface E1 inbound and E0 outbound; however, this presents a security problem for the external interface. If a hacker knew which internal devices were constantly accessing the DMZ servers, he might be able to take advantage of this to try to spoof his way in through the RACL on the external interface; the same RACL is applied outbound on the internal interface. Therefore, I have created two RACLs. The first RACL allows traffic from the internal segment, when sent to the DMZ, to be returned to the internal segment. The second RACL is for traffic leaving the network and returning. By separating the sessions into the two locations that devices access, I am creating a more secure environment.

Configuration Commands

As mentioned at the beginning of this section, you need to configure two named ACLs: One builds the RACL or RACLs, and the other references them to allow returning traffic. You also need to activate them on your router's interface or interfaces. Optionally, you can configure other things, such as the timeout for the idle RACL entries. The following three sections cover the configuration of these components.

Building the RACL

This section focuses on the ACL that you create to build the temporary entries in a RACL. This typically is done when traffic is leaving your network. You build an extended named ACL that restricts what traffic is allowed to leave your network. In this ACL, you specify which traffic you want the Cisco IOS to examine and create temporary ACL entries for. This is done by using a **permit** extended ACL statement that matches on the traffic that you want to have temporary entries created for. In this statement, you add the **reflect** parameter. This statement creates the temporary entries in the specified RACL. Here is the syntax to accomplish this:

```
Router(config)# ip access-list extended internal_ACL_name
Router(config-ext-nacl)# --permit or deny specific connections--
Router(config-ext-nacl)# permit protocol_name
  source_address wildcard_mask [protocol_information] destination_address
  wildcard_mask [protocol_information] reflect RACL_name [timeout #_of_seconds]
Router(config-ext-nacl)# --permit or deny other connections--
```

First, you need to create your extended named ACL with the **ip access-list extended** command.

TIP

When naming your ACL, I recommend using a descriptive name. With RACLs, I include either the placement location of the ACL, such as internal, or the direction of the traffic flow that is being filtered, such as internal-external.

Place your **permit** statement or statements that will match on traffic that you want to build RACL entries for within the ACL. For each of these **permit** statements, you must use the **reflect** keyword and the name of the RACL where the temporary entries will be placed. You also must specify the IP protocol that you want to create RACL entries for, as well as the source and destination: You can be as specific or permissive as you want.

NOTE

The **permit/reflect** statement serves two purposes. First, it builds temporary entries in the specified RACL. Second, it allows the specified traffic to flow through the interface. Remember that at the end of this extended ACL is an implicit deny statement.

Optionally, you can specify the idle timeout for these temporary RACL entries by using the keyword **timeout** followed by the timeout value in seconds. The default timeout is 300 seconds if you omit it. Valid timeout values are 0 to 2,147,483. Setting the value to 0 causes the entry to remain in the RACL list: I highly recommend that you do not do this because it creates a permanent security hole in your perimeter router. Likewise, I do not recommend setting values too high. For UDP and ICMP traffic, 30 to 60 seconds is a good value. However, you might have to tune this on an application-by-application basis. If this is the case, you need a separate **permit/reflect** statement for each unique idle setting. As an example, you might want to create a separate entry for DNS queries and set the timeout for these to a smaller value than other UDP traffic, such as 5 or 10 seconds.

NOTE	It is important to point out that the specified RACL in your extended named ACL does not exist yet. The Cisco IOS dynamically creates it and puts entries in it based on packets matching these **permit/reflect** statements. Plus, you can use the same RACL name for multiple **permit** statements. This places these temporary entries in the same RACL. Typically, I use different RACL names to view the information more easily when troubleshooting, but this is not required.

Restrictive Settings

You can be as specific as you want when matching your outbound session connections. For example, if you want internal users to surf the Internet only with a web browser and allow DNS responses back, you can enter the commands in Example 8-6.

Example 8-6 *Simple RACL Example*

```
Router(config)#  ip access-list extended internal-external
Router(config-ext-nacl)# remark --insert permit or deny specific connections--
Router(config-ext-nacl)# permit tcp any any eq 80 reflect web-only-RACL
Router(config-ext-nacl)# permit udp any any eq 53 reflect dns-only-RACL timeout 10
Router(config-ext-nacl)# remark --insert permit or deny other connections--
```

Example 8-6 instructs the Cisco IOS to create two RACLs that will maintain session information for outbound web connections (web-only-RACL) and DNS queries (dns-only-RACL). Also notice that I set the timeout for the DNS queries to 10 seconds.

Of course, I could have used the same RACL name and put all temporary entries in the same list, as in Example 8-7.

Example 8-7 *Simple Combined RACL Example*

```
Router(config)#  ip access-list extended internal-external
Router(config-ext-nacl)# remark --insert permit or deny specific connections--
Router(config-ext-nacl)# permit tcp any any eq 80 reflect user-RACL
Router(config-ext-nacl)# permit udp any any eq 53 reflect users-RACL timeout 10
Router(config-ext-nacl)# remark --insert permit or deny other connections--
```

In Example 8-7, both the HTTP and DNS queries will be placed in the same RACL (user-RACL).

Permissive Settings

If you want to allow all of your internal users to access the Internet and get returning traffic, you could do something like in Example 8-8.

Example 8-8   *One RACL for All Returning Traffic*

```
Router(config)#  ip access-list extended internal-external
Router(config-ext-nacl)# remark --permit or deny specific connections--
Router(config-ext-nacl)# permit ip any any reflect IP-all-RACL
Router(config-ext-nacl)# remark --permit or deny other connections--
```

In Example 8-8, all outbound IP traffic would create temporary entries in the reflexive ACL called IP-all-RACL. This is a good example of when troubleshooting might become difficult because many temporary entries would exist in this list. If I am allowing all outbound traffic, I typically use a different RACL for each type of traffic, as in Example 8-9.

Example 8-9   *Multiple RACLs for Returning Traffic*

```
Router(config)#  ip access-list extended internal-external
Router(config-ext-nacl)# remark --permit or deny specific connections--
Router(config-ext-nacl)# permit tcp any any reflect tcp-racl
Router(config-ext-nacl)# permit udp any any reflect udp-racl timeout 30
Router(config-ext-nacl)# permit icmp any any reflect icmp-racl timeout 10
Router(config-ext-nacl)# remark --permit or deny other connections--
```

In Example 8-9, I have separated the TCP, UDP, and ICMP traffic into three RACLs: *tcp-racl*, *udp-racl*, and *icmp-racl*, respectively. Therefore, if I am having a problem with a particular protocol, it will be much easier to view my RACL entries by displaying just one particular RACL that contains one protocol than to display one RACL that contains every protocol.

CAUTION   Placement of the **reflect** statements is very important in the processing of the internal ACL. For example, if you do not want users to access a specific resource, make sure that this **deny** statement appears before the corresponding **reflect** statement. Likewise, if you want to create a RACL for certain types of traffic, make sure that no **deny** statement precedes the **reflect** statement that would drop this traffic.

Referencing the RACL

After building your internal extended named ACL, which creates your RACLs, you are ready to reference these temporary entries as traffic flows back into your network. This is done by building a second extended named ACL. In this named ACL, you use the **evaluate** statement to reference your RACLs that were created from the previous internal ACL. Use the following syntax to create your external ACL:

```
Router(config)#  ip access-list extended external_ACL_name
Router(config-ext-nacl)#  remark --permit or deny specific connections--
Router(config-ext-nacl)#  evaluate RACL_name
Router(config-ext-nacl)#  remark --permit or deny other connections--
```

Before you can actually execute the **evaluate** command, you must create the RACL reference with the **permit/reflect** command in your internal ACL. The name of the RACL in the **evaluate** command must match the name of the RACL that you used in the **permit/reflect** command in your internal ACL. If you created multiple RACLs in your internal ACL or ACLs, you must configure a separate **evaluate** command for each RACL.

NOTE   You do not actually create and put entries in the RACL; the Cisco IOS does this automatically. You need to reference the RACL only so that the Cisco IOS processes these entries as traffic returns into your network. Basically, the **evaluate** commands point to the entries in the RACL that the Cisco IOS should use when processing the external extended ACL.

CAUTION   As with the internal ACL, the placement of the **evaluate** statement in the external ACL does matter. When the Cisco IOS processes inbound packets, it examines the first entry in the external ACL. If it does not find a match, it proceeds to the next statement. If the statement is an **evaluate** statement, the Cisco IOS begins processing the first statement in the RACL. If no statements match in the RACL, the Cisco IOS returns to the external ACL and processes the next statement in the extended ACL.

Therefore, if you have a RACL that permits returning traffic, but you place the RACL's **evaluate** statement after a **deny** statement that drops it, the traffic is dropped and the RACL never is processed. In this example, make sure that the **evaluate** statement for the RACL appears before the **deny** statement. Of course, you can use this to your advantage and prevent certain returning traffic by putting the **deny** statement before the **evaluate** command.

ACL Activation

After you have created your internal (**permit/reflect**) and external (**evaluate**) ACLs, you need to activate them by applying them to your router's interface(s). For a two-interface router configuration, this typically is done with the following syntax on the external interface:

```
Router(config)# interface type port_#
Router(config-if)# ip access-group name_of_the_internal_ACL out
Router(config-if)# ip access-group name_of_the_external _ACL in
```

In this example, you apply both of these ACLs on the external interface of the router. In the "Reflexive ACL Examples" section later in this chapter, I go over the two- and three-interface router examples discussed earlier, including how to configure and activate the extended ACLs.

Optional Commands

By default, temporary RACL entries are removed from the RACL when they have been idle for more than 300 seconds. I already showed you how you can adjust this value on a RACL-by-RACL basis with the **permit/reflect** statement in the internal ACL. However, you also can adjust this globally with the following command:

```
Router(config)# ip reflexive-list timeout seconds
```

Valid timeout values are 0 to 2,147,483. Setting the value to 0 causes the entry to remain in the RACL list. Remember my previous warning about setting this value to 0 or to a large number. When you set this value, it affects all RACLs, excluding the ones for which you have configured specific timeout values.

CAUTION   Each temporary entry created in a RACL requires memory to store it. Therefore, you do not want to keep idle connections in there for a long period of time when they are not necessary. A good example of connections that are very brief are DNS queries, HTTP connections, and ICMP messages. I highly recommend that you set the timeout for these values to 60 seconds or less, even if this means creating extra **reflect** entries to accomplish this. For ICMP traffic and DNS queries, 10 seconds is sufficient; for HTTP connections, an idle time between 30–60 seconds is more appropriate.

RACL Verification

After you have configured and activated your extended ACLs, you can verify their operation with the **show access-lists** and **show ip access-list** commands. Example 8-10 shows an example of the output from the **show access-lists** command.

Example 8-10 *Output from the* **show access-lists** *Command*

```
Router# show access-lists
Extended IP access list inbound_access
deny icmp any any
evaluate tcpstuff
evaluate udpstuff

Extended IP access list outbound_access
permit tcp any any reflect tcpstuff
permit udp any any reflect udpstuff

Reflexive IP access list tcpstuff
permit tcp host 200.5.5.5 eq telnet host 192.1.1.1 eq 10638
   (9 matches)  (time left 294 seconds)
```

In Example 8-10 are two extended named ACLs. inbound_access is an external ACL that filters returning traffic with two RACLs, specified in the **evaluate** commands. outbound_access is an internal ACL that has two **reflect** statements that build two RACLs: one for TCP traffic and one for UDP traffic. At the bottom of the display is the RACL for the TCP traffic, called tcpstuff. This ACL currently has only one entry, which allows returning Telnet traffic from 200.5.5.5 to the internal client (192.1.1.1). Notice that that the output from this display does not include the udpstuff RACL; this is because no internal UDP traffic has been examined leaving this network.

Reflexive ACL Examples

Now that you have a basic understanding of the configuration of RACLs, this section shows you some examples that illustrate how to set up RACLs on a router. The following sections contain three examples of the use of RACLs.

Simple RACL Example

In this example (see Figure 8-7), all traffic that originates on the Internet should not be allowed. However, all TCP and UDP returning traffic from the Internet to the internal users should be allowed. Example 8-11 shows a simple RACL example.

Example 8-11 *Simple RACL Example*

```
Router(config)# ip access-list extended internal_ACL
Router(config-ext-nacl)# permit tcp any any reflect tcpstuff_RACL
Router(config-ext-nacl)# permit udp any any reflect udpstuff_RACL timeout 60
Router(config-ext-nacl)# exit
Router(config)# ip access-list extended external_ACL
Router(config-ext-nacl)# evaluate tcpstuff_RACL
Router(config-ext-nacl)# evaluate udpstuff_RACL
Router(config-ext-nacl)# deny ip any any
Router(config-ext-nacl)# exit
Router(config)#  interface ethernet1
Router(config-if)# description  This connects to the Internet
Router(config-if)# ip access-group internal_ACL out
Router(config-if)# ip access-group external_ACL in
```

In Example 8-11, the first extended ACL built, internal_ACL, looks for TCP and UDP sessions and puts these sessions into two RACLs: tcpstuff_RACL and udpstuff_RACL, respectively. This extended ACL is applied outbound on the external interface. The second extended ACL, external_ACL, evaluates traffic coming back in by using the two RACLs; all other traffic is dropped. Remember that placement of the **evaluate** statements is important. In this example, they are placed before the **deny ip any any** statement.

Note that you easily could have placed both TCP and UDP sessions in the same RACL; however, as I pointed out earlier in this chapter, I prefer to separate the traffic, to make troubleshooting easier. By breaking the sessions into separate RACLs, it is easier to view it with the **show access-lists** command (actually, you can view just a specific RACL's entries by using the name of the RACL with this command).

Two-Interface RACL Example

In the "Two-Interface Example" section earlier in this chapter, I discussed an example of ACL placement and operation using Figure 8-7. In this example, I show you the actual configuration of this router with ACLs and RACLs.

Review the access policies discussed in the "Two-Interface Example" section. Example 8-12 shows the configuration to enforce these policies.

Example 8-12 *Two-Interface Configuration Example*

```
Router(config)# ip access-list extended internal_ACL
Router(config-ext-nacl)# permit tcp any any reflect tcp_RACL
Router(config-ext-nacl)# permit udp any any reflect udp_RACL timeout 30
Router(config-ext-nacl)# permit icmp any any reflect icmp_RACL timeout 10
Router(config-ext-nacl)# exit
Router(config)# ip access-list extended external_ACL
Router(config-ext-nacl)# evaluate tcp_RACL
Router(config-ext-nacl)# evaluate udp_RACL
Router(config-ext-nacl)# evaluate icmp_RACL
Router(config-ext-nacl)# permit tcp any host 192.1.1.1 eq 25
Router(config-ext-nacl)# deny ip any any
Router(config-ext-nacl)# exit
Router(config)#  interface ethernet1
Router(config-if)# ip access-group internal_ACL out
Router(config-if)# ip access-group external_ACL in
```

Example 8-12 is very similar to Example 8-11. However, there are two minor differences. First, a temporary RACL is used to allow returning ICMP traffic into the network, where the timeout for this traffic has been reduced from 300 to 30 seconds. Second, external users are allowed access to the internal e-mail server.

Three-Interface RACL Example

In the "Three-Interface Example" section earlier in this chapter, I discussed an example of ACL placement and operation using Figure 8-8. In this example, I show you the actual configuration of this router with ACLs and RACLs. This example is more complex than the previous two.

Review the access policies discussed in the "Three-Interface Example" section. Example 8-13 shows the configuration to enforce these policies. The numbering on the right refers to the numbered explanation that follows Example 8-13.

Example 8-13 *Three-Interface Configuration Example*

```
Router(config)# ip access-list extended internal_ACL
Router(config-ext-nacl)# permit tcp host 192.1.1.1                (1)
  host 192.1.2.1 eq 25 reflect DMZ_RACL
Router(config-ext-nacl)# deny tcp any any eq 25                   (2)
Router(config-ext-nacl)# deny ip host 192.1.1.1 any              (3)
Router(config-ext-nacl)# permit ip any 192.1.2.0 0.0.0.255      (4)
  reflect DMZ_RACL
Router(config-ext-nacl)# permit ip any any                       (5)
Router(config-ext-nacl)# exit
Router(config)# ip access-list extended DMZ_ACL
Router(config-ext-nacl)# permit tcp host 192.1.2.1              (6)
  host 192.1.1.1 eq 25
Router(config-ext-nacl)# evaluate DMZ_RACL                      (7)
Router(config-ext-nacl)# evaluate Internal_returns_RACL         (8)
Router(config-ext-nacl)# exit
Router(config)# ip access-list exit_ACL
Router(config-ext-nacl)# permit tcp host 192.1.2.1 any eq 25   (9)
  reflect DMZ_returns_RACL
Router(config-ext-nacl)# permit udp host 192.1.2.2 any eq 53  (10)
  reflect DMZ_returns_RACL
Router(config-ext-nacl)# permit ip 192.1.1.0 0.0.0.255 any    (11)
  reflect Internal_returns_RACL
Router(config-ext-nacl)# permit tcp host 192.1.2.1 eq 25 any  (12)
Router(config-ext-nacl)# permit udp host 192.1.2.2 eq 53 any
Router(config-ext-nacl)# permit tcp host 192.1.2.3 eq 80 any
Router(config-ext-nacl)# exit
Router(config)# ip access-list extended external_ACL
Router(config-ext-nacl)# permit tcp any host 192.1.2.1 eq 25  (13)
Router(config-ext-nacl)# permit udp any host 192.1.2.2 eq 53
Router(config-ext-nacl)# permit tcp any host 192.1.2.3 eq 80
Router(config-ext-nacl)# evaluate DMZ_returns_RACL            (14)
Router(config-ext-nacl)# evaluate Internal_returns_RACL
Router(config-ext-nacl)# exit
Router(config)# interface ethernet0                            (15)
Router(config-if)# description  Internal Network
Router(config-if)# ip access-group internal_ACL in
Router(config-if)# ip access-group DMZ_ACL out
Router(config-if)# exit
Router(config)# interface ethernet2
Router(config-if)# description  DMZ
Router(config-if)# exit
Router(config)# interface etherent1
Router(config-if)# description  Internet
Router(config-if)# ip access-group exit_ACL out               (16)
Router(config-if)# ip access-group external_ACL in
Router(config-if)# exit
Router(config)# ip reflexive-list timeout 120                  (17)
```

The following is an explanation of the listing in Example 8-13. The numbers refer to the numbers that appear on the right side of Example 8-13:

1 This ACL is used to restrict traffic from leaving the internal segment. The first statement allows e-mail to be sent to the DMZ e-mail server, and allows the return of traffic through the DMZ_RACL.

2 This statement denies any internal machine from sending e-mail directly to the DMZ e-mail server—or any other e-mail server, for that matter.

3 This statement denies the internal e-mail server access to any other DMZ or external device.

4 This statement builds a RACL for traffic flowing from the internal segment to the DMZ. These temporary entries are placed in the DMZ_RACL along with the internal e-mail server's connection to the DMZ's e-mail server. For better security, you might want to break up this single ACL statement into multiple ones, based on protocol, and assign different timeout values for the protocols.

5 This statement allows all other traffic to the Internet from the internal segment.

6 The second named ACL is used to restrict traffic coming from the DMZ and Internet segments to the internal segment. The first statement allows the DMZ e-mail server to forward e-mail to the internal e-mail server.

7 The reference to DMZ_RACL allows the traffic that internal devices sent to the DMZ to return to them.

8 The reference to Internal_returns_RACL allows the traffic that internal devices sent to the Internet to return to them. (See Reference 11 in the Example 8-13).

9 This third ACL is to restrict traffic leaving the network. The first statement allows traffic originated by the DMZ e-mail server to be returned to it (DMZ_returns_RACL).

10 This statement allows DNS queries sent by the DMZ DNS server to the Internet to be returned to it (DMZ_returns_RACL).

11 This statement allows traffic sent by the internal users to be returned to them (Internal_returns_RACL).

12 The next three statements allow the responses of the DMZ servers to be forwarded to the Internet users.

13 This fourth named ACL is used to filter Internet traffic coming into this network. The first three statements allow the Internet to access the e-mail, DNS, and web servers.

14 The references to DMZ_returns_RACL and Internal_returns_RACL allow the traffic that internal devices sent to the Internet to return to them, as well as allows the traffic that the DMZ devices originate to be returned from the Internet. One interesting point to make about Internal_returns_RACL is that it is referenced in *two* named ACLs. This is necessary to allow the returning Internet traffic to flow through both the external ACL (applied inbound on E1) and the DMZ ACL (applied outbound on E0).

15 Ethernet0 is connected to the internal segment. It has two ACLs activated on it. internal_ACL is used to restrict traffic leaving this segment, as well as to build RACLs to allow returning traffic to it. DMZ_returns_RACL allows returning traffic from the DMZ to the internal segment. Ethernet2 is connected to the DMZ segment. Notice that no ACL is applied here; all policies are enforced by the two ACLs on the internal interface and the ACL on the external interface.

16 Ethernet1 is connected to the Internet. It has an ACL applied to it inbound (external_ACL) that restricts traffic into the DMZ and allows returning traffic to the internal users. It also has an ACL applied outbound (exit_ACL) that creates RACL entries and allows Internet queries to be forwarded from the DMZ segment.

17 The last statement in this configuration sets the timeout for all idle connections to 120 seconds. After 120 seconds, an idle connection is removed from the RACL.

TIP   One thing that I definitely recommend monitoring in this configuration is the RACL timeout and the amount of memory that these temporary entries require. If idle entries are causing memory problems, set up separate RACLs for HTTP, ICMP, and DNS query connections, setting the idle timeout for these to 60 seconds or less.

As you can see from this example, setting up a three-interface perimeter router firewall is not an easy task—and this was a very basic configuration. On top of this configuration, you also need to apply the other filtering recommendations discussed in Chapter 7, to provide further protection. You have your work cut out for you.

RACL Configuration

When RACLs first were introduced, I thought that they were a godsend to filtering returning traffic. I was able to successfully use them in many environments. However, the first time I configured a router with three interfaces—internal, external, and DMZ—I spent almost three days getting everything to work correctly. I learned a lot about TCP/IP connections and applications that week, and I spent a lot of time with a protocol analyzer figuring out what port numbers unusual applications were using. In this example, the customer was a small financial institution that was concerned about its Internet connection. It had a DMZ with a couple servers offering e-commerce services. Providing protection for these servers, enforcing their policies, and allowing certain inside users to receive returning traffic was not a simple matter.

From this experience, I learned that you absolutely must understand the customer's policies down to the exact detail: what connections are needed and how these connections operate. I highly recommend that you create a network diagram and draw the different kinds of connections that will be used, including the protocol information used, such as TCP or UDP port numbers. Based on this, you should be able to develop an ACL solution with RACLs to easily accommodate the customer's needs.

Summary

This chapter showed you the basics of configuring RACLs to allow the flow of traffic back into your network. RACLs have advantages over the **established** keyword in an extended ACL because RACL entries are temporary and disappear after either their idle timer expires or, if the connection uses TCP, the connection aborts or is gracefully terminated. RACLs should be used when CBAC is not available.

Next up is Chapter 9, which shows you how to use the Cisco CBAC feature of the Cisco IOS Firewall feature set to configure a stateful firewall function on your router. As you will see in this chapter, CBAC has many more features and functions than reflexive ACLs.

## CHAPTER 9

Context-Based Access Control

In the last chapter, you were introduced to one method of providing stateful filtering with the Cisco IOS: reflexive ACLs (RACLs). This chapter focuses on Context-based Access Control (CBAC), one of the key features in the Cisco IOS Firewall feature set. As you will see at the beginning of this chapter, CBAC has many more features and fewer limitations than RACLs. Cisco recommends that you use CBAC instead of RACLs; you will understand why by the end of this chapter.

CBAC is just one of many features of the Cisco IOS Firewall feature set. The Cisco IOS Firewall also supports other features, including authentication proxy (Chapter 14, "Authentication Proxy") and an intrusion-detection system (Chapter 16, "Intrusion-Detection System"). This chapter focuses only on CBAC, which implements the Cisco IOS Firewall feature set's stateful filtering. I begin by introducing some Cisco IOS Firewall features, and then I discuss features specific to CBAC and how to configure CBAC.

Cisco IOS Firewall Features

The Cisco IOS Firewall feature set is a Cisco IOS add-on that provides enhanced security functions for your Cisco IOS device. It provides more features than a standard stateful firewall, setting it apart from small- or home-office firewall appliances. Basically, the Cisco IOS Firewall feature set enhances the router's security by including features in the Cisco IOS that allow it to perform the functions of an enterprise firewall, such as the Cisco PIX. Here are some of the features included in the Cisco IOS Firewall feature set:

- **CBAC**—Provides stateful application layer filtering, including support for unorthodox protocols and multimedia applications. It can examine supported connections for embedded NAT and PAT information and perform the necessary translations. In addition, it can open additional stateful connections for supported applications, such as FTP and H.323.

- **Port mapping**—Allows the mapping of ports so that CBAC can perform its application inspection correctly, such as assigning HTTP to port 8080 if your web server is processing traffic on this port.

- **Filtering of Java applets**—Filters embedded Java applets on HTTP connections, allowing you to block known malicious sites (this is discussed in Chapter 10, "Filtering Web and Application Traffic").

- **DoS protection**—Detects and prevents Denial of Service (DoS) attacks by limiting the number of connections that a device can set up (this is discussed in Chapter 17, "DoS Protection").

- **Authentication proxy**—Authenticates and authorizes connection requests before permitting the traffic to enter or leave the network by prompting a user for a username and password (this is discussed in Chapter 14).

- **Intrusion-detection system**—Detects and prevents, in real time, 100 of the most common kinds of attacks (this is discussed in Chapter 16).

- **Logging and auditing**—Logs TCP and UDP transactions, and can provide real-time alerts of attacks, including packet and segment header information (this is discussed in Chapter 18, "Logging Events").

- **ACL compatibility**—Offers backward compatibility with other ACL technologies, such as standard, extended, lock-and-key, and timed ACLs.

Of all these features, this chapter focuses only on CBAC.

Supported router platforms of the Cisco IOS Firewall feature set include the SOHO70, SOHO90, 800, uBR900, 1600, 1700, 2500, 2600, 3200, 3600, 3700, 7100, 7200, 7300, 7400, 7500, and 7600 series of routers. Supported switch platforms include the Catalyst 4000, 5000, 6000, and 8850 series of switches.

CBAC Functions

CBAC provides four main functions:

- Filtering traffic
- Inspecting traffic
- Detecting intrusions
- Generating alerts and audits

Filtering Traffic

One of the main functions of CBAC is to filter traffic intelligently, specifically for TCP, UDP, and, recently, ICMP connections. As with RACLs, one of its functions is to allow returning traffic into your network; however, it can be used to filter traffic that originates on either side of your router—internal or external.

Unlike extended ACLs, which can filter only on Layers 3 and 4, and RACLs, which can filter on Layer 5 (session layer) information, CBAC supports application inspection, meaning that it can examine the contents of certain kinds of packets when making its filtering decision. For example, it can examine SMTP commands in an SMTP connection. It also can examine a connection's messages to determine the state of a connection. For example, FTP uses two connections, a control and a data connection. CBAC can examine the control connection, determine that a data connection is being created, and add this connection to its state table. CBAC supports many multimedia, as well as other applications, that perform this function. Likewise, CBAC can examine HTTP connections for Java applets and filter them, if so desired.

Inspecting Traffic

Actually, I already mentioned this feature in the last section: CBAC can inspect application layer information and use this to maintain its stateful firewall function, even for applications that open multiple connections or embed NATed addressing or port information in applications.

This inspection process not only allows returning traffic back into your network, but it also can be used to prevent TCP SYN flood attacks: CBAC can examine the rate at which connections are being made to a service and can shut down these connections if a specified threshold is reached. It also can examine TCP connections to make sure that sequence numbers fall within a certain range, dropping any suspicious packets. Besides examining TCP connections, it can examine traffic for DoS fragment attacks.

Detecting Intrusions

As I mentioned in the last section, CBAC can inspect traffic to implement a stateful firewall, but it also can use this feature to detect certain kinds of DoS attacks. CBAC even can provide protection against SMTP e-mail attacks, limiting the type of SMTP commands that can be sent to your internal e-mail servers. All of these kinds of attacks can cause CBAC to generate logging information about the attack, as well as optionally resetting TCP connections or dropping malicious packets.

Generating Alerts and Audits

CBAC can generate real-time alerts of problems and detected attacks, as well as provide a detailed audit trail of connection requests. For example, you can log all network connection requests, including the IP addresses of the source and destination, the ports used in the connection, the number of bytes sent, and at what time the connection started and ended.

Operation of CBAC

CBAC was introduced in Cisco IOS 12.0(5)T. To keep track of connections that it is monitoring, it builds a state table that contains information about each connection. This table is similar to the state table that the Cisco PIX uses. CBAC monitors TCP, UDP, and ICMP connections and maintains information in the state table for them. CBAC then uses the state table to build dynamic ACL entries to allow returning traffic back through the perimeter router/firewall. This is somewhat similar to RACLs; however, CBAC can inspect application layer information, whereas RACLs cannot. CBAC uses the state table and dynamic ACL entries to detect and prevent certain kinds of DoS attacks, especially those that involve TCP connection flooding.

Basic Operation

Take a look at a simple example to see how CBAC functions. I use the network shown in Figure 9-1 to illustrate this example.

Figure 9-1   *Simple CBAC Operation*

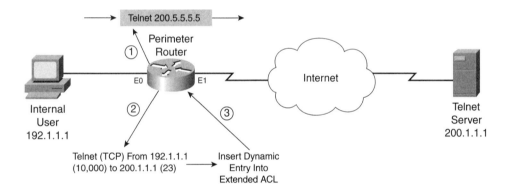

Steps for CBAC Processing:

• Router Inspects Outbound Sessions
• A Statement Is Added to the State Table for the Outbound Telnet Connection
• A Dynamic ACL Entry Is Added on the ACL Applied Inbound on E1

These steps occur in this example:

1 A user initiates an outbound connection, such as a Telnet. If an inbound ACL is applied, this is processed first before any inspection by CBAC. Based on your inspection rules for CBAC, the Cisco IOS might or might not be inspecting the connection. If it is not inspecting the connection, the Cisco IOS allows the packet through; otherwise, the Cisco IOS proceeds to Step 2.

2 The Cisco IOS compares this connection to the entries in its state table: If this connection does not exist, the entry is added; if it exists, the Cisco IOS resets the idle timer for the connection.

3 If this is a new entry, the Cisco IOS adds a dynamic ACL entry on the external interface in the inbound direction, to allow the returning traffic into the network. These dynamic ACL entries are not saved to NVRAM.

Actually, this process appears to be very similar to how RACLs are processed. As with RACLs, CBAC opens temporary openings in your ACLs to allow returning traffic. These entries are created as inspected traffic leaves your network and are removed whenever the connection terminates or the idle timeout period for the connection is reached. As with RACLs, you can specify which protocol or protocols you want to inspect, as well as on which interface and in which direction the inspection should occur.

A new feature was introduced in Cisco IOS 12.3(4)T, called *Firewall ACL Bypass* (FAB). This feature was developed to speed up the Cisco IOS processing of traffic returning to the network. With the FAB feature, the Cisco IOS does not create dynamic ACL entries to allow returning traffic into the network. Instead, the Cisco IOS examines the state table to determine which traffic should be allowed back into the network, which can be handled by fast switching processes such as Cisco Express Forwarding (CEF). If the Cisco IOS does not find a match in the state table, the Cisco IOS uses the ACL applied inbound on the returning interface to enforce policies. By using this process, the router does not have to create and manage dynamic ACL entries on the returning interface: instead, the router only has to check the state table that it maintains. Starting in Cisco IOS 12.3(4)T, the FAB feature automatically is used and cannot be disabled.

NOTE   One nice feature of CBAC is that it is flexible in its configuration, especially in what direction you want to inspect traffic. In the most typical setup, you use CBAC on your perimeter router/firewall to allow returning traffic into your network. However, you can configure CBAC to inspect traffic in two directions—in and out. You might need to do this if you want to protect two parts of your network. In this example, you want both sides to initiate certain connections and allow the returning traffic to reach its originator.

CBAC Enhancements over RACLs

Unlike with RACLs, however, many additional things can occur while the Cisco IOS, using CBAC, is inspecting the traffic on the connection or connections in the state table. I already mentioned one, FAB, in which dynamic ACL entries are no longer necessary to allow returning traffic. This section covers some other enhancements that CBAC has over RACLs.

TCP Traffic

TCP is handled in the same manner with CBAC as is done with RACLs. With TCP, CBAC inspects the connection and examines the control bits in the TCP segment header. If it sees a teardown process (FIN), the Cisco IOS waits 5 seconds for the connection to be torn down gracefully, and then the dynamic ACL entry (before FAB) is removed from the external ACL and the corresponding entry in the state table is removed. If a TCP session is idle longer than 1 hour, the Cisco IOS removes the entry. One unique thing about CBAC, versus RACLs, is that CBAC also monitors the setup of a connection. With CBAC, the Cisco IOS expects the connection to be set up within 30 seconds (this is user-configurable) of seeing the first SYN segment. If the connection is not established during this time period, the Cisco IOS removes the entry from its state table and ACL.

Another difference is that CBAC examines the sequence numbers in TCP connections to make sure that they fall within an expected range. If they do not fall within an expected range, CBAC drops these packets and assumes that a spoofing or DoS attack is occurring.

UDP Traffic

With TCP, it is easy to determine the state of the connection by examining the control bits in the TCP segment header. However, UDP is connectionless, making the inspection process more difficult. As with RACLs, CBAC approximates the life of a UDP connection. It assumes that if no traffic is seen on a UDP connection for more than 30 seconds (this is user-configurable), the connection must have completed; therefore, the Cisco IOS removes the entry in the state table (and the dynamic ACL entry). This is similar to RACLs, with the exception of the default timeout. However, CBAC has one UDP enhancement over RACLs: it also inspects DNS queries and replies. With this feature, CBAC expects that when an internal device generates a DNS query, the remote DNS server will respond with a DNS reply within 5 seconds (this is user-configurable). If a reply is not seen in 5 seconds, the DNS connection entry is removed, to prevent spoofing. Likewise, when the DNS reply is seen from the DNS server, the Cisco IOS immediately removes the entry from its state table (and the dynamic ACL entry). These two enhancements are used to prevent DNS spoofing and DoS attacks.

ICMP Traffic

Inspection of ICMP traffic was introduced in Cisco IOS 12.2(11)YU and was integrated into 12.2(15)T. Before this, CBAC could inspect only TCP and UDP traffic. With ICMP inspection, CBAC can inspect common ICMP message types, including echo request, echo reply, destination unreachable, time exceeded, timestamp request, and timestamp reply messages. CBAC does not inspect other ICMP message types. When inspecting ICMP traffic, the Cisco IOS expects replies to the supported ICMP message types within 10 seconds. If none is seen, the ICMP connection is removed from the state table and the dynamic ACL entry is removed. However, if a response is seen, only the supported message types are allowed (based on the request); other message types are dropped.

Extra Connections

Certain applications, such as FTP and multimedia, open additional connections to transfer information. As mentioned in the last chapter, RACLs either do not handle these connections very well or do not handle them at all. CBAC, on the other hand, supports many of these types of connections. CBAC can inspect the control connection for these applications to determine whether a data connection or other connection is being opened. When CBAC notices the addition of a new connection, it automatically adds this information to its state table (as well as a dynamic ACL entry before FAB) to permit the connection through the router.

Figure 9-2 illustrates how this process is performed with standard, or active, FTP. As you recall from the last chapter, FTP supports two modes: standard and passive. This example focuses only on the use of an internal client using standard FTP to connect to an external server. The client opens a standard FTP connection, with a source port of 10,000, to the FTP server (21). CBAC inspects this connection and adds the appropriate entries to the state table and ACL. Whenever the user needs to download information, the server must open a connection back to the client (with standard FTP only). The user's client software sends the source port to be used for the download to the server on the port 21 connection. CBAC inspects this information, realizes that a new connection will occur, and adds the appropriate entries in the state table and ACL on the returning interface (before FAB). In this example, the client said to use TCP port 10,005 when the server makes the connection from port 20 to the client. CBAC handles this process dynamically, and the traffic for the connection is permitted. I discuss supported protocols for this connection-inspection feature later, in the "Supported Protocols for CBAC" section.

Figure 9-2 *CBAC and FTP*

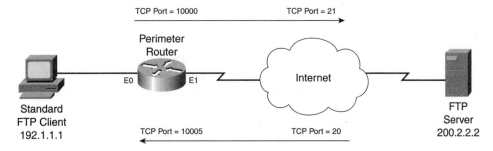

Embedded Addressing Information

With supported applications, CBAC can also inspect connections to see if there is embedded addressing information, such as IP addresses or port numbers, and change these based on information the Cisco IOS has in its address translation table. Let's look at a simple example, shown in Figure 9-3, where the router is using CBAC and is also performing address translation.

Figure 9-3 *CBAC and Address Translation*

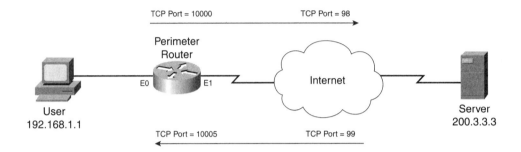

NAT Table

Source IP (Local)	Source IP (Global)
192.168.1.1	192.1.1.2

In this example, I use an imaginary application that uses two connections: one from the client to the server, and one from the server to the client. The router has set up network address translation to statically assign a global (public) address of 192.1.1.2 to the internal client, which is using a private address of 192.168.1.1. When the client initially makes the connection to the server, the Cisco IOS, using CBAC, builds the appropriate entries for the application connection to port 98. Across this connection, the client sends the source port number (10,005) and IP address (192.168.1.1) that the server should use to build the second connection from port 99. Obviously, if the server used this information, the connection would fail because the connection needs to be sent to the public address of 192.1.1.2, not 192.168.1.1.

In the Cisco IOS with FAB, the state table is processed first, then the ACL on the returning interface is processed, and, finally, the address translation occurs (if necessary). CBAC can address this issue by changing the address in the payload on the connection from the client to the server. The server then can respond to the correct address (192.1.1.1), allowing it to connect to the client. In this example, CBAC also would have to use its inspection to dynamically add the second connection to its state table and a dynamic ACL entry to allow the second connection (before FAB). This is similar to what was done in the standard FTP example in the last section. Besides supporting NAT, CBAC can handle PAT. Two restrictions with this feature are as follows:

- The router must be performing the address translation so that CBAC knows how to manipulate the addressing information in the packet payload.

- Not all applications are supported for this feature; with some, only certain types of address translation are supported, such as NAT instead of PAT.

Application Inspection

CBAC even can inspect application layer information to limit the interaction between two devices. A good example of this is the inspection support for SMTP. SMTP is defined in RFC 821 and is the de facto standard for sending e-mail across the Internet. However, SMTP has been hacked in the past and is an insecure protocol. To limit the exposure to your e-mail system, CBAC can inspect the SMTP commands sent between the two e-mail servers on the control connection. This is used to prevent access attacks. This feature is very similar to the Mail Guard feature that the PIX supports. With this feature, CBAC allows only certain SMTP commands. If any other SMTP command is sent, it is denied. The Cisco IOS responds to the sender with an SMTP NOOP message in this instance.

NOTE   Some e-mail systems support Extended SMTP (ESMTP), which provides enhanced functionality between e-mail systems. However, CBAC can inspect only SMTP, not ESMTP, commands. Therefore, if you have an ESMTP server, and outside servers are trying to send ESMTP commands to you, CBAC will deny them. In many cases, the external ESMTP server automatically downgrades itself and uses SMTP commands instead; however, if it does not, the e-mail server will not be capable of sending e-mail to you. Typically, this is a problem not with servers, but with the clients that use SMTP to send or retrieve e-mail messages. If you are inspecting e-mail and experience this problem, disable this CBAC inspection feature. I have had to disable this feature quite often with Microsoft Exchange connections.

DoS Detection and Prevention

CBAC can detect certain kinds of DoS flood attacks. When an attack occurs, the Cisco IOS can take any of the following three actions:

- Block the offending packets
- Protect the internal resource from becoming overloaded with fake connections
- Generate an alert message

To detect DoS attacks, CBAC uses timeout and threshold values to inspect the setup of TCP connections. When TCP connections are being established, they usually do not take more than a second or two. Therefore, if a lot of TCP SYNs are seen from a single source, a threshold can be set to restrict the number of these sessions. In addition, if the connections are not completed within a specific time frame (30 seconds, by default), the Cisco IOS removes this information from its state table and notifies both the source and destination with a TCP RST message on the connection. This is used, especially for your internal resource, to free up these half-open (commonly called *embryonic*) connections. You can define three different thresholds to limit the number of half-open connections:

- Total number of half-open TCP or incomplete UDP sessions
- Total number of half-open TCP or incomplete sessions over a period of time
- Total number of half-open TCP sessions per host

When these thresholds are reached, the Cisco IOS can start dropping incomplete connections that have not been deleted, notify the source and destination that the connections have been torn down (TCP RST), generate an alert, and/or block TCP traffic from the offending device(s). I discuss this CBAC feature more in Chapter 17.

Supported Protocols for CBAC

CBAC can perform inspection for many protocols and applications; however, the depth of its inspection is not necessarily the same for each protocol or application. Here is a list of supported protocols and applications:

- All TCP and UDP sessions, including FTP, HTTP with Java, SMTP, TFTP, and the UNIX R commands, such as rexec, rlogin, and rsh

- ICMP sessions, including echo request, echo reply, destination unreachable, time exceeded, timestamp request, and timestamp reply ICMP messages

- Sun Remote Procedure Calls (RPCs)

- Oracle SQL*Net

- H.323 v1 and v2 applications, including White Pine CU-SeeMe, Netmeeting, and Proshare

- Real-Time Streaming Protocol (RSTP), including applications such as RealNetworks RealAudio G2 player, Cisco IP/TV, and Apple QuickTime 4 software

- Other multimedia applications, including StreamWorks, NetShow, and VDOLive

- Voice over IP (VoIP) protocols, including the Skinny Client Control Protocol (SCCP) and the Session Initiation Protocol (SIP)

All TCP and UDP sessions are supported for inspection, which includes putting a connection's information in a state table and dynamically adding an ACL entry for it (before FAB). For certain applications, such as FTP and SMTP, CBAC can perform additional inspection by restricting the control commands that are executed, fix nontranslated embedded addressing information, and examine control connections to see if additional connections are being set up.

Multimedia applications represent the biggest problem with stateful firewalls because they open multiple connections and sometimes embed addressing information in messages on the control connection. The Cisco IOS CBAC can inspect many of these applications and deal with their quirks, to allow secure connectivity.

RTSP Applications

The Real-Time Streaming Protocol (RTSP), defined in RFC 2326, defines how real-time data streams, such as voice and video, are delivered between devices. It typically is used in applications that need to deploy a large-scale broadcast solution, such as audio and video streaming. Applications that use RTSP include the RealNetwork RealAudio G2 Player, Cisco IP/TV, and Apple QuickTime 4 software.

RTSP uses three types of connections:

- **Control**—Used as the main messaging connection between the client and server. It supports both TCP and UDP; however, CBAC performs inspection only for TCP.

- **Multimedia**—Used to deliver audio, video, or data. These are UDP connections. Either the Real-Time Transport Protocol (RTP) or the Real Data Transport Protocol (RDT) is used to set up and maintain these connections. The Cisco IP/TV and Apple QuickTime 4 products use RTP. RDT was developed by RealNetworks and is used to manage the data connections and retransmission of missing packets. The RealNetwork RealServer G2 product uses RDT.

- **Error**—Can be either a unidirectional or bidirectional UDP connection that the client uses to request missing information or to synchronize audio and/or video streams, to prevent jitter problems.

RTSP clients typically use TCP ports 554 or 8554 to connect to the multimedia server. The client and server then dynamically negotiate the UDP port numbers (1024 to 65,535) for the multimedia streams. Figure 9-4 shows an example of the different types of methods to establish RTSP connections. The top part of this figure shows a connection between a client and server using RTP, the middle part with a client and server using RDT, and the bottom part with a client and server using only a TCP connection for all functions (this typically is used only for small-bandwidth applications).

Figure 9-4   *RTSP Connections*

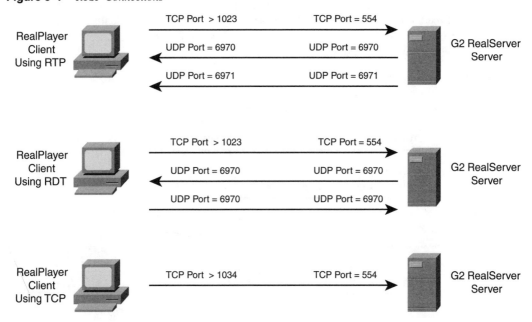

CBAC monitors the control connection to determine when it should add additional connections to its state table, as well as its inbound external ACL (before FAB), and remove the connections.

H.323 Applications

CBAC supports inspection for H.323 version 1 and 2 applications. H.323 defines how to deliver voice, video, and/or data between devices. Unlike RTSP, H.323 is much more complicated. First, either a terminal device can use a server, called a gateway, to find other terminal devices that have content, or it directly can access another terminal device. Second, many more connections are set up between the two terminals when sharing multimedia information.

If a terminal is connecting to a gateway, it opens a TCP connection to port 1720. The gateway then opens a connection back to the terminal, using a dynamically negotiated ports for this second connection that is used to pass control information. The terminal uses this connection to discover the location of other terminals. Based on where the terminal wants to connect, the gateway negotiates the UDP port numbers between the two terminals. The source terminal then initiates the UDP connections to the destination terminal. These UDP connections are used to transport voice, video, and other data payloads. For each of these feeds, there is a separate UDP connection.

Instead of using a gateway, a terminal can connect directly to another terminal, assuming that the destination terminal is configured for this. In this instance, the source terminal opens a TCP connection to port 1720 on the destination terminal, and the remaining UDP multimedia connections that need to be set up are negotiated dynamically, including the port numbers used for these connections. Figure 9-5 illustrates the connections set up directly between two terminals.

Figure 9-5   *H.323 Terminal Connections*

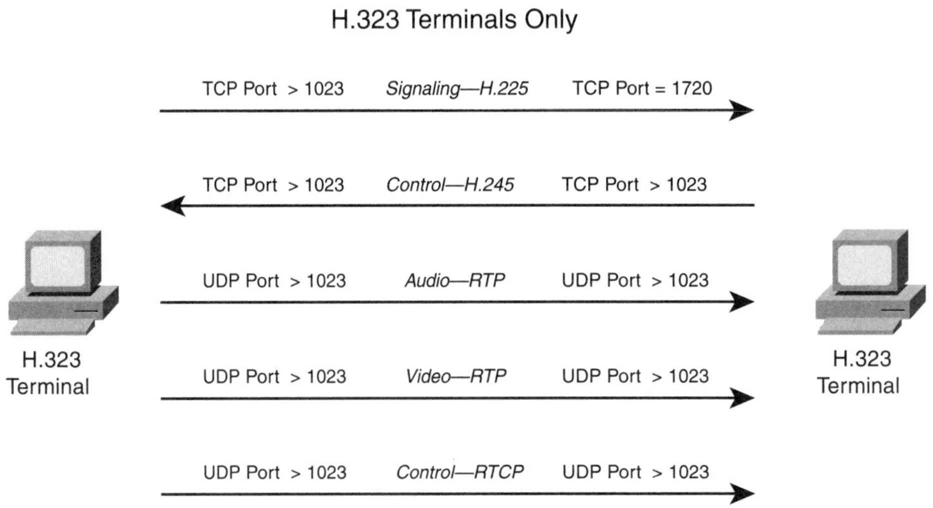

With CBAC, the Cisco IOS inspects the TCP 1720 command connection to determine what additional connections are being established between terminals or gateways. Then it adds the appropriate entry or entries in its state table and dynamically adds the necessary ACL statement(s), before FAB, to allow these additional connections. CBAC also monitors the command connection to determine when the primary or secondary connections no longer are needed, and removes them from the state table and the corresponding dynamic ACL (before FAB) from the inbound external ACL.

Skinny Support

Skinny is a Cisco-proprietary protocol that was developed to support Cisco VoIP phones and their connectivity. With Cisco IP phones, a server runs the CallManager (CM) software. CM has all the phone configurations, as well as their location information. Using DHCP, when a Cisco IP phone boots up, it acquires its IP addressing information as well as the IP address of the CM server.

Figure 9-6 illustrates the connections set up with Skinny. First, the IP phone registers itself with CM (by its IP address) and its identification information. It does this by setting up a TCP connection (port 2000) to CM. This connection remains up until the IP phone is rebooted. If the phone needs additional configuration, CM can function as a TFTP server, holding the phone's configuration on its disk drive. The IP phone then can use TFTP to download its configuration file.

Figure 9-6 *Skinny Connections*

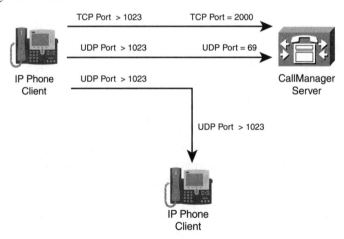

After it has registered with CM, an IP phone can make phone calls to other IP phones. When making a call, the IP phone contacts the CM and tells it the destination phone that it wants to connect to, as well as the source UDP port number that the phone will use. The CM contacts the destination IP phone and informs it of the new connection request. Assuming that the phone is in an on-hook state, the destination IP phone passes back the UDP port number that the source phone should use, which, in turn, the CM passes to the source phone. The source phone then establishes the connection to the destination.

CBAC supports inspection of Skinny connections as of Cisco IOS 12.3(1). With inspection, CBAC inspects the control packets exchanged between the client IP phone and CM. Based on this inspection, CBAC adds (and removes) the necessary entries in the state table and dynamic ACL entries (before FAB) to allow the voice connection to be set up (and torn down) directly between the two IP phones. Some restrictions with Skinny include the following:

- A music-on-hold server, if used, must be installed on the CM: it cannot reside on another device.

- The firewall router with CBAC cannot be the CM because CBAC inspection can inspect only connections going through the router, not connections that terminate on the router.

- The CM and the two IP phones making the connection cannot be on three different networks that are separated by the router/firewall with CBAC. Inspection works only if the three devices are connected to no more than two interfaces on the CBAC router.

SIP Support

SIP is a standards-based protocol that defines the interaction between a VoIP phone, VoIP gateway, and other VoIP phones; it is specified in RFC 2327. SIP defines how to establish, maintain, and tear down phone calls using VoIP.

Figure 9-7 illustrates the connections set up with SIP. First, the client sets up either a TCP or UDP connection to the VoIP gateway (destination port 5060). This is the signaling connection and is used to send call setup and teardown messages to the gateway. After establishing the signaling connection, the VoIP phone can make phone calls. It does this by using the signaling channel to initiate the connection through the gateway. The IP phone sends an unused UDP port greater than 1023 to the gateway, along with the identification of the device that it wants the call. The gateway then contacts the destination IP phone and requests the UDP port number on the destination that the source should use. The gateway passes both the destination IP address and the port number back to the source on the signaling channel. The source IP phone then establishes the phone connection directly to the destination phone. As you can see from this process, the call setup is very similar to that of Skinny.

Figure 9-7   *SIP Connections*

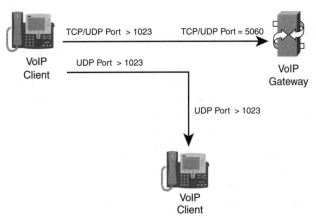

CBAC supports the inspection of SIP connections as of Cisco IOS 12.2(11)YU and 12.2(15)T. CBAC inspects the control packets exchanged between the VoIP phone and VoIP gateway. Based on this inspection, CBAC adds (and removes) the necessary entries in the state table and dynamic ACL entries (before FAB), to allow the voice connection to be set up directly between the two IP phones. Some restrictions with SIP include the following:

- Although SIP supports connections based on DNS names and IP addresses, CBAC supports only connections that specify IP addresses for phone connections. Therefore, the gateway must pass back an IP address of the destination phone.

- SIP supports both TCP and UDP for the signaling connection. However, CBAC supports only UDP (port 5060, by default).

CBAC Performance

Given all of the inspection features that CBAC supports, this can put a large burden on your router, especially in a large network that has many simultaneous sessions that CBAC must maintain. For each session that the router must keep track of, an additional 600 bytes of memory are required to the entry in the state table. If your router must support thousands of connections, your router's memory requirements will be high, as will the CPU cycles needed to handles all of these entries.

CBAC provides for three performance-improvement features, however, to help with reducing the overhead and load on your firewall router:

- Throughput improvement

- Connections per second improvement

- CPU utilization improvement

Throughput Improvement Feature

Throughput, from the CBAC perspective, is defined by the number of packets transferred from one interface to another interface over a 1-second interval. CBAC uses a hash table to perform the lookup process to determine what session a packet is associated with. The issue of using a hashed table is that multiple session entries might match to the same hash value, thereby slowing down the search function of CBAC. When more then one connection entry matches the same hash value, this is called a collision. The more collisions that occur, the longer it takes to find a match, and, thus, the lower your throughput becomes. This is especially true as your connection table becomes larger.

The throughput performance feature of CBAC enables you to dynamically change the size of the hash table that references the connections without having to reboot the router. This feature is new in Cisco IOS 12.2(8)T and is configured using the following command:

```
Router(config)# ip inspect hashtable hash_number
```

The hash number that you configure specifies the number of buckets that the hash table uses. A bucket is basically a reference to one or more sessions. The more buckets you have, the less likely it is that you will experience collisions. The default number of buckets is 1024; this can be changed to 2048, 4096, or 8192.

TIP   The hash table size should be approximately the same number as the total number of concurrent sessions that CBAC is maintaining. If you set the size to a larger size and then later determine that the average number of concurrent sessions is smaller, you dynamically can change the bucket size. Typically, when the number of concurrent sessions falls to below half of the current size, you should adjust the table size downward.

Connections Per Second Improvement Feature

CBAC measures the number of short-lived connections that are created or deleted over a 1-second interval. CBAC can measure only connection-oriented connections. Therefore, only TCP connections are counted; UDP and ICMP are not. Normally, CBAC would process-switch packets for the first few initial TCP packets in adding or removing a connection from the state table. Then packets would be switched normally using whatever switching method was enabled on the router or its interfaces, including CEF. However, the problem with this approach is that it affects the performance of the router, especially if it was hit with hundreds of simultaneous TCP setup or teardown requests.

A good example of this is if your users constantly access Internet web servers. With HTTP, a single downloaded page could include dozens of small HTTP connections, each lasting a second or two. With hundreds of people simultaneously trying to download pages from a website, this seriously could degrade the performance of your router as CBAC is adding and then immediately deleting these connections from the state table.

The connections per second improvement feature reduces the number of packets that have to be processed switched to 1: only the first packet in the session is processed-switched (all packets after that are processed normally). This feature provides a significant boost in performance when your router experiences many short-lived connections, such as HTTP. This feature is new in Cisco IOS 12.2(8)T.

CPU Utilization Improvement Feature

Maintaining a low CPU utilization is important for a router using CBAC, especially when it has to handle hundreds or thousands of sessions. Cisco recently rewrote the code for identifying new sessions and how they are added and removed from the state table, reducing the number of CPU cycles required to process the connection. As mentioned in the discussion of the first feature, Cisco allows you to dynamically change the size of the hash table to reduce the likelihood of collisions that occur when the Cisco IOS is performing a CBAC state table lookup. As mentioned in the last section, the Cisco IOS reduces the number of times that it must perform process switching by doing this only on the first packet of a session. All other packets are switched normally, which means that fewer CPU cycles are required per packet and session. The CPU utilization feature also was introduced in Cisco IOS 12.2(8)T.

CBAC Limitations

Even with all of its features and enhancements, CBAC is not an ultimate firewall solution. In other words, it has limitations and cannot protect you from all kinds of attacks. Actually, this is true of any firewall product. Understanding the limitations of CBAC and the Cisco IOS Firewall feature set will help you better understand whether this solution is a better fit for you network, whether this solution will complement the security solution in your network, and whether a different product would be better for your network.

Here are some of the limitations of CBAC:

- It inspects only the traffic that you specify. This is both an advantage and disadvantage. It enables you to control the overhead that CBAC places on your router, as well as the traffic that is allowed to return. To make it an all-encompassing product, however, you need to configure many inspect statements to fully cover all connection types.

- CBAC is not simple to understand and implement: it requires detailed knowledge of protocols and applications, as well as their operation.

- As with ACLs, the Cisco IOS cannot use CBAC to inspect traffic that the router itself originates.

- CBAC does not inspect packets sent to the router itself. Traffic must flow from one interface to another for inspection to occur.

- CBAC cannot inspect encrypted packets, such as IPSec. However, if the VPN connection terminates on the router, it can inspect traffic entering and leaving the VPN-encrypted tunnel.

- CBAC cannot inspect FTP three-way transfers: it can inspect only passive or standard two-way transfers.

- CBAC does not support inspection for all applications. For certain applications, you need to disable inspection for them to function correctly.

- CBAC supports only process, fast, flow, and CEF switching.

- CBAC ignores ICMP destination unreachable messages.

- The Cisco IOS does not support a stateful failover feature for the state table, as the Cisco PIX does. If a router fails, you can have a redundant router, but the state table is not duplicated between the two. In this instance, the state table must be rebuilt on the second router, causing some connections to fail and requiring users to rebuild those connections.

CBAC Configuration

This section covers the configuration of CBAC for stateful inspection and filtering. Unlike the configuration of RACLs, discussed in the last chapter, the configuration of CBAC is more complicated; there are many more commands with many more options that you either must or can configure.

Following this section, I cover some examples on how you would use CBAC to implement a stateful firewall. Note that this chapter focuses only on the use of CBAC for filtering. I discuss some of CBAC's other inspection features, such as DoS detection and prevention, in Chapter 17.

To simplify the configuration process, I have divided the configuration process into seven simple steps:

Step 1 Determine which interfaces will be internal and external on your router.

Step 2 Create your normal IP ACLs to filter traffic entering and leaving your network. Make sure that you permit the traffic that is to be inspected as it is leaving your network.

Step 3 Change the global timeout values for connections. This is optional.

Step 4 Configure Port Application Mapping (PAM), which specifies the port numbers that CBAC should inspect if the application is using a nonstandard port number, such as HTTP with 8080. This is optional and is required only if your application is using a nonstandard port number.

Step 5 Define your inspection rules. These rules define what entries are added to the state table and what returning traffic is allowed back in. If outbound traffic does not match an inspection rule, the router does not inspect it and treats it as normal traffic.

Step 6   Activate the inspection rule or rules on your router's interface(s). The router then will use CBAC to inspect traffic.

Step 7   Test your configuration by sending traffic through your CBAC router. Even though this is optional, I highly recommend it. The only way that you will find problems is by scrutinizing your configuration and implementation by sending test packets through the router.

CAUTION   Configuring CBAC is not simple. You need to have a very good understanding of how CBAC works, including the inspection process, if you want to reduce the likelihood that you will make configuration mistakes. Configuration mistakes on your part, whether they are inadvertent or the result of trying to get a specific application to work, could open your router and network to security threats. Therefore, take the appropriate amount of time to plan, configure, implement, and test your CBAC policies.

Step 1: Interface Selection

One of the first CBAC tasks that you need to accomplish is to determine which interface is internal and which is external. In this context, internal is where the connections originate, and external is where the returning traffic of these connections will be coming from.

TIP   If you will be configuring two-way CBAC—filtering traffic in two directions—I highly recommend that you first configure one-way CBAC and get this to function correctly before adding the second direction. Two-way configurations are common in intranet and extranet environments.

Step 2: ACL Configuration

In Step 2, you configure your ACLs to filter traffic entering and possibly leaving your network. These ACLs contain many of the filtering suggestions covered in Chapter 7, "Basic Access Lists," such as bogon filtering.

TIP   My recommendation is first to create a basic ACL configuration that allows the necessary traffic into and out of your network, and then add the bogon and other filters for a more robust security solution. This simplifies your CBAC troubleshooting process. After you add your additional filters, continue by adding CBAC to your configuration. This ensures that you easily can narrow any connectivity issues to either your ACL or your CBAC configuration.

After you have configured your filtering ACLs, you need to activate them on your router's interfaces. However, there is one restriction on the use of ACLs and their applications when using CBAC.

On the external interface inbound and the internal interface outbound, only an extended ACL can be applied. For any other situation, you can use either standard or extended ACLs. This means that, for the internal interface inbound and the external interface outbound, you can use either standard or extended ACLs applied in either direction—in or out. Figure 9-8 displays the appropriate use of ACLs.

Figure 9-8 *CBAC and the Application of ACLs*

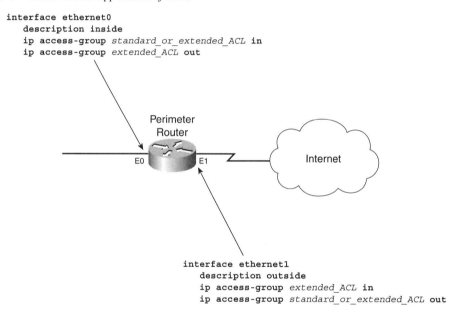

NOTE   Unlike RACLs, CBAC's ACLs can be either named or numbered.

Step 3: Global Timeouts

Optionally, you can change the timeout for connections in the state table (and the dynamic ACL entries, before FAB) with the following CBAC inspection commands:

```
Router(config)# ip inspect tcp synwait-time #_of_seconds
Router(config)# ip inspect tcp finwait-time #_of_seconds
Router(config)# ip inspect tcp idle-time #_of_seconds
Router(config)# ip inspect udp idle-time #_of_seconds
Router(config)# ip inspect dns-timeout #_of_seconds
```

The **ip inspect tcp synwait-time** command specifies how long the Cisco IOS waits for a specific TCP session to be established (to complete the three-way handshake). The default is 30 seconds. If the three-way handshake does not complete by the end of this timeout, the Cisco IOS removes the entry from its state table and the dynamic entry in the ACL (before FAB), and it notifies both parties that the connection has been terminated.

The **ip inspect tcp finwait-time** command specifies how long the Cisco IOS waits to remove an entry from its tables when the source or destination begins the teardown process of a TCP session. The default is 5 seconds. When the Cisco IOS sees that a connection is being torn down, it gives the two devices this time period to tear down the connection before removing the entry from the state table and the corresponding dynamic entry from the ACL (before FAB).

The **ip inspect tcp idle-time** command specifies how long the Cisco IOS maintains an idle TCP connection in its state table. An idle connection is one that is established but has no traffic traversing it. The default is 3600 seconds (1 hour). When the idle period expires, the Cisco IOS removes the entry from the state table and the corresponding dynamic entry from the ACL (before FAB).

The **ip inspect udp idle-time** command specifies how long the Cisco IOS maintains an idle UDP connection in its state table. The default is 30 seconds. After the idle period expires, the Cisco IOS removes the UDP entry from the state table and the corresponding dynamic entry from the ACL (before FAB).

The **ip inspect dns-timeout** command specifies how long the Cisco IOS maintains a DNS query connection in its state table. The default is 5 seconds. When this time period expires, the Cisco IOS removes the DNS query entry from the state table and the corresponding dynamic entry from the ACL (before FAB). This timer supercedes the UDP idle timer. This timer is used to prevent IP spoofing of DNS responses, providing a smaller window for a hacker to spoof DNS responses and, thereby, redirecting an internal device to the wrong service.

NOTE   It is important to point out that CBAC is stateful for TCP connections, but it must approximate UDP and ICMP connections. It does this for "connectionless" sessions by assigning an idle period to them. Also, there is no global timeout command for ICMP traffic; this is configured on an inspection-by-inspection basis and is discussed later.

Step 4: Port Application Mapping

CBAC uses PAM to determine what type of inspection should be performed on a connection. For example, the default application associated with port 25 is SMTP; therefore, CBAC understands, by default, that e-mail is used on this connection and, consequently, can inspect the connection for the appropriate SMTP commands. As another example, the control connection for FTP is TCP 21. Again, CBAC understands that this is used by FTP and performs the appropriate inspection on this connection.

PAM is used to remap ports to or associate additional ports with a specific application so that CBAC can perform the appropriate inspection on the connection. As an example, you might have a web server running on port 8080. By default, CBAC treats this as a normal TCP connection. To have CBAC inspect the connection and treat it as an HTTP connection, you need to associate port 8080 with HTTP.

PAM is the process used to map nonstandard ports to applications so that CBAC can perform the appropriate type of inspection. PAM can be used to associate either TCP or UDP ports to applications. PAM even enables you to assign ports on a host-by-host basis to a specific application. For example, you might have only one HTTP server running on port 8080. You can use PAM to associate only this port on this server for CBAC HTTP application inspection; any other TCP 8080 port on any other device would be treated as a normal TCP connection. With this feature, you greatly reduce the amount of inspection that CBAC has to perform by limiting it to just those devices using the nonstandard ports.

PAM Table

Port mappings are placed in the PAM table, and CBAC uses this table to perform the appropriate inspection on a connection. Three types of entries are used in this table:

- **System-defined entries**—These are the well-known port numbers of applications, such as TCP port 80 for HTTP. These entries cannot be deleted or changed. For example, you cannot assign SMTP port 25 to be inspected on port 80, or HTTP port 80 to 25; however, you can override the system-defined entries on a host-by-host basis (see the last point in this list). Table 9-1 lists the system-defined entries in the PAM table.

- **User-defined entries**—These are applications running on nonstandard port numbers, such as a web server running on ports 8000 or 8080. You easily can create these entries in the PAM table to accommodate all connections with the specified port number. You also can map ranges of ports to a specific application.

- **Host-specific entries**—These are a subset of user-defined entries, where the PAM mapping maps only a connection or connections for a specific host or hosts, but not all connections using the same port number. This enables you to limit the inspection that CBAC does for a specific application. For example, you might have two applications running on port 8080: a web server and a home-grown application. With PAM, you can put an entry in the table for port 8080 for just the web server. This causes CBAC to use HTTP inspection on port 8080 for the web server and normal TCP inspection for 8080 on all other devices.

Table 9-1   *PAM System-Defined Entries*

Application	Port Number
ftp	21
telnet	23
smtp	25

Table 9-1   *PAM System-Defined Entries (Continued)*

Application	Port Number
dns	53
tftp	69
http	80
sunrpc	111
msrpc	135
https	443
exec	512
login	513
shell	514
sql-net	1521
streamworks	1558
h323	1720
netshow	1755
skinny	2000
mgcp	2427
sip	5060
vdolive	7000
realmedia	7070
cuseeme	7648
rstp	554 and 8559

PAM Configuration

Configuring PAM is necessary only if you are running an application on a nonstandard port and want CBAC to inspect this connection. The configuration is straightforward:

```
Router(config)# ip port-map application_name port port_# [list acl_#]
```

First, you must specify the name of the application (supported applications are listed in Table 9-1), followed by the port number. To remap more than one port to an application, repeat the command with the next port number. Optionally, you can associate a standard ACL with the PAM remapping. This standard ACL contains the IP addresses of devices that use the nonstandard port number. Put **permit** entries in the ACL to match on those devices that use the nonstandard port number and **deny** entries for those that do not; remember that there is an implicit deny at the end of this ACL. If you omit the ACL, CBAC assumes that any traffic on the specified port should be inspected per the configured application.

TIP   I have had issues in the past with different versions of the Cisco IOS when I have updated the PAM table and the Cisco IOS did not accept my changes until I saved my configuration and rebooted the router. If you experience this problem, repeat the process I performed.

PAM Verification

After you have configured your port mappings with PAM, you can view them with any of the following commands:

```
Router# show ip port-map
Router# show ip port-map application_name
Router# show ip port-map port port_number
```

Example 9-1 displays the contents of the PAM table.

Example 9-1 *Viewing the PAM Table*

```
Router# show ip port-map
Default mapping: dns          port 53        system defined
Default mapping: vdolive      port 7000      system defined
Default mapping: sunrpc       port 111       system defined
Default mapping: cuseeme      port 7648      system defined
Default mapping: tftp         port 69        system defined
Default mapping: https        port 443       system defined
Default mapping: rtsp         port 8554      system defined
Default mapping: realmedia    port 7070      system defined
Default mapping: streamworks  port 1558      system defined
Default mapping: ftp          port 21        system defined
Default mapping: telnet       port 23        system defined
<--output omitted-->
```

Example 9-1 shows a partial listing of the system-defined entries.

PAM Examples

Now you can take a look at an example where PAM is necessary, using the network shown in Figure 9-9.

Figure 9-9 *PAM Example*

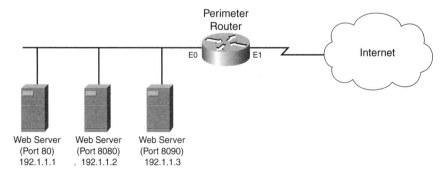

Perimeter
Router

E0   E1

Internet

Web Server   Web Server   Web Server
(Port 80)   (Port 8080)   (Port 8090)
192.1.1.1   . 192.1.1.2   192.1.1.3

Example 9-2 shows the configuration to set up PAM.

Example 9-2 *Using PAM and ACLs to Restrict CBAC Inspection*

```
Router(config)# ip port-map http port 8080 list 1
Router(config)# access-list 1 permit 192.1.1.2
Router(config)# ip port-map http port 8090 list 2
Router(config)# access-list 2 permit 192.1.1.3
```

In Example 9-2, 192.1.1.2 is running a web server on port 8080 and 192.1.1.3 is running a web server on port 8090. The first two commands associate port 8080 HTTP inspection with 192.1.1.2, and the last two commands associate port 8090 HTTP inspection with 192.1.1.3.

Step 5: Inspection Rules

The heart of CBAC is the inspection rules that you define. Inspection rules define what traffic CBAC should inspect. When inspecting traffic, new connections are placed in the state table, and dynamic ACL entries are created (before FAB) to allow for the return of traffic. Inspection can restrict commands executed on a connection, open secondary connections for an application, perform address translation of embedded addressing information, and prevent certain kinds of attacks.

NOTE   By default, there are no predefined inspection rules: You must create them manually. If you do not define an inspection rule for a particular connection, CBAC does not inspect it and this traffic is treated normally.

Inspection Rule Components

The general syntax of an inspection rule is as follows:

```
Router(config)# ip inspect name inspection_name protocol
   [alert {on | off}] [audit-trail {on | off}] [timeout seconds]
```

Inspection rules are created with the **ip inspect name** command. The syntax of the previous command is used for inspections of all types of traffic, with the exception of Java, URLs, and RPCs (I discuss these later in the following sections).

Rules are grouped with an *inspection_name*. This name is similar to the name or number used in an ACL: It associates statements with a particular grouping. Normally, you create one grouping of inspection rules because most companies are concerned about providing a stateful function for a two-interface perimeter router. However, if you need to filter traffic between two networks in an intranet or extranet, or if you have a three-interface router configuration, you typically need to create more than one rule set.

Following the name of the inspection is the name of the protocol or application that you want CBAC to inspect (*protocol*). For protocols and applications, you can specify the following: **cuseeme**, **fragment**, **ftp**, **h323**, **http**, **icmp**, **netshow**, **rcmd** (UNIX R commands), **realaudio**, **rpc**, **rtsp**, **sip**, **skinny**, **smtp**, **sqlnet**, **streamworks**, **tcp**, **tftp**, **udp**, and **vdolive**.

Optionally, you can enable or disable alerts and audits on a per-application or per-protocol basis with the **alert** and **audit** keywords. If you omit these parameters, CBAC uses the default configuration defined with the **ip inspect alert** and **ip inspect audit-trail** commands, respectively. These commands are discussed later in the "Alerts and Audits" section.

The last optional parameter is the **timeout** parameter. If you omit this, it defaults to the timeout value configured with the commands discussed previously in the "Step 3: Global Timeouts" section.

The following sections discuss some of the most important and most common inspection rules that you can configure with CBAC.

Generic TCP and UDP Inspection

You can configure generic TCP and UDP inspection of connections. With generic inspection, CBAC performs only connection inspection: It adds new connections to the state table and a dynamic ACL entry to the external ACL, and removes this information upon termination or timeout of the connection.

With generic inspection, CBAC does not monitor what actually is occurring on the connection, such as what commands are being executed or whether a secondary connection is being negotiated. However, you can configure specific inspection of an application. When you do this, the application inspection, such as FTP, takes precedence over generic TCP and UDP inspection.

NOTE   Basically, TCP and UDP inspection is used to allow returning traffic into your network. However, one additional function of generic TCP inspection is that CBAC examines the sequence numbers in returning segments to ensure that they fall within the configured window range.

Also, 99.9 percent of all traffic that a small company needs to pass through a router configured with CBAC can be accomplished with the inspection of generic TCP and UDP connections, as well as FTP, simplifying your CBAC configuration.

TCP and UDP inspection is done with the following two commands:

```
Router(config)# ip inspect name inspection_name tcp
  [alert {on | off}] [audit-trail {on | off}] [timeout seconds]
Router(config)# ip inspect name inspection_name udp
  [alert {on | off}] [audit-trail {on | off}] [timeout seconds]
```

As you can see, setting up inspection for TCP and UDP is simple.

NOTE	Unlike RACLs, with **ip inspect** statements, you cannot control what traffic within a connection should or should not be inspected. CBAC inspects all traffic covered by an inspection statement.

TIP	If you are using NetMeeting, an H.323 application, you must enable generic TCP inspection as well as H.323 inspection. This is because NetMeeting went beyond the H.323 specification and uses an additional TCP connection that is not defined by H.323. Configuring generic TCP inspection enables CBAC to deal with this additional connection.

ICMP Inspection

As of Cisco IOS 12.2(11)YU and 12.2(15)T, CBAC can inspect ICMP connections. ICMP inspection allows the replies to internal ICMP messages to be returned to the internal device. This is useful when internal network administrators are trying to troubleshoot Layer 3 connectivity problems outside of their network, while still minimizing the exposure from different kinds of ICMP attacks.

NOTE	One limitation of ICMP inspection is that it cannot inspect traceroute implementations that use UDP; many UNIX implementations of traceroute use UDP. You can get around this problem by either enabling generic UDP inspection or specifying the ICMP option in the traceroute program, if this is supported.

Here is the general syntax for ICMP inspection:

```
Router(config)# ip inspect name inspection_name icmp
   [alert {on | off}] [audit-trail {on | off}] [timeout seconds]
```

The default timeout for the return traffic in an ICMP connection is 10 seconds. You can change this by specifying a different value with the optional **timeout** parameter in the **ip inspect name** command. If multiple ICMP messages are sent for the test, the idle timeout starts after the last message.

HTTP Inspection

HTTP inspection can be used in any of the following circumstances:

- Your HTTP server(s) are running on a nonstandard port, such as 8080.
- You want to filter Java applets.
- You want to filter URLs.

To enable inspection for HTTP, use the following configuration:

```
Router(config)# ip inspect name inspection_name http
  [urlfilter] [java-list standard_ACL_#] [alert {on | off}]
  [audit-trail {on | off}] [timeout seconds]
```

The **urlfilter** parameter is used to inspect and filter URLs, and the **java-list** parameter is used to inspect and filter Java applets. I discuss these two options in much more depth in Chapter 10.

RPC Inspection

On a computer, a procedure is a software component running on a system. In Remote Procedure Calls (RPCs), your computer is accessing a procedure on a different computer. RPCs are popular in UNIX environments, with NFS being one of the most common. Even Microsoft uses some RPCs in its software applications.

CBAC can perform inspection on RPCs with the following command:

```
Router(config)# ip inspect name inspection_name rpc
  program-number program_number [wait-time minutes]
  [alert {on | off}] [audit-trail {on | off}] [timeout seconds]
```

Unlike the inspection commands discussed so far, you need to enter the program number of the RPC that you want to inspect. Optionally, you can specify a wait period (**wait-time**), in minutes, that CBAC should use to keep the temporary entry in the state table. This is used to allow more connections from the source to the same destination and port number (but maybe a different RPC). The default is 0 minutes, meaning that the idle timer is used.

SMTP Inspection

CBAC supports application inspection of SMTP connections using the following command:

```
Router(config)# ip inspect name inspection_name smtp
  [alert {on | off}] [audit-trail {on | off}] [timeout seconds]
```

With the activation of SMTP inspection, CBAC filters the SMTP commands on the e-mail connection. CBAC allows only the SMTP commands defined in IETF RFC 821, Section 4.5, through the router; any other SMTP commands are blocked. The allowed SMTP commands include DATA, EXPN, HELO, HELP, MAIL, NOOP, QUIT, RCPT, RSET, SAML, SEND, SOML, and VRFY.

NOTE   SMTP inspection does not support ESMTP. Therefore, if you have enabled SMTP inspection, and your internal e-mail server uses ESMTP and is experiencing e-mail connection problems, you should disable SMTP application inspection for this connection.

Fragment Inspection

CBAC also supports the inspection of fragments with the following command:

```
Router(config)# ip inspect name inspection_name fragment
  max number_of_fragments timeout seconds_to_reassemble
```

The **max** parameter specifies the maximum number of fragmented sessions. The default is 256, but you can change this to 50 to 10,000. In other words, this parameter controls the maximum number of sessions that can contain fragments. Setting this to a large value seriously can affect the performance of the router because it must store all the fragments for these sessions.

The **timeout** parameter specifies for how many seconds the Cisco IOS stores fragments for a session while trying to determine whether the fragments can be reassembled into a packet. The default is 1 second. If the router does not receive all the fragments for a reassembled packet within this time period, CBAC drops the fragments. The Cisco IOS automatically can adjust the timeout value during periods of heavy loads. It does this by examining the number of free connection entries specified by the maximum in the **max** parameter. If there are fewer than 32 connection states, the Cisco IOS divides the time period by half. If there are fewer than 16 connection states, the Cisco IOS automatically changes the time interval to 1 second.

CAUTION   CBAC expects a fragmented packet to arrive in order: The first fragment in the packet should arrive first. If the first fragment is not received first, the Cisco IOS drops the fragments. This can cause problems if an operating system, such as Linux, sends fragments out of order. In the Linux case, the fragments are sent in reverse order. In addition, if load balancing is used between the source and you, the fragments also might arrive out of order. Therefore, I recommend that you not use this inspection feature unless you are under a DoS fragmentation attack: Then enable it.

Skinny Inspection

Skinny inspection is needed only if you are using the Cisco VoIP solution with CM. You need to configure two possible commands:

```
Router(config)# ip inspect name inspection_name skinny
  [alert {on | off}] [audit-trail {on | off}] [timeout seconds]
Router(config)# ip inspect name inspection_name tftp
  [alert {on | off}] [audit-trail {on | off}] [timeout seconds]
```

The first command (**skinny** parameter) is required: It causes CBAC to inspect TCP port 2000 Skinny connections. If you use a TFTP server to download configuration information to your IP phones, you also need to enable inspection for TFTP, which the second configuration command does.

NOTE   There is a configured inactivity timeout for the connection between the IP phone and CM. It is important for the **timeout** value that you specify in your Skinny inspection to be greater than the IP phone–CM timeout period; otherwise, you inadvertently might disconnect an IP phone client. CBAC uses the default timeout for TCP connections for Skinny unless you override them with the **timeout** value parameter (3600 seconds). When CBAC closes a Skinny connection because of inactivity, it sends a TCP RST message to both ends, indicating that the session is being closed. Any phone connections that the IP phone has active will remain active; however, when the user hangs up the phone, the IP phone connection eventually times out after its idle period expires.

Step 6: Inspection Activation

After you have created your inspection rules, you must activate them on your router. As with ACLs, this is done on a router's interface. The **ip inspect** command is used to activate the inspection rule:

```
Router(config)# interface type [slot_#]port_#
Router(config-if)# ip inspect inspection_name {in | out}
```

With the **ip inspect** command, you need to specify the name of the inspection rule grouping, as well as the direction in which you want CBAC to inspect traffic: **in** specifies that inspection of traffic is done as traffic enters the interface, and **out** specifies that it is done as traffic leaves an interface.

The most common implementation of inspection is to activate the inspection rules on the external interface in the outbound direction. This causes CBAC to build temporary ACL entries on the external interface's inbound extended ACL (assuming that your Cisco IOS does not support FAB). If you apply the CBAC inspection rules on an internal interface, you first need to make sure that, for internal traffic, your internal ACL allows the inspected traffic into the router. Second, you activate the inspection rules in the inbound direction, which builds dynamic ACL entries for the extended ACL applied outbound on the outside interface (again, assuming that your Cisco IOS does not support FAB).

Typically, you activate your inspection rules on only one interface on your router. The exception to this is when you need to inspect traffic in two directions, such as in an intranet or extranet environment.

Step 7: Troubleshooting CBAC

After you have configured CBAC, you have three options for monitoring the CBAC inspection process and assisting you in troubleshooting problems:

- **show** commands
- **debug** commands
- Alerts and audits

The best way to test CBAC is to initiate a connection that you know CBAC has been configured to inspect, and then use these tools to verify the inspection process. The following three sections cover these three tools.

show commands

CBAC supports many **show** commands that you can use to view the temporary ACL entries created from the information in the state table, as well as the state table and the operation of CBAC. To view information about CBAC inspection information, use the **show ip inspect** command:

```
Router# show ip inspect [parameter]
```

Table 9-2 displays the optional parameters that you can include with this command.

Table 9-2   **show ip inspect** *Parameters*

Parameter	Explanation
name *inspection_name*	Limits the output of the display to only the inspection rule set that you specified
config	Displays the complete CBAC inspection configuration on the router
interfaces	Displays the inspection rules activated on your router's interface(s)
session	Displays a summary of the connections in the CBAC state table
session [detail]	Displays all the details for connections in the CBAC state table
all	Displays all the information from the options listed in this table

To examine your ACLs, use the following commands:

- **show ip interface**
- **show access-list**
- **show ip access-list**

These commands were discussed in Chapter 7.

NOTE   The important thing to point out about displaying ACLs is that you see both the dynamic CBAC ACL entries (before FAB) and the static entries that you configured in the associated named or numbered extended ACL.

Now take a look at a couple of **show ip inspect** commands. Example 9-3 shows output from the **show ip inspect name inspect_outbound** command.

Example 9-3   *Using the* **show ip inspect name** *Command*

```
Router# show ip inspect name inspect_outbound
show ip inspect name inspect_outbound
Inspection name inspect_outbound
  tcp alert is on audit-trail is off timeout 3600
  udp alert is on audit-trail is off timeout 30
```

In the Example 9-3, you can see the inspection rules configured for the inspection rule set called *inspect_outbound*. With this rule set, TCP and UDP traffic is being inspected, both with their default idle timeouts.

To view the CBAC state table, use the command in Example 9-4.

Example 9-4   *Viewing the CBAC State Table*

```
Router# show ip inspect sessions
Established Sessions
  Session 25A3378 (200.1.1.1:20)=>(192.1.1.2:32704) ftp-data SIS_OPEN
  Session 25A5AC2 (192.1.1.2:32703)=>(200.1.1.1:21) ftp SIS_OPEN
```

In this example, there are two entries in the state table: 192.1.1.2 is inside the network, and 200.1.1.1 is outside. The second entry shows the internal device opening a connection to an external FTP server. The first connection displays the data connection that the FTP server opened back to the internal client. Example 9-5 shows the CBAC dynamic ACL entries created in the inbound extended ACL.

Example 9-5   *Displaying CBAC Dynamic ACL Entries Before FAB*

```
router# show ip access-list
Extended IP access list 100
 permit tcp host 200.1.1.1 eq 21 host 192.1.1.2 eq 32703 (24 matches)
 permit tcp host 200.1.1.1 eq 20 host 192.1.1.2 eq 32704 (88 matches)
<--output omitted-->
```

As you can see from this output, there are two reversed ACL entries to allow the traffic from the FTP server to be sent to the initiating FTP internal client.

Now look at an example of the same internal client opening an H.323v2 connection to an external H.323 server. Example 9-6 shows the entries in the state table on the router.

Example 9-6   *Viewing the CBAC State Table for H.323v2*

```
Router# show ip inspect session
Session 615E2688 (192.1.1.2:38509)=>(200.1.1.2:38509) H323-RTCP-audio SIS_OPEN
Session 615E2688 (192.1.1.2:38408)=>(200.1.1.2:38408) H323-RTP-audio SIS_OPEN
Session 615E2688 (192.1.1.2:38310)=>(200.1.1.2:38310) H323-RTP-video SIS_OPEN
Session 615E2688 (192.1.1.2:38511)=>(200.1.1.2:35611) H323-RTCP-video SIS_OPEN
Session 615E1640 (192.1.1.2:10001)=>(200.1.1.2:1720) H323 SIS_OPEN
```

In this example, you can see all of the H.323 connections set up to download the video and audio streams from the H.323 server application. Example 9-7 shows the ACL entries created from these entries in the state table with a Cisco IOS that does not support FAB.

Example 9-7   *H.323 CBAC Dynamically Added Entries*

```
Router# show ip access-lists
Extended IP access list 100
 permit udp host 200.1.1.2 eq 43509 host 192.1.1.2 eq 39509 (12 matches)
 permit udp host 200.1.1.2 eq 43408 host 192.1.1.2 eq 39408 (381 matches)
 permit udp host 200.1.1.2 eq 43311 host 192.1.1.2 eq 39311 (16 matches)
 permit udp host 200.1.1.2 eq 43510 host 192.1.1.2 eq 39510 (4938 matches)
 permit tcp host 200.1.1.2 eq 1720 host 192.1.1.2 eq 10001 (39 matches)
<--output omitted-->
```

TIP   I like to use one other **show** command, but it is a hidden command (I do not know why). The **show ip inspect stat** command is great for checking out the current, maximum ever, and other counts for connections that CBAC has seen.

debug commands

For more detailed troubleshooting of CBAC, you can use **debug** commands. With **debug** commands, you can see, in real time, the operation of CBAC on your router. Here is the format of the **debug** command for inspection:

```
Router# debug ip inspect parameter
```

Table 9-3 lists the parameters for this **debug** command. Here is the list of application names that you can specify for inspection: **cuseeme**, **dns**, **ftp-cmd**, **ftp-token**, **h323**, **http**, **netshow**, **rcmd**, **realaudio**, **rpc**, **rtsp**, **sip**, **skinny**, **smtp**, **sqlnet**, **streamworks**, **tftp**, and **vdolive**.

Table 9-3   **debug ip inspect** *Parameters*

Parameter	Explanation
tcp	Displays TCP inspection events
udp	Displays UDP inspection events
icmp	Displays ICMP inspection events
application_name	Displays inspection events for the specified application, such as TFTP or SMTP
events	Displays CBAC events, including the processing of packets
object-creation	Displays information about an entry being added to the state table
object-deletion	Displays information about an entry being removed from the state table
function-trace	Displays information about the software functions that CBAC calls
timers	Displays information related to CBAC timers, such as information that the TCP or UDP idle timers are reached
detailed	Displays information about all the CBAC processes on the router

Alerts and Audits

CBAC inspection supports two types of logging functions: alerts and audits. The following two subsections explain how these function and how they are configured.

Alerts

Alerts display messages concerning the operation of CBAC, such as insufficient router resources, DoS attacks, and other threats. Alerts are enabled by default and automatically display on the router's console line. To globally disable alerts, use this command:

```
Router(config)# ip inspect alert-off
```

Remember that you also can disable and enable alerts per inspection rule.

TIP   I highly recommend that you leave alerts enabled. Alerts are useful because they can notify you of network attacks, such as an attack against your e-mail server.

Here is an example of someone trying to send an unapproved SMTP command to an e-mail server:

```
%FW-4-SMTP_INVALID_COMMAND: Invalid SMTP command from initiator
   (200.5.5.5:49387)
```

CBAC can detect a small number of SMTP attacks besides the use of invalid commands, including these:

- Someone trying to send a pipe (|) in the To or From fields of the e-mail message
- Someone trying to send :decode@ in the e-mail header
- Someone trying to use the old SMTP **wiz** or **debug** commands on the SMTP port
- Someone trying to execute arbitrary commands to exploit a bug in the Majordomo e-mail program

Here is an example of an alert being generated when a hacker tries to exploit the SMTP Majordomo bug:

```
02:04:55: %FW-4-TCP_MAJORDOMO_EXEC_BUG: Sig:3107:
   Majordomo Execute Attack - from 200.5.5.5 to 192.1.1.1:
```

Audits

Auditing keeps track of the connections that CBAC inspects, including valid and invalid access attempts. For example, you can see messages when CBAC adds or removes an entry from the state table. The audit record gives some basic statistical information about the connection. Auditing is disabled by default but can be enabled with the following command:

```
Router(config)# ip inspect audit trail
```

Here is an example audit message from CBAC:

```
%FW-6-SESS_AUDIT_TRAIL: tcp session
   initiator (192.1.1.2:32782) sent 22 bytes
   responder (200.1.1.1:23) sent 200 bytes
```

In this example, an audit trail is being created from a Telnet connection initiated from 192.1.1.2.

NOTE   By default, when alerts and audits are enabled, they display messages on the console line. However, you can log this information to other locations, including the router's internal buffer or an external syslog server. These logging concepts are discussed in Chapter 18.

CBAC Removal

If you no longer want to use CBAC on your router, remove it with the following configuration command:

```
Router(config)# no ip inspect
```

This command causes the Cisco IOS to remove all CBAC commands, remove the state table, and remove all temporary ACL entries created by CBAC. This command also resets all timeout and threshold values to their factory defaults.

CAUTION   Disabling CBAC causes all inspection processes to cease. When this is done, the Cisco IOS cannot detect certain kinds of attacks, such as some types of SMTP- and Java-based attacks.

CBAC Examples

DoS detection and prevention with CBAC is discussed in Chapter 17. Here I take a look at some examples of using CBAC for inspection and stateful filtering. Each example has four basic configuration components:

- Defining an extended ACL(s) to filter traffic
- Applying the extended ACL(s) on the appropriate interface(s)
- Defining an inspection rule(s) to allow returning traffic
- Applying the inspection rule(s) to the appropriate interface(s)

You need to configure many other things to secure the router in this example; however, these examples focus on only the previous four core elements in setting up stateful filtering.

Simple Example

Example 9-8 uses three simple inspection rules for TCP, UDP, and ICMP.

Example 9-8 *Setting Up a Simple CBAC Inspection Configuration*

```
Router(config)# ip access-list extended EXTERNAL-ACL
Router(config-ext-nacl)# deny tcp any any log
Router(config-ext-nacl)# deny udp any any log
Router(config-ext-nacl)# deny icmp any any log
Router(config-ext-nacl)# deny ip any any
Router(config)# ip inspect name CBAC-EXAMPLE tcp
Router(config)# ip inspect name CBAC-EXAMPLE udp
Router(config)# ip inspect name CBAC-EXAMPLE icmp
Router(config)# interface ethernet0
Router(config-if)# ip access-group EXTERNAL-ACL in
Router(config-if)# ip inspect CBAC-EXAMPLE out
```

In this example, *EXTERNAL-ACL* is an extended IP ACL that denies all IP traffic. I put in the specific deny statements to log the denied TCP, UDP, and ICMP packets. Also notice that there is no reference to CBAC in the ACL; this is not necessary because CBAC dynamically adds entries at the top of the ACL to allow returning traffic. This is true of a Cisco IOS before FAB; however, with FAB, the Cisco IOS uses the state table to process returning traffic and then the static ACL on the returning interface. Without CBAC, the ACL in this configuration would drop all traffic trying to enter the ethernet0 interface.

Below this are three inspection statements for the rule group called *CBAC-EXAMPLE*: All TCP, UDP, and ICMP traffic is inspected. Ethernet0 is the external interface, where the external ACL is applied inbound and the inspection rules are applied outbound. With this configuration, CBAC knows that inspected traffic leaving the router has dynamic ACL entries automatically added to the top of the applied inbound external ACL (again, before FAB).

NOTE From my perspective, the configuration of CBAC is simpler than that of RACLs. With RACLs, you need two ACLs, and the placement of the **reflect** and **evaluate** entries in the internal and external ACL is critical. With CBAC, you need to worry about only one ACL, and you do not have to worry about where the temporary ACL entries are placed; CBAC takes care of this automatically before FAB or uses the state table only to allow returning traffic with FAB.

To illustrate this further, imagine that an internal user (192.168.1.100) Telnets to an external device (192.168.2.2). Example 9-9 shows the verification on the router of this process.

Example 9-9 *State Table Example Using the Configuration in Example 9-8*

```
Router# show ip inspect sessions
Established Sessions
  Session 82040F2C (192.168.1.100:1289)=>(192.168.2.2:23) tcp SIS_OPEN
```

As you can see, an entry was added to the Cisco IOS state table for the Telnet connection. Example 9-10 shows the display of the ACL information.

Example 9-10 *The ACL, Before FAB, Using the Configuration in Example 9-8*

```
Router# show ip access-list
Extended IP access list EXTERNAL-ACL
  permit tcp host 192.168.2.2 eq telnet host 192.168.1.100 eq 1289 (18 matches)
  10 deny tcp any any log
  20 deny udp any any log
  30 deny icmp any any log
  40 deny ip any any
```

As you can see, the very first line of the ACL is the dynamic Telnet entry that CBAC added from the state table.

NOTE   Before FAB, you see the dynamic ACL entries at the top of the ACL on the returning interface; however, with FAB, you see only the ACL entries that you have configured manually. With FAB, the router uses the state table to allow returning traffic and the ACL to filter other traffic. Even for me, this takes some time to get used to because I always am looking for the temporary dynamic ACL entries to verify the operation of CBAC. With FAB, you need to examine the CBAC state table to verify its operation.

Two-Interface CBAC Example

Figure 9-10 illustrates how to use CBAC in a router that has two interfaces. This example is the same one used in Chapter 8, "Reflexive Access Lists." However, I configure CBAC instead of using RACLs to implement the stateful filtering.

Figure 9-10   *Two-Interface CBAC Example*

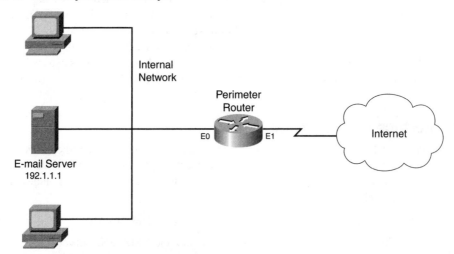

Internal
Network

Perimeter
Router

E0   E1

Internet

E-mail Server
192.1.1.1

In this example, the network has two policies: allow Internet traffic to the internal e-mail server, and allow users access to the Internet. To accomplish this, you need an ACL configuration, such as the following:

- Allow all internal users access to the Internet
- External ACL (apply inbound on E1):
  — Allow returning traffic from the Internet to the internal users
  — Allow Internet traffic to the e-mail server
  — Deny all other traffic

Example 9-11 shows the configuration to enforce these policies.

Example 9-11 *Using CBAC to Implement Policies on a Two-Interface Router*

```
Router(config)# ip access-list extended external_ACL
Router(config-ext-nacl)# permit tcp any host 192.1.1.1 eq smtp
Router(config-ext-nacl)# deny ip any any
Router(config-ext-nacl)# exit
Router(config)# ip inspect name CBAC smtp
Router(config)# ip inspect name CBAC tftp
Router(config)# ip inspect name CBAC ftp
Router(config)# ip inspect name CBAC http
Router(config)# ip inspect name CBAC realaudio
Router(config)# ip inspect name CBAC tcp
Router(config)# ip inspect name CBAC udp
Router(config)# ip inspect name CBAC icmp
Router(config)# ip inspect tcp idle-time 300
Router(config)# interface ethernet1
Router(config-if)# ip inspect CBAC out
Router(config-if)# ip access-group external_ACL in
```

In this example, the *external_ACL* allows only e-mail traffic to be sent to the internal e-mail server (192.1.1.1). All other traffic, by default, is denied. Following the ACL are the inspection rules for the inspection group called CBAC. In this example, TCP, UDP, ICMP, SMTP, TFTP, FTP, HTTP, and RealAudio traffic is being inspected. Next, the TCP idle timer for idle TCP connection has been changed from 3600 seconds to 300 seconds (5 minutes). Finally, the ACL and CBAC are activated on the router's external interface (ethernet1). As you can see from this example, the configuration is straightforward.

Three-Interface CBAC Example

Figure 9-11 illustrates how to use CBAC in a router that has three interfaces. This is the same three-interface example used in the last chapter, where RACLs were used to implement a stateful firewall filtering function. Here is a review of the policies discussed in the last chapter for this network:

- The Internet should be capable of accessing the DMZ e-mail server.
- The Internet should be capable of accessing the DMZ DNS server.

- The Internet should be capable of accessing the DMZ web server.

- The Internet should not be capable of accessing the internal network.

- The internal e-mail server should be capable of accessing only the DMZ e-mail server, nothing else.

- The DMZ e-mail server should be capable of accessing the internal e-mail server to forward mail.

- Internal users should be able to access the Internet and receive replies.

- Internal users should not be able to access the DMZ e-mail server or any external e-mail servers.

Figure 9-11 *Three-Interface CBAC Example*

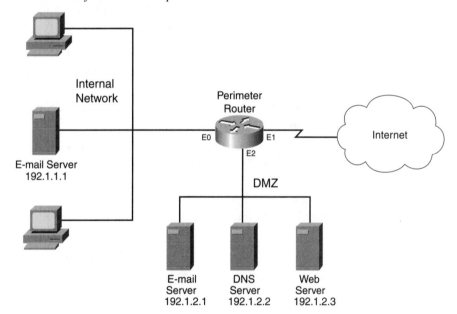

To accomplish these policies, you need three ACLs:

- Internal ACL (apply inbound on E0):
    - Allow internal e-mail server to access DMZ e-mail server
    - Deny internal users to access the DMZ e-mail server and other e-mail servers
    - Deny internal e-mail server from accessing anything else
    - Allow internal users to access all other services (DMZ and Internet)
    - Examine outbound traffic and build the state table entries for new sessions to the DMZ (not a part of the ACL, but part of the CBAC inspection process)
    - Examine outbound traffic and build the state table entries for new sessions to the Internet (not a part of the ACL, but part of the CBAC inspection process)

- DMZ ACL (apply inbound on E2). This restricts traffic from the DMZ to the internal network and the DMZ to the Internet:
  - Allow the DMZ e-mail server to send e-mail to the internal server
  - Allow the DMZ e-mail server to send e-mail to external e-mail servers
  - Allow the DMZ DNS server to query other DNS servers
  - Examine DMZ-related traffic to allow returning traffic from the DMZ to the internal and Internet users (not a part of the ACL, but part of the CBAC inspection process)
- External ACL (apply inbound on E1):
  - Allow Internet users access to the DMZ e-mail server
  - Allow Internet users access to the DMZ DNS server for DNS queries
  - Allow Internet users access to the DMZ web server
  - Examine the traffic sent from the internal network and the DMZ e-mail server to be returned (not a part of the ACL, but part of the CBAC inspection process)

As you can see from the previous list of policies, setup of the ACLs and CBAC is a lot more difficult than in the two-interface CBAC example:

- You need three ACLs: one to restrict traffic coming into the network, one to restrict traffic from the users to the DMZ, and one to restrict traffic from the DMZ to the Internet
- You need a minimum of one, and possibly three, inspection rules, depending on what must be inspected from which interface.

Example 9-12 shows the configuration to enforce these policies.

Example 9-12 *Using CBAC to Implement Policies on a Three-Interface Router*

```
Router(config)# ip access-list extended internal_ACL
Router(config-ext-nacl)# permit tcp host 192.1.1.1            (1)
  host 192.1.2.1 eq smtp
Router(config-ext-nacl)# deny tcp any any eq pop              (2)
Router(config-ext-nacl)# deny tcp any any eq smtp
Router(config-ext-nacl)# deny ip host 192.1.1.1 any          (3)
Router(config-ext-nacl)# permit ip any any                   (4)
Router(config-ext-nacl)# exit
Router(config)#
Router(config)# ip inspect name internal_CBAC smtp audit-trail on (5)
Router(config)# ip inspect name internal_CBAC ftp
Router(config)# ip inspect name internal_CBAC http
Router(config)# ip inspect name internal_CBAC realaudio
Router(config)# ip inspect name internal_CBAC tcp
Router(config)# ip inspect name internal_CBAC udp
Router(config)# ip inspect name internal_CBAC icmp
Router(config)#
Router(config)# ip access-list extended DMZ_ACL
```

Example 9-12 *Using CBAC to Implement Policies on a Three-Interface Router (Continued)*

```
Router(config-ext-nacl)# permit tcp host 192.1.2.1 any eq smtp      (6)
Router(config-ext-nacl)# permit udp host 192.1.2.2 any eq dns       (7)
Router(config-ext-nacl)# exit
Router(config)#
Router(config)# ip inspect name DMZ_CBAC smtp audit-trail on        (8)
Router(config)# ip inspect name DMZ_CBAC http
Router(config)# ip inspect name DMZ_CBAC tcp
Router(config)# ip inspect name DMZ_CBAC udp
Router(config)#
Router(config)# ip access-list extended external_ACL
Router(config-ext-nacl)# permit tcp any host 192.1.2.1 eq smtp      (9)
Router(config-ext-nacl)# permit udp any host 192.1.2.2 eq dns
Router(config-ext-nacl)# permit tcp any host 192.1.2.3 eq http
Router(config-ext-nacl)# exit
Router(config)#
Router(config)# ip inspect name external_CBAC smtp                  (10)
  audit-trail on
Router(config)# ip inspect name external_CBAC ftp
Router(config)# ip inspect name external_CBAC http
Router(config)# ip inspect name external_CBAC realaudio
Router(config)# ip inspect name external_CBAC tcp
Router(config)# ip inspect name external_CBAC udp
Router(config)# ip inspect name external_CBAC icmp
Router(config)#
Router(config)# interface ethernet0                                 (11)
Router(config-if)# description  Internal Network
Router(config-if)# ip access-group internal_ACL in
Router(config-if)# ip inspect internal_CBAC in
Router(config-if)# exit
Router(config)# interface ethernet2                                 (12)
Router(config-if)# description  DMZ
Router(config-if)# ip access-group DMZ_ACL in
Router(config-if)# ip inspect DMZ_CBAC in
Router(config-if)# exit
Router(config)# interface ethernet1                                 (13)
Router(config-if)# description  Internet
Router(config-if)# ip access-group external_ACL in
Router(config-if)# exit
Router(config)# ip inspect tcp synwait-time 15                      (14)
Router(config)# ip inspect tcp idle-time 120
Router(config)# ip inspect udp idle-time 20
```

The following is an explanation of Example 9-12, with reference to the numbering on the right side of the example:

1 internal_ACL is used to filter traffic from the internal segment (connected to ethernet0). The first statement in this ACL allows the internal e-mail server to send e-mail to the DMZ e-mail server.

2 This statement forces the internal clients to send e-mail through the internal e-mail server. In addition, the statement following this one prevents all e-mail connections, minus the e-mail connection listed in the first statement.

3 This statement prevents the internal e-mail server from accessing any other device.

4 All other access from the internal segment to other devices is allowed.

5 The internal_CBAC inspection rules are used to allow traffic for returning sessions to the internal users. In this example, the administrator has determined the protocols that internal people use and has configured the appropriate inspection statements. Notice that the audit trail function has been enabled for SMTP inspection. This is done to provide more information about SMTP connections and possible attacks.

6 The second ACL, DMZ_ACL, is used to filter traffic from the DMZ segment. By default, only two connections are allowed. In this first statement, the DMZ e-mail server is allowed to send e-mail to any e-mail server, including the internal e-mail server and Internet e-mail servers.

7 In the second ACL statement, the DMZ DNS server is allowed to forward DNS queries to other DNS servers.

8 In the second inspection rule set for CBAC, inspection is set up for traffic entering the DMZ segment, allowing for the return of traffic from the DMZ to the internal and Internet segments. Notice that the number of inspection statements is smaller because the applications running on the DMZ are limited.

9 This third ACL is used to filter traffic from the Internet that is trying to access internal resources. Only three statements are configured, allowing access to the DMZ e-mail server, the DMZ DNS server, and the DMZ web server.

10 The third set of CBAC inspection rules allows returning traffic that originally exited the Internet interface. Actually, you could have used the same inspection rule set that I did for the internal interface. However, this adds overhead because some of the traffic is internal to the DMZ, and you do not want these temporary ACL entries to show up on the external interface.

11 This interface is connected to the internal segment and has internal_ACL activated on it as well as the CBAC inspection rule for the internal traffic.

12 This interface is connected to the DMZ segment and has DMZ_ACL activated on it as well as the CBAC inspection rule for the DMZ traffic.

13 This interface is connected to the external (Internet) segment and has external_ACL activated on it.

14 The last set of three statements changes the default idle timeout for connections. The first statement reduces the TCP setup time from 30 to 15 seconds. The second statement reduces the TCP idle timeout from 3600 to 120 seconds (2 minutes). In the third statement, the UDP idle timer is reduced from 30 to 20 seconds.

If you compare this example to the three-interface example in Chapter 8, this example is much cleaner and easier to implement. This is one of the main reasons administrators prefer to use CBAC instead of RACLs.

CBAC and RACLs

When CBAC was introduced, I became a happy convert from the use of RACLs. I originally started building packet-filtering firewalls in the early to mid-1990s. These could filter only on basic Layers 3 and 4 information in a packet. One huge limitation of these filters is that they are good for filtering traffic in one direction but are horrible at filtering traffic in two or more directions. When Cisco introduced RACLs, they provided decent bidirectional filtering. Unfortunately, you had to be a guru in converting your policies to ACLs, especially if you needed to filter traffic among more than two interfaces, as you saw in my three-interface example in Chapter 8, "Reflexive Access Lists." I can remember spending days implementing complex filtering configurations with the help of packet sniffers.

However, with the introduction of CBAC, this issue has been reduced greatly. Along with CBAC, the Cisco IOS Firewall feature set offers many features that enable you to harden your perimeter router and provide a tough defense against a determined hacker. Teaming the Cisco IOS Firewall feature set with other security products, you easily can create a scalable, secure perimeter defense.

Summary

This chapter showed you the basics of using CBAC to implement stateful filtering and inspection of traffic. Cisco recommends CBAC over RACLs when implementing stateful filtering because of the ease of its configuration as well as its enhanced features, including application inspection. With application inspection, CBAC can monitor connections to limit the commands executed on them, to prevent certain kinds of DoS attacks, to detect embedded nontranslated addressing information and translate this information, as well as many other things.

Next up is Chapter 10, which shows you how to filter Java applets and web information using external content filter servers, CBAC, and the Cisco IOS Network-Based Application Recognition (NBAR) feature.

## CHAPTER 10

Filtering Web and Application Traffic

In Chapter 9, "Context-Based Access Control," I discussed how you can use the Cisco CBAC, a feature of the Cisco IOS Firewall feature set, to implement a stateful firewall. This chapter picks up where Chapter 9 left off and focuses on filtering of web and application traffic. As you recall from Chapter 9, one of the features of CBAC is the capability to filter Java applets. This chapter starts by covering how this is done with CBAC. It then expands coverage of HTTP connections by discussing how you can filter web connections using N2H2 and Websense web content filtering servers. This last part of the chapter discusses the Cisco Network-Based Application Recognition (NBAR) feature. NBAR typically is used to implement Quality of Service (QoS). However, this extremely powerful tool also can be used to monitor and filter traffic.

Java Applets

Java applets are scripts that allow a web designer to implement many useful web server features. Java is very popular because of its platform independence: Java applets can be made and run on any machine that supports Java. Given its widespread use and usefulness, however, it has been the target of hackers. With older implementations of Java, hackers successfully downloaded rogue Java code to a user's desktop, allowing the hacker to take control. Sometimes the hacker planted a Trojan horse or worm to control the user's desktop remotely. In other instances, the hacker maliciously deleted user files or erased the entire disk drive.

Java Inspection

Some form of control is necessary to prevent hackers from attacking desktops using Java. Java blocking, or filtering, is the capability to selectively filter Java applets downloaded through HTTP connections. A few solutions are available to you:

- CBAC inspection
- URL filtering
- HTTP proxies

The first solution, CBAC inspection, is the simplest to implement. When configured for Java filtering, CBAC inspection monitors HTTP connections for embedded Java applets. CBAC allows applets from only a list of allowed sites; for all other websites, CBAC blocks the download of the applets. Configuration of friendly and unfriendly Java sites is done with a simple standard ACL. Java inspection gives you more control over the sites that your users access, as well as the content that they can see from Java-enabled sites.

CAUTION   CBAC can inspect Java applets in only open HTTP connections. It cannot inspect Java applets if they have been compressed into a different format, such as .zip or .tar files; if they have been encrypted; or if they have been downloaded through FTP, gopher, or a nonstandard HTTP port that has not been mapped by PAM.

Java Blocking

Chapter 9 briefly covered how CBAC can inspect HTTP traffic and how to configure it. This section expands on how to set up Java filtering with CBAC. Filtering of Java applets is done with HTTP inspection. Use the following command to enable Java applet inspection:

```
Router(config)# ip inspect name inspection_name http
   [java-list standard_ACL_#] [alert {on | off}] [audit-trail {on | off}]
   [timeout seconds]
```

For Java inspection, use a protocol of **http**, and then create a standard IP ACL and reference this ACL in the **ip inspect name** command. The **java-list** parameter specifies the standard IP ACL to use for filtering of applets.

CAUTION   CBAC inspection of Java applets is CPU intensive for the router. Therefore, you should use this feature only if absolutely necessary. My recommendation is to filter all traffic from the website or network that has known malicious Java applets. This can be done with a simple extended ACL statement or statements, which is much less taxing on your router. However, if you need to download web content from a site but you do not trust its Java applets, be forewarned about the burden that you will be placing on your router when CBAC inspects for Java applets.

Java Blocking Example

Take a look at a simple example of setting up CBAC for Java inspection (see Figure 10-1). The administrator at this site found that a new virus was floating around the internal network. After some investigation, the administrator learned that the virus was infiltrating his users' PCs through Java applets from one commonly used web service provider (200.1.1.0/24). Unfortunately, the administrator could not block all HTTP traffic from this site because his internal users needed legitimate access to these web servers. After contacting this web service company about the problem and not getting much help, the administrator decided to use CBAC Java inspection to prevent applets from being downloaded from this site and spreading the virus to his users' computers.

Figure 10-1 *Java Blocking*

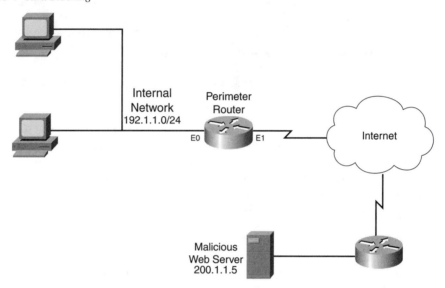

This example focuses only on the Java-blocking component of CBAC. Note that you still need to complete the rest of the configuration based on this company's specific policies. Example 10-1 shows the stripped-down configuration for Java applet filtering.

Example 10-1 *Using CBAC to Filter Java Applets*

```
Router(config)# ip access-list extended EXTERNAL-ACL
Router(config-ext-nacl)# ! <--add other ACL policy statements-->
Router(config-ext-nacl)# deny ip any any
Router(config-ext-nacl)# exit
Router(config)# ip access-list standard JAVA-ACL
Router(config-std-nacl)# deny 200.1.1.0 0.0.0.255
Router(config-std-nacl)# permit any
Router(config-std-nacl)# exit
Router(config)# ip inspect name CBAC-EXAMPLE http java-list JAVA-ACL
Router(config)# ! <--add other CBAC inspection statements-->
Router(config)# interface ethernet0
Router(config-if)# ip access-group EXTERNAL-ACL in
Router(config-if)# ip inspect CBAC-EXAMPLE out
```

In this example, the external ACL filters traffic entering the internal network. Note that I put a place marker where this company will add its ACL statements to implement its specific policies. Below this is a standard named ACL that denies traffic from 200.1.1.0/24 but permits everything else. I have included only one statement in the inspection rules for CBAC, but I added a placeholder for the other CBAC inspection statements needed for implementing a stateful firewall based on this company's policies. Notice that the inspection rule filters Java applets based on the standard ACL, JAVA-ACL, which will deny applets from 200.1.1.0/24 only.

After you have enabled this feature, test it by trying to access web pages from the offending site that uses Java applets. When you do this, CBAC filters the applet and you should see the following alert message (assuming that you have not disabled alerts) on your router's console:

```
%FW-4-HTTP_JAVA_BLOCK: JAVA applet is blocked from
    (200.1.1.5:80) to (192.1.1.22:45323).
```

As you can see from this output, CBAC is blocking applets from the 200.1.1.0/24 network.

NOTE   Java blocking with CBAC is not a scalable solution because it requires you to list which sites are "friendly" or "unfriendly." Typically, you should use this feature to block Java applets from known malicious sites or networks; otherwise, you should use another solution, such as an HTTP proxy or URL filtering with an external policy server. I discuss the latter option in the next section.

URL Filtering

As of Cisco IOS 12.2(11)YU and 12.2(15)T, the Cisco IOS supports URL filtering. One of the problems of using extended ACLs or even CBAC inspection with Java blocking is that your router filters traffic only based on what is in either the ACL or the inspection statement. As an example, imagine that you want to prevent users from accessing pornography, gambling, and peer-to-peer file-sharing sites. Theoretically, you could do this with extended ACLs; however, you would have to know about the IP address of every web page (not just every website). Unfortunately, you cannot screen web pages with normal extended ACLs— only Layer 4 and lower information. Even if you decide to block all pages from these web servers, you easily would have tens of thousands of ACL entries to create and maintain.

Because of these issues, ACLs typically are not used to implement these kinds of policies. Instead, a content-filtering server is used. Cisco currently supports server products from N2H2 (Sentian) and Websense to perform this filtering process. Actually, the content-filtering servers contain the access policies, and your Cisco router uses these external policies to enforce URL access from your users.

NOTE   This section focuses only on how the router accesses and enforces policies stored on an external N2H2 or Websense server. How to install, implement, and maintain these external servers is beyond the scope of this book. For more information on N2H2 products, visit http://www.n2h2.com. For more information about Websense products, visit http://www.websense.com.

Operation of URL Filtering

To help you understand how URL filtering works, take a look at a simple example. The network shown in Figure 10-2 illustrates how URL filtering works.

Figure 10-2 *URL Filtering Process*

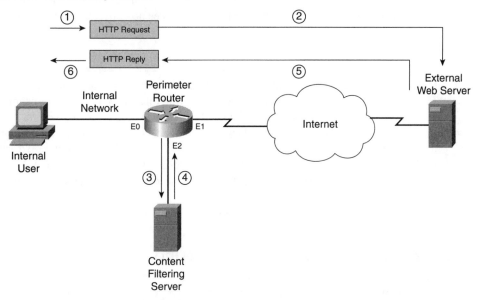

In this example, an internal user sends an HTTP request to download information from an external web server. Here are the steps that occur through the HTTP request and response process, with reference to the numbering in Figure 10-2:

1 The user sends the request, and the router examines it.

2 The router forwards the request to the external server.

3 The router also forwards the request to the content-filtering server to determine whether the access is allowed. Basically, Steps 2 and 3 are occurring almost simultaneously.

4 When the content-filtering server receives the lookup request, it examines its internal database policies to determine the action that the router should take. It then sends the policy action to the router.

5 The response from the content-filtering server typically arrives before the external web server has a chance to return the content that the user was asking for. However, if the external data is returned before the router receives the policy action in Step 4, the router can buffer the returning external web data.

6 The router implements the policy action from the content server: permit or deny the URL data. If the action is to deny the user access, the content-filtering server actually passes back a redirection URL to the user that directs the user to a URL location on

the content-filtering server. The URL contains a message about inappropriate use of the type of content the user was trying to download.

One of the interesting things about this process is that the router allows the initial HTTP request to exit the network instead of first verifying the user's access. This allows the router, in most cases, to receive a response from the content-filtering server before the HTTP reply comes back from the external web server. This produces no noticeable delay in the user's HTTP connection.

CAUTION   I want to stress that URL filtering places a very high burden on your router's processing. Therefore, you should be careful about implementing this on your router. For example, using a low-end router for this process to handle hundreds of internal users might kill your router. In addition, a small delay is added to each connection when verification occurs between the router and the content-filtering server. Choosing the right router platform for URL filtering, as well as the appropriate network design, will make the difference between a solution that provides excellent control over URL access and one that creates connectivity problems for your users.

Advantages and Limitations of URL Filtering

The next two sections cover the advantages and limitations of using a content-filtering server. Obviously, you have much more control over your users' URL access; however, there are downsides to URL filtering.

Advantages of URL Filtering

URL filtering provides many advantages and offers a robust security solution for your network, including the following advantages:

- With a content-filtering server, you more easily can implement your policies based on types of access, such as sports, pornography, gaming, politics, gambling, religion, and other groupings of information. However, you still can define your own access rules and restrictions on a per-host (or per-user) basis.

- Automatic updates can be downloaded to the content servers for new sites that belong to specified categories, as well as the removal of dead links that no longer function. This removes a lot of the management overhead of having to do this process manually.

- You can keep a detailed log on your Websense or N2H2 content server of who is accessing what resources. This is important for accountability when it comes time to identify rule breakers and develop statistics on the type of user web access.

- You can define policies on a per-host or a per-user basis, providing more control over access policies.

- You can define multiple content-filtering servers on your router to provide for redundancy. In this situation, one content-filtering server is defined as the primary, and your router sends all traffic to it. If the primary server is not reachable or is down, your router can use a configured secondary server. If all servers go down, you have the option of either allowing or preventing all HTTP traffic to the router.

- To speed up lookup requests, the router supports an IP cache table that contains a list of IP addresses of web servers that are allowed access by all internal users. You also can define *exclusive domains*: These are domain names that always should be allowed access by your users, such as http://www.cisco.com, http://www.quizware.com, or http://www.boson.com. With the exclusive domain option, you can use wildcard names or enter domain names with partial URL references.

- The Cisco IOS can buffer up to 200 simultaneous HTTP requests, to reduce the likelihood of dropping HTTP connections because of response-time issues between the router and the content-filtering server.

Restrictions of URL Filtering

This section covers the URL filtering restrictions of N2H2 and Websense. You must use only one product: The Cisco IOS does not support both products simultaneously. N2H2 and Websense have the following restrictions:

- You can specify multiple N2H2 or Websense servers for redundancy. However, the Cisco IOS actively uses only one server.

- The setup of URL filtering works with only one content-filtering product: either Websense or N2H2. Cisco does not support the use of both products simultaneously on routers.

- Only TCP is supported for the connection between the router and the N2H2 server (Websense supports both TCP and UDP).

Both N2H2 and Websense support user-based policies based on a user's authentication information, such as a username and password. Normally, this is done with a proxy method to the content-filtering server. However, with the router handling the HTTP access, the Cisco IOS does not retrieve the username from the client. Therefore, by default, the router supports only host (IP address) and global filtering.

Although the Cisco IOS does not support user authentication, Websense and N2H2 do. With both implementations of user authentication, either Microsoft's internal authentication or LDAP is used. Because the router does not support user authentication, these content-filtering products handle this issue in one of two methods:

- When the user initially logs into the Microsoft Windows domain, an installed Websense or N2H2 agent automatically associates users to their IP addresses, which the content-filtering server then can use for filtering requests received from the router.

- The first point has two problems: It requires a user to log out gracefully to keep track of who is using a particular IP address, and it works only with Microsoft Windows. Therefore, a second option is to have the user directly access the N2H2 or Websense server through a web browser connection to authenticate. Alternatively, the first time a user accesses an external web server, the content-filtering server causes the router to redirect the client to the content-filtering server to authenticate first.

URL Filtering Implementation

Setting up URL filtering is a straightforward process. However, you might want to set up or enable configuration options. This section deals with how to set up your router to interact with Websense and N2H2 content-filtering server products. As you will see in this section, CBAC, which performs application layer inspection, is required to perform URL filtering.

NOTE   If you are migrating from one product to another, such as Websense to N2H2 or vice versa, you must remove your configuration component for the old content-filtering server and then add the new one. In other words, the Cisco IOS cannot support both content-filtering products simultaneously.

Content Server Location

One of the first items that you need to deal with in web content filtering on a router is the location of your new content-filtering server: Where should you place this device in your network? One main concern with the router and URL filtering is the response time between the content-filtering server and the router.

As you recall from the "Operation of URL Filtering" section, the router forwards the user's request to the external web server and then sends an access request to the content server. If the external web server's reply comes back to the router before the policy action from the content-filtering server, the router buffers the external server's reply, which introduces delay into the traffic stream and puts an additional burden on the router. The more late responses that your router receives from the content-filtering server, the more of an impact this will have on your throughput.

Therefore, the recommended network design is to put the content server in the same subnet as one of the router's interfaces. However, the more devices that are in the subnet, the more competition there is between these devices when sending traffic through the router on the same interface. Therefore, you need to ensure that there is enough bandwidth between the router and the content-filtering server to handle the communication traffic. In a worst-case situation, you might need a dedicated connection on the router to the filtering server. Figure 10-2 shows an example of connecting the content-filtering server to the same subnet as the router.

URL Filtering Setup

After you have installed the content-filtering software on its server and connected it to the network, you are ready to configure your router to interact with it. The following paragraphs explain the commands that you use to configure your router to use the content-filtering server.

CBAC Inspection

To set up inspection of URLs, you need to configure CBAC for HTTP inspection. This is required to perform URL filtering. Here is the CBAC command:

```
Router(config)# ip inspect name inspection_name http urlfilter
  [java-list ACL_#_or_name]
  [alert {on | off}] [audit-trail {on | off}] [timeout seconds]
```

Note that you must specify the keyword **urlfilter** to enable content filtering for HTTP connections. If you omit this keyword, HTTP inspection is done with Java filtering. The rest of the parameters were discussed in Chapter 9.

TIP   I highly recommended that you specify an ACL to limit the scope of Java or URL filtering. If you do not, your router will have to examine all HTTP connection requests, which is CPU intensive. If you need to inspect all HTTP traffic, make sure that you have purchased the right router model to handle this load.

Server Location

After you enable inspection for HTTP traffic, you must specify the type and location of the content-filtering server. This is required for the router to perform URL filtering. Use this command to specify this information:

```
Router(config)# ip urlfilter server vendor
  {websense | n2h2} IP_address [port port-number] [timeout seconds]
  [retransmit number]
```

The **ip urlfilter server vendor** command specifies how to connect to the content-filtering server. The first parameter that you must specify is what product your content-filtering server is running: **websense** or **n2h2**. Following this is the server's IP address. The remaining four parameters are optional. For an N2H2 server, the default port number is 4005; Websense uses 15,868. If you change the port number during the server installation, you need to reflect that change with the **port** parameter. Following this is the **timeout** value for the server connection. This is the amount of time that the router waits for a response from the content-filtering server; if no response is seen within this time limit, the router uses a second server, if configured. The default timeout is 5 seconds. The router also retransmits requests when a response does not arrive from the server. The default number of retransmissions is 2, but this can be changed with the **retransmit** parameter.

NOTE	You can enter multiple servers, but the first one that you enter becomes the primary server. Therefore, the order of your server entries is important.

URL Cache Size

CBAC uses a URL-filtering cache to store the destination IP addresses of web servers that users are and are not allowed to reach. The more entries the cache can store, the fewer lookups CBAC must perform for the content-filtering server. The default number of entries is 5000, but this can be changed with the following command:

```
Router(config)# ip urlfilter cache #_of_entries
```

The number of entries can range from 0 to 2,147,483,647. Even though you can create very large cache sizes, you must have the appropriate amount of RAM on your router to store this information. You also must configure your content-filtering server to support this option. As this writing, only Websense supports this option.

URL Cache Clearing

The URL cache is cleared in a few ways:

- Every 12 hours, the cache is cleared.
- If the cache reaches 80 percent capacity, the Cisco IOS begins to remove idle entries in the cache at 1-minute intervals until the URL cache capacity falls below 80 percent. A connection is considered idle if it has not been used in the last 10 minutes.
- When doing a cache lookup, CBAC removes all entries that have been idle for more than an hour.
- All entries that have elapsed (based on the content server's configuration) are removed. This is often greater than 15 hours. Therefore, the 12-hour cache clearing typically removes these entries before they have elapsed.

To clear the URL cache table manually, use the following command:

```
Router# clear ip urlfilter cache {IP_address | all}
```

You can clear all entries in the cache with the **all** parameter, or you can clear only entries with the specified destination IP address.

CAUTION	Whenever you make a policy change on the URL content-filtering server, it does not cause the URL cache on the router to be cleared. This can cause policy problems if the content server says to deny certain kinds of traffic, but the router's cache allows it. Therefore, any time that you make policy changes on the content-filtering server, you should log into your router(s) and manually clear the URL cache.

Exclusive Domains

As mentioned in the "Operation of URL Filtering" section, URL filtering places an additional burden on your router, especially if the router constantly must send lookup requests to the content-filtering server. You can reduce the number of lookups in two ways:

- Create a larger cache size.
- Use exclusive domains.

Exclusive domains enable you to define local filtering rules on the router. In this situation, the router first looks at its cache to see if there is a match, then it looks at the locally listed domains, and then it sends a request to the content-filtering server if nothing is found locally on the router. This configuration is very useful for listing sites that always or never should be allowed (and these sites never change). Commonly used sites should be listed. For example, if your network administrators constantly access the Cisco website, include this as a permit action in your exclusive domain configuration.

This is the command to define an exclusive domain:

```
Router(config)# ip urlfilter exclusive-domain
  {permit | deny} domain_name
```

You can specify two actions: **permit** or **deny**. When specifying a domain name, you can be specific by specifying the fully qualified domain name, such as www.quizware.com; a partial domain name, such as .quizware.com; or a fully qualified domain name and a partial URL, such as www.quizware.com/dealgroup. You can list as many domain entries as you want. Example 10-2 shows a simple example of defining two domains that always should be allowed and one that always should be denied.

Example 10-2 *Setting Up Exclusive Domains for URL Filtering*

```
Router(config)# ip urlfilter exclusive-domain permit .cisco.com
Router(config)# ip urlfilter exclusive-domain permit .quizware.com
Router(config)# ip urlfilter exclusive-domain deny .sex.com
```

TIP   If you are experiencing performance problems on your router with URL filtering, look closely at the statistics on your content-filtering server to see which sites constantly are denied or permitted. For these sites, define exclusive domain configurations on the router, thereby reducing the number of lookups to the content-filtering server that the router must perform. I did this once for a customer whose router performance slowed to a crawl when implementing URL filtering. After using this feature, the company hardly noticed the difference in throughput when using the content-filtering server for additional lookups.

Lost Server Connection

Sometimes the Cisco IOS will not be capable of contacting your content-filtering server to authorize users' HTTP connections. For example, you might have to reboot your server because of system patches that you have applied to it. In this situation, the Cisco IOS can take one of two actions concerning HTTP traffic during this blackout period:

- Drop all traffic until the connection between the router and the URL content filter server is restored.

- Permit all traffic until the connection between the router and the URL content filter server is restored.

The default is to drop all traffic. This can be changed with the following command:

```
Router(config)# ip urlfilter allowmode [on | off]
```

on specifies that connection requests should be permitted when the router cannot reach the content-filtering server. **off** specifies that the connections should be dropped.

Whenever your router loses contact with the content-filtering server, an alert message is displayed, along with the status of the allow mode that the router will use. In this example, the router drops traffic until the connection between the router and server is re-established:

```
%URLF-3-ALLOW_MODE: Connection to all URL filter servers are down
  and ALLOW MODE if OFF
```

Maximum Requests

The Cisco IOS temporarily holds up to 1000 pending URL requests. These are requests that the Cisco IOS has sent to the content server and is waiting for a response for. When this limit is reached, new user connection requests are dropped, causing the user's web browser to perform a retransmission. To change the number of pending requests that the Cisco IOS will store, use this command:

```
Router(config)# ip urlfilter max-request #_of_requests
```

The number of requests that you can specify ranges from 1 to 2,147,483,647.

NOTE   The larger you make this number, the more memory your router needs to store pending requests. Therefore, you should tune this by increasing the maximum number of pending requests in small increments so that it does not have a detrimental effect on the router's memory and processing.

Maximum Responses

As mentioned in the "Operation of URL Filtering" section, a router might receive the returning HTTP traffic from the external server before it receives the policy reply from the content-filtering server. In this situation, the router can buffer the HTTP response while waiting for the reply from the filtering server. However, by default, the router buffers only 200 connection responses. This can be changed with this command:

```
Router(config)# ip urlfilter max-resp-pak #_of_responses
```

The number of responses the Cisco IOS can buffer ranges from 0 to 20,000.

NOTE	If you specify 0 as the number of responses that the Cisco IOS stores, the Cisco IOS drops all HTTP server responses received before the authorization reply from the content-filtering server. Be careful about making this value too large because it uses additional memory and requires additional processing on the router to handle the extra buffered packets. Therefore, as in the last section, I recommend that you increase this number in small increments to avoid a detrimental effect on your router.

Alerts

URL-filtering alerts are enabled by default. These alerts display messages when the content-filtering server is not reachable, when all servers are not reachable, or when a URL lookup exceeded the timeout value. Alerts can be disabled or re-enabled with the following command:

```
Router(config)# [no] ip urlfilter alert
```

Example 10-3 shows some common alert messages that the Cisco IOS might display.

Example 10-3 *Examining Cisco IOS Alerts for URL Filtering*

```
%URLF-3-SERVER_DOWN:Connection to the URL filter server      (1)
  192.1.2.2 is down
%URLF-3-ALLOW_MODE:Connection to all URL filter servers      (2)
  are down and ALLOW MODE is OFF
%URLF-5-SERVER_UP:Connection to an URL filter server         (3)
  192.1.2.2 is made, the system is returning
  from ALLOW MODE
%URLF-4-URL_TOO_LONG:URL too long (more than 3072 bytes),    (4)
  possibly a fake packet?
%URLF-4-MAX_REQ:The number of pending request exceeds the    (5)
  maximum limit <1000>
```

The following is an explanation of these messages, with reference to the numbering on the right side of Example 10-3:

1 In this message, the router has lost contact with the content-filtering server (192.1.2.2). If you have configured a secondary server, the router establishes contact with it.

2 If the primary (or secondary) servers fails and no other content-filtering server is available, you will see this message. The router goes into an allow mode, in which all HTTP connections either are allowed or are denied.

3 If CBAC inspection for HTTP has entered the allow mode and then successfully restores connectivity to a content-filtering server, you will see this message.

4 If a URL exceeds 3072 bytes, CBAC generates an alarm indicating that the URL request is being dropped. In most instances, this is a hacker attack trying to gain unauthorized access to your web server by exploiting a bug in the web-application software.

5 If the number of pending URL requests sent to the content-filtering server exceeds the maximum-defined threshold, you will see this message. In this instance, the router drops the user's HTTP connection request.

Many other alert messages exist, but these are the most common ones.

Audits

As with CBAC audits, audits for URL filtering are disabled by default. Enabling audits allows you to log information such as who is making an HTTP connection request and what web server is trying to be accessed. To enable auditing, use the following command:

```
Router(config)# [no] ip urlfilter audit-trail
```

Example 10-4 shows some common auditing messages that you will see with auditing enabled.

Example 10-4 *Examining IDS Audits for URL Filtering*

```
%URLF-6-URL_ALLOWED:Access allowed for URL                      (1)
   http://www.quizware.com; client 192.1.1.12:32828
   server 200.1.1.1:80
%URLF-6-SITE_ALLOWED:Client 192.1.1.12:32834 accessed           (2)
   server 200.1.1.1:80
%URLF-6-URL_BLOCKED:Access denied URL http://www.sex.com;       (3)
   client 192.1.1.12:32983 server 209.81.7.93:80
%URLF-4-SITE-BLOCKED: Access denied for the site                (4)
   `www.gambling.com'; client 12.54.192.6:34557
   server 207.139.179.17:80
```

The following is an explanation of these messages, with reference to the numbering on the right side of Example 10-4:

1 In this message, a client (192.1.1.12) was allowed access to a web server (200.5.5.5). If the destination is not found in the router's local cache, the URL of the user's access is displayed. Only the first 300 bytes of the URL reference are displayed in the message.

2 In this message, a client (192.1.1.12) was allowed access to a web server (200.5.5.1). Unlike the previous message, in this example, the destination was listed in the router's local URL cache, so it did not display the user's URL reference. This reduced overhead on the router.

3 In this message, a client (192.1.1.12) was blocked from accessing a restricted site (www.sex.com). Notice that the URL reference was listed, indicating that this was the first time for accessing this destination.

4 The fourth message is similar to the third one. The main difference is that the message in the third statement was the result of the router getting back a block action from the content-filtering server, whereas the fourth message is the result of the configuration of an exclusive domain on the router. Exclusive domains enable you to specify local policies on the router that define which site(s) are allowed, reducing the overhead of having to contact the content-filtering server.

TIP   Your content-filtering server also has logging capabilities. However, remember that a router caches information about allowing or denying a user's HTTP request, and it uses this information to filter subsequent requests. For this type of filtering, the content-filtering server will not be capable of capturing any logging information of additional connection requests that the router permits or drops, based on the lookups that the router does against its local cache. Therefore, if you want to see every URL-filtering action, you should enable auditing on your router and should forward this information to an external syslog server or the content-filtering server. Be forewarned that this will add an additional burden on your router. More important, you need a lot of disk space if your users generate a lot of HTTP connection requests. Also make sure that your router has the necessary processing power to handle this audit function.

Logging

By default, any log messages generated by CBAC URL filtering are displayed on the console or sent to the router's local buffer or a syslog server, if you have configured these last two options. Another option is to forward these messages to your content-filtering server. This feature enables you to keep all your URL filtering log messages in one location for easy access and monitoring. As I mentioned in the last tip, a content-filtering server does not see log messages for matches that the router finds in its local cache. With this option, you can forward your log messages to the content-filtering server when the router finds a response in the cache. This provides a record of all transactions for users' HTTP connections. This option is disabled by default but can be enabled with the following command:

```
Router(config)# ip urlfilter urlf-server-log
```

CBAC Activation

After you have set up your inspection rules for CBAC, specified the location and type of the URL content-filtering server, and tuned URL filtering, you are ready to activate your CBAC inspection process on your router's interface. This is done with the following configuration:

```
Router(config)# interface type [slot_#]port_#
Router(config-if)#  ip inspect inspection_name {in | out}
```

This configuration was discussed in Chapter 9. When you have activated the inspection group on your router's interface, CBAC begins inspecting URL requests.

URL Filtering Verification

When you have set up and activated URL inspection of HTTP traffic, you can monitor it with various **show** and **debug** commands. The following two sections cover the use of these monitoring and troubleshooting commands.

show Commands

You can use three basic **show** commands to monitor and troubleshoot URL inspection:

- **show ip urlfilter cache**—Displays the destination IP addresses in the router's URL cache

- **show ip urlfilter config**—Displays the URL filter configuration on the router, including the size of the cache, the maximum number of pending requests allowed, the maximum number of buffered packets while waiting for a content server's response, the type of server and its address(es), and other configuration information

- **show ip urlfilter statistics**—Displays URL inspection statistics, including the number of requests sent to and received from the content-filtering server, the number of pending and failed requests, and the number of blocked connections

Take a look at some sample output of these commands. Example 10-5 shows sample output from the **show ip urlfilter cache** command.

Example 10-5 *Using the* **show ip urlfilter cache** *Command*

```
Router# show ip urlfilter cache
Maximum number of entries allowed: 5000
Number of entries cached: 4
IP addresses cached ....
 200.1.1.1
 200.1.1.2
 200.2.2.1
 200.3.3.3
```

The default number of entries allowed in the cache is 5000, which can be seen in Example 10-5. The number of entries in the cache is 4, which is followed by the actual IP addresses of the web servers that your users are trying to access.

Example 10-6 shows sample output from the **show ip urlfilter config** command.

Example 10-6 *Using the* **show ip urlfilter config** *Command*

```
Router# show ip urlfilter config
URL filter is ENABLED
Primary Websense server configurations
============================
Websense server IP address: 192.1.2.1
Websense server port: 15868
Websense retransmit time out: 5 (seconds)
Websense number of retransmit:2
Secondary Websense server configurations:
=============================
None.
Other configurations
===============
Allow mode: OFF
System Alert: ON
```

Example 10-6 *Using the* **show ip urlfilter config** *Command (Continued)*

```
Log message on the router: OFF
Log message on URL filter server:ON
Maximum number of cache entries :5000
Cache timeout :12 (hours)
Maximum number of packet buffers:200
Maximum outstanding requests:1000
```

Here you can see the URL filtering configuration on the router. This router is using a Websense server (192.1.2.1) to perform URL filtering. You also can see that this configuration is using the default values, such as 1000 outstanding requests and 200 buffered HTTP responses.

Example 10-7 shows sample output from the **show ip urlfilter statistics** command.

Example 10-7 *Using the* **show ip urlfilter statistics** *Command*

```
Router# show ip urlfilter statistics
URL filtering statistics
================
Current requests count:30
Current packet buffer count(in use): 12
Current cache entry count: 800
Maxever request count: 1000
Maxever packet buffer count:200
Maxever cache entry count:5000
Total requests sent to URL Filter Server: 38565
Total responses received from URL Filter Server: 38350
Total requests allowed: 38120
Total requests blocked: 238
```

This display has a lot of useful information. The Current Requests Count displays the number of requests (30) that the router has sent to the server and is waiting for a response for. The Current Packet Buffer Count displays the number of HTTP server replies (12) that the router has buffered while waiting for a response from the content-filtering server. The Current Cache Entry Count displays the current number of destination IP addresses (800) that the Cisco IOS has cached in the URL cache table. The Maxever lines display peak values that the system has seen since last powerup. These values typically are used to assist in choosing an appropriate value for the **ip urlfilter cache**, **ip urlfilter packets**, and **ip urlfilter maxrequest** configuration commands.

For instance, the maximum number of simultaneous HTTP authorization requests that the router will handle is 1000. Below these three lines are some totals: the total number of requests that the router has forwarded to the content server for authorization (38,565), the number of responses that the router has received from the content-filtering server (38,350), the number of times the content-filtering server allowed HTTP connections (38,120), and the number of times it denied them (238).

TIP   The **show ip urlfilter statistics** command is a very useful troubleshooting command. Use this command to verify the configuration of your URL filtering. For example, if your packet buffer count is constantly around 180, increase the default buffer size to around 250 with the **ip urlfilter max-resp-pak** command. Likewise, if there is a huge difference between the number of requests that the router sent to the content-filtering server and the number received, track down the problem: Examine the router to make sure that it is not overloaded, examine the content-filtering server to make sure that it is not overloaded, and check the network connection between the router and server to make sure that there is no bandwidth issue (if it is a direct connection between the two devices, make sure that the connection is configured correctly, with the correct speed and full-duplex operation).

debug Commands

You can use three **debug** commands for more detailed troubleshooting of URL-filtering functions:

- **debug ip urlfilter events**—Displays URL-filtering events, such as when a timer event is reached, connection events, and queuing events

- **debug ip urlfilter detailed**—Displays detailed information about the events that the **debug ip urlfilter events** command displays

- **debug ip urlfilter function-trace**—Displays the functions called by the Cisco IOS when performing URL filtering

URL Filtering Example

Now that you have a basic understanding of URL content filtering, take a look at an example of setting this up on your router. Figure 10-3 illustrates this example.

Figure 10-3 *URL Filtering Example*

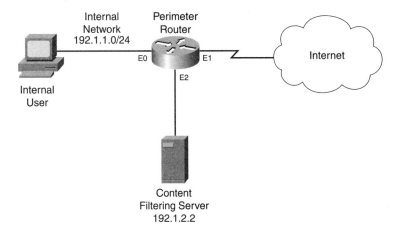

Example 10-8 shows a URL filtering configuration for this network.

Example 10-8 *Simple Configuration of URL Filtering on a Router*

```
Router(config)# ip inspect name RULES http urlfilter          (1)
Router(config)# ip inspect name RULES ftp
Router(config)# ip inspect name RULES smtp
Router(config)# ip inspect name RULES tcp
Router(config)# ip inspect name RULES udp
Router(config)# ip urlfilter server vendor websense 192.1.2.2  (2)
Router(config)# ip urlfilter cache 7000                        (3)
Router(config)# ip urlfilter max-request 1500                  (4)
Router(config)# ip urlfilter max-resp-pack 300                 (5)
Router(config)# ip urlfilter exclusive-domain permit .cisco.com  (6)
Router(config)# ip urlfilter exclusive-domain permit www.quizware.com
Router(config)# ip urlfilter exclusive-domain deny .msn.com
Router(config)# ip urlfilter exclusive-domain deny .aol.com
Router(config)# ip urlfilter audit-trail                       (7)
Router(config)# ip urlfilter alert
Router(config)# ip urlfilter urlf-server-log
Router(config)# ip access-list extended external_ACL
Router(config-ext-nacl)# ! <--enter ACL policies here-->
Router(config-ext-nacl)# deny ip any any
Router(config-ext-nacl)# exit
Router(config)# interface Ethernet1
Router(config-if)# ip inspect RULES out                        (8)
Router(config-if)# ip access-group external_ACL in
```

The following is an explanation of the configuration in Example 10-8, with reference to the numbering on the right side:

1 The first inspection rule in the RULES group specifies inspection for HTTP URL connections.

2 This statement specifies that the content-filtering server is running Websense. Notice that this server is connected directly to the router, providing low latency for requests and replies.

3 This statement increases the default URL cache size from 5000 to 7000. Remember that you should be careful about increasing this value: make sure that you evaluate your router's RAM and processing before increasing URL-filtering performance variables.

4 This statement increases the maximum number of requests from 1000 to 1500; this controls the number of pending requests that the Cisco IOS holds while waiting for responses from the Websense server.

5 This statement increases the maximum number of responses from web servers from 200 to 300 packets.

6 The next four statements set up exclusive domain filtering: All access to all of the Cisco website and www.quizware.com is permitted, and any access to Microsoft's MSN and AOL domain names is denied.

7 The next three commands enable auditing and alerts, and forwarding of URL log messages to the Websense server.

8 The inspection rule (RULES) is enabled on the external interface.

I have added some optional parameters to tune this configuration to work better for this specific network. The only required configurations are Steps 1, 2, and 8.

Network-Based Application Recognition

Network-Based Application Recognition (NBAR) was introduced in Cisco IOS 12.0(5)XE2. NBAR normally is used to implement QoS functions on a router. It ensures that critical applications receive the necessary bandwidth to function correctly. QoS parameters that NBAR can use when setting up QoS for a connection include bandwidth, delay, jitter, and packet loss. This is accomplished by identifying applications or connections and associating them with a class. The Cisco IOS then can use these classes to implement QoS.

Components of QoS

QoS includes the following six components:

- Classification
- Marking
- Congestion management
- Congestion avoidance
- Link-efficiency mechanisms
- Policy and shaping

Classification is used to separate different kinds of traffic into distinct groups. When dealing with QoS, like kinds of traffic typically are grouped together. For example, all voice connections would be placed in a voice classification group, all video applications would be placed in a video classification group, and so on. The traffic is marked based on the classification. For example, if the traffic was Layer 3 traffic, the (Type of Service [ToS]) field in the IP packet header is used to contain the packet's classification or grouping. This is done through the IP Precedence or DSCP method of marking.

When they are marked, this router and other devices beyond this router can use the marking to manage congestion (typically through the use of queuing), avoiding congestion (by dropping low-priority traffic), compressing traffic, and shaping traffic (by enqueuing traffic and sending it out at a constant pace). Obviously, there is a lot more going on with QoS than the brief description I have given.

NBAR and Classification

Classification is the first step in implementing QoS. NBAR can be used to implement classification. NBAR is a Cisco IOS classification engine that inspects packets and classifies them based on their application type. This can be something as simple as examining the TCP or UDP port numbers in the transport header of a segment, or it can as complex as examining information in HTML headers or web content. Basically, NBAR can inspect traffic from Layers 3 through 7. This inspection can look for the following types of information:

- TCP and UDP port numbers in the transport-layer segment header
- Dynamic TCP and UDP port numbers assigned for additional connections for an application, such as FTP (similar to the inspection process that CBAC uses when examining applications that open additional connections)
- Subport information, which is information contained in the application layer data, such as application commands or data types
- Layer 3 IP protocols (other than TCP and UDP)

Classification of traffic with NBAR can be done dynamically or manually. NBAR supports the Protocol Discovery feature, which allows NBAR to discover automatically application protocols that enter or leave an interface. This feature also maintains per-protocol statistics, such as the number of input and output packets and bytes, bit rates, and other statistical information. With manual classification, you define the traffic types that NBAR should examine.

After NBAR has identified an application, the appropriate classification can take place, marking the packet header with the corresponding IP Precedence or DSCP value.

Classification Process

Before I discuss how NBAR can be used for traffic filtering instead of QoS, I need to discuss how NBAR is used to classify traffic. As I already have mentioned, NBAR enables you to classify traffic from information found in Layers 3 through 7 of the OSI reference model. The first step in setting up NBAR is to create classes for traffic that you want NBAR to inspect. You can have NBAR examine many things, such as the application type, specific addresses for connections, data in a connection, and the length of a packet. Based on your matching criteria, NBAR places matching traffic into your specified class (or grouping).

When you have created your classification rules, you create a policy that marks the traffic. For IP traffic, you use IP Precedence to group (classify) the traffic. The IP Precedence standard (and DSCP) uses the bits in the ToS field in an IP packet to classify the traffic. Both of these functions are performed on the ingress interface (as traffic enters your router).

Then you define what action(s) will occur for marked traffic when it leaves a specific egress interface(s) on your router. Normally, with QoS, this affects how the packet is queued up before it is transmitted out the interface. However, you can define other policies for this traffic, such as limiting its bandwidth or even dropping the traffic, based on the classification, of course.

Figure 10-4 illustrates this process.

Figure 10-4 *NBAR Classification Example*

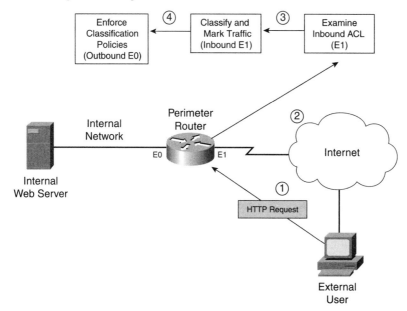

The following steps occur, with reference to the numbering in Figure 10-4:

1 In this example, an external user generates an HTTP query to a web server located on the internal network.

2 The router receives this traffic on its external interface. If an inbound ACL is applied on the external interface, the router processes the ACL.

3 Assuming that the ACL permits the packet, the router uses NBAR to classify and mark the packet. This classification is done in the ingress direction of the external interface. In this case, you need an NBAR classification for HTTP traffic. For QoS purposes, you could classify all HTTP traffic into one grouping; however, if this was for security purposes, you might be looking for specific commands, filenames, or other data in the HTML query request to mark it, such as with a worm, a virus, or a Trojan horse attack. When used for security purposes, you would configure NBAR to drop unwanted or dangerous traffic. If the traffic does not match any of the classification rules, it is not marked (it is not dangerous).

4 After NBAR processes the traffic, it is routed to the egress interface. In this example, this is E0. The router then processes any QoS actions on the packet. I use the term *QoS* loosely here because the Cisco IOS can take many actions when dealing with the packet, such as queuing it up with an appropriate queuing mechanism, shaping it, policing it, and even dropping it. For security purposes, you want to drop the marked

traffic and, possibly log the transaction. If the traffic is not marked, it is treated normally. Finally, if there is an egress ACL on the router's interface, this affects what traffic can exit it.

A few important things must be pointed out about NBAR and classification:

- When the Cisco IOS marks the packets' ToS field with the IP Precedence or DSCP value, this remains in the packet as long as the packet is being routed to the destination (unless another router modifies the ToS value).

- For NBAR to process traffic, the traffic must be seen by two interfaces on your router: The ingress interface classifies and marks the traffic, and the egress interface enforces policies concerning the markings.

- You can apply NBAR classification, marking, and policing in more than one direction of the router. For example, in Figure 10-4, you could set up two different policies: one for traffic entering the network (from E1 to E0) and one for traffic leaving the network (E0 to E1), giving you a lot of flexibility in enforcing security policies.

NBAR and Traffic Filtering

As I mentioned at the beginning of this section, NBAR normally is used to implement QoS policies; however, it easily can be adapted to enforce security policies. You can enforce three basic actions with NBAR when using it for security functions:

- **Filter traffic**—With a filtering policy, NBAR uses an ACL to drop traffic on the egress interface. This requires an extended IP ACL to look for the ToS value marked in the IP header of the packet.

- **Reroute traffic**—With a routing policy, NBAR uses route maps to match on marked traffic to determine how it should be routed. In the case of a security function, you typically route the packet to a null interface on the router, causing the router to drop the packet (I discuss this further in Chapter 15, "Routing Protocol Protection").

- **Log actions**—You can have the router log the filtering action when it drops marked traffic

In this chapter, I focus on the first and third actions. Chapter 15 covers the second option.

Supported Protocols and Applications

NBAR supports the inspection and classification of many different protocols and applications. However, only TCP/IP protocols and applications are supported; protocols such as IPX, AppleTalk, and others are not supported. Table 10-1 lists the TCP/IP protocols that NBAR can classify. Table 10-2 lists the supported applications with static TCP and UDP port numbers. Table 10-3 lists the supported applications with dynamically assigned port numbers. These are applications that use a well-known port number for the control or management connection, but open other connections to deliver information, as FTP does with its data-transfer connection.

Table 10-1 *Supported TCP/IP Protocols*

Protocol Parameter	Protocol Number	Description
icmp	1	Internet Control Message Protocol.
ipinip	4	IP in IP.
egp	8	Exterior Gateway Protocol.
ipsec	50 and 51	IP Security's Encapsulation Security Payload (ESP) and Authentication Header (AH). These two protocols are marked independently.

Table 10-2 *Supported Static Port Numbers*

Application Parameter	Protocol	Port Number	Description
ssh	TCP	22	Secure Shell
pcanywhere	UDP	22	Symantec PCAnywhere
telnet	TCP	23	Telnet
smtp	TCP	25	Simple Mail Transfer Protocol
dns	TCP/UDP	53	Domain Name System
dhcp	UDP	67 and 68	Dynamic Host Configuration Protocol and Bootstrap Protocol
gopher	TCP/UDP	70	Internet Gopher Protocol
finger	TCP	79	Finger User Information Protocol
http	TCP	80	Hypertext Transfer Protocol
kerberos	TCP/UDP	88 and 749	Kerberos Network Authentication Service
pop3	TCP/UDP	110	Post Office Protocol v3
nntp	TCP/UDP	119	Network News Transfer Protocol
ntp	TCP/UDP	123	Network Time Protocol
netbios	TCP/UDP	137 and 139	Microsoft NetBIOS over IP for Windows
netbios	UDP	137 and 138	Microsoft NetBIOS over IP for Windows
imap	TCP/UDP	143 and 220	Internet Message Access Protocol

Table 10-2   *Supported Static Port Numbers (Continued)*

Application Parameter	Protocol	Port Number	Description
snmp	TCP/UDP	161 and 162	Simple Network Management Protocol
bgp	TCP/UDP	179	Border Gateway Protocol
irc	TCP/UDP	194	Internet Relay Chat
ldap	TCP/UDP	389	Lightweight Directory Access Protocol
secure-http	TCP	443	Secure HTTP
syslog	UDP	514	System Logging Utility
printer	TCP/UDP	515	Remote Printer
rip	UDP	520	Routing Information Protocol
secure-nntp	TCP/UDP	563	Secure NNTP
secure-map	TCP/UDP	585 and 993	Secure IMAP
secure-ldap	TCP/UDP	636	Secure LDAP
secure-ftp	TCP	990	Secure FTP
secure-telnet	TCP	992	Secure Telnet
secure-irc	TCP/UDP	994	Secure IRC
secure-pop3	TCP/UDP	995	Secure POP3
socks	TCP	1080	Firewall Security Protocol
notes	TCP/UDP	1352	Lotus Notes
sqlserver	TCP	1433	Microsoft SQL Server
rsvp	UDP	1698 and 1699	Resource Reservation Protocol
l2tp	UDP	1701	L2F and L2TP tunneling protocols for VPNs
pptp	TCP	1723	Microsoft Point-to-Point Tunneling Protocol for VPNs
nfs	TCP/UDP	2049	Network File System
novadigm	TCP/UDP	3460 to 3465	Novadigm Enterprise Desktop Manager (EDM)
pcanywhere	TCP	5631 and 65301	Symantec PCAnywhere
xwindows	TCP	6000 to 6003	X11 X-Windows
cuseeme	TCP/UDP	7648 and 7649	CU-SeeMe Videoconferencing
cuseeme	UDP	24,032	CU-SeeMe Videoconferencing

Table 10-3 *Supported Stateful Applications*

Application Parameter	Protocol	Description
citrix **citrix app**	TCP/UDP	Citrix ICA traffic
ftp	TCP	File Transfer Protocol
exchange	TCP	Microsoft RPC for Exchange
fasttrack	TCP/UDP	P2P file-sharing programs, including Kazaa, Grokster, and Morpheus
gnutella	TCP	P2P file-sharing programs, including BearShare, Gnewtellium, Gnucleus, Gtk-Gnutella, JTella, LimeWire, Morpheus, Mutella, Phex, Qtella, Swapper, XoloX, and XCache
http	TCP	HTTP with inspection of URLs, MIME application types, and host information
napster	TCP	Napster P2P file-sharing programs
kazaa2	TCP	Kazaa P2P file-sharing programs
netshow	TCP/UDP	Microsoft Netshow multimedia program
rcmd	TCP	UNIX R commands: rsh, rlogin, and rexec
realaudio	TCP/UDP	Real Network RealAudio Streaming Protocol (RTSP)
rtp	TCP/UDP	Real-time Transport Protocol
sqlnet	TCP/UDP	Oracle SQL*Net Protocol
streamwork	UDP	Xing Technology Stream Works audio and video application
sunrpc	TCP/UDP	Sun Remote Procedure Calls
tftp	UDP	Trivial File Transfer Protocol
vdolive	TCP/UDP	VDOLive streaming video protocol

The protocols and applications listed in Tables 10-1, 10-2, and 10-3 steadily have been added to NBAR since its inception. Therefore, to have NBAR classify a specific kind of traffic, you might have to either upgrade your Cisco IOS image or load a Packet Description Language Module (PDLM). A PDLM is a specialized module that you can have your Cisco IOS load from Flash to use with NBAR. One nice feature of PDLMs is that they do not require you to upgrade your Cisco IOS or reboot your router. Instead, the Cisco IOS calls them, when needed, from Flash memory. To download PDLMs, visit http://www.cisco.com/pcgi-bin/tablebuild.pl/pdlm; you need a CCO account to do this. Note that PDLMs are a temporary solution to upgrading your Cisco IOS. The newest Cisco IOS images have the necessary inspection function for NBAR built into them and, therefore, do not need PDLMs.

NBAR Restrictions and Limitations

NBAR requires the use of Cisco Express Forwarding. Therefore, only routers that support CEF can support NBAR. Even here, Cisco has not ported NBAR to all of its router platforms. As of this writing, here is a list of routers that support NBAR: 1700, 2600, 3600, 3700, 7100 and 7100 UBR, 7200 and 7200 UBR, 7500 with VIP, and the Catalyst 6500 with the FlexWAN module.

NBAR also has other restrictions, including the following:

- The router cannot examine traffic if the router is either the source or the destination of the traffic.

- The router cannot examine information in subsequent fragments of a packet; it can examine only the first fragment of a packet.

- It can examine only the first 400 bytes of a packet payload.

- It does not support examination of pipelined persistent HTTP requests.

- It cannot examine encrypted traffic, such as HTTPS or IPSec (with IPSec, if the tunnel is terminated on the router but the router is not the endpoint of the traffic, the router can examine the unencrypted traffic using NBAR).

- It can examine only TCP/IP traffic processed by CEF, which excludes IP multicast traffic.

- It cannot examine more than 24 concurrent URLs, hosts, or MIME type matches.

- It is not supported on logical interfaces, such as tunnels or Fast EtherChannels (dialer interfaces are supported in Cisco IOS 12.2[4]T).

- With the 7500 series of routers, the router's processor requires a minimum of 64 MB of RAM.

NOTE   NBAR requires approximately 150 bytes of RAM for each connection that it inspects. To simplify the process for the Cisco IOS, when NBAR is enabled, the Cisco IOS automatically allocates 1 MB of RAM, which supports up to 5000 connections, to NBAR. The Cisco IOS periodically checks the memory usage. If more memory is required, the Cisco IOS dynamically assigns from 200 to 400 kB of RAM for additional connections. If you decide to use NBAR, you first should determine the number of connections that your router will need to support for examination and then make sure that your router has enough memory to hold the connection information.

Basic NBAR Configuration

NBAR is fairly simple to set up. The basic configuration requires you to enable CEF, monitor applications, and classify traffic. You need to perform the following steps:

Step 1   Enable CEF (required).

Step 2 Specify nonstandard ports (optional).

Step 3 Classify traffic (required).

Step 4 Download and install PDLMs (optional).

Step 5 Define a traffic policy (required).

Step 6 Activate the traffic policy on an interface (required).

Step 7 Filter the marked traffic on the opposite interface (required).

The following sections cover the basics of setting up NBAR for traffic filtering.

Step 1: Enable CEF

Before you can use NBAR, your router needs to have CEF enabled. On some routers and switches, this is the default; however, on other devices, you must enable it manually. You use one of two commands to enable (or disable) CEF. For routers that do not support distributed CEF, such as the 1700 or 2600 series, use the following command:

```
Router(config)# ip cef
```

For routers that support distributed CEF (dCEF), such as the 7500 series with VIP modules, use the following command:

```
Router(config)# ip cef distributed
```

You also can disable CEF on an interface-by-interface basis by using this configuration:

```
Router(config)# interface type [slot_#/]port_#
Router(config)# no ip route-cache cef
```

TIP Use the **show ip cef** command to verify that CEF has been enabled on your router.

NOTE The operation and additional configuration of CEF is beyond the scope of this book. For more information about CEF, visit http://www.cisco.com/en/US/products/sw/iosswrel/ps1835/products_configuration_guide_chapter09186a00800ca7cc.html.

Step 2: Specify Nonstandard Ports

Tables 10-2 and 10-3 list the applications that NBAR examines, by default. However, NBAR assumes that these applications run on a specific port number, such as HTTP on port 80. NBAR does not, by default, examine nonstandard ports for applications. Just as with CBAC inspection and PAM, you can tell NBAR to examine applications that are on nonstandard ports. Use the following command to specify an additional port(s) for an application:

```
Router(config)# ip nbar port-map application_name [tcp | udp] port_#
```

Application names can be found in Tables 10-2 and 10-3. If you do not specify a transport layer protocol, it defaults to the ones listed in Tables 10-2 and 10-3. With one command, you can list up to 16 additional port numbers; just list the port numbers on the same command line, but put a space between each port number. Here is a simple example of configuring NBAR to examine for HTTP:

```
Router(config)# ip nbar port-map http tcp 80 8080 8090
```

In this example, I am having NBAR examine these three TCP port numbers for HTTP application information.

NOTE   The **ip nbar port-map** command specifies exactly what port numbers should be examined. Therefore, as with the previous example, if you want to add ports, include the previously examined ports as well as the additional ports that you want NBAR to examine. This command is optional: If all your applications run on the standard port numbers, the configuration of this command is not necessary.

In Cisco IOS 12.3(4)T, Cisco added the User-Defined Custom Application Classification feature to NBAR, which enables you to inspect the payload of packets for string patterns starting at a specified offset. This then can be associated with the **ip nbar port-map** command or the **match protocol** command (discussed in the next section). Here is the syntax for the configuration of this feature:

```
Router(config)# ip nbar port-map custom name payload_byte_offset
  [{ascii string_value | decimal number | hex hexadecimal_value}]
  {source | destination} {tcp | udp} [range] port_#_or_#s
```

You first must give the custom NBAR inspection configuration a unique name. Following this is the offset in the packet payload for the Cisco IOS to begin its inspection. After this you need to specify the type of value to look for: **ascii** indicates a specified string, such as cisco; **decimal** indicates a decimal number; and **hex** indicates a hexadecimal value, such as 0x60. Following the type of value, you need to specify the port information. The **source** and **destination** parameters specify whether the port examined is the source or destination port; this is followed by the protocol (**tcp** or **udp**) and the actual port or range of ports. Here is a simple example to illustrate the NBAR custom protocol configuration:

```
Router(config)# ip nbar port-map custom NewEmailAttack 40
  ascii addressbook destination tcp 25
```

In this example, I have created a custom NBAR inspection rule. This is useful if you are a target to a new type of attack and no patch is out yet to defeat it. In this example, a new e-mail attack has been discovered. In this attack, in the 40th byte of the packet payload is the string addressbook. By using this tool, you easily can look for specific values in the packet payload and then use NBAR to filter these packets.

To view your newly assigned port mappings, use the **show ip nbar port-map** command, as displayed in Example 10-9.

Example 10-9 *Using the* **show ip nbar port-map** *Command*

```
Router# show ip nbar port-map
<--output omitted-->
port-map gnutella           tcp 6346 6347 6348 6349 6355 5634
port-map gopher             udp 70
port-map gopher             tcp 70
port-map http               tcp 80 8080 8090
port-map imap               udp 143 220
port-map imap               tcp 143 220
port-map irc                udp 194
port-map irc                tcp 194
<--output omitted-->
```

Step 3: Classify Traffic

The next step required to set up NBAR is to define a group classification. This classification tells NBAR which protocols and applications should be inspected. The **class-map** command is used to group your NBAR classifications:

```
Router(config)# class-map [match-all | match-any] class_map_name
Router(config-cmap)#
```

The **class-map** command takes you into a subconfiguration mode in which you specify the traffic that should be associated with this classification. When creating the classification, you optionally can specify the **match-all** or **match-any** parameters. The **match-all** parameter specifies that the traffic entering the router must match all of the classifications in the class map for the Cisco IOS to consider it a match. The **match-any** parameter specifies that the traffic has to match only one of the conditions within the class map. If you omit this parameter, it defaults to **match-all**. Following this parameter is the name of the class map. This name can be up to 40 alphanumeric characters in length.

As you can see from the **class-map** syntax, you are taken into a subconfiguration mode in which you specify your conditions for matching of traffic (Router(config-cmap)), specifying what traffic should be associated with this class map. Within the class map, you use the **match** command to specify what traffic should be included for NBAR examination. One of the nice features of the **match** command is that it enables you to match on all different kinds of things in a packet. Here is a list of some of the more common parameters used:

- **access-group**—Specifies an ACL, where matches on permit entries in the ACL are included.

- **class-map**—Specifies another class map to embed within this class map.

- **packet**—Specifies a specific packet length that should be included in the examination. (I discuss how you can use this to detect certain kinds of DoS attacks in Chapter 17, "DoS Protection.")

- **protocol**—Specifies the protocol that NBAR should examine. With some protocols, you can include data information, such as text that the user sends in the application request. This is the most common parameter used with NBAR for security functions.

In this chapter, I focus only on the **match protocol** class map command. The syntax of this command is as follows:

```
Router(config-cmap)# match protocol protocol_name [protocol_options]
```

With this command, you must specify the name of the protocol or application that will be included with NBAR examination; these names can be found in Tables 10-1, 10-2, and 10-3. For certain protocols, you also can include parameter options. If you created a custom NBAR inspection rule, specify the custom name for the *protocol_name*. In this chapter, I focus on just two uses of the **match protocol** command: using NBAR to filter P2P programs and HTML information.

P2P Programs

As I mentioned in Chapter 7, "Basic Access Lists," filtering P2P programs can be very difficult with the use of ACLs, especially because ACLs look at static configuration rules. One advantage of NBAR is that it performs a similar process to CBAC: It can examine the information that is transmitted across a connection, including information that would be used to set up additional connections. NBAR supports this facility for many P2P programs. You can specify a handful of **match** commands to look for P2P programs: **match protocol fasttrack**, **match protocol gnutella**, **match protocol napster**, and **match protocol kazaa2**.

Take a look at the **fasttrack** option first:

```
Router(config-cmap)# match protocol fasttrack
Router(config-cmap)# match protocol fasttrack
  file-transfer regular_expression
```

The first command matches on all FastTrack-related P2P programs, which includes Kazaa, Grokster, and older versions of Morpheus. This command can be used to classify and mark traffic as it leaves your network, allowing your external outbound ACL to drop this traffic. The second command enables you look for P2P connections that contain a specific string in the P2P request.

Here is the syntax to match on Gnutella P2P programs:

```
Router(config-cmap)# match protocol gnutella
Router(config-cmap)# match protocol gnutella
  file-transfer regular_expression
```

The P2P applications that this command can match on include BearShare, Gnewtellium, Gnucleus, Gtk-Gnutella, JTella, LimeWire, newer versions of Morpheus, Mutella, Phex, Qtella, Swapper, XoloX, and XCache.

When specifying the string, you can enter regular expressions. Table 10-4 lists some of the more common regular expressions used. These expressions can be used as a wildcard to match on a string of alphanumeric characters that appear in a character string in the application layer data.

Table 10-4 *Regular Expressions*

Expression	Description
*	Many zeros—any number of characters in this position. For example, *cisco* indicates that the Cisco IOS should look for the keyword cisco anywhere in the string.
?	Match any single character in this position. For example, cis?o indicates that the Cisco IOS should look for three characters, cis, followed by any single character, and then immediately followed by the letter o in the string.
|	Match the character either to the left or to the right of the vertical bar. For example, C|cisco indicates that the Cisco IOS should look for either Cisco or cisco in the string.
(|)	Match the characters to the left or right of the vertical bar. For example, destroy.(jpg | gif) indicates that the Cisco IOS should look for either destroy.jpg or destroy.gif in the string.
[ ]	Match the range of characters specified in the range. For example, cisco[1-3] indicates that the Cisco IOS should look for either cisco1, cisco2, or cisco3 in the string.

A few examples illustrate regular expression matching. In this example, I am matching on all Gnutella traffic:

```
Router(config-cmap)# match protocol gnutella file-transfer "*"
```

In this example, I am matching on any Gnutella traffic that references an MPEG file:

```
Router(config-cmap)# match protocol gnutella file-transfer "*.mpeg"
```

To match on Napster traffic, use the following command:

```
Router(config-cmap)# match protocol napster [non-std]
```

The **non-std** parameter enables you to look for nonstandard Napster port connections. For Kazaa P2P traffic, use the following command:

```
Router(config-cmap)# match protocol kazaa2
```

HTTP Traffic

With NBAR, you can match on HTTP traffic by URL, host name, or MIME type. This is done with the following command:

```
Router(config-cmap)# match protocol http [url URL_string |
    host hostname_string | mime MIME_type]
```

You can use the **url** keyword to match on a full or partial URL in an HTTP request. Take a look at a simple example:

```
Router(config-cmap)# match protocol http url */home/ind*
```

In this example, any URL that contains /home/ind in it would be considered a match.

Here is an example of matching on a host name:

```
Router(config-cmap)# match protocol http host www.quizware.com
```

In this example, if the URL contains www.quizware.com, the packet is considered matched. You can match on partial host names, just like URLs:

```
Router(config-cmap)# match protocol http host *quizware*
```

In this example, any host name with quizware in it would be considered a match.

Finally, you can match on a MIME type. MIME types are used to categorize the type of data, such as a text file, an image file, a video file, and so on. HTML uses these quite extensively to provide presentation layer functions. MIME codes are embedded within HTML text to help the web browser determine how the information should be displayed. With NBAR, you can match on the MIME types, as in this example:

```
Router(config-cmap)# match protocol http mime *jpeg
```

In this example, any MIME type ending in "jpeg" is considered a match. For a list of MIME types, visit ftp://ftp.isi.edu/in-notes/iana/assignments/media-types/media-types.

Step 4: Download PDLMs

When examining certain applications or protocols, you need the correct version of the Cisco IOS that contains the necessary NBAR code. However, if your router does not have the latest or necessary version of the Cisco IOS, you still might be able to use NBAR for the specific application, as long as Cisco has a corresponding PDLM file for it.

PDLMs are small executable code modules used by NBAR. See the "Supported Protocols and Applications" section to find out what PDLM files Cisco supports and where you can download them. The main advantage of using a PDLM is that you do not have to upgrade your Cisco IOS to use the specific NBAR examination feature: Just download the appropriate PDLM file to Flash and then reference it for use by NBAR. In this instance, no reloading of your router is required.

To use a PDLM, you must reference it so that NBAR knows of its existence. Use this command to make the appropriate reference:

```
Router(config)# ip nbar pdlm [location://]PDLM_name
```

In this example, specify the PDLM name. If the PDLM is not in the primary Flash partition, you must specify the optional location.

For example, if you want to examine traffic for Fasttrack applications, but your Cisco IOS version did not support this for NBAR, you could download this PDLM from Cisco into your router's Flash and reference it with the following command:

```
Router(config)# ip nbar pdlm flash://fasttrack.pdlm
```

To see which PDLMs you have enabled on your router, use the **show ip nbar pdlm** command.

Step 5: Define a Traffic Policy

After you have created your class map, you need to assign your policy to it. If you were using NBAR to implement QoS, you would be assigning your QoS policies to the classified traffic. However, because you are dealing with security, you will want to mark the offending packets that you have classified. This is done with a policy. Creating a policy is a three-step process:

Step 1 Define the policy's name.

Step 2 Associate your class map with the policy.

Step 3 Mark the packets that are matched by the class map.

To perform these three steps, use the following configuration:

```
Router(config)# policy-map policy_map_name
Router(config-pmap)# class class_map_name
Router(config-pmap-c)# set [ip] dscp value
```

The last line can be substituted with the following if you prefer to filter on precedence instead of DSCP (for security filtering, this is a matter of personal preference):

```
Router(config-pmap-c)# set [ip] precedence value
```

The policy map name must be unique among all policies and can contain a maximum of 40 alphanumeric characters. When you execute the **policy-map** command, you enter into a subconfiguration mode.

Within the policy map, you include the name of the class map that you created in Step 3 with the **class-map** command. When you execute this command, you enter into a subsubconfiguration mode. Commands that you enter here affect only the specific class map name that you entered.

In this example, you mark the packets that you want to drop, using either DSCP or IP Precedence. For the DSCP or IP Precedence value, make sure that it is greater than 0. This information is placed in the ToS field of the IP header (by default, this field is 0); therefore, any number greater than 0 indicates that you have marked it. If you will use DSCP to handle the marking, use the **set [ip] dscp** command; if you will use IP Precedence to handle the marking, use the **set [ip] precedence** command. It does not matter which of the two commands that you use. Depending on which one you specify, in Step 7, you filter on the appropriate value in your ACL. One other thing to point out is that, as of Cisco IOS 12.2(13)T, you do not need to specify the **ip** keyword in these two set commands. Previous Cisco IOS versions required this keyword.

NOTE A policy map can contain references to multiple class maps; however, your policy map cannot reference more than 64 class maps.

Step 6: Activate the Traffic Policy

After you have set up your policies to mark unwanted or malicious traffic, you need to activate your traffic policies on your router. This is done on one of the router's interfaces. How you want to filter traffic affects the interface that you want to activate NBAR inspection on.

For example, assume that you are worried about the Code Red Worm being downloaded through an HTTP back door on your web servers. In this example, you would apply your policies inbound on the external interface. You then would create an ACL that you would apply outbound on your router's internal interface(s) to filter the marked traffic.

However, you also might be concerned about your internal users accessing the P2P program. In this instance, you would create a second policy and apply it inbound on your internal interface. You then would create an ACL that you would apply outbound on your router's external interface(s) to filter the marked traffic.

To associate a policy map with your router's interface, use the following command:

```
Router(config)# interface type [slot_#]port_#
Router(config-if)# service-policy input policy_map_name
```

You must reference with the **service-policy** Interface command whatever name you specified for your policy map with the **policy-map** command. For QoS purposes, you could specify the direction as either inbound (**input**) or outbound (**output**). However, because you are using NBAR to filter traffic, you apply the policy inbound on the ingress interface and then apply a filtering ACL outbound on the egress interface.

Step 7: Filter Marked Traffic

Now that you have finished setting up and activating your policies, the last step is to set up a filter that will drop the traffic that NBAR marked. If you used DSCP for marking, your ACL statement would use the following syntax:

```
Router(config)# ip access-list extended ACL_name
Router(config-ext-nacl)# <--filtering commands-->
Router(config-ext-nacl)# deny ip any any dscp value [log]
Router(config-ext-nacl)# <--filtering commands-->
```

Note that you can use either a named or a numbered ACL, but you might be restricted to named ACLs if you are using reflexive ACLs. For the DSCP value, enter the value that you specified in the **set dscp** command in your policy map.

If you used IP Precedence for marking, your ACL statement would use the following syntax:

```
Router(config)# ip access-list extended ACL_name
Router(config-ext-nacl)# <--filtering commands-->
Router(config-ext-nacl)# deny ip any any precedence value [log]
Router(config-ext-nacl)# <--filtering commands-->
```

For the precedence value, enter the value that you specified in the **set precedence** command in your policy map.

The last thing that you need to do is activate your ACL; this is done on the opposite interface than where you activated your NBAR policies, and it is applied in the outbound direction.

```
Router(config)# interface type [slot_#]port_#
Router(config-if)# ip access-group ACL_name out
```

This completes your configuration.

NOTE   Remember that, with NBAR policy filtering, the traffic must enter the router on an ingress interface, must be marked (tagged) on this interface, must be forwarded to an egress interface, and must be filtered with an outbound filter on this interface.

NBAR Verification

You can use various commands to verify the configuration and operation of NBAR on your router. Most of the commands are **show** commands, but you can use **debug** in a limited manner to troubleshoot your NBAR configuration.

Class Maps

To view your class map(s), use this command:

```
Router# show class-map [class_map_name]
```

This command displays your class map configuration. Example 10-10 shows sample output of the **show class-map** command.

Example 10-10 *Using the* **show class-map** *Command*

```
Router# show class-map
 Class Map match-any class-default (id 0)
   Match any
 Class Map match-any http-attack (id 1)
   Match protocol http url "*default.ida*"
   Match protocol http url "*root.exe*"
   Match protocol http url "*cmd.exe*"
```

In this example, there are two class maps. The class map called class-default is a catchall class map that the Cisco IOS creates the first time that you create a class map. The second class map, called http-attack, is one that I created. Notice that it is looking for any of the three items in a URL reference.

Policy Maps

To see your policy maps, use the **show policy-map** command:

```
Router# show policy-map [policy_map_name] [interface]
```

Example 10-11 shows sample output of the **show policy-map** command.

Example 10-11 *Using the* **show policy-map** *Command*

```
Router# show policy-map
  Policy Map mark-attack
   Class http-attack
    set dscp 1
```

In this example, there is only one policy on the router, called mark-attack. In this example, the class map of http-attack is included, and any traffic that matches the conditions in the class map has the traffic marked with a DSCP value of 1.

You can include an optional **interface** parameter with this command. This parameter displays what policy maps are activated on which interfaces, as well as statistics for this traffic. Example 10-12 shows sample output of the **show policy-map interface** command.

Example 10-12 *Using the* **show policy-map** *Command with the* **interface** *Parameter*

```
Router# show policy-map interface
 FastEthernet0                                                    (1)

  Service-policy input: mark-attack                               (2)
   Class-map: http-attack (match-any)                             (3)
     19 packets, 7520 bytes
     5 minute offered rate 0 bps, drop rate 0 bps
     Match: protocol http url "*default.ida*"
       0 packets, 0 bytes
       5 minute rate 0 bps
     Match: protocol http url "*root.exe*"                        (4)
       6 packets, 2490 bytes
       5 minute rate 0 bps
     Match: protocol http url "*cmd.exe*"                         (5)
       13 packets, 5030 bytes
       5 minute rate 0 bps
     QoS Set
       dscp 1
         Packets marked 19                                        (6)

   Class-map: class-default (match-any)                           (7)
     101 packets, 12914 bytes
     5 minute offered rate 0 bps, drop rate 0 bps
     Match: any
```

The following are some important points about Example 10-12, with reference to the numbering on the right side of the example:

1 This output deals only with interface Fastethernet0.

2 On this interface, the mark-attack policy has been activated.

3 The mark-attack policy contains two class maps. The first class map is http-attack. Three match rules exist in this class map.

4 This is the second match rule in the class map called http-attack. Notice that six packets (totaling 2490 bytes) have matched on this statement.

5 This is the third match rule in the class map. Thirteen packets (totaling 5030 bytes) have matched this statement.

6 This is the action assigned to matches for the class map called http-attack in the mark-attack policy. In this instance, the DSCP is set to 1 in the IP packet headers. In this example, 19 packets were marked.

7 This is the default class map that the Cisco IOS automatically creates. One nice feature here is that it gives you some basic statistical information about all traffic entering the interface.

Traffic Flow and NBAR

You can get more detailed information about the operation of NBAR with filtering by using a combination of **debug**, **show**, and **clear** commands. For example, you might see that NBAR is filtering traffic, but you want to know the actual mechanics of this filtering. To do this, you first need to enable **debug** for NBAR:

```
Router# debug ip nbar trace #_of_buffers
```

The number of buffers affects how much simultaneous traffic the router can capture. This can be from 50 to 1000.

Unusual to this command is that the output is not displayed on the console. Instead, you must use a **show** command to view it:

```
Router# show ip nbar trace
```

Example 10-13 shows sample output of the **show ip nbar trace** command.

Example 10-13 *Using the* **show ip nbar trace** *Command*

```
Router# show ip nbar trace
Session selected due to match on : Protocol Match (http)
Session contains the following flows :
        192.168.1.100:3381 <--> 192.168.2.2:80(tcp)

Trace[1  ]: A -> B [HTTP-u-url:3] (<< offset = 70) Bound (384+32 >
  384)
Trace[2  ]: B -> A [HTTP-u-client:3]
Trace[3  ]: A -> B [HTTP-u-url:3] (<< offset = 50) Bound (320+32 >
  320)
Trace[4  ]: A -> B [HTTP-u-url:3] (<< offset = 50) (search )
      (search '/?([^ \n\r]*cmd[.]exe)/?([^ \n\r]*root[.]exe)/?
      ([^ \n\r]*default[.]ida)') (add C0A80164D350000 HTTP-u-known
      -server->HTTP-u-known-flow) (add C0A80202500000 TCP->
      HTTP-u-known-server) (add C0A80164D350000 TCP->HTTP-u-known
      -client)
<--outut omitted-->
IP EndPoints:
A : 192.168.1.100:3381/tcp
B : 192.168.2.2:80/tcp
```

In this example, 192.168.1.100 made an HTML request to 192.168.2.2. Notice that in the third trace there was a match on one of the conditions in the class map statement.

Finally, you can clear the information in the buffers with the **clear ip nbar trace** command.

CAUTION   Be forewarned that the **debug ip nbar trace** command is CPU intensive. I recommend using this command to troubleshoot only a flawed NBAR configuration and then immediately disabling it.

NBAR Examples

Now that you have a basic understanding of what NBAR is and how to configure it, take a look at some nifty examples of how you can use NBAR to filter dangerous or unnecessary traffic. Next, you will look at three examples of using NBAR to filter traffic:

- Code Red worm
- Nimda virus/worm
- P2P program usage

The following sections go over these three examples.

NBAR and Code Red

On July 19, 2001, the Code Red worm infiltrated more than 350,000 computers in less than 13 hours. During the peak of its performance, Code Red was infiltrating about 2000 computers per minute. In this instance, a hacker found a coding weakness in Microsoft's Internet Information Server (IIS) versions 4 and 5. The hacker found a URL buffer overflow bug that allowed him to send an HTTP GET request to overflow the buffer, which then allowed him to execute arbitrary code on the web server. When the hole was discovered, the worm copied itself into memory and then attempted to infect other IIS web servers.

About Code Red and Code Red II

Two variations of the Code Red worm were found. In the first variation, a bug in the worm caused it to try to reaffect the same computers constantly. The random-number generator used to target new IP addresses was broken, and the code did not try to detect whether the target machine already was infected.

A different worm by the name of Code Red II found a similar hole in IIS, but only on Windows 2000 computers. Where Code Red I mainly attacked English systems, the Code Red II worm attacked Chinese systems. One of the unique things about the Code Red II worm is that, after a period of time, it intercepted port 80 inbound connections to the IIS server and displayed this message: "Welcome to http://www.worm.com!, Hacked By Chinese!" This was basically a redirect message: The worm did not modify any actual web server files.

What Should I Do?

You should do a few things when dealing with the Code Red I and II worms. Obviously, one of the first things you want to do is to find all IIS servers in your network and download the patch available on the Microsoft website. This sounds somewhat easy, but many products install and use IIS to perform functions other than web browsing, such as remote management and reporting. Even when you patch the servers, the patch prevents the Code Red from only a further infection: The Code Red worm still could be trying to access your network.

Even if you have a firewall in your network, it might not be capable of preventing a Code Red attack. Remember that firewalls typically operate at Layers 3, 4, and sometimes 5. Many firewalls do not have the capability to perform application layer filtering. Therefore, if you are using only extended ACLs to block traffic, and you have an internal IIS server, you are susceptible to attack. Your extended ACL probably is allowing the TCP port 80 connection to the web server.

Using NBAR

With the limitation of ACL filtering, the Cisco IOS has another tool that you can use to prevent the Code Red worm from entering (or leaving) your network: NBAR. NBAR can examine HTTP content and make filtering decisions on it. To understand how Code Red works, you need to take a look at your IIS files. Use the network shown in Figure 10-5 as an example.

Figure 10-5 *Code Red*

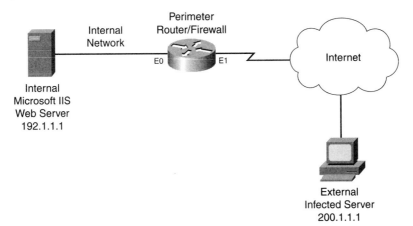

Example 10-14 shows a Code Red entry on the internal server (192.1.1.1).

Example 10-14 *Code Red I Log Entry on the Internal 192.1.1.1 Server*

```
2001-08-01 15:42:13 200.1.1.1 - 192.1.1.1 80 GET /default.ida
NNNNNNNNNNNNNNNNNNNNNNNNNNNNNNNNNNNNNNNNNNNNNNNNNNNNNNNNNNNNNNNNN
NNNNNNNNNNNNNNNNNNNNNNNNNNNNNNNNNNNNNNNNNNNNNNNNNNNNNNNNNNNNNNNNN
NNNNNNNNNNNNNNNNNNNNNNNNNNNNNNNNNNNNNNNNNNNNNNNNNNNNNNNNNNNNNNNNN
NNNNNNNNNNNNNNNNNN%u9090%u6858%ucbd3%u7801%u9090%u6858%ucbd3%u7801%u90
90%u6858%ucbd3%u7801%u9090%u9090%u8190%u00c3%u0003%u8b00%u531b%u53ff%
u0078%u0000%u00=a 403
```

Code Red II is very similar in its footmark, as shown in Example 10-15.

Example 10-15 *Code Red II Log Entry on the Internal 192.1.1.1 Server*

```
2001-08-01 18:52:31 200.1.1.1 - 192.1.1.1 80 GET /default.ida XXXXXXXXXXX
XXXXXXXXXXXXXXXXXXXXXXXXXXXXXXXXXXXXXXXXXXXXXXXXXXXXXXXXXXXXXXXXXXXXXXXXX
XXXXXXXXXXXXXXXXXXXXXXXXXXXXXXXXXXXXXXXXXXXXXXXXXXXXXXXXXXXXXXXXXXXXXXXXX
XXXXXXXXXXXXXXXXXXXXXXXXXXXXXXXXXXXXXXXXXXXXXXXXXXXXXXXXXXXXX%u9090
%u6858%ucbd3%u7801%u9090%u6858%ucbd3%u7801%u9090%u6858%ucbd3%u7801%u9090%
u9090%u8190%u00c3%u0003%u8b00%u531b%u53ff%u0078%u0000%u00=a 403 -
```

Notice that, in both examples, the infected system (200.1.1.1) tries to use the buffer overflow by sending a long URL to 192.1.1.1. One interesting thing about both attacks is that both URL requests contain default.ida in the URL request. In some other minor variations of the Code Red worm, the filename is followed by an .ida extension.

Another interesting thing about Code Red is that it tries to execute the root.exe and cmd.exe files on the IIS server. Therefore, because all of this information is in a URL request on TCP port 80, you easily can detect these kinds of attacks with NBAR.

Code Red Configuration Example

Take a look at an example configuration to filter Code Red I and II. This configuration uses the network shown in Figure 10-5. Example 10-16 displays a simple example of a coding configuration to prevent Code Red (both versions) from entering this network.

Example 10-16 *Using NBAR to Detect Code Red Attacks*

```
Router(config)# class-map match-any code-red-attacks
Router(config-cmap)# match protocol http url "*.ida*"
Router(config-cmap)# match protocol http url "*cmd.exe*"
Router(config-cmap)# match protocol http url "*root.exe*"
Router(config-cmap)# exit
Router(config)# policy-map mark-code-red
Router(config-pmap)# class code-red-attacks
Router(config-pmap-c)# set ip dscp 1
Router(config-pmac-c)# exit
Router(config)# interface ethernet1
Router(config-if)# service-policy input mark-code-red
Router(config-if)# exit
```

continues

Example 10-16 *Using NBAR to Detect Code Red Attacks (Continued)*

```
Router(config)# ip access-list extended block-code-red
Router(config-ext-nacl)# deny ip any any dscp 1 log
Router(config-ext-nacl)# permit ip any any
Router(config-ext-nacl)# exit
Router(config)# interface ethernet0
Router(config-if)# ip access-group block-code-red out
```

This example focuses only on the filtering of Code Red. Obviously, you will want to set up ingress filtering on the external interface. At the beginning of the configuration, a class map called code-red-attacks is created, where the default.ida, cmd.exe, and root.exe strings are looked for in HTTP URL requests—any of these can trigger a match. A policy map called mark-code-red specifies that, for the class map code-red-attacks, matching traffic should be marked with a DSCP value of 1. This policy then is activated on ethernet1 (external interface) in the ingress direction. An ACL is created that drops and logs DSCP 1 marked traffic as packets flow out of the internal interface (ethernet0) in the egress direction.

NOTE   You also can use NBAR with policy-based routing (PBR) to filter the Code Red worm. I discuss how to do this in Chapter 15.

NBAR and Nimda

Nimda is a hybrid form of an attack: It has characteristics of both a virus and a worm. It spread using the following mechanisms:

- When an uneducated user clicked on an e-mail attachment (virus). In some e-mail clients, it ran automatically.

- Using a back door in Microsoft IIS to gain access to the web server.

When Nimda infects a machine, it installs itself and actively finds other machines to infect. It appends JavaScript commands to all locally stored HTML files on the device, including IIS servers. Any person who later attempts to download these pages cause the worm to execute on the machine automatically. As with Code Red, Nimda was not malicious in nature—that is, it did not destroy contents of a machine it infected. However, when Nimda affects a machine, it installs its own SMTP engine to mass-mail itself to other devices and attempts to use TFTP to load files on unaffected systems.

What Should I Do?

Combating Nimda is actually more difficult than combating Code Red, given that Nimda attacks from different directions: e-mail attachments, downloaded JavaScripts, and bugs in IIS. Therefore, you have your work cut out for you when dealing with this hybrid worm/ virus. First, you should make sure that antivirus software is running on every desktop and that they all have the most recent virus-detection files to detect and eradicate Nimda. For your SMTP server, add rules to block the attachments readme.exe and Admin.dll. The JavaScript problem was found in Internet Explorer (IE) 5.0 and 5.01. If you are running either of these versions, apply Service Pack 2 to IE. You also can use NBAR to prevent HTML attacks against your internal IIS servers.

Nimda Configuration Example

Take a look at an example configuration to filter Nimda attacks against IIS web servers. This configuration uses the network shown previously in Figure 10-5. Example 10-17 shows the use of NBAR to drop packets related to the Nimda attack.

Example 10-17 *Using NBAR to Detect Nimda Attacks*

```
Router(config)# class-map match-any nimda-attacks
Router(config-cmap)# match protocol http url "*.ida*"
Router(config-cmap)# match protocol http url "*cmd.exe*"
Router(config-cmap)# match protocol http url "*root.exe*"
Router(config-cmap)# match protocol http url "*readme.eml*"
Router(config-cmap)# exit
Router(config)# policy-map mark-nimda
Router(config-pmap)# class nimda-attacks
Router(config-pmap-c)# set ip dscp 1
Router(config-pmac-c)# exit
Router(config)# interface ethernet1
Router(config-if)# service-policy input mark-nimda
Router(config-if)# exit
Router(config)# ip access-list extended block-nimda
Router(config-ext-nacl)# deny ip any any dscp 1 log
Router(config-ext-nacl)# permit ip any any
Router(config-ext-nacl)# exit
Router(config)# interface ethernet0
Router(config-if)# ip access-group block-nimda out
```

Actually, this example builds upon the Code Red example. The only addition to this configuration is the matching on *readme.eml* in the nimda-attacks class map.

TIP   As you can see from these last two examples—Code Red and Nimda—you can use NBAR to filter many kinds of HTTP-based attacks. I recommend its use to defeat different kinds of virus, worm, and Trojan horse attacks against web servers. With the custom feature introduced in Cisco IOS 12.3(4)T, you can create your own custom NBAR inspections to examine attacks against other services, such as POP3 and SMTP, as well as others.

NBAR and P2P Programs

As I mentioned earlier in Chapter 7, it sometimes can be almost impossible to filter P2P program use by your users, especially for users who are determined to break policies to download and share content. For these users, you can use NBAR to help combat the usage of these programs. If you are concerned about internal users accessing outside file-sharing servers or setting up their own small servers, you can use NBAR to detect the use of these programs, mark the packets, and use an ACL to filter the packets.

Refer back to the network shown previously in Figure 10-5 for how to filter P2P programs with NBAR. Example 10-18 shows a sample configuration that focuses only on the P2P filtering with NBAR.

Example 10-18 *Using NBAR to Block P2P Programs*

```
Router(config)# class-map match-any P2P-usage
Router(config-cmap)# match protocol gnutella
Router(config-cmap)# match protocol gnutella file-transfer "*"
Router(config-cmap)# match protocol fasttrack
Router(config-cmap)# match protocol fasttrack file-transfer "*"
Router(config-cmap)# match napster non-std
Router(config-cmap)# match kazaa2
Router(config-cmap)# match protocol socks
Router(config-cmap)# exit
Router(config)# policy-map mark-P2P
Router(config-pmap)# class P2P-usage
Router(config-pmap-c)# set ip dscp 2
Router(config-pmac-c)# exit
Router(config)# ip access-list extended block-P2P
Router(config-ext-nacl)# deny ip any any dscp 2 log
Router(config-ext-nacl)# ! <--other ACL statements-->
Router(config-ext-nacl)# permit ip any any
Router(config-ext-nacl)# exit
Router(config)# interface ethernet1
Router(config-if)# service-policy input mark-P2P
Router(config-if)# ip access-group block-P2P out
Router(config-if)# exit
Router(config)# interface ethernet0
Router(config-if)# service-policy input mark-P2P
Router(config-if)# ip access-group block-P2P out
```

As you can see from this example, setting up NBAR P2P filtering is simple. First, set up two sets of match statements to examine Fasttrack, Gnutella, Napster, and Kazaa P2P applications. Second, mark these using either IP Precedence or DSCP. Notice that I used a DSCP value of 2.

TIP   Normally, if I am blocking different kinds of things with NBAR, I use different DSCP or Precedence values and different ACL statements so that I can more easily log what I am filtering. For example, I might use a DSCP value of 1 for worms and a DSCP value 2 for P2P programs.

Notice that I have applied the policies inbound on both interfaces, and ACLs outbound on both of these interfaces. Obviously, you need to configure more on this router to secure it, but these statements pertain to just the P2P filtering process.

One important item that I want to point out about this P2P configuration example is that I also am blocking SOCKS traffic. SOCKS commonly is used to tunnel information through HTTP. Therefore, an ingenious user in your network could use SOCKS to tunnel P2P programs through TCP port 80 and easily get around any ACL filtering of NBAR P2P filtering statements on your router. Previously, SOCKS was used to protect a computer's resources. Today other methods, such as commercial-based firewalls, are used. Therefore, tunneling information through TCP port 80 seems very suspicious to me, and I typically block it. Note that you also can do this with an ACL statement instead of using NBAR. If you want to see how SOCKS can be used to tunnel P2P and other information, visit http://www.http-tunnel.com/HT_Products_HTTPTunnelClient.asp.

SOCKS and Tunneling Traffic

I once had a client who knew that internal users were using P2P programs but never actually could detect the usage to confront the individuals. When I heard about this, I laughed to myself because I realized that these users probably were tunneling their traffic in some form or another. In this example, we put a probe on the wire to capture information on SOCKS connections and then analyzed this later. Actually, we were quite surprised at the number of users that we caught doing this. We then used an ACL to block this traffic, and the CIO had a lot of nasty words to say to the rule breakers—one of whom was on her own staff.

Summary

This chapter showed you the basics of filtering URL and application layer information. With CBAC, you can perform very basic Java filtering on connections. The main limitation of this feature is that you can filter applets only based on source IP addresses in packets. Therefore, a better approach to this problem is to use a content-filtering server that allows for better implementation of URL-filtering policies. Cisco supports both Websense and N2H2 products to provide URL content filtering.

For specific kinds of attacks that use HTTP, or for P2P programs, you can use NBAR as an additional tool to filter this traffic. NBAR can be very useful in not just filtering these attacks, but also providing statistical information about the number of attacks (or use).

Next up is Part V, "Address Translation and Firewalls," which shows you how to configure address translation on your Cisco IOS perimeter router/firewall, as well as discusses the issues related to address translation.

## PART V

Address Translation and Firewalls

Chapter 11   Address Translation

Chapter 12   Address Translation Issues

Address Translation

Part IV, "Stateful and Advanced Filtering Technologies," dealt with stateful filtering of traffic as well as filtering of web traffic. This part deals with address translation: why it is necessary, how it is done, problems that address translation introduces, and address-translation features of the Cisco IOS. This chapter focuses on the basics of address translation: the different kinds of address translation available and how they are configured on a Cisco router. The next chapter deals with address translation issues and Cisco IOS features that you can use to solve these problems.

Address Translation Overview

One of the issues that you will face when designing a network is ensuring that all your devices have an IP address. Each device needs an IP address for sending and receiving traffic, as well as for remote management. With a shortage of public IP addresses for accessing the Internet, this presents a problem for assigning addresses to devices to allow communications. Some type of solution is needed.

One of the problems that the Internet faces is IP address depletion. As a long-term solution, IPv6 is addressing this. However, a lot of manpower and money is required to covert from IPv4 to IPv6. As a short-term solution, IETF defined two standards: RFC 1918 and 1631. These standards set aside a range of public IP addresses and allow anyone to use them; they also translate these addresses to public addresses when they leave a company's network. The following sections discuss these standards.

Private Addresses

RFC 1918 sets aside a block of addresses that any network can use, commonly called private addresses. Table 11-1 lists the address class as well as the range of addresses that RFC 1918 sets aside for the class. With this RFC, 1 Class A, 16 Class B, and 256 Class C addresses are set aside for intracompany use. As you can see from this list of addresses, you have more than 17 million at your disposal—more than enough to assign addresses to all your internal devices.

Table 11-1 *RFC 1918 Private Addresses*

Class	Addresses
A	10.0.0.0–10.255.255.255
B	172.16.0.0–172.31.255.255
C	192.168.0.0–192.168.255.255

These addresses work fine for intracompany communications, in which one device in a company accesses another device in the same company. However, using private addresses presents problems when two companies want to share information but they are both using the same private address space. Figure 11-1 shows a simple example of this problem. In this example, two companies, A and B, are both using network 10.0.0.0/8. In Company A, an internal user (A) wants to access a server in Company B. You will notice, that in this example, this presents a problem: Both networks are using network 10.0.0.0/8, and both have overlapping addresses: 10.1.1.1. The two networks cannot communicate with each other.

Figure 11-1 *Overlapping Addresses*

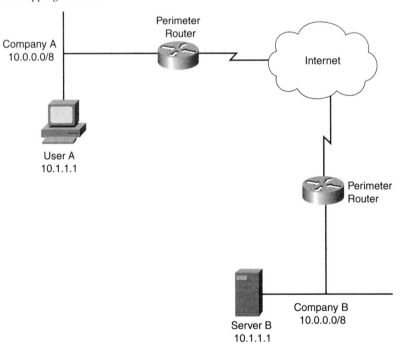

Address Translation

To solve this communication problem, IETF introduced RFC 1631. This RFC defines address translation, translating addressing information in a packet from one number to another. Typically, this is used to translate private addresses to public ones, and vice versa. This translation process commonly is referred to as Network Address Translation (NAT).

You might need to use private IP addresses for these reasons:

- Your current ISP assigned you a limited number of public addresses, but not enough to assign to all of your devices.

- You currently have enough public addresses, but you are changing ISPs and your new ISP will not support your old public address space.

- You need to merge two networks, which, unfortunately, are using the same address space.

- You currently are using someone else's assigned public addresses.

- You want to set up load balancing by using a single virtual IP address to represent multiple devices.

- You want to have better control over traffic entering and leaving your network.

Advantages of Address Translation

Address translation has both its advantages and disadvantages. Take a look at its advantages first:

- You have access to 1 Class A, 16 Class B, and 256 Class C networks, totaling more than 17 million addresses.

- If you change ISPs, your work is simplified. You need to change only the address-translation rules on your address-translation device; you do not have to change addresses on specific devices.

- Your ISP drops packets with private addresses in them, giving you tighter control over traffic leaving your network. If the private addresses are not translated as they leave your network, your ISP drops these packets.

- The internal structure of your network is hidden from outside eyes.

Disadvantages of Address Translation

Address translation also has its share of disadvantages, including the following:

- When performing address translation, your address-translation device introduces delay in the packet stream. The address-translation device must change addressing information in the packet and recompute checksum information.

- The more translations your address translation device needs to support, the greater burden this places on the device. This can create scalability issues in large networks.

- It is more difficult to troubleshoot problems because the source and possibly destination are using translated addresses. Therefore, when you look at an IP address in a packet, you cannot necessarily be sure whether this is the address physically assigned to the device or whether it is a translated address.

- Even though address translation provides tighter security, it allows people to hide their identities through address translation, making it more difficult to track down the source of an attack.

- Some applications embed addressing information in the payload contents. This presents a problem with address-translation devices, which typically translate addressing information only for the IP and, possibly, TCP or UDP headers. If an address-translation device does not translate embedded addressing information, and a device attempts to use the untranslated information, it cannot connect to its destination.

Given the advantages and disadvantages of address translation, you must take care in deciding when you need to use address translation and what it will encompass.

How Address Translation Works

Now that you have a basic understanding of what address translation is, take a look at some of the terms used in address translation, as well as the different kinds of address translation. Many different kinds of devices, such as firewalls, routers, and even servers, can perform address translation (Cisco routers have supported address translation since Cisco IOS 11.2). The following sections will help you become more familiar with these concepts.

Terms Used in Address Translation

Before you can understand how address translation is performed by a device, you first need to become familiar with some terms commonly used with address translation. Table 11-2 explains some basic terms used with address translation; Table 11-3 explains some common types of address translations.

Table 11-2 *Basic Address Translation Terms*

Term	Explanation
Inside	These devices are located inside your network.
Outside	These devices are located outside your network.
Local	These addresses physically are assigned to devices. They are typically private addresses but can be public addresses.
Global	To the outside world, devices appear to be using these addresses. These are public addresses but are not necessarily translated addresses because these devices can be assigned public addresses.
Inside local address	This is an address that either is statically assigned or is assigned through DHCP to your internal device. It can be a public or private address. This is the address that other internal devices in your network see in the source IP address field when viewed inside the network.
Inside global address	This is an address that your internal device appears to be using. It can be assigned by an address-translation device. This is the address that external devices (devices outside your network) see in the source IP address field.
Outside local address	This is an address that an external device is using in its configuration when it generates packets.
Outside global address	This is an address that an external device appears to be using. This is what your devices see in the source IP address field of the remote device's packet.

Table 11-3   *Address Translation Types*

Term	Explanation
Simple translation	One IP address is translated to another IP address; this commonly is called Network Address Translation (NAT).
Extended translation	One IP address and port number are mapped to another IP address and possibly a different port number. This commonly is called Network Address Port Translation (NAPT) or Port Address Translation (PAT).
Static translation	Address translation is configured manually on an address-translation device, mapping one address to another. This also can include port mappings. With port mappings, this commonly is called Port Address Redirection (PAR).
Dynamic translation	Address translation dynamically is performed by an address-translation device by using a pool of addresses. This also can include the dynamic assignment of new port numbers.

Address Translation Terms

In the industry, I commonly see people misuse address translation terms. For example, I see people use the term *NAT* to refer to *NAT* and *PAT*. In reality, NAT refers to an address translation of one IP address to another, whereas PAT refers to translating many IP addresses to a single IP address and making sure that the source port numbers are unique for each of these translations. Be aware that these terms sometimes are used loosely in the industry.

Performing Address Translation

Many different types of address translation exist, as you saw in Table 11-3. This section covers the mechanics and the variations of the different kinds in this table, focusing on specific address translation types.

Network Address Translation

The most common form of address translation is the translation of one IP address to another. Two common forms of this translation exist:

- Changing a source inside local address to a source inside global address

- Changing a destination inside global address to a destination inside local address

You can see how this is done by examining Figure 11-2. In this example, the network on the left is using private addresses (10.0.0.0/8), and the router is performing address translation for these addresses. In Step 1, 10.0.0.1 creates a packet destined for 200.1.1.1. In Step 2, the router receives the packet and performs address translation on the source address. The router first looks at its static configuration for address translation. If it finds a match, it uses the inside global address as the replacement; if not, it uses a dynamic assignment method by checking to see whether this packet should be translated and, if so, what pool of addresses the router should use. In this example, the source IP address was translated from 10.0.0.1 to 192.1.1.1. When the destination device (200.1.1.1) receives the packet in Step 3, it thinks that it is talking to 192.1.1.1 and thus replies to this address. As mentioned earlier, one advantage or disadvantage of this is that the source is anonymous, depending on your view; in this example, the destination has no idea who the real source is. In Step 4, the router receives the packet and performs its address-translation process again. In this instance, though, it changes the destination IP address in the packet header: 192.1.1.1 to 10.0.0.1.

Figure 11-2 *Network Address Translation Example*

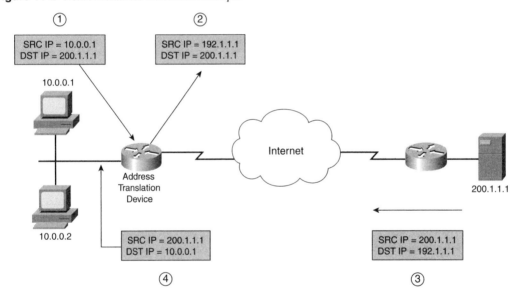

NOTE   One important thing to point out concerning NAT (versus PAT) is that, for each device that sends packets through the address-translation device, you need a separate inside global IP address. For example, if you have simultaneous outbound connections from 500 inside devices, you need 500 global addresses either statically configured or dynamically assigned through an address pool on the address-translation device. Each device needs a unique inside global IP address. Because you might have thousands of internal devices, but only a limited number of public addresses, NAT typically is not used to assign IP addresses for internal devices as they make outbound connections. Instead, NAT is used to assign addresses to devices that external users need access to, such as internal DNS servers, web servers, e-mail servers, FTP servers, and other types of public resources.

Overlapping Addresses

Sometime during your life as a network administrator, you probably will need to connect two networks, but they happen to be using the same address space. Obviously, this creates connectivity problems. As an example, look at Figure 11-3. Companies A and B are using 10.0.0.8/24. This would be okay if both companies used different subnet numbers, with A using 10.1.x.x and Company B using 10.2.x.x. However, as you can see in this example, both companies are using some of the same networks and addresses. This presents a connectivity problem. How can 10.0.0.1 in Company A send information to 10.0.0.1 in Company B?

Figure 11-3 *Overlapping Addresses Example*

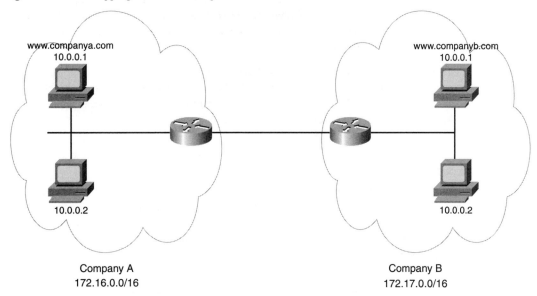

To overcome this problem, you must do one of two things:

- Readdress one of the two networks (or both networks)
- Use address translation

Address translation can be used to solve this problem. In this example, the router connected to Company A translates the local IP addresses to an address in the 172.16.0.0/16 network. Company B's router translates its inside local addresses to 172.17.0.0/16. Therefore, from the two companies' perspectives, the networks look like 172.16.0.0/16 and 172.17.0.0/16. However, there is one issue with this type of address translation: Normally, devices use names to access other devices, and they rely on DNS to resolve names to IP addresses.

Take a closer look at this problem. Assume that the device on Company A (10.0.0.1) wants to access www.companyb.com, which is a web server. It does a DNS lookup, and the DNS server in Company B replies with 10.0.0.1. Company A's device then uses this IP address as a destination and tries to set up a connection to itself. To solve this issue, address-translation devices also need to inspect DNS replies and fix the DNS replies with the appropriate address, commonly referred to as *DNS doctoring*. In this example, Company B's address translation device would have to change the DNS reply address of www.companyb.com from 10.0.0.1 to 172.17.x.x, an address that does not overlap with Company A.

TIP	Use address translation as only a temporary solution when solving overlapping addresses. In other words, use address translation to solve the initial connectivity problem, but begin readdressing one or both networks so that address translation is not necessary. Remember that address translation has its deficiencies. If these networks constantly will be communicating with each other, you want to take address translation out of the picture. Plus, eventually removing address translation makes it much easier to implement, enforce, and troubleshoot your policies.
	Also, many companies require vendors to use specific addresses with the VPN when using extranet VPNs. In this situation, either you or the vendor must translate the addresses. Sometimes this is done for security reasons, but in many cases, it is to ensure that overlapping addressing does not cause a problem.

Address Overloading

Address overloading, commonly called PAT, uses one or more inside global IP address to encompass all inside devices. To differentiate between the different internal connections, PAT ensures that the TCP or UDP source port numbers in the segment header are unique. With this capability, an address-translation device can handle thousands of inside local addresses with a single global address.

NOTE	Theoretically, this would enable you to map 65,536 addresses to a single address because the source port field in a TCP or UDP segment is 16 bits in length. Realistically, though, only about 4000 devices can share a single global IP address because certain port numbers are not used or are not recommended for use. Therefore, if you have 6000 devices that need outside access, you need two inside global addresses for PAT.

Take a look at an example of how address overloading works. In Figure 11-4, the network on the left is using PAT to translate inside local addresses to one inside global address: 192.1.1.1. For the first connection, 10.0.0.1 Telnets to 200.1.1.1 using a source TCP port number of 1024. As you can see from the first entry in the router's address-translation table, the router translated the source IP address to 192.1.1.1 but left the source port number as is because this is the first connection; therefore, no other device is using the same source port number. 10.0.0.1 then makes another Telnet connection to 200.1.1.1. As a source port number, 10.0.0.1 chooses a number greater than 1023 that is not in use; in this instance, it chose 1025. As you can see from the second entry in the address-translation table, the router translated only the source address because the source port number is different from the one used in the first entry. For the third connection, a different device (10.0.0.2) Telnets to the same destination. In this instance, the source port number happens to be the same as the first connection; therefore, the address-translation device changes the source address (10.0.0.2 to 192.1.1.1) as well as the source port number (1024 to 1026). From this translation table, the router easily can determine, based on returning traffic, how it should undo the address-translation process.

Figure 11-4 *Address Overloading Example*

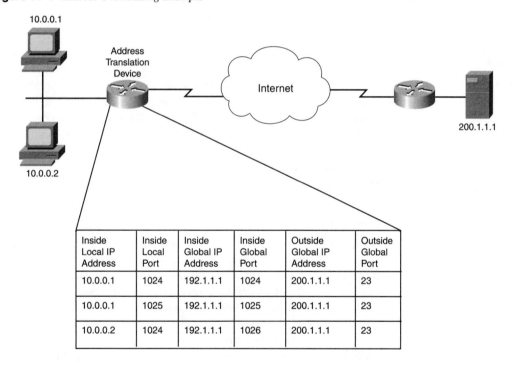

Inside Local IP Address	Inside Local Port	Inside Global IP Address	Inside Global Port	Outside Global IP Address	Outside Global Port
10.0.0.1	1024	192.1.1.1	1024	200.1.1.1	23
10.0.0.1	1025	192.1.1.1	1025	200.1.1.1	23
10.0.0.2	1024	192.1.1.1	1026	200.1.1.1	23

TIP   Note that NAT and PAT are not mutually exclusive. Where NAT is used to perform address translation of inside addresses that external users need to access, PAT typically is used to conserve addresses as inside users access external resources. As an example, assume that your ISP assigned you six public IP addresses. If you had a DNS server, a web server, and an e-mail server, you would need three static NAT configurations for these devices, using up three addresses. This would leave you with three addresses. Assume that you had only 1000 devices that needed access to the Internet. In this example, you could use PAT with one of the remaining public addresses to allow outside access, still leaving you with two spare public IP addresses.

One issue with PAT is that it works fine for traffic that uses TCP and UDP as a transport. However, how can PAT work for applications or protocols that do not use TCP or UDP, such as ping, which uses ICMP? ICMP does not have port numbers. To solve this problem, a vendor typically uses a proprietary mechanism to place identifying information in either the packet header or the payload, to help undo translations for returning traffic. However, this assumes that the destination will include this information in the packet header or payload of returning traffic. Some vendors maintain a state table for this kind of translated traffic, keeping tabs on who generated what, thereby undoing the translation correctly for returning traffic. However, this can pose a problem if two inside devices send the same kind of information to the same destination device. For example, two internal devices simultaneously might ping the same destination device. In this example, the address-translation device could not rely on state information alone to undo the address translation; it would need some type of additional identification information in the returning packets.

CAUTION   PAT works fine with most TCP and UDP connections, but it can experience problems with other types of protocols, such as ICMP, IPSec (with either AH or ESP), PPTP, and others. There is no guarantee that a vendor will support a PAT process for non-TCP and non-UDP connections. In some instances, you might have to use NAT for devices that need to use other protocols, such as IPSec with ESP, when accessing external resources, instead of using PAT.

Traffic Distribution and Load Balancing

One of the commonly forgotten uses of address translation is the traffic distribution feature, commonly called load balancing. As an example, assume that you have a web server that contains content that is very popular on the Internet and that is getting thousands of hits every hour. Because of this traffic, load, the CPU processing on the server is very high and sometimes hits 100 percent, causing it to drop many connection requests and frustrating external users with poor download times. One solution to this problem is to buy a bigger, faster server. However, if you have ever been through this process, it is not simple to buy a new server, migrate the information to the old server, and then swap the old server for the new one.

Traffic distribution in address translation enables you to get around this upgrade process. Instead of swapping out an older server for a newer one, you can purchase a second server and simultaneously use both. At first, you might think that this would cause a problem because both servers have different IP addresses. You could have your DNS server respond in a round-robin fashion, to assign one address to one DNS request, the other address to a second request, and so on. This assumes that your DNS server supports this function; however, one downside to this approach is that the requesting client caches the DNS information and uses it repeatedly. This can lead to a disproportionate amount of traffic being sent to one of the two servers.

A better approach is to have an address-translation device perform this process. In Figure 11-5, the network on the left has two internal web servers that have exactly the same content. The internal DNS server advertises this content as being at 192.1.1.5, even though both servers have the content. When an external device accesses 192.1.1.5 on TCP 80, the address-translation device looks at the last translation that it made and then chooses the next IP address in the server pool for this request. As you can see in this example, the two external users use the two internal servers to obtain the same content.

Figure 11-5 *Traffic Distribution Example*

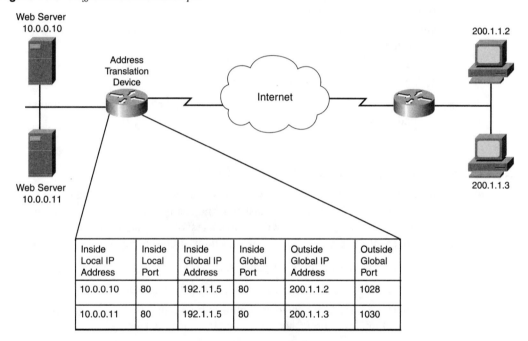

Inside Local IP Address	Inside Local Port	Inside Global IP Address	Inside Global Port	Outside Global IP Address	Outside Global Port
10.0.0.10	80	192.1.1.5	80	200.1.1.2	1028
10.0.0.11	80	192.1.1.5	80	200.1.1.3	1030

CAUTION   Many different kinds of products, including Cisco IOS routers, perform traffic distribution. However, not all of them do this process equally. For example, some solutions just round-robin between the different server addresses, not checking to see if the server is actually available or checking the current load on the server. Some solutions actually check on the server's status and use this when computing how it should perform traffic distribution. Using a Cisco IOS device is probably not the best load-balancing solution: The Cisco local director or content switches would provide a better solution.

Limitations of Address Translation

Even though address translation provides many solutions to your connectivity problems, especially when using private addresses, it does have limitations and restrictions.

For example, as mentioned with PAT, PAT does not work with all types of IP protocols. Here are some common limitations in which address translation might not or will not work:

- Many applications embed IP address and port number information in the payload. Unless an address-translation device is designed to look for this kind of information, these applications will fail when address translation is used. For example, ICMP, SNMP, DNS (replies and zone transfers), BOOTP and DHCP, routing updates, NetBIOS, and multimedia applications commonly include IP addressing in the payload of packets. Chapter 12, "Address Translation Issues," discusses how a Cisco router deals with this issue.

- Address translation will not work if the headers of the packet or the segment are encrypted.

- Some vendors do not support address translation for multicast addresses (the Cisco IOS does, but that is beyond the scope of this book).

There are other limitations, but these three (especially the first) are the most common issues you will find when dealing with address translation.

Address Translation Configuration

The remainder of this chapter focuses on the setup of basic address translation on your router. Some of the issues of address translation and configuration solutions to these issues are left for the next chapter. As you will see in the rest of this chapter, you need to perform two basic steps, no matter what type of address-translation solution(s) you will implement:

- Define your address-translation policies.
- Define which interfaces are considered internal and external.

The following sections cover how to configure address translation for NAT, PAT, port address redirection, overlapping addresses, and basic load balancing.

Configuration of NAT

You can perform NAT translation either statically or dynamically:

- With a static NAT translation, you define a one-to-one mapping of inside local addresses to inside global addresses. Static inside NAT translation typically is done when you have an internal server with a private address, but you want to allow external users to access this service.

- With a dynamic NAT translation, you create a pool of inside global addresses that your internal devices will use when translating their inside local addresses. This typically is used for internal users accessing external resources, especially for connections that experience problems with PAT.

The following two sections discuss how to configure these two types of NAT.

Static NAT

With static NAT, you need to perform two tasks:

Step 1   Define your static translations.

Step 2   Specify which interfaces are internal and external.

To define your static translations, use the **ip nat inside source static** command:

```
Router(config)# ip nat inside source static inside_local_IP_address
   inside_global_IP_address
```

This command creates the static mappings of inside local to inside global addresses. The first IP address that you list is the one that the Cisco IOS examines in the source of the IP packet. If it is found, the Cisco IOS translates the source address to the second address that you listed in this command.

Another form of this command enables you to map one network to another with the following syntax:

```
Router(config)# ip nat inside source static network
   inside_local_IP_network_number inside_global_IP_network_number subnet_mask
```

This command is more user friendly because you do not have to map individual IP addresses: You can map one network to another, address for address. For example, if you have a local network of 192.168.1.0/24 and a global network of 192.1.1.0/24, each host address in the local network is mapped to the corresponding host address in the global network. For example, 192.168.1.1 maps to 192.1.1.1, and 192.168.1.2 maps to 192.1.1.2. For the subnet mask value, you can enter it either in dotted decimal, as in 255.255.255.0, or by number of bits, as in /24.

After you have created your address-translation entries, you must specify what interfaces are considered to be internal (inside) and which are considered external (outside). This is done with the **ip nat {inside | outside}** Interface command:

```
Router(config)# interface type [slot_#/]port_#
Router(config-if)# ip nat {inside | outside}
```

NOTE   By specifying which interfaces are inside and which are outside, you are influencing how address translation is performed by the router.

To help illustrate the use of this command, take a look at the network shown in Figure 11-6. In this example, I want to make two servers inside the network available to the outside world.

Figure 11-6 *Static NAT Example*

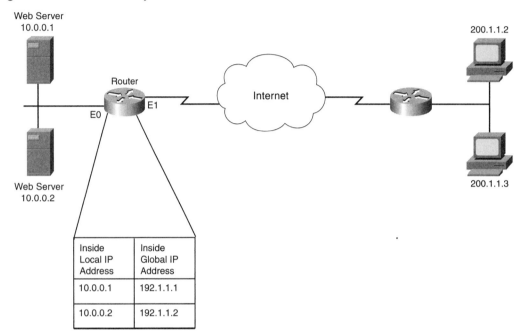

The basic static NAT configuration for this router is displayed in Example 11-1.

Example 11-1 *Basic Example Using Static Inside NAT*

```
Router(config)# ip nat inside source static 10.0.0.1 192.1.1.1
Router(config)# ip nat inside source static 10.0.0.2 192.1.1.2
Router(config)# interface ethernet0
Router(config-if)# ip nat inside
Router(config-if)# exit
Router(config)# interface ethernet1
Router(config-if)# ip nat outside
```

As you can see, 10.0.0.1 is assigned an inside global IP address of 192.1.1.1, and 10.0.0.2 is assigned 192.1.1.2. You can create as many static mappings as you need.

For static NAT, I want to emphasize three important points:

- Make sure that your external ACL, applied inbound, allows traffic to the destination inside global IP addresses, not the inside local addresses. It is important to point out that the router processes the ACL first and then performs the translation.

- Make sure that your DNS server sends the inside global address to requesting outside users.

- If an address is not specified in any translation rule, the Cisco IOS forwards it normally. If you want to prevent packets from entering or leaving your network, use an ACL to filter them.

Dynamic NAT

Configuration of dynamic NAT requires one more step than static NAT. With dynamic NAT, you need to perform the following steps:

Step 1 Define which internal (inside local) addresses are to be translated.

Step 2 Define a pool that specifies the inside global addresses that will be assigned to the inside local addresses.

Step 3 Specify which interfaces are internal and external.

To accomplish Step 1, use the following command:

```
Router(config)# ip nat inside source list standard_IP_access_list_#_or_name
   pool NAT_pool_name
```

The **list** parameter points to a standard IP ACL that specifies which inside local addresses should be translated; any addresses listed with a **permit** statement in the ACL will be translated. The **pool** parameter specifies the global address pool that should be used when performing the translation. This parameter actually points to the **ip nat pool** command that has the list of inside global IP addresses in the pool. With this parameter, specify the name of the NAT pool.

To accomplish Step 2, use the following command:

```
Router(config)# ip nat pool NAT_pool_name beginning_inside_global_IP_address
   ending_inside_global_IP_address {netmask subnet_mask_of_addresses |
   prefix-length #_of_bits}
```

The **ip nat pool** command specifies the list of inside global IP addresses that will be assigned to packets with inside local addresses. You need to name the pool, which must match the name in the **ip nat inside source list** command. Following this, specify the beginning and ending global IP addresses in the pool. Finally, you need to specify the subnet mask associated with the global address pool. This can be done as a dotted-decimal mask (**netmask**) or the number of bits in the mask (**prefix-length**).

NOTE If you do not have enough global addresses in your address pool, the Cisco IOS will not be capable of performing any translations. In other words, the Cisco IOS will not switch dynamically from NAT to PAT based on availability of addresses in this pool. Therefore, you should consider carefully how many addresses you need. You also can manipulate timeouts for addresses so that idle address usage is freed up quicker and made available to other devices that need translation. This is discussed toward the end of this chapter in the section "Setting Timeout Limits."

To accomplish Step 3, use the **ip nat {inside | outside}** command to associate which interface(s) are internal and which are external. This command was discussed previously in the "Static NAT" section.

Now look at a simple example that illustrates the use of dynamic NAT, using the network shown previously in Figure 11-6. As you recall from this example, 10.0.0.1 and 10.0.0.2 were assigned through static NAT, so these are excluded in this configuration. Example 11-2 shows the configuration for the dynamic NAT example.

Example 11-2 *Basic Example Using Dynamic Inside NAT*

```
Router(config)# ip nat inside source list dynamic-nat-addresses    (1)
   pool dynamic-nat-pool
Router(config)# ip access-list standard dynamic-nat-addresses      (2)
Router(config-std-nacl)# deny 10.0.0.1
Router(config-std-nacl)# deny 10.0.0.2
Router(config-std-nacl)# permit 10.0.0.0 0.255.255.255
Router(config-std-nacl)# exit
Router(config)# ip nat pool dynamic-nat-pool 192.1.1.20            (3)
   192.1.1.254 netmask 255.255.255.0
Router(config)# interface ethernet0
Router(config-if)# ip nat inside
Router(config-if)# exit
Router(config)# interface ethernet1
Router(config-if)# ip nat outside
```

Refer to the numbers on the right side of Example 11-2 for this explanation. In Example 11-2, Statement 1 associates the inside local addresses (in standard ACL *dynamic-nat-addresses*) that will be translated to inside global addresses (**pool** *dynamic-nat-pool*). Statement 2 defines the inside local addresses that will be translated. Notice that I am excluding 10.0.0.1 and 10.0.0.2 because these are the two servers that have static translations from the last section; otherwise, any other network 10.0.0.0/8 address will be translated. Statement 3 defines the inside global addresses that local addresses will be translated to. The addresses range from 192.1.1.20 to 192.1.1.254. At the bottom of the code listing is the definition of which interfaces are internal and external.

NOTE   Notice in Example 11-2 that the ACL has an implicit deny at the end, affecting which addresses are translated. Basically, any address in 10.0.0.0/8 is translated, except for 10.0.0.1 and 10.0.0.2; all other addresses are not translated. Cisco recommends that you not have an explicit permit any to allow all addresses to be translated because this can cause connectivity problems in a small number of cases and also creates a security risk.

Also, the two explicit deny statements were not necessary, but I put them there for explanatory purposes. If you have configured both static and dynamic address translation, the Cisco IOS always uses the static configuration before using the dynamic ones.

Configuration of PAT

The configuration of PAT is very similar to the configuration of dynamic NAT. As with dynamic NAT, you perform three configuration steps:

Step 1   Define which internal (inside local) addresses are to be translated.

Step 2   Define a pool that specifies the inside global addresses that will be assigned to the inside local addresses.

Step 3   Specify which interfaces are internal and external.

To accomplish Step 1, use the following command:

```
Router(config)# ip nat inside source list standard_IP_access_list_#_or_name
    pool NAT_pool_name overload
```

This is the same command used with dynamic NAT; the main difference is the use of the **overload** parameter.

If your router has a connection to an ISP, your ISP dynamically is assigning an IP address to your router, and this is the only public address that your ISP is assigning to you, you can use the following command:

```
Router(config)# ip nat inside source list standard_IP_access_list_#_or_name
    interface interface_name overload
```

In this example, the Cisco IOS uses whatever IP address is assigned to your router's external interface to perform PAT. If you use this second option, you do not need to configure an address pool in Step 2, and you can go directly to Step 3.

CAUTION   You should reference the interface name with PAT even if the ISP has assigned you only one address and you have hard-coded this address on your router's external interface. Issues can arise in the Cisco IOS if you reference the IP address on the interface instead of referencing the interface name itself.

To accomplish Step 2, use the following command:

```
Router(config)# ip nat pool NAT_pool_name beginning_inside_global_IP_address
    ending_inside_global_IP_address {netmask subnet_mask_of_addresses | prefix-length
    #_of_bits}
```

The **ip nat pool** command specifies the list of inside global IP addresses that will be assigned to packets with inside local addresses. You need to name of the pool, which must match the name in the **ip nat inside source list** command. Following this, specify the beginning and ending global IP addresses in the pool. For PAT, if you are putting only one IP address in the pool, specify it as both the beginning and ending address. Finally, you need to specify the subnet mask associated with the global address pool.

To accomplish Step 3, use the **ip nat** {**inside** | **outside**} command to associate which interfaces are internal and which are external. This command was discussed previously in the "Static NAT" section.

Now look at a simple example that illustrates the use of dynamic NAT, using use the network shown previously in Figure 11-6. As you recall from this example, 10.0.0.1 and 10.0.0.2 were assigned through static NAT, so they are excluded in this configuration. Example 11-3 shows the configuration for PAT.

Example 11-3 *Basic PAT Configuration*

```
Router(config)# ip nat inside source list dynamic-pat-addresses      (1)
   pool dynamic-pat-pool overload
Router(config)# ip access-list standard dynamic-pat-addresses
Router(config-std-nacl)# permit 10.0.0.0 0.255.255.255
Router(config-std-nacl)# exit
Router(config)# ip nat pool dynamic-pat-pool 192.1.1.19             (2)
   192.1.1.19 netmask 255.255.255.0
Router(config)# interface ethernet0
Router(config-if)# ip nat inside
Router(config-if)# exit
Router(config)# interface ethernet1
Router(config-if)# ip nat outside
```

Refer to the numbers on the right side of Example 11-3 for this explanation. In Example 11-3, Statement 1 associates the inside local addresses (in standard ACL *dynamic-pat-addresses*) that will be translated to inside global addresses (**pool** *dynamic-pat-pool*). Notice the **overload** statement, which indicates that PAT is used. Statement 2 defines the inside global addresses that local addresses will be translated to. In this example, I specified the same address as the beginning and ending address. However, you can specify multiple addresses; in this instance, the **overload** parameter in Statement 1 indicates that PAT is performed. At the bottom of the code listing is the definition of which interfaces are internal and external.

If your ISP assigned you only a single public IP address and did this through DHCP to assign this address to your external interface, the configuration in Example 11-3 would be changed to the configuration in Example 11-4.

Example 11-4 *Basic PAT Configuration Using an Interface*

```
Router(config)# ip nat inside source list dynamic-pat-addresses      (1)
   interface ethernet1 overload
Router(config)# ip access-list standard dynamic-pat-addresses
Router(config-std-nacl)# permit 10.0.0.0 0.255.255.255
Router(config-std-nacl)# exit
Router(config)# interface ethernet0
Router(config-if)# ip nat inside
Router(config-if)# exit
Router(config)# interface ethernet1
Router(config-if)# ip address dhcp                                  (2)
Router(config-if)# ip nat outside
```

Refer to the numbers on the right side of Example 11-4 for this explanation. First, notice in Statement 1 that I reference interface ethernet1 as the address to use for PAT. Second, notice that a global address pool is not needed in this example because the IP address assigned to ethernet1 will be used. Third, Statement 2 specifies that DHCP is used to assign an address to ethernet1; this also can be done through PPP for DSL connections that use PPPoE.

Configuration of Port Address Redirection

In port address redirection (PAR), an address-translation device redirects the connection for traffic directed to one device or port, to a different device or port. A new PAR enhancement, called NAT Default Inside Server, was introduced in Cisco IOS 12.2(13)T. NAT Default Inside Server is an augmentation to Port Static NAT that allows the router to send any requests that it receives from an external host on an unknown port to a default inside server. This was meant to help with people who connected an X-box and other unintelligent networking devices out through a Cisco IOS address-translation device so that the other users on the Internet could connect back to the internal device using a wide range of dynamic ports.

CAUTION   Use NAT Default Inside Server only when you do not know what port or ports need to be forwarded to an internal device. By using this feature, you allow all ports that are not statically redirected to be sent to the default server. Whenever possible, you want to limit your exposure by configuring static translations for PAR instead of using the default inside server option.

PAR is used when your ISP assigns you one public IP address that you have to configure on your perimeter router's external interface, but you want outside users to access services inside your network. In this situation, outside users direct traffic to your router's public address. PAR allows the Cisco IOS to change the addressing information in the packet header to redirect this traffic to an internal device, such as a web or e-mail server.

To set up PAR, use one of the following two commands:

```
Router(config)# ip nat inside source static local_IP_address
   interface external_interface
Router(config)# ip nat inside source static {tcp | udp}
   local_IP_address local_port_# interface external_interface global_port_#
```

With the first command, any traffic sent to the interface specified in the **ip nat inside source static** command is redirected to the inside local IP address. This is useful if all your public services are located on one server. If your public services are spread across multiple servers, you need to use the second command. If you are implementing NAT Default Inside Server, omit the second command in the configuration: You obviously do not know the port number or numbers that external users will use. When you have completed your PAR configuration, you also must specify the location of your interfaces with the **ip nat {inside | outside}** commands.

Take a look at an example in which PAR is useful. In the network in Figure 11-7, this company wants external users to access two internal servers: www (port 80 and 8080) and Telnet (port 23).

Figure 11-7 *PAR Example*

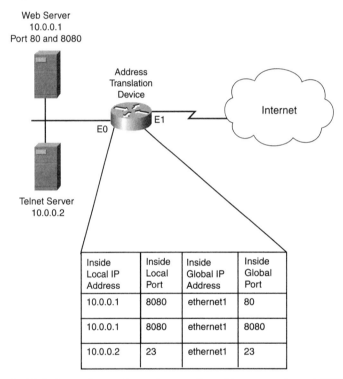

Web Server
10.0.0.1
Port 80 and 8080

Address Translation Device

Internet

Telnet Server
10.0.0.2

Inside Local IP Address	Inside Local Port	Inside Global IP Address	Inside Global Port
10.0.0.1	8080	ethernet1	80
10.0.0.1	8080	ethernet1	8080
10.0.0.2	23	ethernet1	23

Example 11-5 shows the configuration to allow this access through PAR.

Example 11-5 *Simple PAR Configuration*

```
Router(config)# ip nat inside source static tcp 10.0.0.1 8080      (1)
   interface ethernet1 8080
Router(config)# ip nat inside source static tcp 10.0.0.1 8080      (2)
   interface ethernet1 80
Router(config)# ip nat inside source static tcp 10.0.0.2 23        (3)
   interface ethernet1 23
Router(config)# interface ethernet0
Router(config-if)# ip nat inside
Router(config-if)# exit
Router(config)# interface ethernet1
Router(config-if)# ip nat outside
```

Refer to the numbers on the right side of Example 11-5 for this explanation. In Example 11-5, the first three statements set up PAR. Statements 1 and 2 define redirection to the web server. Notice that the internal web server is running on port 8080. The global port numbers have the Cisco IOS look for inbound traffic to either port 80 or 8080, which causes the router to redirect it to 10.0.0.1. The third statement redirects Telnet traffic to 10.0.0.2. One interesting thing about all three of these commands is that they specify the external interface, ethernet1, as the global IP address. If traffic is sent to this address and it does not match the conditions of the three PAR statements, the router itself tries to process the traffic.

NOTE	As of this writing, Cisco has not included a feature that supports dynamic DNS. This feature is useful if your ISP dynamically is assigning your router or firewall with a single IP address, through either DHCP or PPP, but you want external users to access your internal resources to use this address. Some router/firewall products actually go out and update the DNS record information with the new IP address; the Cisco IOS does not support this feature yet, but Cisco has promised that this will be available soon.

Dealing with Overlapping Addresses

Overlapping addresses is a common problem with some networks. Typically, you must deal with overlapping addresses in three situations:

- You are merging two companies that have the same address space.

- A previous administrator addressed your network with someone else's public addresses.

- You are creating a VPN connection to an Extranet partner where either an overlapping address condition exists or one of the parties requires the use of address translation to conform to company security policies.

Of course the long-term solution to this problem is to readdress your network; however, to overcome connectivity problems in the short term, you can resort to address translation to solve your problem.

You can deploy two address-translation solutions for overlapping addresses: static and dynamic. In either solution, you need to perform translation in two directions:

- Inside to outside

- Outside to inside

Take a look at a quick example to illustrate the configuration complexity with overlapping addresses. In Figure 11-8, the network on the right (Company B) has been assigned network 200.1.1.0/24 by the IANA and is the rightful owner of this address space. The network on the left (Company A) also is using this address space. Apparently, before this network was connected to the Internet, a previous administrator randomly choose a Class C network and assigned this address space to all the internal devices. Now Company A wants to connect to the Internet, and its ISP has assigned it a Class C address space: 199.1.1.0/24. In this example, the Company A administrator does not have the time right now to change the addresses that manually were assigned to internal devices. Therefore, the current administrator decided to use address translation as a temporary solution.

Figure 11-8 *Overlapping Addresses and Cisco IOS Configuration*

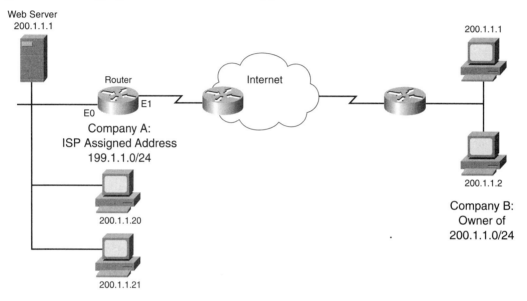

In this example, two translations must occur to solve the overlapping address problem:

- **Inside to outside**—The source addresses of the internal machines must be changed to 199.1.1.x when leaving the network.

- **Outside to inside**—On the off chance that the real owner of 200.1.1.x sends packets to Company A, these addresses must be changed to something else. One common solution is to change these addresses to the ones that the ISP assigned the company on the left. This creates confusion, so sometimes a company uses a private address space. The only issue here is that the internal network needs a route for this network number, which must point to the address-translation device.

The following two sections cover the use of static and dynamic configurations for dealing with overlapping addresses.

Static Translation

When you have overlapping addresses, static translations are used in two situations:

- You have servers on one or both sides that the remote side needs access to.

- You want to statically assign blocks of network addresses manually instead of dynamically, reducing the amount of configuration that needs to be done.

For inside-to-outside translation, use either of the following two commands:

```
Router(config)# ip nat inside source static inside_local_IP_address
  inside_global_IP_address
```

```
Router(config)# ip nat inside source static network inside_local_IP_network_number
  inside_global_IP_network_number subnet_mask
```

These two commands were discussed previously in the "Static NAT" section. For outside-to-inside translation, use either of the following two commands:

```
Router(config)# ip nat outside source static outside_global_IP_address
  inside_local_IP_address [add-route]
```

```
Router(config)# ip nat outside source static network outside_global_IP_network_number
  inside_local_IP_network_number subnet_mask [add-route]
```

As you can see from these two commands, the syntax is slightly different from that of the inside-to-outside configuration. The first address that you list is the address in the source IP address field in the IP packet header; this is what the remote network has placed in this field. The *inside_local_IP* address or network number is the address that this value will be changed to when it is transmitted from the outside interface to the inside interface. The optional **add-route** parameter adds a route for the translated network in the router's routing table.

Take a look at a quick example, based on Figure 11-8, to illustrate how to use static address translation to overcome an overlapping address problem. Example 11-6 shows the configuration for the router in Company A.

Example 11-6 *Basic Static Configuration That Solves Overlapping Addresses*

```
Router(config)# ip nat inside source static                    (1)
  network 200.1.1.0 199.1.1.0 /24
Router(config)# ip nat outside source static                   (2)
  network 200.1.1.0 199.1.1.0 /24
Router(config)# ip route 0.0.0.0 0.0.0.0 205.1.1.1
Router(config)# interface ethernet0
Router(config-if)# ip address 200.1.1.254 255.255.255.0
Router(config-if)# ip nat inside
Router(config-if)# exit
Router(config)# interface ethernet1
Router(config-if)# ip address 205.1.1.2 255.255.255.0
Router(config-if)# ip nat outside
```

Refer to the numbers on the right side of Example 11-6 for this explanation. In the configuration in Example 11-6, Statement 1 converts the inside addresses from 200.1.1.0/24 to 199.1.1.0/24. Statement 2 converts outside addresses from 200.1.1.0/24 to 199.1.1.0/24.

One of the interesting things about this configuration is that, even though it appears confusing, it actually tricks the two networks regarding where the IP addresses—200.1.1.0/24 and 199.1.1.0/24—really are located:

- Even though 199.1.1.0/24 is really Company A, from Company A's perspective, it looks like this network is located at Company B.

- Even though 200.1.1.0/24 is really Company B, these addresses are translated to 199.1.1.0/24 as they enter Company A, making it appear that 199.1.1.0/24 is Company B's addresses.

TIP   As you can see from this example, the overlapping address configuration is confusing. Therefore, I highly recommend that you migrate as quickly as possible from using address translation to solving your connectivity problems with overlapping addresses, to readdressing either one or both networks. Using address translation to solve the problem introduces delay in traffic streams and makes it much more difficult to troubleshoot connectivity problems.

Dynamic Translation

Besides using static address translation to solve overlapping addresses, you can use dynamic address translation. As with static translation, you need to configure translation in both directions.

For inside-to-outside translation, use the configuration discussed in the "Dynamic NAT" section discussed previously. For outside-to-inside translation, use the following configuration syntax:

```
Router(config)# ip nat pool pool_name starting_global_IP_address ending_IP_address
  {netmask subnet_mask_of_addresses | prefix-length #_of_bits}
Router(config)# access-list ACL_# permit source_IP_address [wildcard_mask]
Router(config)# ip nat outside source list ACL_# pool pool_name
```

The **ip nat pool** command creates a pool of addresses that external addresses (**outside**) will be translated to. The **access-list** command specifies which external addresses will be translated; this can be a standard numbered or named ACL. The third command links the ACL and the NAT pool name—in other words, it links the outside addresses (**ip nat outside source list**) that will be translated to addresses specified in the global pool (**ip nat pool**).

Take a look at a quick example, based on Figure 11-8, to illustrate how to use dynamic address translation to overcome an overlapping address problem. Example 11-7 shows the configuration for the router in Company A.

Example 11-7 *Basic Dynamic Configuration That Solves Overlapping Addresses*

```
Router(config)# access-list 1 permit 200.1.1.0 0.0.0.255        (1)
Router(config)# ip nat pool inside-pool 199.1.1.1 199.1.1.127   (2)
  netmask 255.255.255.0
Router(config)# ip nat inside source list 1 pool inside-pool    (3)
Router(config)# ip nat pool outside-pool 199.1.1.128 199.1.1.254 (4)
  netmask 255.255.255.0
Router(config)# ip nat outside source list 1 pool outside-pool  (5)
Router(config)# ip route 0.0.0.0 0.0.0.0 205.1.1.1
Router(config)# interface ethernet0
Router(config-if)# ip address 200.1.1.254 255.255.255.0
Router(config-if)# ip nat inside
```

Example 11-7 *Basic Dynamic Configuration That Solves Overlapping Addresses (Continued)*

```
Router(config-if)# exit
Router(config)# interface ethernet1
Router(config-if)# ip address 205.1.1.2 255.255.255.0
Router(config-if)# ip nat outside
```

Refer to the numbers on the right side of Example 11-7 for the following explanation of the configuration:

1 This statement is used by both inside-to-outside and outside-to-inside translations; it defines the overlapping address space, 200.1.1.0/24

2 This statement defines the address pool that inside addresses (from Company A) will be translated to.

3 This statement associates the inside-to-outside translation: using ACL 1 and **pool** *inside-pool*. In this example internal addresses with any address of 200.1.1.0/24 will be translated to 199.1.1.1–199.1.1.127.

4 This statement defines outside-to-inside translation, specifying the pool of addresses that will be used to translate the Company B's addresses.

5 This statement binds the outside-to-inside translation process: Any source addresses found in ACL 1, as they are entering Company A's network, will be translated to something between 199.1.1.128 and 199.1.1.254.

Overlapping Addresses

The first time I dealt with overlapping addresses, I was nearly pulling out my hair trying to configure a router to perform this successfully. When I looked at the examples from the Ciscos web site, I was confused about why the configurations used the same network number for the address translation for internal and external access. In this instance, the network was using an already assigned public address space (192.x.x.x), and this company's ISP assigned it a new address space (202.x.x.x). With the configuration of address translation, I used 202.x.x.x as the address pool for both directions of translation. It took me a couple of days to straighten out all the problems with this configuration. Based on this experience, I began to readdress the network and update the DNS tables. When everything was set up correctly, I removed the overlapping address configuration. I learned that using address translation to solve overlapping addresses is not a fun and exciting solution—it is a tedious and hair-pulling one.

Configuration of Traffic Distribution

Traffic distribution redirects connection requests to different internal servers for traffic destined to one IP address, thus providing a load-balancing feature. The configuration of traffic distribution is similar to the configuration of dynamic NAT and PAT. With the configuration of traffic distribution, you need to perform three tasks:

Step 1   Create an address pool that has the list of internal servers that will be used for load balancing.

Step 2   Define what address or addresses external devices are using to access the internal resources, and associate this with the pool in Step 1.

Step 3   Specify which interfaces are on the inside and outside.

To accomplish Step 1, use the following command:

```
Router(config)# ip nat pool pool_name beginning_inside_local_IP_address
   ending_inside_local_IP_address {netmask subnet_mask_of_addresses | prefix-length
   #_of_bits} type rotary
```

As you can see from this command, this is similar to configuring NAT or PAT: The main difference is the use of the **type rotary** parameter. This parameter tells the Cisco IOS that it should round-robin the assignment of internal addresses specified in the beginning and ending inside local IP addresses in this command.

To accomplish Step 2, use the following configuration:

```
Router(config)# access-list ACL_# permit IP_address of_internal_server
Router(config)# ip nat inside destination list
   standard_IP_access_list_number_or_name pool pool_name
```

The standard ACL can be either named or numbered. The ACL references the destination IP address (or addresses) that external users are using to access your internal resource: This is the address that your DNS server is sending in DNS replies to the external users. Figure 11-9 shows a simple example, using a virtual IP address (199.1.1.1) to associate with the internal web servers (10.0.0.10 and 10.0.0.11). Using a virtual IP address is a common practice. You need to use this virtual address in your DNS server's resolution record.

Figure 11-9 *Traffic Distribution Example*

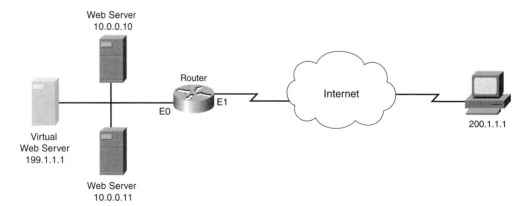

The **ip nat inside destination list** command binds together the ACL and pool name: It tells the Cisco IOS that when traffic is sent to the address or addresses listed in the standard ACL, these destination addresses should be changed to those in the NAT pool, using a round-robin scheme.

Step 3, specifies which of your interfaces are internal and external. This is done with the **ip nat inside** and **ip nat outside** interface commands.

Using Figure 11-9, take a look at an example of configuring traffic distribution. In Example 11-8, 199.1.1.1 is the virtual server IP address; this is the IP address that your DNS server is sending to external users.

Example 11-8 *Basic Traffic Distribution Configuration*

```
Router(config)# ip nat pool inside-hosts 10.0.0.10 10.0.0.11
  prefix-length 24 type rotary
Router(config)# access-list 1 permit 199.1.1.1
Router(config)# ip nat inside destination list 1 pool inside-hosts
Router(config)# interface ethernet0
Router(config-if)# ip nat inside
Router(config-if)# exit
Router(config)# interface ethernet1
Router(config-if)# ip nat outside
```

In Example 11-8, the **ip nat pool** command specifies the two internal servers that will be handling traffic directed to 192.1.1.1. Notice that the **type rotary** parameter specifies that traffic distribution is used. The **access-list** statement specifies the address that external users are using when trying to access the internal web servers: 192.1.1.1. The **ip nat inside destination** command binds together the NAT pool and ACL: When outside users send traffic to 192.1.1.1, it is translated to the addresses in the NAT pool. In this example, the first external connection request will be redirected to 10.0.0.1, the second to 10.0.0.2, the third to 10.0.0.1, and so on. Below this, the location of NAT is specified on the interfaces with the **ip nat {inside | outside}** interface command.

CAUTION   When using this method of traffic distribution with the Cisco IOS, you should be forewarned that the Cisco IOS cannot detect whether one of the servers in the NAT pool has failed, nor can it detect the load on the respective servers. For example, if 10.0.0.10 failed in Figure 11-9, the Cisco IOS still would use this address in load balancing. Therefore, I recommend using this solution only in a very simple setup. Chapter 12 introduces a better solution to this problem.

Configuration of Translation Limits

When the Cisco IOS performs address translation, it stores its translation information in a translation table. These records are kept for a period of time before they are removed. This allows older entries to be aged out, to allow new connections. This is done primarily to age out older idle connections. You can specify two types of limits: the total number of connections and the timeout for connections. The following two sections discuss their configuration.

Setting Connection Limits

By default, there is no preconfigured limit to the number of entries that the Cisco IOS will store in its address translation table. You can specify a limit with the following command:

```
Router(config)# ip nat translation max-entries #_of_entries
```

The number of entries can range from 1 to 2,147,483,647. If you have hard-coded a limit and want to remove the limit (set it back to the factory default), just preface the previous command with the **no** parameter. Unless you are having memory issues on your router, you probably will leave this setting alone.

Setting Timeout Limits

Dynamic address-translation entries time out after their idle period expires. The Cisco IOS actually uses many different timeouts, based on the connection type, to time out idle connections. Here is the command to configure them:

```
Router(config)# ip nat translation timeout_parameter {seconds | never}
```

The timeout parameters, including their default timeout values, are listed in Table 11-4. The timeout value is specified either in a numerical seconds value or in the **never** parameter; the **never** parameter keeps an entry in the translation table until the router is rebooted.

Table 11-4   *Address Translation Types*

Timeout Parameter	Default Timeout (seconds)	Explanation
timeout	86,400	This timeout value applies to all dynamic translations except for address overload translations.
tcp-timeout	86,400	This timeout value applies to all TCP connections.
finrst-timeout	60	This timeout applies to FIN and RST packets, which are used to terminate a TCP connection. When this is reached, the translation entry is removed from the translation table.
syn-timeout	60	This timeout applies to half-open TCP connections (connections that go through the three-way handshake initiation). If a connection is not completed in this time frame, the translation entry is removed from the translation table.
udp-timeout	300	This timeout applies to all UDP idle connections, except for DNS UDP connections.

Table 11-4 *Address Translation Types (Continued)*

Timeout Parameter	Default Timeout (seconds)	Explanation
dns-timeout	60	This timeout applies to all DNS UDP connections.
port-timeout tcp | udp *port_#*	TCP or UDP default	With this parameter, you can specify a specific timeout for a TCP or UDP port number. If it is not configured, the default TCP or UDP timeout is used.
icmp-timeout	60	This timeout applies to all ICMP connections.
pptp-timeout	86,400	This timeout applies to all NAT Point-to-Point Tunneling Protocol (PPTP) connections.

Verifying and Troubleshooting Address Translation

When you have configured address translation on your router, you can use various **show**, **clear**, and **debug** commands to assist you in verifying and troubleshooting address translation. The following three sections cover these commands.

show Commands

To view your address-translation table, which displays static and dynamic entries, use the **show ip nat translations** command:

```
Router# show ip nat translations [esp] [icmp] [pptp] [tcp] [udp]
   [verbose] [vrf vrf_name]
```

Without any options to the **show ip nat translations** command, all entries in the table are displayed. Table 11-5 explains the options for this command.

Table 11-5   **show ip nat translations** *Parameters*

Parameter	Explanation
esp	Displays only the Encapsulation Security Payload (ESP) entries, which are used in IPSec
icmp	Displays only the ICMP entries
pptp	Displays only the PPTP entries
tcp	Displays only the TCP entries
udp	Displays only the UDP entries
verbose	Displays detailed information about each entry, including how long ago the entry was created in the table and how long it has been in use
vrf	Displays only VPN routing and forwarding (VRF) information

Take a look at a few examples of the use of this command. Example 11-9 shows an example of using the **show ip nat translations** command.

Example 11-9 *Using the* **show ip nat translations** *Command*

```
Router# show ip nat translations
Pro   Inside global   Inside local   Outside local  Outside global
---   199.1.1.1       10.0.0.1       ---            ---
---   199.1.1.1       10.0.0.2       ---            ---
```

Notice that Example 11-9 does not contain any port numbers, which shows that the Cisco IOS is performing NAT. If the Cisco IOS was performing PAT, the display would look like Example 11-10.

Example 11-10 *Using the* **show ip nat translations** *Command to Display PAT Connections*

```
Router# show ip nat translations
Pro   Inside global       Inside local      Outside local    Outside global
tcp   199.1.1.1:33348     10.0.0.1:33348    200.1.1.1:23     200.1.1.1:23
tcp   199.1.1.1:33348     10.0.0.2:33349    200.1.1.1:23     200.1.1.1:23
```

Example 11-11 shows sample output when you use the **verbose** parameter.

Example 11-11 *Using the* **verbose** *Parameter in the* **show ip nat translations** *Command*

```
Router# show ip nat translations verbose
Pro   Inside global     Inside local     Outside local    Outside global
tcp   199.1.1.1:2688    10.0.0.20:2688   200.1.1.1:23     200.1.1.1:23
      create 00:00:16, use 00:00:14, left 23:59:45, Map-Id(In): 1, flags:
extended, use_count: 0, entry-id: 3, lc_entries: 0
```

In Example 11-11, only one PAT entry is listed—from an internal device (10.0.0.20 → 199.1.1.1), which created a Telnet to 200.1.1.1. This entry was created 16 seconds ago and has been in use for 14 seconds.

To view statistics regarding the use of address translation, use the following command:

```
Router# show ip nat statistics
```

Example 11-12 shows the output of this command.

Example 11-12 *Using the* **show ip nat statistics** *Command*

```
Router# show ip nat statistics
Total active translations: 1 (0 static, 1 dynamic; 1 extended)   (1)
Outside interfaces:                                              (2)
  Ethernet1
Inside interfaces:
  Ethernet0
Hits: 121  Misses: 4                                            (3)
Expired translations: 3                                         (4)
Dynamic mappings:                                              (5)
-- Inside Source
```

Example 11-12 *Using the* **show ip nat statistics** *Command (Continued)*

```
[Id: 1] access-list 1 pool dynamic-nat-pool refcount 1
 pool dynamic-nat-pool: netmask 255.255.255.0
   start 192.1.1.1 end 192.1.1.1
   type generic, total addresses 1, allocated 1 (100%), misses 0
```

Refer to the numbers on the right side of Example 11-12 for the following explanation of the output. In Example 11-12, Statement 1 shows the total number of active translations. In this example, there are no static translations, one dynamic translation, and one extended translation. An extended translation is one that uses port numbers, as PAT does.

Statement 2 shows which interfaces are associated with the inside and outside of the network. In Statement 3, "Hits," refers to the number of times the Cisco IOS looked in the address-translation table and found a matching entry; "Misses" refers to the number of times that the Cisco IOS did not find a matching entry in the translation table and had to create one. Statement 4 refers to the number of entries that were removed from the translation table because they expired (the corresponding idle timer elapsed).

Statement 5 refers to the address-translation policies that are configured on the router. The **access-list 1 pool dynamic-nat-pool** reference indicates that there has been one match on the ACL, resulting in an address translation. Below this is the address pool used. In this instance, only a single address is listed: 192.1.1.1. The "allocated" reference indicates that one address is being used from the pool and that no misses occur when looking up a reference in the address translation table.

clear Commands

You can remove a dynamically learned entry from the address-translation table using the **clear ip nat translation** command:

```
Router# clear ip nat translation *
Router# clear ip nat translation inside | outside
  global_IP_address local_IP_address
Router# clear ip nat translation protocol inside | outside
  global_IP_address global_port
  local_IP_address local_port
```

The first command removes all dynamic entries from the address-translation table. The second removes either inside or outside entries with the matching global and local address. The third command enables you to remove a specific entry, based on the protocol and port number.

NOTE   The **clear** command cannot remove static entries from the address-translation table. To remove a static entry, you need to preface the respective static NAT configuration mode command with the **no** parameter.

TIP

Any time you make changes in your address-translation policies, I highly recommend that you clear the address-translation table on your router. This forces the router to use the new policies immediately. Actually, I recommend that you clear the address-translation table when you make changes to any policy on the router, including address translation, ACL, CBAC, and other features that implement policies. If you have worked on a Cisco PIX before, you should be familiar with this task.

debug ip nat Command

For troubleshooting, the Cisco IOS supports a **debug** command to examine low-level details. Here is the syntax of this command:

```
Router# debug ip nat [standard_ACL_#] [detailed] [h323] [ipsec]
    [port] [pptp] [route] [sip] [skinny] [vrf]
```

You can qualify the **debug ip nat** command by giving the command a parameter, which then restricts the amount of debug output that the Cisco IOS displays.

Example 11-13 shows the use of this command.

Example 11-13 *Using the* **debug ip nat detailed** *Command*

```
Router# debug ip nat detailed
IP NAT detailed debugging is on
Sep 17 16:30:04.438: NAT*: i: icmp (10.0.0.21, 512) ->          (1)
    (200.1.1.1, 512) [25201]
Sep 17 16:30:04.438: NAT*: s=10.0.0.21->192.1.1.1,             (2)
    d=192.168.2.2 [25201]
Sep 17 16:30:04.442: NAT*: o: icmp (200.1.1.1, 512) ->          (3)
    (192.1.1.1, 512) [25201]
Sep 17 16:30:04.442: NAT*: s=200.1.1.1, d=192.1.1.1->           (4)
    10.0.0.21 [25201]
```

Refer to the numbers on the right side of Example 11-13 for the following explanation of the output. In Statement 1 of this example, an ICMP packet (i) from 10.0.0.21 is being sent to 200.1.1.1 (the router notices that address translation must be performed on this connection, which can be seen based on the NAT* indication). In Statement 2, the Cisco IOS translates the source address from 10.0.0.21 to 192.1.1.1. In Statement 3, an ICMP response is received from the destination (200.1.1.1), and the router notices that it must perform address translation on this packet. Statement 4 shows the address translation occurring, changing the destination address of 192.1.1.1 to 10.0.0.21.

TIP

I cannot begin to stress how useful the **debug ip nat** command is. I have used it numerous times to troubleshoot address translation issues, especially ones with complex filtering configurations. However, this command is CPU intensive and should be disabled immediately after you have found and fixed your problem.

NAT and CBAC Example

Now that you have a basic understanding of NAT, let us talk about how you would use CBAC—or, for that matter, any type of filtering on a router that also has NAT configured on it. In Figure 11-10, the network is using a private address space (192.168.1.0/24), and the ISP has assigned it a Class C public address space: 192.1.1.0/24. However, one restriction of the use of this address space is that two of these addresses must be used for the perimeter router's Ethernet1 connection to the ISP router (192.1.1.1 and 192.1.1.2). Also, the internal network has three services that it wants to allow external users to access: a DNS server, a web server, and an e-mail server.

Figure 11-10 *NAT, CBAC, and Filtering Example*

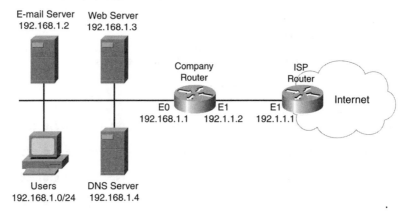

NOTE   To simplify matters, assume that the DNS server is using split DNS. With split DNS, the DNS server has two (or more) sets of resolution entries. Based on the source of the DNS query, the DNS server sends back a specific resolution. In this example, when internal devices request resolution for internal services, the DNS server sends back the appropriate private address (192.168.1.0/24) in the reply. However, when external devices request resolution for internal services, the DNS server sends back the corresponding public address for the service (the one configured through static NAT on the router). This is a common approach to dealing with the use of public and private addresses along with address translation.

In this example, assume that all unnecessary services have been disabled (this was covered in Chapter 4, "Disabling Unnecessary Services"). I use static NAT for the internal services and dynamic NAT for the internal users. Example 11-14 focuses primarily on the configuration for ACL filtering, CBAC, and NAT on the company router.

Example 11-14 *Using ACLs, CBAC, and NAT on a Perimeter Router*

```
Router(config)# ip route 0.0.0.0 0.0.0.0 192.1.1.1
Router(config)#
Router(config)# ip inspect name allow-back-in ftp               (1)
Router(config)# ip inspect name allow-back-in http
Router(config)# ip inspect name allow-back-in realaudio
Router(config)# ip inspect name allow-back-in smtp
Router(config)# ip inspect name allow-back-in tcp
Router(config)# ip inspect name allow-back-in udp timeout 20
Router(config)# ip inspect name allow-back-in vdolive
Router(config)#
Router(config)# ip nat inside source static 192.168.1.2 192.1.1.12 (2)
Router(config)# ip nat inside source static 192.168.1.3 192.1.1.13
Router(config)# ip nat inside source static 192.168.1.4 192.1.1.14
Router(config)#
Router(config)# ip nat pool inside-nat 192.1.1.20 192.1.1.254    (3)
  netmask 255.255.255.0
Router(config)# ip nat inside source list 1 pool inside-nat
Router(config)# access-list 1 permit 192.168.1.0 0.0.0.255
Router(config)#
Router(config)# access-list 100 deny                            (4)
Router(config)# ! <--list of boguns and others
  should be placed here-->
Router(config)# access-list 100 permit icmp any 192.1.1.0 0.0.0.255
  unreachable
Router(config)# access-list 100 permit icmp any 192.1.1.0 0.0.0.255
  echo-reply
Router(config)# access-list 100 permit icmp any 192.1.1.0 0.0.0.255
  packet-too-big
Router(config)# access-list 100 permit icmp any 192.1.1.0 0.0.0.255
  time-exceeded
Router(config)# access-list 100 permit icmp any 192.1.1.0 0.0.0.255
  administratively-prohibited
Router(config)# access-list 100 permit tcp any host 192.1.1.12 eq 25
Router(config)# access-list 100 permit tcp any host 192.1.1.13 eq 80
Router(config)# access-list 100 permit udp any host 192.1.1.14 eq 53
Router(config)# access-list 100 deny ip any any
Router(config)#
Router(config)# interface Ethernet0
Router(config-if)# ip address 192.168.1.1 255.255.255.0
Router(config-if)# ip nat inside
Router(config-if)# exit
Router(config)# interface Ethernet1
Router(config-if)# ip address 192.1.1.2 255.255.255.0
Router(config)# ip access-group 100 in
Router(config)# ip nat outside
Router(config)# ip inspect allow-back-in out                    (5)
```

Refer to the numbers on the right side of Example 11-14 for the following explanation of the configuration. In this example, Statement 1 sets up the inspection for CBAC and then is activated outbound on the external interface, ethernet1, in Statement 5. In Statement 2, three static NAT translations are set up for the e-mail, web, and DNS servers. In Statement 3, these three commands set up dynamic NAT for the inside users. Statement 4 filters ingress traffic from the Internet—I put in a placeholder (a comment with the !) for filtering bogun, private IP, and other addresses. Refer to Chapter 7, "Basic Access Lists," for information on configuring these ACL entries. I then allow certain ICMP messages and traffic to the three internal servers. Everything else is denied. Note that the global addresses are used in the ACL statements, not the addresses that these servers actually have assigned on them. Also, notice that I have enabled NAT on the inside (ethernet0) and outside (ethernet1) interfaces.

As you can see from this example, setting up NAT with other Cisco IOS features is not that difficult. However, one important point to make about this example is that, when you set up filters, you always should use the addresses that show up in the packet headers. For example, notice that in the ingress filter on ethernet1, I specified the destination addresses as the public addresses; this is because the Cisco IOS processes the ACL before it performs NAT:

- For the outside interface, filter on the global addresses.
- For the inside interface, filter on the local addresses.

Also notice that you can use unused addresses off a router's interface for your address translation. In this example, I used unused addresses from 192.1.1.0/24, which is connected to ethernet1. In this instance, the router answers all ARP requests to 192.1.1.0/24 addresses that it has in its address-translation table, basically spoofing or proxying the responses. In this situation, make sure that you do not disable proxy ARP on the router's external (E1) interface.

Summary

This chapter showed you the basics of address translation: its components, how it works, and how to configure it. Many uses of address translation, and many different types, exist. In the most common case, address translation is used to translate private addresses to public addresses as traffic leaves a network, destined for a public network, such as the Internet. Normally, dynamic NAT and PAT are used to handle outbound connections; static NAT and PAR are used to handle inbound connections. As with any solution, address translation provides benefits and has limitations.

Next up is Chapter 12, which shows you some of the issues with address translation and how the Cisco IOS can deal with these issues.

## CHAPTER 12

Address Translation Issues

Chapter 11, "Address Translation," introduced you to the different kinds of address translation and showed you how to configure basic address translation on a Cisco router. It even alluded to some of the problems you will face with address translation, such as embedding addressing information in packet payloads. This chapter focuses on some key issues with address translation and solutions to deal with these issues.

This chapter first discusses issues with embedded addresses and how the Cisco IOS can deal with these when performing address translation. Then it discusses how you can incorporate redundancy into your network when you use address translation, specifically for the address translation device. It next discusses how to perform partial address translation: Sometimes you want to do address translation, but only based on the destination address that the source is accessing. Finally, this chapter discusses a better method of implementing traffic distribution than using the **ip nat** commands discussed in Chapter 11.

Embedded Addressing Information

Probably one of the main problems of address translation is that it breaks certain applications—specifically, those that embed and use addressing information in packet payloads. I talked about this problem with reflexive ACLs in Chapter 8, "Reflexive Access Lists," and CBAC in Chapter 9, "Context-Based Access Control." CBAC has some mechanisms to deal with supported applications to handle a stateful firewall function. CBAC looks for the setup of additional connections by examining the control connection and then adds these extra connections, as appropriate, to its state table. However, if you are using address translation, CBAC does not actually perform the translation. Therefore, if you are using private addresses inside your network, you must use address translation. Your Cisco IOS also must translate embedded address information in packet payloads for applications that have this tendency.

Actually, many applications and protocols embed addressing information in data payloads. This is a small list:

- DNS replies and zone transfers
- Routing updates

- IGMP messages for multicasting
- DHCP and BootP
- Some HTML code
- NetBIOS resolution
- Many NetBIOS applications
- Most multimedia applications
- SQL Server connections

As you can see from this list, quite a few applications exhibit this behavior.

Problem with Embedding Addressing Information

Consider a simple example to see how embedding addressing information in packet payloads can cause connection problems. In Figure 12-1, an external client wants to access data on an Oracle database server using SQL Server for the connection. The network in which the database servers are located uses private addresses.

Figure 12-1 *Embedded Address Example*

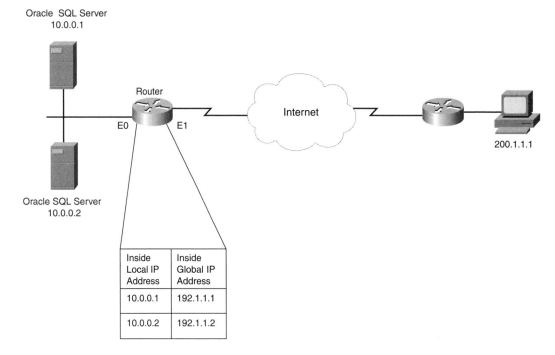

In this example, the data is distributed between two servers. Initially, the external user established a SQL Server connection to 192.1.1.1, the top database server. The router performs the address translation to the internal address that the server is using. When the Oracle server examines the data that the user wants, it realizes that it is on the other internal server, 10.0.0.2. The Oracle server sends back this IP address to the external user in the packet payload (the TCP data portion of the TCP segment). The external user's application then tries to establish a connection to the correct database server, 10.0.0.2.

The problem with this example is that when the router performs address translation, it looks only at the IP header, as well as the TCP and UDP headers (if PAT is being performed). Therefore, the router does not realize that an embedded address (10.0.0.2) needs to be translated in the reply that the top Oracle server sends to the external user. In this example, the external user needs to receive the address of 192.1.1.2 to establish the connection to the second server.

Supported Protocols and Applications

The Cisco IOS can look for embedded addressing information in packet payloads when it performs address translation. The Cisco IOS can examine embedded addressing information for a connection, compare this with the information that it has in its address translation table, and make the appropriate changes. However, not all applications are supported. By default, when the Cisco IOS is configured for address translation, it performs address translation on any packet header information, including the source and destination addresses in the IP header and the port numbers in the TCP and UDP headers. Beyond this point, the Cisco IOS might experience issues with address translation.

However, because many applications embed addressing information in packet payloads, the Cisco IOS supports some applications. On the Cisco IOS, this sometimes is referred to as Application Layer Gateway (ALG) address translation support. Table 12-1 lists the applications that the Cisco IOS examines for embedded addressing information. Cisco constantly is adding applications and protocols to this list.

Table 12-1 *ALG Address Translation Support*

Protocol or Application	Explanation
ICMP	Supports both NAT and PAT. With PAT, because ICMP does not have port numbers, the Cisco IOS uses sequential numbers to associate ICMP traffic with a particular inside device.
FTP	Examines the **PORT** and **PASV** commands in the TCP port 21 connection.
NetBIOS	Supports datagram, name, and session service connection examinations.
RealAudio	Examines additional connection setup requests for both embedded address and port information.

continues

Table 12-1   *ALG Address Translation Support (Continued)*

Protocol or Application	Explanation
CuSeeMe	Examines additional connection setup requests for both embedded address and port information.
StreamWorks	Examines additional connection setup requests for both embedded address and port information.
DNS	Examines DNS replies and translates A and PTR addressing information (discussed in Chapter 11 concerning overlapping addresses). In this instance, if the DNS server is internal and responds with a local instead of a global address, and if the router has a matching static entry in its translation table, the router appropriately translates the addressing information in the DNS reply.
NetMeeting	Supports H.323v2 for NetMeeting 2.x and 3.x, and H.323v1 for 2.x; also supports NetMeeting Directory through Internet Locator Server (ILS), which is used to find other NetMeeting users.
GRE	Examines Generic Route Encapsulation (GRE) tunnel packets, and performs the necessary translation of encapsulated packets.
H.323v2	Examines Alerting, CommunicationModeCommand, Communication-ModeResponse, Facility, FastConnect, OpenLogicalChannel, OpenLogicalChannelAck, Progress, and Setup messages in the control connection. In Cisco IOS 12.2(2)T, it also can examine H.323v2 RAS connections.
H.323v3 and v4	As of Cisco IOS 12.3(1), supports interoperability with H.323v3 and v4, but does not examine any new message types introduced in these new versions.
SIP	Supports SIP as of Cisco IOS 12.2(8)T.
Skinny (SCCP)	Supports Skinny as of 12.1(5)T.
VDOLive	Examines additional connection setup requests for both embedded address and port information.
Vxtreme	Examines additional connection setup requests for both embedded address and port information.

Nonstandard Port Numbers

When examining supported applications for embedded addressing information, the Cisco IOS examines these applications only on their well-known port numbers. For example, the Cisco IOS examines TCP port 21 for FTP. This presents a problem, however, if FTP or other applications are using nonstandard port numbers. For example, you might be using 2021 instead of 21 for FTP. In this example, the Cisco IOS, by default, is not examining port 2021, so it will not translate embedded addressing information on this connection.

Given this issue, the Cisco IOS enables you to specify additional ports that the Cisco IOS should examine for their associated applications. This process, commonly called IP NAT Service, is similar to what PAM does for CBAC, as discussed in Chapter 9. However, whereas PAM is used for stateful connection inspection, IP NAT Service is used to examine supported application connections for embedded addressing information and then appropriately translating this information.

IP NAT Service Configuration

To configure IP NAT Service to examine nonstandard port numbers, us the **ip nat service** command. Here's the syntax of this command:

```
Router(config)# ip nat service list ACL_#_or_name ftp tcp port port_#
Router(config)# ip nat service sip tcp|udp port port_#
Router(config)# ip nat service skinny tcp port port_#
```

For FTP, you first must specify the number or name of a standard ACL. This ACL contains the IP address of the FTP server that has the local address to be translated. This is followed by the nonstandard port number that the FTP server is using.

NOTE   If your FTP server is using the default port as well as a nonstandard port, you must configure IP NAT Service for *both ports*. The address listed in the ACL also must be the inside local address of the server.

Support for nonstandard ports for SIP was added in Cisco IOS 12.2(8)T, allowing the Cisco IOS to listen on SIP messages. The default port number is 5060. Support for Skinny was added in Cisco IOS 12.1(5)T, which listens on Skinny messages on TCP port 2000. You must change this if your CallManager platform is listening on a different port than the default.

NOTE   Unfortunately, as you can see from the previous syntax, IP NAT Service supports only FTP, SIP, and Skinny. Therefore, the Cisco IOS cannot inspect any other application on a nonstandard port number. However, configuring CBAC on your router allows the Cisco IOS to perform address translation for other connection types.

IP NAT Service Example

Example 12-1 shows a sample of using IP NAT Service with FTP.

Example 12-1   *Using IP NAT Service with FTP*

```
Router(config)# ip nat service list 1 ftp tcp port 21
Router(config)# ip nat service list 1 ftp tcp port 2021
Router(config)# access-list 1 permit 10.0.0.1
```

In Example 12-1, the FTP server (10.0.0.1) is using both TCP ports 21 and 2021.

Controlling Address Translation

In the previous chapter, I assumed that you would use a standard ACL to specify the inside local addresses to be translated when leaving the network. The problem with this process is that, in some situations, you want to control when address translation takes place. For example, you might want a particular set of inside local addresses to be translated when they are sent to a particular network number, or to not be translated at all.

Figure 12-2 shows a simple example of a situation in which you might not want to translate addresses. Controlling the use of address translation is common in VPN connections, in which you are using a public network as a transparent transport to tunnel information between your sites. In this example, an IPSec VPN is used to connect the two remote sites. In this instance, when traffic is flowing between the two sites, the addresses should not be translated; however, when traffic from either site goes to other locations in the Internet, it should be translated.

Figure 12-2   *Controlling Address Translation*

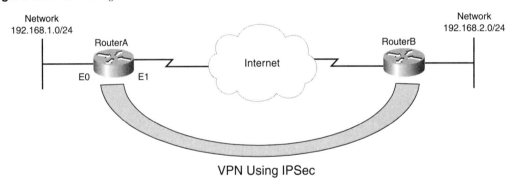

Using ACLs

One of the easiest ways to control address translation is to use ACLs. ACLs are not used to filter traffic in this instance; they are used to specify when addresses should be translated. Chapter 11, "Address Translation," discussed how to use a standard ACL to do this. However, the problem with a standard ACL is that it specifies when traffic should be translated based on where the traffic is coming from: not where it is both coming from and going to.

No restriction states that you must use a standard ACL. Instead, you can use an extended ACL. As an example, you could use the code listing in Example 12-2 to implement address translation control for the network shown in Figure 12-2 for RouterA.

Example 12-2 *Using an Extended ACL in Address Translation*

```
Router(config)# ip nat inside source list dynamic-nat-addresses    (1)
   pool dynamic-nat-pool
Router(config)# ip access-list extended dynamic-nat-addresses      (2)
Router(config-ext-nacl)# deny ip 192.168.1.0 0.0.0.255
   192.168.2.0 0.0.0.255
Router(config-ext-nacl)# permit ip 192.168.1.0 0.0.0.255 any
Router(config-std-nacl)# exit
Router(config)# ip nat pool dynamic-nat-pool 192.1.1.20           (3)
   192.1.1.254 netmask 255.255.255.0
Router(config)# interface ethernet0
Router(config-if)# ip nat inside
Router(config-if)# exit
Router(config)# interface ethernet1
Router(config-if)# ip nat outside
```

Refer to the numbers on the right side of Example 12-2 for the explanation. As you can see from Statement 1, dynamic NAT is used. Statement 2 sets up an extended ACL:

- Any traffic from 192.168.1.0/24 to 192.168.2.0/24 is not translated.
- Any other traffic from 192.168.1.0/24 is translated.

In Statement 3, the NAT pool is defined: Addresses from 192.1.1.20 to 192.1.1.254 are placed in this pool. You will see more examples like this when I discuss VPNs in Part VIII, "Virtual Private Networks."

NOTE   Even though this example used NAT, you also could have used PAT in this configuration.

Using Route Maps: Dynamic Translations

ACLs are only one method that you can use to specify when address translation should occur. The Cisco IOS also supports the use of route maps. Route maps create a fully extended translation entry, which contains the inside and outside local and global addresses, as well as the local and global TCP or UDP port numbers in the translation table. Table 12-2 explains the difference between the entries in the address translation table with ACLs and route maps.

Table 12-2   *ACLs Versus Route Maps*

Translation Method	What Is Translated
ACL (no overload)	Only the local and global IP inside addresses. This is referred to as a *simple* entry in the address translation table.
ACL (with overload)	The local and global addresses, as well as the local and global port numbers.
Route map	The local and global addresses, as well as the local and global port numbers (the same as an ACL with PAT, or overload).

Problems with ACLs and Address Translation

Using ACLs without PAT, or address overloading, can create problems in certain situations. In Figure 12-3, the internal network on the left is using a private address space (10.0.0.0/8) and has a connection to two different ISPs. For ISP1, this network must use the public address space of 192.1.1.0/24 when connecting to its internal network (192.1.2.0/24). For ISP2, the network must use 193.1.1.0/24 when connecting to IPS2's internal network (193.1.2.0/24). RouterA is performing the address translation.

Figure 12-3 *ACLs Versus Route Maps*

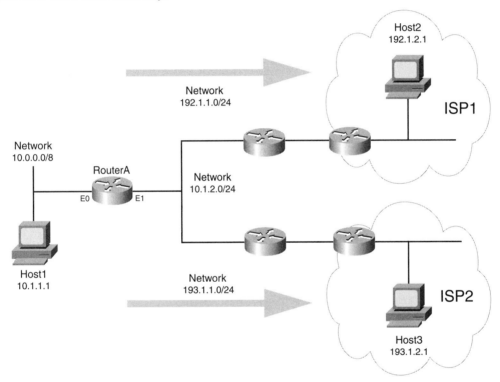

Assume that dynamic NAT is used for outbound traffic and that the configuration uses ACLs. Example 12-3 shows a simplified configuration that RouterA is using.

Example 12-3 *Problems with ACLs and Address Translation*

```
Router(config)# ip nat pool isp1-pool 192.1.1.1 192.1.1.254        (1)
  prefix-length 24
Router(config)# ip nat pool isp2-pool 193.1.1.1 193.1.1.254        (2)
  prefix-length 24
Router(config)# ip nat inside source list isp1-acl pool isp1-pool (1)
Router(config)# ip nat inside source list isp2-acl pool isp2-pool (2)
Router(config)# ip access-list extended isp1-acl                  (1)
Router(config-ext-nacl)# permit ip 10.0.0.0 0.255.255.255
  192.1.2.0 0.0.0.255
```

Example 12-3 *Problems with ACLs and Address Translation (Continued)*

```
Router(config-ext-nacl)# exit
Router(config)# ip access-list extended isp2-acl              (2)
Router(config-ext-nacl)# permit ip 10.0.0.0 0.255.255.255
  193.1.2.0 0.0.0.255
Router(config-ext-nacl)# exit
Router(config)# interface ethernet0
Router(config-if)# ip nat inside
Router(config-if)# exit
Router(config)# interface ethernet1
Router(config-if)# ip nat outside
```

In this example, the statements marked 1 on the right refer to the address translation that occurs between 10.0.0.0/8 and 192.1.2.0/24; statements marked 2 refer to the address translation between 10.0.0.0/8 and 193.1.2.0/24. Notice that this example uses dynamic NAT, not PAT, translation.

Now take a look at a problem that this configuration produces when an internal device, Host1, wants to connect to Host2 in ISP1 and Host3 in ISP2. Assume that Host1 makes an initial connection to Host2, perhaps a Telnet connection. When this occurs, RouterA examines the connection, realizes that an address translation does not exist in the translation table, and creates one:

```
Pro   Inside global   Inside local   Outside local   Outside global
- - -   192.1.1.1       10.1.1.1       - - -           - - -
```

Notice that in the translation table, only the local and global addresses are listed for the translation. This is because this configuration used dynamic NAT without overload, so a simple translation is created.

Assume that after the Telnet connection has been established, Host1 sets up a Telnet to Host3 in ISP2. Can you see what the problem is? When RouterA receives the packets from Host1, it examines the address translation table and sees that there is already an entry for Host1. So, RouterA translates Host1's source address to 192.1.1.1. The problem with this scenario is that Host1 should be translated to 193.1.1.x when sending traffic to 193.1.2.x. In this situation, the router ignores the address translation information in the two ACL statements because an entry already exists in the translation table.

Route Map Configuration

You can use two methods to solve the previous problem: Use address overloading or use route maps. With address overloading, PAT is used, creating an extended entry in the address translation table that includes the local and global inside and outside IP addresses, as well as the local and global inside and outside port numbers. The main problem with address overloading is that it requires the use of PAT, which might cause issues if you really need to use NAT.

Fortunately, route maps also support extended entries but do not require the use of PAT. Normally, route maps are used to implement routing policies on your router, but Cisco has adapted them to be used in other situations, such as address translation. I assume that you are familiar with the general use of route maps on a Cisco IOS router. To reference a route map to use with dynamic NAT, use the following dynamic NAT command:

```
Router(config)# ip nat inside source route-map route_map_name
  pool NAT_pool_name
```

As you can see, this command is similar to the one in which you use an ACL to specify which addresses are translated; the only difference is that you use the **route-map** parameter, along with the name of the route map, instead of the **list** parameter.

Example 12-4 shows a configuration on RouterA that uses route maps to perform address translation for the network shown in Figure 12-3.

Example 12-4 *Using Route Maps to Create Extended Address Translation Entries*

```
Router(config)# ip nat pool isp1-pool 192.1.1.1 192.1.1.254
  prefix-length 24
Router(config)# ip nat pool isp2-pool 193.1.1.1 193.1.1.254
  prefix-length 24
Router(config)# ip nat inside source route-map isp1-map        (1A)
  pool isp1-pool
Router(config)# ip nat inside source route-map isp2-map        (1B)
  pool isp2-pool
Router(config)# route-map isp1-map permit 10                   (2A)
Router(config-route-map)# match ip address isp1-acl
Router(config-route-map)# exit
Router(config)# route-map isp2-map permit 10                   (2B)
Router(config-route-map)# match ip address isp2-acl
Router(config-route-map)# exit
Router(config)# ip access-list extended isp1-acl               (3A)
Router(config-ext-nacl)# permit ip 10.0.0.0 0.255.255.255
   192.1.2.0 0.0.0.255
Router(config-ext-nacl)# exit
Router(config)# ip access-list extended isp2-acl               (3B)
Router(config-ext-nacl)# permit ip 10.0.0.0 0.255.255.255
   193.1.2.0 0.0.0.255
Router(config-ext-nacl)# exit
Router(config)# interface ethernet0
Router(config-if)# ip nat inside
Router(config-if)# exit
Router(config)# interface ethernet1
Router(config-if)# ip nat outside
```

I want to point out a few things concerning this example. Statements 1A and 1B (referring to the numbers on the right side of Example 12-4) associate the internal addresses that should be translated (through a route map) with the global address pool that should be used in the translation. Notice that this example uses dynamic NAT, not PAT, which is just like the previous ACL example. Statements 2A and 2B create the route maps. In this example, for isp1-map, any packets that match isp1-acl should be translated using the associated **ip nat inside source route-map** command. Statements 3A and 3B specify the ACLs used by the two route map commands, which control which packets will be translated.

Now re-examine the connections that Host1 makes and the address translation process that occurs when route maps are used, using the same scenario described in the ACL example.

First, Host1 Telnets to Host2. Assume that this is the first connection from Host1. When this occurs, RouterA notices that no address translation exists, so it creates one:

```
Pro  Inside global    Inside local   Outside local  Outside global
tcp  192.1.1.1:1024   10.0.0.1:1024  192.1.2.1:23   192.1.2.1:23
```

This entry obviously looks different from the one in the ACL example. Remember that ACLs with dynamic NAT create a simple entry, whereas route maps (and ACLs with dynamic PAT) create an extended entry.

Next, Host1 sets up a Telnet connection to Host3. When RouterA receives the first packet of this Telnet connection, it compares this to the entries that the router already has in its translation table. It notices that it does not have an entry for this specific connection, so it adds one:

```
Pro  Inside global    Inside local   Outside local  Outside global
tcp  192.1.1.1:1024   10.0.0.1:1024  192.1.2.1:23   192.1.2.1:23
tcp  193.1.1.1:1025   10.0.0.1:1025  193.1.3.1:23   193.1.3.1:23
```

As you can see from the previous translation table, the bottom entry is the second Telnet, thus solving the connectivity problem: Because the translation has both fully extended entries, the Cisco IOS correctly can translate traffic between the internal host (Host1) and the two external hosts (Host2 and Host3). Of course, you could have used ACLs and PAT to solve this problem, but perhaps PAT would have introduced other connection problems, and using NAT was the preferred solution.

CAUTION   By using route maps, the Cisco IOS creates extended entries in the address translation table, which enables you to set up different address-translation policies with NAT based on the destination address. The only downside of route maps, which is also true of PAT, is that because these configurations create extended entries, you need more memory on your router to store all the entries.

Address Translation and Route Maps

One of my customers needed to use NAT to connect to two other customers; PAT caused problems. However, when performing address translation, one set of translations was to be used for one remote customer, and another set was to be used for the other remote customer. When I set it up, I did not realize that route maps were supported, so I used extended ACLs to match the packets to be translated. I soon found out that when an internal employee tried to access both remote customers, only one worked. It took a day to track down the problem. When I called TAC for a helpful hint, the experts recommended the use of route maps. Since then, I have been a die-hard route-map fan when it comes to setting up address translation. You can do some interesting things with route maps that can't be done with ACLs; I show you one of these things, using the route map **match interface** command, in the next section.

Using Route Maps: Static Translations

The previous section showed you how to use route maps with dynamic NAT. Route maps also are supported with static NAT as of Cisco IOS 12.2(4)T. Currently, static NAT with route maps is supported only for individual address translations; translation of entire network numbers is not supported yet with route maps. To configure static NAT with a route map, use one of the following two commands:

```
Router(config)# ip nat inside source static
  local_IP_address global_IP_address route-map route_map_name [extendable]
Router(config)# ip nat inside source static tcp|udp
  local_IP_address local_port_# global_IP_address global_port_#
  route-map route_map_name [extendable]
```

Typically, the **ip nat inside source static** command is used to translate a small number of entries between your network and two other networks. However, this command provides one interesting parameter: **extendable**. This parameter causes the Cisco IOS to create an extended translation entry in the translation table instead of a simple entry.

Take a look at the use of this parameter by examining the network shown in Figure 12-4. In this example, the network on the left has two Internet connections for redundancy. ISP1 has assigned an IP address space of 192.1.1.0/24. ISP2, which does not support ISP1's address space, has assigned 193.1.1.0/24 to this network. This poses a problem because you need to set up a static translation for the internal web server. Normally, a static statement allows only one translation. In this example, you must choose between 192.1.1.1 translated to 10.0.0.1, or 193.1.1.1 translated to 10.0.0.1 for the web server translation.

Figure 12-4 *Extendable Statics and Route Maps*

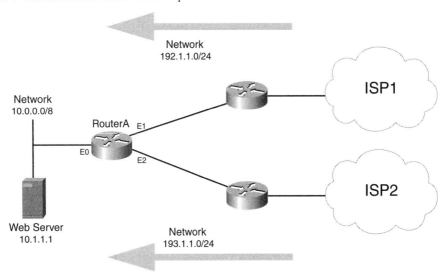

Using the **extendable** parameter, however, you can associate more than one global address with a local address. To solve the address translation problem shown in Figure 12-4 for the internal web server, RouterA's configuration would look like Example 12-5.

Example 12-5 *Using Extendable Static Translations in Route Maps*

```
Router(config)# ip nat inside source static              (1A)
    10.0.0.1 192.1.1.1
    route-map isp1-map extendable
Router(config)# ip nat inside source static              (1B)
    10.0.0.1 193.1.1.1
    route-map isp2-map extendable
Router(config)# route-map isp1-map permit 10             (2A)
Router(config-route-map)# match interface ethernet1
Router(config-route-map)# exit
Router(config)# route-map isp2-map permit 10             (2B)
Router(config-route-map)# match interface ethernet2
Router(config-route-map)# exit
Router(config-ext-nacl)# exit
Router(config)# interface ethernet0
Router(config-if)# ip nat inside
Router(config-if)# exit
Router(config)# interface ethernet1
Router(config-if)# ip nat outside
Router(config-if)# exit
Router(config)# interface ethernet2
Router(config-if)# ip nat outside
```

In this example, Statements 1A and 1B (referring to the numbers on the right side of Example 12-5) specify the static translations of the web server for the two ISPs. Notice that I included the **extendable** parameter: This causes the Cisco IOS to create an extended entry when a user sends traffic to the internal web server. When the web server responds with the HTML information, the Cisco IOS can determine how to undo the translation and send the traffic out the right interface (ISP1 or ISP2) to return the traffic to the user who originated the request.

TIP   One of the interesting things about the route maps in Example 12-5 (Statements 2A and 2B) is that they specify the interface of the inbound traffic, helping the router perform the address translation correctly. In most instances, you have two interfaces on your router connecting to the two ISPs. In this instance, you set up the appropriate address translation (static or dynamic), but you reference the translation with the **match interface** command in your route map configuration. I use this quite often when I have a single router with dual ISPs that require me to use different address spaces.

Address Translation and Redundancy

One of the concerns with any network design is redundancy. The Cisco IOS provides two methods of redundancy for address translation:

● Static NAT redundancy with Hot Standby Router Protocol (HSRP), available Cisco IOS in 12.2(4)T

● Stateful address translation failover, available in Cisco IOS 12.2(13)T

The following sections cover both of these methods.

Static NAT Redundancy with HSRP

Static NAT redundancy with HSRP typically is used in a small network, usually with one subnet or network number, that is connected to two perimeter routers for redundancy. In this situation, the concern is providing redundancy for the internal servers that have private addresses; the perimeter router is performing the address translation function. In a single-router design, if the router fails, external users cannot access the internal resources. To provide redundancy, a second router is added. However, if the primary router fails, the secondary router needs to know that it must perform address translation. This is accomplished using HSRP.

HSRP Redundancy Process

When using HSRP to provide static NAT redundancy, the static NAT configuration is mirrored on the two routers, and the active router processes traffic. HSRP is configured on the default gateways in the subnet, with one configured as the active router and the rest as backup, or standby, routers. A virtual IP address is chosen and assigned to the routers. User devices send traffic to the virtual IP address, which is serviced by the active router. The other routers monitor the active router. If the active router fails, a standby router processes traffic. Note that only static NAT is supported in this configuration, not dynamic NAT; therefore, whatever static NAT commands you configure on the active HSRP router, you also need to configure on the standby router(s).

Look at Figure 12-5 to illustrate how this is set up. In this network, there are two routers. The top router is the active HSRP router, and the bottom one is the standby router. The virtual IP address is 10.0.0.254, which is the default gateway that internal devices use. If the active router fails, within 10 seconds, the standby router promotes itself and processes traffic sent to 10.0.0.254.

Assuming that the ISP assigned you 192.1.1.0/24 and that you had to use this for the external interfaces of your two routers, as shown in Figure 12-5, and also assuming that Internet traffic was trying to reach one of the two statically translated addresses, you have an issue with ARP. For example, assume that an external user was trying to reach 192.1.1.1, the web server. Because the ISP router is connected to 192.1.1.0/24, it performs an ARP for the MAC address of 192.1.1.1. Obviously, this device isn't on this segment; it's the web server at 10.0.0.1. In this situation, the active router responds to the ARP with its BIA address, basically performing a proxy function. Of course, this presents a problem if the active router fails and the standby router is promoted: The ISP still is using the BIA addresses of the active router (that no longer is functioning). To get around this problem, you manually must duplicate the static NAT entries on all HSRP routers, allowing a standby router to assume the responsibility when the active router fails.

Figure 12-5 *Static NAT HSRP Example 1*

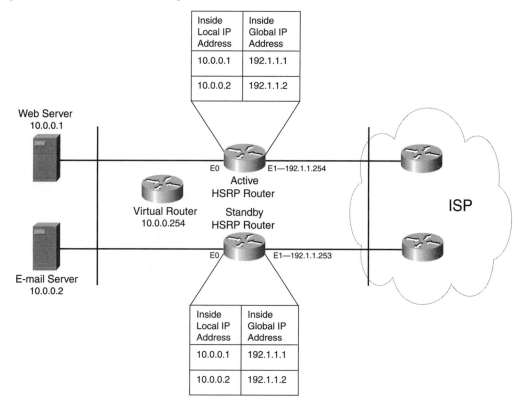

Inside Local IP Address	Inside Global IP Address
10.0.0.1	192.1.1.1
10.0.0.2	192.1.1.2

Inside Local IP Address	Inside Global IP Address
10.0.0.1	192.1.1.1
10.0.0.2	192.1.1.2

NOTE   For the example in Figure 12-5, you must manually configure both sets of static NAT translations on the active and standby routers for failover to occur correctly.

Of course, you might have a network design such as that shown in Figure 12-6. In this example, the network has been assigned 192.1.1.0/24 by the ISP, but the connection from this network to the ISP is using a different address space: 192.2.2.0/24. In this example, you can use HSRP to provide redundancy on both sides of the two redundant routers: on the internal network side and the ISP side. However, for this to function correctly on the ISP side, the ISP must set up a static route to the virtual router IP address. By default, the active router processes all traffic for this next-hop address; if it fails, the standby router promotes itself and processes traffic. But as in the previous example, both HSRP routers still need the same static NAT configuration to provide redundancy.

Figure 12-6 *Static NAT HSRP Example 2*

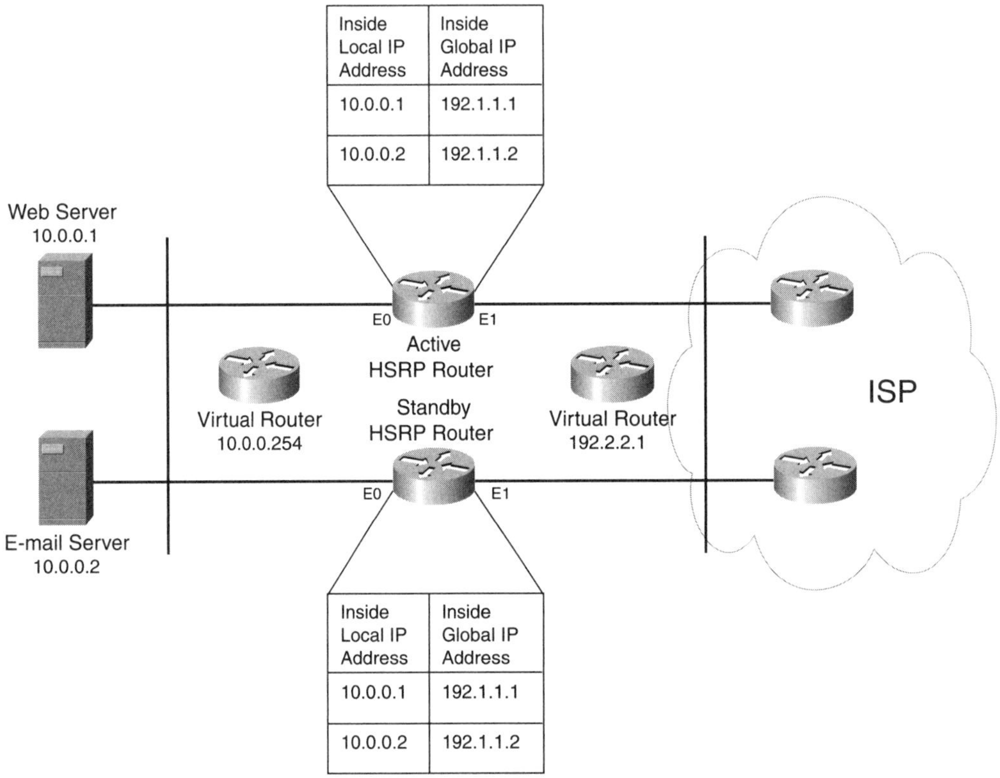

HSRP Redundancy Configuration

To set up static NAT redundancy with HSRP, you must perform two steps:

Step 1 Configure HSRP.

Step 2 Integrate your static NAT configuration with HSRP.

NOTE   I assume that you know how to configure HSRP, so I do not spend time discussing what the various HSRP commands are for, with the exception of how to integrate HSRP with static NAT.

You use these basic commands to configure HSRP:

```
Router(config)# interface type [slot_#/]port_#
Router(config-if)# ip address IP_address subnet_mask          (1)
Router(config-if)# no ip redirects                            (2)
Router(config-if)# standby [group_#] name [HSRP_group_name]   (3)
Router(config-if)# standby [HSRP_group_#] ip IP_address       (4)
```

```
Router(config-if)# standby [group_#] preempt
Router(config-if)# standby [group_#] priority priority_#
Router(config-if)# standby [group_#] track interface decrement_value
```

The only four required Interface commands are marked with numbers on the right side; the last two are optional.

After you have set up HSRP, you are ready to set up NAT. You use these commands to do this:

```
Router(config)# ip nat inside|outside source static
  local_IP_address global_IP_address redundancy HSRP_group_name
Router(config)# interface type [slot_#/]port_#
Router(config-if)# ip nat {inside|outside}
```

The one main difference with the configuration of static NAT is the addition of the **redundancy** parameter. The name of the HSRP group specified here must match the one configured with the **standby name** command.

After you have set up static NAT redundancy with HSRP, you can use the HSRP **show standby** and the address translation **show ip nat translations verbose** commands to verify that this feature is enabled.

HSRP Redundancy Example

Take a look at a configuration example when using HSRP to provide static NAT redundancy. This example uses the network shown previously in Figure 12-5, but it focuses only on the HSRP and address translation configuration. Example 12-6 shows the configuration for the active HSRP router.

Example 12-6 *Using HSRP to Provide Static NAT Redundancy: Active Router*

```
Router(config)# interface ethernet0
Router(config-if)# ip address 10.0.0.253 255.255.255.0
Router(config-if)# no ip redirects
Router(config-if)# ip nat inside
Router(config-if)# standby 1 ip 10.0.0.254
Router(config-if)# standby 1 priority 110
Router(config-if)# standby 1 preempt
Router(config-if)# standby 1 name HSRPGROUP
Router(config-if)# standby 1 track ethernet1
Router(config-if)# exit
Router(config)# interface ethernet1
Router(config-if)# ip address 192.1.1.254
Router(config-if)# ip nat outside
Router(config-if)# exit
Router(config)# ip nat inside source static 10.0.0.1 192.1.1.1
  redundancy HSRPGROUP
Router(config)# ip nat inside source static 10.0.0.2 192.1.1.2
  redundancy HSRPGROUP
```

In Example 12-6, the ethernet0 configuration sets up internal HSRP. At the bottom, notice that the static NAT commands are associated with the HSRP group name.

Example 12-7 shows the configuration for the standby HSRP router.

Example 12-7 *Using HSRP to Provide Static NAT Redundancy: Standby Router*

```
Router(config)# interface ethernet0
Router(config-if)# ip address 10.0.0.252 255.255.255.0
Router(config-if)# no ip redirects
Router(config-if)# ip nat inside
Router(config-if)# standby 1 ip 10.0.0.254
Router(config-if)# standby 1 priority 90
Router(config-if)# standby 1 preempt
Router(config-if)# standby 1 name HSRPGROUP
Router(config-if)# standby 1 track ethernet1
Router(config-if)# exit
Router(config)# interface ethernet1
Router(config-if)# ip address 192.1.1.253
Router(config-if)# ip nat outside
Router(config-if)# exit
Router(config)# ip nat inside source static 10.0.0.1 192.1.1.1
  redundancy HSRPGROUP
Router(config)# ip nat inside source static 10.0.0.2 192.1.1.2
  redundancy HSRPGROUP
```

Notice that the standby router manually had to replicate the two static NAT entries, located at the bottom of the configuration.

Stateful Address Translation Failover

The main problem with static NAT redundancy with HSRP is that it is not a stateful address translation solution: It provides redundancy only for static NAT translations. In other words, if you also are using dynamic address translation, all these translations are lost when the active router fails. This can cause connectivity problems.

Stateful Failover Features and Restrictions

Starting with Cisco IOS 12.2(13)T, Cisco introduced Phase 1 of its stateful address translation failover, referred to as stateful NAT (SNAT). This is Cisco's first step in implementing SNAT. In this solution, two address translation routers are used: a primary, and a backup or backups. These routers commonly are called a translation group. The primary router in the translation group performs active address translations. The backup accepts address translation updates (additions and deletions) from the primary and also checks to make sure that the primary is functioning. If the primary fails, the backup begins processing traffic using its address translation table that was shared with the primary. The address translation information is shared between the primary and backup routers by using a TCP connection.

SNAT even can work with HSRP; however, this process is different than the one described in the previous "Static NAT Redundancy with HSRP" section. Static NAT redundancy with

HSRP provides redundancy for only static translation, not dynamic translation. With SNAT and HSRP, redundancy can be provided for both types of translations.

NOTE   SNAT provides redundancy for dynamic translations; to provide redundancy for static translations, configure the static translations on all routers in the translation group.

Currently, SNAT Phase 1 does not support ALG examination (embedding of addressing information). Therefore, certain applications, such as FTP, NetMeeting, RAS, SIP, Skinny, TFTP, and asymmetrical routing, will not work because they have embedded addresses in packet payloads. SNAT Phase 2 will address this limitation and provide additional redundancy and translation features.

SNAT with HSRP

SNAT can be configured in two ways: with HSRP and without it. The following two sections discuss how to configure both.

To configure SNAT with HSRP, you perform the following steps:

Step 1   Configure HSRP.

Step 2   Configure stateful failover.

Step 3   Configure address translation.

HSRP Configuration

In Step 1, you configure HSRP, typically using these commands:

```
Router(config)# interface type [slot_#/]port_#
Router(config-if)# ip address IP_address subnet_mask          (1)
Router(config-if)# no ip redirects                            (2)
Router(config-if)# standby [group_#] name [HSRP_group_name]   (3)
Router(config-if)# standby [HSRP_group_#] ip IP_address       (4)
Router(config-if)# standby [group_#] preempt
Router(config-if)# standby [group_#] priority priority_#
Router(config-if)# standby [group_#] track interface
  decrement_value
```

The only four required Interface commands are marked here; the last three are optional. Whichever router becomes the active HSRP router processes traffic, adds and removes translations from the address translation table, and updates the other HSRP routers in the group.

HSRP with SNAT Stateful Failover Configuration

After you have set up HSRP, you are ready to set up your stateful failover:

```
Router(config)# ip nat stateful id router_ID_#
Router(config-ipnat-snat)# redundancy HSRP_group_name
Router(config-ipnat-snat-red)# mapping-id mapping_ID_#
```

The **ip nat stateful id** command specifies an identification of the router in the SNAT group. Each router that is participating needs a unique identification number. This number can range from 1 to 2,147,483,647. For example, if two routers will be participating in stateful failover address translation with HSRP, you can use the ID numbers of 1 and 2. The **redundancy** command specifies the name of the HSRP group providing the redundancy; this is configured with the **standby name** command on the router's interface. The **mapping-id** command specifies a number from 1 to 2,147,483,647, to uniquely identify the translations that the active HSRP router will send to the standby router(s). These commands must be configured on all routers in the HSRP group. The main difference in the configuration of the routers is that each router needs a unique router ID; otherwise, the HSRP group name and mapping ID number are the same.

HSRP with SNAT Address Translation Configuration

After you set up stateful failover for address translation, you can proceed with your address translation commands. For static translations, manually configure these on all routers in the HSRP group: Remember that stateful failover applies only to dynamic translations. Next, configure your dynamic translations using the first command and any of the following commands:

```
Router(config)# ip nat pool global_pool_name
  begin_IP_address end_IP_address prefix-length prefix_length
Router(config)# ip nat inside source route-map route_map_name
  pool global_pool_name  mapping-id mapping_ID_# [overload]
Router(config)# ip nat inside source list ACL_#_or_name
  pool global_pool_name mapping-id mapping_ID_# [overload]
```

The **ip nat pool** command defines the global addresses that your local addresses will be translated to; this was discussed in the previous chapter and is a required command. The next two commands specify which local addresses, either through a route map or through an ACL number or name, are to be translated using the global pool. Based on your needs, you configure one of these last two commands. One additional parameter to these two commands is the **mapping-id** command, which tells the Cisco IOS that these dynamic translations are stateful translations. This number must match the mapping ID number in the **mapping-id** command in the **ip nat stateful id** configuration. The last thing you need to do is specify which interfaces are internal and external to the router for address translation by using the **ip nat** {**inside** | **outside**} Interface command.

HSRP and SNAT Stateful Failover Example

Take a look at an example that uses stateful address translation failover with HSRP. In the network shown in Figure 12-7, two routers are used to connect to the same ISP: RouterA and RouterB. This network will use dynamic PAT for the address translation from inside to outside connections.

Figure 12-7 *Stateful Address Translation Failover with HSRP*

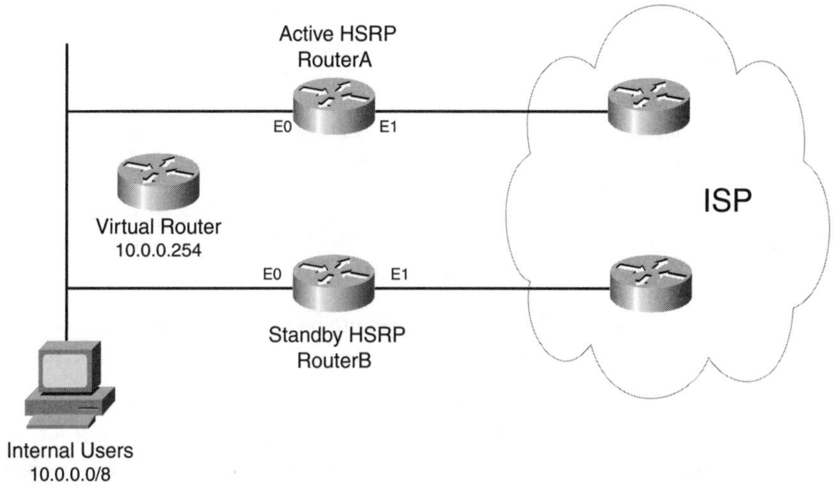

Example 12-8 shows the configuration for RouterA.

Example 12-8 *Using PAT, HSRP, and SNAT on the Active Router*

```
RouterA(config)# interface ethernet0
RouterA(config-if)# ip address 10.0.0.253 255.255.255.0
RouterA(config-if)# ip nat inside
RouterA(config-if)# standby 1 ip 10.0.0.254                       (1)
RouterA(config-if)# standby 1 timers 1 3
RouterA(config-if)# standby 1 priority 150                        (2)
RouterA(config-if)# standby 1 name SNAT-HSRP                      (3)
RouterA(config-if)# standby 1 track ethernet1                     (4)
RouterA(config-if)# exit
RouterA(config)# interface ethernet1
RouterA(config-if)# ip nat outside
RouterA(config-if)# exit
RouterA(config)# ip nat stateful id 1                             (5)
RouterA(config-ipnat-snat)# redundancy SNAT-HSRP
RouterA(config-ipnat-snat-red)# mapping-id 100
RouterA(config-ipnat-snat-red)# exit
RouterA(config)# ip nat pool SNAT-POOL 192.1.1.240 192.1.1.254    (6)
  prefix-length 24
RouterA(config)# ip nat inside source route-map SNAT-MAP         (7)
  pool SNAT-POOL mapping-id 100 overload
RouterA(config)# route-map SNAT-MAP permit 10                     (8)
RouterA(config-route-map)# match ip address SNAT-ACL
RouterA(config)# ip access-list extended SNAT-ACL                 (9)
RouterA(config-ext-nacl)# permit ip 10.0.0.0 0.255.255.255 any
```

Refer to the numbers on the right side of Example 12-8 for the following explanation of the configuration for RouterA:

1 This command assigns the virtual IP address of the default gateway for the internal subnet.

2 This command ensures that RouterA becomes the active router. The default HSRP priority is 100, at which the router with the highest priority becomes the active router, and the next highest the standby.

3 This command configures the name of the HSRP group, which must match the **redundancy** command in Statement 5.

4 This command enables interface tracking on the outside interface. If this interface fails, RouterA demotes itself and allows RouterB to become the active router.

5 These three commands set up stateful failover for address translation. The router ID specified in the **ip nat stateful** command must be different from RouterB's. The **redundancy** command specifies the name of the HSRP group providing the redundancy. The **mapping-id** assigns a mapping number to the dynamic translation entries that will be shared with RouterB.

6 This command specifies the group of global addresses to be used in the translation.

7 This command specifies the local addresses that will be translated, states the global address pool to use for the translation, and specifies that SNAT is used (**mapping-id**) and that PAT is used for the translation (**overload**). Notice that this command references a route map for the local addresses.

8 These two commands specify that the named ACL SNAT-ACL is used to match on the local addresses.

9 This is the ACL that defines the local addresses that should be translated.

Example 12-9 shows the configuration for RouterB.

Example 12-9 *Using PAT, HSRP, and SNAT on the Standby Router*

```
RouterB(config)# interface ethernet0
RouterB(config-if)# ip address 10.0.0.252 255.255.255.0
RouterB(config-if)# ip nat inside
RouterB(config-if)# standby 1 ip 10.0.0.254
RouterB(config-if)# standby 1 timers 1 3
RouterB(config-if)# standby 1 priority 90                        (1)
RouterB(config-if)# standby 1 name SNAT-HSRP
RouterB(config-if)# standby 1 track ethernet1
RouterB(config-if)# exit
RouterB(config)# interface ethernet1
RouterB(config-if)# ip nat outside
RouterB(config-if)# exit
RouterB(config)# ip nat stateful id 2                            (2)
RouterB(config-ipnat-snat)# redundancy SNAT-HSRP
```

Example 12-9 *Using PAT, HSRP, and SNAT on the Standby Router (Continued)*

```
RouterB(config-ipnat-snat-red)# mapping-id 100
RouterB(config-ipnat-snat-red)# exit
RouterB(config)# ip nat pool SNAT-POOL 192.1.1.240 192.1.1.254
  prefix-length 24
RouterB(config)# ip nat inside source route-map SNAT-MAP
  pool SNAT-POOL mapping-id 100 overload
RouterB(config)# route-map SNAT-MAP permit 10
RouterB(config-route-map)# match ip address SNAT-ACL
RouterB(config)# ip access-list extended SNAT-ACL
RouterB(config-ext-nacl)# permit ip 10.0.0.0 0.255.255.255 any
```

Notice that only two differences (besides IP addressing) exist between RouterB and RouterA's configuration. First, because RouterB is the standby router, it has a lower HSRP priority than RouterA (Statement 1); make sure that the standby router has a lower priority than the active one. Statement 2 configures RouterB's stateful address translation ID; this number must be different than RouterA's. Otherwise, the configuration is basically the same.

SNAT Without HSRP

SNAT without HSRP typically is used when the two perimeter routers are not handling default gateway functions for internal hosts (see Figure 12-8). As you can see in this example, the internal hosts are not connected to the two perimeter routers. The two perimeters routers have a direct connection between them, allowing for quicker detection of a failure, as well as dedicated bandwidth for the TCP connection used to share the dynamic address translation entries. An intelligent routing protocol is used to detect failure of the primary router.

Figure 12-8 *Stateful Address Translation Failover Without HSRP*

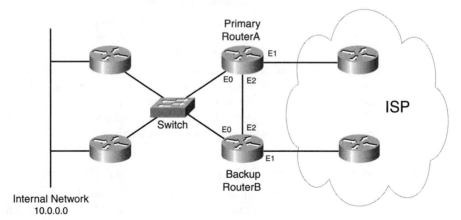

TIP Typically, HSRP is used with stateful failover for address translation when the network is small and the users are connected to the same subnet as the routers. For larger networks, such as the one shown in Figure 12-8, HSRP typically is not used in the failover configuration.

To configure SNAT without HSRP, perform the following steps:

Step 1 Configure stateful failover by defining the primary and backup routers.

Step 2 Configure address translation.

SNAT Stateful Failover Configuration Without HSRP

In Step 1, you configure SNAT. You use these commands for the primary router:

```
Router(config)# ip nat stateful id router_ID_#
Router(config-ipnat-snat)# primary local_IP_address_to_use
Router(config-ipnat-snat-red)# peer backup_router's_IP_address
Router(config-ipnat-snat-red)# mapping-id mapping_ID_#
```

The **ip nat stateful id** command assigns a unique router ID to this router. The **primary** command specifies that this is the primary router; you must specify an IP address on the router that it will use when building the TCP connection to the backup router. The **peer** command specifies the IP address to use to terminate the TCP connection on the backup router. The **mapping-id** command points to the dynamic translation entries that will be shared with the backup router.

You use these commands for the backup router:

```
Router(config)# ip nat stateful id router_ID_#
Router(config-ipnat-snat)# backup local_IP_address_to_use
Router(config-ipnat-snat-red)# peer primary_router's_IP_address
Router(config-ipnat-snat-red)# mapping-id mapping_ID_#
```

This configuration is similar to the primary's configuration. Note that with the **ip nat stateful id** command, you must use a different ID number for the backup than the one assigned to the primary router. Next, the **backup** parameter defines this router as the backup, followed by the local address that this router will use to communicate with the primary router (this is the address listed in the primary's **peer** command). Following this is the peer statement, which specifies the address that the primary router is using (specified in the **primary** statement on the primary router). Finally, the mapping ID number configured here must match the one (or ones) configured on the primary router.

SNAT Address Translation Configuration Without HSRP

Next, you need to configure your address translation commands. The commands are the same as the ones used in the previous "HSRP with SNAT Address Translation Configuration" section, which discussed how to configure stateful failover with HSRP.

Stateful Failover Without HSRP Example

Now that you have a basic understanding of the commands used, take a look at an example to illustrate how to set up stateful address translation failover without using HSRP. This example uses the network shown previously in Figure 12-8. Example 12-10 shows the configuration for RouterA, which is the primary router.

Example 12-10 *Using SNAT Without HSRP on the Primary Router*

```
RouterA(config)# interface ethernet0
RouterA(config-if)# ip address 10.0.0.254 255.255.255.0
RouterA(config-if)# ip nat inside
RouterA(config-if)# exit
RouterA(config)# interface ethernet2
RouterA(config-if)# ip address 192.168.1.254 255.255.255.0          (1)
RouterA(config-if)# exit
RouterA(config)# interface ethernet1
RouterA(config-if)# ip nat outside
RouterA(config-if)# exit
RouterA(config)# ip nat stateful id 1                                (2)
RouterA(config-ipnat-snat)# primary 192.168.1.254
RouterA(config-ipnat-snat-red)# peer 192.168.1.253
RouterA(config-ipnat-snat-red)# mapping-id 100
RouterA(config-ipnat-snat-red)# exit
RouterA(config)# ip nat pool SNAT-POOL 192.1.1.240 192.1.1.254
  prefix-length 24
RouterA(config)# ip nat inside source route-map SNAT-MAP
  pool SNAT-POOL mapping-id 100 overload
RouterA(config)# route-map SNAT-MAP permit 10
RouterA(config-route-map)# match ip address SNAT-ACL
RouterA(config)# ip access-list extended SNAT-ACL
RouterA(config-ext-nacl)# permit ip 10.0.0.0 0.255.255.255 any
```

This configuration is similar to the one that used HSRP. Notice that RouterA (see Statements 1 and 2 on the right side of Example 12-10) uses ethernet2 for the connection to RouterB. Also, in Statement 2, RouterA is configured as the primary.

Example 12-11 shows the configuration of RouterB, the backup router.

Example 12-11 *Using SNAT Without HSRP on the Backup Router*

```
RouterB(config)# interface ethernet0
RouterB(config-if)# ip address 10.0.0.252 255.255.255.0
RouterB(config-if)# exit
RouterA(config)# interface ethernet2
RouterA(config-if)# ip address 192.168.1.253 255.255.255.0
RouterA(config-if)# exit
RouterB(config)# interface ethernet1
RouterB(config-if)# ip nat outside
RouterB(config-if)# exit
RouterA(config)# ip nat stateful id 2
RouterA(config-ipnat-snat)# backup 192.168.1.253
RouterA(config-ipnat-snat-red)# peer 192.168.1.254
```

continues

Example 12-11 *Using SNAT Without HSRP on the Backup Router (Continued)*

```
RouterA(config-ipnat-snat-red)# mapping-id 100
RouterA(config-ipnat-snat-red)# exit
RouterB(config)# ip nat pool SNAT-POOL 192.1.1.240 192.1.1.254
  prefix-length 24
RouterB(config)# ip nat inside source route-map SNAT-MAP
  pool SNAT-POOL mapping-id 100 overload
RouterB(config)# route-map SNAT-MAP permit 10
RouterB(config-route-map)# match ip address SNAT-ACL
RouterB(config)# ip access-list extended SNAT-ACL
RouterB(config-ext-nacl)# permit ip 10.0.0.0 0.255.255.255 any
```

The only major difference between this configuration and the one used by the primary router is the stateful configuration with the **backup** and **peer** commands.

SNAT Verification

When you have finished configuring SNAT on your routers, you can use various commands, in addition to the troubleshooting address translation commands discussed in Chapter 11, to verify and troubleshoot the configuration of SNAT. You can use this basic **show** command to view SNAT information:

```
Router# show ip snat [distributed [verbose] | peer IP_address]
```

The **distributed** parameter enables you to see information about the distributed NAT information, as well as the status of the peer connection. With the **verbose** option, you can see detailed information about the stateful translations themselves (if they exist). If you use the **peer** parameter instead of the **distributed** parameter, you can see information about the TCP connection to the other stateful peer. Example 12-12 shows sample output from this command.

Example 12-12 *Using the* **show ip nat** *Command*

```
Router# show ip snat distributed verbose
Stateful NAT Connected Peers
SNAT: Mode IP-REDUNDANCY :: ACTIVE
 : State READY
 : Local Address 10.0.1.254
 : Local NAT id 1
 : Peer Address 10.0.1.253
 : Peer NAT id 2
 : Mapping List 100
 : InMsgs 384, OutMsgs 385, tcb 0x82BF8BFC, listener 0x0
```

In this command, you can see that SNAT is configured with HSRP (IP-REDUNDANCY) and that this router is the active HSRP router. If this was failover without HSRP, you would see PRIMARY or BACKUP as the specified mode. At the bottom of the display, you can see the number of SNAT messages received and sent between the two routers.

If you want to clear the dynamic address translations used for stateful failover, use the following **clear** command:

```
Router# clear ip snat translation {distributed * |
  peer peer's_IP_address [refresh]}
```

You can clear all the SNAT dynamic translations with the **distributed** * parameter, or just the translations for a specific SNAT peer. With the **peer** parameter on the backup router, you can specify the optional **refresh** parameter, which causes the standby backup router to clear the dynamic SNAT translations in its local address translation table, as well as request a current table update from the active or primary router.

You can clear all the sessions to peer SNAT routers or just a specific session with this command:

```
Router# clear ip snat sessions [* | peer's_IP_address]
```

For detailed troubleshooting of SNAT, use the following command:

```
Router# debug ip snat [detailed]
```

This command enables you to see the actual messages shared between the active/primary and the standby/backup SNAT routers. Example 12-13 shows a sample of the use of this command.

Example 12-13 *Using the* **debug ip snat** *Command*

```
Router# debug ip snat detailed
2w3d:SNAT:Establish TCP peers for PRIMARY
2w3d:SNAT (Send):Enqueuing SYNC Message for Router-Id 1
2w3d:SNAT(write2net):192.168.1.254 <---> 192.168.1.253 send message
2w3d:SNAT(write2net):ver 2, id 100, opcode 1, len 68
2w3d:SNAT (Send):Enqueuing DUMP-REQUEST Message for Router-Id 1
```

In Example 12-13, stateful configuration was set up without HSRP. This router is the primary router. DUMP-REQUEST messages are requests for a dump (complete listing) of the primary's dynamic translation entries.

CAUTION   The **debug ip snat** command is very CPU intensive and should be used only when a small amount of traffic is being translated by the router; otherwise, it might overload the router and cause it to crash, in the worst-case scenario.

Traffic Distribution with Server Load Balancing

As you recall from Chapter 11, you can use NAT to load-balance traffic among multiple internal servers. However, I also mentioned that this feature, configured with **ip nat** commands, has the following limitations:

- It cannot detect whether an internal server in the group fails. This means that the Cisco IOS always will forward traffic to servers in the group, regardless of their operational status.

- It cannot determine loads of the internal servers, so it cannot perform load balancing efficiently.

To deal with these deficiencies, Cisco introduced the Server Load Balancing (SLB) feature in Cisco IOS 12.0(7)XE. As with IP NAT traffic distribution, SLB provides server load balancing, but it does so in a more intelligent manner. With SLB, you define a virtual server on your router, with the virtual server representing a group of real servers, commonly called a server farm. The Cisco IOS takes care of redirecting packets that are directed to the virtual server to the various servers in the server farm. Depending on the platform, such as the Catalyst 6500 switch, this process can be done in hardware.

SLB Process

SLB can operate in one of two redirection modes:

- Directed mode
- Dispatched mode

In directed mode, you assign the virtual server any address that you want. The real servers in the SLB group do not know this address. Instead, the Cisco IOS translates the virtual destination address to an address of one of the real servers by performing NAT. Figure 12-9 illustrates how directed mode works. In this example, a virtual IP address of 192.1.1.1 is used. When Internet users want to access the internal virtual web server, they put 192.1.1.1 in the destination IP address field of the IP header. When the router receives this packet, directed mode causes the Cisco IOS to change 192.1.1.1 to one of the addresses that the internal servers use, recalculate the CRC, and then forward the packet to the internal server. This process is very similar to traffic distribution, discussed in the previous chapter.

Figure 12-9 *SLB: Directed Mode*

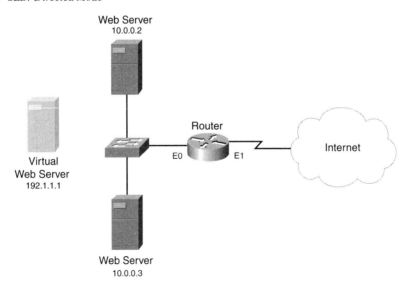

In dispatched mode, which is the default mode for SLB, the real servers know the virtual server address. Actually, the real servers have two IP addresses configured on them: their own personal IP address and the virtual IP address. The virtual IP address is configured as either a loopback address or a secondary IP address. Figure 12-10 illustrates this mode. In the figure, the two file servers have two addresses configured on them: their real address (10.0.0.*x*) and their virtual address (192.1.1.1).

Figure 12-10 *SLB: Dispatched Mode*

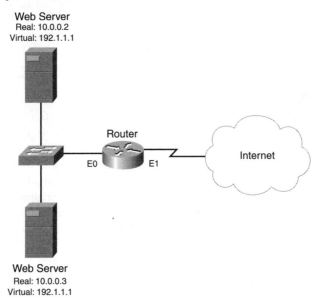

One advantage that dispatched mode has over directed mode is that your router's Cisco IOS does not have to perform address translation on the dispatched packets: It only redirects them, thus maximizing your throughput. With directed mode, the Cisco IOS must change the destination IP address as well recalculate the CRC, which is not necessary in dispatched mode. The limitation of dispatched mode, however, is that the real servers must be connected, through Layer 2, to your router. Of course, if your Layer 3 (perimeter router) device has Layer 2 functionality, as a Catalyst 4000 or 6500 switch with routing functions does, this is less of an issue; if this is not the case, you must connect your router and real servers in the server farm to the same Layer 2 switch. Otherwise, intervening internal routers between your perimeter router and the real servers might not be capable of routing the traffic to the appropriate server. Remember that all of them have the same virtual IP address configured on them. This is the same address in the packet header, so the intermediate routers do not know how to load balance this information. At least if the router is connected directly to the subnet with the server farm, it knows about the real addresses of the server farm and can use the appropriate MAC address found in its ARP table to forward the packet with the virtual address to the correct server.

Load-Balancing Algorithms

This section takes a closer look at the load-balancing process that SLB uses. This process is actually much more sophisticated than what I briefly described in the previous section. The Cisco IOS can use two load-balancing algorithms with SLB:

- Weighted round robin (WRR)
- Weighted least connections (WLC)

Weighted Round Robin

With WRR, the assignment of real servers to handle connections is done on a round-robin fashion: Each real server services a portion of the connections. Because each server might have different performance characteristics, SLB's WRR enables you to assign a weight to a server, basically identifying how many connections that it can handle compared to other servers. For example, assume that the weight on all servers is 1, but for one more powerful server, the weight is 2. In this instance, all of the weighted-1 servers would have one connection assigned to them as the Cisco IOS performs its load balancing. However, when the Cisco IOS reached the weighted-2 server, the Cisco IOS would assign two connections to it. After the Cisco IOS went through the list of real servers, it would start over at the top of the list.

Weighted Least Connections

With WLC, the Cisco IOS examines the number of connections that a real server currently has been assigned. Based on this number, when the Cisco IOS needs to assign a new connection to a real server, it chooses the real server with the fewest number of assigned connections. As with WRR, you can assign a weight to a real server, indicating the likelihood that it can handle more or fewer connections than other servers. The capacity of a real server is the assigned weight of the server divided by the sum of assigned weights of other servers. For example, if a server farm had two servers, with one server (A) having a weight of 1 and the other (B) having a weight of 2, server A would be assigned one third of the connections ($1 / [1 + 2] = 1/3$), whereas server B would be assigned two thirds of the connections ($2 / [1 + 2] = 2/3$).

Other SLB Load-Balancing Features

SLB offers other load-balancing features, including the following:

- **Slow start**—When SLB uses WLC for load balancing, a condition can exist where a real server with no connections can be assigned so many new connections that it is overloaded. This feature prevents this process by controlling the number of new connections redirected to the real server that was just enabled or that became available.

- **Maximum connections**—You can limit the number of active connections that a real server handles in a server group.

- **Port-bound servers**—Based on the TCP or UDP port number of the connection, a specific server group can handle the connection. This enables you to have one server group handle one application, such as www, and another handle a second application, such as FTP.

- **Client-assigned load balancing**—You can limit the access that a client has to a virtual server. For example, you might have two server groups: one for internal clients and one for external clients.

- **Sticky connections**—If a client has an existing connection to a real server, subsequent connection requests from this client can be assigned to the same server. A configurable timer is used so that, even if no current connections exist from the client to the real server, the real server that the client previously used can be assigned again to the client. This feature is useful if you have two server groups, such as one for HTTP and one for HTTPS. In this example, instead of the two real servers from the different groups handling the connection requests for the client, sticky connections allow one real server in just one of the groups to handle the client's connection requests.

- **Automatic server failure detection**—SLB increments a failure counter for a real server when a TCP connection attempt fails for different (not the same) clients. If the number of failed connection requests reaches a predefined threshold, the Cisco IOS dynamically removes the real server from the list of active servers. A server in this state is considered out of service.

- **Automatic server unfail detection**—When a server is removed from the active server list because of a failure detection, no new connections are assigned to it for the length of the predefined retry timer. When this timer expires, SLB puts the real server back on the active server list. If the first new connection to the real server fails, the server again is removed from the active server list.

- **TCP session reassignment**—SLB keeps tabs on every TCP SYN that a client sends when opening up a connection to a real server. If the real server doesn't respond or responds with an RST, the Cisco IOS keeps tabs on the number of times that this occurs. When a predefined threshold is reached, the Cisco IOS assigns the connection request to another server in the server group.

- **SYNGuard**—SLB limits the number of TCP SYNs sent to a virtual server, preventing a DoS SYN flood attack. With this feature, SLB monitors the number of SYNs sent to the virtual server IP address over a defined interval, preventing the number of new connections to a predefined threshold. Any connections above this threshold are dropped.

- **Delay removal of TCP connections**—Because some packets from a TCP session might arrive out of order, when a connection is terminated, SLB maintains the connection information for a short time, ensuring that all packets for the connection have a chance to reach the client or the real server. You can manipulate this delay timer.

- **Dynamic Feedback Protocol (DFP)**—DFP is an SLB protocol that allows the real servers to share status information with the device that is handling the load balancing (the SLB router). DFP is beyond the scope of this book.

- **Stateless backup**—SLB, working with HSRP, allows for a stateless (not stateful) redundancy solution.

SLB Advantages and Limitations

One of the nice features of SLB is that it provides a scalable solution that is easy to maintain. For example, you can add or remove real servers from the group without affecting the function of the virtual server. Plus, when a new real server is added to the server group, the slow start feature ensures that the new server is not overloaded quickly by a flood of new connection requests. Because clients know only about the virtual servers, maintenance is easy: Changes in your configuration are centralized. Plus, clients know only about the virtual address, not the real address of the server, providing extra protection for your server groups. With the SYNGuard feature, SLB can provide a basic level of DoS protection as well.

SLB does have some limitations, however, including the following:

- FTP is supported only in dispatched mode.

- Load balancing is supported only between subnets, not between devices on the same subnet.

- For routers using dispatched mode, the real servers must be connected through Layer 2 to the SLB router.

- For routers, with both directed and dispatched modes, packet switching is not hardware accelerated. The Catalyst 6500 supports hardware acceleration for dispatched mode.

- SLB is supported only on the 2690 series of routers and higher, limiting its usefulness in smaller environments.

SLB Configuration

SLB has a handful of required commands that you must configure to enable it, along with many other optional commands that you can configure. This section breaks down the required and optional configuration tasks.

Required SLB Commands

The first thing that you need to do is specify which real servers will be placed in which server group:

```
Router(config)# ip slb serverfarm server_farm_name
Router(config-slb-sfarm)# real IP_address
Router(config-slb-real)# inservice
```

The **ip slb serverfarm** command creates a grouping of your real servers. The name of the server farm can be up to 15 characters in length. The **real** command specifies the IP address of a real server in the server group. This takes you into a subconfiguration mode, in which the **inservice** command enables the server in the group: Preface the command with the **no** parameter to take it out of service. For more servers, repeat this process with the **real** and **inservice** commands.

After you have created your real server group(s), you need to associate the server farm with a virtual server:

```
Router(config)# ip slb vserver virtual_server_name
Router(config-slb-vserver)# serverfarm server_farm_name
Router(config-slb-vserver)# virtual IP_address {tcp|udp} port_#
  [service service_name]
Router(config-slb-vserver)# inservice
```

The **ip slb vserver** command is used to create the information necessary for your virtual server. You must create a name for the virtual server, which can be up to 15 characters in length. The **serverfarm** command specifies which server farm group is to be used to service traffic sent to the virtual IP address. The virtual IP address for the virtual server is configured with the **virtual** command. You also must specify the protocol used (TCP or UDP), as well as the port number or name of the application that the virtual server handles. Table 12-3 lists valid port names and numbers. The optional **service** parameter specifies that all related connections for a client should be handled by the same real server. Currently, the only choice that you can specify is **ftp**. When you have everything configured, use the **inservice** command to activate the virtual server.

Table 12-3 *Virtual Server Ports*

Virtual Port Name	Virtual Port Number	Description
dns	**53**	Domain Name System
ftp	**21**	File Transfer Protocol
https	**443**	HTTP over SSL
matip-a	**350**	Mapping of Airline Traffic over IP
nntp	**119**	Network News Transport Protocol
pop2	**109**	Post Office Protocol v2

continues

Table 12-3 *Virtual Server Ports (Continued)*

Virtual Port Name	Virtual Port Number	Description
pop3	110	Post Office Protocol v3
smtp	25	Simple Mail Transport Protocol
telnet	23	Telnet
www	80	World Wide Web
	0	All ports

Optional SLB Commands

You can use many optional commands to tune SLB. The section covers many of these commands.

Load-Balancing Algorithm

The default load-balancing algorithm for SLB is WRR. This can be changed with the following configuration:

```
Router(config)# ip slb serverfarm server_farm_name
Router(config-slb-sfarm)# predictor {roundrobin|leastconns}
```

The **roundrobin** command specifies WRR, and the **leastconns** parameter specifies WLC. This command affects all real servers in this server farm group.

Real Server Attributes

These commands affect how SLB interacts with a specified real server in the server farm group:

```
Router(config)# ip slb serverfarm server_farm_name
Router(config-slb-sfarm)# real IP_address
Router(config-slb-real)# faildetect numconns #_of_connections
  [numclients #_of_clients]
Router(config-slb-real)# maxconns maximum_#_of_connections
Router(config-slb-real)# reassign #_of_SYN_requests
Router(config-slb-real)# retry #_of_seconds
Router(config-slb-real)# weight weighting_value
```

These commands affect only the specified real server in the server farm group.

The **faildetect numconns** command specifies the number of consecutive failed connection attempts by a client that cause SLB to take a real server out of service. The default number is 8, but this can range from 1 to 255. Optionally, you can specify the number of unique clients that must have connection failures, along with the total number of failures. The default number of clients is 2, but this can range from 1 to 8.

The **maxconns** command restricts the maximum number of active connections allowed to the real server. This can range from 1 to 4,294,967,295, with 4,294,967,295 as the default.

The **reassign** command specifies the number of consecutive ignored SYNs from a client to a real server that causes SLB to reassign the client's connection to a different real server. SLB waits for 30 seconds for the connection to be established; after this period, SLB removes the connection from its table. The threshold that can be assigned ranges from 1 to 4 SYN requests, with 3 being the default.

The **retry** command specifies the number of seconds that the Cisco IOS should wait after detecting a failed server before a new connection attempt is allowed. This value can range from 0 to 3600 seconds, with 60 seconds as the default. If you specify 0, no new connection attempt is made when a server is considered out of service.

The **weight** command assigns a weight to the real server, which the load-balancing algorithm then uses. This can range from 1 to 155, with 8 as the default weight.

Virtual Server Attributes

These commands affect how SLB interacts with a specified virtual server that is serviced by a server farm group:

```
Router(config)# ip slb vserver virtual_server_name
Router(config-slb-vserver)# client IP_address subnet_mask
Router(config-slb-vserver)# delay #_of_seconds
Router(config-slb-vserver)# idle #_of_seconds
Router(config-slb-vserver)# sticky #_of_seconds [group group_ID]
Router(config-slb-vserver)# synguard #_of_SYNs #_of_milliseconds
Router(config-slb-vserver)# no advertise
```

The **client** command restricts the clients that use the virtual server. By default, all clients (0.0.0.0 0.0.0.0) are allowed to use the virtual server.

The **delay** command specifies the number of seconds that SLB maintains the client's TCP connection in its table after the connection has terminated. This defaults to 10 seconds but can range from 1 to 600.

The **idle** command specifies the number of seconds that SLB keeps an idle connection in its table. The default is 3600 seconds, but this can range from 10 to 65,535.

The **sticky** command specifies the length of time, in seconds, that all the connections from the same client are forwarded to the same real server. By default, this option is disabled. Valid time ranges are 0 to 65,535. The optional **group** parameter associates a virtual server with a group number, which is used to group these connections. The group number ranges from 0 to 255. If more than one virtual server is placed in the same group, services from the same client IP address are handled by the same real server.

The **synguard** command controls the number of TCP SYNs for new connections, to prevent a TCP SYN flood DoS attack. The number of half-open connections can range from 0 to 4,294,967,295. The default is 0, which disables this feature. When it is enabled, the default interval of 100 milliseconds is used to monitor SYN flooding. This can range from 50 to 5000 milliseconds.

The **advertise** command is used to advertise a route to the virtual server address. By default, the Cisco IOS creates a static route for the virtual server address, pointing to interface null0. This ensures that the Cisco IOS will handle the specified virtual server traffic instead of dropping it. To disable this function, use the **no advertise** command.

NAT Configuration

By default, the Cisco IOS uses dispatched mode for servicing the virtual server address. To use directed mode, use the following configuration for the server farm grouping:

```
Router(config)# ip slb serverfarm server_farm_name
Router(config-slb-sfarm)# nat server
```

The **nat server** command enables directed mode for the processing of packets, which causes the Cisco IOS to translate the virtual IP address to the real IP address in the redirection.

SLB Verification

You can use many **show** and **debug** commands to verify and troubleshoot SLB. Table 12-4 lists the **show** commands for SLB.

Table 12-4   *SLB* **show** *Commands*

Command	Description
show ip slb conns [**vservers** *virtserver_name*] [**client** *ip_address*] [**detail**]	Displays all the connections handled by SLB. You can qualify the output with the addition of these parameters.
show ip slb dfp [**agent** *IP_address port_#*] [**detail**] [**weights**]	Displays information about DFP and the real servers using DFP.
show ip slb reals [**vservers** *virtserver_name*] [**detail**]	Displays information about the real servers defined in SLB.
show ip slb serverfarms [**name** *serverfarm_name*] [**detail**]	Displays information about the server farms defined in SLB.
show ip slb stats	Displays statistics about SLB.
show ip slb sticky [**client** *IP_address*]	Displays information about clients' sticky connections.
show ip slb vservers [**name** *virtserver_name*] [**detail**]	Displays information about SLB's virtual servers.

For more detailed troubleshooting, you can use the following **debug** command:

```
Router# debug ip slb {conns | dfp | icmp | reals | all}
```

Table 12-5 displays the options for this command.

Table 12-5   *SLB* **debug** *Commands*

Parameter	Description
conns	Displays messages for connections handled by SLB
dfp	Displays messages about DFP messages
icmp	Displays all ICMP messages used by SLB
reals	Displays all messages for real servers used by SLB
all	Displays all debug messages for SLB

SLB Example

Take a look at a simple example using SLB, using the network shown in Figure 12-11. In this network, two web servers are located off the DMZ interface (ethernet2). The second web server can handle twice as many connections as the first server, so the load-balancing algorithm needs to be adjusted. Assume that the web servers have both their real and virtual addresses configured on them (they're operating in dispatched mode).

Figure 12-11   *SLB Example*

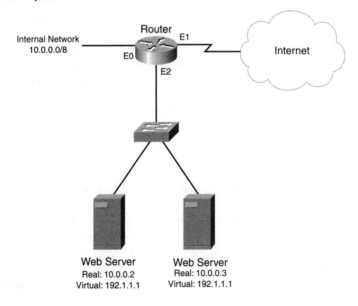

Example 12-14 shows the configuration for this example.

Example 12-14 *Configuring SLB in Dispatched Mode*

```
Router(config)# ip slb serverfarm dmz-web-servers
Router(config-slb-sfarm)# real 10.0.0.2
Router(config-slb-real)# weight 8
Router(config-slb-real)# inservice
Router(config-slb-real)# exit
Router(config-slb-sfarm)# real 10.0.0.3
Router(config-slb-real)# weight 16
Router(config-slb-real)# inservice
Router(config-slb-real)# exit
Router(config)# ip slb vserver internet-web-server
Router(config-slb-vserver)# serverfarm dmz-web-servers
Router(config-slb-vserver)# virtual 192.1.1.1 tcp 80
Router(config-slb-vserver)# inservice
```

As you can see, this example is straightforward. The **ip slb serverfarm** command specifies the real web servers being used: 10.0.0.2 and 10.0.0.3. If you were using directed mode instead of dispatched mode, you would include the **nat service** command here. Notice that, in this example, 10.0.0.3 has twice the weight of 10.0.0.2, indicating that it can handle twice the number of connections. The **ip slb vserver** command creates the virtual server (192.1.1.1) for web traffic.

TIP   One of the interesting things about configuring SLB is that it does not associate the configuration with any particular interface. Therefore, in the example shown in Figure 12-11, external users would use 192.1.1.1 to access the internal servers, and the internal users could use the 10.0.0.2 and 10.0.0.3 address. One problem with this, however, is that the internal users lose load-balancing capabilities. You easily can solve this by creating another virtual server group, placing the two real web servers in the group, and assigning the virtual server an address from 10.0.0.0/8.

Summary

This chapter expanded on the foundation laid in the Chapter 11, discussed some of the issues related to using address translation, and detailed how you can deal with them. One of the biggest problems when using address translation is that some applications, especially NetBIOS and multimedia applications, embed addressing information in the data payload, which typically creates connection problems. The Cisco IOS supports address translation of embedded addressing information in more than a dozen applications. If an application is using a nonstandard port, you also can remap it with the **ip nat service** command.

With extended ACLs, you explicitly can control what traffic gets translated. If you need to perform translations with different sets of global addresses to two or more destinations, though, you must use a solution that creates extended entries, such as PAT or route maps. Route maps are more flexible because you can match on more information in the packet headers, which helps the Cisco IOS to determine if it needs to perform address translation or not on the actual packet.

The Cisco IOS provides for two types of redundancy for address translation solutions: static and dynamic. Static redundancy is provided by HSRP. Dynamic redundancy is implemented using SNAT with either HSRP or a manual primary/backup configuration. This provides a stateful failover process.

As mentioned in the previous chapter, the NAT function of the Cisco IOS provides the capability for traffic distribution, but it has its shortcomings. SLB solves these issues by providing a more scalable and manageable solution. The main limitation of SLB is that it works only on higher-end routers.

Next up is Part VI, "Managing Access Through Routers," which shows you how to authenticate connection requests before allowing them through a router. This part also teaches you how to provide protection for the routing protocol(s) on your router and how to use your routing protocol(s) to provide extra protection for your network.

## PART V

Managing Access Through Routers

Chapter 13   Lock-and-Key Access Lists

Chapter 14   Authentication Proxy

Chapter 15   Routing Protocol Protection

Lock-and-Key Access Lists

One issue that you probably will have to face is allowing your users to access your network remotely, typically through a public network such as the Internet. In most situations, you will use a Virtual Private Network (VPN) to provide for the connectivity. VPNs are discussed in Part VIII, "Virtual Private Networks." However, one limitation that VPNs have is that, after users are connected through a secure connection to your network, they have free reign over internal resources. You could implement an ACL to restrict their traffic, but this ACL applies to all users accessing a resource.

Some mechanism is needed to authenticate users and restrict what resources they can access. Cisco has two solutions to this problem:

- Lock-and-key ACLs
- Authentication proxy

This chapter focuses on lock-and-key ACLs; the next chapter focuses on authentication proxy.

Lock-and-Key Overview

As already discussed in Part III, "Nonstateful Filtering Technologies," you can use ACLs to protect your internal resources from external threats. However, in some situations you might need to allow specific users to other internal resources, but prevent the Internet from reaching these services. Unfortunately, normal ACLs, such as standard and extended ACLs, cannot provide this functionality—they filter only on Layers 3 and 4 and cannot authorize access on a per-user basis. This section details how lock-and-key access lists can help address these limitations.

Lock-and-Key and Normal ACLs

Lock-and-key was Cisco's first solution to the problem of authenticating users on unknown devices. Lock-and-key uses dynamic ACLs, somewhat similar to how Context-Based Access Control (CBAC) and reflexive ACLs work. However, whereas CBAC and reflexive ACLs add ACL entries based on inspected traffic, allowing the return of that traffic into the network, lock-and-key works differently. Lock-and-key requires a user first to authenticate to the router through Telnet or SSH. After being authenticated, specific dynamic ACL entries are activated on the ACL applied to the interface. These entries remain active for a specific period of time and then expire. This enables a user to authenticate and access resources that normally would be denied. Lock-and-key ACLs can be combined with other types of ACLs, such as extended ACLs.

The lock-and-key process is different from a normal extended ACL. With an extended ACL, all the statements are static. Therefore, if you want to allow specific users to access resources inside your network, you must set up a static ACL statement to grant this access; it remains active as long as the ACL is applied to the interface and the interface is up. Of course, if you do not know the IP addresses of these users, you must be fairly promiscuous in allowing a large range of addresses, which might be counter to your security policies. Lock-and-key is a more robust solution because static ACLs have the following characteristics:

- They cannot authenticate individual users.

- They are static and might require you to open a larger hole in your router to allow specific users into your network to access specific resources.

- They are difficult to manage, especially when you must control specific users' access to resources, which also might cause the router to perform excessive processing of ACL statements.

When to Use Lock-and-Key

Lock-and-key, also referred to as dynamic ACL, was introduced to the Cisco IOS in version 11.1, so it has been around for quite a while. Originally, it was developed for dialup access and performed double authentication. With double authentication, the user was authenticated first through PPP's CHAP and then through lock-and-key. Sometimes the terms *double authentication* and *lock-and-key* are used interchangeably; however, lock-and-key is one specific authentication method used within double authentication. Lock-and-key is not restricted to just dialup access, though—it also can be used for LAN access. This chapter focuses on the latter approach.

Lock-and-key typically is used in one of two situations:

- You want restricted access from your network based on a user's identity—with lock-and-key, the user is authenticated first and then granted access.

- You want to control external access to internal resources based on a user's identity.

Lock-and-Key Benefits

Lock-and-key actually works hand in hand with extended ACLs, enhancing their functionality. Lock-and-key benefits include the following:

- Authentication of the users can be centralized on an AAA server.

- Users must provide a username and/or password to authenticate. After they are authenticated, a dynamic ACL entry is activated to allow or restrict additional access.

- Management is simplified because ACL entries are created dynamically based on a user's authentication.

- ACLs are smaller in size, and dynamic entries are added only when a user authenticates, placing a smaller burden of processing the ACL on the router.

- Exposure to your internal resources is limited because dynamic entries are added only when a user authenticates.

Lock-and-Key Process

This section looks at the process that occurs when granting a user access to internal resources when the perimeter router is using lock-and-key. Figure 13-1 illustrates this example.

Figure 13-1 *Lock-and-Key Process*

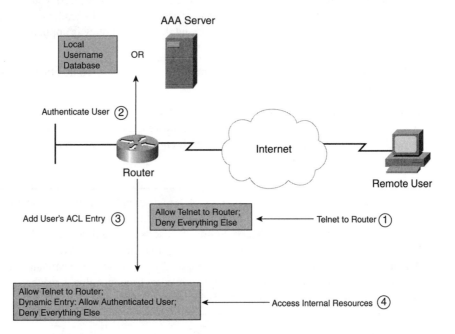

The following is an explanation of the numbered steps in Figure 13-1 that occur during the entire process:

1 A remote user first opens a Telnet or SSH connection to the router. The router's external ACL must permit this connection. The router prompts the user for a username and password, which the user enters.

Caution	Both Telnet and SSH are supported for the authentication. However, for public access to your router performing lock-and-key, I highly recommend that you use SSH instead of Telnet for the authentication connection. This is because SSH encrypts the session, including the password sent to the router. Remember that Telnet sends all traffic, including usernames and passwords, in clear text

2 The router authenticates the connection. Three choices can be used for authentication: the local username database defined with **username** commands, an AAA server using RADIUS or TACACS+, or the **password** command on the VTY lines. If the user fails the authentication, the user is reprompted for the authentication information. If the authentication is successful, the Telnet/SSH connection is *terminated*; the function of the Telnet/SSH connection is for authentication only. After the user has been authenticated, the Telnet/SSH connection no longer is needed, so the router terminates it.

3 After the user successfully authenticates, the Cisco IOS adds a dynamic ACL entry that grants the user access to the configured internal resources. As you will see later in the chapter, you cannot set up per-user access policies. Instead, you define one policy for all your lock-and-key users, and this single policy is applied to all the authenticated users.

4 At this point, the user can access the internal resources that would otherwise be denied (through the dynamic ACL entry).

If users do not authenticate first, they are allowed to access only resources specified in the static external ACL. To access other internal resources, the users first must authenticate through Telnet or SSH. Then the dynamic ACL entry added by the router allows them to access other internal resources.

CAUTION	Lock-and-key is susceptible to IP spoofing. After a user authenticates and opens a temporary hole in the firewall, the hacker can use this address to exploit a spoofing attack (typically, a DoS attack) if the hacker knows the user's source IP address. To prevent this kind of attack, you might want to consider encryption, such as a VPN. The temporary dynamic ACL entry also is not deleted automatically when the user terminates the session. Instead, it remains in the ACL until the dynamic entry timeout value is reached or until the administrator manually clears the entry (whichever happens first).

Lock-and-Key Configuration

Now that you have a basic understanding of how lock-and-key works, the next section takes a look at how to configure it. Lock-and-key uses extended ACLs—actually, you embed a dynamic ACL entry in an extended ACL, and this dynamic ACL entry creates the temporary ACL entry for your authenticated users. Therefore, you need to be very familiar with the configuration and operation of extended ACLs. The following sections discuss how to configure lock-and-key, as well as how to verify your configuration.

Configuration Steps

You must perform three basic steps when setting up lock-and-key:

Step 1   Create your extended ACL. At a minimum, you must permit Telnet or SSH access to the router, as well as put a placeholder entry in the ACL for the dynamic entry that your user's authentication will create.

Step 2   Define your authentication. Lock-and-key supports three methods of authentication: local (the username database), an external AAA server, and the line password. Typically, the line password is not used because all users would use the same password.

Step 3   Enable the lock-and-key authentication method. This occurs on your router's VTY lines. When you enable it, the router can create dynamic ACL entries on its interface ACL that has the lock-and-key ACL reference.

The following sections cover these three steps.

Step 1: Create Your Extended ACL

The first thing you need to do is configure your extended ACL for your router's external interface. The configuration of this ACL is discussed in Chapter 7, "Basic Access Lists." Lock-and-key supports both numbered and named extended ACLs. You must do two things with this ACL:

- The first (or one of the first) entries in the ACL should permit Telnet or SSH access to an IP address on the router that the external users will use. Typically, this is the IP address configured on the external interface.

- Second, you must embed a lock-and-key ACL entry into the ACL. This entry defines what internal resource(s) a user is allowed to access after authenticating.

The following commands create the dynamic lock-and-key ACL entry:

```
Router(config)# access-list ACL_# dynamic dynamic_ACL_name [timeout minutes]
    {deny|permit} IP_protocol source_IP_address src_wildcard_mask
    destination_IP_address dst_wildcard_mask [precedence precedence] [tos TOS]
    [established] [log]
```

or:

```
Router(config)# ip access-list extended ACL_name
Router(config-ext-nacl)# dynamic dynamic_ACL_name [timeout minutes]
    {deny|permit} IP_protocol source_IP_address src_wildcard_mask
    destination_IP_address dst_wildcard_mask [precedence precedence] [tos TOS]
    [established] [log]
```

The **dynamic** keyword in these two ACL methods enables you to specify the name of the dynamic ACL that is to be used. This name must be unique among all named ACLs on the router. The lock-and-key **timeout** parameter is optional. It enables you to specify an absolute timeout for the dynamic entry that an authenticated user creates. The timeout can range from 1 to 9999 minutes.

CAUTION   Two timeouts are associated with dynamic ACL entries for lock-and-key: absolute and idle. The absolute timer is specified in the dynamic ACL entry. If you do not specify a timeout, the default is never to time out the entry. The idle timeout value is specified in the **autocommand** command, which is used to enable lock-and-key authentication on your VTYs. As with the absolute timeout, if you do not specify an idle timeout, the default is never to time out the entry. Therefore, I highly recommend that you configure either an idle or an absolute timeout—or both. Otherwise, if you forget to configure these optional idle parameters, the dynamic ACL entries created will remain in your extended ACL.

Following the **timeout** parameter in the ACL statement, you specify the user's traffic that you want to permit. Normally, you do not know the IP address of the external user (the source); therefore, use the keyword **any**. As you will see in the "Step 3: Enable Lock-and-Key Authentication" section, an option with the **autocommand** command allows the Cisco IOS to replace the keyword **any** with the actual source IP address of the authenticated user.

NOTE   Unfortunately, you can have only one **dynamic** entry in your extended ACL. This ACL entry must encompass all of the external users accessing internal resources. Therefore, some companies set up a bastion host(s) that these users can log into. Lock-and-key can be used to restrict access to the bastion host(s). Users then log into the bastion host to access other resources inside the network. Because of this limitation, many companies prefer to use authentication proxy, discussed in the next chapter. However, if you want external users to access only one resource (or all resources, for that matter), you can accomplish this with a single dynamic ACL entry. Just remember that you can have only one dynamic ACL entry in your extended ACL. Also, this entry typically is placed toward the top of the ACL, to prevent other ACL statements from prematurely dropping the user's traffic.

After you have created your extended ACL with Telnet and/or SSH permission and the dynamic lock-and-key entries, you must activate your ACL on your router's interface with the **ip access-group** command.

The **access-list dynamic-extended** command, shown here, extends the timeout value for lock-and-key entries by 6 minutes:

```
Router(config) access-list dynamic-extended
```

This is an optional command and typically is used when you have a job running that is near its absolute timeout, but the job will not finish in time. By configuring this command on your router, you can extend the timeout value by another 6 minutes.

Here are some important tips regarding the configuration of your lock-and-key ACL:

- You can have only one **dynamic** parameter in the ACL. In some Cisco IOS versions, other **dynamic** parameters are ignored; in others, they are flagged as invalid.

- Use a unique name for the lock-and-key ACL specified with the **dynamic** parameter.

- For the dynamic ACL entry, be as specific as possible regarding what the authenticated users are allowed access to—in other words, it is not recommended that you use the keyword **any** as the destination address.

- Make sure that one of your static ACL entries allows the external users to Telnet (23) and/or SSH (22) into the router.

- If you do not specify an absolute timeout in the dynamic ACL entry, make sure that you specify an idle timeout in the **autocommand** configuration.

- If you specify both an absolute and an idle timeout, make sure that the idle timeout value is smaller than the absolute value. Otherwise, the Cisco IOS might experience problems removing the temporary ACL entry.

- You can combine lock-and-key ACL entries with timed entries, thus restricting outside access to specific dates and times.

- The only values that the router can replace in the temporary ACL entry are the source and destination addresses, assuming that you used the **host** parameter in the **autocommand** command. For the extended ACLs that are applied inbound, the source address is replaced with that of the external user. You also can use lock-and-key to restrict outbound access. In this case, create an extended ACL and apply it outbound on the internal interface. This causes the Cisco IOS to replace the destination keyword **any** with the actual IP address of the internal device.

Here are some important tips about lock-and-key ACLs in general:

- Dynamic entries are removed when the router reboots, when you manually clear the entry, when the idle timeout is reached, or when the absolute timeout is reached. If you save your router's configuration, the dynamic ACL entries that users create when they authenticate are not saved; if your router reboots, however, they easily can be recreated by having the user reauthenticate.

- If you suspect that unauthorized users are trying to authenticate through lock-and-key, enable logging to capture their activity.

Lock-and-Key ACLs

When Cisco first introduced lock-and-key in Cisco IOS 11.1, I thought that it would solve all my per-user authentication problems. Unfortunately, I soon found out that lock-and-key is somewhat restrictive in implementing per-user policies. I had hoped that each user or group could have its own set of defined policies and that these policies would be enforced when the user authenticated. However, lock-and-key allows you to define only one policy statement per ACL, which limits its usefulness in a LAN environment (multiaccess interface). Of course, Cisco intended customers to use lock-and-key to provide double authentication for dialup connections, in which each dialup interface could have a different ACL and, thus, different policies. The appropriate policy (or policies) could be enforced based on the phone number dialed by the user and the line that the user connected to on the router. Normally, I use lock-and-key in small environments, where only a small number of users need authentication and authentication proxy either is not necessary or is not available. In this environment, users need to authenticate only to access a specific host, such as a bastion host. As you will see in the next chapter, authentication proxy uses the same process as lock-and-key; however, it enables you to enforce per-user and per-group policies within the same ACL.

Step 2: Define Your Authentication Method

After you have created your extended ACL with its dynamic entry, you are ready to define your authentication method. Three methods of authentication exist:

- Line password
- Local database
- AAA server

The configuration of the line password is discussed in Chapter 3, "Accessing a Router." The local database and AAA server configuration are discussed in Chapter 5, "Authentication, Authorization, and Accounting."

I highly recommend that you not use the line password method because every user would have to use the same password. This is basically how you would set up authentication with a line password:

```
Router(config)# line vty 0 4
Router(config-line)# login
Router(config-line)# password password
```

To use a local username database, use the following configuration:

```
Router(config)# username user's_name secret user's_password
Router(config)# line vty 0 4
Router(config-line)# login local
```

To set up AAA with TACACS, use the following configuration:

```
Router(config)# aaa new-model
Router(config)# tacacs-server host IP_address
Router(config)# tacacs-server key key
```

```
Router(config)# aaa authentication login authentication_name group tacacs+
Router(config)# line vty 0 4
Router(config-line)# login authentication_name
```

Instead of the last line, you could use this:

```
Router(config-line)# login tacacs
```

Note that RADIUS is not supported with this option.

TIP   When authenticating lock-and-key access, you will want to include all of your VTYs. Typically, this is 0 to 4, but some router models vary. Of the three methods, AAA is the most scalable.

Step 3: Enable Lock-and-Key Authentication

The last thing you need to do is enable lock-and-key authentication on your VTYs. This is accomplished with the following configuration:

```
Router(config)# line vty 0 4
Router(config-line)# autocommand access-enable host [timeout minutes]
```

The **autocommand access-enable** command specifies lock-and-key authentication. When a user successfully authenticates, a temporary ACL entry is inserted into the extended ACL at the **dynamic** parameter placeholder in the extended ACL on the interface where the user is coming into the router. In other words, if you have two external interfaces, the temporary entry is added only on the one interface that the user connects to. Without the **autocommand access-enable** command, the router will not create the temporary ACL entries.

The **host** parameter is optional. By specifying this parameter, however, you cause the Cisco IOS to replace the dynamic ACL entry's keyword **any** with the user's IP address. If the extended ACL is applied inbound, the source keyword **any** is replaced with the user's IP address; if it is applied outbound, the destination keyword **any** is replaced.

CAUTION   If you do not specify the **host** parameter, the Cisco IOS puts the parameters in the dynamic ACL entry in the temporary ACL entry. Therefore, **permit ip any any** in the dynamic entry also would appear in the temporary entry. If you use the **host** keyword, the Cisco IOS replaces one of the keywords, based on the application of the ACL, with the user's IP address, as in **permit** *user_IP* **any**. Always code the keyword **host** in the **autocommand access-enable** command.

The optional **timeout** parameter is used to set the idle timeout for the user's temporary ACL entry. As mentioned in the "Step 1: Create Your Extended ACL" section, if you do not specify an idle timeout, it defaults to no timeout.

Keep in mind these configuration tips regarding the activation of lock-and-key:

- You should secure all your VTYs with the same **autocommand** configuration, to ensure that you are protecting the router (there is one exception to this, covered shortly).

- If you did not configure an absolute timeout in the dynamic ACL entry, make sure that you configure an idle timeout with the **autocommand** command. When configuring an idle timeout, it must be less than the absolute timeout, if configured.

- When using a TACACS+ server to authenticate the user, you should configure the **autocommand** command on the TACACS+ server as a per-user, not per-group, command.

Allowing Remote Administration Access

One problem with the previous approach to securing all your VTYs with the **autocommand** command is that the VTY line is used for lock-and-key user authentication. After the user has authenticated, or when the user fails to authenticate, the Cisco IOS immediately disconnects the user from the router. However, this presents a problem if you want to access the router remotely and perform administration tasks.

Telnet Solution

To solve this problem, set up a semi-backdoor into your router. If you will be using Telnet to access your router remotely, you will perform something like one of the following:

```
Router(config)# line vty last_line_#_plus_1
Router(config-line)# login
Router(config-line)# password password
Router(config-line)# rotary rotary_#
```

or:

```
Router(config)# line vty last_line_#_plus_1
Router(config-line)# login local|tacacs
Router(config-line)# rotary rotary_#
```

The first thing to point out is that you will be creating an additional line number for your VTYs. If you already have VTYs 0 to 4, you use 5 as the VTY number. Second, My preference is to use the second method, not the first, because the second method uses a username and password for authentication instead of just the line password. The third item of note is the function of the **rotary** command. This command removes the Telnet function from port 23 and places it on 3000 + the rotary number. As an example, if the rotary number was 1, you would use a port number of 3001 (instead of 23) for the Telnet connection.

Example 13-1 demonstrates a simple example.

Example 13-1 *Telnet Rotary Example*

```
Router(config)# username richard secret itsasecret
Router(config)# line vty 5
Router(config-line)# login local
Router(config-line)# rotary 1
```

In this example, if you wanted to remotely access the router, you would have to Telnet to the router on port 3001. You also would need to make sure that your router allowed this port number in its inbound ACL on the interface that you would be using to access the router.

CAUTION   If you are determined to use Telnet for remote administration, at least make sure that any type of Telnet access is prohibited from the external interface. In other words, you should use this method only from an internal interface.

SSH Solution

My personal preference is *not* to use Telnet for remote access, but to use SSH instead. Therefore, for all VTYs that you will be using for either remote administration or lock-and-key, specify that only SSH should be used, like this:

```
Router(config)# line vty 0 last_VTY_#
Router(config-line)# transport input ssh
```

Second, perform the configuration in the "Telnet Solution" section. Finally, you must tell the Cisco IOS what port number SSH will use for accessing the router:

```
Router(config)# ip ssh port port_# rotary rotary_#
```

In this command, specify the port number that SSH will use, such as 2000. The rotary number that you specify here must match the rotary number in the **rotary** command configured on your backdoor VTY. With this configuration, SSH will be allowed access to the backdoor VTY only on the configured port number.

Example 13-2 shows a sample of setting up an SSH backdoor.

Example 13-2 *SSH Rotary Example*

```
Router(config)# username richard secret itsasecret
Router(config)# line vty 5
Router(config-line)# login local
Router(config-line)# rotary 1
Router(config-line)# transport input ssh
Router(config-line)# exit
Router(config)# ip ssh port 2000 rotary 1
```

In this example, only SSH access is allowed on VTY 5; plus, to access this VTY, the SSH client needs to use port 2000. Just make sure that any inbound ACL allows this access. If you will use SSH to access the router remotely, you must open this port number in the ACL.

Local Database Solution

A better option to solving remote administration than using rotaries is to use local authentication through the username database. The problem with using rotaries is that you, as an administrator, must remember the port number used for the connection. Instead of having to remember a port number, you can set up two local accounts: one for lock-and-key authentication and one for remote management. In the **username** command for these accounts, you specify when lock-and-key authentication should be used. Example 13-3 shows a sample of setting the local authentication database.

Example 13-3 *Local Authentication Database and Lock-and-Key*

```
Router(config)# username richard1 secret itsasecret
Router(config)# username richard2 secret itsadifferentsecret
Router(config)# username richard2 autocommand access-enable host
```

In this example, the account richard1 is used for remote management, and the account richard2 is used for lock-and-key authentication. With the second account, a second **username** command is used, with the **autocommand access-enable host** parameter. This parameter specifies that when a user authenticates with this account, lock-and-key authentication will take place.

Verification and Troubleshooting

After you have set up lock-and-key, the Cisco IOS supports various commands to verify and troubleshoot your configuration. One of the basic commands that you will use in your troubleshooting is the following:

```
Router# show [ip] access-list
```

Example 13-4 shows output of this command for a user who has not authenticated yet.

Example 13-4 *Verifying Your Lock-and-Key ACL Entries*

```
Router# show access-list
Extended IP access list 100
    10 permit tcp any host 192.168.1.254 eq 22
    20 Dynamic lockandkey permit ip any 192.168.2.0 0.0.0.255
    30 deny ip any any
```

In this example, only SSH access (port 22) is allowed. The dynamic lock-and-key ACL is called lockandkey. It allows a user to access 192.168.2.0/24, once authenticated. Any other traffic is dropped.

To test the connection, the user must use SSH to authenticate. Example 13-5 shows the ACL after a user authenticates.

Example 13-5 *Dynamic ACL Entry Added After Authentication*

```
Router# show access-list
Extended IP access list 150
    10 permit tcp any host 192.168.1.254 eq 22 (200 matches)
    20 Dynamic lockandkey permit ip any any
       permit ip host 200.1.1.1 any
    30 deny ip any any (162 matches)
```

In this example, 200.1.1.1 authenticated, and you can see the corresponding temporary entry that the Cisco IOS created for this user.

If you want to remove a temporary ACL entry manually in your extended ACL, use the **clear access-template** privileged EXEC command.

Lock-and-Key Example

Now that you have a basic understanding of the commands to configure lock-and-key, take a look at an example that uses this feature to restrict access through the router. This example uses the network shown in Figure 13-2. In this example, users will be authenticated before they are allowed access to the Internet from the internal network.

Figure 13-2 *Lock-and-Key External Access Example*

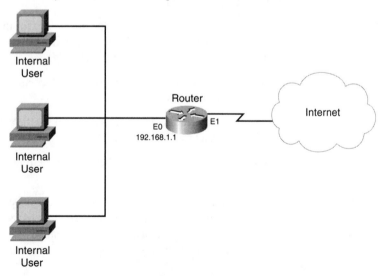

Example 13-6 shows the configuration for the router.

Example 13-6 *Simple Lock-and-Key Authentication Configuration*

```
Router(config)# ip access-list extended allowed-out
Router(confix-ext-nacl)# permit tcp 192.168.1.0 0.0.0.255
                        host 192.168.1.1 eq 22                   (1)
Router(config-ext-nacl)# dynamic dynamic-out permit ip any any   (2)
Router(config-ext-nacl)# deny ip any any
Router(config)# interface etherent0
Router(config-if)# ip address 192.168.1.1 255.255.255.0
Router(config-if)# ip access-group allowed-out in                (3)
Router(config)# username admin1 secret secretadmin1
Router(config)# username user1 secret secret1
Router(config)# line vty 0 4
Router(config-line)# login local                                 (4)
Router(config-line)# transport input ssh
Router(config-line)# autocommand access-enable host timeout 10   (5)
Router(config-line)# exit
Router(config)# line vty 5                                        (6)
Router(config-line)# login local
Router(config-line)# rotary 1
Router(config-line)# transport input ssh
Router(config-line)# exit
Router(config)# ip ssh port 2000 rotary 1
```

The configuration in Example 13-6 focuses only on the lock-and-key configuration. The following is an explanation of this configuration. The numbers on the right side of Example 13-6 correspond to the following numbers:

1 This statement grants SSH access to the internal interface of the router, which is necessary to authenticate the internal users.

2 This statement is the dynamic ACL entry that is the placeholder for the temporary ACL entries after a user is authenticated. Notice that, with the exception of the SSH connection, no traffic is allowed until a user is authenticated.

3 Notice the placement of the ACL—it is on the internal interface applied inbound, which restricts traffic leaving the network.

4 This statement specifies that **username** commands are used for the authentication. The statement below this restricts VTY access to SSH.

5 This statement enables lock-and-key for SSH authentication, setting the idle timer to 10 minutes.

6 This part of the configuration sets up a backdoor so that the administrator can access the router remotely from the internal network. I sometimes use this method instead of specifying lock-and-key in the **username** commands. This makes it more difficult for a hacker to figure out that remote management is allowed (albeit, this is a nonstandard port number).

Note that this example requires a lot more configuration than what is shown, such as an external ACL, address translation, CBAC or reflexive ACLs, and so on. Also note that, unfortunately, because only one user can authenticate, this configuration only allows the first authenticated user access to the Internet; if you remove the host keyword in Reference 5, when one user authenticates, the dynamic ACL entry is activated and all users can access the Internet.

Summary

This chapter showed you the basics of lock-and-key ACLs. Lock-and-key is what I like to call the poor man's version of authentication proxy. Lock-and-key ACLs are used to authenticate a user, opening a temporary hole in your extended ACL filter to grant the user access to other resources. Lock-and-key can use a line password, a local database, or an AAA server to authenticate users, and can authenticate users as their connections either enter or leave the network (or both). Lock-and-key typically is used in a small network that needs to authenticate a specific type of access and when the perimeter router/firewall does not have the Cisco IOS Firewall feature set with authentication proxy installed.

Next is Chapter 14, "Authentication Proxy," which shows you the replacement to lock-and-key ACLs on a router.

## CHAPTER 14

Authentication Proxy

The last chapter discussed how you can use lock-and-key to authenticate users before allowing them access through your perimeter router. As you recall, lock-and-key requires a user first to Telnet into the router to authenticate. Then the Telnet is terminated by the router, and a dynamic ACL entry is created for the user to allow traffic through the router. Lock-and-key is a nifty feature, but it does have limitations:

- It was developed primarily for dialup use, with only one user accessing the router's interface.

- The extended ACL applied to the interface can have only one dynamic entry, which all users must share; this makes it almost impossible to enforce per-user restrictions.

- It requires you to Telnet into the router first, requiring a user's knowledge of the authentication process that must take place first before the user can access resources specified in the dynamic ACL entry.

To overcome these deficiencies, Cisco developed *authentication proxy (AP)*. AP is basically lock-and-key on steroids. It provides the same basic functions as lock-and-key, but it also includes many enhancements that make it more flexible and scalable. Actually, AP and the Cisco PIX's *cut-through proxy (CTP)* are very similar in function. This chapter focuses on the use and configuration of this Cisco IOS Firewall feature.

Introduction to AP

AP is part of the Cisco IOS Firewall feature set and thus requires you to purchase the appropriate Cisco IOS software to access this feature. If you do not have the budget for the Cisco IOS Firewall feature set, you are limited to using lock-and-key for user authentication of connections traveling through the router.

AP enables you to define per-user security access policies that are activated when a user authenticates to the router. For example, you might want to deny all kinds of inbound traffic into your network but open temporary holes in your perimeter router/firewall for specific users. Of course, in many instances, you might not know from what devices these users will be initiating their inbound connections.

AP can deal with this by having the Cisco IOS authenticate users and, based on their authentication, open temporary holes in your router's ACL configuration to allow users to access allowed resources. Unlike with lock-and-key, you can control this access on a per-group or per-user basis. For example, you might have two sets of external users, programmers and network administrators, with two different access policies. When an external user authenticates, the appropriate ACL entries are added to the inbound ACL to allow the user to access the appropriate services. For the programmers, you might set up policies to allow them access to specific development machines; for the network administrators, you might set up access policies to allow them to access specific network-management devices, such as a bastion host.

AP Features

AP first was introduced in Cisco IOS version 12.0(5)T. However, it was limited to performing authentication by HTTP: The user had to use a Java-enabled web browser for authentication. Since then, Cisco has added support for other methods of authentication. These authentication methods are supported:

- HTTP—Cisco IOS 12.0(5)T
- HTTPS (using SSL)—Cisco IOS 12.2(11)YU and 12.2(15)T (you need a Cisco IOS crypto k8 or k9 image to support encryption with HTTPS)
- Telnet—Cisco IOS 12.3(1)
- FTP—Cisco IOS 12.3(1)

As you can see from this list, AP is more flexible than lock-and-key: Lock-and-key supports only Telnet.

AP also supports a form of downloadable ACLs called *access profiles*. AP requires you to use an external AAA server that has the users' accounts and access profiles configured on it. When a user successfully authenticates, the user's access profile is downloaded to the router, where the Cisco IOS includes the access profile as temporary ACL entries in the router's static ACL. Cisco's Cisco Secure ACS product supports access profiles with AP.

AP is compatible with many other Cisco IOS security features, including IDS, CBAC, NAT, and IPSec and VPNs. For example, AP keeps track of incoming HTTP requests to determine whether authentication is needed. If AP sees an abnormally high number of open HTTP requests, this can indicate that the router is under a DoS attack. AP can limit the number of these open requests and drop any requests that go above this threshold.

AP even works with CBAC and NAT; however, if you want to use AP and have NAT configured on your router, Cisco requires you also to use CBAC. NAT can be somewhat tricky with AP. For example, a user might use AP to authenticate using its original address, but NAT then translates this address to another. The concern here is that any temporary dynamic ACL entries created because of the AP authentication should have the correct addressing information. CBAC is needed here because CBAC inspects traffic to make sure that the correct ACL entries are created for the authenticated user.

AP is integrated into AAA, as briefly mentioned in Chapter 5, "Authentication, Authorization, and Accounting." One nice feature of AP and AAA is that you can generate start and stop accounting records for the traffic originating from the authenticated user (this requires the configuration of RADIUS attributes 42, 46, and 47 for both RADIUS and TACACS+ server connections).

Table 14-1 summarizes the features of AP by comparing AP with lock-and-key.

Table 14-1 *AP Versus Lock-and-Key*

Comparator	Authentication Proxy	Lock-and-Key
Authentication connection	HTTP, HTTPS, Telnet, and FTP.	Only Telnet.
User's connection	Can be directed to the router or to one of the previously mentioned services.	Must be directed to the router. After authenticating, the user can use other services dictated by the interface's ACL entries.
Authentication method	AAA authentication and authorization with either TACACS+ or RADIUS.	AAA authentication with TACACS+, RADIUS, or **username** commands.
Temporary ACL location	Defined on the AAA server and downloaded to the router.	Defined as a single dynamic entry in the ACL.
Temporary ACL entries	Each user or group can have its own access profile.	Only a single dynamic ACL entry is used to define all users' policies.

TIP   Cisco recommends that you use lock-and-key if you do not have an AAA server or the Cisco IOS Firewall feature set. I highly recommend that if you need to authenticate users before allowing them through your perimeter router/firewall, you purchase the Cisco IOS Firewall feature set as well as Cisco Secure ACS. This solution provides a more secure and scalable solution than lock-and-key. I commonly refer to lock-and-key as the "poor man's" version of AP.

AP Process

Now that you understand some of the features of AP, this section examines the process that AP uses to authenticate a user and open temporary holes in your ACL.

As you will see later in this chapter, configuring AP is more complex than configuring lock-and-key. One of the things you need to decide is what authentication method or methods are needed: HTTP, HTTPS, Telnet, and/or FTP. My personal recommendation is HTTPS because the connection is encrypted. However, if you are using one-time passwords (OTP), described in Chapter 3, "Accessing a Router," any of these authentication methods is fine.

AP Process Example

Figure 14-1 illustrates the process that takes place with AP. This example assumes that HTTP is used to perform the authentication by the router. As you can see in Figure 14-1, this process is similar to what lock-and-key does during the authentication process, although some differences exist. In this example, the user can cause authentication to occur in one of two methods:

- Open a web connection to the router itself
- Open a web connection to an internal web server

One main difference exists between lock-and-key and AP: AP allows the router to intercept the user's connection (only HTTP, HTTPS, Telnet, and FTP) and perform authentication; after authentication, it allows the router to redirect the user's connection to the resource.

Figure 14-1 *AP Process Example*

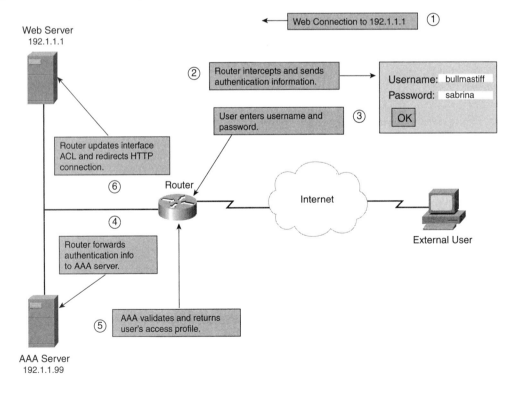

The following is an explanation of the numbered steps in the example shown in Figure 14-1:

Step 1 In this example, the user opens a web connection (HTTP) to the internal web server (192.1.1.1).

Step 2 The router has AP configured, with HTTP as the authentication mechanism, and it intercepts the HTTP connection request. The router sends back a username and password prompt to the user. In the case of HTTP or HTTPS, this is a window that pops up with two text boxes for the username and password.

It is important to point out that if your user has software that blocks pop-ups, this window is not displayed. Therefore, care must be taken to ensure that this window appears on the user's screen.

Step 3 The user must enter a username and password for the appropriate prompts. For HTTP or HTTPS authentication, the user must click the OK button to send the information to the router.

For FTP, if the router is performing redirection and the AAA user account and the FTP server use different usernames and passwords, you can specify both in the username and password prompts. The router then uses the appropriate username/password combination for AAA and for the redirection to the FTP server. When entering the usernames, the user should enter them as **AAA_*username*@*FTP_username***, where the AAA and FTP usernames are separated by the @ symbol. The passwords use the same nomenclature: **AAA_*password*@*FTP_password.***

If you are using one-time passwords, such as token cards, a user can enter the username/password combination up to three times. After this, the user must enter two valid token passwords in succession before the AAA server allows authentication.

Step 4 When the router receives the user's authentication information, it forwards this through TACACS+ or RADIUS to the AAA server.

Step 5 The AAA server authenticates the user. If the user successfully is authenticated, the AAA server sends the user's access profile to the router. The access profile is basically a simplified grouping of ACL statements that define what the user is allowed access to.

Step 6 If the user successfully authenticates, the user receives a pop-up window indicating success (just click the OK button to close it). The router converts the access profile into actual temporary ACL entries that then are activated inbound on the appropriate interface. In this example, this would be inbound on the external interface. The dynamic ACL entries allow the user to access the approved resources. The router actually customizes the user's access profile by placing the user's source IP address in the source field of the ACL entry or entries.

If the router intercepted the HTTP connection, the router redirects the initial connection request to the internal web server.

If the user is not successful in authenticating, the router resends the prompts to the user so that the user can attempt to authenticate again. If the user fails to authenticate after five attempts, the router blocks all new authentication attempts from the user for 2 minutes. This is done to prevent DoS attacks.

One nice feature about this process is that AP enables the router to intercept supported connections, perform authentication, and, for successful authentications, redirect the initial connection request to the appropriate resource.

Of course, the process just described assumes that this is the first time the user initiates a connection. After authentication, the router caches the user's information from the AAA security server and uses this information to determine whether subsequent connections need to be authenticated. The router keeps the cached information for a user as long as traffic is coming to and from the user. If the user is idle for a specified period of time, AP removes the temporary ACL entries and cached information and forces the user to reauthenticate when the user initiates new traffic.

AP Authentication and JavaScript

To provide for secure authentication, AP uses JavaScript. This ensures that the user's username and password are sent to the router instead of accidentally being sent to another web server. Therefore, Cisco highly recommends that JavaScript be enabled for HTTP/HTTPS AP connections on your users' desktops.

However, AP does support authentication without JavaScript, especially in sites that have disabled Java because of security reasons. If JavaScript is disabled, when the user attempts the web connection and the router intercepts it, a pop-up window is opened on the user's desktop that contains the following:

- Instructions on how to enable JavaScript to perform the authentication process automatically

- Instructions on how to manually complete the authentication process and establish the user's web connection

To perform the authentication process manually, follow these steps:

Step 1 Close the pop-up window. Do not click the Done button; instead, click File > Close from the main menu. It is important that you use this process; otherwise, manual authentication will fail.

Step 2 From the user's original web browser window, the user should click the Refresh or Reload button.

If the user's last authentication attempt succeeded, the web page that the user initially was trying to access is displayed. Otherwise, the username/password pop-up window is redisplayed and the user must authenticate again.

CAUTION   Because of the process used with manual authentication, I highly recommend that you explain to your users the process that needs to be done to complete the authentication process successfully. If the user clicks the Done button from the JavaScript warning window, the authentication process will not complete correctly.

AP Usage

AP can be used in many different situations to provide a more secure access method. The following two sections describe when you might want to use AP and where AP typically is deployed.

When to Use AP

AP actually has many practical uses. AP proves useful to your security arrangements in these situations:

- You need to authenticate and authorize external users before allowing them to access specific internal resources, such as a private web server.

- You need to authenticate and authorize internal users before allowing them to access extranet or Internet resources.

- You want to enhance your VPN setup by preauthenticating users before allowing them to set up a VPN connection to your router.

- You need to set up different levels of access on a per-user basis, but you do not necessarily know the IP addresses of the users because these can change on a day-by-day basis (probably because they use PPP or DHCP to acquire their addressing information).

- You need a detailed audit of who connects through the router, how long they were connected, and when these connections occurred.

Where to Use AP

As you saw in the last section, you can use AP to authenticate and authorize access for external users accessing internal resources, as well as internal users accessing external resources. You can configure both of these policies simultaneously on your router.

Figure 14-2 illustrates these policies. In this example, two AP policies have been defined:

- **Internal**—All users must be authenticated before accessing the Internet. Salespeople have complete access, but accounting people are allowed access only to port 80 and ports 8080 through 8099.

- **External**—Any external user who wants to access the internal private web server first must be authenticated.

Figure 14-2 *Where to Use AP*

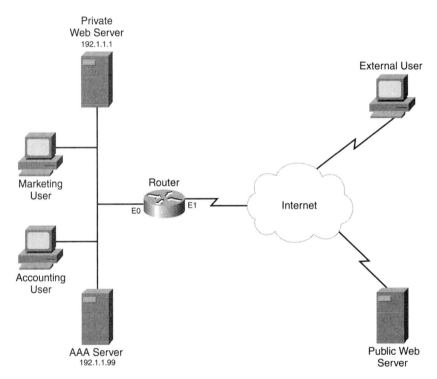

In this example, you create two AP policies: one applied inbound on the internal interface (e0) for the internal users, and one applied inbound on the external interface (e1) for the external users.

Limitations of AP

Despite its advantages, AP has limitations. As with lock-and-key, AP is susceptible to spoofing. After authentication, the router inspects subsequent traffic from the user by examining the user's source IP address. Therefore, if a hacker knows that a user successfully has authenticated, the hacker can compromise the router by executing some form of spoofing attack, taking advantage of this knowledge (and weakness within the mechanics of AP).

Other limitations of AP include these:

- AP works only for traffic traveling through, not to, the router.

- Authentication must occur with HTTP, HTTPS, Telnet, or FTP. These are the most commonly used protocols that provide a mechanism for bidirectional communication, which is why you see only these four methods for authentication on the router. However, after being authenticated, based on any downloaded ACLs, the user can access other resources in the network.

- With HTTP, the Cisco IOS examines only port 80 connections.

- Load balancing with multiple AAA servers is not supported currently with AP.

- If two users are sharing the same device, AP authenticates only the first user, not the second, because AP examines the source IP address in packets to determine whether authentication has been performed.

- As mentioned in the "AP Authentication and JavaScript" section, you can perform authentication without JavaScript, but it is not recommended because it is not as secure.

AP Configuration

The next part of this chapter deals with configuring AP on your Cisco router. Before continuing with the configuration, though, you should meet some prerequisites:

- AP uses AAA to perform authentication and authorization. Make sure that you understand the operation and configuration of AAA discussed in Chapter 5.

- It is highly recommended that you use CBAC (see Chapter 9, "Context-Based Access Control") and ACLs (see Part III, "Nonstateful Filtering Technologies") to complement AP.

- With HTTP and HTTPS authentication, Cisco recommends that you use either Microsoft's Internet Explorer 3.0 or later, or Netscape's Navigator 3.0 or later. Other web browsers might or might not work, so you are on your own if you experience problems with other vendors' web browser products.

When you have met the prerequisites, you are ready to proceed to configuring AP. The following sections discuss the different components that you need to configure:

- Configuring AAA on your router

- Configuring AAA on your AAA server

- Preparing for HTTP and HTTPS (FTP and Telnet do not require special configurations for AP)

- Configuring AP policies

- Tuning AP

- Protecting against access attacks

Configuring AAA on Your Router

One of the first steps is to set up AAA on your router. AAA was covered in Chapter 5, so I do not spend that much time discussing its configuration here. However, one important point to make about AAA and AP is that you must use a TACACS+ or RADIUS server. AP does not support any method of local authentication or authorization.

You will use the following basic AAA commands:

```
Router(config)# aaa new-model                                   (1)
Router(config)# tacacs-server host IP_address                   (2)
  [single-connection] [port port_#] [timeout seconds]
  [key encryption_key]
Router(config)# radius-server host IP_address
  [auth-port port_#] [acct-port port_#] [timeout seconds]
  [retransmit retries]
  [key key_value]
  [alias {hostname|IP_address}]
Router(config)# aaa authentication login default                (3)
  {group radius | group tacacs+ | group server_group}
Router(config)# aaa authorization auth-proxy default            (4)
  {group radius | group tacacs+ | group server_group}
Router(config)# aaa accounting auth-proxy default start-stop    (5)
  {group radius | group tacacs+ | group server_group}
```

Here is a brief explanation of these commands, with reference to the numbering on the right side of the syntax:

1 This command enables AAA.

2 This statement and the next one specify your AAA servers. Remember that you can group your servers with the **aaa group server** command.

3 This command enables AAA authentication.

4 This command enables authorization for AP.

5 This command, which is optional, sets up AAA accounting for AP.

NOTE   If you are setting up AP to verify access from internal users to the outside world and have an ACL applied inbound on the internal interface, you need to allow either RADIUS or TACACS+ communications to the router. RADIUS uses UDP ports 1645 (authentication and authorization) and 1646 (accounting), as well as UDP 1812 and 1813. TACACS+ uses TCP port 49.

Configuring AAA on Your Server

When you have configured AAA on your router, you need to set up AAA on your security server. AP supports the following AAA security servers:

• Cisco Secure ACS 2.1.*x* and later for Windows NT/2000

• Cisco Secure ACS 2.3 for UNIX

- TACACS+ server
- The Ascend RADIUS server
- The Livingston RADIUS server

You need to do a few things on your AAA server:

- Add your users and groups.
- Enable the AP service.
- Create downloadable user profiles that the Cisco IOS converts to ACLs.

The following two sections cover the last two points.

NOTE   The setup of AP on an AAA server is not a simple process, so I briefly discuss it in this chapter. Note, however, that I cover only the use of Cisco Secure ACS for NT/2000 when setting up AP. The version of ACS that I am using is Cisco Secure ACS 3.2. Configuration of other ACS versions and other AAA servers is beyond the scope of this book.

AP Service

By default, the AP service on the Cisco ACS product is disabled. The first thing you need to do is enable it. Enabling it is a two-step process: You need to make changes to the Interface Configuration and Network Configuration sections.

To perform the necessary configuration for the Interface Configuration section, follow these steps:

Step 1   Click the Interface Configuration button in the left-side vertical toolbar.

Step 2   Click the TACACS+ (Cisco IOS) hyperlink in the middle section of the web page.

Step 3   Scroll down to the TACACS+ Services section.

Step 4   In the New Services section, click the closest empty check box and, under the Service column, enter **auth-proxy**.

Step 5   Click the Submit button at the bottom of the window to accept your changes.

In the Network Configuration section, make sure that your router is listed and that the AAA server and router can communicate with each other.

User Authorization Profiles

After you have enabled AP, you need to activate it in the group or groups that your users are associated with that will be using AP. To do this, follow these steps in ACS:

Step 1 Click the Group Setup button in the left-side vertical toolbar.

Step 2 Select the group that you want to add AP to, and click the Edit Settings button.

Step 3 Scroll down to the TACACS+ Settings text box.

Step 4 Toward the bottom of this box, you will find the AP service you just added.

Step 5 Click the check box to the left of the auth-proxy service name.

Step 6 Click the check box to the left of the Custom Attributes description.

Step 7 Beneath the Custom Attributes description is a large text box where you can configure your user authorization profile (UAP) statements. I describe this configuration later.

Step 8 After you have entered your custom attributes, at the bottom of the screen, click the Submit+Restart button.

The UAP in the custom attributes defines what resources a user is authorized to access after being authenticated. Two types of statements exist in a UAP:

```
priv-lvl=15
proxyacl#number=permit protocol any destination_address destination_mask
  protocol_information
```

The **priv-lvl** command assigns the privilege level to the authenticated user. For AP, this must be 15. The **proxyacl#** commands define the UAP—what the user can access after being authenticated. These are basically a simplified access-control entry, which, when the AAA server sends this to the Cisco IOS, the Cisco IOS converts into an ACL statement. Following the **proxyacl#** portion of the command is a statement number. The first statement is numbered 1, the second is 2, and so on. These are used to order your statements. This is followed by an equals sign (=) and then the ACL statement. Note that the format of the ACL statement is the same as that used by entries in a named extended ACL.

NOTE   Make sure that you use the keyword **any** for the source address. When the router receives the UAP entries, the Cisco IOS changes this keyword to the actual source address used by the authenticated user.

Here is a simple UAP example used for the external users in Figure 14-2 trying to access the private web server:

```
priv-lvl=15
proxyacl#1=permit tcp any 192.1.1.1 eq 80
```

This is a straightforward configuration. Note that you can configure multiple **proxyacl#** commands; just make sure that each entry has a unique command number.

Preparing for HTTP or HTTPS

After you have configured AAA on the server and the router, you need to take some preparatory steps on your router to allow AP to occur. As you recall, the Cisco IOS supports HTTP, HTTPS, FTP, and Telnet for authentication and authorization. This means that you need to allow these services in your ACL configuration. For example, if you are setting up AP that uses only HTTPS, and if HTTPS must be done to the router first, you need an entry in the router's inbound ACL that allows the HTTPS (TCP port 443) connection to the router (the destination IP address in the ACL entry should be an address on the router). If you are using other services, you also need to allow these in your ACL entries. Plus, if you are using redirection with HTTP or HTTPS, you need to allow the HTTP/HTTPS connection to the destination service in your ACL entry.

HTTP Configuration Tasks

For HTTP, you need to enable and set up the router's HTTP server. You need to configure these commands on your router:

```
Router(config)# ip http server
Router(config)# ip http authentication aaa
Router(config)# ip http access-class standard_ACL_#
```

The first two commands are necessary. The first command, **ip http server**, enables the router's HTTP server function. The **ip http authentication aaa** command allows the Cisco IOS to use AAA for authentication. The third command is optional: The **ip http access-class** command can be used to restrict certain source addresses to access the router's HTTP server function. This is useful if you will be using AP only to authenticate internal users accessing external resources. In this instance, you know the addresses that the internal clients use. However, for external users, you probably do not know the source addresses, so this command would not be appropriate.

Configuration Tasks for HTTPS

HTTPS was introduced in Cisco IOS 12.2(11)YU and 12.2(15)T. The main advantage that HTTPS has over HTTP, FTP, and Telnet is that information shared across the connection, such as the username and password, is encrypted.

To set up HTTPS for AP, perform the following:

Step 1 Disable the HTTP server:

```
Router(config)# no ip http server
```

Step 2 Enable the HTTPS server function:

```
Router(config)# ip http server-secure
```

Step 3   Enable AAA for the HTTPS server:

```
Router(config)# ip http authentication aaa
```

Step 4   Define a Certificate Authority (CA) trustpoint (optional):

```
Router(config)# ip http secure-trustpoint CA_name
```

In this configuration, the only command that is new is step 4. When two devices are trying to establish a connection, a CA can provide proof of the identities of the two parties, thereby defeating man-in-the-middle or spoofing attacks. Identity information is stored in a certificate, defined in the X.509v3 standard. CAs commonly are used in VPNs as well as secure web transactions. I thoroughly cover the configuration of CAs in Chapter 19, "IPSec Site-to-Site Connections"; refer to this chapter for the router's configuration for a CA.

CAUTION   Note that you do not need to configure a CA to have the router use certificates to verify a device's identity. Instead, you can use HTTPS and have the router generate its own, self-signed certificate. The problem with this approach is that clients can do the same thing. Therefore, if you are very concerned about security, I highly recommend that you set up a CA and have both your router and users use certificates that are used by your own company's CA or a public CA, such as Verisign. With this approach, you can be sure that when a device makes a connection, you can prove the other device's identity.

Configuring AP Policies

After setting up AAA, and, if necessary, preparing the Cisco IOS for HTTP or HTTPS connections, you are ready to define your AP polices and tune AP parameters. To set and activate your AP polices, you need to perform two steps, similar to the steps that you perform when setting up CBAC:

- Define your AP policies.
- Activate your AP policies.

AP Policy Definitions

To define your AP policies, use the following configuration:

```
Router(config)# ip auth-proxy name AP_name {http | ftp | telnet}
    [inactivity-timer minutes] [absolute-timer minutes] [list {ACL_# | ACL_name}]
```

The **ip auth-proxy name** command is used to create your AP policies. If you have more than one interface and you need to define different policies for these interfaces, each policy will have a different AP_name. The name is used to group your policy statements.

Following the name is the authentication method that you want your users to use. For HTTPS, use **http**. If you want to use more than one method, list each method in a separate **ip auth-proxy name** command, but use the same *AP_name*.

Two optional parameters follow. The **inactivity-timer** parameter specifies the number of idle minutes that the user's authentication entries are kept before the Cisco IOS expires them. When they expire, the Cisco IOS removes the entries, which includes any temporary ACL entries that were downloaded from the AAA server. The **absolute-timer** parameter specifies that when the configured time period is reached, whether the user's connection(s) are idle or not, the user's authentication entries are expired and removed. By default, this value is set to 0, which means that only idle connections can be expired. These two timing parameters are used to override the global timing settings for AP (I discuss this command shortly).

CAUTION   When setting the time periods for AP connections, make sure that the time periods are higher than the time periods used by CBAC to expire connections. If the AP timer is smaller, problems can result: AP removes the connections, but CBAC thinks that they are still there, causing the connections to hang. You alleviate this problem by having CBAC remove the entries when the idle time period is reached.

One last optional parameter to this command is the specification of an ACL name or list. This can be a standard or extended ACL. For packets that match **permit** statements in the list, the router performs AP, ensuring that the user is authenticated. This enables you to control which users are authenticated.

Example 14-1 is a simple configuration example, based on the network shown in Figure 14-2, of defining your AP policies. Assume that HTTP is used here for authentication.

Example 14-1 *Simple AP Policy Configuration*

```
Router(config)# ip auth-proxy name internal_users http
Router(config)# ip auth-proxy name external_users http access-list 100
Router(config)# access-list 100 permit tcp any host 192.1.1.1 eq 80
```

As you can see in this example, two policies were defined: one for the internal users and one for the external users. For internal users, all users will be authenticated through HTTP, whereas, only external users trying to access web services on 192.1.1.1 will be authenticated.

AP Policy Activation

When you have created your AP policies, they are not used until activated on your router's interface(s). This is accomplished with the following configuration:

```
Router(config)# interface type [slot_#/]port_#
Router(config-if)# ip auth-proxy AP_name
```

The **ip auth-proxy** command activates the specified AP policy on your router's interface. For example, if you have defined two policies, one for internal users and one for external users, you need to activate the internal policy on all of the internal interfaces, and activate the external policy on all of the external interfaces.

In the previous example, to activate the two AP policies for Figure 14-2, you would use the configuration in Example 14-2.

Example 14-2 *Activating AP*

```
Router(config)# interface ethernet0
Router(config-if)# ip auth-proxy internal_users
Router(config)# interface ethernet1
Router(config-if)# ip auth-proxy external_users
```

Tuning AP

You globally can change two basic items to tune AP for your router: an authentication banner, and idle and absolute timeouts. The authentication banner is displayed during the login process and is similar to the banner created with the **banner motd** command. However, this banner is used only by users being authenticated through AP. Here is the syntax for this command:

```
Router(config)# ip auth-proxy auth-proxy-banner {http | ftp | telnet}
    [stop_character message stop_character]
```

As you can see, the format of this command is similar to that of the **banner motd** command: At the end, you need to specify a stop character at the beginning and ending of your banner message. Notice, however, that this is optional. If you omit the actual banner message, the router's default login banner is used; otherwise, the banner that you specify here is used. With AP, you must specify the authentication type—**http**, **ftp**, or **telnet**—for the banner. Unfortunately, currently there is no method of defining a different banner for different policies. In other words, it is not possible with the current versions of the Cisco IOS to create one banner for internal users and a second banner for external users.

NOTE   If you do not configure an AP banner, no banner is displayed during the AP login process; the user is prompted only for the username and password.

Example 14-3 displays a simple sample of the use of this command.

Example 14-3 *Creating a Banner for AP*

```
Router(config)# ip auth-proxy auth-proxy-banner http #
***Unauthorized use of this system or the network***
***      is prohibited and will be punished to the***
```

Example 14-3 *Creating a Banner for AP (Continued)*

```
***     fullest extent of the law             ***
***To gain access, you must be an authorized user***
***     and must authenticate with an approved  ***
***     username and password                 ***
#
Router(config)#
```

As you can see, you can enter a multiline banner.

As I mentioned with the **ip auth-proxy name** command previously, you can configure two timeouts for users' connections: idle and absolute. Changing these values with the **ip auth-proxy name** command affects only the timeouts for users authenticated with the specific policy name. You globally can set these timeouts with the following two commands:

```
Router(config)# ip auth-proxy inactivity-timer minutes
Router(config)# ip auth-proxy absolute-timer minutes
```

The **inactivity-timer** parameter specifies the number of minutes after a user is idle that the Cisco IOS will remove the user's authentication information, including any dynamic ACL entries that were created from the user's profile downloaded from the AAA server. This number can range from 1 to 2,147,483,647; the default is 60 minutes.

The **absolute-timer** parameter specifies the number of total minutes that the user's information is kept (it does not matter whether the user's connections are idle). This value defaults to 0, which means that the timer is disabled.

Remember my caution in the "AP Policy Definitions" section: Make sure that these timer values are greater than those that CBAC uses. Also, if a user's information is expired and removed, the user must reauthenticate before reaccessing previously authorized resources.

By default, even if you enable AAA accounting for AP, AP will not generate accounting records until you enable it with the following command:

```
Router(config)# ip auth-proxy auth-proxy-audit
```

When you do this and configure AAA accounting, the Cisco IOS creates start/stop records to record the users' authentication activities.

Protecting Against Access Attacks

AP provides a limited solution to protect you against access attacks, called *watch lists*. Watch lists enable you to place blacklisted users on a list, which AP denies access for. The IOS dynamically can learn blacklisted users by examining failed access attempts, or this information can be configured statically.

By default, watch lists are disabled. To enable them, use the following command:

```
Router(config)# ip auth-proxy watch-list enable
```

When it is enabled, AP uses watch lists to block blacklisted users from any further authentication attempts. The Cisco IOS automatically blacklists a person if he tries to authenticate and fails five successive times. You can change this value with this command:

```
Router(config)# ip auth-proxy max-login-attempts maximum_login_#
```

The maximum number of logins can range from 1 to 2,147,483,647.

NOTE   The **ip auth-proxy max-login-attempts** command is actually independent of the watch list feature; it can be used with or without watch lists.

When a user exceeds the maximum number of allowed authentication attempts and watch lists are enabled, the user automatically is blacklisted. By default, a user is blacklisted for 30 minutes. After this time period, the user can attempt authentication again. To change this blocked period, use the following command:

```
Router(config)# ip auth-proxy watch-list expiry-time minutes
```

The expiration, or block, period can range from 1 to 2,147,483,647. When a user is blacklisted, after this expiration time passes, the user automatically is removed from the watch list.

You manually can add and remove devices from the watch list with the following two respective commands:

```
Router(config)# ip auth-proxy watch-list add-item host_IP_address
Router(config)# no ip auth-proxy watch-list add-item host_IP_address
```

Typically, you use the second command if a user accidentally enters the wrong username/ password combination five or more times out of user/keyboard interface problems, and you need to remove that user from the watch list after instructing him what to enter to authenticate.

Verifying and Troubleshooting AP

After you have configured AP, you can use various **show**, **clear**, and **debug** commands to examine and troubleshoot your configuration. The following sections cover the use of these commands.

show Commands

These are the basic **show** commands that you use for AP:

- **show [ip] access-list**—Displays the router's ACLs, including dynamic entries created by AP

- **show ip auth-proxy configuration**—Displays the AP configuration on the router
- **show ip auth-proxy cache**—Displays the status of users who are being authenticated or who have authenticated
- **show ip auth-proxy watch-list**—Displays information in the watch list

I look at the **show ip access-list** command first. Example 14-4 shows a sample of this command before a user has authenticated (this ACL is applied inbound on the external interface).

Example 14-4 *An ACL Before AP Occurs*

```
Router# show ip access-list
Extended IP access list 100
 permit tcp any host 192.1.1.1 eq www
 deny ip any any
```

In Example 14-4, only traffic to the internal web server (193.1.1.1) is allowed. This is required for AP to work. Example 14-5 shows simple output after a user successfully has authenticated.

Example 14-5 *An ACL After AP Occurs*

```
Router# show ip access-list
Extended IP access list 100
! Here are the dynamic ACL entries created from the
!     user's authentication.
 permit icmp host 200.1.1.1 192.1.1.0 0.0.0.255
 permit tcp host 200.1.1.1 192.1.1.2 eq www
 permit tcp any host 192.1.1.1 eq www (64 matches)
 deny ip any any
```

As you can see in Example 14-5, two dynamic ACL entries were created for user 200.1.1.1.

To view your router's AP configuration, use the **show ip auth-proxy** command, as shown in Example 14-6.

Example 14-6 *Viewing Your Router's AP Configuration*

```
router# show ip auth-proxy configuration
Authentication global cache time is 60 minutes
Authentication global absolute time is 0 minutes
Authentication Proxy Rule Configuration
  Auth-proxy name AP-rules
    http list not specified auth-cache-timeout 60 minutes
```

In Example 14-6, only one policy was created: AP-rules. This policy did not specify an ACL and did not change the timers for the policy.

After you have configured AP, have a user initiate a connection that will cause AP to function. When the user authenticates, you can see the authenticated user information with the **show ip auth-proxy cache** command, as shown in Example 14-7.

Example 14-7 *Viewing Authenticated AP Cached User Information*

```
Router# show ip auth-proxy cache
Authentication Proxy Cache
 Client IP 200.1.1.1 Port 32835, timeout 60, state HTTP_ESTAB
```

As you can see in Example 14-7, one user (200.1.1.1) has been authenticated through HTTP (HTTP_ESTAB). HTTP_ESTAB indicates that the client successfully was authenticated through HTTP.

To see information in the watch list, assuming that you have enabled this feature, use the command shown in Example 14-8.

Example 14-8 *Viewing AP's Watch List*

```
Router# show ip auth-proxy watch-list
Authentication Proxy Watch-list is enabled
Watch-list expiry timeout is 30 minutes
Total number of watch-list entries: 2

 Source IP       Type         Violation-count
 201.1.1.1       MAX_RETRY    MAX_LIMIT
 200.1.1.1       CFGED        N/A
Total number of watch-listed users: 2
```

In Example 14-8, the first line of output shows that watch lists are enabled; and the second line shows the expiry timeout. Currently, two entries are in the table. The first entry, 201.1.1.1, was placed there because the user tried to authenticate and failed, exceeding the maximum login threshold. The second entry manually was added to the watch list (CFGED).

clear Commands

This section covers two **clear** commands that AP supports. As I mentioned earlier, authenticated users remain in AP's cache until either the idle or the absolute (if enabled) expire for the user. However, you manually can remove an AP entry from the router's cache by using the following **clear** command:

```
Router# clear ip auth-proxy cache {* | user's_IP_address}
```

If you use the *, all entries are cleared; if you specify a user's IP address, only that IP address is cleared from the router's AP cache. When a user is cleared from the cache, all corresponding dynamic ACL entries are removed and the user must reauthenticate to access previously authorized resources.

The second **clear** command deals with watch lists:

```
Router# clear ip auth-proxy watch-list {user's_IP_address | *}
```

In this example, you can clear a specific user or all users from the watch list (blacklist). This command clears manually entered watch-list entries as well as those that the Cisco IOS dynamically put there because of failed authentication attempts.

debug Commands

For detailed troubleshooting of AP, you can use the **debug ip auth-proxy** command. Here is the syntax for this command:

```
Router# debug ip auth-proxy {ftp | function-trace | http |
   object-creation | object-deletion | tcp | telnet | timer}
```

Table 14-2 describes the parameters for this command.

Table 14-2   *Options for the* **debug ip auth-proxy** *Command*

Parameter	Description
ftp	FTP AP events are shown.
function-trace	AP functions are shown (this command typically is not used, unless by Cisco TAC personnel).
http	HTTP AP events are shown.
object-creation	New AP cache entries are shown.
object-deletion	Removed AP cache entries are shown.
tcp	TCP AP events are shown.
telnet	Telnet AP events are shown.
timer	AP events related to timers are shown.

AP Examples

Now that you have a basic understanding of how to set up AP, I use a couple of examples to illustrate the configuration of AP. The next two sections cover these examples.

Simple AP Example

This first example uses a simple network with simple policies (see Figure 14-3). This example concerns only outside-to-inside access (the next example throws in NAT and CBAC, to make the scenario more complex). This example wants to allow outside access to the public services, but it requires authentication through HTTP to access the private services. Note that the private file server does not support HTTP; therefore, external users must authenticate by using HTTP to connect to the private web server.

Figure 14-3 *Simple AP Example*

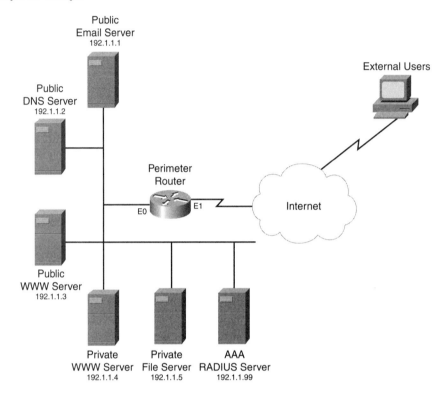

Example 14-9 displays the configuration for the router in Figure 14-3.

Example 14-9 *A Simple AP Configuration Example*

```
Router(config)# aaa new-model                                  (1)
Router(config)# radius-server host 192.1.1.99 key cisco        (2)
Router(config)# aaa authentication login default group radius  (3)
Router(config)# aaa authentication login console-override
  group radius enable
Router(config)# aaa authorization exec default group radius    (4)
Router(config)# aaa authorization auth-proxy default           (5)
  group radius
Router(config)# ip http server                                 (6)
Router(config)# ip http authentication aaa                     (7)
Router(config)# ip auth-proxy inactivity-timer 10              (8)
Router(config)# ip auth-proxy name check-outside http          (9)
  list check-these
Router(config)# ip access-list extended check-these            (10)
Router(config-ext-nacl)# permit tcp any host 192.1.1.4 eq www
```

Example 14-9 *A Simple AP Configuration Example (Continued)*

```
Router(config-ext-nacl)# deny ip any any
Router(config-ext-nacl)# exit
Router(config)# ip access-list extended protect                    (11)
Router(config-ext-nacl)# permit tcp any host 192.1.1.4 eq www
Router(config-ext-nacl)# permit tcp any host 192.1.1.1 eq smtp
Router(config-ext-nacl)# permit udp any host 192.1.1.2 eq dns
Router(config-ext-nacl)# permit tcp any host 192.1.1.3 eq www
Router(config-ext-nacl)# deny ip any any
Router(config-ext-nacl)# exit
Router(config)# interface ethernet1
Router(config-if)# ip access-group protect in                      (12)
Router(config-if)# ip auth-proxy check-outside                     (13)
Router(config-if)# exit
Router(config)# line console 0
Router(config-line)# login authentication console-override         (14)
Router(config-line)# exit
Router(config)# enable secret ocsic
```

Here is an explanation of this example, with reference to the numbering on the right side of Example 14-9:

1 This enables AAA.

2 This defines the RADIUS server used for AAA.

3 This enables login authentication, which is required for AP. However, two commands are used. The first command provides the default method for authentication: RADIUS. The second command is used for console access (see Statement 14) and has a backup method (the privileged EXEC password) if the RADIUS server is not available.

4 If a user is authenticated, only specific authorized users can gain EXEC access to the router. In other words, I do not want to allow external AP users to access the EXEC shell of the router; instead, I define the list of authorized users on the RADIUS server.

CAUTION   It is important that you use this **aaa authorization** command. You definitely do not want any authenticated user access to the shell. AP users should be allowed access only to other services, not the EXEC shell on the router itself.

---

5 Authorization for AP is enabled by using RADIUS—if the RADIUS server is not reachable, the AP users are denied access.

6 This enables the router's HTTP server function.

7 This enables AAA authentication for the HTTP server function.

8 This changes the idle timeout for AP cached information from 60 to 10 minutes.

9 This defines the AP policy: Only HTTP connections listed in the ACL called check-these (see Statement 10) are authenticated. This is important because I want to verify access to the private servers, but I do not want to use AP for the public server.

10 This defines which connections require AP (only those to the private web server).

11 This defines access from the outside world to the inside resources. Notice two things: You must allow the AP connection (the first entry in the ACL), and you should deny anything else, including access to the private file server (this is allowed by the UAP defined on the RADIUS server).

12 This activates the external ACL inbound on the external interface.

13 This activates the AP policy on the external interface.

14 This overrides the default authentication method on the console (below this is the encrypted privileged EXEC password used as the second login method for the console port (see the statement immediately after no. 3).

AP and EXEC Access

As I mentioned in the last Caution note, you always should configure AAA authorization for EXEC access. I once dealt with a client who did not do this. Its configuration allowed users to access an IP address on the router to perform the authentication; however, after authenticating, the user was presented with the user EXEC interface for the router through the web browser. Obviously, this is a serious security risk. When I learned this, I immediately changed the configuration to authorize EXEC access, preventing the AP users from gaining any type of access to the router, with the exception of the AP authentication component. We defined a few exceptions for network administrators within CiscoSecure ACS for Windows 2000.

Complex AP Example: CBAC and NAT

This example uses a more complicated setup in which the router is performing CBAC and NAT, as well as AP. The network in this example is shown in Figure 14-4. In this example, NAT is required because the internal resources are using a private address space: 192.168.1.0/24. Also, CBAC is used to provide a stateful firewall function. For the internal users, all users must be authenticated through HTTP before they can access the Internet: This can be done through an HTTP connection to the router or through an HTTP connection to any Internet web server. Per-user downloadable ACLs are configured on the RADIUS server, defining what specific user groups are allowed to access on the Internet. External users automatically can access the public servers; however, to access the private servers, they first must authenticate through AP by connecting to the private internal web server.

Figure 14-4 *Complex AP Example*

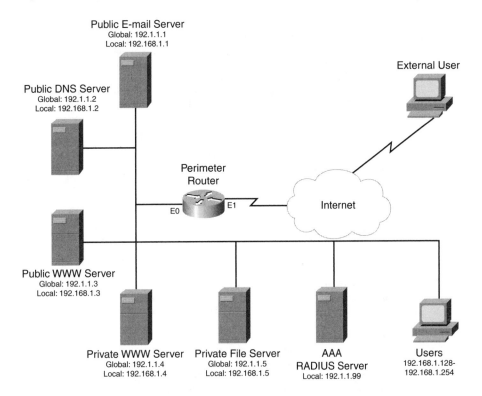

Example 14-10 displays the configuration for the network shown in Figure 14-4.

Example 14-10 *AP Example with CBAC and NAT*

```
Router(config)# ip inspect name CBAC-leaving http              (1)
Router(config)# ip inspect name CBAC-leaving ftp
Router(config)# ip inspect name CBAC-leaving realaudio
Router(config)# ip inspect name CBAC-leaving smtp
Router(config)# ip inspect name CBAC-leaving streamworks
Router(config)# ip inspect name CBAC-leaving udp
Router(config)# ip inspect name CBAC-leaving tcp
Router(config)#
Router(config)# ip inspect name CBAC-entering http             (2)
Router(config)# ip inspect name CBAC-entering ftp
Router(config)# ip inspect name CBAC-entering realaudio
Router(config)# ip inspect name CBAC-entering smtp
Router(config)# ip inspect name CBAC-entering streamworks
Router(config)# ip inspect name CBAC-entering udp
Router(config)# ip inspect name CBAC-entering tcp
Router(config)#
Router(config)# ip nat inside source static                   (3)
   192.168.1.0 192.1.1.0 /24
```

continues

Example 14-10 *AP Example with CBAC and NAT (Continued)*

```
Router(config)#
Router(config)# aaa new-model                                         (4)
Router(config)# radius-server host 192.1.1.99 key cisco               (5)
Router(config)# aaa authentication login default group radius         (6)
Router(config)# aaa authentication login console-override
  group radius enable
Router(config)# aaa authorization exec default group radius           (7)
Router(config)# aaa authorization auth-proxy default                  (8)
  group radius
Router(config)#
Router(config)# ip http server                                        (9)
Router(config)# ip http authentication aaa                           (10)
Router(config)# ip auth-proxy inactivity-timer 60                    (11)
Router(config)# ip auth-proxy name check-outside http                (12)
  list external-AP
Router(config)# ip auth-proxy name check-inside http                 (13)
  list internal-AP
Router(config)#
Router(config)# ip access-list extended external-AP                  (14)
Router(config-ext-nacl)# permit tcp any host 192.1.1.4 eq www
Router(config-ext-nacl)# deny ip any any
Router(config-ext-nacl)# exit
Router(config)#
Router(config)# ip access-list extended internal-AP                  (15)
Router(config-ext-nacl)# permit tcp 192.168.1.128 0.0.0.127
  any eq www
Router(config-ext-nacl)# deny ip any any
Router(config-ext-nacl)# exit
Router(config)#
Router(config)# ip access-list extended protect-from-inside          (16)
Router(config-ext-nacl)# permit tcp 192.168.1.128 0.0.0.127
  any eq www
Router(config-ext-nacl)# deny ip 192.168.1.128 0.0.0.127 any
Router(config-ext-nacl)# permit host ip 192.168.1.1 any eq smtp
Router(config-ext-nacl)# deny ip any any
Router(config-ext-nacl)# exit
Router(config)#
Router(config)# ip access-list extended protect-from-outside         (17)
Router(config-ext-nacl)# permit tcp any host 192.1.1.4 eq www
Router(config-ext-nacl)# permit tcp any host 192.1.1.1 eq smtp
Router(config-ext-nacl)# permit udp any host 192.1.1.2 eq dns
Router(config-ext-nacl)# permit tcp any host 192.1.1.3 eq www
Router(config-ext-nacl)# deny ip any any
Router(config-ext-nacl)# exit
Router(config)#
Router(config)# interface ethernet0
Router(config-if)# description **Inside Interface**
Router(config-if)# ip access-group protect-from-inside in            (18)
Router(config-if)# ip auth-proxy check-inside                        (19)
Router(config-if)# ip inspect CBAC-entering out                      (20)
Router(config-if)# ip nat inside                                     (21)
Router(config-if)# exit
```

Example 14-10 *AP Example with CBAC and NAT (Continued)*

```
Router(config)#
Router(config)# interface ethernet1
Router(config-if)# description **Outside Interface**
Router(config-if)# ip access-group protect-from-outside in     (22)
Router(config-if)# ip auth-proxy check-outside                 (23)
Router(config-if)# ip inspect CBAC-leaving out                 (24)
Router(config-if)# ip nat outside                              (25)
Router(config-if)# exit
Router(config)#
Router(config)# line console 0
Router(config-line)# login authentication console-override     (26)
Router(config-line)# exit
Router(config)# enable secret ocsic                            (27)
```

Here is an explanation of this example, with reference to the numbering on the right side of Example 14-10:

1 This defines the CBAC inspection rule for traffic leaving the network. This is activated on the external interface (ethernet1) in the outbound direction (Statement 24).

2 This defines the CBAC inspection rule for traffic entering the network. This is activated on the internal interface (ethernet0) in the outbound direction (Statement 20).

3 This creates the static translations for the inside private (local) addresses to public (global) addresses: 192.168.1.0/24 to 192.1.1.0/24.

4 This enables AAA.

5 This defines the AAA RADIUS server.

6 This defines authentication for login and console access (console access has a second method, the privileged EXEC password).

7 This defines authorization for EXEC access, thereby restricting AP users from gaining EXEC access on the router. This authorization needs to be defined on the AAA server and should permit only network administrators.

8 This enables AP authorization for AAA through RADIUS.

9 This enables the HTTP server on the router.

10 This enables HTTP authentication for AP users.

11 This increases the AP idle timer to 60 minutes.

12 This creates an AP policy for external users. HTTP is used for the authentication method, and only access to the private web server triggers authentication (external-AP ACL, defined in Statement 14).

13   This creates an AP policy for internal users. HTTP is used for the authentication method, and only internal users (192.168.1.128 to 192.168.1.255) are authenticated (internal-AP, defined in Statement 15). Additional downloadable ACLs can be created for the users' groups to restrict external access.

14   This defines when AP occurs for external users accessing the private web server.

15   This defines when AP occurs when internal users access the Internet.

16   This allows internal devices access to the Internet. The first ACL statement admits the AP. The second statement denies everything else from internal users. However, downloadable ACLs defined on the AAA server can allow users access to other resources. The third statement in the ACL allows the e-mail server to send e-mails to other e-mail servers. This ACL is activated in ethernet0 in the inbound direction (see Statement 18).

17   This filters traffic from the Internet as it enters this network. The first statement allows the AP process to take place to the public server. The next three statements allow external users to the public servers—web, DNS, and e-mail.

18   This activates the ACL that blocks internal traffic from leaving the network.

19   This activates the internal AP policy about restricting internal users from accessing Internet resources.

20   This activates the CBAC inspection rule that allows Internet traffic back through the inside interface as it is sent from internal servers as a reply to external user requests.

21   This specifies the inside interface for NAT.

22   This activates the external ACL on the external interface, blocking Internet traffic.

23   This activates the external AP policy to authenticate users from the Internet.

24   This activates the CBAC inspection rule that allows returning traffic to the Internet.

25   This specifies the outside interface for NAT.

26   This overrides the default AAA login authentication rule to use for console access.

27   This configures the privileged EXEC password, which is used as the second authentication method for console access if the RADIUS server is not reachable.

TIP   As you can see from this example, when you start adding more features to your router's configuration, your task becomes more complex. In this example, I highly recommend that you do the configuration in small pieces. In this example, configure NAT first and then the ACLS, then CBAC, and finally AP.

Summary

This chapter showed you the basics of authentication proxy. Unlike with lock-and-key, you have much more flexibility and control over the authentication and authorization process. When you have different access policies for different users, AP is a better solution than lock-and-key. However, AP requires the use of an external TACACS+ or RADIUS security server. AP enables you to authenticate users through HTTP, HTTPS, Telnet, or FTP with the right version of the Cisco IOS.

Next up is Chapter 15, "Routing Protocol Protection," which shows you how to protect the router's routing protocols, as well as implement solutions to reduce your router and network exposure to attacks through some routing tricks.

## CHAPTER 15

Routing Protocol Protection

This chapter focuses on routing security. Up to this point, I have focused on nonrouting functions, such as using filters to prevent unauthorized access. However, your router will have to perform some basic routing functions, and this brings up concerns related to network failures and service interruptions that a spoofed routing attack might create, as well as access and Denial of Service (DoS) attacks.

Most people assume that if they use static routes, they are protected against routing attacks. However, static routes are not scalable in large internetworks. In these situations, a routing protocol typically is used on the perimeter router to help the router find internal routes. In some cases, you need to advertise and receive routes to an attached ISP(s). Care must be taken when using a routing protocol because the default configuration of a routing protocol does not provide any protection: It is easy to spoof routing updates.

Many routing protocols provide an authentication mechanism to detect and defeat spoofing, but this requires configuration on your part. This chapter focuses on authentication for routing protocols, but it covers some additional tools that you can use to protect you from routing and route spoofing attacks. This chapter covers the following concepts:

- Black hole routing
- Interior gateway protocol (IGP) security
- BGP security
- Reverse-path forwarding (RPF) for unicast traffic

Static and Black Hole Routing

This section covers the use of static routes to provide Layer 3 connectivity, as well as a solution called *black hole routing*, which is an alternative solution to ACLs when you want to drop unwanted traffic.

Static Routes

One of the safest routing solutions for your router is to use static routes to provide for Layer 3 connectivity. These are secure from route spoofing attacks because your router does not rely on routing information being sent and received from other routers: You configure all of the routing information locally on your perimeter router.

Static routes typically are used in these circumstances:

- You have a small number of destinations to configure.
- Only one or two paths exist to each destination.

With static routes, the following is true:

- A default route is used on the perimeter router to reach external resources.
- Specific internal routes are used to reach internal resources.

When using static routes, one of the two following commands is used:

```
Router(config)# ip route destination_network_# [subnet_mask]
  IP_address_of_next_hop_neighbor [administrative_distance] [permanent]
Router(config)# ip route destination_network_# [subnet_mask]
  interface_to_exit [administrative_distance] [permanent]
```

You already should be familiar with these two Cisco router commands. If you want to set up a default route, specify 0.0.0.0 0.0.0.0 for the destination network number and the subnet mask.

Null Routes

Even though static routes are very secure, they present a scalability problem: The more networks that you have, and the more redundant paths that you have to these networks, the more difficult it becomes to manage routing on your router. In this situation, you might have to run a dynamic routing protocol, such as OSPF. However, you can complement a dynamic routing protocol with static routes to provide optimal protection.

One of the concepts that you should be familiar with by now is traffic filtering with ACLs. ACLs enable you to filter packets based on the information contained in their headers. One problem of packet filtering is performance because the router must examine packet headers to make a filtering decision, thus adding some overhead to the processing of the packets.

A complementary solution to both routing and filtering is to use black hole routes. A black hole route is used to forward unwanted or undesirable traffic into a black hole. In Cisco terminology, a special logical interface, called a *null* interface, is used to create the black hole. Static routes are created for destinations that are not desirable, and the static route configuration points to the null interface. Any traffic that has a destination address that has a best match of the black hole static route automatically is dropped. Unlike with ACLs, all switching processes of the Cisco IOS, including CEF, can handle black hole routes without any performance degradation.

Setting up a black hole route is easy because it uses the static route configuration:

```
Router(config)# ip route destination_network_# [subnet_mask] null0
```

Notice that the only unique thing about this command is that the destination interface is null0, the black hole. Any traffic destined to the destination network in the static route command is routed to null0 (that is, it is dropped).

As I mentioned in Chapter 6, "Access List Introduction," and Chapter 7, "Basic Access Lists," you should make your ACLs as short and simple as possible. However, when I discussed how to filter bogon routes in Chapter 7, these ACL commands added quite a bit of length to the ACL. My personal preference is to not use ACLs to filter destination bogon addresses, but instead to use black hole routes.

NOTE   When using the null0 interface for black hole routing, you will want to prevent your router from sending ICMP unreachable messages to the sender of the packet, like this:

```
Router(config)# interface null0
Router(config-if)# no ip unreachables
```

If you do not do this, a hacker can take advantage of this loophole in your configuration to create a DoS attack by flooding your router with black-holed addresses, causing your router to generate an ICMP unreachable message for each packet that the router drops. Hackers like to use this type of DoS attack because many administrators forget to disable ICMP unreachables and inadvertently generate just as much traffic back to the source (which is typically a spoofed address), creating a second DoS attack. By preventing the generation of ICMP unreachable messages, your router silently drops the packets.

CAUTION   Black hole routes drop all traffic sent to the specified destination; there is no granularity of looking at other information to drop traffic. Therefore, this security solution should be used only for known destination addresses that you never want your router to forward traffic to. Based on this information, black hole routing ideally is suited for destination bogon addresses.

Examine the network shown in Figure 15-1. I set up the perimeter router to perform bogon filtering with black hole routers, to give you a better understanding of the configuration.

Figure 15-1 *Black Hole Routing Example*

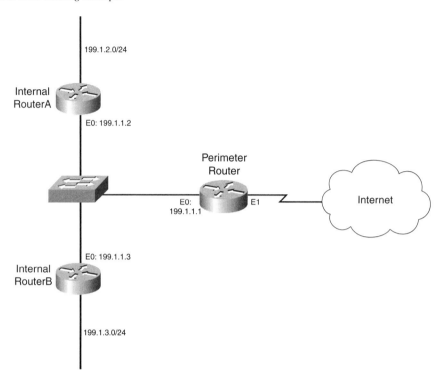

Example 15-1 shows the configuration for the perimeter router in Figure 15-1, focusing on only the black hole routing component.

Example 15-1 *Using Black Hole Routing for Destination Bogon Addresses*

```
Router(config)# interface null0                              (1)
Router(config-if)# no ip unreachables
Router(config-if)# exit
Router(config)#
Router(config)# ip route 199.1.2.0 255.255.255.0 199.1.1.2   (2)
Router(config)# ip route 199.1.3.0 255.255.255.0 199.1.1.3
Router(config)# ip route 0.0.0.0 0.0.0.0 ethernet1
Router(config)#
Router(config)# ip route 1.0.0.0 255.0.0.0 null0             (3)
Router(config)# ip route 2.0.0.0 255.0.0.0 null0
Bouter(config)# ip route 5.0.0.0 255.0.0.0 null0
Router(config)# ip route 7.0.0.0 255.0.0.0 null0
Router(config)# ip route 23.0.0.0 255.0.0.0 null0
Router(config)# ip route 27.0.0.0 255.0.0.0 null0
Router(config)# ip route 31.0.0.0 255.0.0.0 null0
Router(config)# ! <--omitted bogon routes-->
Router(config)# ip route 197.0.0.0 255.0.0.0 null0
Router(config)# ip route 201.0.0.0 255.0.0.0 null0
```

Example 15-1 *Using Black Hole Routing for Destination Bogon Addresses (Continued)*

```
Router(config)# ip route 10.0.0.0 255.0.0.0 null0
Router(config)# ip route 172.16.0.0 255.240.0.0 null0
Router(config)# ip route 192.168.0.0 255.255.0.0 null0
Router(config)# ip route 0.0.0.0 255.0.0.0 null0
Router(config)# ip route 224.0.0.0 240.0.0.0 null0
Router(config)# ip route 240.0.0.0 240.0.0.0 null0
Router(config)# ip route 169.254.0.0 255.255.0.0 null0
Router(config)# ip route 192.0.2.0 255.255.255.0 null0
Router(config)# ip route 127.0.0.0 255.0.0.0 null0
```

In Example 15-1, Statement 1 (referring to the numbers on the right side of Example 15-1) disables ICMP unreachable messages for the black hole routes. The first two statements in Statement 2 set up static routes for the two internal networks, and the third statement is a default route to reach the Internet. All of the statements following Statement 3 are black hole routes.

Policy-Based Routing

Policy-based routing (PBR) is a more flexible alternative to implementing black hole routing than using static routes. I briefly discussed the use of PBR in Chapter 10, "Filtering Web and Application Traffic." In this chapter, I discussed how you can use PBR to mark traffic and then have an ACL drop the traffic. However, there is an alternative solution to dropping the traffic instead of using an ACL: a black hole route.

I do not spend much time discussing the policy commands because many of them were discussed in Chapter 10. To set up PBR for black hole routing, follow these steps:

Step 1   Create an ACL that will match on the packets you have marked (either the DSCP or Type of Service [ToS] field in the IP header).

Step 2   Create a route map that will route the traffic matching the ACL to the null0 interface. Use these commands:

```
Router(config)# route-map route_map_name sequence_#
Router(config-route-map)# match ip address extended_ACL_#_or_name
Router(config-route-map)# set interface null0
```

The **route-map** command creates the route map; give it a descriptive name and a sequence number. The sequence number is used to insert a route map statement into an existing route map. Use the **match ip address** command that points to the ACL in Step 3. The **set interface null0** command specifies where to route the matching packets.

Step 3   Activate the route map on the external interface (if filtering external-to-internal traffic):

```
Router(config)# interface type [slot_#/]port_#
Router(config-if)# ip policy route-map route_map_name
```

It is important to point out here that this is different from what was described in Chapter 10. In Chapter 10, the packets were marked on the ingress interface and were filtered by an ACL on the egress interface: This was necessary because packets cannot be processed twice by an ACL on the same interface. However PBR is a routing function, which occurs after the ACL filtering, so activating your service policies and route map policies on the same interface is correct. Also, PBR supports CEF switching; you do not need to do anything to enable this feature except to configure CEF itself.

Refer back to Figure 15-1 for a couple of examples of using PBR for black hole routing. This first example looks at filtering bogon networks. Example 15-2 shows the configuration.

Example 15-2 *Using PBR for Black Hole Routing*

```
Router(config)# interface null0                                    (1)
Router(config-if)# no ip unreachables
Router(config-if)# exit
Router(config)# ip route 199.1.2.0 255.255.255.0 199.1.1.2
Router(config)# ip route 199.1.3.0 255.255.255.0 199.1.1.3
Router(config)# ip route 0.0.0.0 0.0.0.0 ethernet1
Router(config)#
Router(config)# ip access-list extended bogon-ACL                  (2)
Router(config-ext-nacl)# permit ip 1.0.0.0 0.255.255.255 any
Router(config-ext-nacl)# permit ip 2.0.0.0 0.255.255.255 any
Router(config-ext-nacl)# permit ip 5.0.0.0 0.255.255.255 any
Router(config-ext-nacl)# ! <--output omitted (you need to add the
  rest of the bogons here-->
Router(config-ext-nacl)# deny ip any any
Router(config-ext-nacl)# exit
Router(config)# route-map black-hole 10                            (3)
Router(config-route-map)# match ip address bogon-ACL
Router(config-route-map)# set interface null0
Router(config-route-map)# exit
Router(config)# interface ethernet0
Router(config-if)# ip policy route-map black-hole                  (4)
```

The following is an explanation of Example 15-2, with reference to the numbering on the right side of the configuration:

1 This set of code has the router not generate ICMP unreachable messages and defines the static routes for connectivity.

2 This is a partial ACL that matches on all bogon addresses (I have omitted the complete list, but you can look at the previous example for all of these networks).

3 The route map references the ACL in Step 2 and routes these packets to the null0 interface.

4 The route map is activated on the external interface (with PBR, the matching and
dropping are done on the same interface).

In this next example of using PBR, I change the example used in Chapter 10, where NBAR
was used to drop Code Red packets by using a filter. In this example, I change the configuration
so that, instead of the ACL dropping the packets, PBR is used. Example 15-3 uses the
network in Figure 15-1. I focus only on the policy commands for this configuration.

Example 15-3 *Using PBR to Drop Code Red Packets*

```
Router(config)# class-map match-any code-red-attacks          (1)
Router(config-cmap)# match protocol http url "*.ida*"
Router(config-cmap)# match protocol http url "*cmd.exe*"
Router(config-cmap)# match protocol http url "*root.exe*"
Router(config-cmap)# exit
Router(config)# policy-map mark-code-red                      (2)
Router(config-pmap)# class code-red-attacks
Router(config-pmap-c)# set ip dscp 1
Router(config-pmac-c)# exit
Router(config)# interface ethernet1
Router(config-if)# service-policy input mark-code-red         (3)
Router(config-if)# exit
Router(config)# ip access-list extended match-dscp-ACL        (4)
Router(config-ext-nacl)# permit ip any any dscp 1
Router(config-ext-nacl)# exit
Router(config)# route-map black-hole 10                       (5)
Router(config-route-map)# match ip address match-dscp-ACL
Router(config-route-map)# set interface null0
Router(config-route-map)# exit
Router(config)# interface ethernet1
Router(config-if)# ip policy route-map black-hole             (6)
```

Statements 1, 2, and 3 include the same commands discussed in Chapter 10. Statements 4,
5, and 6 are specifically for PBR. The following is an explanation of Example 15-3 with
reference to the numbering on the right side of the configuration:

1 This class map uses NBAR to match on URL contents.

2 The policy map marks the DSCP field in the IP header for Code Red packets.

3 The policy map is activated on the external interface as traffic enters the perimeter
router from the Internet.

4 The ACL matches on all packets that have the DSCP field set to 1.

5 The route map routes all DSCP = 1 packets to the null0 interface.

6 The route map is activated on the ingress interface (with route maps, you can match
and filter on the same interface).

TIP	If you have a choice between using ACLs to filter traffic and using black hole routing, I definitely recommend the latter, especially if you are using static routes. However, I recommend that you use PBR only in situations in which you already are using it because it does affect the processing cycles of the router. For example, if you already are using it to detect and block Code Red, you might want to use it for other filtering policies as well.

Interior Gateway Protocol Security

If you need to have your perimeter router run an interior gateway protocol (IGP) to learn about internal routes, I highly recommend that, at a minimum, you configure authentication to protect yourself against spoofing attacks. In many cases, using an IGP is a better solution than using static routes, especially considering that IGPs dynamically learn the topology of the network, support multiple redundant paths (for load balancing), and can overcome route outages by learning about alternative paths to a destination.

Need for Routing Protocol Authentication

I once had a contract job for a state government agency in the late 1990s in which I was redesigning the agency's network. It had a T1 line to provide for Internet access and was using RIPv1 as a routing protocol. Intermittently, part of the network lost the connection to the Internet, but the rest of the network still could access the Internet. This typically happened every day from around 10 A.M. to 2 P.M.

After spending a few hours troubleshooting the problem, I determined that actually two default routes were being propagated: one from the T1 router and one from a different device. After careful tracking, I traced the default route back to a UNIX desktop device. Apparently, this user periodically dialed into their personal CompuServe service, which assigned a default route to the UNIX desktop. By default, RIP routing was enabled on the UNIX desktop, causing it to pass the default route to other internally connected routers. Because of the hop count assigned to the CompuServe default route, other internal routers eventually ignored it and used the T1 router's default route; however, routers close to the UNIX box were using the UNIX desktop. Most of the internal traffic was being routed correctly, but some was being routed to CompuServe, which then was dropped.

After this experience, I quickly convinced the company to convert to RIPv2 and implement authentication to prevent this kind of problem from happening again.

Authentication

The main purpose of authentication is to provide verification of the routing contents received by a neighboring router. Authentication enables you to verify whether the received routing update was sent by a valid neighboring router and was received without being tampered with. In other words, it prevents your router from accepting and processing unauthorized or malicious routing updates, which a hacker can use to create a DoS attack.

If you do not use authentication, you are opening yourself up to DoS routing attacks, in which a hacker injects bogus routing information into your router's routing table. A really good hacker could use this opportunity to reroute certain traffic back to him, to implement other kinds of spoofing attacks.

Supported Routing Protocols

Not all routing protocols support authentication. Supported protocols include these:

- Border Gateway Protocol (BGP), which is discussed in the next section
- Intermediate System-to-Intermediate System (IS-IS)
- IP Enhanced Interior Gateway Routing Protocol (EIGRP)
- Open Shortest Path First (OSPF)
- Routing Information Protocol (RIP) version 2

As you can see from this list, RIPv1 and the Cisco IGRP are not included; therefore, I highly recommend that you not use them on your perimeter router.

Authentication Process

A router's routing protocol can employ two forms of authentication:

- Plain text
- Message Digest version 5 (MD5)

The basic difference between these is the same as PPP's PAP and CHAP: PAP sends its authentication information in clear text to a neighboring router and is susceptible to eavesdropping attacks. CHAP uses an MD5 hashing function to send a fixed-length hashed output, not the password, to the remote device.

CAUTION   Authentication with routing protocols is similar to PAP and CHAP. As with PAP, I highly recommend that you not use the plain text form of authentication because the password is sent to the remote router in clear text and is susceptible to eavesdropping attacks.

Plain-Text Process

When using plain-text authentication, the routing protocol used between two routers uses the same authentication key. Some protocols allow the use of multiple keys between the same or different peers, but this depends on the routing protocol. With multiple keys, each key needs a key number for identification purposes. Basically, with plain-text authentication, a router sends a routing update with the key (in clear text) and the key number (if multiple keys are used). When the remote router receives the update, it compares the received key with its own stored key: If the two keys match, the remote router accepts the update; otherwise, it ignores it. Protocols that support plain-text authentication include IS-IS, OSPF, and RIPv2.

MD5 Process

MD5 is a much more secure method of authentication. With MD5, a key also is used, just as with plain text. However, the key is never sent across the network to the remote router; instead, it is used to create a message digest, called a hash value. The key information about the router, such as its IP address, and the routing update are run through the MD5 hashing function, producing a fixed-length result. This result is included with the routing update. The remote peer uses the same key, stored locally; information from the received router; and the received routing update. It runs them through the MD5 hashing function. If its result matches that sent with the routing update, the router can be assured that the router sending the traffic is trusted (used the correct key) and that no one tampered with the packet (only a router with the same key could produce the same message digest). The key itself is never sent across the wire. Routing protocols that support MD5 authentication include IS-IS, OSPF, RIPv2, EIGRP, and BGP.

NOTE	Because of the weaknesses of using plain-text authentication, this book focuses only on using MD5 for authentication.

CAUTION	One word of warning concerning BGP: If a BGP update needs to access a device that performs packet manipulations, including NAT/PAT by an address-translation device, a PIX performing sequence number randomization for TCP, or another form of packet/TCP segment manipulation, this invalidates the MD5 signature and causes the remote BGP peer to ignore the routing update. Therefore, you need to verify that no packet manipulations are occurring between your two BGP peers. If manipulations are occurring, you can resort to using a VPN to tunnel the BGP information between the two peers. Note that you also can use a VPN to transport other routing protocols between peers, but this adds a lot more overhead on your router and should be used as a second solution.

RIPv2

RIPv2 supports both plain-text and MD5 authentication. However, I discuss only the use of MD5 in this book because it is much more secure. You need to configure these commands to implement RIPv2 MD5 authentication:

```
Router(config)# key chain name_of_key_chain
Router(config-keychain)# key key_#
```

```
Router(config-keychain-key)# key-string your_secret_key
Router(config-keychain-key)# exit
Router(config-keychain)# exit
Router(config)# router rip
Router(config-router)# version 2
Router(config-router)# exit
Router(config)# interface [slot_#/]port_#
Router(config-if)# ip rip authentication key-chain name_of_key_chain
Router(config-if)# ip rip authentication mode md5
```

The **key chain** command is used to group your keying information and is given a unique name. Executing this command takes you into a subconfiguration mode, where you enter the key number used to reference the key. Typically, you configure only one key, so most administrators use 1 as the number. This takes you into another subconfiguration mode, where you use the **key-string** command to configure the actual key. Note that you use multiple key numbers in one situation: when you need to change your old key to a new value, but you want to slowly migrate your routers to the new key value.

Within your RIP configuration, you must specify that your router is running version 2 with the **version 2** command. Finally, on each interface on which your router is running RIP, you must activate authentication. This requires the use of two commands. The **ip rip authentication key-chain** command specifies what key to use, and the **ip rip authentication mode md5** command specifies that MD5 authentication is used.

If you are experiencing authentication problems with RIP, use the **debug ip rip** command. After authentication, the **show ip route** command should show at least some of the routes from the neighboring router.

Example 15-4 displays a simple configuration for the perimeter router in Figure 15-1.

Example 15-4 *Authenticating RIPv2 Updates*

```
Perimeter(config)# key chain RIP-KEYS
Perimeter(config-keychain)# key 1
Perimeter(config-keychain-key)# key-string secret-key
Perimeter(config-keychain-key)# exit
Perimeter(config-keychain)# exit
Perimeter(config)# router rip
Perimeter(config-router)# network 199.1.1.0
Perimeter(config-router)# version 2
Perimeter(config-router)# exit
Perimeter(config)# interface ethernet0
Perimeter(config-if)# ip rip authentication key-chain RIP-KEYS
Perimeter(config-if)# ip rip authentication mode md5
```

Use the same configuration for RouterA and RouterB, making sure you that enable RIP authentication on the ethernet0 interfaces of both routers. One thing that can be different on both routers is the name of the key chain; however, the password needs to be the same.

NOTE   When you save your configuration, the keys are hashed and are not stored in clear text, protecting you from eavesdroppers when backing up your router's configuration remotely.

EIGRP

Unlike RIPv2, EIGRP supports only MD5 authentication. The configuration of EIGRP's MD5 authentication is similar to that of RIPv2. You use these commands to set up EIGRP authentication:

```
Router(config)# key chain name_of_key_chain
Router(config-keychain)# key key_#
Router(config-keychain-key)# key-string your_secret_key
Router(config-keychain-key)# exit
Router(config-keychain)# exit
Router(config)# interface [slot_#/]port_#
Router(config-if)# ip authentication key-chain eigrp AS_#
  name_of_key_chain
Router(config-if)# ip authentication mode eigrp AS_# md5
```

As you can see from the configuration, the first part, configuring the **key chain**, is the same as with RIPv2. On the interfaces that are participating in EIGRP, you need to enable authentication. The **ip authentication key-chain eigrp** command specifies the autonomous system (AS) number and the name of the key chain. You also must specify the use of MD5 with the **ip authentication mode eigrp** command. Use the **debug ip eigrp** command to troubleshoot authentication problems.

Example 15-5 shows the configuration of the perimeter router in Figure 15-1 (this example assumes that EIGRP is using AS 65,500).

Example 15-5 *Authenticating EIGRP Updates*

```
Perimeter(config)# key chain EIGRP-KEYS
Perimeter(config-keychain)# key 1
Perimeter(config-keychain-key)# key-string secret-key
Perimeter(config-keychain-key)# exit
Perimeter(config-keychain)# exit
Perimeter(config)# router eigrp 65500
Perimeter(config-router)# network 199.1.1.0
Perimeter(config)# interface ethernet0
Perimeter(config-if)# ip authentication key-chain
  eigrp 65500 EIGRP-KEYS
Perimeter(config-if)# ip authentication mode eigrp 65500 md5
```

As you can see, the configuration is straightforward. The same key and AS number need to be used on RouterA and RouterB.

OSPF

As with RIPv2, OSPF supports both plain-text and MD5 authentication. However, as recommended earlier, you should use MD5 authentication. You use these commands to set up MD5 authentication for OSPF:

```
Router(config)# router ospf process_ID_#
Router(config-router)# area area_# authentication message-digest
Router(config-router)# exit
```

```
Router(config)# interface [slot_#/]port_#
Router(config-if)# ip ospf message-digest-key key_#
  md5 key_value
```

As you can see from the configuration, OSPF's authentication configuration is different from that of RIP or EIGRP. The **area authentication** command is executed under the OSPF routing process (**router ospf** command). Then, for each interface on which you have enabled OSPF, you need to specify authentication with the **ip ospf message-digest-key** command. This command also specifies the key number and key to use with the MD5 algorithm (which allows for different keys for different peers). Use the **show ip ospf neighbor**, **debug ip ospf adj**, and **debug ip ospf events** commands to troubleshoot OSPF authentication.

Example 15-6 shows a simple example of the perimeter router, running OSPF in area 0, between RouterA and RouterB, in Figure 15-1.

Example 15-6 *Authenticating OSPF Updates*

```
Router(config)# router ospf 1
Router(config-router)# network 192.1.1.1 0.0.0.0 area 0
Router(config-router)# area 0 authentication message-digest
Router(config-router)# exit
Router(config)# interface ethernet0
Router(config-if)# ip ospf message-digest-key 1 md5 itsasecret
```

AS you can see from this example, the configuration of OSPF's MD5 authentication is simple.

IS-IS

As with OSPF, IS-IS supports clear-text and MD5 authentication to form a routing neighbor relationship and share routing updates. This section discusses only the use of MD5; however, MD5 authentication in the Cisco IOS is fairly new and requires Cisco IOS 12.2(13)T or later (plus, it is limited to only a few router platforms).

I have divided the configuration task into three groups of configuration tasks.

Step 1   Define your authentication keys and allow receipt of unauthenticated updates.

Step 2   Enable MD5 authentication for the IS-IS routing process.

Step 3   Force IS-IS to use authentication for both sent and received routing updates.

If you have an existing network running IS-IS, it is important to follow these steps to allow uninterrupted transmission from the routers performing authentication to all routers performing (or not performing) authentication.

Group 1 Steps: Authentication Keys

On all your IS-IS routers, configure the following:

```
Router(config)# key chain name_of_key_chain
Router(config-keychain)# key key_#
Router(config-keychain-key)# key-string your_secret_key
Router(config-keychain-key)# exit
Router(config-keychain)# exit
Router(config)# router isis area_tag_#
Router(config-router)# authentication send-only [level-1 | level-2]
```

The first part of the configuration is the same as that used in RIPv2 and EIGRP, where the MD5 hash key is defined (**key-string**). Make sure that you use the same key on each IS-IS router. After you have defined your key, enter the IS-IS routing process and specify the **authentication send-only** command. This command specifies that only routing updates that the router generates will have authentication performed: Any received updates are not authenticated. This enables you to migrate all of your routers so that they all send IS-IS authenticated updates; then you slowly can change your routers over to send and receive authenticated updates. You can qualify authentication by specifying the IS-IS level: 1 or 2. However, if you omit the level specification, the Cisco IOS uses authentication for both levels.

Group 2 Steps: IS-IS Authentication

After you have completed group 1 steps for all your IS-IS routers, you are ready to proceed to the next part of the configuration. Perform the following configuration on all your IS-IS routers:

```
Router(config)# router isis area_tag_#
Router(config-router)# authentication mode md5 [level-1|level-2]
Router(config-router)# authentication key-chain name_of_key_chain
  [level-1 | level-2]
```

These commands enable MD5 authentication for IS-IS on your router. The **authentication mode md5** command specifies MD5 authentication. If you omit the IS-IS level number, both level-1 and level-2 are authenticated through MD5. The **authentication key-chain** command specifies the key to use for the MD5 hashing function.

Group 3 Steps: Using Authentication

You have one last command to complete on all your IS-IS routers:

```
Router(config)# router isis area_tag_#
Router(config-router)# no authentication send-only [level-1|level-2]
```

In this syntax, you want to disable send-only authentication. In other words, you want your router to send authenticated updates as well as authenticate all received updates. The previous configuration performs this process. Make sure that you execute this command on all of your IS-IS routers.

To verify that IS-IS authentication is functioning correctly, use the **show clns neighbors** and **debug isis adj-packets** commands. With authentication functioning correctly, your router should see all IS-IS directly connected neighbors. If you do not see an IS-IS neighbor show up (and it was there before you enabled MD5 authentication), use the **debug isis adj-packets** command for detailed troubleshooting. For specific troubleshooting of IS-IS authentication, use the **debug isis authentication information** command.

IS-IS Authentication Example

Refer back to Figure 15-1 for this next illustration of an IS-IS MD5 authentication example. Example 15-7 shows the configuration steps to perform on the perimeter router.

Example 15-7 *Defining Authentication Keys for IS-IS*

```
Perimeter(config)# key chain ISIS-key
Perimeter(config-keychain)# key 1
Perimeter(config-keychain-key)# key-string secretkey1
Perimeter(config-keychain-key)# exit
Perimeter(config-keychain)# exit
Perimeter(config)# router isis 1
Perimeter(config-router)# authentication send-only
```

When you have completed the configuration in Example 15-7 on the perimeter router, duplicate it on RouterA and RouterB. After this, configure Example 15-8 on the perimeter router.

Example 15-8 *Enable MD5 Authentication for IS-IS*

```
Perimeter(config)# router isis 1
Perimeter(config-router)# authentication mode md5
Perimeter(config-router)# authentication key-chain ISIS-key
```

Again, when you are done with the perimeter router, repeat the Example 15-8 configuration on RouterA and RouterB.

Finally, perform the Example 15-9 configuration on the perimeter router, as well as on RouterA and RouterB.

Example 15-9 *Authentication Both Sent and Received Updates for IS-IS*

```
Router(config)# router isis 1
Router(config-router)# no authentication send-only
```

As you can see from this example, the configuration is more complex than for the other IGPs, but it not that much more difficult.

Other Tools

Besides using authentication, you can use other tools to help secure your routing protocol. This section discusses two tools: passive interfaces and ACL filtering.

Passive Interfaces

Classful routing protocols, such as RIPv1 and IGRP, and classless protocols built upon the foundations of a classful protocol, such as EIGRP, have a quirk in their configuration: You must specify a classful network number under the **router** process with the **network** command. All interfaces that have an address in this network number are included in the routing update. Note that in the newest versions of the Cisco IOS, EIGRP enables you to specify a wildcard mask to be more specific about participating interfaces.

Look at Figure 15-2 as an example. In this network, 191.1.1.0/24 has been broken into four subnets. Assume that the routers in this example are running EIGRP. Even though EIGRP is a classless protocol, it has its roots in IGRP, which is classful. Its configuration is essentially the same as that of IGRP: You configure the classful network number (I am assuming that the Cisco IOS on this router does not support subnet masks for the EIGRP **network** statement.

Figure 15-2 *Classful Routing Example*

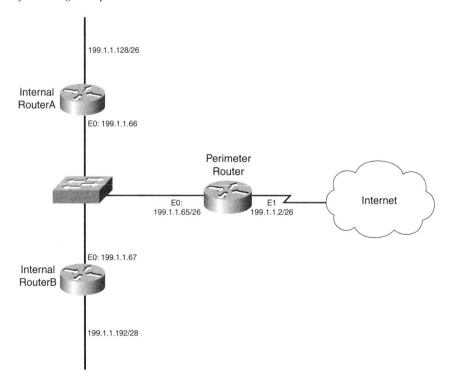

However, in Example 15-10, this creates a problem for the perimeter router.

Example 15-10 *Configuring EIGRP on the Perimeter Router*

```
Perimeter(config)# router eigrp 65500
Perimeter(config-router)# network 192.1.1.0
```

As you can see from Example 15-10, both e0 and e1 are included in the EIGRP process. This creates a problem: You do not want to be advertising your internal routes out of e1 because the ISP—and possibly other devices—might see this information, especially in an ISP-bridged solution connection. Likewise, for RouterA and RouterB, you do not want to be advertising routes to the end stations for the top and bottom network segments. Remember that more attacks occur within than outside your network. Therefore, the less your internal users know about the structure of the network, the harder it becomes for them to mount various attacks.

To prevent your router from generating routing updates on an interface, use the **passive-interface** command:

```
Router(config)# router routing_protocol
  [routing_protocol_information]
Router(config-router)# passive-interface interface_type
  [slot_#/]port_#
```

CAUTION   One important thing to point out concerning the **passive-interface** command is that it prevents the local router only from generating routing updates on the specified interface; the router still will accept routing updates on the interface. Therefore, you need another solution, such as distribution lists or ACL filters, to block incoming routing updates. This is true for RIPv2, but for IS-IS, EIGRP, and OSPF, a neighbor relationship must be established first. Using the **passive-interface** command on interfaces with these routing protocols provides some protection.

Example 15-11 shows an example configuration for the perimeter router in Figure 15-2, assuming that the router is running EIGRP in AS 65,500.

Example 15-11 *Using Passive Interfaces*

```
Router(config)# router eigrp 65500
Router(config-router)# network 192.1.1.0
Router(config-router)# passive-interface e1
```

ACL Filters

As I explained in the last section, passive interfaces prevent the router only from advertising routes on the specified interface; the Cisco IOS still accepts routes on the interface for RIPv2 (however, I always play it safe and use ACLs to restrict updates from routing peers).

To prevent this, you need to configure an interface ACL that blocks routing updates. Table 15-1 displays the IP protocols numbers for the routing protocols.

Table 15-1 *Routing Protocols*

IP Protocol Number	IP Protocol	Other Protocol Information
IP = 9	IGRP	Destination address is 255.255.255.255 (IGRP uses broadcasts)
IP = 88	EIGRP	Destination address is 224.0.0.10 (EIGRP uses multicasts)
IP = 89	OSPF	Destination addresses are 224.0.0.5 and 224.0.0.6 (OSPF uses multicasts)
IP = 124	IS-IS	Destination addresses are 224.0.0.19, 224.0.0.20, and 224.0.0.21 (IS-IS uses multicasts)
UDP = 520	RIPv1	Destination address is 255.255.255.255 (RIPv1 uses broadcasts)
UDP = 520	RIPv2	Destination address is 224.0.0.9 (RIPv2 uses multicasts)
TCP = 179	BGP	Destination address is an address on the router (BGP uses unicast)

Using Figure 15-2 as an example, assume that this network is using RIPv2. To prevent RIPv2 from accepting and receiving routing updates on the external interface (ethernet1), use the configuration in Example 15-12.

Example 15-12 *Protection RIPv2 Routing Updates*

```
Perimeter(config)# router rip
Perimeter(config-router)# version 2
Perimeter(config-router)# network 192.1.1.0
Perimeter(config-router)# passive-interface ethernet1
Perimeter(config-router)# exit
Perimeter(config)# ip access-list extended external-ACL
Perimeter(config-ext-nacl)# ! <--enter your other ACL commands here-->
Perimeter(config-ext-nacl)# deny udp any any eq 520
Perimeter(config-ext-nacl)# ! <--enter your other ACL commands here-->
Perimeter(config-ext-nacl)# exit
Perimeter(config)# interface ethernet1
Perimeter(config-if)# ip access-group external-ACL in
```

As you can see in this example, any RIP traffic that is trying to enter the external interface is blocked.

HSRP

HSRP is the Cisco proprietary default gateway protocol that allows redundancy of default gateways for clients without having to perform additional configuration on the clients. Even though HSRP is not a routing protocol, it serves a routing purpose, so I discuss how to protect HSRP from attacks by showing you how to configure authentication.

Figure 15-3 shows a simple HSRP example. In this example, the network has two perimeter routers, in which the internal users are using a default gateway address of 199.1.1.254, assigned by a DHCP server.

Figure 15-3 *HSRP Example*

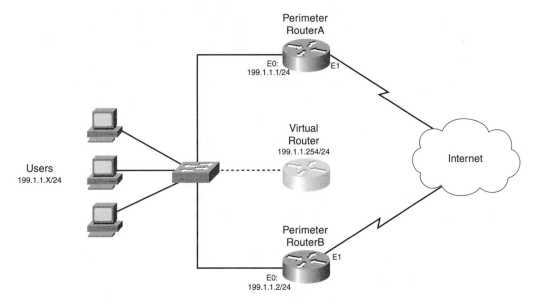

As with the Cisco IOS routing protocols, HSRP supports MD5 authentication as of Cisco IOS 12.3(2)T. The use of authentication prevents spoofing attacks, which can result in a DoS attack. A hacker could subvert the HSRP operation and trick routers in the HSRP group into thinking that the hacker's "router" should be the active router. Thus, all traffic is redirected to the hacker's device, where he can examine it.

NOTE   Even though HSRP supports both clear-text and MD5 authentication, this book focuses only on the use of MD5.

I am assuming that you are already familiar with the configuration of HSRP, so I focus only on the MD5 authentication configuration. Here is the basic configuration of your HSRP router, using MD5 authentication:

```
Router(config)# interface type [slot_#/]port_#
Router(config-if)# ip address IP_address subnet_mask
```

```
Router(config-if)# standby [group_#] ip virtual_IP_address
Router(config-if)# standby [group_#] priority priority
Router(config-if)# standby [group_#] preempt
Router(config-if)# standby track interface_type[slot_#/]port_#
   decrement_value
Router(config-if)# standby [group_#] authentication md5 key-string key
   [timeout seconds]
```

The only new command I am introducing in this configuration is the **standby authentication** command. The key that you specify here must be configured on all HSRP routers in the same HSRP group. If you want to change the HSRP MD5 authentication key, first make sure that you configure the optional **timeout** parameter. This parameter specifies a time period that both the old and new keys are accepted, giving you enough time to configure all of your routers to use the new key.

Instead of configuring the key with the **key-string** parameter in the **standby authentication** command, you can use the following syntax:

```
Router(config)# key chain name_of_key_chain
Router(config-keychain)# key key_#
Router(config-keychain-key)# key-string your_secret_key
Router(config-keychain-key)# exit
Router(config-keychain)# exit
Router(config)# interface type [slot_#/]port_#
Router(config-if)# standby [group_#] authentication md5
   key-chain name_of_key_chain [timeout seconds]
```

When you are done with your configuration, use the **show standby** and **debug standby errors** commands.

Example 15-13 shows a simple configuration example, using Perimeter RouterA in Figure 15-3.

Example 15-13 *Using Authentication with HSRP on RouterA*

```
RouterA(config)# interface ethernet0
RouterA(config-if)# ip address 199.1.1.1 255.255.255.0
RouterA(config-if)# standby 1 ip 199.1.1.254
RouterA(config-if)# standby 1 priority 110
RouterA(config-if)# standby 1 preempt
RouterA(config-if)# standby track ethernet1 50
RouterA(config-if)# standby 1 authentication md5 key-string secret
```

Example 15-14 displays RouterB's configuration.

Example 15-14 *Using Authentication with HSRP on RouterB*

```
RouterB(config)# interface ethernet0
RouterB(config-if)# ip address 199.1.1.2 255.255.255.0
RouterB(config-if)# standby 1 ip 199.1.1.254
RouterB(config-if)# standby 1 priority 100
RouterB(config-if)# standby 1 preempt
RouterB(config-if)# standby 1 authentication md5 key-string secret
```

As you can see from this example, the configuration is straightforward.

BGP Security

This section focuses on securing BGP. In most cases, BGP is used in large networks with two or more Internet connections, where the company needs to have control of traffic leaving and (sometimes) entering the network. One of the issues with BGP is that it does not behave very well in unstable environments. In other words, when there are a lot of changes within BGP, the router must spend a lot of processing to deal with the changes. Without any type of security measures, an ingenious hacker could hijack an external or internal BGP session and wreak havoc on your BGP routing protocol. A hacker easily can generate a DoS attack to subvert your routing information or overcome your router's resources with flapping route information.

As with the IGPs, BGP supports router authentication with MD5. Authentication can be used to prevent spoofing attacks. Another tool, although not security related, is route dampening. In times of heavy routing update changes, you want to ensure that your router is not swamped with handling changes. With a DoS attack, your router might begin missing BGP keepalives, which could cause routing confusion. Route dampening can help with this problem. I discussed bogon filtering at the beginning of this chapter, but BGP also supports this function through the use of prefix lists; with prefix lists, you can restrict what BGP routes your router will accept from a neighbor or neighbors. The following three sections deal with these topics.

Authentication

Of all the routing protocols, setting up MD5 authentication with BGP is the easiest. After you have set up BGP with your peer router and are sending and receiving routes, you should add the following statement to both routers:

```
Router(config)# router bgp AS_#
Router(config-router)# neighbor neighbor's_IP_address
  password password
```

As you can see from this example, setting up authentication is very easy. Just make sure that the password is the same on both routers; otherwise, neither router will accept each other's routing updates. The password can be of mixed case and can be up to 80 characters in length. The first character in the password cannot be a number or a space; however, this is permitted with subsequent characters. MD5 authentication is used to verify the entire BGP TCP segment: This ensures that no tampering is done with the routing updates and routing information contained in the TCP segment.

TIP   When you enable MD5 authentication, the existing TCP connection between the peers is torn down and then rebuilt. Do this during a time of little activity on the router.

CAUTION   Remember my earlier warning about using MD5 authentication and sending routing
updates through devices that change packet header information. For BGP, this would
invalidate the BGP routing updates between peers.

Route Flap Dampening

BGP route flap dampening is a feature that you can enable on your router that helps it
during a time of BGP convergence. With route flap dampening, BGP is more stable and
requires fewer CPU cycles when dealing with flapping routes. A flapping route is a route
that constantly fluctuates, causing a BGP router to generate update messages (adding and
withdrawing the flapping route or routes). Every smart ISP already should be doing this
with BGP configurations.

To set up BGP route flap dampening, add the following command to your BGP
configuration:

```
Router(config)# router bgp AS_#
Router(config-router)# bgp dampening [half_life] [reuse]
  [suppression_limit] [maximum_suppression_time] [route-map route_map_name]
```

Table 15-2 explains the optional parameters for the **bgp dampening** command. Even
though each of these values is optional, all are position-dependent (with the exception of
the **route-map** parameter). Therefore, if you want to change the reuse value, you first must
enter the *half_life* value. To display statistics about flapping routes, use the **show ip bgp
flap-statistics** command. To display dampened BGP routes, use the **show ip bgp
dampened-paths** command.

Table 15-2   *Optional BGP Dampening Parameters*

Parameter	Values	Explanation
half_life	1 to 45 minutes (the default is 15)	Determines how fast the accumulated penalty for a route can decay exponentially, eventually allowing it to be used again. After a route becomes stabilized, the penalty for the route is reduced by half after each half-life period expires. When the penalty value falls below the reuse threshold, the route is used again.
reuse	1 to 20,000 (the default is 750)	When the penalty value for the route falls below this threshold, it is used again by BGP.
suppression_limit	1 to 20,000 (the default is 2000)	When a route is assigned a penalty that exceeds this value, the route is suppressed (dampened).

Table 15-2   *Optional BGP Dampening Parameters (Continued)*

Parameter	Values	Explanation
maximum_suppression_time	1 to 255 minutes (the default is four times the *half_life* parameter value)	This is the maximum amount of time that a route can be suppressed, regardless of the number of times that the route flaps.
route_map_name	Name of route map	This controls which routes BGP dampening is or is not used for.

To help you better understand the process of route dampening, assume that there is a network connected to an ISP using BGP, like that shown in Figure 15-4. In this example, 199.1.7.0/24 is flapping, and the perimeter router has route dampening enabled. When the route flaps enough that its penalty exceeds the configurable suppression limit, the perimeter router stops advertising the route to the ISP. This penalty is decayed using the half-life timer until the reuse limit is reached. When that limit is reached, the perimeter router begins advertising the route again.

Figure 15-4   *BGP Dampening Example*

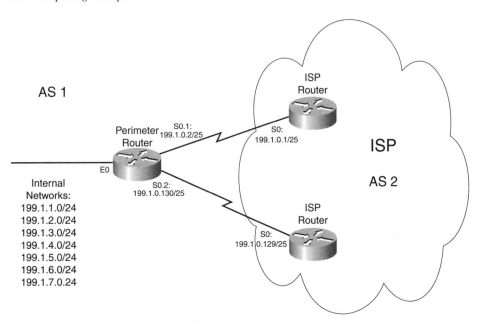

When you have configured route dampening and a BGP peer is reset, the route or routes are withdrawn, but no penalty is applied to the routes. Also, routes external to an AS that were learned from an IBGP peer never are dampened.

BGP Routing Example

To help you better understand how to configure BGP on a router securely, I use the example shown in Figure 15-4 to illustrate a simple solution. The Team Cymru Web Site has an excellent example of setting up BGP in a secure fashion at http://www.cymru.com/Documents/secure-bgp-template.html. Example 15-15 is based on this template and is used to secure BGP running on the perimeter router in Figure 15-4.

Example 15-15 *Securing a BGP Router*

```
Router(config)# router bgp 1
Router(config-router)# no synchronization                     (1)
Router(config-router)# no bgp fast-external-fallover          (2)
Router(config-router)# bgp log-neighbor-changes               (3)
Router(config-router)# bgp dampening route-map                (4)
  varied-dampening
Router(config-router)# network 199.1.0.0 mask 255.255.248.0   (5)
Router(config-router)#
Router(config-router)# neighbor 199.1.0.1 remote-as 2         (6)
Router(config-router)# neighbor 199.1.0.1                     (7)
  soft-reconfiguration inbound
Router(config-router)# neighbor 199.1.0.1 password as2router1 (8)
Router(config-router)# neighbor 199.1.0.1 version 4           (9)
Router(config-router)# neighbor 199.1.0.1 prefix-list         (10)
  bogonlist in
Router(config-router)# neighbor 199.1.0.1 prefix-list         (11)
  announce_out out
Router(config-router)# neighbor 199.1.0.1                     (12)
  maximum-prefix 163000 75
Router(config)#
Router(config-router)# neighbor 199.1.0.129 remote-as 2       (13)
Router(config-router)# neighbor 199.1.0.129
  soft-reconfiguration inbound
Router(config-router)# neighbor 199.1.0.129 password as2router2
Router(config-router)# neighbor 199.1.0.129 version 4
Router(config-router)# neighbor 199.1.0.129 prefix-list bogonlist in
Router(config-router)# neighbor 199.1.0.129
  prefix-list announce_out out
Router(config-router)# neighbor 199.1.0.129
  maximum-prefix 163000 75
Router(config-router)# no auto-summary                        (14)
Router(config-router)# exit
Router(config)#
Router(config)# ip route 199.1.0.0 255.255.248.0 null0        (15)
Router(config)# ip route 199.1.1.0 255.255.255.0 ethernet0    (16)
Router(config)# ip route 199.1.2.0 255.255.255.0 ethernet0
Router(config)# ip route 199.1.3.0 255.255.255.0 ethernet0
Router(config)# ip route 199.1.4.0 255.255.255.0 ethernet0
Router(config)# ip route 199.1.5.0 255.255.255.0 ethernet0
Router(config)# ip route 199.1.6.0 255.255.255.0 ethernet0
Router(config)# ip route 199.1.7.0 255.255.255.0 ethernet0
Router(config)#
Router(config)# ip prefix-list announce_out description only  (17)
  advertise our summarized route
```

Example 15-15 *Securing a BGP Router (Continued)*

```
Router(config)# ip prefix-list announce_out seq 5
  permit 199.1.0.0/21
Router(config)# ip prefix-list announce_out seq 10
  deny 0.0.0.0/0 le 32
Router(config)#
Router(config)# ip prefix-list bogonlist description                (18)
  Block bogons
Router(config)# ip prefix-list bogonlist seq 5
  deny 0.0.0.0/8 le 32
Router(config)# ip prefix-list bogonlist seq 10
  deny 1.0.0.0/8 le 32
Router(config)# ip prefix-list bogonlist seq 15
  deny 2.0.0.0/8 le 32
Router(config)# ip prefix-list bogonlist seq 20
  deny 5.0.0.0/8 le 32
Router(config)# ip prefix-list bogonlist seq 25
  deny 7.0.0.0/8 le 32
Router(config)# ip prefix-list bogonlist seq 30
  deny 10.0.0.0/8 le 32
Router(config)# ! <--other bogons omitted, but you would keep on
  listing them here-->
Router(config)# ip prefix-list bogonlist seq 900                    (19)
  permit 0.0.0.0/0 le 27
Router(config)#
Router(config)# ip prefix-list dampen_long_prefixes                 (20)
 description /24 prefixes longer.
Router(config)# ip prefix-list dampen_long_prefixes seq 5
  permit 0.0.0.0/0 ge 24
Router(config)#
Router(config)# ip prefix-list dampen_medium_prefixes               (21)
  description /22 and /23 prefixes
Router(config)# ip prefix-list dampen_medium_prefixes seq 5
  permit 0.0.0.0/0 ge 22 le 23
Router(config)#
Router(config)# ip prefix-list dampen_short_prefixes                (22)
  description /21 prefixes and shorter
Router(config)# ip prefix-list dampen_short_prefixes seq 5
  permit 0.0.0.0/0 le 21
Router(config)#
Router(config)# ip prefix-list DNS_root_servers                     (23)
  description DNS root server addresses
Router(config)# ip prefix-list DNS_root_servers seq 5
  permit 198.41.0.0/24
Router(config)# ip prefix-list DNS_root_servers seq 10
  permit 128.9.0.0/16
Router(config)# ip prefix-list DNS_root_servers seq 15
  permit 192.33.4.0/24
Router(config)# ip prefix-list DNS_root_servers seq 20
  permit 128.8.0.0/16
Router(config)# ip prefix-list DNS_root_servers seq 25
  permit 192.203.230.0/24
```

continues

Example 15-15 *Securing a BGP Router (Continued)*

```
Router(config)# ip prefix-list DNS_root_servers seq 30
  permit 192.5.4.0/23
Router(config)# ip prefix-list DNS_root_servers seq 35
  permit 192.112.36.0/24
Router(config)# ip prefix-list DNS_root_servers seq 40
  permit 128.63.0.0/16
Router(config)# ip prefix-list DNS_root_servers seq 45
  permit 192.36.148.0/24
Router(config)# ip prefix-list DNS_root_servers seq 50
  permit 193.0.14.0/24
Router(config)# ip prefix-list DNS_root_servers seq 55
  permit 198.32.64.0/24
Router(config)# ip prefix-list DNS_root_servers seq 60
  permit 202.12.27.0/24
Router(config)#
Router(config)# route-map varied-dampening deny 10             (24)
Router(config-route-map)# match ip address prefix-list DNS_root_servers
Router(config-route-map)# exit
Router(config)# route-map varied-dampening permit 20           (25)
Router(config-route-map)# match ip address prefix-list
  dampen_long_prefixes
Router(config-route-map)# set dampening 30 750 3000 60
Router(config-route-map)# exit
Router(config)# route-map varied-dampening permit 30           (26)
Router(config-route-map)# match ip address prefix-list
  dampen_medium_prefixes
Router(config-route-map)# set dampening 15 750 3000 45
Router(config-route-map)# exit
Router(config)# route-map varied-dampening permit 40           (27)
Router(config-route-map)# match ip address prefix-list
  dampen_short_prefixes
Router(config-route-map)# set dampening 10 1500 3000 30
Router(config-route-map)# exit
Router(config)#
Router(config)# ip access-list extended allow_BGP_updates      (28)
Router(config-ext-nacl)# ! <--insert other ACL statements-->
Router(config-ext-nacl)# permit tcp host 199.1.0.1 host 199.1.0.2 eq 179
Router(config-ext-nacl)# permit tcp host 199.1.0.1 eq 179 host 199.1.0.2
Router(config-ext-nacl)# permit tcp host 199.1.0.129 host 199.1.0.130 eq 179
Router(config-ext-nacl)# permit tcp host 199.1.0.129 eq 179 host 199.1.0.130
Router(config-ext-nacl)# access-list 185 deny tcp any any eq 179 log-input
Router(config-ext-nacl)# ! <--insert other ACL statements-->
Router(config-ext-nacl)# exit
Router(config)# interface serial0.1 point-to-point             (29)
Router(config-subif)# ip access-group allow_BGP_updates in
Router(config-subif)# exit
Router(config)# interface serial0.2 point-to-point
Router(config-subif)# ip access-group allow_BGP_updates in
Router(config-subif)# exit
```

The following is an explanation of the configuration in Example 15-15, with reference to the numbering on the right side of the configuration:

1 Does not wait for the IGP to catch up with convergence.

2 Allows for occasional missed keepalives.

3 Logs events regarding BGP neighbors.

4 Specifies the route map to use for dampening. This performs different types of dampening, based on the route in question. These are covered in Statement 23.

5 Reduces CPU utilization by using a **network** statement to advertise the route, along with a null route statement (later) that prohibits the use of the summarized statement by the router itself; it uses the more specific routes. See Statement 16.

6 Configures neighbor 1 in AS 2.

7 Prevents a complete withdrawal of all prefixed routes for neighbor 1 when the **clear ip bgp** command is used, speeding up convergence.

8 Defines the MD5 BGP password, which is used for authentication.

9 Disables negotiation of the BGP version, which speeds up the peering process.

10 Blocks all bogon advertisements in BGP routing updates. These are shown in Statement 18.

TIP   Prefix lists have replaced distribution lists as the preferred filter for BGP on Cisco routers because they are easier on the router's CPU.

---

11 Restricts the advertisement of routes to the ISP, and also prevents the router from becoming a transit network.

12 Prevents the router from trying to receive too many routes from the peer router, causing it to crash. The limit here is a maximum limit (163,000 routes), and 75 is the percentage point at which the Cisco IOS starts generating log messages, indicating a possible problem.

13 This is neighbor 2's configuration, which is basically the same as that of neighbor 1.

14 Disables router auto-summarization.

15 Ensures that the summarized route for the internal network is not used if it is the only route.

16 Involves configuring your internal routing protocol; for a network this small, I am using static routes that point to the appropriate internal network. Obviously, for more than one internal router connected to the perimeter router, you would specify the next-hop address instead of the interface.

17 Uses a prefix list that restricts the router to advertising only the 199.1.0.0/21 summarized route. See Statement 5. Notice that BGP uses prefix lists.

18 Prevents the router from advertising bogon networks. Notice that BGP uses prefix lists.

19 Restricts summarized routes to a /27 or smaller prefix. This ensures that your router is not flooded with more specific routes. Note that you might need to adjust this value to something smaller (less than 27) for a router with smaller memory. If you need more specific paths to make more intelligent choices about reaching a destination, you might need to adjust this to a larger value (greater than 27). This is different for every situation and router.

20 Specifies a prefix list of routes with a prefix of 24 bits or longer. This is used to set up special dampening for the prefixes in Statement 25 (longer prefixes are dampened longer than shorter ones).

21 Specifies a prefix list of routes with a prefix between Statements 22 and 23. This is used to set up special dampening for the prefixes in Statement 26.

22 Specifies a prefix list of routes with a prefix of 21 or less. This is used to set up special dampening for the prefixes (which tend to be more stable) in Statement 27.

23 Specifies a prefix list of DNS root server addresses. This is used for special dampening of these prefixes, ensuring that you do not dampen these. See Statement 24.

24 Ensures that the DNS root servers are never dampened, even if their routes are flapping. Historically, these routes have been stable. See Statement 23.

25 Specifies dampening for /24 and greater prefixes to 60 minutes. See Statement 20.

26 Specifies dampening for /22 to /23 prefixes to 45 minutes. See Statement 21.

27 Specifies dampening for /21 prefixes and smaller to 30 minutes. See Statement 22.

28 Creates an ACL to allow BGP traffic. You need to insert statements before and after these statements. Notice that these statements allow communication only between this router and the two ISP peer routers in AS 2. It is also important to point out that this ACL is an example: No other traffic would be allowed through this ACL, so you would need to tune it appropriately.

29 Activates the ACL on the two point-to-point serial links.

As you can see from this example, setting up BGP, along with security, on your perimeter router is not a task for the faint of heart: It is a very complicated process that requires intimate knowledge of BGP.

Reverse-Path Forwarding (Unicast Traffic)

One useful Cisco IOS tool for preventing IP address spoofing is to use reverse path forwarding (RPF). RPF can be used for both unicast and multicast traffic; however, this book focuses on only unicast traffic. With RPF, the Cisco IOS checks its routing table to determine whether to accept a packet or to drop it. RPF prevents spoofing by examining the source IP address in the packet, the interface, the packet that was received, and routing information in the routing table. If there is a contradiction—for example, the source address is not located off the interface where the router thinks the packet belongs (based on the routing table)—the router drops the packet. Remember that this kind of spoofing is common in many forms of DoS attacks, such as a Smurf attack. Unicast RPF forwards only packets with valid source IP addresses based on information found in the router's routing table. This kind of policy enforcement is common in ISPs.

RPF Process

Refer to Figure 15-5 for this next illustration of RPF. Here is a simplified routing table based on the perimeter router's configuration:

```
199.1.1.0/24    E1
199.1.2.0/24    E0
199.1.3.0/24    E0
199.1.4.0/24    E0
199.1.5.0/24    E0
199.1.6.0/24    E0
199.1.7.0/24    E0
0.0.0.0/0       E1
```

Figure 15-5 *Unicast RPF Example*

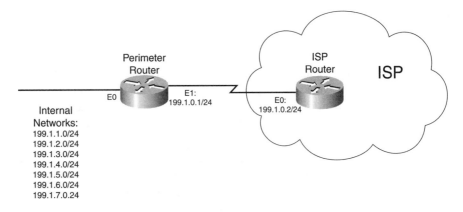

As an example, assume that the perimeter router receives a packet on E0 with an IP address of 199.1.0.5. With RPF, the router knows that this is not valid because 199.1.0.0/25 is located off E1. In this instance, the router drops the packet. Basically, the router compares the source IP address with the routes in the routing table, to make sure that the packet is received off the correct interface. The router matches source IP packets only against best paths (the ones populated in the routing table).

If an inbound ACL is applied to the interface on which RPF is enabled, the router first checks the ACL and then performs its RPF check.

NOTE   For RPF to function, CEF must be enabled on the router. This is because the router uses the Forwarding Information Base (FIB) of CEF to perform the lookup process, which is built from the router's routing table. In other words, RPF does not really look at the router's routing table; instead, it uses the CEF FIB to determine spoofing.

Also, RPF cannot detect all spoofed packets. For the network in this example, the perimeter router cannot determine spoofing from packets received on the external E1 interface if they match the default route statement. Therefore, the more routes your router has in its CEF FIB table, the more likely the router will be capable of detecting spoofing attacks. In addition, RPF cannot detect any spoofed packets that are encapsulated, such as packets encapsulated in GRE, IPSec, L2TP, and other packets.

CAUTION   If you are using BGP on your perimeter router and have configured properties such as local preference and weight, this could affect the best path to the source and thus also could affect the operation of RPF. Therefore, care must be taken when using RPF and BGP.

ACL Enhancements

Unicast RPF forwarding supports ACLs for finer filtering. With the ACL feature, you associate an ACL with RPF. The Cisco IOS then uses the ACL to determine whether the RPF feature should be applied to packets entering the interface. First, RPF is used to determine whether the packet is spoofed. If it is, the Cisco IOS uses the ACL to determine the action performed on the packet. A **permit** statement in the ACL causes the spoofed packet to be allowed; a **deny** statement drops the spoofed packet.

NOTE   Without an associated ACL, RPF automatically drops packets that it believes to be spoofed.

One nice feature with the ACL association is that the Cisco IOS keeps traffic statistics for the Unicast RPF drops. If you add the **log** parameter to your ACL statements, the router creates a log record of spoofed packets (**deny** or **permit** statement matches).

CAUTION	If a DoS spoofing attack is occurring, the attack might drain your router's resources, especially if you are using RPF ACLs with logging enabled. Therefore, care must be taken when using this feature with the ACL **log** parameter.

Statistics

The Cisco IOS keeps track of two types of RPF statistics: global and interface. RPF global statistics can be used to display information about possible attacks against your network, but they are not helpful in determining the source of the attack (which interface). However, you can use the per-interface statistics to determine the source. Two types of per-interface RPF statistics are used:

- **Drops**—Number of spoofed packets that were dropped
- **Suppressed drops**—Number of spoofed packets that were permitted (not dropped because of a match on a **permit** statement in an RPF ACL)

Note that these are general statistics. If you want to see the actual source addresses of packets that are being dropped, you must enable RPF ACL logging.

RPF Usage

RPF works best at the perimeter of your network. If you use it inside your network, it is used best when your routers have more specific routes. With route summarization, a spoofing attack could be in process, and it would be difficult to determine which part of the summarized route the attack is occurring from. For external threats, the more ISPs and companies use RPF, the more likely it is that spoofing attacks can be a thing of the past. However, the more point-of-presence (POP) connections that an ISP has, the more difficult it becomes to use RPF because multiple paths might exist to the source. Using RPF as close to the sources of the addresses as possible is the best solution for ISPs directly connected to their customers.

RPF is deployed best on perimeter routers in networks that have a single connection to the outside world. Of course, RPF will work in multiple-connection environments, as well as with internal routers, but it might not provide the optimum solution in detecting spoofed packets. Figure 15-6 shows an example of the problem that can occur when using RPF in a dual-connection network. In this example, the perimeter router uses interface S0 to send traffic to the remote site. However, using BGP, the Internet has determined that the best path to return the traffic to the network on the left is to send this through S1 on the perimeter router. This creates a problem on the perimeter router with RPF because using its routing table, the router expects this traffic to come through S0. In this instance, the router would drop the returning traffic.

Figure 15-6 *RPF and Dual-Connection Problems*

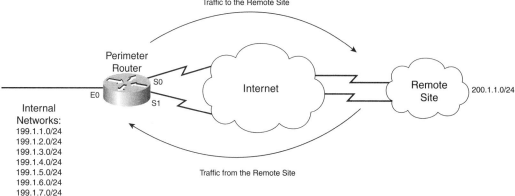

One exception to using RPF for single connections is to use dialup access on an access server. One of the main sources of spoofing attacks is dialup access. By using RPF on your access servers, you can limit your exposure to this method of spoofing attack.

An alternative to RPF is to use ACLs. However, the main problem of ACLs are their performance and day-to-day maintenance. RPF, on the other hand, relies on information from the routing table, which can be built statically or dynamically. With CEF handling the process, you are not taking a performance hit.

RPF Limitations

Despite its advantages and usefulness in detecting and preventing spoofing attacks, RPF has the following limitations:

- RPF requires CEF to function. Routers that do not support CEF or that have it disabled cannot use RPF.

- Your routing table uses asymmetric routes to send traffic to and from a destination. In this situation, different paths are used; this creates problems with RPF by generating false positives for spoofing. Therefore, a single connection to the Internet on the router is the best situation in which to use RPF (you can have multiple connections to the Internet—just make sure that each of these connections is on a separate router).

- RPF typically does not do well when activated on internal interfaces of routers (interfaces connected to the internal network) because of asymmetrical routing issues.

If you have any of these limitations, use ACLs to prevent spoofing attacks instead of RPF.

RPF Configuration

Before you configure RPF, make sure that you perform the following:

- Set up egress filtering: Permit only source addresses that you have assigned, or allow and deny everything else. If you are using RPF, use an egress filter to define egress policies.

- Set up ingress filtering: Deny all bogons and allow only connections to specific internal resources. Also examine source addresses for other anomalies, such as loopback interfaces, RFC 1918 addresses, broadcast addresses, and so on.

- Set up an RPF ACL to handle issues with asymmetric routing if you have dual Internet connections on one router and returning traffic comes from a different network than what it used to reach it.

- Optionally, enable logging on your RPF ACL entries to get a better idea of what traffic is being spoofed.

When you have done this, you are ready to set up unicast RPF. Of all of the features on the router, unicast RPF is one of the easiest to set up. The first thing you need to do is enable CEF:

```
Router(config)# ip cef
```

or

```
Router(config)# ip cef distributed
```

Use one of these two commands based on your router model. Remember that CEF must be enabled to use RPF. The **distributed** parameter is used on certain 7000 series routers and higher to allow line cards to perform express forwarding for those cards that support it, but to still allow the route process to handle normal routing functions, as well as switch traffic to and from legacy line cards.

After you have enabled CEF, you are ready to enable RPF. RPF must be activated on each interface that you want to check for packet spoofing. Typically, this is your router's external interface(s):

```
Router(config)# interface type [slot_#/]port_#
Router(config-if)# ip verify unicast reverse-path [ACL_#_or_name]
```

The optional ACL enables you to specify what actions to take for packets that RPF deems to be spoofed. A **permit** entry in the ACL allows the packet (used to bypass asymmetrical routing issues), and a **deny** entry drops the packet. If you include the **log** parameter in your ACL entries, you can keep track of how often spoofing is occurring.

TIP   If you are using HSRP and you want to disable both RPF and CEF, make sure that you disable RPF first and then disable CEF. Failure to do this in the appropriate order will cause an HSRP failure to occur.

RPF Verification

When you have enabled CEF and RPF, you can verify its configuration with the following command:

```
Router# show cef interface [type [slot_#/]port_#]
  [statistics] [detail]
```

Example 15-16 shows output from the **show cef interface** command.

Example 15-16 *Using the* **show cef interface** *Command*

```
Router# show cef interface serial 2/0/0
Serial2/0/0 is up (if_number 8)
 Internet address is 199.1.1.1/24
 ICMP redirects are never sent
 Per packet loadbalancing is disabled
 IP unicast RPF check is enabled
 Inbound access list is not set
 Outbound access list is not set
 Interface is marked as point-to-point interface
 Packets switched to this interface on linecard are dropped to next slow path
 Hardware idb is Serial2/0/0
 Fast switching type 4, interface type 6
 IP Distributed CEF switching enabled
<--output omitted-->
```

As you can see in this example, RPF is enabled.

Besides using the previous command, you can use others to perform unicast RPF troubleshooting:

- **show ip traffic**—Displays global unicast RPF statistics about drops and suppressed drops.
- **show ip interface**—Displays per-interface unicast RPF statistics.
- **show access-lists**—Displays ACL statistics on matches (as well as logging entries if the **log** parameter has been configured on your ACL statements).

Example 15-17 shows output from the **show ip traffic** command.

Example 15-17 *Using the* **show ip traffic** *Command*

```
Router# show ip traffic
IP statistics:
  Rcvd:  0 total, 0 local destination
         0 format errors, 0 checksum errors, 0 bad hop count
         0 unknown protocol, 0 not a gateway
         0 security failures, 0 bad options, 0 with options
  Opts:  0 end, 0 nop, 0 basic security, 0 loose source route
         0 timestamp, 0 extended security, 0 record route
         0 stream ID, 0 strict source route, 0 alert, 0 other
  Frags: 0 reassembled, 0 timeouts, 0 couldn't reassemble
         0 fragmented, 0 couldn't fragment
```

Example 15-17 *Using the* **show ip traffic** *Command (Continued)*

```
Bcast: 0 received, 0 sent
Mcast: 0 received, 0 sent
Sent:  0 generated, 0 forwarded
Drop:  0 encapsulation failed, 0 unresolved, 0 no adjacency
       0 no route, 0 unicast RPF, 0 forced drop
```

Unicast RPF Example

Use the network shown previously in Figure 15-6 for this next illustration of how to use RPF. As you recall, this example had an asymmetrical routing issue, which inadvertently dropped traffic from a remote site (200.1.1.0/24). Example 15-18 shows the configuration to drop spoofed packets yet allow the asymmetrical routing for 200.1.1.0/24.

Example 15-18 *Using RPF with Asymmetrical Connections*

```
Router(config)# ip cef
Router(config)# ip access-list extended RPF-ACL
Router(config-ext-nacl)# permit ip 200.1.1.0 0.0.0.255
  199.1.0.0 0.0.7.255
Router(config-ext-nacl)# deny ip any any
Router(config-ext-nacl)# exit
Router(config)# interface serial0
Router(config-if)# ip verify unicast reverse-path RPF-ACL
Router(config-if)# exit
Router(config)# interface serial1
Router(config-if)# ip verify unicast reverse-path RPF-ACL
Router(config-if)# exit
```

Summary

This chapter showed you the basics of protecting your routing protocols, as well as using your routing protocols to provide an extra layer of protection on your perimeter router. To prevent routing protocol attacks, you should implement MD5 authentication. Not all routing protocols support this feature, but most do. Previously in this book, I discussed the use of ACLs to drop unwanted traffic, such as bogons. However, this can be done more efficiently with a routing protocol with black hole routing, routing unwanted traffic to the router's null interface. This can be accomplished with a variety of methods, including using static routes, route maps, and prefix lists (only BGP). If your router supports CEF and has a single Internet connection, I highly recommend that you use unicast RPF to prevent spoofing instead of black hole routing because little configuration is needed to set up RPF: It uses the current routing table (CEF FIB) to detect spoofing. In addition, RPF can easily be used with other Cisco IOS features, such as ACL filtering.

Next up is Part VII, "Detecting and Preventing Attacks," which shows you how to detect and prevent DoS and other types of attacks, as well as how to use logging to keep track of attempted and successful attacks.

P A R T VII

Detecting and Preventing Attacks

Chapter 16   Intrusion Detection System

Chapter 17   DoS Protection

Chapter 18   Logging Events

Intrusion-Detection System

Part VI, "Managing Access Through Routers," covered Cisco IOS features and tools that you can use to manage traffic better as it travels through your router. That part focused primarily on authentication: lock-and-key ACLs, authentication proxy, and routing authentication with MD5. This part focuses on detecting and, in some cases, preventing certain kinds of attacks, as well as logging information to help you determine when and how an attack occurred.

This chapter focuses on the capability of the Cisco IOS to detect attacks with the intrusion-detection system (IDS) feature of the Cisco IOS Firewall. The following topics are covered in this chapter:

- IDS introduction
- IDS signatures
- Cisco router IDS solution
- IDS configuration
- IDS examples

IDS Introduction

Intrusion detection is the science—or, in some cases, the art—of detecting network and host attacks. Chapter 1, "Security Threats," discussed the three basic categories of network threats:

- Reconnaissance attacks
- Denial-of-service (DoS) attacks
- Access attacks

IDS solutions attempt to detect and sometimes thwart these three categories of attacks.

IDS Implementations

To detect and prevent attacks, IDS solutions are implemented by one of two methods: profiles or signatures. The following two sections discuss these two methods, including their advantages and limitations.

Profiles

Profile-based systems look for anomalies in traffic. They do this first by capturing traffic under normal circumstances, called a *profile*. They then use the profile to compare it to traffic. A profile contains information about traffic patterns and statistics. Any traffic that does not fit the profile is considered an anomaly and could be a network attack. Because of this process, profile-based systems often are called *anomaly-detection* systems.

One of the main advantages that profile-based systems have is that they have a better likelihood of detecting new kinds of attacks over signature-based systems. For example, assume that a hacker discovers a security hole in a web server and tries to access a special file called access.htm that has been left there by the default installation. This file is never referenced, but it provides back-door management access to the web server. Normally, this should have been removed, but some administrators might have forgotten to do this. This file is never accessed in normal operations, so when a hacker tries to access this file, a profile-based system should raise an alarm because this type of activity is considered an anomaly.

Profile-based systems have some of issues with detecting attacks, however:

- They are prone to a higher level of false readings than signature-based systems because traffic patterns vary. This can be a problem when introducing new applications and devices in the network. Plus, it takes more time to determine whether an attack really occurred or whether it was a false reading, increasing your management overhead.

- Because of changing traffic patterns and network topologies, a lot of time must be spent recreating a current profile, increasing your management.

- When creating the actual profile to compare to traffic, if the captured profile includes an attack, the attack is treated as normal traffic. Therefore, if the attack occurs again and is compared to the profile that contains the attack, the IDS profile device considers this normal and does not raise an alert. Therefore, a lot of care needs to be taken when capturing traffic profiles.

Signatures

Signature-based systems compare traffic to signatures to determine whether an attack is occurring. A signature is basically a grouping of matching criteria (commonly referred to as a template) that the IDS solution should use when determining whether an attack is occurring. Incoming traffic is compared to a list of signatures; if there is a match, an alarm is raised. This type of system is commonly called *misuse detection*.

Unlike profile-based systems, signature systems have fewer false readings because they are looking for very specific things in traffic. As an example, if you know the mechanics of a web server access attack, such as the information contained in a malformed URL, a signature-based system would look for this specific information in HTTP segments.

Signature-based solutions have two main drawbacks, however:

- They can detect only attacks that have been programmed by their installed signatures. If a new attack is discovered, there is a high likelihood that a signature-based solution will not detect the attack. Therefore, you must ensure that your IDS signature solution always has the most up-to-date signatures installed.

- Signature-based solutions have problems when dealing with event horizon attacks, which are attacks that occur over a period of time. A very good hacker might plan reconnaissance and access attacks over a long period of time, making them more difficult to detect: Imagine a ping or port-scan sweep that occurs over a period of hours or days. With a profile-based system, this probably would be flagged as an anomaly. However, a signature-based solution likely would not be capable of detecting this attack because it could not buffer up all of the traffic over a long period of time.

Complications with IDS Systems

As in the last example of dealing with attacks spanning a long period of time, when an IDS system detects a ping sweep or port scan reconnaissance attack, it must look at dozens, if not hundreds, of packets when determining whether an attack is occurring. Because of the limitations of both approaches, an IDS solution might do the following:

- Indicate that an attack is occurring, when there really isn't an attack

- Miss an attack by a hacker because the attack occurred over a long period of time or because the hacker carefully hid the attack among normal traffic patterns

In other words, IDS is not an exact science. Many changes have taken place in IDS solutions in the last few years, and a lot of work still has to be done to improve their effectiveness. Therefore, you should not rely solely on an IDS solution for all your security needs. Instead, an IDS solution should be one part of your security solution and should be complemented by other technologies, such firewalls and VPNs.

NOTE   Some products are a hybrid implementation, containing both signature- and profile-based implementations.

IDS Solutions

Two types of IDS designs exist: network- and host-based solutions. Figure 16-1 shows an example of the two solutions. The next two sections cover these solutions in more depth.

Figure 16-1 *Network- and Host-Based Solutions*

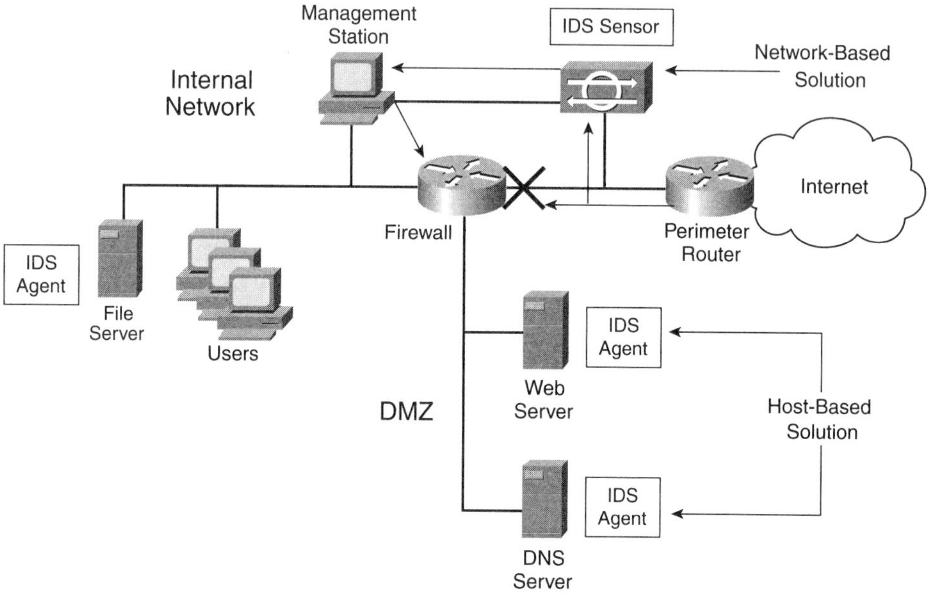

Network-Based Solutions

A network-based solution uses a device called a sensor to monitor traffic on a segment. The sensor examines packets and their contents and determines whether an attack is occurring. Basically, a sensor is an enhanced protocol analyzer: It captures packets that it sees and then compares these packets to the sensor's internal intrusion-detection rules. Cisco offers the following network-based solutions:

- 4200 series hardware sensors
- IDS modules for the Catalyst 6500 switches
- Network Module Cisco IDS (NM-CIDS), which is basically a 4200 sensor in a network module for a Cisco IOS router
- Routers with the Cisco IOS Firewall feature set
- PIX firewalls

Two design philosophies exist concerning network-based IDS solutions: inline and passive monitoring. An inline system has the actual packet traffic pass through the IDS device. One advantage that this design offers is that the IDS device can take a more proactive role in dealing with attacks; however, its main disadvantage is that it tries to perform IDS while also passing traffic between interfaces at wire speeds. Examples of inline designs include the Cisco IOS router and the PIX IDS. Cisco is working on other products in this category.

In a passive-monitoring design, the sensor has an interface attached to the segment that it wants to monitor. This can be accomplished by using a network tap, a hub, or a switched-port analyzer (SPAN) connection on a switch. One advantage of this approach is that the monitoring interface is passive and only receives traffic (only in rare cases will it generate traffic); therefore, it is much less susceptible to an attack than an inline solution is. In some implementations, the sensor itself can take an appropriate action when an attack occurs; in other implementations, a central management solution handles the action. However, the disadvantage of this approach is that the sensor is reacting to the attack after the packets already might have reached the victim. Examples of passive-monitoring IDS devices include the 4200 sensors and the IDS Module for the Catalyst 6500 switches.

A sensor can take these three main actions:

- Log the action or attack (alarm)
- Block the offending traffic (drop)
- Terminate an offending TCP connection (reset)

One of the main advantages of a network-based IDS solution is that it centralizes your IDS process and reduces the number of IDS devices that you need. You put them at critical points in your network, such as your network perimeter and your internal backbone, to monitor traffic.

CAUTION   When choosing a network-based IDS solution, it is important to pick a solution that can handle the analysis of packets at wire speeds. For example, if your sensor is monitoring a 100-Mbps link, but it can process only 50 Mbps of traffic, in some situations, the sensor will drop and miss packets. Therefore, it might miss an attack.

Host-Based Solutions

In a host-based IDS solution, agent software is running on a host system, such as a server or PC. These solutions come with features that include the following:

- Most of these solutions check to make sure that key application and operating system files are not altered.
- Most of these solutions check for unauthorized access.
- Most of these solutions check for appropriate use of the application.
- Some of these solutions check for reconnaissance and DoS attacks.
- All of these solutions create log files, which can be kept locally or forwarded to a central repository (a good centralized solution is important in large IDS deployments).

Host-Based Versus Network-Based

One of the advantages of a host-based system is that it has to handle only traffic sent to the device that it is running on. Sometimes a network-based solution has problems with handling a lot of traffic, and it can be difficult to manage when you need to define per-host IDS policies. However, the main disadvantage of host-based systems is that the more you have, the more difficult they are to manage.

Therefore, a good enterprise solution typically has a mix of both host- and network-based IDS solutions. Sensors are used at the perimeter and backbone of the network, as well as other key access points, such as dialup. This provides a broad range of coverage for the entire network. Agent software is then installed on key hosts to provide extra protection for applications running on the host.

IDS Concerns

To be effective, IDS solutions must be capable of detecting and responding to network and host threats in a real-time manner. However, not every IDS solution fits into every network. This section focuses on some concerns about IDS solutions.

Installed Components

IDS network (sensor) solutions typically have the following components:

- CPU and memory
- Disk space
- Two or more NICs

A hardware sensor is typically a standalone device: It has its own chassis, CPU, RAM, and operating system. The CPU and RAM are critical in an IDS solution because the system might have to process millions of packets per second.

Many popular IDS solutions run on Linux or some variety of UNIX; others run on Microsoft Windows and even proprietary operating systems. For example, the newest Cisco software for its 4200 series sensors runs on top of Linux. A disk drive typically is required to store binary files and logging information. One concern with using a commercial operating system is that it is more susceptible to network attacks than a proprietary operating system; extreme care must be taken in securing the sensor itself, which includes the operating system that it uses.

Because of security risks, many IDS solutions have two NICs (interfaces): One monitors traffic, and one sends logging and reporting information to a central repository. This allows for out-of-band management. You should ensure that the management interface is protected. The sensing interface should not have an IP address; instead, it should be a promiscuous interface that only senses traffic. Some sensors support multiple NICs to monitor multiple segments. One concern with multiple sensing interfaces is the capability of the sensor to process all of its monitored traffic at wire speeds.

Detecting Intrusions

The main purpose of an IDS solution is to detect intrusions. It accomplishes this by examining packets, reassembling fragmented packets into whole packets, and matching these against an installed base of signatures or profiles. The last section mentioned the concern of the sensor being capable of keeping up with the amount of traffic that it needs to process. Another concern is that it have the capability to store packets for a period of time to detect different kinds of attacks, such as those that use fragments. For an IDS solution to detect certain kinds of fragment attacks, it must be capable of storing the fragments and, when it has all the fragments, reassembling them. In large-scale fragment attacks, this requires a lot of memory in the sensor.

Responding to Intrusions

When an attack is detected, an IDS solution should take some kind of action, which can include the following:

- Generate an alarm
- Terminate an offending TCP session
- Drop or block traffic from the offender

All IDS solutions can perform the first action. Depending on the sensor, alarm messages are stored locally, on a management console, or both. An alarm can be construed as a log message, but it differs in the following respects:

- It contains information about the severity of the attack and recommends solutions for dealing with it.
- It can be something as simple as a log message, but it also can take on other means, such as an e-mail, a page, or some other means of communication.

For TCP-based attacks, some sensors can tear down the TCP connection when an attack is detected. This feature commonly is called *TCP reset*. Basically, the sensor sends TCP segments to the victim, closing the session. With Cisco IDS sensors, such as the 4200s, the sensor sends a TCP reset to both the attacker and the victim by spoofing the source and destination addresses of the original packet. Normally, the TCP reset method is coupled with blocking (sometimes called *shunning*). Blocking blocks all traffic from the offender (or the entire network of the offender).

It is important to understand the capabilities of a sensor when making a purchasing decision. One problem with sensors that only generate logs or alarms is that you manually must react to the threat. Sensors that support the TCP reset and shunning or blocking feature enable you to take a more proactive approach when dealing with security threats and attacks.

IDS Signatures

Cisco IDS network-based solutions are signature-based. Basically, a signature is a rule that examines a packet or series of packets for certain contents, such as matches on packet header or data payload information. Signatures are the heart of the Cisco network-based IDS solution. This section focuses on signatures and their implementation.

TIP   It is important to point out that it is not necessarily the number of signatures that makes an IDS signature-based solution good. Instead, it is the flexibility of the signatures in detecting an attack. For example, in one IDS solution, it might take three separate signatures to detect three separate attacks; in a different solution, a single signature might be capable of detecting all three attacks. Flexibility in signatures, as well as the ability to create your own signatures, should be more of a concern when choosing a signature-based IDS solution.

Signature Implementations

Signatures come in two implementations:

- **Context**—Examines the packet header for a match
- **Content**—Examines the packet contents for a match

Context signatures examine only the packet header information when looking for a match. This information can include the IP address fields; the IP protocol field; IP options; IP fragment parameters; IP, TCP, and UDP checksums; IP and TCP port numbers; TCP flags; ICMP message types; and others.

Content signatures, on the other hand, look inside the payload of a packet as well as the packet headers. As an example, many web server attacks send malformed or specific URLs that are contained in application data. As another example, one sendmail reconnaissance attack looks for **EXPN** and **VRFY** commands in the application data (this is covered in the Cisco 3103 signature).

Signature Structures

Besides coming in two implementations, signatures support one of two structures:

- **Atomic**—Examines a single packet for a match
- **Composite**—Examines a stream of packets for a match

An example of a signature that uses an atomic structure is one that examines a TCP segment header for both the SYN and FIN flags. Because this information is contained in the TCP header, and because this is contained in one IP packet, only one packet must be examined to determine whether there is a match.

Some types of attacks, however, are spread across many packets and possibly many connections. A composite structured signature has the sensor examine a stream of packets for a match. An example of a composite signature is one that looks at a series of fragments from the same connection and determines whether the fragments are overlapping (this would be an obvious attack because a real fragmented packet can be reassembled, whereas overlapping fragments cannot).

Basic Classification

In general, there are four basic categories of signatures:

- **Informational (*benign*)**—These signatures trigger on normal network activity, such as ICMP echo requests and the opening or closing of TCP or UDP connections.

- **Reconnaissance**—These signatures trigger on attacks that uncover resources and hosts that are reachable, as well as any possible vulnerabilities that they might contain. Examples of reconnaissance attacks include ping sweeps, DNS queries, and port scanning.

- **Access**—These signatures trigger on access attacks, which include unauthorized access, unauthorized escalation of privileges, and access to protected or sensitive data. Some examples of access attacks include Back Orifice, a Unicode attack against the Microsoft IIS, and NetBus.

- **DoS**—These signatures trigger on attacks that attempt to reduce the level of a resource or system, or to cause it to crash. Examples of DoS attacks include TCP SYN floods, the Ping of Death, Smurf, Fraggle, Trinoo, and Tribe Flood Network.

Cisco Signature Categories

In implementing signatures, Cisco divided the classification of signatures into eight categories, shown in Table 16-1.

Table 16-1   *Cisco Signature Classification Categories*

Signature Series	Description
1000	Signatures on IP header rules, which include IP options, IP fragments, and bad or invalid IP packets
2000	Signatures on ICMP packets, which include ICMP attacks, ping sweeps, and ICMP traffic records
3000	Signatures on attacks using TCP, including TCP host sweeps, TCP SYN floods, TCP port scans, TCP session hijacking, TCP traffic records, TCP applications, e-mail attacks, NetBIOS attacks, and legacy web attacks
4000	Signatures on attacks using UDP, including UDP port scans, UDP applications, and UDP traffic records

continues

Table 16-1 *Cisco Signature Classification Categories (Continued)*

Signature Series	Description
5000	Signatures on web server and browser attacks using HTTP
6000	Signatures on cross-protocol (multiple-protocol) attacks, including distributed DoS (DDoS) attacks, DNS attacks, Loki attacks, authentication attacks, and RPC attacks
8000	Signatures that look for string matches in TCP sessions/applications
10,000	Signatures that trigger on an ACL violation on a Cisco router (match on a **deny** statement)

Cisco Router IDS Solution

The remainder of this chapter focuses on Cisco router IDS capabilities and the configuration of IDS using the Cisco IOS Firewall feature set. The Cisco IOS IDS implementation is suited best for midlevel to higher-level platforms because of the overhead associated with examining packets to detect threats and attacks on perimeter routers. It also can provide a level of protection for remote access and dialup connections. There are four basic reasons for deploying the Cisco IOS Firewall IDS:

- To extend security to your perimeter routers across an enterprise network, especially at branch and regional offices

- To provide a cost-effective IDS solution for small- to medium-size businesses

- To detect external attacks directed at the router itself where a network-based sensor, connected behind the router, cannot detect these attacks

- To implement a one-box perimeter solution

NOTE   The router IDS is not a full-blown IDS solution: Because it is an inline solution, it might affect the performance of the router. Therefore, you need to be careful about enabling it on a router. Also, the router supports a limited number of signatures and, therefore, should be coupled with a network-based IDS solution, such as the 4200 sensors, in medium- to large-size networks.

Signature Support

Whereas the Cisco network-based sensors, such as the 4200, support more than 1000 signatures, the Cisco IOS Firewall IDS feature supports only 100. Because of the limited number of signatures, the Cisco IOS IDS software typically is used at the perimeter of the network and in combination with other IDS solutions, such as dedicated hardware sensors.

For example, if you refer back to Figure 16-1, you can see that the hardware sensor sitting behind the perimeter router never sees the traffic that the perimeter router filters. With the Cisco IOS IDS software, the perimeter router at least can report a small number of attacks that are directed at the perimeter router or that the perimeter router filters; in either case, the hardware sensor behind the perimeter router would never see this traffic anyway. Even though the number of signatures is limited, the Cisco IOS IDS software looks for common attacks and threats. Table 16-2 lists the signatures supported by the Cisco IOS Firewall IDS feature set.

NOTE   More than 40 signatures were added in 12.2(15)T; therefore, if you have an older Cisco IOS version, the number of signatures that the Cisco IOS Firewall feature set supports is actually less than 60. Read the Cisco IOS release notes to determine what signatures are enabled for the Cisco IOS version that you currently are running on your router.

Table 16-2   *Cisco IOS Supported Signatures*

Signature Number	Type	Description
1000	Informational, atomic	Bad options exist in the IP header, or the IP header is incomplete or malformed.
1001	Informational, atomic	Option 7 in the IP header is marked (record the route of the packet).
1002	Informational, atomic	Option 4 in the IP header is marked (timestamp information requested).
1003	Informational, atomic	Option 2 (security) in the IP header is marked. This is obsolete.
1004	Informational, atomic	Option 3 in the IP header is marked (loose source-routing information).
1005	Informational, atomic	Option 8 (SATNET stream identifier) in the IP header is marked. This is obsolete.
1006	Informational, atomic	Strict source routing is requested for the packet.
1100	Attack, atomic	The "more fragments" flag is set to 1, or an offset is indicated in the Offset field.
1101	Attack, atomic	A packet has an IP protocol of 134 or higher. These protocols either are undefined or are reserved and should not be used. (The IP protocol number used to be 101.)

continues

Table 16-2 *Cisco IOS Supported Signatures (Continued)*

Signature Number	Type	Description
1102	Attack, atomic	This indicates a Land.c attack, in which the source and destination addresses are the same.
1104	Attack, compound	127.0.0.1 is detected in the source IP address field.
1105	Attack, compound	A broadcast address (255.255.255.255.) is detected in the source IP address field.
1106	Attack, compound	A multicast address is detected in the source IP address field.
1107	Informational, compound	RFC 1918 addresses are detected.
1202	Attack, compound	The reassembled packet is larger than the specified length or is greater than 65,535 bytes.
1206	Attack, compound	Any fragment (except the last) is less than 400 bytes.
2000	Informational, atomic	The ICMP type field is set to 0 (echo reply).
2001	Informational, atomic	The ICMP type field is set to 1 (host unreachable).
2002	Informational, atomic	The ICMP type field is set to 4 (source quench).
2003	Informational, atomic	The ICMP type field is set to 5 (redirect).
2004	Informational, atomic	The ICMP type field is set to 8 (echo request).
2005	Informational, atomic	The ICMP type field is set to 11 (time exceeded).
2006	Informational, atomic	The ICMP type field is set to 12 (parameter problem in the packet).
2007	Informational, atomic	The ICMP type field is set to 13 (timestamp request).
2008	Informational, atomic	The ICMP type field is set to 14 (timestamp reply).
2009	Informational, atomic	The ICMP type field is set to 15 (information request).
2010	Informational, atomic	The ICMP type field is set to 16 (information reply).
2011	Informational, atomic	The ICMP type field is set to 17 (subnet mask request).
2012	Informational, atomic	The ICMP type field is set to 18 (subnet mask reply).
2150	Attack, atomic	An ICMP packet has the More Fragments flag set to 1, or an offset is indicated in the header.
2151	Attack, atomic	The length in the IP header is set to something larger than 1024 bytes.

Table 16-2   *Cisco IOS Supported Signatures (Continued)*

Signature Number	Type	Description
2154	Attack, atomic	An ICMP packet has the last fragment bit set, and the following is true: ("IP offset" * 8) + "IP data length" > 65,535). This is called the *Ping of Death*.
3038	Attack, compound	A TCP segment does not have the SYN, FIN, ACK, or RST flags set (reconnaissance sweep).
3039	Attack, compound	A fragmented TCP FIN packet was sent to a port less than 1024, called an orphaned FIN.
3040	Attack, atomic	A TCP segment with no bits set is present in the flags field.
3041	Attack, atomic	A TCP segment has both the SYN and FIN bits set.
3042	Attack, atomic	A TCP segment has the FIN bit set but no ACK bit set.
3043	Attack, compound	A fragmented TCP segment has the SYN and FIN bits set.
3050	Attack, compound	Multiple TCP connections have been initiated but have not completed. This looks at only ports 21, 23, 25, and 80.
3100	Attack, compound	This looks for the mail attack against RFC-compliant SMTP servers, such as sendmail.
3101	Attack, compound	E-mail messages have the pipe symbol (l) in the To field.
3102	Attack, compound	E-mail messages have the pipe symbol (l) in the From field.
3103	Attack, compound	E-mail messages have the **expn** or **vrfy** commands.
3104	Attack, compound	E-mail messages have the **wiz** or **debug** commands.
3105	Attack, compound	E-mail messages have :decode@ in the e-mail header.
3106	Attack, compound	An e-mail message has more than 250 (default) Rcpt To lines.
3107	Attack, compound	A bug in Majordomo allows remote users to execute commands on the server.
3150	Attack, compound	The FTP **site** command was executed on an FTP connection.
3151	Informational, compound	The FTP **syst** command was executed on an FTP connection.

continues

Table 16-2   *Cisco IOS Supported Signatures (Continued)*

Signature Number	Type	Description
3152	Attack, compound	The FTP **cwd ~root** command was executed on an FTP connection.
3153	Attack, atomic	In an FTP connection, a **port** command was executed with a different address than the requesting source.
3154	Attack, atomic	A port number less than 1024 or greater than 65,535 was specified on an FTP connection.
3215	Attack, compound	Someone tried to execute a command, using a directory traversal bug, on an IIS web server (IIS DOT DOT EXECUTE attack).
3229	Attack, compound	Someone tried to access the win-c-sample program through a web server.
3233	Attack, compound	An overflow attempt against the CGI-bin count program was detected.
4050	Attack, atomic	The UDP segment length is less than the length in the IP header.
4051	Attack, compound	UDP packets have a source port of 7, 19, or 135 and a destination of 135 (Snork attack).
4052	Attack, compound	UDP traffic was sent to port 7 or 19 (Chargen attack).
4100	Attack, compound	Someone tried to access the /etc/passwd file through TFTP.
4600	Attack, compound	A malformed syslog message was sent to UDP port 514. This is called an Cisco IOS UDP bomb.
5034	Attack, compound	Someone tried to run the newdsn.exe program through an HTTP server.
5035	Attack, compound	An attacker tried to send commands through the CGI-bin program HylaFAX Faxsurvey.
5041	Attack, compound	An attacker tried to execute commands through a CGI-bin script.
5043	Attack, compound	An attacker tried to access scripts on a ColdFusion server.
5044	Attack, compound	An attacker tried to execute commands through the rguest.exe or wguest.exe CGI-bin scripts associated with the Webcom.se Guestbook.
5045	Attack, compound	A CGI-bin script attempted to execute the **xterm -display** command to circumvent a UNIX WWW server.

Table 16-2   *Cisco IOS Supported Signatures (Continued)*

Signature Number	Type	Description
5050	Attack, compound	A .htr buffer overrun attack was detected against a Windows IIS server.
5055	Attack, compound	An HTTP buffer overflow attempt was made using a large username/password combination.
5071	Attack, compound	An attacker tried to access the msacds.dll WWW Windows file to execute commands or view secured files.
5081	Attack, compound	An attacker tried to access the cmd.exe program on a Windows WWW server.
5090	Attack, compound	An attacker tried to access a FrontPage CGI script with a filename ending in 0,0.
5114	Attack, compound	An attacker tried to exploit the Unicode ../ directory movement in WWW IIS.
5116	Attack, compound	An attacker sent shell metacharacters to be executed with the privilege level in the CGI script in Endymion MailMan.
5117	Attack, compound	An attacker attempted to execute code that exploits a vulnerability in phpGroupWare.
5118	Attack, compound	An attacker sent a special HTTP/GET request to upload files to the web server (called the eWave ServletEXEC 3.0C File Upload attack).
5123	Attack, compound	An abnormally large HTTP **GET** request was sent to a web server.
6050	Informational, compound	Someone attempted to access HINFO DNS records on a DNS server.
6051	Informational, compound	A DNS zone transfer with a source port of 53 (legitimate) was detected.
6052	Attack, compound	A DNS zone transfer with a different source port than 53 was detected.
6053	Informational, compound	Someone requested all the records for a DNS server.
6054	Informational, compound	Someone requested the version of a DNS server.
6055	Attack, compound	A DNS inverse query with more than 255 characters was detected, attempting a buffer overflow.

continues

Table 16-2 *Cisco IOS Supported Signatures (Continued)*

Signature Number	Type	Description
6056	Attack, compound	A DNS NXT buffer overflow against a DNS server was detected.
6057	Attack, compound	A DNS SIG buffer overflow against a DNS server was detected.
6062	Informational, compound	A DNS query of type TXT was made with the string Authors.Bind.
6063	Informational, compound	A DNS query type 251 was detected for a zone transfer.
6100	Informational, atomic	Someone tried to register new RPC services on a host.
6101	Informational, atomic	Someone tried to unregister RPC services on a host.
6102	Informational, atomic	An RPC dump request was made to a host.
6103	Attack, atomic	A proxied RPC request was sent to the portmapper process on a host.
6150	Informational, atomic	A request was sent to the portmapper process for the YP server daemon.
6151	Informational, atomic	A request was sent to the portmapper process for the YP bind daemon.
6152	Informational, atomic	A request was sent to the portmapper process for the YP password daemon.
6153	Informational, atomic	A request was sent to the portmapper process for the YP update daemon.
6154	Informational, atomic	A request was sent to the portmapper process for the YP transfer daemon.
6155	Informational, atomic	A request was sent to the portmapper process for the mount daemon.
6175	Informational, atomic	A request was sent to the portmapper process for the rexd daemon.
6180	Informational, atomic	A call was sent to the portmapper process for the rexd daemon. This typically indicates an access attack.
6190	Attack, atomic	A large statd request was sent, probably indicating a buffer overflow attack method.
8000:2101	Attack, atomic	Someone entered the string passwd during an FTP session, probably indicating that someone was trying to download the system's password file.

Router IDS Process

By default, IDS is not enabled on a router that has the Cisco IOS Firewall feature set installed. Instead, you must create audit rules, which specify the signatures that the Cisco IOS should use when looking for suspicious traffic, threats, or attacks. Cisco divides the signatures into two basic categories on the Cisco IOS, based on their severity: informational and attack. You can enable one or both groups. Also, you can selectively enable or disable specific signatures, or specify that a signature be enabled or disabled for a specific host or hosts.

After you have created your audit rule, you need to activate it on the router's interface(s) in an in or out direction. After you do this, IDS is enabled. If you applied the audit rule inbound, all packets are audited entering the interface. Unlike most other features, IDS is performed before any inbound ACL is processed; this enables you to detect external threats coming into your network. If you apply an audit policy outbound on an interface, as long as traffic is permitted into the router and routed to the outbound interface, the audit policy is used. In this case, IDS examines packets before the outbound ACL, if any, is processed on the interface.

When comparing a packet or packets against the router's signatures, the Cisco IOS does it in this order:

1 IP signatures

2 ICMP signatures

3 TCP or UDP signatures (depending on the connection type)

4 Application layer signatures

NOTE One important thing to point out about the matching process is that, as soon as the Cisco IOS finds a match on one signature, it immediately stops looking for any other matches within the same type. However, it continues to look for matches in other modules. For example, if the Cisco IOS finds an IP signature match, it does not look for any other IP signature matches, but it continues on to ICMP. This is different from the Cisco 4200 hardware sensors, which look for all possible signature matches in all categories.

When a router with the firewall IDS enabled detects an attack, it can take one of three actions:

- Generate an alarm, which, by default, is displayed on the console. This alarm also can be sent to a syslog server or to Cisco Secure IDS Director, a centralized management platform.
- For TCP connections, reset them.
- Drop the packet.

<table>
<tr><td>**TIP**</td><td>Cisco highly recommends that you use the reset and drop actions together.</td></tr>
</table>

Even though all 100 signatures are enabled by default, you selectively can disable them if the router is triggering a high number of false positives. You can even disable a signature selectively based on the device that triggered the alarm.

Memory and Performance Issues

I previously discussed some general issues with IDS solutions. This section discusses some issues that are specific to the Cisco IOS and the IDS and its configuration. Obviously, the performance of IDS on a Cisco router depends on many things, including these:

- The processor on the router.
- The amount of memory on the router. For compound signatures, the CBAC allocates memory to maintain not only the state information for the connection, but also internal caching of packets.
- The amount of traffic traveling through the router.
- Whether the router is performing encryption.

<table>
<tr><td>**NOTE**</td><td>Enabling or disabling specific signatures does not impact the performance of IDS on the router. Likewise, interface ACLs do not impact IDS performance. However, if you are using an ACL to determine what packets trigger signatures, there will be a significant impact in the performance of the router.</td></tr>
</table>

IDS Configuration

This section discusses how to set up and verify the operation of IDS. The configuration process requires three steps:

Step 1 Initialization configuration

Step 2 Logging or PostOffice configuration

Step 3 Audit rule configuration and activation

The following sections cover these three steps, as well as how to verify the operation of IDS.

Step 1: Initialization Configuration

You can configure two basic initialization commands for IDS:

```
Router(config)# ip audit po max-events #_of_events
Router(config)# ip audit smtp spam #_of_recipients
```

The **ip audit po max-events** command limits the number of IDS events that the Cisco IOS queues up to send to a remote device. By default, this is 250 events, but this can range from 1 to 65,535. This limit is used to ensure that if a hacker tried to flood a router with a lot of attacks, the router would not overload itself in trying to process all of them. Otherwise, this basically would allow the hacker to create a DoS attack against the router itself.

The **ip audit smtp spam** command is used to limit e-mail spamming that uses mass mailings. With this command, the default number of recipients allowed in an e-mail message is 250. If an e-mail message contains more than this value, the router takes the configured action (I discuss these actions later in the "Global Policies" and "Specific Policies" sections). The number of recipients can range from 1 to 65,535.

Step 2: Logging and PostOffice Configuration

The Cisco IOS can use two methods when logging IDS events: log the information using syslog or log the information using an IDS Director. Using syslog, the Cisco IOS can log information locally (the console or the internal buffer) or remotely (a syslog server). If you want to use the syslog method, you must configure the following IDS statement:

```
Router(config)# ip audit notify log
```

This is the default. If you are using CiscoWorks VMS with Security Monitoring Center (MC), you can forward the router's syslog messages to Security MC, which is used to centralize the repository and reporting of alarm information. When logging informational signatures to the router's console, you also need to execute the following command:

```
Router(config)# logging console info
```

Other methods of using syslog are discussed in Chapter 18, "Logging Events."

Your second logging option is to log information to an IDS Director, which can include Cisco's IDS management console as well as a 4200 series sensor running 3.x. This is more difficult to set up because the IDS Director uses a Cisco-proprietary communication protocol called *PostOffice*. This protocol defines how an agent and management console, as well as two agents, share information with each other. To set up IDS Director communications, use the following syntax:

```
Router(config)# ip audit notify nr-director
Router(config)# ip audit po local hostid host_ID orgid organization_ID

Router(config)# ip audit po remote hostid host_ID orgid organization_ID rmtaddress
  IP_address localaddress IP_address [port port_#] [preference preference_#]
  [timeout seconds] [application {director | logger}]
```

The **ip audit notify nr-director** command enables the logging of IDS events to an IDS Director product. The **ip audit po local** command specifies the PostOffice configuration for the router; the **ip audit po remote** command specifies the configuration for the remote Director device.

With PostOffice, each device needs a unique combination of a host ID and an organization ID. The organization ID is used to group sensors. In smaller companies, normally only a single organization ID is necessary. For enterprise companies, you might have different organization IDs for each division, allowing for easier management of your sensor products. Within each organization, a device needs a unique host ID. This concept is similar to IP addressing, in which you have network numbers and hosts within a network. Both of these IDs range from 1 to 65,535.

For the **ip audit po local** command, you must specify the router's personal ID numbers for the host and organization values. Likewise, you must specify the Director's PostOffice ID information in the **ip audit po remote** command. However, unlike the router's PostOffice configuration, you have to tell your router many more things about the remote Director in the **ip audit po remote** command. After specifying the PostOffice ID of the Director, you need to specify the IP address of the Director and then the IP address that the router will use as its source address (an address on one of its physical or loopback interfaces). The rest of the parameters are optional:

- **port**—By default, PostOffice uses UDP port 45,000, but you can change this (if you do, you also must change it on your other Director and sensor products).

- **preference**—This prioritizes multiple statements, with different IP addresses, for the same Director. The default preference is 1 (highest). Assign the primary addresses a preference of 1; assign secondary addresses a lower preference number.

- **timeout**—This determines the number of seconds that the router waits for the PostOffice reply to be received. The default is 5 seconds.

- **application**—You can specify two application types: **director** (default) or **logger**. With the **director** method, the Cisco IOS uses PostOffice to send IDS messages to a Director product (management platform). This then shows up as an alarm in the management console and also is logged in a file. With the **logger** method, the IDS messages are sent to a Cisco sensor product or to a Director—with either method, only a log message is recorded. Normally, you use this method if you are not using Cisco's Director product for management, but you have Cisco sensors and want to centralize your logging information. Of course, you also easily can do this with syslog.

NOTE   The router's PostOffice identifiers must be configured on the Director device to allow communication between the router and the Director. Also, any time you change the router's PostOffice ID information, you must save your configuration and reboot the router.

Step 3: Audit Rule Configuration and Activation

When you have defined your logging method, you are ready to create your IDS auditing rules. Two sets of commands are used to configure audit rules: global (default actions) and specific.

Global Policies

Global policies are used to take the appropriate actions for matching on signatures, unless a specific rule designates otherwise. To create your global policies, use these two commands:

```
Router(config)# ip audit info {action [alarm] [drop] [reset]}
Router(config)# ip audit attack {action [alarm] [drop] [reset]}
```

As you can see, the two commands specify actions for informational and attack signatures. Each has three possible actions that the router can take:

- **alarm**—Generate an alarm (log), where this is the default action
- **drop**—Drop the packet
- **reset**—For TCP connections, tear down the connection

These commands need to be configured only if you want to change the default action (alarm) and you want the Cisco IOS IDS engine to use the same policy for all traffic of the same signature category.

Specific Policies

Besides globally changing the behavior or IDS, you can create specific IDS auditing policies. Typically, you do this if you have two interfaces on your router—perhaps one connected to the Internet and the other to a remote site—and you want to set up different IDS policies (actions to signature matches) for each interface. Here is the command syntax to set up your specific IDS auditing policies:

```
Router(config)# ip audit name audit_name {info | attack}
   [list standard_ACL_#_or_name] [action [alarm] [drop] [reset]]
```

The first difference between this command and the two global commands is that you must give the policy a name. Following this, specify the signature category: either informational or attack. Optionally, you can specify a standard ACL number or name. With this option, only **permit** source IP address entries in the ACL are used for matching traffic. Remember my earlier warning: Using ACLs with IDS matching severely impacts the performance of the router. Following this are the actions for the specific policy. If you omit the action, it defaults to the action defined in the global policy.

Signature Policies

By default, all signatures are enabled. In some cases, however, you want to disable one or multiple signatures, perhaps because of a high number of false positive matches. You can disable a signature with the following command syntax:

```
Router(config)# ip audit signature signature_#
   {disable | list standard_ACL_#_or_name}
```

You must specify the signature number that you want to disable. Signature numbers were discussed previously in Table 16-2. Following this, you specify one of two parameters. The

disable parameter disables the signature for all IDS auditing policies on the router. The **list** parameter specifies a standard ACL. If a match on the signature occurs and the source IP address matches any of the **deny** entries in the standard ACL, the router takes no action; only **permit** entries will allow the router to perform the configured action for the IDS auditing policy. Again, remember my warning about performance issues when using ACLs with IDS policies.

False Positives

Many IDS solutions enable you to trigger alarms on informational processes, such as pings or DNS zone transfers. This is useful if you have tight control over these things to begin with. However, if these are common occurrences in your network, it becomes much easier to hide a real attack by inserting it into a mass of false positives. I have run into this situation quite a few times, with administrators failing to tune their IDS solutions and receiving thousands of events to track on a daily basis. In some cases, the companies did not even know that they were under attack; in one case, the company already had been attacked successfully.

A good IDS solution brings important events to your immediate attention through a prioritization scheme. However, not all IDS solutions do this; in such cases, searching through lengthy log files for important events becomes difficult, if not impossible, if there are thousands of entries. Therefore, I highly recommend that you tune each IDS solution, disabling signatures that are not necessary or tuning profiles so that the number of false positives is reduced greatly.

Protection Policies

When an IDS alarm is generated because a signature was triggered, the alarm contains a location designator for both the source and destination addresses. IN indicates that the address is internal to the network, and OUT indicates that it is external to the network. Of course, the router does not know internal from external: You must tell the router this. This is done with this configuration:

```
Router(config)# ip audit po protected IP_address [to IP_address]
```

Any address specified in this command is listed as IN as a location designator in the alarm. You can specify a single address or a range of addresses (using the **to** parameter). Note that this command influences only the location tags placed in the alarm message and has no affect on the triggering of signatures.

Policy Activation

After you have defined your IDS audit policies, you must activate them on an interface(s) before your router can use them. Use the following configuration to activate your IDS audit policies:

```
Router(config)# interface type [slot_#/]port_#
Router(config-if)# ip audit audit_name {in | out}
```

You can specify that your policy be activated in the inbound or outbound direction on an interface. If you want to activate a policy in both directions, execute the command twice, specifying **in** for one command and **out** for the other. Normally, you activate your IDS policies inbound on a perimeter router's external interface. After you have activated your IDS policies, the router starts comparing packets to its signature database.

IDS Verification

After you have set up IDS on your router, you can use one **show** command with multiple parameter options to test your IDS configuration:

```
Router(config)# show ip audit { all | configuration | interfaces |
    name audit_name | sessions | statistics}
```

The **all** parameter displays output from all of the other parameters (with the exception of **sessions** and **statistics**). The **configuration** parameter displays how you have configured IDS on your router. The **interfaces** parameter displays which interfaces do and do not have IDS policies activated on them. The **name** parameter displays the configuration of the specified audit policy. The **sessions** parameter displays IDS sessions (Director connections). The **statistics** parameter display statistics about the operation of IDS. Example 16-1 displays sample output with the **all** parameter.

Example 16-1 *Using the* **show ip audit all** *Command*

```
Router# show ip audit all
Event notification through syslog is enabled                    (1)
Event notification through Net Director is disabled
Default action(s) for info signatures is alarm                  (2)
Default action(s) for attack signatures is alarm
Default threshold of recipients for spam signature is 250
PostOffice:HostID:0 OrgID:0 Msg dropped:0
          :Curr Event Buf Size:0  Configured:100
Post Office is not enabled - No connections are active          (3)
Audit Rule Configuration                                        (4)
 Audit name audit_ids
    attack actions alarm drop reset
Interface Configuration
 Interface FastEthernet0                                        (5)
  Inbound IDS audit rule is audit_ids
    attack actions alarm drop reset
  Outgoing IDS audit rule is not set
```

The following is an explanation of the output in Example 16-1, with reference to the numbering on the right side of the example:

1 Syslog is enabled and Director logging is disabled. These are the defaults.

2 These are the actions for the global policies. Notice that they are both set to alarm, which is the default.

3 PostOffice is not configured in this example.

4 This section contains your defined (specific) audit rules. In this example, only one specific policy has been defined: audit_ids. This policy enables only attack signatures, with a response of alarm, drop, and reset for matches on these signatures.

5 The audit_ids policy is enabled on FastEthernet0.

Example 16-2 displays sample output with the **statistics** parameter.

Example 16-2 *Using the* **show ip audit statistics** *Command*

```
Router# show ip audit statistics
Signature audit statistics [process switch:fast switch]
  signature 1107 packets audited: [5:5]
  signature 2004 packets audited: [4:4]
  signature 2150 packets audited: [0:7]
Interfaces configured for audit 1
Session creations since subsystem startup or last reset 0
Current session counts (estab/half-open/terminating) [7:1:1]
Maxever session counts (estab/half-open/terminating) [58:39:3]
Last session created never
Last statistic reset never

Post Office is not enabled - No connections are active
```

In this example, there were matches against three signatures. You also can see the number of packets processed and fast-switched (in the first set of brackets).

If you want to clear your IDS statistics, use the **clear ip audit statistics** command. If you want to clear the IDS configuration on your router completely, use the **clear ip audit configuration** command.

IDS Example

To help you better understand the configuration of the Cisco IOS Firewall IDS feature, take a look at an example. Use the perimeter router in Figure 16-1 as an example. In Example 16-3, alarms should be generated for informational signature matches and alarms, drops, and resets for attacks.

Example 16-3 *Simple IDS Configuration Example*

```
Router(config)# ip audit notify log
Router(config)# ip audit name IDSRULZ info action alarm
Router(config)# ip audit name IDSRULZ attack action alarm drop reset
Router(config)# ip audit signature 2000 disable
Router(config)# ip audit signature 2001 disable
Router(config)# ip audit signature 2002 disable
Router(config)# ip audit signature 2004 disable
Router(config)# ip audit signature 2005 disable
Router(config)# ip audit signature 6051 disable
Router(config)# interface ethernet1
Router(config-if)# ip audit IDSRULZ in
```

In this example, one rule is created (IDSRULZ) that enables the information signatures with a match option of alarm and attack signatures, with actions of alarm, drop, and reset. The following signatures have been disabled:

- 2000 (echo reply)
- 2001 (host unreachable)
- 2002 (source quench)
- 2004 (echo request)
- 2005 (time exceeded)
- 6051 (DNS zone transfers).

These are normal actions and generate a lot of IDS logging records, making it more difficult to see other, more important information.

CAUTION   A common misconfiguration/misunderstanding that I see when administrators enable the Cisco IOS IDS is that they are not aware that portions of the CBAC engine also are enabled. The Cisco internal development team states that enabling components of CBAC is necessary to track half-open sessions for certain signatures. The biggest problem that this creates is that the CBAC inspection process for the **max-incomplete low/high** and 1-minute low/high parameters are set to their default values (these parameters are discussed in Chapter 17, "DoS Protection"). The main problem with the default setting of these parameters is that they are set low for most environments, especially in environments where the router is processing a lot of traffic. Therefore, you need to tune these parameters to appropriate values based on your network's traffic patterns. See Chapter 17 for more information on this topic.

Summary

This chapter showed you the basics of using the IDS feature of the Cisco IOS Firewall feature set. Even though the IDS feature is not a full-blown IDS solution, it provides good coverage for small businesses, as well as an extra level of protection on your perimeter router. Setting up IDS is simple and enables you to examine traffic before an ACL processes it.

Next up is Chapter 17, which shows you how to protect your network from DoS attacks by using various Cisco IOS features.

## CHAPTER 17

DoS Protection

Of the three categories of attacks—reconnaissance, access, and denial-of-service (DoS)—DoS attacks are the easiest to implement yet the hardest to defeat. DoS attacks are based on packet flooding, which uses up bandwidth, CPU, and memory resources on not just the victim device, but also intervening devices, such as routers, switches, and firewalls.

When you are experiencing a DoS attack, one of the first things you need to do is find out the actual kind of DoS attack that is affecting your network. As you will see in the first section of this chapter, a variety of options are available to you, including examining the CPU utilization of your routers, using ACL statements with logging parameters, and using NetFlow.

When you know the kind of DoS attack directed at your network, you can implement an appropriate solution. The remaining sections in this chapter focus on these solutions, including TCP Intercept, CBAC, and rate limiting. Of course, you always can use an ACL to block offending traffic; however, this might introduce other problems, such as the blocking of legitimate traffic. Therefore, in many cases, you need to use other tools, such as the ones discussed in the last half of this chapter, to deal with DoS issues.

Detecting DoS Attacks

A wide variety of DoS attacks can occur. The most common DoS attacks use UDP echos (Fraggle), ICMP echo and echo replies (Smurf), and TCP (TCP SYN flooding). However, you never should assume that the DoS attack that you are experiencing falls under one of these three types: Some do not fall under these categories.

Common Attacks

One of the most common DoS attacks is the Smurf attack, which I covered in Chapter 7, "Basic Access Lists." (Chapter 7 also covered how to use ACLs to deal with the Smurf attack.) In a Smurf attack, the attacker sends a flood of ICMP messages to a reflector or sets of reflectors, with the source IP address in the ICMP echo messages spoofed. The hacker changes these addresses to the address of the actual victim device or devices. The reflectors then innocently reply to the echo messages, inadvertently sending the replies to the victim. In many cases, the source address is a directed broadcast address, allowing the attack to target a network segment instead of a specific host. Based on this information, if you see a large number of ICMP echo replies coming into your network, you probably are experiencing a Smurf attack, or at least a derivative of this kind of attack. Likewise, if you are seeing a large number of packets coming into your network with a directed broadcast address, this would indicate that you are under attack. One method of preventing this is to use the **no ip directed-broadcast** command on your router's interfaces. I discussed this command in Chapter 4, "Disabling Unnecessary Services."

The Fraggle DoS attack is similar to the Smurf attack, except that Fraggle uses UDP echo and echo reply messages instead of ICMP messages. Because UDP echos typically are filtered, Fraggle typically has a less likelihood of having the same impact that Smurf does (I discussed in Chapter 4 how to defeat a Fraggle attack by configuring the **no service tcp-small-servers** and **no service udp small-servers** commands).

The other common attack is a TCP SYN flood attack, in which an attacker tries to overwhelm one or more TCP services running on a machine. The attacker executes this attack by sending a flood of TCP SYN segments to the victim. In most cases, the hacker forges the source address to hide his tracks or possibly to create another DoS attack against a second victim. Therefore, when the server receives the TCP SYNs and tries to complete the three-way handshake, the process fails: The server sends a SYN/ACK response to a bogus or invalid address and, therefore, never gets the final ACK reply in the three-way handshake. During this period, resources are tied up on the server for each of these half-open (commonly called *embryonic*) connections. Because this kind of attack typically is targeted at a specific machine, when you experience a slowing of your server that offers TCP services, such as an e-mail, web, or FTP server, or if one of these servers crashes or halts, this might indicate that it was (and possibly still is) the victim of a TCP SYN flood attack.

Symptoms of Attacks

When your router is experiencing a DoS attack (including worm attacks), either one directed at the router or one in which the router is a transit device, you can look for the following to help you confirm your hunches:

- Your router is seeing an unusually high number of ARP requests.

- Your NAT/PAT address-translation tables have a large number of entries.

- Your router's IP Input, ARP Input, IP Cache Ager, and CEF processes are using abnormally high amounts of memory.

- Your router's ARP, IP Input, CEF, and IPC processes are running at a much higher CPU utilization rate.

TIP   The following sections discuss various methods for detecting and tracing DoS attacks. However, one of the best solutions for detecting DoS attacks is to use an IDS solution. A good IDS solution should tell you exactly the kind of DoS attack that you are facing.

Examining CPU Utilization to Detect DoS Attacks

In any DoS attack situation, the network symptoms that you see typically will be common, such as high CPU utilization on your devices or a high number of certain kinds of packets. Therefore, one of the first things you want to do is to log into your perimeter routers and firewalls and examine their CPU utilization.

On a Cisco router, use the **show processes cpu** command to examine the router's CPU utilization, as shown in Example 17-1.

Example 17-1 *Using the* **show processes cpu** *Command*

```
Router# show processes cpu
CPU utilization for five seconds: 92%/34%; one minute: 90%; five minutes: 45%
 PID Runtime(ms)   Invoked     uSecs   5Sec   1Min   5Min TTY Process
   1          0         1         0  0.00%  0.00%  0.00%   0 Chunk Manager
   2          0       294         0  0.00%  0.00%  0.00%   0 Load Meter
   3       7532      2365      3184  0.00%  0.00%  0.24%   0 Exec
   4          0        13         0  0.00%  0.00%  0.00%   0 DHCPD Timer
   5        800       156      5128  0.00%  0.02%  0.03%   0 Check heaps
   6          0         1         0  0.00%  0.00%  0.00%   0 Pool Manager
<--output omitted-->
```

The shaded line is what you should focus on. Three statistics are listed here:

- **CPU utilization for five seconds**—This is the CPU utilization on the router for the last 5 seconds. The number after the slash (/) is the percentage of CPU time spent at the interrupt level. During an interrupt, the CPU must handle the functions for the process instead of an interface or a specific ASIC (application-specific integrated circuit).

- **One minute**—This is the CPU utilization of the router over the past minute.

- **Five minutes**—This is the CPU utilization of the router over the past 5 minutes.

In Example 17-1, the 5-second utilization is 92 percent and the 1-minute utilization is 90 percent. Notice that the 5-minute utilization is only 45 percent. This probably indicates a brief spike in traffic. If all three of these are at a higher number than normal and are close together in values, such as 75 or 95 percent (depending on your router's baseline, of course), this could indicate a DoS attack. In this situation, you should look at other things on your router to determine whether this is just an anomaly in traffic conditions or a DoS attack.

A derivation of the **show processes cpu** command is the addition of the **history** parameter. This command displays, in an ASCII graphical format, the total CPU usage of the router over 1 minute, 1 hour, and 72 hours. Example 17-2 shows an example of the use of this command.

Example 17-2 *Using the* **show processes cpu history** *Command*

```
Router# show processes cpu history
<-- One minute output omitted -->
    666577686575667667666666766767767676666676676777676666566667
    637801619899351370977199144373235868993274085826964392261
```

continues

Example 17-2 *Using the* **show processes cpu history** *Command (Continued)*

```
100
 90
 80         ** *                       * *       *   * *   *
 70    * * ****# *   ** ***** ***   **** ******   *   *** ***       *
 60   #***##*##*#***#####*#*###*****#*###*#*#*##*#*#**#*#*##*****
 50   ########################################################*
 40   ########################################################
 30   ########################################################
 20   ########################################################
 10   ########################################################
      0....5....1....1....2....2....3....3....4....4....5....5....
           0    5    0    5    0    5    0    5    0    5

                   CPU% per minute (last 60 minutes)
               * = maximum CPU%   # = average CPU%

<-- 72-hour output omitted -->
```

In Example 17-2, the Y-axis of the graph represents CPU utilization, and the X-axis represents the increment period. In this example, I omitted the output for the 1-minute and 72-hour output and listed only the hour output.

The maximum usage, represented by a *, is measured and recorded every second (this is displayed at the very top of a vertical entry). The average usage is measured over a period of 1 second and is represented by a #.

The very top of the graph lists the actual CPU utilization for the 1-minute interval, which fluctuated between 60 and 80 percent utilization.

For worm attacks, examine the following information in the output of the **show process cpu** command: ARP, IP Input, CEF, and IPC processes. Also examine the following information in the output of the **show processes memory** command: IP Input, ARP Input, IP Cache Ager, and CEF processes.

NOTE Of course, looking at the CPU utilization during a DoS attack assumes that you have captured a history of CPU utilization baselines during normal traffic conditions. If you do not have this information and your CPU utilization is running at 75 percent, this might be a normal condition for your router. Therefore, you periodically should gather statistical information about your router, including CPU utilization and the bandwidth utilization on each of its interfaces. This will help you determine whether something abnormal, such as a DoS attack, is directed at your router or is flowing through your router. Also, if your CPU utilization is running at 100 percent because of a severe DoS or worm attack, your router might reload itself. Therefore, you also should check to see if your router periodically is reloading, which could indicate that you are under attack.

Using ACLs to Detect DoS Attacks

One of the most common tools used to detect DoS attacks is ACLs. This is especially true of your perimeter routers and router firewalls because these devices already have ACLs in place to filter traffic. As I mentioned in Chapter 7, you always want to include a **deny ip any any** statement in your ACL at the end. This is not necessary to drop traffic, but it does have the router keep statistics on the number of matches on this statement. This can be useful in determining whether a DoS attack is occurring.

ACL Counters

The first thing you should do is clear the counters for your ACL with the following command:

```
Router# clear access-list counters [ACL_#_or_name]
```

After this, view the ACL in question with the **show access-lists** or **show ip access-list** commands. Example 17-3 shows sample output from the **show access-list** command.

Example 17-3 *Displaying the Counters for ACL Statement Matches*

```
Router# clear access-list counters 100
Router# show access-list 100
Extended IP access list 100
<--output omitted-->
  deny ip any any (3183 matches)
Router#
Router# show access-list 100
Extended IP access list 100
<--output omitted-->
  deny ip any any (7225 matches)
```

Notice in this example that, after I cleared the ACL counters for ACL 100 and then viewed the ACL the first time (right after clearing the ACL counters), the match on the **deny ip any any** statement is 3183, which is relatively high for just a couple of seconds between executing the two commands. Right after executing the first **show** command, I re-executed it. Notice that in the second or two between the execution of the two commands, the number of matches more than doubled. In this example, I was sending a flood of ICMP packets from three devices to one victim device.

Here are some important things to keep in mind about using ACLs to detect a DoS attack:

- In this example, I assumed that the traffic being dropped was the DoS attack. You also need to examine the matches on **permit** entries because your ACL might be permitting the DoS attack, such as a TCP SYN flood. Again, a good baseline of this information should assist you in determining whether a DoS attack is occurring. In other words, you should have gathered ACL statistics in normal traffic periods, and then you can use this to make a comparison.

- Remember that because you are using extended ACLs, you can specify the IP protocol, source and destination addresses, and protocol information, such as TCP and UDP port numbers as well as ICMP message types. This enables you to be as specific as possible in determining a match.

- If the ACL in question is applied to multiple interfaces, remember that the ACL counters are an aggregate of all of the matches on all interfaces on which the ACL has been activated. In this situation, you might want to have a separate named/numbered ACL for each interface.

Specific ACL Entries

Of course, the problem with the previous examination is that you can see that your router is dropping a flood of traffic, but you do not see what traffic the router is dropping. For example, if you do not want to allow any type of ICMP traffic, or even if you want to permit only certain kinds of ICMP traffic, put in the appropriate ACL entries so that, minimally, you can see ACL statistics on matches. Refer to Figure 17-1 for an example. Here, no echo messages should be allowed into the network, and only echo replies to the management station are allowed.

Figure 17-1 *ACL Example*

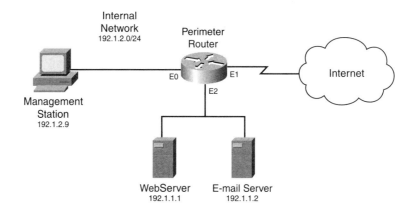

Example 17-4 shows a basic ACL example for this network.

Example 17-4 *A Basic ACL Example*

```
Router(config)# remark Insert other ACL statements here
Router(config)# access-list 100 deny ip any 192.1.1.0 0.0.0.0      (1)
Router(config)# access-list 100 deny ip any 192.1.1.255 0.0.0.0
Router(config)# access-list 100 deny ip any 192.1.2.0 0.0.0.0
Router(config)# access-list 100 deny ip any 192.1.2.255 0.0.0.0
Router(config)# access-list 100 permit icmp any               (2)
  host 192.1.2.9 echo-reply
Router(config)# access-list 100 deny icmp any any echo        (3)
```

Example 17-4 *A Basic ACL Example (Continued)*

```
Router(config)# access-list 100 deny icmp any any echo-reply       (4)
Router(config)# access-list 100 deny udp any any eq echo           (5)
Router(config)# access-list 100 deny udp any eq echo any           (6)
Router(config)# access-list 100 permit tcp any                     (7)
  host 192.1.1.1 eq 80 established
Router(config)# access-list 100 permit tcp any                     (8)
  host 192.1.1.1 eq 80
Router(config)# access-list 100 permit tcp any                     (9)
  host 192.1.1.2 eq 25 established
Router(config)# access-list 100 permit tcp any                     (10)
  host 192.1.1.2 eq 25
Router(config)# remark Insert other ACL statements here
Router(config)# access-list 100 deny ip any any
Router(config)# interface ethernet1
Router(config-if)# ip access-group 100 in
```

This example not only sets up filtering, but it also has specific entries that can be used to detect four DoS attacks: directed broadcast attacks (Statement 1), which are used by many types of DoS attacks; a Smurf attack (Statements 2, 3, and 4); a Fraggle attack (Statements 5 and 6), and TCP SYN floods (Statements 7 and 8):

- For a Smurf attack, if the entries in Statements 2 or 4 are increasing rapidly, this indicates that Smurf reflectors are attacking you (you are the victim). If you are the reflector, you will see entries in Statement 3 rapidly increasing. This is especially true if you do not configure the group of statements in Statement 1. However, to determine this, you would need to enable logging for the ICMP ACL statements, which I discuss in the next section.

- For a Fraggle, attack, if the entries in Statement 5 are increasing, this indicates that you are the victim; a large number of matches against Statement 6 indicates that you are the reflector.

- For a TCP SYN flood attack, you will see the number of matches against Statements 8 and 10 increasing many times over normal baseline numbers. What is unusual about these two ACL statements is that they are normal ACL statements allowing traffic to the e-mail and web servers. However, remember that the Cisco IOS keeps track of the number of matches on all statements, so a large increase in the number of matches for either of these two servers could indicate a TCP SYN flood attack. Because there are many types of TCP flood attacks, using various TCP flags, Statements 7 and 9 look at the other TCP flags for an abnormal number of other TCP messages.

Also, the statements under Statement 1 block traffic sent to the network and directed broadcast addresses of the internal network. These addresses are commonly used in DoS attacks. By having specific entries in your ACL, you can use the **show access-lists** command to determine more easily whether a DoS attack is occurring.

ACL Logging

The main limit of the statistics from the **show access-lists** and **show ip access-list** commands is that they can show you that a high number of hits are occurring against one or a few ACL statements, but this does not tell you who the attacker (or the victim, in some cases) is. One option is to use the **log** or **log-input** parameters at the end of the ACL statements in question. As you recall from Chapter 7, the main difference between these two commands is that the **log-input** parameter displays the input interface of the received packet and the Layer 2 source address in the packet.

CAUTION   In either situation, remember that using either of these two parameters disables CEF switching, which seriously impacts the performance of the router. Therefore, use the log function to pinpoint the attack, including the victim and the attacker, and then remove the **log** or **log-input** parameters from your ACL statement(s).

Smurf Example

For example, assume that the router in Figure 17-1 is under a Smurf attack. When you examine the router's ACL, you notice the output in Example 17-5.

Example 17-5 *Using the* **show access-list** *to Pinpoint a Smurf Attack*

```
Router# show access-list 100
Extended IP access list 100
  <--output omitted-->
  permit icmp any host 192.1.2.9 echo-reply (15 matches)
  deny icmp any any echo (1038 matches)
  deny icmp any any echo-reply (238482 matches)
  deny udp any any eq echo
  deny udp any eq echo any
  <--output omitted-->
```

As you can see in Example 17-5, an inordinate number of ICMP echo reply messages is being denied (remember that only the management station is allowed to ping and receive replies).

To determine the problem, you would modify the ACL statement for the dropped ICMP packets by changing ACL Statement 4 in Example 17-4 to this:

```
Router(config)# access-list 100 deny icmp any any echo reply log-input
```

In this situation, I probably would disable logging to the console but enable logging to the internal buffer (this is discussed in Chapter 18, "Logging Events." Therefore, when there is an inordinate number of log messages, the console interface will not be overwhelmed.

Given the Smurf attack in the example, here is a snippet of the output produced by log messages from a match on the ACL statement:

```
%SEC-6-IPACCESSLOGDP: list 100 denied icmp 201.1.1.1
(Ethernet1) -> 192.1.1.1 (0/0), 1 packet
```

```
%SEC-6-IPACCESSLOGDP: list 100 denied icmp 201.1.1.2
(Ethernet1) -> 192.1.1.1 (0/0), 1 packet
%SEC-6-IPACCESSLOGDP: list 100 denied icmp 201.1.1.9
(Ethernet1) -> 192.1.1.1 (0/0), 1 packet
%SEC-6-IPACCESSLOGDP: list 100 denied icmp 205.8.8.7
(Ethernet1) -> 192.1.1.1 (0/0), 1 packet
%SEC-6-IPACCESSLOGDP: list 100 denied icmp 200.1.1.37
(Ethernet1) -> 192.1.1.1 (0/0), 1 packet
%SEC-6-IPACCESSLOGDP: list 100 denied icmp 201.1.1.1
(Ethernet1) -> 192.1.1.1 (0/0), 1 packet
%SEC-6-IPACCESSLOGDP: list 100 denied icmp 205.8.8.32
(Ethernet1) -> 192.1.1.1 (0/0), 1 packet
%SEC-6-IPACCESSLOGDP: list 100 denied icmp 201.1.1.81
(Ethernet1) -> 192.1.1.1 (0/0), 1 packet
```

In this example, a single host is being attacked: 192.1.1.1. Also notice that most of the ICMP traffic is coming from two networks: 201.1.1.0/24 and 205.8.8.0/24. By using the IANA Whois database (http://www.iana.org), you should be able to see who these addresses belong to. It is important to point out that in a Smurf attack, these are probably not the actual attacker devices, but Smurf reflectors (with Smurf, it is very unlikely that the attacker would use his own address as a source, unless he is a script kiddie). However, at least you have a starting point and should be able to contact the ISPs or administrators who are responsible for these networks so that they can take the appropriate action.

Keep the following items in mind when using logging with ACLs:

- Enabling logging with ACLs can have a small- to medium-size impact on your router, depending on its model. Therefore, I recommend that you be careful using the logging function on routers that are running at 80 percent utilization or higher—especially with ACLs on high-speed interfaces.

- Depending on the version of the Cisco IOS running on your router, logging might affect the switching mode that the router must use to implement the logging function.

- If you are seeing matches against ACL entries in the **show access-list** command, but you are not seeing any entries actually being logged (you have added the **log** parameter to the ACL statement), try clearing the route cache to force packets to be process-switched. Of course, this can cause a lot of traffic to be dropped on a very busy router when it is in the process of rebuilding the cache. To get around this specific problem, use a router that supports CEF.

- ACL logging does not display every packet that matches an ACL entry. Instead, you will see at least the first packet on a match for a session and then packets at periodic intervals. The Cisco IOS uses rate limiting to prevent logging from overloading the router's CPU. It is important to remember that you will not see all packets that match an ACL statement when you have logging enabled.

- During a Smurf attack that involves multiple reflectors, the amount of logging information might be overwhelming. In this instance, set up a separate ACL statement that matches on a single reflector and logging for only this reflector. Typically, this will be multiple devices from a single network, so use an ACL that matched on all of these devices. This helps you determine all of the devices in one reflector site.

TIP   Be as specific as possible in your ACL statements when looking for the DoS attack. Use the
log-input parameter so that you can see the interface where the attack is coming from. If
the router's interface is a multiaccess interface, this information also will include the MAC
address of the next-hop router; use the **show ip arp** *MAC_address* command to see the
router's IP address.

NOTE   The purpose of this section on ACLs was to give you a basic understanding of how to track
down the type of DoS attack. Obviously, you can add or modify ACL entries to determine
the kind of DoS attack you are experiencing.

Damage Limitations

The attacker in a DoS attack wants to affect bandwidth and service levels, so your first
concern should be preventing this traffic from traversing your ISP links. You could set up
an ACL on your perimeter routers to block this traffic, but this stops it only from entering
your network; it does not prevent it from traversing your ISP links.

In this situation, you need to contact your ISP and explain the situation. Hopefully they also
will investigate the problem on their end and either set up a temporary ACL filter to block
the offending traffic or set up rate limiting to reduce the effect that the DoS attack will have.
As I mentioned, this should be a temporary filter: When the attack has been mitigated, these
measures should be removed.

Finding the Attacker

When you are the victim of a DoS attack, tracking down the actual attack, as well as the
perpetrator, can be a difficult and stressful task. Remember that the source addresses in a
DoS attack typically are forged and, therefore, are not very helpful in finding the actual
attacker. Therefore, finding the attacker typically must be done on a hop-by-hop basis, tracing
the attack from one router to the next until you finally arrive at the source of the attack. As you
saw in the "Using ACLs to Detect DoS Attacks" section, this requires administrators possibly
to add ACL entries and/or add logging to specific ACL entries, which can be a complex
process. And because the path of the attack might take you back through multiple ISPs, you
typically must involve law-enforcement agencies to get the kind of cooperation from ISPs and
network administrators that might be necessary to perform this kind of trace.

The Trace Process

Tracing DoS attacks is a straightforward process. In this subsection and the following ones,
I discuss the use of ACLs to perform the trace process. However, other options, such as
NetFlow, can be used as well. I discuss NetFlow after discussing ACLs.

Remember that the source address in the packet probably is spoofed, so you cannot assume anything about the location of the attacker. Therefore, you have your work cut out for you: The actual trace process requires you to trace back, router by router, to the real source of the attack. Figure 17-2 illustrates this process. In this example, the e-mail server (192.1.1.1) is under a DoS attack. The first thing that you would do is to log into RouterA, which I am assuming is the router directly connected to the same segment as the e-mail server. Remember that the DoS attack might be internal, not external, to the network. From here, you would determine which interface the attack is coming from, log into the next-hop router, and perform the same process, tracing this back eventually to the hacker himself.

Figure 17-2 *Tracing Example*

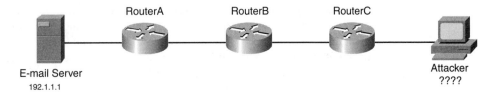

Trace Problems

In a Smurf attack, in which reflectors are used to instigate the attack against a victim, it is fairly easy to determine who the reflectors are. However, when you have found the reflectors, tracing the attack back to the originator of the attack is difficult, if not impossible, because it must be done on a hop-by-hop basis, probably through many different ISPs. Given this tedious process, you face the following problems when tracking down the attacker who instigated the DoS attack:

- Because multiple administrators and networks typically are involved in the trace-back process, it becomes a tedious and slow process tracing back the attack to the real source. Even an unintelligent hacker knows that you will attempt to trace his attack; therefore, the hacker limits the duration of the DoS attack, which might not give you enough time to trace the attack.

- If the attack goes through multiple networks or ISPs, and possibly even through different countries, getting the appropriate assistance could be difficult.

- The attack might be coming from multiple sources, as in a Smurf attack. With a Smurf attack, you need to trace the attack back to each reflector and then, from each reflector, trace the attack back to the real source or sources of the attack.

- The attack might be perpetrated from a hacked computer that was compromised by the hacker. Therefore, finding the actual perpetrator might be impossible unless the hacked computer has detailed logs of unauthorized access to it.

- When you actually track down the DoS attacker, you will face legal and political issues trying to sue for damages in a civil action. You will need detailed proof of the attack to bring criminal actions against the attacker—and this can be very difficult if the attacker is in a different country.

NOTE   Given these problems, you should realize that, in most cases, you will not be able to find the attacker who instigated a DoS attack. Therefore, you should pick your battles. In most cases, you will want to use tools to limit the effect of a DoS attack and attempt to trace back attacks only when they are severe enough to prevent your company from operating or reaching its business goals. Also, if the trace involves multiple companies and ISPs, you typically must get law-enforcement agencies involved to get the information necessary to find the attacker.

Using NetFlow to Detect DoS Attacks

One of the problems of using the **log** or **log-input** parameters with ACL statements is that it is very process-intensive for the router to handle the logging function. Cisco provides another solution, called NetFlow switching. NetFlow enables you to capture statistics of flows traveling through your router. It is a transparent switching method that requires you only to enable it. Unlike ACLs with logging, NetFlow is a switching technology that has much less of an impact on the router. As with ACL logging, you can export NetFlow information to a server, to be examined in more depth.

NetFlow Overview

NetFlow switching is a network-layer switching method that switches packets at high speeds and captures statistics for traffic analysis. It is supported on IP and IP-encapsulated traffic types over a variety of interfaces, including interfaces with input ACLs.

NOTE   NetFlow is not supported on ISL trunk interfaces, ATM and Frame Relay interfaces if more than one input ACL is used, and ATM LANE interfaces.

Cisco developed NetFlow switching to provide the following benefits:

- Processing of ACL statements with little performance penalty (at least, compared to many other switching modes)
- Billing for bandwidth usage in corporate and ISP networks
- Capturing of traffic for network management and capacity planning

NetFlow uses flows to identify traffic. A flow is basically a unidirectional session based on the following fields in an IP packet: IP protocol, source and destination IP address, type of service, source and destination port numbers for TCP and UDP flows, and input interface. When NetFlow identifies a new flow, an entry is added to the NetFlow cache. This entry then is used to switch packets and to perform ACL checking.

NetFlow Configuration

Enabling NetFlow is a simple process. You can use many optional parameters to create a more efficient capturing process for traffic statistics. However, I focus on only the basics of enabling NetFlow, exporting NetFlow statistics, and examining the statistics.

Enabling NetFlow

Enabling NetFlow is done on your router's interface(s). When using it to track down DoS attacks, I recommend that you enable it on an interface or interfaces of your router where you think the source of the DoS attack is originating. Here is the basic configuration to enable NetFlow:

```
Router(config)# interface type [slot_#/]port_#
Router(config-if)# ip route-cache flow
```

The **ip route-cache flow** command enables NetFlow switching on a router's interface. If you have a Cisco router that supports distributed switching, such as the 7500 with RSP and VIP modules, you need to execute one more command on the router's interface:

```
Router(config-if)# ip route-cache distributed
```

This command enables distributed switching with NetFlow.

Exporting NetFlow Data

Optionally, you can export NetFlow statistical data to an external device that supports NetFlow data imports. After you set up the export function, NetFlow information is exported every time a flow expires. A few products on the market, including one from Cisco, can be used to decipher the exported information. You then can use the NetFlow statistical information to generate traffic-analysis reports and graphs. To enable export of NetFlow information, use the following command:

```
Router(config)# ip flow-export IP_address UDP_port_# [version 5]
```

With the **ip flow-export** command, you must specify the IP address of the NetFlow server, as well as the UDP port number used on the server. There are two versions of NetFlow: version 1 and 5. Version 1 is the default if no version number is specified. To export information to a NetFlow server that supports version 5, you must specify the version number in the command. One advantage that version 5 has over version 1 is that version 5 includes a sequence number in each segment. UDP is unreliable, so there is a chance that the NetFlow server will not receive some exported NetFlow packets. Using the sequence number in version 5 allows the NetFlow server to verify that it received all of the NetFlow segments or determine that some are missing.

Examining and Clearing NetFlow Statistics

After you have set up NetFlow, use the **show ip cache flow** command to examine the flows and their statistics:

```
Router# show ip cache [prefix mask] [type number] [verbose] flow
```

The *prefix mask* option displays entries in the cache that match the prefix and subnet mask, limiting your output. Likewise, you can list the specific interface, displaying only the flows for that interface. Example 17-6 displays the output of this command:

Example 17-6 *Using the* **show ip cache flow** *Command*

```
Router# show ip cache flow
IP packet size distribution (33 total packets):                    (1)
   1-32 64   96   128  160 192 224 256 288 320 352 384 416 448 480
   000  000 000 1.00 000 000 000 000 000 000 000 000 000 000 000

   512 544 576 1024 1536 2048 2560 3072 3584 4096 4608
   000 000 000 000  000  000  000  000  000  000  000

IP Flow Switching Cache, 4358208 bytes                             (2)
   1 active, 65535 inactive, 3 added
   68 ager polls, 0 flow alloc failures
   Active flows timeout in 30 minutes
   Inactive flows timeout in 15 seconds
   last clearing of statistics never

Proto Total  Flows  Packets Bytes Packets Active(Sec) Idle(Sec)   (3)
----- Flows  /Sec   /Flow   /Pkt  /Sec    /Flow       /Flow
ICMP     3   0.0       4    100    0.0       0.0       14.1
Total    3   0.0       4    100    0.0       0.0       14.1

SrcIf   SrcIPaddress  DstIf  DstIPaddress  Pr SrcP DstP Pkts       (4)
Et1     200.1.1.1     Et0    192.1.1.1     01 0000 0800   5
```

Here is an explanation of the information in Example 17-6, with reference to the numbering on the right side. Statement 1 displays the percentage of the distribution of packets based on their size. Notice that 100 percent of the packets are in the 128-byte range.

Statement 2 displays some general statistics about NetFlow switching, such as the total number of bytes that the cache table is using, as well as the number of active flows. Also notice that the NetFlow statistics have not been cleared since NetFlow was configured or the router was booted. To clear the flow statistics, use the **clear ip flow stats** command.

Statement 3 displays a section on protocol statistics. Table 17-1 describes these fields. Statement 4 displays the actual flows. Table 17-2 describes these fields.

Table 17-1 *NetFlow Protocol Fields*

Field	Description
Proto	IP protocol name or number, such as ICMP
Total Flows	Total number of flows for this protocol since the statistics last were cleared
Flows/Sec	Average number of flows for the protocol per second for this summary period
Bytes/Pkt	Average number of bytes for the packets associated with this protocol for this summary period

Table 17-1   *NetFlow Protocol Fields (Continued)*

Field	Description
Packets/Sec	Average number of packets per second for this summary period
Active(Sec)/ Flow	Total of all the seconds from the first to last packets of an expired flow, or total flows for this protocol in the summary period
Idle(Sec)/Flow	Total idle time of all seconds since the last packet for this protocol in the summary period

Table 17-2   *NetFlow Flow Fields*

Field	Description
SrcIf	The interface that the packet was received on
SrcIPaddress	The source IP address in the packet
DstIf	The interface that the packet was sent out of
DstIPAddress	The destination address in the packet
Pr	The IP protocol number (1 is ICMP)
SrcP	In hexadecimal, the source port number
DstP	In hexadecimal, the destination port number
Pkts	The number of packets for this flow

NOTE   It is important to point out that the port number information in the output of the **show ip cache flow** command is in hexadecimal. Keep this in mind when looking for particular flows in the cache.

NetFlow and DoS Attacks

Now that you have a basic understanding of how to set up NetFlow and examine its statistics, this section looks at how to use this information to your advantage when trying to determine whether you are experiencing a DoS attack. The next few sections show some examples of different Worm and DoS attacks.

TIP   When you are under a heavy DoS attack, I highly recommend that you use NetFlow instead of ACL logging, to help determine the kind of DoS attack as well as information about where the attack is coming from. If you use ACL logging, there is a chance that the overhead that this adds to your router will overwhelm it, possibly causing it to crash.

W32.Blaster Worm

If you are experiencing high CPU utilization on your router, as well as packet drops on your input interfaces, you might have an infestation of the W32.Blaster worm or one of its derivatives. The W32.Blaster worm appears as UDP traffic on port 69 with high volumes of traffic on ports 135 and 4444. The worm propagates using valid file-sharing ports, such as TFTP and TCP port 135, which is the Microsoft RPC protocol, and Kerberos authentication (TCP port 4444). Blocking these ports can prevent its spread.

Example 17-7 shows a simple example of searching for the W32.Blaster Worm infection/attack, based on the network shown previously in Figure 17-1.

Example 17-7 *Using NetFlow to Track Down the W32.Blaster Worms*

```
Router# show ip cache flow | include 0087
SrcIf    SrcIPaddress    DstIf   DstIPaddress   Pr SrcP DstP    Pkts
Et2      192.1.1.1       Et0     192.1.2.7      06 0B88 0087    1
Et2      192.1.1.1       Et0     192.1.2.9      06 0BF8 0087    1
Et2      192.1.1.1       Et0     192.1.2.23     06 0E80 0087    1
Et2      192.1.1.1       Et0     192.1.2.37     06 0CB0 0087    1
Et2      192.1.1.1       Et0     192.1.2.88     06 0C90 0087    1
```

Notice one interesting thing about the **show** command that I executed: You can use the vertical bar (|) and the **include** parameter to display only the results that match the string that you enter after this parameter. Port 0087, in hexadecimal, is 135 in decimal. To look for TFTP, use the hexadecimal number of 0045; for Kerberos authentication, use 115c.

In the previous output, notice that one device, 192.1.1.1, which is the DMZ web server, is scanning other internal devices using protocol 06 (TCP) with a DstP of 0087 (135—Microsoft RPC). With this information and the number of random port 135 connections it is trying to make to internal devices, you definitely should check out your web server.

TIP   Before beginning, you first should clear the NetFlow statistics and then continually examine the statistics to look for incrementing patterns. This is true for all DoS attacks.

Code Red Worm

At least three variations of the Code Red worm exist. All versions exploit a security vulnerability in the Microsoft IIS web server product by sending a specially formed URI to port 80 on a vulnerable system. Upon a successful attack, the worm replaces the web page of the IIS server with graffiti. In version 1 of the worm, an infected device did one of the following:

- Scanned random IP addresses and passed the infection to other devices
- Launched a DoS attack against 198.137.240.91, which used to be www.whitehouse.gov

One problem with the version 1 worm was that it did not use truly random addresses in its scan process; version 2 does. Version 2 also does not use the hard-coded IP address of the White House's web server; it uses a DNS name and does a DNS lookup to find the address. Both worms suffer the same deficiency: They do not check to see if the devices that they are scanning and trying to infect already are subverted.

Many Cisco products were affected by the amount of traffic that this worm generated. For example, the CSS 11000 content switches, under a heavy worm infestation, experienced memory-allocation errors that required them to be rebooted. Likewise, the 600 DSL routers stopped forwarding traffic until they also were rebooted. Cisco has introduced code fixes for all of its products that experienced problems dealing with this worm.

Because the worm uses a common port, detecting it is slightly more difficult. However, using NetFlow makes your task much easier. Because Code Red spreads itself by looking for vulnerabilities in IIS, you should examine NetFlow information and look for a TCP destination port of 80 (which is 0050 in hexadecimal). The network shown previously in Figure 17-1 illustrates this in Example 17-8.

Example 17-8 *Using NetFlow to Track Down the Code Red Worms*

```
Router# show ip cache flow | include 0050
SrcIf   SrcIPaddress    DstIf   DstIPaddress    Pr SrcP  DstP  Pkts
Et2     192.1.1.1       Et0     192.1.2.3       06 0F9E  0050   1
Et2     192.1.1.1       Et0     192.1.2.9       06 0456  0050   2
Et2     192.1.1.1       Et0     192.1.2.21      06 3001  0050   2
Et2     192.1.1.1       Et0     192.1.2.37      06 B305  0050   1
Et2     192.1.1.1       Et0     192.1.2.38      06 0EEF  0050   1
Et2     192.1.1.1       Et0     192.1.2.88      06 0E75  0050   1
Et2     192.1.1.1       Et0     192.1.2.104     06 1134  0050   2
```

As you can see in this example, there are a few HTTP requests from the web server in the DMZ to internal addresses. If you see an abnormally high number of HTTP requests with the same source address, or if the source address is a web server itself, as is the case here, you have a problem. In this example, the DMZ web server has been attacked successfully and is attempting to spread itself to internal devices.

Smurf Attack

As mentioned throughout this book, the Smurf attack is one of the most common types of DoS attacks because of its simplicity in implementing it on a hacker's behalf. As with worms, you can use NetFlow to track the reflectors and possibly the source(s) of the attack. Example 17-9 shows an example, based on the network shown in Figure 17-1.

Example 17-9 *Using NetFlow to Track Down Smurf Attacks*

```
Router# show ip cache flow | include 0000
SrcIf  SrcIPaddress  DstIf  DstIPaddress  Pr SrcP DstP  Pkts
Et1    201.1.1.1     Et2    192.1.1.1     01 0000 0000   49K
Et1    201.1.1.17    Et2    192.1.1.1     01 0000 0000   50K
Et1    201.1.1.39    Et2    192.1.1.1     01 0000 0000   51K
Et1    201.1.1.104   Et2    192.1.1.1     01 0000 0000   48K
Et1    205.8.8.8     Et2    192.1.1.1     01 0000 0000   31K
Et1    205.8.8.39    Et2    192.1.1.1     01 0000 0000   30K
```

As you can see in this example, two networks seem to be set up as reflectors, attacking the web server on the DMZ (192.1.1.1). Based on this information, you can contact your ISP and the administrators of these networks to take corrective action.

TIP   Besides using NetFlow for tracking down specific attacks, some people at Ohio State University have developed a quick-and-dirty set of tools that uses NetFlow records to detect network and host intrusions. More information about this nifty project can be found at http://www.usenix.org/publications/login/1999-9/osu.html.

CEF Switching

Cisco Express Forwarding (CEF) is a switching mode that was introduced in the Cisco IOS 11.1 and 11.2 software trains and that is available across all 12.0 versions. In traditional Cisco caching solutions, cache entries are built as traffic flows through the router. CEF, on the other hand, mirrors the entire system routing table, alleviating the building on any initial cache. Therefore, CEF handles large amounts of data better than traditional switching and caching methods.

With most DoS attacks, the traffic is sent to one or a handful of victim devices, which does not have any impact on either traditional or CEF switching processes. However, many kinds of SYN flood attacks use random source addresses. The victim or victims of this attack attempt to respond back to the connection attempts, creating a large number of destinations for switching paths. With traditional switching, this would create a performance problem; with CEF, the destinations already have been cached, so there is not as much of an issue dealing with this increased amount of traffic.

When a router is using fast switching on an interface, the CPU must be involved to handle the interrupt requests from the fast-switching interfaces to move traffic from one interface to another. During periods of flooding traffic, this can create a DoS condition on the router itself in which most of its CPU cycles are handling the interface interrupts. You can limit this process by using the **scheduler interval** command:

```
Router(config)# scheduler interval #_of_milliseconds
```

This command causes the router to stop handling interrupt requests at the configured interval and handle other tasks. For example, you might set the value to 250 milliseconds, which tells the Cisco IOS to handle process-level tasks for no more than 250 milliseconds at a time.

Newer Cisco router platforms use the **scheduler allocate** command instead of the **scheduler interval** command:

```
Router(config)# scheduler allocate #_of_milliseconds_of_interrupts
   #_of_milliseconds_of_no_interrupts
```

This command has two parameters: The first parameter specifies the number of milliseconds in which interrupts are handled; the second parameter specifies the number of milliseconds for which interrupts are placed on hold. A common allocation configuration is **scheduler allocate 3000 1000**. With this configuration, interrupts are handled for 3 seconds, but for the next second, the router performs other tasks.

TIP   Cisco has stated that the **scheduler interval** and **scheduler allocate** commands have no negative side effects on the router and should be part of your router's standard configuration.

TCP Intercept

One option for dealing with TCP SYN flood attacks is to implement the Cisco IOS TCP Intercept feature. TCP Intercept enables you to deal with DoS attacks that attempt to take advantage of the weakness in the way that TCP connections establish a session with the three-way handshake. This was discussed in Chapter 1, "Security Threats." This section focuses on how to use TCP Intercept to limit the effectiveness of a TCP SYN food attack that is perpetrated by an attacker.

TCP SYN Flood Attacks

As you recall from Chapter 1, a TCP SYN flood attack is an easy attack to initiate. The attacker sends a flood of TCP SYN segments with no intention of completing the three-way handshake for each of these connections. Typically, the hacker combines this with an IP spoofing attack in which the source addresses in the packet are either invalid or someone else's address. Because these addresses cannot be reached (or, if they are someone else's address, are not responded to), the TCP server being attacked hangs in limbo with these half-open (commonly called *embryonic*) connections. In this situation, the server must wait until the TCP timeout expires for the connection before removing the connection from its local connection table. This creates a problem because it uses up resources on the TCP server, which might deny legitimate TCP connections.

TCP Intercept Modes

TCP Intercept is a Cisco IOS feature that is used to protect TCP services from TCP SYN flood attacks. TCP supports two modes of protection: intercept and watch. The following two sections discuss how these modes operate when dealing with TCP SYN attacks.

Intercept Mode

Intercept mode takes a proactive approach to TCP SYN flood attacks. Figure 17-3 shows an example of a router using intercept mode with TCP Intercept. In intercept mode, the router intercepts all TCP connection requests, as shown in the figure. In this example, an external user is trying to access an internal server using a TCP connection. The router intercepts this request and pretends to be the internal server, completing the connection to the external user. Only upon a successful three-way handshake with the external user (Steps 1 through 3 in Figure 17-3) does the router set up a second TCP connection to the server (Steps 4 through 6). The router then binds the two connections, creating a single connection (Step 7).

Figure 17-3 *TCP Intercept Using Intercept Mode*

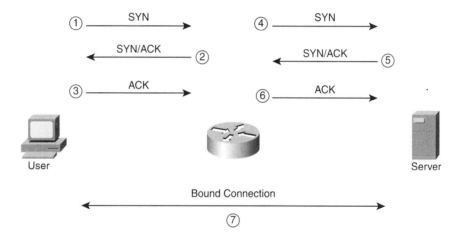

For the most part, this process is transparent to the two devices that make up the final TCP connection. With this approach, if a TCP SYN flood attack is occurring, the router provides a buffer to the internal servers using TCP because they are not affected by the flood: The router deals with the half-open connections, which eventually time out and are removed from the router's TCP connection table. Basically, the router sends an RST to the requesting source device. In the mean time, valid requests are permitted as long as the router successfully can complete the three-way handshake with the external user.

NOTE   One limitation of intercept mode is that any TCP options that are negotiated between the external user and the router (which normally are to the end-server device), such as RFC 1323 window scaling, are not passed from the router to the internal TCP server. This is because the router does not know these options until the first three-way handshake completes with the external user and the router begins the second three-way handshake with the internal TCP server. Typically, this is not a problem because TCP allows for the dynamic negotiation of these parameters during the normal operation of the session.

Watch Mode

Whereas intercept mode takes a proactive approach to dealing with TCP SYN flood attacks, *watch* mode takes a reactive approach. One of the main advantages of intercept mode is that it removes the processing load of TCP SYN floods from the internal server. However, this a double-edged sword because, in most time periods, a TCP SYN flood is not occurring, but the router still is performing the intercept process, placing a heavy burden on it.

To alleviate this problem, you can use TCP Intercept in watch mode. Watch mode takes a passive, or reactive, approach to TCP SYN flood attacks. In watch mode, the router passively watches the setup of TCP connections from users to servers. It monitors these connections, keeping track of embryonic connections that remain in this limbo state. Then it compares this value to a preconfigured timeout value (which defaults to 30 seconds). If a TCP connection does not complete the three-way handshake in this period, the Cisco IOS sends a TCP reset to the server to remove the connection. For an attack that is directed at an internal server using TCP, this removes the half-open connections, thus reducing the load on the server and allowing legitimate connection attempts to be processed.

TCP Intercept Configuration and Verification

Enabling TCP Intercept on your router is a simple process. Only one command is required, but typically you will tune some of the parameters to ensure that TCP Intercept functions smoothly in your environment. The following sections discuss the configuration and verification of TCP Intercept.

Enabling TCP Intercept

The first step in setting up TCP Intercept is to specify which TCP sessions should be intercepted in intercept mode or monitored in watch mode. This is done by using the **ip tcp intercept list** command:

```
Router(config)# ip tcp intercept list extended_ACL_#
```

A couple of important things should be pointed out about this required command. First, this command enables TCP Intercept. Notice that the command is executed at global configuration mode, not on an interface.

Second, you must use an extended ACL to specify which traffic is to be examined by TCP Intercept. As an example, if you want to monitor all TCP setup connections, you would configure something like this:

```
Router(config)# access-list 100 tcp permit tcp any any
Router(config)# ip tcp intercept list 100
```

Typically, this configuration is a bad idea because the router basically would act like a proxy for all inbound and outbound connections.

TIP	When you are setting up TCP Intercept, use it to deal with TCP SYN flood attacks from external users. This is accomplished by configuring an extended ACL for TCP Intercept that refines the traffic that should be monitored. For example, if you have only two servers in your DMZ that use TCP, such as an e-mail server and a web server, set up TCP Intercept to monitor only port 25 traffic to the e-mail server and port 80 traffic to the web server. This greatly reduces the number of TCP connections that the router has to monitor. Because you typically do not know the IP address of the source device, leave it as any.

Defining the Mode

The rest of the TCP Intercept configuration commands are optional. For example, the default mode for TCP Intercept is intercept. If this creates too much of a burden on your router's CPU, you can switch the mode to watch with the following command:

```
Router(config)# ip tcp intercept mode {intercept | watch}
```

Note that you cannot use a mixture of both intercept and watch modes for TCP Intercept, for example, based on the destination address. With TCP Intercept, the mode that it operates in is a global value.

Changing the Timers

You can tune three timers with TCP Intercept: an embryonic timer, a connection reset timer, and a connection idle timer. These can be configured with the three following commands:

```
Router(config)# ip tcp intercept watch-timeout seconds
Router(config)# ip tcp intercept finrst-timeout seconds
Router(config)# ip tcp intercept connection-timeout seconds
```

The **ip tcp intercept watch-timeout** command specifies the maximum length of time that the router will wait, in watch mode, for a TCP connection to complete the three-way handshake. This value defaults to 30 seconds. If the connection is not reached in this time period, the router sends a reset to the server (destination).

When a router with TCP Intercept enabled monitors a connection that is in the process of being torn down, it expects the connection to be torn down within 5 seconds, by default, from the receipt of a reset or FIN exchange. When this time period is reached, the router ceases to manage the connection. You can change this value with the **ip tcp intercept finrst-timeout** command.

When the TCP Intercept is managing TCP connections, it manages a connection only up to 24 hours, by default, for an idle connection. After this, the router drops the connection. You can modify this with the **ip tcp intercept connection-timeout** command.

Changing the Thresholds

In addition to the intercept and watch modes, TCP Intercept uses threshold values to deal with an excessive number of TCP connection attempts during a time of a TCP SYN flood attack. TCP Intercept supports two thresholds: one based on the total number of embryonic connections, and one based on the number of connection requests during the last 1-minute period. You can tune both of these threshold values.

During a time of attack in which your router is seeing an excessive number of connections and one of the two threshold values is reached, the router begins dropping the oldest embryonic connections first (this can be changed with the **drop-mode** parameter, discussed in the next section). For intercept mode, the router reduces the initial retransmission timeout for SYN segments by half. For watch mode, the router reduces the watch time automatically to half of the configured value (if you were using the default of 30 seconds, it becomes 15 seconds).

Aggressive operation of TCP Intercept begins when either of the two thresholds is reached. To specify the values for the maximum embryonic connection threshold, use the following two commands:

```
Router(config)# ip tcp intercept max-incomplete high number
Router(config)# ip tcp intercept max-incomplete low number
```

The **high** parameter specifies when aggressive mode should begin. When this threshold is reached, the router, by default, begins deleting the oldest half-open connections first until it drops enough of these connections to fall below the threshold value specified in the **low** parameter. The default threshold values are 1100 for the **high** parameter and 900 for the **low** parameter.

To specify the values for the expected total number of half-open connection requests in a 1-minute period, use the following two commands:

```
Router(config)# ip tcp intercept one-minute high number
Router(config)# ip tcp intercept one-minute low number
```

The **high** parameter specifies when aggressive mode should begin. When this threshold is reached in a 1-minute measurement period, the router, by default, begins deleting the oldest half-open connections first until it drops enough of these connections to fall below the threshold value specified in the **low** parameter. The default threshold values are 1100 for the **high** parameter and 900 for the **low** parameter.

CAUTION   Be careful about adjusting the threshold values with the **ip tcp intercept max-incomplete** and **one-minute** commands. If you set these values too low, the router might take aggressive action to prevent legitimate connections. This is especially true of the web servers, in which lots of connections are expected when downloading the contents of a web page. Each situation and network is different; you need to establish a baseline before determining what values you should use for the high and low threshold numbers.

Changing the Drop Method

In aggressive mode, the default drop method is to drop the oldest half-open connections first until the number of remaining half-open connections falls below the configured minimum threshold (either total half-open connections or half-open connections in a 1-minute interval). You can change the drop method with the following command:

```
Router(config)# ip tcp intercept drop-mode {oldest | random}
```

The default is **oldest**; by changing it to **random**, TCP Intercept causes the router to randomly drop half-open connections until the number of remaining half-open connections falls below the configured minimum threshold.

Verifying Your Configuration

After you have configured TCP Intercept, you can use two **show** commands and one **debug** command to verify and troubleshoot your configuration. If you want to see general statistics about the operation of TCP Intercept, use the **show tcp intercept statistics** command. Example 17-10 displays sample output of the **show tcp intercept statistics** command.

Example 17-10 *Using the* **show tcp intercept statistics** *Command*

```
Router# show tcp intercept statistics
intercepting new connections using access-list 100
12 incomplete, 5 established connections (total 17)
1 minute connection request rate 2 requests/sec
```

In this example, there are currently 12 half-open connections and 5 established ones. Notice that ACL 100 is used to restrict the traffic that TCP Intercept monitors.

To see the connections that TCP Intercept is monitoring, use the **show tcp intercept connections** command. Example 17-11 displays sample output of the **show tcp intercept connections** command.

Example 17-11 *Using the* **show tcp intercept connections** *Command*

```
Router# show tcp intercept connections
Incomplete:
Client              Server            State    Create    Timeout  Mode
201.1.1.1:33772     200.1.1.30:80     SYNRCVD  00:00:09 00:00:05 I
201.1.1.1:33773     200.1.1.30:80     SYNRCVD  00:00:09 00:00:05 I

Established:
Client              Server            State    Create    Timeout  Mode
201.1.1.2:33771     200.1.1.2:23      ESTAB    00:00:08 23:59:54 I
```

The output of this command is broken into two sections: Incomplete refers to connections that are in an embryonic state; established refers to connections that have completed the three-way handshake. The Client column indicates the source of the connection and the Server column indicates the destination. The connection can be in one of three states:

- **SYNSENT**—The client is attempting to establish a TCP session.
- **SYNRCVD**—The server is responding with a SYN/ACK to the client.
- **ESTAB**—The TCP session has been established, and both devices now can pass data.

The Create column indicates how long it has been since the connection was created. The Timeout column indicates how long the connection has before it times out. Note that the idle times for the two sets of information in this output will be different: The top half is for embryonic connections, and the bottom half is for established idle TCP sessions. The exception to the timeout for established sessions is that, when the session is in the process of being torn down, the idle timer defaults to 5 seconds. The Mode column indicates the mode for TCP Intercept: I is for intercept mode, and W is for watch mode.

For more detailed troubleshooting, you can use the **debug ip tcp intercept** command, which displays the TCP Intercept events occurring on the router. Example 17-12 shows a simple example of the output of this command, with the router in intercept mode.

Example 17-12 *Using the* **debug ip tcp intercept** *Command*

```
Router# debug ip tcp intercept
INTERCEPT: new connection (192.1.1.1:33884) => (200.1.1.2:23)       (1)
INTERCEPT: 192.1.1.1:33884 <- ACK+SYN (200.1.1.2:33884)
INTERCEPT: new connection (192.1.1.1:33885) => (200.1.1.2:23)       (2)
INTERCEPT: 192.1.1.1:33885 <- ACK+SYN (200.1.1.2:33885)
INTERCEPT: retransmit 2 (192.1.1.1:33884) <-                        (3)
           (200.1.1.2:23) SYNRCVD
INTERCEPT: retransmit 2 (192.1.1.1:33885) <-
           (200.1.1.2:23) SYNRCVD
INTERCEPT: new connection (192.1.1.2:32790) => (200.1.1.2:23)       (4)
INTERCEPT: 192.1.1.2:32790 <- ACK+SYN (200.1.1.2:32790)
INTERCEPT: retransmit 4 (192.1.1.1:33884) <-                        (5)
           (200.1.1.2:23) SYNRCVD
INTERCEPT: retransmit 4 (192.1.1.1:33885) <-
           (200.1.1.2:23) SYNRCVD
INTERCEPT: retransmit 2 (192.1.1.2:32790) <-
           (200.1.1.2:23) SYNRCVD
INTERCEPT: 1st half of connection is established                    (6)
           (192.1.1.2:32790) => (200.1.1.2:23)
INTERCEPT: (192.1.1.2:32790) SYN -> 200.1.1.2:23
INTERCEPT: retransmit 2 (192.1.1.2:32790) ->
           (200.1.1.2:23) SYNSENT
INTERCEPT: 2nd half of connection established                       (7)
           (192.1.1.2:32790) => (200.1.1.2:23)
INTERCEPT: (192.1.1.2:32790) ACK -> 200.1.1.2:23
INTERCEPT: retransmit 8 (192.1.1.1:33884) <-                        (8)
           (200.1.1.2:23) SYNRCVD
INTERCEPT: retransmit 8 (192.1.1.1:33885) <-
           (200.1.1.2:23) SYNRCVD
```

continues

Example 17-12 *Using the* **debug ip tcp intercept** *Command (Continued)*

```
INTERCEPT: retransmit 16 (192.1.1.1:33884) <-
           (200.1.1.2:23) SYNRCVD
INTERCEPT: retransmit 16 (192.1.1.1:33885) <-
           (200.1.1.2:23) SYNRCVD
INTERCEPT: retransmitting too long (192.1.1.1:33884) =>          (9)
           (200.1.1.2:23) SYNRCVD
INTERCEPT: 192.1.1.1:33884 <- RST (200.1.1.2:23)
INTERCEPT: retransmitting too long (192.1.1.1:33885) =>
           (200.1.1.2:23) SYNRCVD
INTERCEPT: 192.1.1.1:33885 <- RST (200.1.1.2:23)
```

The following is an explanation of this output, with reference to the numbering on the right side:

1   A new connection arrives from 192.1.1.1 to 200.1.1.1. The router intercepts the connection and responds with a SYN/ACK to 192.1.1.1.

2   A second connection arrives from 192.1.1.1 to the same destination. The router again intercepts this connection and responds with a SYN/ACK to the source (192.1.1.1).

3   The router did not receive an ACK from either request, so the router retransmits the SYN/ACK for the connections.

4   192.1.1.2, a different device, requests a connection to the 200.1.1.2 server. The router intercepts the connection request and responds with a SYN/ACK.

5   The router has not received an ACK from any of the TCP connections, so it retransmits the SYN/ACK for each session request to each source device.

6   The router has received the ACK from the second device, completing the three-way handshake, so the router begins to build a separate connection to the server (200.1.1.1) on behalf of this client.

7   The server responds to the router's connection request with a SYN/ACK, and the router responds with an ACK, completing the three-way handshake.

8   The router still has not received an ACK response for the first two TCP connection requests from 192.1.1.1, so it retransmits the SYN/ACK for these connections.

9   For the two connections request from 192.1.1.1, the connection attempt has exceeded the configured timeout, so the router sends an RST to the source for both of these connection attempts.

TCP Intercept Example

To help you understand TCP Intercept's configuration, reexamine Figure 17-1. In this network, the administrator is concerned about TCP SYN flood attacks against the web server and the e-mail server located in the DMZ. To deal with TCP SYN flood attacks, the administrator has decided to use TCP Intercept in watch mode to monitor connections. Example 17-13 shows the router's configuration for TCP Intercept.

Example 17-13 *Using TCP Intercept to Protect Internal Servers*

```
Router(config)# access-list 100 tcp permit tcp any host 192.1.1.1 eq 80
Router(config)# access-list 100 tcp permit tcp any host 192.1.1.2 eq 25
Router(config)# ip tcp intercept list 100
Router(config)# ip tcp intercept mode watch
Router(config)# ip tcp intercept watch-timeout 20
Router(config)# ip tcp intercept connection-timeout 120
Router(config)# ip tcp intercept max-incomplete high 600
Router(config)# ip tcp intercept min-incomplete low 500
Router(config)# ip tcp intercept one-minute high 800
Router(config)# ip tcp intercept one-minute low 600
```

In this example, TCP Intercept is set up for only the DMZ web and e-mail servers. The mode was changed from intercept to watch, and the watch timeout for connections was changed from 30 to 20 seconds. If a connection is not set up within the 20 seconds, the router sends a reset (RST) to the DMZ server. The idle timeout for TCP connections was changed from 1 day (86,400 seconds) to 2 minutes (120 seconds). This is a more appropriate value, based on the fact that e-mail and especially web server connections are brief and are typically not idle unless there is a connection problem.

Based on the monitoring performed on this network, the administrator chose more appropriate threshold values for the aggressive mode process. Remember, though, that setting these too low can cause half-open legitimate connections to be dropped; setting them too high can allow invalid half-open connections to use up resources on the two DMZ servers. As you can see from this example, setting up TCP Intercept is a simple process.

CBAC and DoS Attacks

Chapter 9, "Context-Based Access Control," discussed how you can use this feature from the Cisco IOS Firewall feature set to implement a stateful firewall function. One thing that I did not cover in Chapter 9 was the capability of CBAC to restrict the number of half-open sessions, which typically is used to prevent TCP SYN flood attacks. This feature is similar to TCP Intercept, but it can examine TCP as well as UDP and ICMP sessions. Of course, with UDP and ICMP, because there is no state machine that defines the setup, maintenance, and removal of a connection, CBAC uses timers instead of connection threshold values. The following sections discuss how you can use CBAC to prevent certain kinds of DoS attacks.

Timeouts and Thresholds

CBAC uses timeouts and thresholds to determine how long state information should be kept for a session and when to drop those sessions, based on them not becoming fully established. Of course, "established" is a defined process when it comes to TCP, in which CBAC can examine the TCP flags to determine the state of the connection. With UDP and ICMP, CBAC must use idle timer limits to approximate when a connection ends. The timeouts and thresholds can be defined globally, as I will show you in this section, or can be done within the actual **ip inspect** command for the traffic that you are inspecting.

TIP   Cisco recommends that you first make changes to the global timeout and threshold values before configuring your inspection rules.

Setting Connection Timeouts

To set the global CBAC timeouts for inspected connections, use the following commands:

```
Router(config)# ip inspect tcp synwait-time seconds
Router(config)# ip inspect tcp finwait-time seconds
Router(config)# ip inspect tcp idle-time seconds
Router(config)# ip inspect udp idle-time seconds
Router(config)# ip inspect dns-timeout seconds
```

These commands were discussed thoroughly in Chapter 9, so I do not go into any more depth about them here.

NOTE   You can override the idle timeouts in the actual inspection commands. When a timeout is configured in an inspection command for an application or protocol, it takes precedence over the global timeout value. Also, there is no global timeout parameter for ICMP traffic: this is configured with the inspection command for ICMP traffic.

Setting Connection Thresholds

As with TCP Intercept, you can set connection thresholds for CBAC inspection. However, unlike TCP Intercept, connection thresholds for CBAC include TCP and UDP traffic. The next two sections discuss the configuration of the threshold values and how CBAC uses them to prevent DoS attacks when an attacker attempts to open an abnormally high number of connections to tie up resources on critical services.

Configuration

Setting up connection thresholds is similar to setting thresholds for TCP Intercept. For CBAC, here are the commands you use:

```
Router(config)# ip inspect max-incomplete high number
Router(config)# ip inspect max-incomplete low number
Router(config)# ip inspect one-minute high number
```

```
Router(config)# ip inspect one-minute low number
Router(config)# ip inspect tcp max-incomplete host number
    block-time minutes
```

You can specify three connection parameter threshold values: maximum half-open sessions, maximum half-open sessions in a 1-minute period, and maximum TCP half-open sessions per host.

The first two commands specify that when the maximum number of half-open sessions reaches the **high** threshold value, CBAC starts dropping the half-open sessions until it reaches the **low** threshold value. The defaults for these thresholds are 500 and 400 half-open sessions, respectively.

The third and fourth commands measure the number of new connection attempts in a 1-minute interval. If the maximum number of new connection attempts reaches the **high** threshold during the time interval, CBAC begins dropping the half-open sessions until it reaches the **low** threshold. The defaults for these thresholds are 500 and 400 half-open sessions, respectively.

Both sets of these parameters are similar to the thresholds defined with TCP Intercept. The one main difference between CBAC and TCP Intercept is the last CBAC command in the previous code listing: **ip inspect tcp max-incomplete host**. This command is a more aggressive command that is used to prevent DoS attacks against a specific host. With this command, CBAC uses two different methods, depending on the value of the **block-time** variable. If the **block-time** variable is set to 0 minutes, when the **host** half-open TCP session limit value is exceeded, CBAC deletes the oldest half-open connection request for every newly requested connection request. However, if the **block-time** value is set to a minute value greater than 0, when the number of half-open sessions exceeds the **host** parameter, CBAC blocks all new connection requests to the host (destination) until the **block-time** period expires.

CAUTION   Be careful about assigning a minute value greater than 0 to the **block-time** value because this also could block legitimate traffic during a DoS attack. My recommendation is to configure a **block-time** value of 0. Also, you need to be very careful about the threshold that you configure for the **host** parameter. Assigning too low of a value for a very busy server could cause CBAC to drop legitimate connection requests.

Half-Open Sessions

One main difference between TCP Intercept and CBAC inspection is that TCP Intercept can be used only to prevent TCP SYN flood attacks. CBAC, however, can prevent DoS attacks for TCP and UDP DoS attacks. The thresholds that CBAC uses are based on the number of half-open sessions. For TCP, a half-open session is one that has not reached an established state; this includes both SYN and SYN/ACK messages (CBAC can detect both kinds of floods). For UDP, a half-open session is one in which no returning traffic is detected.

CBAC DoS Prevention Verification

After you have assigned your timing and threshold parameters, you can use various **show** and **debug** commands (discussed in Chapter 9) to verify your configuration. One option that I mentioned in this chapter is to use audit trails and alerts. Assuming that you have enabled alerts, and you are experiencing a DoS attack, you will see log output similar to the following:

```
%FW-4-ALERT_ON: getting aggressive, count (83/500) current 1-min rate: 501
%FW-4-ALERT_OFF: calming down, count (0/400) current 1-min rate: 271
```

In this example, the first alert message displays the number of half-open sessions (501) and the current limit (500). In the last minute, 271 connection attempts were made. From CBAC's perspective, this is the beginning of a DoS attack. The second message, ALERT OFF, indicates that the number of connections, through both dropping and normal setup completion, has fallen below the minimum threshold (400). In this case, the value is 0, indicating that CBAC dropped some and that the rest were initiated normally.

The combination of both an ON and a OFF message indicates a separate attack. These messages are used for both the maximum number of half-open sessions and the maximum number of new connection attempts in a 1-minute interval.

If a DoS attack is geared at a specific host, you would see the following alert messages:

```
000022: Jan 02 15:42:11.048: %FW-4-HOST_TCP_ALERT_ON:
                        Max tcp half open connections (50)
                        exceeded for host 192.1.1.2
000023: Jan 02 15:42:11.361: %FW-4-BLOCK_HOST:
                        Blocking new TCP connections to host
                        192.1.1.2 for 2 minutes
                        (half-open count 50 exceeded)
000024: Jan 02 15:44:11.372:%FW-4-UNBLOCK_HOST:
                        New TCP connections to host
                        192.1.1.2 no longer blocked
```

In this example, the first message indicates that the maximum number of half-open TCP connections destined to 192.1.1.2 was exceeded (the limit is 50). The second message indicates that the blocking interval was defined at 2 minutes, so subsequent TCP connection requests are denied. The third message indicates that the 2-minute blocking interval has expired and that new connection requests are allowed to 192.1.1.2.

CBAC Example Configuration

You must be careful about changing the half-open session thresholds and timeout values for CBAC. Setting these values too low might cause CBAC to trigger dropping connections during a period of high activity with legitimate traffic. Likewise, setting them too high might put more of a burden on a device during an attack because more half-open sessions are allowed. Example 17-14 shows the configuration for the network in Figure 17-1 to illustrate CBAC's configuration to prevent DoS attacks.

Example 17-14 *Using CBAC to Prevent DoS Attacks*

```
Router(config)# ip inspect tcp synwait-time 20
Router(config)# ip inspect tcp idle-time 60
Router(config)# ip inspect udp idle-time 20
Router(config)# ip inspect max-incomplete high 400
Router(config)# ip inspect max-incomplete low 300
Router(config)# ip inspect one-minute high 600
Router(config)# ip inspect one-minute low 500
Router(config)# ip inspect tcp max-incomplete host 300
  block-time 0
```

In this example, I have modified the timeout for three parameters. The TCP half-open session timeout was modified from 30 to 20 seconds; this is a small network, so connections should complete fairly quickly. I also have modified the idle timeout for TCP connections, changing it from 3600 seconds (1 hour) to 60 seconds; again, most of the connections are either HTTP or SMTP, so they should not be idle for a long period of time. Because UDP is not used very often, I have modified the UDP idle timer from 30 to 20 seconds.

I also have modified the maximum number of half-open connection threshold values to 400 and 300, as well as the 1-minute interval threshold values to 600 and 500. These were configured after monitoring normal activity in this network.

One of the most difficult parameters to figure out is the maximum number of half-open sessions to a host (server). Normally, determining what this parameter should be is very difficult because on several servers, such as e-mail and www, the connection requests can vary wildly from one server to the next; coming up with a valid threshold value that will work with all devices is very difficult. In this instance, there are only two servers—the e-mail server and web server. I set the maximum number of half-open sessions to 300 per destination. This is kind of high for the small network e-mail server, but it is a more appropriate number for the web server (remember that downloading a web page from a web server might involve a dozen or more connection requests).

NOTE   When you are modifying the timeout and threshold values, carefully monitor CBAC to ensure that you are not making the problem worse instead of better. Too often I have seen this situation in real networks.

Also, remember my warning from Chapter 16, "Intrusion Detection System": when you enable IDS on your router, some components of CBAC are enabled to examine application layer information to detect certain kinds of attacks. One of the enabled components include the timeout and thresholds for CBAC; therefore, you will definitely need to tune these to ensure that your router doesn't use the default values, which might be artificially low for your environment, causing legitimate connections to be dropped.

Rate Limiting

With some types of DoS attacks, there's not much you can do to stop the flow of the attack, especially in a distributed DoS (DDos) attack in which the hacker is spoofing the source addresses and using an unsuspecting company or ISP as the reflector in the attack. Tracing this kind of attack to the hacker can be difficult.

In this situation, your first concern should be limiting the impact of the attack on your network, which can be done with rate limiting. Rate limiting enables you to assign a bandwidth restriction to a category of traffic, such as ICMP, UDP, or specific connection types. This section focuses on three solutions for rate limiting: ICMP rate limiting, committed access rate (CAR), and class-based policing (CBP) using Network-Based Application Recognition (NBAR).

TIP   Rate limiting is best used on the ISP's router that connects to your network. In other words, if you are experiencing a flood attack that is saturating your Internet link, implementing rate limiting on your perimeter router will not do much good. Instead, you work with your ISP to put this in place on the ISP's router. Rate limiting is something you configure to restrict the amounts of various outbound traffic. As an example, if you were a reflector in a Smurf attack, you could use rate limiting as a temporary solution to limit the flood of traffic that you are sending to a victim's network. Of course, you will want to try to track down the culprit and stop the attack.

ICMP Rate Limiting

Many attacks create a DoS attack by sending a flood of traffic to a device or devices that do not exist, causing an intervening router to reply back with an ICMP unreachable message for each unknown destination. A good example of this is a worm attack, such as an attack by the SQL Slammer worm. Through this process, the worm, purposefully or inadvertently, tries to find other machines with the same weakness. It typically does this through a ping sweep. Most worms are not intelligent about how they do this: They continually scan the same networks, trying to find the same security hole or holes that the worm used initially to subvert one of your devices.

Using Other Solutions

To prevent the overwhelming number of ICMP unreachables that your router would generate in a worm attack, you can filter the specific kind of traffic, with an ACL that looks for ICMP unreachable messages, like this:

```
Router(config)# <--permit and deny other types of traffic-->
Router(config)# access-list 100 deny icmp any any unreachable
Router(config)# <--permit and deny other types of traffic-->
```

With the SQL Slammer worm attack, you can set up an ACL to block UDP traffic destined to port 1434, like this:

```
Router(config)# <--permit and deny other types of traffic-->
Router(config)# access-list 100 deny udp any any eq 1434
Router(config)# <--permit and deny other types of traffic-->
```

This example blocks all Microsoft SQL traffic and is configured on the external interface of your perimeter router.

NOTE   Of course, if the worm is inside your network, and if either of these two ACLs is applied on your perimeter router inbound on its external interface, these ACLs will not help you much. For these to be effective, you must set up similar ACLs on all or most of your routers throughout your network. Plus, with the first ACL, you might need to allow certain ICMP unreachable messages to specific devices, making this configuration more difficult to implement.

Another possible solution was discussed in Chapter 4, which covered many services that you should disable. One of these is the generation of ICMP unreachable messages by the router. For example, on a perimeter router, you could configure the following on its interfaces (at least, the external interface):

```
Router(config)# interface type [slot_#/]port_#
Router(if-config)# no ip unreachables
```

Again, the problem with this approach is that you need to enable this on all of the routers (and their interfaces) in your network to prevent the generation of ICMP unreachable messages. In many cases, this presents additional problems: For example, it becomes much more difficult to use tools such as ping and traceroute to track down problems because your routers are not generating ICMP unreachable messages.

Using the ICMP Rate-Limiting Feature

Starting in 12.0 of the Cisco IOS, Cisco implemented a default rate limit of one ICMP unreachable packet that a router would generate in a 500-millisecond (ms) interval. This prevents a router from responding to thousands of packets with unreachable destinations with a separate ICMP message for each of these access requests.

In Cisco IOS 12.1, you can tune this operation manually with the following command:

```
Router(config)# ip icmp rate-limit unreachable [df] milliseconds
```

First, notice that this is a global configuration mode command: it applies to any ICMP unreachable message responses on any interface. Second, the **df** parameter is used to restrict the number of ICMP unreachable messages generated by the router when the fragmentation of the packet is needed and the DF bit in the IP packet header is set. Third, you can specify only the time interval for ICMP unreachable messages (in milliseconds).

This can range from 1 to 4,294,967,295. During the specified interval, the Cisco IOS generates only one ICMP unreachable message for the first packet that requires one; for other unreachable events, the router ignores them until the configured time period expires.

Here is a simple example:

```
Router(config)# ip icmp rate-limit unreachable 1000
```

In this example, only one ICMP unreachable message is generated each second.

CAR

The main problem with the **ip icmp rate-limit** command is that it works only for ICMP unreachable messages. To deal with other kinds of traffic, including ICMP unreachables, you can use committed access rate (CAR). CAR enables you to limit traffic entering or leaving an interface, and it can match on any of the following criteria: all IP traffic, IP precedence value, MAC address, or information that matches a **permit** statement in either a standard or an extended ACL.

CAR typically is implemented at the perimeter of your network for egress traffic, and it enables you to have different rate-limiting policies for different types of traffic. For example, you might have different rate limits for ICMP traffic compared to HTTP traffic to a web server.

CAUTION   Using an ACL to specify matching traffic can be process intensive. In addition, if you specify more than one policy, your router will have an additional CPU utilization hit; try to limit the number of policies that you define. Because of these issues, you should use CAR with caution. Typically, I use CAR when I know that I am under attack and want a quick-and-dirty solution to prevent the unwanted traffic while giving valid users and connections the bandwidth that they need. When the attack has been mitigated, I remove the CAR configuration.

CAR Configuration

This section focuses on using CAR to deal with DoS traffic. Here are the commands to set up CAR:

```
Router(config-if)# interface type [slot_#]port_#
Router(config-if)# rate-limit {input | output}
  [access-group [rate-limit] acl-index] bps burst_normal burst_max
  conform-action action exceed-action action
```

Use either a rate-limit, a standard, or an extended ACL to match on the traffic for rate limiting by using one of these three respective commands:

```
Router(config-if)# access-list rate-limit ACL_# {precedence_value |
  MAC_address | mask precedence_mask}
```

or

```
Router(config-if)# access-list ACL_# {deny | permit}
    source_IP_address [source-wildcard_mask]
```

or

```
Router(config-if)# access-list ACL_# {deny | permit} protocol
    source source_wildcard destination destination-wildcard
    [precedence precedence][tos tos] [log]
```

The standard and extended ACLs can be numbered or named.

NOTE   CAR requires that CEF be enabled on your router first.

rate-limit Command

Configuration of CAR is done on a router's interface with the **rate-limit** command. This command specifies the rate policy to be used for the matching traffic. The **input** and **output** parameters specify the direction in which CAR should be performed.

ACL Parameter

Optionally, you can specify an ACL number or name with the **access-group** parameter, which is used to examine specific traffic. You can use three different kinds of ACLs with CAR: rate-limit, standard, and extended (these are listed as the last three separate statements in the previous code examples). A rate-limit ACL enables you to match on a specific precedence value, a range of precedence values, or a specific MAC address. A standard ACL enables you to match on only source IP addresses. An extended ACL enables you to match on many types of traffic, such as the IP protocol, source and destination addresses, source and/or destination protocol information, precedence values, ToS values, and other fields supported by an ACL. The use of the **log** parameter, when combined with CAR, displays the actual matching process, but this is not recommended because of performance issues.

Rate Parameters

Three rate functions are defined in your CAR configuration:

- The average rate, specified in bits per second (bps), for the matching traffic. This is measured by a long-term average of the transmitted rate of traffic on the interface. Traffic under this rate is considered to be conforming.

- The normal burst size, specified in bits per second (bps). This determines how long traffic can burst above the average rate before it is considered nonconforming.

- The excessive burst rate, specified in bits per second (bps). Traffic that exceeds the excessive burst rate is considered nonconforming.

As you can see from these rate parameters, this is similar to Frame Relay's traffic-shaping parameters. However, one important point about the Frame Relay's parameters is that they are used for traffic shaping: CAR's parameters are used for rate limiting.

Rate Actions

When there is a match in an ACL or traffic type, the Cisco IOS can take the actions described in Table 17-3 for conforming (**conform-action** parameter) or nonconforming (**exceed-action** parameter) traffic.

Table 17-3 *CAR Actions*

Action Parameter	Explanation
continue	Evaluates the next **rate-limit** command on the interface
drop	Drops the packet
transmit	Transmits the packet
set prec-continue *precedence_value*	Sets the precedence value in the IP header to the specified value, and then evaluates the next **rate-limit** command on the interface
set prec-transmit *precedence_value*	Sets the precedence value in the IP header to the specified value and transmits the packet

Normally, you use the **continue**, **transmit**, and **set** parameters for conforming traffic; you use the **drop** command for nonconforming traffic. Remember that you are using CAR, in this instance, to limit the effect of DoS attacks. The options of setting a precedence value can be used in further CAR **rate-limit** commands on the interface or by other interfaces on this router or other routers.

Verifying CAR

After you have set up CAR, you can use one of the following three commands to verify its operation:

```
Router# show access-lists
Router# show access-lists rate-limit [ACL_#]
Router# show interfaces [interface_type_and_#] rate-limit
```

Example 17-15 displays sample output using the last command.

Example 17-15 *Using the* **show interfaces rate-limit** *Command for a Specified Interface*

```
Router# show interfaces ethernet2/0 rate-limit
Ethernet2/0
 Input
  matches: access-group rate-limit 100
    params: 64000 bps, 8000 limit, 8000 extended limit
    conformed 0 packets, 0 bytes; action: transmit
    exceeded 0 packets, 0 bytes; action: drop
    last packet: 9383444ms ago, current burst: 0 bytes
    last cleared 01:32:00 ago, conformed 0 bps, exceeded 0 bps
```

In this example, ACL 100 is used to define rate limiting. The average rate is 64,000 bps, and the two burst sizes are set to 8,000 bps, limiting the burst for traffic specified in **permit** statements in ACL 100.

Rate Limiting for ICMP and Smurf Attacks

Now that you have a basic understanding of the configuration of CAR, take a look at a couple of examples of its use for dealing with DoS attacks. In this section, I show you how to use CAR to limit the impact of the Smurf attack. In this example, the customer has a T1 connection and is experiencing a Smurf attack. The customer has talked to the ISP about the problem, and it has decided to implement rate limiting on its interfaces, to limit the scope of the attack as it tries to track down the originator of the attack. Example 17-16 shows the code used on the ISP router.

Example 17-16 *Using CAR on the ISP Router to Rate-Limit Smurf Traffic*

```
ISP(config)# access-list 100 permit icmp any any echo
ISP(config)# access-list 100 permit icmp any any echo-reply
ISP(config)# interface serial0
ISP(config-if)# rate-limit output access-group 100 64000 4000 4000
   conform-action transmit exceed-action drop
```

In Example 17-16, ICMP echos and echo replies are limited to 64 kbps of bandwidth, with a burst size of 4 kbps of bandwidth. Example 17-17 shows the code used on the customer's router.

Example 17-17 *Using CAR on the Customer Router to Rate-Limit Smurf Traffic*

```
Customer(config)# access-list 100 permit icmp any any echo
Customer(config)# access-list 100 permit icmp any any echo-reply
Customer(config)# interface serial0
Customer(config-if)# rate-limit output access-group 100 64000 4000 4000
   conform-action transmit exceed-action drop
```

Notice something interesting about the customer's router configuration: It is the same as the ISP's, applied in the same direction (out). If the attack is being started from the Internet to the company, the customer's configuration is not necessary. However, if the attack is occurring in both directions, possibly because an internal customer device was compromised and used as a reflector, setting up rate limiting in both directions is typically necessary.

TIP   Remember that in DoS flood situations, you need to contact your ISP promptly and have it implement rate limiting in the outbound direction of its router's interface that connects to you. Using the configuration in Example 17-17 on your router still will cause you bandwidth problems on your link to the ISP if the attack is occurring from the outside; however, if your ISP is not cooperative, you can use this configuration on your perimeter router in the ingress direction, restricting the Smurf traffic to your internal devices.

Rate Limiting for TCP SYN and Other TCP Floods

You also can use rate limiting to limit the effect of TCP SYN flood attacks. Example 17-18 shows a configuration for a T1 link, which assumes that the hacker's source IP address is 201.1.1.1.

Example 17-18 *Using CAR to Rate-Limit TCP SYN Floods*

```
Router(config)# access-list 100 deny tcp any host 192.1.1.1 established
Router(config)# access-list 100 permit tcp any host 192.1.1.1
Router(config)# interface serial0
Router(config-if)# rate-limit input access-group 100 8000 4000 4000
  conform-action transmit exceed-action drop
```

Example 17-18 assumes that the configuration is applied on the customer's router. Notice something interesting about the ACL in this example. It uses the **established** keyword to block out all TCP packets except TCP SYN, which is used to establish connections, from being rate limited. Also, it restricts the TCP SYNs from any attacking host to the 192.1.1.1 server; other traffic sent to other internal servers is not rate limited by this configuration.

How to Choose a Rate Limit

If you suspect that you are under a TCP SYN flood or ICMP flood attack, you will want to set up rate limiting for your traffic. If you are not sure of the source of the attack, you can set up rate limiting to the full bandwidth of the link and then use the **show interfaces rate-limit** command to determine how you actually should set the rates in the **rate-limit** command.

Here is a simple example. Assume that you have a T1 connection to the Internet and that you suspect that your web servers in your DMZ are under some kind of TCP SYN flood attack; however, you are not absolutely sure. In this situation, configure CAR (assuming a T1 link) as displayed in Example 17-19.

Example 17-19 *Configuring CAR for a T1 Link*

```
Router(config)# access-list 100 permit tcp any host eq www established
Router(config)# access-list 101 permit tcp any host eq www
Router(config)# interface serial0
Router(config-if)# rate-limit output access-group 100 1544000 64000 64000
  conform-action transmit exceed-action drop
Router(config-if)# rate-limit output access-group 101 64000 16000 16000
  conform-action transmit exceed-action drop
```

In Example 17-19, there are two ACL statements. The first ACL statement looks for any web traffic that is established. The second one looks only for any web traffic. Notice that, with the rate limiting, the first **rate-limit** command allows full bandwidth for already established connections (ACL #101); the second command limits the initial setup of the HTTP connection (the TCP SYNs).

A couple things should be pointed out about this configuration. First, in the first **rate-limit** command, you need to replace the 1,544,000 bps value to match the actual speed of your interface. Second, do not choose arbitrary rate-limiting values for the second **rate-limit** command for the TCP SYN setup of the web connections. Before you define any limits, you should understand your traffic patterns: Putting in a value that is too small or too large might create additional problems. Use the **show interfaces rate-limit** command to tune this process.

TIP   Before implementing CAR, make sure that you have a baseline of traffic flowing through the router under normal circumstances, categorized by traffic type and destination addresses.

Rate Limiting for W32.Blaster Worm

As you might have experienced firsthand, dealing with a worm attack can be a hair-raising experience, especially because most worm attacks either purposefully or inadvertently cause a DoS attack, sucking up bandwidth and causing problems for other applications and services in your network. Assuming that you know the protocols and ports that these worms are using, you can set up rate limiting, using CAR, to limit the bandwidth that they can use.

Consider the W32 Blaster worm as an example. Example 17-20 shows a sample CAR configuration to rate limit the bandwidth to traffic on the ports used by the worm.

Example 17-20 *Using CAR to Rate Limit the W32 Blaster Worm*

```
Router(config)# access-list 199 permit udp any any eq 135
Router(config)# access-list 199 permit udp any any eq 139
Router(config)# access-list 199 permit tcp any any eq 135
Router(config)# access-list 199 permit tcp any any eq 135
Router(config)# access-list 199 permit udp any any eq 445
Router(config)# access-list 199 permit tcp any any eq 445
Router(config)# access-list 199 deny ip any any
Router(config)# interface vlan10
Router(config-if)# rate-limit input access-group rate-limit 199
  256000 64000 64000
  conform-action transmit exceed-action drop
```

NOTE   It is important to point out that you typically are not allowing the previous ports into your network—at least, you should not be. Therefore, this kind of rate limiting typically is done internal to your network on which you have a worm infection that is running rampant. In the previous example, this was done on a 3550 Catalyst switch, to limit the bandwidth for these connections and to limit the impact of the worm. Also make sure that whatever bandwidth limits you have imposed are high enough to allow at least some legitimate traffic of the same type, but low enough to allow other types of traffic. When you have eradicated the worm from your network by updating your antivirus software and applying the appropriate patches, remove the CAR configuration for this traffic because it also can affect legitimate traffic.

NBAR

I discussed NBAR in Chapter 10, "Filtering Web and Application Traffic," and Chapter 15, "Routing Protocol Protection." In Chapter 10, I used NBAR to drop P2P traffic. In Chapter 15, I used NBAR to route unwanted or undesirable traffic to a null interface. You also can use NBAR to limit packet rates of either undesirable traffic or flooding traffic. The configuration of NBAR for rate limiting is actually very similar to using it for policing, with a few minor differences.

NOTE   Cisco recommends using NBAR instead of other rate-limiting features when trying to deal with DoS attacks.

File-Sharing and P2P Programs

I have walked into many environments where P2P programs are using up a lot of a company's bandwidth, but the company's security policy does not explicitly prohibit their use. In one particular situation, many managers and officers of the corporation used these as well as Instant Messenger products and wanted to continue their use, even though they did not really add to the company's bottom line. In this situation, I recommended that the director of networking implement rate limiting for these kinds of products. In this situation, employee file sharing was much slower in their downloads, but employees still were able to access P2P sites, as well as legitimate applications that did not suffer from the burden of these programs.

Smurf Example

Instead of rehashing the syntax of the NBAR configuration commands, which were covered in Chapter 10, I display in this section an example configuration and focus on one new command, **police**, which specifies the policing action to take. This section uses the Smurf attack as an example. Example 17-21 shows the code.

Example 17-21 *Using NBAR to Rate Limit Smurf Traffic*

```
Router(config)# access-list 100 permit icmp any any echo          (1)
Router(config)# access-list 100 permit icmp any any echo-reply
Router(config)# class-map match-any smurf-attacks                 (2)
Router(config-cmap)# match access-group 100
Router(config-cmap)# exit
Router(config)# policy-map mark-smurf                             (3)
Router(config-pmap)# class smurf-attacks
Router(config-pmap-c)# set ip dscp 1
Router(config-pmac-c)# exit
Router(config)# interface ethernet1
```

Example 17-21 *Using NBAR to Rate Limit Smurf Traffic (Continued)*

```
Router(config-if)# description ***To the ISP***
Router(config-if)# service-policy input mark-smurf                    (4)
Router(config-if)# exit
Router(config)# class-map match-any smurf-marked                      (5)
Router(config-cmap)# match dscp 1
Router(config-cmap)# exit
Router(config)# police-map limit-smurfs                               (6)
Router(config-pmap)# class smurf-marked
Router(config-pmap-c)# police 64000 4000 4000
  conform-action transmit exceed-action drop violation drop
Router(config)# interface ethernet0
Router(config-if)# description ***To the Internal Network***
Router(config-if)# service-policy output limit-smurfs                 (7)
```

The following is an explanation of the configuration in Example 17-21, with reference to the numbering on the right side:

1 ACL 100 defines the traffic that I am limiting. Smurf uses ICMP echos and echo replies.

2 The **class-map** command looks for this traffic with the **match access-group** command.

3 The policy map marks all packets matched in the **class-map** command with a DSCP value of 1.

4 The policy map is activated on the perimeter router's external interface, marking traffic as it comes from the Internet and enters this network.

5 Remember that NBAR cannot perform two policies on one interface, such as mark and drop, or mark and limit. Therefore, a separate policy must be created. In Step 5, a second class map is created, looking for the packets (ICMP) that had their DSCP value set to 1.

6 The **police-map** command specifies the policy to be applied to this traffic. In this instance, I first reference the class map, which matches on packets with the DSCP value set to 1. Second, the **police** command is used to enforce rate limiting. This is very similar to CAR's **rate-limit** command. The only difference between this command and the **police** command is that the latter command supports an additional parameter, **violation**, which is optional and specifies the action to take if both the normal and excessive burst sizes are violated. In the previous example, ICMP traffic is limited to an average throughput of 64 kbps, with a burst of 4 kbps. If either of these limits is exceeded, the policy is to drop these excessive ICMP messages.

7 The last step is to activate the second policy map on the router's internal interface (or interfaces, if there is more than one internal interface). After it is activated on the internal interface, the second policy map enforces rate limiting for packets that have their DSCP value set to 1.

Use the **show policy-map interface** command to examine the matching process on Ethernet1 and the policing process on Ethernet0.

As I mentioned in Chapters 10 and 15, NBAR is a multifunctional tool that can be very useful in implementing security measures, which is not what Cisco initially had in mind when offering this feature. Given the last example, you easily can modify it to suite other types of attacks, such as an attack by the SQL Slammer worm. You only need to modify the ACL that looks for the offending traffic.

You even can use this process to limit the bandwidth for other types of traffic that are not necessary for business purposes, such as instant messenger, P2P, and other programs. This approach still allows your users to use these programs, but it limits the bandwidth that they can use. In this situation, however, your first class map looks for the traffic and is applied to the inside interface of your perimeter router, and the policing policy is applied to the external interface.

W32.Blaster Worm Example

In the "CAR" section, I discussed how to use rate limiting to limit the effectiveness of the W32.Blaster worm. I use this worm as an example to set up NBAR to implement rate limiting. Example 17-22 shows the basic configuration for NBAR to rate limit the W32.Blaster worm.

Example 17-22 *Using NBAR to Rate Limit the W32.Blaster Worm*

```
Router(config)# ip nbar port-map netbios1 tcp 135 139 445          (1)
Router(config)# ip nbar port-map netbios2 udp 135 139 445
Router(config)# class-map match-any w32blaster-attack              (2)
Router(config-cmap)# match protocol netbios1
Router(config-cmap)# match protocol netbios2
Router(config-cmap)# exit
Router(config)# policy-map mark-w32blaster                         (3)
Router(config-pmap)# class w32blaster-attack
Router(config-pmap-c)# set ip dscp 1
Router(config-pmac-c)# exit
Router(config)# interface ethernet1
Router(config-if)# description ***To the ISP***
Router(config-if)# service-policy input mark-w32blaster            (4)
Router(config-if)# exit
Router(config)# class-map match-any mark-w32blaster                (5)
Router(config-cmap)# match dscp 1
Router(config-cmap)# exit
Router(config)# police-map limit-w32blaster                        (6)
Router(config-pmap)# class w32blaster-marked
Router(config-pmap-c)# police 64000 4000 4000
  conform-action transmit exceed-action drop violation drop
Router(config)# interface ethernet0
Router(config-if)# description ***To the Internal Network***
Router(config-if)# service-policy output limit-w32blaster          (7)
```

In Statement 1, the first two commands create a custom protocol for NBAR, called netbios, which includes both TCP and UDP ports 135, 139, and 445. Statement 2 points to the custom protocol that you defined for NBAR. All of the other Statements (3 through 7) refer to the same steps that you performed in setting up NBAR for Smurf attacks.

NOTE   Setting up NBAR to rate limit other types of attacks, including other worms, necessitates that you set up rate limiting similar to the Smurf or W32.Blaster configuration.

Summary

This chapter showed you the basics of dealing with DoS attacks. If you suspect that you are under a DoS attack, examine your router's CPU and memory utilization, and look for abnormalities. You also can examine your ACL counters to see if a specific kind of traffic is increasing in an unusual manner. You can use ACL logging to gather more information about the attack, but this is process intensive for the router. In this situation, I recommend using NetFlow to gather information about the attack.

For TCP SYN flood attacks, you can use the router's TCP Intercept feature. However, if you already have the Cisco IOS Firewall feature set installed on your router, use CBAC's timeouts and thresholds to limit the effectiveness of a DoS attack.

In many cases, you need to limit the amount of traffic generated by the DoS attack, to allow legitimate traffic while you track down the culprit of the attack. For ICMP attacks, you can use ICMP rate limiting. You also can use CAR or NBAR.

Next up is Chapter 18, which shows you how to configure your router to produce logging information, as well as how to examine this information.

## CHAPTER 18

Logging Events

This chapter discusses how to set up logging on your perimeter router. Logging is an important process in keeping track of events that occur in your network, especially on your perimeter router. On your perimeter router, you definitely will want to keep track of intrusions and attacks, and the router's logging function can greatly assist in this process.

In this chapter, you learn how to use the various log facilities of a Cisco router, including the console, buffer, and syslog locations. Because timing and time stamps are important for understanding the sequence of events, this chapter covers how to set up time on your router, including manual time settings and the Network Time Protocol (NTP).

New in Cisco IOS 12.3(2)T is the Embedded Syslog Manager (ESM) feature, which allows your router to perform tasks based on the type or severity of a log message. ESM uses Tcl, which provides a lot of flexibility in coding what actions your router will perform. I also discuss other third-party products that you can use to make the management of your log files easier.

These topics are covered in this chapter:

- Basic logging
- Time and date and the Cisco IOS, including manual time configuration and NTP
- Embedded syslog manager
- Additional logging information, including logging tools

Basic Logging

Log messages commonly are referred to as *system error messages* in the Cisco IOS. Each of these messages has a severity level assigned to it, along with a description indicating the seriousness of the problem or event. The Cisco IOS sends logging messages, including output from **debug** commands, to a logging process. By default, this is only the console interface; however, you can log messages to the router's internal buffer; terminal lines, such as the auxiliary and vtys; a syslog server; and an SNMP management station.

Log Message Format

Log messages take the following format on a Cisco IOS device:

```
%<facility>-<severity>-<mnemonic>: <message_text>
```

Here is a simple example:

```
%LINK-5-CHANGED: Interface Ethernet1, changed state to
   administratively down
```

Assuming that you have enabled time stamps, as well as sequence numbers, for your log message, you will see the following, with the sequence number first, followed by the time stamp and then the actual message:

```
000022: Jan 02 15:42:11.048:%LINK-5-CHANGED: Interface Ethernet0,
   changed state to administratively down
```

Adding time stamps and sequence numbers to your router's logging output is discussed in the "Date and Time Stamps" section.

Basic Logging Configuration

You will want to do two basic tasks when setting up logging: enable logging and control the display of logging on your lines. The following two sections discuss these two configuration tasks.

Enabling Logging

By default, logging is enabled on your router for the console line only. Logging must be enabled and configured for any other logging destination. To enable logging, use the following command:

```
Router(config)# logging on
```

Using the **logging on** command, you enable any other configured destination for logging, such as a syslog server or the router's internal buffer, for logging. This command must be enabled before you can log system messages to locations other than the console port; however, you can control individually which processes will receive logging messages with other **logging** commands, as discussed later in the "Logging Destinations" section. For example, if you have configured commands for logging messages to a syslog server but you have not executed the **logging on** command, the Cisco IOS logs messages only to the console line.

Configuring Synchronous Logging

The main purpose of the **logging synchronous** command is to synchronize the logging output for messages and debug output to the router's lines: console, auxiliary, and VTY. For example, one annoying thing about logging events on your router's lines is that you might be typing in a command, and the router displays a message on the line right in the middle of your typing. This message has no bearing on the command that you are typing, and you can continue typing to complete your command; however, this behavior can be annoying.

The main purpose of synchronous logging is to control when messages are displayed on your router's lines. When it is enabled, synchronous logging causes the Cisco IOS to display the message and then perform the equivalent of a ctrl-R, which causes the router to redisplay the information that you have typed on the command line. Example 18-1 shows a simple example of the process without synchronous logging.

Example 18-1 *Displaying Logging Information Without Synchronous Logging*

```
Router(config)# end
Router# show ru
2w2d: %SYS-5-CONFIG_I: Configured from console by consolenning-config
```

Notice how the command **show running-config** was interrupted by a Cisco IOS log message. If you enabled synchronous logging, you would see the output in Example 18-2 instead.

Example 18-2 *Displaying Logging Information with Synchronous Logging*

```
Router(config)# end
Router# show run
2w2d: %SYS-5-CONFIG_I: Configured from console by console
Router# show run
```

In Example 18-2, in the middle of typing the **show running-config** command, a log message was placed on the screen. Then the information that you previously entered on the command-line interface (CLI) is redisplayed.

You can affect the displaying of log messages to your lines with the **logging synchronous** command, shown here:

```
Router(config)# line type #
Router(config-line)# logging synchronous
  [level severity_level | all] [limit #_of_lines]
```

The severity level refers to the severity level of logging messages that are printed asynchronously. Messages with a severity number higher than this value are displayed synchronously (less severe messages); messages with a lower number (more severe) are displayed asynchronously. The default severity level is 2. The **all** parameter causes all messages to be displayed asynchronously, regardless of their assigned security level.

The **limit** parameter specifies how many synchronous messages should be queued up before the router starts dropping new messages. The default value is 20 messages. If the router has to drop messages because it reaches this threshold, you will see the following log message indicating the number of messages that the router had to drop:

```
%SYS-3-MSGLOST #_of_messages due to overflow
```

NOTE	The main disadvantage of synchronous logging is that when your router is generating a lot of messages and you are typing slowly in the CLI, the router must drop any messages above this threshold. Thus, you never will see these messages on your lines. If it is critical that you see these kinds of events, I highly recommend that you log them to either the router's internal buffer, a syslog server, or an SNMP management station.

CAUTION	Be careful about setting large queue limits to nonconsole lines, such as VTYs. If a hacker has access to a VTY on your router and synchronous logging is enabled for your VTYs, the hacker could leave the VTY idle in the middle of a command in the CLI. This would cause the Cisco IOS to fill up the large queue with messages, possibly consuming your router's entire memory. In certain cases, the router stops handling other processes, such as traffic forwarding. In the worst case, the router might reload itself.

Logging Destinations

You can forward logging information to four basic destinations:

- Lines
- Internal buffer
- Syslog server
- SNMP management station

The following sections discuss how to set up logging using these destination options, after covering log messages and security levels.

Severity Levels

Before I discuss logging to the four destination types, I need to cover log messages and security levels. Each log message is associated with a security level, which ranks the seriousness of the message: The lower the number is, the more severe the message is. Severity levels range from 0 (the highest) to 7 (the lowest). Table 18-1 contains an overview of the severity levels. The Parameter column gives the name of the logging level. The Level column lists the corresponding severity level. With the **logging** commands, you can specify the severity by number or name.

NOTE	If you use the **log** keyword in an ACL statement, this output will be displayed on the console only if the severity level is set to 6 or 7.

Table 18-1   *Severity Levels for Logging Messages*

Parameter	Level	Syslog Description	Description
emergencies	0	LOG_EMERG	The system is unusable.
alerts	1	LOG_ALERT	Immediate action is required on your part.
critical	2	LOG_CRIT	A critical condition exists on the router.
errors	3	LOG_ERR	An error condition exists on the router.
warnings	4	LOG_WARNING	A warning condition exists on the router.
notifications	5	LOG_NOTICE	A normal but significant event occurred on the router.
informational	6	LOG_INFO	An informational event occurred on the router.
debugging	7	LOG_DEBUG	This is output from **debug** commands.

One thing that you can control for logging functions is which messages are logged for the four destinations. For example, on the console, you could limit logging to messages at severity level 4 (which displays messages from 0 to 4); but for a syslog server, you could set it to 6 (0 to 6).

Line Logging

Two commands are used for controlling logging messages sent to the router's lines:

```
Router(config)# logging console [severity_level]
Router(config)# logging monitor [severity_level]
```

It is important to point out that the **logging console** command refers to logging to physical TTYs, such as the console and auxiliary lines. The **logging monitor** command refers to logging to logical VTYs, such as Telnet sessions. By default, logging to the console is enabled for all levels; however, you can modify this by changing the severity level in the **logging console** command. Valid severity parameters are listed in the first column of Table 18-1.

Logging to VTYs and the AUX is disabled by default and requires that you either execute the privileged EXEC **terminal monitor** command, which duplicates console logging messages to the VTYs, or configure the **logging monitor** command. If you use the latter approach, you do not need to execute the **terminal monitor** command to see TTY line log output when you initially access a router's VTY. When configuring the **logging monitor** command, if you do not specify the severity level, it defaults to 7 (debug).

Note that, with both commands, you still must enable logging with the **logging on** command.

Because of the processing burden placed on routers to log messages to terminal lines, such as the console, I highly recommend changing the severity level to something higher than debug (lower number). If you need to see messages with lower severity levels, use either the router's internal buffer, a syslog server, or an SNMP management station.

CAUTION   If you disable the **logging on** command in the middle of a process generating error or debug messages, the router might slow down considerably until these messages are displayed on the line of the router. Therefore, be careful about the severity level assigned to logging messages displayed on the console line.

Internal Buffer Logging

One problem of logging messages to TTYs or VTYs is that if you are not actually looking at the screen for the attached line and the message scrolls past the screen and out of your terminal software's history buffer, there is no mechanism to see missed messages. This problem can be alleviated by logging the messages to a destination other than a line.

One solution is to log messages to the router's internal buffer, which is either enabled or disabled by default, depending on the router platform; in most platforms, it is enabled by default. To set up logging to the router's buffer, use the following command:

```
Router(config)# logging buffered [buffer_size | severity_level]
```

This command has two parameters. The *buffer_size* parameter refers to the size, in bytes, that should be allocated to the internal buffer. This can be from 4096 to 4,294,967,295 bytes. To set the buffer size back to the factory default, use the **default logging buffered** command. The *severity_level* parameter refers to the severity level of messages that should be logged, as discussed in Table 18-1. Note that the default size and severity level (typically 7) depend on the router platform model.

CAUTION   Be careful about setting the size of the buffer too large: With many messages, this can cause the router to run out of memory, possibly causing it to crash.

Syslog Server Logging

Enabling logging to a syslog server is slightly more complicated than setting up logging to a line or to the internal buffer, where either no configuration command or a couple of configuration commands are necessary. Here are the basic commands to set up logging to a syslog server:

```
Router(config)# logging on
Router(config)# logging host {IP_address | hostname}
Router(config)# logging trap severity_level
Router(config)# logging source-interface interface_type interface_#
Router(config)# logging origin-id {hostname | ip | string string}
Router(config)# logging facility facility_type
```

The **logging on** command allows logging to nonconsole destinations. The **logging host** command specifies either the IP address, the host name, or the fully qualified domain name (FQDN) of the syslog server. If you enter this command more than once with a different syslog server destination, you can build a list of syslog servers that the router can use. However, the more servers you list, the more duplication of log messages the router must process.

NOTE   Before Cisco IOS 12.2(15)T, trap logging was enabled using the **logging** {*hostname* | *IP_address*} command. Now, use the **logging host** command.

The **logging trap** command specifies the severity level of log messages to send to the syslog server. The default is **informational**; these parameters were discussed in Table 18-1.

By default, whichever interface the router uses to reach the syslog server is the IP address placed in the source IP address field of the IP packet header. To create consistent log entries so that the same address is used on a router, use the **logging source-interface** command. With this command, you must specify the name and number of the interface, as in ethernet 0. This command is necessary only if the router has two or more interfaces to reach the syslog server, but you want to ensure that, for consistency, the same source address is used in the syslog packets. This makes it easier to implement filtering rules to prevent unwanted log messages on the syslog server.

In 12.2(15)T, Cisco added the capability to insert information about the router's identity into the syslog message, making it easier to search for or separate information on the syslog server on a per-router basis. This is accomplished with the **logging origin-id** command, which is disabled by default. Your identification choices are **hostname** (the name configured with the **hostname** command), **ip** (the IP address of the sending interface), and **string** (a string you defined that is used to identify the router). If the string contains spaces, you must enclose it in quotation marks.

The **logging facility** command defines the facility to use on a syslog server running UNIX, where the log messages will be stored. The Cisco IOS supports the facility types listed in Table 18-2.

If you do not specify a facility, it defaults to local7. On a UNIX system, you can specify the location of the log file for the facility that you specify by editing the appropriate configuration file. For example, on a BSD 4.3 UNIX system, edit the /etc/syslog.conf file and create an entry for your facility. Here is a simple example:

```
local7.debugging /usr/adm/logs/router.log
```

Table 18-2 *Syslog Facility Types*

Parameter	Description
auth	Authorization system
cron	Cron facility
daemon	System daemon
kern	Kernel
local0 through **local7**	Locally defined messages (facilities 0 to 7)
lpr	Printer system
mail	E-mail system
news	USENET news
sys9 through **sys14**	System use
syslog	System log
user	User process
uucp	UNIX-to-UNIX copy system

In this example, the facility level is local7 and the **debugging** keyword specifies the syslog logging level. The syslog level affects which levels of messages are stored in the filename that follows: Any message at this severity level or higher is stored in the specified file (/usr/adm/logs/router.log).

To sum up the configuration of a syslog server, see the network shown in Figure 18-1.

Figure 18-1 *Description*

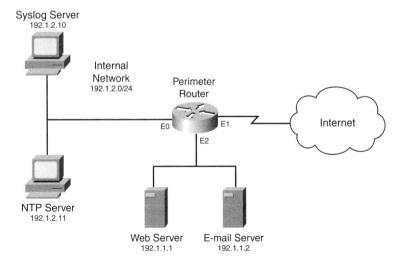

Example 18-3 shows the router's configuration.

Example 18-3 *Setting Up Basic Syslog Logging on a Router*

```
Router(config)# logging on
Router(config)# logging host 192.1.2.10
Router(config)# logging trap informational
Router(config)# logging source-interface ethernet 0
Router(config)# logging origin-id string Perimeter1
```

This example is straightforward. The first command enables logging. The second command specifies the internal syslog server, and the third command sets the logging severity level. The fourth command specifies that the source IP address of ethernet 0 should be used in syslog packets. The last statement sets the origin information to Perimeter1, which appears in the log messages, making it easier to search for log messages from this router.

SNMP Logging

The last location that you can have log messages sent to is an SNMP management station. I briefly discussed the configuration of SNMP in Chapter 3, "Accessing a Router." In this section, I focus only on the configuration of commands to log information to the management station. To enable log messages to be sent to an SNMP management station, you first need to execute the following command:

```
Router(config)# snmp-server enable trap syslog
```

After this, three commands control logging information to the management station:

```
Router(config)# logging on
Router(config)# logging history severity_level
Router(config)# logging history size number
```

I already discussed the use of the first command. The second command specifies the severity level of log messages that should be sent to the SNMP management station. The default level is **warning** (you can see the list of severity levels in Table 18-1). Because SNMP uses UDP, and UDP is unreliable, syslog traps are stored in a history table on the router. At least one syslog message, the most recent one, is stored in the history table (the default is one message). You can increase this up to 500 with the **logging history size** command.

NOTE   Starting with Cisco IOS 12.2(1.4), you can have the Cisco IOS log each NAT translation that it builds by using the **ip nat log translations syslog** command. This can be useful in troubleshooting address-translation problems.

Other Logging Commands

This section covers three miscellaneous logging commands: adding time stamps to log messages, adding sequence numbers to log messages, and rate limiting log messages.

Date and Time Stamps

By default, log messages do not include a date and time stamp. Having a date and time stamp included on each log message is useful in determining when events occurred, especially if you are not sitting in front of the console monitoring the events. To enable date and time stamps, use one of the two following commands:

```
Router(config)# service timestamps {debug | log} uptime
```

or:

```
Router(config)# service timestamps {debug | log} datetime
  [msec] [localtime] [show-timezone] [year]
```

Time stamps can be added to two types of messages: debug and logging messages. The **debug** parameter causes the Cisco IOS to include a time stamp in debug output. The **log** parameter causes the Cisco IOS to include a time stamp in any type of log message. The first command, with the **uptime** parameter, has the Cisco IOS include the amount of time since the router has been up in the message. Here is an example:

```
1w0d: %SYS-5-CONFIG_I: Configured from console by console
```

In this example, the router had been up 1 week and 0 days when this message was generated.

If you want an exact date and time, use the **datetime** parameter. This parameter causes the Cisco IOS to include the date and time along with the message (the date and time are in a UTC format). Here is the standard format: MMM DD HH:MM:SS. When using the **datetime** parameter, you have some optional parameters. The **msec** parameter causes the Cisco IOS to include milliseconds in the message. **localtime** causes the Cisco IOS to display the time based on the time zone configured locally on the router. By default, the year is not included in the time, but using the optional **year** parameter overrides this behavior. The **show-timezone** parameter causes the Cisco IOS to include the time zone name in the output of the date and time. Here is a simple example in which the **log** parameter was used with **datetime**, **localtime**, and **show-timezone:**

```
.May 23 11:13:25 UTC: %SYS-5-CONFIG_I: Configured from console by console
```

You will notice something interesting about the previous message: It begins with a period (.). A log message begins with one of three characters: a blank, an asterisk, or a period. Table 18-3 explains the use of these characters. In the previous example, the router's clock was in sync with an NTP time server, but it lost connectivity to the server, so the router's time might not be exactly correct. Basically, these parameters reflect the authority or reliability of the time source.

Sequence Numbers

Besides adding time stamps to log messages, you can have the Cisco IOS display a sequence number in each message. This is accomplished with the following command:

```
Router(config)# service sequence-numbers
```

Table 18-3 *Log Message Beginning Character*

Parameter	Name	Description
	Blank	The router's clock has been set manually or is in synch with a Network Time Protocol (NTP) time server. (NTP is discussed at the end of this chapter.)
*	Asterisk	The router's clock has not been set or is not in sync with an NTP server.
.	Period	The router's clock was in synch but has lost contact with an NTP server.

Here is an example with both sequence numbers and time stamps enabled:

```
000039: .Dec 30 11:38:541 EST: %SYS-5-CONFIG_I: Configured from
   console by console
```

In this example, the sequence number is 39, indicating the 39th message that was logged.

Rate Limits

Starting in Cisco IOS 12.1(3)T, you can limit the rate of logging messages on a per-second basis with the **logging-rate** command, shown here:

```
Router(config)# logging rate-limit
   {number | all  number | console number} [except severity]
```

By default, no limits are configured on the router. By specifying a number between 1 and 10,000, you are limiting the number of logging messages per second to this value. The **all** keyword, followed by a number, affects all logging and debugging messages. The **console** keyword limits the rate of logging messages to the console. The **except** parameter creates an exception for the messages at the specified severity level and higher.

Example 18-4 shows a simple example of configuring rate limiting for log messages.

Example 18-4 *Configuring Logging Rate Limiting*

```
Router(config)# logging rate-limit console 2 except 2
Router(config)# logging rate-limit 50 except 3
```

In this example, the first command limits logging of messages to two per second to the console, unless the message severity level is between 0 and 2. The second command applies to rate limiting of all other log messages to 50 per second, except for those with a severity level between 0 and 3.

TIP   I highly recommend that you use this command, especially on the console interface, to reduce the overhead that the router must deal with when a flood of messages occurs because of an attack. You can use this command without taking an adverse performance hit.

Logging Verification

After you have configured logging, you can use various **show** commands to verify your logging configuration and operation.

show logging Command

The **show logging** command displays the current state of syslog error and event logging, including any configured syslog server addresses, which types of logging are enabled, and logging statistics. Here is the format of the command:

```
Router# show logging [summary]
```

Example 18-5 shows sample output from this command.

Example 18-5 *Using the* **show logging** *Command*

```
Router# show logging
Syslog logging: enabled (0 messages dropped, 1 messages rate-limited, 0 flushes)
      Console logging: level debugging, 31 messages logged, xml disabled
      Monitor logging: level debugging, 0 messages logged, xml disabled
      Buffer logging: disabled, xml disabled
      Logging Exception size (4096 bytes)
      Count and timestamp logging messages: enabled
      Trap logging: level informational, 187 message lines logged
         Logging to 192.1.2.10, 187 message lines logged
```

In this example, syslog logging has been enabled and one log message has been rate limited. Console and monitoring logging are enabled and set to a severity of debugging. Time stamps also are enabled. At the bottom, you can see that the logging level for traps (syslog) is informational, with a total of 187 messages logged to the syslog server at 192.1.2.10.

If you have enabled logging to the router's internal buffer, you also can see logging messages with the **show logging** command, as in Example 18-6.

Example 18-6 *Using the* **show logging** *Command to View Buffered Log Messages*

```
Router# show logging
Syslog logging:enabled (0 messages dropped, 0 flushes, 0 overruns)
    Console logging: level errors, 32 messages logged, xml disabled
    Monitor logging:level errors, 0 messages logged
    Buffer logging:level debugging, 106 messages logged
    Trap logging:level debugging, 121 message lines logged
       Logging to 192.1.2.10, 121 message lines logged
Log Buffer (6144 bytes):
Dec 11 13:18:49 EDT: NTP: Maxslew = 189739
Dec 11 14:16:42 EDT:%SYS-5-CONFIG:Configured from
    tftp://192.1.2.9/perimeter.cfg
<--output omitted-->
```

To clear the log messages from the internal buffer, use the **clear logging** command.

The **summary** option in the **show logging** command displays counts of messages by type, as in Example 18-7.

Example 18-7 *Using the* **summary** *Parameter with the* **show logging** *Command*

```
Router# show logging summary
+-----+-------+-------+------+-------+-------+-------+------+-------+
  SLOT | EMERG | ALERT | CRIT | ERROR |WARNING| NOTICE| INFO | DEBUG |
+-----+-------+-------+------+-------+-------+-------+------+-------+
|* 0* |   .   |   .   |  .   |   .   |   .   |   .   |  .   |   .   |
|  1  |       |       |      |       |       |       |      |       |
|  2  |       |       |      |   2   |   5   |   48  |      |       |
|  3  |       |       |      |       |       |       |      |       |
|  4  |       |       |      |   1   |   5   |   58  |      |       |
|  5  |       |       |      |       |       |       |      |       |
|  6  |       |       |      |       |       |       |      |       |
|  7  |       |       |      |  19   |   5   |   52  |      |       |
|  8  |       |       |      |       |       |       |      |       |
|  9  |       |       |      |   2   |   5   |   55  |      |       |
| 10  |       |       |      |       |       |       |      |       |
| 11  |       |       |      |   8   |   5   |   67  |      |       |
+-----+-------+-------+------+-------+-------+-------+------+-------+
```

The first column, SLOT, indicates which slot in the chassis the log messages apply to.

NOTE   The **show logging summary** command is supported only for certain router models. In other router models, the **show logging count** command is used, as discussed in the next section.

show logging history Command

The **show logging history** command displays the syslog history table size, the status of the messages in the table, and the messages themselves. Remember that the history table is used to log messages to an SNMP management station. Example 18-8 shows sample output from this command.

Example 18-8 *Using the* **show logging history** *Command*

```
Router# show logging history
Syslog History Table: 1 maximum table entries,
  saving level notifications or higher
0 messages ignored, 0 dropped, 8 table entries flushed,
SNMP notifications not enabled
  entry number 9: SYS-5-CONFIG_I
  Configured from console by console
  timestamp: 1120
```

In this example, the table size is the default value, 1, and any event at a severity level of notification or higher is logged. Eight entries were flushed from the table to make room for new ones. Currently, the latest entry in the table is entry no. 9.

Logging and Error Counts

Starting with Cisco IOS 12.2(8)T, Cisco introduced the Error Log Count feature. This is a useful feature if you are using the router's internal buffer and older messages are being aged out. With this feature, the Cisco IOS still keeps track of the number of occurrences of a particular log message, as well as the last occurrence of the message. This can be useful if the internal buffer cannot hold all of your messages, but the same error or problem continually is recurring and shows up in the output of your error counts. This feature basically supplants the **show logging summary** command discussed in the last section.

Enabling this features is simple. From configuration mode, execute the following command:

```
Router(config)# logging count
```

This command causes the Cisco IOS to count each log message, including the time stamp of the last occurrence for each message type.

After enabling this feature, you can see the error count with the **show logging count** command, as in Example 18-9.

Example 18-9 *Viewing Error Counts for Log Messages*

```
Router# show logging count
Facility        Message Name                            Sev Occur    Last Time
=============================================================================
SYS             BOOTTIME                                 6   1        00:00:15
SYS             RESTART                                  5   1        00:00:14
SYS             CONFIG_I                                 5   2        1d02h
------------    -----------------------------           --------------------
SYS TOTAL                                                    5

LINEPROTO       UPDOWN                                   5   13       00:00:21
------------    -----------------------------           --------------------
LINEPROTO TOTAL                                              13

LINK            UPDOWN                                   3   1        00:00:20
LINK            CHANGED                                  5   12       00:00:10
------------    -----------------------------           --------------------
LINK TOTAL                                                   13
<--output omitted-->
```

In Example 18-9, you can see that the messages are broken down by category.

Time and Date and the Cisco IOS

All Cisco IOS routers support manual and dynamic time services. Time services allow the router to keep track of the current date and time. Having your networking equipment synchronized to the same date and time is important when attempting to troubleshoot problems from syslog messages. This section discusses how to configure time on your router manually, as well as how to use the Network Time Protocol (NTP) to assign the time on your router dynamically. The following sections cover time sources that the router can use and how to configure the date and time manually as well as using NTP.

Router Time Sources

Most Cisco routers have a hardware and software clock, which can be managed separately. The following two sections discuss these two clocks.

Hardware Clock

The hardware clock, often called a system calendar clock, is a battery-powered clock that keeps track of the date and time even when the router is powered off. Most routers have a hardware clock. If no other time source is available, the router uses its hardware clock to provide the date and time. Because the clock is powered by a battery, if the battery dies, the clock defaults to a hard-configured date and time, as shown here:

```
00:00:00.000 UTC Mon Mar 1 1993
```

Software Clock

The router's software clock is the primary source for the date and time. It begins when the router starts up and ends when the router shuts down. Initially, the software clock gets the date and time from the hardware clock, when the router is booting up; however, the software clock can get its date and time from a number of sources, including these:

- NTP
- Simple Network Time Protocol (SNTP)
- CLI commands

Because the software clock can be updated dynamically from a more reliable source, like NTP, it typically has a more accurate date and time than the hardware clock.

The router uses the software clock to provide the date and time to the following services:

- The hardware clock
- NTP, if the router is an NTP server
- Log messages
- Debug messages
- Various **show** commands
- Time ranges in ACLs

The default time zone of the software clock is Coordinated Universal Time (UTC), which also is referred to as Greenwich Mean Time (GMT). However, you can override this with a manual configuration, in which you can specify the router's time zone as well as daylight savings time, sometimes referred to as summer time.

Manual Time and Date Configuration

If the hardware clock's battery is dead and you have no other time source to synchronize your router with, you can manually configure the current date and time after the router boots up. However, you should use this only as a last resort because you would have to change the time setting manually every time the router reboots. The following sections discuss how to configure your router's time settings manually.

Time Zone

As I mentioned at the beginning of this section, the default time zone is UTC. To change the time zone, use the **clock timezone** command, shown here:

```
Router(config)# clock timezone zone_name hours_offset
  [minutes_offset]
```

The *zone_name* parameter is the name of time zone. This is the standard acronym, such as EST for Eastern Standard Time. The *hours_offset* parameter is the number of hours, plus or minus, different from UTC. For example, New York City would be –5. Typically, the *minutes_offset* parameter is not used; however, certain time zones, such as Atlantic Canada Standard Time (AST) is 3.5 hours different from UTC. This is represented as –3 30. Here is a simple example for setting the time zone for a router in Orlando, Florida:

```
Router(config)# clock timezone EST -5
```

TIP   If you will be logging messages from routers in different time zones to a syslog server, Cisco recommends that you use UTC as the time zone on all your routers. This alleviates any confusion about two attacks occurring in two different time zones and determining whether the attacks are occurring simultaneously. This recommendation also applies to troubleshooting problems.

Daylight Saving Time

If your time zone follows daylight saving time (DST), commonly referred to as summer time, you can configure this setting on your router with the **clock summer-time** command. If your time zone uses the standard times and dates for the beginning and end of the summer time clock change, you can use this command to set up DST:

```
Router(config)# clock summer-time zone_name recurring
  [1-4 | first | last] [day month hh:mm day month hh:mm [offset_value]]
```

After you specify the name of the time zone, specify which week the time change occurs: 1 through 4 is the number of the week, **first** is the first week of the month, and **last** is the last week. If you do not specify the week, day, month, and time, it defaults to the standard for the time change. Likewise, if you omit the offset value, it defaults to 60 minutes, which is added to the current time when the first time is reached in the spring, and then is subtracted from the current time when the second time is reached in the fall. Here is a simple example, using the default settings, for Orlando, Florida:

```
Router(config)# clock summer-time EDT recurring
```

If your router uses nonstandard days for changing your clock's time, use either of the following two commands:

```
Router(config)# clock summer-time zone_name date
   month day year hh:mm month day year hh:mm [offset]
```

or:

```
Router(config)# clock summer-time zone_name date
   day month year hh:mm day month year hh:mm [offset]
```

With these two commands, you must specify the exact date and time when summer time begins and ends.

Software Clock Settings

If your router's software clock is synchronized to an external time source, such as an NTP server, it is not necessary to configure the software clock's time settings manually. However, if your router is not synchronized to an external time source, you can manually change the time on the router to set it correctly. This is accomplished with either of the following privileged EXEC commands:

```
Router# clock set hh:mm:ss date month year
```

or:

```
Router# clock set hh:mm:ss month date year
```

Here is a simple example:

```
Router# clock set 12:34:00 November 19 2003
```

If you want to resynchronize the software clock with the hardware clock, use this command:

```
Router# clock read-calendar
```

To view the time and date of the software clock, use the **show clock** command, as in Example 18-10.

Example 18-10 *Viewing the Date and Time of the Software Clock*

```
Router# show clock
12:34:58.015 EST Wed Nov 19 2003
```

The **show clock detail** command displays the current time as well as your clock settings, as shown in Example 18-11.

Example 18-11 *Using the* **show clock detail** *Command*

```
Router# show clock detail
12:35:51.431 EST Wed Nov 19 2003
Time source is user configuration
Summer time starts 02:00:00 EST Sun Apr 4 2004
Summer time ends 02:00:00 EDT Sun Oct 31 2004
```

Hardware Clock Settings

Normally, the only time that the hardware clock is used is initially to give the software clock the correct date and time when the router boots up. After this, the software clock is responsible for ensuring that the hardware clock is updated with the correct time. This way, if you are using NTP and the clock battery in your router is dead, NTP will update the software clock, which, in turn, updates the hardware clock with the correct date and time. The software clock does this at regular intervals.

To change the time of the hardware clock manually, use either of the two following commands:

```
Router# calendar set hh:mm:ss day month year
```

or:

```
Router# calendar set hh:mm:ss month day year
```

Note that the **calendar set** command is not supported on all router models. Use the **show calendar** command to view the time of the hardware clock.

To set the hardware clock from the software clock, use the following command:

```
Router# clock update-calendar
```

Network Time Protocol Overview

NTP, which runs on top of UDP, is an IP protocol used to synchronize time across devices in a network. NTP supports three versions; the newest version, version 3, is defined in RFC 1305. NTP uses a client/server function.

Time Distribution

The server is an authoritative source of time and, as such, should have the most correct time among all devices. This can be supplied by a radio or atomic clock, or even a GPS device. NTP uses the term *stratum* to describe how many hops away the source of time is. For example, a stratum 1 time source is the NTP master server with a reliable clocking mechanism that the server uses to derive time. Each part of your network might have an additional NTP server. These servers are stratum 2 time sources because they derive their time from the

NTP master server. The servers are responsible for giving the time to other lower-stratum servers as well as clients.

NOTE	Cisco routers can be NTP servers. In this function, I highly recommend that you not use the router's hardware clock. Instead, attach an external timing device. Cisco routers do not support radio or atomic clocks for external timing devices, but they do support certain GPS devices. I discuss this later in the "NTP: Server" section.

Distribution of time can be accomplished by the server periodically broadcasting the time or the client requesting the time periodically from the server. When the broadcast method is used in a Layer 2 network, it ensures that, because only one packet is sent, all devices typically have the same time, within a millisecond or so of each other. However, broadcasting has two problems:

- It is easy to spoof, so your timing information could be corrupted.
- It does not work well in a Layer 3 network.

Because of these problems, most NTP implementations have the clients periodically request the time from the server. NTPv3 does support authentication, which greatly reduces the likelihood that a spoofing attack will occur on your timing infrastructure; however, this feature is supported only in client polling, not broadcasting.

Simple Network Time Protocol

A simplified form of NTP, called the Simple Network Time Protocol (SNTP), can be used on clients to derive time, but not to pass time to other devices. For example, when using SNTP, the old (and discontinued) Cisco 1000 series routers, can only accept time from an NTP server; they cannot, in turn, pass the timing information to devices behind them. Unlike the NTP distribution method, SNTP typically provides accuracy of time within 100 milliseconds, and it does not support authentication (NTPv3). Because of these limitations, SNTP should be used only if your router does not support NTPv3.

The remaining part of this section deals with how to configure NTP on your router. I focus on three areas: how to configure your router as a client, how to configure your router as a server, and how to verify your NTP configuration.

Router Client Configuration for NTP

By default, NTP is disabled on all your router's interfaces. Your router, acting as a client, can use two methods to gain the most up-to-date time from an NTP server: periodically polling an NTP server or listening for periodic broadcasts from NTP servers. The following two sections discuss the configuration of both of these services.

Poll-Based Configuration

Clients can use two different polling modes to acquire their timing information from NTP servers:

- Client mode
- Symmetric active mode

In client mode, the client polls all NTP servers in its configuration for the time and then picks one server to use. This mode is a client/server mode, with the router acting as a client. This mode typically is used if the router will not be sending time to other devices. The **ntp server** command is used to specify the information to access the NTP servers.

In symmetric active mode, the router polls the configured time servers for the current time and also sends time to time servers. This mode typically is used to synchronize the group of NTP servers themselves at the same stratum level. The **ntp peer** command is used to specify the other NTP server peers of the router.

TIP   In either mode, a large number of polling requests by a router can affect memory and CPU resources. You should limit the number of peerings that a router has, as well as the number of clients that a router passes time to. In large networks, it is not uncommon to have a hierarchy of time sources to reduce this burden. An alternative solution for large Layer 2 networks is to use broadcasts to disseminate time, as discussed in the next section.

Here is the router command to define other NTP servers:

```
Router(config)# ntp {server | peer} IP_address [version number]
   [key keyid] [source interface] [prefer]
```

If the router is functioning as only a client, use the **server** parameter; otherwise, if the router is acting as a server and is peering to other servers, use the **peer** parameter. Following this is the IP address of the remote NTP server. If you do not specify the version number for NTP, it defaults to 3 (NTPv3). The optional **keyid** parameter references authentication information to be used to verify the server or peer's timing communications. I discuss this later. The **source** parameter specifies what IP address on the router to use as the source address in the IP packet header when sending communications to the remote NTP server. If you omit this parameter, it defaults to the address of the outgoing interface. When you are entering multiple NTP servers, you can use the **prefer** parameter, which specifies that this NTP server is preferred over other servers for synchronization purposes.

NOTE   If you are attempting to use NTPv3 and time synchronization is failing, you might want to try using NTPv2. However, remember that NTPv2 does not support authentication and is thus susceptible to spoofing attacks.

Broadcast-Based Configuration

Broadcast-based synchronization is preferred in larger Layer 2 networks, especially in networks where bandwidth, memory, and CPU resources are limited. Only one mode exists for broadcast-based configuration: broadcastclient mode. Unlike poll-based synchronization, in broadcastclient mode, the client passively listens for NTP broadcasts from an NTP server. Obviously, for this to work, the client and server must be in the same subnet. Enabling broadcastclient mode is done under a router's interface:

```
Router(config)# interface type [slot_#/]port_#
Router(config-if)# ntp broadcast client
Router(config-if)# ntp broadcastdelay microseconds
```

Enable this command only on the interface(s) on which you have NTP servers, to reduce the likelihood of an NTP server spoofing attack. The **ntp broadcast client** command enables the NTP client function on the specified interface to accept time broadcasts from NTP servers. The **ntp broadcastdelay** command is optional. By default, the router compensates for the time delay between the NTP server and the router by adding 3000 microseconds to the NTP servers' advertised time, to adjust for travel delay. You can change this to more accurately affect the delay. This value ranges from 1 to 999,999 microseconds.

SNTP Configuration

SNTP should be used only on routers that do not provide support for NTP. Some Cisco routers that do not provide support for NTP are the 1000, 1600, and 1700 series, depending on the software version running on them.

If your router will be polling the NTP server periodically, use this command:

```
Router(config)# sntp server {IP_address | hostname} [version number]
```

You need to specify only the IP address or hostname of the NTP server. The version number defaults to 1 if you omit it.

If your router will be using time synchronization broadcasts from an NTP server, use this command:

```
Router(config)# sntp broadcast client
```

NOTE   If you configure both of these commands, the router prefers the time from the configured server over broadcasts received from an NTP server. Also, because SNTP does not use authentication, it should be used only as a last resort for a time-synchronization solution.

Router Server Configuration for NTP

Besides performing client functions, a router can be an NTP server. This is very useful in remote office environments, in which the perimeter router at these locations can function as both a client and a server, acquiring timing information from the corporate NTP servers and then, acting as a server, passing this information to the remote office devices behind it.

Distributing Timing Information

I already discussed how to set up peer relationships between routers acting as NTP servers at the same stratum level (**ntp peer** command), as well as how a router can access timing information directly from a server at a higher level (**ntp server** command).

If your router, acting as an NTP server, will be using broadcasts to disseminate timing information, you need to configure the following command on each interface where you want your router to advertise its time synchronization information:

```
Router(config)# interface type [slot_#/]port_#
Router(config-if)# ntp broadcast [version number]
```

If you omit the version, it defaults to 3 (NTPv3).

Configuring an External Clock

As I mentioned at the beginning of the "Time Distribution" section, you can have your router act as an NTP server and obtain clocking information from an externally attached device. You would choose this option if you want your router to be the master NTP server in your network.

Cisco does not support stratum level 1 clocking services, such as atomic or radio clocks; however, it does support certain GPS-based devices (stratum level 2) that you can attach to your router. Your router then can use these devices to obtain timing information, which, in turn, can be redistributed through NTP. When attaching a GPS to a Cisco router, you need a free line. Typically, most administrators do not use the auxiliary port on the router for WAN or CLI communications, so you can attach the GPS device to this.

Not all routers support the attachment of an external clock to them. Cisco supports two types of GPS clocks:

- Trimble Palisade NTP synchronization kit (works only with the 7200 series routers)
- Symmetricom (Telecom-Solutions) GPS clock kit (works only with certain router models)

NOTE   Before you buy a GPS clock for your router, make sure that Cisco supports the GPS product and that your router has the capability to obtain timing information from it—only certain routers support this feature. If your router does not support this feature, you need some other device to use as a master time reference. Most UNIX and Windows server products support external GPS devices.

If you have the Trimble GPS clock and are attaching it to the auxiliary port of a 7200 router, you need to configure the following on your router:

```
Router(config)# line aux 0
Router(config-line)# ntp refclock trimble pps none stratum 1
```

The **ntp refclock** command tells the 7200 that it has a Trimble GPS clock attached. The **pps** parameter indicates the type of pulse-per-second reference support: In the case of Trimble, this is set to **none**. Because this is probably the root time source for your network, you define the time source as a stratum service level of 1.

If you are connecting a Symmetricom GPS product to your router's auxiliary port or TTY line, you use the following configuration:

```
Router(config)# ntp refclock telecom-solutions pps {cts | ri | none}
    [inverted] [pps-offset number]
    [stratum number] [timestamp-offset number]
```

Depending on the Symmetricom GPS product, you need to choose the pulse-per-second (PPS) option as either CTS, RI, or none. The **inverted** option indicates that the PPS pulse is inverted; the **pps-offset** option indicates the PPS pulse offset, in milliseconds. The **stratum** option refers to the NTP stratum level of service that this router will provide as a clock source. This can range from 0 to 15. If this router is the master clock, choose 1. You also can apply an offset to any time stamp that the router generates with the **timestamp-offset** option, which is specified in milliseconds.

Setting Up the NTP Server

If your router will be an authoritative NTP server, as typically would be the case if you attached a GPS unit to it, you must configure the following on your router:

```
Router(config)# ntp master [stratum_level]
```

NOTE	Be careful about using this command in a network that has other master NTP servers. The stratum level appropriately should affect the router's source of clocking information. If this router has the same stratum level of other NTP servers, time-keeping instability issues can arise if the NTP servers do not have their timing information synchronized.

NTP Security

You can take two security measures to create a more secure NTP environment for your router:

- Use access groups to restrict who can access the router's NTP resources.
- Use authentication with the MD5 hashing function to restrict NTP communications between trusted devices.

The following two sections discuss these solutions.

Access Groups

Access groups enable you to define a standard ACL that is used to filter types of NTP messages that the router receives. This feature is useful if your router is an NTP server and you want to restrict NTP access to it. The syntax of the command is as follows:

```
Router(config)# ntp access-group {query-only | serve-only |
    serve | peer} standard_ACL_#
```

Table 18-4 explains the different control options. When matched with a **permit** or **deny** statement in the specified standard ACL, only those communication processes are allowed or prohibited. If you have more than one **ntp access-group** statement defined, the first statement that matches in the first **ntp access-group** statement is used.

Table 18-4 *NTP Access Group Control Options*

Parameter	Description
query-only	Allows only NTP control queries from NTP devices in **permit** statements in the ACL
serve-only	Allows only time requests from NTP devices in **permit** statements in the ACL
serve	Allows time requests and NTP control queries from NTP devices in **permit** statements in the ACL
peer	Allows time requests and NTP control queries, and allows the router to synchronize to servers from NTP devices in **permit** statements in the ACL

Authentication

NTP supports authentication, which is used to validate NTP messages received from another NTP device. This authentication is similar to that used by routing protocols, such as OSPF and EIGRP, and PPP's CHAP. MD5 is used to create a cryptographic checksum, which is attached to the NTP message. A key, known to both sides, is used to create the authentication checksum. When enabled, if the checksum cannot be verified, the NTP message is ignored. One advantage that authentication has over access group control is that access group control is susceptible to IP spoofing attacks. Authentication does not rely on the IP address for authentication—instead, a shared secret key is used.

NOTE Because NTP authentication can be CPU intensive, depending on the router model, this might add a slight slew (where the router's time and the NTP server's time is slightly off) in your router's time value. The slower the router's processor is, the higher the slew value is. If timing is critical, you might want to forego authentication for smaller-end routers and use only access groups.

You need to configure three commands to set up authentication:

```
Router(config)# ntp authenticate
Router(config)# ntp authentication-key key_# md5 key_value
Router(config)# ntp trusted-key key_#
```

The **ntp authenticate** command enables NTP authentication. The **ntp authentication-key** command defines a reference number for the key (*key_#*) as well as the authentication key (the same *key_value* must be configured on the remote NTP device). Finally, the **ntp trusted-key** command specifies which NTP devices should be trusted with authentication, which prevents an accidental synchronization to a system that is not trusted. Notice that a reference number is used. This reference number must match the one used in the **ntp authentication-key** command. By using a key number, you can create multiple keys; this means that you can update keys more easily and can have different keys for different peers.

After you have defined authentication, you need to reference the key number in the **ntp {server | peer}** command, which tells the router which key to use when sending messages to specific peers.

Other NTP Commands

This last section on NTP configuration covers three miscellaneous commands. Earlier, I discussed how to specify the source IP address to be used in communications with other NTP devices (using the **ntp {server | peer}** command). However, you globally can specify the source IP address to use with the following NTP command:

```
Router(config)# ntp source interface
```

If you configure the interface in the **ntp {server | peer}** command, this configuration overrides the global configuration.

For routers that have a hardware clock, you can have the router update the hardware clock from the software clock; however, this is advisable only if the software clock is updated from a reliable NTP source. This is sometimes necessary because the hardware clock can drift slightly over time. To update the hardware clock from the software clock when using NTP, use the following command:

```
Router(config)# ntp update-calendar
```

Chapter 4, "Disabling Unnecessary Services," discussed disabling unnecessary services. With NTP, you can enable or disable it on an interface-by-interface basis. To prevent NTP attacks, disable NTP on interfaces that you will not be using to obtain time. For example, if you have a three-interface router—inside, outside, and DMZ—and your NTP server is off the inside interface, I highly recommend that you disable NTP on the other two interfaces. To disable NTP on an interface, use the following configuration:

```
Router(config)# interface type [slot_#/]port_#
Router(config-if)# ntp disable
```

NTP Verification

After you have configured NTP on your router, you can use various **show** commands to examine your configuration and troubleshoot problems. To see the current time on the router's software clock, use the **show clock** command; to see the time of the hardware clock, use **show calendar**.

NTP Commands

You use two basic commands to examine NTP information:

- **show ntp associations**
- **show ntp status**

The first command displays associations with other NTP devices. Example 18-12 displays sample output from the **show ntp associations** command.

Example 18-12 *Using the* **show ntp associations** *Command*

```
Router> show ntp associations
  address      ref clock    st when  poll reach delay offset  disp
*~192.1.2.11  192.1.2.11   2   31   1024  377    4.1  -8.38   1.5
* master (synced), # master (unsynced), + selected, - candidate,
    ~ configured
```

In Example 18-12, the first set of leading characters displays synchronization information:

- * This router is synchronized to this peer.
- \# This router is almost synchronized to this peer.
- \+ The peer has been selected for possible synchronization.
- \- The peer is a candidate for synchronization.
- \~ The peer has been statically configured.

The address column lists the addresses of the NTP peer devices. The ref clock column lists the addresses for where peers in the address column are getting their time. The st column indicates the stratum level of the peer. The when column indicates the time since the last NTP message was received from this peer. The poll column indicates the polling interval, in seconds, that this router is using to contact the specified peer. The reach column indicates the peer's reachability, in octal. The delay column displays the roundtrip delay, in milliseconds, to the peer. The offset column displays the relative time of the peer's clock to the local router's clock, in milliseconds.

The **show ntp status** command displays the status of NTP on the router. Example 18-13 shows sample output of the **show ntp status** command.

Example 18-13 *Using the* **show ntp status** *Command*

```
Router# show ntp status
Clock is synchronized, stratum 2, reference is 192.1.2.11
nominal freq is 250.0000 Hz, actual freq is 249.9990 Hz, precision is 2**19
reference time is AFE2525E.70597C87 (00:10:39.511 EDT Thu Jan 1 2004)
clock offset is 6.21 msec, root delay is 83.98 msec
root dispersion is 81.96 msec, peer dispersion is 2.02 msec
```

In Example 18-13, the router is synchronized with the NTP server at 192.1.2.11, which provides a stratum level 2 service.

NOTE   I want to point out that NTP updates to time on a device such as a router are done in small incremental changes. Therefore, when you first boot up your router, it might take a while before the router's software clock completely is synchronized with the NTP server. You will see this from the output of the **show ntp status** command. One way to speed up the synchronization is to configure the software clock on the router manually to be close to the time that the NTP server is advertising. I highly recommend this approach if your router has a dead battery for its hardware clock and you need to reboot it: After it has rebooted, manually set the time on the router to speed up the synchronization.

SNTP Command

Only one command is used to verify the configuration and operation of SNTP: **show sntp**. Example 18-14 shows sample output.

Example 18-14 *Verifying SNTP*

```
Router# show sntp
SNTP server      Stratum    Version    Last Receive
192.1.2.11       2          3          00:00:34     Synced  Bcast
Broadcast client mode is enabled.
```

In Example 18-14, one NTPv3 server, 192.1.2.11, provides a stratum level 2 service to this router. This router is learning about the time from this server through local broadcasts.

NTP Configuration Example

Now that you have a basic understanding of NTP and its configuration, take a look at a simple example in which a perimeter router at a corporate network needs to synchronize its time to an internal NTP server. Figure 18-1 is used to illustrate this example. Example 18-15 shows the router's configuration.

Example 18-15 *Configuring NTP on Your Router, Acting as a Client*

```
Router(config)# ntp server 192.1.2.11 key 99 source ethernet0
Router(config)# ntp authenticate
Router(config)# ntp authentication-key 99 md5 55ab8971F
Router(config)# ntp trusted-key 99
Router(config)# ntp update-calendar
Router(config)# access-list 1 permit 192.1.2.11 0.0.0.0
Router(config)# ntp access-group peer 1
Router(config)# interface ethernet1
Router(config-if)# ntp disable
Router(config)# interface ethernet2
Router(config-if)# ntp disable
```

In this example, the NTP server is 192.1.2.11, which is specified in the first command. The next three commands set up authentication and refer back to the first command with the key reference number of 99. Notice that the hash key is 55ab891F, which also must be configured on the NTP server. This router has a hardware clock, so the **ntp update-calendar** command updates the hardware clock from the software clock. The **access-list** and **ntp access-group** commands restrict NTP interaction with only 192.1.2.11. Finally, NTP is disabled on the outside and DMZ interfaces. As you can see, setting up NTP is straightforward.

Time Attack

I once had a client that was using NTP in broadcast mode to disseminate clocking information. One of the internal devices in this client's network was compromised, and the hacker set up shop. One of the things the hacker did was to install an NTP server and set the stratum level of service to 1; he sent broadcasts every 10 seconds, whereas the client's server was doing it every 5 minutes. The hacker used this process to hide his attacks by changing the time (and date, in some circumstances), making it very confusing when examining the log files on the syslog server. It took about 3 weeks before any of the administrators at the client's facility noticed that something unusual was occurring with the logging information and another 2 days to track down the compromised UNIX workstation. From this experience, they changed their NTP time-sharing method to client polling and also set up authentication with NTP, to make it much harder for this kind of problem to occur again.

Embedded Syslog Manager

The Embedded Syslog Manager (ESM), new in Cisco IOS 12.3(2)T, enables you to filter, change the severity level of, route, and customize logging messages on your router. ESM allows logging messages to be logged independently as standard messages, messages formatted using XML, and ESM filtered messages. These messages then can be forwarded to the standard logging destinations: console, internal buffer, and syslog server. By using a separate logging process, ESM ensures that if there is a problem with the ESM filtering modules, the standard logging process will be unaffected.

ESM Overview

As I mentioned in the introduction, ESM is an enhancement, not a replacement, to the existing logging mechanism, including syslog. Both simultaneously can be running on your router. ESM, however, provides enhanced services above and beyond the normal syslog functions of a router.

ESM gives you complete control over the logging process on the router. Before this feature was introduced, if you wanted to perform extra processing on logging events, such as filtering, or have the router take an action for a specific event, you had to write your own scripts and run them against syslog files on a syslog server. With ESM, you can do these tasks on the router itself. Here are some benefits that ESM provides you:

- You can limit the number of syslog messages to prevent a flood of messages in a time of duress or attack.
- You can customize processing of logging messages, such as forwarding specific messages to specific syslog servers.
- You can send e-mail notifications based on a specific log message or message type being generated.
- You can change the security levels for logging messages instead of using the ones that Cisco assigns to the messages.

To perform these functions, ESM uses filter modules, which are scripts written in the Tcl language. Cisco has some predefined scripts that you can use, but you easily can modify these or create your own (assuming that you know Tcl). These scripts can be stored locally on the router, such as in Flash, or on a remote server. The scripts can be stored in plain text or can be precompiled; the latter increases your security because they cannot be edited directly (you can use the tool TclPro to precompile scripts, but other tools are available).

ESM requires Tcl 8.3.4 support, which is available only in Cisco IOS 12.3(2)T and later. Because only Tcl is supported for scripting, you must be proficient in using the Tcl coding language to create your own custom scripts. One limitation with ESM is that it cannot be applied to SNMP logging, such as log messages related to the **snmp-server enable traps syslog** and **logging history** commands.

ESM Filter Modules

Before you can use ESM, you must either create or obtain filtering modules. When you enable ESM, all logging messages first are processed through the referenced ESM filter modules. You can have the router use multiple filter modules, where the modules are processed by the position tag associated with the **logging filter** command. This enables you to enter your **logging filter** commands in any order, but it has the Cisco IOS process them based on the position tag values. When multiple modules are referenced, the output of the first filter module is passed as the input to the second module. If you had a third module, the output of the second module would be passed to the third one.

One component always passed from filter module to filter module is the original logging message. When all filter modules have been processed, the original logging message can be directed to one of three locations: standard, XML, or ESM. With the router's standard logging process, the logging message is directed to the normal destinations: console, buffered, or syslog.

Input Process

Normally, a logging message contains the following variables: facility, severity level, mnemonic, message text, and, optionally, a sequence number and time stamp. However, ESM, preappends a syslog count number to each message. The logging message itself is passed as a Tcl global namespace variable to the filter module. Each component in a logging message is a Tcl global variable, and each of these is prefixed with a double colon (::) when referencing them in the script module. Table 18-5 lists the valid variables that you have access to within a filter module.

Table 18-5 *ESM Filter Module Variables*

Variable	Description
::buginfseq	This is the sequence number of the error message, which can be added to logging messages with the **service sequence-numbers** command.
::clear	This variable contains either event cleared or NULL values.
::facility	This is the name of the facility that generates the message.
::format_string	This is the string to create the original message text. For example, an original message text would be "Configured from %x by %y," where the %x and %y are message arguments. The format string can be passed to the **format** command in Tcl.
::hostname	This is the router's name configured with the **hostname** command. You can add this name to logging messages with the **logging origin-id hostname** command.
::mnemonic	This is the message abbreviation name, such as CONFIG_I or UPDOWN.
::module_position	This is the position number of the filter module in the list of modules. This can be determined by the order of the scripts referenced in the **logging filter** commands.

Table 18-5   *ESM Filter Module Variables (Continued)*

Variable	Description
::msg_args	These are the list of arguments in the format string of the logging message. For example, if the logging message was "%SYS-5-CONFIG_I: Configured from console by console," the format string would be "Configured from %x by %y," where %x and %y are the msg_args.
::orig_msg	This is the original logging message. If you do not want to send the message, have the filter module return a NULL value; otherwise, return this variable (**$::orig_msg**).
::pid	This is the process ID contained in certain logging messages. Look at the **::process** variable for more information.
::process	This is the name of the process and interrupt level, which certain logging messages contain, describing traceback information and internal errors—for example: "-Process= 'Net Background,' ipl= 2, pid= 88."
::severity	This is the severity level of the message, which is from 0 to 7. Within the filter module, you can change this value.
::stream	This is the message stream number and is always set to 2 before the first filter is executed. Here is a standard use of stream numbers: 0—Default message 1—XML tagged message 2—Filtered message 3 to 9—Reserved 10 to 65,535—Available for your use
::syslog_facility	This is the syslog facility that will be used when sending a syslog message to a server. This is a number from 0 to 184, where the default is 184 (local7). You can change this value with the **logging facility** command.
::timestamp	This is the time stamp of the logging message, assuming that time stamps have been enabled with the **service timestamps** command.
::traceback	This is the traceback information in certain logging messages that contain internal errors or tracebacks. See the **::process** variable for more information.
::version	This is the Cisco IOS software version of the router, in this format: "SYS_MAJORVERSION.SYS_MINORVERSION."

Filtering Process

After you have set up ESM, each time the router generates a logging message, the filter modules are processed in the order in which they are referenced, (that is, configured). As each module is processed, it passes its output as input to the next module. Because the Tcl variables in Table 18-5 are global namespace variables, each of these can be changed within your filters and can be used by other filters.

return Statement

Two Tcl global variables automatically are updated by ESM based on the execution of filtering modules: ::orig_msg and ::cli_args (the latter is the arguments passed into the filter module). The ::origin_msg value is set automatically to the return value of the filter module. This is done with the **return** command. For example, if you had a one-line filter module and wanted to pass a value of "This is my new value" to the next filter module, your **return** statement in your first filter module would look like this:

```
return "This is my new value"
```

With this example, the filter module ignores any parameters passed to it and passes the previous text string to the next filter module in the chain.

Here are some other **return** statement examples. With this return statement, all syslog messages are blocked to the ESM stream process:

```
return ""
```

This example sends the value in ::orig_msg to the next module:

```
return $::orig_msg
```

Cisco IOS Commands

You can add Cisco IOS commands to your filter modules by using the Tcl **config** and **exec** commands. For example, assume that you want to add the inbound ACL applied to an interface to your logging message. Assume that the ACL is the one applied to ethernet1, which is also the source address for logging statements to a syslog server. This could be done with the following:

```
set acl_info [exec show ip interface e1 | inc Outbound access list]
puts $acl_info
"  Outgoing access list is not set"
```

In this example, the last line is the output passed to the syslog message.

NOTE   More information on TCL scripting can be found on the Cisco website in the "Cisco IOS Scripting with Tcl" guide. Just do a search for this string.

Example Filter Modules

Cisco provides some sample Tcl scripts on its website for ESM filter modules; however, Cisco does not support all of these scripts. The phrase "buyer beware" applies. Some of the example scripts include the following:

- Escalating the severity level of a message
- Counting messages
- Creating XML tags
- Associating logging messages to a stream ID
- Sending an e-mail alert

As I mentioned at the beginning of this section on ESM, this chapter does not provide an in-depth study of the configuration of Tcl scripts. To give you a flavor of scripting, however, I look at two scripts included on the Cisco website: email.txt and email_guts.txt.

The email.txt script creates an e-mail message with the logging message. Here are the guts of this script:

```
# Usage:  Provide email address as CLI argument.  Set email server IP in
#         email_guts.tcl
# Namespace: email
if { [info exists email::init] == 0 } {
   source flash:/email_guts.tcl
}
# Check for null message
if { [string length $::orig_msg] == 0} {
    return ""
   }
if { [info exists ::msg_args] } {
   if { [string compare -nocase CONFIG_I $::mnemonic ] == 0 } {
               email::sendmessage $::cli_args $::mnemonic \
               [string trim $::orig_msg]
   }
}
return $::orig_msg
```

One argument that you must pass to this script is the e-mail address where you want e-mail messages sent.

The email_guts.txt script specifies the e-mail server's IP address, as well as the from and friendly strings:

```
# Usage: Set email host IP, from, and friendly strings below.
#
namespace eval email {
    set sendmail(smtphost) 192.1.1.2
    set sendmail(from) $::hostname
    set sendmail(friendly) $::hostname
    proc sendmessage {toList subject body} {
        variable sendmail
        set smtphost $sendmail(smtphost)
        set from $sendmail(from)
        set friendly $sendmail(friendly)
        set sockid [socket $smtphost 25]
## DEBUG
```

```
set status [catch {
        puts $sockid "HELO $smtphost"
        flush $sockid
        set result [gets $sockid]
        puts $sockid "MAIL From:<$from>"
        flush $sockid
        set result [gets $sockid]
        foreach to $toList {
            puts $sockid "RCPT To:<$to>"
            flush $sockid
        }
        set result [gets $sockid]
        puts  $sockid "DATA "
        flush $sockid
        set result [gets  $sockid]
        puts  $sockid "From: $friendly <$from>"
        foreach to $toList {
            puts $sockid "To:<$to>"
        }
        puts  $sockid "Subject: $subject"
        puts  $sockid "\n"
        foreach line [split $body "\n"] {
            puts  $sockid " $line"
        }
        puts  $sockid "."
        puts  $sockid "QUIT"
        flush $sockid
        set result [gets  $sockid]
} result]
        catch {close $sockid }
    if {$status} then {
        return -code error $result
    }
}
} ;# end namespace email
set email::init 1
```

Introduction to ESM Setup and Configuration

After you have created your filter modules for ESM, put them in a place where the router can locate them through a URL-style syntax. I recommend that you put the Tcl scripts (filter modules) in the router's Flash. When this is done, you need to perform the following steps:

Step 1   Reference each filter module with a separate **logging filter** command.

Step 2   Use the **logging {console | buffered | monitor | host} filtered** command to use your ESM filter modules. Optionally, configure other **logging** commands, such as **logging source-interface** and **logging origin-id**.

Step 3   Verify your configuration with the **show logging** command.

The following sections cover the configuration in more depth.

Specifying Filter Modules

The first thing that you must do is reference your filter modules. This is done using the **logging filter** command:

```
Router(config)# logging filter filter_url [position_#]
  [args filter_arguments]
```

The *filter_url* parameter specifies the location of the filter module. If the module is stored locally in the router's Flash, use **flash:** or **slot0:** as the source. If it is stored remotely, use either **ftp:, rcp:,** or **tftp:**. For a remote location, the filter URL should also contain the IP address of the module, as well as the directory in which the module is located. For locally and remotely stored modules, you need to specify the name of the module. The extension of these scripts is either .txt for a plain, noncompiled Tcl script or .tcl for a precompiled Tcl script.

Following the URL specification is the position number of the filter module during the filtering process. If you omit the position number, the router processes filter modules in the order in which you configure them. For each filter module that you have, you need a separate **logging filter** command. Finally, the optional **args** parameter specifies any arguments that you want to pass to the filter (in the filter, you need to reference these arguments if you want to use them). For example, you could pass an e-mail address to a script by using this syntax: **args richard@quizware.com**. If you have multiple arguments, separate the arguments by a space. Note that if the script is set up to accept an argument already, you do not need to preface the argument with the **args** parameter.

Here is a simple example of referencing a compiled script stored in the router's Flash:

```
Router(config)# logging filter flash:/email.tcl richard@quizware.com
```

Using Filter Modules

Next, you must tell your router to use the filter modules that you specified with the **logging filter** command. This is done using the following commands:

```
Router(config)# logging [console | buffered | monitor] filtered
  [severity_level]
Router(config)# logging host {IP_address | hostname} filtered
  [stream stream_ID]
```

In the first **logging** command, the optional *severity_level* parameter specifies that logging messages at that severity level or higher (lower number) will be processed by the filter modules. Note that the severity level specified in the **logging console**, **logging buffered**, and **logging monitored** commands takes precedence over the severity level specified in this command.

In the second command, the optional **stream** parameter can be used to direct logging messages to a specific syslog host. As an example, you could specify that all severity level 5 messages should have a stream ID of 7 associated with them; then, with the **stream** parameter, you could have the appropriate **logging host** command process these logging messages.

Example 18-16 shows a simple example that e-mails a message for any messages logged to the console with a severity level of 0 to 3.

Example 18-16 *Sending an E-mail Message Based on Logging Severity Levels*

```
Router(config)# logging filter slot0:/email.tcl richard@quizware.com
Router(config)# logging filter slot0:/email_guts.tcl
Router(config)# logging console filtered 3
```

Verifying Your ESM Configuration

After you have configured your ESM filters, you can use the **show logging** command to verify your configuration. Example 18-17 shows a sample output of this command based on Example 18-16.

Example 18-17 *Using the* **show logging** *Command to Verify Your ESM Configuration*

```
Router# show logging
Syslog logging: enabled(0 messages dropped, 12 messages rate-limited,
   0 flushes, 0 overruns, xml disabled, filtering enabled)
   Console logging: level debugging, 32 messages logged, xml disabled,
     filtering enabled
   Monitor logging: level warnings , 0 messages logged, xml disabled,
     filtering disabled
   Buffer logging: level debugging, 839 messages logged, xml disabled,
     filtering disabled
   Logging Exception size (8192 bytes)
   Count and timestamp logging messages: disabled

Filter modules:
     slot0:/email.tcl richard@quizware.com
     slot0:/email_guts.tcl

Log Buffer (8192 bytes):

*Jan 5 12:49:02.513: %SYS-5-CONFIG_I: Configured from console
   by console
<--output omitted-->
```

Additional Logging Information

Now that you have logging set up, your most difficult task is to make sense of logging information found in your logging messages. I discussed some of this in the previous chapter related to DoS attacks. In this chapter, I give only an overview of what you should look for in your log files, as well as additional tools that you can use to make this process easier.

What to Look For

At a base level, every day you should look at the following items concerning your log files:

- How many total messages were recorded in yesterday's log file?

  Is this more or less than the day before? You should have a baseline developed that shows, on average, the number of entries per day or based on the day of week. If there is a huge discrepancy, scrutinize the logging process and the log file to look for any problems or issues.

- How many messages did you have for each severity level in yesterday's log file?

  Again, you should have a baseline for this information and should examine any major discrepancies.

- Are you seeing any new types of messages in your log files that you rarely see?

  If so, again, you should scrutinize these log messages.

- If you are logging ACL entries, what are the top 10 denied IP addresses?

  Look at not only the top 10 denied IP addresses, but also the network numbers that these are from. If there is a pattern here, you might want to block the entire network in question.

- If you are logging ACL entries, is there a major increase on the number of matches of a particular **permit** or **deny** statement?

  If so, this might indicate that a security weakness was found in an application or operating system, or a new worm is attacking your network. If you see a major increase in the number of matches of a particular ACL statement, definitely investigate this discrepancy and take the appropriate action.

TIP   Also examine CPU utilization and memory use on your router, as discussed in the previous chapter.

Additional Tools

Many additional tools are available to help you with your logging process. I briefly focus on three third-party tools that you can use to help you with your logging and syslog process. Many are available, and you can easily create your own tools to examine your log files with scripting tools such as Tcl, Perl, and others.

Rotating Syslog Log Files

Every day (or more often, if necessary) you should rotate the syslog server's log files. Then periodically, you should archive old syslog files. A syslog file that is being rotated out should have the date in its name, as well as a descriptive term. For example, if you have separate log files for three perimeter routers, I would use the following syntax for the rotated filenames: *router_name.date*.log (or something similar).

One package that I have used is logrot. It does what its name implies: It rotates log files. Logrot was built to work with CiscoWorks log files on Sun Solaris and Windows systems. You can find information for logrot at http://sourceforge.net/project/showfiles .php?group_id=25401&package_id=79001. Of course, you easily can create your own script to perform log rotation; I have done this many times using simple shell script commands.

However, no matter what product you use, you need to automate the rotation process. On UNIX systems, you can do this by using the kron process. On a Windows 2000 system, you can use the *Scheduled Tasks* tool. To do this, go to Start, > Programs, > Accessories, > System Tools, > Scheduled Tasks; then double-click the Add Schedule Task icon. This brings up the Schedule Task wizard, where you easily can point to your log file rotation program and schedule how often it should run.

Examining Log File Contents

You can use a variety of programs to examine and monitor the contents of your syslog server's log files. The following sections cover some of the commonly used ones.

cislog

One simple log file report program that I have used is cislog, which is useful for monitoring syslog files for Cisco products. It is actually a set of Perl scripts that can monitor the following information:

- **acl-report.pl**—This Perl script summarizes the deny messages based on top source IP addresses, the most active destination ports, and the most active protocol types.

- **dial-report.pl**—This Perl script lists the users and their addresses, as well as when they dialed into the router.

- **router-report.pl**—This Perl script summarizes the log messages created by Cisco routers and produces information such as a summary of the top log message types, successful Telnet attempts, and which sources entered configuration mode.

- **switch-report.pl**—This Perl script performs the same function as the router-report.pl, but for Catalyst switches.

The great thing about these tools is that they are written in Perl. If you are proficient in programming in Perl, you can use these scripts as a starting point and can add enhancements to them to meet your specific needs. cislog can be found at http://sourceforge.net/project/ showfiles.php?group_id=25401&package_id=34535.

swatch

Another popular log file–processing utility is swatch, which standards for Simple WATCHer. This software can be found at http://swatch.sourceforge.net/. One advantage that swatch has over other log file checkers is that it actively scans your log files for new messages and then takes an action based on the message that was newly recorded. Its one main downside is that it runs only on Linux/UNIX platforms; Windows currently is not supported. I have used swatch quite often because of its ease in customization to look for specific things and then take appropriate actions on these matches.

fwlogwatch

A third popular tool is fwlogwatch, which runs on many Linux/UNIX platforms as well as Windows (through Cygwin). fwlogwatch can detect and process log entries from multiple platforms, including Linux ipchains, netfilter, and iptables; Solaris/BSD/Irix/HP-UX ipfilter; Cisco IOS and PIX logs; NetScreen Windows XP firewall; Elsa Lancom's router; and Snort IDS. All of these log entries can be in the same file, and the log file can be compressed using gzip. Other features include these:

- Resolves for protocols, services, and host names
- Lookups against the whois database for easy access to contact information of administrators of remote networks
- Inclusion or exclusion of hosts, ports, chains, and targets
- Support for multiple languages
- Intelligent search capabilities based on log field columns
- Generation of output in plain text and HTML, as well as the capability to send reports by e-mail
- Real-time processing of log files, including instant notifications by e-mail, winpopup, or any other method that you can configure through a shell script
- Support for antispoofing and IPv6

For more information on fwlogwatch, visit http://cert.uni-stuttgart.de/projects/fwlogwatch/.

Summary

This chapter showed you the basics of logging on your Cisco perimeter router. Without logging, it becomes almost impossible to determine whether your network or router is under attack. Setting up logging with the **logging** commands is a simple and straight-forward process, even with the configuration of extra features such as NTP and ESM.

Next up is Part VIII, "Virtual Private Networks," which shows you how to establish secure connections between your perimeter routers across a public network.

PART **VIII**

Virtual Private Networks

Chapter 19   IPSec Site-to-Site Connections

Chapter 20   IPSec Remote Access Connections

19

IPSec Site-to-Site Connections

This chapter and the next one cover some basics of VPN connectivity on your perimeter router. Because of space constraints in this book, I have decided to focus on two types of VPN connections: IPSec site-to-site (or LAN-to-LAN, sometimes referred to as L2L) and remote-access IPSec connections. I assume that you are already somewhat familiar with the IPSec standard and its components. Because a perimeter router is used in many cases to terminate VPN connections, I have included two chapters in this book on this topic. For more detailed information related to VPNs with Cisco products, look for my upcoming book *The Complete Cisco VPN Configuration Guide* (Cisco Press, 2005), which discusses in depth the setup and troubleshooting of VPNs using the Cisco 3000 series concentrators, routers, PIX firewalls, and software clients.

This chapter covers the following topics:

- IPSec preparation
- IKE Phase 1: the management connection
- IKE Phase 2: the data connections
- IPSec troubleshooting
- IPSec L2L connection example

IPSec Preparation

Before you begin the configuration of IPSec connections on your perimeter router, you need to do some background investigative work. You need to gather important information about how IPSec connections will be established, lay out a network design, allow for IPSec in your design, and then begin your implementation. The following two sections discuss this process.

Basic Tasks

When designing an IPSec solution, you go through eight different steps:

Step 1 **Handle design and policy issues**—Here, you lay out which routers will be terminating IPSec connections, what types of IPSec connections will be used (L2L and/or remote access), and how the IPSec connections will be protected (authentication methods, encryption algorithms, hashing functions, and so on).

Step 2   **Allow for IPSec traffic**—On your perimeter router and other routers and firewalls performing filtering, you need to allow IPSec connections to the appropriate source(s) and destination(s).

Step 3   **Configure IKE Phase 1 management-connection policies**—You must define the IKE Phase 1 policies that will be used to protect the management connection between your two IPSec devices. The management connection is used to build IPSec data connections in IKE Phase 2. These policies include the type of authentication that will be used to authenticate the peer's identities (preshared keys, RSA encrypted nonces, or RSA signatures), the encryption algorithm used, the hashing function used, the lifetime of the management connection, and the Diffie-Hellman key group to be used to create the shared secret key (this is used to share keying information securely for other processes, such as with the 3DES encryption key or the MD5 hashing function key).

Step 4   **Define what traffic is to be protected by the IPSec connection**—On Cisco routers, a crypto ACL is used to define what traffic is to be protected between two IPSec peers. Basically, a crypto ACL is an ACL with **permit** statements in it that identify the data traffic, in IKE Phase 2, that is to be protected.

Step 5   **Create your transform set(s)**—A transform set defines the protocols and algorithms that are used to protect the data traffic in IKE Phase 2. Protocols include the Authentication Header (AH) and the Encapsulation Security Payload (ESP). Algorithms include DES, 3DES, AES, and null for encryption, and SHA or MD5 for hashing functions. The transform also defines the method for terminating a connection: tunnel or transport mode. For low-bandwidth connections, you also can specify LZS compression.

Step 6   **Build a crypto map**—A crypto map binds together all of your IPSec components to build secured connections, called security associations (SAs). This includes information such as who the remote peer is (its IP address or fully qualified domain name [FQDN]), the transform set and crypto ACL to use, and other configuration information. For remote-access connections, you need to build a special type of crypto map called a dynamic crypto map; in addition, you need to define your client policies, such as split tunneling, local IP address assignment, and other client functions.

Step 7   **Activate your crypto map**—After you have built your crypto map, the router will not use it until you activate it on one or more of the router's interfaces. For a perimeter router, this typically is the router's external or public interface.

Step 8   **Test your IPSec connection**—In the last step, you test your IPSec connection by generating traffic that will trigger your routers to build the management (IKE Phase 1) and data (IKE Phase 2) connections. You can use many **show** and **debug** commands to help troubleshoot this process.

As you can see from this list, you have your work cut out for you.

External ACL

Whether your perimeter router will be terminating an IPSec connection or an internal device will be performing this function, the perimeter router's ACL on the external interface must allow IPSec traffic. You probably need to permit three connections for each peer that is connecting:

- IKE Phase 1 traffic: UDP port 500
- IKE Phase 2 traffic: AH and ESP packets

Here is a simple breakdown on the ACL commands to use:

```
Router(config)# access-list ACL_# permit udp
  source_address wildcard_mask destination_address wildcard_mask eq isakmp
Router(config)# access-list ACL_# permit ahp
  source_address wildcard_mask destination_address wildcard_mask
Router(config)# access-list ACL_# permit esp
  source_address wildcard_mask destination_address wildcard_mask
Router(config)# interface type [slot_#/]port_#
Router(config-if)# ip access-group ACL_# in
```

To allow the IKE Phase 1 connection between the two peers, you need to allow UDP port 500 traffic, which the first ACL statement in this code listing does. If your perimeter router is terminating the connection, put your router's IP address as the destination address. For security purposes, if you know the IP address of the remote IPSec peer, configure this instead of using the keyword **any** as the source address in the ACL statement. The second ACL statement applies to AH connections, and the third one applies to ESP connections.

NOTE   In most situations, AH is not used with IPSec connections because it breaks when these packets are sent through an intermediate address-translation device. AH protects the IP header and payload contents with an integrity checksum value (ICV), and an address-translation device changes address information in the IP and, possibly, the transport layer head; this breaks the ICV value. Therefore, if you are not using AH, do not allow it in your ACL statement. ESP, on the other hand, does not protect the IP header contents—it protects only the encapsulated payload (which could be an encapsulated IP packet, if the IPSec connection is functioning in tunnel mode, as discussed in the "Transform Set" section later in this chapter).

TIP   For remote-access IPSec connections, you typically do not know the IP address of the peer until the peer makes first contact. Therefore, your ACL must be somewhat promiscuous in the use of the keyword **any** for the source IP address. If this is a concern, configure the router to allow specific L2L connections and force remote-access users to use authentication proxy. Then have your AAA server download the appropriate ACL entry to allow the user's IPSec remote-access connection.

IKE Phase 1: Management Connection

This book focuses on setting up IPSec connections that use only ISAKMP/IKE. The combination of these two protocols provides the framework for building IPSec connections, including the sharing of keying information for algorithms and functions.

The Internet Security Association and Key Management Protocol (ISAKMP), defined in RFC 2408, defines the message format, the mechanics of a key-exchange protocol, and the negotiation process to build an SA for IPSec. However, ISAKMP does not define how keys should be managed or how they are shared between the two IPSec peers. IKE is used to solve these two problems.

Internet Key Exchange (IKE), defined in RFC 2409, negotiates security protocols and the exchange of keying information to build an SA to a remote IPSec peer. IKE is a hybrid protocol, combining ISAKMP and the Oakley and Skeme key exchange methods. IKE completes the ISAKMP protocol, filling in what ISAKMP does not define or do. Oakley and Skeme have five defined key groups. Of these groups, Cisco routers supports three groups. Group 1 uses a 768-bit key, group 2 uses a 1024-bit key, and group 5 uses a 1536-bit key for keying information. For the actual key creation, IKE uses Diffie-Hellman (DH) to create the public/private key combination that will allow the creation of an SA between two IPSec peers. DH is used to share information securely between the two peers before any management connection in IKE Phase 1 is built.

One optional solution is to not use ISAKMP/IKE to build IPSec connections. If you choose this route, you need to configure manually everything that ISAKMP/IKE does dynamically; however, this is beyond the scope of this book.

NOTE   It is very common in the industry for people to loosely use the terms *ISAKMP* and *IKE*. The combination of these protocols builds secure connections between devices. This is accomplished in two phases: Phase 1 and Phase 2. In this chapter and the next, I refer to the two phases as IKE Phase 1 and 2, which also includes ISAKMP.

Enabling ISAKMP/IKE

On a Cisco router that has IPSec as a component of the Cisco IOS, ISAKMP/IKE is enabled by default. If your router is not using IPSec, I recommend that you disable it with the following command:

```
Router(config)# no crypto isakmp enable
```

You easily can re-enable it by removing the **no** parameter from this command.

Defining IKE Phase 1 Policies

To move data between two devices, three connections are built between the two IPSec peers:

- **One bidirectional IKE Phase 1 connection**—I commonly refer to this as the management connection. The peers use this connection to negotiate policy information for the data connections that will be built in IKE Phase 2.

- **Two unidirectional IKE Phase 2 connections**—I commonly refer to these as the data connections. To move data between two peers, two unidirectional connections are built: from peer A to peer B, and from peer B to peer A. These connections protect the actual user's data, such as a Telnet, e-mail, or FTP traffic.

Policy Commands

To build an IKE Phase 1 management connection, you must specify policies that will define how this connection is to be protected. If all peers have the same capabilities, you need only one policy that will be applied to all peers. However, if you have two peers with different capabilities (for example, one supports 3DES encryption and the other supports DES), you must create two separate policies.

You define these items in your IKE Phase 1 policies:

- The type of authentication (**authentication** command)
- The encryption algorithm (**encryption** command)
- The DH group number (**group** command)
- The hash function (**hash** command)
- The lifetime for the management SA that is being negotiated (**lifetime** command)

Creating a Policy

To create an IKE Phase 1 policy, use the following command:

```
Router(config)# crypto isakmp policy priority_#
Router(config-isakmp)#
```

The **crypto isakmp policy** command creates an IKE Phase 1 policy, where the *priority_#* parameter specifies the policy number: It binds together the policy statements for this policy. This number can range from 1 to 10,000. The lower the number is, the higher the policy priority is. This number plays an important role in determining which policy should be used between two peers. When determining which policy to use, both IPSec peers share their list of IKE Phase 1 policies with the other. These policies then are compared from highest to lowest priority (where 1 is the highest-priority policy, if configured). The first policy that the peer accepts is the one used for the current management session. If no policy is found to match between the two peers, a management connection is not built and, therefore, no data connections are built.

TIP

> The peer processes the policies in the order of their priority, so you always should give the most secure policy the highest priority (lowest number) and the least secure policy the lowest priority (highest number).

Specifying Policy Parameters

You probably noticed in the last coding example that the **crypto isakmp policy** command takes you into a subconfiguration mode, where you enter your specific IKE Phase 1 policies. The *priority_#* of this command groups the policy statements, similar to what a number or name does for an ACL. Here are the policy commands that you can define for your IKE Phase 1 management connection:

```
Router(config)#  crypto isakmp policy priority_#
Router(config-isakmp)# authentication {rsa-sig | rsa-encr | pre-share}
Router(config-isakmp)# encryption {des | 3des | aes | aes 192 | aes 256}
Router(config-isakmp)# hash {md5 | sha}
Router(config-isakmp)# group {1 | 2 | 5}
Router(config-isakmp)# lifetime #_of_seconds
```

The **authentication** command specifies the type of authentication to use when validating the identity of the remote IPSec peer. There are three choices. **rsa-sig** specifies that certificates and a Certificate Authority (CA) are used for authentication (this is the default method). **rsa-encr** specifies that RSA encrypted nonces are used. **pre-share** specifies that a single preshared key is used. RSA signatures are the most secure and scalable, but this is also the slowest method and the most difficult to set up initially. If you specify **rsa-encr**, you need to generate your own public and private key combination, as well as give your public key to the remote peer and manually configure the remote peer's public key on your router. Configuring preshared keys is the simplest method; however, because it uses only a single key for authentication, it should be used only for a small number of L2L connections. The configuration of these authentication methods is discussed later in the "IKE Phase 1 Peer Authentication" section.

The encryption algorithm used to encrypt the information for the management connection is configured using the **encryption** command. DES uses a 56-bit key, and 3DES uses a 168-bit key. Depending on the type, AES uses either a 128-, 192-, or 256-bit key. The default encryption algorithm, if not specified, is **des**, which is the weakest form of encryption; AES is the strongest.

Hashing functions are used to verify that packets are not altered by a device between the two peers. Hashing functions create an integrity checksum value that the remote end uses to validate that the packet contents have not been tampered with. Two hashing functions are supported: MD5 (128-bit signature) and SHA (160-bit signature). The signature created by these functions is the ICV value. SHA is more secure, but MD5 is quicker in its computation. The default is SHA if you omit the **hash** command from your policy configuration.

Cisco IOS routers support three DH key groups: 1, 2, and 5. Group 1 keys are 768 bits in length, group 2 keys are 1024 bits, and group 5 keys are 1536 bits. The default is group 1 if you do not configure the **group** command. Also, the default lifetime of the management connection is 86,400 seconds (1 day); you can change this value with the **lifetime** command. By default, when making a connection to a remote peer, the peer that has the lowest time value is used.

TIP

Some IPSec devices require that the lifetime parameters match on the two peers. If they do not match, the management SA will not form. Cisco devices, on the other hand, use the smaller lifetime value between the two peers. Therefore, when building a management SA to a non-Cisco device, I highly recommend that you configure the lifetime value on your Cisco router to match the non-Cisco device's timeout.

Policy Verification

To view your IKE Phase 1 policies, use the **show crypto isakmp policy** command, as shown in Example 19-1.

Example 19-1 *Using the* **show crypto isakmp policy** *Command*

```
Router# show crypto isakmp policy
Protection suite priority 1
  encryption algorithm:   DES - Data Encryption Standard (56 bit keys)
  hash algorithm: Message Digest 5
  authentication method:  preshared Key
  Diffie-Hellman Group:   #2 (1024 bit)
  lifetime:        86400 seconds, no volume limit
Default protection suite
  encryption algorithm:   DES - Data Encryption Standard (56 bit keys).
  hash algorithm:         Secure Hash Standard
  authentication method:  Rivest-Shamir-Adleman Signature
  Diffie-Hellman group:   #1 (768 bit)
  lifetime:               86400 seconds, no volume limit
```

In Example 19-1, the highest-ranking policy (the priority is 1). The encryption algorithm is DES, the default; the hash function is MD5; the authentication method is preshared keys; the DH group is 2; and the lifetime is 1 day. Note that the router has a default ISAKMP policy that is preconfigured on the router; this is shown at the bottom of the output of Example 19-1.

IKE Phase 1 Peer Authentication

In your IKE Phase 1 policy configuration, one of the policies that you can configure is the authentication method with the **authentication** command. IPSec supports three authentication methods:

- Preshared keys
- RSA encrypted nonces
- Digital certificates (RSA signatures)

The configuration of all three of these methods is covered later in this section after the coverage of the peer identity type.

Identity Type

Before I discuss how to configure the three different authentication methods, I need to discuss a peer's identity type. You use an identity type to identify a peer on your router. Three identity types exist: the IP address of the peer, the peer's name, and the peer's distinguished name (DN). You first must determine which of these three types you will use in identifying your IPSec peers. Here is the command to specify the identity type:

```
Router(config)#  crypto isakmp identity {address | hostname | dn}
```

As you can notice from this command, it is a global configuration mode command, so it applies to all IPSec configurations. If you do not configure this command, the default is to specify a peer by its IP address. This command affects how you configure the identity of the peer in other IPSec commands.

If you specify the **hostname** parameter, you can specify a FQDN for the remote peer or statically configure the name resolution with the **ip host** command. I recommend using dynamic DNS resolution only if the remote peer is acquiring its IP address dynamically, which then is updated automatically in a DNS server's resolution table. I prefer not to use DNS because it is susceptible to session hijacking. If the peer has more than one IP address, I recommend using the **hostname** parameter and then statically configuring name resolution with the **ip host** command, with which you can specify more than one IP address for a device. This provides a method of redundancy if the first IP address of the peer is not reachable.

The **dn** parameter specifies the use of the distinguished name of the device from the router certificate. Either **dn** or **hostname** is necessary if you will be deploying DN-based crypto maps.

Authentication with Preshared Keys

When creating your IKE Phase 1 policies, if you configured authentication to be **pre-share** in the **authentication** command, authentication is accomplished by assigning the same key to both peers. Depending on the identity type defined on your router, you use one of these two commands:

```
Router(config)#  crypto isakmp key the_key address IP_address_of_peer
```

or:

```
Router(config)#  crypto isakmp key the_key hostname hostname_of_peer
```

The key can be an alphanumeric value up to 128 characters in length. If you specify an IP address of 0.0.0.0 for the **address** parameter, this is treated as a wildcard; all remote peers must use this key when authenticating. I highly recommend that you not use this trick because, if one peer becomes compromised, all your peers are compromised. Instead, I recommend that you configure a different authentication key for each remote peer.

To view your preshared keys, use the **show crypto isakmp key** command.

Authentication with RSA Encrypted Nonces

As you saw in the last section, configuring preshared key authentication is a simple process. However, because it uses a single symmetric key value for authentication, it is less secure than RSA encrypted nonces, which uses asymmetric keys (public and private).

If you specified your IKE Phase 1 authentication method with **authentication rsa-encr** in your ISAKMP policy configuration, you need to perform four steps to set up your RSA public/private key authentication:

Step 1   Create your router's personal RSA public/private keys.

Step 2   Share your router's public key with your peer.

Step 3   Get your peer's public key and configure it on your router.

Step 4   Verify the key that you configured for your peer.

RSA Manual Key Generation

To create a public/private key combination on your router, you first must give your router a unique FQDN with the **hostname** and **ip domain-name** commands. After this, you can generate your public/private keys with the following command:

```
Router(config)# crypto key generate rsa [usage-keys]
```

If you use the optional **usage-key** parameter, two sets of public/private key combinations are created: one for the signature and one for encryption. However, only one set of public/private keys is needed for IPSec authentication purposes, so you can omit this parameter.

Example 19-2 shows a simple example of generating your RSA public/private keys for encrypted nonces.

Example 19-2 *Creating RSA Keys for RSA Encrypted Nonces*

```
Router(config)# hostname richard
richard(config)# ip domain-name quizware.com
richard(config)# crypto key generate rsa
The name for the keys will be: richard.quizware.com
Choose the size of the key modulus in the range of 360 to 2048
for your Signature Keys. Choosing a key modulus greater than 512
may take a few minutes.
How many bits in the modulus[512]?
Generating RSA keys.... [OK].
richard(config)#
```

Example 19-2 shows how to configure your router to generate a single public/private RSA key combination. Notice that you are prompted for a modulus value, which affects the strength of the keys: The bigger the modulus is, the stronger the security of the keys will be. However, the longer the modulus is, the longer it takes to create a key pair. For example, on a 2500 router, using a 512-bit modulus takes about 20 seconds to generate the key-pair; however, if you changed the modulus to 2048 bits, it would take about an hour for the 2500 to generate the public/private key pair.

After you have generated your public/private key-pair combination, you can view your router's public key with the **show crypto key mypubkey rsa** command. If you used the **usage-keys** parameter when creating your keys, you will see two public keys. You need to give these key to your remote IPSec peer out of band. In other words, do not e-mail this to the peer because it will be traversing a public network and is susceptible to eavesdropping. Example 19-3 shows an example of this command.

Example 19-3 *Viewing Your Router's RSA Public Keys*

```
richard# show crytpo key mypubkey rsa
% Key pair was generated at: 07:06:28 UTC Oct 21 2001
Key name: richard.quizware.com
 Usage: Signature Key
 Key Data:
  105C311D 06039B86 1898F70D 01010105 00789B00 3048CBA1 0123E23B
  55D6AB22 11AEF1B0 ADCE18A6 432101C5 129D99E4 64987820 847EABC9
  D3214E4C 55179DD2 991AA8A9 FA603DD2 1234A6F8 FED76E28 D5DEF221
  B583D7A4 71020301 0201
```

NOTE   You cannot view your router's private keys, nor can you back them up to a remote server, such as with Trivial File Transfer Protocol (TFTP). Therefore, if your router fails and you replace it, you need to generate new keys for the new router and share the new public key with your current peers.

Peer Key Configuration

After your peer has generated his public/private keys, you need to obtain his public key out of band and then configure this on your router. To configure the peer's public key on your router, use the following configuration:

```
Router(config)#  crypto key pubkey-chain rsa
Router(config-pubkey-chain)# {addressed-key | named-key}
  {IP_address | host_name} [encryption | signature]
Router(config-pubkey-key)# key-string the_key
Router(config-pubkey-key)# quit
```

First, you need to enter the public key configuration mode by entering the **crypto key pubkey-chain rsa** command; notice that the prompt changed to (config-pubkey-chain).

Here, based on the identity type configured on the router, you use either the **addressed-key** or **named-key** commands. With the **addressed-key** command, you need to configure the IP address of the remote peer; with the **named-key** command, enter the peer device's name (typically a FQDN). Following this, you optionally can specify which type of key it is. If you generated two sets of keys with the **usage-keys** parameter with the **crypto key generate rsa** command, you need to configure both. If you do not specify the type of key, it defaults to signature. This takes you into a sub-subconfiguration mode, where you need to enter the peer's public key with the **key-string** command. With this command, the peer's key can be entered on multiple lines. When you are finished entering the peer's key, on a blank line, enter the **quit** command. Example 19-4 shows how to configure your peer's RSA public key.

Example 19-4 *Entering a Peer's RSA Public Key*

```
Router(config)#  crypto key pubkey-chain rsa
Router(config-pubkey-chain)# addressed-key 200.1.1.1 signature
Router(config-pubkey-key)# key-string
Router(config-pubkey-key)# 105C311D 06039B86 1898F70D 01010105
Router(config-pubkey-key)# 00789B00 3048CBA1 0123E23B 55D6AB22
Router(config-pubkey-key)# 11AEF1B0 ADCE18A6 432101C5 129D99E4
Router(config-pubkey-key)# 64987820 847EABC9 D3214E4C 55179DD2
Router(config-pubkey-key)# 991AA8A9 FA603DD2 1234A6F8 FED76E28
Router(config-pubkey-key)# D5DEF221 B583D7A4 71020301 0201
Router(config-pubkey-key)# quit
```

As you can see from Example 19-4, I entered the peer's public key on multiple command lines.

To view any peer's public key that you have configured on your router, use the following command:

```
Router#  show crypto key pubkey-chain rsa
 [name host_name | address IP_address]
```

Authentication with Certificates

Of the three types of IKE Phase 1 authentication, certificates provides the most security and scalability; however, they are also the most difficult to implement and troubleshoot. This section provides a brief overview of certificates and certificate authorities (CAs), as well as how to configure IPSec certificate authentication on your router.

Certificates and CAs

A certificate contains information to authenticate a device. Unlike preshared keys and RSA encrypted nonces, in which only two devices—the peers—are involved in the authentication process, a third device called the CA plays a role with certificates and IPSec. A CA is a trusted third-party device used to validate the identity of a peer. It typically is used with IPSec, but it also is used with e-commerce applications that use Secure Socket Layer (SSL). The CA's role in the authentication process is to act as the keeper of digital certificates.

The ITU-T X.509v3 standard defines the format and contents of a digital certificate. Digital certificates contain information about a device that can be used to authenticate it and contain three basic pieces of information:

- **The CA's public key**—The CA uses its private key to sign the digital certificate (including its contents). Another device then can use the public key of the CA to verify the authenticity and integrity of the certificate because only the public key of the CA can be used to validate the CA's signature (also on the certificate). Because this process uses the CA's public key to perform verification, you should obtain the CA's key out of band; if you obtain it in-band, verify with the administrator of the CA that the public key was not altered during transit across a public network.

- **The identity of the IPSec device**—This is some form of identification information that is used to uniquely identify the source of the public key. This can be a name, an address, a company name, a serial number, an IP address, or some other type of information. In most products, each certificate is assigned a unique serial number, which then is used to differentiate among different certificates.

- **The public key of the IPSec device**—This key, along with its private key (created by using the RSA algorithm), is used to create and validate the authentication information. The public key is used by any other device to validate the identity of the IPSec device associated with this certificate. Each IPSec device uses its personal private key to create a digital signature, which is placed on the device's personal certificate; only the public key of this device can validate the signature.

To provide redundancy when using certificates and CAs, a CA can implement one or more registration authorities (RAs). RAs act as proxies for CAs. RAs cannot generate certificates for devices, but they can pass out existing certificates for validation purposes, as well as Certificate Revocation Lists (CRLs), discussed later.

Cisco IOS routers support the following CA products, among others:

- Baltimore Technologies Unicert
- Entrust public-key infrastructure (PKI)
- Microsoft Windows 2000 and 2003 Certificate Services
- Verisign OnSite

I have used both Microsoft products with great success.

Simple Certificate Enrollment Protocol

The Simple Certificate Enrollment Protocol (SCEP) is one of two methods that you can use to obtain certificate information on your router. SCEP occurs in-band and provides a quick way of obtaining a certificate. The alternative method is manual: You generate certificate information and send this out of band to the administrator of the CA. The administrator generates a certificate for you and sends this back to you out of band. Then you manually put this into your IPSec device. Because the manual method is very work intensive and does not scale well, most network administrators prefer to use SCEP.

SCEP defines how an IPSec device and a CA interact when obtaining their initial certificate information. SCEP originally was developed by Cisco, Entrust, Microsoft, Netscape, Sun, and Verisign; it is currently in a draft state with Internet Engineering Task Force (IETF). It supports both the PKCS #7 and #10 standards (#7 defines how to encrypt, sign, and format certificate enrollment messages, and #10 defines how to handle multiple certificates in one request).

Certificate Revocation List

Basically, a CRL contains a list of revoked certificates, including their serial numbers. Here are some common reasons why a certificate might be revoked:

- A change was made in your security policy.
- Your device's private key was compromised.
- Your device is being taken permanently out of service.

A CRL is used to speed up the process of reauthenticating devices when their IKE Phase 1 management connection expires and needs to be rebuilt. When your router gets the peer's certificate initially and builds the management connection, your router caches the peer's certificate in memory. A CRL can be used to validate that the peer's certificate that you have cached is still current and valid. Without a CRL, when the management connection is about to expire and your router and peer need to rebuild the connection, the two devices must recontact the CA and request each other's personal certificate again. The problem with this process is that if the CA has a few million certificates, as would be the case in a public CA device, this could take a few seconds for the lookup to occur, adding delay in the rebuilding of the management connection. Instead, the two peers can ask the CA for a CRL; the CA can respond with this instantaneously because it does not require a special lookup. The two devices then can check to see if their peer is listed in the CRL: If it is not, the peer's certificate that they have cached is valid; otherwise, they need to request an updated certificate from the CA for the peer.

Certificate Enrollment and Configuration Process

Now that you have a basic overview of the components involved in using certificates for authentication in IKE Phase 1, you can go through the following steps to obtain certificate information on your router:

Step 1 Check your NVRAM usage. Your router's personal certificate and the CA and RA certificates are stored in NVRAM, and you might not have enough memory to hold them. (Use the **crypto ca certificate query** command.)

Step 2   Set the correct date and time on your router to interact with the CA. This is important for validating your certificate when the CA sends this to you. (Use the **clock timezone** and **clock set** commands or, preferably, Network Time Protocol (NTP).)

Step 3   Configure a unique FQDN on your router. (Use the **hostname** and **ip domain-name** commands.)

Step 4   Create your RSA public/private keys. (Use the **crypto key generate rsa** command.) The CA places your router's public key in the certificate, and the private key is used to sign authentication information during the IKE Phase 1 authentication process.

Step 5   Specify the location of the CA so that your router can reach it to obtain and validate certificates. (Use the **crypto ca {identity | trustpoint}** and **enrollment url** commands.)

Step 6   Obtain the CA's root certificate and verify the CA's signature on it. (Use the **crypto ca authenticate** command.)

Step 7   Obtain your router's own identity certificate from the CA. (Use the **crypto ca enroll** command.)

Step 8   Verify your certificate information. (Use the **show crypto ca certificates** command.)

Step 1: Check NVRAM Usage

The following certificate information is stored in NVRAM:

- The CA's certificate
- Your router's own certificate
- If the CA supports an RA, the RA's two certificates
- One CRL if there is no RA, or multiple CRLs if there is at least one RA

If you use the **show crypto ca certificates** command after obtaining certificate information, you quickly will see that each certificate is not small. Because certificate information is stored in NVRAM, this can be an issue. If your router does not have enough NVRAM to store this information, you need to execute the following command:

```
Router(config)# crypto ca certificate query
```

This command causes the router not to store the certificate information in NVRAM; instead, every time the router boots up, it goes out to the CA and automatically obtains it.

CAUTION   The problem with acquiring certificate information each time that the router boots up is that this process is susceptible to man-in-the-middle attacks.

Step 2: Specify Your Router's Name

Configuring your router's name information is straightforward. Use the following commands:

```
Router(config)#  hostname router's_name
Router(config)#  ip domain-name domain_name
```

Step 3: Configure the Correct Date and Time

To configure the correct date and time, use the following commands:

```
Router(config)#  clock timezone time_zone_name UTC_hour_offset
  [minute_offset]
Router#  clock set HH:MM:SS day name_of_month year
```

Of course, you can use NTP. Both these commands and NTP were discussed in Chapter 18, "Logging Events."

Step 4: Generate Your Keys

When you have configured your router's identity and have set the correct date and time, you are ready to create your router's public/private key combination:

```
littledog(config)#  crypto key generate rsa
```

Use the **show crypto key mypubkey rsa** command to view your router's personal public key(s). These commands were discussed previously.

Step 5: Specify Your Certificate Authority

Now that you have created your public/private key combination, you can specify how to access the CA. Here are the commands to do this:

```
Router(config)#  ip host CA_name IP_address
Router(config)#  crypto ca identity|trustpoint CA_name
Router(config-ca-identity)#  enrollment url URL_and_CGI_bin_location
Router(config-ca-identity)#  enrollment retry-period #_of_minutes
Router(config-ca-identity)#  enrollment retry-count #_of_times
Router(config-ca-identity)#  enrollment mode ra
Router(config-ca-identity)#  crl optional
```

The first command is not necessary if you are using DNS to resolve the CA's name to an IP address. The **crypto ca identity** or **trustpoint** commands are used to take you into a subconfiguration mode where you can configure the access parameters for the CA. In older versions of the Cisco IOS, you need to use the **identity** parameter, but in 12.2 and later versions, you use **trustpoint**.

The only required command within this subconfiguration mode is **enrollment url**, which specifies the URL location of the CA. Example 19-5 shows an example when accessing Verity's CA product.

Example 19-5 *Specifying the Access for the Verity CA Product*

```
quizware(config)#  crypto ca identity ca.verity.com
quizware(config-ca-identity)#  enrollment url
  http://ca.verity.com/cgi-bin
```

Example 19-6 shows an example accessing a Microsoft CA.

Example 19-6 *Specifying the Access for the Microsoft CA Product*

```
quizware(config)#  crypto ca identity ca.quizware.com
quizware(config-ca-identity)#  enrollment url
  http://ca.quizware.com/certsrv/mscep/mscep.dll
```

The administrator of the CA will tell you the correct URL locator to use.

The rest of the commands are optional. For example, you can specify the retry period with the **enrollment retry-period** command. This specifies how often the router resends its request to the CA when it does not get a response; the default is 1 minute. You also can specify how many times the router resends a request to the CA when the CA is not responding. By default, the router continues to do so until it gets a response. You can set the number of times with the **enrollment retry-count** command. If your CA supports an RA for redundancy, you need to tell your router this with the **enrollment mode ra** command. Your router is also configured to request a CRL automatically whenever it has a peer's certificate information in memory and wants to build a new connection when an old one is expiring. You can override this behavior with the **crl optional** command, which, if the CRL is not available, causes the router to go ahead and set up the IKE Phase 1 management connection without verifying that the certificate has been revoked. The default behavior is for the router to not rebuild the connection unless it can get a CRL from the CA (or the RA).

CRL Problems

I have experienced problems with CAs in which no CRL is created on the CA. In this situation, the management connection failed to be built. When examining output from the router's **debug** commands, it was not obvious that this was the problem. It took me a handful of days tinkering around to pinpoint this problem. When I fixed this problem, the management connection was established successfully. As I have found numerous other times when building IPSec connections, following a laid-out plan and performing things step by step helps simplify the troubleshooting process.

Step 6: Validate the CA's Identity

When you have established the identity of the CA, you need to obtain the CA's personal certificate and validate it. This is accomplished with the following command, assuming that you are using SCEP:

```
Router(config)#  crypto ca authenticate CA's_name
```

This command has the router retrieve the CA's certificate and then has you verify the CA's signature on the certificate. This process uses SCEP. Example 19-7 shows how to obtain the CA's certificate and validate it.

Example 19-7 *Obtaining the CA's Certificate and Validating It*

```
Router(config)# crypto ca authenticate ca.quizware.com
Certificate has the following attributes:
Fingerprint: 9871 A1E2 FF13 C1D0 0159
Do you accept this certificate? [yes/no] yes
Router#
```

You must answer yes or no to accept the certificate. Before you accept it, you should call the administrator of the CA and verify the signature, to ensure that it was not tampered with as it was sent from the CA to your router (a man-in-the-middle attack).

Step 7: Retrieve the Router's Personal Certificate

After you have retrieved the CA's certificate, you can go ahead and request that the CA send your router its own certificate. This process uses SCEP. Here is the command to request the router's personal certificate:

```
Router(config)#  crypto ca enroll CA's_name
```

You first are prompted for a password. This password is required and is used if you need to revoke the certificate, which reduces the likelihood of anybody calling the CA administrator and revoking a certificate. If you are using a public CA, write down this password and store it in a secure location. Without this password, you cannot revoke the router's certificate when needed.

Optionally, you can include the router's serial number or IP address as part of the certificate information. If you do this, it takes 5 to 45 seconds to get a certificate request, through SCEP, back from the CA (assuming that the CA is set up to grant certificates automatically).

If the result is successful, you should see this message:

```
%CRYPTO-6-CERTRET: Certificate received from Certificate Authority
```

If there is a problem, you will see this:

```
%CRYPTO-6-CERTREJ: Certificate enrollment request was rejected by
   Certificate Authority
```

This message indicates either that the CA rejected your request or that there is a configuration problem.

After you successfully retrieve your certificate, save your configuration, including the CA and router's certificates to NVRAM, with the **copy running-config startup-config** command. Note that the **crypto ca enroll** command and your prompt responses are not stored in NVRAM. Therefore, if you forget to save your configuration to NVRAM before the router reboots, you must go through this process again after the router comes back up.

Example 19-8 displays an example of using this command.

Example 19-8 *Obtaining Your Router's Identity Certificate*

```
quizware(config)# crypto ca enroll ca.quizware.com
% Start certificate enrollment ..
% Create a challenge password. You will need to verbally provide
    this password to the CA Administrator in order to revoke your
    certificate. For security reasons your password will not be saved
    in the configuration. Please make a note of it.
Password: mysecretpass
Re-enter password: mysecretpass
% The subject name in the certificate will be: quizware.quizware.com
% Include the router serial number in the subject name? [yes/no]: yes
% The serial number in the certificate will be: 1234567890
% Include an IP address in the subject name [yes/no]? yes
Interface: ethernet0
Request certificate from CA [yes/no]? yes
% Certificate request sent to Certificate Authority
% The certificate request fingerprint will be displayed.
% The 'show crypto ca certificate' command will also show the fingerprint.
quizware(config)#   Fingerprint: 01234567 89ABCDEF 01234567 89ABCDEF
%CRYPTO-6-CERTRET: Certificate received from Certificate Authority
quizware(config)#
```

As you can see, the router successfully acquired a certificate.

Step 8: Verify Your Router's Certificate Configuration

After you have acquired the personal certificates for the CA and your router, you can view the certificates with the **show crypto ca certificates** command, displayed in Example 19-9.

Example 19-9 *Viewing Certificates on Your Router*

```
quizware# show crypto ca certificates
Certificate
  Subject Name
    Name: quizware.quizware.com
    IP Address: 192.1.1.1
    Serial Number: 123456789
  Status: Pending
  Key Usage: General Purpose
    Fingerprint: 12AE7BCD F98513D2 A34DECB1 557891A2 00000000
CA Certificate
  Status: Available
  Certificate Serial Number: 9815321EA5DCABEF1A23F76B891C92421
  Key Usage: Not Set
<--output omitted-->
```

Notice that the status in this example is *pending*. This means that the CA has received the request but has not generated a certificate for you. In this situation, the administrator of the CA probably has automatic certificate approval disabled and must manually approve your certificate request.

Removing Your Router's Certificate

If you need to remove a certificate on your router, first view the specific certificate that you want to remove with the **show crypto ca certificates** command. Typically, you do this if your certificate has expired and you need to get a new certificate, or if you are taking this router permanently out of service. You need to know the device's FQDN in the certificate, as well as the serial number of the certificate. Next, perform the following:

```
Router(config)# crypto ca certificate chain device's_FQDN
Router(config-cert-chain)# no certificate device's_serial_#
```

The **crypto ca certificate chain** command takes you into a certificate subconfiguration mode. The **no certificate** command deletes the specific certificate.

If you no longer will be using a CA for authentication and you want to remove this configuration from your router, you first must delete the certificates for the router and the CA. After this, you need to remove the CA's configuration with the following command:

```
Router(config)# no crypto ca {identity | trustpoint} CA's_name
```

Removing Your Router's RSA Keys

If you need to remove the RSA keys on your router, perhaps to generate new ones, use the following command:

```
Router(config)# crypto key zeroize rsa
```

If the public/private key combination is used with a certificate, you need to delete the certificate first and then delete the keys.

To remove your peers' public keys that you manually have configured, first display the peer's public key information and then delete it. Based on the identity type defined in the **crypto isakmp identity** command, you use either the **no named-key** or **no addressed-key** commands. Here are the actual commands:

```
Router# show crypto key pubkey-chain rsa
Router(config)# crypto key pubkey-chain rsa
Router(config-pubkey-chain)# no named-key fully_qualified_peer_name
  [encryption | signature]
```

or:

```
Router(config-pubkey-chain)# no addressed-key IP_address_of_peer
  [encryption | signature]
```

Typically, you must perform this process if your IPSec peer has regenerated its RSA encrypted nonces keys. In this situation, you need to delete the peer's old public key and enter the new one. You must choose the appropriate key command based on the identity type configured on your router when removing the peer's public key.

IKE Phase 2: Data Connection

IKE Phase 2 is responsible for building two unidirectional data connections between the two peers. You need to perform the following things:

Step 1   Build a crypto ACL that defines what traffic is to be protected.

Step 2   Create a transform set that defines how the traffic is to be protected in the crypto ACL.

Step 3   Create a separate crypto map entry for each IPSec peer, which binds all of the IPSec information together.

Step 4   Activate the crypto map on your router's interface.

Step 5   Verify your configuration.

This section covers the basics of entering the commands to allow this process to occur.

Step 1: Building a Crypto ACL

The purpose of a crypto ACL is to define which traffic is to be protected by IPSec. Basically, a crypto ACL is an extended ACL with **permit** statements that define what traffic is to be protected. Whatever ACL you create on one peer must be mirrored on the other peer. For example, if you have the following statement on PeerA:

```
PeerA(config)# access-list 109 permit ip 192.168.1.0 0.0.0.255
   192.168.2.0 0.0.0.255
```

you must have this statement on PeerB:

```
PeerA(config)# access-list 110 permit ip 192.168.2.0 0.0.0.255
   192.168.1.0 0.0.0.255
```

Notice that the addressing information is reversed on the two sides (the ACL number or name does not have to match). If you do not configure a mirrored crypto ACL, in most cases, the setup of the data connection will fail. One interesting thing to point out about the crypto ACL is that it is not applied to any interface on the router; instead, it is activated within a crypto map entry for the peer that the traffic is destined to.

Here are some rules that apply to incoming traffic for a crypto ACL:

- If the traffic is supposed to be protected (specified in the crypto ACL) and it is not, the router drops the packets.

- If the traffic is not supposed to be protected and it is not protected, the router forwards the traffic normally.

- If the traffic is not supposed to be protected and it is IPSec traffic, the router forwards it normally (the router assumes that this IPSec traffic is for some other internal device).

These rules apply to outgoing traffic for a crypto ACL:

- If the traffic matches a crypto ACL entry, the router applies the information in the appropriate crypto map entry, to protect it.
- If the traffic does not match a crypto ACL entry, the router forwards the traffic normally.

CAUTION I highly recommend that you not use the keyword **any** for the source or destination address in a crypto ACL entry. This causes the router to treat all traffic from the source or destination as protected traffic, which can cause connectivity problems. Therefore, be as specific as possible about the traffic that is protected. This also helps reduce the processing required on your router to deal with the encryption and decryption of traffic.

NOTE If your router is handling NAT as well as IPSec connections, for outgoing traffic, router does NAT first and then the IPSec protection. Therefore, the crypto ACL should have the translated (global) address in the source address field of the ACL statement. For inbound traffic, the router handles the IPSec part first and then NAT (if necessary).

Step 2: Creating a Transform Set

Whereas the crypto ACL defines what data traffic is to be protected, a transform set defines how the data traffic is to be protected. To create a transform set, use the following command:

```
Router(config)# crypto ipsec transform-set name_of_transform_set
   transform_#1 [transform_#2 [transform_#3] [transform #4]]]
Router(config-crytpo-trans)# mode {tunnel | transport}
```

Each transform set must have a unique name. The following sections discuss the parameters that you can use to create your transform sets.

Transform Set Protection Parameters

Following the name of the transform set, you can list up to four transforms. A transform defines the protection method. Table 19-1 lists the valid transforms that you can use in your transform set. The first column lists the security protocol. To make it more readable, I have divided the table into four sections of rows; you can choose one transform from each section to be a part of your transform set. For example, you cannot have both **ah-md5-hmac** and **ad-sha-hmac** because they are from the same security protocol. Here is another invalid one: **ah-md5-hmac**, **esp-des**, and **esp-null**. This is invalid because it has two ESP encryption algorithms. However, you could have **esp-md5-hmac** and **esp-3des** in the same transform set because they are different security protocols (from different sections of the table).

Table 19-1   *Protection Transforms*

Security Protocol	Parameter	Description
AH integrity	**ah-md5-hmac**	AH packet integrity checking with MD5
AH integrity	**ah-sha-hmac**	AH packet integrity checking with SHA
ESP integrity	**esp-md5-hmac**	ESP packet integrity checking with MD5
ESP integrity	**esp-sha-hmac**	ESP packet integrity checking with SHA
ESP encryption	**esp-null**	ESP with no encryption
ESP encryption	**esp-des**	ESP with DES encryption
ESP encryption	**esp-3des**	ESP with 3DES encryption
ESP encryption	**esp-aes**	ESP with AES encryption
ESP encryption	**esp-aes192**	ESP with AES 192 encryption
ESP encryption	**esp-aes256**	ESP with AES 256 encryption
Compression	**comp-lzs**	Compression with Lempel-Ziv-Stac (LVS)

Transform Set Connection Modes

With IPSec, you can use two connection modes to pass protected data: tunnel and transport. Figure 19-1 shows an example of these two modes. The bottom shows an example of transport mode. In transport mode, the real source and destination devices perform the protection: in this case, it is the two PCs (192.1.2.1 and 200.1.2.1). Looking at the IP header of these packets, you can see the source and destination's IP addresses. Transport mode typically is used for a small number of point-to-point protected connections.

Figure 19-1   *IPSec Connection Modes*

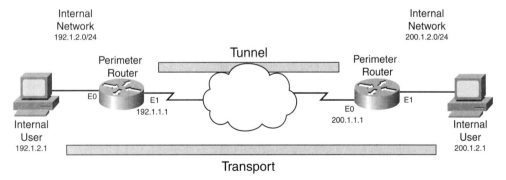

However, if you need to protect traffic between two networks, transport mode does not scale well: tunnel mode is more useful in this situation. In tunnel mode, the actual source and destination do not perform the protection; instead, an intermediate device, such as a router, firewall, or VPN concentrator, performs the protection function, as in the top connection shown in Figure 19-1 (between the two routers). Actually, the devices on the two internal networks are completely unaware of the fact that the two perimeter routers are protecting their traffic through IPSec. IP packets between the two networks are encapsulated in a packet by the perimeter routers. The new packet header includes the IP addresses of the two perimeter routers, and the original, encapsulated IP packet maintains its packet-header information (actually, the entire original packet is protected).

Tunnel mode provides these advantages:

- It centralizes the configuration of IPSec policies.

- It provides scalability because you can choose from a wide variety of IPSec platforms to build the L2L tunnels.

- Because the original IP packet is encapsulated, you can transport private IP addressing across a public network. In addition, your internal addressing scheme is hidden from prying eyes in the public network, assuming that one of your transforms is ESP encryption.

When you execute the **crypto ipsec transform-set** command, you are taken into a subconfiguration mode for your transform set. The **mode** command specifies the mode of the connection. If you do not configure the connection mode, it defaults to **tunnel**. Transport mode is used on routers on which a point-to-point connection is needed, such as from your router to a syslog or TFTP server, or for a GRE tunnel; however, in most cases, you will be using tunnel mode.

Transform Set Verification

After you have configured your transform set or sets, you can view them with the **show crypto ipsec transform-set** command, as displayed in Example 19-10.

Example 19-10 *Viewing Your Router's Transform Sets*

```
Router# show crypto ipsec transform-set
Transform set ESP-ONLY: { esp-3des esp-sha-hmac  }
  will negotiate = { Tunnel,  },
Transform set AH-AND-ESP: { ah-sha-hmac  }
  will negotiate = { Tunnel,  },
  { esp-3des esp-md5-hmac  }
  will negotiate = { Tunnel,  },
```

In Example 19-10, there are two transform sets: One is called ESP-ONLY, and the other is AH-AND-ESP. The transform set ESP-ONLY uses 3DES for encryption and SHA for packet authentication with ESP. The transform set AH-AND-ESP uses SHA for AH packet authentication, MD5 for ESP packet authentication, and 3DES for ESP encryption. Both transforms are using tunnel mode.

Step 3: Creating a Crypto Map

A crypto map ties together all of the IKE Phase 2 components to build protected data connections to remote peers. A crypto map contains the following information:

- The name or address of the remote IPSec peer.

- The local address that the router should use when sending traffic to the remote IPSec peer. By default, this is the interface that traffic exits to reach the remote peer. However, if your router has two physical interfaces by which the remote peer can reach you, you might want to set up a loopback interface and specify the address on this interface for use with IPSec source and termination points.

- Which data traffic should be protected to the remote IPSec peer, specified in a crypto ACL.

- The transform set to use to protect the data traffic.

- The lifetime of the data connections.

Crypto Map Rules

Crypto maps cannot be created haphazardly: You must follow rules when building a crypto map. For example, a crypto map must contain the following information for an L2L connection:

- It must contain the IP address of the remote peer.

- It must contain the method of negotiation: manual or dynamic ISAKMP/IKE (this book covers only the dynamic method).

- It must contain the traffic that should be protected (this crypto ACL needs to be mirrored on the remote peer).

- Crypto ACLs should not overlap between different entries of a crypto map (this is a common problem I have seen in troubleshooting IPSec connections to multiple peers).

- At least one matching transform set must exist on the remote peer.

If you do not have this information for an L2L connection, the appropriate SAs are not built. SAs that are built are assigned an index number, called a Security Parameter Index (SPI) value. This number uniquely identifies the connection between the peers, and this value is placed in the AH and ESP headers of the IPSec packets. When SAs are built between the two peers (one bidirectional management SA for IKE Phase 1, and two unidirectional data SAs for IKE Phase 2), the components of the IKE Phase 1 policies and the crypto map define what is to be protected and how it is protected. The router uses the SPI values to determine what information in these components to use for the protection or verification of a connection.

Crypto Map Types

Basically two types of crypto maps exist:

- **Static map**—This type of map is used for L2L connections when you know the connection information for the remote peer and when your router will be initiating the connection to the remote peer.

- **Dynamic map**—This type of map is used for remote-access connections and L2L connections when the remote peer is establishing the connection to you and you do not know, up front, what information the peer will be using to protect the connection. A good example of this is a remote peer that acquires its address from its ISP through Dynamic Host Configuration Protocol (DHCP) or PPPoE. In this example, you do not know the peer's IP address until it connects to the ISP and then connects to you. In this situation, you cannot use a static map because a static map requires you to know, up front, the IP address of the peer.

This chapter focuses only on static crypto maps; the next chapter, "IPSec Remote-Access Connections," discusses dynamic crypto maps.

A crypto map can have one or more entries in it. You need more than one entry in your crypto map if the any of the following is true:

- You need connections to multiple peers (sites).

- You want different types of protection to the same or different peers.

- You are using manual ISAKMP. With manual ISAKMP, the crypto ACL where you specify protected traffic can have only the **permit** statement in it. If you need multiple **permit** statements, you need a separate crypto map entry for each **permit** statement.

Static Crypto Map Entries

Now take a look at creating static crypto map entries in your crypto map. To create a static crypto map entry, use the following command:

```
Router(config)#  crypto map name_of_crypto_map sequence_#
  {ipsec-isakmp I ipsec-manual I cisco}
Router(config-crypto-map)#
```

A crypto map is like an ACL, in that a crypto map can have multiple entries in it. And like a named ACL, the crypto map must be given a name to bind these entries to the crypto map. This name must be unique among all names of crypto maps on your router. Typically, you have to create only one crypto map, but it might have several entries in it.

Following the name of the crypto map, you give it a sequence number. This identifies the specific entry for the crypto map. The router uses these sequence numbers to determine what parameters to use for protection for a particular peer. The sequence numbers are important because the router processes them from lowest to highest numbered. Therefore, the most secure entry should have the lowest sequence number, and the least secure entry should have the highest sequence number. When a remote peer makes a connection to your router, your router processes these in order until it finds a match for the peer. If no match is found, no IPSec connections are built between the two peers.

After you have entered a sequence number, you must specify the method of negotiation. You have three options:

- **ipsec-isakmp**—This method uses ISAKMP/IKE to negotiate the security parameters, including keying information.

- **ipsec-manual**—This method requires you manually to configure the ISAKMP/IKE parameters, including the packet authentication and encryption keys to use. (This method should be used only if the remote side does not support ISAKMP/IKE; this book does not cover this option.)

- **cisco**—This method uses the old Cisco VPN technology called Cisco Encryption Technology (CET). Cisco has replaced CET with IPSec.

Upon entering the negotiation method, press the Enter key to move into a subconfiguration mode where you can enter the information to protect the data SA.

Entry Commands

For static crypto map entries that use ISAKMP/IKE, here is the basic configuration to use for a specific entry:

```
Router(config)# crypto map name_of_crypto_map seq_#  ipsec-isakmp
Router(config-crypto-map)# match address ACL_#_or_name
Router(config-crypto-map)# set peer hostname_or_IP_address
Router(config-crypto-map)# set transform-set
  name_of_transform_set1 [name_of_transform_set2...set6]
Router(config-crypto-map)# set pfs [group1 | group2 | group5]
Router(config-crypto-map)# set security-association lifetime
  seconds #_of_seconds
Router(config-crypto-map)# set security-association lifetime
  kilobytes #_of_kilobytes
```

For a static crypto map entry, three commands are required: **match address**, **set peer**, and **set transform-set**. The **match address** command specifies the traffic to be protected. With this command, you reference your crypto ACL.

The **set peer** command specifies either the IP address or the name of the remote peer to which the router will be making IPSec connections. You can list more than one of these commands for multiple peers. However, this is only for redundancy; the router uses the peer in the first **set peer** command that you configure and uses other peers only if the first peer is not reachable. If you want to set up more than one connection to a peer, you need to create multiple crypto map entries.

NOTE   I recommend not using the name option for a peer unless you statically configure name resolution with the **ip host** command. Remember that DNS can be easily hijacked.

The **set transform set** command specifies the transform set to use to protect the IKE Phase 2 data connection to this peer. You can list up to six transform sets. The order in which you list them is important: The remote peer looks for a matching transform set based on the order in which you entered the transforms. Therefore, make sure that you configure the most secure transform first and the least secure last. Typically, with L2L connections, you control the protection used on the routers at both ends. In this case, you need to configure only one transform and specify it here.

The **set pfs** command is optional. PFS stands for Perfect Forward Secrecy. When you enable this option, you are specifying that DH should be used to exchange the keying information instead of the existing IPSec connection. DH's advantages are that if the old connection was compromised, keying information will not be sent across it, and that DH is more secure than the connection-encryption algorithms because of the key size used. However, the downside of using PFS is that it adds delay because the DH connection must be built. Only three DH groups are supported: groups 1, 2, and 5. If you omit the group designation, it defaults to **group1**, which is the least secure (group 5 is the most secure).

You can associate two lifetime values with your IKE Phase 2 data connections. You can configure these on a peer-by-peer basis or globally. Configuring these timeout values in a crypto map entry overrides the global values. The two lifetimes are based on time, in seconds, and in kilobytes transferred. The default lifetime in seconds is 3600 (1 hour), which you can override with the **set security-association lifetime seconds** crypto map command. The default lifetime for amount of data transferred is 4,608,000 KB; you can override this with the **set security-association lifetime kilobytes** command. When either of these lifetimes is almost reached, the router begins building new data connections to replace the ones that are just about to expire.

If you want to set these lifetimes globally instead of tuning them for each IPSec connection, use the following two global configuration mode commands:

```
Router(config)# crypto ipsec security-association lifetime
  seconds #_of_seconds
Router(config)# crypto ipsec security-association lifetime
  kilobytes #_of_kilobytes
```

Any timeout specified in a crypto map entry overrides the globally defined values.

Step 4: Activating a Crypto Map

After you have created a crypto map, you need to activate it. Activation is accomplished just like activating an ACL: You activate it on an interface. With crypto maps, only one crypto map can be activated on a router's interface. However, you can have the same or different crypto maps activated on different router interfaces. Normally, you need to create only a single crypto map and activate this on your router's public, or external, interface. However, if your perimeter router has two public interfaces, you can activate the same crypto map on multiple interfaces.

To activate your crypto map on an interface, use the following command:

```
Router(config)# interface type [slot_#/]port_#
Router(config-if)# crypto map name_of_the_crypto_map
```

By default, when you have activated a crypto map on your router's interface, the router uses the IP address on this interface as the source IP address in its IPSec packets. If your router has two public interfaces, for example, and you want your router to use the same IP address for both interfaces (perhaps a loopback interface), use the following command:

```
Router(config)#  crypto map name_of_the_crypto_map
  local-address name_of_interface
```

For example, if you have a loopback0 interface and want the router to use this as the source (and termination point) of its IPSec transmissions, you would configure the following:

```
Router(config)# crypto map MYMAP local-address loopback0
```

Note that you still would apply the crypto map to the physical interfaces connected to the public network.

Step 5: Verifying a Crypto Map Configuration

To verify your crypto map configuration, use the following command:

```
Router#  show crypto map [{interface interface_name] |
  tag crypto_map_name}]
```

This command displays your crypto map configuration. Optionally, the **interface** parameter lists only the crypto map activated on the specified interface. The **tag** parameter displays only the specified crypto map name. Example 19-11 shows an example of the use of the **show crypto map** command.

Example 19-11 *Viewing Your Crypto Maps*

```
Router# show crypto map
Crypto Map: "MYMAP" idb: Ethernet1 local address: 192.1.1.1
Crypto Map "MYMAP" 10 ipsec-isakmp
  Peer = 200.1.1.1
  Extended IP access list 100
    access-list 100 permit ip
      source: addr = 192.168.1.0/255.255.255.0
      dest:   addr = 192.168.2.0/255.255.255.0
  Current peer: 200.1.1.1
  Security-association lifetime:
    4608000 kilobytes/3600 seconds
  PFS (Y/N): N
  Transform sets={ RemotePeerTransform, }
```

In this example, the crypto map is applied to interface ethernet1, and the local IP address used for IPSec communications is 192.1.1.1. There is only one entry in this crypto map, called MYMAP, with a sequence number of 10. The peer specified is 200.1.1.1, and the crypto ACL is 100, which protects traffic between the local network (192.168.1.0/24) and the remote network (192.168.2.0/24). Below this are the lifetime values for this peer, whether or not PFS is used, and the list of transform sets used. In this example, only one transform set is used: RemotePeerTransform.

IPSec Connection Troubleshooting

Probably one of the most difficult things to troubleshoot on a router is IPSec connections that just do not want to work, no matter what you try to do. In my upcoming book *The Complete Cisco VPN Configuration Guide* (Cisco Press, 2005), I devote a separate chapter for troubleshooting for Cisco IOS routers, PIX firewalls, and the 3000 series concentrators. In this section, I cover only the very basics of troubleshooting IPSec VPN connections.

TIP	To troubleshoot IPSec connection problems, you must be familiar with how IPSec connections are set up and the negotiation process that occurs between peers. Many times I have used **show** and **debug** commands on Cisco devices to troubleshoot problems, only to find out that the problem I was experiencing was not showing up in the output of these commands. Of course, this has happened only a handful of times. In most instances, the output of **debug** commands will pinpoint the problem. Only through an intimate knowledge of IPSec was I able to diagnose these oddball problems correctly. Plus, to understand the output of the **debug** commands, which is quite copious, you must understand the process that IPSec goes through in establishing connections. Therefore, if you will be working with IPSec and VPNs quite a bit, I definitely recommend that you pick up a book on VPNs that explains in detail not only how IPSec connections are set up, but also how to read diagnostic information from commands such as **debug**.

Examining SAs

As you recall from the "Defining IKE Phase 1 Policies" section, earlier in this chapter, three connections are set up in IPSec: one bidirectional management connection during IKE Phase 1, and two unidirectional data connections during IKE Phase 2.

To view the IKE Phase 1 management connections, use the **show crypto isakmp sa** command. Example 19-12 shows sample **show crypto isakmp sa** output.

Example 19-12 *Viewing the IKE Phase 1 Management Connection*

```
Router# show crypto isakmp sa
dst          src        state     conn-id   slot
200.1.1.1    192.1.1.1  QM_IDLE         3      0
```

When troubleshooting, this is the first command that you should use to determine whether you have an IKE Phase 1 management connection to the remote peer. The state column in this output displays the status of the management connection. If it says QM_IDLE, this indicates that the router was successful in establishing a connection to the remote peer. Table 19-2 describes the various states of the connection that you can see in this column.

Table 19-2 *IPSec Connection States*

ISAKMP/IKE Mode	State	Description
IKE Phase 1 Main Mode	MM_NO_STATE	During IKE Phase 1 main mode, the management SA was created on the router, but nothing has been negotiated with the remote peer.
	MM_SA_SETUP	During IKE Phase 1 main mode, both IPSec peers successfully negotiated the IKE policy parameters.
	MM_KEY_EXCH	During IKE Phase 1 main mode, the DH exchange occurred, and a shared secret key was generated.
	MM_KEY_AUTH	During IKE Phase 1 main mode, the authentication of the identity of both peers was successful, and IKE Phase 2 now can begin.
IKE Phase 1 Aggressive Mode	AG_NO_STATE	During IKE Phase 1 aggressive mode, the management SA was created on the router, but nothing has been negotiated with the remote peer.
	AG_INIT_EXCH	During IKE Phase 1 aggressive mode, both IPSec peers successfully negotiated the IKE policy parameters, and the DH exchange occurred, with a shared secret key being generated.
	AG_AUTH	During IKE Phase 1 aggressive mode, the authentication of the identity of both peers was successful, and IKE Phase 2 can begin.
IKE Phase 2 Quick Mode	QM_IDLE	This completes IKE Phase 1 and the beginning, and possibly the ending of IKE Phase 2.

To view the IPSec data that SAs built in IKE Phase 2, use the **show crypto ipsec sa** command. Example 19-13 shows sample output from this command.

Example 19-13 *Viewing the IKE Phase 2 Data Connections*

```
Router# show crypto ipsec sa
interface: Ethernet1                                              (1)
   Crypto map tag: IPSECMAP, local addr. 192.1.1.1

   local  ident (addr/mask/prot/port):                           (2)
                   (192.1.1.1/255.255.255.255/0/0)
   remote ident (addr/mask/prot/port):
                   (200.1.1.1/255.255.255.255/0/0)
   current_peer: 200.1.1.1
     PERMIT, flags={origin_is_acl,}
   #pkts encaps: 20, #pkts encrypt: 20, #pkts digest 20          (3)
   #pkts decaps: 20, #pkts decrypt: 20, #pkts verify 20
   #send errors 0, #rcv errors 0
     local crypto endpt.: 192.1.1.1,                             (4)
        remote crypto endpt.: 200.1.1.1
     path mtu 1500, media mtu 1500
     current outbound spi: 20890A6E

     inbound esp sas:                                            (5)
      spi: 0x257A1038(628756536)
        transform: esp-sha-hmac, esp-3des,
        in use settings ={Tunnel, }
        slot: 0, conn id: 14, crypto map: IPSECMAP
        sa timing: remaining key lifetime (k/sec): (4607999/3600)
        IV size: 8 bytes
        replay detection support: Y
     inbound ah sas:
     outbound esp sas:
      spi: 0x20890A6E(545852014)
        transform: esp-sha-hmac, esp-3des,
        in use settings ={Tunnel, }
        slot: 0, conn id: 15, crypto map: IPSECMAP
        sa timing: remaining key lifetime (k/sec): (4607999/3600)
        IV size: 8 bytes
        replay detection support: Y
     outbound ah sas:
```

The following is a brief explanation of the output in Example 19-13, with reference to the numbering on the right side:

1 On Ethernet1, the crypto map named IPSECMAP is enabled, and the IP address that this router uses for IPSec communications is 192.1.1.1.

2 The local and remote ident lines display the peers involved in the connection.

3 If the connection successfully has been set up, you should see the number of packets that were encapsulated and encrypted, that had an ICV value attached to them when set to the remote peer, and the opposite when received from the remote peer.

4 These are the local and remote endpoints for the IPSec connection, as well as the MTU used.

5 There will be two sets of SAs for each tunnel: inbound and outbound. Inbound is from the remote peer to this router. Outbound is from this router to the remote peer. For both inbound and outbound, there are two sections: one for ESP and one for AH. In this example, there is nothing listed under AH, indicating that AH is not used to protect the connection. I examine one of these sections, *inbound esp sas*, to explain some of the information found for a connection. First, notice that each of these connections has a unique SPI value. For the inbound ESP SA, the transform parameters used to protect it are ESP SHA and 3DES encryption. The connection mode is tunnel mode.

The **show crypto engine connections** command is also a useful troubleshooting tool. It enables you to examine information about the encryption and decryption process. Here are some parameters that you can use with this command:

- **active**—View the active connections using **encryption/decryption**.
- **dh**—View the DH connections.
- **dropped-packet**—View information about dropped packets.
- **flow**—View flow table entries.

Using debug Commands

You can use many **debug** commands to troubleshoot the setup and maintenance of IPSec SAs. Here is a basic list of **debug** commands:

- **debug crypto engine**—Troubleshoots the encryption and decryption process by the router
- **debug crypto isakmp**—Troubleshoots IKE Phase 1 connections
- **debug crypto key-exchange**—Troubleshoots key exchange problems, including DH
- **debug crypto pki transactions**—Troubleshoots public key infrastructure (PKI) certificate problems, including the enrollment and verification process
- **debug crypto ipsec**—Troubleshoots IKE Phase 2 connections

Most IPSec problems are related to the negotiation process in IKE Phase 1, so I briefly look at the output of the **debug crypto isakmp** command. Example 19-14 shows sample output.

Example 19-14 *Using the* **debug crypto isakmp** *Command*

```
Router# debug crypto isakmp
15:31:51: ISAKMP (8): beginning Main Mode exchange
15:31:51: ISAKMP (8): processing SA payload. message ID = 0
15:31:51: ISAKMP (8): Checking ISAKMP transform 1 against          (1)
  priority 100 policy
15:31:51: ISAKMP: encryption 3DES-CBC
15:31:51: ISAKMP: hash SHA
15:31:51: ISAKMP: default group 2
15:31:51: ISAKMP: auth pre-share
15:31:51: ISAKMP (8): atts are acceptable. Next payload is 0        (2)
15:31:51: ISAKMP (8): SA is doing pre-shared key authentication     (3)
```

Example 19-14 *Using the* **debug crypto isakmp** *Command (Continued)*

```
15:31:52: ISAKMP (8): processing KE payload. message ID = 0
15:31:52: ISAKMP (8): processing NONCE payload. message ID = 0
15:31:52: ISAKMP (8): SKEYID state generated
15:31:52: ISAKMP (8): processing ID payload. message ID = 0
15:31:52: ISAKMP (8): processing HASH payload. message ID = 0
15:31:52: ISAKMP (8): SA has been authenticated              (4)
15:31:52: ISAKMP (8): beginning Quick Mode exchange,         (5)
 M-ID of 767162845
15:31:52: ISAKMP (8): processing SA payload.
 message ID = 767162845
15:31:52: ISAKMP (8): Checking IPSec proposal 1              (6)
15:31:52: ISAKMP: transform 1, ESP_3DES
15:31:52: ISAKMP: attributes in transform:
15:31:52: ISAKMP: encaps is 1
15:31:52: ISAKMP: SA life type in seconds
15:31:52: ISAKMP: SA life duration (basic) of 3600
15:31:52: ISAKMP: SA life type in kilobytes
15:31:52: ISAKMP: SA life duration (VPI) of 0x0 0x46 0x50 0x0
15:31:52: ISAKMP: authenticator is HMAC-SHA
15:31:52: ISAKMP (8): atts are acceptable.                   (7)
15:31:52: ISAKMP (8): processing NONCE payload.
 message ID = 767162845
15:31:52: ISAKMP (8): processing ID payload.
 message ID = 767162845
15:31:52: ISAKMP (8): processing ID payload.
 message ID = 767162845
15:31:52: ISAKMP (8): Creating IPSec SAs
15:31:52: inbound SA from 200.1.1.1 to 192.1.1.1
 (proxy 200.1.1.1 to 192.1.1.1 )
15:31:52: has spi 134123537 and conn_id 10 and flags 4
15:31:52: lifetime of 3600 seconds
15:31:52: lifetime of 4608000 kilobytes
15:31:52: outbound SA from 192.1.1.1 to 200.1.1.1
 (proxy 192.1.1.1 to 200.1.1.1)
15:31:52: has spi 88123189 and conn_id 11 and flags 4
15:31:52: lifetime of 3600 seconds
15:31:59: lifetime of 4608000 kilobytes
```

The following is a brief explanation of the output in Example 19-14, with reference to the numbering on the right side:

1 In this reference, the two peers have exchanged their IKE Phase 1 policies, and this router is comparing the remote peer's first policy (policy 1) to the local policy 100.

2 In this example, I was lucky and the first policy matched (atts are acceptable).

3 Because identity authentication was specified as preshare in the matching ISAKMP policy, this is being performed now.

4 The preshared key authentication was successful, completing IKE Phase 1.

5 IKE Phase 2 begins.

> **6** The crypto map transform sets are being compared between the two peers.
>
> **7** A match was found on the first pair of transform sets, and now one data SA is created in each direction.

Clearing Connections

Two basic **clear** commands exist: One deals with IKE Phase 1, and the other deals with IPSec SAs. To clear your active IKE Phase 1 management connections, use the **clear iskamp sa** command:

```
Router# clear crypto isakmp [connection_ID]
```

If you omit the connection_ID, all management connections are deleted. To delete a specific connection, specify the connection's connection_ID. This can be found in the conn-id column of the output of the **show crypto isakmp sa** command.

To remove all IPSec connections on your router, use the privileged EXEC **clear crypto sa** command. You should clear your connections any time you make a policy change to your IPSec configuration. Instead of deleting all of your IPSec SAs, you can modify this command by adding another parameter to restrict the connections that are deleted. Here are the variations of this command:

- **clear crypto sa peer** {*IP_address* | *host_name*}—Removes all SAs specific to a single IPSec peer

- **clear crypto sa map** *crypto_map_name*—Removes all SAs specific to the named crypto map

- **clear crypto sa entry** *dest_IP_address protocol spi_#*—Removes a specific SA to a particular IPSec peer

- **clear crypto sa counters**—Clears your SA traffic counters only (not the actual SAs)

L2L Example

To help you better understand the setup of an L2L connection, I will show you an example. This example uses the network in Figure 19-2 for this L2L connection. In this example, two sites need to connect across the Internet using an IPSec L2L connection between two perimeter routers.

Figure 19-2 *L2L Example*

For this example, the IPSec policies are as follows:

- **Peers**—192.1.1.1 and 200.1.1.1
- **ISAKMP/IKE policy**—3DES for encryption, SHA for packet authentication, DH group 2 keys, lifetime of 1 hour
- **Protected traffic**—Anything between 192.168.1.0/24 and 192.168.2.0/24
- **Connection method**—Tunnel
- **Data transforms**—ESP 3DES encryption and ESP SHA packet authentication

Example 19-15 shows RouterA's configuration.

Example 19-15 *RouterA's L2L Configuration*

```
RouterA(config)# access-list 100 permit udp host 200.1.1.1      (1)
  host 192.1.1.1 eq isakmp
RouterA(config)# access-list 100 permit esp host 200.1.1.1
  host 192.1.1.1
RouterA(config)# remark <--include other ACL statements for
  ACL 100-->
RouterA(config)# crypto isakmp policy 10                        (2)
RouterA(config-isakmp)# authentication pre-share
RouterA(config-isakmp)# encryption 3des
RouterA(config-isakmp)# group 2
RouterA(config-isakmp)# lifetime 3600
RouterA(config-isakmp)# exit
RouterA(config)# crypto isakmp key 123RouterL2L address 200.1.1.1 (3)
RouterA(config)# access-list 101 permit ip 192.168.1.0 0.0.0.255 (4)
  192.168.2.0 0.0.0.255
RouterA(config)# crypto ipsec transform-set RouterBtransform    (5)
  esp-sha-hmac esp-3des
RouterA(config)# crypto map IPSECMAP 100 ipsec-isakmp           (6)
RouterA(config-crypto-map)# match address 101
RouterA(config-crypto-map)# set peer 200.1.1.1
RouterA(config-crypto-map)# set transform-set RouterBtransform
RouterA(config-crypto-map)# exit
RouterA(config)# access-list 102 deny ip 192.168.1.0 0.0.0.255  (7)
  192.168.2.0 0.0.0.255
RouterA(config)# access-list 102 permit ip 192.168.1.0 0.0.0.255
  any
RouterA(config)# ip nat inside source list 102                  (8)
  interface Ethernet1 overload
RouterA(config)# interface ethernet0
RouterA(config-if)# ip nat inside
RouterA(config-if)# exit
RouterA(config)# interface ethernet1                            (9)
RouterA(config-if)# ip nat outside
RouterA(config-if)# ip access-group 100 in
RouterA(config-if)# ip address 192.1.1.1
RouterA(config-if)# crypto map IPSECMAP
```

The following is a brief explanation of RouterA's configuration in Example 19-15, with reference to the numbering on the right side:

1 This ACL allows ISAKMP/IKE and ESP traffic between the two routers. You obviously need to add many more statements to this ACL, to allow other types of connections.

2 ISAKMP policy 10 defines the parameters used to secure the IKE Phase 1 management connection.

3 Because preshared keys are used for identity authentication, the **crypto isakmp key** command specifies the preshared key; this must match the key value on RouterB.

4 ACL 101 is the crypto ACL, specifying that traffic between 192.168.1.0/24 and 192.168.2.0/24 should be protected.

5 The IKE Phase 2 data connections should be protected with ESP with SHA packet authentication and 3DES encryption.

6 There is only one entry in the crypto map: 100. This entry specifies the traffic to be protected (ACL 101), the remote peer (200.1.1.1), and the transform set to protect the traffic (RouterBtransform).

7 ACL 102 is used to specify when address translation is to be performed. In this example, it is disabled between 192.168.1.0/24 and 192.168.2.0/24, but it is enabled when 192.168.1.0/24 tries to reach any other Internet destination.

8 PAT is used for address translation with ACL 102.

9 On the interface, the protection ACL is applied (100) and the crypto map is activated (IPSECMAP).

Example 19-16 shows RouterB's configuration.

Example 19-16 *RouterB's L2L Configuration*

```
RouterB(config)# access-list 100 permit udp host 200.1.1.1
  host 192.1.1.1 eq isakmp
RouterB(config)# access-list 100 permit esp host 200.1.1.1
  host 192.1.1.1
RouterB(config)# remark <--include other ACL statements for
  ACL 100-->
RouterB(config)# crypto isakmp policy 10
RouterB(config-isakmp)# authentication pre-share
RouterB(config-isakmp)# encryption 3des
RouterB(config-isakmp)# group 2
RouterB(config-isakmp)# lifetime 3600
RouterB(config-isakmp)# exit
RouterA(config)# crypto isakmp key 123RouterL2L address 192.1.1.1
RouterB(config)# access-list 101 permit ip 192.168.2.0 0.0.0.255
  192.168.1.0 0.0.0.255
RouterB(config)# crypto ipsec transform-set RouterAtransform
  esp-sha-hmac esp-3des
```

Example 19-16 *RouterB's L2L Configuration (Continued)*

```
RouterB(config)# crypto map IPSECMAP 100 ipsec-isakmp
RouterB(config-crypto-map)# match address 101
RouterB(config-crypto-map)# set peer 192.1.1.1
RouterB(config-crypto-map)# set transform-set RouterAtransform
RouterB(config-crypto-map)# exit
RouterA(config)# access-list 102 deny ip 192.168.2.0 0.0.0.255
  192.168.1.0 0.0.0.255
RouterA(config)# access-list 102 permit ip 192.168.2.0 0.0.0.255
  any
RouterA(config)# ip nat inside source list 102
  interface Ethernet1 overload
RouterA(config)# interface ethernet0
RouterA(config-if)# ip nat inside
RouterA(config-if)# exit
RouterB(config)# interface ethernet 1
RouterB(config-if)# ip nat outside
RouterB(config-if)# ip access-group 100 in
RouterB(config-if)# ip address 200.1.1.1
RouterB(config-if)# crypto map IPSECMAP
```

As you can see from RouterB's configuration, it is very similar to RouterA's.

NOTE   If you have static translations, you need to use route maps and possibly loopback interfaces to resolve address-translation issues with the VPN. An example of this can be found at http://www.cisco.com/en/US/tech/tk583/tk372/technologies_configuration_example09186a0080094634.shtml.

Summary

This chapter showed you the basics of setting up L2L connections between Cisco IOS routers. With L2L connections, you need to handle design and policy issues, allow for IPSec traffic, configure your IKE Phase 1 management connection policies, define what data traffic is to be protected by IPSec, create your data transforms, build a crypto map, activate your crypto map, and test your configuration. Even with a simple example as I explained at the end of the chapter, you must perform a lot of configuration tasks to set up your L2L connection. This chapter provided a brief overview of the process, but you might have to do many other things, depending your router's setup and your connection needs, to set up the L2L connection (however, this is beyond the scope of this book).

Next up is Chapter 20, which shows you how to set up IPSec remote-access client VPN connections to your router.

## CHAPTER 20

IPSec Remote-Access Connections

This chapter covers the basic of using a Cisco router to terminate IPSec remote-access connections. Although the setup of remote-access connections can involve many different types of remote-access clients, such as IPSec, L2TP, PPTP, software and hardware, client and server, and others, I focus only on using a Cisco router to terminate IPSec remote-access connections. Look to my upcoming book *The Complete Cisco VPN Configuration Guide* (Cisco Press, 2005), for more information about remote-access VPNs with Cisco products.

This chapter covers the IPSec remote-access connection-setup process for setting up the EasyVPN server on a Cisco router, and gives an example of the EasyVPN server configuration on a router.

Remote Access Overview

IPSec remote access is used to connect remote-access clients, such as a PC or small office, home office (SOHO) device (a small-end router or firewall appliance) to a corporate network. Figure 20-1 shows a simple example. In a remote-access VPN connection, the client has two IP addresses: one assigned to the NIC and one assigned by the VPN corporate device.

In Figure 20-1, the remote-access PC has an IP address that the ISP assigned to its NIC, by either DHCP, PPPoE, or PPP (dialup), and one that the corporate office VPN router assigned it internally. The client uses ESP tunnel mode to send packets to the corporate office network. The original IP packet has a source address that internally was assigned (192.168.1.100) and a destination address of the corporate network (192.168.1.0/24) when sent to the corporate network. ESP tunnel mode encapsulates this packet and adds a new IP header, where the source address is the ISP-assigned address for the source (200.1.1.1) and the destination address is (192.1.1.1), the corporate office VPN router. However, when the client sends packets to other destinations, such as Internet sites, it uses normal IP packets with its ISP-assigned address as the source.

NOTE	One of the interesting things about this scenario is that, from the corporate office's perspective, the client looks like it is attached directly to the 192.168.1.0/24 network, when, in reality, it is connected through a VPN across a public network.

Figure 20-1 *Remote-Access VPN Example*

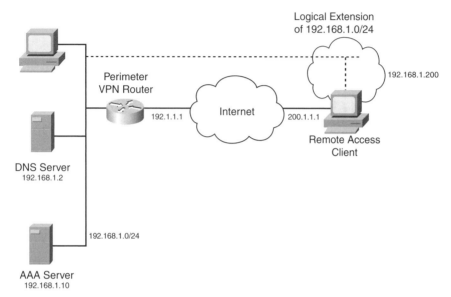

You have a lot of management and policy flexibility in this design. Typically, access policies are defined on the corporate side and are pushed down to the client. Information that the corporate device can assign to the client includes the internal IP address, DNS and WINS server addresses, the domain name, filtering and split tunneling policies, and many other items. In addition, when it comes to authentication, you can have the VPN corporate device perform authentication of the client or pass off the authentication to a AAA server, like the one shown in Figure 20-1.

EasyVPN Introduction

EasyVPN is a feature that Cisco developed to make the deployment of remote-access VPNs a simple process. It provides for consistent policies and key management, centralizing your administration and simplifying your configuration. EasyVPN has two components:

- EasyVPN server (EVS)
- EasyVPN client (EVC) or remote (EVR)

The EVS component is responsible for terminating the remote-access VPN connection at the corporate site. This can be an IOS-based router (12.2[8]T and later), a PIX firewall (FOS 6.0 and later), or the 3000 series concentrators (version 3.0 and later). For large numbers of remote-access client connections, both Cisco and I recommend the use of a VPN concentrator. Typically, routers are used for site-to-site connections. VPN concentrators support many more VPN features than IOS routers or PIX firewalls; however, for site-to-site connections and a small number of remote-access connections, an IOS router is an ideal solution, especially if you already have a router in place that can perform this process.

The EVC component is responsible for initiating the VPN connection. Cisco devices that can perform the function of a client include the VPN 3002 hardware client; the 800, 900, and 1700 series routers (IOS 12.2[15]T for Phase 2 support); and the PIX 501 firewall (FOS 6.2). The Cisco Secure and Unity 3.*x* and 4.*x* software clients also can perform the role of a client. One of the interesting things about the EVC is that some of Cisco's smaller-end routers can perform the function of a client. This provides more flexibility on your part because you can define access policies on your EVS and have these pushed down to your EVC router.

EasyVPN IPSec Support

EasyVPN uses IPSec to establish remote-access connections. Here are the IPSec components that EasyVPN supports:

- **ISAKMP/IKE**—Only dynamic support for ISAKMP/IKE is supported. Manual configuration is not.
- **Authentication methods**—Only RSA signatures and preshared keys are supported.
- **Encryption algorithms**—DES, 3DES, AES, AES-192, AES-256, and null (for data connections only) are supported.
- **Hashing functions**—MD5 and SHA are supported.
- **Diffie-Hellman (DH) key groups**—Groups 2 and 5 are supported.
- **Data-connection parameters**—ESP in tunnel mode and LZS compression are supported.

The following items are not supported:

- Digital Signature Standard (DSS) authentication
- Diffie-Hellman (DH) group 1 keys
- Authentication Header (AH) protocol
- Encapsulation Security Payload (ESP) transport mode
- Manual keying with ISAKMP/IKE
- Perfect forward secrecy (PFS)

EasyVPN Features

EasyVPN features include the following:

- **Policy push**—As I already mentioned, you can define policies on your EVS and have these pushed down to your EVCs.
- **Group and user policies**—You can implement group and user policies. Group policies apply to a group of devices or users, and user policies apply to a single device or user. With groups, you can more easily segregate your clients into appropriate categories and then apply policies on a group-by-group basis.

- **XAUTH authentication**—Remote access supports two types of authentication: device and user. I discussed the three different methods of performing device authentication in Chapter 19, "IPSec Site-to-Site Connections": preshared keys, RSA encrypted nonces, and RSA signatures (digital certificates). Remote access supports a second type of authentication, called user, or XAUTH, authentication, which enables you to give each user a username and password. This has an advantage over device authentication because the authentication information is stored on the device. As an example, if a user's laptop is stolen and you were using only device authentication, the thief who stole the laptop would have access to your network because he would not have to enter manually the authentication information—it is already stored on the device. XAUTH adds another layer of protection. With policy push, you can prevent the user from storing the user's password on the user device. Therefore, even if the user's device was compromised or stolen, the perpetrator still cannot access your corporate network using a VPN unless that hacker also knows the user's personal username and password.

- **Split tunneling**—Split tunneling is the capability to assign a policy that defines what is and is not tunneled through the remote-access VPN connection. The default policy is to force the client to send all traffic to the central site, through the VPN, and then have the central site forward the traffic. However, in certain cases, this does not make sense, especially if the information that the remote client wants is located at the local ISP or on a local LAN segment. Split tunneling enables you to assign tunneling policies on the EVS and push these policies down to the client.

- **Split DNS**—Split DNS is similar to split tunneling, and the two typically are used together. Split DNS allows a client to have two sets of DNS servers: one set for accessing services through the VPN connection, and another set for accessing services outside the VPN connection (the Internet).

- **IKE mode config**—IKE mode config allows the EVS to assign configuration information to the client. This configuration information includes the client's internal IP address, DNS server addresses, WINS server addresses, a domain name, filtering policies and restrictions, split tunneling, and other configuration and policy components.

- **IKE dead peer detection (DPD)**—DPD allows an EVS or EVC to detect a device failure at the other end of the VPN connection. Basically, IKE DPD is a remote-access VPN keepalive function. This is very useful for dialup clients that are prone to connection drops. In this situation, an EVS quickly can detect that a client is no longer there and can remove its connection information. Likewise, this feature provides redundancy for clients. If the client detects that its current EVS is no longer reachable, the client can initiate a connection to a secondary EVS. Note that DPD also can be used for LAN-to-LAN (L2L) connections.

- **Initial contact**—Initial contact is used when an EVC unexpectedly becomes disconnected from an EVS, and the EVC attempts to reconnect to the EVS. Without this feature, the EVS would not allow the new connection because the EVS assumes that the client already is connected (by a dead connection). Initial contact allows the EVS to remove the old security associations (SAs) for the EVC and build new ones.

- **NAT transparency (NAT-T)**—NAT-T, introduced in IOS 12.2(13)T, is an IPSec component that allows remote-access connections to be established through an address-translation device, specifically one that uses Port Address Translation. It accomplishes this by encapsulating the IPSec (ESP) packets in a UDP segment, using destination port 4500. To detect whether an address-translation device exists between the two IPSec devices, the two peers send a payload of hashes to each other: If both ends can verify the payload hashes, no translation was performed and the IPSec connection is set up normally; otherwise, if the payload hashes are invalidated, the peers automatically use NAT-T. The address-translation detection process takes place during IKE Phase 1; the use of NAT-T takes place in IKE Phase 2. NAT keepalives are generated by the two peers to ensure that the address-translation entry for the devices remains in the address-translation table on the address-translation device.

IPSec Remote-Access Connection Process

Setup for an IPSec remote-access connection is more complex than that for an L2L connection. Basically, when setting up an IPSec remote access connection, seven steps occur:

1 The EVC initiates an IPSec connection to the EVS.

2 The EVC sends its IKE Phase 1 policies to the EVS.

3 The EVS looks for a matching IKE Phase 1 policy and builds the management connection.

4 The EVS performs XAUTH for user authentication.

5 Using IKE mode config, the EVS downloads policies to the EVC.

6 The EVS uses reverse-route injection (RRI) to build a route for the EVC.

7 The EVS and EVC share transforms to build an IKE Phase 2 data connection.

The following sections cover these steps in more depth.

Step 1: The EVC Initiates an IPSec Connection

In Step 1, the client initiates the IPSec connection to the server. The same kinds of things that occur with an L2L connection in this step also occur with the remote-access client. Based on the client's authentication configuration, the client uses one of the two following connection modes:

- **Aggressive mode**—Used if the client is configured for preshared keys. (When using this mode, Cisco recommends that your client device have a unique host name and that the identity type be configured for host name, not IP address. On Cisco EVC routers, this is done with the **crypto isakmp identity hostname** command.)

- **Main mode**—Used if the client is configured for certificates using RSA signatures.

Step 2: The EVC Sends the IKE Phase 1 Policies

In Step 2, the client creates a list of its IKE Phase 1 policies. This is done by having the client generate all possible combinations of parameters for IKE Phase 1 components that it supports (and that are supported by EasyVPN). These parameters include encryption algorithms, hashing functions, DH groups, and authentication methods. For example, assume that the client supports the following:

- **Encryption algorithms**—DES, 3DES
- **Hash functions**—SHA, MD5
- **DH group**—2
- **Authentication**—RSA signatures

Here is the list of policies that the client would create based on the supported IKE Phase 1 parameters previously listed:

- 3DES, SHA, DH 2, RSA signatures
- 3DES, MD5, DH 2, RSA signatures
- DES, SHA, DH 2, RSA signatures
- DES, MD5, DH 2, RSA signatures

This process reduces the manual configuration of these policy lists on the client. The client then sends its list of IKE Phase 1 policy permutations to the server.

Step 3: The EVS Accepts an IKE Phase 1 Policy

In Step 3, the server accepts one of the client's IKE Phase 1 policy proposals. The server does this by comparing its own IKE Phase 1 policies with the client's policies, starting with the server's highest-priority policy (the one with the lowest number). Based on this process, make sure that the server's list of policies has the most secured policies in the highest-priority policies, and the least secured policies with the lowest-priority policies.

When a match is found, the associated authentication method is used to perform device authentication. If the device authentication is successful, the management connection is built, completing IKE Phase 1.

Step 4: The EVS Authenticates the User

In Step 4, the server performs XAUTH, authenticating the user using the client. XAUTH is used to ensure that an authorized user is using the client device. The client sends its username and password to the server. The server can authenticate the user using a local username database or can forward the authentication information to a AAA server, such as Cisco Secure ACS. Assuming that the user is authenticated successfully, the process continues to Step 5.

Step 5: The EVS Performs IKE Mode Config

In Step 5, the server downloads (pushes) configuration and policy information to the client using IKE mode config. This information includes the following:

- Internal address of the client
- Domain name
- DNS server addresses
- WINS server addresses
- Split tunneling policies
- Split DNS policies
- List of backup servers
- Firewall filtering policies

Besides this information, many other components are shared in IKE mode config. This information is based on the group that the user belongs to, as well as the user's configuration itself: Both are defined on the server.

Step 6: The EVS Handles Routing with RRI

In Step 6, the server uses RRI to create a static route to reach a client's internal IP address. RRI is necessary unless you are using generic route encapsulation (GRE) between the client and the server. RRI routes then can be redistributed to a routing protocol, such as OSPF, and advertised to the rest of the server's network.

Two types of RRI exist: client and network RRI. Figure 20-2 shows an example of the two types. Typically, when a client connects, such as with EVC_A and EVC_B, the EVS assigns a single IP address to the client. This host address is advertised, through RRI and redistribution, to a dynamic routing protocol such as OSPF at the EVS site.

However, with some types of clients, such as a 3002 or a small-end router or PIX firewall, this can pose a problem. For example, how do devices behind the EVC reach the corporate network? Cisco accomplishes this by providing two connection modes: client and network extension modes. In client mode, the EVC, such as EVC_B, uses PAT on the assigned internal address, translating its local devices to this assigned address: Any address in 192.168.1.0/24 is translated to 172.16.199.1 through PAT, making the network behind EVC_B appear as one logical device (EVC_B). In network extension mode, the client's locally connected network addresses are left as they are, as is the case with EVC_C. Typically, client mode is used when devices on the EVS side do not need to access resources on the EVC side; the EVC devices only need to access corporate resources. Network extension mode is used when both sides of the tunnel need to access resources on the other side and, therefore, the EVC-side devices need unique IP addresses.

Figure 20-2 *RRI Example*

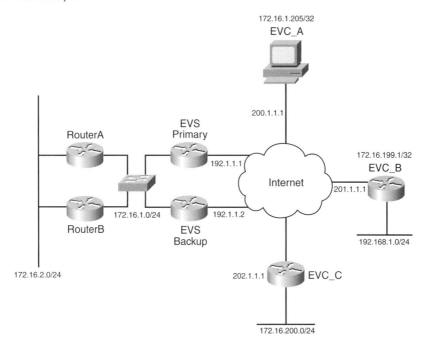

In either situation, RRI helps internal devices find the respective remote-access client. In client extension mode, the EVS builds a host address route. In network extension mode, the EVC shares with the EVS the locally connected route, and the EVS builds a network static route. Through redistribution, the EVS then can advertise these static routes to other routers so that other devices at the central site can reach any type of remote-access client.

The static routes that RRI creates are temporary ones. When the VPN connection is lost or terminated, the associated RRI static route is removed. With these temporary static routes, RRI allows the router to act as a proxy, responding to ARP requests to the VPN clients when an internal machine is trying to reach the remote client's internal address. Since the EVS needs to respond to local ARP requests for destination EVCs, you need to ensure that proxy ARP is enabled on your router's internal interface(s).

NOTE   RRI is not necessary if you have only one EVS. RRI is used when there is more than one EVS and there might be issues surrounding which EVS an internal device should use to reach a remote client. If you are using static routes on your EVS pointing to your clients, you do not need RRI; likewise, if you have a GRE tunnel to share routing information between the EVC and EVS, you do not need RRI. Therefore, RRI is optional, depending on your setup.

Step 7: The IPSec Devices Build the Data Connections

In Step 7, the two IPSec peers share their IKE Phase 2 policies (transforms) and attempt to build the two unidirectional data connections. Again, the client sends all possible permutations of transform sets based on its capabilities. Assuming that the two sides can find a matching transform set, the two unidirectional data connections are built and IKE Phase 2 completes. At this point, the two sides can send user traffic to each other.

IPSec Remote-Access EVS Setup

Now that you have a basic understanding of how a remote-access connection is built, I discuss how you would use a router as an EVS, including how to configure it to support remote-access IPSec clients. The following sections discuss the configuration details of this process. Again, I focus only on the basics of this configuration.

Configuration Process

When setting up IPSec remote-access connections on your EVS router, you perform these basic tasks:

Task 1—Define your AAA policies for authentication of devices (preshared keys and RSA signatures) and users (XAUTH).
Task 2—Define the group information for your remote-access clients, which includes the policies for the groups.
Task 3—Create your IKE Phase 1 policies.
Task 4—Create your dynamic crypto map, which is used for remote-access connections.
Task 5—Create your static crypto map, which includes the dynamic crypto map as an entry (the static crypto map references the dynamic crypto map).
Task 6—Verify your configuration to ensure that your client connections are correct.

The following sections cover these tasks.

Task 1: Authentication Policies

To perform client authentication for remote access, you can have your router perform XAUTH authentication locally or forward authentication requests to an AAA server. In either method, you need to enable AAA:

```
Router(config)# aaa new-model
```

If you will have the router perform the authentication, you configure the following command for each user:

```
Router(config)# username username secret password
```

This command was discussed in Chapter 3, "Accessing a Router."

For an AAA server, you need to configure one of the two following commands, based on whether you are using TACACS+ or RADIUS as your security protocol.

If you are using TACACS+, use this command:

```
Router(config)# tacacs-server host IP_address [single-connection]
  [port port_#] [timeout seconds] [key encryption_key]
```

If you are using RADIUS, use this command:

```
Router(config)# radius-server host IP_address [auth-port port_#] [acct-port port_#]
  [timeout seconds] [retransmit retries] [key key_value]
  [alias {hostname|IP_address}]
```

These commands were discussed in Chapter 5, "Authentication, Authorization, and Accounting."

With either local or remote authentication, you need to set up AAA authentication and authorization with the following two commands:

```
Router(config)# aaa authentication login authen_list_name method
Router(config)# aaa authorization network author_list_name method
```

The **aaa authentication login** command handles XAUTH user authentication. Do not use the keyword **default** for the *authen_list_name* because this affects all login methods. Instead, give it a unique name, which you will reference later in your remote-access configuration (in the **crypto map** *dynamic_map_name* **client authentication list** command). The methods that you can list are **group tacacs**, **group radius**, or **local**.

The **aaa authorization network** command handles the authorization of the remote-access IPSec connection. This *author_list_name* must match the *list_name* in the **crypto isakmp client configuration group** command, discussed later.

NOTE   The *author_list_name* in the **aaa authorization network** command is the name of the group. Your users who belong to this group must configure this group name on their client.

Task 2: Group Policies

After setting up AAA, you can go ahead and define your users' group policies. For each group, you can configure the following information:

```
Router(config)# ip local pool IP_pool_name
  beginning_IP_address ending_IP_address
Router(config)# crypto isakmp client configuration group
  author_list_name [max-users #_of_users] [max-logins #_of_logins]
Router(config-isakmp-group)# pool IP_pool_name
Router(config-isakmp-group)# key pre_shared_key
Router(config-isakmp-group)# domain domain_name
Router(config-isakmp-group)# dns 1st_server_IP 2nd_server_IP
Router(config-isakmp-group)# wins 1st_server_IP 2nd_server_IP
```

```
Router(config-isakmp-group)# split-dns domain-name
Router(config-isakmp-group)# acl ACL_#_or_name
Router(config-isakmp-group)# include-local-lan
Router(config-isakmp-group)# firewall are-u-there
Router(config-isakmp-group)# access-restrict interface_name
Router(config-isakmp-group)# save-password
```

The **ip local pool** command creates an address pool of internal addresses that will be assigned to your remote-access clients. The pool must have a unique pool name, and you must list the beginning and ending IP addresses in the pool. You will reference this in your group configuration.

The **crypto isakmp client configuration group** command creates your remote-access group. Note that you must enter the group name here, which needs to match the *author_list_name* in the **aaa authorization network** command discussed previously. When a client initiates a remote-access connection, it passes the group name to the server (router), and the server uses this to apply the policies from the respective group to the user's access. The optional **max-users** parameter is used to restrict the number of connections to a remote access group. This value can range from 1 to 5000. The optional **max-logins** parameter restricts the maximum number of simultaneous logins for the specified group. This can range from 1 to 10. These last two parameters are new in IOS 12.3(4)T.

NOTE   With preshared keys and device authentication, the client must manually configure the group name on its device; however, this option does not exist for certificate authentication. In this case, for the EVS to understand what group the user device belongs to, you need to make sure that the department, or Organizational Unit (OU), field on the client's certificate contains the name of the group.

When you execute the **crypto isakmp client configuration group** command, you enter a subconfiguration mode where you can enter the group's policies:

- EVCs that are connecting in client mode need to be assigned an internal IP address. The pool that you use for these addresses was defined previously by the **ip local pool** command; you reference that pool here with the **pool** command.

- If your IKE Phase 1 policy states that you will use preshared keys, you need to configure the **key** command with the group's preshared key value. Otherwise, if you are using certificates, you omit this value.

- The **domain** command specifies the DNS domain name to assign to the remote-access client.

- With the **dns** command, you can assign up to two DNS server IP addresses to the client. With the **wins** command, you can assign up to two WINS server addresses.

- The **split-dns** command is new in 12.3(4)T and enables you to specify which domains the DNS servers in the **dns** command should be used in. For example, if you specify a domain name of quizware.com in the **split-dns** command, only this domain uses the DNS servers in the **dns** command for resolutions. Basically, these DNS resolutions are tunneled across the IPSec connection; otherwise, the EVC uses the DNS servers locally assigned to it for resolution.

- The **acl** command specifies a name or number of an ACL. Any traffic matching a **permit** statement in this ACL must be protected; anything else is ignored, from an IPSec perspective. This is used to set up split tunneling on the EVC, and it protects specified traffic to the central site and allows unprotected access to other sites. The default is that all traffic must be sent to the EVS when the IPSec tunnel is up between the EVC and EVS.

- The **include-local-lan** command is new in 12.3(2)T and is an alternative to split tunneling with the **acl** command. The **include-local-lan** parameter allows the client to perform split tunneling where access to its local LAN segment is allowed in an unprotected fashion, but all other traffic must be sent to the central site's EVS. This allows the EVC to access local resources. One restriction with this command is that you must use an AAA RADIUS server for the authenticated user.

- The **firewall are-u-there** command is new in IOS 12.3(2)T. This command implements the Are You There (AYT) VPN feature, where the EVS has the software EVC check for the existence of a local firewall. Supported client firewalls include Black Ice and Zone Alarm. If you configure this option and the client device does not have a supported firewall operational, the EVS drops the connection. (The EVS probes this information from the EVC.) One nice thing about the Cisco VPN 3.x and 4.x clients is that they already have a stripped-down version of ZoneAlarm integrated into the client software, called Cisco Integrated Client (CIC). The use of this feature adds more security to your VPN solution; however, it does require that you use RADIUS authentication for users in this group. Another feature of AYT is that when this policy is pushed down to the client, the Cisco client software periodically checks to make sure that the client is there. If it is not, the Cisco client does not allow outbound traffic until the client enables the supported firewall product.

- The **access-restrict** command is new in 12.2(13)T and enables you to restrict the termination of a client's IPSec connection to a specific interface. This command has bearing only if you have applied the crypto map that this group's configuration is associated with to multiple interfaces on your router. You can define multiple restricted interfaces, if that is necessary. Note that this command works only if the users in this group all are being authenticated with RADIUS.

- The **save-password** command, new in IOS 12.3(2)T, allows the client to store the XAUTH (user) password locally on the client device. The default is to not allow this to occur, and I highly recommend that you leave it this way for PC or laptop clients. However, for PIX, router, or 3002 clients, you need to enable this option. Therefore, if you have a mixture of both types of clients, create at least two groups: one for the PC and laptop clients, and the other for the hardware clients. This command requires the use of AAA authentication through RADIUS.

Task 3: IKE Phase 1 Policies

After you define your remote-access groups, you are ready to move to your IKE Phase 1 policies. Many of the commands discussed in the previous chapter are also used here. First, you need to configure an IKE Phase 1 policy that matches the capabilities of the clients in your remote-access group(s). This is accomplished with the following commands, which were covered in the previous chapter:

```
Router(config)# crypto isakmp policy priority_#
Router(config-isakmp)# authentication {rsa-sig | rsa-encr | pre-share}
Router(config-isakmp)# encryption {des | 3des | aes | aes 192 | aes 256}
Router(config-isakmp)# hash {md5 | sha}
Router(config-isakmp)# group {2 | 5}
Router(config-isakmp)# lifetime #_of_seconds
```

One important item to point out about this configuration is the last command: **lifetime**. Many software EVCs do not specify the lifetime, which means that the lifetime of the EVS is used. You can control this value with the **lifetime** command. Also remember that at least one policy on the EVC must match one policy on the EVS.

You can use three additional IKE Phase 1 commands for remote-access connections:

```
Router(config)# crypto isakmp keepalive #_of_seconds #_of_retries_seconds
Router(config)# crypto isakmp xauth timeout #_of_seconds
Router(config)# crypto isakmp nat keepalive #_of_seconds
```

The **crypto isakmp keepalive** command, new in IOS 12.2(8)T, implements DPD and specifies two parameters: the number of seconds and the length of the retry period. The number of seconds can range from 10 to 3600 and specifies how often DPD messages are sent to the EVC. If the queried EVC does not reply to the EVS's DPD query, the EVS waits for the time period specified by the #_of_retries_seconds parameter. For example, if the two values are 60 and 10, respectively, the EVS sends DPD messages every 60 seconds. When a reply is missed for one of the messages, the EVS router tries sending the message again in 10 seconds.

The **crypto isakmp xauth timeout** command specifies the length of time that the client user has to enter a username and password during XAUTH authentication. This value can range from 5 to 90 seconds, with the default at 60 seconds.

The **crypto isakmp nat keepalive** command specifies the polling period if NAT-T is being used by the peers. Note that you do not need to enable NAT-T; if your IOS is 12.2(13)T or later, the NAT-T feature is enabled by default. In this instance, the two peers test the connection between themselves to detect whether any address translation is occurring between them: If this is true, the two peers automatically use NAT-T; otherwise, normal IPSec data connections are built between the two peers. Your only option with NAT-T is to specify the number of seconds that keepalives should be generated, to ensure that the address translation entry on the address-translation device stays active. The value can range from 5 to 3600 seconds. By default, NAT keepalives are not sent between the two peers. Use the **show crypto ipsec sa** command to verify whether your IPSec data connections are using NAT-T. If they are using NAT-T, the tunnel mode for the SA will be *UDP-encaps*.

Task 4: Dynamic Crypto Maps

You must complete two tasks to establish the unidirectional data connections in IKE Phase 2: create a dynamic crypto map and reference the dynamic crypto map in a static map configuration. Static crypto maps are used with L2L connections, in which you know the remote peer's identity and capabilities. However, static crypto maps do not work well when some of the connection parameters are unknown and will not be known until the remote device connects to the router.

Overview of Dynamic Crypto Maps

Dynamic crypto maps are used for remote-access connections when you typically do not know the peer's identity or capabilities until connection time. For example, you typically do not know a remote-access client's IP address if the client is connecting through a dialup, cable modem, or DSL connection from an ISP. Dynamic crypto maps should be used to accept inbound connections from remote-access clients; they cannot initiate outbound connections as a static crypto map entry can. Plus, they require the use of dynamic ISAKMP/IKE to perform the negotiation of parameters.

Actually, a dynamic crypto map is like an embedded crypto map. As mentioned earlier, with your remote-access VPN connection, you use two maps: a static and a dynamic one. The dynamic crypto map specifies the parameters to use to protect the client's remote access connection. Only one crypto map can be applied to a router's interface, and you might need to have both remote-access and L2L connections. Cisco gets around this problem by referencing the dynamic crypto map within a static crypto map by creating a separate entry in the static crypto map for the dynamic map (thus the reference to "embedded").

The "dynamic" in dynamic crypto map implies that when the remote-access client initiates the connection to the server, the server dynamically learns the connection parameters to use for the connection—thus the term *dynamic*. Because you typically do not know a lot of the connection information for the EVC, you must make sure that this static map reference is assigned the lowest priority (highest crypto map entry or sequence number). In other words, you want to use the dynamic entry as only a last resort: Use the static entries for L2L connections and then the last entry or entries for remote-access connections.

Creating a Dynamic Crypto Map

To create a dynamic crypto map, use the following command:

```
Router(config)# crypto dynamic-map dynamic_crypto_map_name sequence_#
Router(config-crypto-map)#
```

The dynamic crypto map must be given a unique name among all dynamic crypto maps on the router. As with static crypto maps, you can have multiple entries within a dynamic map. Each entry needs a unique sequence number. These sequence numbers are processed from lowest to highest numbers. Therefore, make sure that when you configure your security parameters for the map entries, you put the most secure parameters in the lowest-numbered entry.

Most of the commands that you can configure for a static map entry are also available for a dynamic map entry, including those listed in Table 20-1. Based on the information listed in this table, in most cases, the only command that you configure in a dynamic crypto map entry is the **set transform-set** command. Remember that this command specifies the transform(s) to use to protect the data connection, such as ESP in tunnel mode using 3DES encryption and MD5 for packet authentication. The EVS figures out all other parameters that are not listed in the dynamic crypto map when the client connects to it.

Table 20-1   *Dynamic Crypto Map Commands*

Command	Use	Other Information
set transform-set	Required	This specifies the transform set to use for the remote-access clients. It is the only required parameter.
match-address	Optional	This command specifies the ACL to use to define what traffic is to be protected. Because the client address or addresses are not know until connection time, this command is used rarely. If you use this command, your ACL can have only one **permit** entry. If the ACL has more than one of these entries, the first one is processed and the rest are ignored.
set peer	Optional	This command specifies the identity of the peer. Because this typically is unknown until connection time with a remote-access connection, it is used rarely.
set pfs	Optional (not supported for EVCs)	This command specifies the use of DH to share new keying information for rebuilding expiring data connections. Cisco does not support this with its EVCs.
set security-association lifetime	Optional	This command specifies the lifetime of the data SA, in seconds or kilobytes. This command also is supported in Global Configuration mode.
reverse-route [remote-peer]	Optional	This command adds a static route for the internal address of the remote-access client. Using the **remote-peer** option adds both the client's public address and the internal address as static routes to the router's routing table.

TIP   About the only time you would use the optional parameters in Table 20-1 is for an L2L connection in which one router has a statically configured IP address and the other router has a dynamic address. In this situation, you would configure the statically addressed router with both a static and a dynamic crypto map (it does not know the remote peer's identity), and the dynamically addressed router with a static crypto map (it knows the remote peer's identity)

To create a transform set, use the following command:

```
Router(config)# crypto ipsec transform-set name_of_transform_set
   transform_#1 [transform_#2 [transform_#3]]
```

Refer to Table 19-1 in Chapter 19 for the details of the parameters for this command.

Most parameters are not known for remote-access clients (except how you will protect them with a transform), so your configuration will look like this:

```
Router(config)#  crypto dynamic-map map_name sequence_#
Router(config-crypto-map)#  set transform-set transform_set_name(s)
Router(config-crypto-map)#  reverse-route
```

In reality, the **reverse-route** command is necessary only if you have two or more EVS routers at the central site handling remote-access connections; otherwise, you can omit this command.

Using a Dynamic Crypto Map

After building your dynamic crypto map, you need to reference it in a static crypto map entry by using the following command:

```
Router(config)# crypto map static_crypto_map_name sequence_# ipsec-isakmp
   dynamic dynamic_crypto_map_name
```

As you can see from this command, this is basically the same as a static crypto map entry; the only difference is the **dynamic** parameter at the end, along with the name of the dynamic crypto map.

NOTE   Remember to use a sequence number that is numerically higher than that of your static crypto map entries, giving it the lowest priority from a policy comparison standpoint.

Verifying a Dynamic Crypto Map

After you have created your dynamic crypto map, you can view it with the following command:

```
Router# show crypto dynamic-map [tag dynamic_crypto_map_name]
```

Optionally, you can list the name of the dynamic crypto map to limit your output with the **tag** parameter. Example 20-1 displays sample output from this command.

Example 20-1 *Using the* **show crypto dynamic-map** *Command*

```
Router# show crypto dynamic-map
Crypto Map Template "EASYVPN" 900
        No matching address list set.
        Current peer: 0.0.0.0
        Security association lifetime:
                        4608000 kilobytes/3600 seconds
        PFS (Y/N): N
        Transform sets={ transdynamic-1, transdynamic-2, }
```

As you can see in Example 20-1, only two transforms were defined for the dynamic crypto map called *EASYVPN*: *transdynamic-1* and *transdynamic-2*.

Task 5: Static Crypto Map

The last step in your configuration is to configure your static crypto map. Here are the commands you use:

```
Router(config)# crypto map static_map_name client authentication
  list authen_list_name
Router(config)# crypto map static_map_name isakmp authorization
  list author_list_name
Router(config)# crypto map static_map_name client configuration
  address initiate|respond
Router(config)# crypto map static_map_name sequence_#
  ipsec-isakmp dynamic dynamic_map_name
Router(config)# interface type [slot_#/]port_#
Router(config-if)# crypto map static_map_name
```

The first command in this configuration, **crypto map client authentication**, references the use of the **aaa authentication login** command discussed earlier for XAUTH authentication: It specifies how authentication is to be done for remote-access clients. The *authen_list_name* here must match the *authen_list_name* in the **aaa authentication login** command.

The **crypto map isakmp authorization** command references the **aaa authorization network** command, specifying that authorization should be done for remote-access VPN connections. The *author_list_name* in both these commands must match.

The **crypto map client configuration address** command allows the router to assign information to the remote-access client. If you specify the **initiate** parameter, the router can assign addressing and policy information to the client without the client's prompting. The **respond** parameter has the router wait for the client's prompt for this information and then has the router respond with the policy information. If you are not sure whether the client will prompt for policy information, configure this command twice: once with the **initiate** parameter and once with the **respond** parameter.

I already discussed how to associate the dynamic crypto map in a static map entry in the last section with the **crypto map ipsec-isakmp dynamic** command. Remember to place the dynamic crypto map reference as the highest sequence number so that L2L crypto map entries have a higher priority. Finally, you must activate the static crypto map on the router's public interface or interfaces with the **crypto map** command.

Task 6: Remote-Access Verification

The same **show** and **debug** commands discussed in the previous chapter for verifying and troubleshooting IPSec L2L connections apply to remote-access connections. However, you can use one additional command for verification and troubleshooting:

```
Router# show crypto session {group | summary}
```

The **group** parameter has the IOS display the remote-access groups that are currently active on the router (there is a current connection to a user in a group). Example 20-2 shows sample output from the **show crypto session group** command.

Example 20-2 *Using the* **show crypto session group** *Command*

```
Router# show crypto session group
 Group:    Connections
 quizware: 2
```

In this example, there are two current user connections in the group called quizware.

The **summary** parameter shows the users that are connected for each of the groups defined on the EVS, which is new in IOS 12.3(4)T. Example 20-3 shows sample output from the **show crypto session summary** command.

Example 20-3 *Using the* **show crypto session summary** *Command*

```
Router# show crypto session summary
 Group quizware has 2 connections
  User (Logins)
  richard (1)
  natalie (1)
```

In Example 20-3, there are two connections in the group called quizware: one for the user richard and one for the user natalie.

IPSec Remote Access Example

To help you understand the configuration of IPSec remote access on a router, review Figure 20-1, which I use for the following example. Example 20-4 displays a sample configuration for the router shown in Figure 20-1.

Example 20-4 *Setting up a Simple Configuration on an EVS for Remote Access*

```
Router(config)# aaa new-model                                        (1)
Router(config)# aaa authentication login vpnauthenticate local
Router(config)# aaa authorization network quizware local
Router(config)# username richard secret hispassword
Router(config)# username natalie secret herpassword
Router(config)# crypto isakmp policy 10                              (2)
Router(config-isakmp)# encryption 3des
Router(config-isakmp)# hash md5
Router(config-isakmp)# authentication pre-share
Router(config-isakmp)# group 2
Router(config-isakmp)# exit
Router(config)# crypto isakmp keepalive 20 10                        (3)
Router(config)# crypto isakmp xauth timeout 45
Router(config)# ip local pool quizware_pool                          (4)
                    192.168.1.200 192.168.1.254
Router(config)# crypto isakmp client configuration group quizware    (5)
Router(config-isakmp-group)# key quizwarekey
Router(config-isakmp-group)# pool quizware_pool
Router(config-isakmp-group)# domain quizware.com
Router(config-isakmp-group)# dns 192.168.1.2
Router(config-isakmp-group)# split-dns quizware.com
Router(config-isakmp-group)# include-local-lan
Router(config-isakmp-group)# exit
Router(config)# crypto ipsec transform-set easyclients              (6)
                    esp-3des esp-sha-hmac
Router(config)# crypto dynamic-map dynamic_map 10                   (7)
Router(config-crypto-map)# set transform-set easyclients
Router(config-crypto-map)# exit
Router(config)# crypto map static_map client authentication         (8)
                    list vpnauthenticate
Router(config)# crypto map static_map isakmp authorization          (9)
                    list quizware
Router(config)# crypto map static_map client configuration          (10)
                    address respond
Router(config)# crypto map static_map client configuration
                    address initiate
Router(config)# crypto map static_map 999 ipsec-isakmp              (11)
                    dynamic dynamic_map
Router(config)# access-list 100 permit udp any                      (12)
                    host 192.1.1.1 eq isakmp
Router(config)# access-list 100 permit esp any
                    host 192.1.1.1
Router(config)# access-list 100 permit udp any
                    host 192.1.1.1 eq 4500
Router(config)# remark <--include other ACL statements
                       for ACL 100-->
Router(config)# interface ethernet1                                 (13)
Router(config-if)# ip address 192.1.1.1 255.255.255.0
Router(config-if)# ip access-group 100 in
Router(config-if)# crypto map static_map
```

The following is an explanation of the configuration in Example 20-4, with reference to the numbering on the right side:

1 The first three **aaa** commands enable AAA, define authentication for remote access, and specify the remote-access group called quizware, respectively. The two **username** commands set up user accounts for XAUTH.

2 The IKE Phase 1 policy defines 3DES encryption, an MD5 hash function, device authentication with preshared keys, and DH group 2 keys.

3 IKE DPD is defined with a keepalive interval of 20 seconds and a retry period of 10 seconds. The XAUTH authentication timeout period has been changed to 45 seconds.

4 An internal address pool for remote-access clients includes addresses from 192.168.1.200 to 192.168.1.254.

5 The quizware remote-access group is defined. The preshared key for this group is set to quizwarekey, and the address pool assigned to this group is the one defined in the **ip local pool** command: quizware_pool. The domain name is defined as quizware.com, and the DNS server is 192.168.1.2. Split DNS is set up so that the remote-access VPN connection is used to resolve any devices within quizware.com and the user's local DNS configuration is used to resolve other names. The **include-local-lan** allows split tunneling for only the remote-access user's local LAN segment: All other traffic must be tunneled to the central site.

6 A transform set is built for the remote-access clients, specifying only the ESP protocol with 3DES encryption and SHA as a hashing protocol.

7 A dynamic crypto map, called dynamic_map, specifies the transform set for remote-access clients.

8 Remote-access VPN authentication list (vpnauthenticate) from the **aaa authentication login** command is tied to the static crypto map.

9 The remote-access group from the **aaa authorization network** command, quizware, is associated with the static crypto map.

10 These two commands allow the router to respond to IKE mode requests, as well as to initiate them to a client.

11 The remote-access dynamic crypto map is referenced in a static crypto map entry. Notice that I have given the entry a higher number, just in case I decide later to add L2L connections, which should have a lower number than this.

12 This ACL is used to allow remote-access users to terminate their IPSec connections on the router. Notice that the source address is unknown and, therefore, is specified as **any**. Also, the third statement, with UDP port 4500, allows remote-access connections from EVCs that need to use NAT-T.

13 The static crypto map is activated on the router's public interface.

As you can see from this example, this simple configuration for remote-access users is more complicated than an L2L configuration.

EasyVPN Deception

EasyVPN is a marketing term developed by someone at Cisco to attempt to make the setup of remote-access VPNs seem easy. Actually, there is nothing "easy" about setting up and troubleshooting any type of VPN connection, remote access or L2L. The first time I set up a remote-access VPN on a Cisco router, it took me more than a day to get everything running correctly. Based on this experience, I prefer to use Cisco remote-access concentrators for remote access, and, in many cases, L2L connections. The concentrators support all of the VPN functions of the router, plus a lot more—especially when it concerns remote-access features and functions, such as SSL VPNs. In addition, the concentrators support an easy-to-use GUI interface. When you compare the cost of a concentrator with SEP cards to a comparable 7200 with VPN accelerator cards, the concentrators are a better, more scalable VPN purchase. About the only time I use routers for VPN connections is when they already exist in the network and I need to support only a small number of VPN connections. If I need to support a lot of connections, especially remote access, I prefer to use a concentrator. However, Cisco is making strides in simplifying the configuration of VPNs with its VPN Device Manager (VDM), Security Device Manager (SDM), and Router Management Console (MC)—the latter is a part of CiscoWorks VMS.

Summary

This chapter showed you the basics of setting up remote-access IPSec connections using EasyVPN with an EVS and an EVC. EasyVPN enables you to control policy decisions and push these decisions down to the client. Unlike L2L connections, a remote-access connection supports both user (XAUTH) and device authentication. Configuration of XAUTH requires the use of AAA.

In a remote-access connection, the EVC initiates the connection to the EVS and sends its IKE Phase 1 policies. The EVS finds a matching policy, and the management connection is built. The EVS then performs user authentication using XAUTH. Upon successful authentication, the EVS sends configuration and policy information to the EVC through IKE Mode Config. The EVS then uses RRI to add a static route for the EVC to its local routing table, which can be redistributed through a dynamic-routing protocol. Finally, the EVC and EVS build the two unidirectional data connections during IKE Phase 2.

Next up is Part IX, "Case Study," which wraps up the book and puts many of the features and tools discussed in this book to work in a real-life example.

PART IX

Case Study

Chapter 21   Case Study

Case Study

This chapter is different from the rest of the chapters in this book. From Chapter 3, "Accessing a Router," onward, each chapter discussed security issues and the Cisco IOS features that you could use to deal with these issues, including configuration commands. Each chapter included examples of using these commands in a networking environment.

This chapter does not introduce any new material. Instead, it focuses on implementing the concepts and features discussed in this book in a case-study environment.

Company Profile

The network shown in Figure 21-1 illustrates this case study. The company in this network has two sites—a corporate and branch office—as well as remote access users that connect through the Internet. The following sections discuss the necessary requirements for these components.

Corporate Office

The corporate office has five segments and two routers: RouterA, which is a perimeter router, and RouterB, which is an internal router. The following two sections cover the roles of the two routers and the network segments.

Perimeter Router

The perimeter router is RouterA and is a 3745. Because of security issues, secure access to this router should be set up and restrictions should be placed on who can access this router. RouterA has three interfaces. E0/0 connects to the company's ISP through a cable-modem connection. It is assigned an IP address of 192.1.1.1. The 192.1.1.0/24 network has been assigned by the ISP to this company, but two of these addresses must be used between this company and the ISP. In this case, 192.1.1.1 is assigned to RouterA, and 192.1.1.254 is assigned to the ISP's router.

Figure 21-1 *Case Study Network*

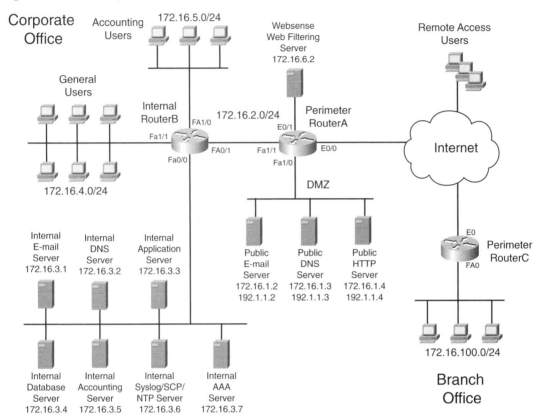

FA1/0 connects to the company's DMZ segment. This segment houses a public e-mail server, a DNS server, and an HTTP server. All of these devices have a private address from the network 172.16.1.0/24; however, the perimeter router performs address translation so that these are reachable from users on the Internet.

All internal users should be able to access the DMZ devices and the Internet. However, the company is concerned about web surfing. Interface E0/1 on the perimeter router is a dedicated connection to a content-filtering device.

The public e-mail server acts as a bridge between the internal e-mail server and the SMTP e-mail servers on the Internet. This company uses a standard SMTP e-mail software package and is concerned about the security of the server.

The public DNS server resolves DNS names of the DMZ devices for Internet users. In other words, it resolves the names of the DMZ devices to 192.1.1.x addresses. Note that no internal devices use this DNS server for resolution to access other internal devices. In other words, an internal device would use the internal DNS server when accessing DMZ devices.

The public web server houses public web page information for Internet users, as well as a small e-commerce section where the company sells a few e-book documents. Because of issues of security with the online transactions, SSL is used to transmit an Internet user's personal credit card information (both HTTP and HTTPS are used for access to this server).

Interface FA1/1 of the perimeter router connects to the internal router. The network number used is 172.16.2.0/24. The only two devices on this segment are the two routers.

Internal Router

The perimeter router has a dedicated connection to the internal router, also a 3745, on subnet 172.16.2.0/24. The internal router is responsible for interconnecting the company's internal segments at the corporate site, as well as implementing traffic-flow policies. This router should restrict access to the EXEC shell and use a secure method of access.

The FA0/0 interface of this router connects to the company's server farm, where there are seven servers. An internal e-mail server handles the distribution of all internal e-mail of the users and is a forwarding point of e-mail to the public e-mail server on the DMZ. The DMZ then handles any type of Internet e-mail access.

An internal DNS server handles resolution for all internal devices. However, if the name to be resolved is not an internal device (at either the corporate or branch office sites), the internal DNS server forwards the name-resolution request to the appropriate server.

The internal application server is used as a repository of the company's applications. The more critical applications used by company employees are located on this server. The front end is an HTTP with secure socket layer (HTTPS) web server for these applications. The internal database server is used by most users in the company and holds the data used by the company's critical applications on the internal application server. Access to this server should be restricted to only the application server.

The accounting department's server also is located on this segment. Because of the sensitive nature of this information, care must be taken in who can access this server. The application that runs on this server uses a nonstandard port (TCP 2501) for network access.

The syslog/SCP/NTP (secure copy) server handles remote logging for devices, including the three routers: RouterA, RouterB, and RouterC. It also uses SCP to store configurations and images of devices. This server also serves as the master time source for the network. The last server on the server farm segment is a Cisco Secure ACS AAA server. It handles all AAA functions for the network, including router access.

Two other network segments are connected to this router. Interface FA1/0 is connected to the accounting users. These users need access to all servers in the server farm except the syslog server. Interface FA1/1 is connected to the general user population. These users should be able to access all of the servers in the server farm except the accounting and syslog servers. These users should not be able to access the accounting user segment.

Branch Office

This company has one branch office, which has an existing Internet connection through a 1721 router and a cable modem setup. To save money, the company wants to use a VPN to connect the branch office to the corporate office site. The branch office has only users; all servers are located at the corporate site. Because of security issues, all branch-office traffic must be sent to the corporate site through the VPN before going anywhere else. Because there are only a few dozen users at this site, this will not cause a performance issue. An ISDN dialup connection between these two sites serves as a backup if the cable modem connection fails (the configuration of this is not covered in the case study).

Remote-Access Users

Some of the company's personnel work at home in the evenings, and a few salespeople also work on the road a lot. Because of these issues, a VPN is needed to provide a secure connection between these users to the corporate site through the Internet. Local LAN and Internet access should be allowed for these users, but a software firewall should be installed on their PCs, and all traffic sent to the corporate site should be protected. Remote-access users will be using the subnets 172.16.252.0/24 (network administrators), 127.16.253.0/24 (accounting users), and 172.16.254.0/24 (general users).

Proposal

The following lists the proposals that will be incorporated into the security design of this network:

- All unnecessary services on all three routers should be disabled. This will be done manually. SSH will be used on all routers for access (Telnet should be blocked). Only network administrators (172.16.4.12, 172.16.4.13, 172.16.4.14, and 172.16.4.15) should be allowed EXEC access.

- Each administrator should have a separate account to access the routers. AAA is used to set up authentication of access to the routers. All command executions and system events should be logged. A back-door account should be set up on each router, in case the AAA server is not reachable. The AAA server used will be Cisco Secure ACS with TACACS+ as the security protocol. Even the branch office router will be set up for AAA.

- Normal extended ACLs will be used for implementing the policy restrictions on the internal routers. Normal extended ACLs also will be used on RouterC, the branch-office router.

- The perimeter router, RouterA, will use a combination of normal extended ACLs and Context-Based Access Control (CBAC) for filtering. Inspection should be set up for e-mail as well as HTTP. The internal router will use CBAC also to allow returning traffic from the outside and to inspect SMTP traffic.

- Web filtering through the Websense server will be implemented on the perimeter router.

- Address translation needs to be configured on the perimeter router. Static translations are needed for the DMZ devices and dynamic translations for all other internal devices accessing the Internet. For VPN connections, address translation should be disabled.

- Because of the small number of subnets, static routes should be used for routing. Reverse-path forwarding should be used to prevent certain kinds of spoofing attacks.

- IDS is implemented on both the corporate and branch-office perimeter routers, to provide enhanced protection. Attacks should be logged to a syslog server, and TCP reset should be used for TCP connection attacks.

- CBAC will be used to protect against connection attacks, including TCP SYN flooding.

- Because of the limited use of ICMP and UDP for Internet access, the company is concerned about DoS attacks with these protocols. It has decided to implement rate limiting through NBAR.

- NTP will be used to synchronize devices. The internal syslog server also serves as the master NTP time source, and authentication is used to verify a device's identity. All three routers will log syslog messages, with time stamps, to the syslog server. For RouterC at the branch office, these messages should be encrypted.

- A site-to-site IPSec VPN should be used to protect traffic between the branch and corporate offices. All branch traffic must traverse this connection, including traffic destined to the Internet. Device authentication is done with preshared keys.

- To handle remote-access users, Easy VPN is implemented. There are three groups of users: admin, accounting, and users. The admin group includes the network administrators. The accounting group includes remote-access accounting personnel, and the appropriate restrictions should be applied to these people. The users group includes all other employees. A software firewall is required for these users to access the Internet; all traffic sent to the corporate site should be protected.

Case Study Configuration

Now that I have defined the policies for this network, I can explain the configuration for the three routers. I start with a basic configuration on each router and then explain, proposal by proposal, the rest of the configuration.

Basic Configuration

Before I begin with the configuration of the security features on the three routers, I first show you the base configuration of the routers. Example 21-1 shows RouterA's configuration.

Example 21-1 *RouterA's Initial Configuration*

```
Router(config)# hostname RouterA
RouterA(config)# interface ethernet0/0
RouterA(config-if)# description Internet Connection
RouterA(config-if)# ip address 192.1.1.1 255.255.255.0
RouterA(config-if)# exit
RouterA(config)# interface ethernet0/1
RouterA(config-if)# description WebSense Filtering Server
RouterA(config-if)# ip address 172.16.6.1 255.255.255.0
RouterA(config-if)# exit
RouterA(config)# interface fastethernet1/0
RouterA(config-if)# description DMZ Segment
RouterA(config-if)# ip address 172.16.1.1 255.255.255.0
RouterA(config-if)# exit
RouterA(config)# interface fastethernet1/1
RouterA(config-if)# description Internal Network
RouterA(config-if)# ip address 172.16.2.1 255.255.255.0
RouterA(config-if)# exit
```

NOTE   The DDR configuration for RouterA is not shown here, but it is necessary for a backup connection between RouterA and RouterC. Routing information is added in the "Routing" section, discussed later in this chapter.

Example 21-2 shows RouterB's configuration.

Example 21-2 *RouterB's Initial Configuration*

```
Router(config)# hostname RouterB
RouterB(config)# interface fastethernet0/0
RouterB(config-if)# description Server Farm
RouterB(config-if)# ip address 172.16.3.254 255.255.255.0
RouterB(config-if)# exit
RouterB(config)# interface fastethernet0/1
RouterB(config-if)# description To the Perimeter Router
RouterB(config-if)# ip address 172.16.2.254 255.255.255.0
RouterB(config-if)# exit
RouterB(config)# interface fastethernet1/0
RouterB(config-if)# description Accounting Users
RouterB(config-if)# ip address 172.16.5.254 255.255.255.0
RouterB(config-if)# exit
RouterB(config)# interface fastethernet1/1
RouterB(config-if)# description General Users
RouterB(config-if)# ip address 172.16.4.254 255.255.255.0
RouterB(config-if)# exit
```

Example 21-3 shows RouterC's configuration.

Example 21-3 *RouterC's Initial Configuration*

```
Router(config)# hostname RouterC
RouterC(config)# interface ethernet0
RouterC(config-if)# description Internet Connection
RouterC(config-if)# ip address 200.1.1.1 255.255.255.0
RouterC(config-if)# exit
RouterC(config)# interface fastethernet0
RouterC(config-if)# description Internal Segment
RouterC(config-if)# ip address 172.16.100.1 255.255.255.0
RouterC(config-if)# exit
```

Unnecessary Services and SSH

Example 21-4 displays the configuration done on RouterA to disable all unnecessary services and to enable SSH. Note that, for the most part, the same configuration has been applied to RouterB and RouterC.

Example 21-4 *Disabling Services on RouterA*

```
RouterA(config)# no cdp run                                          (1)
RouterA(config)# no service tcp-small-servers
RouterA(config)# no service udp-small-servers
RouterA(config)# no ip finger
RouterA(config)# no ip identd
RouterA(config)# no service finger
RouterA(config)# no ip source-route
RouterA(config)# no ftp-server enable
RouterA(config)# no ip http server
RouterA(config)# no ip http secure-server
RouterA(config)# no snmp-server community public RO
RouterA(config)# no snmp-server community private RW
RouterA(config)# no snmp-server enable traps
RouterA(config)# no snmp-server system-shutdown
RouterA(config)# no snmp-server trap-auth
RouterA(config)# no snmp-server
RouterA(config)# no ip domain-lookup
RouterA(config)# no ip bootp server
RouterA(config)# no service dhcp
RouterA(config)# no service pad
RouterA(config)# no boot network
RouterA(config)# no service config
RouterA(config)# banner motd $                                      (2)
THIS QuizWare COMPUTING SYSTEM IS FOR AUTHORIZED
OFFICIAL USE ONLY. Unauthorized use or use for other than official
THE DEAL GROUP, INC. business is a violation of State and Federal LAW

Individuals using this computing system are subject to having all
of their activities on this system monitored and recorded without
further notice. Auditing of users may include keystroke monitoring.
```

continues

Example 21-4 *Disabling Services on RouterA (Continued)*

```
Any individual who uses this system expressly consents to such
monitoring and is advised that information about their use of the
system may be provided to State and Federal law enforcement or
other authorities if evidence of criminal or other unauthorized
activity is found.
$
RouterA(config)# interface ethernet0/0                          (3)
RouterA(config-if)# no ip directed-broadcast
RouterA(config-if)# no ip unreachable
RouterA(config-if)# no ip redirect
RouterA(config-if)# no ip mask-reply
RouterA(config-if)# exit
RouterA(config)# interface ethernet0/1
RouterA(config-if)# no ip directed-broadcast
RouterA(config-if)# no ip unreachable
RouterA(config-if)# no ip redirect
RouterA(config-if)# no ip mask-reply
RouterA(config-if)# exit
RouterA(config)# interface fastethernet1/0
RouterA(config-if)# no ip directed-broadcast
RouterA(config-if)# no ip unreachable
RouterA(config-if)# no ip redirect
RouterA(config-if)# no ip mask-reply
RouterA(config-if)# exit
RouterA(config)# interface fastethernet1/1
RouterA(config-if)# no ip directed-broadcast
RouterA(config-if)# no ip unreachable
RouterA(config-if)# no ip redirect
RouterA(config-if)# no ip mask-reply
RouterA(config-if)# exit
RouterA(config)# service tcp-keepalives-in                      (4)
RouterA(config)# service tcp-keepalives-out
RouterA(config)# ip domain-name quizware.com                    (5)
RouterA(config)# crypto key generate rsa
RouterA(config)# access-list 1 permit 172.16.4.12 0.0.0.3       (6)
RouterA(config)# access-list 1 deny any
RouterA(config)# line vty 0 4                                   (7)
RouterA(config-line)# login
RouterA(config-line)# access-class 1 in
RouterA(config-line)# transport input ssh
RouterA(config-line)# transport output ssh
```

The following is a brief explanation of Example 21-4, with reference to the numbering on the right side:

1 The first part of this configuration disables all unnecessary services, such as TCP and UDP small servers, finger, source routing, SNMP, and others.

2 This part of the configuration assigns a login banner to the router, explaining the valid usage of the router.

3 This section disables unnecessary services on the router's interfaces, such as proxy ARP, ICMP unreachables and redirects, and others. Typically, this is necessary only on the perimeter router's external interface, but by doing this on other interfaces, you are providing a more secure router—especially if attacks are occurring from inside your network. Note that proxy ARP is not disabled on any of the router's interface because devices of the other interfaces might need to send traffic to the remote access VPN users and the Internet users need to access the internal devices represented, statically and dynamically, by global addresses.

4 With these two commands, the router monitors network TCP connections, such as SSH, to and from the router by generating keepalives. The advantage that these commands provide is that, if an SSH connection, for instance, is aborted abnormally, the keepalive function detect this and immediately removes the bad connection, freeing up the router's VTY line.

5 These two commands (as well as the **hostname** command from the last section) allow SSH access by generating the public and private keys used for encryption.

6 This standard numbered ACL is used to restrict access to the VTYs, which are the management stations. Notice that this ACL is activated in the **line vty** configuration below.

7 This configuration applies to the VTYs. The management ACL is activated, and only SSH access is allowed in or out of the router through the VTYs.

The configuration for RouterB and RouterC is basically the same as that for RouterA.

TIP　　If your router is running a Cisco IOS that supports the AutoSecure feature, discussed in Chapter 4, "Disabling Unnecessary Services," I recommend using this feature instead of manually disabling unnecessary services. In particular, the manual approach requires you to disable many things, and you might forget to disable an item or two.

AAA

Next up is the configuration of AAA to secure access to the three routers. A Cisco Secure ACS server (172.16.3.7) is used to centralize AAA functions, found on the server farm segment. All user accounts are defined here, but a back door is set up for console access, just in case there is a reachability problem to the AAA server.

Example 21-5 shows the AAA configuration for RouterA.

Example 21-5 *Setting up AAA on RouterA*

```
RouterA(config)# aaa new-model                               (1)
RouterA(config)# tacacs-server host 172.16.3.7 single-connection
  key AAA_QuizWare
```

continues

Example 21-5 *Setting up AAA on RouterA (Continued)*

```
RouterA(config)# username backdoor secret QuizWareAccess      (2)
RouterA(config)# aaa authentication login console_access      (3)
  group tacacs+ local
RouterA(config)# aaa authentication login default
  group tacacs+
RouterA(config)# aaa authentication enable default            (4)
  group tacacs+ local
RouterA(config)# aaa authentication username-prompt "Password:"  (5)
RouterA(config)# aaa authentication password-prompt "Password:"
RouterA(config)# aaa authentication fail-message ##
Invalid authentication, please reenter
#_
RouterA(config)# aaa authentication attempts login 1          (6)
RouterA(config)# line console 0                               (7)
RouterA(config-line)# login authentication console_access
```

The following is an explanation of RouterA's configuration in Example 21-5, with reference to the numbering on the right side:

1 AAA is enabled, and the TACACS+ protocol and server are specified.

2 A back-door account is set up, in case the AAA server is not reachable.

3 The first **aaa authentication login** command specifies two authentication methods. TACACS+ and the local username database are associated with the *console_access* list name. This then is referenced on the console line. The second **aaa authentication login** command specifies the default method of authentication for lines that do not specify a specific method, such as the VTYs or auxiliary lines.

4 The **aaa authentication enable** command specifies authentication for privileged EXEC access.

5 The first two commands set both the username and the password prompt to Password:, which is used to trick someone not familiar with the router's login process. The third command specifies the fail message that should be displayed upon an authentication failure. Notice that it's blank because I don't want a hacker to know that I'm using the username and password description trick.

6 The number of authentication login attempts is set to 1. If a user cannot authenticate on the first try, the connection is disabled and that user must re-establish the connection to try again.

7 The console line is associated with the **aaa authentication login** command with the name *console_access*, which allows both the TACACS+ and the local username database authentication methods.

The configuration for RouterB and RouterC is the same as that for RouterA. However, there is one issue with the branch-office router. When RouterC contacts the AAA server, its source address is E0, the public interface and the destination is the AAA server. In this case, the AAA server has a private address. You can solve this problem in two ways.

The first (and less preferable) solution is to set up a NAT translation on RouterA for the AAA server, giving the AAA server a public address. The main problem with this solution is that you need to open a small hole in RouterA's ACL on its public interface, and all TACACS+ traffic is sent across the Internet in the clear. Of course, TACACS+ encrypts the payload of the packet, but someone sniffing on the wire will know about the TACACS+ connection and might try to use this information to break into your network.

The second (and more preferable solution) is to use a VPN. However, there is still a problem: The source address of the TACACS+ packets is E0 (the public interface); unfortunately, this cannot be secured with a VPN because this is a termination point for the VPN connection. To get around this problem, you can set up a generic routing encapsulation tunnel between RouterC and either RouterA or RouterB. By using the GRE tunnel, the source of the TACACS+ transmission will be the tunnel interface, which can be protected by the tunnel.

In this example, I assume that the GRE tunnel is between RouterC and RouterA, where all traffic at the branch office will use the GRE tunnel. Example 21-6 shows RouterC's configuration.

Example 21-6 *Setting up a GRE Tunnel on RouterC*

```
RouterC(config)# interface tunnel0
RouterC(config-if)# ip address 172.16.99.2 255.255.255.0
RouterC(config-if)# tunnel source Ethernet0
RouterC(config-if)# tunnel destination 192.1.1.1
RouterC(config-if)# exit
```

The GRE tunnel is necessary to protect the AAA traffic between RouterC and the corporate site. I also have decided to use the GRE connection for all traffic between these two sites, which simplifies the VPN setup.

NOTE   The GRE tunnel is also necessary to have the traffic sent to the corporate site and then out to the Internet. If this was not necessary, a better solution would be to have RouterC source the TACACS+ transmissions from FastEthernet0 with the **ip tacacs source-interface** (or **ip radius source-interface**) command. Then you could ensure that this IP address was included in the IPSec crypto ACL to protect this traffic.

Example 21-7 shows RouterA's configuration (the internal router).

Example 21-7 *Setting up a GRE Tunnel on RouterA*

```
RouterA(config)# interface tunnel0
RouterA(config-if)# ip address 172.16.99.1 255.255.255.0
RouterA(config-if)# tunnel source Ethernet0/0
RouterA(config-if)# tunnel destination 200.1.1.1
```

Routing will be set up in the "Routing" section later in the chapter. I show you how to protect this traffic with a VPN in the "Site-to-Site VPN" section.

NOTE   For a small number of users, I probably would not use an AAA server. However, some features, such as authentication proxy, require it. In this example, you might want to add authentication proxy to authenticate remote-access VPN users, so you would need an AAA server. However, this topic is not covered in this case study.

In this example, you need to set up the Cisco Secure ACS server, including the three routers, as network devices; create a group for the network administrators; and then create your administrator accounts. When you are done, make sure that you test connectivity between the routers and the AAA server, especially for accounting. Use the **debug** commands discussed in Chapter 5, "Authentication, Authorization, and Accounting," to help troubleshoot any connectivity problems.

Access Control Lists

This section discusses the ACLs that you will use to filter traffic. I start with the most complex configuration: RouterA. With the perimeter router, I primarily am concerned about the kind of traffic coming into it from the Internet. Example 21-8 shows a sample configuration of this ACL.

Example 21-8 *Setting up an ACL on RouterA to Filter Internet Traffic*

```
RouterA(config)# ip access-list extended ingress-filter
RouterA(config-ext-nacl)# remark Unassigned IANA addresses
RouterA(config-ext-nacl)# deny ip 1.0.0.0 0.255.255.255 any
RouterA(config-ext-nacl)# deny ip 2.0.0.0 0.255.255.255 any
RouterA(config-ext-nacl)# deny ip 5.0.0.0 0.255.255.255 any
RouterA(config-ext-nacl)# deny ip 7.0.0.0 0.255.255.255 any
RouterA(config-ext-nacl)# deny ip 23.0.0.0 0.255.255.255 any
RouterA(config-ext-nacl)# deny ip 27.0.0.0 0.255.255.255 any
RouterA(config-ext-nacl)# deny ip 31.0.0.0 0.255.255.255 any
RouterA(config-ext-nacl)# deny ip 36.0.0.0 0.255.255.255 any
RouterA(config-ext-nacl)# deny ip 37.0.0.0 0.255.255.255 any
RouterA(config-ext-nacl)# deny ip 39.0.0.0 0.255.255.255 any
RouterA(config-ext-nacl)# deny ip 41.0.0.0 0.255.255.255 any
RouterA(config-ext-nacl)# deny ip 42.0.0.0 0.255.255.255 any
RouterA(config-ext-nacl)# deny ip 49.0.0.0 0.255.255.255 any
RouterA(config-ext-nacl)# deny ip 50.0.0.0 0.255.255.255 any
RouterA(config-ext-nacl)# deny ip 58.0.0.0 0.255.255.255 any
RouterA(config-ext-nacl)# deny ip 59.0.0.0 0.255.255.255 any
RouterA(config-ext-nacl)# deny ip 60.0.0.0 0.255.255.255 any
RouterA(config-ext-nacl)# deny ip 70.0.0.0 0.255.255.255 any
RouterA(config-ext-nacl)# deny ip 71.0.0.0 0.255.255.255 any
RouterA(config-ext-nacl)# deny ip 72.0.0.0 0.255.255.255 any
```

Example 21-8 *Setting up an ACL on RouterA to Filter Internet Traffic (Continued)*

```
RouterA(config-ext-nacl)# deny ip 73.0.0.0 0.255.255.255 any
RouterA(config-ext-nacl)# deny ip 74.0.0.0 0.255.255.255 any
RouterA(config-ext-nacl)# deny ip 75.0.0.0 0.255.255.255 any
RouterA(config-ext-nacl)# deny ip 76.0.0.0 0.255.255.255 any
RouterA(config-ext-nacl)# deny ip 77.0.0.0 0.255.255.255 any
RouterA(config-ext-nacl)# deny ip 78.0.0.0 0.255.255.255 any
RouterA(config-ext-nacl)# deny ip 79.0.0.0 0.255.255.255 any
RouterA(config-ext-nacl)# deny ip 83.0.0.0 0.255.255.255 any
RouterA(config-ext-nacl)# deny ip 84.0.0.0 0.255.255.255 any
RouterA(config-ext-nacl)# deny ip 85.0.0.0 0.255.255.255 any
RouterA(config-ext-nacl)# deny ip 86.0.0.0 0.255.255.255 any
RouterA(config-ext-nacl)# deny ip 87.0.0.0 0.255.255.255 any
RouterA(config-ext-nacl)# deny ip 88.0.0.0 0.255.255.255 any
RouterA(config-ext-nacl)# deny ip 89.0.0.0 0.255.255.255 any
RouterA(config-ext-nacl)# deny ip 90.0.0.0 0.255.255.255 any
RouterA(config-ext-nacl)# deny ip 91.0.0.0 0.255.255.255 any
RouterA(config-ext-nacl)# deny ip 92.0.0.0 0.255.255.255 any
RouterA(config-ext-nacl)# deny ip 93.0.0.0 0.255.255.255 any
RouterA(config-ext-nacl)# deny ip 94.0.0.0 0.255.255.255 any
RouterA(config-ext-nacl)# deny ip 95.0.0.0 0.255.255.255 any
RouterA(config-ext-nacl)# deny ip 96.0.0.0 0.255.255.255 any
RouterA(config-ext-nacl)# deny ip 97.0.0.0 0.255.255.255 any
RouterA(config-ext-nacl)# deny ip 98.0.0.0 0.255.255.255 any
RouterA(config-ext-nacl)# deny ip 99.0.0.0 0.255.255.255 any
RouterA(config-ext-nacl)# deny ip 100.0.0.0 0.255.255.255 any
RouterA(config-ext-nacl)# deny ip 101.0.0.0 0.255.255.255 any
RouterA(config-ext-nacl)# deny ip 102.0.0.0 0.255.255.255 any
RouterA(config-ext-nacl)# deny ip 103.0.0.0 0.255.255.255 any
RouterA(config-ext-nacl)# deny ip 104.0.0.0 0.255.255.255 any
RouterA(config-ext-nacl)# deny ip 105.0.0.0 0.255.255.255 any
RouterA(config-ext-nacl)# deny ip 106.0.0.0 0.255.255.255 any
RouterA(config-ext-nacl)# deny ip 107.0.0.0 0.255.255.255 any
RouterA(config-ext-nacl)# deny ip 108.0.0.0 0.255.255.255 any
RouterA(config-ext-nacl)# deny ip 109.0.0.0 0.255.255.255 any
RouterA(config-ext-nacl)# deny ip 110.0.0.0 0.255.255.255 any
RouterA(config-ext-nacl)# deny ip 111.0.0.0 0.255.255.255 any
RouterA(config-ext-nacl)# deny ip 112.0.0.0 0.255.255.255 any
RouterA(config-ext-nacl)# deny ip 113.0.0.0 0.255.255.255 any
RouterA(config-ext-nacl)# deny ip 114.0.0.0 0.255.255.255 any
RouterA(config-ext-nacl)# deny ip 115.0.0.0 0.255.255.255 any
RouterA(config-ext-nacl)# deny ip 116.0.0.0 0.255.255.255 any
RouterA(config-ext-nacl)# deny ip 117.0.0.0 0.255.255.255 any
RouterA(config-ext-nacl)# deny ip 118.0.0.0 0.255.255.255 any
RouterA(config-ext-nacl)# deny ip 119.0.0.0 0.255.255.255 any
RouterA(config-ext-nacl)# deny ip 120.0.0.0 0.255.255.255 any
RouterA(config-ext-nacl)# deny ip 121.0.0.0 0.255.255.255 any
RouterA(config-ext-nacl)# deny ip 122.0.0.0 0.255.255.255 any
RouterA(config-ext-nacl)# deny ip 123.0.0.0 0.255.255.255 any
RouterA(config-ext-nacl)# deny ip 124.0.0.0 0.255.255.255 any
RouterA(config-ext-nacl)# deny ip 125.0.0.0 0.255.255.255 any
```

continues

Example 21-8 *Setting up an ACL on RouterA to Filter Internet Traffic (Continued)*

```
RouterA(config-ext-nacl)# deny ip 126.0.0.0 0.255.255.255 any
RouterA(config-ext-nacl)# deny ip 197.0.0.0 0.255.255.255 any
RouterA(config-ext-nacl)# deny ip 201.0.0.0 0.255.255.255 any
RouterA(config-ext-nacl)# remark RFC 1918 private addresses
RouterA(config-ext-nacl)# deny ip 10.0.0.0 0.255.255.255 any
RouterA(config-ext-nacl)# deny ip 172.16.0.0 0.15.255.255 any
RouterA(config-ext-nacl)# deny ip 192.168.0.0 0.0.255.255 any
RouterA(config-ext-nacl)# remark Other bogons
RouterA(config-ext-nacl)# deny ip 224.0.0.0 15.255.255.255 any
RouterA(config-ext-nacl)# deny ip 240.0.0.0 15.255.255.255 any
RouterA(config-ext-nacl)# deny ip 0.0.0.0 0.255.255.255 any
RouterA(config-ext-nacl)# deny ip 169.254.0.0 0.0.255.255 any
RouterA(config-ext-nacl)# deny ip 192.0.2.0 0.0.0.255 any
RouterA(config-ext-nacl)# deny ip 127.0.0.0 0.255.255.255 any
RouterA(config-ext-nacl)# remark Allow IPSec access for
  site-to-site connections
RouterA(config-ext-nacl)# permit udp any host 192.1.1.1 eq isakmp
RouterA(config-ext-nacl)# permit esp any host 192.1.1.1
RouterA(config-ext-nacl)# permit udp any host 192.1.1.1 eq 4500
RouterA(config-ext-nacl)# permit gre host 200.1.1.1 host 192.1.1.1
RouterA(config-ext-nacl)# remark Allow access to DMZ servers
RouterA(config-ext-nacl)# permit tcp any host 192.1.1.2 eq 25
RouterA(config-ext-nacl)# permit udp any host 192.1.1.3 eq 53
RouterA(config-ext-nacl)# permit tcp any host 192.1.1.4 eq 80
RouterA(config-ext-nacl)# remark Deny all other traffic
RouterA(config-ext-nacl)# deny ip any any
RouterA(config-ext-nacl)# exit
RouterA(config)# interface ethernet0/0
RouterA(config-if)# ip access-group ingress-filter in
```

As you can see from Example 21-8, this is very similar to Example 7-22, shown previously in Chapter 7, "Basic Access Lists." The main difference here is that IPSec access is allowed (discussed later in the "Site-to-Site VPN" and "Remote-Access VPNs" sections), as is access to the specific services on the servers in the DMZ section. One thing that I want to point out about this configuration is that the previous ACL needs to allow NAT-T traffic (UDP 4500) for some remote-access users who are connecting to the perimeter router through an address-translation device. The GRE tunnel between RouterA and RouterC also needs to be permitted, even though this traffic is encrypted. This is because the ACL is processed twice: before and after the traffic is unencrypted. The next section discusses the use of CBAC to allow returning traffic through this router to internal devices.

I also have added one additional ACL to restrict access from internal users to the DMZ segment, as displayed in Example 21-9.

Example 21-9 *Restricting Traffic to the DMZ Segment on RouterA*

```
RouterA(config)# ip access-list extended DMZ-filter
RouterA(config-ext-nacl)# remark Allow access to DMZ servers
RouterA(config-ext-nacl)# permit tcp any host 172.16.1.2 eq 25
RouterA(config-ext-nacl)# permit udp any host 172.16.1.3 eq 53
```

Example 21-9 *Restricting Traffic to the DMZ Segment on RouterA (Continued)*

```
RouterA(config-ext-nacl)# permit tcp any host 172.16.1.4 eq 80
RouterA(config-ext-nacl)# remark Deny all other traffic
RouterA(config-ext-nacl)# deny ip any any
RouterA(config-ext-nacl)# exit
RouterA(config)# interface FastEthernet1/0
RouterA(config-if)# ip access-group DMZ-filter out
```

This ACL applies to any traffic exiting the DMZ interface, including internal and Internet traffic, even though these same statements already are included in the public interface's ingress filter. This ACL is necessary to restrict any type of traffic from exiting this interface. Also notice that I am using the local addresses in the filter because this is what is assigned on the devices on the DMZ.

The configuration of RouterB is shorter, but its policy implementation is much different. Example 21-10 shows RouterB's configuration.

Example 21-10 *Configuring RouterB's Filtering Policies*

```
RouterB(config)# ip access-list extended server-farm-filter
RouterB(config-ext-nacl)# remark Restrict access to the email server
RouterB(config-ext-nacl)# permit tcp 172.16.0.0 0.0.255.255
  host 172.16.3.1 eq 25
RouterB(config-ext-nacl)# remark Restrict access to the DNS server
RouterB(config-ext-nacl)# permit udp 172.16.0.0 0.0.255.255
  host 172.16.3.2 eq 53
RouterB(config-ext-nacl)# remark Restrict access to the application
  server
RouterB(config-ext-nacl)# permit tcp 172.16.0.0 0.0.255.255
  host 172.16.3.3 eq 443
RouterB(config-ext-nacl)# remark Deny access to the database server
RouterB(config-ext-nacl)# deny ip any host 172.16.3.4
RouterB(config-ext-nacl)# remark Protect the accounting server
RouterB(config-ext-nacl)# permit tcp 172.16.5.0 0.0.0.255
  host 172.16.3.5 eq 2501
RouterB(config-ext-nacl)# permit tcp 172.16.253.0 0.0.0.255
  host 172.16.3.5 eq 2501
RouterB(config-ext-nacl)# deny ip any host 172.16.3.5
RouterB(config-ext-nacl)# remark Protect the SCP server service
RouterB(config-ext-nacl)# permit tcp host 172.16.3.254
  host 172.16.3.6 eq 22
RouterB(config-ext-nacl)# permit tcp host 172.16.2.1
  host 172.16.3.6 eq 22
RouterB(config-ext-nacl)# permit tcp host 172.16.99.2
  host 172.16.3.6 eq 22
RouterB(config-ext-nacl)# remark Protect the syslog server service
RouterB(config-ext-nacl)# permit udp host 172.16.3.254
  host 172.16.3.6 eq 514
RouterB(config-ext-nacl)# permit udp host 172.16.2.1
  host 172.16.3.6 eq 514
RouterB(config-ext-nacl)# permit udp host 172.16.99.2
  host 172.16.3.6 eq 514
```

continues

Example 21-10 *Configuring RouterB's Filtering Policies (Continued)*

```
RouterB(config-ext-nacl)# remark Protect the NTP server service
RouterB(config-ext-nacl)# permit tcp any host 172.16.3.6 eq 123
RouterB(config-ext-nacl)# remark Deny all other traffic to the
  Syslog/SCP/NTP server
RouterB(config-ext-nacl)# deny ip any host 172.16.3.6
RouterB(config-ext-nacl)# exit
RouterB(config)# interface FastEthernet0/0
RouterB(config-if)# ip access-group server-farm-filter out
RouterB(config-if)# exit
RouterB(config)# ip access-list extended user-filter
RouterB(config-ext-nacl)# remark Restrict access to the accounting
  segment, but allow everything else
RouterB(config-ext-nacl)# deny ip any 172.16.5.0 0.0.0.255
RouterB(config-ext-nacl)# permit ip any any
RouterB(config-ext-nacl)# exit
RouterB(config)# interface FastEthernet1/1
RouterB(config-if)# ip access-group user-filter in
RouterB(config-if)# exit
RouterB(config)# ip access-list extended other-filter
RouterB(config-ext-nacl)# remark Deny all traffic--CBAC will allow
  returning traffic
RouterB(config-ext-nacl)# permit tcp host 172.16.1.2
  host 172.16.3.1 eq 25
RouterB(config-ext-nacl)# permit ip host 172.16.99.2
  172.16.3.6 0.0.0.254
RouterB(config-ext-nacl)# permit ip host 172.16.2.1
  172.16.3.6 0.0.0.254
RouterB(config-ext-nacl)# permit ip 172.16.99.0 0.0.0.255
  172.16.3.0 0.0.0.255
RouterB(config-ext-nacl)# permit ip 172.16.100.0 0.0.0.255
  172.16.3.0 0.0.0.255
RouterB(config-ext-nacl)# permit ip 172.16.252.0 0.0.0.255
  172.16.3.0 0.0.0.255
RouterB(config-ext-nacl)# permit ip 172.16.253.0 0.0.0.255
  172.16.3.0 0.0.0.255
RouterB(config-ext-nacl)# permit ip 172.16.254.0 0.0.0.255
  172.16.3.0 0.0.0.255
RouterB(config-ext-nacl)# deny ip any any
RouterB(config-ext-nacl)# exit
RouterB(config)# interface FastEthernet0/1
RouterB(config-if)# ip access-group other-filter in
RouterB(config-if)# exit
```

This configuration has three ACLs. The server-farm-filter ACL filters traffic as it exits the server-farm interface and is destined to the servers. One interesting item to point out is the syslog and SCP section for RouterC. Notice that the source address is the GRE tunnel interface for RouterC. To ensure that RouterC uses the tunnel interface, the code example for RouterC has the necessary static route. As I mentioned in the last section for AAA, this is necessary to protect RouterC's traffic with the site-to-site VPN.

The user-filter ACL is used to ensure that traffic from the user segment is blocked from the accounting segment. The other-filter ACL, by default, blocks all traffic coming from the perimeter router except for e-mail traffic from the e-mail server, remote access and the site-to-site VPN traffic (which is allowed to the server-farm segment), and management traffic from RouterA and RouterC. CBAC permits returning traffic, originally sent from the internal devices, as shown in the next section.

Of the three routers, RouterC's configuration is the simplest. Example 21-11 shows RouterC's configuration.

Example 21-11 *Configuring RouterC's Filter*

```
RouterC(config)# ip route 172.16.3.6 255.255.255.255 tunnel0
RouterC(config)# ip access-list extended ingress-filter
RouterC(config-ext-nacl)# remark Allow Site-to-Site IPSec access
RouterC(config-ext-nacl)# permit udp host 192.1.1.1 host 200.1.1.1 eq 500
RouterC(config-ext-nacl)# permit esp host 192.1.1.1 host 200.1.1.1
RouterC(config-ext-nacl)# permit gre host 192.1.1.1 host 200.1.1.1
RouterC(config-ext-nacl)# remark Deny all other traffic
RouterC(config-ext-nacl)# deny ip any any
RouterC(config-ext-nacl)# exit
RouterC(config)# interface Ethernet0
RouterC(config-if)# ip access-group ingress-filter in
```

As I mentioned previously, the static route is used to allow management traffic from RouterC to be protected by the site-to-site VPN connection through the GRE tunnel to RouterB. The ACL allows only IPSec traffic between RouterA and RouterC; all other traffic is denied. Remember that all of the branch office's traffic must use the site-to-site VPN connection to the corporate office; therefore, the ACL allows only IPSec traffic. Also, the GRE tunnel is required to allow RouterA to perform address translation on the branch office's traffic as it comes out the GRE tunnel and before it is sent out to the Internet.

CBAC and Web Filtering

The Cisco IOS Firewall feature set is installed on RouterA and RouterB. With RouterC, this is not necessary because all of the branch-office traffic is sent through the IPSec tunnel to RouterA. RouterC needs only a Cisco IOS that includes IPSec.

As you recall, CBAC was discussed in Chapter 9, "Context-Based Access Control." This section covers only the stateful filtering configuration of CBAC, as well as filtering with Websense. Other CBAC commands are discussed later. I start with RouterA's CBAC configuration, as displayed in Example 21-12.

Example 21-12 *Configuring CBAC on RouterA*

```
RouterA(config)# ip access-list extended ICMP-filter          (1)
RouterA(config-ext-nacl)# remark Allow management ICMP, deny others
RouterA(config-ext-nacl)# permit icmp 172.16.4.12 0.0.0.3 any
RouterA(config-ext-nacl)# deny icmp any any
RouterA(config-ext-nacl)# permit ip any any
RouterA(config)# ip inspect name CBAC-A1 smtp                 (2)
RouterA(config)# ip inspect name CBAC-A1 ftp
RouterA(config)# ip inspect name CBAC-A1 tcp
RouterA(config)# ip inspect name CBAC-A1 udp
RouterA(config)# ip inspect name CBAC-A1 icmp
RouterA(config)# ip inspect name CBAC-A1 http urlfilter       (3)
RouterA(config)# ip inspect tcp synwait-time 15              (4)
RouterA(config)# ip inspect tcp idle-time 300
RouterA(config)# ip inspect udp idle-time 20
RouterA(config)# ip urlfilter server vendor Websense 172.16.6.2  (5)
RouterA(config)# ip urlfilter cache 7000
RouterA(config)# ip urlfilter max-request 1500
RouterA(config)# ip urlfilter max-resp-pack 350
RouterA(config)# ip urlfilter alert
RouterA(config)# interface Ethernet0/0                       (6)
RouterA(config-if)# ip access-group ICMP-filter out
RouterA(config-if)# ip inspect CBAC-A1 out
RouterA(config-if)# exit
RouterA(config)# ip inspect name CBAC-A2 smtp                (7)
RouterA(config)# ip inspect name CBAC-A2 ftp
RouterA(config)# ip inspect name CBAC-A2 tcp
RouterA(config)# interface FastEthernet1/0
RouterA(config-if)# ip inspect CBAC-A2 in
```

The following is an explanation of the configuration in Example 21-12, with reference to the numbering on the right:

1 In this example, an ACL is configured to restrict outbound traffic. Basically, only the management devices are allowed to send out ICMP traffic. However, all other types of traffic are permitted.

2 A CBAC inspection rule called CBAC-A1 is created, which inspects SMTP, FTP, HTTP, TCP, UDP, and ICMP traffic as it exits the public interface (the only traffic denied outbound is ICMP traffic from nonmanagement devices).

3 This CBAC inspection rule allows for URL filtering of HTTP traffic by the Websense server.

4 Some of the timeout parameters are changed for inspection. The longest that CBAC will wait for TCP sessions to be established is 15 seconds. The idle timeout for TCP and UDP sessions also is changed to 300 seconds and 20 seconds, respectively.

5 This is the Websense configuration. The **ip urlfilter cache** statement increases the default URL cache size from 5000 to 7000. The **ip urlfilter max-request** statement increases the maximum number of requests from 1000 to 1500. This controls the

number of pending requests that the Cisco IOS holds while waiting for responses from the Websense server. The **ip urlfilter max-resp-pack** statement increases the maximum number of responses from the public web server from 200 to 350 packets.

6 The outbound ICMP filter is applied on the public interface as well as CBAC inspection (inspecting traffic as it leaves the router).

7 This second CBAC rule grouping allows traffic from the DMZ segment to be returned to these servers.

Example 21-13 shows the internal router's CBAC configuration.

Example 21-13 *Configuring CBAC on RouterB*

```
RouterB(config)# ip inspect name CBAC-B smtp
RouterB(config)# ip inspect name CBAC-B ftp
RouterB(config)# ip inspect name CBAC-B http
RouterB(config)# ip inspect name CBAC-B tcp
RouterB(config)# ip inspect name CBAC-B udp
RouterB(config)# ip inspect name CBAC-B icmp
RouterB(config)# ip inspect tcp synwait-time 15
RouterB(config)# ip inspect tcp idle-time 180
RouterB(config)# ip inspect udp idle-time 20
RouterB(config)# interface FastEthernet0/1
RouterB(config-if)# ip inspect CBAC-B out
```

The inspection rule for CBAC on RouterB is CBAC-B. This is the basically the same CBAC configuration as used on RouterA, with the exception of the ICMP filter and Websense. In this example, anyone can use ICMP traffic within the internal network, but RouterA allows only management users to use ICMP to access the Internet.

NOTE   If you are concerned about cost, you might want to implement reflexive ACLs on the internal router instead of using CBAC. However, remember that CBAC provides application inspection, such as inspection of e-mail commands, whereas reflexive ACLs cannot (session layer only). With the perimeter router, you must use CBAC because this company needs to have Websense inspect URLs.

Address Translation

As you can see from this case study, the network is using a private Class B network: 172.16.0.0. Therefore, address translation is needed to allow internal devices to access the Internet. Two types of address translation are required: static, for the public DMZ servers; and dynamic, for the users. In this network, RouterA performs address translation. Example 21-14 shows the necessary address-translation configuration for RouterA.

Example 21-14 *Setting up Address Translation on RouterA*

```
RouterA(config)# ip nat inside source static 172.16.1.2 192.1.1.2 (1)
RouterA(config)# ip nat inside source static 172.16.1.3 192.1.1.3
RouterA(config)# ip nat inside source static 172.16.1.4 192.1.1.4
RouterA(config)# ip nat inside source list dynamic-pat-addresses  (2)
  pool dynamic-nat-pool overload
RouterA(config)# ip access-list extended dynamic-pat-addresses    (3)
RouterA(config-ext-nacl)# deny ip 172.16.0.0 0.0.255.255
  172.16.0.0 0.0.255.255
RouterA(config-ext-nacl)# permit ip 172.16.0.0 any
RouterA(config-ext-nacl)# exit
RouterA(config)# ip nat pool dynamic-pat-pool 192.1.1.250          (4)
  192.1.1.253 netmask 255.255.255.0
RouterA(config)# interface fastethernet1/0                         (5)
RouterA(config-if)# ip nat inside
RouterA(config-if)# exit
RouterA(config)# interface fastethernet1/1
RouterA(config-if)# ip nat inside
RouterA(config-if)# exit
RouterA(config)# interface ethernet0/1
RouterA(config-if)# ip nat inside
RouterA(config-if)# exit
RouterA(config)# interface tunnel0
RouterA(config-if)# ip nat inside
RouterA(config-if)# exit
RouterA(config)# interface ethernet0/0
RouterA(config-if)# ip nat outside
```

The following is an explanation of the code listing in Example 21-14, with reference to the numbering on the right side:

1 These three static NAT commands perform address translation for the three DMZ servers.

2 The **ip nat inside source list** command defines dynamic PAT.

3 The **ip nat inside source list** command references this ACL to define when dynamic PATH should be performed. In this example, PAT is performed for all addresses except for connections between company devices (172.16.0.0/16). This is necessary for access from the corporate site to the remote-access VPN devices, as well as for access to the two networks (172.16.99.0/24 and 172.16.100.0/24) at the branch office.

4 The **ip nat pool** command defines the global addresses used by PAT for address translation.

5 Interface ethernet0/0 is defined as "outside" for NAT and the other three interfaces (ethernet0/1, fastethernet0/0, and fastethernet0/1), as well as the GRE tunnel, are designated as "inside." The Websense server connection is included because this company bought a subscription from Websense for automatic updates, which this server polls for on a weekly basis, so address translation is necessary. You also can use a static translation, if you want.

The previous configuration has one problem as it relates to VPN connections. The configuration specifies when to disable address translation for dynamic PAT; however, there are three static NAT configurations, and these are performed before the crypto map is applied. Therefore, the global IP addresses are used when sent to devices at the end of the VPN connections. In this situation, I want all internal devices to use their private addresses when communicating with each other. As an example, assume that the public web server (172.16.1.4 to 192.1.1.4) needs to send traffic to a remote-access user, such as 172.16.252.1. In this situation, the perimeter router changes the source address of the web server from 172.16.1.4 to 192.1.1.4 because the static NAT translation command specifies this translation.

To get around this problem, you can set up a configuration trick. As you recall from Chapter 12, "Address Translation Issues," address translation is enabled with the interface command **ip nat inside** and **ip nat outside**. When traffic comes into an inside interface and immediately exits an outside interface, the address-translation policies that you have defined take effect. This trick requires you to introduce a third interface into the configuration, which is a loopback interface. I use a simple example to explain how this works. For example, assume that the public web server sends traffic to 172.16.252.1. The perimeter router receives the traffic on an interface designated as inside for NAT (interface fa0/0). Policy routing states that this traffic is forwarded to the loopback interface, which has no NAT configuration, so NAT is not performed. The router then determines that, from the loopback interface, the traffic must use the VPN connection on the public interface to reach the remote-access user. In this example, the loopback interface lacks any NAT configuration, and the external interface is designated as outside for NAT. Because the loopback interface is not designated as inside, no static address translation is performed.

Example 21-15 shows the configuration that you need to add to RouterA to implement this address-translation policy.

Example 21-15 *Bypassing NAT on RouterA When Sending Traffic to Remote-Access Users*

```
RouterA(config)# ip access-list extended no-static-NAT          (1)
RouterA(config-ext-nacl)# remark From the email server to the VPN devices
RouterA(config-ext-nacl)# permit ip host 172.16.1.2 172.16.252.0 0.255.255.255
RouterA(config-ext-nacl)# permit ip host 172.16.1.2 172.16.253.0 0.255.255.255
RouterA(config-ext-nacl)# permit ip host 172.16.1.2 172.16.254.0 0.255.255.255
RouterA(config-ext-nacl)# remark From the DNS server to the VPN devices
RouterA(config-ext-nacl)# permit ip host 172.16.1.3 172.16.252.0 0.255.255.255
RouterA(config-ext-nacl)# permit ip host 172.16.1.3 172.16.253.0 0.255.255.255
RouterA(config-ext-nacl)# permit ip host 172.16.1.3 172.16.254.0 0.255.255.255
RouterA(config-ext-nacl)# remark From the web server to the VPN devices
RouterA(config-ext-nacl)# permit ip host 172.16.1.4 172.16.252.0 0.255.255.255
RouterA(config-ext-nacl)# permit ip host 172.16.1.4 172.16.253.0 0.255.255.255
RouterA(config-ext-nacl)# permit ip host 172.16.1.4 172.16.254.0 0.255.255.255
RouterA(config-ext-nacl)# exit
RouterA(config)# interface loopback0                            (2)
RouterA(config-if)# ip address 172.16.98.1 255.255.255.0
RouterA(config-if)# exit
RouterA(config)# route-map no-NAT permit 10                     (3)
```

continues

Example 21-15 *Bypassing NAT on RouterA When Sending Traffic to Remote-Access Users (Continued)*

```
RouterA(config-route-map)# match ip address no-static-NAT
RouterA(config-router-map)# set interface loopback0
RouterA(config-router-map)# exit
RouterA(config)# route-map no-NAT permit 20
RouterA(config-router-map)# exit
RouterA(config)# interface fastethernet1/0                    (4)
RouterA(config-if)# ip policy route-map no-NAT
```

The following is an explanation of the configuration in Example 21-15, with reference to the numbering on the right side:

1 This ACL defines matches for traffic from any of the DMZ servers to any of the company's VPN devices' remote-access internal addresses. Note that I did not include the branch office, even though it is also using a VPN connection to reach the corporate site. Because the GRE tunnel on interface tunnel0 is defined as inside for NAT, NAT translation does not take place between the corporate site and the branch office.

2 A loopback interface is created for the temporary hop between the DMZ servers and the VPN devices.

3 The route map specifies the ACL in Step 1, which causes the Cisco IOS to forward traffic from the DMZ servers to the loopback interface before being forwarded to the VPN devices. If there is no match in the ACL, the DMZ traffic is routed normally.

4 The route map is activated on the DMZ interface.

NOTE   The configuration in Example 21-15 is necessary only if you have static address-translation commands and you want to disable the translation on a connection-by-connection basis, as with VPNs. In addition, switching packets through source routing like this causes every packet that matches the route map to be process-switched, which is far more CPU intensive than other switching methods supported by the router. Take care to list only the exact packets that need this function and to do this only if absolutely necessary.

Routing

This section covers the routing and routing protection configuration used on these routers. First, because this network is small, static routes are used for connectivity. Example 21-16 shows an example of RouterA's static route configuration.

Example 21-16 *Setting up Routing on RouterA*

```
RouterA(config)# ip route 0.0.0.0 0.0.0.0 192.1.1.254
RouterA(config)# ip route 172.16.3.0 255.255.255.0 172.16.2.254
RouterA(config)# ip route 172.16.4.0 255.255.255.0 172.16.2.254
RouterA(config)# ip route 172.16.5.0 255.255.255.0 172.16.2.254
RouterA(config)# ip route 172.16.100.0 255.255.255.0 tunnel0
```

Notice that I am using the GRE tunnel to reach the branch office.

Here is the routing configuration for RouterB:

```
RouterB(config)# ip route 0.0.0.0 0.0.0.0 172.16.2.1
```

Here is the routing configuration for RouterC:

```
RouterC(config)# ip route 192.1.1.1 255.255.255.255 200.200.200.2
RouterC(config)# ip route 0.0.0.0 0.0.0.0 tunnel0
```

RouterC has a default route pointing to the tunnel interface to reach all networks, with one exception. To build the GRE tunnel, RouterC needs to be capable of accessing the tunnel destination, 192.1.1.1. I have added a host route pointing to RouterC's ISP router to access RouterA across the Internet.

NOTE   If you are experiencing performance problems across the VPN connection between the branch office and corporate sites, it probably is related to the MTU size used for packets. In this example, remember that you have two tunnels and two sets of overhead: IPSec and GRE. You should adjust the MTU size on your branch-office devices to around 1400 bytes (I am assuming that Ethernet is used in this calculation).

To prevent internal spoofing attacks, I implement Reverse-Path Forwarding (RPF) on all three routers. My ACL on the perimeter router's external interface prevents external spoofing (blocks the private addresses, of which I am using 172.16.0.0/24), so I use RPF here to prevent internal spoofing. Example 21-17 shows the configuration for RouterA.

Example 21-17 *Using RPF on RouterA to Prevent Internal Spoofing*

```
RouterA(config)# ip cef
RouterA(config)# interface ethernet0/1
RouterA(config-if)# ip verify unicast reverse-path
RouterA(config-if)# exit
RouterA(config)# interface fastethernet1/0
RouterA(config-if)# ip verify unicast reverse-path
RouterA(config-if)# exit
RouterA(config)# interface fastethernet1/1
RouterA(config-if)# ip verify unicast reverse-path
RouterA(config-if)# exit
```

First, you must enable CEF. After this, for each interface on which you want to enable RPF, you must execute the **ip verify unicast reverse-path** command. For RouterB, enable RPF on all four of its interfaces; for RouterC, do so on both the internal and external interface.

Intrusion-Detection System

Because RouterA has the Cisco IOS Firewall feature set, as an added protection mechanism, I implement an IDS on it to help detect some common attacks against the router itself as well as the corporate network. Some people consider loading up the Cisco IOS Firewall feature set on RouterC at the branch office to take advantage of this feature; however, the only traffic that RouterC allows is the IPSec traffic from RouterA, so I am a lot less concerned about attacks against the branch office.

NOTE   If you are really concerned about attacks, put IDS network sensors at the corporate and branch office locations. At the corporate office, attach a sensor to a T-tap between the cable modem and RouterA, as well as to the server-farm segment. However, that assumes that you are very concerned about security and network and host attacks.

Example 21-18 shows the IDS configuration used on the perimeter router.

Example 21-18 *Setting up IDS on RouterA*

```
RouterA(config)# ip audit notify log
RouterA(config)# ip audit name IDSRULE attack action alarm drop reset
RouterA(config)# ip audit name IDSRULE info action alarm
RouterA(config)# interface ethernet0/0
RouterA(config-if)# ip audit IDSRULE in
```

In Example 21-18, I have enabled logging of IDS events, which I log to the syslog server (discussed in the "NTP and Syslog" section) with the **ip audit notify log** command. There are two IDS rules: The first one enables the attack signatures; the responses are alarm, drop, and reset connections. The second one enables alarms for the informational signatures. This rule is activated on the perimeter router's external interface.

Connection Attacks and CBAC

This company is concerned about connection attacks, especially against e-mail and web servers. I have decided to set connection limits, using CBAC, on the perimeter router to limit these attacks.

Example 21-19 shows an example configuration.

Example 21-19 *Configuring CBAC Thresholds on RouterA to Prevent Connection Floods*

```
RouterA(config)# ip inspect max-incomplete high 700
RouterA(config)# ip inspect max-incomplete low 550
RouterA(config)# ip inspect one-minute high 800
RouterA(config)# ip inspect one-minute low 650
```

In this code, I modified the maximum number of half-open connection threshold values to 700 and 550, and I changed the one-minute interval threshold values to 800 and 650. These values were configured after monitoring normal activity in this network. I previously configured the CBAC timeouts in the "CBAC and Web Filtering" section.

Rate Limiting

Another concern of this company is to limit the bandwidth that ICMP and UDP traffic can use. The company has contacted its ISP at both the corporate and branch office sites to have it set up rate limiting of these protocols. At the corporate and branch office, the ISP limits ICMP traffic to 64 kbps and UDP traffic to 96 kbps.

Besides preventing external DoS attacks, the company wants to ensure that certain protocols have enough bandwidth when sending traffic to the Internet. Important traffic includes SMTP, DNS, VPN, and HTTP. All other traffic is not as important and should be limited to 256 kbps, with a burst of 32 kbps, in the outbound direction at the corporate site. I use NBAR to set this up. Example 21-20 shows the configuration for this rate limiting, which was discussed in Chapter 17, "DoS Protection."

Example 21-20 *Setting up Traffic Rate Limiting on RouterA*

```
RouterA(config)# access-list 111 deny tcp any any eq 25        (1)
RouterA(config)# access-list 111 deny udp any any eq 53
RouterA(config)# access-list 111 deny udp any any eq 500
RouterA(config)# access-list 111 deny esp any any
RouterA(config)# access-list 111 deny udp any any eq 4500
RouterA(config)# access-list 111 deny tcp any any eq 80
RouterA(config)# access-list 111 permit ip any any
RouterA(config)# class-map match-any non-important-traffic      (2)
RouterA(config-cmap)# match access-group 111
RouterA(config-cmap)# exit
RouterA(config)# policy-map mark-non-important-traffic          (3)
RouterA(config-pmap)# class non-important-traffic
RouterA(config-pmap-c)# set ip dscp 1
RouterA(config-pmac-c)# exit
RouterA(config)# interface ethernet0/1                          (4)
RouterA(config-if)# service-policy input mark-non-important-traffic
RouterA(config-if)# exit
RouterA(config)# interface fastethernet1/0
```

continues

Example 21-20 *Setting up Traffic Rate Limiting on RouterA (Continued)*

```
RouterA(config-if)# service-policy input mark-non-important-traffic
RouterA(config-if)# exit
RouterA(config)# interface fastethernet1/1
RouterA(config-if)# service-policy input mark-non-important-traffic
RouterA(config-if)# exit
RouterA(config)# class-map match-any marked-traffic              (5)
RouterA(config-cmap)# match dscp 1
RouterA(config-cmap)# exit
RouterA(config)# police-map limit-traffic                        (6)
RouterA(config-pmap)# class marked-traffic
RouterA(config-pmap-c)# police 256000 32000 32000
  conform-action transmit exceed-action drop violation drop
RouterA(config)# interface ethernet0/0
RouterA(config-if)# service-policy output limit-traffic          (7)
```

The following is an explanation of the configuration in Example 21-20, with reference to the numbering on the right side:

1 ACL 111 defines the traffic that I am limiting. Notice that I am not limiting e-mail (25), DNS (53), ISAKMP for IPSec (500), ESP, NAT-T (UDP 4500), or HTTP (80): The **permit** statement at the end matches on everything else.

2 The **class-map** command looks for this traffic with the use of the **match access-group** command.

3 The policy map marks all packets matched in the **class-map** command with a DSCP value of 1.

4 The policy map is activated on the perimeter router's internal interfaces, marking traffic as it comes from the DMZ, Websense, or internal segments.

5 Remember that NBAR cannot perform two policies on one interface, such as mark and drop, or mark and limit. Therefore, a separate policy must be created. In Step 5, a second class map is created, looking for the packets that had their DSCP value set to 1.

6 The **police-map** command specifies the policy to be applied to this traffic. In this instance, I first reference the class map, which matches on packets with the DSCP value set to 1. Second, the **police** command is used to enforce rate limiting. Marked traffic is limited to an average throughput of 256 kbps, with a burst of 32 kbps. If either of these limits is exceeded, the policy is to drop the excessive traffic.

7 The last step is to activate the second policy map on the perimeter router's external interface. When it is activated on the external interface, the second policy map will enforce rate limiting for packets that have their DSCP value set to 1.

NOTE	You also can use CAR for rate limiting; however, Cisco recommends using NBAR because it performs better.

NTP and Syslog

NTP is used to synchronize the time on the routers. The internal syslog server (172.16.3.6) acts as the master NTP source and uses authentication to verify any device's identity before sharing time information with it.

Example 21-21 displays the configuration necessary to set up NTP on RouterA.

Example 21-21 *Configuring NTP on RouterA*

```
RouterA(config)# ntp server 172.16.3.6 key 32 source fastethernet0/1
RouterA(config)# ntp authenticate
RouterA(config)# ntp authentication-key 32 md5 78ba12ac
RouterA(config)# ntp trusted-key 32
RouterA(config)# ntp update-calendar
RouterA(config)# access-list 19 permit 172.16.3.6 0.0.0.0
RouterA(config)# ntp access-group peer 19
RouterA(config)# ntp source fastethernet0/1
RouterA(config)# interface ethernet0/0
RouterA(config-if)# ntp disable
RouterA(config-if)# exit
RouterA(config)# interface ethernet0/1
RouterA(config-if)# ntp disable
RouterA(config-if)# exit
RouterA(config)# interface fastethernet1/0
RouterA(config-if)# ntp disable
RouterA(config-if)# exit
```

In Example 21-21, the NTP server is 172.16.3.6, which is specified in the first command. The next three commands set up authentication and refer back to the first command with the key reference number of 32. Notice that the encryption/decryption key is 78ba12ac, which also must be configured on the NTP server. This router has a hardware clock, so the **ntp update-calendar** command updates the hardware clock from the software clock. The **access-list** and **ntp access-group** commands restrict NTP interaction with only 172.16.3.6. Following this, the source interface of the packets is set to the internal interface (172.16.2.0/16). Finally, NTP is disabled on the outside, DMZ, and Websense interfaces.

The configuration of RouterB and RouterC is basically the same; however, for security purposes, you should configure a separate key and then disable NTP on interfaces that are not used to acquire time. On RouterB, this is all interfaces except 172.16.3.0/24; on

RouterC, this is both physical interfaces (not the GRE tunnel). In addition, on RouterC, the tunnel interface should be the source of NTP transmissions.

After setting up NTP, all three routers will use syslog to send messages to the syslog server (172.16.3.6) on the server-farm segment. Example 21-22 shows the syslog configuration on RouterA

Example 21-22 *Configuring Access to a Syslog Server on RouterA*

```
RouterA(config)# service timestamps log datetime
RouterA(config)# logging on
RouterA(config)# logging host 172.16.3.6
RouterA(config)# logging trap informational
RouterA(config)# logging source-interface fastethernet1/1
RouterA(config)# logging origin-id string Perimeter
```

In Example 21-22, time stamps are enabled for logging messages. All messages also are sent out the internal interface (fastethernet0/1). The name included in the message is Perimeter.

Example 21-23 shows the configuration for RouterB.

Example 21-23 *Configuring Access to a Syslog Server on RouterB*

```
RouterB(config)# service timestamps log datetime
RouterB(config)# logging on
RouterB(config)# logging host 172.16.3.6
RouterB(config)# logging trap informational
RouterB(config)# logging source-interface fastethernet0/0
RouterB(config)# logging origin-id string Internal
```

Example 21-24 shows the configuration for RouterC.

Example 21-24 *Configuring Access to a Syslog Server on RouterC*

```
RouterC(config)# service timestamps log datetime
RouterC(config)# logging on
RouterC(config)# logging host 172.16.3.6
RouterC(config)# logging trap informational
RouterC(config)# logging source-interface tunnel0
RouterC(config)# logging origin-id string Branch
```

One interesting thing to point out about this example is that the source of syslog traffic is the IP address on the tunnel0 interface.

Site-to-Site VPN

This network contains one site-to-site IPSec VPN connection: between the perimeter router at the corporate site and the branch-office router. As you recall from the "Proposal" section earlier, all branch-office traffic, including any traffic destined to the Internet, must traverse this connection. Here are the IKE Phase 1 components used for the management connection:

- **Device authentication**—Preshared keys, where the key used is 123QuizWare321
- **Encryption**—3DES
- **Hash function**—SHA
- **DH group**—Group 2
- **Lifetime**—Default

Here are the IKE Phase 2 components used for the data connection:

- **ESP mode**—Tunnel
- **ESP encryption**—3DES
- **ESP packet authentication**—SHA
- **Lifetime**—Default

I start with RouterA's configuration. Example 21-25 shows the IPSec configuration for the site-to-site connection to RouterC.

Example 21-25 *Setting the Corporate Office Site-to-Site Connection on RouterA*

```
RouterA(config)# crypto isakmp policy 100                       (1)
RouterA(config-isakmp)# authentication pre-share
RouterA(config-isakmp)# encryption 3des
RouterA(config-isakmp)# hash sha
RouterA(config-isakmp)# group 2
RouterA(config-isakmp)# exit
RouterA(config)# crypto isakmp key 123QuizWare321              (2)
  address 200.1.1.1 no-xauth
RouterA(config)# access-list 119 permit gre host 200.1.1.1    (3)
  host 192.1.1.1
RouterA(config)# crypto ipsec transform-set Routertransform   (4)
  esp-sha-hmac esp-3des
RouterA(config-crytpo-trans)# mode tunnel
RouterA(config-crytpo-trans)# exit
RouterA(config)# crypto map IPSECMAP 100 ipsec-isakmp         (5)
RouterA(config-crypto-map)# match address 119
RouterA(config-crypto-map)# set peer 200.1.1.1
RouterA(config-crypto-map)# set pfs group2
RouterA(config-crypto-map)# set transform-set Routertransform
RouterA(config-crypto-map)# exit
RouterA(config)# interface ethernet0/0                         (6)
RouterA(config-if)# crypto map IPSECMAP
RouterA(config-if)# exit
```

The following is a breakdown of RouterA's configuration in Example 21-25, with reference to the numbering on the right side:

1 ISAKMP policy 100 defines the protection for the management connection.

2 The key for RouterC (200.1.1.1) is defined as 123QuizWare321. Because this router supports both remote access and site-to-site connections, the **no-xauth** parameter ensures that this key will not be used for XAUTH remote-access user connections; it will be used for only the site-to-site connection.

3 The crypto ACL specifies that the GRE tunnel traffic is to be protected (which is basically all traffic between the corporate site and the branch-office routers).

4 The transform set Routertransform specifies that ESP SHA and ESP 3DES, in tunnel mode, are to be used for protection.

5 The crypto map IPSECMAP has one entry in it for site-to-site connections. The crypto ACL (119) is referenced for the protected traffic, the peer is specified (200.1.1.1 — RouterC), PFS is used to share keying information when the data connections are about to expire, and the Routertransform set is specified for the protection of the data connections.

6 The crypto ACL is activated.

NOTE   Before Cisco IOS 12.2(13)T, you had to activate the crypto ACL on both the physical interface and the tunnel interface. With Cisco IOS 12.2(13)T and later, you need to apply the crypto map on only the physical interface. Actually, Cisco recommends that you apply the crypto map on only the physical interface in this instance, even though I never have experienced issues when applying it to both interfaces.

Example 21-26 shows the configuration for RouterC.

Example 21-26 *Setting the Branch Office Site-to-Site Connection on RouterA*

```
RouterC(config)# crypto isakmp policy 100
RouterC(config-isakmp)# authentication pre-share
RouterC(config-isakmp)# encryption 3des
RouterC(config-isakmp)# hash sha
RouterC(config-isakmp)# group 2
RouterC(config-isakmp)# exit
RouterC(config)# crypto isakmp key 123QuizWare321 address 192.1.1.1 no-xauth
RouterC(config)# access-list 119 permit gre host 192.1.1.1 host 200.1.1.1
RouterC(config)# crypto ipsec transform-set Routertransform esp-sha-hmac esp-3des
RouterC(config-crytpo-trans)# mode tunnel
RouterC(config-crytpo-trans)# exit
RouterC(config)# crypto map IPSECMAP 100 ipsec-isakmp
RouterC(config-crypto-map)# match address 119
RouterC(config-crypto-map)# set peer 192.1.1.1
RouterC(config-crypto-map)# set pfs group2
RouterC(config-crypto-map)# set transform-set Routertransform
RouterC(config-crypto-map)# exit
```

Example 21-26 *Setting the Branch Office Site-to-Site Connection on RouterA (Continued)*

```
RouterC(config)# interface ethernet0
RouterC(config-if)# crypto map IPSECMAP
RouterC(config-if)# exit
```

As you can see from Example 21-26, the setup of the site-to-site connection is almost the same as for RouterA. There are three differences, which I have shaded:

- The address in the preshared key statement is RouterA's.
- The crypto ACL is mirrored.
- The peer in the crypto map is RouterA.

TIP	In most cases, I perform the configuration on one router, paste it onto a text editor, edit it for the second router, and then paste the configuration into the second router, simplifying the configuration process.

Remote-Access VPNs

The last section of this chapter covers how to set up the remote-access VPN connectivity. As I mentioned at the beginning of the chapter, a few of the company's personnel periodically use the Internet to connect to the company. Because of security issues, an IPSec VPN is used. Easy VPN is used for the configuration.

Local LAN and Internet access is allowed for these users, but a software firewall should be installed on their PCs, and any traffic destined for the corporate office should be protected. Therefore, I need to configure split-tunneling. Remote-access users will be using the subnets 172.16.252.0/24 (network administrators), 127.16.253.0/24 (accounting users), and 172.16.254.0/24 (general users), so I need to set up three different groups with three different address pools. This is necessary to implement internal filtering policies on the routers, if necessary. The names of these groups are admin, accounting, and users.

Example 21-27 shows the basic configuration on RouterA, which terminates the remote-access VPN connections.

Example 21-27 *Setting up Remote-Access VPN Connectivity on RouterA*

```
RouterA(config)# aaa authentication login vpnauthenticate          (1)
  group tacacs
RouterA(config)# aaa authorization network admin group tacacs
RouterA(config)# aaa authorization network accounting group tacacs
RouterA(config)# aaa authorization network users group tacacs
RouterA(config)# crypto isakmp policy 200                          (2)
RouterA(config-isakmp)# encryption 3des
```

continues

Example 21-27 *Setting up Remote-Access VPN Connectivity on RouterA (Continued)*

```
RouterA(config-isakmp)# hash md5
RouterA(config-isakmp)# authentication pre-share
RouterA(config-isakmp)# group 2
RouterA(config-isakmp)# exit
RouterA(config)# crypto isakmp keepalive 20 10                    (3)
RouterA(config)# crypto isakmp xauth timeout 45
RouterA(config)# ip local pool admin_pool                        (4)
  172.16.252.1 172.16.252.254
RouterA(config)# ip local pool accounting_pool 172.16.253.1 172.16.253.254
RouterA(config)# ip local pool users_pool 172.16.254.1 172.16.254.254
RouterA(config)# crypto isakmp client configuration group admin   (5)
RouterA(config-isakmp-group)# key adminkeya13
RouterA(config-isakmp-group)# pool admin_pool
RouterA(config-isakmp-group)# domain quizware.com
RouterA(config-isakmp-group)# dns 172.16.3.2
RouterA(config-isakmp-group)# split-dns quizware.com
RouterA(config-isakmp-group)# acl 131
RouterA(config-isakmp-group)# firewall are-u-there
RouterA(config-isakmp-group)# exit
RouterA(config)# crypto isakmp client configuration             (6)
  group accounting
RouterA(config-isakmp-group)# key acctkeyf21
RouterA(config-isakmp-group)# pool accounting_pool
RouterA(config-isakmp-group)# domain quizware.com
RouterA(config-isakmp-group)# dns 172.16.3.2
RouterA(config-isakmp-group)# split-dns quizware.com
RouterA(config-isakmp-group)# acl 131
RouterA(config-isakmp-group)# firewall are-u-there
RouterA(config-isakmp-group)# exit
RouterA(config)# crypto isakmp client configuration group users  (7)
RouterA(config-isakmp-group)# key userskeyd7a
RouterA(config-isakmp-group)# pool users_pool
RouterA(config-isakmp-group)# domain quizware.com
RouterA(config-isakmp-group)# dns 172.16.3.2
RouterA(config-isakmp-group)# split-dns quizware.com
RouterA(config-isakmp-group)# acl 131
RouterA(config-isakmp-group)# firewall are-u-there
RouterA(config-isakmp-group)# exit
RouterA(config)# access-list 131 permit any                      (8)
  172.16.0.0 0.0.255.255
RouterA(config)# crypto ipsec transform-set easyclients          (9)
  esp-3des esp-sha-hmac
RouterA(config)# crypto dynamic-map dynamic_map 100              (10)
RouterA(config-crypto-map)# set transform-set easyclients
RouterA(config-crypto-map)# exit
RouterA(config)# crypto map IPSECMAP client authentication       (11)
  list vpnauthenticate
RouterA(config)# crypto map IPSECMAP isakmp authorization        (12)
  list admin
```

Example 21-27 *Setting up Remote-Access VPN Connectivity on RouterA (Continued)*

```
RouterA(config)# crypto map IPSECMAP isakmp authorization
  list accounting
RouterA(config)# crypto map IPSECMAP isakmp authorization
  list users
RouterA(config)# crypto map IPSECMAP client configuration        (13)
  address respond
RouterA(config)# crypto map IPSECMAP 999 ipsec-isakmp            (14)
  dynamic dynamic_map
```

The following is an explanation of RouterA's configuration in Example 21-27, with reference to the numbering on the right:

1 The **aaa authentication login** command sets up a login method called vpnauthenticate, which is used for XAUTH authentication. The user accounts for XAUTH are defined on the Cisco Secure ACS server (this is not shown in the case study). The three **aaa authorization network** commands define the remote-access groups for the three types of people establishing remote-access connections. This is necessary to be able to match up the users to the appropriate groups.

2 A separate IKE Phase 1 policy is defined for the remote-access users. The main difference between the site-to-site policy and this one is that this one uses MD5 for packet authentication.

3 IKE DPD is defined with a keepalive interval of 20 seconds and a retry period of 10 seconds. The XAUTH authentication time period is changed to 45 seconds.

4 Three address pools are created here—one for each remote-access group. I use this approach because it gives me more flexibility in implementing internal filtering policies, such as still allowing remote-access accounting people to access the internal accounting server, while denying other remote-access people to this server.

5 The first **crypto isakmp client configuration** command defines the policies for the remote-access admin group. Each group has its own unique preshared key. I have defined the DNS server as the internal device; I also have configured split tunneling (**acl**), where ACL 131 in Step 8 specifies that traffic sent to 172.16.0.0/16 is to be protected; all other traffic can be sent in clear text to the local LAN segment or to the Internet. I am assuming that the users are using the Cisco 3.6.3 VPN client or higher with the Cisco Integrated Client (CIC) firewall enabled. If this is not so, the **firewall are-u-there** command will prevent access (note that Black Ice and ZoneAlarm also are supported firewalls).

6 This is the remote-access configuration for the accounting group. It is basically the same as the configuration for the admin group, with the exception of the preshared key and the address pool.

7 This is the remote-access configuration for the users group, which all users of this company use except the network administrators and the accounting personnel. It is basically the same as the configuration for the admin group, with the exception of the preshared key and the address pool.

8 ACL 131 defines the split tunneling policy for the **acl** command in each remote-access group. This statement specifies that any traffic from the remote-access clients sent to 172.16.0.0/16 must be protected.

9 I have set up a separate transform set for the remote-access users. This gives me more flexibility later if I decide to make changes to how the remote-access data connections are protected.

10 For remote-access users, I need to create a dynamic crypto map. In this instance, because all remote-access users are using the same client (they all have the same IPSec capabilities), I need only one entry. Here is where I specify the remote-access clients' transform set.

11 For the static crypto map that I created in the last section, I specify that XAUTH authentication is needed for remote-access clients.

12 The next three commands specify that, for the static crypto map, authorization should occur for the three remote-access user groups.

13 The **crypto map client configuration** command allows the router to respond with the IKE Mode Config information to the remote-access clients. The **initiate** parameter is not necessary because the Cisco VPN 3.6.3 and later clients initiate the process by asking for the mode configuration information.

14 Finally, the dynamic map needs to be referenced in the static crypto map. The important thing here is that the map entry must be higher than all of the site-to-site connection entries. As you recall from the last section, the site-to-site connection had an entry number of 100, and in this configuration, the dynamic map has an entry number of 999.

As you can see from this configuration, the more groups you have, the more complex the configuration becomes. As I mentioned in Chapter 20, "IPSec Remote-Access Connections," I prefer to use the Cisco VPN 3000 concentrators when I need to set up a large number of users and groups. In this case, because the network is small and the number of users is small, I used the existing perimeter router to handle this function.

Summary

This chapter showed you a case study using the many security features discussed in this book. By no means is this the only possible solution to the given problem; however, the goal of this chapter is to show you how to implement Cisco security features in an integrated manner. As you will learn, each networking situation has its own set of unique problems and issues, as well as possible solutions.

TIP   As you can see from this case study, even though the network is small, the configuration is quite complex. Therefore, I highly recommend that you implement one component at a time, making the setup and troubleshooting process easier. As a final note, good luck with your security endeavors!

INDEX

A

AAA, 201
  accounting, 226–227
    broadcast accounting, 229–230
    configuring, 227
    enabling, 227–229
    suppressing null username records, 229
    troubleshooting, 230
  authentication, 213–214
    login banners, 218–219
    method lists, 214–215
    privileged EXEC shell access, 217
    user EXEC shell access, 216–217
    username and password prompts, 218
  authorization, 222
    configuring, 222
    example of, 225
    restricting command execution, 223–224
    troubleshooting, 224
  centralizing, 203
    server groupings, 208
    server protocol example configuration, 211–212
    with RADIUS, 205–208
    with TACACS+, 203–205
  configuring, 202
    on perimeter routers, case study, 817–820
  functions of, 202
aaa accounting command, 227
aaa authentication login command, 216
aaa authorization command command, 225
aaa new-model command, 204
absolute command, creating time ranges, 286
absolute timer (lock-and-key), 556
access, controlling, 43
access attacks, 22–24
  data manipulation attacks, 24–25
  session attacks, 25–29
    masquerading attacks, 26
    preventing, 28–29
    repudiation attacks, 28
    session-hijacking attacks, 26–27
    session-replay attacks, 26
access profiles, 568
access-class command, 123

accessing Cisco routers, 117
  aging password authentication, 113–114
  local access, 118–120
  no password authentication, 111–112
  OTPs, 114–115
  privileged EXEC mode, 146–152
  remote access, 121–145
  static password authentication, 112–113
  token card services, 115–117
access-restrict command, 796
accounting, 226–227
  broadcast accounting, 229–230
  configuring, 227
  enabling, 227–229
  suppressing null username records, 229
  troubleshooting with debug aaa accounting command, 230
acl command, 796
ACLs (access control lists), 237–238, 259–260
  accounting
    defining thresholds, 294
    filtering information, 293–294
    limiting transit records, 294–295
  activating, 252
  bogon addresses
    egress filtering, 305–307
    ingress filtering, 302–305
  configuring
    on internal routers, case study, 823–825
    on perimeter routers, case study, 820–823
  controlling address translation, 514–515
  creating, 250–251
  deleting entries from, 261
  detecting DoS attacks, 665–672
  editing, 252–253
  example, 238
  extended, 264
    named extended ACLs, 273
    numbered extended ACLs, 264–272
    three-interface router example, 275–278
    two-interface router example, 273–275
  fragments, filtering, 282–285
  lock-and-key, 551–552
    configuring, 555–560
    example, 563–564
    operation, 553–554

remote administration access,
560–562

troubleshooting, 562–563

when to use, 552

logging updates, 291

threshold, changing, 291–292

violations, accounting, 292–293

monitoring rcp command usage, 327

placement of, 248–249

preventing attacks

fraggle attacks, 310–311

smurf attacks, 308–310

TCP SYN floods, 307–308

processing, 241

conditions, 241

rules, 246–247

statement order, 243–246

RACLs, 351

building, 358

configuring, 365–374

examples of, 374–378

filtering returning traffic, 359–360

limitations of, 361–364

removing entries, 360–361

traffic processing, 357

versus extended ACLs, 352–356

remarks, 251

adding, 290

securing routing protocols, 613–614

sequenced

configuring, 296–298

deleting entries, 299

inserting entries, 300–301

resequencing, 298–299

standard, 260

examples of, 263–264

named standard ACLs, 262–263

numbered standard ACLs, 261–262

timed, 285

activating time ranges, 287

creating time ranges, 285–287

distributed, 287–288

example configuration, 288–289

Trojan horse attacks, blocking, 325–326

turbo, configuring, 295–296

types of, 240–241

verifying configuring, 278–280

wildcard masks, converting from subnet masks,
254–256

activating

ACLs, 252

AP policies, 580–581

CBAC inspection rules, 410

crypto maps, 773

time ranges for timed ACLs, 287

adding remarks to ACLs, 290

address overloading, 480–481

address translation

configuring on perimeter routers, case study,
827–830

connection limits, configuring, 500

controlling

with ACLs, 514–515

with route maps, 517

with route maps with dynamic NAT,
515–519

with route maps with static NAT,
520–521

dynamic translation, 477

embedded addressing information,
509–510

ALG support, 511–512

supported protocols, 511

extended translation, 477

IP NAT Service, 512

configuring, 513–514

limitations of, 484

NAT, 474–477

configuring, 484–488

global addresses, 476

local addresses, 476–477

overlapping addresses, 479

static NAT redundancy with HSRP,
522–526

with CBAC, configuring, 505–507

overlapping addresses, configuring, 493–497

PAR, configuring, 491, 493

PAT, 480–481

configuring, 489–491

private addresses, 473–474

simple translation, 477

SNAT, 526
    configuring with HSRP, 527–531
    configuring without HSRP, 531–534
    verifying configuration, 534–535
static translation, 477
statistics, displaying, 502–503
timeout limits, configuring, 500–501
traffic distribution, 482
    configuring, 498–499
translation table entries, removing, 503–504
troubleshooting with debug ip nat
    command, 504
verifying with show commands, 501–502
address-translation firewalls, 72
    advantages of, 75
    applications of, 76
    filtering process, 72–75
    limitations of, 75–76
administering firewall systems, 101
agents (DDoS attacks), 317
AGFs (application gateway firewalls), 64
    advantages of, 70
    applications of, 72
    authentication methods, 66–67
    authentication process, 65–66
    CGFs, 67–68
    cut-through proxy firewalls, 69–70
    limitations of, 70–71
aging password authentication, 113
    susceptibility to eavesdropping attacks, 114
AIM (AOL Instant Messenger), filtering, 333–334
alerts
    CBAC, 383
    URL filtering, 437
alerts (CBAC), configuring, 414
ALG (Application Layer Gateway), address
    translation support, 511–512
amplification attacks, 310
    amplifiers, discovering, 313–314
    disabling directed broadcasts, 311
    filtering directed broadcasts, 311, 313
    victims, discovering, 313–314
anomaly-based IDS solutions, 93
antispoofing, 327
AP (authentication proxy), 567
    AAA, configuring, 576
    access profiles, 568

applications of, 573–574
authentication process, 570–572
banners, creating, 582–583
configuring, 575
    AAA server configuration, 576–579
    policies, activating, 580–581
    preparing for HTTP/HTTPS, 579–580
example configuration, 587–594
features, 568–569
JavaScript, 572–573
limitations of, 574–575
troubleshooting
    with clear commands, 587
    with debug commands, 587
    with show commands, 584–586
tuning, 582–583
versus lock-and-key, 569
watch lists, configuring, 583–584
Apple iChat, filtering, 338
application attacks, 31
application inspection, CBAC, 389
applications
    Apple iChat, blocking use of, 338
    file-sharing, filtering, 338–341, 343–347
    ICQ, blocking use of, 334–335
    IM, blocking use of, 333–334
    MSN Messenger, blocking use of, 335
    Yahoo! Messenger, blocking use of, 336–338
applying dynamic crypto maps, 800
are-u-there command, 796
assigning
    privilege levels to commands, 146–149
    static passwords to auxiliary line, 119
    static passwords to console line, 118
attacks
    access, 22–24
        data manipulation attacks, 24–25
        session attacks, 25–29
    amplification, discovering intended victims,
        313–314
    DDoS, 317–319
        agents, 317
        client, 317
        handler, 317
        Stacheldraht, 322–323
        TFN, 319–320
        TFN2K, 320

Trinity, 324
Trinoo, 321–322
DoS, 31–33
    detecting, 661–662, 665–676
    preventing, 33–34
    Smurf, 677
    symptoms, 662–664
feint, 318
Land.c, 304
reconnaissance, 19, 314
    eavesdropping attacks, 20–21
    preventing with egress traffic filtering,
        315–316
    preventing with ingress ICMP filtering,
        315
    preventing with traceroute, 316
    scanning attacks, 19–20
TCP SYN flood, preventing with TCP Intercept,
    679–686
Trojan horses, 29–31, 325
    blocking with ACLs, 325–326
    detecting, 325
    monitoring rcp command usage with
        ACLs, 327
viruses, 29–31
worms, 29–31
AudioGalaxy, filtering, 345–346
audits (CBAC)
    configuring, 414
    URL filtering, 438–439
authentication, 213–214
    aging password configuration, 113
        susceptibility to eavesdropping, 114
    basic configuration example, 156–158
    centralizing, 24
    example of, 220–221
    for local Cisco router access, 120
    login banners, 153–154, 218–219
        configuring, 154–156
    MD5, configuring
        on BGP, 617
        on EIGRP, 608
        on HSRP, 615–616
        on IS-IS, 609–611
        on OSPF, 608–609
        on RIP, 606–607
    method lists, 214–215
    no password configuration, 111–112

NTP, 728–729
of IGPs, 604
    MD5 authentication, 606
    plain-text authentication, 605
passwords
    encrypting, 152–153
    OTPs, 114–115
privileged EXEC shell access, 217
static password configuration, 112–113
token card services, 115–117
troubleshooting, 219–220
user EXEC shell access, 216–217
username and password prompts, 218
authorization, 222
    configuring, 222
    example of, 225
    restricting command execution, 223–224
    troubleshooting, 224
AutoSecure feature, 184
    configuring, 187–188
    forwarding plane, 186
    management plane, 185
    sample script, 188–198
    verifying configuration, 198
auxiliary line
    assigning passwords, 119
    configuring access to Cisco routers, 119

B

banners, 153–154, 218–219
    AP authentication banners, creating, 582–583
    configuring, 154–156
BGP (Border Gateway Protocol), 617
    MD5 authentication, caveats, 606
    MD5 authentication, configuring, 617
    route flap dampening, configuring, 618–619
    secure configuration example, 620–624
black hole routing, configuring, 598–604
blocking
    applications, 332–333
        Apple iChat, 338
        ICQ, 334–335
        IM, 333–334
        MSN Messenger, 335
        Yahoo! Messenger, 336–338

bogons, 302
  egress filtering, 305–307
  ingress filtering, 302–305
Stacheldraht attacks, 322–323
TFN attacks, 320
TFN2K attacks, 320
Trinity attacks, 324
Trinoo attacks, 321–322
Trojan horse attacks with
  ACLs, 325–326
bogons, 301
  blocking, 302
  egress filtering, 305–307
  IANA listing, 301
  ingress filtering, 302–305
BootP, disabling, 170
broadcast accounting, 229–230
broadcast-based NTP configuration, 725
building RACLs, 358, 368–374

C

capturing accounting information, 226–229
  broadcast accounting, 229–230
  suppressing null username records, 229
CAR (committed access rate), limiting DoS attack
  damage, 694–698
CAs (Certificate Authorities), 29
  configuring HTTPS access to Cisco routers,
    134–139
case studies
  branch offices, 812
  corporate offices
    internal routers, 811
    perimeter routers, 809–811
  internal routers
    ACL configuration, 823–825
    CBAC configuration, 827
    configuring, 814
  perimeter routers
    AAA configuration, 817–820
    ACL configuration, 820–823
    address-translation configuration,
      827–830
    CBAC configuration, 825–826
    CBAC threshold configuration, 833

configuring, 813–814
    IDS configuration, 832
    NTP configuration, 835
    rate limiting configuration, 833–834
    remote access VPNs configuration,
      839–842
    RPF configuration, 831
    site-to-site VPNs configuration,
      836–838
    static route configuration, 830
    sylog configuration, 836
  proposals, 812–813
  remote access users, 812
  unnecessary services, disabling, 815–817
CBAC (Context-Based Access Control)
  alerts, 383
    configuring, 414
  audits, configuring, 414
  configuring, 398–399
    ACL creation, 400
    global timeouts, 400–401
    inspection rules, 405–410
    interface selection, 399
    on internal routers, case study, 827
    on perimeter routers, case study, 825–826
    PAM, 401–405
  enhancements exclusive to, 385
    application inspection, 389
    DoS detection and prevention,
      389–390
    embedded addressing information,
      387–388
    extra connections, 387
    ICMP traffic, 386
    TCP traffic, 385–386
    UDP traffic, 386
  example configuration, 691
    of inspection rules, 415–417
    three-interface configuration,
      418, 420–422
    two-interface configuration, 417–418
  flexibility of configuration, 385
  inspection rules
    activating, 410
    configuring, 405–409
  intrusion detection, 383
  Java inspection, 426

configuring, 426
  example, 426–428
limitations of, 397–398
misconfiguration, preventing, 399
operation, 383–385
PAM
  configuring, 401–403
  example configuration, 405
  verifying configuration, 404
performance, 395
  connections per second, 396–397
  CPU utilization, 397
  throughput, 396
preventing DoS attack, 690
removing from router, 415
state table, changing connection timeouts,
  400–401
supported protocols, 390
  H.323, 392–393
  RTSP, 390
  SIP, 394–395
  Skinny, 393–394
thresholds, 687
  configuring on perimeter routers, case
    study, 833
  connection thresholds, 688–689
timeouts, 687
  connection timeouts, 688
traffic filtering, 382–383
traffic inspection, 383
troubleshooting, 410
  with debug commands, 413–415
  with show commands, 411–413
URL inspection
  alerts, 437
  audits, 438–439
  configuring, 433–435
  example, 443–444
  logging, 439
  maximum requests, 436
  maximum responses, 436
  troubleshooting, 442
  verifying, 440–441
with NAT, configuring, 505–507
CDP (Cisco Discovery Protocol), disabling,
  162–163, 173
CEF (Cisco Express Forwarding), 678–679

centralizing AAA, 203
  authentication processes, 24
  server groupings, 208
  server protocol example configuration,
    211–212
  with RADIUS, 205–208
  with TACACS+, 203–205
CGFs (connection gateway firewalls), 67–68
challenge-based authentication, 116
Chargen, 32
cipher suites, 131
Cisco IOS Firewall feature set, 103–104
  features, 381–382
Cisco IOS Firewalls, application of, 105–106
Cisco IOS IDS, 644
  configuring, 652–656
  example configuration, 658–659
  performance issues, 652
  signature support, 645–650
  verifying configuration, 657–658
Cisco IOS Software
  ALG address translation support, 511–512
  applications of, 102
  real server attributes, 542–543
  SLB, 536–537
    configuring, 541–544
    example configuration, 545–546
    limitations of, 540
    load balancing algorithms, 538
    load balancing features, 539–540
    verifying configuration, 544
  virtual server attributes, 543–544
Cisco routers, 79–80
  accessing, 117
  privileged EXEC access, 146
    assigning privilege levels, 146–149
    local authentication database,
      150–152
    password levels, 146, 149–150
  remote access
    via HTTPS, 130–139
    via SNMP, 139–145
    via SSH, 123–127
    via VTY lines, 121–123
    via web browser, 127–130
  user EXEC access
    local access, 118–120
    remote access, 121

Cisco Secure ACS authentication server, token card
support, 117
clear commands
removing translation table entries,
503–504
troubleshooting AP, 587
clearing URL filtering cache, 434
clear-text passwords, 118–119
CLI configuration, SDM, 99
client (DDoS attacks), 317
Code Red worm, 676–677
filtering, 463–466
commands
aaa accounting, 227
aaa authentication login, 216
aaa authorization, 225
aaa new-model, 204
access-class, 123
clear, 503–504
crypto ca trustpoint, 135
debug aaa accounting, 230
debug aaa authentication, 219–220
debug aaa authorization, 224
debug ip nat, 504
debug ip scp, 232
debug ip snat, 535
debug radius, 211
debug tacacs, 209
enable secret, 149
ip access-list log-update threshold, 291
ip http secure-client-auth, 136
ip nat pool, 496
ip nbar port-map, 453
ip slb serverfarm, 541
logging synchronous line configuration, 118
no ip inspect, removing CBAC from router, 415
passive-interface, 613
privilege levels, assigning, 146–149
radius-server host, 207
radius-server timeout, 207
rcp, monitoring usage with ACLs, 327
security authentication failure rate, 198
security passwords min-length, 198
show, verifying address translation, 501–502
show access-list compiled, 295–296
show ip http server secure status, 137
show logging, 716–717

show logging history, 717
show ntp associations, 730
show ntp status, 730–731
show privilege, 150
show sntp, 731–732
show tacacs, 209
snmp server-group, 144
snmp-server community, 141
tacacs-server host, 205
comparing
Cisco PIX and Cisco IOS firewall solutions,
105–106
lock-and-key and AP, 569
RADIUS and TACACAS+, 212–213
computer technology weaknesses, 13
network equipment, 15
network protocols, 13
operating systems, 14–15
conditions (ACLs), 241
configuration autoloading, disabling, 172–173
configuring
AAA, 202
ACLs, 250–251
accounting, 292–295
remarks, 251
verifying configuration, 278–280
address translation
connection limits, 500
of overlapping addresses, 493–497
timeout limits, 500–501
AP, 575
AAA, 576
AAA server configuration, 576–579
example configuration, 587–594
policies, activating, 580–581
preparing for HTTP/HTTPS, 579–580
watch lists, 583–584
authentication, example, 156–158
authorization, 222
AutoSecure, 187–188
sample script, 188–198
verifying configuration, 198
basic logging, 706
black hole routing, 599–601
with PBR, 601–604
CBAC, 398–399
alerts, 414

audits, 414
connection thresholds, 688–689
connection timeouts, 688
creating ACLs, 400
flexibility of, 385
global timeouts, 400–401
inspection rules, 405–410
interface selection, 399
PAM, 401–405
verifying configuration, 410–415
Cisco IOS IDS, 652–656
ESM, 738–740
internal router, case study, 814
IP NAT Service, 513–514
IPSec site-to-site connections,
747–748
external ACL, 749
IKE phase 1, 750–753
IKE phase 1 peer authentication, 753–765
IKE phase 2 data connection, 766–774
Java inspection, 426
lock-and-key, 555–560
logging, synchronous logging, 706–708
login banners, 154–156
manual time and date, 720–722
MD5 authentication
on BGP, 617
on EIGRP, 608
on HSRP, 615–616
on IS-IS, 609–611
on OSPF, 608–609
on RIP, 606–607
NAT, 484–486
dynamic NAT, 487–488
with CBAC, 505–507
NBAR, 451–453
filtering marked traffic, 459
group classifications, 454–455
HTTP traffic filtering, 457
P2P program filtering, 455–469
PDLMs, downloading, 457
policies, 458–459
verifying configuration, 460–463
NTP, 725
authentication, 728–729
broadcast-based configuration, 725
client configuration, 723

example, 731–732
poll-based configuration, 724
restricting resources, 728
server configuration, 725–727
PAR, 491–493
passive interfaces, 612–613
PAT, 489–491
perimeter routers, case study, 813–814
RACLs, 365, 368–374
interface selection, 365–368
route flap dampening on BGP, 618–619
RPF, 629
verifying configuration, 630–631
SCP, 231
sequenced ACLs, 296–298
SLB, 541–544
SNAT
with HSRP, 527–531
without HSRP, 531–534
static crypto maps, 801
static NAT, redundancy with HSRP, 524–526
timed ACLs, example, 288–289
traffic distribution, 498–499
turbo ACLs, 295–296
URL filtering, 432–434
alerts, 437
audits, 438–439
cache, clearing, 434
exclusive domains, 435
logging, 439
maximum requests, 436
maximum responses, 436
with CLI, SDM, 99
connection thresholds, configuring on CBAC,
688–689
connections
embryonic, 13
timeouts, configuring on CBAC, 688
connections per second feature (CBAC), 396–397
console line, assigning passwords, 118
content filtering, 81. *See also* URL filtering
controlling
access to resources, 43
address translation
with ACLs, 514–515
with route maps, 517

with route maps with dynamic NAT,
515–519
with route maps with static NAT, 520–521
cost benefit analysis of security measures, 8
CPU hogging, 31
CPU utilization feature of CBAC, 397
creating
ACLs, 250–251
AP authentication banners, 582–583
dynamic crypto maps, 799–800
time ranges for timed ACLs, 285
with absolute command, 286
with periodic command, 286–287
transform sets, 800
CRLs, troubleshooting, 762
crypto ca trustpoint command, 135
crypto isakmp nat keepalive command, 797
crypto isakmp xauth timeout command, 797
crypto maps, 771–773
CSI (Computer Security Institute), 16
cut-through proxy firewalls, 69–70

D

data manipulation attacks, 24–25
DDoS attacks, 317–319
agents, 317
client, 317
handler, 317
Stacheldraht, blocking, 322–323
TFN, 319
blocking, 320
TFN2K, blocking, 320
Trinity, blocking, 324
Trinoo, blocking, 321–322
debug aaa accounting command, 230
debug aaa authentication command, 219
debug aaa authorization command, 224
debug commands
troubleshooting AP, 587
troubleshooting CBAC, 413–415
troubleshooting URL filtering, 442
debug ip nat command, 504
debug ip scp command, 232
debug ip snat command, 535
debug radius command, 211

debug tacacs command, 209
defining ACL accounting thresholds, 294
deleting entries from ACLs, 261
sequenced ACLs, 299
Deloder worm, 330
denying
fragments through ACLs, 282
traffic from a specific device, 283
design guidelines for firewall systems, 81
adhering to security policy, 81
DMZs, 85
internal DMZs, 90–91
multiple DMZs, 89
single DMZs, 87–89
traffic flow, 85–87
keeping it simple, 82
layered defense approach, 83–84
using the correct device, 82–83
designing security solutions, 34
Cisco security wheel, 35–37
destinations of logging messages
internal buffer logging, 710
line logging, 709–710
SNMP logging, 713
syslog server logging, 710–713
detecting
DoS attacks, 661–662
symptoms, 662–664
with ACLs, 665–672
with NetFlow, 672–676
intrusions with CBAC, 383
devices
amplifiers, 310
firewall component, 92
IDS component, 92–93
perimeter routers, 91
placement of firewall components, 94
enhanced firewall system design,
96–98
simple firewall system design, 95–96
token cards, 115–116
Cisco Secure ACS authentication server
support, 117
synchronization with token card
server, 117
VPNs component, 92
DHCP, disabling, 171

directed broadcasts
  disabling, 176, 311
  filtering, 311–313
disabling
  directed broadcasts, 311
  ICMP unreachables for black hole routes, 599
disabling unnecessary services, 815–817
  global services, 161
    BootP, 170
    CDP, 162–163
    configuration autoloading, 172–173
    DHCP, 171
    DNS name resolution, 169–170
    finger, 164–165
    FTP, 167
    HTTP, 167
    IdentD, 165
    IP source routing, 166
    PAD, 172
    SNMP, 168–169
    TCP small servers, 163–164
    TFTP, 167
    UDP small servers, 163–164
  interface services, 173
    directed broadcasts, 176
    ICMP messages, 177–180
    MOP, 181
    Proxy ARP, 174–176
    unused interfaces, 182
    VTYs, 181–182
  with AutoSecure, 184
    forwarding plane, 186
    management plane, 185
disaster recovery plans, 11–12
discovering intended amplification attack victims, 313–314
displaying
  address translation statistics, 502–503
  connection timeouts for local access, 121
  sequence numbers in log messages, 714–715
distributed timed ACLs, 287–288
distribution of time, configuring, 722–723
DMZs, 85
  internal DMZ designs, 90–91
  multiple DMZ designs, 89
  single DMZ designs, 87, 89
  traffic flow, 85–87

DNS doctoring, 479
DNS name resolution, disabling, 169–170
DoS attacks, 31–33
  detecting, 661–662
    with ACLs, 665, 667–672
    with NetFlow, 672–676
  fraggle, preventing with ACLs, 310–311
  Land.c, 304
  preventing with CBAC, 33–34, 389–390, 690
  rate limiting, 692
    CAR, 694–698
    ICMP rate limiting, 692–693
    NBAR, 700–703
  smurf
    preventing with ACLs, 308, 310
    via amplification, preventing, 311–313
  Smurf attacks, 677
  symptoms of, 662–664
  TCP SYN floods, preventing with ACLs, 307–308
downloading PDLMs, 457
dropped packets, logging, 279
dropping fragments, 283
dynamic ACLs. *See* lock-and-key ACLs
dynamic address translation, 477
dynamic crypto maps
  applying, 800
  creating, 799–800
  verifying, 800
dynamic NAT
  configuring, 487–488
  route maps, configuring, 515–519
dynamic translation of overlapping addresses
  configuring, 496–497

E

EasyVPN, 786
  EVS
    RRI, 791–792
      setup process, 793–802
    features, 787–789
    IPSec supportt, 787
eavesdropping attacks, 20–21
editing ACLs, 252–253
eDonkey, filtering, 346–347

egress filtering
of bogon addresses, 305–307
of ICMP traffic, 315–316
EIGRP (Enhanced IGRP), configuring MD5
authentication, 608
e-mail bombs, 28–31
embedded addressing information, 509–510
ALG support, 511–512
IP NAT Service, 512
configuring, 513–514
supported protocols, 511
embryonic connections, 13, 389
enable authentication, 217
enable secret command, 149
enabling security policies across diverse
platforms, 6–7
encryption
passwords, 152–153
SCP, 231
configuring, 231
example of, 232–233
troubleshooting, 232
types of, 22
enforcing
security policies, 11
traffic filtering with NBAR, 447
enhanced features of CBAC, performance, 395
connections per second, 396–397
CPU utilization, 397
throughput, 396
enhanced firewall system design, 96–98
enhancements to CBAC, 385
application inspection, 389
DoS detection and prevention, 389–390
embedded addressing information, 387–388
extra connections, 387
ICMP traffic, 386
TCP traffic, 385–386
UDP traffic, 386
Error Log Count feature (Cisco IOS), 718
ESM (Embedded Syslog Manager), 705, 732–733
configuring, 738–740
filter modules, 733–734
example, 737–738
variables, 734–736
input process, 734–735

evaluate statement, placement of in external
ACLs, 372
EVC (EasyVPN client), 786
EVS (EasyVPN server), 786
RRI, 791–792
setup process, 793–799
examining
log file contents, 742–743
TCP control information, 57–59
examples
of ACLs, 263–264
of AP, 587, 589–594
of authentication, 220–221
of authorization, 225
of BGP configuration, 620–624
of CBAC
inspection rules, 415–417
three-interface CBAC, 418–422
two-interface CBAC, 417–418
of configuring basic authentication, 156–158
of disabling unnecessary services on perimeter
routers, 183–184
of extended ACLs
three-interface routers, 275–278
two-interface routers, 273–275
of fragment filtering, 283–285
of IPSec remote-access, 802–805
of IPSec site-to-site connections, 780–783
of Java inspection, 426–428
of lock-and-key ACLs, 563–564
of NBAR, 463
Code Red worm, 463–466
Nimda, 466–467
of NTP configuration, 731–732
of PAM configuration, 405
of RACLs, 374–375
three-interface RACLs, 375–378
two-interface RACLs, 375
of RPF configuration, 631
of SCP, 232–233
of SLB configuration, 545–546
of TCP Intercept configuration, 686–687
of timed ACL configuration, 288–289
of URL filtering, 443–444
exclusive domains, 431
configuring, 435

extended ACLs, 264
  named extended, 273
  numbered extended, 264–266
    filtering ICMP traffic, 271–272
    filtering TCP traffic, 267–269
    filtering UDP traffic, 269–271
  policies, configuring, 275
  three-interface router example, 275–278
  two-interface router example, 273–275
  versus RACLs, 352–356
extended address translation, 477
external threats, 17

F

FAB (Firewall ACL Bypass), 385
features
  of AP, 568–569
  of CBAC, performance enhancements,
    395–397
  of EasyVPN, 787–789
feint attacks, 318
file-sharing applications, filtering, 332–333,
  338–339
  AudioGalaxy, 345–346
  eDonkey, 346–347
  Gnutella, 343
  IMesh, 343–344
  Kazaa, 341–343
  Morpheus, 341–343
  Napster, 340–341
  WinMX, 344–345
filter modules (ESM), 733–734
  example, 737–738
  variables, 734–736
filtering
  ACL accounting information, 293–294
  Apple iChat application, 338
  bogon addresses with ACLs
    egress filtering, 305–307
    ingress filtering, 302–305
  directed broadcasts, 311, 313
  file-sharing applications, 338–339
    AudioGalaxy, 345–346
    eDonkey, 346–347

  Gnutella, 343
  IMesh, 343–344
  Kazaa, 341–343
  Morpheus, 341–343
  Napster, 340–341
  WinMX, 344–345
ICQ applications, 334–335
IM applications, 332–334
Java, 426–428
marked traffic (NBAR), 459
MSN Messenger applications, 335
returning traffic with RACLs, 359–360
URLs, 428
  advantages of, 430–431
  alerts, 437
  audits, 438–439
  cache, clearing, 434
  configuring, 432–434
  example, 443–444
  exclusive domains, 435
  logging, 439
  maximum requests, 436
  maximum responses, 436
  operation, 429–430
  restrictions, 431–432
  troubleshooting, 442
  verifying, 440–441
web traffic
  Code Red worm, 463–466
  Nimda, 466–467
with ACLs, 237–238, 259–260
  conditions, 241
  example, 238
  extended, 264–278
  matches, 241
  placement of, 248–249
  rules, 246–247
  standard, 260–264
  statement order, 243–246
with CBAC, 382–383
with NBAR, 447
Yahoo! Messenger applications, 336–338
finger, disabling, 164–165
firewalls systems, 43
  address translation, 72
    advantages of, 75
    applications of, 76

filtering process, 72–75
limitations of, 75–76
administering, 101
AGFs, 64
advantages of, 70
applications of, 72
authentication methods, 66–67
authentication process, 65–66
CGFs, 67–68
cut-through proxy firewalls, 69–70
limitations of, 70–71
component placement, 94
design considerations, 98–99
enhanced firewall system design, 96–98
simple firewall system design, 95–96
content filtering, 81
defining, 42
design guidelines, 81
adhering to security policy, 81
DMZs, 85–91
keeping it simple, 82
layered defense approach, 83–84
using the correct device, 82–83
host-based, 76
advantages of, 77–78
applications of, 79
hybrid, 79–80
intrusion-detection, 80
packet-filtering, 47–48
activating, 51
advantages of, 51
applying rules, 48
examining TCP control information, 58–59
filtering decisions, 49–50
limitations of, 52–53
typical applications, 53
stateful, 53–54
advantages of, 61
advantages over packet-filtering firewalls, 54
applications of, 64
limitations of, 61–64
non-stateful protocols, 62
state table, 59–60
flags, 57
flexibility of CBAC configuration, 385

forwarding plane (AutoSecure), 186
fraggle attacks, preventing with ACLs, 310–311
Fraggle DoS attack, 662
fragments, 280–281
configuring CBAC inspection rules, 409
dropping, 283
filtering, 281–282
example, 283–285
on stateful firewalls, 281
FTP, disabling, 167
functions of AAA, 202

G

generating SNMP traps, 141
global adresses, 476
global services, disabling, 161
BootP, 170
CDP, 162–163
configuration autoloading, 172–173
DHCP, 171
DNS name resolution, 169–170
finger, 164–165
FTP, 167
HTTP, 167
IdentD, 165
IP source routing, 166
PAD, 172
SNMP, 168–169
TCP small servers, 163–164
TFTP, 167
UDP small servers, 163–164
Gnutella, filtering, 343
goals of security, 7
group classifications, defining for NBAR, 454–455

H

H.323, CBAC support, 392–393
handler (DDoS attacks), 317
hardware clock, 719
headless chicken syndrome, 12
host-based firewalls, 76
advantages of, 77
limitations of, 78–79

host-based IDS solutions, 94, 639
host-specific entries (PAM), 402
HSRP (Hot Standby Router Protocol), 614
    MD5 authentication, configuring, 615–616
    SNAT configuration, 527–528, 530–531
    static NAT redundancy, 522–526
HTTP traffic fitltering
    access to Cisco routers, configuring 128–130
    CBAC inspection rules, configuring, 407–408
    disabling, 167
    NBAR configuration, 457
HTTPS, configuring access to Cisco routers,
    130–131
    with CA, 134–139
    with no CA, 132–134
hybrid firewalls, 79–80

I

IANA (Internet Assigned Numbers Authority)
    web site, 301
ICMP (Internet Control Message Protocol)
    CBAC handling of, 386
    configuring CBAC inspection rules, 407
    disabling, 177–180
    egress traffic filtering, 315–316
    ingress traffic filtering, 315
    mask replies, disabling, 180
    rate limiting, 692–693
    redirects, disabling, 178–179
    traffic filtering with numbered extended ACLs,
        271–272
    unreachables, disabling, 177–178
        for black hole routes, 599
ICQ (instant messaging) applications
    filtering, 334–335
IdentD, disabling, 165
idle timer (lock-and-key), 556
IDS (intrusion detection systems), 92–93
    anomoly-based, 93
    Cisco IOS IDS, 644
        configuring, 652–654, 656
        example configuration, 658–659
        performance issues, 652
        signature support, 645–650

verifying configuration,
    657–658
configuring on perimeter routers,
    case study, 832
false positives, 656
host-based solutions, 94, 639
installed components, 640
network-based solutions, 94, 638–639
profiles, 636
responses to intrusions, 641
signature-based solutions, 93
signatures, 637, 642
    categories of, 643–644
    implementing, 642
    structures, 642–643
IGPs (interior gateway protocols)
    authentication, 604
        MD5, 606
        plain-text, 605
    EIGRP, MD5 authentication, 608
    IS-IS, MD5 authentication, 609–611
    OSPF. MD5 authentication, 608–609
    RIP, MD5 authentication, 606–607
IM (instant messaging) applications, filtering,
    332–334
IMesh, filtering, 343–344
implementing firewall features, 101
importance of monitoring, 36
include-local-lan command, 796
informs (SNMP), generating, 141
ingress filtering
    of bogon addresses, 302–305
    of ICMP traffic, 315
insecure CDP interfaces, disabling, 173
inserting entries in sequenced ACLs, 300–301
inspection rules, CBAC, 383, 405–406
    activating, 410
    example configuration, 415–417
    fragments, 409
    HTTP traffic, 407–408
    ICMP traffic, 407
    RPCs, 408
    Skinny, 409
    SMTP traffic, 408
    TCP/UDP traffic, 406–407
intended amplification attack victims,
    discovering, 313–314

interface services, disabling, 173
  directed broadcasts, 176
  ICMP messages, 177–180
    mask replies, 180
    redirects, 178–179
    unreachables, 177–178
  MOP, 181
  Proxy ARP, 174–176
  unused interfaces, 182
  VTYs, 181–182
internal buffer logging, 710
internal routers
  ACL configuration, case study, 823–825
  basic configuration, case study, 814
  CBAC configuration, case study, 827
  in corporate office, 811
internal threats, 17
intrustion detection, 80
  CBAC, 383
ip access-list log-update threshold
  command, 291
IP accounting, ACL configuration, 292–293
  defining thresholds, 294
  filtering accounting information, 293–294
  limiting transit records, 294–295
IP address spoofing, preventing with RPF, 625–627
IP blocking, 33
ip http secure-client-auth command, 136
ip inspect dns-timeout command, 401
ip inspect tcp finwait-time command, 401
ip inspect tcp idle-time command, 401
ip inspect tcp synwait-time command, 401
ip inspect udp idle-time command, 401
ip nat pool command, 496
IP NAT Service, 512
  configuring, 513–514
ip nbar port-map command, 453
ip slb serverfarm command, 541
IP source routing, disabling, 166
IPSec
  EasyVPN support, 787
  EVS
    remote-access verification, 802
    setup process, 793–800
  remote access, 785–786
    connection process, 789–793
    example, 802–805

site-to-site connections
  configuring, 747–748
  example, 780–783
  external ACL, configuring, 749
  IKE phase 1, 750–765
  IKE phase 2, data connection, 766–774
  troubleshooting, 775–780
IRC (Internet Relay Chat) servers, susceptibility to
  smurf attacks, 310
IRR (Internet Routing Registry), 314
IS-IS (Intermediate System-to-Intermediate
  System), configuring MD5 authentication,
  609–611

J

Java filtering, CBAC inspection
  configuring, 426
  example, 426–428
JavaScript, enabling for AP connections, 572–573

K

Kazaa, filtering, 341, 343
keystroke-capturing programs, 113
KISS principle, firewall system design guideline, 82

L

L2L *See* IPSec, site-to-site connections.
Land.c, 32, 304
LANguard Network Security Scanner, 19
layered defense approach to firewall system design,
  83–84
layers of OSI reference model, 46
limitations
  of address translation, 484
  of AP, 574–575
  of CBAC, 397–398
  of NBAR, 451
  of RACLs, 361
    application issues, 362
    FTP, 363
    passive FTP, 364
    stateful issues, 362

of RPF for spoofing prevention, 628
of SLB, 540
of SNAT, 526
limiting ACL accounting transit records, 294–295
line logging, 709–710
link encryption, 22
load balancing, 482. *See also* traffic distribution
    SLB, 536–537
        algorithms used, 538
        configuring, 541–544
        example configuration, 545–546
        features, 539–540
        limitations, 540
        real server attributes, 542–543
        verifying configuration, 544
        virtual server attributes, 543–544
local access to Cisco routers, 118–119
    authentication methods, 120
    via auxiliary line, 119
    via console port, 118
local adresses, 476–477
local authentication database, 150–152
locating source of amplification attacks, 313–314
lock-and-key ACLs, 551–552
    configuring, 555–560
    example, 563–564
    operation, 553–554
    remote administration access, 560–562
    troubleshooting, 562–563
    versus AP, 569
    when to use, 552
logging, 705
    CBAC
        alerts, 414
        audits, 414
    configuring, 706
    destinations, 708
    displaying sequence numbers, 714–715
    dropped packets, 279
    Error Log Count feature (Cisco IOS), 718
    ESM, 733
        configuring, 738–740
        filter modules, 733–738
        input process, 734–735
    examining log file contents, 742–743
    internal buffer logging, 710
    line logging, 709–710

rate limiting, 715–716
severity levels, 708–709
show logging command, 716–717
show logging history command, 717
SNMP logging, 713
synchronous logging, configuring, 706–708
syslog server logging, 710–713
timestamping messages, 714
updates
    adding to ACLs, 291
    threshold, changing, 291–292
URL filtering messages, 439
violations, accounting on ACLs, 292–293
    accounting thresholds, defining, 294
    filtering accounting information, 293–294
    transit records, limiting, 294–295
logging synchronous line configuration command, 118
login authentication, 216–217
login banners, 153–154, 218–219
    configuring, 154–156
login connection timeouts, overriding, 120–121

M

management plane (AutoSecure), 185
managing firewall systems, 101
manual time and date configuration, 720–722
maps, creating, 800
mask replies (ICMP), disabling, 180
masquerading attacks, 26
MD5 authentication, configuring, 606
    BGP, 606, 617
    EIGRP, 608
    HSRP, 615–616
    IS-IS, 609–611
    OSPF, 608–609
    RIP, 606–607
method lists, 214–215
Microsoft RPC service, susceptibility to worms, 330–332
misconfiguration of CBAC, preventing, 399

monitoring
    importance of, 36
    rcp command usage with ACLs, 327
MOP, disabling, 181
Morpheus, filtering, 341, 343
MOTD banners, creating AP authentication banners, 582–583
MSN Messenger applications, filtering, 335

N

Nachi worm, 331
named extended ACLs, 273
named standard ACLs, 262–263
Napster, filtering, 340–341
NAT (Network Address Translation), 474–475, 477
    configuring, 484–486
    Default Inside Server, 491
    dynamic NAT, configuring, 487–488
    global addresses, 476
    local addresses, 476–477
    overlapping addresses, 479
    static NAT, redundancy with HSRP, 522–526
    troubleshooting with debug ip nat
        command, 504
    with CBAC, configuring, 505–507
NBAR, 444
    configuring, 451–453
    examples, 463
        Code Red worm, 463–466
        Nimda, 466–467
    group classifications, configuring, 454–455
    HTTP traffic filtering, configuring, 457
    limiting DoS attack damage, 700–703
    marked traffic, filtering, 459
    P2P program filtering
        configuring, 455–456
        example, 467, 469
    PDLMs, 450
        downloading, 457
    policies, configuring, 458
    policy maps, associating with router
        interface, 459
    restrictions, 451
    supported protocols and applications,
        447–450
    traffic classification, 445–446

    traffic filtering, 447
    verifying configuration, 460–463
Nessus, 19
NetFlow, detecting DoS attacks, 672–676
network-based IDS solutions, 94, 638–639
Nimda, filtering, 466–467
no ip inspect command, removing CBAC from
    router, 415
no password authentication, 111–112
non-stateful protocols, 62
notifications (SNMP), 141
NTP (Network Time Protocol)
    configuring on perimeter routers,
        case study, 835
    example configuration, 731–732
null interfaces, black hole routes, 598
    configuring, 599, 601
numbered extended ACLs, 264–266
    ICMP traffic, filtering, 271–272
    TCP traffic, filtering, 267–269
    UDP traffic, filtering, 269–271
numbered standard ACLs, 261–262

O

opening ports with packet-filtering firewalls, 56
operating systems, weaknesses in, 14
OSI reference model, 45–46
OSPF (Open Shortest Path First), configuring MD5
    authentication, 608–609
OTPs (one-time passwords), 114–115
    susceptibility to eavesdropping
        attacks, 115
overlapping addresses
    address translation, configuring, 493
        dynamic translation, 496–497
        static translation, 494–496
    DNS doctoring, 479
overriding login connection timeouts, 120–121

P

P2P program filtering
    AudioGalaxy, 345–346
    eDonkey, 338–339, 346–347

Gnutella, 343
IMesh, 343–344
Kazaa, 341–343
Morpheus, 341–343
NBAR configuration, 455–456, 467–469
Napster, 340–341
WinMX, 344–345
packet encryption, 22
packet filtering
ACLs
accounting information, filtering, 293–294
accounting thresholds, defining, 294
logging updates, 291–292
logging violations, accounting, 292–293
remarks, adding, 290
transit records, limiting, 294–295
denying traffic from a specific device, 283
fragments, 281–282
dropping, 283
example, 283–285
sequenced ACLs
configuring, 296–298
deleting entries, 299
inserting entries, 300–301
resequencing, 298–299
timed ACLs, 285
activating time ranges, 287
creating time ranges, 285–287
distributed, 287–288
example configuration, 288–289
turbo ACLs, 295–296
packet fragmentation and reassembly attacks, 32
packet sniffers, 21
Packet Storm website, 317
packet-filtering firewalls, 47–48
activating, 51
advantages of, 51
applying rules, 48
examining TCP control information, 58–59
filtering decisions, 49–50
limitations of, 52–53
opening ports, 56
typical applications, 53
packets
dropped, logging, 279
fragments, 280–281
CBAC inspection rules, configuring, 409
filtering, 282

PAD (packet assember/disassembler), disabling, 172
PAM (Port Application Mapping), 401
configuring, 403
entry types, 402
example configuration, 405
verifying configuration, 404
PAR (port address redirection), configuring, 491–493
passive interfaces, securing routing protocols, 612–613
passive-interface command, 613
passwords
clear-text, 118–119
encrypting, 152–153
prompts, 218
PAT (Port Address Translation), 480–481
configuring, 489–491
PBR (policy-based routing), black hole routing, 601–604
PDLMs (Packet Description Language Modules), 450
downoading, 457
PenguiNet SSH, 124
performance of CBAC, 395
connections per second feature, 396–397
CPU utilization, 397
throughput performance feature, 396
perimeter routers, 91
AAA configuration, case study, 817–820
ACL configuration, case study, 820–823
address-translation configuration, case study, 827–830
basic configuration, case study, 813–814
CBAC configuration, case study, 825–826
thresholds, 833
IDS configuration, case study, 832
in corporate office, 809, 811
NTP configuration, case study, 835
rate limiting configuration, case study, 833–834
remote-access VPN configuration, case study, 839, 841–842
restricting
access to, 111
command execution, 223–224
RPF configuration, case study, 831

site-to-site VPN configuration, case study, 836–838

static route configuration, case study, 830

sylog configuration, case study, 836

unnecessary services, disabling, 183–184

periodic command, creating time ranges, 286–287

personal firewalls, 76

    advantages of, 77

    applications of, 79

    limitations of, 78

ping of death attacks, 32

placement

    of ACLs, 248–249

    of firewall components, 94

        design considerations, 98–99

        enhanced firewall system design, 96–98

        simple firewall system design, 95–96

plain-text authentication of routing protocols, 605

planning for security, 6

policies

    AP, activating, 580–581

    configuring with extended ACLs, 275

    enabling across diverse platforms, 6–7

    enforcing, 11

    weaknesses in, 9–10

        lack of change management, 11

        lack of disaster recovery plan, 11–12

policy maps

    associating with router interface, 459

    defining for NBAR, 458

poll-based NTP configuration, 724

ports, opening with packet-filtering firewalls, 56

port-scanning utilities, 19

preventing

    amplification attacks

        disabling directed broadcasts, 311

        filtering directed broadcasts, 311, 313

    CBAC misconfiguration, 399

    DoS attacks, 33–34

    eavesdropping attacks, 21

    fraggle attacks with ACLs, 310–311

    reconnaissance attacks

        egress ICMP traffic filtering, 315–316

        ingress ICMP traffic filtering, 314–315

    session attacks, 28–29

smurf attacks with ACLs, 308, 310

spoofing with RPF, 625–628

TCP SYN flood attacks

    with TCP Intercept, 679–686

    with ACLs, 307–308

private addresses, 473–474

privileged EXEC access, 146

    assigning privilege levels, 146–149

    local authentication database, 150–152

    password levels, 149–150

    passwords, 146

    securing shell access, 217

processing ACLs, 241

    conditions, 241

    matches, 241

    rules, 246–247

    tatement order, 243–246

profile-based IDS systems, 636

protocols supported by CBAC, 390

    H.323, 392–393

    RTSP, 390

    SIP, 394–395

    Skinny, 393–394

Proxy ARP, disabling, 174–176

Q-R

QoS, NBAR classification, 445–446

RACLs (reflexive ACLs), 351. *See also* CBAC

    and CBAC, 423

    building, 358

    configuring, 365, 368–374

        interface selection, 365–368

    examples of, 374–375

        three-interface RACLs, 375–378

        two-interface RACLs, 375

    filtering returning traffic, 359–360

    limitations of, 361

        application issues, 362

        FTP, 363

        passive FTP, 364

        stateful issues, 362

    removing entries, 360–361

    traffic processing, 357

    versus extended ACLs, 352–356

RADIUS (Remote Access Dial-In User Service)
centralizing AAA security policies,
205–208
server groupings, 208
server protocol example configuration,
211–212
limitations of, 206
troubleshooting, 210
versus TACACS+, 212–213
radius-server host command, 207
radius-server timeout command, 207
rate limiting, 692
configuring on perimeter routers, case study,
833–834
ICAR, 694–698
ICMP rate limiting, 692–693
log messages, 715–716
NBAR, 700–703
rcp command, monitoring use with ACLs, 327
reconnaissance attacks, 19, 314
eavesdropping attacks, 20–21
keystroke-capturing programs, 113
preventing
with egress ICMP traffic filtering,
315–316
with ingress ICMP traffic
filtering, 315
with traceroute, 316
scanning attacks, 19–20
redirects (ICMP), disabling, 178–179
remarks (ACLs), 251
adding, 290
remote access to Cisco routers, 121
lock-and-key secured routers,
560–562
privileged EXEC access, 146
assigning privilege levels, 146–149
local authentication database, 150–152
password levels, 149–150
passwords, 146
via HTTPS, 130–139
configuring with CA, 134–139
configuring with no CA, 132–134
HTTPS connection components, 131
via SNMP, 139–141
v1 and v2 configuration, 141–143
v3 configuration, 143–145

via SSH, 123
client connections, 127
server configuration, 124–125
server example, 126
via VTY lines, 121, 123
via web browser, 127–130
remote access VPNs, Easy VPNs, 786
features, 787–789
IPSec support, 787
remote-access connection process (IPSec),
789–793
remote-access VPNs, configuring on perimeter
routers, case study, 839–842
removing
ACL entries, 261
CBAC from router, 415
IPSec connections from router, 780
RACL entries, 360–361
translation table entries with clear command,
503–504
repudiation attacks, 28
rerouting attacks, 32
resequencing sequenced ACLs, 298–299
restricting
access to perimeter routers, 111
command execution on perimeter router,
223–224
NTP resources, 728
RFC 1631, address translation, 474
RIP, configuring MD5 authentication, 606–607
rotating syslog files, 741
route flap dampening, configuring on BGP, 618–619
route maps, controlling address translation, 517
with dynamic NAT, 515–519
with static NAT, 520–521
router time sources
hardware clock, 719
software clock, 719
routing protocols
BGP, 617
MD5 authentication, configuring, 617
route flap dampening, configuring,
618–619
secure configuration example, 620–624
EIGRP, MD5 authentication, 608
IGPs
authentication, 604

MD5 authentication, 606
plain-text authentication, 605
IS-IS, MD5 authentication, 609–611
OSPF, MD5 authentication, 608–609
RIP, MD5 authentication, 606–607
securing
with ACLs, 613–614
with passive interfaces, 612–613
RPCs (Remote Procedure Calls), configuring CBAC
inspection rules, 408
RPF (reverse-path forwarding), 626
configuring, 629, 831
limitations of, 628
per-interface statistics, 627
preventing IP spoofing, 625–627
verifying configuration, 630–631
RRI (reverse route injection), 791–792
RTSP, CBAC support, 390

S

save-password command, 796
scanning attacks, 19–20
SCEP (Simple Certificate Enrollment
Protocol), 758
SCP (secure copy), 231
configuring, 231
example of, 232–233
troubleshooting, 232
SDM (Security Device Manager), 99
security authentication failure rate
command, 198
security passwords min-length command, 198
security wheel, 35–37
segments (TCP), fragmentation, 280–281
sequenced ACLs
configuring, 296–298
deleting entries, 299
inserting entries, 300–301
resequencing, 298–299
services, blocking, 332–333
Apple iChat, 338
ICQ, 334–335
IM, 333–334
MSN Messenger, 335
Yahoo! Messenger, 336–338

session attacks, 25–29
masquerading attacks, 26
preventing, 28–29
repudiation attacks, 28
session-hijacking attacks, 26–27
session-replay attacks, 26
session-hijacking attacks, 26–27
session-replay attacks, 26
severity levels of logging messages,
708–709
show access-list compiled command, 295–296
show commands
troubleshooting AP, 584–586
troubleshooting CBAC, 411–413
verifying address translation, 501–502
verifying URL filtering configuration,
440–441
show ip http server secure status command, 137
show logging command, 716–717
show logging history command, 717
show ntp associations command, 730
show ntp status command, 730–731
show privilege command, 150
show sntp command, 731–732
show tacacs command, 209
shunning, 33
signature-based IDS solutions, 93
signatures, 637, 642
categories of, 643–644
implementing, 642
structures, 642–643
simple address translation, 477
simple CBAC example, 415–417
simple firewall system design, 95–96
SIP (Session Initiation Protocol), CBAC support,
394–395
site-to-site VPNs, configuring on perimeter routers,
case study, 836–838
Skinny protocol
CBAC support, 393–394
configuring CBAC inspection rules, 409
SLB (Server Load Balancing), 536–537
configuring, 541–544
example configuration, 545–546
limitations of, 540
load balancing algorithms, 538
load balancing features, 539–540

verifying configuration, 544
real server attributes, 542–543
virtual server attributes, 543–544
SMTP (Simple Mail Transfer Protocol), configuring
CBAC inspection rules, 408
smurf attacks, 32, 661, 677
preventing with ACLs, 308–310
preventing with amplification
disabling directed broadcasts, 311
filtering directed broadcasts, 311–313
SNAT (stateful NAT), 526
configuring with HSRP, 527–531
configuring without HSRP, 531–534
verifying configuration, 534–535
SNMP (Simple Network Management Protocol)
disabling, 168–169
logging, 713
remote access to Cisco routers, 139–141
v1 and v2 configuration, 141–143
v3 configuration, 143–145
traps, specifying destinations, 145
snmp-server community command, 141
snmp-server group command, 144
SNTP (Simple Network Time Protocol), 723
authentication, 728–729
broadcast-based configuration, 725
client configuration, 723
configuring, 725
poll-based configuration, 724
restricting resources, 728
server configuration, 725–727
social engineering, 23
SOCKS traffic, filtering with NBAR, 469
software clock, 719
sources of amplification attacks, locating, 313–314
spamming, 28
spoofing, preventing with RPF, 625–627
SQL Slammer worm, 328–329
SSH (Secure Shell)
DoS attacks, vulnerability of Cisco IOS
Software, 127
remote access to Cisco routers, 123
client connections, 127
server configuration, 124–125
server example, 126
SSL (Secure Sockets Layer), configuring remote
access to Cisco routers, , 130–139

Stacheldraht attacks, blocking, 322–323
standard ACLs, 260
examples of, 263–264
named standard ACLs, 262–263
numbered standard ACLs, 261–262
starting up AutoSecure, 187–188
state table
CBAC, changing connection timeouts, 400–401
stateful firewalls, 59–60
stateful firewalls, 53–54
advantages of, 61
advantages over packet-filtering firewalls, 54
applications of, 64
fragments, filtering, 281
limitations of, 61
multiple application connections, 63
non-stateful protocols, 62
state table size, 64
state table, 59–60
static address translation, 477
static crypto maps, configuring, 801
static NAT
redundancy with HSRP, 522–526
route maps, configuring, 520–521
static password authentication, 112–113
static routing, 597–598
configuring on perimeter routers,
case study, 830
static translation of overlapping addresses,
configuring, 494–496
statistics of address translation, displaying, 502–503
structured threats, 17
subnet masks, converting to wildcard masks,
254–256
supported protocols on CBAC, 390
H.323, 392–393
RTSP, 390
SIP, 394–395
Skinny, 393–394
sylog, configuring on perimeter routers,
case study, 836
symptoms of DoS attacks, 662–664
synchronous logging, configuring, 706–708
syslog files, rotating, 741
syslog server logging, 710–713
System-defined entries (PAM), 402

T

TACACS+
    centralizing AAA security policies, 203–205
        server groupings, 208
        server protocol example configuration, 211–212
    troubleshooting, 209–210
    versus RADIUS, 212–213
tacacs-server host command, 205
TCP (Transmission Control Protocol)
    CBAC handling of, 385–386
    configuring CBAC inspection rules, 406–407
    control information, examining, 57–59
    segments, fragmentation, 280–281
    traffic filtering with numbered extended ACLs, 267–269
    weaknesses in, 13
TCP Intercept, 679
    example, 686–687
    preventing TCP SYN flood attacks, 679–686
TCP small servers, disabling, 163–164
TCP SYN flood attacks, 32, 662
    preventing with ACLs, 307–308
technologies, weaknesses of, 13
    network equipment, 15
    network protocols, 13
    operating systems, 14–15
TFN (tribe flood network) attacks, 319
    blocking, 320
TFN2k (tribe flood network 2K) attacks, blocking, 320
TFTP (Trivial File Transfer Protocol), disabling, 167
threats, types of, 17
three-interface CBAC, example configuration, 418–422
three-interface RACLs, example, 375–378
threshold of ACL logging, changing, 291–294
throughput performance feature of CBAC, 396
time and date configuration, 720–722
time-based authentication, 115
timed ACLs, 285
    activating time ranges, 287
    creating time ranges, 285
        with absolute command, 286
        with periodic command, 286–287

        distributed, 287–288
        example configuration, 288–289
timeout limits, translation table configuration, 500–501
timestamping logging messages, 714
TIS Firewall Toolkit, 48
token card services, 115–117
traceroute, preventing reconnaissance attacks, 316
tracking intended amplification attack victims and perpetrators, 313–314
traffic classification, implementing with NBAR, 445–446
traffic distribution, 482
    configuring, 498–499
traffic filtering, 237–238, 259–260
    ACL processing, 241
        conditions, 241
        matches, 241
        rules, 246–247
        statement order, 243–246
    example, 238
    CBAC, 382–383
    extended ACLs, 264
        named extended ACLs, 273
        numbered extended ACLs, 264–272
        three-interface router example, 275–278
        two-interface router example, 273–275
    implementing with NBAR, 447
    placement of ACLs, 248–249
    RACLs
        configuring, 365–374
        examples of, 374–378
        filtering returning traffic, 359–360
        limitations of, 361
          application issues, 362
          FTP, 363–364
          stateful issues, 362
        removing entries, 360–361
    standard ACLs, 260
        examples of, 263–264
        named standard ACLs, 262–263
        numbered standard ACLs, 261–262
traffic inspection, CBAC, 383
transform sets, 131
    creating, 800
transit records for ACL accounting, limiting, 294–295

translation tables
    connection limits, configuring, 500
    removing entries with clear commands,
        503–504
    timeout limits, configuring, 500–501
traps
    generating, 141
    specifying destinations, 145
Trinity attacks, blocking, 324
Trinoo attacks, blocking, 321–322
Trojan horses, 29–31, 325
    blocking with ACLs, 325–326
    detecting, 325
    monitoring rcp command usage with ACLs, 327
troubleshooting
    accounting with debug aaa accounting
        command, 230
    address translation with debug ip nat
        command, 504
    AP
        with clear commands, 587
        with debug commands, 587
        with show commands, 584–586
    authentication, 219
        with debug aaa authentication, 220
    authorization, 224
    CBAC, 410
        with debug commands, 413–415
        with show commands, 411–413
    CRLs, 762
    IPSec site-to-site connections, 775–778
        debug commands, 778–780
    lock-and-key ACLs, 562–563
    RADIUS, 210
    SCP, 232
    TACACS+, 209–210
    URL filtering, 442
tuning AP performance, 582–583
turbo ACLs, 295
    configuring, 295–296
two-interface CBAC, example configuration,
    417–418
two-interface RACLs, example of, 375

U

UAPs (user authorization profiles), 578
UDP (User Datagram Protocol)
    CBAC handling of, 386
    configuring CBAC inspection rules, 406–407
    traffic filtering with numbered extended ACLs,
        269–271
UDP small servers, disabling, 163–164
unauthorized access attacks, 23–24
unicast RPF
    configuring, 629
    example configuration, 631
    preventing IP spoofing, 625–627
        limitations, 628
        per-interface statistics, 627
    verifying configuration, 630–631
unidirectional connections
    filtering, RACLs, 351
unnecessary services, disabling, 815–817
    global services, 161
        BootP, 170
        CDP, 162–163
        configuration autoloading, 172–173
        DHCP, 171
        DNS name resolution, 169–170
        finger, 164–165
        FTP, 167
        HTTP, 167
        IdentD, 165
        IP source routing, 166
        PAD, 172
        SNMP, 168–169
        TCP small servers, 163–164
        TFTP, 167
        UDP small servers, 163–164
    interface services, 173
        directed broadcasts, 176
        ICMP messages, 177–180
        MOP, 181
        Proxy ARP, 174–176
        unused interfaces, 182
        VTYs, 181–182
    with AutoSecure feature, 184
        forwarding plane, 186
        management plane, 185

unreachables (ICMP), disabling, 177–178
    for black hole routes, 599
unstructured threats, 17
unused interfaces, disabling, 182
URL filtering, 428
    advantages of, 430–431
    alerts, 437
    audits, 438–439
    cache, clearing, 434
    configuring, 432–434
    example, 443–444
    exclusive domains, configuring, 435
    logging, 439
    maximum requests, 436
    maximum responses, 436
    operation, 429–430
    restrictions, 431–432
    troubleshooting, 442
    verifying, 440–441
user EXEC access
    local access, 118–119
        authentication methods, 120
        via auxiliary line, 119
        via console port, 118
    remote access, 121
        via HTTPS, 130–139
        via SNMP, 139–145
        via SSH, 123–127
        via VTY lines, 121, 123
        via web browser, 127–130
    securing shell access, 216–217
User-Defined Custom Application Classification
    feature (NB AR), 453
User-Defined Custom Application Classification
    feature (NBAR), 453
user-defined entries (PAM), 402
username and password prompts, 218

V

verifying
    ACL configuration, 278–280
    address translation with show commands,
        501–502
    AutoSecure configuration, 198

    CBAC configuration, 410
        with debug commands, 413–415
        with show commands, 411–413
    Cisco IOS IDS configuration, 657–658
    dynamic crypto maps, 800
    NBAR configuration, 460–463
    PAM configuration, 404
    RPF configuration, 630–631
    SLB configuration, 544
    SNAT configuration, 534–535
    URL filtering configuration, 440–441
viruses, 29–31
    worms, 327
        Deloder worm, 330
        Microsoft RPC service, susceptibility to,
            330–332
        SQL Slammer worm, 328–329
VPNs, 92, 786–789
VTY lines
    configuring access to Cisco routers, 119
    disabling, 181–182
    login connection timeouts, overriding, 120–121
    remote access to Cisco routers, 121–123

W

W32.Blaster worm, 676
W32.Welchia worm, 331
watch lists, configuring, 583–584
weaknesses
    in computer technologies, 13
        network equipment, 15
        network protocols, 13
        operating systems, 14–15
    in equipment configurations, 15–16
    in policy definitions, 9–10
        lack of change management, 11
        lack of disaster recovery plan, 11–12
web browsers, remote access to Cisco routers,
    127–130
web traffic
    Code Red worm, filtering, 463–466
    Java inspection, 426–428
    Nimda, filtering, 466–467
    URL filtering, 428
        advantages of, 430–431

alerts, 437
audits, 438–439
configuring, 432–435
example, 443–444
logging, 439
maximum requests, 436
maximum responses, 436
operation, 429–430
restrictions, 431–432
troubleshooting, 442
verifying, 440–441
websites
IANA, 301
Packet Storm, 317
wildcard masks (ACLs), 254–256
WinMX, filtering, 344–345
WinNuke, 33
worms, 29–31, 327
Code Red, 676–677
Deloder worm, 330
Microsoft RPC service, susceptibility to,
330–332
Nachi, 331
SQL Slammer worm, 328–329
W32.Blaster, 676
W32.Welchia, 331

X-Y-Z

Yahoo! Messenger, filtering, 336–338

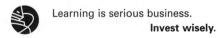

SEARCH THOUSANDS OF BOOKS FROM LEADING PUBLISHERS

Safari® Bookshelf is a searchable electronic reference library for IT professionals that features more than 2,000 titles from technical publishers, including Cisco Press.

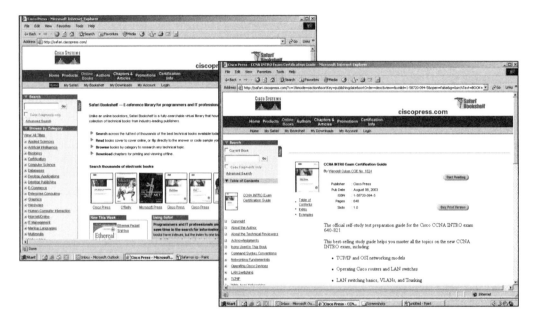

With Safari Bookshelf you can

- **Search** the full text of thousands of technical books, including more than 70 Cisco Press titles from authors such as Wendell Odom, Jeff Doyle, Bill Parkhurst, Sam Halabi, and Karl Solie.

- **Read** the books on My Bookshelf from cover to cover, or just flip to the information you need.

- **Browse** books by category to research any technical topic.

- **Download** chapters for printing and viewing offline.

With a customized library, you'll have access to your books when and where you need them—and all you need is a user name and password.

TRY SAFARI BOOKSHELF FREE FOR 14 DAYS!

You can sign up to get a 10-slot Bookshelf free for the first 14 days.
Visit **http://safari.ciscopress.com** to register.

CISCO SYSTEMS

Cisco Press

3 STEPS TO LEARNING

STEP 1

STEP 2

STEP 3

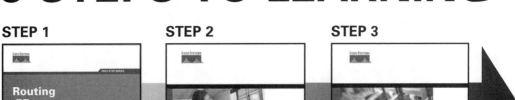

First-Step

Fundamentals

Networking
Technology Guides

STEP 1 **First-Step**—Benefit from easy-to-grasp explanations.
No experience required!

STEP 2 **Fundamentals**—Understand the purpose, application,
and management of technology.

STEP 3 **Networking Technology Guides**—Gain the knowledge
to master the challenge of the network.

NETWORK BUSINESS SERIES

The Network Business series helps professionals tackle the
business issues surrounding the network. Whether you are a
seasoned IT professional or a business manager with minimal
technical expertise, this series will help you understand the
business case for technologies.

Justify Your Network Investment.

Look for Cisco Press titles at your favorite bookseller today.

Visit **www.ciscopress.com/series** for details on each of these book series.

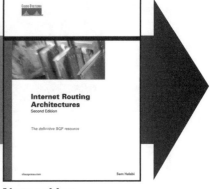

☐ **YES!** I'm requesting a **free** subscription to *Packet*™ magazine.

☐ No. I'm not interested at this time.

☐ Mr.
☐ Ms.

First Name (Please Print)   Last Name

Title/Position (Required)

Company (Required)

Address

City   State/Province

Zip/Postal Code   Country

Telephone (Include country and area codes)   Fax

E-mail

Signature (Required)   Date

☐ I would like to receive additional information on Cisco's services and products by e-mail.

1. Do you or your company:
- A ☐ Use Cisco products
- B ☐ Resell Cisco products
- C ☐ Both
- D ☐ Neither

2. Your organization's relationship to Cisco Systems:
- A ☐ Customer/End User
- B ☐ Prospective Customer
- C ☐ Cisco Reseller
- D ☐ Cisco Distributor
- E ☐ Integrator
- F ☐ Non-Authorized Reseller
- G ☐ Cisco Training Partner
- I ☐ Cisco OEM
- J ☐ Consultant
- K ☐ Other (specify): _____

3. How many people does your entire company employ?
- A ☐ More than 10,000
- B ☐ 5,000 to 9,999
- c ☐ 1,000 to 4,999
- D ☐ 500 to 999
- E ☐ 250 to 499
- f ☐ 100 to 249
- G ☐ Fewer than 100

4. Is your company a Service Provider?
- A ☐ Yes
- B ☐ No

5. Your involvement in network equipment purchases:
- A ☐ Recommend
- B ☐ Approve
- C ☐ Neither

6. Your personal involvement in networking:
- A ☐ Entire enterprise at all sites
- B ☐ Departments or network segments at more than one site
- C ☐ Single department or network segment
- F ☐ Public network
- D ☐ No involvement
- E ☐ Other (specify): _____

7. Your Industry:
- A ☐ Aerospace
- B ☐ Agriculture/Mining/Construction
- C ☐ Banking/Finance
- D ☐ Chemical/Pharmaceutical
- E ☐ Consultant
- F ☐ Computer/Systems/Electronics
- G ☐ Education (K–12)
- U ☐ Education (College/Univ.)
- H ☐ Government—Federal
- I ☐ Government—State
- J ☐ Government—Local
- K ☐ Health Care
- L ☐ Telecommunications
- M ☐ Utilities/Transportation
- N ☐ Other (specify): _____

CPRESS

PACKET

Packet magazine serves as the premier publication linking customers to Cisco Systems, Inc. Delivering complete coverage of cutting-edge networking trends and innovations, *Packet* is a magazine for technical, hands-on users. It delivers industry-specific information for enterprise, service provider, and small and midsized business market segments. A toolchest for planners and decision makers, *Packet* contains a vast array of practical information, boasting sample configurations, real-life customer examples, and tips on getting the most from your Cisco Systems' investments. Simply put, *Packet* magazine is straight talk straight from the worldwide leader in networking for the Internet, Cisco Systems, Inc.

We hope you'll take advantage of this useful resource. I look forward to hearing from you!

Cecelia Glover
Packet Circulation Manager
packet@external.cisco.com
www.cisco.com/go/packet

PACKET